D0397279

MAR 1981
RECEIVED
McKusick
Law Library

LITTLE, BROWN AND COMPANY

Law School Casebook Series

The Employment Relation and the Law. Edited by BENJAMIN AARON, Professor of Law and Director, Institute of Industrial Relations, University of California at Los Angeles

Antitrust Analysis: Problems, Text, Cases. PHILLIP AREEDA, Professor of Law, Harvard University

Land Ownership and Use: Cases, Statutes, and Other Materials. CURTIS J. BERGER, Professor of Law, Columbia University

International Law: Cases and Materials. Second Edition. WILLIAM W. BISHOP, JR., Professor of Law, University of Michigan

Federal Income, Estate and Gift Taxation. Third Edition. BORIS I. BITTKER, Southmayd Professor of Law, Yale University

Jurisdiction and Judgments: Cases and Statutes. WILLIAM WIRT BLUME, Professor of Law, University of California, Hastings College of Law, and CHARLES W. JOINER, Associate Dean and Professor of Law, University of Michigan

Pleading and Joinder: Cases and Statutes. WILLIAM WIRT BLUME, Professor of Law, University of California, Hastings College of Law, and JOHN W. REED, Dean and Professor of Law, University of Colorado

Estate Planning. Third Edition. A. JAMES CASNER, Associate Dean and Weld Professor of Law, Harvard University

Cases and Text on Property. A. JAMES CASNER, Associate Dean and Weld Professor of Law, Harvard University, and W. BARTON LEACH, Story Professor of Law, Harvard University

International Legal Process. ABRAM CHAYES, Professor of Law, Harvard University, THOMAS EHRLICH, Professor of Law, Stanford University, and ANDREAS F. LOWENFELD, Professor of Law, New York University

Cases and Materials on Debtor and Creditor. VERN COUNTRYMAN, Professor of Law, Harvard University

The Lawyer in Modern Society. VERN COUNTRYMAN, Professor of Law, Harvard University, and TED FINMAN, Professor of Law, University of Wisconsin

Law and Medicine: Text and Source Materials on Medico-Legal Problems. WILLIAM J. CURRAN, Professor of Legal Medicine, Boston University; Lecturer in Legal Medicine, Harvard Law School

Trade Regulation: Cases and Materials. FRANK ELKOURI, Professor of Law, University of Oklahoma

Political and Civil Rights in the United States. Third Edition. THOMAS I. EMERSON, Lines Professor of Law, Yale University, DAVID HABER, Professor of Law, Rutgers University, and NORMAN DORSEN, Professor of Law and Director of the Arthur Garfield Hays Civil Liberties Program, New York University

Cases and Materials on Family Law. CALEB FOOTE, Professor of Law and Criminology, University of California at Berkeley, ROBERT J. LEVY, Professor of Law, University of Minnesota, and FRANK E. A. SANDER, Professor of Law, Harvard University

Oil and Gas Taxation: Cases and Materials. SIMON M. FRANK, formerly Professor of Law, University of Houston, C. W. WELLEN, formerly Lecturer in Law, University of Houston, and OWEN LIPSCOMB of the Texas Bar

Cases and Materials on Corporations. ALEXANDER H. FREY, Algernon Sidney Biddle Professor of Law, University of Pennsylvania, C. ROBERT MORRIS, Professor of Law, University of Minnesota, and JESSE CHOPER, Professor of Law, University of California at Berkeley

Constitutional Law: Cases and Other Problems. Third Edition. PAUL A. FREUND, Carl M. Loeb University Professor, Harvard University, ARTHUR E. SUTHERLAND, Bussey Professor of Law, Harvard University, MARK DE WOLFE HOWE, late Charles Warren Professor of American Legal History, Harvard University, and ERNEST J. BROWN, Professor of Law, Harvard University

Cases and Materials on Torts. CHARLES O. GREGORY, John B. Minor Professor of Law, University of Virginia, and HARRY KALVEN, JR., Professor of Law, University of Chicago

Land-use Planning: A Casebook on the Use, Misuse, and Re-use of Urban Land. CHARLES M. HAAR, Professor of Law, Harvard University

Administrative Law: Cases and Materials. Third Edition. LOUIS L. JAFFE, Byrne Professor of Administrative Law, Harvard University, and NATHANIEL L. NATHANSON, Professor of Law, Northwestern University

Trials and Appeals: Cases, Text, Statutes, Rules, and Forms. CHARLES W. JOINER, Associate Dean and Professor of Law, University of Michigan

Constitutional Law: Cases and Materials. Third Edition. PAUL G. KAUPER, Professor of Law, University of Michigan

Contracts: Cases and Materials. FRIEDRICH KESSLER, Sterling Professor of Law, Yale University, and MALCOLM PITMAN SHARP, Professor of Law, Emeritus, University of Chicago

Basic Business Associations: Cases, Text and Problems. ELVIN R. LATTY, William R. Perkins Professor of Law, Duke University, and GEORGE T. FRAMPTON, Professor of Law, University of Illinois

Cases and Text on the Law of Wills. Second Edition, 1960 Revision. W. BARTON LEACH, Story Professor of Law, Harvard University

Legislation: Cases and Materials. FRANK C. NEWMAN, Professor of Law, University of California at Berkeley, and STANLEY S. SURREY, formerly Jeremiah Smith, Jr., Professor of Law, Harvard University

Criminal Law and Its Processes: Cases and Materials. MONRAD G. PAULSEN, Professor of Law, Columbia University, and SANFORD H. KADISH, Professor of Law, University of California at Berkeley

Family Law: Cases and Materials. MORRIS PLOSCOWE, Adjunct Associate Professor of Law, New York University, and DORIS JONAS FREED, of the New York and Maryland Bars

Problems and Materials on Decedents' Estates and Trusts. EUGENE F. SCOLES, Professor of Law, University of Illinois, and EDWARD C. HALBACH, JR., Dean and Professor of Law, University of California at Berkeley

Cases and Other Materials on Civil Procedure. AUSTIN W. SCOTT, Dane Professor of Law, Emeritus, Harvard University, and ROBERT B. KENT, Professor of Law, Boston University

Select Cases and Other Authorities on the Law of Trusts. AUSTIN W. SCOTT, Dane Professor of Law, Emeritus, Harvard University, and AUSTIN W. SCOTT, JR., late Professor of Law, University of Colorado

An Introduction to Criminal Justice: Text and Cases. ORVILL C. SNYDER, Professor of Law, Emeritus, Brooklyn Law School

The Civil Law System: Cases and Materials for the Comparative Study of Law. ARTHUR TAYLOR VON MEHREN, Professor of Law, Harvard University

The Law of Multistate Problems: Cases and Materials on Conflict of Laws. ARTHUR TAYLOR VON MEHREN, Professor of Law, Harvard University, and DONALD THEODORE TRAUTMAN, Professor of Law, Harvard University

Cases on Contracts. SAMUEL WILLISTON, late Dane Professor of Law, Harvard University, Revised Sixth Edition by WILLIAM T. LAUBE, A. F. and May T. Morrison Professor of Law, University of California at Berkeley

Labor Relations and the Law. Third Edition. Edited by JERRE WILLIAMS, Rex G. and Edna Heflin Baker Professor of Constitutional Law, University of Texas, and BENJAMIN AARON, Professor of Law and Director, Institute of Industrial Relations, University of California at Los Angeles

Law School Textbook Series

American Civil Procedure. WILLIAM WIRT BLUME, Professor of Law, University of California, Hastings College of Law

Readings in Jurisprudence and Legal Philosophy. MORRIS R. COHEN, late Professor of Law, City College of New York, and FELIX S. COHEN, late Visiting Professor of Law, City College of New York, and Visiting Lecturer, Yale University

The Elements of Law. THOMAS E. DAVITT, S.J., Professor of Jurisprudence, Marquette University

Handbook of Modern Equity. Second Edition. WILLIAM Q. DE FUNIAK, Professor of Law, University of San Francisco

Judicial Control of Administrative Action. Abridged Student Edition. LOUIS L. JAFFE, Byrne Professor of Administrative Law, Harvard University

Civil Procedure. FLEMING JAMES, JR., Lafayette S. Foster Professor of Law, Yale University

Trial Tactics and Methods. ROBERT E. KEETON, Professor of Law, Harvard University

Securities Regulation. Student Edition. LOUIS LOSS, William Nelson Cromwell Professor of Law, Harvard University

Effective Legal Research: Student Edition Revised. MILES O. PRICE, Professor of Law and Law Librarian, Emeritus, Columbia University, and HARRY BITNER, Professor of Law and Law Librarian, Cornell University

Scott's Abridgment of the Law of Trusts. AUSTIN W. SCOTT, Dane Professor of Law, Emeritus, Harvard University

Handbook of Law Study. FERDINAND FAIRFAX STONE, W. R. Irby Professor of Law and Director of Institute of Comparative Law, Tulane University

Materials on the Lawyer's Professional Responsibility. WILLIAM M. TRUMBULL, Professor of Law, Emeritus, Northwestern University

LITTLE, BROWN AND COMPANY
Law Book Division

Editorial Board

A. JAMES CASNER, CHAIRMAN
Weld Professor of Law, Harvard University

FRANCIS A. ALLEN
Dean and Professor of Law, University of Michigan

BORIS I. BITTKER
Southmayd Professor of Law, Yale University

CLARK BYSE
Professor of Law, Harvard University

HARRY KALVEN, JR.
Professor of Law, University of Chicago

W. BARTON LEACH
Story Professor of Law, Harvard University

A. LEO LEVIN
Professor of Law and Vice Provost, University of Pennsylvania

FRANK C. NEWMAN
Professor of Law, University of California at Berkeley

HERBERT L. PACKER
Professor of Law and Vice Provost, Stanford University

WILLIS L. M. REESE
Charles Evans Hughes Professor of Law and Director, Parker School
of Foreign and Comparative Law, Columbia University

LABOR RELATIONS AND THE LAW

THIRD EDITION

Compiled by a Group of Teachers
and Practitioners of Labor Law
Known as the Labor Law Group Trust
Under the Editorship of

JERRE S. WILLIAMS

CO-CHAIRMAN, LABOR LAW GROUP TRUST

LITTLE, BROWN AND COMPANY
Boston   1965   *Toronto*

COPYRIGHT, ©, 1948, 1950, 1953 BY ROBERT E. MATHEWS
COPYRIGHT, ©, 1957, 1960, 1965 BY THE LABOR LAW GROUP TRUST

ALL RIGHTS RESERVED, INCLUDING THE RIGHT TO REPRODUCE
THIS BOOK OR PORTIONS THEREOF IN ANY FORM

LIBRARY OF CONGRESS CATALOG CARD NO. 65–25408

Third Printing

*Published simultaneously in Canada
by Little, Brown & Company (Canada) Ltd.*
PRINTED IN THE UNITED STATES OF AMERICA

To Our Colleague

W. Willard Wirtz

Lawyer, Teacher, Scholar, Arbitrator, Member of the Cabinet of the President of the United States, this book is respectfully dedicated.

McKUSICK LAW LIBRARY
UNIVERSITY OF SOUTH DAKOTA
VERMILLION, SOUTH DAKOTA

Foreword

It is the hope of the Labor Law Group that this Third Edition of Labor Relations and the Law marks an additional significant step following in the tradition of the prior labor law teaching materials which the Group has prepared.

To trace the origins of this volume one must go back almost twenty years — to December of 1946. It was then that W. Willard Wirtz, at that time a member of the Northwestern University Law Faculty, presented a paper at a round table at the annual meeting of the Association of American Law Schools.[1] The topic for discussion was "A New Prospectus for Labor Law."

Professor Wirtz's presentation was so critical of the inadequacies of the teaching materials of those days, so challenging and imaginative as to the possibilities of an approach that would be both more constructive and more realistic, that it immediately captured the interest of the participants. Accordingly, they took to the floor of the Association a request to authorize the holding of a conference on the teaching of labor law.

The newly elected Round Table Council directed themselves towards obtaining a grant to finance this proposal. Within the next few months they had elicited the interest of the Carnegie Corporation of New York.[2] By means of a substantial grant, and with the hospitable cooperation of the University of Michigan Law School, they were able to hold a two-week conference at Ann Arbor during June of 1947. This was known as the "Conference on the Training of Law Students in Labor Relations." [3]

Each morning speakers discussed the adequacies and inadequacies of the training of young law graduates for practice in the field of labor relations. Lawyers and economists, labor and management attorneys, and national figures of long service in the public interest comprised the list of distinguished speakers. The audience was composed of teachers from thirty-two law schools, who each afternoon in small round tables discussed the comments made at the morning session.

A majority of the law teachers in attendance later expressed the desire

[1] His paper was later published as On Teaching Labor Law, 42 Ill. L. Rev. 1 (1947).

[2] It should be understood, of course, that the Corporation has not endorsed, by virtue of this grant, any of the statements or views contained in any of the volumes to which its generous grant has contributed.

[3] A complete transcript of the proceedings of this Conference was later distributed to the library of each law school belonging to the Association.

to make the fullest possible use of their experience by compiling a set of teaching materials that would, they hoped, reflect the points of view that had most impressed them at the Conference. As time went on, and materials took shape, changes took place in the list of cooperating editors, some dropped out and others, some of whom had not been present at Ann Arbor, became participants. First identified as "a group of teachers and practitioners of Labor Law," these persons ultimately established a common law trust, procured recognition of tax exempt status, and assumed the name of the "Labor Law Group."

Ordinarily it is of little interest to users of a book to know anything of the procedure whereby it was constructed, tested, and finally released for publication. However, the editorial activities of the Labor Law Group in preparing the five volumes that have now been published is so unique as to justify a brief description. Characteristically, work on each volume commenced with a conference of as many of the editors as could attend to block out in broad outline the subject matter to be dealt with. Thereafter, this broad definition of coverage was broken down into a succession of parts and each was entrusted to a small committee. After preparing, through correspondence, lists of sub-topics and of the principal cases and notes deemed suitable for each part, these committees met for a week end and prepared their materials for circulation in mimeographed form among the other participants. These were then put in temporary binding for experimental classroom use. Comments were elicited from all users; these too were circulated, and a conference was held for re-examination of materials in the light of these suggestions and criticisms. In the case of the original volume of Labor Relations and the Law, this entire process was repeated, but with reassignments of committee membership, before its final publication in 1953. All of the preparation of the preliminary editions and the first published edition was under the general editorship of Robert E. Mathews.

This pattern, adjusted to variations in subject matter, was used for The Employment Relation and the Law (1957), Benjamin Aaron, Editor, as well as the Second Edition of Labor Relations and the Law (1960), Donald H. Wollett and Benjamin Aaron, Editors. Meanwhile, a third volume, Readings on Labor Law, had been produced (1955), but it was a collection of articles and was scarcely susceptible to this procedure. It was compiled by the late Charles A. Reynard, with such suggestions as others in the Group were able to contribute.

There have been, of course, other books before these which have been produced by several persons working cooperatively. But the contribution made by the present series is far more than in number of participants. The feature that is here unique is the jointness of the total product. It is no mere aggregation of individual compilations; rather, the thought of all participants has contributed to every portion of the whole. The product is greater than the sum total of its individual contributions, for each has been weighed, considered, and remolded by a group consensus.

It is hoped that it will not seem out of place to mention another feature that characterizes this series of books. It indeed reflects the interest and dedication of the participating editors that during the nineteen years that most of them have worked together, at no time has any of them received any share in the royalties. On the contrary, the immense amount of time that has been involved has been contributed without compensation. It has often been contributed at actual personal expense, occasioned by the necessity of refusing other employment in order to meet editorial commitments. All royalties have been held in trust to defray out-of-pocket costs entailed partly by research and clerical aid, but chiefly by group or committee conferences. In a sense, this would seem to constitute a financial self-perpetuation; more accurately, it is a continuing sequence of publications made possible by the dedication of the editors to the ever recurring challenge to provide materials that will contribute to the education of abler lawyers, better qualified to serve not merely their clients but the public good.

When these materials were first published there were two aspects that made the original volume unique. One was the inclusion of extensive foreign law notes for comparative use to throw sharper light on the state of American law. The editors acknowledge their indebtedness for this to Dr. Arthur Lenhoff of the University of Buffalo. For various reasons beyond the control of the editors, it has been necessary to reduce these foreign law references in both the Second and the Third Editions. This in no sense reflects a change in viewpoint, however, for the editors hope that foreign labor law material will continue to be emphasized and, indeed, expanded in the event of publication of later editions.

A second unique aspect is the use of a continuing series of episodic problems illustrative of a typical progression of organizational efforts, from the initial approach in an unorganized company through a history of negotiation efforts that finally culminate in a collective agreement. As the story proceeds, other episodes illustrate the use of economic force by both management and labor. Throughout this whole series there runs a sequence of representation and unfair labor practice proceedings.

Perhaps no other area in the curriculum is adapted to a single continuing narrative of this sort; but in the labor relations field there is a cycle of events that is so frequent as to be typical. It starts at the very birth of organizational effort and terminates in the mature and stable relationship of a soundly administered agreement. It is this recurring sequence that is pictured here in a succession of incidents factually set out in the history of a fictitious enterprise, the Enderby Rubber Company.

This device lends itself admirably to class discussion. Student attention can be focused on these developing facts, and the conduct of the participants — whose names recur through every episode — raises a long array of issues which can be dealt with in classroom discussion in the light of the decisions of the National Labor Relations Board, of courts, and of arbitrators, that are interspersed throughout. This pattern, first introduced twelve years ago, has been found so productive as, in somewhat edited and modernized form, to justify its continuation in this Third Edition.

This new edition of Labor Relations and the Law is not merely an up-dating of the materials contained in the Second Edition. Just as the Second Edition was a substantial revision of the First, this Third Edition also is largely a new work. Since the publication of the Second Edition, the members of the Labor Law Group have become increasingly concerned with the fragmentation of the typical law school approach to labor law. As the relationship between employer and employee has matured, it has become increasingly obvious that this relationship constitutes a whole environment in which management and labor must get along together and work with each other. Yet, the traditional course in labor law has considered only that portion of the work environment which has to do with the setting up of the collective bargaining relationship. There has been little or no concern over the substantive issues involved in collective bargaining, especially as they relate to the broad programs of social welfare legislation which are inextricably a part of the entire labor management relationship in a modern industrial plant.

These considerations led the Labor Law Group to the conclusion that there must be a consideration of such matters as wage and hour legislation, pension and retirement programs, unemployment compensation, health insurance, and workmen's compensation if a full understanding of the relationship between management and labor is to be achieved. The major innovation in the Third Edition, then, is the introduction of materials designed to round out the full labor management picture by relating the collective bargaining process to these other matters, which are as vital a part of the relationship as is the process of bargaining itself.

The Group has also attempted to sense the meaning of current developments in labor relations and project them into the future. Substantial emphasis has been placed upon the problems of automation and the effective utilization of manpower. In addition, a new section considers public employment, as developments move toward authorizing public employees to be represented by organizations of their own choosing in dealing with the public bodies which hire them.

The Third Edition also carries further the trend, noticeable in the Second Edition, of placing less emphasis upon factual data and more upon materials designed for teaching through raising pertinent issues in the classroom.

The book is divided into five parts. Part I undertakes to present a brief historical survey of the development of labor law and at the same time to pose the current critical issues in labor-management relations. Economic information concerning the current status of the worker in our society is given, and a brief survey of the various statutory contributions to the entire work environment is made. This survey includes reference to such statutes as the Federal Wage and Hour Law, the Civil Rights Act of 1964, unemployment compensation and old age and survivor's insurance, and other similar legislation. Finally, this part discusses the current issues resulting from technological advance.

Part II is concerned with the organization and setting up of collective bargaining. Permissible and prohibited conduct of both employers and unions is the subject of detailed inquiry. In addition to the use of the series of Enderby Company problems mentioned above, this part contains as an innovation another problem teaching device, which summarizes a series of past cases and then relates that summary to a current unresolved issue.   A separate section of this part poses the fundamental issues involved in federalism or "pre-emption," although related materials are found throughout the book.

Part III has to do with the collective bargaining process after it has been established.   The duty to bargain in good faith is first considered. Then the subjects of bargaining are taken up in detail.   Included in this portion of Part III is a consideration of the relationship to collective bargaining of such matters as pensions and retirement benefits, the Federal Wage and Hour Law, unemployment compensation, workmen's compensation, and health and medical care.   Union security issues, as they are established in collective bargaining and controlled by law, are then considered.   Finally, the public interest in collective bargaining becomes the object of attention through materials exploring the labor dispute which has a serious impact on the general public, the relationship of labor unions to the antitrust laws, and the rights and obligations of public employees in undertaking to establish a collective bargaining relationship with their public employers.

Part IV considers the administration of the collective bargaining agreement once it has been made.   Here there is emphasis upon the grievance procedure and the arbitration process.   As the latest developments reveal, attention must be directed toward the relationship between the National Labor Relations Board and the courts and the grievance and arbitration process.   Finally, consideration is given to the protection of the rights of the individual in the collective bargaining process.

Part V presents materials relating to the quite recent and highly important legal developments designed to protect the rights of individual union members within their unions, and the reciprocal rights of unions to be free from improper disruptions of their valid activities by individual employees.   The passage of the Labor-Management Reporting and Disclosure Act of 1959 created an entirely new era in protecting the union member in the democratic processes within his union and from oppression by his union.   The detailed application of this far-reaching statute is the subject of consideration in this part.   Also, Title VII of the Civil Rights Act of 1964, in establishing the principle of equal employment opportunities without discrimination based upon race, religion, national origin, or sex, is the subject of materials designed to highlight the process of ensuring that the individual worker does not get lost in the group activity of labor and management in their collective bargaining relationship.

This Third Edition of Labor Relations and the Law began to take shape in June of 1963, at a three-day conference held at the Ohio State University College of Law in Columbus.   At that time the members of the Labor Law Group invited several teachers and other experts in the labor relations field to meet with them and discuss the modernization of labor law teaching materials.   It was at this meeting that the Group decided that effective labor law teaching materials today must include such legislative matters as wage and hour laws, unemployment compensation, workmen's compensation, pensions, and other similar benefits. By the conclusion of this meeting, a general tentative outline of the Third Edition had been developed. Task forces for each of the five parts in the outline were selected.

The next year was spent in developing precise and detailed outlines of the contents of each of the five parts. These outlines were reproduced and sent to each member of the Group in the spring of 1964. At a meeting held at the University of Texas Law School in June of 1964, each outline was gone over in detail by the entire Group, and substantial revisions were made. Since that meeting, the time has been spent in actually preparing the materials.

Not all members of the Group have been able to participate actively in the preparation of this volume. The active editors consist of the committee members for each of the five parts. They are, Part I: Professor Alfred W. Blumrosen of Rutgers University, Chairman, Professor Alexander H. Frey of the University of Pennsylvania, Donald H. Wollett, Esq., of the New York City Bar; Part II, Professor Richard S. Sullivan of Boston College, Chairman, Professor Cornelius J. Peck of the University of Washington, Dean Ivan C. Rutledge of Ohio State University; Part III: Professor Kurt L. Hanslowe of Cornell University, Chairman, Professor Howard Lesnick of the University of Pennsylvania, Professor Don W. Sears of the University of Colorado; Part IV, Professor Herbert L. Sherman, Jr., of the University of Pittsburgh, Chairman, Professor William P. Murphy of the University of Missouri, Edwin R. Teple, Esq., of the Cleveland Bar and Lecturer at Western Reserve University; Part V, Professor Benjamin Aaron of the University of California, Los Angeles, Chairman, Professor Robert F. Koretz of Syracuse University, Professor Walter E. Oberer of Cornell University.

In addition to these particular assignments, special appreciation must be given to Professor Robert E. Mathews, who, as mentioned previously, served as the General Editor in developing the First Edition of these materials. In spite of other demands, he has been a constant source of guidance and aid in the preparation of this Third Edition, particularly to the undersigned as the General Editor. Further, except for the mention of his own important role, he supplied those portions of this foreword which detail the origins of the Labor Law Group and the development and content of the first two editions of Labor Relations and the Law. Further recognition must also be given to Dean Rutledge, who not only participated fully as a committee member in preparing Part II of these materials, but also undertook the all-important tasks of compiling the table of cases and the index for this volume. The thanks of the entire Group also go to Professor Duncan MacIntyre of Cornell University, who aided in the preparation of a substantial portion of Part III. The thanks of the cooperating editors are expressed to Mr. Rodney Robertson, General Manager, Law Book Department, Little, Brown & Company, and his staff, for their cooperation in the publication of this book under great press of time.

Finally, the members of the Labor Law Group express their tremendous respect, admiration, and appreciation to one of their number, W. Willard Wirtz. Earlier in this foreword there was described the role that Willard Wirtz played in inaugurating the chain of events which led to the development of the various teaching materials by the Labor Law Group. Following those initial days, he participated actively in all of the conferences and all of the work of the Labor Law Group in the preparation of the first two editions. The press of his duties as Under Secretary of Labor and then Secretary of Labor is the only thing that kept him from complete and active participation in the preparation of this Third Edition. We respectfully dedicate this volume to Willard Wirtz in appreciation of his great contributions and his delightful companionship in these Group endeavors.

Jerre S. Williams

Austin, Texas
June, 1965

Labor Law Group

Benjamin Aaron, University of California, Los Angeles
Alfred W. Blumrosen, Rutgers University
Abner Brodie, University of Wisconsin
Aaron A. Caghan, Attorney, United States Department of Labor
Alexander H. Frey, University of Pennsylvania
Carl H. Fulda, University of Texas
Kurt L. Hanslowe, Cornell University
Robert L. Howard, University of Missouri
Robert Koretz, Syracuse University
Howard Lesnick, University of Pennsylvania
Pierre R. Loiseaux, University of Texas
Robert E. Mathews, Ohio State University
Jay W. Murphy, University of Alabama
William P. Murphy, University of Missouri
Walter E. Oberer, Cornell University
Cornelius J. Peck, University of Washington
William G. Rice, Jr., Attorney, Madison, Wisconsin
Ivan C. Rutledge, Ohio State University
Don W. Sears, University of Colorado
Herbert L. Sherman, Jr., University of Pittsburgh
Richard S. Sullivan, Boston College
Clyde W. Summers, Yale University
Edwin R. Teple, Attorney, Cleveland, Ohio
Bertram F. Willcox, Cornell University
Jerre S. Williams, University of Texas
W. Willard Wirtz, Secretary of Labor, Washington, D.C.
Donald H. Wollett, Attorney, New York City

Table of Contents

PART I

LABOR RELATIONS: A PERSPECTIVE

PART II

ESTABLISHMENT AND MAINTENANCE OF
COLLECTIVE BARGAINING

PART III

COLLECTIVE BARGAINING: PROCESS AND SCOPE

PART IV

THE ADMINISTRATION OF THE LABOR AGREEMENT INCLUDING THE DUTY OF FAIR REPRESENTATION

PART V

THE INDIVIDUAL: EQUAL EMPLOYMENT OPPORTUNITY
AND HIS RELATIONSHIP TO THE UNION

Table of Cases

Principal cases are indicated by italic page references, while cases cited in the text and footnotes are designated by roman numbers.

LABOR RELATIONS AND THE LAW

Throughout this book, where there are footnotes in quoted material — that is, cases, articles, and so forth — the original numbers have been retained. Editor's notes are numbered beginning with 1 at the start of each part. Whenever these notes are keyed to quoted material they are signed "Ed."

PART ONE

Labor Relations: A Perspective

A. The Problem of an Individual Worker in an Industrial Society

John Martin came to work in the bituminous coal fields of West Virginia around the beginning of the twentieth century. He worked underground about fifty-two hours per week. His pay was based on a per-ton rate, but the checking of this tonnage was done by company personnel who often counted 2600 to 3000 pounds per ton. His pay averaged 20 cents an hour. The mine was not unionized, and Martin knew from the talk of other miners that union men would be quickly discharged by the company. One night Martin was visited at home by a United Mine Workers representative who said he was trying to organize the mines so that the West Virginia miners could have the same pay and working conditions as in the mines in Ohio and Illinois. Martin agreed to join the union, but on condition that this be kept quiet. Later his superintendent asked if he had joined and he said, "No," for fear of discharge. "Any union man will be fired on the spot," the superintendent told him.

In 1906, the miners struck for recognition of their union. Martin struck with them. The strike included bloody battles between the miners and private police employed by the mine operators. An injunction was finally issued against the strike and it collapsed. Martin was not allowed to return to work. A mine superintendent told him, "No damned union man is going to work here again." Martin could not find employment in any of the other mines in the area. For ten years, he did odd jobs in the West Virginia coal towns. When World War I created increased demand for coal, he was able to get back into the mines. The struggle for unionization was about where he had left it. He now worked at a rate which produced 38 cents per hour. In Illinois, the UMW had secured some safety provisions, and in the Pennsylvania, Ohio, and Illinois fields the miners had hired their own checkweigh men. Martin worked in the mines until 1923, witnessing renewed but abortive attempts at union organization efforts by the UMW. In 1923, he began to cough seriously, and was diagnosed as having silicosis. He went to a lawyer who told him to get out of the mine for his health's sake, but to forget about suing the mine operators for whom he had worked. "First of all, there may be no common law liability for occupational diseases. Secondly, if there is any such liability, it is based on negligence, and the owner is not negligent if dust is one of the ordinary risks of mining, and thirdly, you knew this might happen when you went into the mines, so you cannot recover." Martin asked the lawyer about workmen's compensation, and was told that it did not cover occupational diseases.

Martin left the mines again. During the depression which began in 1929, he was among the 25 per cent of the national labor force which was unemployed. In 1933, United Mine Workers' organizers flooded West Virginia, and successfully unionized the mines in a short period of time. In 1936, his silicosis arrested, Martin returned to the mines. His average hourly rate was now 80 cents. From then until his retirement in late 1953, Martin worked under mining conditions which constantly improved. His hourly wage was $1.16 in 1946, $1.55 in 1950, and $1.88 in 1953. During World War II, Martin watched his union leader, John L. Lewis, defy government orders designed to continue coal production without wage increases which might upset the national economy.

At the end of World War II, the first fruits of union concern for older workers emerged from negotiations between Lewis and the government, which was then operating the mines. The negotiations established a health, welfare, and pension program, to be financed by a royalty payment of 5 cents per ton on each ton of coal mined. This rate was increased to 40 cents per ton by 1952. From the fund thus developed, pensions would be paid and a system of hospitals would be established in the coal-producing regions of the country.

The union, which had never opposed the introduction of costly mechanical and automatic devices in the industry, watched as the increased capital cost of coal production meant that the number of miners decreased, the productivity of the remaining miners increased, and the level of coal production remained nearly constant. As a part of this process, Martin retired in late 1953, and then had some difficulty collecting his pension when the trustees changed the eligibility requirements.

The wave of retirements had made room in the coal industry for Martin's son, Harry, who began to work in the mines when he returned from military service in 1946. His future as a miner was precarious, however, and with the advent of another type of automatic equipment he was finally laid off in 1955. He sought employment elsewhere in the mines, living on his unemployment compensation. This expired after twenty-six weeks. Harry then took odd jobs. But jobs were scarce, and he finally had to seek welfare assistance. In the early 1960's, Harry heard of some government plans to revitalize the Appalachian region, but he saw nothing of this. In 1960, both he and his now ailing aged father were notified that men unemployed for more than one year could no longer have free UMW hospital services because the royalties, now up to 40 cents per ton, were not sufficient to support the hospital program. Later, he heard that the hospital chain had been transferred to the Presbyterian Church. Also, in 1960, his father received word that the pension benefits he had been receiving would be reduced from $100 to $75 per month.

B. The Legal Background Concerning the Organization of Workers

1. *Union Organization and the Common Law*

a. THE NATURE OF THE "FREEDOM" TO ORGANIZE

HITCHMAN COAL & COKE CO. v. MITCHELL

Supreme Court of the United States, 1917
245 U.S. 229, 38 Sup. Ct. 65, 62 L. Ed. 260

MR. JUSTICE PITNEY delivered the opinion of the court.

This was a suit in equity, commenced October 24, 1907, in the United States Circuit (afterwards District) Court for the Northern District of West Virginia, by the Hitchman Coal & Coke Company, a corporation organized under the laws of the State of West Virginia, against certain citizens of the State of Ohio, sued individually and also as officers of the United Mine Workers of America. . . .

Plaintiff owns about 5,000 acres of coal lands situate at or near Benwood, in Marshall County, West Virginia, and within what is known as the "Pan Handle District" of that State, and operates a coal mine thereon, employing between 200 and 300 men, and having an annual output, in and before 1907, of about 300,000 tons. At the time of the filing of the bill, and for a considerable time before and ever since, it operated its mine "non-union," under an agreement with its men to the effect that the mine should be run on a non-union basis, that the employees should not become connected with the Union while employed by plaintiff, and that if they joined it their employment with plaintiff should cease. The bill set forth these facts, inter alia, alleged that they were known to defendants and each of them, and "that the said defendants have unlawfully and maliciously agreed together, confederated, combined and formed themselves into a conspiracy, the purpose of which they are proceeding to carry out and are now about to finally accomplish, namely: to cause your orator's mine to be shut down, its plant to remain idle, its contracts to be broken and unfulfilled, until such time as your orator shall submit to the demand of the Union that it shall unionize its plant, and having submitted to such demand unionize its plant by employing only union men who shall become subject to the orders of the Union," etc. The general object of the bill was to obtain an injunction to restrain defendants from interfering with the relations existing between plaintiff and its employees in order to compel plaintiff to "unionize" the mine.

A restraining order having been granted, followed by a temporary injunction, the served defendants filed answers, and thereupon made a motion to modify the injunction, which was refused. 172 Fed. Rep. 963. An appeal taken by defendants from this order was dismissed by the Circuit Court of Appeals. 176 Fed. Rep. 549. . . .

The District Court based its decision upon two grounds: (1) That the organization known as the United Mine Workers of America, and its branches, as conducted and managed at the time of the suit and for many years before, was a common-law conspiracy in unreasonable restraint of trade, and also and especially a conspiracy against the rights of non-union miners in West Virginia; and (2) That the defendants, in an effort to compel the plaintiff to enter into contractual relations with the Union relating to the employment of labor and the production of coal, although having knowledge of express contracts existing between plaintiff and its employees which excluded relations with the Union, endeavored by unlawful means to procure a breach of these contracts by the employees.

A brief recital of previous transactions between the parties becomes material. The Union is a voluntary and unincorporated association which was organized in the year 1890 in the States of Ohio and Indiana, and afterwards was extended to other States. . . .

From 1897 to 1906 what were known as joint interstate conferences were held annually or biennially between officials of the Union and representatives of the operators in the "Central Competitive Field" (which includes Western Pennsylvania, Ohio, Indiana, and Illinois, but not West Virginia), for the purpose of agreeing upon the scale of wages and the conditions of employment in that field. In addition there were occasional conferences of the same character affecting other States and districts.

Plaintiff's mine is within the territorial limits of Sub-district No. 5 of District No. 6. Coal-mining operations were commenced there in the early part of the year 1902, and the mine was operated "non-union" until April, 1903, when, under threats from the Union officials, including defendants Watkins and Sullivan, that a certain unionized mine in Ohio, owned by the same proprietors, would be closed down if the men at the Hitchman were not allowed to organize, plaintiff consented to the unionization of the latter mine. This went into effect on the 1st of April, 1903, and upon the very next day the men were called out on strike because of a disagreement with the company as to the basis upon which mining should be paid for.

[The strike was settled in May, after Hitchman had been placed under financial pressures because it could not supply coal to the Baltimore & Ohio Railroad. In the spring of 1904, there was another strike over wages. Thereafter, there was no further difficulty until March, 1906, when the agreement between the UMW and the operators in the Central Competitive Field expired. The Hitchman contract expired at the same time. Strikes ensued throughout the bituminous coal region. The Hitchman mine operated for a while under a temporary agreement which continued the old wage scale, but provided that any increases which were later agreed upon would be made retroactive. On April 15, 1906, a Vice President of the sub-district of the union came to the mine and called the workers out on strike.]

About the 1st of June a self-appointed committee of employees called upon plaintiff's president, stated in substance that they could not remain longer on strike because they were not receiving benefits from the Union, and asked upon what terms they could return to work. They were told that they could come back, but not as members of the United Mine Workers of America; that thenceforward the mine would be run non-union, and the company would deal with each man individually. They assented to this, and returned to work on a non-union basis. Mr. Pickett, the mine superintendent, had charge of employing the men, then and afterwards, and to each one who applied for employment he explained the conditions, which were that while the company paid the wages demanded by the Union and as much as anybody else, the mine was run non-union and would continue so to run; that the company would not recognize the United Mine Workers of America; that if any man wanted to become a member of that union he was at liberty to do so; but he could not be a member of it and remain in the employ of the Hitchman Company; that if he worked for the company he would have to work as a non-union man. To this each man employed gave his assent, understanding that while he worked for the company he must keep out of the Union.

Since January, 1908 (after the commencement of the suit), in addition to having this verbal understanding, each man has been required to sign an employment card expressing in substance the same terms. This has neither enlarged nor diminished plaintiff's rights, the agreement not being such as is required by law to be in writing.

Under this arrangement as to the terms of employment, plaintiff operated its mine from June 12, 1906, until the commencement of the suit in the fall of the following year. . . .

In fact, all coal mines in the Panhandle and elsewhere in West Virginia, except in a small district known as the Kanawha field, were run "non-union," while the entire industry in Ohio, Indiana, and Illinois was operated on the "closed-shop" basis, so that no man could hold a job about the mines unless he was a member of the United Mine Workers of America. Pennsylvania occupied a middle ground, only a part of it being under the jurisdiction of the Union. Other States need not be particularly mentioned.

The unorganized conditions of the mines in the Panhandle and some other districts was recognized as a serious interference with the purposes of the Union in the Central Competitive Field, particularly as it tended to keep the cost of production low, and, through competition with coal produced in the organized field, rendered it more difficult for the operators there to maintain prices high enough to induce them to grant certain concessions demanded by the Union. This was the subject of earnest and protracted discussion in the annual international convention of the U.M.W.A. held at Indianapolis, Indiana, in the month of January, 1907, . . .

[Reports made to the convention disclosed that some 400,000 miners had struck, that district settlements, rather than an over-all industry settlement, had been entered into, and that the membership of the UMW had suffered a major decline.]

. . . In the course of the discussion the purpose of organizing West Virginia in the interest of the unionized mine workers in the Central Competitive Field, and the probability that it could be organized only by means of strikes, were repeatedly declared and were disputed by nobody. All who spoke advocated strikes, differing only as to whether these should be nation-wide or sectional. Defendant Lewis, in his report, recommended an abandonment of the policy of sectional settlements which had been pursued in the previous year. This recommendation, interpreted as a criticism of the policy pursued under the leadership of President Mitchell in the settlement of the 1906 strike, was the subject of long and earnest debate, in the course of which Lewis said: "When we organize West Virginia, when we organize the unorganized sections of Pennsylvania, we will organize them by a strike movement." And again, towards the close of the debate: "No one has made the statement that we can organize West Virginia without a strike." Defendant Green took part, favoring the view of Mr. Lewis that strikes should be treated nationally instead of sectionally. In the course of his remarks he said: "I say to you, gentlemen, one reason why I opposed the policy that was pursued last year was because over in Ohio we were peculiarly situated. We had West Virginia on the south and Pennsylvania on the east, and after four months of a strike in eastern Ohio we had reached the danger line. We felt keenly the competition from West Virginia, and during the suspension our mines in Ohio chafed under the object lesson they had. They saw West Virginia coal go by, train-load after train-load passing their doors, when they were on strike. This coal supplied the markets that they should have had. There is no disguising the fact, something must be done to remedy this condition. Year after year Ohio has had to go home and strike in some portion of the district to enforce the interstate agreement that was signed up here. . . . I confess here and now, that the overwhelming sentiment in Ohio was that a settlement by sections would not correct the conditions we complained of. Now, something must be done; it is absolutely necessary to protect us against the competition that comes from the unorganized fields east of us." Mr. Mitchell opposed the view of defendant Lewis, reiterating an opinion, repeatedly expressed before, that West Virginia and the other unorganized fields, "would not be thoroughly organized except as the result of a successful strike"; but declaring that "they will not be organized at all, strike or no strike, unless we are able to support the men in those fields from the first day they lay down their tools. . . .

The discussion continued during three days, and at the end of it the report of a committee which expressed disagreement with Vice President Lewis' opposition to sectional settlements and recommended "a continuation in the future of the same wise, conservative business-like policies" that had been pursued by President Mitchell, was adopted by a viva voce vote.

The plain effect of this action was to approve a policy which, as applied to the concrete case, meant that in order to relieve the union miners of Ohio, Indiana, and Illinois from the competition of the cheaper product of the non-union mines of West Virginia, the West Virginia mines should be "organized" by means of strikes local to West Virginia, the strike benefits to be paid by assessments upon the union miners in the other States mentioned, while they remained at work.

[Following the convention, Hughes, a union organizer, was sent into the panhandle of West Virginia to conduct an organizing campaign at the Hitchman and neighboring mines, Glendale and Richland.]

The evidence shows that he had distinct and timely notice that membership in the Union was inconsistent with the terms of employment at all three mines, and a violation of the express provisions of the agreement at the Hitchman and Glendale.

Having unsuccessfully applied to Koch and McKinley [company managers] for their cooperation, Hughes proceeded to interview as many of the men as he could reach and to hold public meetings in the interest of the Union. There is clear and uncontradicted evidence that he did not confine himself to mere persuasion, but resorted to deception and abuse. In his public speeches he employed abusive language respecting Mr. Pickett, William Daugherty, and Jim Jarrett.[1] He prophesied, in such a way that ignorant, foreign-born miners, such as he was addressing, naturally might believe him to be speaking with knowledge, that the wages paid by the Hitchman would be reduced unless the mine was unionized. The evidence as to the methods he employed in personally interviewing the miners, while meagre, is significant. Myers, a Hitchman miner, testified: "He told me that he was a good friend of Mr. Koch, and that Mr. Koch had nothing against having the place organized again. He said he was a friend of his, and I made the remark that I would ask Mr. Koch and see if it was so; and he said no, that was of no use because he was telling me the truth." He did not confine his attentions to men who already were in plaintiff's employ, but in addition dissuaded men who had accepted employment from going to work.

A highly significant thing, giving character to Hughes' entire course of conduct, is that while his solicitation of the men was more or less public, as necessarily it had to be, he was careful to keep secret the number and the names of those who agreed to join the Union. . . . Pickett, the mine superintendent, had learned of only five men at the Glendale who were inclined to join Hughes' movement; but when these were asked to remain outside of the mine for a talk, fifteen other men waited with them,

---

[1] Mr. Pickett was superintendent of the Hitchman and Glendale mines, and it was with him that the miners made their agreements to refrain from membership in the Union; Daugherty and Jarrett were miners at the Hitchman, and had been, respectively, President and Financial Secretary of the local union at the time of the 1906 strike, when the local deserted the U.M.W.A.

and upon being reminded that while the company would not try to prevent them from becoming members of the Union, they could not be members and at the same time work for the Glendale Company, they all accepted this as equivalent to a notice of discharge. And, as has been stated, the owner of the Richland, while repeatedly threatened with unionization, was kept in the dark as to the progress made by the organizer amongst his employees until the mine was actually shut down.

The question whether Hughes had "power or authority" to shut down the Hitchman mine is beside the mark. We are not here concerned with any question of ultra vires, but with an actual threat of closing down plaintiff's mine, made by Hughes while acting as agent of an organized body of men who indubitably were united in a purpose to close it unless plaintiff would conform to their wishes with respect to its management, and who lacked the power to carry out that purpose only because they had not as yet persuaded a sufficient number of the Hitchman miners to join with them, and hence employed Hughes as an "organizer" and sent him to the mine with the very object of securing the support of the necessary number of miners. They succeeded with respect to one of the mines threatened (the Richland), and preparations of like character were in progress at the Hitchman and the Glendale at the time the restraining order was made in this cause.

If there be any practical distinction between organizing the miners and organizing the mine, it has no application to this case. Unionizing the miners is but a step in the process of unionizing the mine, followed by the latter almost as a matter of course. Plaintiff is as much entitled to prevent the first step as the second, so far as its own employees are concerned, and to be protected against irreparable injury resulting from either. . . .

In short, at the time the bill was filed, defendants, although having full notice of the terms of employment existing between plaintiff and its miners, were engaged in an earnest effort to subvert those relations without plaintiff's consent, and to alienate a sufficient number of the men to shut down the mine, to the end that the fear of losses through stoppage of operations might coerce plaintiff into "recognizing the union" at the cost of its own independence. . . .

What are the legal consequences of the facts that have been detailed?

That the plaintiff was acting within its lawful rights in employing its men only upon terms of continuing non-membership in the United Mine Workers of America is not open to question. Plaintiff's repeated costly experiences of strikes and other interferences while attempting to "run union" were a sufficient explanation of its resolve to run "non-union," if any were needed. But neither explanation nor justification is needed. Whatever may be the advantages of "collective bargaining," it is not bargaining at all, in any just sense, unless it is voluntary on both sides. The same liberty which enables men to form unions, and through the union to enter into agreements with employers willing to agree, entitles other men to remain independent of the union and other employers to agree with them to employ no man who owes any allegiance or obligation to the union. In the latter case, as in the former, the parties are entitled to be protected by the law in the enjoyment of the benefits of any lawful agreement they may make. This court repeatedly has held that the employer is as free to make non-membership in a union a condition of employment, as the working man is free to join the union, and that this is a part of the constitutional rights of personal liberty and private property, not to be taken away even by legislation, unless through some proper exercise of the paramount police power. Adair v. United States, 208 U.S. 161, 174; Coppage v. Kansas, 236 U.S. 1, 14. In the present case, needless to say, there is no act of legislation to which defendants may resort for justification.

Plaintiff, having in the exercise of its undoubted rights established a working agreement between it and its employees, with the free assent of the latter, is entitled to be protected in the enjoyment of the resulting status, as in any other legal right. That the employment was "at will," and terminable by either party at any time, is of no consequence. In Truax v. Raich, 239 U.S. 33, 38, this court ruled upon the precise question as follows: "It is said that the bill does not show an employment for a term, and that under an employment at will the complainant could be discharged at any time for any reason or for no reason, the motive of the employer being immaterial. The conclusion, however, that is sought to be drawn is too broad. The fact that the employment is at the will of the parties, respectively, does not make it one at the will of others. The employee has manifest interest in the freedom of the employer to exercise his judgment without illegal interference or compulsion, and, by the weight of authority, the unjustified interference of third persons is actionable although the employment is at will." (Citing many cases.)

In short, plaintiff was and is entitled to the good will of its employees, precisely as a merchant is entitled to the good will of his customers although they are under no obligation to continue to deal with him. The value of the relation lies in the reasonable probability that by properly treating its employees, and paying them fair wages, and avoiding reasonable grounds of complaint, it will be able to retain them in its employ, and to fill vacancies occurring from time to time by the employment of other men on the same terms. The pecuniary value of such reasonable probabilities is incalculably great, and is recognized by the law in a variety of relations. [Citations omitted.]

The right of action for persuading an employee to leave his employer is universally recognized — nowhere more clearly than in West Virginia — and it rests upon fundamental principles of general application, not upon the English statute of laborers. [Citations omitted.]

We turn to the matters set up by way of justification or excuse for defendants' interference with the situation existing at plaintiff's mine.

The case involves no question of the rights of employees. Defendants have no agency for plaintiff's employees, nor do they assert any disagreement or grievance in their behalf. In fact, there is none; but, if there were, defendants could not, without agency, set up any rights that employees might have. The right of the latter to strike would not give to defendants the right to instigate a strike. The difference is fundamental.

It is suggested as a ground of criticism that plaintiff endeavored to secure a closed non-union mine through individual agreements with its employees, as if this furnished some sort of excuse for the employment of coercive measures to secure a closed union shop through a collective agreement with the Union. It is a sufficient answer, in law, to repeat that plaintiff had a legal and constitutional right to exclude union men from its employ. But it may be worth while to say, in addition: first, that there was no middle ground open to plaintiff; no option to have an "open shop" employing union men and non-union men indifferently; it was the Union that insisted upon closed-shop agreements, requiring even carpenters employed about a mine to be members of the Union, and making the employment of any non union man a ground for a strike; and secondly, plaintiff was in the reasonable exercise of its rights in excluding all union men from its employ, having learned, from a previous experience, that unless this were done union organizers might gain access to its mine in the guise of laborers.

Defendants set up, by way of justification or excuse, the right of workingmen to form unions, and to enlarge their membership by inviting other workingmen to join. The right is freely conceded, provided the objects of the union be proper and legitimate, which we assume to be true, in a general sense, with respect to the Union here in question. Gompers v. Bucks Stove & Range Co., 221 U.S. 418, 439. The cardinal error of defendants' position lies in the assumption that the right is so absolute that it may be exercised under any circumstances and without any qualification; whereas in truth, like other rights that exist in civilized society, it must always be exercised with reasonable regard for the conflicting rights of others. Brennan v. United Hatters, 73 N.J.L. 729, 749. . . .

Now, assuming defendants were exercising, through Hughes, the right to invite men to join their Union, still they had plain notice that plaintiff's mine was run "non-union," that none of the men had a right to remain at work there after joining the Union, and that the observance of this agreement was of great importance and value both to plaintiff and to its men who had voluntarily made the agreement and desired to continue working under it. Yet defendants, far from exercising any care to refrain from unnecessarily injuring plaintiff, deliberately and advisedly selected that method of enlarging their membership which would inflict the greatest injury upon plaintiff and its loyal employees. Every Hitchman miner who joined Hughes' "secret order" and permitted his name to be entered upon Hughes' list was guilty of a breach of his contract of employment and acted a lie whenever thereafter he entered plaintiff's mine to work. Hughes not only connived at this, but must be deemed to have caused and procured it, for it was the main feature of defendants' plan, the sine qua non of their programme. Evidently it was deemed to be necessary, in order to "organize the Panhandle by a strike movement," that at the Hitchman, for example, man after man should be persuaded to join the Union, and having done so to remain at work, keeping the employer in ignorance of their number and identity, until so many had joined that by stopping work in a body they could coerce the employer and the remaining miners to "organize the mine," that is, to make an agreement that none but members of the Union should be employed, that terms of employment should be determined by negotiation not with the employees but with union officers — perhaps residents of other States and employees of competing mines — and that all question in controversy between the mine operator and the miners should likewise be settled with outsiders.

True, it is suggested that under the existing contract an employee was not called upon to leave plaintiff's employ until he actually joined the Union, and that the evidence shows only an attempt by Hughes to induce the men to *agree* to join, but no attempt to induce them to violate their contract by failing to withdraw from plaintiff's employment after *actually joining.* . . .

But the facts render it plain that what the defendants were endeavoring to do at the Hitchman mine and neighboring mines cannot be treated as a bona fide effort to enlarge the membership of the Union. There is no evidence to show, nor can it be inferred, that defendants intended or desired to have the men at these mines join the Union, *unless they could organize the mines.* Without this, the new members would be added to the number of men competing for jobs in the organized districts, while non-union men would take their places in the Panhandle mines. Except as a means to the end of compelling the owners of these mines to change their method of operation, the defendants were not seeking to enlarge the union membership.

In any aspect of the matter, it cannot be said that defendants were pursuing their object by *lawful* means. The question of their intentions — of their bona fides — cannot be ignored. It enters into the question of malice. As Bowen, L.J., justly said, in the Mogul Steamship Case, 23 Q.B. Div. 613, "Intentionally to do that which is calculated in the ordinary course of events to damage, and which does, in fact, damage another in that other person's property or trade, is actionable if done without just cause or excuse." And the intentional infliction of such damage upon another, without justification or excuse, is malicious in law. [Citations omitted.] Of course, in a court of equity, when passing upon the right of injunction, damage threatened, irremediable by action at law, is equivalent to damage done. And we cannot deem the proffered excuse to be a *"just* cause or excuse," where it is based, as in this case, upon an assertion of conflicting rights that are sought to be attained by unfair methods, and for the very purpose of interfering with plaintiff's rights, of which defendants have full notice.

Another fundamental error in defendants' position consists in the assumption that all measures that may be resorted to are lawful if they are "peaceable" — that is, if they stop short of physical violence, or coercion through fear of it. In our opinion, any violation of plaintiff's legal rights contrived by defendants for the purpose of inflicting damage, or having that as its necessary effect, is as plainly inhibited by the law as if it involved a breach of the peace. A combination to procure concerted breaches of contract by plaintiff's employees constitutes such a violation. [Citations omitted.]

The present is not a case of merely withholding from an employer an economic need — as a supply of labor — until he assents to be governed by union regulations. Defendants have no supply of labor of which plaintiff stands in need. By the statement of defendant Lewis himself, made in his formal report to the Indianapolis convention of 1907, out of more than 370,000 coal miners in the States of Pennsylvania, Maryland, Virginia, and West Virginia, less than 80,000 (about 22 per cent.) were members of the Union. Considering the Panhandle separately, doubtless the proportion was even smaller, and the supply of non-union labor ample. There is no reason to doubt that if defendants had been actuated by a genuine desire to increase the membership of the Union without unnecessary injury to the known rights of plaintiff, they would have permitted their proselytes to withdraw from plaintiff's employ when and as they became affiliated with the Union — as their contract of employment required them to do — and that in this event plaintiff would have been able to secure an adequate supply of non-union men to take their places. It was with knowledge of this, and because of it, that defendants, through Hughes as their agent, caused the new members to remain at work in plaintiff's mine until a sufficient number of men should be persuaded to join so as to bring about a strike and render it difficult if not practically impossible for plaintiff to continue to exercise its undoubted legal and constitutional right to run its mine "non-union."

It was one thing for plaintiff to find, from time to time, comparatively small numbers of men to take vacant places in a going mine, another and a much more difficult thing to find a complete gang of new men to start up a mine shut down by a strike, when there might be a reasonable apprehension of violence at the hands of the strikers and their sympathizers. The disordered condition of a mining town in time of strike is matter of common knowledge. It was this kind of intimidation, as well as that resulting from the large organized membership of the Union, that defendants sought to exert upon plaintiff, . . .

Defendants' acts cannot be justified by any analogy to competition in trade. They are not competitors of plaintiff; and if they were their conduct exceeds the bounds of fair trade. Certainly, if a competing trader should endeavor to draw custom from his rival, not by offering better or cheaper goods, employing more competent salesmen, or displaying more attractive advertisements, but by persuading the rival's clerks to desert him under circumstances rendering it difficult or embarrassing for him to fill their places, any court of equity would grant an injunction to restrain this as unfair competition.

Upon all the facts, we are constrained to hold that the purpose entertained by defendants to bring about a strike at plaintiff's mine in order to compel plaintiff, through fear of financial loss, to consent to the unionization of the mine as the lesser evil, was an unlawful purpose, and that the methods resorted to by Hughes — the inducing of employees to unite with the Union in an effort to subvert the system of employment at the mine by concerted breaches of the contracts of employment known to be in force there, not to mention misrepresentation, deceptive statements, and threats of pecuniary loss communicated by Hughes to the men — were unlawful and malicious methods, and not to be justified as a fair exercise of the right to increase the membership of the Union. . . .

Respecting the sweep of the injunction, we differ somewhat from the result reached by the District Court.

So far as it restrains — (1) Interfering or attempting to interfere with plaintiff's employees for the purpose of unionizing plaintiff's mine without its consent, by representing or causing to be represented to any of plaintiff's employees, or to any person who might become an employee of plaintiff, that such person will suffer or is likely to suffer some loss or trouble in continuing in or in entering the employment of plaintiff, by reason of plaintiff not recognizing the Union, or because plaintiff runs a non-union mine; (2) Interfering or attempting to interfere with plaintiff's employees for the purpose of unionizing the mine without plaintiff's consent, and in aid of such purpose knowingly and wilfully bringing about the breaking by plaintiff's employees of contracts of service known at the time to exist with plaintiff's present and future employees; (3) Knowingly and wilfully enticing plaintiff's employees, present or future, to leave plaintiff's service on the ground that plaintiff does not recognize the United Mine Workers of America or runs a non-union mine, etc.; (4) Interfering or attempting to interfere with plaintiff's employees so as knowingly and wilfully to bring about the breaking by plaintiff's employees, present and future, of their contracts of service, known to the defendants to exist, and especially from knowingly and wilfully enticing such employees, present or future, to leave plaintiff's service without plaintiff's consent; (5) Trespassing on or entering upon the grounds and premises of plaintiff or its mine for the purpose of interfering therewith or hindering or obstructing its business, or with the purpose of compelling or inducing, by threats, intimidation, violent or abusive language, or persuasion, any of plaintiff's employees to refuse or fail to perform their duties as such; and (6) Compelling or inducing or attempting to compel or induce, by threats, intimidation, or abusive or violent language, any of plaintiff's employees to leave its service or fail or refuse to perform their duties as such employees, or compelling or attempting to compel by like means any person desiring to seek employment in plaintiff's mine and works from so accepting employment therein; — the decree is fully supported by the proofs. But it goes further, and awards an injunction against picketing and against acts of physical violence, and we find no evidence that either of these forms of interference was threatened. The decree should be modified by eliminating picketing and physical violence from the sweep of the injunction. . . .

MR. JUSTICE BRANDEIS, dissenting. . . .

First: The alleged illegality of the United Mine Workers of America under the law of West Virginia.

The United Mine Workers of America does not appear to differ essentially in character and purpose from other international unions which, like it, are affiliated with the American Federation of Labor. Its membership is said to be larger than that of any other; and it may be more powerful. But the common law does not limit the size of unions or the degree to which individual workmen may by union increase their bargaining power. As stated in Gompers v. Bucks Stove & Range Co., 221 U.S. 418, 439: "The law, therefore, recognizes the right of workingmen to unite and to invite others to join their ranks, thereby making available the strength, influence and power that come from such association." We do not find either in the decisions or the statutes of West Virginia anything inconsistent with the law as declared by this court. The union is not an unlawful organization, and is not in itself an unlawful conspiracy. We have no occasion to consider the legality of the specific provisions contained in its constitution or by-laws. . . .

Second: The alleged illegality of the United Mine Workers of America under the Federal Anti-Trust Act. . . .

Third: The alleged conspiracy against the West Virginia Mines.

It was doubtless the desire of the United Mine Workers to unionize every mine on the American continent and especially those in West Virginia which compete directly with the mines of Western Pennsylvania, Ohio, Indiana, and other States already unionized. That desire and the purpose to effect it were not unlawful. They were part of a reasonable effort to improve the condition of workingmen engaged in the industry by strengthening their bargaining power through unions; and extending the field of union power. No conspiracy to shut down or otherwise injure West Virginia was proved, nor was there any averment in the bill of such conspiracy, or any issue otherwise raised by the pleadings which justified the consideration of that question by the District Court.

Fourth: "Unionizing plaintiff's mine without plaintiff's consent."

The fundamental prohibition of the injunction is against acts done "for the purpose of unionizing plaintiff's mine without plaintiff's consent." Unionizing a shop does not mean inducing the employees to become members of the union. It means inducing the employer to enter into a collective agreement with the union governing the relations of the employer to the employees. Unionizing implies, therefore, at least *formal* consent of the employer. Both plaintiff and defendants insisted upon exercising the right to secure contracts for a closed shop. The plaintiff sought to secure the *closed non-union shop* through individual agreements with employees. The defendants sought to secure the *closed union shop* through a collective agreement with the union. Since collective bargaining is legal, the fact that the workingmen's agreement is made not by individuals directly with the employer, but by the employees with the union and by it, on their behalf, with the employer, is of no significance in this connection. The end being *lawful,* defendant's efforts to unionize the mine can be illegal, only if the methods or means pursued were unlawful; unless indeed there is some special significance in the expression "unionizing without plaintiff's consent."

It is urged that a union agreement curtails the liberty of the operator. Every agreement curtails the liberty of those who enter into it. The test of legality is not whether an agreement curtails liberty, but whether the parties have agreed upon some thing which the law prohibits or declares otherwise to be inconsistent with the public welfare. The operator by the union agreement binds himself: (1) to employ only members of the union; (2) to negotiate with union officers instead of with employees individually the scale of wages and the hours of work; (3) to treat with the duly constituted representatives of the union to settle disputes concerning the discharge of men and other controversies arising out of the employment. These are the chief features of a "unionizing" by which the employer's liberty is curtailed. Each of them is legal. To obtain any of them or all of them men may lawfully strive and even strike. And, if the union may legally strike to obtain each of the things for which the agreement provides, why may it not strike or use equivalent economic pressure to secure an agreement to provide them?

It is also urged that defendants are seeking to "coerce" plaintiff to "unionize" its mine. But coercion, in a legal sense, is not exerted when a union merely endeavors to induce employees to join a union with the intention thereafter to order a strike unless the employer consents to unionize his shop. Such pressure is not coercion in a legal sense. The employer is free either to accept the agreement or the disadvantage. Indeed, the plaintiff's whole case is rested upon agreements secured under similar pressure of economic necessity or disadvantage. If it is coercion to threaten to strike unless plaintiff consents to a closed union shop, it is coercion also to threaten not to give one employment unless the applicant will consent to a closed non-union shop. The employer may sign the union agreement for fear that *labor* may not be otherwise obtainable; the workman may sign the individual agreement for fear that *employment* may not be otherwise obtainable. But such fear does not imply coercion in a legal sense.

In other words an employer, in order to effectuate the closing of his shop to *union* labor, may exact an agreement to that effect from his employees. The agreement itself being a lawful one, the employer may withhold from the men an economic need — employment — until they assent to make it. Likewise an agreement closing a shop to *non-union* labor being lawful, the union may withhold from an employer an economic need — labor — until he assents to make it. In a legal sense an agreement entered into, under such circumstances, is voluntarily entered into; and as the agreement is in itself legal, no reason appears why the general rule that a legal end may be pursued by legal means should not be applied. Or, putting it in other words, there is nothing in the character of the agreement which should make *unlawful* means used to attain it, which in other connections are recognized as *lawful.*

Fifth: There was no attempt to induce employees to violate their contracts.

The contract created an employment at will; and the employee was free to leave at any time. The contract did not bind the employee *not* to join the union; and he was free to join it at any time. The contract merely bound him to withdraw from plaintiff's employ, if he joined the union. There is evidence of an attempt to induce plaintiff's employees to *agree* to join the union; but none whatever of any attempt to induce them to violate their contract. Until an employee actually joined the union he was not, under the contract, called upon to leave plaintiff's employ. There consequently would be no breach of contract until the employee both joined the union *and* failed to withdraw from plaintiff's employ. There was no evidence that any employee was persuaded to do that or that such a course was contemplated. What perhaps was intended was to secure agreements or assurances from individual employees that they would join the union when a large number of them should have consented to do so; with the purpose, when such time arrived, to have them join the union together and strike — unless plaintiff consented to unionize the mine. Such a course would have been clearly permissible under the contract.

Sixth: Merely persuading employees to leave plaintiff's employ or others not to enter it was not unlawful.

To induce third persons to leave an employment is actionable if done maliciously and without justifiable cause although such persons are free to leave at their own will. Truax v. Raich, 239 U.S. 33, 38; Thacker Coal Co. v. Burke, 59 W. Va. 253. It is equally actionable so to induce others not to enter the service. The individual contracts of plaintiff with its employees added nothing to its right in this connection, since the employment was terminable at will.

As persuasion, considered merely as a means, is clearly legal, defendants were within their rights if, and only if, their interference with the relation of plaintiff to its employees was for justifiable cause. The purpose of interfering was confessedly in order to strengthen the union, in the belief that thereby the condition of workmen engaged in mining would be improved; the bargaining power of the individual workingman was to be strengthened by collective bargaining; and collective bargaining was to be ensured by obtaining the union agreement. It should not, at this day, be doubted that to induce workingmen to leave or not to enter an employment in order to advance such a purpose is justifiable when the workmen are not bound by contract to remain in such employment. . . .

MR. JUSTICE HOLMES and MR. JUSTICE CLARKE concur in this dissent.

b.   THE CRIMINAL CONSPIRACY DOCTRINE

The first recorded "labor relations" case in this country was one in which a group of journeymen shoemakers in Philadelphia were indicted, convicted, and fined $8 each when they "did combine, conspire and con-

federate, and unlawfully agree together . . . that they . . . would not
. . . work . . . but at certain large prices and rates," Philadelphia Cordwainers' Case of 1806 (Commonwealth v. Pullis, Phila. Mayor's Court), 3
Commons and Gilmore, A Documentary History of American Industrial
Society 59-248 (1910). The pattern which was developed here, involving
the identification of the most common activity of employee groups as a
"criminal conspiracy," was followed in eight of the ten similar cases which
arose during the next twenty years in Pennsylvania, Maryland, New York,
and Massachusetts. See Nelles, Commonwealth v. Hunt, 32 Colum. L.
Rev. 1128, 1166 (1932).

In the charge which Moses Levy, one of the judges of the Mayor's
Court in Philadelphia and its Recorder, made to the jury in the Cord-
wainers' Case he summed up "the law" as follows (3 Commons and
Gilmore at 228-233):

"It is proper to consider, is such a combination consistent with the principles of our law, and injurious to the public welfare? The usual means
by which the prices of work are regulated, are the demand for the article
and the excellence of its fabric. Where the work is well done, and the demand is considerable, the prices will necessarily be high. Where the work
is ill done, and the demand is inconsiderable, they will unquestionably be
low. . . . To make an artificial regulation, is not to regard the excellence
of the work or quality of the material, but to fix a positive and arbitrary
price, governed by no standard, controlled by no impartial person, but
dependent on the will of the few who are interested; this is the unnatural
way of raising the price of goods or work. . . . It is an unnatural, artificial means of raising the price of work beyond its standard, and taking an
undue advantage of the public. Is the rule of law bottomed upon such
principles, as to permit or protect such conduct? Consider it on the footing of the general commerce of the city. Is there any man who can calcu-
late (if this is tolerated) at what price he may safely contract to deliver
articles, for which he may receive orders, if he is to be regulated by the
journeymen in an arbitrary jump from one price to another? . . . Can he
fix the price of his commodity for a future day? It is impossible that any
man can carry on commerce in this way. There cannot be a large contract entered into, but what the contractor will make at his peril. He
may be ruined by the difference of prices made by the journeymen in
the intermediate time. . . . Consider these circumstances as they affect
trade generally. Does this measure tend to make good workmen? No:
it puts the botch incapable of doing justice to his work, on a level with
the best tradesman. The master must give the same wages to each.
Such a practice would take away all the excitement to excel in workman-
ship or industry. Consider the effect it would have upon the whole community. If the masters say they will not sell under certain prices, as the
journeymen declare they will not work at certain wages, they, if persisted
in, would put the whole body of the people into their power. Shoes and
boots are articles of the first necessity. If they could stand out three or
four weeks in winter, they might raise the price of boots to thirty, forty,
or fifty dollars a pair, at least for some time, and until a competent supply

could be got from other places. In every point of view, this measure is pregnant with public mischief and private injury . . . tends to demoralize the workmen . . . destroy the trade of the city, and leaves the pockets of the whole community to the discretion of the concerned. . . .

"It is in the volumes of the common law we are to seek for information in the far greater number, as well as the most important causes that come before our tribunals. . . . It says there may be cases in which what one man may do with [out] offence, many combined may not do with impunity. It distinguishes between the object so aimed at in different transactions. If the purpose to be obtained, be an object of individual interest, it may be fairly attempted by an individual . . . Many are prohibited from combining for the attainment of it.

"What is the case now before us? . . . A combination of workmen to raise their wages may be considered in a two fold point of view: one is to benefit themselves . . . the other is to injure those who do not join their society. The rule of law condemns both. If the rule be clear, we are bound to conform to it even though we do not comprehend the principle upon which it is founded. We are not to reject it because we do not see the reason of it. It is enough, that it is the will of the majority. It is law because it is their will — if it is law, there may be good reasons for it though we cannot find them out. But the rule in this case is pregnant with sound sense and all the authorities are clear upon the subject. Hawkins, the greatest authority on the criminal law, has laid it down, that a combination to maintaining one another, carrying a particular object, whether true or false, is criminal. . . ."

The historical development of the criminal conspiracy doctrine is traced in Landis and Manoff, Cases on Labor Law, c. 1 (1942).

Another factor in the evolution of the criminal conspiracy doctrine was suggested in People v. Faulkner, 4 Commons and Gilmore, A Documentary History of American Industrial Society 315 et seq. (1910), decided in the court of Oyer and Terminer of New York City in 1836. Tailors had struck first for wages and then (after they had received substantial increases) for a kind of seniority system. Highhanded tactics were used against employers of "dungs," tailors who took work when more senior tailors were without jobs. The trial was on an indictment for conspiring to injure trade and commerce (based on a New York statute) and was apparently not based on another indictment for "riot, and assault and battery." The result in the case was virtually certain in view of the conviction a year earlier of a group of bootmakers who had engaged in similar tactics. People v. Fisher, 14 Wend. 9 (N.Y. 1835). The tailors were convicted of conspiracy. In imposing fines totaling $1150, Judge Edwards addressed the tailors at length, in part as follows (4 Commons and Gilmore at 330-331):

"Associations of this description are of recent origin in this country. Here, where the government is purely paternal, where the people are governed by laws of their own creating; where the legislature proceeds with a watchful regard to the welfare not only of the whole, but of every class of society; where the representatives ever lend a listening ear to the complaints of their constituents, it has not been found necessary or proper to subject any portion of the people to the control of self-created societies. Judging from what we have witnessed within the last year, we should be led to the conclusion that the trades of the country, which contribute immeasurably to its wealth, and upon which the prosperity of a most valuable portion of the community hinges, [are] rapidly passing from the control of the supreme power of the state into the hands of private societies. . . . Every American knows, or ought to know, that he has no better friend than the laws, and that he needs no artificial combination for his protection. . . . They [the "private societies" of the journeymen groups] are of foreign origin, and I am led to believe are mainly upheld by foreigners. . . .

"Self-created societies are unknown to the constitution and laws, and will not be permitted to rear their crest and extend their baneful influence over any portion of the community."

Judge Edwards' suggestion that private group activity constituted an improper intrusion into the relationship between the individual and the state denied the principle of pluralism which has since become a commonplace explanation for certain aspects of American government. See, for example, Horn, Groups and the Constitution (1956); Kariel, The Decline of American Pluralism (1961); Miller, Private Governments and the Constitution (1959); Prestus, The Organizational Society (1962); Blumrosen, Group Interests in Labor Law, 13 Rutgers L. Rev. 432 (1959); Friedman, Corporate Power, Government by Private Groups and the Law, 57 Colum. L. Rev. 155 (1957); Jaffe, Law Making by Private Groups, 51 Harv. L. Rev. 201 (1937); Wirtz, Government by Private Groups, 13 La. L. Rev. 440 (1953).

Judge Edwards' observation that the union movement of his time was largely supported by "foreigners" was as questionable as his paternalistic view of American government in which the association was not to intervene and mediate between the individual and the state. Alexis de Toqueville was touring America about the time Judge Edwards lectured the tailors. Of the associational life of the nation, he wrote, in his Democracy in America 319 (Oxford ed. 1947):*

"The political associations that exist in the United States are only a single feature in the midst of the immense assemblage of associations in that country. Americans of all ages, all conditions, and all dispositions, constantly form associations. They have not only commercial and manufacturing companies, in which all take part, but associations of a thousand other kinds — religious, moral, serious, futile, extensive or restricted, enormous or diminutive. . . . The English often perform great things singly; whereas the Americans form associations for the smallest undertakings. It is evident that the former people consider associations as a powerful means of action, but the latter seem to regard it as the only means they have of acting.

"Thus the most democratic country on the face of the earth is that in

* Reprinted with permission of the Oxford University Press.

McKUSICK LAW LIBRARY
UNIVERSITY OF SOUTH DAKOTA
VERMILLION, SOUTH DAKOTA

which men have in our time carried to the highest perfection the art of pursuing in common the object of their common desires, and have applied this new science to the greatest number of purposes. Is this the result of accident? or is there in reality any necessary connection between the principle of association and that of equality? Aristocratic communities always contain, among a multitude of persons who by themselves are powerless, a small number of powerful and wealthy citizens, each of whom can achieve great undertakings single-handed. In aristocratic societies men do not need to combine in order to act, because they are strongly held together. . . . Among democratic nations, on the contrary, all the citizens are independent and feeble; they can do hardly anything by themselves, and none of them can oblige his fellow men to lend him their assistance. They all, therefore, fall into a state of incapacity, if they do not learn voluntarily to help each other."

The courts' application of the criminal conspiracy doctrine to early employee group activities eventually aroused a storm of public protest. The people felt that the courts had overreached their authority. The public concern was not limited to working groups; it included also those who voted Federalist, wanted high tariffs, and owned mills and factories which would be closed if labor feeling grew too strong. Labor was already recognized as a strong, if not cohesive, economic and political force.

These were undoubtedly among the considerations which prompted the Supreme Judicial Court of Massachusetts, in 1842, to set aside the conviction (for criminal conspiracy) of seven members of the Boston Journeymen Bootmakers' Society who had indicated that they would refuse to work in shops where nonmembers of the Society were employed at less than the scheduled rate (obtained by the Society in a recent strike) of $2 per pair of boots. Commonwealth v. Hunt, 4 Metc. 111 (1842). The court, while not rejecting the doctrine of criminal conspiracy as being inapplicable to organized employee activity, cut the heart from the old approach by insisting that it was the *purpose* of the concerted action rather than the fact of such concert itself which was important. Chief Justice Shaw wrote (p. 129): "The manifest intention of the association is, to induce all those engaged in the same occupation to become members of it. Such a purpose is not unlawful. It would give them a power which might be exerted for useful and honorable purposes, or for dangerous and pernicious ones. If the latter were the real and actual object, and susceptible of proof, it should have been specially charged. . . . In this state of things, we cannot perceive, that it is criminal for men to agree together to exercise their acknowledged rights, in such a manner as best to subserve their own interests."

In the same volume of the Massachusetts reports, Justice Shaw decided Farwell v. Boston and Worcester Railroad Corp., 4 Metc. 49 (Mass. 1842), adopting the "fellow servant rule," which denied an employee recovery against his employer for injuries caused by the negligence of another employee. This rule and the hardships which it imposed on employees was replaced seventy years later by a series of Workmen's Compensation and Employer Liability Laws. In adopting the fellow servant rule, which had previously been developed in only one English case and accepted in a South Carolina decision, Justice Shaw wrote in terms which seem equally applicable to his decision in Commonwealth v. Hunt (p. 58):

"In considering the rights and obligations arising out of particular relations, it is competent for courts of justice to regard considerations of policy and general convenience, and to draw from them such rules as will, in their practical application, best promote the safety and security of all parties concerned." [1]

Commonwealth v. Hunt foreshadowed the demise of the criminal law prohibitions on union organizing activities. State v. Donaldson, 32 N.J.L. 151 (Sup. Ct. 1867), is one of the last reported cases involving the doctrine. It was repudiated by the New Jersey Legislature in 1883.

C. TORT LIABILITY OF UNIONS

After the Civil War, legality of union action was litigated in tort actions for money damages. The issue raised in these cases concerned the extent to which associations could restrain the operation of the "free market place" by regulating prices, supply of labor, and the terms of employment. The first cases involved a combination of employers. Master Stevedores' Assn. v. Walsh, 2 Daly 1 (N.Y.C.P. 1867), held that an incorporated association of master stevedores (who were the entrepreneurs of that business) could penalize any member of the association who charged less than the association's schedule of prices. The New York Court of Common Pleas declared that, "It is better for the law to leave such matters to the action of the parties interested — to leave master workmen or journeymen free to form what associations they please in relation to the rate of compensation, so long as they are voluntary." The labor cases in the Cordwainers tradition were distinguished as involving coercion of nonmembers of the group.

In Walker v. Cronin, 107 Mass. 555 (1871), a union program of permitting its members (shoemakers) to work only in shops which provided acceptable terms and conditions of employment was held an actionable tort. In this and other cases of the period, the courts developed the principle that organized labor's pressures constitute a "prima facie tort." If there was "intentional infliction of harm" on employers or on nonunion employees, which there invariably was, this was "in itself wrong." But there might be "justifiable cause" shown, and then this was a defense. If the purpose of the "infliction of harm" was the procuring of higher wages, this was an instance of justifiable cause as far as most courts were concerned, and therefore the strike was not tortious but only "com-

---

[1] See Nelles, Commonwealth v. Hunt, 32 Colum. L. Rev. 1128 (1932). See also Gregory, Labor and the Law 27-29 (2d rev. ed. 1958); Schlesinger, The Age of Jackson 339-341 (1945). (This is the first editor's footnote in Part I. Editor's notes are numbered beginning with 1 at the start of each Part. Whenever these notes are keyed into quoted material they are signed Ed. The original numbers have been retained for all notes in quoted material.) — ED.

petition." Some courts felt the same way about action designed to enlarge union membership; others, notably those in Massachusetts, considered such strikes to be "without justification" and therefore a sufficient basis for recovery of damages.

d. ORGANIZED LABOR AND THE EQUITY COURTS

Toward the end of the nineteenth century another phase of judicial participation in the evolution of the employment relationship was initiated. Labor activities which had first been considered as the subject of criminal proceedings, and then as torts, were identified, almost suddenly, as matters enjoinable in the equity courts.

It was only by accident that the courts in this country stumbled into a departure from what had always been the English rule against the issuance of injunctions in labor disputes. It is apparently true that the American practice developed as a by-product of the fact that so many railroads were in receivership in the 1880's and 1890's, under the control of agents of the courts of equity. When the railroad employees struck for something or other, the equity court's traditional weapon was turned on them. The technique worked so well and so quickly that it was almost immediately applied to strikes at plants where the equity court had no interest until the strike broke.

In Vegelahn v. Guntner, 167 Mass. 92 (1896), the Massachusetts court issued an injunction against any kind of picketing by a union which was seeking only higher wages and shorter hours. These "purposes" were apparently considered legitimate, but the fact that here there was picketing as well as a refusal to work prompted the court to throw its weight on the side of the employer. If there was picketing, the court reasoned, there was bound to be more serious trouble, and it was deemed best to nip it in the bud.

Justice Holmes dissented, noting (pp. 105-106) the "numberless instances [in which] the law warrants the intentional infliction of temporal damage," particularly in the area of commerce and business. The reason, he said, "is that the doctrine generally has been accepted that free competition is worth more to society than it costs, and that on this ground the infliction of the damage is privileged." He spoke particularly of the difficulties judges have when they seek to introduce their personal standards of "justification" into determinations as to what activities in this area are proper and what are improper. "The true grounds of decision are considerations of policy and social advantage, and it is vain to suppose that solutions can be attained merely by logic and the general propositions of law which nobody disputes. Propositions as to public policy rarely are unanimously accepted. . . ."

Thus the rules of the substantive law concerning the right of employees to organize emerged out of tort law as developed by equity courts and applied in proceedings initiated by employers seeking to enjoin union activity. Of this era of the law, Professor Gregory has written:[*]

* Gregory, Labor and the Law 102-103 (2d rev. ed. 1958). Reprinted with the permission of W. W. Norton Company.

"[P]erhaps the most alarming feature of the labor injunction, . . . was the ease with which its use increasingly tempted judges to dispense with any well-founded independent theory of illegality. . . . They came to look at much of organized labor's economic coercive activity as enjoinable in itself, without bothering to find or to state in their opinions that it was also unlawful. This was an unfortunate tendency which fed on itself. It seemed to lead many courts to grant sweeping injunctions on the basis of personal or class dislike of organized labor's economic program instead of in accordance with settled standards of law. A process of this sort lent itself admirably to the use of the illegal purpose doctrine.

". . . [S]ince no generally recognized body of law existed, aside from that governing various specific types of conduct, by which to judge the legality of purposes and contexts, many courts asked to issue injunctions unfortunately slipped into the custom of using as standards their own notions of what they believed to be good or bad as a matter of policy. In this way too many judges began to think of labor union activity as something enjoinable in itself. . . . This unwholesome state of affairs, where labor unionists never knew just where they stood under the shadow of a brooding and undefined judicial power, involved an almost certain threat of suppression to most of organized labor's bargaining and organizational program, without benefit of any legislative declaration of policy or, indeed, of any rules of the game that might be called law."

The procedures under which injunctions were issued often failed to afford unions a fair opportunity to establish a defense prior to the issuance of the writ. These procedures included the issuance of injunctions ex parte, on affidavits of a type which many adjudged utterly untruthworthy. See Judge Amidon's opinion in Great Northern Ry. v. Brosseau, 286 Fed. 414 (D.N.D. 1923); Frankfurter and Green, The Labor Injunction (1930).

e. JUDICIAL REACTION TO THE BEGINNINGS OF LEGISLATIVE REFORM

Near the turn of the century, a spirit of progressivism crossed the land, bringing with it certain legislative reforms. See Mowry, The Era of Theodore Roosevelt and the Birth of Modern America, 1900-1912, c. 4, 5 (1958). Among these reforms were statutes designed to protect employees from the doctrines of negligence, contributory negligence, assumption of risk, and fellow servant. These rules minimized the opportunity of employees to recover damages for injuries sustained in the course of their employment. A series of employer liability acts abolished contributory negligence and assumption of risk and in other ways made it easier for employees to recover damages for work-connected injuries. Perhaps the most famous, certainly the most significant, of these statutes at the current time is the Federal Employer's Liability Act, 35 Stat. 65, as amended, 45 U.S.C. §§51-60, which governs work-connected injuries in railroad employment, and, by statutory extension, injuries to seamen. 41 Stat. 1007, 46 U.S.C. §688. By 1910, however, it was clear that attempts to modify the common law through the Employer Liability Acts did not meet the problem of industrial accidents, and the states began to enact Workmen's Compensation Acts. These statutes abandoned negligence as the basis of liability and adopted instead the concept of an automatic right to recover a limited amount for a work-connected injury. See page 515 infra; Somers and Somers, Workmen's Compensation, c. 1, 2 (1954).

From this same spirit of progressive legislation emerged statutes from Congress and some seventeen states protecting the rights of some employees to join a union against employer decisions not to hire or to discharge employees because of their union affiliation. These statutes denied the employer the right to operate under a policy of having only nonunion employees. Some states also attempted to restrict the power of equity courts to enjoin union activity.

One statute which recognized the employee's right to join a union without losing his job was the Erdman Act of 1898, 30 Stat. 424, adopted by Congress to regulate labor relations of railroad employees. It came before the Supreme Court in Adair v. United States, 208 U.S. 161 (1908), a case later relied on by the majority in Hitchman. In Adair, the Court held that Congress lacked power under the interstate commerce clause to regulate labor relations on the railroads.[2] The Court also held that the restriction on the employer's right to operate a nonunion shop violated the due process clause of the Fifth Amendment. Justice Harlan wrote (pp. 175, 178-179):

"It was the legal right of defendant, Adair — however unwise such a course might have been — to discharge Coppage because of his being a member of a labor organization, as it was the legal right of Coppage, if he saw fit to do so — however unwise such a course on his part might have been — to quit the service in which he was engaged, because the defendant employed some persons who were not members of a labor organization. In all such particulars the employer and the employe have equality of right, and any legislation that disturbs that equality is an arbitrary interference with the liberty of contract which no government can legally justify in a free land. . . .

"But what possible legal or logical connection is there between an employe's membership in a labor organization and the carrying on of interstate commerce? Such relation to a labor organization cannot have, in itself and the eye of the law, any bearing upon commerce with which the employe is connected by his labor and services. Labor associations, we assume, are organized for the general purpose of improving or bettering the conditions and conserving the interests of its members as wage-earners — an object entirely legitimate and to be commended rather than condemned. But surely those associations as labor organizations have nothing to do with interstate commerce as such. One who engages in the service of an interstate carrier will, it must be assumed, faithfully perform his duty, whether he be a member or not a member of a labor organization. His fitness for the position in which he labors and his diligence in

---

[2] Compare, on the commerce clause issue, Loewe v. Lawlor, 208 U.S. 274 (1908), infra page 36.

the discharge of his duties cannot in law or sound reason depend in any degree upon his being or not being a member of a labor organization. It cannot be assumed that his fitness is assured, or his diligence increased, by such membership, or that he is less fit or less diligent because of his not being a member of such an organization. *It is the employe as a man and not as a member of a labor organization who labors in the service of an interstate carrier.* Will it be said that the provision in question had its origin in the apprehension, on the part of Congress, that . . . if it did not insert in the statute some such provision as the one here in question, members of labor organizations would, by illegal or violent measures, interrupt or impair the freedom of commerce among the States? We will not indulge in any such conjectures. . . ."

In Coppage v. Kansas, 236 U.S. 1 (1915), the Supreme Court invalidated a Kansas statute which prohibited employers from entering into and enforcing employment contracts that precluded union membership so long as the employee worked for the employer (the so-called "Yellow Dog" contract). The Court, through Justice Pitney, wrote (pp. 16-18): "The Act, as the construction given to it by the state court shows, is intended to deprive employers of a part of their liberty of contract, to the corresponding advantage of the employed and the upbuilding of the labor organizations. But no attempt is made, or could reasonably be made, to sustain the purpose to strengthen these voluntary organizations, any more than other voluntary associations of persons, as a legitimate object for the exercise of the police power. They are not public institutions, charged by law with public or governmental duties, such as would render the maintenance of their membership a matter of direct concern to the general welfare. If they were, a different question would be presented.

"As to the interest of the employed, it is said by the Kansas Supreme Court (87 Kansas, p. 759) to be a matter of common knowledge that 'employes, as a rule, are not financially able to be as independent in making contracts for the sale of their labor as are employers in making contracts of purchase thereof.' No doubt, wherever the right of private property exists, there must and will be inequalities of fortune; and thus it naturally happens that parties negotiating about a contract are not equally unhampered by circumstances. This applies to all contracts, and not merely to that between employer and employe. Indeed a little reflection will show that wherever the right of private property and the right of free contract co-exist, each party when contracting is inevitably more or less influenced by the question whether he has much property, or little, or none; for the contract is made to the very end that each may gain something that he needs or desires more urgently than that which he proposes to give in exchange. And, since it is self-evident that, unless all things are held in common, some persons must have more property than others, it is from the nature of things impossible to uphold freedom of contract and the right of private property without at the same time recognizing as legitimate those inequalities of fortune that are the necessary result of the exercise of those rights. But the Fourteenth Amendment, in declaring that a State shall not 'deprive any person of life, liberty or property without due process of law,' gives to each of these an equal sanction; it recognizes 'liberty' and 'property' as co-existent human rights, and debars the States from any unwarranted interference with either.

"And since a State may not strike them down directly it is clear that it may not do so indirectly, as by declaring in effect that the public good requires the removal of those inequalities that are but the normal and inevitable result of their exercise, and then invoking the police power in order to remove the inequalities, without other object in view. The police power is broad, and not easily defined, but it cannot be given the wide scope that is here asserted for it, without in effect nullifying the constitutional guaranty." [3]

A new one-volume work which emphasizes labor history in this century is Taft, Organized Labor in American History (1964). Of the aftermath of the Hitchman decision, Taft wrote (pp. 360-361):[*] "Employers, who in many instances had been compelled during wartime to recognize unions or deal with them, were anxious to throw off the shackles imposed by such organizations. The design of employers is evident in other industries and in their general attitude toward organized labor. In carrying out their plans they were aided greatly by the decisions of the U.S. Supreme Court and the conservative mood that took possession of the country. . . .

"The employer offensive in general, as well as in particular industries, was supported by the attitude of the courts and conservative opinion. In a series of decisions beginning with the Hitchman case, the U.S. Supreme Court made it more difficult for labor organizations to carry on defensive or offensive campaigns against employers. . . .

"On January 21, 1921, a national conference of state Manufacturers' associations, meeting in Chicago, suggested that industry be run on the 'American Plan,' i.e., a shop which does not deal with the union.

"Some employers were not satisfied with the definition and A. M. Glossbrenner of the Indiana Manufacturers' Association declared, 'we will not employ an individual in any part of the plant that does not sign an individual contract in which it is expressed that he is not and will not become a member of a labor organization while in our employ.' The open-shop policy meant even more. Testifying before the Legislative (Lockwood) Committee of New York state investigating building costs, Eugene Grace, the head of the Bethlehem Steel Corporation, claimed his company would not sell fabricated steel to union builders and contractors in the New York and Philadelphia area.

"Grace admitted that the Structural Iron Workers' Union had not discriminated against nonunion products, but he nevertheless held his policy was in the public interest. According to President William H. Barr, in '1,300 cities of this country Chambers of Commerce have rec-

[3] See Rodes, Due Process and Social Legislation in the Supreme Court — A Post-Mortem, 33 Notre Dame Law. 5 (1957). — ED.

[*] Reprinted with the permission of Harper and Row, publishers.

ommended the open shop.' Practically every industrial center developed an 'American Plan' open-shop organization. In Seattle the Associated Industries was organized in March 1919 by open-shop employers desiring to spread the American Plan. In January of the following year, the Associated Industries of Detroit adopted the American Plan of Employment which declared for full discretion on the terms of employment by the employer. The National Open Shop Association, which sought to establish local units, advised its potential members that the 'work must be clothed with the utmost secrecy, as we have found that publicity usually beats our purpose. For this reason you can feel assured that we will treat the matter in strict confidence.'

"The Associated Employers of Indianapolis initiated the movement to combine the loosely organized employer groups into a unified whole, and many employers' groups were induced to support the movement. Others were especially organized to promote it.

"The propaganda materials of all the groups sponsoring the American Plan of Employment stressed the need for giving the employer full control in industry, decried the practices of organized labor, especially limitation of output and union security, and urged generally that employers eliminate the unions from their properties. Open-shop organizations were active in virtually every community."

NOTE

For reference purposes, the classic history of trade unionism is the four-volume work by Commons, History of Labour in the United States (1918-1935).

f. TRADE UNION ACTIVITY AND THE ANTITRUST LAWS

AMERICAN STEEL FOUNDRIES v. TRI-CITY CENTRAL TRADES COUNCIL
Supreme Court of the United States, 1921
257 U.S. 184, 42 Sup. Ct. 72, 66 L. Ed. 189

[American Steel Foundries operated a steel products plant in Granite City, Illinois, which normally employed 1600 men. The plant closed in November, 1913. When the plant reopened in April, 1914, the company re-employed about 350 men, 150 of whom were skilled tradesmen such as electricians, crane men, mill hands, machinists, and blacksmiths. The men were rehired in the order of company preference from among those who applied at the gate. The company then announced that the wages of the skilled employees were to be cut from two to ten cents per hour below the rates prevailing prior to the November shutdown. The Tri-City Central Trades Council, composed of thirty-seven craft unions in Granite City and two adjoining towns, sought to negotiate with the company to re-establish the old wage rates. The plant manager refused to negotiate with them on the grounds that he ran an "open shop" and did not recognize organized labor.   On April 22, the Council declared a strike and established a picket line outside of the plant.   Only two employees struck.   In May, the company sought an injunction against the picketing.   A temporary restraining order was issued.   At the trial which followed, there was sharply conflicting testimony as to whether the picket line had been conducted in a threatening manner, whether assaults had been committed by pickets on employees entering the plant, and whether union officials had participated in threatening demonstrations and in the assaults.   After the hearing, a final decree was entered enjoining the union perpetually from the use of persuasion, intimidation, threats, and suggestions of violence to interfere with any employee of American Steel Foundries or any person seeking to secure employment with ASF, from congregating in the vicinity of the plant, and "from picketing or maintaining at or near the premises of the complainant, or on the streets leading to the premises of said complainant, any picket or pickets, and from doing any acts or things whatever in furtherance of any conspiracy or combination among them, or any of them, to obstruct, or interfere with said American Steel Foundries, its officers, agents or employees, in the free and unrestrained control and operation of its plant, foundry and property and the operation of its business."

The union appealed, objecting especially to the injunction against efforts to persuade persons not to work at ASF, to the prohibition against assembling in the neighborhood of the plant and against picketing.   The Circuit Court of Appeals struck the word "persuasion" from the injunction, and qualified the prohibition against picketing by adding the words, "in a threatening manner."   The company appealed to the Supreme Court.]

MR. CHIEF JUSTICE TAFT delivered the opinion of the court. . . .

The first question in the case is whether §20 of the Clayton Act, October 15, 1914, c. 323, 38 Stat. 738,[4] is to be applied in this case. . . .

It has been determined by this court that the irreparable injury to property or to a property right, in the first paragraph of §20, includes injury to the business of an employer, and that the second paragraph applies only in cases growing out of a dispute concerning terms or conditions of employment, between an employer and employee, between employers and employees, or between employees, or between persons employed and persons seeking employment, and not to such dispute between an employer and persons who are neither ex-employees nor seeking employment.   Duplex Printing Press Co. v. Deering, 254 U.S. 443. Only two of the defendants, Cook and Churchill, who left at the time of the strike, can invoke in their behalf §20.   We must, therefore, first consider the propriety of the decree as against them, and then as against the other defendants.

The prohibitions of §20, material here, are those which forbid an injunction against, first, recommending, advising or persuading others by

4 Relevant sections of the Clayton Act, including Section 20, are reproduced in the Reference Supplement, page 120. — ED.

peaceful means to cease employment and labor; second, attending at any place where such person or persons may lawfully be for the purpose of peacefully obtaining or communicating information, or peacefully persuading any person to work or to abstain from working; third, peaceably assembling in a lawful manner and for lawful purposes. This court has already called attention in the Duplex Case to the emphasis upon the words "peaceful" and "lawful" in this section. 254 U.S. 443, 473. It is clear that Congress wished to forbid the use by the federal courts of their equity arm to prevent peaceable persuasion by employees, discharged or expectant, in promotion of their side of the dispute, and to secure them against judicial restraint in obtaining or communicating information in any place where they might lawfully be. This introduces no new principle into the equity jurisprudence of those courts. It is merely declaratory of what was the best practice always. Congress thought it wise to stabilize this rule of action and render it uniform.

The object and problem of Congress in §20, and indeed of courts of equity before its enactment, was to reconcile the rights of the employer in his business and in the access of his employees to his place of business and egress therefrom without intimidation or obstruction, on the one hand, and the right of the employees, recent or expectant, to use peaceable and lawful means to induce present employees and would-be employees to join their ranks, on the other. If, in their attempts at persuasion or communication with those whom they would enlist with them, those of the labor side adopt methods which however lawful in their announced purpose inevitably lead to intimidation and obstruction, then it is the court's duty which the terms of §20 do not modify, so to limit what the propagandists do as to time, manner and place as shall prevent infractions of the law and violations of the right of the employees, and of the employer for whom they wish to work.

How far may men go in persuasion and communication and still not violate the right of those whom they would influence? In going to and from work, men have a right to as free a passage without obstruction as the streets afford, consistent with the right of others to enjoy the same privilege. We are a social people and the accosting by one of another in an inoffensive way and an offer by one to communicate and discuss information with a view to influencing the other's action are not regarded as aggression or a violation of that other's rights. If, however, the offer is declined, as it may rightfully be, then persistence, importunity, following and dogging become unjustifiable annoyance and obstruction which is likely soon to savor of intimidation. From all of this the person sought to be influenced has a right to be free and his employer has a right to have him free.

The nearer this importunate intercepting of employees or would-be employees is to the place of business, the greater the obstruction and interference with the business and especially with the property right of access of the employer. Attempted discussion and argument of this kind in such proximity is certain to attract attention and congregation of the curious, or, it may be, interested bystanders, and thus to increase the obstruction as well as the aspect of intimidation which the situation quickly assumes. In the present case the three or four groups of picketers, were made up of from four to twelve in a group. They constituted the picket lines. Each union interested, electricians, cranemen, machinists and blacksmiths, had several representatives on the picket line, and assaults and violence ensued. They began early and continued from time to time during the three weeks of the strike after the picketing began. All information tendered, all arguments advanced and all persuasion used under such circumstances were intimidation. They could not be otherwise. It is idle to talk of peaceful communication in such a place and under such conditions. The numbers of the pickets in the groups constituted intimidation. The name "picket" indicated a militant purpose, inconsistent with peaceable persuasion. The crowds they drew made the passage of the employees to and from the place of work, one of running the gauntlet. Persuasion or communication attempted in such a presence and under such conditions was anything but peaceable and lawful. When one or more assaults or disturbances ensued, they characterized the whole campaign, which became effective because of its intimidating character, in spite of the admonitions given by the leaders to their followers as to lawful methods to be pursued, however sincere. Our conclusion is that picketing thus instituted is unlawful and can not be peaceable and may be properly enjoined by the specific term because its meaning is clearly understood in the sphere of the controversy by those who are parties to it. . . .

A restraining order against picketing will advise earnest advocates of labor's cause that the law does not look with favor on an enforced discussion of the merits of the issue between individuals who wish to work, and groups of those who do not, under conditions which subject the individuals who wish to work to a severe test of their nerve and physical strength and courage. But while this is so, we must have every regard to the congressional intention manifested in the act and to the principle of existing law which it declared, that ex-employees and others properly acting with them shall have an opportunity, so far as is consistent with peace and law, to observe who are still working for the employer, to communicate with them and to persuade them to join the ranks of his opponents in a lawful economic struggle. Regarding as primary the rights of the employees to work for whom they will, and, undisturbed by annoying importunity or intimidation of numbers, to go freely to and from their place of labor, and keeping in mind the right of the employer incident to his property and business to free access of such employees, what can be done to reconcile the conflicting interests?

Each case must turn on its own circumstances. It is a case for the flexible remedial power of a court of equity which may try one mode of restraint, and if it fails or proves to be too drastic, may change it. We think that the strikers and their sympathizers engaged in the economic struggle should be limited to one representative for each point of ingress and egress in the plant or place of business and that all others be enjoined from congregating or loitering at the plant or in the neighboring streets by which access is had to the plant, that such representatives should have the right of observation, communication and persuasion but with special admonition that their communication, arguments and appeals shall not be abusive, libelous or threatening, and that they shall not approach individuals together but singly, and shall not in their single efforts at communication or persuasion obstruct an unwilling listener by importunate following or dogging his steps.   This is not laid down as a rigid rule, but only as one which should apply to this case under the circumstances disclosed by the evidence and which may be varied in other cases.   It becomes a question for the judgment of the Chancellor who has heard the witnesses, familiarized himself with the locus in quo and observed the tendencies to disturbance and conflict.   The purpose should be to prevent the inevitable intimidation of the presence of groups of pickets, but to allow missionaries.

With these views, it is apparent that we can not sustain the qualification of the order of the District Court which the Circuit Court of Appeals made.   That court followed the case of Iron Molders' Union v. Allis-Chalmers Co., 166 Fed. 45, and modified the order of the District Court which enjoins defendants "from picketing or maintaining at or near the premises of the complainant, or on the streets leading to the premises of said complainant, any picket or pickets" by adding the words "in a threatening or intimidating manner."   This qualification seems to us to be inadequate.   In actual result, it leaves compliance largely to the discretion of the pickets.   It ignores the necessary element of intimidation in the presence of groups as pickets.   It does not secure practically that which the court must secure and to which the complainant and his workmen are entitled.   The phrase really recognizes as legal that which bears the sinister name of "picketing" which it is to be observed Congress carefully refrained from using in §20.

The second important question in the case is as to the form of decree against the Tri-City Trades Council and the other defendants.   What has been said as to picketing applies to them, of course, as fully as to the ex-employees, but how as to the injunction against persuasion?

The argument made on behalf of the American Foundries in support of enjoining persuasion is that the Tri-City Central Trades Council and the other defendants being neither employees nor strikers were intruders into the controversy, and were engaged without excuse in an unlawful conspiracy to injure the American Foundries by enticing its employees, and, therefore, should be enjoined.

It is to be noted, that while there was only one member of the unions of the Trades Council who went out in the strike, the number of skilled employees then engaged by the Foundries was not one-quarter of the whole number of men who would be engaged when it was in full operation. . . .   It is thus probable that members of the local unions were looking forward to employment when complainant should resume full operation and even though they were not ex-employees within the Clayton Act, they were directly interested in the wages which were to be paid.

Is interference of a labor organization by persuasion and appeal to induce a strike against low wages under such circumstances without lawful excuse and malicious? We think not. Labor unions are recognized by the Clayton Act as legal when instituted for mutual help and lawfully carrying out their legitimate objects. They have long been thus recognized by the courts. They were organized out of the necessities of the situation. A single employee was helpless in dealing with an employer. He was dependent ordinarily on his daily wage for the maintenance of himself and family. If the employer refused to pay him the wages that he thought fair, he was nevertheless unable to leave the employ and to resist arbitrary and unfair treatment. Union was essential to give laborers opportunity to deal on equality with their employer. They united to exert influence upon him and to leave him in a body in order by this inconvenience to induce him to make better terms with them. They were withholding their labor of economic value to make him pay what they thought it was worth. The right to combine for such a lawful purpose has in many years not been denied by any court. The strike became a lawful instrument in a lawful economic struggle or competition between employer and employees as to the share or division between them of the joint product of labor and capital. To render this combination at all effective, employees must make their combination extend beyond one shop. It is helpful to have as many as may be in the same trade in the same community united, because in the competition between employers they are bound to be affected by the standard of wages of their trade in the neighborhood. Therefore, they may use all lawful propaganda to enlarge their membership and especially among those whose labor at lower wages will injure their whole guild. It is impossible to hold such persuasion and propaganda without more, to be without excuse and malicious. The principle of the unlawfulness of maliciously enticing laborers still remains and action may be maintained therefor in proper cases, but to make it applicable to local labor unions, in such a case as this, seems to us to be unreasonable. . . .

The counsel for the Steel Foundries rely on two cases in this court to support their contention. The first is that of Hitchman Coal & Coke Co. v. Mitchell, 245 U.S. 229. The principle followed in the Hitchman Case can not be invoked here. . . . The unlawful and deceitful means used were quite enough to sustain the decision of the court without more. The statement of the purpose of the plan is sufficient to show the remoteness of the benefit ultimately to be derived by the members of the International Union from its success and the formidable country-wide and dangerous character of the control of interstate commerce sought. The circumstances of the case make it no authority for the contention here.

Duplex Printing Press Co. v. Deering, 254 U.S. 443, also cited, can have no bearing here. . . . It [involved] a palpable effort on the part of the International Association of Machinists to institute a secondary boycott, that is, by coercion, to use the right of trade of persons having nothing to do with the controversy between the Duplex Company and the Machinist's Union, and having no interest in it, to injure the Duplex Company in its interstate trade. This was decided not to be within §20 of the

Clayton Act, but was held, following the case of Loewe v. Lawlor, 208 U.S. 274, to be an unlawful combination in restraint of interstate trade. The Hitchman Case was cited in the Duplex Case, but there is nothing in the ratio decidendi of either which limits our conclusion here or which requires us to hold that the members of a local labor union and the union itself do not have sufficient interest in the wages paid to the employees of any employer in the community to justify their use of lawful and peaceable persuasion to induce those employees to refuse to accept such reduced wages and to quit their employment. For this reason, we think that the restraint from persuasion included within the injunction of the District Court was improper, and in that regard the decree must also be modified. In this we agree with the Circuit Court of Appeals.

MR. JUSTICE BRANDEIS concurs in substance in the opinion and the judgment of the court.

MR. JUSTICE CLARKE dissents.[5]

NOTE

Before 1890 there was no federal antitrust law. There was, however, in each state an ancient law which treated as unenforceable certain contracts "in restraint of trade." This was inherited from the common law of England, which had consistently frowned on combinations, whether by merchants or by workers, to raise prices or lower the supply of goods. The ruling class in England had been the landowning class; the judges, generally sharing the opinions of that class, looked with alarm on the cornering of a market, which tended to increase the cost of living of those who owned the land.[6] In addition to the courts' refusal to enforce any agreement between the participants in any such contract or conspiracy, there were historical precedents for punishments of a criminal nature.[7]

Then in 1890 the federal Sherman Act, 26 Stat. 209, 15 U.S.C. §§1, 2, was passed. It made criminal any contract, combination, or conspiracy in restraint of trade or commerce, interstate or foreign; also any monopolization, or any attempt or conspiracy to monopolize any such trade or commerce.

As Professor Gregory says, "Everyone knew why the act was passed in 1890. It was in response to popular demand aroused by the fear of gigantic industrial and commercial enterprises which threatened to seize control of the *manufacturing and marketing of consumer goods of all kinds.*" (Emphasis supplied.)[8] Whether this statute was ever intended to apply to any of the concerted activities of workers has been, and still is, matter for hot debate. But one thing is clear: it was never intended

---

[5] For contemporary comment on the American Steel Foundries case, see Gregory, Labor and the Law c. 7 (2d rev. ed. 1958); Blumrosen, Group Interests in Labor Law, 13 Rutgers L. Rev. 432, 438 (1959). — ED.

[6] The history of English governmental regulation of the employment relationship is discussed in 2 Holdsworth, A History of English Law 459-464 (3d ed. 1923).

[7] See Gregory, Labor and the Law 200-205 (2d rev. ed. 1958).

[8] Id. at 202.

to apply to their banding together to obtain better wages or hours or working conditions. This, which may be thought of as a "primary" and "economic" banding together, has not been held or seriously claimed to be within the criminal offenses created by the Sherman Act. In other words, the views of Recorder Levy expressed in the Philadelphia Cordwainers' Case (see page 19 supra) have never been thought to have been made a part of federal antitrust law. This is simply not the kind of restraint on competition at which that statute was aimed. That such a banding together can be "monopolistic" in a broad sense of that term must be conceded. But it is not the sort of monopolistic combination, for fatter profits, which was intended. Granting that a powerful union may have extensive control over a labor market, it does not seek, typically, to use that control in order to make the most money possible for itself and its members. Note, for an illustration of this difference, that the insistence upon a union scale of wages and hours is conduct different from that which would be expected of a monopolistic profit-making business. Such an organization would seek to get the best terms possible from each enterprise or firm, whereas union policy is typically aimed at standardization.

But with respect to such banding together to utilize techniques like the "secondary boycott," the story has been quite a different one. Although during its first eighteen years the statute was not applied to any such activity, in 1908, in the first great labor case, it was. In the famous Danbury Hatters' Case, Loewe v. Lawlor, 208 U.S. 274 (1908), and, in a later stage, 235 U.S. 522 (1915), the United Hatters of North America, AFL, had sought to unionize the shop of a Connecticut hat manufacturer by inducing strikes at his factory and by boycotting his products, his dealers, and his customers throughout the nation, all causing an alleged $80,000 of damage. The AFL had cooperated in this effort by urging all its members not to buy hats manufactured by the Connecticut concern. The interstate character of the business was clear. The Court held that the activities were an illegal boycott and that the prohibitions of the Sherman Act covered a combination of this sort by labor as well as by capital. Questions of motive or justification, as possibly bearing on the reasonableness of the restraint, received no consideration. Pursuant to the Sherman Act the damages were trebled, to reach $240,000. The resulting judgment was enforced mercilessly against poor workers and their families, simply because of their membership in the offending unions. Naturally, these cruel results stirred a storm of public protest.

It led to an effort by Congress to ameliorate the situation by the enactment in 1914 of Sections 6 and 20 of the Clayton Act, 38 Stat. 731, 15 U.S.C. §17; 38 Stat. 738, 29 U.S.C. §52. Section 6 provides that the labor of a human being is not a commodity or article of commerce, and excludes from antitrust law coverage unions and union activities and persons "lawfully carrying out the legitimate objects thereof." Section 20 places drastic limitations, or limitations sounding drastic, on the granting of injunctions in labor disputes (as apparently broadly defined) "unless necessary to prevent irreparable injury to property." It ends with the phrase "nor shall any of the acts specified in this paragraph be considered or held to be violations of any law of the United States." But this section too is peppered, in its second paragraph, with the phrases and words, "peaceful means," "lawfully," "peacefully," "by peaceful and lawful means," "peaceably," "lawful purposes," describing the conduct which may not be enjoined.

In Duplex Printing Co. v. Deering, 254 U.S. 443 (1921), the Supreme Court emasculated Sections 6 and 20 of the Clayton Act. The complainant manufactured printing presses in Michigan and installed them at the purchasers' places of business. At least 80 per cent of the company's output was sold outside Michigan. After a strike had failed to unionize the complainant's factory (the only nonunion establishment of its kind in the country) the International Association of Machinists decided to boycott the complainant's presses. In furtherance of this plan, the Machinists, with the assistance of affiliated unions, threatened repair shops, trucking companies, and customers of the complainant with sympathetic strikes. Federal jurisdiction was grounded both on diversity of citizenship and on the federal antitrust laws. A majority of the Court ruled that this conduct was an enjoinable violation of the federal antitrust statutes. The Clayton Act was considered applicable, although it had been enacted after the events which had given rise to the litigation. Justice Pitney, speaking for the majority, held that the Clayton Act did not prevent an injunction. He reached this result on the basis of a "duplex" rationale: (1) that the Clayton Act dealt, in spite of the breadth of its definition of a labor dispute, solely with disputes between an employer and his own employees; and (2) that words in the statute such as "lawful" and "peaceful" showed that the statute dealt solely with the kinds of conduct which would have been lawful anyhow, without any statute at all. The case is chiefly remembered now for the classic dissent by Justice Brandeis, with Justices Holmes and Clarke concurring. This relied, so far as the common law was involved, upon the justification of economic self-interest; and so far as the statutes were concerned, it took exception to the majority's narrow readings of the statutory intent.

Despite the suggestion in the Tri-City case that the antitrust laws were applicable only to "secondary" as distinct from "primary" union activity, the Court applied the Sherman Act against some primary union activity. In the two Coronado Coal cases, United Mine Workers v. Coronado Coal Co., 259 U.S. 344 (1922), and 268 U.S. 295 (1925), the United Mine Workers had struck against a nonunion mine which was operating in a unionized area where other operators complained of its unfair competition. The strike was patterned with criminal violence and substantial destruction of property, the burning of tipples and coal cars, and the dynamiting of the mine. In the first Coronado case, the Court held (259 U.S. at 411) that a violation of the Sherman Act was not proved by a mere showing that union activity had the effect of reducing interstate commerce even by unlawful means. There must be proof that the union "intended to restrain commerce" or that its action "has necessarily such a direct, material and substantial effect to restrain it that the intent must reasonably be inferred." Upon retrial of the case additional evidence was introduced to satisfy the Court that at least as to the local union, "the purpose of the destruction was to stop the production of non-union coal and prevent its shipment to markets of other states . . . where it would, by competition, tend to reduce the prices of the commodity and injuriously affect the maintenance of wages for union labor in competing mines." 268 U.S. at 310.

2. The Legislative Era

a. THE RAILWAY LABOR ACT

During the 1920's, Congress had been experimenting with new and more specialized procedures for the resolution of labor disputes on the railroads. From this experience came the pattern for legislation which, in the 1930's, would regulate labor relations in virtually all industry. The nation was barely into the great depression when this new type of legislation came before the Supreme Court.

TEXAS & NEW ORLEANS R. CO. v. BROTHERHOOD OF RAILWAY CLERKS

Supreme Court of the United States, 1930
281 U.S. 548, 50 Sup. Ct. 427, 74 L. Ed. 1034

[The Brotherhood began to represent clerks of the defendant railroad in 1918. In 1925 the railroad instigated the formation of a new union of its clerks, the "Association of Clerical Employees-Southern Pacific Lines," and intimidated and coerced employees to leave the Brotherhood and join the Association. Railroad employees were allowed to solicit memberships for the Association on company time, and to charge to the railroad expenses of recruiting Association members. Leading representatives of the Brotherhood were discharged, and their passes canceled. The District Court granted a temporary injunction against the railroad to prevent it from interfering with, influencing, intimidating, or coercing employees in their selection of representatives under the Railway Labor Act of 1926. After issuance of the injunction, the railroad recognized the Association as the representative of its clerical employees, relying on a showing that a majority of the clerks had signed authorization cards for the Association. The railroad then denied recognition to the Brotherhood. Alleging that this act violated the injunction, the Brotherhood sought to have the railroad punished for contempt of the court order.]

MR. CHIEF JUSTICE HUGHES delivered the opinion of the Court. . . . In proceedings to punish for contempt, the District Court decided that the Railroad Company and certain of its officers who were defendants had violated the order of injunction and completely nullified it. The Court directed that, in order to purge themselves of this contempt, the Railroad Company and these officers should completely "disestablish the Association of Clerical Employees," as it was then constituted as the recognized representative of the clerical employees of the Railroad Company, and should reinstate the Brotherhood as such representative, until such time as these employees by a secret ballot taken in accordance with the further direction of the Court, and without the dictation or interference of the Railroad Company and its officers, should choose other representatives. The order also required the restoration to service and to stated privileges of certain employees who had been discharged by the Railroad Company. 24 F.2d 426. Punishment was prescribed in case the defendants did not purge themselves of contempt as directed.

On final hearing, the temporary injunction was made permanent. 25 F.2d 873. At the same time, a motion to vacate the order in the contempt proceedings was denied. 25 F.2d 876. The Circuit Court of Appeals affirmed the decree, holding that the injunction was properly granted and that, in imposing conditions for the purging of the defendants of contempt, the District Court had not gone beyond the appropriate exercise of its authority in providing for the restoration of the status quo, 33 F.2d 13. This Court granted a writ of certiorari. 280 U.S. 550.

The bill of complaint invoked subdivision third of section 2 of the Railway Labor Act of 1926 (c. 347, 44 Stat. 577), which provides as follows:

"Third. Representatives, for the purposes of this Act, shall be designated by the respective parties in such manner as may be provided in their corporate organization or unincorporated association, or by other means of collective action, without interference, influence, or coercion exercised by either party over the self-organization or designation of representatives by the other."

The controversy is with respect to the construction, validity and application of this statutory provision. . . .

It is unnecessary to review the history of the legislation enacted by Congress in relation to the settlement of railway labor disputes, as earlier efforts culminated in Title III of the Transportation Act, 1920 (c. 91, 41 Stat. 456, 469) the purpose and effect of which have been determined by this Court. In Pennsylvania Railroad Company v. United States Railroad Labor Board, 261 U.S. 72, the question was whether the members of the Railroad Labor Board as constituted under the provisions of the Transportation Act, 1920, had exceeded their powers. The Court held that the Board had jurisdiction to hear and decide a dispute over rules and working conditions upon the application of either side, when the parties had failed to agree and an adjustment board had not been organized. The Board also had jurisdiction to decide who might represent the employees in the conferences contemplated by the statute and to make reasonable rules for ascertaining the will of the employees in this respect. Interference by injunction with the exercise of the discretion of the Board in the matters committed to it, and with the publication of its opinions, was decided to be unwarranted. The Court thought it evident that Congress considered it to be "of the highest public interest to prevent the interruption of interstate commerce by labor disputes and strikes," and that its plan was "to encourage settlement without strikes, first by conference between the parties; failing that, by reference to adjustment boards of the parties' own choosing," and, if this proved to be ineffective, "by a full hearing before a National Board" organized as the statute provided. But the Court added: "The decisions of the Labor Board are not to be enforced by process. The only sanction of its decision is to be the force of public opinion invoked by the fairness of a full hearing, the intrinsic justice of the conclusion, strengthened by the official prestige of the Board, and the full publication of the violation of such decision by any party to the proceeding." It was said to be the evident thought of Congress "that the economic interest of every member of the Public in the undisturbed flow of interstate commerce and the acute inconvenience to which all must be subjected by an interruption caused by a serious and widespread labor dispute, fastens public attention closely on all the circumstances of the controversy and arouses public criticism of the side thought to be at fault." Id. pp. 79, 80. The Court concluded that the Labor Board was "to act as a Board of Arbitration," but that there was "no constraint" upon the parties "to do what the Board decides they should do except the moral constraint of publication of its decision." Id. P. 84.

The provisions of Title III of the Transportation Act, 1920, were again before the Court in Pennsylvania Railroad System and Allied Lines Federation No. 90 v. Pennsylvania Railroad Company, 267 U.S. 203. This was a suit by a union to enjoin the Railroad Company from carrying out an alleged conspiracy to defeat the provisions of the legislation establishing the Railroad Labor Board. The complainants, the Court said, sought "to enforce by mandatory injunction a compliance with a decision of the Board"; and the Court held that "such a remedy by injunction in a court, it was not the intention of Congress to provide." Id. p. 216. The Court pointed out that "the ultimate decision of the Board, it is conceded, is not compulsory, and no process is furnished to enforce it." It was in the light of these conclusions as to the purport of the statute that the Court considered the freedom of action of the Railroad Company. The Court said that the Company was using "every endeavor to avoid compliance with the judgment and principles of the Labor Board as to the proper method of securing representatives of the whole body of its employees," that it was "seeking to control its employees by agreements free from the influence of an independent trade union," and, so far as concerned its dealing with its employees, was "refusing to comply with the decisions of the Labor Board." But the Court held that this conduct was within the strict legal rights of the Railroad Company and that Congress had not intended to make such conduct legally actionable. Id. p. 217.

It was with clear appreciation of the infirmity of the existing legislation, and in the endeavor to establish a more practicable plan in order to accomplish the desired result, that Congress enacted the Railway Labor Act of 1926. It was decided to make a fresh start. The situation was thus described in the report of the bill to the Senate by the Committee on Interstate Commerce (69th Cong., 1st sess., Sen. Rep. No. 222): "In view of the fact that the employees absolutely refuse to appear before the labor board and that many of the important railroads are themselves opposed to it, that it has been held by the Supreme Court to have no power to enforce its judgments, that its authority is not recognized or respected by the employees and by a number of important railroads, that the President has suggested that it would be wise to seek a substitute for it, and that the party platforms of both the Republican and Democratic Parties in 1924 clearly indicated dissatisfaction with the provisions of the transportation act relating to labor, the committee concluded that the time had arrived when the labor board should be abolished and the provisions relating to labor in the transportation act, 1920, should be repealed."

The bill was introduced as the result of prolonged conferences between representative committees of railroad presidents and of executives of railroad labor organizations, and embodied an agreement of a large majority of both.[2]   The provisions of Title III of the Transportation Act, 1920, and also the Act of July 15, 1913 (c. 6, 38 Stat. 103) which provided for mediation, conciliation and arbitration in controversies with railway employees, were repealed.

While adhering in the new statute to the policy of providing for the amicable adjustment of labor disputes, and for voluntary submissions to arbitration as opposed to a system of compulsory arbitration, Congress buttressed this policy by creating certain definite legal obligations.   The outstanding feature of the Act of 1926 is the provision for an enforceable award in arbitration proceedings.   The arbitration is voluntary, but the award pursuant to the arbitration is conclusive upon the parties as to the merits and facts of the controversy submitted.   (Section 9.) . . . Petition for the impeachment of the award may be made upon the grounds that the award does not conform to the substantive requirements of the Act or to the stipulation of the parties, or that the proceedings were not in ac-

---

[2] In the report of the bill by the Committee on Interstate and Foreign Commerce to the House of Representatives, it was said (69th Cong. 1st sess., H. R. Rep. No. 328):

"The bill was introduced as the product of negotiations and conferences between a representative committee of railroad presidents and a representative committee of railroad labor organization executives, extending over several months, which were concluded with the approval of the bill, respectively, by the Association of Railway Executives and by the executives of 20 railroad labor organizations.   As introduced, it represented the agreement of railway managements operating over 80 per cent of the railroad mileage and labor organizations representing an overwhelming majority of the railroad employees."

The committee of the Senate on Interstate Commerce reported to the Senate on this point, as follows (69th Cong., 1st sess., Sen. Rep. No. 222):

"The railroads favoring the bill appeared before the committee through their representatives and advocated it.   None of the railroads opposing the bill appeared either in person or by any representative.   The bill was agreed to also by all the organizations know as 'standard recognized railway labor organizations,' 20 in number, and these appeared by their representatives before the committee in advocacy of the bill."

cordance with the Act or were tainted with fraud or corruption. . . . Thus it is contemplated that the proceedings for the amicable adjustment of disputes will have an appropriate termination in a binding adjudication, enforceable as such.

Another definite object of the Act of 1926 is to provide, in case of a dispute between a carrier and its employees which has not been adjusted under the provisions of the Act, for the more effectual protection of interstate commerce from interruption to such a degree as to deprive any section of the country of essential transportation service. (Section 10.) In case the Board of Mediation established by the Act, as an independent agency in the executive branch of the Government, finds that such an interruption of interstate commerce is threatened, that Board is to notify the President, who may thereupon in his discretion create an emergency board of investigation to report, within thirty days, with respect to the dispute. The Act then provides that "After the creation of such board and for thirty days after such board has made its report to the President, no change, except by agreement, shall be made by the parties to the controversy in the conditions out of which the dispute arose." (Id.) This prohibition, in order to safeguard the vital interests of the country while an investigation is in progress, manifestly imports a legal obligation. The Brotherhood insists, and we think rightly, that the major purpose of Congress in passing the Railway Labor Act was "to provide a machinery to prevent strikes." Section 10 is described by counsel for the Brotherhood as "a provision limiting the right to strike," and in this view it is insisted that there "is no possible question that Congress intended to make the provisions of Section 10 enforceable to the extent of authorizing any court of competent jurisdiction to restrain either party to the controversy from changing the existing status during the sixty-day period provided for the emergency board." . . .

It is thus apparent that Congress, in the legislation of 1926, while elaborating a plan for amicable adjustments and voluntary arbitration of disputes between common carriers and their employees, thought it necessary to impose, and did impose, certain definite obligations enforceable by judicial proceedings. The question before us is whether a legal obligation of this sort is also to be found in the provisions of subdivision third of Section 2 of the Act providing that "Representatives for the purposes of this Act, shall be designated by the respective parties . . . without interference, influence, or coercion exercised by either party over the self-organization or designation of representatives by the other."

It is at once to be observed that Congress was not content with the general declaration of the duty of carriers and employees to make every reasonable effort to enter into and maintain agreements concerning rates of pay, rules and working conditions, and to settle disputes with all expedition in conference between authorized representatives, but added this distinct prohibition against coercive measures. This addition can not be treated as superfluous or insignificant, or as intended to be without effect. Ex parte Public National Bank, 278 U.S. 101, 104. While an affirmative declaration of duty contained in a legislative enactment may be of imper-

fect obligation because not enforceable in terms, a definite statutory prohibition of conduct which would thwart the declared purpose of the
legislation cannot be disregarded. The intent of Congress is clear with
respect to the sort of conduct that is prohibited. "Interference" with
freedom of action and "coercion" refer to well understood concepts
of the law. The meaning of the word "influence" in this clause may be
gathered from the context. Noscitur a sociis. Virginia v. Tennessee,
148 U.S. 503, 519. The use of the word is not to be taken as interdicting
the normal relations and innocent communications which are a part of
all friendly intercourse, albeit between employer and employee. "Influence" in this context plainly means pressure, the use of the authority or
power of either party to induce action by the other in derogation of what
the statute calls "self-organization." The phrase covers the abuse of relation or opportunity so as to corrupt or override the will, and it is no more
difficult to appraise conduct of this sort in connection with the selection
of representatives for the purposes of this Act than in relation to well-
known applications of the law with respect to fraud, duress and undue
influence. If Congress intended that the prohibition, as thus construed,
should be enforced, the courts would encounter no difficulty in fulfilling
its purpose, as the present suit demonstrates.

In reaching a conclusion as to the intent of Congress, the importance
of the prohibition in its relation to the plan devised by the Act must
have appropriate consideration. Freedom of choice in the selection of
representatives on each side of the dispute is the essential foundation of
the statutory scheme. All the proceedings looking to amicable adjustments and to agreements for arbitration of disputes, the entire policy of
the Act, must depend for success on the uncoerced action of each party
through its own representatives to the end that agreements satisfactory
to both may be reached and the peace essential to the uninterrupted
service of the instrumentalities of interstate commerce may be maintained. There is no impairment of the voluntary character of arrangements for the adjustment of disputes in the imposition of a legal obligation not to interfere with the free choice of those who are to make such
adjustments. On the contrary, it is of the essence of a voluntary scheme,
if it is to accomplish its purpose, that this liberty should be safeguarded.
The definite prohibition which Congress inserted in the Act can not
therefore be overridden in the view that Congress intended it to be ignored. As the prohibition was appropriate to the aim of Congress, and
is capable of enforcement, the conclusion must be that enforcement was
contemplated.

The absence of penalty is not controlling. The creation of a legal
right by language suitable to that end does not require for its effectiveness the imposition of statutory penalties. Many rights are enforced for
which no statutory penalties are provided. In the case of the statute in
question, there is an absence of penalty, in the sense of specially prescribed punishment, with respect to the arbitral awards and the prohibition of change in conditions pending the investigation and report of an
emergency board, but in each instance a legal obligation is created and

the statutory requirements are susceptible of enforcement by proceedings appropriate to each. The same is true of the prohibition of interference or coercion in connection with the choice of representatives. The right is created and the remedy exists. Marbury v. Madison, 1 Cranch 137, 162, 163.

We entertain no doubt of the constitutional authority of Congress to enact the prohibition. The power to regulate commerce is the power to enact "all appropriate legislation" for its "protection and advancement" (The Daniel Ball, 10 Wall. 557, 564); to adopt measures "to promote its growth and insure its safety" (County of Mobile v. Kimball, 102 U.S. 691, 696, 697); to "foster, protect, control and restrain" (Second Employers' Liability Cases, 223 U.S. 1, 47). Exercising this authority, Congress may facilitate the amicable settlement of disputes which threaten the service of the necessary agencies of interstate transportation. In shaping its legislation to this end, Congress was entitled to take cognizance of actual conditions and to address itself to practicable measures. The legality of collective action on the part of employees in order to safeguard their proper interests is not to be disputed. It has long been recognized that employees are entitled to organize for the purpose of securing the redress of grievances and to promote agreements with employers relating to rates of pay and conditions of work. American Steel Foundries v. Tri-City Central Trades Council, 257 U.S. 184, 209. Congress was not required to ignore this right of the employees but could safeguard it and seek to make their appropriate collective action an instrument of peace rather than of strife. Such collective action would be a mockery if representation were made futile by interferences with freedom of choice. Thus the prohibition by Congress of interference with the selection of representatives for the purpose of negotiation and conference between employers and employees, instead of being an invasion of the constitutional right of either, was based on the recognition of the rights of both. The petitioners invoke the principle declared in Adair v. United States, 208 U.S. 161, and Coppage v. Kansas, 236 U.S. 1, but these decisions are inapplicable. The Railway Labor Act of 1926 does not interfere with the normal exercise of the right of the carrier to select its employees or to discharge them. The statute is not aimed at this right of the employers but at the interference with the right of employees to have representatives of their own choosing. As the carriers subject to the Act have no constitutional right to interfere with the freedom of the employees in making their selections, they cannot complain of the statute on constitutional grounds. . . .

Decree affirmed.

MR. JUSTICE McREYNOLDS did not hear the argument and took no part in the decision of this case.

NOTE

In 1934, Congress again amended the Railway Labor Act. This was because of a belief that continued interference by carriers with the right of their employees to join or organize unions of their own choice and to designate them as their bargaining representatives, and continued denial by carriers of the authority of the representatives so chosen, were major causes of labor disputes. The amendments specifically prohibited carriers from interfering "in any way" (including the company-union device) with the right of their employees to organize and bargain collectively through representatives of their own choosing, and recognized that employees have the right to designate as their representatives persons who are not in the employ of the carrier. Further, the amendments stated that the principle of majority rule would determine which bargaining agent, if any, a particular craft or class of employees wanted. §2, Third and Fourth. They provided that the National Mediation Board should investigate representation questions, determine which representative had majority support among the particular group of employees, and certify it. §2, Ninth. The amendments also directed carriers to "treat with" the certified representative as the representative of the craft or class for the purposes of collective bargaining. §2, Ninth.

In a landmark decision, Virginian Ry. v. System Federation No. 40, 300 U.S. 515 (1937), the United States Supreme Court held that the amended Act, while it did not require agreement, did impose the affirmative and judicially enforceable duty to meet and confer, to listen, and to make reasonable efforts to compose differences and to reach agreement, as well as the negative duty not to "treat with" any other representative for the purpose of collective bargaining. In addition to directing the carrier to recognize and bargain with the petitioning union (which had been certified, after an election, by the National Mediation Board) as the representative of its mechanical department employees, the Court restrained the railroad from interfering with coercing, or influencing the employees in their free choice of a collective bargaining representative.

b. THE NORRIS-LAGUARDIA ACT

The political events leading up to the adoption of federal anti-injunction legislation are described in Taft, Organized Labor in American History 414-415 (1964):*

"The general labor movement gained an outstanding legislative victory with the passage of the Norris-LaGuardia Act regulating the issuance of injunctions in labor disputes by the federal courts. At the suggestion of the AFL, Senator Henrik Shipstead in December 1927 introduced a simple bill limiting the use of the injunction. After hearings by a subcommittee of the Senate Committee on the Judiciary, it submitted a bill in June 1928 which approached the question 'from a new point of view, that of definitely specifying the procedure to be followed in labor cases.' This was followed by the inclusion of planks in both the Republican and Democratic national platforms of 1928 pledging relief from the abuse of injunctions. . . .

"During 1929 and 1930, the interest in the labor injunctions declined,

* Reprinted with the permission of Harper and Row, publishers.

but the AFL and others interested in this measure renewed their activity in the following year. In January 1931 the National Committee on Labor Injunctions, with former Federal District Judge Charles F. Amidon as chairman, was formed to promote the legislation. The committee had more than four hundred members, many of them distinguished lawyers and public men. When the Seventy-second Congress met on December 7, 1931, the federation strongly urged adoption of an anti-injunction measure. It passed the House of Representatives by a vote of 363 to 13, the Senate by 75 to 5, and was signed by President Hoover on March 23, 1932. The final vote does not, however, reflect the strength of the opposition. It was no exaggeration when the executive council announced 'that it really represents the outstanding legal accomplishment of the American Federation of Labor.' The law limited the issuance of injunctions in labor disputes by the federal courts, prohibited court injunctions against certain otherwise legal activities of unions, granted a jury trial to defendants in contempt cases committed outside of the court room, and compelled a change of venue when requested."

The Norris-LaGuardia Act thus destroyed the power of the federal courts to issue injunctions in connection with most labor disputes. Examine the statute[9] to see how the Congress met the various complaints which had arisen concerning both the substantive law developed by the federal courts and the procedures used by these courts in the issuance of injunctions. The basic framework is found in Sections 2,3,4,7, and 13 of the Act.

C. THE NATIONAL INDUSTRIAL RECOVERY ACT

The depression of the early thirties brought into sharp relief the disparity between the organized power of industry (to keep prices up — among other things) and the lonely weakness of individual wage earners, who were also consumers. Less than 10 per cent of the American work force was organized.

In 1933, the National Industrial Recovery Act, 48 Stat. 195, was adopted by Congress, and there followed a period of frantic experimentation with attempted federal control of prices, wages, and hours. In the course of this trying and erring, there was added to the NIRA a provision, Section 7(a), which contained the following:

". . . (1) That employees shall have the right to organize and bargain collectively through representatives of their own choosing, and shall be free from the interference, restraint, or coercion of employers of labor, or their agents, in the designation of such representatives or in self-organization or in other concerted activities for the purpose of collective bargaining or other mutual aid or protection; (2) that no employee and no one seeking employment shall be required as a condition of employment to join any company union or to refrain from joining, organizing or assisting a labor organization of his own choosing . . ."

In August, 1933, President Roosevelt established, by Executive Order, a

[9] The text of this statute is printed in the Reference Supplement, page 114.

National Labor Board composed of seven members (three employer members, three labor members, with Senator Wagner as chairman). The Board's function was never clearly identified or recognized: it was to "enforce" Section 7(a); it was also to put out the fire of strikes which sprang from the resentment of groups of employees against the fairly general ignoring by employers of the statutory policy pronouncement in Section 7(a). Very little else was accomplished by the Board.

Under the NIRA, union membership, particularly in the coal industry, expanded rapidly. West Virginia, which had been the focus of many unsuccessful organizing drives and of much bitter violence, came into the United Mine Workers fold during the summer of 1933. See Taft, Organized Labor in American History, c. 33 (1964).

In 1934, Senator Wagner tried to get through Congress a bill (Labor Disputes Bill of 1934) which would have put teeth into Section 7(a) and have provided effective machinery for the enforcement of the principle it embodied. Congress could not reach agreement on this bill, although there was reaffirmation of the Section 7(a) principle in Public Resolution No. 44. So the President again used his executive powers, this time to set up a National Labor Relations Board composed of three "public" members, expert in the labor relations field, with provision made for a considerable staff and field organization. The Board's authority was more clearly defined than in the case of the earlier board: to investigate serious labor disputes and alleged violations of Section 7(a); and to hold elections in which employees could freely select "representatives of their own choosing."

This first National Labor Relations Board was short-lived, for in May, 1935, the Supreme Court found the NIRA unconstitutional in Schechter Poultry Corp. v. United States, 295 U.S. 495 (1935). Even during the Board's brief life, its efforts were continually frustrated by lack of power to compel compliance with its orders.

d. THE BITUMINOUS COAL CONSERVATION ACT

Almost immediately after the Schechter decision Congress passed a modified version of the NIRA, to apply specifically to the coal industry, which had been jointly sponsored by elements in the coal industry and the United Mine Workers. This statute declared that the regulation of competition in the coal industry was a matter of public interest. It created a Commission consisting of representatives of producers of two thirds of the national tonnage production of coal and more than one half of the mine workers. Prices of coal were to be fixed, and the wages, hours, and working conditions in the mines were to be regulated. This Act was declared unconstitutional on multiple grounds in Carter v. Carter Coal Co., 298 U.S. 238 (1936), in which the Court said, inter alia (p. 311):

"The power conferred upon the majority is, in effect, the power to regulate the affairs of an unwilling minority. This is legislative delegation in its most obnoxious form; for it is not even delegation to an official or an official body, presumptively disinterested, but to private persons whose interests may be and often are adverse to the interests of others in the same business. The record shows that the conditions of competition differ among the various localities. In some, coal dealers compete among themselves. In other localities, they also compete with the mechanical production of electrical energy and of natural gas. Some coal producers favor the code; others oppose it; and the record clearly indicates that this diversity of view arises from their conflicting and even antagonistic interests. The difference between producing coal and regulating its production is, of course, fundamental. The former is a private activity; the latter is necessarily a governmental function, since, in the very nature of things, one person may not be intrusted with the power to regulate the business of another, and especially of a competitor. And a statute which attempts to confer such power undertakes an intolerable and unconstitutional interference with personal liberty and private property. The delegation is so clearly arbitrary, and so clearly a denial of rights safeguarded by the due process clause of the Fifth Amendment, that it is unnecessary to do more than refer to decisions of this court which foreclose the question. . . ."

e.   THE NATIONAL LABOR RELATIONS ACT
OF 1935 — THE WAGNER ACT

The demise of the NIRA as a result of the Schechter decision led not only to the Bituminous Coal Act, but to the adoption of a National Labor Relations Act of 1935, called the Wagner Act. This statute, enacted one month after the Schechter decision, adopted Section 7(a) of the old NIRA as the heart of a new national labor relations policy. The experience of the Board under the NIRA was to prove invaluable in this next step in the development of the law. Deriving directly from Section 7(a) of the NIRA, Section 7 of the NLRA provided that "Employees shall have the right to self-organization, to form, join, or assist labor organizations, to bargain collectively through representatives of their own choosing, and to engage in concerted activities for the purpose of collective bargaining or other mutual aid or protection." But where Congress in 1933 and 1934 had stopped with a pronouncement of principle, it went on in 1935 to provide for the effectuation of that principle. The statutory pattern it established has remained, with one major change in 1947, the pattern of federal regulation of collective bargaining ever since.[10]

First, a three-man National Labor Relations Board (enlarged to five in 1947) was set up, with provision made for staff and field organization, to administer the new law. §§3-6.

Second, provision was made in Section 9 for the conducting by the Board of elections by which employees would select "representatives of their own choosing" for bargaining purposes. The exercise of this function came to be known as the handling of "representation" procedures and cases.

10 The text of this statute, as subsequently amended, is printed in the Reference Supplement, page 17.

Third, the new Act identified five sets of employer practices which were deemed inimical to the exercise of the rights specified in Section 7. These were listed, in Section 8, as "unfair labor practices." Chief among them were employer discrimination against employees because of their union activity and employer "refusal to bargain" with a properly authorized collective bargaining agent. Section 10 of the Act prescribed the procedures for Board determination of cases involving alleged unfair labor practices, and for enforcement of its orders that such practices, if found, be stopped and that restitution be made. Provision for review of Board orders by the United States Courts of Appeals was included in Section 10. The National Lawyers Committee of the American Liberty League took the position that the Act "constitutes an illegal interference with the individual freedom of employees. . . ." The committee concluded, ". . . we have no hesitance in considering it is unconstitutional and that it constitutes a complete departure from constitutional and traditional theories of government." The constitutionality of the substance of the regulatory measure was tested before the Supreme Court in 1937.

NATIONAL LABOR RELATIONS BOARD v. JONES & LAUGHLIN STEEL CORP.

Supreme Court of the United States, 1937
301 U.S. 1, 57 Sup. Ct. 615, 81 L. Ed. 893

Mr. Chief Justice Hughes delivered the opinion of the Court.

In a proceeding under the National Labor Relations Act of 1935, the National Labor Relations Board found that the respondent, Jones & Laughlin Steel Corporation, had violated the Act by engaging in unfair labor practices affecting commerce. The proceeding was instituted by the Beaver Valley Lodge No. 200, affiliated with the Amalgamated Association of Iron, Steel and Tin Workers of America, a labor organization. The unfair labor practices charged were that the corporation was discriminating against members of the union with regard to hire and tenure of employment, and was coercing and intimidating its employees in order to interfere with their self-organization. The discriminatory and coercive action alleged was the discharge of certain employees.

The National Labor Relations Board, sustaining the charge, ordered the corporation to cease and desist from such discrimination and coercion, to offer reinstatement to ten of the employees named, to make good their losses in pay, and to post for thirty days notices that the corporation would not discharge or discriminate against members, or those desiring to become members, of the labor union. As the corporation failed to comply, the Board petitioned the Circuit Court of Appeals to enforce the order. The court denied the petition, holding that the order lay beyond the range of federal power. 83 F.2d 998. We granted certiorari. . . .

The procedure in the instant case followed the statute. The labor union filed with the Board its verified charge. The Board thereupon issued its complaint against the respondent alleging that its action in discharging the employees in question constituted unfair labor practices affecting commerce within the meaning of §8, subdivisions (1) and (3), and §2, subdivisions (6) and (7) of the Act. Respondent, appearing specially for the purpose of objecting to the jurisdiction of the Board, filed its answer. Respondent admitted the discharges, but alleged that they were made because of inefficiency or violation of rules or for other good reasons and were not ascribable to union membership or activities. As an affirmative defense respondent challenged the constitutional validity of the statute and its applicability in the instant case. Notice of hearing was given and respondent appeared by counsel. The Board first took up the issue of jurisdiction and evidence was presented by both the Board and the respondent. Respondent then moved to dismiss the complaint for lack of jurisdiction; and, on denial of that motion, respondent in accordance with its special appearance withdrew from further participation in the hearing. The Board received evidence upon the merits and at its close made its findings and order.

Contesting the ruling of the Board, the respondent argues (1) that the Act is in reality a regulation of labor relations and not of interstate commerce; (2) that the Act can have no application to the respondent's relations with its production employees because they are not subject to regulation by the federal government; and (3) that the provisions of the Act violate §2 of Article III and the Fifth and Seventh Amendments of the Constitution of the United States.

[The Court first held that the commerce clause permitted Congress to regulate the activities of the employer.]

Second. The unfair labor practices in question. — The unfair labor practices found by the Board are those defined in §8, subdivisions (1) and (3). . . .

Thus, in its present application, the statute goes no further than to safeguard the right of employees to self-organization and to select representatives of their own choosing for collective bargaining or other mutual protection without restraint or coercion by their employer.

That is a fundamental right. Employees have as clear a right to organize and select their representatives for lawful purposes as the respondent has to organize its business and select its own officers and agents. Discrimination and coercion to prevent the free exercise of the right of employees to self-organization and representation is a proper subject for condemnation by competent legislative authority. Long ago we stated the reason for labor organizations. We said that they were organized out of the necessities of the situation; that a single employee was helpless in dealing with an employer; that he was dependent ordinarily on his daily wage for the maintenance of himself and family; that if the employer refused to pay him the wages that he thought fair, he was nevertheless unable to leave the employ and resist arbitrary and unfair treatment; that union was essential to give laborers opportunity to deal on an equality with their employer. American Steel Foundries v. Tri-City Central Trades Council, 257 U.S. 184, 209. We reiterated these views when we had under consideration the Railway Labor Act of 1926. Fully recognizing the legality of collective action on the part of employees in order to safeguard their proper interests, we said that Congress was not required to ignore this right but could safeguard it. Congress could seek to make appropriate collective action of employees an instrument of peace rather than of strife. We said that such collective action would be a mockery if representation were made futile by interference with freedom of choice. Hence the prohibition by Congress of interference with the selection of representatives for the purpose of negotiation and conference between employers and employees, "instead of being an invasion of the constitutional right of either, was based on the recognition of the rights of both." Texas & N.O.R. Co. v. Railway Clerks [see page 38 supra]. We have reasserted the same principle in sustaining the application of the Railway Labor Act as amended in 1934. Virginian Railway Co. v. System Federation, No. 40 [300 U.S. 515 (1937)].

[The Court then held that the regulation could be applied to production workers.]

Fourth. Effects of the unfair labor practice in respondent's enterprise.
. . . Experience has abundantly demonstrated that the recognition of the right of employees to self-organization and to have representatives of their own choosing for the purpose of collective bargaining is often an essential condition of industrial peace. Refusal to confer and negotiate has been one of the most prolific causes of strife. This is such an outstanding fact in the history of labor disturbances that it is a proper subject of judicial notice and requires no citation of instances. The opinion in the case of Virginian Railway Co. v. System Federation, No. 40, supra, points out that, in the case of carriers, experience has shown that before the amendment, of 1934, of the Railway Labor Act "when there was no dispute as to the organizations authorized to represent the employees and when there was a willingness of the employer to meet such representative for a discussion of their grievances, amicable adjustment of differences had generally followed and strikes had been avoided." That, on the other hand, "a prolific source of dispute had been the maintenance by the railroad of company unions and the denial by railway management of the authority of representatives chosen by their employees." The opinion in that case also points to the large measure of success of the labor policy embodied in the Railway Labor Act. But with respect to the appropriateness of the recognition of self-organization and representation in the promotion of peace, the question is not essentially different in the case of employees in industries of such a character that interstate commerce is put in jeopardy from the case of employees of transportation companies. And of what avail is it to protect the facility of transportation, if interstate commerce is throttled with respect to the commodities to be transported!

These questions have frequently engaged the attention of Congress and have been the subject of many inquiries. The steel industry is one of the great basic industries of the United States, with ramifying activities affecting interstate commerce at every point. The Government aptly refers to the steel strike of 1919-1920 with its far-reaching consequences. The fact that there appears to have been no major disturbance in that industry in the more recent period did not dispose of the possibilities of future and like dangers to interstate commerce which Congress was entitled to foresee and to exercise its protective power to forestall. It is not necessary again to detail the facts as to respondent's enterprise. Instead of being beyond the pale, we think that it presents in a most striking way the close and intimate relation which a manufacturing industry may have to interstate commerce and we have no doubt that Congress had constitutional authority to safeguard the right of respondent's employees to self-organization and freedom in the choice of representatives for collective bargaining.

Fifth. The means which the Act employs. — Questions under the due process clause and other constitutional restrictions. — Respondent asserts its right to conduct its business in an orderly manner without being subjected to arbitrary restraints. What we have said points to the fallacy in the argument. Employees have their correlative right to organize for the purpose of securing the redress of grievances and to promote agreements with employers relating to rates of pay and conditions of work. Texas & N.O.R. Co. v. Railway Clerks, supra; Virginian Railway Co. v. System Federation, No. 40. Restraint for the purpose of preventing an unjust interference with that right cannot be considered arbitrary or capricious. The provision of §9(a) that representatives, for the purpose of collective bargaining, of the majority of the employees in an appropriate unit shall be the exclusive representatives of all the employees in that unit, imposes upon the respondent only the duty of conferring and negotiating with the authorized representatives of its employees for the purpose of settling a labor dispute. This provision has its analogue in §2, Ninth, of the Railway Labor Act which was under consideration in Virginian Railway Co. v. System Federation, No. 40, supra. The decree which we affirmed in that case required the Railway Company to treat with the representative chosen by the employees and also to refrain from entering into collective labor agreements with anyone other than their true representative as ascertained in accordance with the provisions of the Act. We said that the obligation to treat with the true representative was exclusive and hence imposed the negative duty to treat with no other. We also pointed out that, as conceded by the Government, the injunction against the Company's entering into any contract concerning rules, rates of pay and working conditions except with a chosen representative was "designed only to prevent collective bargaining with anyone purporting to represent employees" other than the representative they had selected. It was taken "to prohibit the negotiation of labor contracts generally applicable to employees" in the described unit with any other representative than the one so chosen, "but not as precluding such individual contracts" as the Company might "elect to make directly with individual employees." We think this construction also applies to §9(a) of the National Labor Relations Act.

The Act does not compel agreements between employers and employees. It does not compel any agreement whatever. It does not prevent the employer "from refusing to make a collective contract and hiring individuals on whatever terms" the employer "may by unilateral action determine." The Act expressly provides in §9(a) that any individual employee or a group of employees shall have the right at any time to present grievances to their employer. The theory of the Act is that free opportunity for negotiation with accredited representatives of employees is likely to promote industrial peace and may bring about the adjustments and agreements which the Act in itself does not attempt to compel. . . . The Act does not interfere with the normal exercise of the right of the employer to select its employees or to discharge them. The employer may not, under cover of that right, intimidate or coerce its employees with respect to their self-organization and representation, and, on the other hand, the Board is not entitled to make its authority a pretext for interference with the right of discharge when that right is exercised for other reasons than such intimidation and coercion. The true purpose is the subject of investigation with full opportunity to show the facts. It would seem that when employers freely recognize the right of their employees to their own organizations and their unrestricted right of representation there will be much less occasion for controversy in respect to the free and appropriate exercise of the right of selection and discharge.

The Act has been criticised as one-sided in its application; that it subjects the employer to supervision and restraint and leaves untouched the abuses for which employees may be responsible; that it fails to provide a more comprehensive plan, — with better assurances of fairness to both sides and with increased chances of success in bringing about, if not compelling, equitable solutions of industrial disputes affecting interstate commerce. But we are dealing with the power of Congress, not with a particular policy or with the extent to which policy should go. We have frequently said that the legislative authority, exerted within its proper field, need not embrace all the evils within its reach. The Constitution does not forbid "cautious advance, step by step," in dealing with the evils which are exhibited in activities within the range of legislative power. . . .

The order of the Board required the reinstatement of the employees who were found to have been discharged because of their "union activity" and for the purpose of "discouraging membership in the union." That requirement was authorized by the Act. §10(c). . . .

Our conclusion is that the order of the Board was within its competency and that the Act is valid as here applied. The judgment of the Circuit Court of Appeals is reversed and the cause is remanded for further proceedings in conformity with this opinion.

JUSTICES MCREYNOLDS, VANDEVANTER, SUTHERLAND and BUTLER dissented.

FREY, DEMOCRACY, FREE ENTERPRISE, AND COLLECTIVE BARGAINING*

Democracy and freedom of enterprise are the cornerstones of our political and economic structure, and any conditions that threaten the perma-

* Alexander Hamilton Frey, Algernon Sidney Biddle Professor of Law, Uni-

nence of these basic institutions are matters of the gravest concern to the vast majority of the American people.

Democracy is a concept that arises out of *group* existence. To an individual living completely alone, democracy would have no personal significance. The term applies only to the relations of an individual to others in his group. The very idea of a group connotes a number of individuals associated together for the achievement of some common objective. The people of the United States are a vast continental community and *as a group* they have one dominant desire to which all else is subordinate, namely, that each member of the group shall have the maximum individual freedom that is consistent with like freedom for every other member of the group. "Democracy" is the term by which we Americans summarize this group objective, for when we express our belief in democracy, it is our underlying belief in this great ideal and its eternal rightness that we seek in shorthand fashion to express.

But the attainment of this degree of freedom for each devolves responsibilities upon all. For ascertaining the special function which each individual shall perform as his contribution to our democratic objectives, we have adopted two procedures: governmental and nongovernmental.

But only a very small part of the specialized tasks which our group objectives necessitate do we expressly delegate to "government." In keeping with our American conviction as to the basic importance of individual liberty, we have for the most part refrained from prescribing individual functions. So, in general, we privilege each to determine for himself what activity he will engage in, what contribution he will make to the welfare of the group.

This privilege of each American to determine for himself, free from dictation by government, what contribution he will make to the well-being of the national group, to select the uses to which his labor or his property is to be subjected, is in essence what is denoted by the term "freedom of enterprise." Obviously, if we are to be free from governmental dictation as to the production and distribution of economic goods, there must be some process whereby a decision is reached as to what each one of us shall contribute to the national economic pool, and as to what each one of us shall receive in return. In the United States these all-important questions have in general always been determined by a process of bargaining.

All over the United States, day in and day out, individuals or groups or associations are negotiating, bartering, dickering, contracting, buying and selling, lending and borrowing, renting and leasing, producing and distributing, supplying and demanding, all upon terms and under conditions reciprocally accepted — in short, bargaining. Out of this unending welter of bargaining come food, shelter, clothing, amusements, the cost of

versity of Pennsylvania Law School. This essay is based in considerable part upon material appearing in the Introductory Chapter of Frey's Cases on Labor Law 1-6 (1941), and in an article by the same author, The Logic of Collective Bargaining and Arbitration, 12 Law & Contempt. Prob. 264-280 (1947). — ED.

living, inflation, deflation, wealth, poverty, success, failure — freedom of enterprise.

The antithesis of freedom of enterprise is dictation by government: economic decisions proclaimed by governmental fiat instead of emerging from an untrammeled bargaining process. Experience demonstrates, however, that even in the United States, enterprise is not entirely free and that government does from time to time intervene.

Thus we have come to recognize that it is the proper function of those whom we denominate "government" not only to specialize in certain delegated tasks such as police and fire protection, road building, education, postal service, etc., but also to intervene and exercise a measure of control over the activities of the self-chosen specialists whenever either the security or the liberty of numbers of people is threatened. The threat may come from within or from without the nation, but from whatever source, whenever it occurs, an emergency exists and the vast majority of the members of the national group will favor governmental action or control.

Whenever government intervenes to protect the security or liberty of some, it destroys the liberty, actual or potential, of others. There is always this price which the group must pay whenever it establishes a new rule or delegates a new power.

For the preservation of our system of freedom of enterprise it is essential to minimize conditions that will be regarded by the majority of the people as emergencies justifying governmental intervention. In any given transaction there may be a considerable disparity between the bargaining powers of buyer and seller without any noteworthy effect upon our economy. Some inequality of bargaining power is the rule rather than the exception, and our free-enterprise system does not, and cannot reasonably be expected to, concern itself with minor advantages that may accrue to the stronger party. But if there is an absence of bargaining power, or if a pronounced disparity of bargaining power develops as to a significant class of buyers (or sellers), then experience has taught that government will intervene, either by dictating to buyer and seller the terms of the sale (thus removing it from the traditional process of free enterprise), or by attempting to improve the bargaining power of the weaker side, so that the bargaining process, and the free-enterprise system, may continue to function without the injustice inherent in inequality. (Infancy laws, usury statutes, and fiduciary standards are traditional examples; so, too, are temporary controls on rents, commodities, wages, etc., when emergency conditions disrupt the normal balance of bargaining power.)

Whatever the subject matter of the transaction may be, a "bargaining" situation does not obtain between a buyer and a seller unless each is able to force upon the other some concession, some abandonment of a preferred position. The seller can exert very little pressure with respect to the terms of the sale unless there is some degree of scarcity, some limitation upon the supply of that which he seeks to sell. This is the first essential of "bargaining power." If the seller is offering something for which the buyer is willing to pay a price, i.e., which it is advantageous to the buyer to purchase at some price, the ultimate price which the seller receives, whether he controls all or only a fraction of the supply, depends upon the respective resources with which each of the parties can withstand a deadlock. In other words, if the seller has no capital, if he must sell to live — even in the extreme case where he controls the entire supply — he must accept the best terms offered, however far below what he regards as a "fair" price. Without some resources at the seller's command, there is no element of "give and take" in the situation. This is the second essential of "bargaining power."

Since "bargaining" is the core of freedom of enterprise, those who lack one or both of these essentials of bargaining power are in reality not within the framework of the system, and if such persons constitute a considerable class of buyers or sellers, the deficiency must be eliminated, or governmental intervention to promote their interests may be anticipated, with the attendant danger of a chain reaction resulting in extensive inroads upon the free-enterprise system.

The Industrial Revolution, i.e., the mechanization of the processes of production and the introduction of the factory system, brought about conditions which have terminated the ability of any but the most highly skilled workers to bargain individually with their employers on a basis of equality. In earlier times employer and employee generally belonged to the same community, attended the same church, participated in the same political activities, and were not very far removed in the economic scale. There was no great surplus of labor; if the terms of employment offered to a given employee by his employer where unsatisfactory, more likely than not they would talk face to face and reach an accord. Or if the terms were regarded by the employee as utterly unreasonable, he could do odd jobs for others, farm on his own land, and look forward to the security of at least subsistence for himself and his family for an indefinite period. And eventually either his employer would feel the need of his services sufficiently to modify his former offer, or the employee would find other satisfactory work in the same community.

But with the coming of the Industrial Revolution all this was changed. Great cities developed which were the centers of the factory system. The individual worker and his employer grew farther and farther apart socially and economically. The favorable atmosphere for personal conferences and adjustment of disputes disappeared. Mass production methods resulted in huge concentrations of labor and in a great increase in the percentage of jobs not requiring skilled work. Thus unskilled workers are today the vast majority of those employed or seeking employment, and their labor has little or no element of scarcity. Moreover, whether skilled or unskilled, the individual factory worker normally has no capital with which to withstand a "buyers' strike." He owns no land, has no tools, and hence has few resources with which he and his family can hope to survive an extended deadlock with his employer over terms of employment. Furthermore, labor cannot be preserved and held for a more favorable market: a worker cannot tomorrow sell today's unexpended labor. Nor does the labor of an individual worker have the fluidity that attaches to most commodities or to credit seeking a market: a workman in Philadelphia does not have the resources with which to avail himself of an opportunity for employment that may exist in Chicago or even in Pittsburgh. He and his family are effectively bound to a limited geographical area of job opportunity; and within this area the job opportunities may, as in many a mill town, all be controlled by a single employer.

This unfavorable bargaining position of the individual worker has been greatly accentuated by the phenomenal growth in the use of the corporation as a device for conducting business enterprises, both large and small. In the commercial world the corporation has become much the most important employer of labor. Many persons, however, are still accustomed to think of labor problems in terms of the relations between an individual small businessman and his few employees. One so conditioned is very apt to overlook the most significant factors behind the current labor movement, factors arising out of the present commanding and expanding position of the modern corporation in national affairs. Although the law conceives of a corporation, for many purposes, as an entity — a single fictitious person — it is patent that the influential corporations are in fact huge combinations of persons, strongly equipped for bargaining purposes on all fronts.

In short, under modern industrial conditions the individual worker is powerless to bargain on an equal basis with his employer with respect to the terms of his employment. Acting alone, he has no practical alternative but to accept the terms offered to him. And this unfavorable bargaining position is reflected in the development of the case law relating to the economic hazards which confront the individual worker. He has no job security, no protection from discharge without "cause." Where any ambiguity exists, or if the term is indefinite, courts tend to construe employment contracts not as contracts for a term but as a hiring at will. The individual worker is not only unable to insure job security for himself; he is also powerless to influence the amount or frequency of his wage payments, to resist if his employer demands of him an excessive number of hours of labor, or to force his employer to install safety devices and other protections against industrial accidents.

If it be conceded that under modern industrial conditions the individual worker, acting alone, has little or no bargaining power, then it must be recognized that he will endeavor to foster his interests by acting in concert with his fellow workers. To labor leaders and other students of labor problems the desirability of organizations through which workers can bargain collectively is axiomatic, for labor unions can do much to offset the lack of bargaining power of the individual member. In the first place, they provide a medium for concerted action by which the supply of labor available to an employer may be restricted, so that even unskilled labor in an era of unemployment will have some scarcity value. Secondly, their treasuries constitute a potential source of that minimum of capital which the individual worker must have if he is to be able to resist at all when deadlocked with his employer over terms and conditions of employment. Thus, through unionization, the individual worker is enabled to secure at least a measure of the two essentials of bargaining power.

If workers fail in their efforts to bring themselves within the framework of our free-enterprise system by achieving collective bargaining power — and they had failed signally prior to the passage of the National Labor Relations Act in 1935 — then governmental intervention to promote the interests of a group of such proportions may be anticipated. Apparently the Congress and various state legislatures ultimately came to regard the unequal bargaining position of the individual worker as an emergency justifying legislative attention. They might have attempted by legislative fiat to force upon employers and employees prescribed wages, hours, prices, and other standards. But in a society such as ours, dedicated to the perpetuation of a system of free enterprise, the function of government is not to displace that system but to protect it, and fortunately government has elected to put its faith in the ability of labor and capital voluntarily to reach agreements that in the long run will be in the best interests of society. Accordingly, the Federal Government has thus far sought to safeguard the individual worker in interstate commerce not by dictating the wages to be paid to him, but by facilitating the development of organization through which he may achieve the only kind of realistic freedom of enterprise available to him, namely, collective bargaining.

There can be little doubt that if the collective bargaining endeavor fails significantly to bring about substantial equality of bargaining power between employers, and employees,[1] the government will be forced to attempt to aid whichever is the weaker side by dictating wages to be paid and received. Dictation by government of the terms of any scale (even the establishment of "floors" and "ceilings") tends to set off a chain of governmental actions which increasingly restrict the areas of free enterprise. This is particularly true with respect to the establishment of labor costs by governmental fiat, for in order to effectuate its wage policy the government would find it had also to concern itself with other costs and with prices, which in turn would involve profits, and the investment of capital, and the use of property, and the myriad decisions which are now reached by the traditional process of free bargaining.

If the alternatives are substantial equality of bargaining power for the individual employee in relation to his employer through the device of collective bargaining, or governmental dictation of wages and a congeries of related interests, then collective bargaining emerges as a potential bulwark of the free-enterprise system, and labor unions are seen as organizations having significance to society as well as to their own members. An understanding of the factors without which collective bargaining cannot succeed is of the utmost importance to the preservation of our national economy.

Since individual workers can bring themselves within the framework of our free-enterprise system only by bargaining collectively, the first essen-

[1] Collective bargaining might fail either because employers succeed in reducing unions to an impotent state, or because unions become so powerful and arrogant as to make a mockery of bargaining negotiations.

tial is that employers shall bargain with their employees only on a collective and not on an individual basis. Even though a group of workers form an organization and agree to negotiate only as a unit with a given employer or potential employer, they do not in fact achieve any bargaining power with reference to that employer so long as he is able to obtain an adequate supply of competent employees on his own terms by dealing individually with other, unorganized workers. Hence, if there is a sincere desire to have labor relations determined by a genuine bargaining process, and not by governmental fiat, it is necessary either that employers voluntarily refrain from dealing with individual workers for their labor except on terms that have emerged from collective bargaining negotiations, or that employers be precluded from engaging in such individual transactions by virtue of the organization of substantially all available workers as members of one or more labor unions through which they will bargain collectively only.

The suggested self-restraint is hardly likely to occur: each employer (even corporations employing huge aggregates of workers) will discount the danger of eventual governmental intervention on a national scale because of the absence of genuine bargaining in his plant; each employer will convince himself that the terms and conditions of employment which he will unilaterally establish if the opportunity presents itself are fair and reasonable. Accordingly, it is difficult to escape the conclusion that bargaining as to labor relations can exist only if employers cannot obtain adequate supplies of labor except by first negotiating terms and conditions of employment with an association of workers organized to bargain collectively.

Even if the employer has, however, no choice but to deal with one union representing all of his employees or potential employees in a given bargaining unit,[2] this does not place the employer in the unfair position of a would-be buyer of a commodity which has been monopolized by a single seller. The monopolistic commodity seller has many potential buyers to pit against one another, they being unorganized, while each individual buyer has, by hypothesis, no alternate seller with whom to deal.[3] A labor union is a bargaining agency only if the workers comprising it act as one man in selling their labor. The difficulty or impossibility

[2] A bargaining unit is not a union; it is a group of jobs. It may be the jobs connected with a particular machine or operation; it may be the jobs of a particular craft, such as painters; it may be the jobs in a particular department of a plant; it may be clerical jobs or production jobs; it may be all nonsupervisory jobs in a given plant or in all the plants of the employer. Collective bargaining cannot proceed until the bargaining unit has been determined, whether by prior practice or custom, decision of an administrative agency, or agreement of the parties.

[3] Except where labor is involved, individual sellers and individual buyers are in general deemed to have comparable bargaining power. Hence, when unions of commodity sellers have been formed, government has sought, through antitrust statutes, to restore the bargaining process by breaking up such combinations. With respect to individual sellers of labor, government has attempted, through labor relations statutes, to re-establish the bargaining process by stimulating the development of unions of such sellers.

which an employer encounters in finding another group of employees, when all are organized, is thus matched by the difficulty or impossibility which the union members, as a unit, encounter in finding another employer. The first element of bargaining equality is therefore present, i.e., the opportunities for the buyer to buy and the seller to sell elsewhere are equal.

This unitary aspect of organized workers is an essential element of collective bargaining. There can be no bargaining as to the sale of labor without the right to strike and to lock out. Unless those available for work in a given bargaining unit are permitted to act in concert in refusing to work on the job or jobs involved in the bargaining unit, and unless the employer is permitted to withhold job opportunities from the members of the bargaining unit as a group, a bargaining condition as to labor relations cannot exist.

Outside the field of labor relations, the equivalent of a strike or a lockout is a normal element in the bargaining process. When buyer A (usually a corporation) is unable to reach an accord with seller X (usually another corporation), buyer A refuses to deal further with seller X, or vice versa, and each seeks a seller or a buyer elsewhere. But, as indicated above, when a bargaining impasse occurs between an employer and a union, resulting in a strike or a lockout, there is normally no other seller (i.e., the entire group of workers involved in the bargaining unit) for the buyer (i.e., the employer) to turn to, and there is no other employer from whom the workers as a body can obtain employment. The accuracy of this statement is not affected by the fact that a few employees, as individuals, may be able to get some kind of temporary work elsewhere, or that the employer may be able to obtain a trickle of replacements for individual workers. If a strike develops in any plant in which the organized workers constitute a sizable segment of the community, the possibility of other jobs or other workers being obtained on a substantial scale is illusory. Consequently, so long as the deadlock continues, the parties have no alternatives but to wait each other out, or to resume negotiations with each other.

The vast body of consumers constituting the public has a very real interest in not having the production of coal, steel, transportation, automobiles, housing, food, and goods and services of many other sorts interrupted while employers and employees engaged in such production slug out their differences over labor relations. Consequently, there are recurring proposals for federal or state legislation aimed at precluding strikes and lockouts, at least in those situations in which the public interest is vitally affected. If such an inroad on collective bargaining should ever be ordained, the omnivorous character of the concept of a "vitally affected" public interest can readily be imagined. But very few members of the public fully comprehend that there is no bargaining power available to most workers in modern industry unless those who can perform the jobs in a given bargaining unit are able to act as one man, and unless that "one man" is given the privilege which any individual has of refusing to work upon the terms or under the conditions proffered. Too many employers are unmindful of the long-range probability that the absence of collective bargaining as to labor relations will lead to the destruction of their freedom of enterprise and the emergence of some form of state socialism or planned economy.

Here, then, is a perplexing dilemma: strikes which materially affect the production or distribution of essential commodities are inimical to the public interest, but legislation which curtails the right to strike, thus in effect eliminating collective bargaining, is not an expedient way to protect the public interest, for the consequences of the cure may too readily be worse than the disease.

It is of the utmost importance constantly to bear in mind that the basic purpose of collective bargaining is not the process of negotiating and dickering, but the reaching of an agreement between labor and management. Toward the achievement of this purpose the strike, or the possibility thereof, fulfills an essential function. Strikes occur when the parties have failed to reach agreement, i.e., when collective bargaining has not achieved its purpose. A strike thrusts both ways — it visits financial detriment upon both the employer and his employees. Hence it ultimately renders each side more amenable to compromise, more willing to recede somewhat from a position that may have contributed to the impasse. In the realm of labor relations the free-enterprise system can exist only if strikes, actual or potential, are permitted to fulfill this function. Here then is the real dilemma: the public has admittedly an interest in the production lost through strikes; it also has an interest in the preservation and strengthening of the free-enterprise system of which voluntary agreement is the core. Which interest is, or should be, paramount?

SIMONS, SOME REFLECTIONS ON SYNDICALISM [1]
52 Journal of Political Economy 1 (1944)

Students of social science must fear popular approval; evil is with them when all men speak well of them. If there is any set of opinions by the advocacy of which a newspaper can increase its sales, then the student . . . is bound to dwell on the limitations and defects and errors, if any, in that set of opinions; and never to advocate them unconditionally even in an ad hoc discussion. It is almost impossible

---

[1] Author's note: The manuscript of this article was prepared in 1941. It was designed, not for publication, but as an exercise in formulating some persuasions or prejudices which kept creeping into discussions of other subjects or problems. Later, several friends looked at the manuscript. Some of them, though not all, questioned the presumption against publication. So the matter was referred to the editors. After they decided to publish, one insert and a few footnotes were added to the original draft.

[Henry C. Simons was Professor of Economics at the University of Chicago. This article is reprinted here with the permission of the copyright owner, the Journal of Political Economy. It has been reduced to less than half its original length for the purpose of this volume. The deletions have been of paragraphs, of sentences, and, in a few instances, of phrases. All deletions are indicated by ellipsis points. — Ed.]

for a student to be a true patriot and to have the reputation of being
one at the same time.

—ALFRED MARSHALL [2]

Questioning the virtues of the organized labor movements is like at-
tacking religion, monogamy, motherhood or the home. . . . One simply
cannot argue that organization is injurious to labor; one is either for labor or against it, and the test is one's attitude toward unionism. But let
me indicate from the outset that my central interest, and the criterion in
terms of which I wish to argue, is a maximizing of aggregate labor income
and a minimizing of inequality. If unionism were good for labor as a
whole, that would be the end of the issue for me, since the community
whose welfare concerns us is composed overwhelmingly of laborers.

Our problem here, at bottom, is one of broad political philosophy. . . .
What we generally fail to see is the identity of interest between the
whole community and enterprises seeking to keep down costs. Where
enterprise is competitive — and substantial, enduring restraint of competition in product markets is rare — enterprisers represent the community
interest effectively; indeed, they are merely intermediaries between consumers of goods and sellers of services. Thus we commonly overlook the
conflict of interest between every large organized group of laborers and
the community as a whole. . . .

All the grosser mistakes in economic policy, if not most manifestations
of democratic corruption, arise from focusing upon the interests of people
as producers rather than upon their interests as consumers, i.e., from
acting on behalf of producer minorities rather than on behalf of the
whole community as sellers of services and buyers of products. One gets
the right answers usually by regarding simply the interests of consumers,
since we are all consumers; and the answers reached by this approach are
presumably the correct ones for laborers as a whole. But one doesn't
get elected by approaching issues in this way! People seldom vote in
terms of their common interests, whether as sellers or as buyers. . . .

I am arguing . . . as an advocate of the elaborate mixed system of traditional economic liberalism. The essence of this practical political philosophy is a distrust of all concentrations of power. No individual may
be trusted with much power, no organization, and no institution save the
state itself. . . .

Monopoly power must be abused. It has no use save abuse. Some
people evidently have believed that labor organizations should have monopoly powers and be trusted not to use them. Collective bargaining, for
the Webbs, was evidently a scheme whereby labor monopolies were to
raise wages to competitive levels, merely counteracting monopsony[11]
among buyers, but eschewing further exercise of organizational powers.

[2] Quoted in A. C. Pigou, Economics in Practice (London, 1935), pp. 10-11.
[11] A situation where a single buyer (as distinguished from a producer or seller),
or several buyers acting in unison, control substantially the entire demand for a
commodity. See Wilcox, Investigation of Concentration of Economic Power,
TNEC Monograph No. 21, p. 10 (1940). — ED.

A trade-unionism, affecting wages and working rules only within such limits, and doing all the many other good things that unions can do, would be a blessing all around. No one could seriously question its merits in the abstract. But monopsony in the labor market is, I think, very unsubstantial or transitory; and it is romantic and unreasonable to expect organizations to exercise powers only within limits consistent with the common interest. All bargaining power is monopoly power. Such power, once attained, will be used as fully as its conservation permits and also used continuously for its own accretion and consolidation. . . .

I do not assert that our only monopoly problems lie in the labor market. . . . It is shameful to have permitted the growth of vast corporate empires, the collusive restraint of trade by trade-associations, and the gross abuse of patent privilege for extortion, exclusion, and output restriction. But enterprise monopoly is also a skin disease, easy to correct when and if we will, and usually moderate in its abuses, since its powers are necessarily small, and since the danger of political reckoning is never very remote. Enterprise monopoly, enjoying very limited access to violence and facing heavy penalties for unfair methods against rivals, is always plagued by competition, actual and potential, and must always operate against a deeply hostile, if lethargic, attitude of courts, legislatures, and the public. . . . The proper remedies here are not very difficult technically or politically.

Labor monopolies are, now or potentially, a different kind of animal. . . . If governments have tolerated flagrant violations of law by employers, they are nearly impotent to enforce laws against mass minorities even if majority opinion permitted it. Thus, unions may deal with scabs in ways which make even Rockefeller's early methods seem polite and legitimate. They have little to fear from chiselers in their own midst; and they have now little to fear from Congress or the courts. . . .

I am here arguing merely the classical case for free trade, free markets, and free occupational migration. The argument is equally sound whether invoked against external or internal barriers, against governmental restrictions on trade, or against those imposed by private monopolies. . . . The public interest demands free exchange and free movement of workers among occupations. Above all, it demands the easiest possible access by workers in low-wage occupations to highly productive and unusually remunerative employment. Unionism implies ability of established workers in high-wage areas and occupations to insulate themselves from competition, excluding inexperienced new workers and qualitatively inferior labor from their markets. . . .[8]

[8] . . . Incidentally, I am wholly intolerant of the apology usually made, for labor monopolies and for almost every particular racket, that "everyone is doing it." A prominent educator is alleged recently to have said, also by way of apology: "There is no public interest any more; there are only interests." If such statements are true, moral or realistic, we should all make careers in the army and assert that military dictatorship is the only feasible foreign policy and the only means to internal peace or prosperity! Another implication is that nothing should be done about anything until everything has been done about everything else.

Labor demands may be rationalized and popularized as demands for a larger share of earnings — as part of a contest over the shares of labor and capital in particular outputs. But enterprises remain essentially inter-mediaries between sellers of services and buyers of product. The sem-blance of struggle between labor and capital conceals the substantial con-flict between a labor monopoly and the community; between organized workers and consumers; and especially between established workers in more remunerative occupations and workers elsewhere. The masses of the unorganized and unorganizable lose as consumers; they lose by being denied access to higher-wage areas; and they lose by an artificial abun-dance of labor in the markets where they must sell, i.e., by being forced to compete with workers who should have been drawn off into the higher-wage occupations. . . .[12]

If we are to preserve modern industrial production without totalitarian control, we must solve the problem of private investment. . . . Every new enterprise and every new investment must now pay heavy tribute to labor (and other monopolies) in acquiring its plant and equipment; and it faces the prospect of increasing extortion in its efforts to utilize facilities after they are constructed. . . .

We face a real problem in economic inequality. This problem can be handled easily and without serious diseconomies, if one is not hysterically in a hurry, by progressive taxation of income and inheritance. Merely by repairing a few structural flaws in our income tax, we could assure steady reduction of inequality in property incomes and continuous correction of wide disparities in non-property incomes. But radicals and powerseekers have little interest in such dull, peaceful, orderly, efficient, gradualist methods. So they have simply ignored critical issues in tax reform and plumped for labor organization. . . .

Few Americans will straightforwardly espouse syndicalism or look with approval on Il Duce's corporative state. Few likewise will face the patent fact that we are rushing pell-mell toward and into the political order in the United States. Our formal political structure, of course, retains its traditional character. Our legislators, state and federal, still represent geographic sections of the nation. But alongside this formal political structure arises now a structure of powerful organizations of labor, im-mune to prosecution as monopolies and largely immune to the proscrip-tions or penalties of other laws. . . .

[12] One may recognize the possibility that, with wide or universal organization of workers, federations of unions might enforce some moderation of wage de-mands and of exclusive, restrictive practices among the labor aristocracies. Such internal discipline among and between unions is a real contingency in small, homogeneous nations like Sweden (especially if complemented by a strong free-trade tradition). In a vast nation or a culturally heterogeneous population, the possibility may be dismissed as utterly unsubstantial. Moreover, the develop-ment of such effective "regulation" would involve radical constitutional change in the political system, i.e., reduction of the Congress or national legislature to a status not unlike that of the British crown.
It is interesting to note that Swedish co-operatives have at times discharged functions of our Anti-Trust Division — which is not a decisive reason for abolish-ing that agency here!

The intricate pluralism of modern democracies is, of course, a commonplace among students of sociology and politics. . . . But . . . we have never faced the kind of minority problem which widespread, aggressive, national and regional unions and their federations present. . . . Peaceful strikes, even in the absence of overt violence or intimidation, are a meaningless conception when they involve disruption of an elaborate production process with intricate division of labor. What is obvious in the case of railways and utilities is similarly true of coal-mining, steel production, and ultimately of every important industry and occupation. . . .

The obvious struggle within particular industries over division of earnings tends largely to obscure the more substantial identity of interest and functional complementarity of labor and employer organizations. Popularly regarded and defended as counterpoises to industrial concentration or enterprise monopoly, unions in fact serve mainly to buttress effective monopoly in product markets where it already obtains, and to call it into existence when it does not. . . .

While extremely ill-informed, I know of no instance where a powerful union has proposed reduction of a monopolistic product price or given real support, singly or in federations, to anti-trust policy. On the other hand, N.I.R.A., like extreme tariff protection, was strongly supported by organized labor. The formal and enforced cartelization of the coal industry may be credited largely to U.M.W. . . . If labor remains and becomes increasingly cartelized along industry lines, enterprises must be similarly organized for bargaining purposes — not only to present a united front and to recoup wage-increases from consumers but because labor itself will prefer, demand, and, in any case, compel such employer organization. . . .

We must alter our labor policy or abandon our anti-trust policy — as English businessmen so urgently recommend. If one big union is a fait accompli in, say, the automotive industry, that industry is all through as a competitive sector of our economy — and damned to full cartelization, if not to General Motors. . . . If labor is tightly cartelized or syndicalized, enterprises must adjust themselves to the political realities. . . .

It is easy to argue that the whole problem is so hard and ominous politically that no effort should be made to solve or even see it. . . . I maintain that it is immoral to take such absolute dilemmas seriously. . . .

With free trade the world can gradually be welded into a securely peaceful, democratic whole; with it, we may work miracles in monetary and political co-operation, in raising standards everywhere by economic integration and by relatively unrestricted movements both of goods and of investment funds. . . . But there can be no free world trade without free internal trade in the dominant post-war nation. . . . Free trade among collectivisms is a meaningless conception. . . . There can be no really free access to raw materials produced by monopolists or cartels, or to raw materials produced by workers organized to price their services monopolistically.

Given free internal trade . . . we can prosper far more abundantly as part of a world economy and can lead the whole world into durable prosperity and peace. Thus, I submit that the peace will be won or lost in the field of American domestic economic policy . . . on issues in the field of labor policy. . . .

The peace will be won or lost on the simple issue of economic disarmament. The extreme nationalism of high protection, quota limitations, exchange controls, and bilateral trading must be swept away, at least among the leading protagonists in the present conflict. But movement in this direction cannot come unless there is wholesale economic disarmament also within these nations. As nations, we must abandon the contest for dominance and subjugation, finding our proper places in a close-knit, integrated world economy whose markets and commodities are freely and equally available to all. As individuals, we must find and make our places in a domestic system of free exchange, instead of organizing into occupational or industrial states to pursue domestically a power contest which is the analogue of war among nations, and perhaps its most important cause.[12]

JAFFE, LAW MAKING BY PRIVATE GROUPS*
51 Harvard Law Review 201, 250-253 (1937)

With the Carter Coal case [supra page 47] we must compare the Virginian Railway case [relied on in Jones & Laughlin, supra page 49] in which the majority rule for collective bargaining was upheld. How does it differ? In the latter all persons in the class have a formal vote. There is less likelihood of the oppression of the minority or of nonrepresented groups. But it is like the Carter case in that the majority secure the power to negotiate a contract which will be binding on all members of the class. Here there is no standard. Indeed, it is difficult to see what the standard could be; nor is there administrative control. And where regulation proceeds from private contract, as in the Fair Trade Acts permitting the fixing of resale prices, the Court, with its traditional preference for such regulation, finds that it violates no constitutional prohibition. There a manufacturer of an article — and large manufacturers are prone to "follow" each other and so arrive at a uniform fixed price throughout the field — fixes the price at which the retailer is to sell and the consumer to buy. But where government specifically delegates overt and positive power to an entire group as in the Bituminous Coal Act then the Court is more sensitive to oppression and may strike it down. Will a standard of action save it? It surely can do no harm, but if the likelihood of oppression is seriously entertained by the Court, neither will it do

---

[12] For another vigorous critique of federal labor policy see Petro, The Labor Policy for the Free Society (1957). A rejoinder to Petro's analysis can be found in Willcox, The Labor Policy of a Free Society; A Review, 11 Ind. & Lab. Rel. Rev. 272 (1958); Wollett, Book Review, 36 Texas L. Rev. 252 (1957). — ED.

* Louis L. Jaffe, Professor of Law, Harvard University. Reprinted with the permission of the editors of the Harvard Law Review, copyright 1937 by the Harvard Law Review Association.

much good. A group of producers is given, for example, a power to fix a minimum price to buyers. Would it not be an empty protection to require that the price be "reasonable?" For even assuming that this standard has meaning, there is absent, as suggested above, disinterested administration. The logical implication of the demand for a standard is that there be at some point a public administrative control. Where oppression cannot be otherwise avoided, sound political theory would demand such control. It might be thought that in every case such a control is advisable if only to resolve a doubt. But the values to be derived from self-government, which I have discussed above, may in this way be lessened; indeed, to do away with public administrative control may have been the prime purpose of the delegation to the private group. The judgment as to when such a control is advisable or necessary would seem to be one for Congress to make. The extent to which devices for self-government can be used with safety and profit is, par excellence, a matter for experiment to be carried on under the surveillance of the legislature. Anticipated danger should not in itself bring down the doom of unconstitutionality. But the Carter Coal Co. decision shows that in certain cases, at least, concessions must be made to the judicial demand for safeguards, and here a measure of public control should suffice to meet that demand, though a number of courts find not even that control enough and so close the door entirely to the use of these devices.

In all that has gone before it may have seemed to the reader that there has been a naïve assumption that these groups and their numbers are completely benevolent, that within them no member will be oppressed and that the group will deal fairly with the world. It is undoubtedly true that the doctrinal writers who have propounded the need for group autonomy have either been unaware of, or have deliberately ignored (in true propaganda fashion), the problem of controlling the exercise of autonomous powers. In dwelling on the beauties of co-operation in our society the wishful thinker may exaggerate the uniformities of the units composing industrial groups. It is undeniable that almost any imaginable group given extensive powers may oppress the minority of the group and exploit other groups. To what extent this will be so is, of course, largely a matter of speculation as to a future situation, and it may be that the controls must be evolved through experiment. Recent experience has demonstrated these dangers in nearly every field. In agriculture a mutual policy of crop restriction in the interests of the landowner may be oppressive to share tenants at whose expense the restriction may be carried on; a policy of price and production regulation in the marketing of an agricultural product may be seized upon by powerful distributors, or distributors allied with dominant producing interests, to destroy the competitive position of small producers, e.g., a small producer by eliminating costly overhead may be able, legitimately, to sell at a price which could not cover these costs for the bigger producer; regulations imposing minimum price may put the small producer out of business. The same effects were widely complained of in connection with the administration of industrial codes under the National Industrial Recovery

Act. In these situations there is also the interest of the public, difficult to
define or evaluate, and having no effective organization. In the past it
has been possible to assume that within the ranks of labor there is no
conflict. It is still true in considerable degree that what a majority of a
given industrial labor group desires is likely to be for the interest of the
entire group. But there are disquieting signs of danger to the rank and
file from corrupt labor bureaucracies, and many might be alarmed at the
prospect of placing in their hands coercive instruments enabling them to
perpetuate their hegemony by corrupt deals with management. Indeed,
our entire economy is honeycombed with violent and bitter intra and
inter group conflict.

Do these dangers mean that the entire concept of group participation
in whatever form is inadvisable politically and outlawed constitutionally?
Mr. Justice Sutherland in the Carter Coal Co. case adverted to the antagonistic interests within the coal industry and deduced the proposition
that "in the very nature of things, one person may not be entrusted with
the power to regulate the business of another". In reply it may be urged
that we are presented with a choice of evils. The power of special interests pervades our entire legal and governmental structure. Once given
the fact that a phase of our economic life is to be regulated, it must be
understood that these interests will, in one way or another, be effective, be
it in the legislative or in the administrative process. Under both the
Recovery Act and the Agricultural Adjustment Act — particularly as it
related to marketing — the initiative in proposing a scheme came from
some group in the industry, and expectably this group would be the dominant group, the organized group. The possibility was great that its ideas
would be written into law. Such representation, though not necessarily
covert, is unofficial and irresponsible. As amended the Agricultural Adjustment Act requires a vote of ratification by the interested producers
before a marketing scheme can become law. It is true that in certain
instances this may, by giving it the use of a coercive sanction, increase the
power of the dominant group. It is true also that a veto may be of little
use without leadership and organization, and that it is of the very nature
of the inferior groups that they lack these things. But admitting these
limitations on the value of democratic procedures, both here and in general, it is still true that the franchise provides the unorganized groups —
who may even be a majority — with an opportunity which without it
they do not have. It is much more feasible to rally specialized groups
than a mass of undifferentiated voters. Granted that the less powerful
components of a group might be in a position where they must accept
some plan, they may still wring concessions; and the possibility of this
may in a measure control the original drafting.

Courts must not strike down lightly legislative plans for group participation in law making and government. The machine must be harnessed
and run by those who can best run it; and individual will must find
employment and expression. For these ends the legislature may legitimately consider that public administration in some cases is inadequate
acting alone and in others a positive and unnecessary embarrassment. In

a world imperatively needing organization the risk of granting power in some form is inevitable. The devices here suggested do not violate the genius and tradition of our law; and indeed, if sound political judgment goes into their making, may reinforce and underscore the democratic pattern of our institutions. "If we would guide by the light of reason, we must let our minds be bold."

BLUMROSEN, UNION-MANAGEMENT AGREEMENTS WHICH HARM OTHERS*
10 Journal of Public Law 345, 345-346 (1962)

Our labor laws urge unions and management to adjust their differences through the process of collective bargaining. As union and management officials accept this principle, they may decide to join forces and achieve their objectives at the expense of competitors, workers or the public. Those who are injured by these union-management decisions may seek legal protection. This crystallizes a conflict between legal policies in support of collective bargaining which indicates a broad area of freedom for union-management agreement and policies which would require union and management to recognize other interests. . . .

Our attitude toward the power of union and management acting jointly will be a reflection of our attitude toward powerful private groups in our society. The critical role played in the destiny of individuals, groups and the nation by the union, the corporation, the church and the professional association has given rise to great concern. We have mixed feelings about such power in the hands of private groups.

We respect free action. Free private decision is the goal of many of our legal and political institutions, the object of much of our public philosophy. Decisions of private groups are entitled to respect in our system of values simply because they are reached by the process of free private decision. Furthermore, our distrust of centralized government leads us to applaud these private groups as power centers of sufficient independence to restrain possible excesses of government.

But we are troubled when private groups exercise power without any required responsibility toward the broader community. We wonder if our distrust of government is actually a distrust of those who hold power. If so, perhaps privately exercised power should be subjected to restrictions analogous to those imposed on government. Such restraints must come, directly or indirectly, from government itself. Thus we wish government to regulate private power while the private power centers are justified as a check on government. In this rough sense, we have imported a "balance of power" concept into our view of the relation between government and group. Having "politicized" the relation, we should not be surprised to find private power attempting to influence those in government who would regulate it.

But ambivalence and uncertainty concerning the proper relation

* Alfred W. Blumrosen, Professor of Law, Rutgers University. Reprinted with the permission of the editors of the Journal of Public Law.

among government, group and individual may have an important virtue. Uncertainty means that experimentation is permissible; that the painful process of thoughtfully considering all elements of emerging problems may play an important, perhaps decisive, role in their resolution. Therefore careful analysis of each problem is urgently required. The evolution of sound, legal relationships between group and group, government and group, and individual and group must have an adequate foundation which requires: (1) an understanding of the realities to be regulated, (2) general legal concepts which can be brought to bear on this reality, (3) decisions on a policy level as to how conflicting interests should be adjusted and (4) legal doctrines which can translate these policy decisions into requirements for specific action on the part of those concerned.

J. I. CASE CO. v. NLRB

Supreme Court of the United States, 1944
321 U.S. 332, 64 Sup. Ct. 576, 88 L. Ed. 762

MR. JUSTICE JACKSON delivered the opinion of the Court.

This case was heard by the National Labor Relations Board on stipulated facts which so far as concern present issues are as follows:

The petitioner, J. I. Case Company, at its Rock Island, Illinois, plant, from 1937 offered each employee an individual contract of employment. The contracts were uniform and for a term of one year. The Company agreed to furnish employment as steadily as conditions permitted, to pay a specified rate, which the Company might redetermine if the job changed, and to maintain certain hospital facilities. The employee agreed to accept the provisions, to serve faithfully and honestly for the term, to comply with factory rules, and that defective work should not be paid for. About 75% of the employees accepted and worked under these agreements.

According to the Board's stipulation and finding, the execution of these contracts was not a condition of employment, nor was the status of individual employees affected by reason of signing or failing to sign the contracts. It is not found or contended that the agreements were coerced, obtained by any unfair labor practice, or that they were not valid under the circumstances in which they were made.

While the individual contracts executed August 1, 1941 were in effect, a C.I.O. union petitioned the Board for certification as the exclusive bargaining representative of the production and maintenance employees. On December 17, 1941 a hearing was held, at which the Company urged the individual contracts as a bar to representation proceedings. The Board, however, directed an election which was won by the union. The union was thereupon certified as the exclusive bargaining representative of the employees in question in respect to wages, hours, and other conditions of employment.

The union then asked the Company to bargain. It refused, declaring that it could not deal with the union in any manner affecting rights and obligations under the individual contracts while they remained in effect.

It offered to negotiate on matters which did not affect rights under the individual contracts, and said that upon the expiration of the contracts it would bargain as to all matters. Twice the Company sent circulars to its employees asserting the validity of the individual contracts and stating the position that it took before the Board in reference to them.

The Board held that the Company had refused to bargain collectively, in violation of Sec. 8(5) of the National Labor Relations Act, and that the contracts had been utilized, by means of the circulars, to impede employees in the exercise of rights guaranteed by Sec. 7 of the Act, with the result that the Company had engaged in unfair labor practices within the meaning of Sec. 8(1) of the Act. It ordered the Company to cease and desist from giving effect to the contracts, from extending them or entering into new ones, from refusing to bargain and from interfering with the employees; and it required the Company to give notice accordingly and to bargain upon request.

The Circuit Court of Appeals, with modification not in issue here, granted an order of enforcement. The issues are unsettled ones important in the administration of the Act, and we granted certiorari. In doing so we asked counsel, in view of the expiration of the individual contracts and the negotiation of a collective contract, to discuss whether the case was moot. In view of the continuing character of the order we think it is not, and will examine the merits.

Contract in labor law is a term the implications of which must be determined from the connection in which it appears. Collective bargaining between employer and the representatives of a unit, usually a union, results in an accord as to terms which will govern hiring and work and pay in that unit. The result is not, however, a contract of employment except in rare cases; no one has a job by reason of it and no obligation to any individual ordinarily comes into existence from it alone. The negotiations between union and management result in what has often been called a trade agreement, rather than in a contract of employment. Without pushing the analogy too far, the agreement may be likened to the tariffs established by a carrier, to standard provisions prescribed by supervising authorities for insurance policies, or to utility schedules of rates and rules for service, which do not of themselves establish any relationships but which do govern the terms of the shipper or insurer or customer relationship whenever and with whomever it may be established. Indeed, in some European countries, contrary to American practice, the terms of a collectively negotiated trade agreement are submitted to a government department and if approved become a governmental regulation ruling employment in the unit.

After the collective trade agreement is made, the individuals who shall benefit by it are identified by individual hirings. The employer, except as restricted by the collective agreement itself and except that he must engage in no unfair labor practice or discrimination, is free to select those he will employ or discharge. But the terms of the employment already have been traded out. There is little left to individual agreement except the act of hiring. This hiring may be by writing or by word of mouth or may be implied from conduct. In the sense of contracts of hiring, individual contracts between the employer and employees are not forbidden, but indeed are necessitated by the collective bargaining procedure.

But, however engaged, an employee becomes entitled by virtue of the Labor Relations Act somewhat as a third party beneficiary to all benefits of the collective trade agreement, even if on his own he would yield to less favorable terms. The individual hiring contract is subsidiary to the terms of the trade agreement and may not waive any of its benefits, any more than a shipper can contract away the benefit of filed tariffs, the insurer the benefit of standard provisions, or the utility customer the benefit of legally established rates.

Concurrent existence of these two types of agreement raises problems as to which the National Labor Relations Act makes no express provision. We have, however, held that individual contracts obtained as the result of an unfair labor practice may not be the basis of advantage to the violator of the Act nor of disadvantage to employees. National Licorice Co. v. Labor Board, 309 U.S. 350. But it is urged that where, as here, the contracts were not unfairly or unlawfully obtained, the court indicated a contrary rule in Labor Board v. Jones & Laughlin Steel Corp., 301 U.S. 1, 44-45, and Virginian Ry. Co. v. System Federation, 300 U.S. 515. Without reviewing those cases in detail it may be said that their decisions called for nothing and their opinions contain nothing which may be properly read to rule the case before us. The court in those cases recognized the existence of some scope for individual contracts, but it did not undertake to define it or to consider the relations between lawful individual and collective agreements, which is the problem now before us.

Care has been taken in the opinions of the Court to reserve a field for the individual contract, even in industries covered by the National Labor Relations Act, not merely as an act or evidence of hiring, but also in the sense of a completely individually bargained contract setting out terms of employment because there are circumstances in which it may legally be used, in fact, in which there is no alternative. Without limiting the possibilities, instances such as the following will occur: Men may continue to work after a collective agreement expires and, despite negotiation in good faith, the negotiation may be deadlocked or delayed; in the interim express or implied individual agreements may be held to govern. The conditions for collective bargaining may not exist; thus a majority of the employees may refuse to join a union or agree upon or designate bargaining representatives, or the majority may not be demonstrable by the means prescribed by the statute, or a previously existent majority may have been lost without unlawful interference by the employer and no new majority have been formed. As the employer in these circumstances may be under no legal obligation to bargain collectively, he may be free to enter into individual contracts.

Individual contracts, no matter what the circumstances that justify their execution or what their terms, may not be availed of to defeat or delay the procedures prescribed by the National Labor Relations Act looking to collective bargaining, nor to exclude the contracting employee from a duly ascertained bargaining unit; nor may they be used to forestall bargaining or to limit or condition the terms of the collective agreement. "The Board asserts a public right vested in it as a public body, charged in the public interest with the duty of preventing unfair labor practices." National Licorice Co. v. Labor Board, 309 U.S. 350, 364. Wherever private contracts conflict with its functions, they obviously must yield or the Act would be reduced to a futility.

It is equally clear since the collective trade agreement is to serve the purpose contemplated by the Act, the individual contract cannot be effective as a waiver of any benefit to which the employee otherwise would be entitled under the trade agreement. The very purpose of providing by statute for the collective agreement is to supersede the terms of separate agreements of employees with terms which reflect the strength and bargaining power and serve the welfare of the group. Its benefits and advantages are open to every employee of the represented unit, whatever the type or terms of his pre-existing contract of employment.

But it is urged that some employees may lose by the collective agreement, that an individual workman may sometimes have, or be capable of getting, better terms than those obtainable by the group and that his freedom of contract must be respected on that account. We are not called upon to say that under no circumstances can an individual enforce an agreement more advantageous than a collective agreement, but we find the mere possibility that such agreements might be made no ground for holding generally that individual contracts may survive or surmount collective ones. The practice and philosophy of collective bargaining looks with suspicion on such individual advantages. Of course, where there is great variation in circumstances of employment or capacity of employees, it is possible for the collective bargain to prescribe only minimum rates or maximum hours or expressly to leave certain areas open to individual bargaining. But except as so provided, advantages to individuals may prove as disruptive to industrial peace as disadvantages. They are a fruitful way of interfering with organization and choice of representatives; increased compensation, if individually deserved, is often earned at the cost of breaking down some other standard thought to be for the welfare of the group, and always creates the suspicion of being paid at the long-range expense of the group as a whole. Such discriminations not infrequently amount to unfair labor practices. The workman is free, if he values his own bargaining position more than that of the group, to vote against representation; but the majority rules, and if it collectivizes the employment bargain, individual advantages or favors will generally in practice go in as a contribution to the collective result. We cannot except individual contracts generally from the operation of collective ones because some may be more individually advantageous. Individual contracts cannot subtract from collective ones, and whether under some circumstances they may add to them in matters covered by the collective bargain we leave to be determined by appropriate forums under the laws of contracts applicable, and to the Labor Board if they constitute unfair labor practices.

It is also urged that such individual contracts may embody matters that are not necessarily included within the statutory scope of collective bargaining, such as stock purchase, group insurance, hospitalization, or medical attention. We know of nothing to prevent the employee's, because he is an employee, making any contract provided it is not inconsistent with a collective agreement or does not amount to or result from or is not part of an unfair labor practice. But in so doing the employer may not incidentally exact or obtain any diminution of his own obligation or any increase of those of employees in the matters covered by collective agreement.

Hence we find that the contentions of the Company that the individual contracts precluded a choice of representatives and warranted refusal to bargain during their duration were properly overruled. It follows that representation to the employees by circular letter that they had such legal effect was improper and could properly be prohibited by the Board. . . .

[The Court proceeded to consider a subsidiary point turning on the form of the Board's order, and then directed that the form be modified.]

As so modified the decree is affirmed.

MR. JUSTICE ROBERTS is of the opinion that the judgment should be reversed.

STEELE v. LOUISVILLE & NASHVILLE RAILROAD CO.

Supreme Court of the United States, 1944
323 U.S. 192, 65 Sup. Ct. 226, 89 L. Ed. 173

MR. CHIEF JUSTICE STONE delivered the opinion of the Court.

The question is whether the Railway Labor Act, 48 Stat. 1185, 45 U.S.C. secs. 151 et seq., imposes on a labor organization, acting by authority of the statute as the exclusive bargaining representative of a craft or class of railway employees, the duty to represent all the employees in the craft without discrimination because of their race, and, if so, whether the courts have jurisdiction to protect the minority of the craft or class from the violation of such obligation.

The issue is raised by demurrer to the substituted amended bill of complaint filed by petitioner, a locomotive fireman, in a suit brought in the Alabama Circuit Court against his employer, the Louisville & Nashville Railroad Company, the Brotherhood of Locomotive Firemen and Enginemen, an unincorporated labor organization, and certain individuals representing the Brotherhood. The Circuit Court sustained the demurrer, and the Supreme Court of Alabama affirmed. 245 Ala. 113, 16 So.(2d) 416. We granted certiorari, 322 U.S. 722, the question presented being one of importance in the administration of the Railway Labor Act.

The allegations of the bill of complaint, so far as now material, are as follows: Petitioner, a Negro, is a locomotive fireman in the employ of respondent Railroad, suing on his own behalf and that of his fellow employees who, like petitioner, are Negro firemen employed by the Railroad. Respondent Brotherhood, a labor organization, is, as provided under sec. 2, Fourth of the Railway Labor Act, the exclusive bargaining representative of the craft of firemen employed by the Railroad and is recognized as such by it and the members of the craft. The majority of the firemen employed by the Railroad are white and are members of the Brotherhood, but a substantial minority are Negroes who, by the constitution and ritual of the Brotherhood, are excluded from its membership. As the membership of the Brotherhood constitutes a majority of all firemen employed on respondent Railroad, and as under sec. 2, Fourth, the members, because they are the majority, have the right to choose and have chosen the Brotherhood to represent the craft, petitioner and other Negro firemen on the road have been required to accept the Brotherhood as their representative for the purposes of the Act.

On March 28, 1940, the Brotherhood, purporting to act as representative of the entire craft of firemen, without informing the Negro firemen or giving them opportunity to be heard, served a notice on respondent Railroad and on twenty other railroads operating principally in the southeastern part of the United States. The notice announced the Brotherhood's desire to amend the existing collective bargaining agreement in such manner as ultimately to exclude all Negro firemen from the service. By established practice on the several railroads so notified only white firemen can be promoted to serve as engineers, and the notice proposed that only "promotable," i.e., white, men should be employed as firemen or assigned to new runs or jobs or permanent vacancies in established runs or jobs.

On February 18, 1941, the railroads and the Brotherhood, as representative of the craft, entered into a new agreement which provided that not more than 50% of the firemen in each class of service in each seniority district of a carrier should be Negroes; that until such percentage should be reached all new runs and all vacancies should be filled by white men; and that the agreement did not sanction the employment of Negroes in any seniority district in which they were not working. The agreement reserved the right of the Brotherhood to negotiate for further restrictions on the employment of Negro firemen on the individual railroads. On May 12, 1941, the Brotherhood entered into a supplemental agreement with respondent Railroad further controlling the seniority rights of Negro firemen and restricting their employment. The Negro firemen were not given notice or opportunity to be heard with respect to either of these agreements, which were put into effect before their existence was disclosed to the Negro firemen. . . .

Protests and appeals of petitioner and his fellow Negro firemen, addressed to the Railroad and the Brotherhood, in an effort to secure relief and redress, have been ignored. Respondents have expressed their intention to enforce the agreement of February 18, 1941 and its subsequent modifications. The Brotherhood has acted and asserts the right to act as exclusive bargaining representative of the firemen's craft. It is alleged that in that capacity it is under a duty and obligation imposed by the Act to represent the Negro firemen impartially and in good faith; but instead, in its notice to and contracts with the railroads, it has been hostile and disloyal to the Negro firemen, has deliberately discriminated against them, and has sought to deprive them of their seniority rights and to drive them out of employment in their craft, all in order to create a monopoly of employment for Brotherhood members. . . .

The Supreme Court of Alabama took jurisdiction of the cause but held on the merits that petitioner's complaint stated no cause of action. It pointed out that the Act places a mandatory duty on the Railroad to treat with the Brotherhood as the exclusive representative of the employees in a craft, imposes heavy criminal penalties for willful failure to comply with its command, and provides that the majority of any craft shall have the right to determine who shall be the representative of the class for collective bargaining with the employer. See Virginian R. Co. v. System Federation, 300 U.S. 515, 545. It thought that the Brotherhood was empowered by the statute to enter into the agreement of February 18, 1941, and that by virtue of the statute the Brotherhood has power by agreement with the Railroad both to create the seniority rights of petitioner and his fellow Negro employees and to destroy them. It construed the statute, not as creating the relationship of principal and agent between the members of the craft and the Brotherhood, but as conferring on the Brotherhood plenary authority to treat with the Railroad and enter into contracts fixing rates of pay and working conditions for the craft as a whole without any legal obligation or duty to protect the rights of minorities from discrimination or unfair treatment, however gross. Consequently it held that neither the Brotherhood nor the Railroad violated any rights of petitioner or his fellow Negro employees by negotiating the contracts discriminating against them. . . .

But we think that Congress, in enacting the Railway Labor Act and authorizing a labor union, chosen by a majority of a craft, to represent the craft, did not intend to confer plenary power upon the union to sacrifice, for the benefit of its members, rights of the minority of the craft, without imposing on it any duty to protect the minority. Since petitioner and the other Negro members of the craft are not members of the Brotherhood or eligible for membership, the authority to act for them is derived not from their action or consent but wholly from the command of the Act. Section 2, Fourth provides: "Employees shall have the right to organize and bargain collectively through representatives of their own choosing. The majority of any craft or class of employees shall have the right to determine who shall be the representative of the craft or class for the purposes of this Act. . . ." Under secs. 2, Sixth and Seventh, when the representative bargains for a change of working conditions, the latter section specifies that they are the working conditions of employees "as a class." Section 1, Sixth of the Act defines "representative" as meaning "Any person or . . . labor union . . . designated either by a carrier or group of carriers or by its or their employees, to act for it or them." The use of the word "representative," as thus defined and in all the contexts in which it is found, plainly implies that the representative is to act on behalf of all the employees which, by virtue of the statute, it undertakes to represent.

By the terms of the Act, sec. 2, Fourth, the employees are permitted to act "through" their representative, and it represents them "for the purposes of" the Act. Sections 2 ,Third, Fourth, Ninth. The purposes of the Act declared by Sec. 2 are the avoidance of "any interruption to commerce or to the operation of any carrier engaged therein," and this aim is sought to be achieved by encouraging "the prompt and orderly settlement of all disputes concerning rates of pay, rules, or working conditions." Compare Texas & New Orleans R. Co. v. Brotherhood of Clerks, 281 U.S. 548, 569. These purposes would hardly be attained if a substantial minority of the craft were denied the right to have their interests considered at the conference table and if the final result of the bargaining process were to be the sacrifice of the interests of the minority by the action of a representative chosen by the majority. The only recourse of the minority would be to strike, with the attendant interruption of commerce, which the Act seeks to avoid.

Section 2, Second, requiring carriers to bargain with the representative so chosen, operates to exclude any other from representing a craft. Virginian R. Co. v. System Federation, supra, 545. The minority members of a craft are thus deprived by the statute of the right, which they would otherwise possess, to choose a representative of their own, and its members cannot bargain individually on behalf of themselves as to matters which are properly the subject of collective bargaining. Order of Railroad Telegraphers v. Railway Express Agency, 321 U.S. 342, and see under the like provisions of the National Labor Relations Act, J. I. Case Co. v. Labor Board, 321 U.S. 332, and Medo Photo Supply Corp. v. Labor Board, 321 U.S. 678. . . .

Unless the labor union representing a craft owes some duty to represent non-union members of the craft, at least to the extent of not discriminating against them as such in the contracts which it makes as their representative, the minority would be left with no means of protecting their interests or, indeed, their right to earn a livelihood by pursuing the occupation in which they are employed. While the majority of the craft chooses the bargaining representative, when chosen it represents, as the Act by its terms makes plain, the craft or class, and not the majority. The fair interpretation of the statutory language is that the organization chosen to represent the craft is to represent all its members, the majority as well as the minority, and it is to act for and not against those whom it represents. It is a principle of general application that the exercise of a granted power to act in behalf of others involves the assumption toward them of a duty to exercise the power in their interest and behalf, and that such a grant of power will not be deemed to dispense with all duty toward those for whom it is exercised unless so expressed.

We think that the Railway Labor Act imposes upon the statutory representative of a craft at least as exacting a duty to protect equally the interests of the members of the craft as the Constitution imposes upon a legislature to give equal protection to the interests of those for whom it legislates. Congress has seen fit to clothe the bargaining representative with powers comparable to those possessed by a legislative body both to create and restrict the rights of those whom it represents, cf. J. I. Case Co. v. Labor Board, supra, 335, but it has also imposed on the representative a corresponding duty. We hold that the language of the Act to which we have referred, read in the light of the purposes of the Act, expresses the aim of Congress to impose on the bargaining representative of a craft or class of employees the duty to exercise fairly the power conferred upon it in behalf of all those for whom it acts, without hostile discrimination against them.

This does not mean that the statutory representative of a craft is barred from making contracts which may have unfavorable effects on some of the members of the craft represented. Variations in the terms of the contract based on differences relevant to the authorized purposes of the contract in conditions to which they are to be applied, such as differences in seniority, the type of work performed, the competence and skill with which it is performed, are within the scope of the bargaining representation of a craft, all of whose members are not identical in their interest or merit. Cf. Carmichael v. Southern Coal Co., 301 U.S. 495, 509-510, 512 and cases cited; Washington v. Superior Court, 289 U.S. 361, 366; Metropolitan Casualty Co. v. Brownell, 294 U.S. 580, 583. Without attempting to mark the allowable limits of differences in the terms of contracts based on differences of conditions to which they apply, it is enough for present purposes to say that the statutory power to represent a craft and to make contracts as to wages, hours and working conditions does not include the authority to make among members of the craft discriminations not based on such relevant differences. Here the discriminations based on race alone are obviously irrelevant and invidious. Congress plainly did not undertake to authorize the bargaining representative to make such discriminations. Cf. Yick Wo v. Hopkins, 118 U.S. 356; Yu Cong Eng v. Trinidad, 271 U.S. 500; Missouri ex rel. Gaines v. Canada, 305 U.S. 337; Hill v. Texas, 316 U.S. 400.

The representative which thus discriminates may be enjoined from so doing, and its members may be enjoined from taking the benefit of such discriminatory action. No more is the Railroad bound by or entitled to take the benefit of a contract which the bargaining representative is prohibited by statute from making. In both cases the right asserted, which is derived from the duty imposed by the statute on the bargaining representative, is a federal right implied from the statute and the policy which it has adopted. It is the federal statute which condemns as unlawful the Brotherhood's conduct. "The extent and nature of the legal consequences of this condemnation, though left by the statute to judicial determination, are nevertheless to be derived from it and the federal policy which it has adopted." Deitrick v. Greaney, 309 U.S. 190, 200-201; Board of County Commissioners v. United States, 308 U.S. 343; Sola Electric Co. v. Jefferson Co., 317 U.S. 173, 176-7; cf. Clearfield Trust Co. v. United States, 318 U.S. 363.

So long as a labor union assumes to act as the statutory representative of a craft, it cannot rightly refuse to perform the duty, which is inseparable from the power of representation conferred upon it, to represent the entire membership of the craft. While the statute does not deny to such a bargaining labor organization the right to determine eligibility to its membership, it does require the union, in collective bargaining and in making contracts with the carrier, to represent non-union or minority union members of the craft without hostile discrimination, fairly, impartially, and in good faith. Wherever necessary to that end, the union is required to consider requests of non-union members of the craft and expressions of their views with respect to collective bargaining with the employer and to give to them notice of and opportunity for hearing upon its proposed action. . . .

We conclude that the duty which the statute imposes on a union representative of a craft to represent the interests of all its members stands on no different footing and that the statute contemplates resort to the usual judicial remedies of injunction and award of damages when appropriate for breach of that duty.

The judgment is accordingly reversed and remanded for further proceedings not inconsistent with this opinion.

Reversed.

NOTES

1. The National Labor Relations Act was but one of a series of New Deal measures dealing with labor relations. Others included:

(a) *The Social Security Act.* The Social Security Act of 1935, 49 Stat. 620, 42 U.S.C., c. 7, established a national retirement pension program financed by employee and employer contributions. The statute provides for the payment of retirement benefits to persons who have been employees or were self-employed for specific periods of time, beginning at certain specified ages. Its constitutionality was upheld in Helvering v. Davis, 301 U.S. 619 (1937).

The Act, as it has been amended over the years, now provides for retirement and death benefits to be paid to workers over the age of sixty-two which had, in 1964, a minimum payment of $32 per month and a maximum family benefit of $254 per month. Benefit payments are made to retired workers, with increased amounts if children under eighteen are being cared for. In case of death of a worker covered by the statute, survivors' benefits are paid to his widow and children under eighteen. Disability benefits were introduced into the Act in 1950.

The payments are, in theory, financed from a tax on employers, employees, and self-employed persons. This tax, for employers, employees each, is now scheduled to be 4⅛ per cent of covered payroll in 1966-1967 and 4⅜ per cent in and after 1968.

Legislative efforts to engraft a general medical care program into the Social Security system had, as of the fall of 1964, not been successful. For a general discussion of the Social Security Act, see Social Security Administration, Social Security in the United States (1959); Social Security Administration, The Social Security Act: Its First Twenty-five Years (1960); Schottland, The Social Security Program in the United States (1963).

(b) *Unemployment compensation.* When the various private and public relief systems proved inadequate to provide for the nearly 25 per cent of the work force which was unemployed during the depression which began in 1929, proposals were made in many states for the adoption of unemployment insurance systems. No such legislation was passed, however, for fear of jeopardizing the competitive position of that state's industry. As part of the Social Security Act, a tax was imposed on payrolls, most of which was to be rebated to the states if they adopted Unemployment Compensation Acts which met certain federal standards. The result was the passage in all states of Unemployment Compensation Acts, within a few months. The constitutionality of the federal Act was upheld in Steward Machine Co. v. Davis, 301 U.S. 548 (1937).

The state statutes pay benefits which range from $26 to $55 per week to persons who have had the requisite employment history, are now unemployed, and are prepared to accept employment. Benefits are paid for varying periods, the most common being twenty-six weeks. A worker may be disqualified from receiving all or part of the benefit payments for several reasons, including discharge for work-connected misconduct, quitting without good cause, refusing to seek or accept suitable work, or because his unemployment is related to a labor dispute. See U. S. Department of Labor, Comparison of State Unemployment Insurance Laws as of January, 1960, BES No. U-141.

(c) *Wage and hour laws.* Minimum wages and the rule of time and one half for overtime in excess of forty hours per week were established through the adoption in 1938 of the Fair Labor Standards Act, 52 Stat. 1060, 29 U.S.C. §201. In addition, wages, hours, and working conditions in connection with government supply contracts were regulated under the Walsh-Healey Act, 49 Stat. 2036, 41 U.S.C. §35 (1936).

The Fair Labor Standards Act originally provided for a minimum wage of 25 cents per hour. It is now up to $1.25. Coverage of the Act has been expanded over the years so that it now covers some 26 million workers. It also requires payment of time and one half for overtime. It prohibits the selling of goods in the channels of interstate commerce which were made with child labor. See Bureau of National Affairs, The New Wage and Hour Law (1961).

2. The theory of the Wagner Act, recognizing employees' rights to organize, bargain collectively, and engage in concerted activities, was in

obvious conflict with the theory of the decisions applying the Sherman Act to union activities (see page 29 supra).[13]   The task of harmonizing the two philosophies was undertaken by the Supreme Court, beginning with Apex Hosiery Co. v. Leader, 310 U.S. 469 (1940).[14]   Apex Hosiery Company annually produced $5,000,000 worth of hosiery at its Philadelphia factory from raw materials shipped to it from outside the state. More than 80 per cent of its product was regularly shipped in interstate commerce, such shipments constituting less than 3 per cent of the total national product.   When the company refused to accede to a closed-shop demand, the union ordered a strike.   Although only eight Apex employees were then members of the union, assistance was rendered by the union employees of other local factories.   Under the direction of Leader, the union president, the plant was forcibly seized and a so-called sit-down strike maintained.   Machinery was destroyed and during the period of unlawful occupation the strikers repeatedly refused to permit the shipment of $800,000 worth of finished hosiery, 80 per cent of which was on interstate order.   Business was thus suspended for more than three months.   The Court held that a treble damage suit under the antitrust laws was not available to the complainant.   The following points are important highlights of the opinion by Justice Stone:

(a) Defendants' activities substantially restrained and were intended to restrain interstate transportation, but

(b) The issue is whether this is the kind of restraint at which the Sherman Act is directed.

(c) Common law background, legislative history, and prior distinguishable decisions of the Court show that a violation requires a restraint on commercial competition in the marketing of goods and services.   Complainant must therefore show a restraint which has, or is intended to have, an effect on market prices or otherwise deprives purchasers or consumers of the advantages which they derive from competition.

Chief Justice Stone wrote: ". . . successful union activity, as for example consummation of a wage agreement with employers, may have some influence on price competition which is based on differences in labor standards.   Since, in order to render a labor combination effective it must eliminate the competition from non-union made goods, . . . an elimination of price competition based on differences in labor standards is the objective of any national labor organization.   But this effect on competition has not been considered to be the kind of curtailment of price competition prohibited by the Sherman Act."   Id. at 503-504.   In a footnote supporting the above statement, he wrote: "Federal legislation aimed at protecting and favoring labor organizations and eliminating the competition of employers and employees based on labor conditions regarded as substandard, . . . supports the conclusion that Congress does

---

[13] See Blumrosen, Group Interests in Labor Law, 13 Rutgers L. Rev. 432, 446-452 (1959).

[14] For comment on the Apex case, see Gregory, The Sherman Act v. Labor, 8 U. Chi. L. Rev. 222 (1941); Landis, The Apex Case, 26 Cornell L.Q. 191 (1941).

not regard the effects upon competition from such combinations and standards as against public policy or condemned by the Sherman Act." Id. at 504. Justice Stone then summarized the Norris-LaGuardia Act, the Wagner Act, the Public Contracts Act, and the Fair Labor Standards Act. "This series of acts," he concluded, "clearly recognizes that combinations of workers eliminating competition among themselves, and restricting competition among their employers based on wage cutting are not contrary to the public policy." Ibid.

A "labor lawyer" might, nevertheless, inquire concerning the Apex decision whether (a) the result would have been different if the volume of complainant's business approximated 10 per cent of the national total; (b) the Duplex case, supra, is satisfactorily distinguishable; or (c) a local strike to eliminate the use of certain types of labor-saving machinery is permissible.

The final step in freeing unions from the antitrust laws was taken in United States v. Hutcheson, 312 U.S. 219 (1941).[15] In this case the Carpenters, who were engaged in a jurisdictional work dispute with the Machinists, attempted to further their position by local strikes called against Anheuser-Busch, Inc. (brewers), and several contractors who were engaged in the erection of additional facilities for Anheuser-Busch and its adjoining tenant. The strike was supplemented by picketing the Anheuser-Busch plant and the plant of the nearby tenant and the construction projects, and by the nationwide circularization of a request that union members and their friends refrain from buying and drinking Anheuser-Busch beer. The Court held that a Sherman Act *indictment* was demurrable. As noted above, Justice Stone thought that the Apex case was applicable — at least if aided by some free-speech concepts. Justice Frankfurter, however, in delivering the opinion of the Court chose much broader grounds. He viewed the Norris-LaGuardia Act as a congressional interpretation of the Clayton Act, saying (p. 231): "Therefore, whether trade union conduct constitutes a violation of the Sherman Law *is to be determined only by reading the Sherman Law and section 20 of the Clayton Act and the Norris-LaGuardia Act as a harmonizing text of outlawry of labor conduct.*" (Emphasis supplied.)

Thus the application of the Sherman Act to union activities was substantially circumscribed.

In Columbia River Packers v. Hinton, 315 U.S. 143 (1942), fishermen who leased boats and sold the fish caught to processors formed a union which bargained collectively with the processors to fix the price. Members sold only to processors who had union contracts, and processors under contract bought only from union members. One processor who refused to contract with the union was boycotted. He sought an injunction under the Sherman Act. The Court held that this was not a labor dispute within the Norris-LaGuardia Act but was a dispute be-

---

[15] For comment on the Hutcheson decision, see Cavers, And What of the Apex Case Now? 8 U. Chi. L. Rev. 516 (1941); Nathanson and Wirtz, The Hutcheson Case: Another View, 36 Ill. L. Rev. 41 (1941).

tween businessmen over the sale of a commodity. There was no employer-employee relationship, but a combination in restraint of trade.

In Hunt v. Crumboch, 325 U.S. 821 (1945), the Teamsters had called a strike to compel all truckers hauling for A & P to join the union. The plaintiff, a trucking partnership, continued hauling for A & P in spite of the strike. Violence occurred, a union member was killed, and one of the partners was tried for murder but acquitted. The Teamsters finally won the closed-shop agreement with A & P but then refused to allow the partners to join and prevented them from hauling for A & P or any other unionized firm. The Court held that although the union's conceded object was to drive the plaintiff out of business by means of a secondary boycott, there was no violation of the Sherman Act.

If the union boycott is a part of a joint union-employer combination aimed at eliminating competitors, the union may still be subject to the antitrust laws. Local No. 3 of the IBEW combined with manufacturers of electrical equipment and contractors in New York City to control the New York market by refusing to deal with outsiders. In Allen Bradley Co. v. Local 3, IBEW, 325 U.S. 797 (1945), the Court held that the union lost its immunity when it acted in combination with business groups.

3. The Wagner Act remained in effect without change for twelve years. These were years of vigorous administration of the Act by the Board, with substantial confirmation of most of the Board's policies by the Supreme Court. The membership of the labor unions multiplied several times over. Collective bargaining became the general practice in the country, at least in the manufacturing industries. But this was also a period of gathering opposititon to some of the policies developed by the Board under the Act; there was a natural counterreaction to the fast-increasing bargaining power of labor; and a division appeared, too, within the ranks of labor itself.[16]

At the time the NLRA was passed, organized labor consisted almost entirely of unions affiliated with the American Federation of Labor. Many AFL unions traditionally gained status as the bargaining agent in particular plants by putting sufficient economic pressure on the employer to force him into agreement. The wishes of the employees involved were often ignored or at least not regarded as decisive. The emphasis of the NLRA on employee preference and free choice in the selection or rejection of bargaining representatives disturbed this organizational technique. But the requirement of employer neutrality and the absence of any restrictions on unions in influencing employees made the statute appear to be a net gain to the AFL unions.

However, the Congress of Industrial Organizations was formed in 1936 and struggles began to arise between AFL and CIO affiliates over the organization of workers. The NLRA, which concerned itself with em-

[16] For excellent historical reviews, see Bernstein, The New Deal Collective Bargaining Policy (1950); Millis and Brown, From the Wagner Act to Taft-Hartley (1950).

ployer-employee disputes over organization, was not designed to handle interunion conflicts. Employers, hemmed off by the policy of neutrality, frequently found themselves in the middle of bitter jurisdictional quarrels. They were hamstrung by the statute from resolving the dispute by throwing their weight on the side of one of the disputants, and they were frequently subjected to severe economic pressures by one or both of the unions which were seeking collective bargaining status. This development, and the failure of the statute to meet it, created considerable dissatisfaction on the part of some employers and some AFL unions with the terms and the administration of the NLRA.

After World War II there was a sharp swerve to the right on socioeconomic matters generally. The first manifestation of this shift in public sentiment in Congress took place in the battle over the adoption of the Employment Act of 1946, 60 Stat. 23, 15 U.S.C. §1021. Anticipating significant manpower problems with the reconversion of the economy to a peacetime basis, and anxious to avoid a recurrence of the depression of the 1930's, the Senate passed a bill calling for "full employment" as a primary national policy, and implementing that policy with a national budgetary program which would insure sufficient governmental activity, including spending, to provide employment for those who wished it, if private enterprise could not generate "full" employment.

Opponents in the House of Representatives succeeded in watering down the legislation so that it no longer provided any implementing mechanism for the policy of "creating and maintaining, in a manner calculated to foster and promote free competitive enterprise and the general welfare, conditions under which there will be afforded useful employment opportunities, including self-employment, for those able, willing and seeking to work, and to promote maximum employment, production and purchasing power." [17]

Under this statute, the President's Council of Economic Advisors was created, and its annual reports to the President on the state of the nation's economic health have provided the documentation for many economic proposals in the last eighteen years.

f. THE LABOR MANAGEMENT RELATIONS ACT OF 1947 — THE TAFT-HARTLEY ACT

The change in public sentiment on socio-economic matters referred to immediately above was reflected also in the public attitude toward organized labor. With a membership of 15 million in 1947, as compared with 3 million in 1933, unions were thought by many to have attained a degree of power that menaced collective bargaining, individ-

---

[17] The intellectual environment in which the Employment Act was debated is described in Chamberlain, Labor 470-472 (1958). The entire legislative process involved in the passage of the Act is described in Bailey, Congress Makes a Law (1950).

uals, minority groups, and the political status quo. It was believed in some quarters that the War Labor Board, the Labor Relations Board, the Wage and Hour Division of the Department of Labor, and the Conciliation Service, through a strong prolabor bias, had accelerated these developments. The dynamic unionization of millions of unskilled workers in the mass production industries was especially disturbing. The arrogant abuses of power by some labor leaders had lessened public confidence in union responsibility. Communism was feared to have gained control of a number of unions and to be threatening others. Sentiment was growing for government control of unions to protect the public interest. And a fraction of management had initiated antiunion campaigns.

As a result of these and other factors the Labor Management Relations Act (Taft-Hartley) was passed in 1947.[18] The preamble of the original NLRA was modified to limit the blame for labor disputes obstructing and burdening commerce to *some* employers and to extend the blame to the conduct of *some* unions. §1. The employer unfair labor practices were retained, with some modification because of the regulation of union security agreements, but were made less restrictive by giving employers a greater privilege to speak freely in labor controversies than had been permitted by the original statute. §§8(a) and (c). The freedom of unions to exercise economic pressures on employers and employees was restricted for the first time by forbidding certain union unfair labor practices. §8(b).

Under the original NLRA, employees had the privilege of rejecting unionization and choosing to remain unorganized. This privilege was expressly spelled out by the amendments as a right and was protected against union restraint and coercion except when a certain type of union-shop agreement was in existence. §§7, 8(b)(1).

Under the original statute employers were privileged to enter into closed-shop, union-shop, maintenance-of-membership, and other types of union secuity contracts, even though such agreements required employees to be union members and encouraged membership in one union and discouraged membership in others. The amendments limited this privilege to certain types of union-shop and maintenance-of-membership agreements, and unions were prohibited from attempting to cause illegal employer discrimination. §§2(a)(3), 8(b)(2). Probably the most important single effect of these changes was to outlaw the closed-shop agreements which had become common in many of the industries that were characterized by collective bargaining. The obligation to bargain collectively, which had been imposed by the original statute only on employers, was extended to unions. §8(b)(3). In both cases, a refusal to bargain was made an unfair labor practice.

In addition, unions were prohibited from engaging in certain types of secondary strikes, from engaging in strikes to force an employer to recognize any union other than the one certified by the Board as the bar-

[18] The text of the statute, as subsequently amended, is printed in the Reference Supplement, page 17.

gaining agent in his plant, and from striking to force an employer to assign jurisdiction over particular work tasks to one union rather than to another. §§8(b)(4)(A), (B), (C), and (D). Moreover, the Board was empowered and directed to resolve such jurisdictional disputes. §10(k).

An effort was made to regulate the admission policies of unions by prohibiting, under certain circumstances, the imposition of excessive or discriminatory fees. §8(b)(5). Featherbedding practices were restricted to some extent by prohibiting unions from extorting payments from employers for work not performed. §8(b)(6).

Administratively, the statute was so amended that the NLRB's functions became almost entirely judicial. The Board was increased from three members to five, and its administrative and prosecuting functions were vested in a General Counsel. §§3, 4.

The Taft-Hartley Act not only amended the Wagner Act, but also marked the extension of federal legislation into new areas of labor relations which had previously been regulated, if at all, by state law. For example, Congress decreed that collective bargaining contracts were to be enforceable in the federal courts against unions, which were to be treated henceforth as suable entities. §301. Congress also restricted payments to union officials, §302; provided for civil actions in addition to unfair labor practice sanctions against secondary boycotts, §303; and restricted political contributions and expenditures of unions. §304. In Title II of the Act, the Federal Mediation and Conciliation service was strengthened, and Congress indicated its support for arbitration processes. §203(d). So-called "National Emergency Disputes" were to be subject to an eighty-day cooling-off period before any strike which imperiled the national health or safety. During that time, a panel was to evaluate the dispute and make findings of fact, but not recommendations, and the employees were to vote on the employer's last offer. §206.

In addition, states were permitted to adopt "right-to-work" laws which would prohibit any form of compulsory union membership. §14(b). Under the aegis of this section some nineteen states, tending to be those less industrialized, adopted and enforced "right to work" laws during this period.[19]

LINCOLN FEDERAL LABOR UNION v. NORTHWESTERN IRON & METAL CO.

Supreme Court of the United States, 1949
335 U.S. 525, 69 Sup. Ct. 251, 93 L. Ed. 212

MR. JUSTICE BLACK delivered the opinion of the Court.

Under employment practices in the United States, employers have sometimes limited work opportunities to members of unions, sometimes to non-union members, and at other times have employed and kept their

[19] See Sultan, The Union Security Issue, in Public Policy and Collective Bargaining 88 (Shister, Aaron, and Summers, eds. 1962).

workers without regard to whether they were or were not members of a union. Employers are commanded to follow this latter employment practice in the states of North Carolina and Nebraska. A North Carolina statute and a Nebraska constitutional amendment[1] provide that no person in those states shall be denied an opportunity to obtain or retain employment because he is or is not a member of a labor organization. To enforce this policy North Carolina and Nebraska employers are also forbidden to enter into contracts or agreements obligating themselves to exclude persons from employment because they are or are not labor union members.[2]

These state laws were given timely challenge in North Carolina and Nebraska courts on the ground that insofar as they attempt to protect non-union members from discrimination, the laws are in violation of rights guaranteed employers, unions, and their members by the United States Constitution. . . . All of these contentions were rejected by the State Supreme Courts and the cases are here on appeal under §237 of the Judicial Code, 28 U.S.C. §344 (now 28 U.S.C. §1257). . . .

It is contended that the North Carolina and Nebraska laws deny unions and their members equal protection of the laws and thus offend the equal protection clause of the Fourteenth Amendment. Because the outlawed contracts are a useful incentive to the growth of union membership, it is said that these laws weaken the bargaining power of unions and correspondingly strengthen the power of employers. This may be true. But there are other matters to be considered. The state

---

[1] Section 2 of Chapter 328 of the North Carolina Session Laws, enacted in 1947, reads as follows:

"Any agreement or combination between any employer and any labor union or labor organization whereby persons not members of such union or organization shall be denied the right to work for said employer, or whereby such membership is made a condition of employment or continuation of employment by such employer, or whereby any such union or organization acquires an employment monopoly in any enterprise, is hereby declared to be against the public policy and an illegal combination or conspiracy in restraint of trade or commerce in the State of North Carolina."

Nebraska in 1946 adopted a constitutional amendment, Art. XV, §13 of which reads as follows:

"No person shall be denied employment because of membership in or affiliation with, or resignation or expulsion from a labor organization or because of refusal to join or affiliate with a labor organization; nor shall any individual or corporation or association of any kind enter into any contract, written or oral, to exclude persons from employment because of membership in or nonmembership in a labor organization."

[2] Shops that refuse to employ any but union members are sometimes designated as "closed shops," sometimes as "union shops." Contracts which obligate an employer to employ none but union members are sometimes designated as union security agreements, closed shop contracts or union shop contracts. There is also much dispute as to the exact meaning of the term "open shop." See Encyclopedia of Social Sciences, Vol. 3 (1930), pp. 568-569. There is such an important difference in emphasis between these different labels that we think it better to avoid use of any of them in this opinion.

laws also make it impossible for an employer to make contracts with company unions which obligate the employer to refuse jobs to union members. In this respect, these state laws protect the employment opportunities of members of independent unions. See Wallace Corporation v. Labor Board, [323 U.S. 248]. This circumstance alone, without regard to others that need not be mentioned, is sufficient to support the state laws against a charge that they deny equal protection to unions as against employers and non-union workers. . . .

It is contended that these state laws deprive appellants of their liberty without due process of law in violation of the Fourteenth Amendment. Appellants argue that the laws are specifically designed to deprive all persons within the two states of "liberty" (1) to refuse to hire or retain any person in employment because he is or is not a union member, and (2) to make a contract or agreement to engage in such employment discrimination against union or non-union members. . . .

. . . [T]he decisive question under the due process contention . . . is: Does the due process clause forbid a state to pass laws clearly designed to safeguard the opportunity of non-union workers to get and hold jobs, free from discrimination against them because they are non-union workers?

There was a period in which labor union members who wanted to get and hold jobs were the victims of widespread employer discrimination practices. Contracts between employers and their employees were used by employers to accomplish this anti-union employment discrimination. Before hiring workers, employers required them to sign agreements stating that the workers were not and would not become labor union members. Such anti-union practices were so obnoxious to workers that they gave these required agreements the name of "yellow dog contracts." This hostility of workers also prompted passage of state and federal laws to ban employer discrimination against union members and to outlaw yellow dog contracts.

In 1907 this Court in Adair v. United States, 208 U.S. 161, considered the federal law which prohibited discrimination against union workers. Adair, an agent of the Louisville & Nashville Railroad Company, had been indicted and convicted for having discharged Coppage, an employee of the railroad, because Coppage was a member of the Order of Locomotive Firemen. This Court there held, over the dissents of Justices McKenna and Holmes, that the railroad, because of the due process clause of the Fifth Amendment, had a constitutional right to discriminate against union members and could therefore do so through use of yellow dog contracts. The chief reliance for this holding was Lochner v. New York, 198 U.S. 45, which had invalidated a New York law prescribing maximum hours for work in bakeries. This Court had found support for its Lochner holding in what had been said in Allgeyer v. Louisiana, 165 U.S. 578, a case on which appellants here strongly rely. There were strong dissents in the Adair and Lochner cases.

In 1914 this Court reaffirmed the principles of the Adair case in Coppage v. Kansas, 236 U.S. 1, again over strong dissents, and held that a

Kansas statute outlawing yellow dog contracts denied employers and employees a liberty to fix terms of employment. For this reason the law was held invalid under the due process clause.

The Allgeyer-Lochner-Adair-Coppage constitutional doctrine was for some years followed by this Court. It was used to strike down laws fixing minimum wages and maximum hours in employment, laws fixing prices, and laws regulating business activities. See cases cited in Olsen v. Nebraska, 313 U.S. 236, 244-246, and Osborn v. Ozlin, 310 U.S. 53, 66-67. And the same constitutional philosophy was faithfully adhered to in Adams v. Tanner, 244 U.S. 590, a case strongly pressed upon us by appellants. In Adams v. Tanner, this Court with four justices dissenting struck down a state law absolutely prohibiting maintenance of private employment agencies. The majority found that such businesses were highly beneficial to the public and upon this conclusion held that the state was without power to proscribe them. Our holding and opinion in Olsen v. Nebraska, supra, clearly undermined Adams v. Tanner.

Appellants also rely heavily on certain language used in this Court's opinion in Wolff Packing Co. v. Court of Industrial Relations, 262 U.S. 522. In that case the Court invalidated a state law which in part provided a method for a state agency to fix wages and hours. See Wolff Co. v. Industrial Court, 267 U.S. 552, 565. In invalidating this part of the state act, this Court construed the due process clause as forbidding legislation to fix hours and wages, or to fix prices of products. The Court also relied on a distinction between businesses according to whether they were or were not "clothed with a public interest." This latter distinction was rejected in Nebbia v. New York, 291 U.S. 502. That the due process clause does not ban legislative power to fix prices, wages and hours as was assumed in the Wolff case, was settled as to price fixing in the Nebbia and Olsen cases. That wages and hours can be fixed by law is no longer doubted since West Coast Hotel Co. v. Parrish, 300 U.S. 379; United States v. Darby, 312 U.S. 100, 125; Phelps Dodge Corp. v. Labor Board, 313 U.S. 177, 187.

This Court beginning at least as early as 1934, when the Nebbia case was decided, has steadily rejected the due process philosophy enunciated in the Adair-Coppage line of cases. In doing so it has consciously returned closer and closer to the earlier constitutional principle that states have power to legislate against what are found to be injurious practices in their internal commercial and business affairs, so long as their laws do not run afoul of some specific federal constitutional prohibition, or of some valid federal law. See Nebbia v. New York, supra at 523-524, and West Coast Hotel Co. v. Parrish, supra at 392-395, and cases cited. Under this constitutional doctrine the due process clause is no longer to be so broadly construed that the Congress and state legislatures are put in a strait jacket when they attempt to suppress business and industrial conditions which they regard as offensive to the public welfare.

Appellants now ask us to return, at least in part, to the due process philosophy that has been deliberately discarded. Claiming that the Federal Constitution itself affords protection for union members against discrimination, they nevertheless assert that the same Constitution forbids a state from providing the same protection for non-union members. Just as we have held that the due process clause erects no obstacle to block legislative protection of union members, we now hold that legislative protection can be afforded non-union workers.

Affirmed.[20]

MR. JUSTICE FRANKFURTER, concurring. . . .

The coming of the machine age tended to despoil human personality. It turned men and women into "hands." The industrial history of the early Nineteenth Century demonstrated the helplessness of the individual employee to achieve human dignity in a society so largely affected by technological advances. Hence the trade union made itself increasingly felt, not only as an indispensable weapon of self-defense on the part of workers but as an aid to the well-being of a society in which work is an expression of life and not merely the means of earning subsistence. But unionization encountered the shibboleths of a pre-machine age and these were reflected in juridical assumptions that survived the facts on which they were based. Adam Smith was treated as though his generalizations had been imparted to him on Sinai and not as a thinker who addressed himself to the elimination of restrictions which had become fetters upon initiative and enterprise in his day. Basic human rights expressed by the constitutional conception of "liberty" were equated with theories of laissez faire.[1] The result was that economic views of confined validity were treated by lawyers and judges as though the Framers had enshrined them in the Constitution. This misapplication of the notions of the classic economists and resulting disregard of the perduring reach of the Constitution led to Mr. Justice Holmes' famous protest in the Lochner case against measuring the Fourteenth Amendment by Mr. Herbert Spencer's Social Statics. 198 U.S. 45, 75. Had not Mr. Justice Holmes' awareness of the impermanence of legislation as against the permanence of the Constitution gradually prevailed, there might indeed have been "hardly any limit but the sky" to the embodiment of "our economic or moral beliefs" in that Amendment's "prohibitions." Baldwin v. Missouri, 281 U.S. 586, 595.

The attitude which regarded any legislative encroachment upon the existing economic order as infected with unconstitutionality led to disrespect for legislative attempts to strengthen the wage-earner's bargaining power. With that attitude as a premise, Adair v. United States, 208 U.S. 161, and Coppage v. Kansas, 236 U.S. 1, followed logically enough; not

---

[20] For subsequent confirmation of Justice Black's view, see Ferguson v. Skrupa, 372 U.S. 726 (1963). — ED.

[1] Of course, theory never wholly squared with the facts. Even while laissez faire doctrines were dominant, State activity in economic affairs was considerable. See Handlin, Commonwealth: A Study of the Role of Government in the American Economy, Massachusetts, 1774-1861 (1947); Hartz, Economic Policy and Democratic Thought: Pennsylvania, 1776-1860 (1948).

even Truax v. Corrigan, 257 U.S. 312, could be considered unexpected. But when the tide turned, it was not merely because circumstances had changed and there had arisen a new order with new claims to divine origin. . . .

Unions are powers within the State. Like the power of industrial and financial aggregations, the power of organized labor springs from a group which is only a fraction of the whole that Mr. Justice Holmes referred to as "the one club to which we all belong." The power of the former is subject to control, though, of course, the particular incidence of control may be brought to test at the bar of this Court. E.g., Northern Securities Co. v. United States, 193 U.S. 197; North American Co. v. S. E. C., 327 U.S. 686. Neither can the latter claim constitutional exemption. Even the Government — the organ of the whole people — is restricted by the system of checks and balances established by our Constitution. The designers of that system distributed authority among the three branches "not to promote efficiency but to preclude the exercise of arbitrary power." Mr. Justice Brandeis, dissenting in Myers v. United States, 272 U.S. 52, 293. Their concern for individual members of society, for whose well-being government is instituted, gave urgency to the fear that concentrated power would become arbitrary. It is a fear that the history of such power, even when professedly employed for democratic purposes, has hardly rendered unfounded.

If concern for the individual justifies incorporating in the Constitution itself devices to curb public authority, a legislative judgment that his protection requires the regulation of the private power of unions cannot be dismissed as insupportable. A union is no more than a medium through which individuals are able to act together; union power was begotten of individual helplessness. But that power can come into being only when, and continue to exist only so long as, individual aims are seen to be shared in common with the other members of the group. There is a natural emphasis, however, on what is shared and a resulting tendency to subordinate the inconsistent interests and impulses of individuals. From this, it is an easy transition to thinking of the union as an entity having rights and purposes of its own. An ardent supporter of trade unions who is also no less a disinterested student of society has pointed out that "As soon as we personify the idea, whether it is a country or a church, a trade union or an employers' association, we obscure individual responsibility by transferring emotional loyalties to a fictitious creation which then acts upon us psychologically as an obstruction, especially in times of crisis, to the critical exercise of a reasoned judgment." Laski, Morris Cohen's Approach to Legal Philosophy, 15 U. of Chi. L. Rev. 575, 581 (1948).

The right of association, like any other right carried to its extreme, encounters limiting principles. See Hudson County Water Co. v. McCarter, 209 U.S. 349, 355. At the point where the mutual advantage of association demands too much individual disadvantage, a compromise must be struck. See Dicey, Law and Public Opinion in England 465-66 (1905).

When that point has been reached — where the intersection should fall — is plainly a question within the special province of the legislature. . . .

NOTE

During the decade of the 1950's there were gradual legislative expansions of much of the legislation of the 1930's. The Fair Labor Standards Act was amended to embrace more persons within its coverage, and the hourly minimum wages went up from 75 cents, in 1949, to $1.25 as a result of the 1961 amendments. Social Security coverage was broadened to include self-employed persons, and the level of benefits was increased. During two recessions or "readjustments" in the 1950's Congress "bailed out" state unemployment compensation funds which were running perilously low and thereby persuaded some states to extend the period of coverage of the unemployment compensation laws beyond the usual twenty-six weeks to take care of urgent unemployment problems. For a survey of the current law, see Schottland, The Social Security Program in the United States (1963).

In 1958, largely as a result of Senator Douglas' urging, Congress adopted a statute which entered yet another field of labor relations, the Welfare and Pensions Disclosure Act, to try to regulate and protect employee interests in the booming field of welfare plans. The Act lacked enforcement elements, and was strengthened by subsequent amendments.[21]

g. THE LABOR MANAGEMENT REPORTING AND DISCLOSURE ACT OF 1959 — THE LANDRUM-GRIFFIN ACT

In the late 1950's, largely as a result of dramatization by Senator McClellan of certain abuses by union officers of the power they had acquired, Congress was prodded into the regulation of still another area of labor relations, the internal affairs of labor organizations. Spurred by concern for undemocratic practices within unions, and after much political maneuvering, the Labor Management Reporting and Disclosure Act of 1959 was adopted.[22]

Title I of the law purports to guarantee to union members equal participation in union affairs, freedom of speech and assembly, reasonable and uniform dues, initiation fees, and assessments, freedom to sue unions and their officers, and fair treatment in disciplinary cases. Title II requires the disclosure by unions, their officers, and their employees of de-

[21] Bureau of National Affairs, Federal-State Regulation of Welfare Funds 1-39 (rev. ed. 1961).
[22] The text of this statute is printed in the Reference Supplement, page 51. The political activity leading up to the adoption of the Act is vividly described in McAdams, Power and Politics in Labor Legislation (1964).

tailed information about financial dealings, operation of trusteeships, and private arrangements with employees. (Similar, though less stringent, requirements are imposed on employers and their agents.) Title III regulates the manner in which union trusteeships may be established and maintained, and protects the rights of members of organizations placed under trusteeship. Title IV similarly regulates the conduct of union elections, and is designed to insure the fairness of such elections, the right of equal participation as candidates and voters of all qualified union members, and the means by which illegal elections may be challenged or set aside. Title V imposes fiduciary responsibilities upon union officers and representatives, disqualifies convicted criminals and former Communists from eligibility for union office for fixed periods of time, and requires that certain union officers be bonded for the faithful discharge of their duties.

There came up for consideration by Congress in the course of the 1959 legislation, the question of making further amendments to the National Labor Relations Act; and Title VII was eventually included for this purpose. These amendments did not change the basic pattern of the NLRA provisions, as amended in 1947. Section 7 was not altered. One change was made in the provisions covering the organization and general procedures of the Board. §3. The procedures for the handling of representation cases were left the same, except in one minor respect. The principal amendments were in connection with the union unfair labor practice provisions. §§8(b)(4), 8(b)(7), and 8(e). Restrictions on secondary boycotts were strengthened, "organizational picketing" was limited, the representation election was placed more in the forefront of the legislative scheme for identifying labor union representatives, and so-called "hot cargo" contracts were proscribed.

h. ECONOMIC LEGISLATION OF THE 1960's

In the 1960's, the pace of legislation relating to labor relations has quickened. In 1962, Michael Harrington's The Other America received widespread publicity as national concern for problems of poverty was focused on areas within the nation which lagged behind the rest of the country in economic growth. In 1961, the Area Development Act, 75 Stat. 47, 42 U.S.C. §2501, was passed by Congress to stimulate economic activity in these "depressed areas." And the following year, the Manpower Development and Training Act, 76 Stat. 23, as amended 42 U.S.C. §2571, was adopted to further the attempt to upgrade the skills and talents of unemployed workers. One consequence of the latter statute has been the series of annual Manpower Reports of the President which bring together statistical tables and Department of Labor thinking concerning national manpower development and needs. The beginnings of a comprehensive governmental program of assistance to unemployed or underemployed persons in obtaining skills necessary to find employment, and in stimulating the economy so that employment would be available, were crystallized in the Economic Cooperation Act of 1964, the so-called "anti-poverty" Act, 78 Stat. 508, 42 U.S.C. §2701. This Act, through a number of different steps and approaches, aims at stimulating levels of employment and levels of skills to man that employment. An "equal pay" amendment was added to the FLSA in 1963 to eliminate wage differentials based on sex, 77 Stat. 56, 29 U.S.C. §206 (d).

i. THE CIVIL RIGHTS ACT OF 1964

The year 1964 saw the culmination of a drive for racial equality in employment which had been going on since the early 1940's when, to avert a march on Washington, President Roosevelt established a Fair Employment Practices Commission by Executive Order 8802, 6 Fed. Reg. 3109 (1941).

When Congress considered labor legislation in 1947 and again in 1959, moves were made to include prohibitions on racial discrimination by both unions and employers. Congress declined to accept such proposals in both instances. See Blumrosen, Legal Protection Against Exclusion from Union Activities, 22 Ohio St. L.J. 21, 27-29 (1961).

Meanwhile, some twenty states in the industrial North and West had adopted Fair Employment Practices Acts. See Bamberger and Levin, The Right to Equal Treatment: Administrative Enforcement of Anti-discrimination Legislation, 74 Harv. L. Rev. 526 (1961). These laws, with their emphasis on "education" rather than "enforcement," were of limited effectiveness. Norgren and Hill, Toward Fair Employment (1964); Blumrosen, Antidiscrimination Laws in Action in New Jersey: A Law-Sociology Study, 19 Rutgers L. Rev. 187 (1965).

During most of this period, Presidential Committees on Equal Employment Opportunity, operating under Executive Order, dealt with discrimination by employers who were government contractors. See 1961 U.S. Commission on Civil Rights Report, Employment, cc. 1, 4 (1961). In 1964, the culmination of a drive for federal civil rights legislation in general carried with it Title VII of the Civil Rights Act, Public Law 88-352, 78 Stat. 241, 42 U.S.C. §2000e, which prohibits discrimination in employment practices by unions and employers, and establishes procedures for implementing the rights granted.

C. THE ECONOMIC CONTEXT

It is impossible in a few pages to provide all of the significant data necessary for an understanding of the economic context within which labor and social legislation is operative. The following materials are intended only to provide some background information and to suggest other avenues of exploration.

TABLE I. NATIONAL INCOME, BY TYPE OF INCOME: 1929 AND 1963 [23]

| | In Billions Current Dollars | | Percent of Total | | |
	1929	1963	1929	1963	Net Change
Total National Income	87.8	478.4	100.0	100.0	
Compensation of Employees:	51.1	340.4	58.2	71.1	12.9
Wages and Salaries	50.4	312.3	57.4	65.2	7.8
Supplements	0.7	28.0	.8	5.8	5.0
Proprietors Income	14.8	50.5	16.8	10.5	— 6.3
Business and Professional	8.8	37.7	10.0	7.8	— 2.2
Farm	6.0	12.8	6.8	2.6	— 4.2
Rental Income of Persons:	5.4	12.1	6.2	2.5	— 3.7
Corporate Profits	10.1	51.3	11.4	10.9	— 0.5
Net Interest	6.4	24.1	7.3	5.0	— 2.3

[23] U.S. Dept. of Commerce, Bureau of the Census, Statistical Abstract of the United States, 1964, p. 326; U.S. Dept. of Labor, American Workers Fact Book 94 (1960).

TABLE II. FAMILY PERSONAL INCOME RECEIVED BY EACH FIFTH AND TOP FIVE PERCENT OF FAMILIES AND UNATTACHED INDIVIDUALS, 1929-1962 [24]

| | | | Percentage of Income | | | |
Rank by Size of Income	1929	1935-6	1941	1947	1958	1962
Lowest Fifth		4.1	4.1	5.0	4.7	4.6
	12.5 [25]					
Second Fifth		9.2	9.5	11.0	11.1	10.9
Third Fifth	13.8	14.1	15.3	16.0	16.3	16.3
Fourth Fifth	19.3	20.9	22.3	22.0	22.4	22.7
Highest Fifth	54.4	51.7	48.8	46.0	45.5	45.5
Top 5%	30.0	26.5	24.0	20.9	20.2	19.6
			Average Income (Current Dollars)			
Lowest Fifth		337	450	1,023	1,459	1,662
	725					
Second Fifth		749	1,044	2,275	3,478	3,966
Third Fifth	1,606	1,146	1,694	3,308	5,106	5,938
Fourth Fifth	2,252	1,708	2,463	4,542	7,016	8,241
Highest Fifth	6,327	4,216	5,396	9,483	14,254	16,505
Top 5%	13,960	8,654	10,617	17,226	25,276	28,482

[24] U.S. Dept. of Commerce, Bureau of the Census, Statistical Abstract of the United States, 1964, p. 337; Historical Statistics 166 (1960).
[25] Average of both lowest and second fifth in both tables. — ED.

TABLE III. MEMBERSHIP IN NATIONAL AND INTERNATIONAL UNIONS WITH
HEADQUARTERS IN THE UNITED STATES, 1900-1962[26]

	1900	1910	1920	1930	1935	1940	1945	1950	1955	1960	1962
Number of Affiliated Unions											
AFL	82	120	110	104	109	105	102	107	139	134	130
CIO	—	—	—	—	—	42	40	30			
Total Membership (1,000)	791	2,116	5,034	3,682	3,728	8,944	14,796	15,000	17,749	18,117	17,630
Percent of total labor force	2.5	—	12.5	7.25	6.7	15.5	21.9	22.0	24.4	23.3	22.2
Percent of total non-agricultural labor force	—	—	—	10.3	13.4	27.2	35.3	31.9	33.6	31.4	29.7
AFL (1,000)	548	1,562	4,079	2,961	3,045	4,247	6,931	7,143	16,062	15,072	14,835
CIO (1,000)	—	—	—	—	—	3,625	6,000	5,000			
Independents (1,000)	243	554	955	671	683	1,072	1,865	2,600	1,688	3,045	2,794

[26] U.S. Dept. of Commerce, Bureau of the Census, Statistical Abstract of the United States, 1964, p. 247; Historical Statistics 97 (1960).

TABLE IV. WORK STOPPAGES, 1927-1963 [27]

Year	Total	Workers involved		Man-days idle	
		Number (1,000)	Percent of total employed	Number (1,000)	Percent of estimated working time
1963........	3,362	941	2.0	16,100	0.13
1962........	3,614	1,230	2.7	18,600	0.16
1961........	3,367	1,450	3.2	16,300	0.14
1960........	3,333	1,320	3.0	19,100	0.17
1959........	3,708	1,880	4.3	69,000	0.61
1958........	3,694	2,060	4.8	23,900	0.22
1957........	3,673	1,390	3.1	16,500	0.14
1956........	3,825	1,900	4.3	33,100	0.29
1955........	4,320	2,650	6.2	28,200	0.26
1954........	3,468	1,530	3.7	22,600	0.21
1953........	5,091	2,400	5.6	28,300	0.26
1952........	5,117	3,540	8.8	59,100	0.57
1951........	4,737	2,220	5.5	22,900	0.23
1950........	4,843	2,410	6.9	38,800	0.44
1949........	3,606	3,030	9.0	50,500	0.59
1948........	3,419	1,960	5.5	34,100	0.37
1947........	3,693	2,170	6.5	34,600	0.41
1946........	4,985	4,600	14.5	116,000	1.43
1945........	4,750	3,470	12.2	38,000	0.47
1944........	4,956	2,120	7.0	8,720	0.09
1943........	3,752	1,980	6.9	13,500	0.15
1942........	2,968	840	2.8	4,180	0.05
1941........	4,288	2,360	8.4	23,000	0.32
1940........	2,508	577	2.3	6,700	0.10
1939........	2,613	1,170	4.7	17,800	0.28
1938........	2,772	688	2.8	9,150	0.15
1937........	4,740	1,860	7.2	28,400	0.43
1936........	2,172	789	3.1	13,900	0.21
1935........	2,014	1,120	5.2	15,500	0.29
1934........	1,856	1,470	7.2	19,600	0.38
1933........	1,695	1,170	6.3	16,900	0.36
1932........	841	324	1.8	10,500	0.23
1931........	810	342	1.6	6,890	0.11
1930........	637	183	0.8	3,320	0.05
1929........	921	289	1.2	5,350	0.07
1928........	604	314	1.3	12,600	0.17
1927........	707	330	1.4	26,200	0.37

[27] U.S. Dept. of Commerce, Bureau of the Census, Statistical Abstract of the United States, 1964, p. 249; Historical Statistics 99 (1960).

TABLE V.   MANUFACTURES — GENERAL STATISTICS FOR ESTABLISHMENTS, BY EMPLOYEE SIZE-CLASS: 1958 [28]

[Numbers in thousands; money figures in millions of dollars. Excludes Alaska and Hawaii]

Number of Employees in Firm	Establish- ments	Employees	Payroll	Value Added by Mfg.	New Capital Expenditures
1-10	156 (52.4%)	558 (3.6%)	2,035 (2.8%)	4,376 (3.1%)	510 (5.6%)
11-49	93 (31.2%)	2,078 (13.6%)	8,673 (11.7%)	15,927 (11.2%)	988 (10.9%)
50-99	22 (7.3%)	1,513 (9.8%)	6,416 (8.7%)	12,024 (8.5%)	607 (6.7%)
100-249	16 (5.4%)	2,497 (16.2%)	10,938 (14.8%)	21,162 (15%)	1,165 (12.8%)
250-499	6 (2.1%)	2,150 (14%)	9,709 (13.2%)	19,291 (13.7%)	1,122 (12.4%)
500-999	3 (0.9%)	1,893 (12.3%)	9,176 (12.4%)	18,103 (12.8%)	1,198 (13.2%)
1000 and over	1 (0.7%)	4,695 (30.5%)	26,832 (36.3%)	50,387 (36.7%)	3,486 (38.4%)
Totals	298	15,394	73,750	141,270	9,076

[28] U.S. Dept. of Commerce, Bureau of the Census, Statistical Abstract of the United States, 1964, p. 769.

TABLE VI.   AVERAGE DURATION OF UNEMPLOYMENT AND PERCENT DISTRIBUTION OF TOTAL AND LONG-TERM UNEMPLOYMENT, BY SEX AND AGE, 1963 [29]

Sex and age	Average duration of unemploy- ment (in weeks)	Percent distribution		
		Total unemployed	Unemployed 15 weeks and over	Unemployed 27 weeks and over
Both sexes: Number.....	14.0	4,166,000	1,088,000	553,000
Percent		100.0	100.0	100.0
14 to 24 years..........	10.3	39.3	27.7	25.0
25 to 44 years..........	13.5	33.7	34.4	31.8
45 to 64 years..........	19.2	24.0	32.8	36.7
65 years and over........	26.8	3.0	5.1	6.5
Male.................	15.5	60.9	65.7	69.3
14 to 24 years..........	11.3	23.1	17.8	16.8
25 to 44 years..........	14.4	19.9	21.2	20.4
45 to 64 years..........	21.0	15.5	22.6	26.4
65 years and over........	29.7	2.3	4.1	5.6
Female	11.7	39.1	34.3	30.7
14 to 24 years..........	8.8	16.2	9.9	8.2
25 to 44 years..........	12.2	13.8	13.2	11.4
45 to 64 years..........	16.0	8.4	10.2	10.3
65 years and over........	16.8	.7	.9	.9

Detail may not add to totals because of rounding.

[29] U.S. Dept. of Labor, Report on Manpower Requirements, Resources, Utilization, and Training 28 (1964).

TABLE VII.   UNEMPLOYMENT RATES, BY YEARS OF SCHOOL COMPLETED, MARCH 1962 [30]

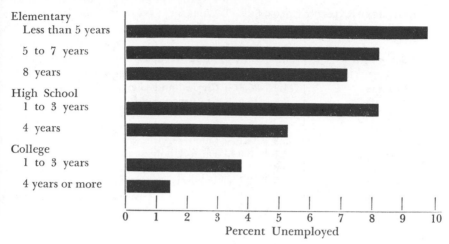

Percent Unemployed

[30] Id. at 32.

TABLE VIII.   UNEMPLOYMENT RATES FOR OCCUPATION GROUPS, 1963 [31]

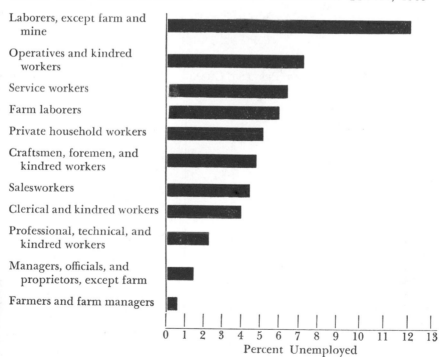

Percent Unemployed

[31] Id. at 25.

TABLE IX [32]

Sex and age	White	Non-white	Major occupation group	White	Non-white
			UNEMPLOYMENT RATES OF EXPERIENCED WORKERS, BY COLOR AND OCCUPATION, 1963		
UNEMPLOYMENT RATES, BY COLOR, SEX, AND AGE, 1963					
Male	4.7	10.6	All occupation groups	4.4	9.3
14 to 19 years..........	14.2	25.4	Clerical and sales workers	3.9	7.4
20 to 24 years..........	7.8	15.6	Craftsmen and foremen..	4.6	8.2
25 to 34 years..........	3.9	9.5	Operatives	6.9	11.1
35 to 44 years..........	2.9	8.0	Private household workers	3.1	7.7
45 to 54 years..........	3.3	7.1	Other service workers...	5.3	10.0
55 years and over.......	4.1	8.0	Farm laborers and fore-		
Female	5.8	11.3	men	5.0	7.1
14 to 19 years..........	13.6	33.1	Laborers, except farm		
20 to 24 years..........	7.4	18.8	and mine............	11.0	15.2
25 to 34 years..........	5.8	11.7			
35 to 44 years..........	4.6	8.2			
45 to 54 years..........	3.9	6.1			
55 years and over.......	3.4	4.6			

[32] Id. at 105.

TABLE X.   YEAR-TO-YEAR PERCENT CHANGE IN OUTPUT PER MAN-HOUR, 1947-63 [33]

Period	Total private economy	Agriculture	Nonagricultural industries
1947-48....................	3.5	18.7	2.1
1948-49....................	2.9	− 4.7	3.7
1949-50....................	7.2	13.9	5.3
1950-51....................	2.5	− 1.1	1.6
1951-52....................	2.2	9.2	1.3
1952-53....................	4.1	11.3	2.7
1953-54....................	1.8	7.2	1.6
1954-55....................	4.5	3.6	4.3
1955-56....................	.1	2.2	− .4
1956-57....................	3.5	6.7	2.8
1957-58....................	2.5	9.3	1.8
1858-59....................	3.6	− .2	3.6
1959-60....................	1.9	6.3	1.6
1960-61....................	3.3	5.9	2.9
1961-62....................	3.9	3.4	3.8
1962-63....................	3.5	7.4	3.0

[33] Id. at 47.

D. TECHNOLOGICAL CHANGE

It has been clear for some time that the rate and quality of technological change, as that change has been transmitted through the economic system, pose perhaps the major problem for the United States in the 1960's in the field of employment and manpower. The literature in connection with this problem is enormous,[34] and it would be presumptuous to attempt any thorough exposition of its ramifications here. The material which follows undertakes only to identify some of the main lines of development which are occurring through unions, through employers, through collective bargaining, and by government, as the changes in technology foster the emergence of a national manpower policy.

1. *The Problem*

SOME MANPOWER IMPLICATIONS OF TECHNOLOGICAL CHANGE

U.S. Department of Labor, Report on Manpower Requirements, Resources, Utilization, and Training 61-62 (1964)

The rapid pace and pervasiveness of technological change in American industry are apparent from this brief review of major trends. The technological revolution continues to affect all segments of the economy, but some much more than others.

The factors which will stimulate or impede the extension of automation and other new developments, and the probable manpower consequences of these developments, are now being studied by the Department of Labor and many research organizations. At this point, conclusions as to the net effect of current technological trends on employment levels would be speculation. It is obvious, however, that important shifts in manpower requirements are in process, with forced readjustments for large numbers of workers and serious implications for the education and training both of the present work force and of young people still in school.

---

[34] Much of the best writing in the area has been compiled in Staff of Subcommittee on Employment and Manpower, Senate Committee on Labor and Public Welfare, Exploring the Dimensions of the Manpower Revolution, 88th Cong., 2d Sess. (Comm. Print, 1964), 1 of Selected Readings in Employment and Manpower (1964). Another collection of basic source material is Philipson, ed., Automation: Implications for the Future (1962). Another is Dunlop, ed., Automation and Technological Change (1962). Recent experience dealing with automation is discussed in Somers, Cushman, and Weinberg, eds., Adjusting to Technological Change (1963).

The popular word "automation," used to describe the process of technological change, was apparently coined by D. S. Harder of the Ford Motor Company in 1946. It first appeared in print in LeGrand, Ford Handles by Automation, American Machinist 107 (Oct. 21, 1948). See Killingsworth, Automation in Manufacturing, in I.R.R.A. Annual Proceedings 20 (1958).

Occupational effects of several broad types can be discerned. These are briefly outlined below. It must be emphasized, however, that the conclusions indicated are provisional, subject to amplification and verification by further research.

OCCUPATIONAL CHANGES

One of the most evident occupational effects of current technological changes is their impact on *unskilled and semiskilled jobs.* The increasing mechanization of materials handling has eliminated much manual labor in the lifting, movement, and loading of goods. Factory jobs involving direct step-by-step manipulation of equipment or materials or manual tending of machinery are also becoming relatively fewer, because of the introduction of automatic machinery.

In some instances, the level of skill required to operate new machinery is no higher than that for the old operation. This is true, for example, of the men who feed, watch the operations of, and remove completed products from new automatic threading machines in a nut and bolt factory; and of those performing parallel functions on an automated line for the production of resistors in a new electronics plant. Occasionally the new job requires only that the person watch a light panel and push a button on signal.

But situations of this type do not negate the general finding that current technology is tending to restrict employment in jobs with low skill demands. While semiskilled operators are required for an automatic machine, they are likely to be few in number — far fewer than the operatives replaced by the machine. And in highly automated systems, where feeding of the machine and removal of products from it are handled mechanically, the manual aspects of operators' work may be eliminated altogether. On the other hand, a continued rise in the general level of income may mean more jobs for parking lot attendants, gardeners, hedgemen, and home repair mechanics, all of whom are relatively unskilled.

For *production workers,* the typical job of the future will probably be that of machine monitor. A good many operators of highly automated equipment already have this function. They may have responsibility for supervising complexes of automatic equipment (sometimes a battery of machines), for controlling an integrated system of conveyors and processing machines from a remote station, or for monitoring an elaborate instrument control panel and recording information for interpretation. More and more, the operator is becoming a skilled watchman, with functions demanding patience, alertness to malfunctioning, a sense of responsibility for costly equipment, and a better educational background than was needed in the past by factory operatives.

Maintenance and repair workers qualified to service and repair electronic equipment, instruments, and automated machinery have a growing field of employment. Plants that automate attempt to keep this costly equipment operating as nearly continuously as possible, thereby providing more employment for maintenance workers in most of the major areas of technological change discussed earlier in this chapter.

More and better training is required for the maintenance positions in enterprises adopting this new, complex equipment — especially because of the combination of electronic, electro-mechanical, and sometimes even hydraulic operations involved in the machine-and-control systems. Thus, many instrument repairmen and business-machine servicemen need post-high school education in engineering fundamentals, mechanics, or electronics, as well as intensive occupational training, to service the complex instruments and office machines coming into use. Maintenance electricians and appliance servicemen will need more technical education in order to handle a growing number and variety of electronic devices. Similarly, in some other skilled trades — including those of machinist, tool and diemaker, electroplater, and plumber and pipefitter — technological advances are introducing new technical requirements.

Among *office workers,* electronic data processing is eliminating many routine jobs and reducing the repetitive aspects of other jobs. Electronic data processing is having its greatest effects on detailed, repetitive manual work in functions such as accounting, addressing, billing, inventory control, payrolls, and other recordkeeping. Many clerical occupations — especially those of a service character, such as bank teller, complaint clerk, receptionist, and secretary — continue unaffected by automation.

Most of the new EDP jobs, on the other hand, are at a higher level. Those of the programmer and systems analyst are in the professional category, while most of the console and peripheral equipment operators are in the upper level of clerical work. Thus, considering both the jobs eliminated and those created, the net result of a changeover to electronic data processing is likely to be a somewhat higher average level for employees in the offices affected. There is evidence also that electronic data processing, in eliminating many of the routine elements of office jobs, enlarges employees' personal responsibility, requires greater accuracy in office work, and imposes the necessity for workers to meet more precise deadlines. Under some circumstances, the conditions of work for clerical employees under electronic data processing may become more similar to those of factory workers.

The evidence is still far from conclusive regarding the general effects of automation on *managerial personnel.* In some instances, however, the introduction of electronic data processing and the accompanying reorganization of managerial functions have led to reduced staffs in the lower and middle echelons of management.

In *scientific and engineering professions,* a notable effect of recent scientific and technological advances has been the creation of new specialties. Such fields as cryogenics, bionics, ultrasonics, computer technology, and microelectronics were little known a decade ago. The development of computers has also been one of the main factors in the great postwar expansion in the mathematics profession and has had a revolutionary effect in many other scientific and engineering fields. Interdisciplinary training of engineers and other professional workers and revision of engineering curricula are proposed to meet industry's emerging needs.

2.　The Response of Collective Bargaining

BOK, AUTOMATION, PRODUCTIVITY AND MANPOWER PROBLEMS*
2, 13-19 (1964)

1. There are no statistics which disclose the unemployment resulting from automation or from other sources of increased productivity. But increased productivity is relevant to the problem of unemployment since the rate at which productivity rises, together with increases in the size of the labor force, help determine the pace at which the economy must grow in order to reduce unemployment to the desired minimum.

2. Although future trends in productivity cannot be predicted with certainty, there is a distinct possibility that productivity in the non-agricultural sector may rise at a moderately faster rate over the next 5-10 years than it has during the post-war period.

3. It is also possible that productivity will rise at a still more rapid rate in the 1970's, although predictions to this effect are highly speculative.

4. Regardless of the rate at which productivity increases in broad sectors of the economy, there will continue to be a number of industries in which productivity rises more rapidly than demand; employment in these industries will therefore decline, and significant problems of displacement may result. . . .

There are no available statistics which separate the effects of automation from those of the various other factors which affect productivity. For this reason, . . . [there] follows . . . an analysis of the effects of increased productivity rather than automation per se. . . .

The discussion . . . is limited to the methods which *private parties* have employed to achieve higher levels of productivity "without sacrifice of human values."

1. *Advance Notice:* A large number of collective bargaining agreements require notice prior to layoff, but the notice period is generally no longer than a week. A few recent agreements require notification several months or more prior to the introduction of new equipment, and many employers have voluntarily given substantial notice of impending technological changes. Employees can often be informed long before automated equipment is introduced, since the decision to automate is customarily made months and even years prior to installation. A substantial period of notice is frequently desirable since certain programs of adjustment, notably training and placement schemes, will take considerable time to prepare and implement. Published accounts of actual ex-

*Derek Bok, Professor of Law, Harvard Law School, Consultant to the President's Committee on Labor Management Policy. The excerpt is taken from a discussion paper prepared for that Committee.

perience with advance notice are distinctly favorable. Consultation with the union and the employees has . . . done much to dispel rumors, reduce resistance to change and permit careful planning of adjustment programs. Despite expectations to the contrary, advance notice has generally not affected morale adversely or caused the premature departure of significant numbers of employees.[1] No information is available as to the extent to which competitive considerations deter employers from giving advance notice.

2. *Avoiding Layoffs:*

a. *Attrition:* A few collective bargaining agreements require that reductions in force be accomplished through attrition or at some fixed rate which will minimize layoffs. Employers have often decided on their own initiative to introduce new equipment gradually in order to allow the work force to diminish by attrition. There are many examples in which substantial reductions in force have been achieved with virtually no layoffs through the application of this principle.

The employer may find attrition unattractive if the rate of turnover is not rapid enough in relation to the desired reduction in force to avoid retaining workers whose services are no longer necessary. On the other hand, the rate of attrition may be accelerated in a manner satisfactory to the employees if other programs of adjustment are in effect, such as the early retirement and transfer plans discussed below.

b. *Early Retirement:* If many employees are advanced in years, an early retirement plan may help to achieve a substantial reduction in force without layoffs. But unless increased benefits are provided to compensate for the unavailability of social security payments, few workers will agree to retire prematurely. Those who do so will frequently count on obtaining other jobs, in which case unemployment in the community may not be reduced. The cost of increasing pension benefits to satisfactory levels is often substantial, but several companies have provided such increases in recent years.

c. *Work Spreading:* There are several techniques for spreading work. Provisions for temporary reductions in the work week are widespread but serve largely to adjust to sporadic cutbacks in production. Premium rates for overtime are almost universal in collective bargaining agreements, and there are indications that certain unions may make efforts to place still further limits on overtime. Extended vacation plans have recently been introduced, notably in the steel industry, and reductions in hours have been widely discussed as a bargaining objective. Work-spreading plans result in greater leisure time, but their primary purpose today is to create more jobs. Increases in labor costs, among other factors, place practical limits on the degree to which employment can be increased by these methods. Moreover, the success of these schemes in creating jobs will also depend on whether employees

---

[1] Many employees may refrain from quitting prematurely either because they do not wish to forfeit severance benefits or because other programs of adjustment have been introduced which provide some assurance that prolonged unemployment will not result following the installation of new equipment.

"moonlight" when free time is available and whether employers will respond to the increased labor costs by hastening the introduction of labor-saving devices. The problem of moonlighting is probably not substantial unless the reduction in hours is pronounced. The effect of work spreading on the introduction of labor-saving devices is not clearly understood, and presumably varies considerably from one situation to another.

d. *Retraining:* Retraining is a valuable technique for minimizing layoffs in the event of automation, since employees can usually learn to operate the new equipment without undue difficulty. Where more complex jobs are involved, some employers have encountered a reluctance among employees to undergo retraining or to operate the new equipment. There have also been cases in which inadequate education has disqualified a substantial fraction of the employees from training programs. These problems, however, do not pose a serious problem unless a large proportion of the employees must undergo retraining in order to preserve their jobs.

e. *Transfer and Relocation:* When large reductions in force take place through automation or other causes, there are often no jobs in the plant for which the employees may be trained. In large companies, this problem may be overcome to some extent by providing for transfer to other plants. Transfer may create conflicts among employees if the jobs and seniority rights of workers at the other plant are placed in jeopardy. Various compromises have been devised to meet this problem, ranging from placing the transferring employee at the bottom of the seniority list at the new plant, to giving him a right to "bump" employees with less seniority. Apart from questions of seniority, employees may simply not wish to move to the new plant. Various inducements have been provided in recent years to overcome resistance to transfer, including reimbursement for moving expenses and an option to return within a stipulated time if the new location or job seem unsatisfactory. Varied success has been achieved with transfer programs, but some firms have persuaded up to 50% of the laid off employees to move long distances to a new plant.

3. *Minimizing the Burden of Unemployment:*

a. *Severance Pay:* Severance pay is provided in 30% of all major collective agreements. The amount paid will generally vary according to length of service. Severance pay provides only temporary relief against unemployment, and the payments tend to be small for junior employees, who are the most likely to be laid off. On the other hand these benefits (like early retirement plans) often provide great assistance to older workers who may be seriously handicapped by their age in securing new employment. Various studies involving plant closings suggest that severance pay is often used to repay debts rather than to defray the cost of finding and preparing for a new job. Some recent agreements, however, have provided that employees may draw against severance benefits prior to layoff to pay for training and other costs of finding new work.

b. *Vesting of Pension Rights:* Vesting provisions have grown rapidly since 1955 and now appear in more than two-thirds of all private pension plans (covering 60% of all workers with pension rights). Such provisions commonly permit vesting when the employee reaches the age of 40 or 45 years, provided he has accumulated a minimum of service (usually 15 years). The employees most likely to be laid off are those without sufficient service to permit their pension rights to vest. These workers will suffer economic loss upon being laid off unless they can transfer the pension to their new employer. This is generally possible only in the case of transfer between firms covered by the same multi-employer pension plan.

4. *Facilitating New Employment:* Several employers and unions have attempted to train workers for new jobs and to find employment for them. When training has been conducted on a continuing basis, as in various programs conducted in craft unions, considerable success has been achieved in equipping workers to adapt to changing skill requirements and employment opportunities. Programs devised rapidly to meet some particular crisis have encountered much greater difficulty. Such programs may be stymied by the fact that few jobs are available in the local area. The education and aptitudes of the workers may severely limit the range of jobs for which they can be trained. Difficulties may arise in predicting what kind of jobs will be available when the training period ends. Company, union and even community facilities may not suffice for the type of training required. A critical problem is the lack of some central repository where a comprehensive listing of job openings can be obtained together with data regarding the skills and experience of employees seeking work. Without this information, as representatives of the Armour Fund point out, ". . . it is extremely difficult for private groups . . . to mount a broadly effective placement campaign." . . .

Several recent developments suggest new areas for exploration in connection with private methods of adjustment:

1. *Review of Certain Internal Plant Rules:* Rules relating to seniority, transfer, promotion, etc., help to determine the characteristics of the men who are laid off; their age, skill and breadth of experience. Much is now known about the bearing these characteristics have on the ability of employees to find new jobs. In some cases, these considerations could be reflected more effectively in the rules governing seniority, etc., but it is increasingly recognized that these questions are highly complex and must be explored before layoffs are imminent. Reviews of this kind have been conducted recently in the steel industry, resulting in revisions which promise to increase the protection given to more senior employees and broaden the opportunities for workers to develop new skills without interfering with the efficiency of the enterprise.

2. *Industry Surveys:* In Canada, government subsidies are provided to encourage unions and employers to study the long range possibilities of technological change in their respective industries and the relation of these changes to training needs and possible cutbacks in employment.

Under the auspices of the Armour Committee, studies have recently been conducted in this country concerning the economic prospects of the meatpacking industry and skill requirements for certain types of automated equipment. Moreover, a tripartite commission has caused a manpower profile to be made of the operating work force in the railroad industry to determine the age, skills and experience of the employees who may be affected by technological change. A similar study is now being made in the East Coast Longshore Industry by the U.S. Department of Labor. Such studies are still few in number, but the information derived from work of this kind seems directly relevant to a decision whether to emphasize training, early retirement, attrition, transfer or some combination of these alternatives in devising programs of adjustment.

3. *Education and Training:* In attempting to operate a placement program for workers laid off in Oklahoma City, the Armour Company found that three months did not suffice to develop a training program which would equip employees for many of the jobs available in the community. This experience underscores the need for establishing training programs on a continuing basis which will provide employees with basic skills. Training of this kind is already conducted by industry on a broader scale than in other countries. On the other hand, a recent nationwide survey reports that only 1.5 million employees are currently engaged in programs which will provide them with a marketable skill. In the view of many experts, this number could be substantially increased. Moreover, programs recently introduced by the Steelworkers and by certain companies and unions in the Los Angeles area illustrate the opportunities which exist for working with educational and civic institutions (perhaps capitalizing on extended vacation plans) to encourage programs of instruction covering a broader range of subject matter. . . .

The private programs discussed in this section have an indispensable role to play in the process of adjustment to technological change. In a large and complex economy, the problems of displacement and adjustment are too vast to be undertaken by any single agency. Moreover, in the course of many independent efforts by private parties, experimentation and improvisation will take place which may in turn enlarge our understanding of how to deal effectively with the more difficult aspects of training, placement, relocation, etc. In addition, management and union officials are uniquely situated to select the methods of adjustment that are best suited to the situation at hand. Flexibility of this kind is essential for the techniques of adjustment that are called for will vary from one case to another depending on the characteristics of the employees involved, the situation in the local labor market, and the outlook and structure of the firm itself.[35]

Despite these advantages, private methods of adjustment cannot be expected to provide a total solution to the problems of displacement:

1. Private methods of adjustment are not sufficient to counteract un-

[35] See Kennedy, Automation Funds and Displaced Workers (1963). — Ed.

employment in the economy as a whole.　Extended vacations and reductions in hours may increase employment, but various factors tend to limit the number of jobs which can be created by these techniques. Programs of attrition, transfer, placement, and training assist employees in avoiding layoffs and finding new jobs; in so doing, these programs may help to alleviate frictional unemployment but they can do little to diminish the number of employees without jobs.

2.　Although private programs contribute in several ways to help individuals find new jobs, they cannot adequately cope with the problem of hard-core unemployment.　In the first place, private agreements seldom provide unemployment benefits of any kind beyond a limited period after layoff.　Second, private programs are oriented toward assisting those already employed rather than individuals such as new entrants into the labor force who encounter difficulty in finding a job.　Third, long-term unemployment often results not so much from insufficient training as from a lack of basic education, which only the State can normally provide.

3.　Very few private methods of adjustment extend to more than a small fraction of the labor force.　Collective bargaining has provided the most important stimulus for the creation of these plans, but less than one-third of the labor force is covered by collective agreements.　Even among this segment of employees, only 30% are protected by severance pay, only 11% by supplemental unemployment benefits, and only a handful of agreements make provision for interplant transfer and relocation allowances. While much can be done to encourage the spread of these devices, there are impressive obstacles to overcome.　Many firms are too small to undertake training programs; others are forced to innovate in order to meet severe competition and will therefore feel unable either to finance costly programs of adjustment or to wait long enough to effect reductions in force through attrition; still other firms will simply be unwilling, for one reason or another, to undergo the trouble and expense of providing suitable programs of adjustment.

3.　*Governmental Response to Problems of Technological Change: The Emergence of a National Manpower Policy*

If, as the preceding material suggests, collectively bargained approaches to problems of unemployment resulting from technological change are inadequate to cope with the full impact of inevitable developments, what plans and programs are emerging in government to meet the need?　Since 1960, a bewildering array of plans, executive orders, administrative proposals, congressional committee reports, and statutes have been adopted, promulgated, and amended.　Out of this welter of activity the outline of a national manpower policy is emerging. The most comprehensive govermental attempt to pull together the threads of these various programs into a coherent policy is a committee report of the U.S. Congress. Senate Committee on Labor and Public Welfare, Subcommittee on Employment and Manpower, Toward Full Employment: Proposals for a Comprehensive Employment and Manpower Policy in the United States, 88th Cong., 2d Sess. (Comm. Print, 1964). Said the majority report of the committee (p. 7):

"Employment policy, as the term is used in this report, refers to those policies designed to influence the over-all level of employment in the economy. Manpower policy relates to the development of manpower resources and the matching of available manpower with the available jobs. Policy implies more than the existence of programs and practices which have some impact on the problem at hand. A policy requires the explicit recognition of goals and the formulation of a coherent program for realization of those goals. The Employment Act of 1946 established the basis for an employment policy in the United States, but little has been done subsequently to give meaning to the Act. At no time prior to 1961 can the United States be said to have had a real manpower policy."

The policy which seems to be emerging has infinitely complex variations which can only be suggested here in outline form:

(1) Gathering, organizing, and disseminating information and ideas concerning national manpower problems. Before one can begin to solve a problem, he must recognize and define it. In this task, the gathering together in organized form of manpower statistics and projections has been a fundamental prerequisite. The vehicle by which this has been most successfully done is the annual Manpower Report of the President, initiated under the Manpower Development and Training Act of 1962. These reports, prepared largely in the Department of Labor, have become the basic source material for the consideration of manpower problems and have helped to organize these problems into manageable categories for thought and action. In addition, the congressional committee testimony which lies behind the report "Toward Full Employment," mentioned above, provides much source material.[36]

(2) Making the U.S. Employment Service a national manpower agency. The increasingly rapid reorganization of the labor force has put a heavy strain on the job information and placement facilities of the country. One method of improving the operation of the job market itself is to improve the performance of its primary mechanism, the U.S. Employment Service. Internal administrative changes have been made (see Toward Full Employment), and legislative and executive reforms have been proposed.[37]

(3) Improving the recruitment, training, and placement functions of apprenticeship training programs. Such programs, if existing at all, have often been casual and disorganized. Improvement has become the ob-

[36] Staff of Senate Committee on Labor and Public Welfare, Nation's Manpower Revolution, pts. 1-9, 88th Cong., 1st Sess. (Comm. Print, 1963). See also Gordon, U.S. Manpower and Employment Policy, 87 Mo. Labor Rev. 1314 (1964).

[37] See Haber and Cruger, The Role of the United States Employment Service in a Changing Economy (1964).

jective of the Department of Labor, Bureau of Apprenticeship Training.[38]

(4) Development of training programs to provide educable people with skills which will enable them to perform needed functions. This phase of manpower activities is currently operating through three governmental programs. It is the prime objective of the Manpower Development and Training Act of 1962 (76 Stat. 23, as amended, 42 U.S.C. §2571), and one objective of the 1961 Area Redevelopment Act (75 Stat. 47, 42 U.S.C. §2501).[39] The first year's activities revealed that its primary area of achievement lay in improving the capabilities of those workers who were close to being satisfactory in the first instance in terms of age, race, education, and prior work experience.[40] Amendments to the MDTA adopted in 1963 were aimed at allowing the benefits of MDTA programs to flow to those who were more on the fringe of the acceptable labor force.

The primary thrust of the Economic Opportunity Act of 1964 (78 Stat. 508, 42 U.S.C. §2701) is to provide job openings which will carry with them the opportunity for the holders to become self-sufficient contributories to the labor force. The Act envisions programs aimed especially at the problems of youth (Title I) and other programs designed to meet needs of adults for education and training (Title II). The program has several other objectives. See S. Rep. No. 1218, 88th Cong., 2d Sess. (1964).

(5) Regional economic development. This is the objective of the 1961 Area Redevelopment Act (75 Stat. 47, 42 U.S.C. §2501). Area development consists of a cluster of projects. A disadvantaged geographical area develops a comprehensive economic improvement plan, and then identifies specific projects of both public and private dimensions. The federal government will then assist with funds and technical advice to improve the economic tone of the area. See Levitan and Shepard, Technological Change and the Community, in Adjusting to Technological Change (Somers, Cushman, and Weinberg, eds. 1963). See also Roe v. Kervick, 42 N.J. 191, 199 A.2d 834 (1964), for a consideration of the problems of municipal government law which emerge under the Area Redevelopment Act.

(6) Stimulation of small business through a variety of loan and technical assistance programs as well as attempting to assure small business an appropriate share of defense business. This program is operated through the United States Department of Commerce as well as through the Defense Department. See Small Business Administration Annual Report to the President, 1-55 (1963).

(7) Taking into account the manpower implications of tariff reduc-

[38] See An Assessment of Apprenticeship, 87 Mo. Labor Rev. 18, 143, 391, 625 (1964).

[39] See U.S. Dept. of Labor, Report of the Secretary of Labor on Manpower Research and Training (1964).

[40] U.S. Dept. of Labor, Manpower Evaluation Report No. 1, Training Disadvantaged Groups (1963).

tion decisions. The Trade Expansion Act of 1962 (76 Stat. 872, 19 U.S.C. §1801) includes provisions (19 U.S.C. §§1931-1951) for adjustment, retraining, and relocation allowances for employees of at least three years' seniority whose jobs are abolished as a result of the adverse effects of increased imports. The allowances can run up to one year in most cases.

(8) Proposals for work spreading and income guarantees. Among the ideas which have evolved in the early 1960's to meet problems of technological change on the governmental level have been those concerned with work spreading and income guarantees. Work spreading proposals have included the encouragement of early retirement by reduction of the entitlement age for social security benefits, reduction of the standard work week from forty to thirty-five hours or less by amendment of the Fair Labor Standards Act, and reduction of the use of overtime by increasing FLSA overtime rates from time and one half to double time.

Income guarantee proposals have ranged from increasing the level of social security benefits to the provision by government of an assured annual income to all citizens. The 1964 Report of the President's Council of Economic Advisors, p. 77, estimated that for 11 billion dollars (the amount of the 1963 tax cut) every family in the nation could be assured an income of not less than $3000 per year. But the Council quickly dismissed this proposal as not touching the roots of poverty.

NOTE

The coordination of the various programs through a central office, the Office of Economic Opportunity, is provided in Title VI of the Anti-Poverty Act, in the office of the Director. See 42 U.S.C. §2961.

4. *Organized Labor's Policy in Response to Market and Technological Conditions: The Case of the United Mine Workers*

The use of economic power by unions must be understood within a complex economic context. This context includes world market conditions, the economic condition of the nation, the industry, and the particular employers which are involved in a labor relations controversy. The economic context includes the technological foundation upon which the productive processes are established. Union policy decisions in relation to the market and technological conditions are of the greatest importance. No single approach to these problems has been taken by American unionism. Some unions have resisted technological change; others, including the United Mine Workers, have welcomed it. Some unions have ignored market conditions; others, including the United Mine Workers, have been intimately concerned with these conditions. The following materials, dealing with the United Mine Workers' policy on these and related matters, are intended to illustrate the richness of the interaction between unionism, the market, and the technology.

The contemporary attitude of the union toward technological change is described in Baratz, The Union and the Coal Industry 71-72 (1955):*

"John L. Lewis has been called, among other things, 'the best salesman [the machinery industry] ever had.' The implication is, of course, that rising wage rates have caused coal producers to substitute machinery for labor.

"There seems little room for doubt that the United Mine Workers wants the mines mechanized. The union president said in 1947: 'The UMWA . . . [takes] the position that the only way in which the standard of living could be increased . . . would be by increasing the productivity and lowering the unit costs and utilizing the genius of science and the automatic machine . . . and the usage of power to do the work of human hands, and the UMW educated its membership through the years to an acceptance of that policy. . . .

" 'As the result of that policy, the UMW . . . declared that the miners had a right to participate, through increased wages and shorter hours and improved safety and better conditions, in the increased productive efficiency of the industry, holding that there were three parties to the profit by increased proficiency and greater production: (a) the investor who was given a larger return and a more secure investment; (b) the mine worker who would get higher wages and shorter hours, improved safety conditions; and (c) the consumer of the product who could buy this product at a lower unit cost. . . .'

"The union will accept mechanization so long as it shares in the benefits accruing initially to the operators. This is a long-standing policy, first appearing when machine differentials were being established in the early 1900's. There have been rumblings from the ranks against mechanization, particularly during the depression of the 1930's. The objections were easily overruled.

"The union's current strategy is easy to describe. By raising wage rates (and labor costs per ton) and by eliminating regional wage-rate differentials, heavy pressure to mechanize will be brought to bear on all firms, especially the relatively high-cost operations. Since the union insists that it must share in the benefits of mechanization, the increased use of machines will enable the union to exact even higher wage rates or shorter hours or both. Higher wage rates, in brief, encourage mechanization, which permits still higher wage rates. Seemingly the cycle could go on indefinitely, limited only by the financial capacity of firms to install machines and by the ingenuity of mining machinery manufacturers to devise ever more efficient equipment. The actual limits are set, of course, by the level and elasticity of demand for coal."

The result of this approach has been the transformation of the industry from low capital cost to high capital cost operation, particularly in the Southern regions, including West Virginia, which were slow to mechanize. See Baratz, supra, at 123. This has meant, among other things, that the productivity per man hour has dramatically increased, as the following table indicates:

* Reprinted by permission of the Yale University Press.

BITUMINOUS COAL PRODUCTIVITY AND EMPLOYMENT [41]

Year	Tons Per Man Day	Total Tons (in millions)	Employed
1900	2.98	212	304,375
1910	3.46	417	555,533
1920	4.00	568	639,537
1930	5.06	467	493,202
1940	5.19	460	439,075
1950	6.77	516	415,582
1952	7.42	467	335,000
1959	12.22	412	180,000

[41] Baratz, The Union and the Coal Industry 40-43 (1955); Kennedy, supra note 35, at 16.

ADAMS, TECHNOLOGY AND PRODUCTIVITY IN BITUMINOUS COAL, 1949-1959*

84 Monthly Labor Review 1081, 1081-1082 (1961)

Since 1949, the bituminous coal industry has engaged in a rapid modernization program in an attempt to improve its competitive position in postwar energy markets. A consequence of these efforts has been an impressive increase in output per man-hour and, conversely, a sharp reduction in labor requirements per ton.

In spite of the importance of this basic industry, it shared little of the general prosperity of the 1950's. While industrial output and employment rose, coal production had a downward trend and employment fell almost continuously. Falling demand for coal was due largely to technological changes in other industries; changes that altered fuel consumption patterns forced coal out of several of its major markets and hampered its growth in those that were retained. For example, dieselization of the railroads wiped out their demand for coal as a fuel for motive power. The welded-steel pipeline and the resultant intercontinental transportation of petroleum and natural gas were responsible for substantial losses in the retail market which includes space heating. At the same time, increases in combustion efficiency, which allowed more energy to be secured from a ton of coal, dampened the demand for coal in markets where there was little competition from other fuels. Simultaneously, less fuel energy was required per unit of goods and services produced as a result of changes in the organization of industrial production.

While the demand for coal was falling rapidly, the capacity to produce coal was falling much more slowly. The selling price of coal remained almost constant, but the prices of materials, supplies, labor, and other input factors were rising sharply. Profits, although fluctuating widely from year to year, were also in a generally downward trend. Against this background of falling demand and rising production costs, the coal industry, with full support of the United Mine Workers of America (Ind.) intensified a mechanization program that had begun many years before

* This article is by Robert T. Adams.

A variety of new machines were developed and introduced along with appropriate new mining techniques. Concurrently, the industry made other changes, such as internal reorganization of some of the larger coal producing companies and the expansion of cooperative membership organizations including those engaged in market and industrial research and development.

The result of these combined efforts was an 85-percent increase in output per production worker man-hour in the decade following 1949. The average annual rate of increase of 6.4 percent was more than double the rate of any previous decade. In terms of output per all-employee man-hour, the rise was only slightly less.

The dramatic rise in output per man-hour in bituminous coal mining stands out when compared with changes that occurred in the rest of the economy. Between 1949 and 1959, the rise in output per man-hour of all employees in bituminous coal advanced twice as fast as in the total private economy and almost three times as fast as in the nonfarm sector. While increases as large as that in mining are often recorded in newly developing industries, they are seldom attained by those that have reached maturity. They are, however, invariably accompanied by problems as well as benefits.

As production declined and unit labor requirements were reduced, employment fell sharply. The average number of production workers in the industry fell by three-fifths, to less than 150,000 in 1959. This decline left the industry with only one-fourth as many workers as were employed during 1923, the alltime high of bituminous coal employment. One result of this contraction of the work force was an increase in the average age of employed mineworkers. According to records of the Bureau of Old-Age and Survivors Insurance, the median age of coal miners in 1957 was 42 years compared with 37 years in U.S. industry as a whole.

Mechanization of bituminous coal mining also significantly changed the job structure and the work involved in mining. Increasing proportions of mineworkers were employed, particularly after World War II, in administrative, professional, and clerical jobs, in processing work above ground, and in maintenance, transportation, and supervision underground rather than in direct production at the face of the coal seam.

NOTE

Both the policy of advancing technological improvement and that of eliminating the low wage competitor were furthered by the introduction of a royalty payment on each ton of coal produced, which would go into a fund from which health, welfare, and pension programs would be financed. Initial battles over the establishment of the funds are described in Kennedy, Automation Funds and Displaced Workers, c. 2 (1963). The fund was created in 1946 through negotiations between the union and the government, which was then in control of the bituminous coal mines. In 1946, the royalty rate was 5 cents per ton. It was doubled in 1947 and again in 1948. In the 1950 Bituminous Coal Agreement it was raised to 30 cents and in 1952 to its present 40 cents per ton. The following cases suggest some problems which have arisen in connection with the various union policies set out above.

KOSTY v. LEWIS

United States Court of Appeals, District of Columbia, 1963
319 F.2d 744, certiorari denied, 375 U.S. 964 (1964)

McGowan, Circuit Judge.

A problem arising in the administration of the United Mine Workers of America Welfare and Retirement Fund of 1950 is the subject of this appeal. It is prosecuted by a member of the union who brought suit to compel the payment of a retirement pension which the Trustees of the Fund had denied him. After a trial to the District Court, his action was dismissed. An understanding of the issues to be resolved requires an examination of (1) the nature and origin of the Fund, including the provisions made for its administration, (2) the circumstances of the appellant in relation to his claim of eligibility for a pension, and (3) the function and scope of judicial review in a matter of this kind.

I . . .

At their second meeting on April 5, 1950, the Trustees adopted Resolution No. 10, providing a monthly pension for retired employees. Resolution No. 10 promulgated regulations (stated to be "subject to amendment, revocation and revision at the discretion of the Trustees") prescribing eligibility requirements and covering other administrative aspects of the pension system. In order to be eligible, an applicant for a pension was required to have (1) attained the age of 60, (2) retired by permanently ceasing work in the Bituminous Coal Industry after May 28, 1946, (3) been employed for at least one year immediately preceding his retirement, and (4) completed 20 years of service in the Coal Industry.

On January 28, 1953, the Trustees adopted Resolution No. 30, which superseded Resolution No. 10 as the governing regulation with respect to pension eligibility requirements. The new resolution was made effective forthwith, that is to say, January 29, 1953. The significant change which it made, for purposes of this proceeding, was to prescribe that the requisite 20 years of service must have taken place within the 25-year period immediately preceding the filing of a pension application. A few weeks later, on March 13, 1953, the Trustees, by Resolution No. 31, amended Resolution No. 30, retroactively effective as of January 29, 1953, by enlarging from 25 to 30 years the period immediately preceding application within which the 20 years of service must have occurred. This change was perpetuated in a further amending resolution, No. 32, adopted by the Trustees on May 12, 1953.

I I

The appellant, at the age of 65 years and five months, retired on June 26, 1953, and promptly thereafter filed his application for a pension on the form provided by the Fund. The application recited a total of over 31 years of service in the coal industry, comprised of two non-consecutive periods. The first of these was from 1906 to 1924 as an employee of Bethlehem Mines Corporation; the second was from 1940 to 1953 as an employee of Stineman Coal & Coke Company.

The administrative files of the Fund relating to this application, which were put in evidence in the District Court, showed that appellant's application was denied for the reason that it did not appear that appellant had had 20 years of service in the 30-year period immediately preceding the filing of the application, as required by Resolution No. 30, as amended. . . .

The appellant's second period of employment — from 1941 to 1953 — was conceded by the Trustees, but, in response to interrogatories, the Trustees stated that they had no information as to whether the appellant had or had not been employed as a coal miner from 1906 to 1924. At the trial appellant testified at length with respect to this first period of employment, stating that it had ended because he had received an injury in the course of his employment. This testimony was corroborated by that of another miner who had worked with appellant at the same mine throughout the entire period from 1906 to 1924. The Trustees offered no evidence of any kind contradicting this testimony, and made no effort to impeach the witnesses on this point.

The trial judge found that Resolution No. 10 imposed "no restriction as to the period of time in which those 20 years of service had to be completed." This finding seems fully justified by the language of Resolution No. 10, and the Trustees make no contrary contention. Since appellant was over the age of 60 at the time Resolution No. 10 was adopted, he could have qualified for a pension thereunder at any time by a simple election to stop working. He was not bound to do so, however, because Resolution No. 10 did not impose any requirement that an employee, otherwise qualified for a pension thereunder, was obligated to terminate his employment and take his pension.

The record shows explicitly, from the testimony of the neutral Trustee, that no notice of any kind was given by the Trustees of their purpose to change the eligibility requirements. As has been noted, the amending resolution was effective immediately upon its adoption. Thus, appellant, at the age of 65, found his existing eligibility abruptly terminated, and he was confronted with the necessity of amassing approximately $8\frac{1}{2}$ years additional service in order to qualify under the new rule. The trial judge concluded that, under these circumstances, there was no evidence of arbitrary or capricious conduct on the part of the Trustees vis-à-vis the appellant, and that his claim for relief had not been established.

III . . .

The institutional arrangements creating this Fund and specifying the purposes to which it is to be devoted are cast expressly in fiduciary form; and the Trustees, like all fiduciaries, are subject to judicial correction in a proper case upon a showing that they have acted arbitrarily or capriciously towards one of the persons to whom their trust obligations run.

I V

The question before us, then, is: Was the court below right in determining, on the facts of record, that the abrupt alteration by the Trustees of the eligibility requirements was not an arbitrary or capricious action in its impact upon appellant?

Counsel for appellant have pressed two principal contentions upon us as warranting reversal of the decision of the District Court. One is couched in terms of "vested rights," and consists of the claim that appellant, prior to the adoption of the revised eligibility requirements, had possessed in substance fully matured rights entitling him to a pension, and that these rights could not lawfully be divested. Essential to this argument is the assertion that that element of eligibility in Resolution No. 10 involving actual retirement from work is not to be placed in the same scale with the other requirements, such as length of service and age — that it should be regarded as a "procedural rule" rather than one of a substantive character, and thereby be waived or disregarded in appraising the degree to which pension rights have become vested in one who meets all of the other standards laid down as essential to eligibility.

In the view we take of the case, however, we find it neither necessary nor illuminating to approach the problem by reference to these well-worn legal slogans. We recognize that the Trustees have been accorded wide latitude in specifying from time to time *what* the eligibility qualifications shall be. Our concern is, rather, with *how* changes in the qualifications are made. Stated another way, our interest here is directed to the reasonableness of the opportunity afforded to mature pension eligibility under current standards where all that is lacking is the actual termination of employment, rather than in debating whether such eligibility should be regarded in substance as already having been matured.

This brings us to appellant's second major contention, which is that the Trustees acted arbitrarily in altering the eligibility requirement in respect of years of service without prior notice of any kind or the provision of an opportunity rationally calculated to give appellant an opportunity to elect between taking his pension or continuing in employment subject to the new requirement. It is clear from the nature of the testimony given by the neutral Trustee at the trial that the Trustees felt themselves under no obligation of any kind in this regard. This testimony was simply that no notice of any kind was afforded, which is another way of saying that the Trustees looked upon employees situated as was appellant as continuing to work in the coal industry at their peril in terms of the possibility that pension eligibility might be wiped out for all practical purposes at any moment by the sudden action of the Trustees in changing the requirements. We do not believe that the concededly broad grant of authority to the Trustees was this broad. To hold otherwise would make this particular grant wholly out of harmony with the other features of the trust agreement, which reflect the fiduciary character of the responsibilities devolved upon the Trustees in respect of employees who had devoted substantial segments of their lives to the coal industry.

We do not deny the authority of the Trustees to revise pension eligibility requirements in the light of their experience. Flexibility of this kind seems especially necessary for the operation of this Fund, tied as it is to the fluctuating fortunes of the coal industry. But trial and error, where trust relationships are involved, operate within some limitations of fundamental fairness. These were, in our judgment, exceeded here by the failure of the Trustees to accord any notice or period of grace which would have afforded some reasonable possibility for an employee like appellant to have elected to retire and take the pension available immediately prior to the change. We do not say that actual notice to each employee of his opportunity so to elect would be necessary to defeat a claim, since there may be problems of identification and communication which the Trustees may not be able to overcome in every case, although no point of this kind is made on their behalf in the record of this case. We do say that it was clearly not beyond the capacity or resources of the Trustees to have devised some system of publicity for the impending change which reasonable men would regard as having fulfilled their fiduciary undertakings. To have made no effort at all in such direction entitled this appellant to claim with reason that he has been exposed to arbitrary and capricious action by those who owed him adherence to a different — and higher — standard of conduct. . . .

The case is remanded to the District Court with directions to enter judgment for the appellant in accordance with this opinion.

PENNINGTON v. UNITED MINE WORKERS OF AMERICA

United States Court of Appeals, Sixth Circuit, 1963
325 F.2d 804

SHACKELFORD MILLER, JR., Circuit Judge.

This is an action by . . . Trustees of the United Mine Workers of America Welfare and Retirement Fund, hereinafter referred to as Trustees against the . . . Phillips Brothers Coal Company, a partnership, hereinafter referred to as Phillips. The Trustees seek to recover

$55,982.62 as royalty payments alleged to be due and unpaid pursuant to the terms of a trust provision contained in a wage agreement between United Mine Workers of America, . . . and Phillips. . . .

The complaint alleges that on or about October 1, 1953, Phillips and the Union entered into the National Bituminous Coal Wage Agreement of 1950, as amended [in 1952, 1955, and 1956, under which] Phillips was required to pay into the Welfare Fund the sum of 40 cents per ton on each ton of coal produced for use or sale. The parties have stipulated the amount of tonnage of coal so produced during the period of October 1, 1953, through December 31, 1958, which was subject to the 40 cents per ton royalty, that Phillips made royalty payments thereon pursuant to the Wage Agreements in the total amount of $2,227.70, and that the amount of royalty which was not paid on said total production was $55,982.62, being the amount sued for.

There is no contention by the defendants that the Wage Agreements were not executed by the partnership, but it is contended by them that they were invalid and that no liability exists for the unpaid royalties.

The answer alleges that the agreements were entered into by Phillips by reason of duress on the part of UMW, which conducted a program of terrorism in the section in which Phillips' mine was located, with the result that the agreements were unwillingly executed because Phillips knew that they would not be permitted to operate their coal mine unless said agreements were signed.

The answer further alleges that UMW and certain large producers of coal entered into a conspiracy, the purpose of which was to place financial burdens upon Phillips and other small operators similarly situated that could not possibly be paid out of funds realized from the operation of the mine, and such mines, thus being unable to meet the demands, would be closed down, either through violence or suits such as the present one, leaving the business of shipping coal in interstate commerce and to the government agencies to the large coal operators; that UMW and the large coal companies conspired to increase such financial burdens by increasing the wage scale, both by modifications of the Wage Agreement and by having the Walsh-Healey Act apply to the coal industry and have the minimum wage determined thereunder; and that such conspiracy and the acts thereunder were in violation of Sections 1 and 2 of the Sherman Anti-Trust Act, Sections 1 and 2, Title 15 United States Code. . . .

By an amended answer and cross claim Phillips alleges that in contrast to the disputes which existed between the large coal-producing companies of the country and UMW during the period of World War II and the postwar period, there has been no dispute of any consequence between these parties since 1950, that the alleged conspiracy commenced in 1950, and that it has been implemented by additional understandings between the parties to make more effective the activities in restraint of trade. It specifically alleges that the Union agreed to the termination of employment for thousands of its members because of the mechanization of mines, that it would not protest the closing down of mines which could not be mechanized and that it would go along with the understanding that the coal industry would be confined to a comparatively few companies and the miners employed would be reduced drastically; that as a consequence of this understanding, membership of the United Mine Workers has decreased from 500,000 to 150,000; that the Union agreed that it would not make special agreements with the small operators in the Kentucky and Tennessee region, which would give consideration to local conditions and the particular coal seams mined by the operators, but would have a standard agreement for all operators; that the Union agreed that in the planned mechanization program it would aid in the financing which would become necessary to attain the mechanization of the mines of the large companies; that the large coal-producing companies agreed with the Union that they would not protest the demands of the Union with respect to wage increases so long as the companies were able to match those increases by increased productivity through mechanization; that the companies agreed that there would be no protests from them over the Union's use of the Welfare Fund for its own purposes and in furtherance of its organizing efforts; that under the 1958 Wage Agreement it was required that all signatory operators refrain from buying or marketing nonunion coal; and that the Union and the large companies agreed that they would do all things possible to restrain the production, marketing and sale of nonunion coal.

By another amended cross claim Phillips claims damages for the period commencing four years prior to the filing of the original cross claim on February 14, 1958, the period of damage to end December 31, 1958, at which time the cross plaintiffs ceased to do business, as limited by the four-year limitation provided by Section 15b, Title 15 United States Code. . . .

. . . UMW filed its answer in which it denies that it joined in any conspiracy in restraint of trade or commerce in violation of the Sherman Act, or that it monopolized or attempted to monopolize or conspire with any other person or group of persons to monopolize any part of the trade or commerce among the several states. Affirmatively, it alleges that by virtue of Section 6 of the Clayton Act, Section 17, Title 15 United States Code, it is exempt from the provisions of Sections 1 and 2 of the Sherman Act. It contends that it is a labor organization within the meaning of Section 6 of the Clayton Act and it acted as such for its members in the negotiations for the execution of the Wage Agreements and that during the period of time involved herein its acts were motivated by legitimate labor goals and for the purpose of securing union standards of wages and better conditions of employment for its members, thus qualifying for the exemption provided by the Act.

The claim of the Trustees against Phillips and Phillips' cross claim against the Union were consolidated for trial by jury. Following a trial of some four and one-half weeks the case was submitted to the jury.

[The jury found that the trustees had engaged in a combination or conspiracy to restrain interstate commerce unreasonably beyond the exemption created for labor organizations and had proximately caused $90,000 damage to Phillips Brothers Company.]

The District Judge ruled that there was no material or substantial evidence to support the finding of the jury that the Trustees of the Welfare Fund, as distinguished from the Union, engaged in a combination or conspiracy to unreasonably restrain trade or monopolize or attempt to monopolize commerce among the several states and ordered that the verdict of the jury in so finding be set aside. . . .

Phillips has appealed from the judgment against it . . .

The District Judge overruled the motion of the Union for judgment notwithstanding the verdict and, in the alternative, for a new trial, and entered judgment for Phillips against the Union in the amount of $270,000.00, being three times the amount of damages awarded by the jury, and also included in the judgment the additional sum of $55,000.00 as a reasonable amount of attorneys' fees to be awarded and assessed in accordance with the applicable statutes, thus making a total award in the favor of Phillips in the amount of $325,000.00. The Union has taken an appeal from this judgment . . . Although some question about this may have existed prior to 1945, the Supreme Court held in that year that although an exemption exists in cases where a labor union acts alone in furtherance of its own purposes, it does not exist in cases where a labor union combines with a nonlabor organization to restrain competition in, or to monopolize the marketing of, goods in interstate commerce. Allen Bradley Co. v. Local Union No. 3, etc., 325 U.S. 797. See also: United Brotherhood of Carpenters, etc. v. United States, 330 U.S. 395, 400; Los Angeles Meat & Provision Drivers Union v. United States, 371 U.S. 94, 99-101. The District Judge was not in error in refusing to dismiss the cross claim or to direct a verdict for the Union on this ground, and in submitting to the jury under a proper instruction the question whether the Union acted alone in carrying out the legitimate objects of labor unions, or aided, cooperated, conspired or combined with business groups in order to accomplish purposes which the antitrust laws prohibit. . . .

The Union's main contention on this appeal is that the evidence was insufficient to take the case to the jury on the allegations of the cross claim that it conspired with certain large coal producing companies to restrain trade in the bituminous coal industry among the several states or to monopolize the trade in such industry among the several states, and that it was error for the District Judge to overrule its motions for a directed verdict and for judgment notwithstanding the verdict.

In support of the basic theory of the cross claim that UMW and the major coal companies conspired to eliminate the smaller and weaker companies thus leaving the industry to the major coal companies alone, the following background was given to the jury. After World War II the economics of the Bituminous Coal Industry became unstable by reason of the fact that there was more coal being produced than the markets required; that before 1950 the major coal producers and the union were in agreement that the major problem of the industry was over-production and that the growth of smaller independent and nonunion producers was contributing to the problem; that the major companies and the Union disagreed on how the problem should be handled; that on its side the Union was contending that the answer was to cut down on the working time of the producers; that the Union urged a three-day work week; that for many months before the 1950 contract was signed the Union took the initiative on this question and directed the working time of the men in the industry; that this domination of the men in the industry was interfered with by the passage of the new Taft-Hartley Act; that the Union's efforts to maintain closed shops and to maintain a Union controlled welfare fund were challenged and in some instances were defeated in the Courts by the major coal companies; that the major coal companies were opposed to the Union's dictating the working time of the men in the industry because it cut into profits.

Phillips contends that a marked change occurred in the relations of the Union and the major coal companies in 1950 as disclosed in their bargaining relations before and after that year; that the understanding at the time of the signing of the 1950 Wage Agreement was that the major coal companies were to decide on the working time for their employees; that this was a surrender on the part of the Union of its previous policy of seeking to control the economics of the industry by controlling the working time; that the understanding was that the problem of stabilizing the economics of the industry was to be taken care of by eliminating the smaller and weaker companies, leaving the industry to the major coal companies alone.

The following history of the Wage Agreements between UMW and the coal operators show the increased financial burden placed upon the operators over the period of 1945 through 1958.

UMW and mine operators have negotiated collective bargaining agreements since UMW's beginning in 1890 until the present time. Failure of collective bargaining purposes to function led to work stoppages and seizures and operations of the mines by the Federal Government on five occasions during 1943 through 1946. The National Bituminous Coal Wage Agreement of 1945 terminated pursuant to its terms on March 30, 1946. Collective bargaining between the Secretary of the Interior and UMW resulted in a contract increasing wages $1.85 per day, establishing a welfare and retirement fund of 5 cents per ton on all coal produced for use or for sale and continuing the nine-hour day with overtime for work in excess of seven hours per day and thirty-five hours per week.

Ensuing disputes thereafter resulted in UMW terminating the agreement, but negotiations were resumed and a new agreement was entered into effective July 1, 1947, which increased wages $1.20 a day, reduced the work day to eight hours and increased payments to the welfare fund to 10 cents per ton. Following the resignation of the Welfare Fund's neutral trustee and a disagreement of the remaining two trustees with respect to pension payments, the UMW announced that the operators had dishonored the contract and a nationwide strike began in March 1948. The President invoked Taft-Hartley's national emergency provisions, a Board of Inquiry held hearings and injunction proceedings to enjoin the strike were instituted.

A new agreement was executed on June 25, 1948, which provided for an increase of $1.00 per day in wages and raised the royalty payment to the welfare fund to 20 cents per ton. . . .

The 1952 agreement . . . raised basic daily wages $1.90 to $18.25, and increased fund payments . . . to 40 cents a ton. . . .

The 1958 agreement . . . provided a two-step $2.00 a day wage increase, which brought basic wages as of April 1, 1959, to $24.25 daily. Vacation pay was raised $20.00 to a total of $200.00 for a fourteen-day period.

The campaign to impose the wage contracts upon the smaller non-union mines was intense after 1950. In areas of strong resistance mobs and terrorism were used. One or more of the major coal companies assisted in closing the operations of the principal union competitor of UMW in the bituminous coal labor field. We think the evidence supports the contention of Phillips that the Union knew that the weaker companies could not meet the increased costs of wages and welfare fund payments required by the successive wage agreements and that they would fall by the wayside by reason thereof, and that the increased costs in the successive agreements were geared to the abilities of the major coal companies to mechanize and not have their profits affected by the increased costs.

There was also evidence that before signing the Wage Agreement in October 1953 Phillips told the UMW representative that it was a new company just starting out and that it could not pay the wage scale or the 40 cents a ton to the Welfare Fund, and that the representative told them that they could work out their own working arrangements with their employees and pay whatever they could to the Welfare Fund. To its knowledge, no employee of the partnership belonged to the Union at that time and the Union did not represent the employees, although the Union succeeded in organizing the company later.

With respect to suits against coal operators in Tennessee for unpaid royalties, two suits were filed in 1954, no suits were filed in 1955, one suit was filed in 1956, no suits were filed in 1957, thirty-nine suits were filed in 1958, thirty-eight of which were pending as of December 1, 1960, when the tabulation was made, and seven suits were filed in 1959. It was the established policy of the Trustees to make no discounts or reductions or settlements for less than the full amount owed, irrespective of the economic condition of the operator. Many of the small operators were unable to meet the increased labor costs under the Wage Agreement and the payments to the Welfare Fund, and discontinued operations. Phillips strongly stresses the heavy increase in the litigation in 1958. The present action was filed against it on January 6, 1958. . . .

The 1952 Wage Agreement contained a clause which provided that the signatory operators would not buy, sell or deal in coal mined by companies that did not pay the same labor costs as contained in the Wage Agreement. The major coal companies had the practice of frequently buying coal from the smaller companies to apply on their large long-term contracts. This market was eliminated for those small companies that could not operate under the provisions of the Wage Agreement.

There was evidence showing that UMW acquired [substantial stock and financial interests in two coal companies, which totaled over $25,000,000.]

It was not unreasonable for the jury to conclude from these facts that it was the purpose of the UMW to have a very material voice, if not the dominant one, in determining the policies and operations of these two major coal companies, which, as is hereinafter pointed out are charged with playing an important role in the alleged conspiracy.

The evidence showed the large growth of the Tennessee Valley Authority steam plants, generating electricity by steam. The use of coal by TVA increased from 500,000 tons in 1950 to approximately 20,000,000 tons in 1956. The TVA plants were designed for the use of coal only. TVA buys coal under term and spot market bids. The spot market involves small orders of coal to be delivered in a short period of time, which offers definite advantages to small companies with weak financial resources, which can thus avoid long-term commitments. About seventy-five percent of TVA coal is bought on term contracts and about twenty-five per cent on spot contracts. In 1955 UMW and two of the large coal producing companies successfully sought a determination by the Secretary of Labor of a minimum wage in the coal industry under the Walsh-Healey Act. The minimum wage determined was materially higher, in most instances twice as high, than the minimum wage determined in any other industry under the Walsh-Healey Act. This minimum wage determination prevented Phillips from bidding on the TVA term market, although it left open to Phillips for the time being the TVA spot market.

We believe that the following evidence is relevant on this phase of the case. At the 1956 Convention of the Union, President John L. Lewis introduced Secretary of Labor Mitchell, who, in the course of his remarks, spoke as follows: ". . . As you know, about a year ago the Secretary of Labor, for the first time in history, found a minimum wage in the coal industry which controlled the wages that were to be paid to workers who worked on government contracts. We purposely sought that determination in order to exclude from government bidding those non-union mines which are a detriment to the industry. And I think by and large we have succeeded, . . . Twenty-five per cent, at the moment, of the TVA purchases are made under contracts less than $10,000.00, which excepts such purchases from the determination of the Walsh-Healey Act. I have set in motion a study of the TVA purchasing policy to see if there is any evasion of the Walsh-Healey determination on the part of TVA. . . .

"I propose to continue this enforcement policy, because I believe it is in the interest not only of the worker but is in the interest of the fair employer to prevent the chiseling, nonunion employer from competing in the market place with fair employers who hire union labor."

President Lewis, responding at the end of the speech, said:

"I am sure that the Chair voices the sentiments in the mind of every delegate in expressing our appreciation of the address of the distinguished Secretary of Labor. His personal assurance of his intention to fairly treat the men of the coal industry is bulwarked and borne out by his attitude in the entire period of three and a half years of his incumbency of that office."

Although this evidence was objected to by the Union, it was admitted by the District Judge with the cautionary admonition that the Secretary of Labor couldn't say anything that would prejudice the rights of the UMW unless the UMW authorized him to say it, or unless the UMW approved what he said, or ratified what he said, or acquiesced in what he said. We are of the opinion that this evidence was not improperly received.

Contracts for less than $10,000.00 were not subject to the wage determination of the Walsh-Healey Act. Phillips sold coal on the TVA spot market under contracts for less than $10,000.00, thus avoiding the wage determination of the Walsh-Healey Act. About the end of 1956 the price of coal on the spot market began to decline, which continued through 1957 and 1958, finally reaching a very low figure in 1958. During 1956, 1957 and 1958 Pittsburg-Midway Coal Co., Peabody Coal Co., West Kentucky Coal Co. and Nashville Coal Co., four of the large coal producing companies, made large offerings of tonnage on the TVA spot market at generally declining prices, with a number of such bids being successful. There was evidence that West Kentucky coal was sold extensively in the middle western market, most of it up and down the Mississippi Valley, that the middle western utility market had held up well, but that the distress coal which was for sale by West Kentucky Coal Co. and Nashville Coal Co. was for the most part thrown into the TVA market rather than the other market. [West Kentucky Coal was one of the companies in which the UMW had financial interests.] There was also evidence that West Kentucky Coal Co., Nashville Coal Co. and Peabody Coal Co. did not make an analysis of the profit on the coal sold to TVA, the President of Peabody Coal Co. stating that he was "afraid to look at some of them." There was also evidence that the heavy offerings of West Kentucky coal on the TVA spot market would have the effect of bearing down on the price heavily.

We believe it was a reasonable deduction which the jury could make that the wage determination for the coal industry under the Walsh-Healey Act and the dumping of West Kentucky coal on the TVA spot market materially and adversely affected the operations of Phillips in the important TVA market, thus contributing to the elimination of the company as a competitor to the large coal producing companies operating in that area, including the West Kentucky Coal Company, in which the UMW had such a dominant interest. . . .

UMW contends that the District Judge erred in admitting evidence with reference to the Walsh-Healey prevailing wage determination and having TVA comply therewith, and in charging the jury concerning UMW's efforts to obtain Walsh-Healey prevailing wage determinations and to have TVA enforce such wages. It relies upon Eastern Railroad Presidents Conference v. Noerr Motor Freight, Inc., 365 U.S. 127. It was held in that case that no violation of the Sherman Act can be predicated upon mere attempts to influence the passage or enforcement of laws, and that the Sherman Act does not prohibit two or more persons from associating together in an attempt to persuade the legislature or the executive to take particular action with respect to a law that would produce a restraint or monopoly.

With respect to the Walsh-Healey Act, the District Judge charged the jury:

"Any approach to the Secretary of Labor, which was designed to raise the minimum wages to be paid by coal operators doing business with the TVA or other governmental agencies, was not a violation of the antitrust laws. Therefore, you will not give any consideration whatever to this approach to or meeting with the Secretary of Labor, unless you find that the approach to the Secretary of Labor was a part of the conspiracy to get the prevailing wages establish (*sic*) in the coal industry so high as to drive the small operators out of business."

UMW contends that although the first part of this instruction was in accordance with the ruling in the Noerr case, it was error to qualify the instruction by the concluding words, "unless you find. . . ."

The District Judge also instructed the jury that it was no violation of the anti-trust law for the Union or the coal operators to urge the TVA to abide by the spirit and letter of the Walsh-Healey Act or to modify its methods of buying coal, "unless the parties so urged the TVA to modify its policies in buying coal for the purpose of driving the small operators out of business." The qualifying words in this instruction are likewise complained of.

We do not construe the Noerr ruling as creating an unlimited exemption to Sections 1 and 2 of the Sherman Anti-Trust Act. We believe that the Noerr ruling had reference to conduct which in good faith looked to the enforcement of the law or a modification of an existing policy, unaccompanied by a purpose or intent to further a conspiracy to violate a statute. It is the illegal purpose or intent inherent in the conduct which vitiates the conduct which would otherwise be legal. We find no error in the two instructions complained of.

[After considering other objections, the court affirmed the judgment against the UMW, and also affirmed the decision of the District Judge in directing a verdict in favor of the trustees for the amount due the welfare fund.]

E. The Relation Between Union Economic and Political Activity

UNITED STATES v. INTERNATIONAL UNION, UNITED AUTOMOBILE WORKERS

Supreme Court of the United States, 1957
352 U.S. 567, 77 Sup. Ct. 529, 1 L. Ed. 2d 563

[The United Automobile Workers union was indicted in the Federal District Court in Detroit, Michigan, for violation of 18 U.S.C. §610. The indictment alleged that the general treasury of the union defrayed the expenses of a program televised over commercial station WJBK in Detroit. The program supported democratic candidates for the U.S. Congress in the primary and general elections in 1954. The government alleged that this payment constituted an "expenditure" prohibited by the statute, which reads:

"It is unlawful for any national bank, or any corporation organized by authority of any law of Congress, to make a contribution or expenditure in connection with any election to any political office, or in connection with any primary election or political convention or caucus held to select candidates for any political office, or for any corporation whatever, or any labor organization to make a contribution or expenditure in connection with any election at which Presidential and Vice Presidential electors or a Senator or Representative in, or a Delegate or Resident Commissioner to Congress are to be voted for, or in connection with any primary election or political convention or caucus held to select candidates for any of the foregoing offices, or for any candidate, political committee, or other person to accept or receive any contribution prohibited by this section."

Prior to trial, the union moved to dismiss the indictment because (1) it failed to state an offense under the statute and (2) the statute was, on its face and as applied, offensive to the constitutional rights of the union, "in that the statute (i) abridges freedom of speech and of the press and the right peaceably to assemble and to petition; (ii) abridges the right to choose senators and representatives guaranteed by Article I §2 and the Seventeenth Amendment; (iii) creates an arbitrary and unlawful classification and discriminates against labor organizations in violation of the Fifth Amendment, and (iv) is vague and indefinite and fails to provide a reasonably acertainable standard of guilt in violation of the Fifth and Sixth Amendments."

The District Court, following United States v. CIO, 335 U.S. 106 (1948), dismissed the indictment, holding that the payments did not constitute an "expenditure" within the meaning of the statute. 138 F. Supp. 53 (1956). Under 18 U.S.C. §3731, the Criminal Appeals Act, the government took a direct appeal to the Supreme Court.

During oral argument, counsel for the union made the following statement to the Court:

"For a hundred years, if Your Honors please, we have been engaged in political activity. Our own union Constitution, from its first day, urges it. One cannot draw a line between bargaining and politics. Bargaining is supplemented by legislation and legislation is supplemented by bargaining.

"Now, you cannot split legislation from bargaining. At the bargaining table we get Blue Cross and Blue Shield and at the Congress we ask for national health insurance to supplement it.

"In Congress we get unemployment compensation, and at the bargaining table we supplement it with supplementary unemployment payment. This is as one, what you have here, the bargaining and the legislative process."]

MR. JUSTICE FRANKFURTER delivered the opinion of the Court. . . . Speaking broadly, what is involved here is the integrity of our electoral process, and, not less, the responsibility of the individual citizen for the successful functioning of that process. This case thus raises issues not less than basic to a democratic society.

The concentration of wealth consequent upon the industrial expansion in the post-Civil War era had profound implications for American life. The impact of the abuses resulting from this concentration gradually made itself felt by a rising tide of reform protest in the last decade of the nineteenth century. The Sherman Law was a response to the felt threat to economic freedom created by enormous industrial combines. The income tax law of 1894 reflected congressional concern over the growing disparity of income between the many and the few.

No less lively, although slower to evoke federal action, was popular feeling that aggregated capital unduly influenced politics, an influence not stopping short of corruption. The matter is not exaggerated by two leading historians: "The nation was fabulously rich but its wealth was gravitating rapidly into the hands of a small portion of the population, and the power of wealth threatened to undermine the political integrity of the Republic." 2 Morison and Commager, The Growth of the American Republic (4th ed. 1950), 355. In the '90's many States passed laws requiring candidates for office and their political committees to make public the sources and amounts of contributions to their campaign funds and the recipients and amounts of their campaign expenditures. The theory behind these laws was that the spotlight of publicity would discourage corporations from making political contributions and would thereby end their control over party policies. But these state publicity laws either became dead letters or were found to be futile. . . .

Concern over the size and source of campaign funds so actively entered the presidential campaign of 1904 that it crystallized popular sentiment for federal action to purge national politics of what was conceived to be the pernicious influence of "big money" campaign contributions. A few days after the election of 1904, the defeated candidate for the presidency said:

"The greatest moral question which now confronts us is, Shall the trusts and corporations be prevented from contributing money to control or aid in controlling elections?" . . .

Grist was added to the reformers' mill by the investigation of the great life insurance companies conducted by the Joint Committee of the New York Legislature, the Armstrong Committee, under the guidance of Charles Evans Hughes. The Committee's report, filed early in 1906, revealed that one insurance company alone had contributed almost $50,000 to a national campaign committee in 1904 and had given substantial amounts in preceding presidential campaigns. The Committee concluded:

"Contributions by insurance corporations for political purposes should be strictly forbidden. Neither executive officers nor directors should be allowed to use the moneys paid for purposes of insurance in support of political candidates or platforms. . . ."

Less than a month later the Committee on Elections of the House of Representatives began considering a number of proposals designed to cleanse the political process. Some bills prohibited political contributions by certain classes of corporations; some merely required disclosure of contributions; and others made bribery at elections a federal crime. The feeling of articulate reform groups was reflected at a public hearing held by the Committee. . . . Samuel Gompers, President of the American Federation of Labor . . . said, with respect to the publicity bill:

"Whether this bill meets all of the needs may be questioned; that is open to discussion; but the necessity for some law upon the subject is patent to every man who hopes for the maintenance of the institutions under which we live. It is doubtful to my mind if the contributions and expenditures of vast sums of money in the nominations and elections for our public offices can continue to increase without endangering the endurance of our Republic in its purity and in its essence.

". . . If the interests of any people are threatened by corruption in our public life or corruption in elections, surely it must of necessity be those, that large class of people, whom we for convenience term the wageworkers.

"I am not in a mood, and never am, to indulge in denunciations or criticism, but it does come to me sometimes that one of the reasons for the absence of legislation of a liberal or sympathetic or just character, so far as it affects the interest of the wage-earners of America, can be fairly well traced with the growth of the corruption funds and the influences that are in operation during elections and campaigns. . . . I am under the impression that the patience of the American workingmen is about exhausted —" . . .

President Roosevelt's annual message of 1906 listed as the first item of congressional business a law prohibiting political contributions by corporations. 41 Cong. Rec. 22. Shortly thereafter, in 1907, Congress provided:

"That it shall be unlawful for any national bank, or any corporation organized by authority of any laws of Congress, to make a money contribution in connection with any election to any political office. It shall also be unlawful for any corporation whatever to make a money contribution in connection with any election at which Presidential and Vice-

Presidential electors or a Representative in Congress is to be voted for or any election by any State legislature of a United States Senator." 34 Stat. 864. As the historical background of this statute indicates, its aim was not merely to prevent the subversion of the integrity of the electoral process. Its underlying philosophy was to sustain the active, alert responsibility of the individual citizen in a democracy for the wise conduct of government.

This act of 1907 was merely the first concrete manifestation of a continuing congressional concern for elections "free from the power of money."

[Justice Frankfurter then traced the gradual strengthening during the next years of the laws, particularly §313, relating to political expenditures and contributions.]

The need for unprecedented economic mobilization propelled by World War II enormously stimulated the power of organized labor and soon aroused consciousness of its power outside its ranks. Wartime strikes gave rise to fears of the new concentration of power represented by the gains of trade unionism. And so the belief grew that, just as the great corporations had made huge political contributions to influence governmental action or inaction, whether consciously or unconsciously, the powerful unions were pursuing a similar course, and with the same untoward consequences for the democratic process. Thus, in 1943, when Congress passed the Smith-Connally Act to secure defense production against work stoppages, contained therein was a provision extending to labor organizations, for the duration of the war, §313 of the Corrupt Practices Act. 57 Stat. 163, 167. The testimony of Congressman Landis, author of this measure, before a subcommittee of the House Committee on Labor makes plain the dominant concern that evoked it:

"The fact that a hearing has been granted is a high tribute to the ability of the Labor Committee to recognize the fact that public opinion toward the conduct of labor unions is rapidly undergoing a change. The public thinks, and has a right to think, that labor unions, as public institutions should be granted the same rights and no greater rights than any other public group. My bill seeks to put labor unions on exactly the same basis, insofar as their financial activities are concerned, as corporations have been on for many years. . . .

". . . One of the matters upon which I sensed that the public was taking a stand opposite to that of labor leaders was the question of the handling of funds of labor organizations. The public was aroused by many rumors of huge war chests being maintained by labor unions, of enormous fees and dues being extorted from war workers, of political contributions to parties and candidates which later were held as clubs over the head of high Federal officials. . . ."

Despite §313's wartime application to labor organizations Congress was advised of enormous financial outlays said to have been made by some unions in connection with the national elections of 1944. The Senate's Special Committee on Campaign Expenditures investigated, inter alia, the role of the Political Action Committee of the Congress of Industrial

Organizations. The Committee found "no clear-cut violation of the Corrupt Practices Act on the part of the Political Action Committee" on the ground that it had made direct contributions only to candidates and political committees involved in state and local elections and federal primaries, to which the Act did not apply, and had limited its participation in federal elections to political "expenditures," as distinguished from "contributions" to candidates or committees. S. Rep. No. 101, 79th Cong., 1st Sess. 23. The Committee also investigated, on complaint of Senator Taft, the Ohio C.I.O. Council's distribution to the public at large of 200,000 copies of a pamphlet opposing the re-election of Senator Taft and supporting his rival. In response to the C.I.O.'s assertion that this was not a proscribed "contribution" but merely an "expenditure of its own funds to state its position to the world, exercising its right of free speech . . . ," the Committee requested the Department of Justice to bring a test case on these facts. Id., at 59. It also recommended extension of §313 to cover primary campaigns and nominating conventions. Id., at 81. A minority of the Committee, Senators Ball and Ferguson, advocated further amendment of §313 to proscribe "expenditures" as well as "contributions" in order to avoid the possibility of emasculation of the statutory policy through a narrow judicial construction of "contributions." Id., at 83. [In this and the following year, the House Special Committee to Investigate Campaign Expenditures reached similar conclusions.] Early in 1947 the Special Committee to Investigate Senatorial Campaign Expenditures in the 1946 elections, the Ellender Committee, urged similar action to "plug the existing loophole," S. Rep. No. 1, Part 2, 80th Cong., 1st Sess. 38-39, and Senator Ellender introduced a bill to that effect.

Shortly thereafter, Congress again acted to protect the political process from what it deemed to be the corroding effect of money employed in elections by aggregated power. Section 304 of the labor bill introduced into the House by Representative Hartley in 1947, like the Ellender bill, embodied the changes recommended in the reports of the Senate and House Committees on Campaign Expenditures. It sought to amend §313 of the Corrupt Practices Act to proscribe any "expenditure" as well as "any contribution," to make permanent §313's application to labor organizations and to extend its coverage to federal primaries and nominating conventions. The Report of the House Committee on Education and Labor, which considered and approved the Hartley bill, merely summarized §304, H.R. Rep. No. 245, 80th Cong., 1st Sess. 46, and this section gave rise to little debate in the House. See 93 Cong. Rec. 3428, 3522. Because no similar measure was in the labor bill introduced by Senator Taft, the Senate as a whole did not consider the provisions of §304 until they had been adopted by the Conference Committee. In explaining §304 to his colleagues, Senator Taft, who was one of the conferees, said:

"I may say that the amendment is in exactly the same words which were recommended by the Ellender committee, which investigated expenditures by Senators in the last election. . . . In this instance the words of the Smith-Connally Act have been somewhat changed in effect so as to plug up a loophole which obviously developed, and which, if the courts had permitted advantage to be taken of it, as a matter of fact, would absolutely have destroyed the prohibition against political advertising by corporations. If 'contribution' does not mean 'expenditure,' then a candidate for office could have his corporation friends publish an advertisement for him in the newspapers every day for a month before election. I do not think the law contemplated such a thing, but it was claimed that it did, at least when it applied to labor organizations. So, all we are doing here is plugging up the hole which developed, following the recommendation by our own Elections Committee, in the Ellender bill." 93 Cong. Rec. 6439. After considerable debate, the conference version was approved by the Senate, and the bill subsequently became law despite the President's veto. It is this section of the statute that the District Court held did not reach the activities alleged in the indictment. . . .

For our purposes, the indictment charged appellee with having used union dues to sponsor commercial television broadcasts designed to influence the electorate to select certain candidates for Congress in connection with the 1954 elections.

To deny that such activity, either on the part of a corporation or a labor organization, constituted an "expenditure in connection with any [federal] election" is to deny the long series of congressional efforts calculated to avoid the deleterious influences on federal elections resulting from the use of money by those who exercise control over large aggregations of capital. More particularly, this Court would have to ignore the history of the statute from the time it was first made applicable to labor organizations. As indicated by the reports of the Congressional Committees that investigated campaign expenditures, it was to embrace precisely the kind of indirect contribution alleged in the indictment that Congress amended §313 to proscribe "expenditures." It is open to the Government to prove under this indictment activity by appellee that, except for an irrelevant difference in the medium of communication employed, is virtually indistinguishable from the Brotherhood of Railway Trainmen's purchase of radio time to sponsor candidates or the Ohio C.I.O.'s general distribution of pamphlets to oppose Senator Taft. Because such conduct was claimed to be merely "an expenditure [by the union] of its own funds to state its position to the world," the Senate and House Committees recommended and Congress enacted, as we have seen, the prohibition of "expenditures" as well as "contributions" to "plug the existing loophole."

Although not entitled to the same weight as these carefully considered committee reports, the Senate debate preceding the passage of the Taft-Hartley Act confirms what these reports demonstrate. A colloquy between Senator Taft and Senator Pepper dealt with the problem confronting us:

MR. PEPPER. Does what the Senator has said in the past also apply to a radio speech? If a national labor union, for example, should believe that it was in the public interest to elect the Democratic Party instead of the

Republican Party, or vice versa, would it be forbidden by this proposed act to pay for any radio time, for anybody to make a speech that would express to the people the point of view of that organization?

"MR. TAFT. If it contributed its own funds to get somebody to make a speech, I would say they would violate the law.

"MR. PEPPER. If they paid for the radio time?

"MR. TAFT. If they are simply giving the time, I would say not; I would say that is in the course of their regular business.

"MR. PEPPER. What I mean is this: I was not assuming that the radio station was owned by the labor organization. Suppose that in the 1948 campaign, Mr. William Green, as president of the American Federation of Labor, should believe it to be in the interest of his membership to go on the radio and support one party or the other in the national election, and should use American Federation of Labor funds to pay for the radio time. Would that be an expenditure which is forbidden to a labor organization under the statute?

"MR. TAFT. Yes." 93 Cong. Rec. 6439. . . .

United States v. C.I.O., 335 U.S. 106, presented a different situation. The decision in that case rested on the Court's reading of an indictment that charged defendants with having distributed only to union members or purchasers an issue, Vol. 10, No. 28, of "The CIO News," a weekly newspaper owned and published by the C.I.O. That issue contained a statement by the C.I.O. president urging all members of the C.I.O. to vote for a certain candidate. Thus, unlike the union-sponsored political broadcast alleged in this case, the communication for which the defendants were indicted in C.I.O. was neither directed nor delivered to the public at large. The organization merely distributed its house organ to its own people. The evil at which Congress has struck in §313 is the use of corporation or union funds to influence the public at large to vote for a particular candidate or a particular party.

Our holding that the District Court committed error when it dismissed the indictment for having failed to state an offense under the statute implies no disrespect for "the cardinal rule of construction, that where the language of an act will bear two interpretations, equally obvious, that one which is clearly in accordance with the provisions of the constitution is to be preferred." Knights Templars' Indemnity Co. v. Jarman, 187 U.S. 197, 205. The case before us does not call for its application. Here only one interpretation may be fairly derived from the relevant materials. The rule of construction to be invoked when constitutional problems lurk in an ambiguous statute does not permit disregard of what Congress commands.

Appellee urges that if, as we hold, 18 U.S.C. §610 embraces the activity alleged in the indictment, it offends several rights guaranteed by the Constitution. The Government replies that the actual restraint upon union political activity imposed by the statute is so narrowly limited that Congress did not exceed its powers to protect the political process from undue influence of large aggregations of capital and to promote individual responsibility for democratic government. Once more we are confronted with the duty of being mindful of the conditions under which we may enter upon the delicate process of constitutional adjudication.

The impressive lesson of history confirms the wisdom of the repeated enunciation, the variously expressed admonition, of self-imposed inhibition against passing on the validity of an Act of Congress "unless absolutely necessary to a decision of the case." Burton v. United States, 196 U.S. 283, 295. Observance of this principle makes for the minimum tension within our democratic political system where "scarcely any question arises . . . which does not become, sooner or later, a subject of judicial debate." 1 De Tocqueville, Democracy in America (4th Am. ed. 1843), 306. . . .

Refusal to anticipate constitutional questions is peculiarly appropriate in the circumstances of this case. First of all, these questions come to us unillumined by the consideration of a single judge — we are asked to decide them in the first instance. Again, only an adjudication on the merits can provide the concrete factual setting that sharpens the deliberative process especially demanded for constitutional decision. Finally, by remanding the case for trial it may well be that the Court will not be called upon to pass on the questions now raised. . . .

Counsel are prone to shape litigation, so far as it is within their control, in order to secure comprehensive rulings. This is true both of counsel for defendants and for the Government. Such desire on their part is not difficult to appreciate. But the Court has its responsibility. Matter now buried under abstract constitutional issues may, by the elucidation of a trial, be brought to the surface, and in the outcome constitutional questions may disappear. Allegations of the indictment hypothetically framed to elicit a ruling from this Court or based upon misunderstanding of the facts may not survive the test of proof. For example, was the broadcast paid for out of the general dues of the union membership or may the funds be fairly said to have been obtained on a voluntary basis? Did the broadcast reach the public at large or only those affiliated with appellee? Did it constitute active electioneering or simply state the record of particular candidates on economic issues? Did the union sponsor the broadcast with the intent to affect the results of the election? As Senator Taft repeatedly recognized in the debate on §304, prosecutions under the Act may present difficult questions of fact. . . . We suggest the possibility of such questions, not to imply answers to problems of statutory construction, but merely to indicate the covert issues that may be involved in this case.

Enough has been said to justify withholding determination of the more or less abstract issues of constitutional law. Because the District Court's erroneous interpretation of the statute led it to stop the prosecution prematurely, its judgment must be reversed and the case must be remanded to it for further proceedings not inconsistent with this opinion.

Mr. Justice Douglas, with whom The Chief Justice [Warren] and Mr. Justice Black join, dissenting.

We deal here with a problem that is fundamental to the electoral process and to the operation of our democratic society. It is whether a union can express its views on the issues of an election and on the merits of the candidates, unrestrained and unfettered by the Congress. The principle at stake is not peculiar to unions. It is applicable as well to associations of manufacturers, retail and wholesale trade groups, consumers' leagues, farmers' unions, religious groups and every other association representing a segment of American life and taking an active part in our political campaigns and discussions. It is as important an issue as has come before the Court, for it reaches the very vitals of our system of government.

Under our Constitution it is We The People who are sovereign. The people have the final say. The legislators are their spokesmen. The people determine through their votes the destiny of the nation. It is therefore important — vitally important — that all channels of communication be open to them during every election, that no point of view be restrained or barred, and that the people have access to the views of every group in the community. . . .

. . . To draw a constitutional line between informing the people and inciting or persuading them and to suggest that one is protected and the other not by the First Amendment is to give constitutional dignity to an irrelevance. Any political speaker worth his salt intends to sway voters. . . .

Finally, the Court asks whether the broadcast was "paid for out of the general dues of the union membership or may the funds be fairly said to have been obtained on a voluntary basis." Behind this question is the idea that there may be a minority of union members who are of a different political school than their leaders and who object to the use of their union dues to espouse one political view. This is a question that concerns the internal management of union affairs. To date, unions have operated under a rule of the majority. Perhaps minority rights need protection. But this way of doing it is, indeed, burning down the house to roast the pig. All union expenditures for political discourse are banned because a minority might object. . . .

If minorities need protection against the use of union funds for political speech-making, there are ways of reaching that end without denying the majority their First Amendment rights.

First Amendment rights are not merely curtailed by the construction of the Act which the Court adopts. Today's ruling abolishes First Amendment rights on a wholesale basis. Protection of minority groups, if any, can be no excuse. The Act is not "narrowly drawn" to meet that abuse.

Some may think that one group or another should not express its views in an election because it is too powerful, because it advocates unpopular ideas, or because it has a record of lawless action. But these are not justifications for withholding First Amendment rights from any group — labor or corporate. Cf. United States v. Rumely, 345 U.S. 41. First Amendment rights are part of the heritage of all persons and groups in this country. They are not to be dispensed or withheld merely because we or the Congress thinks the person or group is worthy or unworthy.

These constitutional questions are so grave that the least we should do is to construe this Act, as we have in comparable situations (United States

v. C.I.O., supra; United States v. Rumely, 345 U.S. 41; United States v. Harriss, 347 U.S. 612), to limit the word "expenditure" to activity that does not involve First Amendment rights.

NOTES

1. On remand, the case was tried to a jury. The District Judge was required to frame instructions based on the opinion you have just read. His charge is quoted in Lane, Political Expenditures by Labor Unions, 9 Lab. L.J. 725, 733 (1958). It included the following statement:

" 'Was the broadcast paid for out of the general dues of the union membership?'

"If the question had ended there, the answer would be unquestionably 'Yes' because the plaintiff charges and the defendant admits that the broadcasts were paid for out of the general dues of the union membership. But in arriving at what it thought Congress must have meant by passing this Act, the Supreme Court question doesn't end there. It goes on to ask you to determine not only was the broadcast paid for out of the general dues of the union membership, but

" '— may the funds used be fairly said to have been obtained on a voluntary basis?'

"If — that last part — if by that is meant passing of the hat for voluntary contributions by individual members approached by some committee or otherwise, then this, what happened here, was not voluntary, because it came out of the dues. There was no passing of the hat or anything like that. But I believe that the word 'fairly' was put in there for some reason. The Supreme Court does not usually use words recklessly. It said — and here I quote from part of the question —

" '— or may the funds be fairly said to have been obtained on a voluntary basis?'

"So in deciding whether or not the funds used may be fairly said to have been obtained on a voluntary basis, you have a right to take into consideration the fact that these men, in 1954, were delegates to a convention just like any other convention and just like any other delegates. They represented others. The whole membership couldn't go to the convention any more than the whole membership of some fraternal organization can go to a convention. They send delegates. And at the convention in 1953 these delegates, acting for the UAW membership, voted as they had on previous conventions, authority for their governing board to use part of the dues for this educational program that the governing board had used and was preparing to use in the future."

The jury acquitted.

2. For subsequent Supreme Court decisions dealing with organized political activity, see NAACP v. Button, 371 U.S. 415 (1963); Brotherhood of Railway Trainmen v. Virginia, 377 U.S. 1 (1964); New York Times v. Sullivan, 376 U.S. 254 (1964).

3. The related problem of the right of employees under a union shop agreement with respect to the political use of union dues is considered in

Part V, infra page 973, in connection with the case of International Assn. of Machinists v. Street, 367 U.S. 740 (1961). In that case the Court distinguished funds used for political purposes from those used for other ends. The problem of a remedy against improper political expenditures of dues was discussed in the following terms (p. 772): "We also think that a blanket injunction against all expenditures of funds for the disputed purposes, even one conditioned on cessation of improper expenditures, would not be a proper exercise of equitable discretion. Nor would it be proper to issue an interim or temporary blanket injunction of this character pending a final adjudication. The Norris-LaGuardia Act, 47 Stat. 70, 29 U.S.C. §§101-115, expresses a basic policy against the injunction of activities of labor unions. . . .

". . . Moreover, the fact that these expenditures are made for political activities is an additional reason for reluctance to impose such an injunctive remedy. Whatever may be the powers of Congress or the States to forbid unions altogether to make various types of political expenditures, as to which we express no opinion here, many of the expenditures involved in the present case are made for the purpose of disseminating information as to candidates and programs and publicizing the positions of the unions on them. As to such expenditures an injunction would work a restraint on the expression of political ideas which might be offensive to the First Amendment. For the majority also has an interest in stating its views without being silenced by the dissenters."

Justice Frankfurter rejected the distinction between "political" use of union dues and the use of dues for the purposes of collective bargaining, stating (p. 814): "It is not true in life that political protection is irrelevant to, and insulated from, economic interests. It is not true for industry or finance. Neither is it true for labor. It disrespects the wise, hardheaded men who were the authors of our Constitution and our Bill of Rights to conclude that their scheme of government requires what the facts of life reject. As Mr. Justice Rutledge stated: 'To say that labor unions as such have nothing of value to contribute to that process [the electoral process] and no vital or legitimate interest in it is to ignore the obvious facts of political and economic life and of their increasing interrelationship in modern society.' "

PART TWO

Establishment and Maintenance of Collective Bargaining

A. PATTERNS OF REPRESENTATION

1. *Administrative Action*

a. NATURE OF THE BARGAINING UNIT

ENDERBY PROBLEM 1

The Enderby Rubber Company operates an automobile tire and miscellaneous rubber products plant on the outskirts of Chicago. The company employs approximately 1000 men and women, the work force being divided roughly as follows:

Production and maintenance employees — Tire Division	500
Production and maintenance employees — Miscellaneous Rubber Goods Division	350
Foremen	50
Clerical	75
Executive	25

There has been no collective bargaining on behalf of the Enderby employees.

A committee of five employees sends a letter to Mr. Leslie White, the Industrial Relations Manager of the Enderby Company, advising him that a majority of the workers in the plant have become members of the United Rubber, Cork, Linoleum and Plastic Workers of America, AFL-CIO, and that this union has established Local 417 for the employees of the plant. The letter asks that the company recognize Local 417 and start immediately on the negotiation of a collective bargaining agreement.

In response to White's request the committee, accompanied by George Layton, a representative of the international office of the union, goes to White's office for a conference.

White asks the committee how many members the local has. The answer is, "We've got over half the men lined up." White asks for a list of the members. The committee refuses. White calls attention to the fact that all the members of the committee are from the Tire Division. Layton answers that the union has many members in both the Tire Division and the Miscellaneous Division and that it also has substantial support among the clerical employees. Layton adds, however, that the union does not claim to represent the foremen or the executive personnel. After further discussion, White tells the committee that he will "talk the matter over with some of our people," and suggests a meeting for the following Monday.

At the Monday meeting, White tells the committee that the company "has decided not to recognize Local 417 as the bargaining representative for the employees of the plant unless and until the NLRB conducts an election and certifies the United Rubber Workers as the bargaining agent." Oliver Curme, one of the employees, who has been elected president of Local 417, reverses the position taken by Layton at the previous meeting and offers to submit membership cards to White for a cross-check against the company's employment records. White refuses this offer, stating that he does not trust such evidence, and he reaffirms his position that the company will not negotiate with the union until it has been certified.

Curme, obviously irritated by White's position, retorts, "My people aren't going to like this," and he adds, "There may be some trouble in the plant."

Three days later Local 417 files a petition with a regional office of the NLRB under Section 9(c) of the NLRA, requesting that the union be certified as the representative of "all production, maintenance, and clerical employees of the Enderby Rubber Company, Chicago plant."

Shortly after this petition is filed, the Enderby Employees Association, an unaffiliated union, which also claims support among the Enderby employees, files a petition with the Board requesting that it be "certified as the representative of all employees in the Miscellaneous Rubber Goods Division at the Enderby Chicago Plant."

A few days later the NLRB directs that a hearing be held on each petition and that the matter be consolidated.

Shortly thereafter, O'Doul, Plant Superintendent of the Enderby Company, approaches three employees, Kane, Alston, and Jones, at their workbench. O'Doul tells the three men that the company is about to submit a sealed bid in an effort to get a government contract and that it wishes to know, in order to estimate its future labor costs with the greatest possible accuracy, the extent to which Local 417 has support among the employees. O'Doul assures the three employees that their answers will in no way prejudice their employment with the company.

O'Doul then asks each of them whether he is a member of Local 417. Each of the three employees tells O'Doul, "That is none of your business." O'Doul thereupon warns the men that unless they answer his questions truthfully, he will consider them to be insubordinate and will recommend their discharge, and repeats the question. The three employees still refuse to answer. Two days later White sends discharge slips to Kane and Alston. Jones, who is the senior employee in the department and has an excellent work record, receives no notice, nor is he disciplined in any other way.

Five days later, O'Doul calls all of the employees together about twenty minutes before closing time and makes a short speech in the company club room, in the course of which he says: "Under the NLRA you have a right to belong to a union, either Local 417, the Enderby Employees Association, or any other labor organization. However, you also have a right not to belong to any union. Personally, I do not think you need a union. You are already receiving pensions, life insurance, sickness and accident benefits, vacation with pay, Christmas bonuses, and you have wages that are as high as any in the industry. I know that you are too smart to join a union and pay dues and fees for something you are already getting for nothing. However, under the law, I have to admit that you are entitled to join a union if that is what you want to do. I would like to say one final thing. If you decide to join or vote for a union, I hope that you will choose the Enderby Employees Association. It is not tied in with any national labor organization and is led by local people who understand our problems in this plant. I am sure that the company would prefer to deal with our own people, and I am sure that you would get better representation."

The following week the NLRB regional office holds the scheduled hearing. At the outset of the hearing Local 417 makes an offer to prove that the Enderby Employees Association has been the beneficiary of company support in violation of Section 8(a)(2). The hearing officer's disposition of this offer of proof and the transcript of the representation hearing follow.

HEARING OFFICER HOLT: The hearing will be in order.

This is a formal hearing in the matter of the Enderby Rubber Company and Local 417, United Rubber, Cork, Linoleum and Plastic Workers of America, AFL-CIO, and the Enderby Employees Association, consolidated cases numbered 45 RC 2015 and 45 RC 2027 before the National Labor Relations Board. The Hearing Officer appearing for the National Labor Relations Board is Harold Holt.

Will counsel please state their appearances for the record?

For the Company?

MR. BLAIR: Blair & Morgan, by Harold L. Blair, 768 Congress Street, Chicago, Illinois.

HEARING OFFICER: For the Petitioner Rubber Workers?

MR. COOPER: Cooper & Cooper, by Daniel X. Cooper, 42 LaSalle Boulevard, Chicago, Illinois.

HEARING OFFICER: For the Petitioner Employees Association?

MR. ENDICOTT: Robert M. Endicott, 16 Milk Street, Chicago, Illinois.

HEARING OFFICER: Are there any other persons, parties, or labor organizations in the hearing room at this time who claim an interest in this proceeding?

(The Hearing Officer hears no response.)

I wish to inform all parties that the Official Reporter makes the only official transcript of these proceedings, and all citations in briefs or arguments must refer to the official record.

After the close of the hearing, any party wishing to have corrections made in the record may file his proposed corrections with the regional office, either by way of stipulation or motion.

Statements of reasons in support of motions or objections should be as concise as possible. I wish to stress the fact that all matter that is spoken in the hearing room is recorded by the Official Reporter while the hearing is in session. In the event that any of the parties wish to make off-the-record remarks, requests to make such remarks should be directed to the Hearing Officer, and not to the Official Reporter.

Objections and exceptions may upon appropriate request be permitted to stand to an entire line of questioning. Automatic exceptions will be allowed to all adverse rulings. Five copies of all pleadings submitted during the hearing are to be filed with the Hearing Officer.

The sole objective of the Hearing Officer here is to ascertain the respective positions of the parties and to obtain a full and complete factual record upon which the Board may discharge its duties under Section 9 of the National Labor Relations Act, as amended. The services of the Hearing Officer are equally at the disposal of all parties to the proceeding in developing such material evidence.

At this time I offer in evidence as Board's Exhibit No. 1 the following papers in this proceeding which I shall designate for the record as follows:

(a) Petition in Case No. 45 RC 2015 for Certification of Representatives, Pursuant to Section 9(c) of the National Labor Relations Act, as amended, filed November 16, and signed by Oliver M. Curme, on behalf of Local 417, United Rubber, Cork, Linoleum and Plastic Workers.

(b) Petition in Case No. 45 RC 2027 for Certification of Representatives, Pursuant to Section 9(c) of the National Labor Relations Act, as amended, filed November 18, and signed by Robert M. Endicott, for the Enderby Employees Association.

(c) Order consolidating cases Nos. 45 RC 2015 and 45 RC 2027 for purposes of hearing, dated November 20, and signed by John Alter, Regional Director.

(d) Notice of Representation Hearing in the instant case signed by John Alter, Regional Director, and dated November 23.

(e) Affidavit of Service of the aforementioned papers executed by Mary Smith, before Joan O'Brien, designated Agent, together with appended postal registry return receipts showing service of the said papers, dated November 23.

Is there any objection to the receipt of these documents in evidence?

MR. BLAIR: No objection.

MR. COOPER: No objection.

MR. ENDICOTT: No objection.

HEARING OFFICER: The Hearing Officer hearing no objection, the documents referred to are received in evidence as Board's Exhibit No. 1.

HEARING OFFICER: Are there any motions to intervene in these proceedings to be submitted to the Hearing Officer at this time? This does not include parties or persons who have been served with formal notice by registered mail of the hearing in this case.

(The Hearing Officer hears no response.)

Off the record.

HEARING OFFICER: On the record.

Now with respect to the Company's business. The Enderby Rubber Company is an Illinois corporation with its principal place of business located at Chicago, Illinois. It is engaged in the manufacture and distribution of rubber and plastic products. It annually ships finished goods valued in excess of $1,000,000 directly to states of the United States other than the state of Illinois.

Mr. Blair, is that a fair statement of the business and operations of the Company?

MR. BLAIR: Yes.

HEARING OFFICER: On behalf of the Company do you admit that the Company is engaged in interstate commerce within the meaning of the National Labor Relations Act, as amended?

MR. BLAIR: I do.

HEARING OFFICER: Will the Company furnish a payroll and cooperate with the Board in the holding of any election which the Board may direct?

MR. BLAIR: It will.

HEARING OFFICER: Is the correct and legal name of the Company that by which it has been designated in these proceedings, to wit: The Enderby Rubber Company? Is "Company" spelled out?

MR. BLAIR: It is.

HEARING OFFICER: Mr. Cooper, is the correct name of the Petitioner Rubber Workers that which appears on the petition filed in this case, to wit: Local 417, United Rubber, Cork, Linoleum and Plastic Workers of America, AFL-CIO?

MR. COOPER: It is.

HEARING OFFICER: Mr. Endicott, is the correct name of the Petitioner Employees Association, the Enderby Employees Association?

MR. ENDICOTT: It is.

HEARING OFFICER: Can it be stipulated that both of the petitioners herein, the United Rubber Workers, Local 417, affiliated with the AFL-CIO, and the Enderby Employees Association, unaffiliated, are labor organizations within the meaning of the National Labor Relations Act, as amended?

Do you so stipulate, Mr. Blair, on behalf of the Company?

MR. BLAIR: I do.

HEARING OFFICER: Do you so stipulate, Mr. Endicott, on behalf of the Petitioner Employees Association?

MR. ENDICOTT: I do.

HEARING OFFICER: Do you stipulate, Mr. Cooper, on behalf of the Petitioner Rubber Workers?

MR. COOPER: I stipulate that the Rubber Workers Local 417 is a labor organization within the meaning of the Act. I do not stipulate that the Enderby Employees Association is a labor organization.

HEARING OFFICER: All right. We have a stipulation with respect to the Rubber Workers and after I dispose of certain preliminary matters, we will take evidence on the status of the Enderby Employees Association.

Off the record.

HEARING OFFICER: On the record. Gentlemen, can we agree to the two following stipulations?

(a) On October 29, the Petitioner Rubber Workers, Local 417, in writing requested recognition as the bargaining agent for the employees in the requested unit. The Company refused to grant recognition unless and until the Petitioner was certified by the National Labor Relations Board.

(b) The Enderby Employees Association on November 18, by the filing of a petition with the Regional Office requested recognition as bargaining agent for the employees in the unit sought by it, and the employer declined to recognize the Association unless and until it is certified by the National Labor Relations Board.

MR. BLAIR: I am perfectly agreeable to the proposed stipulation.

MR. ENDICOTT: I so stipulate.

MR. COOPER: I agree to the first of the two proposed stipulations, namely, the one regarding the Rubber Workers' petition. However, I do not agree to the second stipulation regarding the Enderby Employees Association. There is no evidence that the Association made a demand upon the employer.

HEARING OFFICER: The objection will be overruled, Mr. Cooper. The filing of the petition by the Association is sufficient evidence of a demand.

HEARING OFFICER: Mr. Blair, what is the over-all employment in the plant?

MR. BLAIR: One thousand employees.

HEARING OFFICER: Can you break this down into employees as distinguished from executives and supervisors?

MR. BLAIR: Yes. There are 850 production and maintenance employees; 500 are employed in the tire division of the Company and 350 are employed in our miscellaneous rubber goods division. Of the balance, 75 are clerical employees, 50 are foremen, and we have 25 executives.

HEARING OFFICER: Has the Company any presently existing or recently expired contracts with any labor organizations, covering any employees in the requested units?

MR. BLAIR: No.

HEARING OFFICER: Does the Company anticipate a substantial increase or decrease in its employment roll insofar as the requested units are concerned, within the next sixty to ninety days?

MR. BLAIR: No.

HEARING OFFICER: The unit petitioned for by the Rubber Workers is as follows:

> "All production, maintenance and clerical employees of the Enderby Rubber Company, Chicago plant, excluding guards, executives and supervisors as defined in the Act."

What is your position with respect to the requested unit, Mr. Blair, on behalf of the employer?

Mr. Blair: The unit, as sought, is clearly inappropriate on three grounds. In the first place, as I understand it, the unit as petitioned for, includes the miscellaneous division.

Hearing Officer: Mr. Cooper, is that correct?

Mr. Cooper: Yes.

Mr. Blair: The miscellaneous division, as the evidence will show, is entirely separate and distinct from the tire division. It includes employees of different skills than those in the tire division, uses different equipment and is separately housed. There is no community of interest between these two groups. Secondly, the fire hose department, which is in the miscellaneous division, is not properly included within units of either the miscellaneous and tire divisions together or the miscellaneous division taken alone. And finally, the clerical employees have nothing in common with the production and maintenance employees and should not be properly included with them in any unit. As I understand it, the Hearing Officer merely desires our position at this time. I shall give the full reasons in support of this position when the evidence is in.

Hearing Officer: Thank you, Mr. Blair. Mr. Endicott, what is the position of the Association?

Mr. Endicott: Well, I'm not a lawyer but I do feel that the miscellaneous rubber goods division is a separate unit and should be treated separately. I hadn't thought about the clerical employees and whatever the Board decides on that is O.K. with the Association. I do not agree, however, with Mr. Blair that the fire hose department would not properly be included in the miscellaneous division. I do agree that it would be improper to include that department with the tire division.

Hearing Officer: You are an employee of the Enderby Rubber Company, Mr. Endicott?

Mr. Endicott: Yes.

Hearing Officer: And you are not represented by counsel?

Mr. Endicott: No.

Hearing Officer: As I understand it, you take the position that the unit requested by the Rubber Workers, which would include the miscellaneous division, is inappropriate. You take no position with respect to the inclusion or exclusion of clerical employees? It is also your claim that the employees in the fire hose department, which is now located in the miscellaneous division, would be properly included in a unit confined to the miscellaneous division.

Mr. Endicott: That's correct.

Hearing Officer: I might add, Mr. Endicott, that since you are not represented by counsel, if at any time during the hearing you fail to understand some of the more technical points which arise, or if you are unable to develop some of the issues which seem to be important to you, feel free to call upon the Hearing Officer to assist you. As I stated in opening this hearing, the services of the Hearing Officer are at the disposal of all of the parties in developing material evidence. This is a nonadversary proceeding in the nature of an investigation and I make this suggestion to you since it is my obligation to obtain a full and complete record.   For this reason, it often becomes necessary for the Hearing Officer to participate in the proceedings regardless of whether the parties are represented by counsel or not.   Mr. Cooper, on behalf of the Rubber Workers, what is your position?   Just briefly.

MR. COOPER: As stated in our petition, the Rubber Workers take the position that the miscellaneous division and the tire division constitute one appropriate unit.   Neither group constitutes a craft unit and the degree of skills involved does not justify separate units.   Incidentally, I might add that we are unaware of any real differences so far as the employees in the so-called fire hose department are concerned.   With respect to the clerical employees, it is our position that they are factory clericals, not office clericals, and have an identity of interest with the production and maintenance employees.   I might add that perhaps our unit description does not make this entirely clear.   Therefore, I should like to move to amend the petition by inserting the word "factory" before the word "clerical" in the unit requested.

HEARING OFFICER: Any objection, Mr. Blair?

MR. BLAIR: No objection to the Motion to Amend, but this does not alter my position, previously stated, that the clericals should not be a part of the appropriate unit.

HEARING OFFICER: That is understood.

HEARING OFFICER: Mr. Endicott, do you have any objection to this amendment?

MR. ENDICOTT: No sir.

HEARING OFFICER: The Motion to Amend will be allowed.   The unit as sought by the Rubber Workers will now read:

> "All production, maintenance and factory clerical employees of the Enderby Rubber Company, Chicago plant, excluding guards, executives and supervisors as defined in the Act."

Mr. Blair, just to keep the record straight, how many of the 75 clericals are strictly office workers and how many work in sections of the plant other than the main office?

MR. BLAIR: They are all office workers, but in direct answer to your question and without departing from my original position, I will say that about 12 clericals work in the main office.   The balance are located outside of the main office.

HEARING OFFICER: The unit sought by the Enderby Employees Association reads as follows:

> "All employees in the Miscellaneous Rubber Goods Division at the Enderby Chicago Plant."

I assume, Mr. Endicott, that you do not intend to seek those employees who, by statute, may not properly be included?

MR. ENDICOTT: That's right.

HEARING OFFICER: Off the record.

HEARING OFFICER: On the record.   During the off-the-record discussion the Hearing Officer explained the statutory exclusions to Mr. Endicott. Accordingly, I now entertain your motion, Mr. Endicott, to provide for the statutory exclusions by adding to your unit description "excluding guards, executives and supervisors within the meaning of the Act." Any objections, Mr. Blair?

MR. BLAIR: No sir.

HEARING OFFICER: Mr. Cooper?

MR. COOPER: No.

HEARING OFFICER: The motion is granted and the unit as now sought by the Association reads:

> "All employees in the Miscellaneous Rubber Goods Division at the Enderby Chicago Plant, excluding guards, executives and supervisors within the meaning of the Act."

Mr. Blair, what is your position with respect to the unit sought by the Association?

MR. BLAIR: It is inappropriate so far as it contains clerical employees and the employees who are employed in the fire hose department.

HEARING OFFICER: Mr. Cooper?

MR. COOPER: It is inappropriate for reasons which I have already stated.

HEARING OFFICER: Now, gentlemen, before we proceed to take evidence with respect to the appropriateness or inappropriateness of the units sought, I should like to dispose of the matter of the Association's status as a labor organization. Mr. Endicott, will you or any officer of the Association whom you may choose, take the witness stand?

ROBERT M. ENDICOTT

a witness called by and on behalf of the Board, being first duly sworn, was examined and testified as follows:

HEARING OFFICER: Mr. Endicott, what is your relationship to the Petitioner Enderby Employees Association?

THE WITNESS: I am President of the Enderby Employees Association.

HEARING OFFICER: Mr. Endicott, what is the purpose of your Association?

THE WITNESS: We formed a group to represent the employees of the miscellaneous division to deal with the Company. The employees of the miscellaneous division want to act as a unit in dealing with the employer. Our Association will take up grievances, wages, hours of work and other working conditions with the employer, on behalf of all the employees of the miscellaneous division.

HEARING OFFICER: Do you intend to do anything else?

THE WITNESS: Well, yes. When we iron out these things, we will put them in a written contract between the Association and the Company.

HEARING OFFICER: Mr. Blair?

MR. BLAIR: No questions.

HEARING OFFICER: Mr. Cooper?

MR. COOPER: Yes. May I ask how many authorization cards the Association submitted in support of its petition?

HEARING OFFICER: As you undoubtedly know, Mr. Cooper, we require that the Petitioner submit a showing of interest of 30 percent of the total employees in the unit requested before the petition is processed. This is an administrative matter and is not open to attack at the representation hearing.[1]

MR. COOPER: Well, I am familiar with the Board's rulings in this respect, but I am not sure that I have ever understood them. Ordinarily, I would not bring up the subject but it has come to my attention that some of the authorization cards obtained by the Association were obtained by coercion and others were forged.

HEARING OFFICER: Mr. Cooper, this is not the proper forum to raise such questions. Had you desired to present any evidence to the Regional Director along the lines you have just mentioned, you would have been free to do so and the matter would have been carefully investigated by an inquiry separate and apart from this formal hearing. Again, I repeat, this is an administrative matter and not subject to litigation here.

MR. COOPER: Well, I suppose I will have to accept that and I don't want to be argumentative but it seems odd to me. What if one card was forged and the Association only had a 30 percent showing to start with, this would mean that they did not meet their 30 percent showing of interest.

HEARING OFFICER: I don't want to get into a further discussion on this point with you, Mr. Cooper, but I should point out to you that the reason for the 30 percent showing is that the Board does not want to put an employer through hearings and elections if the union can only organize a few employees and only demonstrate a minimal showing of interest. In the hypothetical case you just recited, suppose the Association only had a 29 percent uncoerced showing of interest. In the final analysis, the secret election which is provided for by the Act would disclose this, so that nobody would be hurt. Please proceed with your cross-examination, if you have any, of the witness.

CROSS-EXAMINATION

Q. (By Mr. Cooper) Mr. Endicott, are you one of the founders of the Association?

A. Yes.

Q. And how did you happen to form this organization just at this time?

MR. BLAIR: I object.

HEARING OFFICER: What is the purpose of the question, Mr. Cooper? What are you seeking to prove?

MR. COOPER: I intend to show that this is a company-instigated, company-dominated and company-assisted organization.

HEARING OFFICER: The objection will be sustained, Mr. Cooper. The only issue involved in the witness's testimony is whether the Enderby Employees Association is a labor organization.

MR. COOPER: All right. I then desire to make an offer of proof. If this

---

[1] Compare NLRA §9(e)(1). According to NLRB, 23d Ann. Rep. 14 (1958), intervenors are not required to show their interest by a 30 percent authorization, if they seek the same unit as petitioners. — ED.

witness were permitted to respond to my questions, I would elicit from him testimony which would establish that the Association sprang up after the Rubber Workers commenced organizational activity among the Enderby employees; that the organization was formed as a direct result of the suggestion of management, more than the suggestion, the request of management; that thereafter management instructed the Association committee not only in procedural requirements, such as the drawing up of bylaws and a constitution, but also in the actual filing of the instant petition. Management also assisted the committee actively, on company time and premises, in signing up employees on authorization cards. The Enderby Employees Association is strictly a creature of the employer and violates the policies, purposes and statutory requirements of the National Labor Relations Act. It is not and it cannot be a labor organization within the meaning of the law.

MR. BLAIR: I object to this combined speech and offer of proof on the grounds that the speech is out of order and that the offer of proof is improper. An offer of proof cannot be properly made on cross-examination. If Mr. Endicott were Mr. Cooper's witness, such an offer might be in order. He is not Mr. Cooper's witness and Mr. Cooper cannot know what his testimony will be.

HEARING OFFICER: In any event, I shall reject the offer of proof without going into the technical aspects of Mr. Blair's objection. The Board will not accept evidence of an unfair labor practice in a representation hearing.[2]

MR. COOPER: Very respectfully, Mr. Hearing Officer, I am not making this offer of proof technically in connection with any unfair labor practice charge. It is made in connection with the procedural provisions of the National Labor Relations Act as they relate to the conduct of representation hearings. I am not seeking to prove that either the Enderby Rubber Company or the Enderby Employees Association has violated any provision of Section 8 of the national law. I do seek to show what is the fact, that the company domination and assistance which has taken place makes the Enderby Employees Association an improper party here, so far as the term "labor organization" is relevant to Section 9 of the national law; and in this connection I call your attention to the General Shoe doctrine,[3] which I submit to you makes my offer of proof quite valid. If company interference which falls short of an unfair labor practice will invalidate an election, certainly a company-dominated association is not a proper election petitioner.

HEARING OFFICER: Same ruling, Mr. Cooper. This is not the place to

[2] In Times Square Stores Corp., 79 N.L.R.B. 361 (1948), the Board held that the statutory scheme of separation of functions of the General Counsel and the Board precludes it from deciding unfair labor practice questions in a representation proceeding. See also Marine Optical Manufacturing Co., 92 N.L.R.B. 571 (1950). — ED.

[3] In General Shoe Corp., 77 N.L.R.B. 124 (1948), the Board held that an employer's conduct in calling twenty to twenty-five employees into his office during working hours to listen to intemperate antiunion statements is grounds for setting aside an election even though it does not constitute an unfair labor practice. — ED.

file unfair labor practice charges. Do you have any further questions for this witness?

MR. COOPER: None. You will note my exceptions?

HEARING OFFICER: That will not be necessary. You have an automatic exception to all adverse rulings.

HEARING OFFICER: You are excused, Mr. Endicott.

MR. ENDICOTT: Gosh, maybe I do need a lawyer.

HEARING OFFICER: Please, gentlemen. There will be a ten-minute recess.

HEARING OFFICER: On the record. Gentlemen, during the off-the-record discussion at the conclusion of the recess, it was decided that the employer's industrial relations manager, Mr. White, would be in the best position to furnish factual data with respect to the unit questions. Of course, you may, after he has concluded his testimony, produce witnesses either to add to his testimony or refute it. Mr. Blair, would you have Mr. White take the witness stand?

MR. BLAIR: Mr. White, will you take the stand please?

LESLIE R. WHITE

a witness called for and on behalf of the employer, having been duly sworn, was examined and testified as follows:

HEARING OFFICER: Tell the reporter your name and address please.

THE WITNESS: Leslie R. White, 97 Rockaway Road, Leominster, Illinois.

HEARING OFFICER: What is your occupation, Mr. White?

THE WITNESS: I am Industrial Relations Manager of the Enderby Rubber Company, at Chicago, Illinois.

DIRECT EXAMINATION

Q. (By Mr. Blair) How long has the Chicago Plant of the Enderby Rubber Company been in existence?

A. About thirty-nine years, sir. In one form or another.

Q. Well, now could you tell us something of the nature of its original business?

A. Yes sir. The Company was originally organized in 1920 for the purpose of manufacturing fire hose. It acquired at that time a part of its present location in Chicago.

Q. Fire hose continues to be a part of the Company's production?

A. Yes, a very important part.

Q. Now, at some time the Company began the manufacture and distribution of tires, rubber tires?

A. That is correct. We expanded our facilities and began tire production some time in 1927.

Q. Does the Company manufacture anything except fire hose and tires? By the way, Mr. White, I assume we are talking about automobile tires.

A. Oh, our tire division also produces truck tires, tractor tires and tires for planes as well as bicycles.

Q. I see. So you have a tire division and a fire hose division?

A. Well, not precisely. We have a tire division and a miscellaneous division. The fire hose department is a part of the so-called miscellaneous division.

Q. What other products are manufactured by the miscellaneous division?

A. Well, we manufacture various types of plastic products and materials.

HEARING OFFICER: What would be the nature of this plastics production, Mr. White?

WITNESS: Oh, we have a quite varied production of plastics. Floor and wall tile, paneling for automobiles, planes, refrigerators, radio and television casing and equipment, advertising displays. We also produce such items as various types of plastic cloth, patent handbags, etc.

HEARING OFFICER: What is a patent handbag?

WITNESS: Well, it looks like alligator but it isn't and it's cheaper.

Q. (By Mr. Blair) When did the Company begin the manufacture of these plastic items, Mr. White?

A. In 1948. At that time we established our so-called miscellaneous rubber goods division.

Q. Will you state the circumstances under which this division was set up?

A. Well, up until that time we had been exclusively concerned with the manufacture of fire hose and tires, the fire hose business being the original concern of the Company. Perhaps I should say at this time that the rubber used in making this hose is compounded in accordance with a secret formula which has been handed down in the Rudow family, the principal stockholder in the Enderby Company. The making of the hose itself is a fairly specialized art. For some years we had not been too satisfied with housing this operation with the tire division. Sometime in 1947 a furniture factory adjacent to our plant closed its doors. The building, a large two-story structure, was put up for sale rather reasonably. The Enderby Board of Directors discussed purchasing it for the purpose of further plant expansion but primarily with the object of transferring to it the fire hose department. At the same time it was decided to further diversify our production by getting into the plastics business. I might say that many of our long-term customers so far as the tire division was concerned had become interested in some of the by-products of the plastics field, and we felt that here was an opportunity to meet this new demand. In any event, the furniture factory was acquired in 1948, the staff of our fire hose department was transferred and the plastics department was started with new personnel. We called the entire operation the miscellaneous rubber goods division.

Q. What is manufactured on the first floor of the miscellaneous division building?

A. Principally plastic parts, pieces and materials such as I have previously described.

Q. Does this work require a high degree of skill?

A. No. It is what we call a line operation. Actually we were able to utilize the services of the employees who had been laid off when the furniture company ceased its operations. We were able to train them for the work and most of them are still with us.

Q. How many people are employed in the plastics department?

A. Right now, approximately 240 production and maintenance employees.

Q. Now you have described the employment of these people, Mr. White, as something of a straight line operation.

A. Yes sir.

Q. And I take it that you would describe their work as involving a comparatively low degree of skill?

A. Yes, I would.

Q. Could you describe in more detail the operation which takes place in the plastics department?

A. Well, sir, we are equipped so as to be practically integrated in the plastics field. With reference to almost all of our products we commence processing with the basic raw materials, by using a Banbury mixing machine. Our operations thereafter include the usual ones. We have machinery and facilities for injection moldings, compression molding, extruding, laminating, spreading, grinding, pressing and polishing, spraying, etc.

Q. And there is no particular degree of skill required for these operations and the use of this machinery?

A. None that comparatively brief on-the-job training will not provide.

HEARING OFFICER: Mr. White, what about the design of some of these plastic articles which you have previously mentioned? I think, for example, of that — what was it? — that patent handbag.

WITNESS: Sir, I think you should understand that all of our production in the plastics department is on order. We do not manufacture generally, that is, we do not turn out what I might call shelf items. As a consequence, we receive from the party who orders the production, a design, model or template and our production of that item is then scheduled to this particular model. The various types of machinery which I have mentioned are mechanically adjustable to meet the requirements of the design.

HEARING OFFICER: I see. Now how many foremen are employed in the plastics department?

WITNESS: At the present time, sir, there are, let's see, 7.

HEARING OFFICER: Do you have an office force located in the building with the plastics department?

WITNESS: Well, sir, there is one small office which is used by the superintendent of the department.

HEARING OFFICER: Does he have an office force?

WITNESS: No sir, he does not. All of the office work is done in the main building; that is, in the main office which is located in the old tire division building.

HEARING OFFICER: Thank you. You may continue your examination, Mr. Blair.

Q. (By Mr. Blair) Is the first floor of the miscellaneous building entirely devoted to plastics production?

A. No, not entirely.   For the past couple of years we have been turning out rubber mats upon which typewriters and other pieces of office equipment may be placed.

Q. Is this operation a part of your plastics department?

A. Well, I suppose we treat it that way.   We have no separate personnel or supervision for it.   The work is done by the same employees and some of these mats are laminated to plastic bases or edged with colored plastic.

Q. And the work requires no particular or different skills?

A. Oh, definitely not.   The operations are rather simple.

Q. Now, do we have the entire picture so far as the first floor of miscellaneous is concerned?

A. Yes sir.   We are considering the manufacture of certain types of rubber footwear, but it's only an idea at this time.

Q. I see.   Mr. White, what about the fire hose operation?   This department is on the second floor of the miscellaneous building?

A. That is correct.

Q. Is this operation a skilled operation?

A. Comparatively speaking, it certainly is.

Q. Comparing it with what?

A. Comparing it with the plastics department, I would call it highly skilled.   Comparing it with the tire division, I would say it was an operation which demanded about the same skill.   Our basic rubber composition here is a unique one and produces a material which requires particular care in introducing the fibrous materials.   New employees in this department require much more on-the-job training than is necessary in the plastics department.   Furthermore, in a sense, everything is built on our secret formula.   The people on this work must be carefully screened.   We really consider them to be confidential employees.[4]

HEARING OFFICER: How many people are employed in the fire hose department?

WITNESS: Just now, we have exactly 100 excluding the superintendent, foremen, and clericals.

HEARING OFFICER: There is just one superintendent?

WITNESS: Yes sir.

HEARING OFFICER: And he is exclusively concerned with the fire hose department?

WITNESS: Yes sir.

HEARING OFFICER: How many foremen are employed in this department?

---

[4] As a matter of policy, the NLRB excludes from bargaining units employees who perform confidential services for their employer, and employees whose interests are closely allied with those of management.   Confidential employees are those who assist and act in a confidential capacity to persons who formulate, determine, and effectuate management policies in the field of labor relations. Managerial employees are those in executive positions with authority to formulate and effectuate management policies.   See NLRB, 23d Ann. Rep. 41-43 (1958). — ED.

WITNESS: We have, let's see — 14.

HEARING OFFICER: And how many of the employees have actual contact with the secret process?

WITNESS: Three.

HEARING OFFICER: These are foremen, I assume?

WITNESS: That is correct.

HEARING OFFICER: You have certain machines in the fire hose department?

WITNESS: Yes, sir, we have the machinery which is used in compounding our basic material and then the usual extruding and laminating machinery which is common to the manufacture of hose.

HEARING OFFICER: I see. Who is responsible for the maintenance of the machinery and equipment in the plastics and fire hose departments?

WITNESS: Well, in plastics we have 6 regular so-called maintenance people and 3 in fire hose.

HEARING OFFICER: These are included in your enumeration of the people employed in the several departments?

WITNESS: That is correct, sir.

HEARING OFFICER: Is there any office on the second floor connected with the fire hose department?

WITNESS: Yes sir, there is one small office for the superintendent. The set-up is the same as in the plastics department on the first floor.

HEARING OFFICER: Thank you. You may inquire, Mr. Blair.

Q. (By Mr. Blair) Who handles the labor relations policies for these departments?

A. I do. At the top level for the entire Chicago plant.

Q. Do the employees in these departments enjoy certain benefits?

A. Yes, many benefits. The best in the business.

MR. COOPER: I object to the characterizations and move that except for the answer "yes" they be stricken.

HEARING OFFICER: They may go out.

Q. What benefits do the employees enjoy?

A. Insurance, vacation, accident and health, sick leave.

Q. Is there any seniority?

A. Yes. Seniority in layoffs and recalls.

Q. Is this seniority plant-wide? Or is it confined to the departments?

A. No. The tire division has its seniority and miscellaneous has its seniority.

Q. Does plastics have a seniority as distinguished from fire hose?

A. Yes.

Q. Is there any interchange of employees between the tire division and the miscellaneous rubber goods division?

A. No.

Q. Between the plastics department and the fire hose department?

A. No.

Q. Is there any common supervision?

A. No. We have our own superintendent at the tire division and separate superintendents as I have previously stated in the plastics and fire hose departments.

Q. Now will you describe the operations of the tire division?

A. Yes. This is a comparatively highly skilled operation as distinguished from the plastics department and about the same skilled operation as that of the fire hose department. The intricacies of curing the tire by placing it in a tire mold require substantial aptitude and a good deal of experience. The same is true of finishing. We have the usual Banbury, mill mixing, calendering, bias machines; band machines, bead formers, tire line machines such as models 40 and 50, bag-o-matics and curing machines. These all require skilled operation.

Q. How many people are employed in the tire division?

A. Right now, just 494 production and maintenance men.

Q. These do not include foremen?

A. No sir. There are 29 foremen in the tire division.

Q. And the tire division has its own superintendent?

A. Yes sir.

HEARING OFFICER: I gather that the main office of the plant is located in the building which houses the tire division?

WITNESS: Yes sir. Just inside the main entrance and to your right.

HEARING OFFICER: Now, I believe that you have previously testified that there are 12 clericals employed in this office?

WITNESS: Yes sir, they are made up of a telephone operator-receptionist, utility clerks, records clerk and stenographers.

HEARING OFFICER: Now where are the other clericals employed?

WITNESS: We have a group of 35 IBM operators who work in one room on the second floor of the tire division building, but they record statistics for both plants.

HEARING OFFICER: Do they have separate supervision?

WITNESS: Yes, they do.

HEARING OFFICER: Where are the other clericals located?

WITNESS: Well, in addition we have clerks who work with each group, that is, in the tire division in the main plant and on the plastics and fire hose floors in the new building. There are, let's see, 28 in all. Their work is directly related to the various operations performed by the production and maintenance workers. There are receiving clerks, shipping clerks, stock and utility clerks in this group.

HEARING OFFICER: How are these clerks allocated between the various departments, Mr. White?

WITNESS: If I could look at this. Just a minute, sir. There are 14 in tire, 7 in plastics and 7 in fire hose.

HEARING OFFICER: Thank you. Do you have any further questions, Mr. Blair?

MR. BLAIR: No sir, not at this time.

HEARING OFFICER: You may cross-examine, Mr. Cooper.

CROSS-EXAMINATION

Q. (By Mr. Cooper) Mr. White, how far are these several buildings of the Enderby plant removed from each other?

A. Oh, I'd say about 25 yards.

Q. Are they physically joined?

A. There is a tunnel.

Q. If the operations are separate, what is the tunnel used for?

A. So that the superintendents, foremen, clerks and, where necessary, the employees can go to the main office without going outside the building.

Q. Is it correct to state that all of the employees in the Chicago plant are involved in the manufacture of plastic or rubber products?

A. Yes.

Q. Have any of these employees been trained especially in trade schools outside the plant? Is there an apprenticeship program involved in any of the jobs in either division?

A. Just on-the-job training.

Q. That was not the question. Is any apprenticeship program in the traditional sense involved?

A. No formal apprenticeship, if that's what you mean.

Q. Just the instruction which would be required in the case of any new employee on any new job — correct?

A. Well, it's a question of degree. There is a great difference between the instruction and training in the tire division and the plastics work.

Q. One takes longer than the other?

A. Yes. One is skilled and one is unskilled.

Q. Well, let's take three men who were just graduated from high school, all of average intelligence and physical well-being. What would be required of one of these men who starts in the tire division?

A. It would take perhaps just a year to train such a man before he would be proficient in the skill required for a majority of the jobs.

Q. And the other high school graduate in the plastics department? How long would it take to train him?

A. Perhaps a month or two. It's a straight line operation. I'd say a month or two in each operation. There are, oh, six or seven operations.

Q. And in the fire hose department?

A. Again I'd have difficulty in answering this question. Three months might be sufficient if the right man were employed. We must get more mature men for this operation — they need to be patient and painstaking rather than possessed of dexterity or of unusual trade skill. This is work which a man could not be trained for outside the plant. It is strictly on-the-job training.

Q. So that, actually, if a child possessed the patience of a mature man he could perform this operation?

A. Well, patience and mature judgment, yes. Patience and mature dependability are the prime requisites in the basic manufacture of the fire hose.

Q. Are there any state licenses required for any of these positions?

A. No.

Q. Now, Mr. White, you have mentioned several times the importance of your secret formula to this fire hose operation?

A. Yes sir.

Q. How many of the employees in the fire hose department have actual contact with this formula?

A. Well, to a certain extent they all do.

Q. You mean, they all are entrusted with knowledge of this formula?

A. No. They are not — but they work in regular contact with the product of the formula.

Q. How many are actually entrusted with knowledge of the formula?

A. Well, we have three such employees.

Q. And these are foremen?

A. Yes sir, that is true.

Q. I see. Do any of your employees in the production end of the miscellaneous or tire divisions have special degrees as an incident of their jobs?

A. No.

Q. With respect to employment benefits, isn't it true that all benefits apply equally to all employees of both divisions?

A. Well, no. Some men receive longer vacations than others, some higher wages and the like.

Q. Isn't that because of the various job classifications and the length of service?

A. Yes.

Q. So that, actually, all benefits apply equally to all production employees?

A. I don't quite understand it that way.

Q. Well, all right, let's break it down. When an employee has been with the Company one year he receives a week's vacation, is that correct?

A. Yes.

Q. And that applies to all of the production and maintenance employees whatever their department or division?

A. Yes.

Q. After five years' service, two weeks' vacation, right?

A. Yes.

Q. So the only difference in vacation benefits would be where one man was with the Company longer than the other?

A. Yes.

Q. So that, actually, they receive the same program of benefits?

A. Yes.

Q. And the same type of formula would apply to insurance benefits?

A. Yes.

Q. And wages are dependent upon job classification?

A. Yes.

Q. And the only difference between the men in the tire division and the miscellaneous is that higher wage classifications are involved in the tire division?

A. By and large, yes. The greater the skill, the higher the classification.

Q. But, isn't it true that there are some classifications in the tire division which are on a level with those in the miscellaneous division?

A. Well, yes. There are some jobs which require little skill in the tire division.

Q. Such as the utility jobs, repairing flaws, stocking the bank machines and salvaging scrap where miscuts occur?

A. Yes. All of those jobs.

Q. They require little or no skill?

A. That's correct.

Q. And their classification is a great deal lower than your experienced men either in the fire hose or plastics end of the miscellaneous division?

A. That's true, but they constitute only a small percentage of the employee complement of the tire division. The actual operators in the tire division are quite skilled.

Q. Well, how do these actual operators acquire this great skill?

A. Mostly experience and training.

Q. And the training comes about by instructions and experience on the job performing the operation, correct?

A. I suppose that's so.

Q. Will you describe this training?

A. Well, the men have to be instructed in the operation of the various kinds of machinery. Probably three weeks is a sufficient learning period for most machines. Some of the jobs, however, such as operating the 4-roll calender, might take as much as six months.

Q. So that becoming a skilled operator is really just a matter of time?

A. I wouldn't say that; there must be a native aptitude.

Q. How many years have you been personnel director here?

A. Fifteen.

Q. Is there any probationary period for an employee in the tire division?

A. Well, we have taken men on trial.

Q. Other than misconduct, how many employees have been discharged for reasons other than misconduct during the past fifteen years?

A. Not many. We screen them pretty well on hire.

Q. Can you name any?

A. Not offhand.

Q. So that, in fifteen years you cannot name a single man who was discharged because of ineptitude either soon after he came to work in the tire division or during his employment with the company?

A. No. Not offhand. But we have found that many people can't master certain operations.

Q. Isn't it fair to say that no special talent is required for this work — just experience gained in time?

MR. BLAIR: I object to this. It calls for a conclusion and is argumentative.

HEARING OFFICER: He may answer. Overruled.

A. Special talent is required, Mr. Cooper. On-the-job training and experience are not sufficient.

Q. And isn't it true that the only difference between your production employees is that they perform different functions of the production work involved?

A. I can't go along with that, Mr. Cooper. There are different skills involved and degrees of those skills.

Q. Now, Mr. White, you mentioned a while ago that there is a departmental seniority system at the plant?

A. That is correct.

Q. And employees are never transferred between departments?

A. That is correct. There may have been, over the years, one or two occasions where we did employ a man in one department who had previously been employed in another but I wouldn't describe this as seniority transfer.

Q. I see. Now, as regards your departmental seniority system, it is based on length of service within the department?

A. No sir. Not strictly length of service. Length of service, granted skill and ability are equal.

Q. And this test is applicable within each department?

A. Yes sir, it is.

Q. There is no difference between the respective seniority systems applicable to the various departments?

A. No sir, there is not.

Q. Now, turning to the clerical employees — there are 12 office clericals in the plant?

A. No sir, that is not correct. There are 75 office clericals in the plant.

Q. Twelve of these 75 office clericals work in the main office?

A. That is so.

Q. They are never interchanged? There is no interchange of this pool of clericals with the others?

A. No sir, there is not.

Q. And there are 35 IBM machine operators located on the second floor of the tire division building?

A. That is correct. We refer to them as our statistical department.

Q. These statisticians have been especially trained for machine operation?

A. Yes, they have all received IBM schooling.

Q. Are they ever transferred to other jobs?

A. Well, that does occasionally happen. Once in a while when work is slack we may require some of these machine operators to perform other clerical duties.

Q. And what would be the nature of such other clerical duties?

A. Oh, they might assist the shipping and stock and utility clerks in the various departments.

Q. Now your receiving clerks, shipping clerks, stock and utility clerks, etc., their work is directly related to the operations performed by the production and maintenance workers? There are 28?

A. Yes, that is true, in a sense.

Q. Would you describe their duties for us?

A. Well, they do work with the production employees. I suppose for the most part they perform what you might call manual labor. The shipping and receiving clerks are required to make records, to prepare receipts for apparatus and materials coming into their particular departments. They must see that the equipment and production are properly identified and tagged for transfer and outgoing shipments. They make shipping arrangements of a mechanical nature with trucking companies and railroads. They collect and distribute reports within the departments and back and forth to the statistical department, occasionally to the main office.

Q. They have nothing like a home office removed from the production and maintenance employees?

A. No sir, they do not.

Q. Their working schedule is the same as the production and maintenance employees?

A. Yes, they have the same standard working day and work week.

Q. How about the other clericals? Those in the main office and I think you called it the statistical department?

A. The clericals in the main office arrive at work one-half hour later than the production and maintenance employees.

Q. What about the IBM machine operators?

A. Their hours are the same as the production and maintenance employees.

Q. All the clericals except the 12 employed in the main office arrive when the first shift goes to work?

A. That is correct.

Q. Thank you, Mr. White. I have no further questions at this time.

HEARING OFFICER: Mr. Blair, do you wish to examine?

MR. BLAIR: Yes, I have a number of questions here for Mr. White but I would like to make a suggestion. We have heard testimony here today about machinery described as Banbury, extruding, laminating, calendering, banding, milling, bead forming and tire line equipment which was identified as models 40 and 50. I wonder if it would not be a very helpful thing if we took a view of the premises so to speak. I am sure that the Company would welcome such a visit and I very respectfully suggest that an on-the-scene view of our operations would be very helpful to the Hearing Officer.

MR. COOPER: I have no objection to that, Mr. Hearing Officer, and I would go along with that suggestion. Possibly we could postpone the hearings at this time and meet in that main office which Mr. White has described, say tomorrow morning?

MR. ENDICOTT: I'd be agreeable.

HEARING OFFICER: Off the record.

HEARING OFFICER: On the record. Thank you, Mr. White. You are excused. The hearing is adjourned until 2 P.M. tomorrow.

During a somewhat lengthy recess on the second day of the hearing, representatives of the company, Local 417, and the Enderby Employees Association found that their disagreement was not quite so substantial as the developing record might seem to indicate. There was mutual concession that the employees in the various departments and divisions of the company could be grouped as follows:

Miscellaneous Division	
Production and Maintenance	
Plastics Department	250
Fire Hose Department	100
Clerical	
Plastics Department	7
Fire Hose Department	7
Foremen	
Plastics Department	7
Fire Hose Department	14
Superintendents	
Plastics Department	1
Fire Hose Department	1
Tire Division	
Production and Maintenance	500
Clerical	14
Foremen	29
Superintendent	1
Statistical Department	
Clerical	35
Main Office	
Clerical	12

Although White was somewhat insistent that Cooper was minimizing the comparative skills of the employees in the several departments, he finally made it clear that the company was quite willing to accept the choice of the employees as between the competing unions. After some discussion with Curme, Cooper suggested that two voting groups could be set up. Under this arrangement the production and maintenance and clerical employees in the Miscellaneous Division would be given a choice between Local 417, the Enderby Employees Association, or neither; the production and maintenance and clerical employees in the Tire Division (including those working in the statistical department) would be allowed to choose between Local 417 and no union. In the event that Local 417 obtained a majority of the votes cast by both groups it would become the bargaining agency for both divisions. Should the Enderby Employees

Association obtain a majority in the Miscellaneous Division it would become the representative of all the nonsupervisory employees in both the plastics and fire hose departments. White expressed some reluctance about including the statistical department in the Tire Division vote and argued that the thirty-five clerical employees should be allowed to determine by majority vote whether they wished to be represented by Local 417. Cooper indicated that he had some doubt whether the Regional Director of the National Labor Relations Board would approve any arrangement which gave the clericals in the statistical department such a choice. He finally agreed to White's amendment of his proposal, and the parties subsequently drafted this arrangement on the regional office's consent election form.

NOTES

1. Referring to NLRA §9(c)(4), would it have been lawful for the regional office to suggest and the parties to use the consent election form after the filing of a petition but before, and assuming the parties could agree, in lieu of, a hearing? If that could be done, what purpose did the hearing here serve?

Assuming that no petition had ever been filed, would Section 9(a) stand in the way of informal execution of the Cooper-White arrangement by calling on a state agency, for example, or the Honest Ballot Association, instead of the NLRB? "In the instant case the election was held under the auspices of a responsible State government agency and it is not contended that the election was affected by any irregularities. In these circumstances we shall accord the same effects [under Section 9(c)(3)] as we would attach to a determination of representatives based upon an election conducted by the Board. [So the petition is dismissed.]" T-H Products Co., 113 N.L.R.B. 1246, 1247 (1955). Compare Bartenders Union and Fowler Hotel, 138 N.L.R.B. 1315, 1316-1317 (1962). Does Section 9(b), in any event, necessitate resort to the Board?

2. "Absent a history of collective bargaining at the plant involved, where A union seeks a small unit of employees and B union seeks a more comprehensive unit including the employees sought by A, the Board, if it concludes that the employees desired by A could either be a separate unit or part of the all-inclusive unit requested by B, directs a 'Globe' election. . . . The employees sought by A are set up as a separate voting group — A, B, and 'neither' are placed on the ballot. The remaining employees are established as another voting group with B on the ballot in a yes-no vote. If the employees sought by A vote for A, this is indicative of their desires as to the form of unit they want — the Board will find them to be a separate appropriate unit and certify A in that unit. If they vote for B, however, they also indicate the type of unit they want — a more comprehensive unit — and if B receives a majority vote in the residual voting group, the Board will certify B in a large single unit composed of the 2 voting groups, finding that unit to be appropriate. This is usually done where A union desires a craft unit and B union desires an industrial unit,

absent a history of collective bargaining." Feldesman, Representation Cases Decided Under Taft-Hartley Act, 22 L.R.R.M. 31, 41 (1948).

Does the Cooper-White arrangement come within the formula of the Globe Stamping Co. case, 3 N.L.R.B. 294 (1937)? Why is the problem of the thirty-five clerical employees in the "statistical department" not obviated by "Globing" them too?

What are the variations in "Globing," including those arising from application of the limitations (added in 1947) contained in Sections 9(b)(1) and 9(b)(2)?

The Globe election procedure is also discussed in Note, 6 U. Chi. L. Rev. 673 (1939). Compare Arenwald and Landay, Representation Problems Under the New York State Labor Relations Act, 8 id. 471, 483-489 (1941).

3. The Canadian Industrial Relations and Disputes Investigation Act, 1948, §8, provides: "Where a group of employees of an employer belong to a craft or group exercising technical skills, by reason of which they are distinguishable from the employees as a whole and the majority of the group are members of one trade union pertaining to such craft or other skills, the trade union may apply to the Board subject to the provisions of section seven of this Act, and shall be entitled to be certified as the bargaining agent of the employees in the group if the group is otherwise appropriate as a unit for collective bargaining."

4. See NLRA §14(c), which was added by the LMRDA of 1959, and NLRB, 28th Ann. Rep. 34-35 (1964). The question of the Board's authority to decline to exercise its power was much litigated but not definitively settled until this amendment in 1959, which also countered the doctrine of Guss v. Utah Labor Relations Board, 353 U.S. 1 (1957), that even if the Board declined to act in a labor dispute "affecting interstate commerce" under NLRA, the states were without authority to assume jurisdiction. The effect of this amendment upon the applicability of state law is discussed in Aaron, The Labor Management Reporting and Disclosure Act, II, 73 Harv. L. Rev. 1086, 1097-1098 (1960). The proviso against declining jurisdiction refers to standards announced by the Board on October 2, 1958. The standards expanded the area of the cases the Board could accept. As set forth in NLRB, 23d Ann. Rep. §8 (1958), these minimum requirements to establish Board jurisdiction were established:

"1. *Non-retail enterprises:* $50,000 outflow or inflow, directly or indirectly into interstate commerce.

"2. *Office buildings:* Gross revenue of $100,000 of which $25,000 or more is derived from organizations that meet any of the standards.

"3. *Retail concerns:* $500,000 gross volume of business.

"4. *Instrumentalities, links and channels of interstate commerce:* $50,000 from interstate (or linkage) part of enterprise, or from services performed for employers in commerce.

"5. *Public utilities:* $250,000 gross volume, or meet non-retail standards.

"6. *Transit systems:* $250,000 gross volume except taxicabs, as to which the retail test shall apply.

"7. *Newspapers and communication systems:* $100,000 gross volume for radio, television, telegraph and telephone; $200,000 gross volume for newspapers.

"8. *National defense:* Substantial impact on national defense.

"9. *Business in the Territories and District of Columbia:* Above standards apply in Territories; all businesses in District of Columbia are subject to jurisdiction regardless of interstate volume.

"10. *Associations:* Regarded as single employer.

"Direct outflow refers to goods shipped or services furnished by the employer outside the State. Indirect outflow includes sales within the State to users meeting any standard except solely an indirect inflow or indirect outflow standard. Direct inflow refers to goods or services furnished directly to the employer from outside the State in which the employer is located.

"Indirect inflow refers to the purchase of goods or services which originated outside the employer's State but which he purchased from a seller within the State. Direct and indirect outflow may be combined, and direct and indirect inflow may also be combined, to meet the $50,000 requirement. However, outflow and inflow may not be combined."

5. Prior to the 1959 amendments, Section 9 contained provisions that prohibited the Board from investigating a petition or issuing a complaint on behalf of a labor organization unless it had complied with certain filing requirements. Some of them were intended to protect unions from Communist domination. Officers were required to file affidavits of nonmembership in the Communist Party and nonbelief in overthrow of the United States government "by force or by any illegal or unconstitutional methods." Section 201(d) of the LMRDA relieved the NLRB of all responsibility for administering requirements that labor organizations file certain information with the federal government. This responsibility was vested in the Secretary of Labor, but the non-Communist affidavit was dropped, and in its stead were enacted the provisions of LMRDA §504 (held unconstitutional in Brown v. United States, 334 F.2d 488 (9th Cir.), cert. granted, 379 U.S. 899 (1964)). In Alto Plastics Manufacturing Corp., 136 N.L.R.B. 850 (1962), the Board held that it had no authority to withhold its processes from the petitioner on the ground that it was a "paper union" and its contracts were "sweetheart" contracts. It suggested however that failure to fulfill statutory obligations on the part of a certified union would justify a motion to revoke the certification. (See page 925 infra.) Compare the concluding clause in Section 9(b), concerning guard's unions.

6. A striking contrast between our labor relations law and the systems found elsewhere is the unique use in our country of the device of the exclusive bargaining representative in the appropriate unit. For example, Western European countries do not have this device of certifying a bargaining representative. Each union represents its own members and only its own members. But to understand how these other systems of labor control function when ours is so deeply committed to the exclusive bargaining representation principle, other significant differences between

those systems and our own must also be realized. The typical pattern of collective bargaining in Europe consists of nationwide bargaining between an association of employers and an association of trade unions. These two groups may be limited to a single industry. But in some countries they are the only respective employer and trade union groups engaged in bargaining for the entire country. In this latter instance the bargaining is somewhat comparable to the situation which would exist in this country if the National Association of Manufacturers or the U.S. Chamber of Commerce bargained out a basic wage for the whole nation with the AFL-CIO. Usually then, this bargain is subject to governmental approval. In general see Strumthal, Contemporary Collective Bargaining in Seven Countries (1957).

Under this wholly different structure of collective bargaining where do the details of the employment relationship take shape, such matters as employee discipline and discharge, show-up pay, pensions, hours of work and shift schedules, seniority, vacation pay, and scheduling? Most of these matters are the subject either of legislative control or of a form of bargaining with "work councils." As far as legislation is concerned, the European tradition is for much greater regulation of the various details of the employer-employee relationship by statutory law. This body of labor law is typically called Social Law or Social Security Law and is virtually all the labor law that exists in those countries. See Symposium, Comparative Labor Law and Law of the Employment Relation, 18 Rutgers L. Rev. 233 (1964). This symposium consists of some of the papers delivered at the Fifth International Congress for Social Law and Social Security, Lyons, France, September, 1963.

Where such details of the employment relationship are not set by statute, they develop out of the negotiations between employers and "work councils." These bodies are elected by the employees independent of union affiliation. Their organization and powers usually are prescribed by law. One of their major functions is to work out the details of the relationship with the employer as either an implementation of or "watchdog" function over the statutory law, or concerning matters to which the law does not apply. Another function is to represent individual employees in grievances with the employer, a function usually performed by the exclusive bargaining representative in our system. See page 941 infra. On the role of work councils see Ramm, Works Councils in the Member States of the European Economic Community, in Labour Law in Europe with Special Reference to the Common Market, Int. & Comp. L.Q. Supp. Pub. No. 5, p. 39 (1962).

Does not the national nonlocal role typically played by trade unions in other countries constitute one explanation for the political, religious, or social orientation of such organizations? Are the more rigid classes in the social structure of those other countries another reason for the different pattern? Are not work councils more democratic than trade unions? But would not work councils lead to more worker intrusion in management decisions, as does occur in some Western European countries? Is the greater extent of statutory regulation of the work relationship a danger to economic freedom, or is a greater danger to be found in the detailed regulation of the collective bargaining process and of unions which we have in this country?

b. THE MULTI-LOCATION UNIT

INSURANCE AGENTS' PROBLEM

The Industrial Life Insurance Company of Rhode Island has offices in Providence, Cranston, Woonsocket, Pawtucket, Newport, and Westerly. Each agent is employed under a comprehensive written contract, uniform throughout the company, which does business in all the East Coast states except Virginia. This contract reflects the centralized determination of employer policy toward employees, which is made at the home office in Providence. Each of the other offices has a manager, who initially recruits agents subject to home office approval after independent investigation of the applicant. All absences from work are reported to the home office, paychecks are written there, etc. The office manager can suspend for no more than three days, but only the home office can discharge, and the manager's exercise of the power to suspend is limited to situations of compelling emergency.

The Pawtucket office was organized in the 1940's by an AFL federal local union based primarily in Massachusetts. At one time this union had a collective agreement with the company, on the basis of voluntary recognition. This local became part of the AFL's Insurance Agents Council, and it subsequently affiliated with the Insurance Agents International Union, AFL, renamed after merger with a CIO counterpart, Insurance Workers International Union, AFL-CIO. This union has continued to undertake representation of the Pawtucket employees, but from 1951 to the present time, 1961, has been unable to conclude an agreement. The company, however, has not refused to deal with it.

At the Providence office an organization has been formed under the name Association of Debit Agents. It is the beneficiary of some funds for organization sufficient to mount a state-wide campaign of modest proportions, beginning in 1961, except that the Pawtucket employees would probably vote AFL-CIO or no union rather than ADA. Indeed, preliminary surveys indicate that optimum strategy might be to concentrate on Providence and defer organization of the rest of the state. Most of the employees in the Cranston office, for example, are presently antiunion. However, the company, it is assumed, would not grant further union recognition without an election, except on a state-wide basis.

Relevant to the situation at Industrial Life Insurance Company is the 1944 case of Metropolitan Life Insurance Co., 56 N.L.R.B. 1635. It held that employees of the company at Akron and Toledo did not constitute two separate appropriate units, and said that the AFL's competitors, the CIO (United Office and Professional Workers) at Cleveland and an independent union (International Union of Life Insurance Agents) at Cincinnati, could not prevail on the basis of city-wide units pending a later showing as to the possibility of state-wide organization. At pp. 1639-1640 the Board said:

"Organization among insurance agents is comparatively recent, but is steadily growing. The tendency of such organization is toward state-wide units. [The Prudential Insurance Company, known familiarly to the agents as 'Pru,' is organized on a state-wide basis, except at Toledo, where the NLRB less than six months earlier had found a unit appropriate.] In the instant case, since the Federation, the Independent, and the C.I.O. are all actively engaged in a broad organizational program in Ohio, and since it may reasonably be anticipated that one of these organizations may in the near future extend its membership to state-wide proportions, we are of the opinion that it will not effectuate the policies of the Act to set up city-wide units for employees of the Company in Ohio at this time."

Fifteen years later, in 1959, Member Fanning, concurring specially in Life Insurance Co. of Virginia, 123 N.L.R.B. 610, said (p. 613): "I would not reaffirm the Metropolitan Life Insurance Company decision." He said the record in the case before him showed that the 1944 prediction as to insurance agents' organization had not been fulfilled and that decision had been a major obstacle to organization. But Chairman Leedom and Member Rodgers, on the basis of the Metropolitan case, denied a unit for the Danville, Virginia, office. Member Joseph A. Jenkins agreed, but solely on the ground that the union admitted its only reason for asking for the Danville office was its lack of resources to organize on a broader basis. Member Fanning concurred on the ground that the conditions of employment did not vary from city to city but were uniform throughout the company, and the company's administrative structure did not encompass the city as a component unit.

As of 1961, Member Bean, who did not participate, had been replaced by Chairman McCulloch, an appointee of President Kennedy. Member Jenkins had been succeeded by another Kennedy appointee, Member Brown. So the Board consisted of Chairman McCulloch, the holdover members, Rodgers, Leedom, and Fanning, and Member Brown. How would you have advised the ADA?

The following materials, although subsequent to the time of decision for ADA, are intended to shed further light on the questions raised.

Quaker City Life Insurance Co., 134 N.L.R.B. 960, decided December 5, 1961, Members Rodgers and Leedom dissenting, in effect adopted the Fanning analysis of the 1944 case, concluding (p. 962):

"Obviously when the purpose for which a rule which has been established fails, the rule should fail. This is especially so with respect to a rule which unfairly prejudices the collective-bargaining rights of employees. Accordingly, in the future, the Board's policy will be not to preclude the organization of insurance agents into units of less than employerwide or statewide scope, and we shall apply our normal unit principles to the cases as they arise."

In this case a campaign by the AFL-CIO union to organize the employer's agents at Alexandria, Norfolk, and Richmond had culminated in a petition for a separate unit in Alexandria. The Court of Appeals sustained the Board's determination that the Alexandria office was an appropriate unit. 319 F.2d 690 (4th Cir. 1963). At p. 693 the court said:

"It appears clear on the facts involved in the instant case that the Board's choice of a single office unit of debit insurance agents should not be disturbed by us. The job specifications of the agents are highly standardized, their working conditions are very similar, and the office operates in an isolated manner, with little or no contact with other branch offices. There is no administrative office operating between the local offices and the main office. The District Manager has at least some control over the operating conditions of each employee. We cannot say that a single office unit is an arbitrary choice as an appropriate unit since substantial evidence on the record as a whole supports the decision of the N.L.R.B."

But Judge Boreman, dissenting on this point, wrote (p. 696):

"The Board then concluded that since the underlying reason for the adoption of the rule of the Metropolitan case had failed, the rule itself must also fail. The instant case reeks with consideration of extent of organization. It is quite clear that the Board's decision . . . is that it is easier to organize small local district offices one at a time . . . than it is to organize the state-wide or company-wide group as a single unit. This appears to me to be nothing less than a return to the heretofore unacceptable and outlawed practice of establishing provisional units which were admittedly based on the extent of organization and a circumvention of the express prohibition of the statute under the guise of a policy change. To require the Company to bargain separately with a representative of the employees in each district office, as organization of each small unit may succeed, can result in nothing but confusion and turmoil."

Is the avoidance of "confusion and turmoil" one of the standards for determining an appropriate unit? Section 9(b) speaks in terms of assuring employees the "fullest freedom in exercising the rights guaranteed by this Act." What is the scope of judicial review? After the above-quoted passage from the majority opinion, the court cited Section 10(e), among other materials.

In Metropolitan Life Insurance Co. v. NLRB, 327 F.2d 906 (1st Cir. 1964), the employer contested the certification of a unit consisting of the agents at its district office in Woonsocket, contending that the only appropriate unit would be all its offices in the United States, or all in its New England territory, or all eight of its Rhode Island offices. The court recounted the Board determinations in four Metropolitan cases and one Equitable Life Insurance case. The Equitable unit consisted of two district offices in Cleveland, Ohio, and another in Lorain, Ohio, twenty-eight miles away. The Cleveland Metropolitan unit consisted of six offices in the city and three suburban offices eight or nine miles away. In a Metropolitan case arising in Delaware, the Board certified a representative for two of the three district offices of the company in the state. (This determination is reviewed in the passage quoted below from the Third Circuit.) The Board approved a unit for the Metropolitan district office in Sioux City, Iowa, which also included two offices under its administrative control in Fargo, N.D., 284 miles away, and Sioux Falls, S.D., 120 miles away. In a Metropolitan Chicago unit, the Board included all thirty-three district offices within the city limits, six of them serving territories beyond the city limits. There were also fourteen suburban offices, three of them serving areas within Chicago, but they were not included.

The First Circuit in the Woonsocket case wrote (p. 910):

"Why there should be a community of interest among Metropolitan's agents working from both city and suburban offices in Cleveland but no community of interest among its agents working in both city and suburban offices in Chicago is not explained by the Board majority and is beyond our comprehension.

"The Board majority in this case did not discuss what weight, if any, it gave to the factor of extent of union organization. Nor indeed has this majority done so in any of its decisions since Quaker City.

"Looking at its actions, however, we have not found a single instance since Quaker City wherein the majority of the Board refused the debit insurance agent unit petitioned for by the Union. We would not consider this fact alone decisive for we would hesitate to assume that the Board was subservient to the Union. Yet we believe this fact is entitled to considerable weight in the light of the testimony of the Union's vice-president in Metropolitan's Cleveland case [made part of the record in this case], that if the Union did not succeed in organizing on a broader basis it would as a matter of policy petition for a unit 'on a district basis.' Indeed it is apparent that the Union followed this policy in the present case for . . . it was only after lack of success in its state-wide attempt that it sought and received the Board's acceptance of the single district office in Woonsocket.

"In short, the Union naturally wants units in which it can win elections [5] and on the basis of the Board majority's actions, which speak more clearly than its words, it seems to us evident that in this case the Board majority in keeping with its apparent practice in recent years has given the Union the unit it wants. In the absence of any statement by the Board majority of any other rational basis for its varying unit determinations, we can only conclude that the two member Board minority is correct in its charge that the majority has indeed reverted to its pre-1944 policy. . . ."

The Supreme Court vacated this judgment for remand to the Board, in order to have the Board's explanation for the decision in and distinctions among the insurance agents' cases, rather than the rationalizations of counsel in the brief and argument before the Supreme Court. NLRB v. Metropolitan Life Insurance Co., 380 U.S. 438 (1965).

In the Third Circuit case, involving the Metropolitan offices in Dela-

---

[5] According to the Bureau of National Affairs, Survey of White-Collar Organizing for 1963, 55 L.R.R.M. 83 (1964), counting success in organizing by the number of employees in units where NLRB elections were won, the Insurance Workers, AFL-CIO, had the greatest success in 1963 of any white-collar organization, with 1405 employees, although it won only eight out of fourteen elections. — ED.

ware, it appears that the office not included in the unit is in Dover and the other two are in the Wilmington area, some forty-six miles away. Approving the unit, the court said:

"[W]e believe the effect of 9(c)(5) is to require the Board to determine whether a unit is in and of itself appropriate, apart from the extent to which the employees are organized. Whether the employees were controlled by the extent of their organization when they petitioned the Board is not the issue. . . . The extent to which the Union failed to organize should not determine the appropriateness of the group it did organize. . . . The grouping of the two district offices was founded in part on cogent geographical considerations." [6]

The Board majority sees its position concerning insurance agents as no less than part of an integral policy extending to other industries. In P. Ballentine & Sons, 141 N.L.R.B. 1103 (1963), the emloyer had twelve branch offices for distributing beer on the East Coast from Rhode Island to the District of Columbia. The unit sought was the salesmen at the Newark, N.J., branch.

In overruling a previous decision[7] involving the same employer and one of the petitioning unions, the Board said (p. 1107):

"To effectuate the clear mandate of Section 9, the Board, in Dixie Belle Mills, Sav-on Drugs, and Quaker City Life Insurance Company, has recently reemphasized its long-standing policy *not* to compel labor organizations to seek representation in the most comprehensive grouping unless an appropriate unit compatible with that requested does not exist."

It went on to conclude that each branch was equivalent to a single plant, enjoying a Section 9(b) presumption of appropriateness.

Dixie Belle Mills, Inc., 139 N.L.R.B. 629 (1962), presented what the dissenter described as "an uncommonly high degree of integration" between operations under the same employer of chenille mills twenty miles apart. But the petitioning union obtained direction of an election for production and maintenance employees at one of the mills, the union having disclaimed any desire to proceed in a larger unit. The majority pointed especially (p. 632) to: "The degree of autonomy in the operations at the [one plant], the lack of a substantial interchange of employees between [the two plants], the geographical separation . . . , the absence of any bargaining history, and the fact that no labor organization seeks to represent a multi-plant unit."

Sav-on Drugs, Inc., 138 N.L.R.B. 1032 (1962), like P. Ballentine, squarely overruled prior decisions. In this instance, however, the prior decisions represented a settled rule that the appropriate unit in retail chainstores, absent unusual circumstances, should embrace employees of all stores located within the employer's administrative division or geographic area. As Member Brown put it, in an address at St. Louis:[8] "In

---

[6] Metropolitan Life Insurance Co. v. NLRB, 328 F.2d 820 (3d Cir. 1964). The Sixth Circuit agreed, sustaining the Cleveland unit determination. 330 F.2d 62 (1964). — Ed.

[7] 120 N.L.R.B. 86 (1958).

[8] 55 L.R.R.M. 93, 94 (1964).

other words, insurance and retail chain store employees have now been given the same rights as employees in other businesses. . . ." Member Rodgers, dissenting in Sav-on Drugs, referred to the multistore principle as having stood since 1948, grounded in the centralization of chainstore personnel policy, and other patterns covering more than a single store and creating (p. 1036), "a singular community of interests for employees in such multistore groups."

In Singer Sewing Machine Co. v. NLRB, 329 F.2d 200 (4th Cir. 1964), a certificate had been issued for a representative of the employees of Singer in its Pittsburgh City District retail shops. Singer had tried to prove (p. 205): "that the Regional Director first determined that a unit based mainly on a geographical basis, i.e., Allegheny County, Pennsylvania, was the appropriate one, that he informed the Union, which then attempted to organize the remaining three shops in Allegheny County not included in the Pittsburgh City District, but, when the Union failed to organize these shops, the Regional Director reverted to the Pittsburgh City District as the appropriate unit . . . Assuming, as we must, that the witnesses will testify as their evidence was proferred, we believe that their testimony would show that extent of organization was the controlling factor in the unit determination and it would be no answer to the invalidity of an order having such a basis that the other factors . . . would support the unit determination which was made."

Finally, in Overnite Transportation Co. v. NLRB, 327 F.2d 36 (4th Cir. 1963), the same court had sustained the board in granting a union request for a unit of automobile mechanics and helpers, excluding other maintenance workers such as parts clerks, tire repairmen, and other service employees. At p. 40, the court said:

"The Company reasons that because the union's motive in petitioning for a craft unit was based upon the extent to which it had successfully organized the employees therein, it necessarily follows that the Board was similarly motivated. . . . [T]o ascribe the same motivation to the Board would require us to find that the Board ignored all relevant evidence. . . . We find no justification to hold that the Board acted with such duplicity."

C. THE CRAFT UNIT

AMERICAN POTASH & CHEMICAL CORP.[9]
National Labor Relations Board, 1954
107 N.L.R.B. 1418

[The employer manufactures basic chemicals by a continuous flow process. Each of the plants is interdependent and no part of the operation can be separately performed. The Chemical Workers petitioned for a unit of all production and maintenance workers, and the employer, the Mine Workers, and the Smelter Workers supported this request for a plantwide unit. The IBEW sought to sever all electricians in the engi-

[9] See NLRA §§9(b)(1) and (2). — ED.

neering and maintenance departments, the Operating Engineers sought a separate unit of the power division, and the IAM sought three separate units consisting of (1) pump packers and oilers, (2) riggers and crane engineers, and (3) toolroom helpers.]

In support of their unit contentions, the Employer, the Chemical Workers, the Smelter Workers, and the Mine Workers contend that the operations at this plant demonstrate the same type of integration as that involved in basic steel, and involve a portion of an industry engaged in producing basic, rather than consumer, products. For these and related reasons, they urge that the Board's National Tube doctrine be applied to the chemical industry or, at least, to the basic chemical industry. . . .

. . . [A]fter full consideration of all the contentions advanced and a balancing of all the equities, we feel that the right of separate representation should not be denied the members of a craft group merely because they are employed in an industry which involves highly integrated production processes and in which the prevailing pattern of bargaining is industrial in character. We shall, therefore, not extend the practice of denying craft severance on an industry-wide basis.

That practice, first adopted in National Tube, and thereafter applied in other cases, would, if applied to other industries, result in the emasculation of the principle of craft independence which clearly and emphatically Congress intended to preserve. However, as we do not deem it wise or feasible to upset a pattern of bargaining already firmly established, we shall continue to decline to entertain petitions for craft or departmental severance in those industries to which the Board has already applied National Tube and where plantwide bargaining prevails. We deem it sufficient for the purposes of this case to make it clear that the National Tube doctrine will not be further extended, and that the practice of denying craft severance in industry after industry on the so-called integration of operations theory will not be further followed.

Accordingly, we find that the intent of Congress will best be effectuated by a finding, and we so find, that a craft group will be appropriate for severance purposes in cases where a true craft group is sought and where, in addition, the union seeking to represent it is one which traditionally represents that craft.

In requiring that the union seeking severance must be the one which traditionally represents that craft we are taking cognizance of the fact that there are unions which have devoted themselves to the special problems of the various craft employees, thereby demonstrating that the interests of these craft employees are distinctive and traditionally recognized.

In adopting this new rule, we have given grave consideration to the argument of employer and union groups that fragmentation of bargaining units in highly integrated industries which are characteristic of our modern industrial system can result in loss of maximum efficiency and sometimes afford an opportunity for jurisdictional disputes as to work assignments. We are cognizant of the disruptive economic and social conditions that can and sometimes do occur as the result of craft existence in industrial plants, as where, for example, a small cohesive craft group, by striking, closes down a large industrial plant employing thousands of workers. The alternative, however, is to deny crafts separate representation, and experience has shown that this approach, which was predominant under the American Can decision, was no less productive of labor unrest.

The lesson which we draw is that, consistent with the clear intent of Congress, it is not the province of this Board to dictate the course and pattern of labor organization in our vast industrial complex. If millions of employees today feel that their interests are better served by craft unionism, it is not for us to say that they can only be represented on an industrial basis or for that matter that they must bargain on strict craft lines. All that we are considering here is whether true craft groups should have an opportunity to decide the issue for themselves. We conclude that we must afford them that choice in order to give effect to the statute. Whatever may be lost in maximum industrial efficiency, and experience has not shown that this loss is measurably greater than that which flowed from the rigid doctrine of American Can, is more than compensated for by the gain in industrial democracy and the freedom of employees to choose their own unions and their own form of collective bargaining.

In adopting our new rule, we wish to make it clear that the requirement that the unit sought to be severed must be a true craft group will be rigidly enforced in cases where severance is sought on that basis. We propose to exercise great care in making certain that in the administration of this rule only groups exercising genuine craft skills will be embraced within the ambit of the rule, and that the requirements will not be relaxed over a period of time. We feel that the problem is one of administration rather than concept. We are also of the opinion that under the rule we are adopting fewer groups will be severed but that, at the same time, the principle of craft independence will be maintained.

In our opinion a true craft unit consists of a distinct and homogeneous group of skilled journeymen craftsmen, working as such, together with their apprentices and/or helpers. To be a "journeymen craftsman" an individual must have a kind and degree of skill which is normally acquired only by undergoing a substantial period of apprenticeship or comparable training. An excellent rule-of-thumb test of a worker's journeyman standing is the number of years' apprenticeship he has served — the generally accepted standards of which vary from craft to craft. We will, however, recognize an experience equivalent where it is clearly demonstrated to exist. In addition, to meet the requirements for severance under the Board's new rule, we shall require that all craftsmen of the same type in any plant, except those in traditional departmental units, must be included in the unit. By like token, employees who may work in association with the craft but not in the direct line of progression in the craft will be excluded. All the craftsmen included in the unit must be practitioners of the same allied craft. Furthermore, such craftsmen must be primarily engaged in the performance of tasks requiring the exercise of their craft skills.

In this connection, we also recognize that the equities of employees in certain other minority groups, though lacking the hallmark of craft skill, may also require that they be treated as severable units. Many employers have functionally distinct departments containing employees identified with traditional trades or occupations distinct from that of other employees and who have common special interest in collective bargaining for that reason. As we have already indicated in our discussion of craft groups, there are unions which have devoted themselves to the special problems of these employees in functionally distinct departments, indicating that their interests are distinctive and traditionally recognized. The circumstances in which this situation exists are strictly limited in character and extent, and the Board does not propose to allow petitioners seeking severance to use this concept as a basis for establishing extent-of-organization units or for fragmentizing plantwide units into departments wherever craft severance cannot be established. This does not provide by any means a substitute basis for avoiding our craft-unit criteria. Here again the problem is one of administration rather than concept, and, while we feel that we must accord recognition to the historically established separate interests of certain departmental groups which have by tradition and practice acquired craft-like characteristics, we shall require strict proof that (1) the departmental group is functionally distinct and separate and (2) the petitioner is a union which has traditionally devoted itself to serving the special interest of the employees in question. In this situation, as in craft-severance cases, the petitioner must assume the burden of establishing the facts which justify severing a smaller unit from the plantwide unit in existence in the plant. When such a union requests a departmental unit of the type it traditionally represents, we may find that it is entitled to severance.

With these principles in mind, we now turn to an examination of the specific units requested.

The IBEW's Request

The IBEW requests a unit of all electricians, including leadmen, construction and maintenance electricians, and linemen, excluding (by agreement with the Operating Engineers) the powerhouse electrician and all other employees. The Employer maintains an apprenticeship program for electricians, required by the State of California. Employees who are not first-class journeymen electricians progress from the classification of electrician by successfully completing a 4-year apprenticeship program. Thus the electricians here possess the special training of members of a craft. Of the employees classified as electricians, some work in the plant, others are assigned to the village construction and maintenance forces, and yet others work in the special motor-repair shop. Those who work in village maintenance install wiring and electrical devices in new village construction and repair village electrical equipment. They work in teams with other craftsmen. The plant electricians repair, install, and disconnect motors, switches, electrical control panels, and other devices

used to control electrical currents.   The repair-shop electricians disman-
tle electrical motors which have been removed from operation, rewinding
them, if necessary, replacing required parts, reassembling and testing
them.   Both the plant and repair-shop electricians also work with other
craftsmen on some of these tasks.   The record establishes, however, that
only electricians connect or disconnect electrical circuits.

The IBEW contends, and we agree, that the electricians here comprise
a traditional craft group, performing distinctive and typical craft tasks.
Moreover, the Petitioner is a labor organization which historically and
traditionally represents this craft.   Under these circumstances, we find
that electricians may constitute a separate appropriate unit if they so desire.

The Operating Engineers' Request

The Operating Engineers seeks to sever a unit of all employees under
the supervision of the general foreman of the power division of the engineering department.   There is no apprenticeship program for any of the
power-division employees and the Employer does not require any special
training for any of these employees except the switchboard operator.
None of them is required to be licensed.   The power-division employees
are classified as boilerroom helpers, filtermen, water tenders, firemen, refrigeration engineer, fuel oil tender, and switchboard operators.   The
line of progression is from the lowest to the highest classification, but the
record does not establish the length of on-the-job training required to
qualify employees for progressive transfers.

Although it seems clear that the power-division employees are not
craftsmen, and we so find, it is equally clear that they constitute an appropriate departmental unit.   Moreover, they are requested by the union
which historically and traditionally represents such a powerhouse unit.
Under these circumstances, we find that the power-division employees
may constitute a separate appropriate unit if they so desire.

The IAM's Request

The IAM seeks to sever three units: All pump packers and oilers in the
engineering division, all riggers and crane engineers in the engineering
division, and all toolroom keepers.   There is no apprenticeship program
covering any of these employees.   They are all unskilled and perform
routine and repetitive work.   Machinists, boilerroom mechanics, and utility men regularly pack pumps and the operating personnel of the power
division and production employees do routine oiling and lubricating.
The riggers do less than half of the rigging work in the plant.   Certain
craft helpers also work in the toolroom as keepers.   Under these circumstances, none of the three constitutes by any standard an appropriate
unit.   We conclude that the IAM was here seeking to sever units which it
may have deemed possibly tenable but which were in fact based upon its
extent of organization.   Accordingly, we shall dismiss the IAM's petitions.

We shall at this time direct elections in the following voting groups:

(1) All electricians, including leadmen and apprentices . . .

(2) All power-division employees, including switchboard operators, firemen, refrigerating engineer, refrigeration oilers, water tenders, filtermen, boilerroom helpers, and fuel oil tenders . . .

(3) All of the hourly paid employees of the Company at its Trona, California, plant, in the production village maintenance and housing divisions, mercantile, supplies, and engineering departments . . .

However, in view of our finding that one of the factors supporting the appropriateness of separate representation for voting groups (1) and (2) is that the petitioners seeking to represent these groups are labor organizations which traditionally represent such employees (in this case, the IBEW and the Operating Engineers), we find it necessary to modify the procedure for tallying the votes cast in Globe-type elections. We shall provide that if a majority of the employees in voting group (1) or (2) select the union seeking to represent them separately, those employees will be taken to have indicated their desire to constitute a separate bargaining unit and the Regional Director conducting the election is instructed to issue a certification of representatives to the labor organization seeking and selected by the employees in each group for such unit, which the Board, in such circumstances, finds to be appropriate for purposes of collective bargaining. On the other hand, if a majority of the employees in voting groups (1) or (2) do not vote for the union which is seeking to represent them in a separate unit, that group will appropriately be included in the production and maintenance unit and their votes shall be pooled with those in voting group 3,[12] and the Regional Director conducting the election is instructed to issue a certification of representatives to the labor organization selected by a majority of the employees in the pooled group, which the Board, in such circumstances, finds to be a single unit appropriate for purposes of collective bargaining.

[The opinions of Member Murdock, concurring in part and dissenting in part, and Member Peterson dissenting in part are omitted.]

NOTES

1. How does the general rule of American Potash differ from the New York craft proviso: "In any case where the majority of employees of a particular craft . . . shall so decide the Board shall designate such [craft as an appropriate unit]" (N.Y. Labor Relations Act §705(2))?

2. Suppose there is a history of plantwide bargaining in the industry, but the plant in question is new. Would it make any difference that the employer is also new to the industry? In either event, it seems, the Na-

[12] The Board hereby adopts the recommendations made by Board Members Murdock and Peterson in their dissent in Pacific Intermountain Express Co., 105 N.L.R.B. 480. If the votes are pooled, they are to be tallied in the following manner: The votes for the union seeking the separate unit shall be counted as valid votes, but neither for nor against any union seeking to represent the more comprehensive unit; all other votes are to be accorded their face value, whether for representation in a union seeking the comprehensive group or for no union.

tional Tube doctrine could apply. Kaiser Aluminum & Chemical Corp., 119 N.L.R.B. 695 (1957). But under the American Potash limitation, the only industries to which National Tube applies are basic steel, basic aluminum, lumber, and wet milling. See Permanente Metals Corp., 89 N.L.R.B. 804 (1950); Weyerhaeuser Timber Co., 87 N.L.R.B. 1076 (1949); Corn Products Refining Co., 80 N.L.R.B. 362 (1948).

Conversely, the American Potash requirement of a "true craft" group is applicable although the plant is new and the question is whether a new craft unit shall be approved. Reynolds Metals Co., 108 N.L.R.B. 821 (1954). In this case, since the skills were held insufficient, the applicability of National Tube was not reached.

3. Could it be argued that the American Potash limitation itself violates Section 9(b)(2) in restricting National Tube to the four industries in which plantwide bargaining history had been held determinative? The Board's refusal to consider the high degree of integration of manufacturing processes in plate glass has been condemned as arbitrary, in view of its treatment of the other four industries. NLRB v. Pittsburgh Plate Glass Co., 270 F.2d 167 (4th Cir. 1959), cert. denied, 361 U.S. 943 (1960).

In American Can Co., 13 N.L.R.B. 1252 (1939), the Board denied craft severance to Operating Engineers, Firemen & Oilers, and the IBEW, all AFL unions, because the Steel Workers Organizing Committee (CIO) had a year earlier won a plantwide election and subsequently obtained a collective agreement. The Senate Committee on Labor and Public Welfare, reporting on language that became Section 9(b)(2), said: "This overrules the American Can rule." S. Rep. No. 105, 80th Cong., 1st Sess. 25 (1947). And it added (p. 12): "Since the decision [in American Can], where the Board refused to permit craft units to be "carved out" from a broader bargaining unit already established, the Board, except under unusual circumstances, has virtually compelled skilled artisans to remain parts of a comprehensive plant unit. The committee regards the application of this doctrine as inequitable."

In National Tube Co., 76 N.L.R.B. 1199 (1948), the Board nevertheless denied craft severance to bricklayers in the steel industry. It expressly declined to place "particular stress" upon a prior certification, but did have regard to the bargaining history of National Tube, its corporate superior, United States Steel, and as seen above, the entire basic steel industry. In American Potash, it turns out, the Board was mindful in some sense of three more industries.

4. If the dominant characteristic of a departmental unit is community of interest, taking into account location, supervision, duties, and benefits of employees, are these considerations absent from craft units? Suppose a union is well qualified as a craft union and seeks to sever a unit of that craft from one plant to a multiplant unit of production and maintenance workers. This was denied in General Motors Corp., 120 N.L.R.B. 1215 (1958). Similarly multicraft units are inappropriate for severance either as craft or departmental units. Mesta Machine Co., 120 N.L.R.B. 1791 (1958). However, maintenance units may in fact be multicraft units.

Under the American Cyanamid case, 131 N.L.R.B. 909 (1961), a maintenance unit may be "Globed" as equally appropriate to an inclusive production and maintenance unit, though absence of a bargaining history on the basis of the larger unit does not necessarily establish its appropriateness.

5. The "traditional representative" craft test may apply only to severance and not to new-unit cases. Industrial Rayon Corp., 128 N.L.R.B. 514 (1960), enforcement denied, 291 F.2d 809 (4th Cir. 1961). Moreover, an exception favors a new union organized specifically for the purpose of seeking severance. Friden Calculating Machine Co., 110 N.L.R.B. 1618 (1954). Would this exception apply if the petitioner turned out to have been formed by and to be "fronting" for an unqualified union? See Iowa Packing Co., 125 N.L.R.B. 1408 (1959), denying severance.

NLRB, 27TH ANNUAL REPORT
77-78 (1963)

. . . The wishes of the employees concerned, as ascertained in self-determination elections, are taken into consideration where (1) specifically required by the Act, or (2) in the Board's view, representation of an employee group in a separate unit or a larger unit is equally appropriate, or (3) the question of a group's inclusion in an existing unit rather than continued nonrepresentation is involved.[10]

In cases where a question of representation existed in the historical unit and the incumbent union sought to include a previously unrepresented fringe group not sought by any other union on a different basis, the Zia [108 N.L.R.B. 1134 (1954)] rule provided that [they] would not be included in the historical unit without first ascertaining [their desires]. . . .

The majority held in the D. V. Displays case [134 N.L.R.B. 568 (1961), Members Rodgers and Leedom dissenting] that the Board now[11] will direct only one election which will include all the employees in the unit found to be appropriate.

THE HALF BROTHERS PROBLEM

A carpet and floor covering wholesaler has dealt with the Office Employees' Union for three years as representative of eleven or so office clerical employees. Not represented are two employees, a porter-clerk, and an inside salesman. The porter-clerk serves as janitor and messenger for the

---

[10] However, no severance is granted for decertification, Campbell Soup Co., 111 N.L.R.B. 234 (1955), and accordingly there is no option to vote "no union" in a craft severance election, American Tobacco Co., 115 N.L.R.B. 218 (1956). — Ed.

[11] Overruling Zia and reinstating Waterous Co., 92 N.L.R.B. 76 (1950), which in turn overruled Petersen & Lytle, 60 N.L.R.B. 1070 (1945). See Cohen, Self-determination Elections Among Previously Unrepresented Employees in Fringe Groups: a Re-examination, 50 Geo. L. J. 187 (1961). — Ed.

office. The salesman works in the same building as the office employees, in a sample room, and does no "outside" selling.

The Teamsters seek to represent all thirteen employees. The Office Employees, intervening, seek continued representation of the eleven clerks, typists, stenographers, and switchboard and accounting machine operators.

May the Board direct separate elections in the two groups, notwithstanding the D. V. Displays case, supra? Note that the incumbent does not seek to represent the more inclusive group. Consider also that the Board has a categorical rule against one-man units.

Assume that separate elections are directed (with only the choice between Teamsters and no union presented to the salesman and porter-clerk). Formulate instructions on how the Regional Director should make his certificate in each of the voting patterns displayed in the table below. "O" means Office Employees, "T" Teamsters, "N" no union, "P" porter-clerk, and "S" salesman.

| Old-unit Votes | | | Fringe | | Pool | | |
O	T	N	P	S	O	T	N
11	0	0	T	T	11	2	0
11	0	0	N	N	11	0	2
0	0	11	T	T	0	2	11
6	5	0	T	T	6	7	0
6	5	0	N	T	6	6	1
0	5	6	T	T	0	7	6
0	6	5	N	N	0	6	7

Compare the solution in Felix Half & Brother, Inc., 132 N.L.R.B. 1523 (1961). What disadvantage would Office Employees suffer by amending its petition to include the larger unit?

d.   EXCLUDED GROUPS
(1)   In General

NLRB, 27TH ANNUAL REPORT
71-76 (1963)

AGRICULTURAL LABORERS

A continuing rider to the Board's appropriation act requires the Board to determine "agricultural labor" status so as to conform to the definition of the term "agriculture" in section 3(f) of the Fair Labor Standards Act. . . . [I]t is the Board's policy "to follow wherever possible" the interpretation of section 3(f) by the Department of Labor. Thus, relying on the rulings of the Department of Labor, the Board held that processing and marketing employees of a dairy farm were not "agricultural laborers," because all eggs handled and 90 percent of the milk processed were produced elsewhere, not on the employer's farm. . . .

INDEPENDENT CONTRACTORS

. . .

A Board majority held that drivers who had previously been employees of a toy and novelty distributor had not been converted to independent contractors by virtue of their individual franchise contracts with the employer. The majority found that the employer reserved to itself the right to control the manner and means by which the drivers performed their work, and left little room for the drivers to make decisions which would govern their profit and loss. . . .

SUPERVISORS

. . . In the past, the Board has followed the policy . . . that employees who spend a regular and substantial part of their time performing supervisory duties on a seasonal basis are supervisors and are excluded. . . . Upon reconsideration . . . a Board majority revised [this] policy to include these seasonal supervisors in the unit, but only with respect to their rank-and-file duties, and to permit them to vote regardless of their employee status at the time of the election.[12] . . .

. . . The fact that individuals have been included in a contract unit does not preclude the Board from excluding them as supervisors.

NOTES

1. The history of Board determination and statutory amendment concerning supervisory personnel is an illuminating one.

In the 1930's it was exceptional for unions to seek to organize supervisory employees, so almost as a matter of course they were excluded from the units then being established. But whether they would be entitled to separate recognition was a question not long in coming, to be resolved affirmatively by the Board in Union Collieries Coal Co., 41 N.L.R.B. 96 (1942), then negatively, as a matter of inappropriate unit, in Maryland Drydock Co., 49 N.L.R.B. 733 (1943), after Member Houston succeeded Member Leiserson (on the three-man board). Finally, however, Member Houston joined Chairman Millis in favor of a foreman's unit, and this determination was sustained in Packard Motor Car Co. v. NLRB, 330 U.S. 485 (1947). The effect of the exclusion of supervisors in the 1947 amendments, resulting in the present form of NLRA §§2(3) and 2(11), is explained in H.R. Rep. No. 245, 80th Cong., 1st Sess. 17 (1947):

"The bill does not forbid anyone to organize. It does not forbid any employer to recognize a union of foremen. Employers who, in the past,

---

12 With this shift in doctrine in 1962 (Great Western Sugar Co., 137 N.L.R.B. 551), compare Berea Publishing Co., 140 N.L.R.B. 516 (1963), which reinstated a 1951 precedent that an employee who works in the unit less than half time (although working for the same employer outside the unit for the balance of his time) is to be included in the unit as if he were a part-time employee. — ED

have bargained collectively with supervisors may continue to do so. What the bill does is to say what the law always has said until the Labor Board, in the exercise of what it modestly calls its 'expertness,' changed the law: That no one, whether employer or employee, need have as his agent one who is obligated to those on the other side, or one whom, for *any* reason, he does not trust."

Compare the following language from Safeway Stores, Inc. v. Retail Clerks International Assn., 41 Cal. 2d 567, 575, 261 P.2d 721, 726 (1953), concerning a strike, after the 1947 amendments, for inclusion of store managers in the unit:

"It is eminently proper that management supervisors, the store managers in this case, be kept free from the divided loyalty that would be engendered by compulsory membership in the defendant local unions. . . .

"Confronted with the responsibility of declaration where as here there is no constitutional or legislative guide on the subject we hold that the trial court was correct in deciding that the coercion sought to be exercised by the defendants under the circumstances of this case was not reasonably related to any legitimate interest of organized labor; that the activities of the defendants were not in the furtherance of any proper labor objective, and that as a matter of sound public policy were within the equity jurisdiction of the court."

2. Section 2(2) of the NLRA excludes all governmental units from the definition of the term "employer". It follows that public employees are not covered by the statute and are not entitled to claim its protections in attempts to secure organizational and bargaining rights. A substantial body of law has been developing out of the press of governmental employees for collective bargaining. See the material infra page 742.

(2)　Independent Contractors

When is a person pursuing an "independent calling" or engaged in 'business for himself"? Is "right of control" really a test or is it a label for a conclusion? Part of the history of the 1947 amendment to the definition of "employee" is contained in H.R. Rep. No. 245, 80th Cong., 1st Sess. 18 (1947):

"An 'employee', according to all standard dictionaries, according to the law as the courts have stated it, and according to the understanding of almost everyone, with the exception of members of the National Labor Relations Board, means someone who works for another for hire. But in the case of National Labor Relations Board v. Hearst Publications, Inc., 322 U.S. 111 (1944), the Board expanded the definition of the term 'employee' beyond anything that it ever had included before, and the Supreme Court, relying upon the theoretic 'expertness' of the Board, upheld the Board. In this case the Board held independent merchants who bought newspapers from the publisher and hired people to sell them to be 'employees'. The people the merchants hired to sell the papers were 'employees' of the merchants, but holding the merchants to be 'employees' of the publisher of the papers was most far reaching. It must be presumed that when Congress passed the Labor Act, it intended words it used to have the meanings that they had when Congress passed the act, not new meanings that, 9 years later, the Labor Board might think up. In the law, there always has been a difference, and a big difference, between 'employees' and 'independent contractors'. 'Employees' work for wages or salaries under direct supervision. 'Independent contractors' undertake to do a job for a price, decide how the work will be done, usually hire others to do the work, and depend for their income not upon wages, but upon the difference between what they pay for goods, materials, and labor and what they receive for the end result, that is, upon profits. It is inconceivable that Congress, when it passed the act, authorized the Board to give to every word in the act whatever meaning it wished. On the contrary, Congress intended then, and it intends now, that the Board give to words not far-fetched meanings but ordinary meanings. To correct what the Board has done, and what the Supreme Court, putting misplaced reliance upon the Board's expertness, has approved, the bill excludes 'independent contractors' from the definition of 'employees'."

For an attack on the right of control test that argues for consideration also of opportunity for profit or loss, amount of investment, and degree of skill, as well as control and statutory purpose (whether under NLRA, Jones Act, Fair Labor Standards Act, or Social Security Act), see Broden, General Rules Determining the Employment Relationship Under Social Security Laws: After Twenty Years an Unsolved Problem, 33 Temp. L.Q. 307, 381 (1960). In United Insurance Co. v. NLRB, 304 F.2d 86 (7th Cir. 1962), the administrative conclusion that debit insurance agents of United were employees was set aside, because under this company they determined when they would work, and they paid their own expenses, including assistants' salaries, travel, bonding, rent, postage, and telephone, out of commissions from collected premiums. The same court of appeals in NLRB v. Phoenix Mutual Life Insurance Co., 167 F.2d 983 (1948), had relied upon a noncontributory pension plan, full-time representation of the company, and other factors to reject the argument that life insurance salesmen were independent contractors. Both cases, as well as cases from other circuits, strongly suggest that in applying the independent contractor exclusion the scope of judicial review approaches independence of the administrative judgment.

Truck drivers who are also selling goods recurrently present the same kind of problem. In International Brotherhood of Teamsters v. Oliver, 358 U.S. 283 (1959), a collective agreement regulated leasing of trucks to carriers by owner-drivers, including the terms of rental payments. As the Court saw the history and purpose of these regulations, they were so related to protection of the wage scale as to be "obviously not price fixing but wages." P. 294. But in National Van Lines, Inc. v. NLRB, 273 F.2d 402 (7th Cir. 1960), a case involving NLRA §2(3)," the court wrote (p. 407): "Oliver was concerned with the interpretation of a collective bargaining agreement between a group of local labor unions and a group of interstate motor carriers and whether a state antitrust law could be applied to prohibit the parties from carrying out its terms. We fail to see its relevance here."

Did counsel for the Board err in appealing to the Oliver case as authority that truck owners could be employees of a corporation for which they had agreed to drive? Under the National Van Lines contract the drivers paid their expenses such as for hiring help, payroll taxes, loss of or damage to trailers furnished by National. National, however, had its insignia painted on the tractors, approved all drivers, paid half the cost of drivers' uniforms, assigned the runs, and paid certain taxes, license fees, and insurance premiums.

For a review of the authorities and another rejection in a newspaper carrier case of the Board's application of the right of control test, see NLRB v. A. S. Abell Co., 327 F.2d 1 (4th Cir. 1964). With Northwestern Mutual Life Insurance Co. v. Tone, 125 Conn. 183, 4 A.2d 640 (1939), holding that insurance agents are not employees for unemployment compensation purposes, contrast Republic Life Insurance Co. v. Dobson, 204 Okla. 5, 226 P.2d 402 (1950), holding that they are employees under the Selective Service Act.

Is it possible that some of the owner-drivers were neither "employees" nor "independent contractors" but "supervisors"? See Deaton Truck Line, Inc. v. NLRB, 337 F.2d 697 (5th Cir. 1964).

NOTE

Are the variations in policy supporting the exclusions in NLRA §2(3) of governmental employees, independent contractors, and supervisors such as to warrant differences in legal restrictions upon their organizational activities? Compare the status of agricultural and domestic workers. See Morin, The Organizability of Farm Labor in the United States, 68-70 (1952); Report of the President's Commission on Migratory Labor 105-118 (1951).

2. *Litigation*
a.   INTRODUCTION

The total cases "closed" by the NLRB ranged from 14,779 in 1958 to 24,678 in the year ending June 30, 1963.[13] However, this administrative activity includes dispositions by agreement and unilateral action, such as stipulations for consent elections and disclaimer of interest in representation, or withdrawal of charges of unfair labor practice or their settlement or adjustment. The number of "decisions" in contested matters growing out of the 24,678 cases in 1963 was only 3340, of which the Regional Directors made 2034, in representation cases. Among the 1306 made by the Board were 227 in representation cases and 587 in unfair practice cases.

[13] The unfair labor practice complaint cases have increased from less than half to 55 per cent. NLRB, 28th Ann. Rep. 23 (1964).

The others included 116 post-election questions and forty work assignment questions under Section 8(b)(4)(D).[14]

In fiscal 1963 there were four Supreme Court cases, 198 cases in the courts of appeals, and 238 in the district courts.[15] The district court cases reflect litigation under NLRA §§10(j) and 10(l). The 10(j) injunction is discretionary, and the Board invoked it only seventy-seven times up to June 30, 1963, but this reflects an average of about three a year before 1961 and fourteen since then.[16]

The two widely differing procedures under the National Labor Relations Act, the representation procedures under Section 9 and the unfair labor practice procedures under Section 10, must be kept clearly separate. As a matter of convenience, the NLRB calls representation cases "R" cases and unfair labor practice cases "C" cases. The procedures in R cases are shown throughout the materials on administrative action, supra. The procedures in C cases are here described.

The procedure in a C case begins with the filing of a charge. The Rules provide that any person may file a charge, and person is defined in accordance with the statutory definition, Sections 102.1 and 102.9, in NLRB, Rules and Regulations and Statements of Procedure, Series 8 (1962).

The charge, like the petition, is filed in a regional office, where it is assigned a file number.[17] Should a representation proceeding involving the same parties be pending, the general practice is to postpone any election, in the absence of a request to proceed by the charging party, until the charge is investigated.[18] Conversely, if a charge is filed under Section 8(b)(7), but a petition is also filed within such time as to constitute a defense, the processing of the petition will supersede the charge. However, in this case, the deliberative processes of Section 9 do not apply and the Board (through the regional office) is directed to conduct an expedited election.[19]

---

[14] Id. at 21.

[15] Id. at 22-24.

[16] Id. at 184, Table 18; McCulloch, The Development of Administrative Remedies, 14 Lab. L.J. 339, 346 (1963).

[17] The region, designated by the first element of the number, is where the charged unfair practice occurred. The letters separating the digits in the number characterize the case: CE for violations of §8(e), CA for employer violations (other than CE cases), CP for violations of §8(b)(7), CD for §8(b)(4)(D), CC for §8(b)(4)-(A)-(C), and CB for union violations (other than CE, CD, and CC cases). Petitions have the same scheme except that RC applies to petitions under §9(c)(1)-(A)(i), RD for §9(c)(1)(A)(ii), RM for §9(c)(1)(B), and UD for §9(e)(1). A petition when a charge under §8(b)(7) is on file is merely designated by R (preceded by the number of the region and followed by the individual file number).

[18] In Holt Bros., 146 N.L.R.B. No. 45 (1964), a charge under §8(e) is held not to block the election because although true it would not necessarily imply interference with employee choice.

[19] Under §9, if informal investigation and negotiation are not suspended by the filing of a charge, or terminated by agreement or disclaimer of interest, the formal steps are: direction of a hearing, direction of election (or dismissal of the petition, finding that no question concerning representation exists), rulings

The investigation of the charge may reveal that the events upon which it is based are more than six months old or that it is nonmeritorious, whereupon the charging party may be persuaded to withdraw the charges, or they may be dismissed.[20] Or it may be revealed that the same matter has been submitted to arbitration, whereupon further investigation would generally be suspended pending the outcome of that process.[21] If a complaint issues under Sections 8(b)(4)(A), (B), or (C), 8(b)(7), or 8(e), a district court suit for a preliminary injunction must also be brought.[22]

Although the charging party can appeal from refusal to issue a complaint to the General Counsel, NLRB, Rules and Regulations, Series 8 (1962), §102.19, the decision of the General Counsel is not reviewable in the courts as a "final order," General Drivers v. NLRB, 179 F.2d 492 (10th Cir. 1950). Conversely, the issuance of a complaint does not bind the Board to accept jurisdiction.[23]

If the charges are found to be meritorious and settlement efforts fail, a complaint issues unless Section 10(k) is applicable. In that event, if there is no voluntary adjustment or agreement upon methods for voluntary adjustment, and it appears to the Regional Director that the Board should determine the dispute, a hearing officer is designated and a hearing is held, upon the record of which the Board makes an award or other disposition. If subsequently the Regional Director is not satisfied that the parties are complying, he issues a complaint under Section 8(b)(4)(D). NLRB, Statements of Procedure, Series 8, Subpart F (1962).

When the complaint issues, a notice of hearing accompanies it, and the respondent is required to file an answer. There is provision for intervention and the charging party usually intervenes. Although the General Counsel has ultimate control of amendments to the complaint and negotiations for settlement, the charging party has the right to an opportunity to be heard, once a complaint has issued. Marine Engineers' Beneficial Assn. v. NLRB, 202 F.2d 546 (3d Cir. 1953). And it has been held that failure to object to the admission of evidence addressed to issues outside the complaint and answer leaves the question of amendment to conform

---

on challenged ballots and objections to the election, and certification of a representative (or certification of no-union results, or direction of a runoff or return). Under §8(b)(7) the Regional Director conducts the election in an administratively determined unit, without a hearing. If no unit is appropriate, investigation of the charge is resumed.

[20] Most cases are concluded in the regional offices. In the year ending June 30, 1963, for example, 38.7 per cent of the charges filed were withdrawn, 17.5 per cent settled or adjusted prior to the complaint-issuance stage, and almost 30 per cent dismissed. Only 905 cases, or less than 6 per cent, reached the Board members for decision. NLRB, 28th Ann. Rep. 10-11 (1964).

[21] Even after the complaint is issued, the Board may defer. Dubo Manufacturing Corp., 142 N.L.R.B. 431 (1963).

[22] Comparison of §§10(j) and (1) discloses that in CA and CB cases the Board has discretion to seek an injunction, but the Regional Director has discretion in CD cases, and in CP cases an injunction should not be sought if there is also a meritorious charge under §8(a)(2).

[23] See Haleston Drug Stores v. NLRB, 187 F.2d 418 (9th Cir.), cert. denied, 342 U.S. 815 (1951), and compare the proviso in §14(c)(1).

to proof within the discretion of the Board.   Frito Co. v. NLRB, 330 F.2d 458 (9th Cir. 1964).

The trial examiner assigned to preside at the hearing is governed by the Federal Rules of Civil Procedure, so far as practicable, in ruling on evidence.   He is authorized to hold conferences for settlement or simplification of issues by consent of the parties, to administer oaths, and in general to regulate the course of the hearing.   His decision at the conclusion of the hearing contains a summary of the evidence, his findings and conclusions, and a recommended order.   The transcript of the hearing contains his rulings at the hearing, and the record includes the briefs of the parties.   The order becomes the order of the Board unless within twenty days after service of the decision exceptions to it are filed.   If exceptions are filed, supporting briefs may be filed, and if request is made the Board grants oral argument in cases of exceptional interest.

The order may dismiss the complaint for administrative reasons, or on the merits.   If the complaint is sustained in whole or in part the order will typically require that the respondent (a) cease and desist from the practice, (b) take specified affirmative action to remedy the evil effects of the practice, (c) post a conspicuous notice of the contents of the order, and (d) report the details of its compliance to the Regional Director.

TABLE I.   INCIDENCE OF VIOLATIONS FOUND —
BOARD DECISIONS[24]

| | 1958 | | | 1963 | | |
	Total	*Violations*	*Per Cent*	*Total*	*Violations*	*Per Cent*
Against Employers	177	150	85	700	551	79
Against Unions	176	135	77	205	171	83

Judicial review of the order may occur as an incident to enforcement proceedings or, if the respondent assumes the initiative, by a petition for review.[25]   Compare the venue options under Sections 10(e) and 10(f), and visualize the possible race to the courthouse.

The principal cases which follow in the remainder of Part II and a portion of Part III afford a thorough coverage of the nature and scope of the procedures for review of NLRB unfair labor practice determinations in the federal courts of appeal.   The leading case on the extent to which the findings of fact by the Board are binding upon the reviewing court is Universal Camera Corp. v. NLRB, 340 U.S. 474 (1951).   Here the Court made clear that the "substantial evidence rule" as applied to other administrative tribunals and codified in Section 10(e) of the Administrative Procedure Act applied equally to the National Labor Relations Board. Without attempting to define "substantial evidence," the court said (p. 490) that "courts must now assume more responsibility for the reasonableness and

[24] NLRB, 23d and 28th Ann. Reps. (1959, 1964).
[25] See Office Employees v. NLRB, cited infra page 203, for an example of the use of the review petition to attack the Board's administrative dismissal of a complaint.

fairness of Labor Board decisions than some courts have shown in the past." In discussing the weight to be given the findings of the trial examiner, and the effect of the Board's reversing an examiner, the Court said that the Board could reject his findings even though they were not "clearly erroneous." Reviewing courts, however, should give the examiner's report "such probative force as it intrinsically commands." P. 495.

b. THE ESTABLISHMENT OF BARGAINING RELATIONSHIPS BY UNFAIR LABOR PRACTICE LITIGATION

JOY SILK MILLS, INC. v. NLRB

United States Court of Appeals, District of Columbia Circuit, 1950
185 F.2d 732, certiorari denied, 341 U.S. 914 (1951)

[During a brief strike concerned with certain grievances other than recognition, thirty-eight out of the fifty-two employees of the Joy Silk Mills at Hartsville, S.C., signed cards designating the Textile Workers of America (AFL) as collective bargaining representative. On September 24, 1948, four days after the strike was settled, Jacobs, the union's director in Atlanta, telephoned Gilbert, the company's president, to discuss recognition. On September 30, at a conference where Jacobs, Gilbert, the company's attorney, and an NLRB field examiner were present, Jacobs offered Gilbert a check of the union's membership cards, but instead plans were laid for a consent election on October 19. Gilbert instructed his supervisors not to interfere with union activities and posted a notice advising the employees of their right to vote freely. Before October 19, however, Gilbert and some of his supervisors made various promises to improve working conditions and engaged in interrogation concerning union activity coupled with suggestions of loss of benefits if the union won the election. When the union lost, it immediately filed objections, which led the Regional Director to set aside the election and order another one. Then the union withdrew its representation petition and filed charges under Sections 8(a)(1) and (5). The Board found the promises and interrogation contrary to Section 8(a)(1) and also that there had been a violation of Section 8(a)(5). The company petitioned the District of Columbia Court of Appeals to set aside the order of the Board. The order directed the company to cease and desist from the unfair practices, including the refusal to bargain collectively with the Textile Workers as the exclusive representative of the production and maintenance employees, and upon request "to bargain collectively with the Textile Workers of America."]

WASHINGTON, Circuit Judge. . . .

Was there a refusal to bargain collectively in violation of Section 8(a)(5) of the Act? Before there can be a wrongful refusal to bargain, there must have been a request to bargain by the union. N.L.R.B. v. Columbian Enameling & Stamping Co., 306 U.S. 292. The Board concluded that such a request was made by Jacobs in the telephone conversation with Gilbert on September 24. Jacobs testified that he had requested recognition of the union as collective bargaining agent, stating that the union had been authorized to represent the employees; and that he had suggested a cross-check of membership cards with the payroll, by an impartial person, to prove the authorization. He further testified that Gilbert declined both requests, stating he wished to consult his attorney; that he thought the matter had been settled by an election held two years previously, which the union had lost; and that in any event he preferred to have the Board handle the matter. Gilbert testified that no request to bargain was made and that Jacobs merely said he had enough employees to petition the Board for an election if Gilbert wouldn't agree to a consent election. Jacobs also testified that at the meeting of September 30, he suggested negotiating a contract to obviate the necessity of an election. Again there was contradictory testimony. The trial examiner chose to believe Jacobs' version of the conversations, finding Gilbert mistaken in his recollection, and concluded that there had been a request to bargain; these findings were affirmed by the Board. The circumstances of the conversations corroborate this conclusion to some extent. But apart from that, credibility of witnesses is a matter for Board determination, and not for this court. Nor must the request to bargain be in haec verba, so long as there was one by clear implication. The Labor-Management Relations Act "is not a statute of frauds or an act prescribing the formalities of conveyancing. No seal or writing is required by its terms. Nor is any special formula or form of words."

The question presented is then whether Gilbert's refusal to bargain was permissible under the Act. It has been held that an employer may refuse recognition to a union when motivated by a good faith doubt as to that union's majority status. North Electric Mfg. Co. v. N.L.R.B., 6 Cir., 123 F.2d 887; N.L.R.B. v. Chicago Apparatus Co., 7 Cir., 116 F.2d 753. When, however, such refusal is due to a desire to gain time and to take action to dissipate the union's majority, the refusal is no longer justifiable and constitutes a violation of the duty to bargain set forth in Section 8(a)(5) of the Act. N.L.R.B. v. Federbush Co., 2 Cir., 121 F.2d 954, 956; N.L.R.B. v. Remington Rand, Inc., 2 Cir., 94 F.2d 862, 868-869. The Act provides for election proceedings in order to provide a mechanism whereby an employer acting in good faith may secure a determination of whether or not the union does in fact have a majority and is therefore the appropriate agent with which to bargain. Another purpose is to insure that the employees may freely register their individual choices concerning representation. Certainly it is not one of the purposes of the election provisions to supply an employer with a procedural device by which he may secure the time necessary to defeat efforts toward organization being made by a union. Thus, the problem now before us narrows down to whether or not the evidence warrants the Board's inference that the refusal of recognition was in fact motivated by bad faith.

We think that there was "substantial" evidence, viewing the entire record, from which the Board could conclude that the original refusal of recognition was in bad faith. Cf. N.L.R.B. v. Consolidated Machine Tool Corp., 2 Cir., 163 F.2d 376, certiorari denied 332 U.S. 824. The employer engaged in coercive activities immediately preceding the election. Interference commenced only five days after the consent election had been agreed upon. The time lapse between the first request to bargain and the election was only 26 days. In view of the totality of the evidence, it is a reasonable conclusion that the employer did not suddenly suffer a change of heart. "We are in a field where subtleties of conduct may play no small part . . ." N.L.R.B. v. Express Publishing Co., 312 U.S. 426, 437. Neither the Board nor the courts can read the minds of men. As the Board has stated: "In cases of this type the question of whether an employer is acting in good or bad faith at the time of the refusal is, of course, one which of necessity must be determined in the light of all relevant facts in the case, including any unlawful conduct of the employer, the sequence of events, and the time lapse between the refusal and the unlawful conduct." Petitioner has transgressed the bounds of permissible conduct to a sufficient extent to permit the Board to conclude that its refusal to bargain was as ill-intentioned as its other actions. . . .

There remains for consideration whether the Board's order should be enforced in full or should be modified in some respects.

First, as to that portion of the order relating to the refusal to bargain: If the Board is correct in its finding that the employer refused to bargain in violation of Section 8(a)(5), its order that the employer bargain collectively with the union is within its authority, and is amply sustained by precedent. This is true despite the fact that the union lost the consent election. The Board has concluded that the union's loss of strength was due to petitioner's coercive activities. It has also concluded that prior to the engagement in that coercion the union had a large majority. The Board is specifically empowered "to take such affirmative action . . . as will effectuate the policies of this chapter." 29 U.S.C.A. §160(c). It has been consistently held by the Supreme Court that where an employer refuses to bargain collectively with a majority union, and the union loses its majority status because of the employer's coercive activities, suffering the loss of an election, it is appropriate for the Board to order the employer to bargain with the union. Franks Bros. Co. v. N.L.R.B., 321 U.S. 702; N.L.R.B. v. P. Lorillard Co., 314 U.S. 512; N.L.R.B. v. Bradford Dyeing Assn., 310 U.S. 318, 339-340. . . .

The decision in Franks Bros. Co. v. N.L.R.B., supra, appears controlling, and the order of the Board is entitled to be enforced in the respect just discussed.

As to that portion of the order requiring the petitioner to cease and desist from refusing to bargain, what has been said above is equally applicable, and the order must likewise be enforced. . . .

Wilber K. Miller, Circuit Judge, dissents, being of the view that no part of the Board's order should be enforced.

NOTE

Is the order to bargain a certification of the Textile Workers? A certification under Section 9 must ordinarily be respected for one year, although in Rocky Mountain Phosphates, 138 N.L.R.B. 292 (1962), the

Board held that when the employer knew the certified union was defunct and that another union had a clear majority, he violated the Act in refusing to bargain with the new union even though the certification year had more than three months to run. In NLRB v. Warren Co., 350 U.S. 107 (1955), the Court held that when an order to bargain has been embodied in a decree of enforcement, the employer is liable to contempt sanctions for failure to bargain fairly for a reasonable length of time, even though the union does not in fact have majority status in the plant. And compare "certify" in Sections 9(c)(1) and (e)(1), "facts certified" in Section 9(d), "certified" in Section 8(b)(4)(C), and "currently certified" in Section 8(b)(7).

BERNEL FOAM PRODUCTS CO. and TEXTILE WORKERS UNION OF AMERICA, AFL-CIO
National Labor Relations Board, 1964
146 N.L.R.B. No. 161

[Ryan, the union representative, having obtained authorization cards from fifty-three of the eighty-eight production and maintenance workers, telephoned Bernel, the company president and requested recognition. Bernel refused, declining Ryan's offer to turn the cards over to a clergyman for verification. The next day, November 12, 1962, he attended a meeting of the union and again refused until the union was certified following an NLRB election. On the union's petition an election was scheduled for December 3. On November 30, the last working day before the election, Bernel met with the employees, and on election day the company circulated certain leaflets. After the union lost the election, it filed the charges that are the subject of the instant complaint. The trial examiner found, and the Board agreed, that attending the union meeting with the union's consent was not a violation of Section 8(a)(1), but that certain statements of Bernel on November 30 and certain contents of the leaflets did violate Section 8(a)(1). The opinion signed by Chairman McCulloch and Members Fanning and Brown continues:]

In reaching its conclusion in [Aiello Dairy Farms, 110 N.L.R.B. 1365 (1954), overruling M. H. Davidson Co., 94 N.L.R.B. 142 (1951), and intervening decisions] that, since the union had proceeded to an election and lost, it could no longer assert its majority status by filing an 8(a)(5) charge, the Board relied basically on two considerations which we are persuaded are not grounded in logic or upon a proper interpretation of the policies of the Act. The reasons given were that the union would thereby be (1) pursuing inconsistent procedures in seeking to prove its majority, and (2) circumventing Board policy against holding elections while 8(a)(5) charges are pending thus causing expenditure of public funds in useless and repetitive procedures.

With respect to the first basis, we would point out that, although both procedures may be available to the union in given circumstances and may have as a common element establishment of a union's majority status as employee representative, the unfair labor practice and the representation proceedings are not inconsistent. The latter may establish the union's majority as of the day of the election, but it does not resolve the union's majority status on the date demand for recognition and bargaining was made and refused — which is the determination made in the former proceeding. Neither are they grounded in contradictory assertions of fact. In situations where both procedures are available, it is the refusal to bargain which generates initiation of the election procedure. And, although in filing a representation petition the union asserts as a formal matter that a question concerning representation exists, as a practical matter, the union has not altered its position that it represents the employees and is entitled to recognition. Rather, it is stating the employer's assertion of such a question and seeking an election as a means of proving that there is no validity in that assertion. As these are not inconsistent procedures, there is no basis for applying such a concept of election of remedies as was established in Aiello.

Moreover, the so-called "choice" which the union is forced to make under Aiello between going to an election or filing an 8(a)(5) charge is at best a Hobson's choice. Although an election is a relatively swift and inexpensive way for the union to put the force of law behind its majority status, the procedure is highly uncertain entailing the real possibility that because of conduct by the employer no fair election will be held. That this danger is not imaginary is amply demonstrated by the fact that in both Aiello and the instant case, as in many similar cases, the election was set aside on the basis of the employer's unlawful conduct. On the other hand, although in pursuing an 8(a)(5) charge a union does not risk the effect upon its majority of later unlawful conduct on the part of the employer, such a proceeding is considerably more complicated, consumes more time during which employees are denied the representation they desire, and involves greater expense. Since this difficult and rather dubious "choice" is created by the employer's unlawful conduct, there is no warrant for imposing upon the union which represents the employees an irrevocable option as to the method it will pursue in seeking vindication of the employees' representation rights while permitting the offending party to enjoy at the expense of public policy the fruits of such unlawful conduct. The fact that in an election a vote favorable to the union may obviate for it the necessity for pursuing the unfair labor practice route does not, in our view, warrant requiring that the union forfeit the right to request that the effect upon it of the employer's unlawful conduct be rectified when it develops that such conduct has been sufficiently onerous to interfere with the election and to cause a substantial deterioration in the union's status.

In addition, where the conduct engaged in is found to be of a type which makes a fair election impossible the election is set aside and regarded as a nullity. There is absolutely no basis for holding the participating union alone bound by an election which has been declared a nullity. Either the election is not a nullity or the union is not bound thereby. To hold, as our dissenting colleague would, that by participating initially in an ultimately void election the union irrevocably committed itself to the representation proceeding and, therefore, may seek a remedy only in another election, overlooks the fact that an election is not a remedy either in statutory concept or in reality. On the contrary, experience has demonstrated that a vast majority of the re-run elections' results favor the party which interfered with the original election. This clearly demonstrates the lingering effect of unacceptable electioneering conduct. Thus, in a majority of the cases another election can hardly be said to be an adequate remedy for the employer's unlawful refusal to recognize the employees' designated majority representative which was followed by conduct which interfered with the employees' freedom of choice. To ignore such conduct, as the Aiello doctrine of option and waiver does, is incompatible with the statutory mandate. Indeed, it lends the Board's procedures as a tool to thwart the statutory rights of the majority of the employees involved and subverts the very purpose of the Act. It is to be hoped that an approach which denies an employer any benefit from its unlawful refusal to bargain will remove the motive for demanding unnecessary elections and diminish efforts to undermine the will of the employees by interfering with their freedom of choice.

As to (2), we do not find persuasive the reasoning that the Aiello rule is justified on the grounds that to hold otherwise would permit the union to abuse the Board's processes by causing it to "expend time and public funds in useless and repetitive proceedings." Although we are in agreement that "useless and repetitive proceedings" are to be avoided, we do not agree that prosecution of an 8(a)(5) charge in such circumstances is either useless or repetitive. . . .

Our dissenting colleague argues that the Aiello rule is a "fundamentally fair approach" because "once having made its choice, the union must stick to it." This view, in our opinion, relegates the Board to the role of a detached observer in a game being played between a union and an employer. If this, indeed, were the Board's function, we might agree that the Union, having lost the election, could not fairly charge that it had won the game. However, a proceeding under Section 8(a)(5) of the Act is not a game. . . . We cannot agree that the basic question presented here is one of "balancing the scales" either toward the union or employer. Rather, the issue is one of providing an adequate remedy for conduct which has been specifically proscribed by Congress.

In view of the foregoing, the Aiello decision and subsequent decisions to the same effect are hereby overruled.

3. The Trial Examiner concluded, and we agree, that Respondent's conduct constituted a refusal to bargain with the Union in violation of Section 8(a)(5) of the Act under the Board's decision in Snow & Sons [134 N.L.R.B. 709 (1961)]. In that case, the Board held that where an employer entertains no reasonable doubt either with respect to the appropriateness of the proposed unit or the union's representative status and seeks a Board-directed election without a valid ground therefor, he has failed to fulfill the bargaining requirements under the Act and thereby

violates 8(a)(5), even though the employer did not embark upon a program of interference to dissipate the union's majority. . . .

The Trial Examiner rejected, however, the General Counsel's contention that the Respondent's conduct also violated Section 8(a)(5) of the Act under the Board's decision in Joy Silk. . . .

In disagreement with the Trial Examiner, we find that Respondent's refusal to bargain with the Union was motivated by a desire to create the opportunity to dissipate the Union's majority. In reaching this conclusion, we rely on the facts that (1) Respondent refused to recognize the Union without any reasonable basis for doubting the Union's majority, rejecting its offer of proof and insisting upon an election, and (2) shortly before the election Respondent engaged in unlawful conduct consisting of promises of benefit to employees and a suggestion that they form a shop union or shop committee, which conduct, we find was designed to induce employees to repudiate the Union. Accordingly, we find that Respondent's refusal to recognize the Union was motivated by its desire to gain time in which to undermine the Union's majority status and that such conduct is violative of Section 8(a)(5) of the Act.

As the 8(a)(5) issue was fully litigated at the hearing, and as we have found that Respondent violated Section 8(a)(5) of the Act, we shall order Respondent to recognize the Union as the collective bargaining agent of its employees in the appropriate unit. . . .

[Member Jenkins concurred on the ground that as the unfair practices in question had not taken place until shortly before the election the union was not fully aware of them in proceeding with the election. Hence he would rely on Joy Silk Mills, supra page 187, and would not reach the Aiello issue. Member Leedom concurred in part and dissented in part.]

C. CHALLENGES TO ADMINISTRATIVE DECISION BY INDEPENDENT COURT ACTION

LEEDOM v. KYNE
Supreme Court of the United States, 1958
358 U.S. 184, 79 Sup. Ct. 180, 3 L. Ed. 2d 210

MR. JUSTICE WHITTAKER delivered the opinion of the Court.

Section 9(b)(1) of the National Labor Management Relations Act, §9, 49 Stat. 453, 29 U.S.C. §159(b)(1), provides that, in determining the unit appropriate for collective bargaining purposes, "the Board shall not (1) decide that any unit is appropriate for such purposes if such unit includes both professional employees and employees who are not professional employees unless a majority of such professional employees vote for inclusion in such unit." The Board, after refusing to take a vote among the professional employees to determine whether a majority of them would "vote for inclusion in such unit," included both professional and nonprofessional employees in the bargaining unit that it found appropriate. The sole and narrow question presented is whether a Federal District Court has jurisdiction of an original suit to vacate that determination of the Board because made in excess of its powers.

The facts are undisputed. Buffalo Section, Westinghouse Engineers Association, Engineers and Scientists of America, a voluntary unincorporated labor organization, hereafter called the Association, was created for the purpose of promoting the economic and professional status of the nonsupervisory professional employees of Westinghouse Electric Corporation at its plant in Cheektowaga, New York, through collective bargaining with their employer. In October 1955, the Association petitioned the National Labor Relations Board for certification as the exclusive collective bargaining agent of all nonsupervisory professional employees, being then 233 in number, of the Westinghouse Company at its Cheektowaga plant, pursuant to the provisions of §9 of the Act, 29 U.S.C. §159. A hearing was held by the Board upon that petition. A competing labor organization was permitted by the Board to intervene. It asked the Board to expand the unit to include employees in five other categories who performed technical work and were thought by it to be "professional employees" within the meaning of §2(12) of the Act, 29 U.S.C. §152(12). The Board found that they were not professional employees within the meaning of the Act. However, it found that nine employees in three of those categories should nevertheless be included in the unit because they "share a close community of employment interest with [the professional employees, and their inclusion would not] destroy the predominantly professional character of such a unit." The Board, after denying the Association's request to take a vote among the professional employees to determine whether a majority of them favored "inclusion in such unit," included the 233 professional employees and the nine nonprofessional employees in the unit and directed an election to determine whether they desired to be represented by the Association, by the other labor organization, or by neither. The Association moved the Board to stay the election and to amend its decision by excluding the nonprofessional employees from the unit. The Board denied that motion and went ahead with the election at which the Association received a majority of the valid votes cast and was thereafter certified by the Board as the collective bargaining agent for the unit.

Thereafter respondent, individually, and as president of the Association, brought this suit in the District Court against the members of the Board, alleging the foregoing facts and asserting that the Board had exceeded its statutory power in including the professional employees, without their consent, in a unit with nonprofessional employees in violation of §9(b)(1) which commands that the Board "shall not" do so, and praying, among other things, that the Board's action be set aside. The defendants, members of the Board, moved to dismiss for want of jurisdiction and, in the alternative, for a summary judgment. The plaintiff also moved for summary judgment. The trial court found that the Board had disobeyed the express command of §9(b)(1) in including nonprofessional employees and professional employees in the same unit without the latter's consent, and in doing so had acted in excess of its powers to the injury of the professional employees, and that the court had jurisdiction to grant the relief prayed. It accordingly denied the Board's motion and granted the plaintiff's motion and entered judgment setting aside the Board's determination of the bargaining unit and also the election and the Board's certification. 148 F. Supp. 597.

On the Board's appeal it did not contest the trial court's conclusion that the Board, in commingling professional with nonprofessional employees in the unit, had acted in excess of its powers and had thereby worked injury to the statutory rights of the professional employees. Instead, it contended only that the District Court lacked jurisdiction to entertain the suit. The Court of Appeals held that the District Court did have jurisdiction and affirmed its judgment. 101 App. D.C. 398, 249 F.2d 490. Because of the importance of the question and the fact that it has been left open in our previous decisions, we granted certiorari, 355 U.S. 922.

Petitioners, members of the Board, concede here that the District Court had jurisdiction of the suit under §24(8) of the Judicial Code, 28 U.S.C. §1337, unless the review provisions of the National Labor Management Relations Act destroyed it. In American Federation of Labor v. National Labor Relations Board, 308 U.S. 401, this Court held that a Board order in certification proceedings under §9 is not "a final order" and therefore is not subject to judicial review except as it may be drawn in question by a petition for enforcement or review of an order made under §10(c) of the Act, restraining an unfair labor practice. But the Court was at pains to point out in that case that "[t]he question [there presented was] distinct from . . . whether petitioners are precluded by the provisions of the Wagner Act from maintaining an independent suit in a district court to set aside the Board's action because contrary to the statute . . ." Id., 308 U.S. at page 404. The Board argued there, as it does here, that the provisions of the Act, particularly §9(d), have foreclosed review of its action by an original suit in a District Court. This Court said: "But that question is not presented for decision by the record before us. Its answer involves a determination whether the Wagner Act, insofar as it has given legally enforceable rights, has deprived the district courts of some portion of their original jurisdiction conferred by §24 of the Judicial Code, 28 U.S.C.A. §41. It can be appropriately answered only upon a showing in such a suit that unlawful action of the Board has inflicted an injury on the petitioners for which the law, *apart from the review provisions of the Wagner Act,* affords a remedy. This question can be properly and adequately considered only when it is brought to us for review upon a suitable record." Id., 308 U.S. at page 412. (Emphasis added.)

The record in this case squarely presents the question found not to have been presented by the record in American Federation of Labor v. National Labor Relations Board, supra. This case, in its posture before us, involves "unlawful action of the Board [which] has inflicted an injury on the [respondent]." Does the law, "apart from the review provisions of the . . . Act," afford a remedy? We think the answer surely must be yes. This suit is not one to "review," in the sense of that term as used in the

Act, a decision of the Board made within its jurisdiction. Rather it is one to strike down an order of the Board made in excess of its delegated powers and contrary to a specific prohibition in the Act. Section 9(b)(1) is clear and mandatory. It says that, in determining the unit appropriate for the purposes of collective bargaining, "the Board *shall not* (1) decide that any unit is appropriate for such purposes if such unit includes both professional employees and employees who are not professional employees unless a majority of such professional employees vote for inclusion in such unit." (Emphasis added.) Yet the Board included in the unit employees whom it found were not professional employees, after refusing to determine whether a majority of the professional employees would "vote for inclusion in such unit." Plainly, this was an attempted exercise of power that had been specifically withheld. It deprived the professional employees of a "right" assured to them by Congress. Surely, in these circumstances, a Federal District Court has jurisdiction of an original suit to prevent deprivation of a right so given.

In Texas & New Orleans R. Co. v. Brotherhood of Railway & S.S. Clerks, 281 U.S. 548, 549, it was contended that, because no remedy had been expressly given for redress of the congressionally-created right in suit, the Act conferred "merely an abstract right which was not intended to be enforced by legal proceedings." Id., 281 U.S. at page 558. This Court rejected that contention. It said: "While an affirmative declaration of duty contained in a legislative enactment may be of imperfect obligation because not enforceable in terms, a definite statutory prohibition of conduct which would thwart the declared purpose of the legislation cannot be disregarded . . . If Congress intended that the prohibition, as thus construed, should be enforced, the courts would encounter no difficulty in fulfilling its purpose . . . The definite prohibition which Congress inserted in the act can not therefore be overridden in the view that Congress intended it to be ignored. As the prohibition was appropriate to the aim of Congress, and is capable of enforcement, the conclusion must be that enforcement was contemplated." Id., 281 U.S. at pages 568, 569. And compare Virginian R. Co. v. System Federation, 300 U.S. 515.

In Switchmen's Union of North America v. National Mediation Board, 320 U.S. 297, this Court held that the District Court did not have jurisdiction of an original suit to review an order of the National Mediation Board determining that all yardmen of the rail lines operated by the New York Central system constituted an appropriate bargaining unit, because the Railway Labor Board had acted within its delegated powers. But in the course of that opinion the Court announced principles that are controlling here. "If the absence of jurisdiction of the federal courts meant a sacrifice or obliteration of a right which Congress had created, the inference would be strong that Congress intended the statutory provisions governing the general jurisdiction of those courts to control. That was the purport of the decisions of this Court in Texas & New Orleans R. Co. v. Brotherhood of Railway & S.S. Clerks, 281 U.S. 548, and Virginian R. Co. v. System Federation No. 40, 300 U.S. 515. In those cases it was apparent that but for the general jurisdiction of the federal courts there would be no remedy to enforce the statutory commands which Congress had written into the Railway Labor Act. The result would have been that the 'right' of collective bargaining was unsupported by any legal sanction. That would have robbed the Act of its vitality and thwarted its purpose." Id., 320 U.S. at page 300.

Here, differently from the Switchmen's case, "absence of jurisdiction of the federal courts" would mean "a sacrifice or obliteration of a right which Congress" has given professional employees, for there is no other means, within their control (American Federation of Labor v. National Labor Relations Board, supra), to protect and enforce that right. And "the inference [is] strong that Congress intended the statutory provisions governing the general jurisdiction of those courts to control." 320 U.S. at page 300. This Court cannot lightly infer that Congress does not intend judicial protection of rights it confers against agency action taken in excess of delegated powers. Cf. Harmon v. Brucker, 355 U.S. 579; Stark v. Wickard, 321 U.S. 288; American School of Magnetic Healing v. McAnnulty, 187 U.S. 94.

Where, as here, Congress has given a "right" to the professional employees it must be held that it intended that right to be enforced, and "the courts . . . encounter no difficulty in fulfilling its purpose." Texas & New Orleans R. Co. v. Brotherhood of Railway & S.S. Clerks, supra, 281 U.S. at page 568.

The Court of Appeals was right in holding, in the circumstances of this case, that the District Court had jurisdiction of this suit, and its judgment is affirmed.

Mr. Justice Brennan, whom Mr. Justice Frankfurter joins, dissenting.

The legislative history of the Wagner Act, and of the Taft-Hartley amendments, shows a considered congressional purpose to restrict judicial review of National Labor Relations Board representation certifications to review in the Courts of Appeals in the circumstances specified in §9(d), 29 U.S.C. §159(d). The question was extensively debated when both Acts were being considered, and on both occasions Congress concluded that, unless drastically limited, time-consuming court procedures would seriously threaten to frustrate the basic national policy of preventing industrial strife and achieving industrial peace by promoting collective bargaining.

The Congress had before it when considering the Wagner Act the concrete evidence that delays pending time-consuming judicial review could be a serious hindrance to the primary objective of the Act — bringing employers and employees together to resolve their differences through discussion. Congress was acutely aware of the experience of the predecessor of the present Labor Board under the National Industrial Recovery Act, which provided that investigations and certifications by the Board could be brought directly to the courts for review. Such direct review was determined by the Congress to be "productive of a large measure of industrial strife . . ." and was specifically eliminated in the Wagner Act. Although Congress recognized that it was necessary to determine employee representatives before collective bargaining could begin, Congress concluded that the chance for industrial peace increased correlatively to how quickly collective bargaining commenced. For this reason Congress ordained that the courts should not interfere with the prompt holding of representation elections or the commencement of collective bargaining once an employee representative has been chosen. Congress knew that if direct judicial review of the Board's investigation and certification of representatives was not barred, "the Government can be delayed indefinitely before it takes the first step toward industrial peace." Therefore, §9(d) was written to provide "for review in the courts only after the election has been held and the Board has ordered the employer to do something predicated upon the results of the election." After the Wagner Act was passed, a proposed amendment to allow judicial review after an election but before an unfair labor practice order was specifically rejected. In short, Congress set itself firmly against direct judicial review of the investigation and certification of representatives, and required the prompt initiation of the collective-bargaining process after the Board's certification, because of the risk that time-consuming review might defeat the objectives of the national labor policy. See American Federation of Labor v. National Labor Relations Board, 308 U.S. 401, 409-411; Madden v. Brotherhood and Union of Transit Employees, 4 Cir., 147 F.2d 439, 158 A.L.R. 1330.

When the Taft-Hartley amendments were under consideration, employers complained that because §9(d) allowed judicial review to an employer only when unfair labor practice charges were based in whole or in part upon facts certified following an investigation of representatives, these "cumbersome proceedings" meant that the employer could have review only by commiting an unfair labor practice "no matter how much in good faith he doubted the validity of the certification." A House amendment therefore provided for direct review in the Courts of Appeals of Board certifications on appeal of any person interested, as from a final order of the Board. Opponents revived the same arguments successfully employed in the Wagner Act debates . . . Both sides recognized that the House amendment would produce a fundamental change in the law. The Senate rejected the House amendment; the amendments proposed by that body continued only the indirect and limited review provided in original §9(d). In conference, the Senate view prevailed. . . .

The Court today opens a gaping hole in this congressional wall against direct resort to the courts. The Court holds that a party alleging that the Board was guilty of "unlawful action" in making an investigation and certification of representatives need not await judicial review until the situation specified in §9(d) arises, but has a case immediately cognizable by a District Court under the "original jurisdiction" granted by 28 U.S.C. §1337 of "any civil action or proceeding arising under any Act of Congress regulating commerce.". . .

There is nothing in the legislative history to indicate that the Congress intended any exception from the requirement that collective bargaining begin without awaiting judicial review of a Board certification or the investigation preceding it. Certainly nothing appears that an exception was intended where the attack upon the Board's action is based upon an alleged misinterpretation of the statute. The policy behind the limitation of judicial review applies just as clearly when the challenge is made on this ground. Plainly direct judicial review of a Board's interpretation of the statute is as likely to be as drawn out, and thus as frustrative of the national policy, as is review of any other type of Board decision. That appears from the timetable in Inland Empire District Council, etc. v. Millis, 325 U.S. 697. That case also involved a challenge in a District Court to a statutory interpretation by the Board in a representation proceeding. The Court held that it was not necessary to reach the question of the District Court's jurisdiction since it had not been shown that the Board's interpretation of the pertinent statute was erroneous. But over two years elapsed while the question was being litigated. The hearing which led to the certification was held in May 1943 and this Court's decision was announced on June 11, 1945.

If there be error in the Board's statutory interpretation here, although there was none in Inland Empire Council, I ask, again, where even a scintilla of evidence is to be found that Congress intended an exception to permit direct judicial review for Board errors in statutory interpretation, obvious or debatable? Of course, there is none. . . .

I daresay that the ingenuity of counsel will, after today's decision, be entirely adequate to the task of finding some alleged "unlawful action," whether in statutory interpretation or otherwise, sufficient to get a foot in a District Court door under 28 U.S.C. §1337. Even when the Board wins such a case on the merits, as in Inland Empire Council, while the case is dragging through the courts the threat will be ever present of the industrial strife sought to be averted by Congress in providing only drastically limited judicial review under §9(d). Both union and management will be able to use the tactic of litigation to delay the initiation of collective bargaining when it suits their purposes. . . .

It is no support for the Court's decision that the respondent union may suffer hardship if review under 28 U.S.C. §1337 is not open to it. The Congress was fully aware of the disadvantages and possible unfairness which could result from the limitation on judicial review enacted in §9(d). The House proposal for direct review of Board certification in the Taft-Hartley amendments was based in part upon the fact that, under the Wagner Act, the operation of §9(d) was "unfair to . . . the union that loses, which has no appeal at all no matter how wrong the certification may be; [and to] the employees, who also have no appeal . . ." Congress nevertheless continued the limited judicial review provided by §9(d) because Congress believed the disadvantages of broader review to be more serious than the difficulties which limited review posed for the parties. Furthermore, Congress felt that the Board procedures and the limited review provided in §9(d) were adequate to protect the parties.

The Court supports its decision by stating that Switchmen's Union of North America v. National Mediation Board, supra, "announced principles that are controlling here." This is true, but I believe that those principles lead to, indeed compel, a result contrary to that reached by the Court. In that case, the Switchmen's Union sought to challenge in a District Court the certification of an employee representative by the National Mediation Board under the Railway Labor Act, 45 U.S.C. §151 et seq. The Board certified the Brotherhood of Railroad Trainmen as representative for all the yardmen of the rail lines operated by the New York Central system. The Switchmen's Union contended that yardmen of certain designated parts of the system should be permitted to vote for separate representatives instead of being compelled to take part in a system-wide election. The Board rejected this contention of the Switchmen's Union upon the ground that the Railway Labor Act did not authorize the Board to determine a unit of less than the entire system. The Board's interpretation was that the "Railway Labor Act vests the Board with no discretion to split a single carrier . . ." Switchmen's case, 320 U.S. at page 309. This Court held that the action of the Switchmen's Union was not cognizable in a District Court. The Court held that the Railway Labor Act, read in the light of its history, disclosed a congressional intention to bar direct review in the District Courts of certifications by the Mediation Board. This was held notwithstanding the fact that the certification was based on an alleged misinterpretation of the Act.

This same reasoning has striking application in this case. The National Labor Relations Act provides that the Labor Board "shall decide in each case . . . the unit appropriate for the purposes of collective bargaining," §9(b), but also provides that the Board "shall not . . . decide that any unit is appropriate . . . if such unit includes both professional employees and employees who are not professional employees unless a majority of such professional employees vote for inclusion in such unit . . ." §9(b)(1). The Board, in making the certification in dispute, has interpreted these provisions as requiring the approval of the professional employees of a mixed bargaining unit of professionals and nonprofessionals only when the professionals are a minority in the unit, since only in such a case would they need this protection against the ignoring of their particular interests. This interpretation is the basis of respondent union's complaint in its action under 28 U.S.C. §1337 in the District Court. But an alleged error in statutory construction was also the basis of the District Court action in the Switchmen's case. Thus the two cases are perfectly parallel. And just as surely as in the case of the Mediation Board under the Railway Labor Act, the Congress has barred District Court review of National Labor Relations Board certifications under the Labor Management Relations Act. The history of the controversy over direct judicial review which I have canvassed shows with a clarity perhaps not even as true of the Mediation Board that the National Labor Relations Board was the "precise machinery," 320 U.S. at page 301, selected by Congress for the purpose of determining a certification and that "there was to be no dragging out of the controversy into other tribunals of law." Id., 320 U.S. at page 305. Congress evidenced its will definitely and emphatically "by the highly selective manner in which Congress . . . provided for judicial review of administrative orders or determinations under the Act." Id., 320 U.S. at page 305. Review is confined to review in a Court of Appeals in the circumstances specified in §9(d). . . .

I would reverse and remand the case to the District Court with instructions to dismiss the complaint for lack of jurisdiction of the subject matter.

NOTES

1. Consider Section 9(d) and Pittsburgh Plate Glass Co. v. NLRB, 313 U.S. 146 (1941), a case illustrating judicial review of the Board's unit determination by this method. The employer objected to the Board's determination that a multiplant unit of production and maintenance workers was appropriate. When the certified union was denied recognition, the Board found the employer guilty of refusal to bargain. The employer defended on the ground that the duty to bargain runs only to the representative in an appropriate unit, so the issue for the Court under Section 10(f) was whether the Board had exceeded its power to determine the appropriate unit. In this case the Board was sustained in its refusal at the C case hearing to permit the employer to present evidence that had been withheld from the R case hearing where the unit determination was first made.

This position is distinguished in cases like Singer Sewing Machine Co. v. NLRB, 329 F.2d 200 (4th Cir. 1964), when the evidence is not available at the time of the R case hearing. Under Board practice, the trial examiner is bound by the unit determination made on the basis of the R case hearing. Hence there seem to be six critical omissions, any one of which could waive an objection to the unit determination: failure to insist upon a hearing, failure to maintain the objection before the hearing examiner, failure to appeal from the Regional Director to the Board under the Rules and Regulations, Series 8 (1962), §102.67(c), failure to maintain the objection at the C case hearing before the trial examiner, failure to preserve the exception before the Board, and failure to maintain it in court. See Rockwell Manufacturing Co. v. NLRB, 330 F.2d 795 (7th Cir. 1964), sustaining the Board's refusal to grant a hearing on objections to an election where no material issue of fact was tendered, and finding the Board's prospective change of rules neither arbitrary nor capricious, whereby misconduct in an election campaign after filing the petition but before a stipulation for certification upon a consent election would not be considered since it occurred prior to the rule change effective September 17, 1962. See also NLRB v. Ideal Laundry and Dry Cleaning Co., 330 F.2d 712 (10th Cir. 1964), denying enforcement because of denial of a hearing on representation issues. There had been an R case hearing, but after the election the Regional Director had made a further ex parte investigation.

2. In Kyne, was the Board's counsel well advised not to contest the finding of the trial court that the Board exceeded its powers? Consider the bases for making such a finding when the unit determination process

consists of the application of broad, nebulous standards to collective bargaining potentialities in the light of ever-changing industrial techniques and ever-shifting political forces, both within the union movement and in the larger labor market place.

The Fourth Circuit, in the extent-of-organization Singer Sewing Machine case, supra Note 1, conceded that there is a general limitation on judicial review of quasi-judicial proceedings against attempting to probe mental processes of administrators. United States v. Morgan, 313 U.S. 409 (1941). However, it held that this limitation is lifted when the regulated party makes a prima facie showing of misconduct by the administrator. Hence, since Singer had made such a showing, it was entitled to have the Board's field examiner testify whether he had sought by pretext to get names of employees outside the Pittsburgh City District, and Section 102.118 of the Rules and Regulations, Series 8 (1962), requiring permission from the General Counsel, would not protect him.

In Metropolitan Life Insurance Co., 147 N.L.R.B. No. 84 (1964), granting a unit of agents and insurance consultants at the district office at Holyoke, Mass., the Board, apparently reacting to judicial criticism, expressly disclaimed having been controlled in the Woonsocket (First Circuit) case by extent of organization, and engaged in argument purporting to support the conclusion that in the Holyoke case Section 9(c)(5) was not being violated.

3. The Court has had two occasions to respond to Justice Brennan's "gaping hole" observation in his Kyne dissent. In McCulloch v. Sociedad Nacional de Marineros de Honduras, 372 U.S. 10, 16-17 (1963), it said:

"We are not of course precluded from reexamining the jurisdiction of the District Court in Sociedad's action, merely because no challenge was made by the parties. Mitchell v. Maurer, 293 U.S. 237, 244 (1934). . . . [W]e hold that the action falls within the limited exception fashioned in Leedom v. Kyne, 358 U.S. 184 (1958). In that case judicial intervention was permitted since the Board's order was 'in excess of its delegated powers and contrary to a specific prohibition in the Act.' Id., at 188. While here the Board has violated no specific prohibition in the Act, the overriding consideration is that the Board's assertion of power to determine the representation of foreign seamen aboard vessels under foreign flags has aroused vigorous protests from foreign governments and created international problems for our Government. Important interests of the immediate parties are of course at stake. But the presence of public questions particularly high in the scale of our national interest because of their international complexion is a uniquely compelling justification for prompt judicial resolution of the controversy over the Board's power. No question of remotely comparable urgency was involved in Kyne, which was a purely domestic adversary situation. The exception recognized today is therefore not to be taken as an enlargement of the exception in Kyne."

But in Boire v. Greyhound Corp., 376 U.S. 473 (1964), a suit against a Regional Director instituted in the Southern District of Florida, the Court, reversing judgments granting and affirming the grant of an injunction, said (pp. 481-482):

"The respondent makes no claim that this case is akin to Sociedad Nacional. The argument is, rather, that the present case is one which falls within the narrow limits of Kyne. . . . The respondent points out that Congress has specifically excluded an independent contractor from the definition of 'employee.' . . . It is said that the Board's finding that Greyhound is an employer of employees who are hired, paid, transferred and promoted by an independent contractor, is therefore, plainly in excess of the statutory powers delegated to it by Congress. This argument, we think, misconceives both the import of the substantive federal laws and the painstakingly delineated procedural boundaries of Kyne.

"[Substantively, there is no contention here that the employees in question are independent contractors.] And whether Greyhound [as well as the independent contractor Floors, Inc.] possessed sufficient indicia of control to be an 'employer' is essentially a factual issue, unlike the question in Kyne, which depended solely upon construction of the statute. The Kyne exception is a narrow one, not to be extended to permit plenary District Court review of Board orders in certification proceedings whenever it can be said that an erroneous assessment of the particular facts before the Board has led it to a conclusion which does not comport with the law. Judicial review in such a situation has been limited by Congress to the Court of Appeals, and then only under the conditions explicitly laid down in §9(d) of the Act.'"

4. With the cases in the preceding note, compare Hotel Employees v. Leedom, 147 F. Supp. 306 (D.D.C. 1957). In this case, a petition for representation by a hotel employees union was dismissed by the NLRB on the ground that the Board consistently had declined jurisdiction over the hotel industry. Claiming a violation of constitutional rights resulting from unfair discrimination and of their right to represent under the NLRA, the union brought suit in the federal district court for a declaratory judgment and injunctive relief. The district judge dismissed the suit on the ground that the NLRB's determination to decline jurisdiction over the hotel industry was unassailable. This decision was reversed, per curiam, by the U.S. Supreme Court, 358 U.S. 99 (1958). The Court said the suit could not be dismissed on the asserted ground that the NLRB had the right to exclude the hotel industry as an industry from coverage. The Court relied on Office Employees v. NLRB, 353 U.S. 313 (1957), which held that the NLRB could not exempt unions as a class from being employers under the statute as to their own employees.

3. *Multi-Employer Organization*

ENDERBY PROBLEM 2
(See page 139 supra for Enderby Problem 1)

Several days after adjournment of the hearing described in Problem 1, Blair received a confidential memorandum from White. Excerpts appear below:

"As you know the company has been an active member of the Mid-Western Rubber Manufacturers Association for some years, . . . and in the interest of our competitive position we have followed very closely the economic adjustments which the Association has bargained for the organized members. . . .

"The current activity of the Rubber Workers raises some problems which are frankly not solved by the legal niceties of fitting an appropriate local unit to our work force. . . . Whatever choice the Board makes (and I haven't much illusion here) we just can't survive unless we remain rationally competitive. . . . If forced into this union business we have no intention of pricing ourselves out of the market, and believe me that would not be difficult.

". . . Nor, if the Rubber Workers should come in, do our plans involve any attempt to blunder along alone. . . .

"In an effort to think our situation through we have been mulling over future possibilities and alternatives. . . . Some of our people are asking bothersome questions. . . . You will appreciate that the answers could have direct bearing on the kind of total response which we are to make to the present union campaign. . . .

"1. The existing Association bylaws delegate to the Association the power and authority to represent the members in collective bargaining. If Local 417 is certified can we take the position that all contract negotiations must be conducted exclusively with the Association?

"2. How far can we push the foregoing position? E.g., if the union refuses to cooperate can we anticipate a strike over the matter by effecting layoffs?

"3. The other eight members of the Association have contracts with other locals of the United Rubber Workers and it has been the policy of the Association to work toward a uniform master agreement. We have complete confidence in the Association; . . . and reason to believe, despite the Local 417 petition, that the union's national officers would be favorably disposed toward a unit comprising the Association's membership. Assuming it could be engineered what would be the legal advantages and disadvantages of such a unit. . . . We understand that the courts allow associations to protect themselves by lockouts. . . . But what is the unemployment compensation picture in such situations?

"I realize that as usual you may need more specific information. . . . Don't hesitate to inquire. Incidentally, your friend O'Doul says we missed the boat by not taking a position at the hearing that the only appropriate unit would be the Association. Quite a fellow . . ."

NLRB v. TRUCK DRIVERS LOCAL 449
Supreme Court of the United States, 1957
353 U.S. 87, 77 Sup. Ct. 643, 1 L. Ed. 2d 676

[Eight employers in the linen supply business in Buffalo, New York, comprise the membership of the Linen and Credit Exchange. For thirteen years the Exchange and the union have bargained on a multiple-employer basis. In 1953, negotiations failed. The union put into effect a "whipsawing" plan by striking one of the Exchange members. The other seven members as a countermove laid off their drivers, notifying the union that the drivers of all members would be recalled when the union ended its strike at the one. The union filed charges claiming that this lockout violated Sections 8(a)(1) and (3). The Board held that the lockout was defensive and privileged in nature rather than retaliatory and unlawful. The Court of Appeals reversed, holding that in the absence of unusual economic necessity, a lockout violated the Act.]

MR. JUSTICE BRENNAN delivered the opinion of the Court. . . .

Legislative history of the Wagner Act, 49 Stat. 449, indicates that there was no intent to prohibit strikes or lockouts as such. The unqualified use of the term "lock-out" in several sections of the Taft-Hartley Act is statutory recognition that there are circumstances in which employers may lawfully resort to the lockout as an economic weapon. This conclusion is supported by the legislative history of the Act.

We are not concerned here with the cases in which the lockout has been held unlawful because designed to frustrate organizational efforts, to destroy or undermine bargaining representation, or to evade the duty to bargain. Nor are we called upon to define the limits of the legitimate use of the lockout.[19] The narrow question to be decided is whether a temporary lockout may lawfully be used as a defense to a union strike tactic which threatens the destruction of the employer's interest in bargaining on a group basis.

The Court of Appeals rejected the preservation of the integrity of the multi-employer bargaining unit as a justification for an employer lockout.[20] The court founded this conclusion upon its interpretation of the Taft-Hartley Act and its legislative history. After stating that "[m]ulti-employer bargaining has never received the express sanction of Congress," the court reasoned that because at the time of the enactment of the Taft-Hartley Act the Board had never "gone to the extreme lengths to which it now seeks to go in order to maintain the 'stability of the employer unit,' " Congress cannot be said to have given legislative approval to the present Board action. The court concluded that "Congress must have intended that such a radical innovation be left open for consideration by the joint committee it set up under §402 of the Act to study, among other things, 'the methods and procedures for best carrying out the collective-bargaining processes, with special attention to the effects of industry-wide or regional bargaining upon the national economy.' "[22]

[19] We thus find it unnecessary to pass upon the question whether, as a general proposition, the employer lockout is the corollary of the employees' statutory right to strike.

[20] As previously noted, the Board decision is based in part on a finding that the preservation of employer solidarity justifies a lockout as a defense to a whipsaw strike.

[22] The opinion of the Court of Appeals may be interpreted as rejecting employer solidarity as a justification for a lockout on the ground that the Union strike constituted a withdrawal by the Union from the multi-employer bargaining unit. The Court of Appeals vigorously argued that a union should be accorded the same freedom of voluntary withdrawal from a multi-employer bargaining unit as the Board has accorded to individual employers. But that question is not presented by this case, and we expressly reserve decision until it is

We cannot subscribe to this interpretation. Multi-employer bargaining long antedated the Wagner Act, both in industries like the garment industry, characterized by numerous employers of small work forces, and in industries like longshoring and building construction, where workers change employers from day to day or week to week. This basis of bargaining has had its greatest expansion since enactment of the Wagner Act because employers have sought through group bargaining to match increased union strength. Approximately four million employees are now governed by collective bargaining agreements signed by unions with thousands of employer associations. At the time of the debates on the Taft-Hartley amendments, proposals were made to limit or outlaw multi-employer bargaining. These proposals failed of enactment. They were met with a storm of protest that their adoption would tend to weaken and not strengthen the process of collective bargaining and would conflict with the national labor policy of promoting industrial peace through effective collective bargaining.

The debates over the proposals demonstrate that Congress refused to interfere with such bargaining because there was cogent evidence that in many industries the multi-employer bargaining basis was a vital factor in the effectuation of the national policy of promoting labor peace through strengthened collective bargaining. The inaction of Congress with respect to multi-employer bargaining cannot be said to indicate an intention to leave the resolution of this problem to future legislation. Rather, the compelling conclusion is that Congress intended "that the Board should continue its established administrative practice of certifying multi-employer units, and intended to leave to the Board's specialized judgment the inevitable questions concerning multi-employer bargaining bound to arise in the future."

Although the Act protects the right of the employees to strike in support of their demands, this protection is not so absolute as to deny self-help by employers when legitimate interests of employees and employers collide. Conflict may arise, for example, between the right to strike and the interest of small employers in preserving multi-employer bargaining as a means of bargaining on an equal basis with a large union and avoiding the competitive disadvantages resulting from nonuniform contractual terms. The ultimate problem is the balancing of the conflicting legitimate interests. The function of striking that balance to effectuate national labor policy is often a difficult and delicate responsibility, which the Congress committed primarily to the National Labor Relations Board, subject to limited judicial review.

The Court of Appeals recognized that the National Labor Relations Board has legitimately balanced conflicting interests by permitting lockouts where economic hardship was shown. The court erred, however, in

---

properly before us. The facts here clearly show that the Union strike was not an attempt to withdraw from the multi-employer bargaining unit. On the contrary, the Union continued to carry on negotiations with the Exchange until an agreement was reached and signed.

too narrowly confining the exercise of Board discretion to the cases of economic hardship. We hold that in the circumstances of this case the Board correctly balanced the conflicting interests in deciding that a temporary lockout to preserve the multi-employer bargaining basis from the disintegration threatened by the Union's strike action was lawful.

Reversed.

NLRB v. BROWN

Supreme Court of the United States, 1965
380 U.S. 278, 85 Sup. Ct. 980, 13 L. Ed. 2d 839

MR. JUSTICE BRENNAN delivered the opinion of the Court.

The respondents, who are members of a multiemployer bargaining group, locked out their members in response to a whipsaw strike against another member of the group. They and the struck employer continued operations with temporary replacements. The National Labor Relations Board found that the struck employer's use of temporary replacements was lawful under Labor Board v. Mackay Radio & Telegraph Co., 304 U.S. 333, but that the respondents had violated §§8(a)(1) and (3) of the National Labor Relations Act by locking out their regular employees and using temporary replacements to carry on business. 137 N.L.R.B. 73. The Court of Appeals for the Tenth Circuit disagreed and refused to enforce the Board's order. 319 F.2d 7. We granted certiori, 375 U.S. 962. We affirm the Court of Appeals.

Five operators of six retail food stores in Carlsbad, New Mexico, make up the employer group. The stores had bargained successfully on a group basis for many years with Local 462 of the Retail Clerks International Association. Negotiations for a new collective agreement to replace the expiring one began in January 1960. Agreement was reached by mid February on all terms except the amount and effective date of a wage increase. Bargaining continued without result, and on March 2 the Local informed the employers that a strike had been authorized. The employers responded that a strike against any member of the employer group would be regarded as a strike against all. On March 16, the union struck Food Jet, Inc., one of the group. The four respondents, operating five stores, immediately locked out all employees represented by the Local, telling them, and the Local, that they would be recalled to work when the strike against Food Jet ended. The stores, including Food Jet, continued to carry on business by using management personnel, relatives of such personnel, and a few temporary employees; all of the temporary replacements were expressly told that the arrangement would be discontinued when the whipsaw strike ended. Bargaining continued until April 22 when an agreement was reached. The employers immediately released the temporary replacements and restored the strikers and locked out employees to their jobs. . . .

The Board's decision does not rest upon independent evidence that the respondents acted either out of hostility toward the Local or in reprisal for the whipsaw strike. It rests upon the Board's appraisal that the respondents' conduct carried its own indicia of unlawful intent, thereby establishing, without more, that the conduct constituted an unfair labor practice. It was disagreement with this appraisal, which we share, that led the Court of Appeals to refuse to enforce the Board's order. . . .

In the circumstances of this case we do not see how the continued operations of respondents and their use of temporary replacements any more implies hostile motivation, nor how it is inherently more destructive of employee rights, than the lockout itself. Rather, the compelling inference is that this was all part and parcel of respondents' defensive measure to preserve the multiemployer group in the face of the whipsaw strike. Since Food Jet legitimately continued business operation, it is only reasonable to regard respondents' action as evincing concern that the integrity of the employer group was threatened unless they also managed to stay open for business during the lockout. For with Food Jet open for business and respondents' stores closed, the prospect that the whipsaw strike would succeed in breaking up the employer association was not at all fanciful. The retail food industry is very competitive and repetitive patronage is highly important. Faced with the prospect of a loss of patronage to Food Jet, it is logical that respondents should have been concerned that one or more of their number might bolt the group and come to terms with the Local, thus destroying the common front essential to multiemployer bargaining. The Court of Appeals correctly pictured the respondents' dilemma in saying, "If . . . the struck employer does choose to operate with replacements and the other employers cannot replace after lockout, the economic advantage passes to the struck member, the nonstruck members are deterred in exercising the defensive lockout, and the whipsaw strike . . . enjoys an almost inescapable prospect of success." 319 F.2d, at 11. Clearly respondents' continued operations with the use of temporary replacements following the lockout was wholly consistent with a legitimate business purpose.

Nor are we persuaded by the Board's argument that justification for the inference of hostile motivation appears in the respondents' use of temporary employees rather than some of the regular employees. It is not commonsense, we think, to say that the regular employees were "willing to work at the employers' terms." 137 N.L.R.B., at 76. It seems probable that this "willingness" was motivated as much by their understandable desire to further the objective of the whipsaw strike — to break through the employers' united front by forcing Food Jet to accept the Local's terms — as it was by a desire to work for the employers under the existing unacceptable terms. As the Board's dissenting members put it, "These employees are willing only to receive wages while their brethren in the rest of the associationwide unit are exerting whipsaw pressure on one employer to gain benefits that will ultimately accrue to all employees in the associationwide unit, including those here locked out." 137 N.L.R.B., at 78. Moreover, the course of action to which the Board would limit the respondents would force them into the position of aiding and abetting the success of the whipsaw strike and consequently would render "largely illusory," 137 N.L.R.B., at 78-79, the right of lockout recognized by Buffalo

Linen; the right would be meaningless if barred to nonstruck stores that find it necessary to operate because the struck store does so.

The Board's finding of a §8(a) (1) violation emphasized the impact of respondents' conduct upon the effectiveness of the whipsaw strike. It is no doubt true that the collective strength of the stores to resist that strike is maintained, and even increased, when all stores stay open with temporary replacements. The pressures on the employees are necessarily greater when none of the union employees is working and the stores remain open. But these pressures are no more than the result of the Local's inability to make effective use of the whipsaw tactic. Moreover, these effects are no different from those that result from the legitimate use of any economic weapon by an employer. Continued operations with the use of temporary replacements may result in the failure of the whipsaw strike, but this does not mean that the employers' conduct is demonstrably so destructive of employee rights or so devoid of significant service to any legitimate business and that it cannot be tolerated consistently with the Act. Certainly then, in the absence of evidentiary findings of hostile motive, there is no support of the conclusion that respondents violated §8(a)(1). . . .

We recognize that, analogous to the determination of unfair practices under §8(a)(1), when an employer practice is inherently destructive of employee rights and is not justified by the service of important business ends, no specific evidence of intent to discourage union membership is necessary to establish a violation of §8(a)(3). This principle, we have said, is "but an application of the common-law rule that a man is held to intend the foreseeable consequences of his conduct." Radio Officers Union v. Labor Board, [347 U.S. 17 (1954)]. . . . But where, as here, the tendency to discourage union membership is comparatively slight, and the employer's conduct is reasonably adapted to achieve legitimate business ends or to deal with business exigencies, we enter into an area where the improper motivation of the employer must be established by independent evidence. . . .

. . . While the use of temporary nonunion personnel in preference to the locked-out union members is discriminatory, we think that any resulting tendency to discourage union membership is comparatively remote, and that this use of temporary personnel constitutes a measure reasonably adapted to the effectuation of a legitimate business. Here discontent on the part of the Local's membership in all likelihood is attributable largely to the fact that the membership was locked out as the result of the Local's whipsaw stratagem. But the lockout itself is concededly within the rule of Buffalo Linen. We think that the added dissatisfaction and resultant pressure on membership attributable to the fact that the nonstruck employers remain in business with temporary replacements is comparatively insubstantial. First, the replacements were expressly used for the duration of the labor dispute only; thus, the displaced employees could not have looked upon the replacements as threatening their jobs. At the most the union would be forced to capitulate and return its members to work on terms which, while not as desirable as hoped for, were still better than under the old contract. Second, the membership, through its control of union policy, could end the dispute and terminate the lockout at any time simply by agreeing to the employers' terms and returning to work on a regular basis. Third, in light of the union-shop provision that has been carried forward into the new contract from the old collective agreement, it would appear that a union member would have nothing to gain, and much to lose, by quitting the union. Under all these circumstances, we cannot say that the employers' conduct had any great tendency to discourage union membership. Not only was the prospect of discouragement of membership comparatively remote, but the respondents' attempt to remain open for business with the help of temporary replacements was a measure reasonably adapted to the achievement of a legitimate end — preserving the integrity of the multi-employer bargain unit. . . .

It is argued, finally, that the Board's decision is within the area of its expert judgment and that, in setting it aside, the Court of Appeals exceeded the authorized scope of judicial review. This proposition rests upon our statement in Buffalo Linen that in reconciling the conflicting interests of labor and management the Board's determination is to be subjected to "limited judicial review." 353 U.S., at 96. When we used the phrase "limited judicial review" we did not mean that the balance struck by the Board is immune from judicial examination and reversal in proper cases. Courts are expressly empowered to enforce, modify or set aside, in whole or in part, the Board's orders, except that the findings of the Board with respect to questions of fact, if supported by substantial evidence on the record considered as a whole shall be conclusive. . . . Reviewing courts are not obliged to stand aside and rubber stamp their affirmance of administrative decisions that may seem inconsistent with a statutory mandate or that frustrate the congressional policy underlying a statute. . . . Of course due deference is to be rendered to agency determinations of fact, so long as there is substantial evidence to be found in the record as a whole. But where, as here, the review is not of a question of fact, but of judgment as to the proper balance to be struck between conflicting interests, "[t]he deference owed to an expert tribunal cannot be allowed to slip into a judicial inertia which results in the unauthorized assumption by an agency of major policy decisions properly made by Congress." American Shipbuilding Corp. v. Labor Board, 380 U.S. 300, 318.

[The judgment of the Court of Appeals is affirmed because the order rested on "an erroneous legal foundation."]

MR. JUSTICE GOLDBERG, whom The Chief Justice joins, concurring. . . .

There would be grave doubts as to whether locking out and hiring permanent replacements is justified by any legitimate interest of the non-struck employers, for Buffalo Linen makes clear that the test in such a situation is not whether parity is achieved between struck and nonstruck employers, but rather, whether the nonstruck employer's actions are necessary to counteract whipsaw effects of the strike and to preserve the employer bargaining unit. Since in this case the nonstruck employers did nothing more than hire temporary replacements, an activity necessary to counter whipsawing by the union and to preserve the bargaining unit, I agree that, applying Buffalo Linen, that the judgment of the Court of Appeals should be affirmed.

MR. JUSTICE WHITE, dissenting.

[The Justice propounds the following questions, answering them in the negative:

Does Buffalo Linen establish an unqualified right of employers in a multiemployer unit to lock out?

Can it be assumed that a struck employer operating with replacements is at the same disadvantage vis-a-vis the nonstruck employers as an employer whose operations are totally shut down by the union?

Is the Board's finding that there was no economic necessity for the nonstruck employers to shut down irrelevant?

Is the disparity between the struck employer who resumes operations and the nonstruck employers who choose to lock out to maintain a united front caused by the whipsawing of the union?

Should the nonstruck employer enjoy an exception to the rule that an employer may not displace union members with nonunion members solely on account of union membership?

Does the process of temporary replacement with nonunion men have only a slight tendency to discourage union membership?]

NOTES

1. Williams, The Labor Dispute Qualification — A Primer and Some Problems, 8 Vand. L. Rev. 338, 365-369 (1955), argues that defining lockout is an impossible task, and advocates as a test which side is seeking to alter the status quo. It should be noted, however, that he is considering a definition which relates to unemployment compensation rights during labor disputes. An exception favorable to compensation when the employer is the aggressor in the dispute, trying "to deprive employees of some advantage they already possess," apparently obtains in Connecticut, California, and Utah, although not applicable in the case of a Buffalo Linen type of lockout in California and Utah. See Segal, Some Comments on Illicit Lockouts, N.Y. U. 16th Annual Conf. on Labor 41, 54-55 (Christensen ed. 1963). A kind of judicial neutrality disdains to enter upon the merits of the dispute. Compare Lewis, The Law of Unemployment Compensation in Labor Disputes, 13 Lab. L.J. 174, 176-178, 179-183 (1962). In what sense, if at all, is NLRA law binding in the administration of a state unemployment compensation statute? Only when that statute makes "lawfulness" of employer or employee conduct relevant to eligibility for benefits? Compare the program for policy reconciliation in a closely related area proposed by Mandelker, Refusals to Work and Union Objectives in the Administration of Taft-Hartley and Unemployment Compensation, 44 Cornell L.Q. 477 (1959).

2. The Board considers that an association is the employer for a multiemployer unit, even though under the association rules any of the mem-

bers at their meeting prior to negotiations may orally indicate whether they wish to be bound, when there has been a substantial history of bargaining on the association basis. Hoisting and Portable Engineers and Cascade Employers Assn., 141 N.L.R.B. 469 (1963). In Great Atlantic and Pacific Tea Co., 145 N.L.R.B. 361 (1963), the Board found it unnecessary to decide whether the union and several employers merely by agreeing to bargain jointly could forthwith establish a unit after a history of single-employer bargaining, since the union had not so agreed. In any event, the employers' agreement among themselves was not sufficient. Compare Arden Farms, 117 N.L.R.B. 318 (1957), granting a single-employer unit in the absence of multi-employer bargaining history on the ground that such units are presumptively appropriate, though the employers and one of the two unions claiming representative status favored the multi-employer unit. Can a labor organization, under these rules, prevent the establishment of multi-employer bargaining?

The next year after Arden Farms, the Board took up the question of conversion from multi-employer to single-employer bargaining:

"We would [because of the importance of timing] refuse to permit the withdrawal of an employer or a union from a duly established multi-employer bargaining unit, except upon adequate written notice given prior to the date set by the contract for modification, or to the agreed upon date to begin the multi-employer negotiations. Where actual bargaining negotiations based upon the existing multi-employer unit have begun, we would not permit, except on mutual consent, an abandonment of the unit . . . absent unusual circumstaces." Retail Associates, Inc., 120 N.L.R.B. 388, 395 (1958).

In Morand Bros. Beverage Co. v. NLRB, 190 F.2d 576 (7th Cir. 1951), the group history was that of annual negotiations between representatives of employer associations and representatives of the union, with submission to the membership on both sides for ratification, and separate but identical documents for the union and each association member. The Board, having found that either single-employer units or an association-wide unit was appropriate, found violations based upon an association-wide lockout that followed a bargaining strike against one of the members. The Court of Appeals, addressing the issue whether the union was engaged in protected activity, found substantial evidence to support the finding that the motive in striking one member was, and was understood to be, economic, i.e., to obtain a contract, not to force the company to select a different bargaining representative. The opinion of the court (pp. 581-582) states:

"With respect to the Union's submission of its proposed contract to the individual petitioners, after negotiations with the Associations' Labor Committees had been stalemated, we believe that, in view of the fact that past contracts, although negotiated by the Associations, had been signed by petitioners individually and the fact that petitioner was free at any time to withdraw from the association to which it belonged and bargain on its own behalf (see Section 8(b)(4)(A) of the Act, this cannot be said to have been an unfair labor practice. Certainly, the fact that identical contracts were sent to the entire membership of the Associations, though perhaps indicative of a Union belief that the Associations' members might be less adamant than their Labor Committees had been, is hardly consistent with a refusal, on the part of the Union, to continue bargaining on an association-wide basis. [Nor is the union's continuing to meet with the associations' representatives after initiating its appeal to individual members.] Consequently, although we do not indorse the Board's reasoning to the effect that, once negotiations have been stalemated, a union may utterly disregard the employer unit with which it has theretofore bargained and proceed to fashion a new unit for bargaining purposes, we do approve its conclusion that the Union here did not violate Sections 8(b)(1)(B) or 8(b)(3) of the Act."

In Ice Cream Drivers Local 717 and Ice Cream Council, Inc., 145 N.L.R.B. 865 (1964), the Board found that the purpose of a series of strikes was to force the remaining members of an association (the others having voluntarily withdrawn from multi-employer bargaining) to revoke their selection of the Council as their representative, and that the union thereby violated Section 8(b)(1)(B).

3. The Board has found the cooperation of employers to resist work stoppages in support of grievances covered by arbitration also to be of concern to the unit as a whole. The stoppages were not authorized by the responsible unions, but the Board intimated that it was not impressed by their vigor in resisting them. The employer group, represented by the Publishers' Association of New York City, threatened shutdown of all members and in two instances actually carried it out, but the suspension was so effective in terminating the stoppage that there were no lost wages and no employee was told to leave the premises. The Court of Appeals affirmed dismissal of the complaint against the employers. New York Mailers Union v. NLRB, 327 F.2d 292 (2d. Cir. 1964).

4. On the lockout as the reciprocal to the strike see American Ship Building Co. v. NLRB infra, p. 413.

B. Employer Conduct Affecting the Establishment of Collective Bargaining

1. *Domination and Assistance*

PROBLEM ON EMPLOYEE REPRESENTATION

James N. Thusiast, a vice-president of the Cabot Carbon Company, has sent a letter to Harold L. Blair, which says in part: "[I]t is a little-known fact that the success of our 'employee committees' in our Southwestern Division went a long way towards relieving the embarrassment of the planners at the War Production Board in Washington, who, apparently unconscious of the relationship between tire production and carbon black, had neglected to include us in their systems of priorities. For a while there, tires in the ETO were so short that we were actually carrying on our processes in French plants. But that's another story. Our Reno Stinson, Director of Industrial Relations for our Southwestern Division, when Washington discovered us became Chairman of the WPB Committee representing the carbon-black industry. They were setting up these labor-management committees that both we and our union people were watching with fingers crossed.

"At one extreme were the employees, fortunately few in our organization, who regard the employer as the traditional enemy, more than capable of taking care of himself, and who consider any idea of aid to the enemy ridiculous. They would look upon this scheme as merely a disguised company union. Some of our people thought these committees were a reflection upon their administrative and executive ability, and at best that labor was not capable of making a worthwhile contribution in the managerial field. Anyway, we went ahead, electing employee representatives from each plant in the division, Stinson drafted by-laws for employee committees to be established at each of the plants, employees and management approved the by-laws and a copy of them went to WPB. Stinson testified at a Labor Board hearing that he considered himself a WPB representative in providing the leadership for working out these plans.

"Many of the wartime committees were organized simply as a gesture of complying with the WPB request. Some, like ours, though, were so beneficial that they remained as an apparently permanent feature of the productive machine.

"Our thinking on the general policies that could be considered keys to successful operation can be stated under eight heads. They are that labor and management will work together to improve production; that the work of the job production committee shall neither duplicate, conflict with nor replace recognized procedures for grievance-handling and other collective-bargaining matters; that the activities of the production committee shall be of mutual benefit to management and labor and not further the special interests of either group; that neither management nor labor shall sustain losses as a result of the work of the committee; that management representatives will be given sufficient authority to secure prompt decisions on committee recommendations; that labor representatives will be comparable in number with the management representatives and will have sufficient prestige and authority to secure full cooperation of the workers on committee programs; that labor and management shall each choose its own representatives, and if there is a recognized collective-bargaining agent, it shall name the labor representatives; and that the scope of the committee's work and the authority delegated to it will be clearly defined, provision being made for adjustments as new problems arise. We gave our committees consideration of safety, increased efficiency of production, conservation of supplies, materials, and equipment, encouragement of ingenuity and initiative, and at non-union plants or departments handling the grievances of employees. Bond drives, housing, and transportation (car-pooling, in view of gasoline and tire rationing) were discontinued with the end of the war.

"With us, the system was not as permanent as it seemed. We had to discontinue it as a result of charges filed in November 1954 by the Chemical Workers Union. Purely, I may add, for the sake of a bargaining advantage, which did not as it finally worked out help them a bit. It hurt us, though; when we had to give up our committees we lost a part of the program for employees that had proved workable and mutually beneficial both in our unionized and in our non-union plants in the Southwestern Division. It was conceded all around, as it had to be, that our policy is not anti-union and never has been, and grievance handling was entrusted to the committees only at the unorganized plants. Although the Court of Appeals accepted, the Supreme Court rejected our argument that the proviso to Section 9(a) was ample authority for our program. I believe the Supreme Court referred to a passage in the legislative history declaring that the conference agreement made no change in the definition of labor organization from what was in the Wagner Act. It also placed emphasis upon the rejection of Section 8(d)(3) in the Hartley Bill as it came from the House, which we argued was superfluous in light of the language of Section 9(a) as the measure was finally enacted. . . .

"The new system I would like to set up would depend upon the cooperation of the union in organized plants. It would not handle any grievances in any plant, and would be responsible only for the development of ideas and programs to improve efficiency and eliminate waste. In organized plants the union would nominate six candidates, of which three could be elected, and in unorganized plants the employees would choose three representatives by any orderly process they might wish. Management representatives would be strictly enjoined never to negotiate with, promise, or make commitments to employee members, or do other than explore and investigate ideas and report back to top management. . . .

"No elections would be held in plants where a majority of employees were opposed to the plan. In organized plants the union, of course, would speak for the employees. . . .

"So if there are any legal pitfalls in the direction of our thinking, I would like to be advised when I see you next month. . . ."

What advice should Blair offer? The Carbon Company case, NLRB v. Cabot Carbon Co., is reported at 360 U.S. 203 (1959), and includes these passages from pp. 212-214:

"The Court of Appeals was therefore in error in holding that company-dominated employee Committees . . . are not 'labor organizations' . . . simply because they do not 'bargain with' employers in 'the usual concept of collective bargaining.' [In 1935 a proposal to substitute "bargaining collectively" for "dealing" was not adopted. It is plain from the bylaws of the committees that at nonunion plants they handled employee grievances.] This alone brings those Committees squarely within the statutory definition of 'labor organizations.'

"Moreover, although none of the Employee Committees attempted to negotiate any formal bargaining contract [they nevertheless] made proposals and requests respecting such matters as seniority, job classification, job bidding, working schedules, holidays, vacations, sick leave, a merit system, wage corrections, and improvement of working facilities and conditions. [Also, with the central committee, composed of chairmen of the plant committees, the industrial relations director conducted negotiations on a wide range of issues. That is, he discussed with them their proposals, granting some and rejecting others.]"

INTERNATIONAL LADIES' GARMENT WORKERS' UNION v. NLRB

Supreme Court of the United States, 1961
366 U.S. 731, 81 Sup. Ct. 1603, 6 L. Ed. 2d 762

MR. JUSTICE CLARK delivered the opinion of the Court. . . .

In October 1956 the petitioner union initiated an organizational campaign at Bernhard-Altmann Texas Corporation's knitwear manufacturing plant in San Antonio, Texas. No other labor organization was similarly engaged at that time. During the course of that campaign, on July 29, 1957, certain of the company's Topping Department employees went on strike in protest against a wage reduction. That dispute was in no way related to the union campaign, however, and the organizational efforts were continued during the strike. Some of the striking employees had signed authorization cards solicited by the union during its drive, and, while the strike was in progress, the union entered upon a course of negotiations with the employer. As a result of those negotiations, held in New York City where the home offices of both were located, on August 30, 1957, the employer and union signed a "memorandum of understanding." In that memorandum the company recognized the union as exclusive bargaining representative of "all production and shipping employees." The union representative asserted that the union's comparison of the employee authorization cards in its possession with the number of eligible employees representatives of the company furnished it indicated that the union had in fact secured such cards from a majority of employees in the unit. Neither employer nor union made any effort at that time to check the cards in the union's possession against the employee roll, or otherwise, to ascertain with any degree of certainty that the union's assertion, later found by the Board to be erroneous, was founded on fact rather than upon good-faith assumption. The agreement, containing no union security provisions, called for the ending of the strike and for certain improved wages and conditions of employment. It also provided that a "formal agreement containing these terms" would "be promptly drafted . . . and signed by both parties within the next two weeks."

Thereafter, on October 10, 1957, a formal collective bargaining agreement, embodying the terms of the August 30 memorandum, was signed by the parties. The bargaining unit description set out in the formal contract, although more specific, conformed to that contained in the prior memorandum. It is not disputed that as of execution of the formal contract the union in fact represented a clear majority of employees in the appropriate unit. In upholding the complaints filed against the employer and union by the General Counsel, the Board decided that the employer's good-faith belief that the union in fact represented a majority of employees in the unit on the critical date of the memorandum of understanding was not a defense, "particularly where, as here, the Company made no effort to check the authorization cards against its payroll records." 122 N.L.R.B. 1289, 1292. Noting that the union was "actively seeking recognition at the time such recognition was granted," and that "the Union was [not] the passive recipient of an unsolicited gift bestowed by the Company," the Board found that the union's execution of the August 30 agreement was a "direct deprivation" of the nonconsenting majority employees' organizational and bargaining rights. At pp. 1292, 1293, note 9. Accordingly, the Board ordered the employer to withhold all recognition from the union and to cease giving effect to agreements entered into with the union; the union was ordered to cease acting as bargaining representative of any of the employees until such time as a Board-conducted election demonstrated its majority status, and to refrain from seeking to enforce the agreements previously entered.

The Court of Appeals . . . distinguished our decision in Labor Board v. Drivers Local Union No. 639, 362 U.S. 274, on the ground that there was involved here neither recognitional nor organizational picketing. The court held that the bona fides of the parties was irrelevant except to the extent that it "was arrived at through an adequate effort to determine the true facts of the situation." [280 F.2d] at p. 622.

At the outset, we reject as without relevance to our decision the fact that, as of the execution date of the formal agreement on October 10, petitioner represented a majority of the employees. As the Court of Appeals indicated, the recognition of the minority union on August 30, 1957, was "a fait accompli depriving the majority of the employees of their guaranteed right to choose their own representative." 280 F.2d, at 621. It is, therefore, of no consequence that petitioner may have acquired by October 10 the necessary majority if, during the interim, it was acting unlawfully. Indeed, such acquisition of majority status itself might indicate that the recognition secured by the August 30 agreement afforded petitioner a deceptive cloak of authority with which to persuasively elicit additional employee support.

Nor does this case directly involve a strike. The strike which occurred was in protest against a wage reduction and had nothing to do with petitioner's quest for recognition. Likewise, no question of picketing is presented. Lastly, the violation which the Board found was the grant by the employer of exclusive representation status to a minority union as distinguished from an employer's bargaining with a minority union for its members only. Therefore, the exclusive representation provision is the vice in the agreement, and discussion of "collective bargaining," as distinguished from "exclusive recognition," is pointless. Moreover, the insistence that we hold the agreement valid and enforceable as to those employees who consented to it must be rejected. On the facts shown, the agreement must fail in its entirety. It was obtained under the erroneous claim of majority representation. Perhaps the employer would not have entered into it if he had known the facts. Quite apart from other conceivable situations, the unlawful genesis of this agreement precludes its partial validity.

In their selection of a bargaining representative, §9(a) of the Wagner Act guarantees employees freedom of choice and majority rule. . . . Bernhard-Altmann granted exclusive bargaining status to an agency selected by a minority of its employees, thereby impressing that agent upon the nonconsenting majority. There could be no clearer abridgment of §7 of the Act, assuring employees the right "to bargain collectively through representatives of their own choosing" or "to refrain from" such activity. It follows, without need of further demonstration, that the employer activity found present here violated §8(a)(1) of the Act which prohibits employer interference with, and restraint of, employee exercise of §7 rights. Section 8(a)(2) of the Act makes it an unfair labor practice for an employer to "contribute . . . support" to a labor organization. The law has long been settled that a grant of exclusive recognition to a minority union constitutes unlawful support in violation of that section, because the union so favored is given "a marked advantage over any other in securing the adherence of employees," Labor Board v. Pennsylvania Greyhound Lines, 303 U.S. 261, 267. In the Taft-Hartley Law, Congress added §8(b)(1)(A) to the Wagner Act, prohibiting, as the Court of Appeals held, "unions from invading the rights of employees under §7 in a fashion comparable to the activities of employers prohibited under §8(a)(1)." 280 F.2d, at 620. It was the intent of Congress to impose upon unions the same restrictions which the Wagner Act imposed on employers with respect to violations of employee rights.

The petitioner, while taking no issue with the fact of its minority status on the critical date, maintains that both Bernhard-Altmann's and its own good-faith beliefs in petitioner's majority status are a complete defense. . . . We find nothing in the statutory language prescribing scienter as an element of the unfair labor practices here involved. The act made unlawful by §8(a)(2) is employer support of a minority union. Here that support is an accomplished fact. More need not be shown, for, even if mistakenly, the employees' rights have been invaded. It follows that prohibited conduct cannot be excused by a showing of good faith.

This conclusion, while giving the employee only the protection assured him by the Act, places no particular hardship on the employer or the union. It merely requires that recognition be withheld until the Board-conducted election results in majority selection of a representative. The Board's order here, as we might infer from the employer's failure to resist its enforcement, would apparently result in similarly slight hardship upon it. We do not share petitioner's apprehension that holding such conduct unlawful will somehow induce a breakdown, or seriously impede the progress of collective bargaining. If an employer takes reasonable steps to verify union claims, themselves advanced only after careful estimate — precisely what Bernhard-Altmann and petitioner failed to do here — he can readily ascertain their validity and obviate a Board election. We fail to see any onerous burden involved in requiring responsible negotiators to be careful, by cross-checking, for example, well-analyzed employer records with union listings or authorization cards. Individual and collective employee rights may not be trampled upon merely because it is inconvenient to avoid doing so. Moreover, no penalty is attached to the violation. Assuming that an employer in good faith accepts or rejects a union claim of majority status, the validity of his decision may be tested in an unfair labor practice proceeding. If he is found to have erred in extending or withholding recognition, he is subject only to a remedial order requiring him to conform his conduct to the norms set out in the Act, as was the case here. No further penalty results. We believe the Board's remedial order is the proper one in such cases. Labor Board v. District 50, U.M.W., 355 U.S. 453.

Affirmed.

MR. JUSTICE DOUGLAS, with whom MR. JUSTICE BLACK concurs, dissenting in part.

I agree that, under the statutory scheme, a minority union does not have the standing to bargain for all employees. That principle of representative government extends only to the majority. But where there is no majority union, I see no reason why the minority union should be disabled from bargaining for the minority of the members who have joined it. Yet the order of the Board, now approved, enjoins petitioner union from acting as the exclusive bargaining representative "of any of the employees," and it enjoins the employer from recognizing the union as the representative of "any of its employees."

We have indicated over and again that, absent an exclusive agency for bargaining created by a majority of workers, a minority union has standing to bargain for its members. . . .

. . . In Edison Co. v. Labor Board, 305 U.S. 197, a union, the Brotherhood of Electrical Workers, was allowed to act as a bargaining representative for the employees who were its members, even though they were a minority. The Court said, ". . . in the absence of such an exclusive agency the employees represented by the Brotherhood, even if they were a minority, clearly had the right to make their own choice." Id., 237. Maintenance of the status of a minority union, until an election was held, might well serve the purpose of protecting commerce "from interruptions and obstructions caused by industrial strife." Id., 237. A decree requiring the employer to cease recognizing the Brotherhood as the exclusive representative of its members was modified:

"The contracts do not claim for the Brotherhood exclusive representation of the companies' employees but only representation of those who are its members, and the continued operation of the contracts is necessarily subject to the provision of the law by which representatives of the employees for the purpose of collective bargaining can be ascertained in case any question of 'representation' should arise. We construe [the order] as having no more effect than to provide that there shall be no interference with an exclusive bargaining agency if one other than the [union] should be established in accordance with . . . the Act." Id., 239.

It was in that tradition that we recently sustained the right of a minority union to picket peacefully to compel recognition. Labor Board v. Drivers Local Union, 362 U.S. 274. There a minority union sought to compel exclusive representation rights. To be sure, this Court recognized in that case that "tension exists between . . . [the] right to form, join or assist labor organizations and [the] right to refrain from doing so." Id., 280.   But when a minority union seeks only to represent its own, what provision of the Act deprives it of its right to represent them, where a majority have not selected another union to represent them? . . .

Honoring a minority union — where no majority union exists or even where the activities of the minority union do not collide with a bargaining agreement — is being respectful of history.   Long before the Wagner Act, employers and employees had the right to discuss their problems.   In the early days the unions were representatives of a minority of workers. The aim — at least the hope — of the legislation was that majority unions would emerge and provide stabilizing influences.   Yet I have found nothing in the history of the successive measures, starting with the Wagner Act, that indicates any purpose on the part of Congress to deny a minority union the right to bargain for its members when a majority have not in fact chosen a bargaining representative.

I think the Court is correct insofar as it sets aside the exclusive recognition clause in the contract.   I think it is incorrect in setting aside the entire contract.   First, that agreement secured valuable benefits for the union's members regarding wages and hours, work standards and distribution, discharge and discipline, holidays, vacations, health and welfare fund, and other matters.   Since there was no duly selected representative for all the employees authorized in accordance with the Act, it certainly was the right of the employee union members to designate the union or any other appropriate person to make this contract they desired.   To hold the contract void as to the union's voluntary members seems to me to go beyond the competency of the Board under the Act and to be unsupported by any principle of contract law.   Certainly there is no principle of justice or fairness with which I am familiar that requires these employees to be stripped of the benefits they acquired by the good-faith bargaining of their designated agent.   Such a deprivation gives no protection to the majority who were not members of the union and arbitrarily takes from the union members their contract rights.

Second, the result of today's decision is to enjoin the employer from dealing with the union as the representative of its own members in any manner, whether in relation to grievances or otherwise, until it is certified as a majority union.   A case for complete disestablishment of the union cannot be sustained under our decisions.   While the power of the Board is broad, it is "not limitless."   Labor Board v. Mine Workers, 355 U.S. 453, 458.   Thus a distinction has been taken between remedies in situations where a union has been dominated by the employer and where unions have been assisted but not dominated.   Id., 458-459.

The present case is unique.   The findings are that both the employer and the union were in "good faith" in believing that the union represented a majority of the workers.   Good-faith violations of the Act are nonetheless violations; and the present violation warrants disestablishment of the union as a majority representative.   But this good-faith mistake hardly warrants full and complete disestablishment, heretofore reserved for flagrant violations of the Act. Its application here smacks more of a penalty than of a remedial measure.

I think this union is entitled to speak for its members until another union is certified as occupying the bargaining field. That is its common-law right in no way diluted or impaired by the Act.

NOTES

1. What remedy would they approve? An extreme sanction, "disestablishment," renders an organization permanently ineligible for recognition on motion of the employer or for a place on the ballot, regardless of majority status and complete emancipation from the employer. Before 1947 an organization not affiliated with the AFL or the CIO was invariably disestablished, while an affiliated union would merely be disqualified until it might be certified by the Board. In Carpenter Steel Co., 76 N.L.R.B. 670 (1948), the Board announced its new policy to apply the same standards to affiliated and independent unions, and in any case where "an employer's unfair labor practices were limited to interference and support and never reached the point of dominating" to eschew disestablishment and order only "that recognition be withheld until certification." Disestablishment, according to Board theory, includes reimbursement by the employer of dues and other exactions under illegal arrangements to which the employer is a party, regardless of individual coercion of employees. See NLRB, 27th Ann. Rep. 105-106 (1963). In a rival-union situation, appropriate relief may include a direction to bargain with the disfavored union, if its majority status was subverted by the unfair labor practice. International Assn. of Machinists v. NLRB, 311 U.S. 72 (1940).

2. The Hartley Bill proposed a Section 8(d)(3), which did not win favorable action in the Senate, specifying that it would not be an unfair practice for the employer to form or maintain "a committee of employees and [to discuss] with it matters of mutual interest, including grievances, wages, hours of employment, and other working conditions, if the Board has not certified or the employer has not recognized" a Section 9 representative.

In Golden State Bottling Co., 147 N.L.R.B. No. 47 (1964), where the employer forced the employees to elect new union officers to sign a contract in accordance with the employer's offer, a Board panel rejected the trial examiner's conclusion of domination, finding only interference.

The court rejected the Board's conclusion of domination in NLRB v. Prince Macaroni Manufacturing Co., 329 F.2d 803 (1st Cir. 1964), criticizing it for using purely objective standards and pointing out that there was no evidence tending to show that the Employees' Committee, initially formed at the company president's suggestion as a means of settling a strike in 1941, had not been an effective organ for advancing the interests of the employees, or that they were not satisfied with its performance. It agreed, however, that it was unlawful for the employer to organize and supervise the elections of committee members, although there was nothing to show that they were not conducted fairly. On the other hand, domination is not established by the fact of meetings on company property and time without deduction from pay, or company publication of the minutes instead of the execution of written agreements, or the committee's lack of a source of revenue.

3. Chicago Rawhide Manufacturing Co. v. NLRB, 221 F.2d 165, 167 (7th Cir. 1955):

" 'Support' is proscribed because, as a practical matter, it cannot be separated from influence. A line must be drawn, however, between support and cooperation. Support, even though innocent, can be identified because it constitutes at least some degree of control or influence. Cooperation only assists the employees or their bargaining representative in carrying out their independent intention. If this line between cooperation and support is not recognized, the employer's fear of accusations of domination may defeat the principal purpose of the Act, which is cooperation between management and labor."

The Board dismissed Section 8(a)(2) allegations showing that the employer met a group of strikers and discussed their grievances and the possible formation of a committee, but made no concessions, promises, or threats, and did not treat with the group as a representative. Burrell Metal Products Corp., 134 N.L.R.B. 921 (1961).

4. Lodge 916 of the International Association of Machinists, AFL-CIO, won bargaining rights at the Texas Bolt Company and concluded an agreement effective from September, 1959, to March 31, 1960. When this agreement expired, negotiations broke down, and the Machinists became inactive. About a year later District 37 of the United Steelworkers of America began an organizing campaign. Shortly after the drive began three employees took legal-sized yellow sheets, headed "Names of Men who are interesting [*sic*] in Joining Texas Bolt Local Union," around the plant for signatures. This activity took place during working hours and yielded enough signatures to warrant consulting a lawyer, on whose advice the name "Independent Steel Workers Union" was adopted and a petition for NLRB election filed. The plant manager answered an inquiry to the effect that personally he thought the Independent Union was a good idea, and the plant superintendent, also in response to an inquiry, said the Independent Union would be better than having an outside union come in and the president of the company would probably go along with it more than he would with an outside union. On hotly contested but substantial evidence the trial examiner recommended and the Board adopted a finding that the three employees were supervisors, and the Independent was found to be dominated. The court enforced disestablishment. Texas Bolt Co., 135 N.L.R.B. 1188 (1962), 313 F.2d 761 (5th Cir. 1963).

5. Assistance in the form of entering into a contract with one of several rival unions, including the incumbent, may constitute an unfair labor practice under the Board's Mid-West Piping doctrine. 63 N.L.R.B. 1060 (1945). The principle stated is that it is an unfair labor practice to extend recognition when a "real question concerning representation" exists, since when rival claims are being made there is a high risk that employees

will sign cards for more than one union, and the formal election process is more reliable than the employer's determination. The Board requires that a real question exist, but may find it though no petition had been filed. Novak Logging Co., 119 N.L.R.B. 1573 (1958). Some courts of appeal, however, are inclined to stress the employer's good faith, or due diligence to ascertain the majority status, rather than the mere existence of the question concerning representation. See, for example, Iowa Beef Packers v. NLRB, 331 F.2d 176 (8th Cir. 1964), and cases cited at 182. Does the principal case foreclose this emphasis? Apparently the Fifth Circuit, for example, regards the principal case as relevant to the rival-union situation. NLRB v. Signal Oil & Gas Co., 303 F.2d 785 (5th Cir. 1962). For an attack on the premise that recognition is necessarily coercive, see Getman, The Midwest Piping Doctrine: An Example of the Need for Reappraisal of Labor Board Dogma, 31 U. Chi. L. Rev. 292 (1964).

6. Note the special disabilities incurred by a violation of Section 8(a)(2), under Sections 8(b)(7) and 10(1), added in 1959.

7. The Board applies Mid-West Piping to the construction industry under the parenthetical exception for assisted unions in Section 8(f). Oilfield Maintenance Co., 142 N.L.R.B. 1384 (1963).

8. To what extent will the employer be held responsible for the conduct of (a) supervisors and (b) others? Under the Wagner Act it was held that instead of a strict application of respondeat superior the Board must take into account whether employees would have just cause to believe agents professing to serve a union were acting for management, and that the Act enunciates a clear legislative policy to free the bargaining process from all taint of employer influence. International Assn. of Machinists v. NLRB, 311 U.S. 72 (1940). The Taft-Hartley Act substituted in Section 2(2) for "acting in the interest of the employer" the phrase "acting as an agent of an employer," and added Section 2(13). (Contrast Norris-La Guardia Act §6.) The purpose of Section 2(13), as stated in H.R. Rep. No. 510, 80th Cong., 1st Sess. 36 (1947), was to make employers and labor organizations alike subject to "the ordinary common law rules of agency."

The apparent authority of a supervisor may be sufficient to cover threats in contravention of his instructions, rendering the employer liable. Aladdin Industries, 147 N.L.R.B. No. 167 (1964). Subsequent general expressions of employer neutrality, albeit from superior officers, do not cancel out prior threats of supervisors. Green Fire Brick Co. v. NLRB, 326 F.2d 910 (8th Cir. 1964). One court has observed that strict principles of agency do not apply to activities within a union by supervisors. Local 636, Plumbers v. NLRB, 287 F.2d 354 (D.C. Cir. 1961).

Section 201(b) of LMRDA imposes reporting requirements upon "every person who pursuant to any agreement or arrangement with an employer undertakes" certain activities having an object in connection with rights under NLRA §7. Supervisors, regular officers, and employees are as such exempt from this requirement, but an employer may be held responsible for the conduct of nonemployees as well as nonsupervisory employees under NLRA §8. In Austin Concrete Works, 132 N.L.R.B. 184 (1961), the employee's activities for which the employer was held responsible were compensated on a per diem basis. He was not a supervisor, but his per diem pay was to aid the campaign against the union.

On the other hand, although a nonsupervisory employee was charged with reporting on the moral character of job applicants and on employees who stayed too long in the restroom, her coercive speech was not to be imputed to the employer, in the absence of evidence showing that she was regarded as a management spokesman, or that the speech was authorized or ratified by the employer. Cabinets, Inc., 130 N.L.R.B. 1378 (1961). But an employee does not have to be at the supervisory level to reflect the attitude of management. A plant floorlady without authority to hire and fire may have duties that are such as to justify that inference. NLRB v. Des Moines Foods, Inc., 296 F.2d 285 (8th Cir. 1961).

When the municipal police chief and assistant plant superintendent went to the house of an employee and the chief promised $50, payment of hospital bills, and exemption from arrest to "whip" the union's representative, the employer was held responsible for the subsequent severe beating, although the superintendent remained silent throughout the occurrence. NLRB v. Dorsey Trailers, 179 F.2d 589 (5th Cir. 1950). A newspaper not otherwise related to the employer nevertheless caused the employer to be found guilty of interference by an editorial containing threats, where the employer had copies mailed to employees. NLRB v. Bibb Manufacturing Co., 188 F.2d 825 (5th Cir. 1951). But it has been held that although an employer is party to an exclusive hiring-hall agreement responsibility for unlawful discrimination in its administration by the union is not extended to the employer, absent notice or probable cause for employer inquiry into the nature of the difficulty in which the job applicant is involved. Lummus Co. v. NLRB, 339 F.2d 728 (D.C. Cir. 1964).

2. Plant Rules and Discipline

ENDERBY PROBLEM 3

(See page 203 supra for Enderby Problem 2)

Prior to the NLRB election, the following additional events occurred:

On December 20, White called employee Robert Endicott, President of Enderby Employees Association, to his office and questioned him closely about the strength of Local 417 in the Miscellaneous Division. Endicott was somewhat evasive but professed not to be worried over the outcome of the election. White then impressed on Endicott that a victory by Curme's union and subsequent push for higher wages would require the company to increase radically the amount of mechanization in the Plastics Department. He closed the interview by remarking that he was relying on Endicott's "often demonstrated common sense and concern for the welfare of his fellow employees." About a week later several strangers were brought into the Plastics Department by the superintendent and for several days made an obviously careful study of various operations. Then on January 12, White posted the following notice: "To all our employees. The company does not contemplate at this time any substantial change in production processes."

For a number of years the Enderby Company has had a rule prohibiting the distribution of any literature in any place on company property on the ground that it constitutes a littering nuisance and a fire hazard. Prior to the beginning of the morning shift on January 15, O'Doul discovered Jones (the employee who survived the earlier altercation with O'Doul) placing a union membership card on each working place in the Statistical Department. There were no other employees present. O'Doul promptly collected the cards and told Jones to report to the main office. Jones protested that it was a well-known fact that Endicott had been allowed to distribute literature on behalf of the Enderby Employees Association. A heated argument ensued during which Jones referred to O'Doul as "an Irish slave trader." Jones was subsequently discharged for repeated insubordination.

The following day each employee received a personal letter from White. This communication reviewed the progress which the particular employee had made with the company, compared the Enderby wage structure with those of competitors, and claimed that in the few instances where the Rubber Workers union had succeeded in establishing somewhat higher rates the improvement had been accompanied by the substitution of machinery for employees. White finally requested that the employee think carefully before he was "lured into voting to prefer machines to people."

January 27, White addressed an assembly of the employees during the morning shift. In this speech White reiterated the theme of his earlier letters. He concluded his talk by stating that top management was particularly anxious that he make two things clear. First, whatever the outcome of the election, the company would, as usual, put into effect the selective merit increases which it customarily gave on February 15. Secondly, the company would always be prepared to "cope with the irresponsibility of a strike, or for that matter, any scatterbrained union mismanagement."

Layton then went to White and accused him of making a speech which "doctored up phony statistics furnished by the company's master, the Midwestern Rubber Manufacturers Association." He demanded an opportunity to address the employees in reply on company time and property. White refused, suggesting that the company was "not in the business of financing debates and that Layton should use the free platform at the union hall."

Several days later the election was held as scheduled and both the United Rubber Workers and the Enderby Employees Association were defeated.

In addition to the materials in this subsection, refer also to subsection 3, Persuasion, infra page 242, and Enderby Problem 1, supra page 139.

EDWARD G. BUDD MANUFACTURING CO. v. NLRB
United States Court of Appeals, Third Circuit, 1943
138 F.2d 86

BIGGS, Circuit Judge. . . .

The complaint, as subsequently amended, alleges that the petitioner, in September, 1933, created and foisted a labor organization, known as the Budd Employee Representation Association, upon its employees and thereafter contributed financial support to the Association, and dominated its activities. The amended complaint also alleges that in July, 1941, the petitioner discharged an employee, Walter Weigand, because of his activities on behalf of the union . . .

The case of Walter Weigand is extraordinary. If ever a workman deserved summary discharge it was he. He was under the influence of liquor while on duty. He came to work when he chose and he left the plant and his shift as he pleased. In fact, a foreman on one occasion was agreeably surprised to find Weigand at work and commented upon it. Weigand amiably stated that he was enjoying it. He brought a woman (apparently generally known as the "Duchess") to the rear of the plant yard and introduced some of the employees to her. He took another employee to visit her and when this man got too drunk to be able to go home, punched his time-card for him and put him on the table in the representatives' meeting room in the plant in order to sleep off his intoxication. Weigand's immediate superiors demanded again and again that he be discharged, but each time higher officials intervened on Weigand's behalf because as was naïvely stated he was "a representative" (of the Association, found to be a dominated union). In return for not working at the job for which he was hired, the petitioner gave him full pay and on five separate occasions raised his wages. One of these raises was general; that is to say, Weigand profited by a general wage increase throughout the plant, but the other four raises were given Weigand at times when other employees in the plant did not receive wage increases.

The petitioner contends that Weigand was discharged because of cumulative grievances against him. But about the time of the discharge it was suspected by some of the representatives that Weigand had joined the complaining CIO union. One of the representatives taxed him with this fact and Weigand offered to bet a hundred dollars that it could not be proved. On July 22, 1941, Weigand did disclose his union membership to the vice-chairman (Rattigan) of the Association and to another representative (Mullen) and apparently tried to persuade them to support the union. Weigand asserts that the next day he, with Rattigan and Mullen, were seen talking to CIO organizer Reichwein on a street corner. The following day, according to Weigand's testimony, Mullen came to Weigand at the plant and stated that he, Mullen, had just had an interview with Personnel Director McIlvain and Plant Manager Mahan. According to Weigand, Mullen said to him, "Maybe you didn't get me in a jam."

And, "We were seen down there." The following day Weigand was discharged.

As this court stated in National Labor Relations Board v. Condenser Corp., . . . 3 Cir., 128 F.2d at page 75, an employer may discharge an employee for a good reason, a poor reason or no reason at all so long as the provisions of the National Labor Relations Act are not violated. It is, of course, a violation to discharge an employee because he has engaged in activities on behalf of a union. Conversely an employer may retain an employee for a good reason, a bad reason or no reason at all and the reason is not a concern of the Board. But it is certainly too great a strain on our credulity to assert, as does the petitioner, that Weigand was discharged for an accumulation of offenses. We think that he was discharged because his work on behalf of the CIO had become known to the plant manager. That ended his sinecure at the Budd plant. The Board found that he was discharged because of his activities on behalf of the union. The record shows that the Board's finding was based on sufficient evidence. . . .

NOTES

1. The Fifth Circuit, in NLRB v. Tex-O-Kan Flour Mills Co., 122 F.2d 433, 438 (1941), said that a cease and desist order generally "costs no money and only warns to observe a right which already existed; evidence *short of demonstration* may easily justify such an order." (Emphasis supplied.) What then of an order requiring payment of money, reinstatement on the job, or some other affirmative act? In NLRB v. Walton Manufacturing Co., 369 U.S. 404 (1962), the Court remanded a case to the Fifth Circuit because of doubt whether a special rule had been applied in deciding if there was sufficient evidence to support an order of reinstatement with back pay, holding that the Tex-O-Kan distinction is erroneous under Universal Camera Corp. v. NLRB (see page 186 supra).

Justices Frankfurter and Harlan, dissenting, did not agree that the court below was applying a more stringent rule for reinstatement cases, and argued for the Fifth Circuit's evidentiary practice, applicable to any trier of fact, to accept plausible, uncontradicted, unimpeached testimony. Apparently the principle is that when the proponent (here, General Counsel) has no substantial evidence to the contrary, such testimony is binding, and it is not enough for "impeachment" that the witness testifying to a business reason for discrimination (discipline or layoff) is an official of the employer. See NLRB v. Florida Citrus Canners Co-op, 311 F.2d 541, 543 (5th Cir. 1963).

On remand (322 F.2d 187), the court of appeals assured the Board that it was "whipping a dead horse . . . dead for years," but conceded that Walton does present a Tex-O-Kan problem and that Tex-O-Kan had been quoted in the Walton opinion before the appeal to the Supreme Court. Applying Universal Camera as the Supreme Court had clarified it, nine more employees were held entitled to reinstatement.

2. During an organizational campaign, management hears that an employee is threatening to dynamite the plant if the campaign is unsuccessful. Acting on an honest but mistaken belief in the truth of the rumor, the employer discharges the employee. Does this constitute an unfair labor practice under Section 8(a)(1)? See NLRB v. Burnup and Sims, Inc., 379 U.S. 21 (1964). Would it violate Section 8(a)(3)? Suppose management later discovered its mistake and did nothing? Or, discovering its mistake, offered reinstatement?

REPUBLIC AVIATION CORP. v. NLRB
NLRB v. LE TOURNEAU CO.
Supreme Court of the United States, 1945
324 U.S. 793, 65 Sup. Ct. 982, 89 L. Ed. 1372

MR. JUSTICE REED delivered the opinion of the Court.

In the Republic Aviation Corporation case, the employer, a large and rapidly growing military aircraft manufacturer, adopted, well before any union activity at the plant, a general rule against soliciting which read as follows: "Soliciting of any type cannot be permitted in the factory or offices." The Republic plant was located in a built-up section of Suffolk County, New York. An employee persisted after being warned of the rule in soliciting union membership in the plant by passing out application cards to employees on his own time during lunch periods. The employee was discharged for infraction of the rule and, as the National Labor Relations Board found, without discrimination on the part of the employer toward union activity.

Three other employees were discharged for wearing UAW-CIO union steward buttons in the plant after being requested to remove the insignia. The union was at that time active in seeking to organize the plant. The reason which the employer gave for the request was that, as the union was not then the duly designated representative of the employees, the wearing of the steward buttons in the plant indicated an acknowledgment by the management of the authority of the stewards to represent the employees in dealing with the management and might impinge upon the employer's policy of strict neutrality in union matters and might interfere with the existing grievance system of the corporation.

The Board was of the view that wearing union steward buttons by employees did not carry any implication of recognition of that union by the employer where, as here, there was no competing labor organization in the plant. The discharges of the stewards, however, were found not to be motivated by opposition to the particular union, or, we deduce, to unionism.

The Board determined that the promulgation and enforcement of the "no solicitation" rule violated §8(1) of the National Labor Relations Act as it interfered with, restrained and coerced employees in their rights under §7 and discriminated against the discharged employee under §8(3). It determined also that the discharge of the stewards violated §8(1) and 8(3). As a consequence of its conclusions as to the solicitation and the wearing of the insignia, the Board entered the usual cease and desist order and directed the reinstatement of the discharged employees with back pay and also the rescission of "the rule against solicitation in so far as it prohibits union activity and solicitation on company property during the employees' own time." 51 N.L.R.B. 1186, 1189. The Circuit Court of Appeals for the Second Circuit affirmed, 142 F.2d 193, and we granted certiorari, 323 U.S. 688, because of conflict with the decisions of other circuits.

In the case of Le Tourneau Company of Georgia, two employees were suspended two days each for distributing union literature or circulars on the employees' own time on company owned and policed parking lots, adjacent to the company's fenced-in plant, in violation of a long standing and strictly enforced rule, adopted prior to union organization activity about the premises, which read as follows: "In the future, no Merchants, Concern, Company, or Individual or Individuals will be permitted to distribute, post, or otherwise circulate handbills or posters, or any literature of any description, on Company property without first securing permission from the Personnel Department."

The rule was adopted to control littering and petty pilfering from parked autos by distributors. The Board determined that there was no union bias or discrimination by the company in enforcing the rule.

The company's plant for the manufacture of earthmoving machinery and other products for the war is in the country on a six thousand acre tract. The plant is bisected by one public road and built along another. There is one hundred feet of company-owned land for parking or other use between the highways and the employee entrances to the fenced enclosures where the work is done, so that contact on public ways or on non-company property with employees at or about the establishment is limited to those employees, less than 800 out of 2100, who are likely to walk across the public highway near the plant on their way to work, or to those employees who will stop their private automobiles, buses or other conveyances on the public roads for communications. The employees' dwellings are widely scattered.

The Board found that the application of the rule to the distribution of union literature by the employees on company property which resulted in the lay-offs was an unfair labor practice under §8(1) and 8(3). Cease and desist, and rule rescission orders, with directions to pay the employees for their lost time, followed. 54 N.L.R.B. 1253. The Circuit Court of Appeals for the Fifth Circuit reversed the Board, 143 F.2d 67, and we granted certiorari because of conflict with the Republic case. 323 U.S. 698.

These cases bring here for review the action of the National Labor Relations Board in working out an adjustment between the undisputed right of self-organization assured to employees under the Wagner Act and the equally undisputed right of employers to maintain discipline in their establishments. Like so many others, these rights are not unlimited in the sense that they can be exercised without regard to any duty which the existence of rights in others may place upon employer or employee. Opportunity to organize and proper discipline are both essential elements in a balanced society.

The Wagner Act did not undertake the impossible task of specifying in precise and unmistakable language each incident which would constitute an unfair labor practice. On the contrary, that Act left to the Board the work of applying the Act's general prohibitory language in the light of the infinite combinations of events which might be charged as violative of its terms. Thus a "rigid scheme of remedies" is avoided and administrative flexibility within appropriate statutory limitations obtained to accomplish the dominant purpose of the legislation. Phelps Dodge Corp. v. Labor Board, 313 U.S. 177, 194. So far as we are here concerned, that purpose is the right of employees to organize for mutual aid without employer interference. This is the principle of labor relations which the Board is to foster.

The gravamen of the objection of both Republic and Le Tourneau to the Board's orders is that they rest on a policy formulated without due administrative procedure. To be more specific it is that the Board cannot substitute its knowledge of industrial relations for substantive evidence. The contention is that there must be evidence before the Board to show that the rules and orders of the employers interfered with and discouraged union organization in the circumstances and situation of each company. Neither in the Republic nor the Le Tourneau cases can it properly be said that there was evidence or a finding that the plant's physical location made solicitation away from company property ineffective to reach prospective union members. Neither of these is like a mining or lumber camp where the employees pass their rest as well as their work time on the employer's premises, so that union organization must proceed upon the employer's premises or be seriously handicapped. . . .

In the Republic Aviation Corporation case the evidence showed that the petitioner was in early 1943 a non-urban manufacturing establishment for military production which employed thousands. It was growing rapidly. Trains and automobiles gathered daily many employees for the plant from an area on Long Island, certainly larger than walking distance. The rule against solicitation was introduced in evidence and the circumstances of its violation by the dismissed employee after warning was [sic] detailed.

As to the employees who were discharged for wearing the buttons of a union steward, the evidence showed in addition the discussion in regard to their right to wear the insignia when the union had not been recognized by the petitioner as the representative of the employees. Petitioner looked upon a steward as a union representative for the adjustment of grievances with the management after employer recognition of the stewards' union. Until such recognition petitioner felt that it would violate its neutrality in labor organization if it permitted the display of a steward button by an employee. From its point of view, such display represented to other employees that the union already was recognized.

No evidence was offered that any unusual conditions existed in labor relations, the plant location or otherwise to support any contention that conditions at this plant differed from those occurring normally at any other large establishment.

The Le Tourneau Company of Georgia case also is barren of special circumstances. The evidence which was introduced tends to prove the simple facts heretofore set out as to the circumstances surrounding the discharge of the two employees for distributing union circulars.

These were the facts upon which the Board reached its conclusions as to unfair labor practices. The Intermediate Report in the Republic Aviation case, 51 N.L.R.B. at 1195, set out the reason why the rule against solicitation was considered inimical to the right of organization.[6] This was approved by the Board. Id., 1186. The Board's reasons for concluding that the petitioner's insistence that its employees refrain from wearing steward buttons appear at page 1187 of the report.[7] In the Le Tourneau Company case the discussion of the reasons underlying the findings was much more extended. 54 N.L.R.B. 1253, 1258, et seq. We insert in the note below a quotation which shows the character of the Board's opinion.[8] Furthermore, in both opinions of the Board full citation of authorities was given, including Matter of Peyton Packing Co., 49 N.L.R.B. 828, 50 N.L.R.B. 355, hereinafter referred to.

[6] 51 N.L.R.B. 1195: "Thus, under the conditions obtaining in January 1943, the respondent's employees, working long hours in a plant engaged entirely in war production and expanding with extreme rapidity, were entirely deprived of their normal right to 'full freedom of association' in the plant on their own time, the very time and place uniquely appropriate and almost solely available to them therefor. The respondent's rule is therefore in clear derogation of the rights of its employees guaranteed by the Act."

[7] We quote an illustrative portion. 51 N.L.R.B. 1187-88: "We do not believe that the wearing of a steward button is a representation that the employer either approves or recognizes the union in question as the representative of the employees, especially when, as here, there is no competing labor organization in the plant. Furthermore, there is no evidence in the record herein that the respondent's employees so understood the steward buttons or that the appearance of union stewards in the plant affected the normal operation of the respondent's grievance procedure. On the other hand, the right of employees to wear union insignia at work has long been recognized as a reasonable and legitimate form of union activity, and the respondent's curtailment of that right is clearly violative of the Act."

[8] 54 N.L.R.B. at 1259-60: "As the Circuit Court of Appeals for the Second Circuit has held, 'It is not every interference with property rights that is within the Fifth Amendment . . . Inconvenience, or even some dislocation of property rights, may be necessary in order to safeguard the right to collective bargaining.' The Board has frequently applied this principle in decisions involving varying sets of circumstances, where it has held that the employer's right to control his property does not permit him to deny access to his property to persons whose presence is necessary there to enable the employees effectively to exercise their right to self-organization and collective bargaining, and in those decisions which have reached the courts, the Board's position has been sustained. Similarly, the Board has held that, while it was 'within the province of an employer to promulgate and enforce a rule prohibiting union solicitation during working hours,' it was 'not within the province of an employer to promulgate and enforce a rule prohibiting union solicitation by an employee outside of working hours, although on company property,' the latter restriction being deemed an unreasonable impediment to the exercise of the right to self-organization."

The Board has fairly, we think, explicated in these cases the theory which moved it to its conclusions in these cases. The excerpts from its opinions just quoted show this. The reasons why it has decided as it has are sufficiently set forth. We cannot agree, as Republic urges, that in these present cases reviewing courts are left to "sheer acceptance" of the Board's conclusions or that its formulation of policy is "cryptic." See Eastern-Central Assn. v. United States, 321 U.S. 194, 209.

Not only has the Board in these cases sufficiently expressed the theory upon which it concludes that rules against solicitation or prohibitions against the wearing of insignia must fall as interferences with union organization, but, in so far as rules against solicitation are concerned, it had theretofore succinctly expressed the requirements of proof which it considered appropriate to outweigh or overcome the presumption as to rules against solicitation. In the Peyton Packing Company case, 49 N.L.R.B. 828, at 843, hereinbefore referred to the presumption adopted by the Board is set forth.[10]

. . . We perceive no error in the Board's adoption of this presumption. The Board had previously considered similar rules in industrial establishments and the definitive form which the Peyton Packing Company decision gave to the presumption was the product of the Board's appraisal of normal conditions about industrial establishments. Like a statutory presumption or one established by regulation, the validity, perhaps in a varying degree, depends upon the rationality between what is proved and what is inferred.

In the Republic Aviation case, petitioner urges that irrespective of the validity of the rule against solicitation, its application in this instance did not violate §8(3) . . . because the rule was not discriminatorily applied against union solicitation but was impartially enforced against all solicitors. It seems clear, however, that if a rule against solicitation is invalid as to union solicitation on the employer's premises during the employee's own time, a discharge because of violation of that rule discriminates within the meaning of §8(3) in that it discourages membership in a labor organization.

Republic Aviation Corporation v. National Labor Relations Board is affirmed.

[10] 49 N.L.R.B. at 843-44: "The Act, of course, does not prevent an employer from making and enforcing reasonable rules covering the conduct of employees on company time. Working time is for work. It is therefore within the province of an employer to promulgate and enforce a rule prohibiting union solicitation during working hours. Such a rule must be presumed to be valid in the absence of evidence that it was adopted for a discriminatory purpose. It is no less true that time outside working hours, whether before or after work, or during luncheon or rest periods, is an employee's time to use as he wishes without unreasonable restraint, although the employee is on company property. It is therefore not within the province of an employer to promulgate and enforce a rule prohibiting union solicitation by an employee outside of working hours, although on company property. Such a rule must be presumed to be an unreasonable impediment to self-organization and therefore discriminatory in the absence of evidence that special circumstances make the rule necessary in order to maintain production or discipline."

National Labor Relations Board v. Le Tourneau Company of Georgia
is reversed.

MR. JUSTICE ROBERTS dissents in each case.

NLRB v. BABCOCK AND WILCOX CO.
NLRB v. SEAMPRUFE, INC.
RANCO, INC. v. NLRB
Supreme Court of the United States, 1956
351 U.S. 105, 76 Sup. Ct. 679, 100 L. Ed. 975

MR. JUSTICE REED delivered the opinion of the Court.

In each of these cases the employer refused to permit distribution of
union literature by nonemployee union organizers on company-owned
parking lots. The National Labor Relations Board, in separate and unrelated proceedings, found in each case that it was unreasonably difficult
for the union organizer to reach the employees off company property and
held that, in refusing the unions access to parking lots, the employers had
unreasonably impeded their employees' right to self-organization in violation of §8(a)(1) of the National Labor Relations Act . . .

. . . These holdings were placed on the Labor Board's determination
in Le Tourneau Company of Georgia, 54 N.L.R.B. 1253. In the Le
Tourneau case the Board balanced the conflicting interests of employees
to receive information on self-organization on the company's property
from fellow employees during nonworking time, with the employer's right
to control the use of his property and found the former more essential in
the circumstances of that case. Recognizing that the employer could restrict employees' union activities when necessary to maintain plant discipline or production, the Board said: "Upon all the above considerations,
we are convinced, and find, that the respondent, in applying its 'no-
distributing' rule to the distribution of union literature by its employees
on its parking lots has placed an unreasonable impediment on the freedom of communication essential to the exercise of its employees' right to
self-organization." Le Tourneau Company of Georgia, 54 N.L.R.B.
1262. This Court affirmed the Board. Republic Aviation Corp. v.
NLRB, 324 U.S. 793, 801 et seq. The same rule had been earlier and
more fully stated in Peyton Packing Co., 49 N.L.R.B. 828, 843-844.

The Board has applied its reasoning in the Le Tourneau case without
distinction to situations where the distribution was made, as here, by nonemployees. Carolina Mills, 92 N.L.R.B. 1141, 1149, 1168-1169. The fact
that our Le Tourneau case ruled only as to employees has been noted by
the Courts of Appeal in NLRB v. Lake Superior Lumber Corp., 6 Cir.,
167 F.2d 147, 150, and NLRB v. Seamprufe, Inc., 10 Cir., 222 F.2d at page
860.

In these present cases the Board has set out the facts that support its
conclusions as to the necessity for allowing nonemployee union organizers
to distribute union literature on the company's property. In essence they
are that nonemployee union representatives if barred would have to use
personal contacts on streets or at home, telephones, letters or advertised

meetings to get in touch with the employees. The force of this position in respect to employees isolated from normal contacts has been recognized by this Court and by others. See Republic Aviation Corp. v. NLRB, supra, 324 U.S. at page 799, note 3; NLRB v. Lake Superior Lumber Corp., supra, 167 F.2d at page 150. We recognize too, that the Board has the responsibility of " 'applying the Act's general prohibitory language in the light of the infinite combinations of events which might be charged as violative of its terms.' " NLRB v. Stowe Spinning Co., 336 U.S. 226, 231. We are slow to overturn an administrative decision.

It is our judgment, however, that an employer may validly post his property against nonemployee distribution of union literature if reasonable efforts by the union through other available channels of communication will enable it to reach the employees with its message and if the employer's notice or order does not discriminate against the union by allowing other distribution. In these circumstances the employer may not be compelled to allow distribution even under such reasonable regulations as the orders in these cases permit.

This is not a problem of always open or always closed doors for union organization on company property. Organization rights are granted to workers by the same authority, the National Government, that preserves property rights. Accommodation between the two must be obtained with as little destruction of one as is consistent with the maintenance of the other. The employer may not affirmatively interfere with organization; the union may not always insist that the employer aid organization. But when the inaccessibility of employees makes ineffective the reasonable attempts by nonemployees to communicate with them through the usual channels, the right to exclude from property has been required to yield to the extent needed to permit communication of information on the right to organize.

The determination of the proper adjustments rests with the Board. Its rulings, when reached on findings of fact, supported by substantial evidence on the record as a whole, should be sustained by the courts unless its conclusions rest on erroneous legal foundations. Here the Board failed to make a distinction between rules of law applicable to employees and those applicable to nonemployees.

The distinction is one of substance. No restriction may be placed on the employees' right to discuss self-organization among themselves, unless the employer can demonstrate that a restriction is necessary to maintain production or discipline. Republic Aviation Corp. v. NLRB, 324 U.S. 793, 803. But no such obligation is owed nonemployee organizers. Their access to company property is governed by a different consideration. The right of self-organization depends in some measure on the ability of employees to learn the advantages of self-organization from others. Consequently, if the location of a plant and the living quarters of the employees place the employees beyond the reach of reasonable union efforts to communicate with them, the employer must allow the union to approach his employees on his property. No such conditions are shown in these records.

The plants are close to small well-settled communities where a large percentage of the employees live. The usual methods of imparting information are available. . . . The various instruments of publicity are at hand. Though the quarters of the employees are scattered they are in reasonable reach. The Act requires only that the employer refrain from interference, discrimination, restraint or coercion in the employees' excercise of their own rights. It does not require that the employer permit the use of its facilities for organization when other means are readily available . . .

MR. JUSTICE HARLAN took no part in the consideration or decision of these cases.

NOTE

Is Section 8(c) relevant to the issues canvassed in the preceding cases?

The Administrative Procedure Act §7(c), first sentence, 60 Stat. 241 (1946), as amended, 5 U.S.C. §1006(c), says: "Except as statutes otherwise provide, the proponent of a rule or order shall have the burden of proof." Must the Board in striking down a nondiscriminatory no-solicitation rule make a finding based upon substantial evidence in the record that the employees have inadequate alternative means of communication? "[T]his would simply be an incitement to litigation and casuistry," says one court of appeals, in a case involving solicitation by employees on their own time. NLRB v. United Aircraft Corp., 324 F.2d 128, 130 (2d Cir. 1963), cert. denied, 376 U.S. 951 (1964). Nor does the Board depend upon evidence in the record in setting up presumptions for rules applicable to employees. In Stoddard-Quirk Manufacturing Co., 138 N.L.R.B. 615 (1962), where a majority distinguished between solicitation and distribution of literature, the presumption favorable to freedom for literature was limited to nonworking areas of the plant, primarily by examining the precedents. The two dissenters were told that their argument that small-plant conditions make it virtually impossible to circulate union literature anywhere except at work benches "defies all experience," but neither opinion argued from the record. (The Board was unanimous that solicitation in working areas is presumptively protected.)

May the employer and incumbent union agree to a ban on solicitation for the term of the collective bargaining agreement? NLRB v. Gale Products Co., 337 F.2d 390 (7th Cir. 1964), denying enforcement, holds such an agreement a good defense to Section 8(a)(1) allegations.

MAY DEPARTMENT STORES CO.

National Labor Relations Board, 1962
136 N.L.R.B. 797, enforcement denied, 316 F.2d 797 (6th Cir. 1963)

The Respondent owns and operates two department stores in the Greater Cleveland, Ohio, area. During the year 1959 and 1960, the Joint Petitioners campaigned to organize the Respondent. During this time the Respondent had in effect and enforced a broad no-solicitation rule which prohibited, inter alia, union solicitation in the selling areas of the store during the employees' working and non-working time. The Respondent's enforcement of this rule, as such, is not alleged by the General Counsel as a violation or as interference with the election. Just prior to the election held on April 28, 1960, at a time when it was enforcing its no-solicitation rule, the Respondent made noncoercive antiunion speeches to massed assemblies of employees on company property and thereafter denied the Union's request for equal opportunity and time to address the same employees. It is the theory of the General Counsel that the refusal to grant the Union's request to reply, on these uncontested facts, constitutes a violation of Section 8(a)(1) of the Act and also warrants setting aside the election. We agree with the position taken by the General Counsel.

In the Bonwit Teller case,[5] the employer had in effect a no-solicitation rule which forbade solicitation during working and non-working time on the selling floors of the department store. The employer made preelection antiunion speeches to the employees in the selling areas but refused the Union's request for an opportunity to reply on equal terms. The Board found that such refusal interfered with the employees' organizational rights guaranteed by Section 7, in violation of Section 8(a)(1), and ordered the employer to cease and desist from such refusals. The Court of Appeals for the Second Circuit upheld the Board's finding of the violation.[6] In substance the Second Circuit reasons as follows: "The Board, however, has allowed retail department stores the privilege of prohibiting all solicitation within the selling areas of the store during both working and non-working hours, [citations and footnote omitted]. Bonwit Teller chose to avail itself of that privilege and, having done so, was in our opinion required to abstain from campaigning against the Union on the same premises to which the Union was denied access; if it should be otherwise, the practical advantage to the employer who was opposed to unionization would constitute a serious interference with the right of his employees to organize.[7]

In our opinion, the Board and court holding in the Bonwit Teller case, which we consider to be legally sound, squarely controls the issue in the present case.

Each of the contending parties herein relies upon Livingston Shirt Corporation[8] as supporting its respective position. The Bonwit Teller case itself, as noted, dealt with department store situations. Thereafter, for a time, the Board also applied the doctrine of Bonwit Teller to establishments other than retail department stores. However, in the Livingston

---

[5] Bonwit Teller, Inc., 96 N.L.R.B. 608 [1951].

[6] Bonwit Teller, Inc. v. NLRB, 197 F.2d 640 (C.A. 2 [1952]), cert. denied, 345 U.S. 905 [1953].

[7] Id. at 645. See also NLRB v. American Tube Bending Co., Inc., 205 F.2d 45 (C.A. 2 [1953]), enf'g 102 N.L.R.B. 735, wherein the Second Circuit made it clear that its decision in Bonwit Teller gave the union a right of reply precisely because the broad rule was permitted.

[8] 107 N.L.R.B. 400 (1953).

Shirt case, the Board modified its approach to the problem in the following terms:

"Accordingly, we are convinced that absent special circumstances as hereinafter indicated, there is nothing improper in an employer refusing to grant to the union a right equal to his own in his plant. We rule therefore that, *in the absence of either an unlawful broad no-solicitation rule (prohibiting union access to company premises on other than working time) or a privileged no-solicitation rule (broad, but not unlawful because of the character of the business)* [citing Marshall Field and Co., 98 N.L.R.B. 88], an employer does not commit an unfair labor practice if he makes a preelection speech on company time and premises to his employees and denies the union's request for an opportunity to reply. (Emphasis supplied.)

"Our holding here finds support in the recent decision of the Second Circuit Court of Appeals in the American Tube Bending case [cited supra note 7], in which it explicated its view of permissible employer conduct within the scope of the Bonwit Teller doctrine."

We find no basis for the Respondent's contention that in Livingston Shirt the Board overruled the Bonwit Teller doctrine as it applies to department stores with broad but privileged no-solicitation rules. It is clear that this latter situation was expressly excluded from the statement of allowable employer conduct. . . .

However, the Respondent, in the alternative, maintains that certain decisions of the Supreme Court control and resolve the instant case. The Respondent contends in record argument and brief that the Nutone[13] and Babcock & Wilcox[14] cases stand for the proposition that retail store employers may (1) enforce a broad but privileged rule; (2) make antiunion speeches to massed assemblies of employees; and (3) at the same time deny to organizing unions a similar right to reply.

We do not agree. Indeed, we believe that those decisions delineating the extent to which an employer can restrict the organizational activities of employees and nonemployees on its premises require the result we have reached herein. The no-solicitation rule enforced by Respondent is one which seriously impaired the right of employees to discuss union organization on company premises during nonworking as well as working time and thus created an imbalance in the opportunities for organizational communication. Respondent's rule is broader than the valid rule involved in the Nutone case, which restricted employees' discussion of such matters only during their working time, but left them free to discuss and evaluate such matters during their nonworking time. Thus Respondent's rule, albeit privileged, involved a significantly greater restriction on employees' self-organization rights than did the rule involved in Nutone.

In Nutone the Supreme Court discussed the right of an employer to enforce against its employees a no-solicitation rule relating only to working time, while itself engaging in an antiunion campaign during such

[13] NLRB v. United Steelworkers of America (NuTone, Inc.), 357 U.S. 357 [1958].
[14] NLRB v. Babcock & Wilcox Company, 351 U.S. 105 [supra, p. 233].

time. It noted that the question at issue in such cases was whether "such conduct to any considerable degree created an imbalance in the opportunities for organizational communication." While holding that no such imbalance was shown therein, the Court indicated that the result might have been different had "the employees, or the union on their behalf, requested the employer, himself engaging in antiunion solicitation, to make an exception to the rule for pro-union solicitation." Further, it indicated that even absent such a request, the employer's conduct might properly have been deemed unlawful, had it "truly diminished the ability of the labor organizations involved to carry their messages to the employees. *Just as that is a vital consideration in determining the validity of a no-solicitation rule, . . . it is highly relevant in determining whether a valid rule has been fairly applied."* (Emphasis supplied.)

Applying these principles, we find that a glaring "imbalance in opportunities for organizational communication" was created by Respondent's enforcement of the broad rule against union discussion during nonworking time as well as during working time, while it was engaged in utilizing such time to bring its antiunion message to the employees. By such conduct Respondent seized for itself the most advantageous circumstances in which to present to employees its side of the organizational question. It spoke to them in massed assemblies during working time, thus gaining the not inconsiderable benefit flowing from the utilization of the employment relationship for such purposes, and insuring that its message would reach all of its employees in the most carefully thought out and coherent form for maximum effectiveness. At the same time it relegated the Union and its employee supporters to relatively catch-as-catch-can methods of rebuttal, such as home visits, advertised meetings on the employees' own time, telephone calls, letters, and the various mass media of communication. While it is true that the Supreme Court in Babcock & Wilcox held that an employer may normally put a union to the task of organizing employees through such channels, it indicated that such right was not absolute, but was limited to those circumstances where the effectiveness of such channels of communication was not diminished by employer conduct, or by other circumstances.

The normal effectiveness of such channels stems not alone from the ability of a union to make contact with employees, away from their place of work, but also from the availability of normal opportunities to employees who have been contacted to discuss the matter with their fellow employees at their place of work. The place of work is the one place where all employees involved are sure to be together. Thus it is the one place where they can all discuss with each other the advantages and disadvantages of organization, and lend each other support and encouragement. Such full discussion lies at the very heart of the organizational rights guaranteed by the Act, and is not to be restricted, except as the exigencies of production, discipline, and order demand. It is only where opportunities for such discussion are available, limited, of course, by the need to maintain production, order and discipline, that the election procedures established in the Act can be expected to produce the peaceful resolution of representation questions on the basis of a free and informed choice. Where such discussion is not allowed, the normal channels of communication become clogged and lose their effectiveness. In such circumstances, the balance in "opportunities for organizational communication" is destroyed by an employer's utilization of working time and place for its antiunion campaign. Accordingly, while Respondent was under no obligation to forego utilizing such time and place for its antiunion campaign, we find that it was under an obligation to accede to the Union's request to address the employees under similar circumstances. Only by such action could it maintain the balance which the Supreme Court deemed so important a factor in this area. Respondent's failure to accede to the Union's request seriously impaired the employees' ability to learn of the advantages of union organization from others, and to discuss such advantages among themselves. It thereby interfered with their rights of self-organization as guaranteed in Section 7 of the Act.

Accordingly, we find that Respondent's conduct, as discussed above, violated Section 8(a)(1) of the Act and interfered with the conduct of the election of April 28, 1961. We shall therefore set aside that election and direct a new election. . . .

Member Rodgers, dissenting:

I would adopt the recommendations of the Trial Examiner in their entirety. I would dismiss the allegation of the complaint that Respondent violated Section 8(a)(1) of the Act and would find without merit the allegation that the Employer engaged in conduct which affected the results of the election. . . .

In finding that this refusal by the Employer is a violation of the law, my colleagues are reviving a rule known as the "equal opportunity" doctrine, which doctrine is, in my opinion, contrary to the first amendment to the Constitution, Section 8(c) of the Act, and decisions of the Board and courts.

The Board is holding that because the Employer has used his own property, and his own time, to speak to a voluntary meeting of his employees in an uncoercive and lawful manner concerning unionization, the Employer must, under penalty of law, make his property and the time of his employees, for which he pays, available to the Union for the purpose of organizing his employees. They do so in an opinion which contains not a single allusion to Section 8(c) of the Act, and which relies exclusively on the well-known but discredited Bonwit Teller case. . . .

Whatever latent vitality may have inhered in that part of the Livingston opinion on which the majority relies . . . has been extinguished by court decisions. Soon after the Livingston decision, the Court of Appeals for the Sixth Circuit had occasion to consider and reject the application by the Board of the Bonwit Teller rule to a department store, in F. W. Woolworth Co.,[23] in circumstances identical to the instant case. . . .

Moreover, the Supreme Court later found no violation of the Act in a case in which an employer had not observed his own rule. As the Board

[23] NLRB v. F. W. Woolworth Co., 214 F.2d 78 (C.A. 6), June 3, 1954, one judge dissenting, denying enforcement of 102 N.L.R.B. 581.

said in the Walton[26] case, the Supreme Court in the Nutone case indicated that the following factors are relevant in determining whether "a valid rule has been fairly applied": (1) The employees must request the employer to make an exception to the rule for prounion solicitation, even though the employer is engaging in antiunion solicitation and in effect violating the rule himself, because if the employer voluntarily offers the use of his facilities and the time of his employees for prounion solicitation he subjects himself to a possible charge of violation of Section 8(a)(2) of the Act; (2) because such a rule is presumptively valid both as to promulgation and enforcement, the union involved has to show that enforcement of the rule is an "unreasonable impediment" to organization in that it cannot effectively carry its message to the employees in any other way.

As noted above, in considering cases of this type, the Supreme Court has approached the problem of whether, and in what circumstances, an employer may prohibit union solicitation on its premises as a problem of balancing the employees' need for communication on the subject of union organization with an employer's exercise of his property rights. Because in the view of the Court mechanical answers that the doors must always be open or closed to unions will not suffice, the Court has evolved the criteria set forth above for establishing "the concrete basis for appraising the significance of the employer's conduct," [28] which the Court had found wanting in the Board decisions which it reviewed. I do not believe the attempted distinction by my colleagues, on the ground that the rule here, though lawful, is broader than the rules in the Nutone case, warrants the conclusion that the Court would view the problem in the instant case as a problem of an essentially different type.

In stating that there exists in this case an "imbalance in the opportunities for organizational communication," [30] my colleagues have framed their conclusion in the language used by the Supreme Court, in the Nutone case. However, they have made none of the supporting findings which the Court has indicated are necessary to establish the basis for such a conclusion in cases of this type. . . .

My colleagues have neither considered the existence of alternative channels, nor evaluated their possible effectiveness. They summarily discard all methods other than a talk by the Union to the employees on company time and premises as being "relatively catch-as-catch-can methods." It is therefore readily apparent that their finding of an "imbalance in the opportunities for organizational communication" is predicated solely on the denial to the Union of a channel of communication used by the Employer.

The Trial Examiner found no proof that the usual channels of communication existent in a modern metropolitan area were unavailable for use by the Union. It is clear that the Union had available and extensively used television and radio to broadcast half-hour and hour programs and

---

26 Walton Manufacturing Company, 126 N.L.R.B. 697.
28 See NLRB v. United Steelworkers of America (NuTone, Inc.), 357 U.S. 357, at 364.
30 See 357 U.S. 357, at 362.

spot announcements. Beginning about August 1958, the Union passed handbills at the downtown store every week, or every other week, until the election in April 1960. To some extent, the Union attempted to and did publish newspaper advertisements. Ninety-four percent of the employees of the downtown store live within 10 miles of the store, and 87 percent of the employees of the suburban store live within 5 miles of the store. It is apparent that, in these circumstances, it would have been feasible and reasonable for the Union to utilize home visits and telephone solicitations, which it did to some extent use. It would also have been feasible for the union to have mailed literature to the 1,250 employees whose names and addresses the Union possessed. It is further apparent that the Union had, by August 1959, 8 months before the election, secured authorization cards from at least 30 percent of approximately 1,000 of the employees, in support of the first petition which it filed. This indicates the practical effectiveness of the media on communication which the Union had chosen to utilize. . . .

Member Leedom, dissenting:

Under the principles established in the Nutone case, which I deem dispositive of the issues in this case, the enforcement of a valid no-solicitation rule by an employer who is at the same time engaging in antiunion solicitation may not constitute an unfair labor practice in the absence of substantial evidence that, when all alternative reasonably available channels of communication are considered, the ability of the union to carry its message to the employees has been truly diminished. Unlike the majority, I do not think such a true diminution can be established merely by showing that as a general proposition department store employees can be more easily reached through the avenues of communication open to their employer than through the avenues open to a union. As I find in this record no evidence of true diminution, I would find that the complaint should be dismissed and the objections to the election should be overruled.

NOTES

1. Why is the rule against solicitation on nonworking time in selling areas not attacked? Would a policy of neatness and prevention of littering justify a rule against distribution of literature? Monolith Portland Cement Co., 94 N.L.R.B. 1358 (1951), for this reason sanctioned a rule against passing leaflets. In NLRB v. Rockwell Manufacturing Co., 271 F.2d 109 (3d Cir. 1959), the court denied enforcement of a Board decision declaring invalid a rule prohibiting distribution of literature in the plant parking lot. The court recognized a company interest in order, cleanliness, and discipline, and found a failure to show that there were no other effective channels for telling the union's side of the story. A plant rule against union buttons may be justified where necessary to maintain discipline in an incendiary situation. Caterpillar Tractor Co. v. NLRB, 230 F.2d 357 (7th Cir. 1956); Boeing Airplane Co. v. NLRB, 217 F.2d 369 (9th Cir. 1954). Compare Kimble Glass Co., 113 N.L.R.B. 577

(1955), aff'd, 230 F.2d 484 (6th Cir. 1956). Or union buttons may be barred to protect the employer's impression on customers by use of livery. NLRB v. Harrah's Club, 337 F.2d 177 (9th Cir. 1964).

2. In NLRB v. Stowe Spinning Co., 336 U.S. 226 (1949), it was held to be an unfair labor practice for an employer, in a company-owned town, to deny the union use of the only suitable meeting hall in the town while making it generally available to other groups. Would it be an unfair labor practice for the employer to close the hall to all groups, including the union? Compare Marsh v. Alabama, 326 U.S. 501 (1946), holding unconstitutional an employer's rule against pamphlet distribution on the streets of the company-owned town. In Joseph Bancroft & Sons Co., 140 N.L.R.B. 1288 (1963), an election was set aside because of no-trespassing rules applicable to company-owned housing adjacent to the plant and occupied by about one eighth of the eligible voters.

3.   *Persuasion*

If a plant rule denies to the union an avenue of approach to the employees, what bearing should this have upon the lawfulness of the employer's use of the same channel of communications in a campaign to persuade employees to oppose the union? The Supreme Court for the first time addressed itself to this issue in the NuTone case, and its companion, the Avondale Mills case, both of which were decided sub nom. NLRB v. United Steelworkers of America, 357 U.S. 357 (1958). The Court characterizes as "very narrow and almost abstract" the question whether it is an unfair labor practice for an employer to enforce an otherwise valid no-solicitation rule against the employees, while the company itself uses the methods of persuasion forbidden to the employees by the rule.

The opinion all but declines to answer the question, in calling attention to the Board's duty to appraise carefully the interest of both sides in each case and its special understanding of these situations. There was no evidence of the effect of the rule on the ability of the union to deliver its message, and the union had not requested that the rule be suspended or modified during the campaign. The opinion notes of these aspects of the case, and the Board's order dismissing an allegation of discriminatory enforcement of the rule is sustained.

Mr. Chief Justice Warren, who was with the majority in NuTone, dissented in Avondale Mills, in part because the only expression of view carried on by the employer was a series of threats. Hence he would have enforced the Board's order against Avondale Mills, while affirming the Board's dismissal of part of the complaint in NuTone, since certain dis charges and interrogations found to be unfair labor practices were unrelated to enforcement of the no-solicitation rule. Although the speech in NuTone was antiunion in tenor, it was protected by Section 8(c). Thus to him the exercise of free speech, regardless of what channels are used cannot be burdened with a duty to redress an imbalance in opportunities for communication. This position may be related to the broader issue a to the relationship between the content of communications and the circumstances of their utterance.

Consider, for example, in addition to the question of obtaining the means of communication, this observation of Judge Learned Hand in NLRB v. Federbush Co., 121 F.2d 954, 957 (2d Cir. 1941): "Words are not pebbles in alien juxtaposition; they have only a communal existence; and not only does the meaning of each interpenetrate the other, but all in their aggregate take their purport from the setting in which they are used, of which the relation between the speaker and the hearer is perhaps the most important part. What to an outsider will be no more than the vigorous presentation of a conviction, to an employee may be the manifestation of a determination which it is not safe to thwart. The Board must decide how far the second aspect obliterates the first."

NLRB v. VIRGINIA ELECTRIC & POWER CO.
Supreme Court of the United States, 1941
314 U.S. 469, 62 Sup. Ct. 344, 86 L. Ed. 348

[The company interrogated employees concerning their union activities and engaged in espionage. Furthermore, its president told the employees that a union was "entirely unnecessary." Subsequently the company posted a bulletin which, while conceding that the employees had the right to join a union, laid emphasis on the right to continue bargaining on an individual basis. "For the last fifteen years this Company and its employees have enjoyed a happy relationship of mutual confidence and understanding . . . and during this period there has not been any labor organization . . ." A few weeks thereafter the company, in response to several requests for improved working conditions, told the employees to choose representatives to meet with company officials for discussion of the Wagner Act. At these meetings officers of the company read speeches which pointed out the awkwardness of individual bargaining and urged conducting negotiations through representatives chosen by the employees. "In view of your request to bargain directly with the Company, and in view of your right to self-organization as provided in the law, it will facilitate negotiations if you will proceed to set up your organization, select your own officers and adviser, adopt your own by-laws and rules, and select your representatives to meet with the Company officials whenever you desire."

Following this, meetings for an "inside" union, arranged with the cooperation of company supervisors, were held on company property and in some cases on company time. Membership applications, many of which were signed on company time, were distributed widely. As soon as a majority of the employees had signed up, the company recognized the Independent (which had adopted a constitution during the interim) and signed a contract which provided for a wage increase, a closed shop, and a checkoff. Meetings of the "outside" union, affiliated with the CIO, were kept under surveillance, employees were warned against "messing with the CIO" under penalty of discharge, and one employee, a CIO member who had spoken openly in opposition to an "inside" union, was discharged for union activities.]

MR. JUSTICE MURPHY delivered the opinion of the Court. . . .

The Board specifically found that the bulletin of April 26 and the speeches of May 24 "interfered with, restrained and coerced" the Company's employees in the exercise of their rights guaranteed by §7 of the Act. The Company strongly urges that such a finding is repugnant to the First Amendment. Neither the Act nor the Board's order here enjoins the employer from expressing its view on labor policies or problems, nor is a penalty imposed upon it because of any utterances which it has made. The sanctions of the Act are imposed not in punishment of the employer but for the protection of the employees. The employer in this case is as free now as ever to take any side it may choose on this controversial issue. But certainly conduct, though evidenced in part by speech, may amount in connection with other circumstances to coercion within the meaning of the Act. If the total activities of an employer restrain or coerce his employees in their free choice, then those employees are entitled to the protection of the Act. And in determining whether a course of conduct amounts to restraint or coercion, pressure exerted vocally by the employer may no more be disregarded than pressure exerted in other ways. For "Slight suggestions as to the employer's choice between unions may have telling effect among men who know the consequences of incurring that employer's strong displeasure." International Association of Machinists v. National Labor Relations Board, 311 U.S. 72, 78.

If the Board's order here may fairly be said to be based on the totality of the Company's activities during the period in question, we may not consider the findings of the Board as to the coercive effect of the bulletin and the speeches in isolation from the findings as respects the other conduct of the Company. If the Board's ultimate conclusion is based upon a complex of activities, such as the anti-union background of the Company, the activities of Bishop, Edwards' warning to the employees that they would be discharged for "messing with the C.I.O.," the discharge of Mann, the quick formation of the Independent, and the part which the management may have played in that formation, that conclusion would not be vitiated by the fact that the Board considered what the Company said in conjunction with what it did. The mere fact that language merges into a course of conduct does not put that whole course without the range of otherwise applicable administrative power. In determining whether the Company actually interfered with, restrained, and coerced it employees, the Board has a right to look at what the Company has said, as well as what it has done.

But, from the Board's decision, we are far from clear that the Board here considered the whole complex of activities, of which the bulletin and the speeches are but parts, in reaching its ultimate conclusion with regard to the Independent. The Board regarded the bulletin on its face as showing a marked bias against national unions by implying that strikes and unrest are caused by the organizational campaigns of such bodies, by stressing the "happy relationship of mutual confidence and understanding" prevailing in the absence of organization since the defeat of the Amalgamated in 1922, and by emphasizing the negative "right" of the employees to refrain from exercising their rights guaranteed under the Act, after paying "lip service" to those rights. Summing up its conclusions, the Board said: "We interpret the bulletin as an appeal to the employees to bargain with the respondent directly, without the intervention of any 'outside' union. We find that by posting the bulletin the respondent interfered with, restrained, and coerced its employees in the exercise of the rights guaranteed in §7 of the Act."

The Board was of the view that the speeches delivered in the meetings of May 24 provided the impetus for the formation of a system-wide organization, that they reemphasized the Company's distaste for "outside" organizations by referring to the bulletin, and that, after quoting the provision of the Act forbidding employer domination of labor organizations, they suggested that the employees select their "own" officers, and adopt their "own" by-laws and rules. The Board's finding was: "We find that at the May 24 meetings the respondent urged its employees to organize and to do so independently of 'outside' assistance, and that it thereby interfered with, restrained, and coerced its employees in the exercise of the rights guaranteed in §7 of the Act."

It is clear that the Board specifically found that those utterances were unfair labor practices, and it does not appear that the Board raised them to the stature of coercion by reliance on the surrounding circumstances. If the utterances are thus to be separated from their background, we find it difficult to sustain a finding of coercion with respect to them alone. The bulletin and the speeches set forth the right of the employees to do as they please without fear of retaliation by the Company. Perhaps the purport of these utterances may be altered by imponderable subtleties at work which it is not our function to appraise. Whether there are sufficient findings and evidence of interference, restraint, coercion, and domination without reference to the bulletin and the speeches, or whether the whole course of conduct evidenced in part by the utterances was aimed at achieving objectives forbidden by the Act, are questions for the Board to decide upon the evidence.

Here, we are not sufficiently certain from the findings that the Board based its conclusion with regard to the Independent upon the whole course of conduct revealed by this record. Rather it appears that the Board rested heavily upon findings with regard to the bulletin and the speeches the adequacy of which we regard as doubtful. We therefore remand the cause to the Circuit Court of Appeals with directions to remand it to the Board for a redetermination of the issues in the light of this opinion. We do not mean to intimate any views of our own as to whether the Independent was dominated or suggest to the Board what its conclusion should be when it reconsiders the case. Since the Board rested the remainder of its order in large part on its findings with respect to the domination of the Independent, we do not at this time reach the other parts of the Board's order, including the command that the checked-off dues and assessments should be refunded.

Reversed and remanded.

MR. JUSTICE ROBERTS and MR. JUSTICE JACKSON took no part in the consideration or decision of this case.

[Upon remand, the Board found that in view of the totality of conduct of the company, the bulletin and speeches amounted to unfair labor practices. Upon appeal the Supreme Court affirmed, 319 U.S. 533 (1943).]

NOTES

1. How does Section 8(c), added in 1947, affect the Virginia Electric test for utterances that violate the Act? It "appears to enlarge somewhat the protection previously accorded by the original statute and to grant immunity beyond that contemplated by the free speech guaranties of the Constitution" in that noncoercive antiunion remarks of an employer may not be admissible even to show motive. NLRB, 13th Ann. Rep. 45, 49 (1948). "The practice which the Board has had in the past of using speeches and publications of employers concerning labor organizations and collective bargaining arrangements as evidence, no matter how irrelevant or immaterial, that some later act of the employer had an illegal purpose gave rise to the necessity for this change in the law." H.R. Rep. No. 510, 80th Cong., 1st Sess. 45 (1947), from the statement of the House Managers in the conference committee. The language of Section 8(c) is "no more than a restatement of the principle embodied in the First Amendment." NLRB v. LaSalle Steel Co., 178 F.2d 829, 835 (7th Cir. 1949), cert. denied, 339 U.S. 963 (1950); NLRB v. Bailey Co., 180 F.2d 278, 280 (6th Cir. 1950); Great Western Broadcasting Corp. v. NLRB, 310 F.2d 591, 599 (9th Cir. 1962).

2. Is an announcement privileged? A representation? A statement of legal position? A prediction? A question? In NLRB v. Servette, 377 U.S. 46 (1964), warnings that handbills would be distributed in front of noncooperating stores were held not to be "threats" within the meaning of Section 8(b)(4), because the distribution of handbills was protected by the statute, and the Court pointed out that this protection would be undermined if warnings that the union would do what was protected could be treated as a violation. Compare NLRB v. Exchange Parts Co., 375 U.S. 405 (1964), in which announcement of a new system for computing wages which was more favorable to the employees, so timed as to dissuade employees from voting for the union, was held a violation of Section 8(a)(1), although the policy had been decided upon earlier by management, and it was, in accordance with the announcement, put into effect unconditionally on a permanent basis. Section 8(c) was not explicitly argued, but the Court said: "[T]he absence of conditions or threats pertaining to the particular benefits conferred would be of controlling significance only if it could be presumed that no question of additional

benefits or renegotiation of existing benefits would arise in the future; and, of course, no such presumption is tenable." 375 U.S. at 410.

Suppose that the union on the day before the election circulates leaflets stating falsely: "Not long ago beryllium poisoning claimed the lives of many workers in this industry and in our plant"; and misstating comparisons with benefits under union contracts at other plants. To these statements add that on election day 90 percent of the employees received a denial in leaflets from the employer, distributed fifteen minutes before they voted. Is the issue whether knowledge of the falsity of its propaganda can be imputed to the union (or employer, as the case may be)? Whether the employees relied on the representations? Whether the subjects of the representations were important? Whether those subjects are emotion-inflaming? Whether those subjects are relevant to the choice embodied in the vote? Whether the employer (or union, as the case may be) had an opportunity to reply? Whether an effective reply was made? Whether the matter was such that a reply could refute it if false? NLRB v. Trancoa Chemical Corp., 303 F.2d 456 (1st Cir. 1962), reproves the NLRB for arguing in effect that it is too busy to hold unions up to high standards in election campaigns. The conclusion of the court is that the Board erred in overruling objections to an election by counting on the employees to evaluate misrepresentations not amounting to forgery and other campaign trickery when there was opportunity to refute them. According to the court, falseness becomes particularly significant when it is intentional. The significance is that deliberate falsification evidences the importance of the matter in affecting an election; else why falsify?

Another decision concluding that the Board did not scrutinize the campaign closely enough for misstatements was NLRB v. Houston Chronicle Co., 300 F.2d 273 (5th Cir. 1962). The challenged statement was a letter from the union exaggerating Guild wages at a newspaper in San Antonio. It was sent two days before election, and the day before the election the employer sent a telegram challenging its assertions.

The court agreed with the Board doctrine that gives weight to whether the promulgating party had special knowledge, increasing the likelihood of reliance, and whether there was rebuttal or opportunity therefor. It also approved the Board's propositions that misrepresentation need not be deliberate, in view of the effect on employees whether deliberate or otherwise, and that absent fraud or coercion the Board does not attempt to police and censor the utterances of the parties. However, said the court, these are merely useful factual tests to determine whether the election reflects the desires of the employees, free of improper influence. The court concluded that the employer's reply was ineffectual and the union had such special knowledge as to inspire reliance.

3. A Board majority of 3-to-2 in Plochman and Harrison — Cherry Lane Foods, Inc., 140 N.L.R.B. 130 (1962), placed stress on the inflammatory use of a moving picture, a production depicting union violence, entitled "And Women Must Weep." The rationale relied upon characterization of the cinematographer's art as here employed to document false

descriptions of the union in a last-minute prepotent appeal to reject thuggery. In Storkline Corp., 142 N.L.R.B. 875 (1963), one of the numerous "And Women Must Weep" cases setting aside elections, the impact of the moving picture was likened (p. 878) to the use of the picture of a prominent labor leader dancing with a partner of a different race, and other exploitations of the racial theme. The Board was referring to the "powerful emotional force" of the propaganda in Sewell Manufacturing Co., 138 N.L.R.B. 66 (1962).

An employer's speech asserted that customers buy on the basis of price and dependability, that the employer is the sole supplier for some customers, and that the employer has been told it "would not continue to be the sole source of supply if [it] became unionized, due to the ever present possibility of a work stoppage due to strikes or walkouts." Is this a representation, a threat, or a prediction? Is classification in these terms helpful? Or if one customer, for which the employer was the sole supplier, had so stated, would the employer's statement be, as the trial examiner and reviewing court held, a substantial, correct, and accurate report, neither coercive nor deliberately false or misleading? Union Carbide Corp. v. NLRB, 310 F.2d 844 (6th Cir. 1962). The NLRB had held that these statements were in the form of a prediction but contained a clear threat of loss of employment if the employees selected the union. 136 N.L.R.B. 95, 97 (1962). In NLRB v. Transport Clearings, Inc., 311 F.2d 519 (5th Cir. 1962), the court denies enforcement to part of an order against telling employees that they are putting all jobs in jeopardy by engaging in union activity but enforces another part against threatening employees that the operation would close and the girls would be walking the streets if the union came in, citing with approval NLRB v. Morris Fishman & Sons, Inc., 278 F.2d 792 (3d Cir. 1960), distinguishing between a threat to close the plant and an economic prophecy that the plant will close, if the employer signs a contract with the union.

4. *"The union is against your best interests.* If the union wins the election, an outsider will negotiate or make demands upon the Company for you. There is no law that requires that I agree to anything he desires or says. * There is only one way that a union representative can enforce his demands upon the Company. This is by calling a strike. When you strike, you will lose your wages and possibly your job. The Company is free to hire someone to take your place while you are striking and when the strike is over there may not be a job for you.

"The union question is not whether it is good for great numbers of men in the mass of employment industries, but whether it is best for you, your job and your family at *this* Company. Pretty generally in small companies the employees have refused to go along with union methods. They recognize that their jobs and earnings, including overtime, depends upon the company's ability to sell their product in the competitive market. *You know that under union methods we would not have been able to operate with continuous employment for you during the past year. Good pay checks depend upon continuous full time employment."

What language in the foregoing passages taken from a letter sent to all employees by the management three days before the election would be most questionable? Does their context save these statements? A Board panel majority found the language following the asterisk in each paragraph repugnant to NLRA §8(a)(1), but the court held it protected by Section 8(c). Texas Industries, Inc. v. NLRB, 336 F.2d 128 (5th Cir. 1964). The court said that the passages in the second paragraph were not threatening either in terms or, in view of the context, in substance. The statements in the first paragraph were held protected as merely stating the employer's legal rights and indicating that it might pursue them.

5. In Lord Baltimore Press, 142 N.L.R.B. 328 (1963), the employer stated that it did not intend to recognize a certain union because the Board had erred in directing the election in an inappropriate unit, explaining that if the election went pro-union the process of getting to the court of appeals to vindicate its position might take several years. Then followed an appeal to vote against the union. The explanation that the unit was inappropriate was preceded by an argument that the union in question would sacrifice the interests of these employees to those in commercial printing, a different industry. The Board, one member dissenting and two not participating, set aside the election, rejecting a "narrow legalistic approach" and refusing to "consider words in isolation." It found a "careful juxtaposition of foreboding possibilities" to convey "the futility of choosing the Petitioner." The opinion recognizes that its conclusion, like those in Oak Manufacturing Co., 141 N.L.R.B. 1323 (1963), Dal-Tex Optical Co., 137 N.L.R.B. 1782 (1962), and Sewell Manufacturing Co., 138 N.L.R.B. 66 (1962), was based upon a re-examination of the scope of campaign material.

"[I]f a union got in and we started negotiations . . . everything would be wiped clean, [employees would lose some benefits, in particular the present vacation plan, and would have to] start from scratch." A Section 8(a)(1) order was enforced because of this employer message in NLRB v. Marsh Supermarkets, 327 F.2d 109 (7th Cir. 1963), the opinion remarking that the language in Dal-Tex Optical "went further" than that quoted above. In Trent Tube Co., 147 N.L.R.B. No. 60 (1964), however, a Board majority of 3-to-2 held that the election results should be certified although the employer had used the expression "bargaining starts from scratch" early in the campaign, without repetition, and the statement was followed by apt responses to the employer's campaign. Compare the dissenter's position in Oak Manufacturing that "You have everything to gain and nothing to lose by voting 'No' " could not reasonably be construed as a veiled threat because it was part of a reply to union propaganda. See NLRB v. Realist, Inc., 328 F.2d 840 (7th Cir.), cert. denied, 377 U.S. 994 (1964), sustaining the setting aside of the election on grounds of a veiled threat to move operations out of the state and propagation of the idea that it would be futile to choose the union in order to obtain greater benefits. The dissenting judge would have invoked Section 8(c), but the majority accepted the "laboratory conditions" standard for elections, first set forth in General Shoe Corp., 77 N.L.R.B. 124 (1948).

Overruling prior cases, Blue Flash Express Co., 109 N.L.R.B. 591 (1954), holds that it is not per se unlawful for an employer to interrogate employees about their views or activities concerning organization. The courts have generally required more than a Board holding that the interrogation in question was an unfair labor practice. For instance, the Second Circuit asserts that it imposes "fairly severe standards": (1) whether there is a history of employer hostility; (2) whether the questioner appears, from the nature of the information sought, to be preparing reprisals against individuals; (3) how high in the management hierarchy the questioner is; (4) whether the place of questioning was in the boss's office; and (5) whether the reply was truthful. Bourne v. NLRB, 332 F.2d 47 (2d Cir. 1964). According to Beaver Valley Canning Co. v. NLRB, 332 F.2d 429 (8th Cir. 1964), isolated questions about union activity without suggestion of hostility to the union "fall squarely within the free speech" protection of the Act.

On the procedure for soliciting employees for copies of their affidavits given to Board agents, in preparation for litigation, see W. T. Grant Co. v. NLRB, 337 F.2d 447 (7th Cir. 1964).

PEERLESS PLYWOOD CO.
National Labor Relations Board, 1953
107 N.L.R.B. 427

The Board issued its Decision and Direction of Election on May 13, 1953. Two days later, the Regional Director completed arrangements for holding the election during the morning of May 26, 1953. On May 20, 1953, the Petitioner wrote a letter to the Employer requesting equal time and facilities in the event that the Employer made a speech to the employees on Employer time and property. The Employer denied the Petitioner's request on May 22, 1953, stating that it did not have a "no-solicitation" rule and that therefore the Board's ruling in the Bonwit Teller case did not apply.

The election was held between 9:30 A.M. and 10:15 A.M., on May 26, 1953. On the afternoon of May 25, less than 24 hours before the election, the Employer assembled the employees on its property in order to have them listen to a prepared speech about the election delivered by the secretary-treasurer of the Employer. After the speech was read, mimeographed copies of it were distributed to the employees present. The speech was non-coercive in character.

The Regional Director recommended that the objections be sustained and the election set aside because, "it is now established Board policy that if the employer utilizes company time and property to campaign against the union he may not deny the union an opportunity to reply under the same circumstances." The Employer challenges the conclusion and recommendation of the Regional Director. It argues that the Petitioner held a meeting at its own hall on the evening of May 25, at which it had ample opportunity to present its side of the case to the employees at the last available moment, and to answer the arguments put forth by the

Employer at a meeting on the Employer's premises that afternoon. It also asserts that it has never had a "no-solicitation" rule and the opportunity afforded the Petitioner to present its side of the case to employees has been unrestricted.

Under the Board's broad Bonwit Teller doctrine, this election would have been set aside because the employer made a speech to his employees prior to an election and denied the union an opportunity to use his premises to make a speech in reply. This would have been done regardless of the timing of the employer's speech, so long as it was pre-election, and regardless of whether or not the employer had a broad no-solicitation rule.

In our decision in the Livingston Shirt case [107 N.L.R.B. 400], the majority of the Board reverses the broad Bonwit Teller decision. In that case we hold that, in the absence of either a privileged or an unlawful broad no-solicitation rule, an employer does not commit an unfair labor practice if he makes a non-coercive speech to his employees and denies the union an opportunity to reply on company premises.

We are now called upon to decide what our rule shall be in an election case in the light of our Livingston Shirt decision. We have abandoned the Bonwit Teller doctrine in complaint cases. But this does not, however, dispose of the problem as it affects the conduct of an election. It is our considered view, based on experience with conducting representation elections, that last-minute speeches by either employers or unions delivered to massed assemblies of employees on company time have an unwholesome and unsettling effect and tend to interfere with that sober and thoughtful choice which a free election is designed to reflect. We believe that the real vice is in the last-minute character of the speech coupled with the fact that it is made on company time whether delivered by the employer or the union or both. Such a speech, because of its timing, tends to create a mass psychology which overrides arguments made through other campaign media and gives an unfair advantage to the party, whether employer or union, who in this manner obtains the last most telling word.

When viewed in this light, it is plain that the situation is aggravated rather than equalized by an attempted application of the Bonwit Teller doctrine to elections. In an attempt to achieve equality, the effect of Bonwit Teller was to create a further imbalance by giving an advantage to the party who, by virtue of making a speech on company time only a few hours before the election, thereby was accorded the last most effective word.

Accordingly, we now establish an election rule which will be applied in all election cases. This rule shall be that employers and unions alike will be prohibited from making election speeches on company time to massed assemblies of employees within twenty-four hours before the scheduled time for conducting an election. Violation of this rule will cause the election to be set aside whenever valid objections are filed.

We institute this rule pursuant to our statutory authority and obligation to conduct elections in circumstances and under conditions which will insure employees a free and untrammeled choice. Implicit in this rule is our view that the combined circumstances of (1) the use of Company time for pre-election speeches and (2) the delivery of such speeches on the eve of the election tend to destroy freedom of choice and establish an atmosphere in which a free election cannot be held. Also implicit in the rule is our judgment that non-coercive speeches made prior to the proscribed period will not interfere with a free election, inasmuch as our rule will allow time for their effect to be neutralized by the impact of other media of employee persuasion.

This rule is closely akin to, and no more than an extension of, our longstanding rule prohibiting electioneering by either party at or near the polling place. We have previously prescribed space limitations, now we prescribe time limitations as well. This rule arises from the same concept and has the same purpose of keeping our elections free. It is this same purpose which has led us recently to prohibit the use of sound trucks for the purpose of projecting voice propaganda into the polling place although the trucks are physically located outside the proscribed polling area. Likewise it is this same purpose which caused us in another recent decision to set aside an election because an atmosphere of terror was created by individual employees, although their conduct could not be attributed either to the union or the employer.

We believe that the application of this same concept of fair and free elections to speeches on company time on the very eve of an election will have a salutary effect, will not give undue advantage to any party, and will afford employees an opportunity to exercise their franchise in an atmosphere more truly conducive to freedom of choice.

This rule will not interfere with the rights of unions or employers to circulate campaign literature on or off the premises at any time prior to an election, nor will it prohibit the use of any other legitimate campaign propaganda or media. It does not, of course, sanction coercive speeches or other conduct prior to the twenty-four hour period, nor does it prohibit an employer from making (without granting the union an opportunity to reply) campaign speeches on company time prior to the twenty-four hour period, provided, of course, such speeches are not otherwise violative of Section 8(a)(1). Moreover, the rule does not prohibit employers or unions from making campaign speeches on or off company premises during the twenty-four hour period if employee attendance is voluntary and on the employees' own time.

In this case, as the Employer delivered its speech to employees on company time less than 24 hours in advance of the election, we find that a free and untrammeled expression of employees' desires was thereby prevented. . . . We shall accordingly set aside the results of the May 26 election and direct a new one to be conducted in accordance with our new rule.

Member Murdock, dissenting in part and concurring in part:

While I agree that the election held in this proceeding on May 26, 1953 should be set aside and a new election held, I strongly dissent from the basis on which the majority reaches this result. The majority opinion, in my considered judgment, errs in substituting the new 24 hour rule announced herein for the Board's established doctrines concerning employer pre-election speeches. In accord with my dissenting opinion in the Livingston Shirt case, I would herein reaffirm those principles set forth in Bonwit Teller and succeeding decisions which have, this day, been overruled by my colleagues, but which in my view are the only proper bases for setting this election aside. . . .

In closing I would note that even if the Bonwit Teller doctrine is abandoned as a basis for finding unfair labor practices, as the majority has done in the Livingston Shirt decision, it does not necessarily follow that the doctrine must or should be abandoned as a basis for setting elections aside. If this Board has the power, as the majority believes, to tell the employer that he cannot make a speech at all on company time and premises within 24 hours of an election, under pain of having the election set aside, then certainly it could not be argued that the Board does not have the power to tell the employer that if he elects to make such a speech at any time during the period preceding the election and does not grant the union's request for an opportunity to speak under similar circumstances, the Board will set aside the election. . . .

Accordingly, adhering to the Bonwit Teller doctrine in representation cases, as the Employer herein delivered an antiunion speech to its employees on company time and property and thereafter denied an equal opportunity to the Petitioner to express its views, I would find that the Employer interfered with the free choice of its employees. On that basis alone I agree with the result reached in the majority opinion in setting aside the election and directing a new election.

NOTES

1. Speeches during nonworking time are not within the 24-hour rule. Falmouth Co., 115 N.L.R.B. 1533 (1956). Is the adjudicative procedure employed in the establishment of the 24-hour rule, and in thus construing its reach, an appropriate way to regulate the election process? It has been charged that the adjudicative procedure is "demonstrably wrong" when used to set up quantitative rules for assertion of jurisdiction by the NLRB. Peck, The Atrophied Rule-Making Powers of the National Labor Relations Board, 70 Yale L.J. 729 (1961). "To insist upon one form of action [rule-making] to the exclusion of the other [adjudication] is to exalt form over necessity. . . . [T]he choice . . . is one that lies primarily in the informed discretion of the administrative agency." SEC v. Chenery Corp., 332 U.S. 194, 202-203 (1947).

2. Only objections grounded in the period beginning with the filing of the petition for election are considered by the Board. Ideal Electric & Manufacturing Co., 134 N.L.R.B. 1275 (1961); Goodyear Tire & Rubber Co., 138 N.L.R.B. 453 (1962).

3. In Great Atlantic & Pacific Tea Co., 140 N.L.R.B. 133 (1962), a management official held individual interviews in isolated areas of the plant with about 7 per cent of the employees. The Board found that this

destroyed the requisite laboratory conditions for a free election and directed a new one. One member, dissenting, would permit noncoercive individual conversations anywhere but at "the locus of final authority," rather than confining the place for such employer solicitation substantially to the work station of the employee being interviewed.

4.   Tenure and Compensation

ENDERBY PROBLEM 4

(*See page 224 supra for Enderby Problem 3*)

Several months after the election Endicott approached White with reference to a persistent rumor that a substantial layoff had been scheduled for the Miscellaneous Division. White was most affable and jokingly inquired whom Endicott represented. White indicated that the company was working on a program that could require a work load adjustment in plastics but until the plans were completed it would be a waste of time to talk about them. He spoke vaguely of an important government subcontract "that will really make all of us put out." A week later seventy-five of the older and better paid employees in the Plastics Department were laid off. This action was accompanied by a bulletin which informed the employees that a contract with General Titanics Corporation required substantial alteration of plastic methods and therefore some temporary unemployment.

Endicott promptly questioned White about the details of the changes and pointed out that the selections for layoff were not in line with the long-existing seniority system, "last in first out, skill and ability being equal." White refused to discuss the matter, or indeed, give any information. He curtly observed that the company could hardly be expected to discuss its production schedules with a union which had recently been rejected by the employees. Endicott, somewhat unsure of his position, consulted Curme. The latter was most hostile and told Endicott to "stew in your own juice."

Endicott was now under increasing political pressure within the Enderby Association. He therefore called a strike to protest the company's action in laying off the seventy-five employees. Both he and White were surprised when a majority of the employees in the Miscellaneous Division responded to the strike call.

The company found it difficult to replace the strikers. White rejected the temporary expedient of trying to fill some of the jobs by transferring employees from the Tire Division. Curme had been looking for a popular issue and such transfers would involve too much risk of spreading the strike. Furthermore, White was aware that Local 417 had not abandoned its interest in organizing Enderby. He had recently turned down an application for employment in the Tire Division when he discovered that the applicant was both a friend of Layton and former organizer with the Rubber Workers Union. A notice from the company advising each striker that he risked permanent replacement was not too effective; the assurance of a permanent job failed to attract the necessary complement of new employees.

Some weeks later the company announced a program under which strike replacements and strikers who left the strike and returned to their jobs would have preferred seniority in the event of future layoffs. As White subsequently remarked, "the announcement worked like a charm." About half the strikers returned to work and the replacement of 50 per cent of the others took place. Endicott urged in vain that the company's promise would prove just as illusory as the former seniority system. Within a week Endicott received notice of his discharge.

At this time Curme was getting ready to file another election petition at Enderby. The fact, however, that a substantial number of the replaced strikers had recently become members of Local 417 forced his hand. Curme therefore advised Dan Cooper, the union attorney, that he contemplated a strike in the Tire Division in protest of the superseniority program which Enderby had promulgated. He inquired what effect such a strike would have on the processing of an election petition and what would be the voting status of strikers, replacements and employees on layoff in the Tire and Miscellaneous Divisions. He "wanted the whole picture." Cooper said that it seemed to him that the real problem was whether a strike in Tire would be a sensible tactic. Curme repeated his request, indicating that he would take care of tactics if Cooper would handle the law.

NLRB v. MACKAY RADIO & TELEGRAPH CO.

Supreme Court of the United States, 1938
304 U.S. 333, 58 Sup. Ct. 904, 82 L. Ed. 1381

[The Mackay Company's headquarters in New York City was bargaining there with American Radio Telegraphists Association; its San Francisco office was bargaining with Local 3 of the same national. The negotiations bogged down. The national officers decided on a general strike. Local 3's representative in New York so informed his local; and the local's officers called the San Francisco employees out at midnight on Friday, October 4, 1935. The company, to maintain service, brought in replacements from Los Angeles, Chicago, and New York. The strike was unsuccessful throughout the country. The San Francisco strikers, by Monday, had become fearful of losing their jobs forever. One telephoned the company's local supervisor, who said the company would take the men back — except, he said, that the company had had to promise permanent San Francisco jobs to eleven of the replacements it had brought in, and these must not be ousted against their will. The supervisor then called a meeting of the strikers. But in doing so he omitted eleven men who he said would have to apply for reinstatement, subject to the approval of the company's New York office. Thirty-six attended the meeting, including a few of the eleven, who had happened to hear about it. The superintendent reiterated his statements about return to work, and also about the eleven. A resolution to return at once was carried, and most did return.

Then, or shortly thereafter, six of the eleven in question took their places and resumed their work without challenge, as only five of the replacements wanted to stay in San Francisco. The five strikers not reinstated, all of whom were prominent in the union and in the strike, reported for work at various times during the next three days, but were told there were no openings. They were asked to file applications which would be considered for any future vacancies. After three weeks of waiting, the secretary of Local 3 filed a charge of violations of Sections 8(1) and (3). The Board issued its complaint alleging that the company's discharge of the five violated Section 8(1) and also, because discriminatory, violated Section 8(3). Later, it found that the refusals to reinstate the five men were equivalent to discharges, and issued its usual order including full reinstatement of the five with back pay, posting of notices, and so forth.

In the Court of Appeals for the Ninth Circuit, the court set the Board's order aside.]

MR. JUSTICE ROBERTS delivered the opinion of the Court. . . .

Second. Under the findings the strike was a consequence of, or in connection with, a current labor dispute as defined in Sec. 2(9) of the Act. That there were pending negotiations for the execution of a contract touching wages and terms and conditions of employment of point-to-point operators cannot be denied. But it is said the record fails to disclose what caused these negotiations to fail or to show that the respondent was in any wise in fault in failing to comply with the union's demands; and, therefore, for all that appears, the strike was not called by reason of fault of the respondent. The argument confuses a current labor dispute with an unfair labor practice defined in §8 of the Act. True there is no evidence that respondent had been guilty of any unfair labor practice prior to the strike, but within the intent of the Act there was an existing labor dispute in connection with which the strike was called. The finding is that the strike was deemed "advisable in view of the unsatisfactory state of negotiations" in New York. It was unnecessary for the Board to find what was in fact the state of the negotiations in New York when the strike was called, or in so many words that a labor dispute as defined by the Act existed. The wisdom or unwisdom of the men, their justification or lack of it, in attributing to respondent an unreasonable or arbitrary attitude in connection with the negotiations, cannot determine whether, when they struck, they did so as a consequence of or in connection with a current labor dispute.

Third. The strikers remained employees under Sec. 2(3) of the Act which provides: "The term 'employee' shall include . . . any individual whose work has ceased as a consequence of, or in connection with, any current labor dispute or because of any unfair labor practice, and who has not obtained any other regular and substantially equivalent employment . . ." Within this definition the strikers remained employees for the purpose of the Act and were protected against the unfair labor practices denounced by it.

Fourth. It is contended that the Board lacked jurisdiction because re-

spondent was at no time guilty of any unfair labor practice. Section 8 of the Act denominates as such practice action by an employer to interfere with, restrain, or coerce employees in the exercise of their rights to organize, to form, join or assist labor organizations, and to engage in concerted activities for the purpose of collective bargaining or other mutual aid or protection, or "by discrimination in regard to . . . tenure of employment or any term or condition of employment to encourage or discourage membership in any labor organization: . . ." There is no evidence and no finding that the respondent was guilty of any unfair labor practice in connection with the negotiations in New York. On the contrary, it affirmatively appears that the respondent was negotiating with the authorized representatives of the union. Nor was it an unfair labor practice to replace the striking employees with others in an effort to carry on the business. Although Section 13 provides, "Nothing in this Act shall be construed so as to interfere with or impede or diminish in any way the right to strike," it does not follow that an employer, guilty of no act denounced by the statute, has lost the right to protect and continue his business by supplying places left vacant by strikers. And he is not bound to discharge those hired to fill the places of strikers, upon the election of the latter to resume their employment, in order to create places for them. The assurance by respondent to those who accepted employment during the strike that if they so desired their places might be permanent was not an unfair labor practice nor was it such to reinstate only so many of the strikers as there were vacant places to be filled. But the claim put forward is that the unfair labor practice indulged by the respondent was discrimination in reinstating striking employees by keeping out certain of them for the sole reason that they had been active in the union. As we have said, the strikers retained, under the Act, the status of employees. Any such discrimination in putting them back to work is, therefore, prohibited by §8.
    . . . The Board found, and we cannot say that its finding is unsupported, that, in taking back six of the eleven men and excluding five who were active union men, the respondent's officials discriminated against the latter on account of their union activities and that the excuse given that they did not apply until after the quota was full was an afterthought and not the true reason for the discrimination against them.
    As we have said, the respondent was not bound to displace men hired to take the strikers' places in order to provide positions for them. It might have refused reinstatement on the ground of skill or ability, but the Board found that it did not do so. It might have resorted to any one of a number of methods of determining which of its striking employees would have to wait because five men had taken permanent positions during the strike, but it is found that the preparation and use of the list, and the action taken by the respondent, were with the purpose to discriminate against those most active in the union. There is evidence to support these findings.
    Sixth. The Board's order does not violate the Fifth Amendment. The respondent insists that the relation of employer and employee ceased at the inception of the strike. The plain meaning of the Act is that if men

strike in connection with a current labor dispute their action is not to be construed as a renunciation of the employment relation and they remain employees for the remedial purposes specified in the Act. We have held that, in the exercise of the commerce power, Congress may impose upon contractual relationships reasonable regulations calculated to protect commerce against threatened industrial strife. . . .

Seventh. The affirmative relief ordered by the Board was within its powers and its order was not arbitrary or capricious. . . .

. . . On the basis of the findings, five men who took part in the strike were discriminated against in connection with a blanket offer to reinstate striking employees. The Board enjoined further discrimination against employees by reason of union affiliation, but it could not grant complete relief in respect of the five men short of ordering that the discrimination be neutralized by their being given their former positions and reimbursed for the loss due to their lack of employment consequent upon the respondent's discrimination. . . .

The judgment of the Circuit Court of Appeals is reversed and the cause is remanded to that court for further proceedings in conformity with this opinion.

Reversed.

MR. JUSTICE CARDOZO and MR. JUSTICE REED took no part in the consideration or decision of this case.

NOTES

1. The Board's present position is that refusal of an employee to cross a picket line at the premises of an employer other than his own is, like striking, a concerted activity under Section 7, but that in the absence of evidence of animus against the union, the dismissal of such an employee is privileged as a means of continuing the interrupted business relationship. Redwing Carriers, 137 N.L.R.B. 1545, review denied, 325 F.2d 1011 (D.C. Cir. 1963), cert. denied, 377 U.S. 905 (1964). Since such refusals constitute a Section 7 activity, the Board argues that the employer must honor an unconditional application for employment by such dismissed employees, if their jobs are still open. One court disagrees: In NLRB v. L. G. Everist, Inc., 334 F.2d 312 (8th Cir. 1964), it was held that on this issue the Board is making an unrealistic distinction between discharge and denial of reinstatement, just as it did in NLRB v. Rockaway News Co., 345 U.S. 71 (1953), when the refusal to cross the picket line was a breach of the collective bargaining agreement. The court said (p. 75): "Substantive rights and duties in the field of labor-management do not depend upon verbal ritual reminiscent of medieval real property law."

Nevertheless, it appears that a "deadline" letter warning a striker that he will be replaced, as in Robinson Freight Lines, 114 N.L.R.B. 1093 (1955), is regarded as more clearly lawful than one enclosing "all monies due" the striker, as in Liberty Electronics Corp., 138 N.L.R.B. 1074 (1962). May the employer advertise for permanent replacements before the strike begins but after it has been threatened?

2. The Act does not prohibit an effective discharge for joining a strike in violation of the terms of the collective bargaining agreement. NLRB v. Sands Manufacturing Co., 306 U.S. 332 (1939). Or for unlawful acts such as assault or trespass, as in the "sit-down" strike. Such discharge terminates the wrongdoer's status as an employee of that employer and justifies denial of reinstatement. NLRB v. Fansteel Corp., 306 U.S. 240 (1939). It is irrelevant that the lawlessness is collateral to the policies of the Act, e.g., a strike that violates the mutiny statute. Southern Steamship Co. v. NLRB, 316 U.S. 31 (1942).

The Board has devised a doctrine it describes as "condonation" to fit the case of an employer who denies reinstatement without having "discharged" such wrongdoers, or though they had been discharged, negotiation for settlement or other evidence shows that the misconduct in question is not now, if it ever was, treated as cause for discharge. "Condonation" thus serves as a passport to relief for an employee whose activities are unlawful but related to a strike, if the employer shows that the "slate is wiped clean" in so far as the unlawfulness is concerned. Thereafter, denial of unconditional application to return to work may be found to be discriminatory, and an unfair labor practice. See Confectionery Drivers Local 805 v. NLRB, 312 F.2d 108 (2d Cir. 1963). But the employer is not required to treat all the participants in the strike alike; the conduct of the ringleaders may not be "condoned" even though the slate is wiped clean as to aiders and abetters. NLRB v. E. A. Laboratories, 188 F.2d 885 (2d Cir. 1951).

3. In addition to unlawful discrimination in reinstatement, the employer may commit an unfair practice by attaching unlawful conditions to reinstatement, for example, requiring clearance from the union where clearance, under a valid union-shop contract, was to be on some nonfinancial basis. See Confectionery Drivers Local 805 v. NLRB, 312 F.2d 108 (2d Cir. 1963). Such conditions in effect amount to a denial of reinstatement and start the running of liability for back pay. Contrast the doctrine of Volney Felt Mills, Inc., 70 N.L.R.B. 908 (1946), that to award back pay to strikers for any period prior to their unconditional application to return to work, even if they are on a strike provoked by flagrant unfair labor practices of the employer, does not effectuate the policy of the Act to minimize industrial strife.

Does the Board's remedial power extend to an order to hire applicants for employment discriminated against in violation of the Act, as well as an order to reinstate strikers whose applications to return to work have been unlawfully denied? See NLRA §10(c), the phrase authorizing "affirmative action, including reinstatement of *employees* with or without back pay" (emphasis supplied), and §2(3). Upholding this power in Phelps Dodge Corp. v. NLRB, 313 U.S. 177 (1941), the Court said that the word "including" does not lend itself to a meaning so destructive as to withdraw such authority from the Board. So to interpret it would be "to shrivel a versatile principle to an illustrative application."

The same case also confirmed the power to order reinstatement of a victim of discrimination although he had obtained other substantially

equivalent employment, when such an order was felt necessary to effectuate the policies of the Act.

To frustrate the strategy of guilty employers in withholding reinstatement, calculating that there will probably be earnings from other employment to reduce the liability for back pay, the Board devised a formula, approved in NLRB v. Seven-Up Bottling Co., 344 U.S. 344 (1953).
Under this formula, collateral earnings in one calendar quarter may not
be counted against back-pay liability in another.

Compare the remedy in Section 10(j). Could it be invoked to prevent
an employer from benefiting from wrongful denial of reinstatement?
Should the General Counsel be required to publish the number of instances of waiver of reinstatement as incident to back-pay settlements?
Ascertainment of the amount of pay due is not a part of the principal
proceeding on a complaint, but if it becomes the subject of formal controversy the moving document is usually a "specification," heard before a
trial examiner as in complaint cases. NLRB, Rules and Regulations,
Series 8, §§102.52-102.59 (1962).

4. It has been held that the pressure of an economic strike may be met
by contracting out work formerly performed by strikers, and no prior negotiation with their representatives is required. NLRB v. Abbott Publishing Co., 331 F.2d 209 (7th Cir. 1964); Hawaii Meat Co. v. NLRB, 321
F.2d 397 (9th Cir. 1963).

NLRB v. ERIE RESISTOR CORP.

Supreme Court of the United States, 1963
373 U.S. 221, 83 Sup. Ct. 1139, 10 L. Ed. 2d 308

MR. JUSTICE WHITE delivered the opinion of the Court.

The question before us is whether an employer commits an unfair labor
practice under §8(a) of the National Labor Relations Act, 61 Stat. 136,
29 U.S.C. §158 when he extends a 20-year seniority credit to strike replacements and strikers who leave the strike and return to work. . . .

Erie Resistor Corporation and Local 613 of the International Union of
Electrical, Radio and Machine Workers were bound by a collective bargaining agreement which was due to expire on March 31, 1959. In January 1959, both parties met to negotiate new terms but, after extensive
bargaining, they were unable to reach agreement. Upon expiration of
the contract, the union, in support of its contract demands, called a strike
which was joined by all of the 478 employees in the unit.[2]

The company, under intense competition and subject to insistent demands from its customers to maintain deliveries, decided to continue production operations. Transferring clerks, engineers and other nonunit
employees to production jobs, the company managed to keep production
at about 15% to 30% of normal during the month of April. On May 3,
however, the company notified the union members that it intended to
begin hiring replacements and that strikers would retain their jobs until

[2] In addition to these employees, 450 employees in the unit were on layoff
status.

replaced. The plant was located in an area classified by the United States Department of Labor as one of severe unemployment and the company had in fact received applications for employment as early as a week or two after the strike began.

Replacements were told that they would not be laid off or discharged at the end of the strike. To implement that assurance, particularly in view of the 450 employees already laid off on March 31, the company notified the union that it intended to accord the replacements some form of super-seniority. At regular bargaining sessions between the company and union, the union made it clear that, in its view, no matter what form the super-seniority plan might take, it would necessarily work an illegal discrimination against the strikers. As negotiations advanced on other issues, it became evident that super-seniority was fast becoming the focal point of disagreement. On May 28, the company informed the union that it had decided to award 20 years additional seniority both to replacements and to strikers who returned to work, which would be available only for credit against future layoffs and which could not be used for other employee benefits based on years of service. The strikers, at a union meeting the next day, unanimously resolved to continue striking now in protest against the proposed plan as well.

[The strike was settled by an agreement that left unresolved the company's replacement and job assurance policy. All but 129 strikers were returned to their jobs, but by May, 1960, pursuant to the superseniority policy, many of them had been laid off in a reduction in force.]

We think the Court of Appeals erred in holding that, in the absence of a finding of specific illegal intent, a legitimate business purpose is always a defense to an unfair labor practice charge. Cases in this Court dealing with unfair labor practices have recognized the relevance and importance of showing the employer's intent or motive to discriminate or to interfere with union rights. But specific evidence of such subjective intent is "not an indispensable element of proof of violation." Radio Officers v. Labor Board, 347 U.S. 17, 44. "Some conduct may by its very nature contain the implications of the required intent; the natural foreseeable consequences of certain action may warrant the inference. . . . The existence of discrimination may at times be inferred by the Board, for 'it is permissible to draw on experience in factual inquiries.' " Teamsters Local v. Labor Board, 365 U.S. 667, 675.

Though the intent necessary for an unfair labor practice may be shown in different ways, proving it in one manner may have far different weight and far different consequences than proving it in another. When specific evidence of a subjective intent to discriminate or to encourage or discourage union membership is shown, and found, many otherwise innocent or ambiguous actions which are normally incident to the conduct of a business may, without more, be converted into unfair labor practices. Labor Board v. Jones & Laughlin Steel Corp., 301 U.S. 1, 46 (discharging employees); Associated Press v. Labor Board, 301 U.S. 103, 132 (discharging employees); Phelps Dodge Corp. v. Labor Board, 313 U.S. 177 (hiring employees). . . .

The Board made a detailed assessment of super-seniority and, to its experienced eye, such a plan had the following characteristics:

(1) Super-seniority affects the tenure of all strikers whereas permanent replacement, proper under Mackay, affects only those who are, in actuality, replaced. It is one thing to say that a striker is subject to loss of his job at the strike's end but quite another to hold that in addition to the threat of replacement, all strikers will at best return to their jobs with seniority inferior to that of the replacements and of those who left the strike.

(2) A super-seniority award necessarily operates to the detriment of those who participated in the strike as compared to nonstrikers.

(3) Super-seniority made available to striking bargaining unit employees as well as to new employees is in effect offering individual benefits to the strikers to induce them to abandon the strike.

(4) Extending the benefits of super-seniority to striking bargaining unit employees as well as to new replacements deals a crippling blow to the strike effort. At one stroke, those with low seniority have the opportunity to obtain the job security which ordinarily only long years of service can bring, while conversely, the accumulated seniority of older employees is seriously diluted. This combination of threat and promise could be expected to undermine the strikers' mutual interest and place the entire strike effort in jeopardy. The history of this strike and its virtual collapse following the announcement of the plan emphasize the grave repercussions of super-seniority.

(5) Super-seniority renders future bargaining difficult, if not impossible, for the collective bargaining representative. Unlike the replacement granted in Mackay which ceases to be an issue once the strike is over, the plan here creates a cleavage in the plant continuing long after the strike is ended. Employees are henceforth divided into two camps: those who stayed with the union and those who returned before the end of the strike and thereby gained extra seniority. This breach is reemphasized with each subsequent layoff and stands as an ever-present reminder of the dangers connected with striking and with union activities in general.

In the light of this analysis, super-seniority by its very terms operates to discriminate between strikers and non-strikers, both during and after a strike, and its destructive impact upon the strike and union activity cannot be doubted. The origin of the plan, as respondent insists, may have been to keep production going and it may have been necessary to offer super-seniority to attract replacements and induce union members to leave the strike. But if this is true, accomplishment of respondent's business purpose inexorably was contingent upon attracting sufficient replacements and strikers by offering preferential inducements to those who worked as opposed to those who struck. We think the Board was entitled to treat this case as involving conduct which carried its own indicia of intent and which is barred by the Act unless saved from illegality by an overriding business purpose justifying the invasion of union rights. The Board concluded that the business purpose asserted was insufficient to insulate the super-seniority plan from the reach of §8(a)(1) and §8(a)(3), and we turn now to a review of that conclusion.

The Court of Appeals and respondent rely upon Mackay as precluding the result reached by the Board but we are not persuaded. Under the decision in that case an employer may operate his plant during a strike and at its conclusion need not discharge those who worked during the strike in order to make way for returning strikers. It may be, as the Court of Appeals said, that "such a replacement policy is obviously discriminatory and may tend to discourage union membership." But Mackay did not deal with super-seniority, with its effects upon all strikers, whether replaced or not, or with its powerful impact upon a strike itself. Because the employer's interest must be deemed to outweigh the damage to concerted activities caused by permanently replacing strikers does not mean it also outweighs the far greater encroachment resulting from super-seniority in addition to permanent replacement.

We have no intention of questioning the continuing vitality of the Mackay rule, but we are not prepared to extend it to the situation we have here. To do so would require us to set aside the Board's considered judgment that the Act and its underlying policy require, in the present context, giving more weight to the harm wrought by super-seniority than to the interest of the employer in operating its plant during the strike by utilizing this particular means of attracting replacements. We find nothing in the Act or its legislative history to indicate that super-seniority is necessarily an acceptable method of resisting the economic impact of a strike, nor do we find anything inconsistent with the result which the Board reached. On the contrary, these sources are wholly consistent with, and lend full support to, the conclusion of the Board. . . .

While Congress has from time to time revamped and redirected national labor policy, its concern for the integrity of the strike weapon has remained constant. . . .

Accordingly, in view of the deference paid the strike weapon by the federal labor laws and the devastating consequences upon it which the Board found was and would be precipitated by respondent's inherently discriminatory super-seniority plan, we cannot say the Board erred in the balance which it struck here. . . . The matter before the Board lay well within the mainstream of its duties. It was attempting to deal with an issue which Congress had placed in its hands and "where Congress has in the statute given the Board a question to answer, the courts will give respect to that answer." Labor Board v. Insurance Agents [361 U.S. 477], at 499. Here, as in other cases, we must recognize the Board's special function of applying the general provisions of the Act to the complexities of industrial life. Republic Aviation Corp. v. Labor Board, 324 U.S. 793, 798; Phelps Dodge Corp. v. Labor Board, supra, at 194, and of "(appraising) carefully the interests of both sides of any labor-management controversy in the diverse circumstances of particular cases" from its special understanding of "the actualities of industrial relations." Labor Board v. United Steelworkers [357 U.S. 357], at 362-363. "The ultimate problem is the balancing of the conflicting legitimate interests. The function of striking that balance to effectuate national labor policy is often a difficult and delicate responsibility, which the Congress committed primarily to the National Labor Relations Board, subject to limited judicial review." Labor Board v. Truck Drivers Union, 353 U.S. 87, 96.

Consequently, because the Board's judgment was that the claimed business purpose would not outweigh the necessary harm to employee rights — a judgment which we sustain — it could properly put aside evidence of respondent's motive and decline to find whether the conduct was or was not prompted by the claimed business purpose. We reverse the judgment of the Court of Appeals and remand the case to that court since its review was a limited one and it must now reach the remaining questions before it, including the propriety of the remedy which at least in part turns upon the Board's construction of the settlement agreement as being no barrier to an award not only of reinstatement but of back pay as well.

MR. JUSTICE HARLAN, concurring.

I agree with the Court that the Board's conclusions respecting this 20-year "superseniority" plan were justified without inquiry into the respondents' motives. However, I do not think that the same thing would necessarily be true in all circumstances, as for example with a plan providing for a much shorter period of extra seniority. Being unsure whether the Court intends to hold that the Board has power to outlaw all such plans, irrespective of the employer's motives and other circumstances, or only to sustain its action in the particular circumstances of this case, I concur in the judgment.

NLRB, 28TH ANNUAL REPORT [26]
54-55 (1964)

The Board has adopted the rule that the voting eligibility status of an economic striker may be forfeited by action [such as accepting other permanent employment] which evinces an intention to abandon interest in his struck job regardless of the outcome of the strike [but] an economic striker will be presumed to retain his voting eligibility, notwithstanding his acceptance of new employment, unless the party challenging his vote affirmatively establishes that the striker has abandoned his struck job. However, acceptance of other employment, even without informing the new employer that only temporary employment is sought, will not of itself be sufficient to establish abandonment. . . .

Similarly, the Board will presume that replacements for economic strikers are permanent employees and eligible to vote. To rebut this presumption, the party challenging the eligibility of a replacement must affirmatively establish that the replacement was not employed on the struck job on a permanent basis.

Generally, permanent replacements . . . are eligible to vote only if employed on the eligibility and election dates. [According to a Board

[26] Omitted footnotes refer principally to W. Wilton Wood, Inc., 127 N.L.R.B. 1675 (1960); Greenspan Engraving Corp., 137 N.L.R.B. 1308 (1962); and Pacific Tile & Porcelain Co., 137 N.L.R.B. 1358 (1962). — Ed.

majority the exception in favor of replacements when the strike occurs after the issuance of the direction of election does not apply to] the ordinary situation of a strike arising before the election was directed, [so] striker replacements who were not employed on the eligibility date were ineligible to vote.

NOTE

What is the Board's choice, when the statutory twelve months may run while the parties are arguing about the question concerning representation? In Kingsport Press, Inc., 146 N.L.R.B. No. 137 (1964), before briefs were filed the Board directed an election to save the eligibility of economic strikers. It said that when the briefs came in they could be considered as though on motion for reconsideration. See Kingsport Press, Inc. v. McCulloch, 336 F.2d 753 (D.C. Cir. 1964), sustaining dismissal of an action to enjoin the election for lack of jurisdiction.

NLRB v. RAPID BINDERY, INC.
United States Court of Appeals, Second Circuit, 1961
293 F.2d 170

WATERMAN, Circuit Judge.

The National Labor Relations Board, pursuant to Section 10(e) of the National Labor Relations Act (N.L.R.A.), 29 U.S.C.A. §160(e), has petitioned this court for enforcement of its order of April 15, 1960 issued against the respondents Rapid Bindery, Inc. (Rapid) and Frontier Bindery Corporation (Frontier).

Until March 1959 Rapid operated a bindery plant in Dunkirk, N.Y. The source of its work was Greater Buffalo Press, Inc. (Buffalo), a commercial printer. Buffalo's printing plant was located in Buffalo, N.Y. Buffalo did some of its own bindery work and subcontracted the remainder of it to Rapid. For reasons to be developed later in this opinion, Rapid became unable adequately to service Buffalo. Thereupon, the sole shareholders of Rapid, J. Walter Koessler and his brother Kenneth Koessler, together with William Hammond, an officer of Rapid acting as trustee for members of the Koessler family, formed a new entity, Frontier. Frontier's plant was in Tonawanda, N.Y. It began as a partnership but was later incorporated, all the stock being owned by the two Koesslers and by Hammond as trustee. This led the trial examiner, whose findings and conclusions were accepted in toto by the Board, to find as a fact that Frontier was the alter ego of Rapid. That finding is clearly correct. Moreover, Buffalo and the Great Lakes Color Printing Corp. (hereinafter Great Lakes) from which Rapid rented space at Dunkirk were also owned and controlled by these same individuals. Therefore there emerges from the Board's record a picture of an integrated printing operation controlled by the Koesslers. Based upon these facts the trial examiner treated the case as one where there had been a transfer by a single entity of work from one plant to another, followed by the subsequent abandonment of the old plant. . . . During the course of the hearing the examiner appeared to concede the economic necessity of the removal from Dunkirk by discouraging evidence tending to prove it. However, from the evidence that was admitted it is clear that the transfer of operations from Dunkirk was indeed economically necessary. Despite this, the examiner found that the move was not made solely for economic reasons but was made "in an atmosphere redolent with hostility toward the Union, and for the purpose of discouraging membership in it," and consequently that the respondents violated §8(a)(3). . . .

. . .[W]e agree with the Board that the failure to give notice to the union of the move and failure to discuss the treatment to be accorded displaced employees was a violation of §8(a)(5). We also find that the record contains substantial evidence to support the Board's determination that the respondents committed an unfair labor practice within the purview of §8(a)(1). We will grant enforcement to as much of the Board's order as deals with the §8(a)(1) and §8(a)(5) violations.

Rapid proved that the Dunkirk operation had been an unsuccessful one almost from its inception. For some time prior to the final decision to abandon operations there the Koesslers had been actively seeking a new plant. Rapid was located in little more than a railroad shed appended to the Great Lakes plant. The floor plan was long and narrow and unsuitable for bindery operations. Prior to the fall of 1958 the space had become inadequate. A competent work force was difficult to maintain in Dunkirk. The evidence was that within the span of one year the corporation had been forced to hire 232 individuals in order to maintain a work force of 40. Many overtime hours were required, hours that would not have been necessary if a full complement of employees could have been constantly maintained. Although Rapid did some work for Great Lakes, the bulk of the work it did was for Buffalo, and Rapid's costs were enhanced because of the transportation expense between the two cities of Buffalo and Dunkirk.

Then in the Fall of 1958 at about the time Union appeared on the scene Buffalo obtained a large commercial printing job for the preparation of catalogs from its customer, Western Auto Stores. This job was substantially larger than anything Buffalo had previously undertaken and the bindery work required for it was also sizable. It was obvious to respondents that Rapid could not do the job. Rapid lacked both space and a sufficient work force, and the transportation costs would have been exorbitant. Moreover, it was stated that the post office in Dunkirk could not handle the heavy mailings involved in Western Auto's plan for its catalog distribution. However, the examiner found that the decision to move from Dunkirk was not finally decided upon until after Union came on the scene. The record supports this finding. Union's petition for recognition as bargaining agent was filed with the Board on October 6, 1958. A consent election was agreed to on October 13. The election was conducted by the Board on October 30. On November 6 Union was certified. The examiner accepted Kenneth Koessler's testimony that management's decision to move was not finally made until early November. . . .

Pursuant to the decision respondents had finally made in early November part of Rapid's plant was moved to Frontier's facilities at Tonawanda on or about December 3, 1958. This was about a month after the certification of Union. At Tonawanda there were none of the disadvantages suffered at Dunkirk. Frontier had sufficient floor space so that work could be performed there efficiently. It was located in a suburb of the City of Buffalo and transportation costs were thereby substantially reduced. There was no post office problem and a large labor force was available. . . .

Rapid's plant was finally fully closed on March 1, 1959 when Buffalo withdrew from Rapid all of its remaining bindery work. Buffalo was forced to do this because Buffalo's Canadian customer for whom the work was being done had a clause in its union contract that required such work to be done by the Mailer's Union, a different international Union than the one certified at Rapid.

Upon the facts so found the Board is of the opinion that the respondents violated §8(a)(3) at two junctures. The first was in December when a part of the machinery was moved from Rapid at Dunkirk to Frontier at Tonawanda. The second was when Rapid's Dunkirk operation was totally abandoned. Rapid sought to justify these moves on the ground of sound economic need. In our view the record supports the employer's contentions. The Board's position appears to be that a move by management when that move is required for sound business reasons is nevertheless an unfair labor practice if the move is accelerated or reinforced by contemporaneous employer differences with a union. This position is not supported by the language of the Act or by the decisional law interpreting that language. . . .

In those situations where a change or discontinuance of business operations is dictated by sound financial or economic reasons the courts have refused to find that §8(a)(3) has been violated even though the employer action may have been accelerated by union activity. NLRB v. Lassing, 6 Cir., 1960, 284 F.2d 781, certiorari denied 1961, 366 U.S. 909; NLRB v. R. C. Mahon Co., 6 Cir., 1959, 269 F.2d 44; NLRB v. Houston Chronicle Pub. Co., 5 Cir., 1954, 211 F.2d 848. In Lassing an employer had been toying with the idea of terminating its own transportation of the gas it produced in favor of utilizing a common carrier for this purpose, and had determined that any further increase in costs would dictate such a move. A union demand for recognition of three of its drivers foreshadowed just such an increase. The discontinuance of private carriage in favor of common was not found to be violative of §8(a)(3). NLRB v. R. C. Mahon Co., supra, was a similar situation. There plant guards were discharged for reasons of economy and the employer hired an independent contractor to supply it with plant protection.

The case of NLRB v. Houston Chronicle Pub. Co., supra, where the background situation was as redolent with animosity as it was in the instant case, is closest on its facts to our case. There the Board found violations of §§8(a)(3), 8(a)(5) and 8(a)(1) when the employer changed its system of newspaper delivery from one which it controlled to one operated by independent contractors. As here, the corporation produced testimony to show that the change was required by economic necessity; but in the case before us that testimony was not challenged. There it was. Nevertheless, on review the Court of Appeals held that the Board's finding that the employer's act had been illegally motivated was not supported by substantial evidence, and that the real motivation was the one of economic necessity.

It is our view that the record before us does not support the inference drawn from it by the Board that Rapid's move was motivated by the desire to avoid its obligations to Union. All of the evidence points to motivation for sound business reasons. Though there may have been animosity between Union and Rapid, animosity furnishes no basis for the inference that this was the preponderant motive for the move when convincing evidence was received demonstrating business necessity. The decided cases do not condemn an employer who considers his relationship with his plant's union as only one part of the broad economic picture he must survey when he is faced with determining the desirability of making changes in his operations.

A word is perhaps necessary with respect to the questions presented by the final abandonment of Rapid's Dunkirk operations. Though the December movement of machinery to Frontier appears clearly justifiable for valid economic reasons, the Board claims that the final abandonment at Dunkirk resulted from the pressure brought to bear on Rapid by the Canadian customer and that submission to this pressure was illegal and violated the Act. The Board argues that this caused Rapid to discriminate against Union in favor of the Mailer's Union. It relies on NLRB v. Hudson Motor Car Co., 6 Cir., 1942, 128 F.2d 528, for the proposition that employer discrimination between unions for sound economic reasons is illegal. However, Hudson is not in point. In that case there were two unions in the employer's plant. Each represented certain employees. Because of threats and pressure brought upon Hudson by a favored union, it was discriminating against the other. This is an entirely different situation from the one before us. Rapid's continued life depended on business which it could no longer do unless it acceded to a legitimate demand made by a customer who conditioned its contract upon Rapid's compliance. Inability to comply with the demand of the Canadian customer put Rapid out of business. This situation was not within the control of Rapid whose employees were not members of the Mailer's Union, or of Buffalo, some of whose employees were. . . .

The remedies chosen by the Board are too broad for the violations that were properly found.

Those portions of the order that direct the respondents to cease and desist from interfering with the employees' exercise of their guaranteed rights are clearly proper in view of the finding of §8(a)(1) violations.

The portion of the order that requires an offer of employment to the displaced employees is proper in view of our holding that there had been a §8(a)(5) violation.

However, the portion of the order that requires respondent Frontier to recognize Union as the exclusive bargaining representative at the Frontier plant in Tonawanda is not proper inasmuch as Union does not appear to represent any of the employees in the Tonawanda plant. If it later should happen that a substantial number of Rapid's employees accept employment in Tonawanda or that a substantial number of Frontier's employees designate Union as their representative, Union could properly petition the Board for another election at that plant.

Moreover, the portions of the order should not be enforced that require respondents to make the employees whole by paying them allegedly lost wages and certain contingent traveling expenses. These order provisions are based upon the §8(a)(3) violations that the Board found and which we have struck down. We hold that the move was motivated by sound economic reasons and it is our view that any obligation due to Rapid's employees will be fulfilled by offering them jobs at the Frontier plant in Tonawanda.

NOTE

In NLRB v. Exchange Parts Co., supra page 246, the Court said that Section 8(a)(1) prohibits "conduct immediately favorable to employees which is undertaken with the express purpose of impinging upon their freedom of choice for or against unionization and is reasonably calculated to have that effect." So the unconditional bestowal of a wage increase during an election campaign was held a violation, like the promise of favors expressly conditioned on leaving the union in Medo Photo Supply Corp. v. NLRB, 321 U.S. 678 (1944). The corresponding analysis of a disadvantage, in the Erie Resistor example of superseniority for replacements, was borrowed from general intent doctrine in the law of crimes and compounded with the balancing-of-interests model. By this approach the Court reached the conclusion that because the claimed business purpose would not outweigh the harm to employee rights, evidence of motive was properly excluded. What if the claimed justification is going out of business?

In Textile Workers Union v. Darlington Manufacturing Co., 380 U.S. 263 (1965), the Court, per Mr. Justice Harlan, at page 273, said: "We hold here only that when an employer closes his entire business, even if the liquidation is motivated by vindictiveness towards the union, such action is not an unfair labor practice." However, a discriminatory partial closing may afford employer leverage for discouraging the free exercise of rights under Section 7 among remaining employees similar to those in the cases of the runaway shop and the temporary closing. In such cases, there are remedies open to the Board that include reinstatement of the discharged employees in other parts of the business. Hence, a partial closing is an unfair labor practice under Section 8(a)(3) "if motivated by a purpose to chill unionism in any of the remaining plants of the single employer and if the employer may reasonably have foreseen that such closing will likely have that effect." (p. 275). In that case, it was held that the findings of the Board were defective, in that they contained nothing on the purpose and effect of the closing of the Darlington plant with respect to employees in other plants comprising the single enterprise controlled by the family of Roger Milliken. The judgment of the Court of Appeals was therefore vacated to remand the case to the Board for further findings on the issue of purpose and effect of the permanent closing of the Darlington plant. The Court compared the unqualified character of the right to go out of business with the right of employees to quit their employment permanently, even if motivated by a desire to ruin the employer, notwithstanding restrictions on engaging in a strike.

NLRB v. WASHINGTON ALUMINUM CO.
Supreme Court of the United States, 1962
370 U.S. 9, 82 Sup. Ct. 1099, 8 L. Ed. 2d 298

Mr. Justice Black delivered the opinion of the Court.

The Court of Appeals for the Fourth Circuit, with Chief Judge Soboloff dissenting, refused to enforce an order of the National Labor Relations Board directing the respondent Washington Aluminum Company to reinstate and make whole seven employees whom the company had discharged for leaving their work in the machine shop without permission on claims that the shop was too cold to work in.[1] . . .

January 5, 1959, was an extraordinarily cold day for Baltimore, with unusually high winds and a low temperature of 11 degrees followed by a high of 22. When the employees on the day shift came to work that morning, they found the shop bitterly cold, due not only to the unusually harsh weather, but also to the fact that the large oil furnace had broken down the night before and had not as yet been put back into operation. As the workers gathered in the shop just before the starting hour of 7:30, one of them, a Mr. Caron, went into the office of Mr. Jarvis, the foreman, hoping to warm himself but, instead, found the foreman's quarters as uncomfortable as the rest of the shop. As Caron and Jarvis sat in Jarvis' office discussing how bitingly cold the building was, some of the other machinists walked by the office window "huddled" together in a fashion that caused Jarvis to exclaim that "[i]f those fellows had any guts at all, they would go home!" When the starting buzzer sounded a few moments later, Caron walked back to his working place in the shop and found all the other machinists "huddled there, shaking a little, cold." Caron then said to these workers, ". . . Dave (Jarvis) told me if we had any guts, we

---

[1] 291 F.2d 869. The Court of Appeals also refused to enforce another Board order requiring the respondent company to bargain collectively with the Industrial Union of Marine & Shipbuilding Workers of America, AFL-CIO, as the certified bargaining representative of its employees. Since the Union's status as majority bargaining representative turns on the ballots cast in the Board election by four of the seven discharged employees, the enforceability of that order depends upon the validity of the discharges being challenged in the principal part of the case. Our decision on the discharge question will therefore also govern the refusal-to-bargain issue.

would go home . . . I am going home — it is too damned cold to work." Caron asked the other workers what they were going to do and, after some discussion among themselves, they decided to leave with him. One of these workers, testifying before the Board, summarized their entire discussion this way: "And we had all got together and thought it would be a good idea to go home; maybe we could get some heat brought into the plant that way." As they started to leave, Jarvis approached and persuaded one of the workers to remain at the job. But Caron and the other six workers on the day shift left practically in a body in a matter of minutes after the 7:30 buzzer. . . .

When the company's general foreman arrived between 7:45 and 8 that morning, Jarvis promptly informed him that all but one of the employees had left because the shop was too cold. The company's president came in at approximately 8:20 A.M. and, upon learning of the walk-out immediately said to the foreman, ". . . if they have all gone, we are going to terminate them." After discussion "at great length" between the general foreman and the company president as to what might be the effect of the walkout on employee discipline and plant production, the president formalized his discharge of the workers who had walked out by giving orders at 9 A.M. that the affected workers should be notified about their discharge immediately, either by telephone, telegram or personally. This was done.

On these facts the Board found that the conduct of the workers was a concerted activity to protest the company's failure to supply adequate heat in its machine shop, that such conduct is protected under the provision of §7 of the National Labor Relations Act which guarantees that "Employees shall have the right . . . to engage in . . . concerted activities for the purpose of collective bargaining or other mutual aid or protection," and that the discharge of these workers by the company amounted to an unfair labor practice under §8(a)(1) of the Act . . .

In denying enforcement . . . the majority of the Court of Appeals took the position that because the workers simply "summarily left their place of employment" without affording the company an "opportunity to avoid the work stoppage by granting a concession to a demand," their walkout did not amount to a concerted activity protected by §7 of the Act. On this basis, they held that there was no justification for the conduct of the workers in violating the established rules of the plant by leaving their jobs without permission and that the Board had therefore exceeded its power in issuing the order involved here because §10(c) declares that the Board shall not require reinstatement or back pay for an employee whom an employer has suspended or discharged "for cause."

We cannot agree that employees necessarily lose their right to engage in concerted activities under §7 merely because they do not present a specific demand upon their employer to remedy a condition they find objectionable. The language of §7 is broad enough to protect concerted activities whether they take place before, after, or at the same time such a demand is made. To compel the Board to interpret and apply that language in the restricted fashion suggested by the respondent here would only tend to frustrate the policy of the Act to protect the right of workers to act together to better their working conditions. Indeed, as indicated by this very case, such an interpretation of §7 might place burdens upon employees so great that it would effectively nullify the right to engage in concerted activities which that section protects. The seven employees here were part of a small group of employees who were wholly unorganized. They had no bargaining representative and, in fact, no representative of any kind to present their grievances to their employer. Under these circumstances, they had to speak for themselves as best they could. As pointed out above, prior to the day they left the shop, several of them had repeatedly complained to company officials about the cold working conditions in the shop. These had been more or less spontaneous individual pleas, unsupported by any threat of concerted protest, to which the company apparently gave little consideration and which it now says the Board should have treated as nothing more than "the same sort of gripes as the gripes made about the heat in the summertime." The bitter cold of January 5, however, finally brought these workers' individual complaints into concert so that some more effective action could be considered. Having no bargaining representative and no established procedure by which they could take full advantage of their unanimity of opinion in negotiations with the company, the men took the most direct course to let the company know that they wanted a warmer place in which to work. So, after talking among themselves, they walked out together in the hope that this action might spotlight their complaint and bring about some improvement in what they considered to be the "miserable" conditions of their employment. This we think was enough to justify the Board's holding that they were not required to make any more specific demand than they did to be entitled to the protection of §7.

Although the company contends to the contrary, we think that the walkout involved here did grow out of a "labor dispute" within the plain meaning of the definition of that term in §2(9) of the Act, which declares that it includes "any controversy concerning terms, tenure or conditions of employment. . . ." The findings of the Board, which are supported by substantial evidence and which were not disturbed below, show a running dispute between the machine shop employees and the company over the heating of the shop on cold days — a dispute which culminated in the decision of the employees to act concertedly in an effort to force the company to improve that condition of their employment. The fact that the company was already making every effort to repair the furnace and bring heat into the shop that morning does not change the nature of the controversy that caused the walkout. At the very most, that fact might tend to indicate that the conduct of the men in leaving was unnecessary and unwise, and it has long been settled that the reasonableness of workers' decisions to engage in concerted activity is irrelevant to the determination of whether a labor dispute exists or not. Moreover, the evidence here shows that the conduct of these workers was far from unjustified under the circumstances. The company's own foreman expressed the opinion that the shop was so cold that the men should go home. This statement by the foreman but emphasizes the obvious — that is, that the conditions of coldness about which complaint had been made before had been so aggravated on the day of the walkout that the concerted action of the men in leaving their jobs seemed like a perfectly natural and reasonable thing to do.

Nor can we accept the company's contention that because it admittedly had an established plant rule which forbade employees to leave their work without permission of the foreman, there was justifiable "cause" for discharging these employees, wholly separate and apart from any concerted activities in which they engaged in protest against the poorly heated plant. Section 10(c) of the Act does authorize an employer to discharge employees for "cause" and our cases have long recognized this right on the part of an employer. But this, of course, cannot mean that an employer is at liberty to punish a man by discharging him for engaging in concerted activities which §7 of the Act protects. And the plant rule in question here purports to permit the company to do just that for it would prohibit even the most plainly protected kinds of concerted work stoppages until and unless the permission of the company's foreman was obtained. . . .

[These activities were not unlawful, violent, in breach of contract, disloyal or indefensible by any recognized standard of conduct.]

We hold therefore that the Board correctly interpreted and applied the Act to the circumstances of this case and it was error for the Court of Appeals to refuse to enforce its order. The judgment of the Court of Appeals is reversed and the cause is remanded to that court with directions to enforce the order in its entirety.

Mr. Justice Frankfurter and Mr. Justice White took no part in the consideration or decision of this case.

NOTES

1. Was the winter morning walkout a strike? See LMRA §502. If it is "protected activity" what, if anything, follows from Section 502? In NLRB v. Fruin-Colnon Construction Co., 330 F.2d 885 (8th Cir. 1964), the order required reinstatement of employees who refused to work in a mine shaft under hazards of falling rock and water, and slippery footing, although there was in effect a collective agreement containing a "no-strike" clause. The court denied enforcement, holding that there was no reasonable basis for belief that conditions were abnormally dangerous. It expressly refused to follow the doctrine of NLRB v. Knight Morley Corp., 251 F.2d 753 (6th Cir. 1957), cert. denied, 357 U.S. 927 (1958), that only a good-faith belief is required.

2. Are "quickie" walkouts protected activity when there is no unusual condition in the shop? What bearing has the absence of sanction from the Section 9 representative (the "wildcat" aspect), as distinct from breach of agreement? In NLRB v. R. C. Can Co., 328 F.2d 974 (5th Cir. 1964), an international union, the Steelworkers, was the certified representative. Its negotiations, prolonged for some time, were being obstructed by the company's insistence on scheduling for convenience of the company's at-

torney. Eight of approximately fifty employees in the unit left the plant premises at the morning coffee break, held a conference at a bowling alley, and returned an hour later with crude signs "On Strike." The union representative persuaded them to make an unconditional offer to return to work. Acceptance of the offer was deferred on the pretext of investigating the situation. The court by a vote of 2-to-1 enforced the order against the company, the judges dividing on whether the objects of the activity and its tactics were in conflict with the policy and procedure previously resolved by the union. The majority found substantial evidence to support the Board's conclusion that the activity was protected in that both the union and the hotheads wanted to get the employer to confer, and that the union had not resolved against using the strike to achieve this object. Contrast NLRB v. Sunbeam Lighting Co., 318 F.2d 661 (7th Cir. 1963), predicating the denial of enforcement on the lack of substantial evidence that a majority joined the concerted activity. See Cox, The Right to Engage in Concerted Activities, 26 Ind. L.J. 319, 332-333 (1951).

C. Union Conduct Affecting the Establishment of Collective Bargaining

1. *Picketing*

ENDERBY PROBLEM 5
(*See page 254 supra for Enderby Problem 4*)

Curme did not find Cooper's analysis of voting rights at Enderby too satisfactory. "Full of careful lawyer's talk," he reported to Layton. He was more disturbed, however, by a growing suspicion that a recent general wage increase throughout the plant, as well as the improved working schedule in the Tire Division, had weakened the union's position. He dropped the idea of a strike and decided to postpone the filing of an election petition.

Several days after this decision Local 417 stationed four members in front of the Enderby plant.

Two of these representatives carried signs which read: "Enderby Co Unfair to Senior Citizens. Local 417 Protests."

The other two members distributed handbills which were addressed "To the Public" and accused the company of arbitrarily discharging older employees in the absence of a union contract. These handbills were given to any person who would take them; and since no work stoppage occurred most of them were regularly received by Enderby employees a they entered and left the plant.

The first two days of this conduct, all truck drivers employed by othe companies refused to pick up or deliver at the Enderby plant. No member of Local 417, however, requested this refusal; and normal operation were resumed on the third day when Layton finally succeeded in convinc ing officers of the Teamster locals that the truck operators were hurting the union. Thereafter, there were occasional delays in critical deliveries, "which," White told Blair, "can hardly be attributed to natural causes."

During the next month Local 417 also continued to solicit membership on the company premises and scheduled more frequent organizational meetings at the union hall. Blair advised White that it would be a waste of time and money to take any legal steps against the union campaign — "to keep his collar buttoned and let the Rubber Workers hang themselves."

Then, before and after their respective shifts, many members of Local 417 began to distribute in front of retail stores and filling stations leaflets which read as follows: "We Ask You! Can you rely on the integrity of an unfair product? Local 417 United Rubber Workers protests the Enderby Company's treatment of its senior employees."

White immediately discharged seven union officers for engaging in this "indefensible conduct." The union promptly called a strike but only about 200 workers walked out.

For the next week there was considerable massing of strikers at the main plant gate at the start and close of the shifts. Some of the non-strikers were jostled, all of them were called scabs and derided with profane epithets. Truck drivers refused to attempt deliveries. Finally the company secured an injunction which prohibited any and all assembly before any entrance to the plant.

Thereafter the strike quickly collapsed and all of the strikers applied for reinstatement. The company refused to reinstate twelve of them on the ground that they had been leaders of the group which had "illegally massed at the plant gate."

Upon learning of this action by the company twenty-five other strikers refused to return to work unless all the strikers were reinstated.

The company then filled the jobs of the twelve men whom it had refused to reinstate and the twenty-five men remaining on strike. Curme again sought legal advice from Cooper.

THORNHILL v. ALABAMA

Supreme Court of the United States, 1940
310 U.S. 88, 60 Sup. Ct. 736, 84 L. Ed. 1093

[Thornhill was convicted under a complaint phrased substantially in terms of the Alabama Code of 1923, §3448: "Loitering or picketing forbidden. — Any person or persons, who, without a just cause or legal excuse therefor, go near to or loiter about the premises or place of business of any other person . . . engaged in a lawful business, for the purpose, or with the intent of influencing, or inducing other persons not to trade with, buy from, sell to, have business dealings with, or be employed by such persons . . . or who picket the works or place of business of such other persons . . . for the purpose of hindering, delaying, or interfering with or injuring any lawful business or enterprise of another, shall be guilty of a misdemeanor; but nothing herein shall prevent any person from soliciting trade or business for a competitive business." The testimony showed that during a strike the employer scheduled a resumption of operations and on the day appointed Thornhill approached an employee and told him that "they" were on strike and did not want anybody to go up there and work, and that Thornhill did not threaten or appear angry to the employee, who was not put in fear but did go back to his house. Thornhill was one of six to eight pickets patrolling on company land, but the company had never demanded that men stay off. Thornhill objected that the statute was repugnant to the United States Constitution, but his conviction was affirmed, and the Supreme Court granted certiorari.]

MR. JUSTICE MURPHY delivered the opinion of the Court. . . .

First. The freedom of speech and of the press, which are secured by the First Amendment against abridgment by the United States, are among the fundamental personal rights and liberties which are secured to all persons by the Fourteenth Amendment against abridgment by a State.

The safeguarding of these rights to the ends that men may speak as they think on matters vital to them and that falsehoods may be exposed through the process of education and discussion is essential to free government. Those who won our independence had confidence in the power of free and fearless reasoning and communication of ideas to discover and spread political and economic truth. Noxious doctrines in those fields may be refuted and their evil averted by the courageous exercise of the right of free discussion. Abridgment of freedom of speech and of the press, however, impairs those opportunities for public education that are essential to effective exercise of the power of correcting error through the processes of popular government. Compare United States v. Carolene Products Co., 304 U.S. 144, 152-153n. Mere legislative preference for one rather than another means for combating substantive evils, therefore, may well prove an inadequate foundation on which to rest regulations which are aimed at or in their operation diminish the effective exercise of rights so necessary to the maintenance of democratic institutions. It is imperative that, when the effective exercise of these rights is claimed to be abridged, the courts should "weigh the circumstances" and "appraise the substantiality of the reasons advanced" in support of the challenged regulations. Schneider v. State, 308 U.S. 147, 161, 162.

Second. The section in question must be judged upon its face. . . .

Proof of an abuse of power in the particular case has never been deemed a requisite for attack on the constitutionality of a statute purporting to license the dissemination of ideas. Schneider v. State, 308 U.S. 147, 162-165; Hague v. C.I.O., 307 U.S. 496, 516; Lovell v. Griffin, 303 U.S. 444, 451. . . . The power of the licensor against which John Milton directed his assault by his "Appeal for the Liberty of Unlicensed Printing" is pernicious not merely by reason of the censure of particular comment but by reason of the threat to censure comments on matters of public concern. It is not merely the sporadic abuse of power by the censor but the pervasive threat inherent in its very existence that constitutes the danger to freedom of discussion. See Near v. Minnesota, 283 U.S. 697,

713. . . . . The existence of such a statute, which readily lends itself to harsh and discriminatory enforcement by local prosecuting officials, against particular groups deemed to merit their displeasure, results in a continuous and pervasive restraint on all freedom of discussion that might reasonably be regarded as within its purview. It is not any less effective or, if the restraint is not permissible, less pernicious than the restraint on freedom of discussion imposed by the threat of censorship. . . .

Third. Section 3448 has been applied by the state courts so as to prohibit a single individual from walking slowly and peacefully back and forth on the public sidewalk in front of the premises of an employer, without speaking to anyone, carrying a sign or placard on a staff above his head stating only the fact that the employer did not employ union men affiliated with the American Federation of Labor; the purpose of the described activity was concededly to advise customers and prospective customers of the relationship existing between the employer and its employees and thereby to induce such customers not to patronize the employer. . . . The statute as thus authoritatively construed and applied leaves room for no exceptions based upon either the number of persons engaged in the proscribed activity, the peaceful character of their demeanor, the nature of their dispute with an employer, or the restrained character and the accurateness of the terminology used in notifying the public of the facts of the dispute.

The numerous forms of conduct proscribed by Section 3448 are subsumed under two offenses: the first embraces the activities of all who "without just cause or legal excuse" "go near to or loiter about the premises" of any person engaged in a lawful business for the purpose of influencing or inducing others to adopt any of certain enumerated courses of action; the second, all who "picket" the place of business of any such person "for the purpose of hindering, delaying or interfering with or injuring any lawful business or enterprise of another." It is apparent that one or the other of the offenses comprehends every practicable method whereby the facts of a labor dispute may be publicized in the vicinity of the place of business of an employer. The phrase "without just cause or legal excuse" does not in any effective manner restrict the breadth of the regulation; the words themselves have no ascertainable meaning either inherent or historical. . . . An intention to hinder, delay or interfere with a lawful business, which is an element of the second offense, likewise can be proved merely by showing that others reacted in a way normally expectable of some upon learning the facts of a dispute. The vague contours of the term "picket" are nowhere delineated. . . . In sum, whatever the means used to publicize the facts of a labor dispute, whether by printed sign, by pamphlet, by word of mouth or otherwise, all such activity without exception is within the inclusive prohibition of the statute so long as it occurs in the vicinity of the scene of the dispute.

Fourth. We think that Section 3448 is invalid on its face.

The freedom of speech and of the press guaranteed by the Constitution embraces at the least the liberty to discuss publicly and truthfully all matters of public concern without previous restraint or fear of subsequent punishment. The exigencies of the colonial period and the efforts to secure freedom from oppressive administration developed a broadened conception of these liberties as adequate to supply the public need for information and education with respect to the significant issues of the time. . . . Freedom of discussion, if it would fulfill its historic function in this nation, must embrace all issues about which information is needed or appropriate to enable the members of society to cope with the exigencies of their period.

In the circumstances of our times the dissemination of information concerning the facts of a labor dispute must be regarded as within that area of free discussion that is guaranteed by the Constitution. Hague v. C.I.O., 307 U.S. 496; Schneider v. State, 308 U.S. 147, 155, 162-163. See Senn v. Tile Layers Union, 301 U.S. 468, 478. It is recognized now that satisfactory hours and wages and working conditions in industry and a bargaining position which makes these possible have an importance which is not less than the interests of those in the business or industry directly concerned. The health of the present generation and of those as yet unborn may depend on these matters, and the practices in a single factory may have economic repercussions upon a whole region and affect widespread systems of marketing. The merest glance at state and federal legislation on the subject demonstrates the force of the argument that labor relations are not matters of mere local or private concern. Free discussion concerning the conditions in industry and the causes of labor disputes appears to us indispensable to the effective and intelligent use of the processes of popular government to shape the destiny of modern industrial society. The issues raised by regulations, such as are challenged here, infringing upon the right of employees effectively to inform the public of the facts of a labor dispute are part of this larger problem. We concur in the observation of Mr. Justice Brandeis, speaking for the Court in Senn's case (301 U.S. at 478): "Members of a union might, without special statutory authorization by a State, make known the facts of a labor dispute, for freedom of speech is guaranteed by the Federal Constitution."

It is true that the rights of employers and employees to conduct their economic affairs and to compete with others for a share in the products of industry are subject to modification or qualification in the interests of the society in which they exist. This is but an instance of the power of the State to set the limits of permissible contest open to industrial combatants. See Mr. Justice Brandeis in 254 U.S. at 488. It does not follow that the State in dealing with the evils arising from industrial disputes may impair the effective exercise of the right to discuss freely industrial relations which are matters of public concern. A contrary conclusion could be used to support abridgment of freedom of speech and of the press concerning almost every matter of importance to society.

The range of activities proscribed by Section 3448, whether characterized as picketing or loitering or otherwise, embraces nearly every practicable, effective means whereby those interested — including the employees directly affected — may enlighten the public on the nature and causes of a labor dispute. The safeguarding of these means is essential to the securing of an informed and educated public opinion with respect to a matter which is of public concern. It may be that effective exercise of the means of advancing public knowledge may persuade some of those reached to refrain from entering into advantageous relations with the business establishment which is the scene of the dispute. Every expression of opinion on matters that are important has the potentiality of inducing action in the interests of one rather than another group in society. But the group in power at any moment may not impose penal sanctions on peaceful and truthful discussion of matters of public interest merely on a showing that others may thereby be persuaded to take action inconsistent with its interests. Abridgment of the liberty of such discussion can be justified only where the clear danger of substantive evils arises under circumstances affording no opportunity to test the merits of ideas by competition for acceptance in the market of public opinion. We hold that the danger of injury to an industrial concern is neither so serious nor so imminent as to justify the sweeping proscription of freedom of discussion embodied in Section 3448.

The State urges that the purpose of the challenged statute is the protection of the community from the violence and breaches of the peace, which, it asserts, are the concomitants of picketing. The power and the duty of the State to take adequate steps to preserve the peace and to protect the privacy, the lives, and the property of its residents cannot be doubted. But no clear and present danger of destruction of life or property, or invasion of the right of privacy, or breach of the peace can be thought to be inherent in the activities of every person who approaches the premises of an employer and publicizes the facts of a labor dispute involving the latter. We are not now concerned with picketing en masse or otherwise conducted which might occasion such imminent and aggravated danger to these interests as to justify a statute narrowly drawn to cover the precise situation giving rise to the danger. Compare American Foundries v. Tri-City Council, 257 U.S. 184, 205. Section 3448 in question here does not aim specifically at serious encroachments on these interests and does not evidence any such care in balancing these interests against the interest of the community and that of the individual in freedom of discussion on matters of public concern.

It is not enough to say that Section 3448 is limited or restricted in its application to such activity as takes place at the scene of the labor dispute. "[The] streets are natural and proper places for the dissemination of information and opinion; and one is not to have the exercise of his liberty of expression in appropriate places abridged on the plea that it may be exercised in some other place." Schneider v. State, 308 U.S. 147, 161, 163; Hague v. C.I.O., 307 U.S. 496, 515-516. The danger of breach of the peace or serious invasion of rights of property or privacy at the scene of a labor dispute is not sufficiently imminent in all cases to warrant the legislature in determining that such place is not appropriate for the range of activities outlawed by Section 3448.

Reversed.

MR. JUSTICE MCREYNOLDS is of the opinion that the judgment below should be affirmed.

INTERNATIONAL BROTHERHOOD OF TEAMSTERS, LOCAL 695 v. VOGT, INC.

Supreme Court of the United States, 1957
354 U.S. 284, 77 Sup. Ct. 1166, 1 L. Ed. 2d 1347

[The employer operated a gravel pit in Wisconsin, where it employed fifteen to twenty men. The union sought to organize these men but failed. It then set up a picket line with signs reading: "The men on this job are not 100% affiliated with A.F.L." In consequence, drivers of truck companies refused to cross the line. The trial court did not make the finding requested by the employer that the picketing had been for the purpose of coercing him to compel his employees to join the union, but it enjoined the picketing on the ground that there was no "labor dispute" within the meaning of the Wisconsin anti-injunction Act. The Wisconsin Supreme Court at first reversed, relying on A.F.L. v. Swing, 312 U.S. 321 (1941), for its conclusion that picketing could not constitutionally be enjoined merely because of the absence of a "labor dispute." Upon reargument, the court withdrew its original opinion. Although the trial court had refused to make the finding requested by the employer, the state supreme court, noting that the facts as to which the request was made were undisputed, drew the inference as to the purpose of the picketing and itself made the finding. It then held that since such a purpose is unlawful under the state labor law which makes it an unfair labor practice for an employee, individually or in concert with others, to "coerce, intimidate or induce any employer to interfere with any of his employees in the enjoyment of their legal rights," the injunction was properly issued.

MR. JUSTICE FRANKFURTER delivered the opinion of the Court. . . .

We are asked to reverse the judgment of the Wisconsin Supreme Court, which to a large extent rested its decision on that of the Supreme Judicial Court of Maine in Pappas v. Stacey [151 Me. 36, 116 A.2d 497 (1955)] . . . When an appeal from that decision was filed here, this Court granted appellee's motion to dismiss for lack of a substantial federal question. 350 U.S. 870. Since the present case presents a similar question, we might well have denied certiorari on the strength of our decision in that case. In view of the recurrence of the question, we thought it advisable to grant certiorari, 352 U.S. 817, and to restate the principles governing this type of case.

It is inherent in the concept embodied in the Due Process Clause that its scope be determined by a "gradual process of judicial inclusion and exclusion," Davidson v. New Orleans, 96 U.S. 97, 104. Inevitably, therefore the doctrine of a particular case "is not allowed to end with its enunciation, and . . . an expression in an opinion yields later to the impact of facts unforeseen." Jaybird Mining Co. v. Weir, 271 U.S. 609, 619 (Brandeis, J., dissenting). . . .

Although the Court had been closely divided in the Senn case [Senn v. Tile Layers Protective Union, Local 5, 301 U.S. 468], three years later, in passing on a restrictive instead of a permissive state statute, the Court made sweeping pronouncements about the right to picket in holding unconstitutional a statute that had been applied to ban all picketing, with "no exceptions based upon either the number of persons engaged in the proscribed activity, the peaceful character of their demeanor, the nature of their dispute with an employer, or the restrained character and the accurateness of the terminology used in notifying the public of the facts of the dispute." Thornhill v. Alabama, 310 U.S. 88, 99. As the statute dealt at large with all picketing, so the Court broadly assimilated peaceful picketing in general to freedom of speech, and as such protected against abridgment by the Fourteenth Amendment.

These principles were applied by the Court in A.F.L. v. Swing, 312 U.S. 321, to hold unconstitutional an injunction against peaceful picketing, based on a State's common-law policy against picketing when there was no immediate dispute between employer and employee. . . .

Soon, however, the Court came to realize that the broad pronouncements, but not the specific holding, of Thornhill had to yield "to the impact of facts unforeseen," or at least not sufficiently appreciated . . . Cases reached the Court in which a State had designed a remedy to meet a specific situation or to accomplish a particular social policy. These cases made manifest that picketing, even though "peaceful," involved more than just communication of ideas and could not be immune from all state regulation. . . .

The implied reassessments of the broad language of the Thornhill case were finally generalized in a series of cases sustaining injunctions against peaceful picketing, even when arising in the course of a labor controversy, when such picketing was counter to valid state policy in a domain open to state regulation. The decisive reconsideration came in Giboney v. Empire Storage & Ice Co., 336 U.S. 490. A union, seeking to organize peddlers, picketed a wholesale dealer to induce it to refrain from selling to nonunion peddlers. The state courts, finding that such an agreement would constitute a conspiracy in restraint of trade in violation of the state antitrust laws, enjoined the picketing. The Court affirmed unanimously. . . .

The following Term, the Court decided a group of cases applying and elaborating on the theory of Giboney. In Hughes v. Superior Court, 339 U.S. 460, the Court held that the Fourteenth Amendment did not bar use of the injunction to prohibit picketing of a place of business solely to secure compliance with a demand that its employees be hired in percentage to the racial origin of its customers. . . . The Court also found it immaterial that the state policy had been expressed by the judiciary rather than by the legislature. . . .

[The Court reviewed Teamsters Union v. Hanke, 339 U.S. 470; Building Service Employees v. Gazzam, 339 U.S. 532; Plumbers Union v. Graham, 345 U.S. 192.]

This series of cases, then, established a broad field in which a State, in enforcing some public policy, whether of its criminal or its civil law, and whether announced by its legislature or its courts, could constitutionally enjoin peaceful picketing aimed at preventing effectuation of that policy.

In the light of this background, the Maine Supreme Judicial Court in 1955 decided, on an agreed statement of facts, the case of Pappas v. Stacey [supra]. From the statement, it appeared that three union employees went on strike, and picketed a restaurant peacefully "for the sole purpose of seeking to organize other employees of the Plaintiff, ultimately to have the Plaintiff enter into collective bargaining and negotiations with the Union . . ." Maine had a statute providing that workers should have full liberty of self-organization, free from restraint by employers or other persons. [Me. Rev. Stat. Ann., c. 30, §15 (1954).] The Maine Supreme Judicial Court drew the inference from the agreed statement of facts that "there is a steady and exacting pressure upon the employer to interfere with the free choice of the employees in the matter of organization. To say that the picketing is not designed to bring about such action is to forget an obvious purpose of the picketing — to cause economic loss to the business during noncompliance by the employees with the requests of the union." It therefore enjoined the picketing, and an appeal was taken to this Court.

The whole series of cases . . . allowing, as they did, wide discretion to a State in the formulation of domestic policy, and not involving a curtailment of free speech in its obvious and accepted scope, led this Court, without the need of further argument, to grant appellee's motion to dismiss the appeal in that it no longer presented a substantial federal question. 350 U.S. 870.

The Stacey case is this case. As in Stacey, the present case was tried without oral testimony. As in Stacey, the highest state court drew the inference from the facts that the picketing was to coerce the employer to put pressure on his employees to join the union, in violation of the declared policy of the State. (For a declaration of similar congressional policy see §8 of the Taft-Hartley Act, 61 Stat. 29 U.S.C. §158.) The cases discussed above all hold that, consistent with the Fourteenth Amendment, a State may enjoin such conduct.

Of course, the mere fact that there is "picketing" does not automatically justify its restraint without an investigation into its conduct and purposes. State courts, no more than state legislatures, can enact blanket prohibitions against picketing. Thornhill v. Alabama and A.F.L. v. Swing, supra. The series of cases following Thornhill and Swing demonstrate that the policy of Wisconsin enforced by the prohibition of this picketing is a valid one. In this case the circumstances set forth in the opinion of the Wisconsin Supreme Court afford a rational basis for the inference it drew concerning the purpose of the picketing. . . .

Affirmed.

MR. JUSTICE WHITTAKER took no part in the consideration or decision of this case.

MR. JUSTICE DOUGLAS, with whom THE CHIEF JUSTICE and MR. JUSTICE BLACK concur, dissenting.

The Court has now come full circle. . . .

. . . [W]here . . . there is no rioting, no mass picketing, no violence, no disorder, no fisticuffs, no coercion — indeed nothing but speech — the principles announced in Thornhill and Swing should give the advocacy of one side of a dispute First Amendment protection.

The retreat began when, in International Brotherhood of Teamsters Union v. Hanke, 339 U.S. 470, four members of the Court announced that all picketing could be prohibited if a state court decided that that picketing violated the State's public policy. The retreat became a rout in Local Union No. 10, United Ass'n of Journeymen, Plumbers and Steamfitters, etc. v. Graham, 345 U.S. 192. It was only the "purpose" of the picketing which was relevant. The state court's characterization of the picketers' "purpose" has been made well-nigh conclusive. Considerations of the proximity of picketing to conduct which the State could control or prevent were abandoned, and no longer was it necessary for the state court's decree to be narrowly drawn to proscribe a specific evil. . . .

Today, the Court signs the formal surrender. State courts and state legislatures cannot fashion blanket prohibitions on all picketing. But, for practical purposes, the situation now is as it was when Senn v. Tile Layers Union, 301 U.S. 468, was decided. State courts and state legislatures are free to decide whether to permit or suppress any particular picket line for any reason other than a blanket policy against all picketing. I would adhere to the principle announced in Thornhill. I would adhere to the result reached in Swing. I would return to the test enunciated in Giboney — that this form of expression can be regulated or prohibited only to the extent that it forms an essential part of a course of conduct which the State can regulate or prohibit. I would reverse the judgment below.[27]

NOTES

1. Justice Douglas in his dissent in Vogt refers to International Brotherhood of Teamsters v. Hanke, 339 U.S. 470 (1950), as the case in which the "retreat" away from the Court's protecting picketing as free speech began. In this case, unionized employees of used-car lots picketed the Hanke lot because it did not follow a ban on remaining open at night and on Saturdays and Sundays. This ban was part of a contract negotiated by the union with the automobile dealers of the community. The Hanke lot had no employees as it was staffed wholly with the Hanke family. The Court held that the picketing was not constitutionally protected and could be outlawed by the state. The decision was 5-to-3, and there

[27] Compare NLRB v. Fruit and Vegetable Packers and Warehousemen, Local 760, page 335 infra. — ED.

was no majority opinion. Was the union picketing to force the Hankes to do something illegal? Does this make any difference? In what way, if any, was this case a "retreat" from Thornhill? In which case, Hanke or Vogt, is the action of the state in barring picketing more easily justified against a claim of constitutional privilege in the picketing?

2. The amended Wisconsin anti-injunction act, Wis. Stat. §103.51 (1945), did not prevent relief in the principal case although the initial state statute was the forerunner of broad federal legislation.

". . . [N]o court of the United States, as herein defined, shall have jurisdiction to issue any restraining order or temporary or permanent injunction in a case involving or growing out of a labor dispute, except in a strict conformity with the provisions of this Act . . . ."

With these words, Congress in 1932 declared its determination to eliminate the evils of labor injunctions in the federal courts. The Norris-LaGuardia Act,[28] is not based on the power of Congress to regulate interstate commerce, but on the power granted to Congress by Article III of the Constitution to regulate the jurisdiction of inferior federal courts. The application of the statute does not depend on the kind of business involved but on the court in which the suit is brought.

A careful reading of its fifteen sections discloses in specific detail the design to prohibit the issuance of injunctions in most labor disputes and to prevent procedural abuses in those situations where an injunction might be issued. Perhaps more important, however, is the Act's firm endorsement of a policy favorable to collective organization and bargaining and the requirement of a general attitude of non-intervention by the courts. The basic framework of the legislative restriction is found in Sections 13, 7, and 4, *taken in that order.*

A number of states have enacted legislation substantially modeled on the Norris-LaGuardia Act. Compare Hawaii Rev. Laws §908-1 (1963 Supp.); Ind. Ann. Stats. §40-501 (1952); La. Rev. Stat. §23:821 (1950); Md. Ann. Code, art. 100 (1957); Minn. Stats. Ann. §185.07 (1946); N.J. Rev. Stat. §2A:15-51 (1951); N.Y. Civ. Practice Act §876-a; Ore. Rev. Stat. §662.010 (1959); Pa. Stat. Ann., tit. 43, §206a (Purdon, 1952); Utah Code Ann. §34-1-23 (1953); Wash. Rev. Code §49:32:010 (1958). But the pattern of state law generally is far from uniform, and the prevalence of injunctions in state courts despite these statutes is examined in Document No. 7, State Court Injunctions, Report of the Subcommittee on Labor and Public Welfare, 82 Cong., 1st Sess. (1951), summarized in 73 Mo. Labor Rev. 59 (1951).

The legislative progression in Massachusetts is interesting. There the original statute was primarily modeled on Section 7 of the federal law; but its failure to include the restrictive provisions of Section 4 left the courts free to apply their common law concepts as to the propriety of the union conduct. Simon v. Schwachman, 301 Mass. 573, 18 N.E.2d (1938) Subsequent amendments, however, expanded the definition of labor dispute and attempted to coordinate judicial intervention with the evolving

[28] See page 45 supra. The text of the Act is printed in the Reference Supplement at page 114.

collective bargaining process by the technique of defining certain "lawful" and "unlawful" disputes and boycotts. Mass. Ann. Laws, c. 149, §20C (1957). More recently the legislature has provided a three-judge court for cases arising under this statute. Mass. Ann. Laws, c. 212, §30 (1963 Supp.).

3. What is a "case involving or growing out of a labor dispute"? Consider the following:

(a) In 1937, a CIO union attempted to organize Zirkin's eleven fur workers, but only two joined. When Zirkin refused to recognize the CIO union, it called a strike and picketed the premises. The other nine fur workers, without any interference or coercion by Zirkin, joined an AFL union, which was thereupon recognized as the bargaining representative. After an agreement was signed, the CIO engaged in mass picketing, accompanied by threats and assaults to compel Zirkin to rescind his recognition and void the contract. The AFL union obtained an injunction in the federal district court, which found there was no "labor dispute" within the meaning of the Norris-LaGuardia Act. The CIO appealed. See Fur Workers Union, Local 72 (CIO) v. Fur Workers Union (AFL), 105 F.2d 1 (D.C. Cir. 1939), aff'd per curiam, 308 U.S. 522 (1939).

(b) The plaintiff bought a house from a nonunion building contractor, built by him as part of a housing development. The Building Trades Council maintained a picket line across the only entrance to the development from the highway. When the plaintiff tried to have his house connected with gas and electricity, the employees of the Long Island Lighting Company refused to cross the picket line because it would have resulted in their expulsion from their union. Compare Schivera v. Long Island Lighting Co., 296 N.Y. 26, 69 N.E.2d 233 (1946), with Muncie Building Trades Council v. Umbarger, 215 Ind. 13, 17 N.E.2d 828 (1938).

(c) The Order of Railroad Telegraphers voted to strike in aid of a demand that no existing position be abolished without its consent. See Order of Railroad Telegraphers v. Chicago & N.W.R. Co., 362 U.S. 330 (1960). Compare Brotherhood of Railroad Trainmen v. Chicago River & Indiana R. Co., 353 U.S. 30 (1957).

(d) Employees of the Metropolitan Transit Authority were represented by the Carmen's Union. The enabling Act establishing the Authority provides in part that "with respect to hours of employment, rates of wages, salaries, hours, working conditions, health benefits, pensions and retirement allowances" the employees of the Authority shall be governed by the laws relating to "street railway companies" rather than the laws governing "public employees." When the Authority made certain work assignments allegedly in derogation of the union's bargaining position, a strike was called. Compare Hansen v. Commonwealth, 344 Mass. 214, 181 N.E.2d 843 (1962).

(e) Processors of yellow grease purchased and picked up the raw material directly, using their own employee drivers. They also purchased part of their supply from independent peddlers whose earnings consist of the difference between the price at which they bought and the price at which they resold to the processors. A union representing the processors' employees organized the peddlers and thereafter fixed the peddler's purchase and sale prices and allocated their customers. Processors were coerced into dealing exclusively with the union peddlers by threat of labor trouble, and nonunion peddlers were forced out of business. The government attacked this activity as violative of the federal antitrust laws and as part of the relief sought an order excluding the independent peddlers from membership in the union. See Norris-LaGuardia Act §4(b); compare Los Angeles Meat & Provision Drivers Union v. United States, 371 U.S. 94 (1962).

(f) A collective bargaining agreement deprived certain employees of benefits on a racial basis. These employees sued to enjoin the union and employer from complying with the discriminatory clauses. See Graham v. Brotherhood of Locomotive Firemen & Enginemen, 338 U.S. 232 (1949); compare New Negro Alliance v. Sanitary Grocery Co., 303 U.S. 552 (1938).

(g) Sinclair Refining Co. v. Atkinson, 370 U.S. 195 (1962), infra page 882.

NLRB v. DRIVERS, CHAUFFEURS, HELPERS, LOCAL UNION NO. 639

Supreme Court of the United States, 1960
362 U.S. 274, 80 Sup. Ct. 706, 4 L. Ed. 2d 710

MR. JUSTICE BRENNAN delivered the opinion of the Court.

The question in this case is whether peaceful picketing by a union, which does not represent a majority of the employees, to compel immediate recognition as the employees' exclusive bargaining agent, is conduct of the union "to restrain or coerce" the employees in the exercise of rights guaranteed in §7, and thus an unfair labor practice under §8(b)(1)(A) of the National Labor Relations Act, as amended by the Taft-Hartley Act.

Curtis Bros., Inc., has a retail store and a warehouse in Washington, D.C., in which it carries on a moving, warehousing and retail furniture business. In 1953 respondent Teamster Local 639 was certified by the National Labor Relations Board, following a Board-conducted election, to be the exclusive representative of the Company's drivers, helpers, warehousemen and furniture finishers. However, when the Local called a strike over contract terms in February 1954 only nine of 21 employees in the unit left their jobs and Curtis Bros. replaced the nine with new employees. The strike continued but the Local gradually lost membership, and when after a year Curtis Bros. petitioned the Board to conduct another election, the Local wrote the Board that it did not claim to represent a majority of the employees. The Board nevertheless ordered another election, 114 N.L.R.B. 116, which was held in October 1955, and the then employees of the unit voted 28 to one in favor of "no union."

A month after the election, in November 1955, the Local withdrew a picket line which had been maintained before the employees' entrance to the warehouse during the period from February 1954. However, picketing at the customers' entrance to the retail store was continued, but limited to not more than two pickets at any time. The pickets were orderly at all times and made no attempt to prevent anyone from entering the store. They simply patrolled before the entrance carrying signs reading on one side, "Curtis Bros. employs nonunion drivers, helpers, warehousemen and etc. Unfair to Teamsters Union No. 639 AFL," and on the other side, "Teamsters Union No. 639 AFL wants employees of Curtis Bros. to join them to gain union wages, hours, and working conditions."

After this picketing continued for about six months, Curtis Bros. made it the subject of an unfair labor practice charge against the Local for alleged violation of §8(b)(1)(A). A complaint issued which alleged, in substance, that the picketing was activity to "restrain or coerce" the employees in the exercise of §7 rights, and thus an unfair labor practice under §8(b)(1)(A), because it was "recognitional" picketing, that is, picketing designed to induce Curtis Bros. to recognize the Local as the exclusive bargaining agent for the employees, although the union did not represent a majority of the employees.

The Trial Examiner recommended that the complaint be dismissed on the ground that the Local's peaceful picketing, even if "recognitional," was not conduct to "restrain or coerce." The Board, one member dissenting, disagreed and entered a cease-and-desist order, 119 N.L.R.B. 232. On review at the instance of the Local, the United States Court of Appeals for the District of Columbia Circuit, by a divided court, set aside the Board's order, holding that §8(b)(1)(A) "is inapplicable to peaceful picketing, whether 'organizational' or 'recognitional' in nature. . . ." 274 F.2d 551, 552. Because of the importance of the question in the administration of the Act, we granted certiorari. 359 U.S. 965.

After we granted certiorari, the Congress enacted the Labor-Management Reporting and Disclosure Act of 1959, which, among other things, adds a new §8(b)(7) to the National Labor Relations Act. It was stated by the Board on oral argument that if this case arose under the 1959 Act, the Board might have proceded against the Local under §8(b)-(7). This does not, however, relegate this litigation to the status of an unimportant controversy over the meaning of a statute which has been significantly changed. For the Board contends that new §8(b)(7) does not displace §8(b)(1)(A) but merely "supplements the power already conferred by Section 8(b)(1)(A)." It argues that the Board may proceed against peaceful "recognitional" picketing conducted by a minority union in more situations than are specified in §8(b)(7) and without regard to the limitations of §8(b)(7)(C). . . .

We first consider §8(b)(1)(A) in the light of §13, as amended, which provides, in substance, that the Taft-Hartley Act shall not be taken as restricting or expanding either the right to strike or the limitations or qualifications on that right, as these were understood prior to 1947, unless "specifically provided for" in the Act itself. The Wagner Act conferred upon the Board wide authority to protect strikers from employer retaliation. However, the Court and the Board fashioned the doctrine that the Board should deny reinstatement to strikers who engaged in strikes which were conducted in an unlawful manner or for an unlawful objective. See for example Southern S.S. Co. v. Labor Board, 316 U.S. 31; Labor Board v. Fansteel Metallurgical Corp., 306 U.S. 240; Labor Board v. Sands Mfg. Co., 306 U.S. 332; and American News Co., 55 N.L.R.B. 1302. These are the "limitations or qualifications" on the right to strike referred to in §13. . . . Therefore, since the Board's order in this case against peaceful picketing would obviously "impede" the right to strike, it can only be sustained if such power is "specifically provided for" in §8(b)(1)(A), as added by the Taft-Hartley Act. To be sure, §13 does not require that the authority for the Board action be spelled out in so many words. Rather, since the Board does not contend that §8(b)(1)(A) embodies one of the "limitations or qualifications" on the right to strike, §13 declares a rule of construction which cautions against an expansive reading of that section which would adversely affect the right to strike, unless the congressional purpose to give it that meaning persuasively appears either from the structure or history of the statute. Therefore, §13 is a command of Congress to the courts to resolve doubts and ambiguities in favor of an interpretation of §8(b)(1)(A) which safeguards the right to strike as understood prior to the passage of the Taft-Hartley Act.

The Board asserts that the very general standard in §8(b)(1)(A) vests power in the Board to sit in judgment upon, and to condemn, a minority union's resort to a specific economic weapon, here peaceful picketing. The structure of §8(b), which defines unfair labor practices, hardly supports the Board's claims. Earlier this Term we pointed out that "Congress has been rather specific when it has come to outlaw particular economic weapons on the part of unions." Labor Board v. Insurance Agents' International Union, 361 U.S. 477, 498. We referred to §8(b)(4) as illustrative of the congressional practice. In the context of a union's striking to promote enlarged membership, Congress there explicitly prohibited a union's resort to the secondary boycott, to the strike to force employers or self-employed persons to join unions, and, very pertinent here, to the "recognitional" strike where another union is certified. Plainly if the Board's interpretation is sustained, §8(b)(1)(A) largely overlaps at least this last-mentioned prohibition, namely §8(b)(4)(C), to the extent of making it almost redundant. But the Court has rejected an argument that a provision of §8(b)(4) is a repetition of the prohibitions of §8(b)(1)(A). In International Brotherhood of Electrical Workers v. Labor Board, 341 U.S. 694, the Court, in holding that a peaceful strike to promote self-organization was proscribed by §8(b)(4)(A) if its objective was to "induce or encourage" a secondary boycott, contrasted the language of the two subsections and labeled the words "restrain or coerce" in §8(b)(1)(A) a "restricted phrase" to be equated with "threat or reprisal or force or promise of benefit." Id., at 701-703.

In the sensitive area of peaceful picketing Congress has dealt explicitly with isolated evils which experience has established flow from such picketing. Therefore, unless there is the clearest indication in the legislative history of §8(b)(1)(A) supporting the Board's claim of power under that

Section, we cannot sustain the Board's order here. We now turn to an examination of the legislative history.

In the comprehensive review of union practices leading up to the enactment of the Taft-Hartley Act, picketing practices were subjected to intensive inquiry by both House and Senate Labor Committees. The Senate bill as brought to the floor by the Senate Labor Committee regulated organizational activity in specified situations. Proposed §8(b)(4)(3), now §8(b)(4)(C), of the law, made "recognitional" picketing of a primary employer unlawful only where "another labor organization has been certified as the representative" of his employees. Section 8(b)(4)(2), now §8(b)(4)(B), prohibited attempts to force recognition through secondary pressure.

However, five members of the Senate Labor Committee, including Senators Taft and Ball, believed that the Senate bill did not go far enough in the regulation of practices employed by unions for organizational purposes. These Senators introduced on the floor a proposed amendment to the Committee bill. The amendment as originally phrased was the counterpart of §8(a)(1) applicable to employers; it would have made it an unfair labor practice for a labor organization "to interfere with" as well as "to restrain or coerce . . . employees in the exercise of the rights guaranteed in section 7 . . . ." The words "interfere with" were dropped during the debate, but except for this change, the amendment became §8(b)-(1)(A). . . .

. . . The plainest indication negating an intention to restrict the use by unions of methods of peaceful persuasion, including peaceful picketing, is seen in the comments of Senator Taft near the close of the debate. He said:

"It seems to me very clear that so long as a union-organizing drive is conducted by persuasion, by propaganda, so long as it has every legitimate purpose, the Board cannot in any way interfere with it. . . ." 93 Cong. Rec. 4434. . . .

"The effect of the pending amendment is that the Board may call the union before them, exactly as it has called the employer, and say, 'Here are the rules of the game. You must cease and desist from coercing and restraining the employees who want to work from going to work and earning the money which they are entitled to earn.' The Board may say, 'You can persuade them; you can put up signs; you can conduct any form of propaganda you want to in order to persuade them, but you cannot, by threat of force or threat of economic reprisal, prevent them from exercising their right to work.' As I see it, that is the effect of the amendment." 93 Cong. Rec. 4436. . . .

". . . The cease-and-desist order will be directed against the use of threats and coercion. It will not be directed against the use of propaganda or the use of persuasion, or against the use of any of the other peaceful methods of organizing employees.

"Mr. President, I can see nothing in the pending measure which . . . would in some way outlaw strikes. It would outlaw threats against employees. It would not outlaw anybody striking who wanted to strike. It would not prevent anyone using the strike in a legitimate way, conducting peaceful picketing, or employing persuasion. All it would do would be to outlaw such restraint and coercion as would prevent people from going to work if they wished to go to work." Ibid.

This approach in the Senate is in sharp contrast to the House view, which was that picketing should be strictly circumscribed. . . .

But the House conferees abandoned the House bill in conference and accepted the Senate proposal. H.R. Conf. Rep. No. 510 on H.R. 3020, 80th Cong., 1st Sess. 42. They joined in a Conference Report which stated that "the primary strike for recognition (without a Board certification) was not prohibited." Id., at 43. . . .

We conclude that the Board's interpretation of §8(b)(1)(A) finds support neither in the way Congress structured §8(b) nor in the legislative history of §8(b)(1)(A). Rather it seems clear, and we hold, that Congress in the Taft-Hartley Act authorized the Board to regulate peaceful "recognitional" picketing only when it is employed to accomplish objectives specified in §8(b)(4); and that §8(b)(1)(A) is a grant of power to the Board limited to authority to proceed against union tactics involving violence, intimidation, and reprisal or threats thereof — conduct involving more than the general pressures upon persons employed by the affected employers implicit in economic strikes. . . .

Affirmed.

[Justice Stewart, joined by Justices Frankfurter and Whittaker, would follow the suggestion of the Solicitor General and remand the case to the Board for reconsideration in the light of the 1959 legislation, enacted after the writ of certiorari was granted in this case.]

DAYTON TYPOGRAPHICAL UNION NO. 57 v. NLRB
United States Court of Appeals, District of Columbia Circuit,
1963, 326 F.2d 634

[Picketing in this case began many months before the effective date of the 1959 amendments. However, this aspect of the case, on which the dissent of Judge Fahy is based, is not reproduced here. The picketing began, along with a strike, after the employer had declined to recognize or bargain with a union, pending a determination by NLRB election under an employer-filed petition. The union had signed up thirty-five of the fifty-one employees in the shop, had advised that it was not in compliance with the anti-Communist affidavit requirements then in effect, and had offered to submit to an election conducted by any reputable local citizen chosen by the employer. During the strike and picketing, the Board held a hearing and directed an election, but later granted the employer leave to withdraw the petition, which the union did not oppose. The anti-Communist affidavit requirements came to an end on September 14, 1959, with the effective date of the amendments (even before then, under United Mine Workers v. Arkansas Oak Flooring Co., 351 U.S. 62 (1956), the employer was held obliged to grant recognition if there was no

bona fide dispute as to the existence of the majority representative).
Nevertheless, the union never did file a petition for representation or an
unfair labor practice charge, but continued to picket for recognition and
bargaining. The Board found a violation of Section 8(b)(7)(C) under its
Blinne Construction Co. case, International Hod Carriers, 135 N.L.R.B.
1153 (1962), and the union petitions for review.]

WASHINGTON, Circuit Judge. . . .

We think it clear that Section 8(b)(7), as reported by the Conference
and as enacted by Congress, reflects a conscious and intentional acceptance by the Senate conferees — and by Congress — of the House-spon-
sored requirement for current certification of a union, and a conscious
and intentional abandonment by the Senate conferees — and by Congress — of the Senate-sponsored provision which would have exempted
unions having majority status, even though not certified, from the ban
on picketing imposed by Section 8(b)(7). Cf. Mastro Plastics Corp. v.
National Labor Relations Board, 350 U.S. 270 at 288-289, and National
Labor Relations Board v. Drivers Local Union, 362 U.S. 274, 288-289. In
the circumstances, we are unable to read into the statute, contrary to its
actual language and the legislative intent, an exemption for non-
complying uncertified unions representing a majority of the employees.

The Union suggests also that the picketing here should not be treated
as having as one of its objects "forcing or requiring" the employer to
recognize the Union when the employer was already required by Sections
8(a)(5) and 9(a) of the Act to recognize a majority union. However, before the picketing commenced the employer had refused to carry out its
statutory obligation, assuming for present purposes that the obligation
was fully established. In such circumstances the peaceful picketing, accompanied by the distribution of leaflets which attacked the employer's
refusal to recognize and bargain with the Union, necessarily had as an
objective "requiring," if not "forcing," the employer to meet its asserted
legal obligation. The Trial Examiner indeed found that the picketing
was "for the purposes of forcing the Company to recognize the Union and
to bargain collectively" with it. The Board adopted the finding.

True, in National Labor Relations Board v. Drivers Local Union, supra, the Supreme Court held that the words "to restrain or coerce" in
Section 8(b)(1)(A) of the Act do not apply to peaceful picketing not
involving "violence, intimidation, and reprisal or threats thereof." 362
U.S. at 290.

It by no means follows, however, that the words "forcing or requiring"
in the new Section 8(b)(7) are to be construed as not applicable to peaceful picketing. The Second Circuit in National Labor Relations Board v.
Local 239, International Brotherhood of Teamsters, 289 F.2d 41 (2d Cir.
1961), cert. denied, 368 U.S. 833 (1961), declined so to construe those
words. There are important structural differences between the two sections. Section 8(b)(1)(A), 29 U.S.C. §158(b)(1)(A) (1958), does not use
the word "picketing" at all: it declares that it shall be an unfair labor
practice for a labor organization "to restrain or coerce (A) employees in
the exercise of the rights" guaranteed in Section 7. The clear implication

is that only an actual restraint or coercion of some kind is proscribed, not the passive attempt to influence involved in peaceful picketing — as we and the Supreme Court held. In contrast, Section 8(b)(7) refers in terms to picketing which has an object of "forcing or requiring" an employer to recognize an uncertified union. Unlike Section 8(b)(1), it is the purpose of the picketing, rather than the means used, which is decisive. It is hardly debatable that an object or aim of peaceful recognitional picketing must be to "require," if not to force, the employer to recognize the union. . . .

We turn now to the contention that the Union may not be found to have committed the unfair labor practice described by Section 8(b)(7) of the Act, where the picketing was not only for the purpose of recognition, but also to protest unfair labor practices of the employer alleged to be in violation of Section 8(a)(1) and (5) of the Act.

The Union has not charged the employer with unfair labor practices under Section 8(a)(1) and (5), and no finding that it was guilty of such practices has been made. We will, however, assume for present purposes that the Company has engaged in the unfair practices described in Section 8(a)(1) and (5).

It is clear that prior to the 1959 Act a union could lawfully picket to protest an unfair labor practice of the employer. Mastro Plastics v. National Labor Relations Board, 350 U.S. 270; United Mine Workers of America v. Arkansas Oak Flooring Co., 351 U.S. 62. The question we have here is whether the 1959 Act — and in particular Section 8(b)(7) — circumscribes or qualifies that right in cases where another aim or object of the picketing is recognition or organization. We must look both at the Act itself and the legislative materials at hand. . . .

. . . Instead of making any unfair labor practice of the employer a complete defense to an 8(b)(7) charge as in S.1555 — or a complete defense to an application for a temporary restraining order under Section 10(1) and a complete defense to a complaint under Section 10(b) as in the proposed Senate resolution — the provision enacted emerged only as a ban against application under Section 8(b)(7) for a restraining order if an 8(a)(2) charge against the employer had been filed and found meritorious. We can only conclude that the Conference and the Congress considered and deliberately abandoned the thought of making every employer unfair labor practice a blanket defense to an 8(b)(7) charge. In such circumstances, we cannot construe the enactment as intended to have that effect. . . . It is certainly to be supposed that if any of the House conferees were of the view that any other employer unfair labor practice was a defense against, or would remove, the ban imposed by Section 8(b)(7) on organizational or recognitional picketing, some statement to that effect would have been made. None has been cited to us nor has our research disclosed any. We are unable to conclude that the House conferees conceded in conference that unfair practice picketing could lawfully continue beyond the 30-day period fixed by Section 8(b)(7) if such picketing also had any organizational or recognitional objective, or that either the Senate or the House intended that such picketing would be permitted under the 1959 Act.

We read National Labor Relations Board v. Drivers Local Union, 362 U.S. 274, as directly supporting our conclusion here. . . . [T]here, unlike the position taken by the Senate, the House view "was that picketing should be strictly circumscribed" but "the House conferees abandoned the House bill in conference and accepted the Senate proposal." 362 U.S. at 288, 289. The Supreme Court concluded in this posture that Section 8(b)(1)(A) as enacted was not intended to circumscribe picketing in the manner originally put forward by the House but abandoned in conference, and that the words "to restrain or coerce" used in the section did not apply to peaceful picketing to compel immediate recognition but only to "union tactics involving violence, intimidation, and reprisal or threats thereof." 362 U.S. at 290. Conversely, in our case the House view prevailed, and the Senate provision which would have exempted unfair practice picketing from the limited ban imposed by Section 8(b)(7) was abandoned in conference and was not enacted. We are not free to write in such an exemption, contrary to the congressional decision not to include it, no matter how desirable we ourselves might think such a result would be. . . .

In considering the reasonableness and constitutionality of the congressional action in adopting Section 8(b)(7), an important factor is the practical impact of the requirements of the section. Are those requirements unduly oppressive in actual operation? The answer to this question is partly to be found in the manner in which the section is administered by the Board. In this connection, the Board said in the Blinne case, 135 N.L.R.B. at pp. 1165-66:

". . . the fears that the statutory requirement for filing a timely petition will compel a union which has been the victim of unfair labor practices to undergo a coerced election are groundless. No action will be taken on that petition while unfair labor practice charges are pending, and until a valid election is held pursuant to that petition, the union's right to picket under the statutory scheme is unimpaired.

"On the other side of the coin, it may safely be assumed that groundless unfair labor practice charges in this area, because of the statutory priority accorded Section 8(b)(7) violations, will be quickly dismissed. Following such dismissal an election can be directed forthwith upon the subsisting petition, thereby effectuating the congressional purpose. Moreover, the fact that a timely petition is on file will protect the innocent union, which through a mistake of fact or law has filed a groundless unfair labor practice charge, from a finding of an 8(b)(7)(C) violation. . . ."

In its brief in the present case, the Board says:

"In terms of the facts of this case, the Union could have preserved its right to continue picketing by filing a timely representation petition and a Section 8(a)(5) charge. If, as it asserts, the Company refused to recognize it although the Company did not have a good faith doubt as to the Union's majority status, the refusal was violative of Section 8(a)(5), and a complaint would presumably have issued on the charge. In that event, no election would have been held on the petition, and the Union would have been free to continue picketing pending a resolution of the Section 8(a)(5) issue. On the other hand, had investigation of the Section 8(a)-(5) charge proved it to be without merit, the petition would have protected the Union against having its picketing enjoined until an election had first been conducted, and, if the Union won the election, it would, of course, have remained free to continue picketing." (Pp. 39-40; footnotes omitted.) The Board's brief further states:

"The Board views a meritorious 8(a)(5) charge and a representation petition as mutually inconsistent, for the latter presupposes that a question concerning representation exists whereas the former presupposes that it does not. Accordingly, if a complaint has issued on an 8(a)(5) charge, the Board will ordinarily not entertain a representation petition, or will dismiss one that may have been filed, involving the same employees, rather than hold the petition, pending remedial action, as it does in the case of other employer unfair labor practices. See Aiello Dairy Farms, 110 N.L.R.B. 1365, 1366-1367.[29] However, it does not follow, as petitioner assumes, that, had it filed both a petition and an 8(a)(5) charge, the Board, at least in the circumstances of an 8(b)(7)(C) case, would have required it to make a choice between whether it wanted to proceed on the petition or on the charge. Rather, there is every reason to believe that the petition would have been held pending an investigation of the 8(a)-(5) charge, and dismissed only if it were decided to issue a complaint thereon.

"Since a meritorious Section 8(a)(5) charge in effect moots a representation petition, the Board has held that, if a complaint alleging a refusal to bargain in violation of Section 8(a)(5) has issued, it would not find picketing for recognition purposes violation of Section 8(b)(7)(C) even though a representation petition had not been filed within a reasonable time from the commencement of the picketing. For, in these circumstances, the filing of a representation petition could not serve as the basis for an election; it would only be dismissed. Blinne, supra, 135 N.L.R.B. No. 121, p. 17, n. 24. But, the Union which files a Section 8(a)(5) charge alone, without coupling it with a representation petition, takes the risk that, if no complaint issues on the charge, there would be no bar to proceeding to enjoin the picketing under Section 8(b)(7)(C)." (Pp. 40-41, n. 42).

We rely upon these representations in reaching our conclusion here that Section 8(b)(7) is not in fact oppressive in operation, or unduly restrictive of the rights given to labor by the Federal labor legislation generally. A ban on organizational or recognitional picketing only is effected, and that in narrowly defined circumstances. A majority union may continue its recognitional picketing beyond the permitted reasonable period, not to exceed 30 days, if it files a timely petition for an election. If it also claims unfair labor practices on the part of the employer, it may

[29] But see Bernel Foam Products Co. and Textile Workers Union of America, AFL-CIO, supra page 190. — Ed.

file charges with the General Counsel of the Board. Whether or not the General Counsel chooses to issue a complaint on such charges, the union is protected. If no complaint on the unfair practice charge is issued, the union will still be free to continue its picketing and may, in the proceedings on its petition for an election, bring to the attention of the Board the effect of the claimed unfair labor practices on the prospects of holding a free and fair election. In such a case, the Board, if it considers that the unfair practices of the employer make a fair election impossible, would and should defer such election until it can be conducted in an atmosphere devoid of unfair pressures. On the other hand, if the General Counsel elects in his discretion to issue a complaint against the unfair labor practice of the employer, the petition for an election may, and in our view ordinarily should, be held in abeyance until the unfair practice charge is adjudicated and corrected. The picketing could lawfully continue. Then the fair election contemplated by the statute and decisions can be held.

The Board has indicated, however, that it makes a distinction between an 8(a)(5) violation and other unfair labor practices of the employer. If a complaint issues on an 8(a)(5) violation, the Board will not view picketing as violating Section 8(b)(7) and will dismiss the petition for an election if one has already been filed. We add to this that if the Board on its own initiative has dismissed the petition for an election, a union which has also filed an unfair labor practice charge under Section 8(a)(5) should not, and in our view will not, suffer. It may continue picketing without violating Section 8(b)(7), since it has filed a petition for an election. Regardless of whether or not the Board retains the petition the union is in compliance with the statute.

So viewed and so enforced, we think Section 8(b)(7) is without constitutional infirmity. The petitioner union urges that it is being driven to pursue public remedies, and is being deprived of its traditional private remedy of self-help. But in fact, as we have seen, a union which follows the Board's pattern of administration as outlined above can pursue its picketing — for recognitional as well as unfair labor practice purposes — without interruption or illegality. We think it clear that at all times after the effective date of Section 8(b)(7) the petitioner union had a course of action open to it by which it could have continued to picket without infringement of Section 8(b)(7)(C) — a course which could not have harmed its interests, and which would have comported with the congressional purpose of solving industrial disputes through the processes of the Board. The regulation of picketing imposed by Section 8(b)(7) thus appears to us to be far from severe, and well within the authority of Congress. . . .

For these reasons, the order of the Board will be affirmed.

NOTES

1. The "truthfully advising the public" proviso applies only to subparagraph (C). NLRB v. Local 182, International Brotherhood of Teamsters, 314 F.2d 53 (2d Cir. 1963). It applies, notwithstanding a recogni-

tional object, if informing the public is also a purpose. Smitley v. NLRB, 327 F.2d 351 (9th Cir. 1964). If the union, in addition to informing the public, is signaling economic pressure from organized labor as such, the proviso does not apply. Local 3, IBEW and Jack Picoult, 144 N.L.R.B. 5 (1963). Would the proviso be a defense if the union sought to prevent interruptions of pickups and deliveries, but during twelve weeks at eighteen stores there were three delivery stoppages, two work delays, and "several" delivery delays? The Board's conclusion that this was not "an effect" limiting the proviso was affirmed in Barker Bros. Corp. v. NLRB, 328 F.2d 431 (9th Cir. 1964).

2. In view of assaults and other picket-line misconduct, though characterized as trivial by the trial examiner, twenty-six days before filing a petition was held an unreasonably long time. District 65, Retail, Wholesale Union and Eastern Camera & Photo Corp., 141 N.L.R.B. 991 (1963). Filing a petition is ineffectual as a defense to subparagraph (C) allegations if the "employer" is a principal contractor having no employees, since an election is not feasible; and even in the construction industry, Section 8(f) sanctions only the voluntary negotiation of pre-hire agreements. Local 542, International Union of Operating Engineers and R. S. Noonan, Inc., 142 N.L.R.B. 1132 (1963), enforced, 331 F.2d 99 (3d Cir. 1964). In a case where there were employees, but the petition was filed "weeks before the commencement of picketing," the General Counsel suspended investigation of a Section 8(b)(7)(C) charge, deferring to the expedited election processes under the Board's Rules §102.75. See NLRB General Counsel, Report on Case-Handling Developments at NLRB, 57 Lab. Rel. Rep. (L.R.R.M.) 162, 163 (1964). This report covers the calendar quarter ending September 30, 1964.

"While we do not condone a practice of Union striking and picketing an employer within two days after demanding recognition, it nevertheless appears . . . that the refusal to recognize . . . was not in the requisite good faith." NLRB v. Shurett, 314 F.2d 43 (5th Cir. 1963).

3. Picketing for reinstatement of an employee, whether lawfully discharged or not, or in protest of an unfair practice of the employer (other than denial of recognition itself), or in protest of the nonunion or even the rival-union labor standards of the picketed employer is held not necessarily organizational or recognitional in purpose. United Automobile Workers and Fanelli Ford Sales Co., 133 N.L.R.B. 1468 (1961), overruling Lewis Food Co., 115 N.L.R.B. 890 (1956); Teamsters Local 200 and Bachman Furniture Co., 134 N.L.R.B. 670 (1961); Houston Building and Construction Trades Council and Claude Everett Construction Co., 136 N.L.R.B. 321 (1962); and under Section 8(b)(4)(C), Local 41, International Hod Carriers and Calumet Contractors Assn., 133 N.L.R.B. 512 (1961). For an effective criticism of the Board's "disingenuous humility" in failing either to search for the union's genuine interest in the labor conditions in question or, in the interest of administrative convenience, to take area-standards picketing as recognitional, see Meltzer, Organization Picketing and the NLRB: Five on a Seesaw, 30 U. Chi. L. Rev. 78 (1962).

Picketing may be within Section 8(b)(7)(C) although the "employer" has no employees. If the principal contractor subcontracts work instead of using employees to perform any of it, picketing to obtain an agreement that the subcontractors will assign work within the jurisdiction of the union to its members is recognitional. See the Noonan case, supra.

2. *Cause for Discharge*

NLRB v. LOCAL UNION 1229, INTERNATIONAL BROTHERHOOD OF ELECTRICAL WORKERS

Supreme Court of the United States, 1953
346 U.S. 464, 74 Sup. Ct. 172, 98 L. Ed. 195

MR. JUSTICE BURTON delivered the opinion of the Court.

The issue before us is whether the discharge of certain employees by their employer constituted an unfair labor practice, within the meaning of §§8(a)(1) and 7 of the Taft-Hartley Act, justifying their reinstatement by the National Labor Relations Board. For the reason that their discharge was "for cause" within the meaning of §10(c) of that Act, we sustain the Board in not requiring their reinstatement.

In 1949, the Jefferson Standard Broadcasting Company (here called the company) was a North Carolina corporation engaged in interstate commerce. Under a license from the Federal Communications Commission, it operated, at Charlotte, North Carolina, a 50,000-watt radio station, with call letters WBT. It broadcast 10 to 12 hours daily by radio and television. The television service, which it started July 14, 1949, representing an investment of about $500,000, was the only such service in the area. Less than 50% of the station's programs originated in Charlotte. The others were piped in over leased wires, generally from New York, California or Illinois from several different networks. Its annual gross revenue from broadcasting operations exceeded $100,000 but its television enterprise caused it a monthly loss of about $10,000 during the first four months of that operation, including the period here involved. Its rates for television advertising were geared to the number of receiving sets in the area. Local dealers had large inventories of such sets ready to meet anticipated demands.

The company employed 22 technicians. In December 1948, negotiations to settle the terms of their employment after January 31, 1949, were begun between representatives of the company and of the respondent Local Union No. 1229, International Brotherhood of Electrical Workers, American Federation of Labor (here called the union). The negotiations reached an impasse in January 1949, and the existing contract of employment expired January 31. The technicians, nevertheless, continued to work for the company and their collective-bargaining negotiations were resumed in July, only to break down again July 8. The main point of disagreement arose from the union's demand for the renewal of a provision that all discharges from employment be subject to arbitration and the company's counterproposal that such arbitration be limited to the facts material to each discharge, leaving it to the company to determine whether those facts gave adequate cause for discharge.

July 9, 1949, the union began daily peaceful picketing of the company's station. Placards and handbills on the picket line charged the company with unfairness to its technicians and emphasized the company's refusal to renew the provision for arbitration of discharges. The placards and handbills named the union as the representative of the WBT technicians. The employees did not strike. They confined their respective tours of picketing to their off-duty hours and continued to draw full pay. There was no violence or threat of violence and no one has taken exception to any of the above conduct.

But on August 24, 1949, a new procedure made its appearance. Without warning, several of its technicians launched a vitriolic attack on the quality of the company's television broadcasts. Five thousand handbills were printed over the designation "WBT TECHNICIANS." These were distributed on the picket line, on the public square two or three blocks from the company's premises, in barber shops, restaurants and busses. Some were mailed to local businessmen. The handbills made no reference to the union, to a labor controversy or to collective bargaining. They read:

"IS CHARLOTTE A SECOND-CLASS CITY?"

"You might think so from the kind of Television programs being presented by the Jefferson Standard Broadcasting Co. over WBTV. Have you seen one of their television programs lately? Did you know that all the programs presented over WBTV are on film and may be from one day to five years old? There are no local programs presented by WBTV. You cannot receive the local baseball games, football games or other local events because WBTV does not have the proper equipment to make these pick ups. Cities like New York, Boston, Philadelphia, Washington receive such programs nightly. Why doesn't the Jefferson Standard Broadcasting Company purchase the needed equipment to bring you the same type of programs enjoyed by other leading American cities? Could it be that they consider Charlotte a second-class community and only entitled to the pictures now being presented to them?

"WBT TECHNICIANS"

This attack continued until September 3, 1949, when the company discharged ten of its technicians, whom it charged with sponsoring or distributing these handbills. The company's letter discharging them tells its side of the story.

September 4, the union's picketing resumed its original tenor and, September 13, the union filed with the Board a charge that the company, by discharging the above-mentioned ten technicians, had engaged in an unfair labor practice. The General Counsel for the Board filed a complaint based on those charges and, after hearing, a trial examiner made detailed findings and a recommendation that all of those discharged be reinstated with back pay. 94 N.L.R.B. 1507, 1527. The Board found that one of the discharged men had neither sponsored nor distributed the "Second-Class City" handbill and ordered his reinstatement with back pay. It then found that the other nine had sponsored or distributed the handbill and held that the company, by discharging them for such conduct, had not engaged in an unfair labor practice. The Board, accordingly, did not order their reinstatement. One member dissented. Id., at 1507 et seq. Under §10(f) of the Taft-Hartley Act, the union petitioned the Court of Appeals for the District of Columbia Circuit for a review of the Board's order and for such a modification of it as would reinstate all ten of the discharged technicians with back pay. That court remanded the cause to the Board for further consideration and for a finding as to the "unlawfulness" of the conduct of the employees which had led to their discharge. 91 U.S. App. D.C. 333, 202 F.2d 186. We granted certiorari because of the importance of the case in the administration of the Taft-Hartley Act. 345 U.S. 947.

In its essence, the issue is simple. It is whether these employees, whose contracts of employment had expired, were discharged "for cause." They were discharged solely because, at a critical time in the initiation of the company's television service, they sponsored or distributed 5,000 handbills making a sharp, public, disparaging attack upon the quality of the company's product and its business policies, in a manner reasonably calculated to harm the company's reputation and reduce its income. The attack was made by them expressly as "WBT TECHNICIANS." It continued ten days without indication of abatement. The Board found that —

"It [the handbill] occasioned widespread comment in the community, and caused Respondent to apprehend a loss of advertising revenue due to dissatisfaction with its television broadcasting service.

"In short, the employees in this case deliberately undertook to alienate their employer's customers by impugning the technical quality of his product. As the Trial Examiner found, they did not misrepresent, at least wilfully, the facts they cited to support their disparaging report. And their ultimate purpose — to extract a concession from the employer with respect to the terms of their employment — was lawful. That purpose, however, was undisclosed; the employees purported to speak as experts, in the interest of consumers and the public at large. They did not indicate that they sought to secure any benefit for themselves, *as employees,* by casting discredit upon their employer." 94 N.L.R.B., at 1511.

The company's letter shows that it interpreted the handbill as a demonstration of such detrimental disloyalty as to provide "cause" for its refusal to continue in its employ the perpetrators of the attack. We agree.

Section 10(c) of the Taft-Hartley Act expressly provides that "No order of the Board shall require the reinstatement of any individual as an employee who has been suspended or discharged, or the payment to him of any back pay, if such individual was suspended or discharged for cause." There is no more elemental cause for discharge of an employee than disloyalty to his employer. It is equally elemental that the Taft-Hartley Act seeks to strengthen, rather than to weaken, that cooperation, continuity of service and cordial contractual relation between employer and employee that is born of loyalty to their common enterprise.

Congress, while safeguarding, in §7, the right of employees to engage in "concerted activities for the purpose of collective bargaining to engage mutual aid or protection," did not weaken the underlying contractual bonds and loyalties of employer and employee. The conference report that led to the enactment of the law said:

". . . [T]he courts have firmly established the rule that under the existing provisions of section 7 of the National Labor Relations Act, employees are not given any right to engage in unlawful or other improper conduct. . . .

". . . Furthermore, in section 10(c) of the amended act, as proposed in the conference agreement, it is specifically provided that no order of the Board shall require the reinstatement of any individual or the payment to him of any back pay if such individual was suspended or discharged for cause, and this, of course, applies with equal force whether or not the acts constituting the cause for discharge were committed in connection with a concerted activity." H.R. Rep. No. 510, 80th Cong., 1st Sess. 38-39.

This has been clear since the early days of the Wagner Act. In 1937, Chief Justice Hughes, writing for the Court, said:

"The Act does not interfere with the normal exercise of the right of the employer to select its employees or to discharge them. The employer may not, under cover of that right, intimidate or coerce its employees with respect to their self-organization and representation, and, on the other hand, the Board is not entitled to make its authority a pretext for interference with the right of discharge when that right is exercised for other reasons than such intimidation and coercion." Labor Board v. Jones & Laughlin, 301 U.S. 1, 45-46. See also, Labor Board v. Fansteel Corp., 306 U.S. 240, 252-258; Auto. Workers v. Wisconsin Board, 336 U.S. 245, 260-263.

Many cases reaching their final disposition in the Courts of Appeals furnish examples emphasizing the importance of enforcing industrial plant discipline and of maintaining loyalty as well as the rights of concerted activities. The courts have refused to reinstate employees discharged for "cause" consisting of insubordination, disobedience or disloyalty. In such cases, it often has been necessary to identify individual employees, somewhat comparable to the nine discharged in this case, and to recognize that their discharges were for causes which were separable from the concerted activities of others whose acts might come within the protection of §7. . . .

The legal principle that insubordination, disobedience or disloyalty is adequate cause for discharge is plain enough. The difficulty arises in determining whether, in fact, the discharges are made because of such a separable cause or because of some other concerted activities engaged in for the purpose of collective bargaining or other mutual aid or protection which may not be adequate cause for discharge. Cf. Labor Board v. Peter Cailler Kohler Co., 130 F.2d 503.

In the instant case the Board found that the company's discharge of the nine offenders resulted from their sponsoring and distributing the "Second-Class City" handbills of August 24-September 3, issued in their name as the "WBT TECHNICIANS." Assuming that there had been no pending labor controversy, the conduct of the "WBT TECHNICIANS" from August 24 through September 3 unquestionably would have provided adequate cause for their disciplinary discharge within the meaning of §10(c). Their attack related itself to no labor practice of the company. It made no reference to wages, hours, or working conditions. The policies attacked were those of finance and public relations for which management, not technicians, must be responsible. The attack asked for no public sympathy or support. It was a continuing attack, initiated while off duty, upon the very interests which the attackers were being paid to conserve and develop. Nothing could be further from the purpose of the Act than to require an employer to finance such activities. Nothing would contribute less to the Act's declared purpose of promoting industrial peace and stability.

The fortuity of the coexistence of a labor dispute affords these technicians no substantial defense. While they were also union men and leaders in the labor controversy, they took pains to separate those categories. In contrast to their claims on the picket line as to the labor controversy, their handbill of August 24 omitted all reference to it. The handbill diverted attention from the labor controversy. It attacked public policies of the company which had no discernible relation to that controversy. The only connection between the handbill and the labor controversy was an ultimate and undisclosed purpose or motive on the part of some of the sponsors that, by the hoped-for financial pressure, the attack might extract from the company some future concession. A disclosure of that motive might have lost more public support for the employees than it would have gained, for it would have given the handbill more the character of coercion than of collective bargaining. Referring to the attack, the Board said "In our judgment, these tactics, in the circumstances of this case, were hardly less 'indefensible' than acts of physical sabotage." 94 N.L.R.B., at 1511. In any event, the findings of the Board effectively separate the attack from the labor controversy and treat it solely as one made by the company's technical experts upon the quality of the company's product. As such, it was as adequate a cause for the discharge of its sponsors as if the labor controversy had not been pending. The technicians, themselves, so handled their attack as thus to bring their discharge under §10(c).

The Board stated "We . . . do not decide whether the disparagement of product involved here would have justified the employer in discharging the employees responsible for it, had it been uttered in the context of a conventional appeal for support of the union in the labor dispute." Id., at 1512, n.18. This underscored the Board's factual conclusion that the attack of August 24 was not part of an appeal for support in the pending dispute. It was a concerted separable attack purporting to be made in the interest of the public rather than in that of the employees.

We find no occasion to remand this cause to the Board for further specificity of findings. Even if the attack were to be treated, as the Board has not treated it, as a concerted activity wholly or partly within the scope of those mentioned in §7, the means used by the technicians in conducting the attack have deprived the attackers of the protection of that section, when read in the light and context of the purpose of the Act.

Accordingly, the order of the Court of Appeals remanding the cause to the National Labor Relations Board is set aside, and the cause is remanded to the Court of Appeals with instructions to dismiss respondent's petition to modify the order of the Board.

It is so ordered.

MR. JUSTICE FRANKFURTER, whom MR. JUSTICE BLACK and MR. JUSTICE DOUGLAS join, dissenting.

The issue before us is not whether this Court would have sustained the Board's order in this case had we been charged by Congress, as we could not have been, "with the normal and primary responsibility for granting or denying enforcement of Labor Board orders." Labor Board v. Pittsburgh S.S. Co., 340 U.S. 498, 502. The issue is whether we should reverse the Court of Appeals, which is so charged, because that court withheld immediate decision on the Board's order and asked the Board for further light. That court found that the Board employed an improper standard as the basis for its decision. The Board judged the conduct in controversy by finding it "indefensible." The Court of Appeals held that by "giving 'indefensible' a vague content different from 'unlawful,' the Board misconceived the scope of the established rule." 91 U.S. App. D.C. 333, 335, 202 F.2d 186, 188. Within "unlawful" that court included activities which "contravene . . . basic policies of the Act." The Court of Appeals remanded the case for the Board's judgment whether the conduct of the employees was protected by §7 under what it deemed "the established rule."

On this central issue — whether the Court of Appeals rightly or wrongly found that the Board applied an improper criterion — this Court is silent. It does not support the Board in using "indefensible" as the legal litmus nor does it reject the Court of Appeal's rejection of that test. This Court presumably does not disagree with the assumption of the Court of Appeals that conduct may be "indefensible" in the colloquial meaning of that loose adjective, and yet be within the protection of §7.

Instead, the Court, relying on §10(c) which permits discharges "for cause," points to the "disloyalty" of the employees and finds sufficient "cause" regardless of whether the handbill was a "concerted activity" within §7. Section 10(c) does not speak of discharge "for disloyalty." If Congress had so written that section, it would have overturned much of the law that had been developed by the Board and the courts in the twelve years preceding the Taft-Hartley Act. The legislative history makes clear that Congress had no such purpose but was rather expressing approval of the construction of "concerted activities" adopted by the Board and the courts. Many of the legally recognized tactics and weapons of labor would readily be condemned for "disloyalty" were they employed between man and man in friendly personal relations. In this connection it is significant that the ground now taken by the Court, insofar as it is derived from the provision of §10(c) relating to discharge "for cause," was not invoked by the Board in justification of its order.

To suggest that all actions which in the absence of a labor controversy might be "cause" — or, to use the words commonly found in labor agreements, "just cause" — for discharge should be unprotected, even when such actions were undertaken as "concerted activities, for the purpose of collective bargaining," is to misconstrue legislation designed to put labor on a fair footing with management. Furthermore, it would disregard the rough and tumble of strikes, in the course of which loose and even reckless language is properly discounted.

"Concerted activities" by employees and dismissal "for cause" by employers are not dissociated legal criteria under the Act. They are like the two halves of a pair of shears. Of course, as the Conference Report on the Taft-Hartley Act said, men on strike may be guilty of conduct "in connection with a concerted activity" which properly constitutes "cause" for dismissal and bars reinstatement. But §10(c) does not obviate the necessity for a determination whether the distribution of the handbills here was a legitimate tool in a labor dispute or was so "improper," as the Conference Report put it, as to be denied the protection of §7 and to constitute a discharge "for cause." It is for the Board, in the first instance, to make these evaluations, and a court of appeals does not travel beyond its proper bounds in asking the Board for greater explicitness in light of the correct legal standards of judgment.

The Board and the courts of appeals will hardly find guidance for future cases from this Court's reversal of the Court of Appeals, beyond that which the specific facts of this case may afford. More than that, to float such imprecise notions as "discipline" and "loyalty" in the context of labor controversies, as the basis of the right to discharge, is to open the door wide to individual judgment by Board members and judges. One may anticipate that the Court's opinion will needlessly stimulate litigation.

Section 7 of course only protects "concerted activities" in the course of promoting legitimate interests of labor. But to treat the offensive handbills here as though they were circulated by the technicians as interloping outsiders to the sustained dispute between them and their employer is a very unreal way of looking at the circumstances of a labor controversy. Certainly there is nothing in the language of the Act or in the legislative history to indicate that only conventional placards and handbills, headed by a trite phrase such as "UNFAIR TO LABOR," are protected. In any event, on a remand the Board could properly be asked to leave no doubt whether the technicians, in distributing the handbills, were, so far as the public could tell, on a frolic of their own or whether this tactic, however unorthodox, was no more unlawful than other union behavior previously found to be entitled to protection.

It follows that the Court of Appeals should not be reversed.

NOTES

1. Suppose that employees while engaged in a valid economic strike propagandize to the effect that the company's product made during the strike may be inferior because of the lack of skill of employees making the product? In Patterson-Sargent Co. and United Gas Workers, AFL-CIO, 115 N.L.R.B. 1627 (1956), striking employees were discharged by the company for handing out handbills during the strike which read:

"BEWARE PAINT SUBSTITUTE"

"The employees of the Patterson-Sargent Company in Cleveland who manufacture paint under the brand of B.P.S., were forced on strike by the company. As a result, there is not being manufactured any paint at the Patterson-Sargent Company in Cleveland by the well trained, experienced employees who have made the paint you have always bought.

"This is a warning that you should make certain that any B.P.S. paint you buy is made by the regular employees who know the formulas and the exact amount of ingredients to put into paint. If you should happen to get paint which is made by any other than the regular well trained, experienced workers, it might not do for you what you want it to do. It could peel, crack, blister, scale or any one of many undesirable things that would cause you inconvenience, lost time and money.

"Stop! Think! Is it worth your while to risk spending your good money for a product which might not be what you are accustomed to using? You will be informed when you can again buy B.P.S. paint which is made by the regular employees in Cleveland."

The trial examiner found that the handbill was false. The Board, however, said that it was immaterial whether the handbill was false or not, and upheld the right of the employer to discharge under the Jefferson Standard case.

In Hoover Co. v. NLRB, 191 F.2d 380 (6th Cir. 1951), denying enforcement of 90 N.L.R.B. 1614 (1950), employees who were discharged for instituting a consumer boycott against the employer's product were denied reinstatement. The court said (pp. 389-390): "An employee cannot work and strike at the same time. . . . He cannot collect wages for his employment, and, at the same time, engage in activities to injure or destroy his employer's business. . . . It is a wrong done to the company for employees, while being employed and paid wages by a company, to engage in a boycott to prevent others from purchasing what their employer is engaged in selling and which is the very thing their employer is paying them to produce. An employer is not required, under the Act, to finance a boycott against himself."

2. Does the principal case allow a species of conduct that is not cause

for discharge but is nevertheless unprotected? As previously seen, if the employer has committed no unfair labor practice and the strike is economic, either discharge for cause or activity unprotected would, even if the job were unfilled, lead to the conclusion in the absence of "condonation" that there was no unfair labor practice in denial of reinstatement.

In NLRB v. Thayer Co., 213 F.2d 748 (1st Cir.), cert. denied, 348 U.S. 883 (1954), the court hit upon an important analytical difference between the reinstatement of economic strikers and the reinstatement of unfair labor practice strikers: "[W]here . . . the strike was caused by an unfair labor practice, the power of the Board to order reinstatement is not necessarily dependent upon a determination that the strike activity was a 'concerted activity' within the protection of Section 7. . . . It ordinarily may be assumed that the Board will balance the severity of the employer's unfair labor practice . . . against whatever employee misconduct may have occurred in the course of the strike." 213 F.2d at 753, 755.

The chronology in Kohler Co., 148 N.L.R.B. No. 147 (1964), helps to depict the nature of the issue:

1933 — Recognition of company-dominated union (KWA).
1934 — Violent strike, (old) Labor Board election with KWA winning over AFL.
1950 — First UAW organizing drive.
1951 — KWA wins election over UAW.
1952 — UAW supporter discharged for organizational activities, KWA affiliates with UAW, UAW wins Labor Board Election and loses all company assistance, strike voted. Company stockpiles coal, food, ammunition, builds watchtowers, buys shotguns and tear gas guns, and enters into agreement with UAW.
1953 — Wage reopener negotiations, strike voted, preparations as in 1952, and agreement.
1954 — Impasse in negotiations for new contract, and strike, with mass picketing, assaults, beginning April 5. Company grants a 3-cent increase on June 1 and subsequently discharges certain strikers, including 44 for mass picketing, 12 for assaults or demonstrations at homes of nonstrikers, and 12 for instigating misconduct.
1960 — Board on August 26 finds strike economic until June 1, 1954, converted to unfair practice strike by company violations then and thereafter, denies reinstatement to all 77 discharged for cause, but orders reinstatement of all other strikers except those permanently replaced prior to June 1, 1954. UAW on September 1 unconditionally applies for reinstatement of some 1800 strikers, including those replaced prior to June 1, 1954, and the 77 discharged for cause.
1962 — Court of Appeals on January 26 sustains UAW contentions that inferences against the company from pre-1953 events were erroneously ignored in concluding that the strike was economic in its inception, and that in denying reinstatement to the 77, the doctrine of Thayer was erroneously ignored.

1964 — On September 30, some 10½ years later, Board holds strike to be
against unfair labor practices from its inception, orders reinstatement of 57 named strikers and all who may have been replaced
prior to June 1, 1954 (in addition to those awarded reinstatement in 1960).

Under the Thayer doctrine, the Board held that seventeen employees
were discharged for misconduct so flagrant as to preclude reinstatement as
a measure to effectuate the policies of the Act.   Member Brown would
have reinstated eight of these on the ground that the violence of the assaults of which they were guilty was not so flagrant considering the pro-
vocative circumstances.   Member Leedom, who had been on the Board in
1960, adhered to the 1960 conclusions except that in his application of
Thayer, four employees (of the seventy-seven) were entitled to reinstatement.   Since he would not find that the strike was an unfair practice
strike from the beginning he found no occasion to apply Thayer to evaluate the mass picketing that occurred prior to June 1, 1954, which the
majority found insufficient to bar reinstatement.   The majority held that
the liability for back pay should be tolled from September 1, 1960, to
January 26, 1962.

In general, the Board thus tolerated mass picketing and demonstrations
at the homes of nonstrikers, in the absence of striking blows or kicks or
threatening harm to family members.   Compare NLRB v. Fansteel Metallurgical Corp., 306 U.S. 240, 253 (1939), holding as to reinstatement of
sit-down strikers: "To justify such conduct because of the existence of a
labor dispute or of an unfair labor practice would be to put a premium
on resort to force instead of legal remedies and to subvert the principles of
law and order which lie at the foundations of society."

According to one author, commenting in 1960, the Board's "delay,
muddied issues, distorted findings of fact, and perverted conclusions of
law" in the Kohler case justified his call for its abolition in particular,
and in general a return from administrative agencies to the courts of law.
Petro, The Kohler Strike: Union Violence and Administrative Law 110
(1961).

3.   Secondary   Pressures

ENDERBY PROBLEM 6
(See page 274 supra for Enderby Problem 5)

Herbert Krask Associates successfully bid on a contract for a substantial
addition to the building which houses the Miscellaneous Division at Enderby.   Work started on this project shortly after the events described in
the previous Problem.

Enderby's contract with Krask called in part for the installation of floor
and wall tile manufactured by Enderby.   Such tile had previously been
used by contractors on other Krask jobs without protest from any employee or union representative.   Representatives of Local 417 called on

Krask and threatened to "cause trouble" unless he stopped using Enderby tile. When Krask refused, Local 417 resumed the picketing and handbilling in front of the Enderby plant as described in Problem 5. The distribution of the handbills addressed "To the Public" was extended to the gate used exclusively by Krask and its subcontractors.

Members of Local 7, Tilelayers Union, who were employed by the McGrath Company, a subcontractor, refused to install Enderby tile. They protested that the tile "is nonunion and has been pre-trimmed by Enderby for most areas of installation, work always performed by the tilelayers on the job." The contract between the unions affiliated with the local building trades council and Krask contained a provision reading as follows: "The company agrees that it will not subcontract work to a nonunion subcontractor, a subcontractor who is currently involved in a labor dispute, or a subcontractor who has not agreed to Section 36(b) of the area agreement." The contract between Local 7 and McGrath contained Section 36(b), which reads: "The company agrees that it will not require its employees to ready for installation or to install nonunion materials."

McGrath attempted to perform its contractual obligation to Krask by hiring nonunion tilelayers. Local 7 stationed a picket at the gate. The picket carried a sign stating: "McGrath Company Unfair. Local 7, Tilelayers Union." All of the building tradesmen walked off the job, and the project was shut down.

The shutdown of the building project gave new life to the Local 417 campaign. Nonemployee representatives of the union visited selected retail outlets handling Enderby products and asked the managers to stop temporarily the selling of Enderby products. For the most part the retailers refused to give the requested cooperation; a few of them pointed out that as Enderby franchise dealers they depended largely or entirely on such sales. When the dealer refused, the union promptly placed several pickets before the customer entrance of the store. These representatives carried placards which read: "Local 417, United Rubber Workers: Enderby products are unfair. Please do not buy Enderby products." While such picketing continued, sales of Enderby products fell off substantially and all of the picketed dealers noticed an appreciable decline in the sales volume of other items. There was, however, no work stoppage of any kind attendant on this union activity except in the case of Ducks Department Store. There, after the picketing began, Smithers, a nonunion clerk, refused to handle Enderby mats and was immediately discharged.

White was further disheartened by occurrences at the Enderby plant. Truck drivers were again refusing to pick up and deliver, but Local 417 was evidently making no effort to correct the situation. When White angrily asserted that the trucking companies were "in conspiracy with Hoffa's people to choke Enderby for the benefit of the Rubber workers," Blair patiently pointed to a recently negotiated provision in contracts with the Teamster locals: ". . . It shall not be cause for discharge or disciplinary action in the event an employee refuses to enter upon any property involved in any labor dispute or refuses to go through or work behind any picket line . . ." White tartly rejoined that this language confirmed the existence of a conspiracy and that he couldn't understand how it could be legal. He sharply questioned Blair about a truck trailing incident which had taken place the previous day. An Enderby truck had crossed the city to make a critical delivery of tires at a customer's warehouse. Representatives of Local 417 had followed in a car and then stood alongside the truck with "To the Public" handbills at the unloading point. It was necessary for the customer's supervisory help to unload the truck when the employees in the shipping and receiving department (members of the Teamsters Union) refused to handle the tires.

Within several weeks the Enderby Company put the following plan into operation: 200 employees in the Tire Division were laid off because of the company's difficulty getting supplies and scheduling deliveries. The work which these employees ordinarily would have done was subcontracted to Good Deal Tire Company. Although Enderby owns 20 per cent of the stock in Good Deal and is also a substantial creditor, this company is a member of the Midwest Tire Manufacturers Association and regularly contracts with Local 666, United Rubber Workers. Officers of this local are extremely hostile to Oliver Curme, whom they regard as "a kind of bull in a china shop." The then current agreement with Local 666 provided in part: "No employee shall, without the consent of the union, be required to perform any service which but for the existence of a strike or lockout between a labor union and any other person would be performed by the employees of such person."

When work under the subcontract with Enderby started at Good Deal, representatives of Local 417 began to picket the plant with signs: "Good Deal unfair. Does work of locked-out employees. Local 417, United Rubber Workers." Some of the Good Deal employees walked out and thereafter teamsters, on the instruction of their union officers, refused to cross the picket line. A few days later Local 666 charged Good Deal with a flagrant breach of contract and successfully called a total strike.

The Enderby Company immediately filed unfair labor practice charges against Locals 417, 666, and the Teamsters Union. Blair also started an action against Local 7, Tilelayers Union, in the federal district court.

LOCAL 761, INTERNATIONAL UNION OF ELECTRICAL, RADIO AND MACHINE WORKERS, AFL-CIO v. NLRB

Supreme Court of the United States, 1961
366 U.S. 667, 81 Sup. Ct. 1285, 6 L. Ed. 2d 592

MR. JUSTICE FRANKFURTER delivered the opinion of the Court.

Local 761 of the International Union of Electrical, Radio and Machine Workers, AFL-CIO was charged with a violation of §8(b)(4)(A) of the Taft-Hartley Act . . . upon the following facts.

General Electric Corporation operates a plant outside of Louisville, Kentucky, where it manufactures washers, dryers, and other electrical household appliances. The square-shaped, thousand-acre, unfenced plant is known as Appliance Park. A large drainage ditch makes ingress and egress impossible except over five roadways across culverts, designated as gates.

Since 1954, General Electric sought to confine the employees of independent contractors, described hereafter, who work on the premises of the Park, to the use of Gate 3-A and confine its use to them. The undisputed reason for doing so was to insulate General Electric employees from the frequent labor disputes in which the contractors were involved. Gate 3-A is 550 feet away from the nearest entrance available for General Electric employees, suppliers, and deliverymen. Although anyone can pass the gate without challenge, the roadway leads to a guard-house where identification must be presented. Vehicle stickers of various shapes and colors enable a guard to check on sight whether a vehicle is authorized to use Gate 3-A. Since January 1958, a prominent sign has been posted at the gate which states: "Gate 3-A For Employees Of Contractors Only — G.E. Employees Use Other Gates." On rare occasions, it appears, a General Electric employee was allowed to pass the guard-house, but such occurrence was in violation of company instructions. There was no proof of any unauthorized attempts to pass the gate during the strike in question.

The independent contractors are utilized for a great variety of tasks on the Appliance Park premises. Some do construction work on new buildings; some install and repair ventilation and heating equipment; some engage in retooling and rearranging operations necessary to the manufacture of new models; others do "general maintenance work." These services are contracted to outside employers either because the company's employees lack the necessary skill or manpower, or because the work can be done more economically by independent contractors. The latter reason determined the contracting of maintenance work for which the Central Maintenance department of the company bid competitively with the contractors. While some of the work done by these contractors had on occasion been previously performed by Central Maintenance, the findings do not disclose the number of employees of independent contractors who were performing these routine maintenance services, as compared with those who were doing specialized work of a capital-improvement nature.

The Union, petitioner here, is the certified bargaining representative for the production and maintenance workers who constitute approximately 7,600 of the 10,500 employees of General Electric at Appliance Park. On July 27, 1958, the Union called a strike because of 24 unsettled grievances with the company. Picketing occurred at all the gates, including Gate 3-A, and continued until August 9 when an injunction was issued by a Federal District Court. The signs carried by the pickets at all gates read: "Local 761 On Strike G.E. Unfair." Because of the picketing, almost all of the employees of independent contractors refused to enter the company premises.

Neither the legality of the strike or of the picketing at any of the gates except 3-A is in dispute, nor that the picketing was other than peaceful in nature. The sole claim is that the picketing before the gate exclusively used by employees of independent contractors was conduct proscribed by §8(b)(4)(A).

The Trial Examiner recommended that the Board dismiss the complaint. He concluded that the limitations on picketing which the Board had prescribed in so-called "common situs" cases were not applicable to the situation before him, in that the picketing at Gate 3-A represented traditional primary action which necessarily had a secondary effect of inconveniencing those who did business with the struck employer. He reasoned that if a primary employer could limit the area of picketing around his own premises by constructing a separate gate for employees of independent contractors, such a device could also be used to isolate employees of his suppliers and customers, and that such action could not relevantly be distinguished from oral appeals made to secondary employees not to cross a picket line where only a single gate existed.

The Board rejected the Trial Examiner's conclusion, 123 N.L.R.B. 1547. It held that since only the employees of the independent contractors were allowed to use Gate 3-A, the Union's object in picketing there was "to enmesh these employees of the neutral employers in its dispute with the Company" thereby constituting a violation of §8(b)(4)(A) because the independent employees were encouraged to engage in a concerted refusal to work "with an object of forcing the independent contractors to cease doing business with the Company."

The Court of Appeals for the District of Columbia granted enforcement of the Board's order, 278 F.2d 282. Although noting that a fine line was being drawn, it concluded that the Board was correct in finding that the objective of the Gate 3-A picketing was to encourage the independent-contractor employees to engage in a concerted refusal to perform services for their employers in order to bring pressure on General Electric. Since the incidence of the problem involved in this case is extensive and the treatment it has received calls for clarification, we brought the case here. . . .

[Section 8(b)(4)(A)] could not be literally construed; otherwise it would ban most strikes historically considered to be lawful, so-called primary activity . . . Thus the section "left a striking labor organization free to use persuasion, including picketing, not only on the primary employer and his employees but on numerous others. Among these were secondary employers who were customers or suppliers of the primary employer and persons dealing with them . . . and even employees of secondary employers so long as the labor organization did not . . . 'induce or encourage the employees of any employer to engage, in a strike or a concerted refusal in the course of their employment' . . ." National Labor Relations Board v. Local 294, International Brotherhood of Teamsters, 2 Cir., 284 F.2d 887, 889 . . .

Important as is the distinction between legitimate "primary activity" and banned "secondary activity," it does not present a glaringly bright line. The objectives of any picketing include a desire to influence others from withholding from the employer their services or trade . . . But picketing which induces secondary employees to respect a picket line is not the equivalent of picketing which has an object of inducing those employees to engage in concerted conduct against their employer in order to force him to refuse to deal with the struck employer. . . .

However difficult the drawing of lines more nice than obvious, the statute compels the task. Accordingly, the Board and the courts have attempted to devise reasonable criteria drawing heavily upon the means to which a union resorts in promoting its cause. . . .

The nature of the problem, as revealed by unfolding variant situations, inevitably involves an evolutionary process for its rational response, not a quick, definitive formula as a comprehensive answer. And so, it is not surprising that the Board has more or less felt its way during the fourteen years in which it has had to apply §8(b)(4)(A), and has modified and reformed its standards on the basis of accumulating experience. . . .

II

The early decisions of the Board following the Taft-Hartley amendments involved activity which took place around the secondary employer's premises. . . . The board found this to be illegal secondary activity. . . . In contrast, when picketing took place around the premises of the primary employer, the Board regarded this as valid primary activity [Ryan Construction Corp., 85 N.L.R.B. 417]. Thus, the Board eliminated picketing which took place around the situs of the primary employer — regardless of the special circumstances involved — from being held invalid secondary activity under 8(b)(4)(A).

However, the impact of the new situations made the Board conscious of the complexity of the problem by reason of the protean forms in which it appeared. This became clear in the "common situs" cases — situations where two employers were performing separate tasks on common premises. The Moore Dry Dock case [Sailors' Union of the Pacific, 92 N.L.R.B. 547] . . . laid out the Board's new standards in this area. There, the union picketed outside an entrance to a dock where a ship, owned by the struck employer, was being trained and outfitted. Although the premises picketed were those of the secondary employer, they constituted the only place where picketing could take place; furthermore, the objectives of the picketing were no more aimed at the employees of the secondary employer — the dock owner — than they had been in [Ryan]. The Board concluded, however, that when the situs of the primary employer was "ambulatory" there must be a balance between the union's right to picket and the interest of the secondary employer in being free from picketing. It set out four standards for picketing in such situations which would be presumptive of valid primary activity; (1) that the picketing be limited to times when the situs of dispute was located on the secondary premises, (2) that the primary employer be engaged in his normal business at the situs, (3) that the picketing take place reasonably close to the situs, and (4) that the picketing clearly disclose that the dispute was only with the primary employer. These tests were widely accepted by reviewing federal courts. . . . As is too often the way of law or, at least, of adjudiciations, soon the Dry Dock tests were mechanically applied so that a violation of one of the standards was taken to be presumptive of illegal activity. For example, failure of picket signs clearly to designate the employer against whom the strike was directed was held to be violative of §8(b)(4)(A). . . .

[After discussing Board decisions applying the Dry Dock tests to picketing at premises owned by the primary employer but occupied in part by other employers, the Court continued:] Where the work done by the secondary employees is unrelated to the normal operations of the primary employer, it is difficult to perceive how the pressure of picketing the entire situs is any less on the neutral employer merely because the picketing takes place at property owned by the struck employer. The application of the Dry Dock tests to limit the picketing effects to the employees of the employer against whom the dispute is directed carries out the "dual congressional objectives of preserving the right of labor organizations to bring pressure to bear on offending employers in primary labor disputes and of shielding unoffending employers and others from pressures in controversies not their own." National Labor Relations Board v. Denver Building & Const. Trades Council . . . 341 U.S. at page 692. . . .

III

From this necessary survey of the course of the Board's treatment of our problem, the precise nature of the issue before us emerges. With due regard to the relation between the Board's function and the scope of judicial review of its rulings, the question is whether the Board may apply the Dry Dock criteria so as to make unlawful picketing at a gate utilized exclusively by employees of independent contractors who work on the struck employers' premises. The effect of such a holding would not bar the union from picketing at all gates used by the employees, suppliers, and customers of the struck employer. Of course an employer may not, by removing all his employees from the situs of the strike, bar the union from publicizing its cause. . . . The basis of the Board's decision in this case would not remotely have that effect, nor any such tendency for the future.

The Union claims that if the Board's ruling is upheld, employers will be free to erect separate gates for deliveries, customers, and replacement workers which will be immunized from picketing. This fear is baseless. The key to the problem is found in the type of work that is being performed by those who use the separate gate. It is significant that the Board has since applied its rationale, first stated in the present case, only to situations where the independent workers were performing tasks unconnected to the normal operations of the struck employer — usually construction work on his buildings. In such situations, the indicated limitations on picketing activity respect the balance of competing interests that Congress has required the Board to enforce. On the other hand, if a separate gate were devised for regular plant deliveries, the barring of picketing at that location would make a clear invasion on traditional primary activity of appealing to neutral employees whose tasks aid the employer's everyday operations. The 1959 Amendments to the National Labor Relations Act, which removed the word "concerted" from the boycott provisions, included a proviso that "nothing contained in this clause (B) shall be construed to make unlawful, where not otherwise unlawful, any primary strike or primary picketing." . . . The proviso was directed against the fear that the removal of "concerted" from the statute might be interpreted so that "the picketing at the factory violates section 8(b)(4) (A) because the pickets induce the truck drivers employed by the trucker not to perform their usual services where an object is to compel the trucking firm not to do business with the . . . manufacturer during the strike." Analysis of the bill prepared by Senator Kennedy and Representative Thompson, 105 Cong. Rec. 16589.

In a case similar to the one now before us, the Court of Appeals for the Second Circuit sustained the Board in its application of §8(b)(4)(A) to a separate gate situation. "There must be a separate gate marked and set apart from other gates; the work done by the men who use the gate must be unrelated to the normal operations of the employer and the work must be of a kind that would not, if done when the plant were engaged in its regular operations, necessitate curtailing those operations." United Steelworkers of America, AFL-CIO v. National Labor Relations Board, 2 Cir. [289 F.2d 591, 595 (1961)]. These seem to us controlling considerations.

I V

The foregoing course of reasoning would require that the judgment below sustaining the Board's order be affirmed but for one consideration, even though this consideration may turn out not to affect the result. The legal path by which the Board and the Court of Appeals reached their decisions did not take into account that if Gate 3-A was in fact used by employees of independent contractors who performed conventional maintenance work necessary to the normal operations of General Electric, the use of the gate would have been a mingled one outside the bar of §8(b)-(4)(A). In short, such mixed use of this portion of the struck employer's premises would not bar picketing rights of the striking employees. While the record shows some such mingled use, it sheds no light on its extent. It may well turn out to be that the instances of these maintenance tasks were so insubstantial as to be treated by the Board as de minimis. We cannot here guess at the quantitative aspect of this problem. It calls for Board determination. For determination of the questions thus raised, the case must be remanded by the Court of Appeals to the Board.

Reversed.

THE CHIEF JUSTICE and MR. JUSTICE BLACK concur in the result.

[The dissenting opinion of Mr. Justice Douglas is omitted.]

NOTE

A railroad spur serves a plant on a right-of-way granted by the plant to the railroad. A gate in the fence surrounding the plant has to be opened for switching operations, and is not used otherwise. In a strike at the plant may picketing be carried on at this gate? Yes, according to United Steelworkers v. NLRB, 376 U.S. 492, 498 (1964): "It seems clear that the rejection of the Board's position in General Electric leaves no room for the even narrower approach of the Court of Appeals in this case [that lawful picketing must appeal to employees of the primary employer]."

LOCAL 861, INTERNATIONAL BROTHERHOOD OF ELECTRICAL WORKERS and PLAUCHE ELECTRIC, INC.

National Labor Relations Board, 1962
135 N.L.R.B. 250

[A wholesale and retail tire concern agreed with Plauche to have certain electrical work done at the premises of the tire company, and Plauche did the work in the manner agreed.]

Respondent picketed in front of the entrance of U.S. Tire on October 6 and until some time in the early afternoon of October 7. During the picketing, Plauche's employees on the job, Bonin, Arnaud and Duhon, worked inside the U.S. Tire premises. There were no interruptions of any kind. The picket sign stated: "Plauche Electric, Inc., is attempting to destroy working conditions established through negotiations by the IBEW, Local Union 861. No dispute with any other contractor." When Plauche's employees left for lunch and a coffee break, the picketing continued. There was no picketing at Plauche's office.

Plauche maintains an office in the area to which his employees, as a normal requirement, report in the morning to be dispatched by truck to the job and report back in the evening. On occasion, an employee will return to the office during the course of the day for the purpose of picking up a tool or materials. On the first day of picketing at U.S. Tire, Arnaud and Duhon reported to the office and then went to the job. Bonin went directly to the job for a short time, having been delayed by a hospital visit and then went directly home. The other two reported back to the office at the end of the first day. Arnaud went back to the office for a short time on the morning of the first day. On the second day, all three reported to the office at the start of the work day. Duhon worked at U.S. Tire only part of the day. All three left the job at 6 P.M., well after the pickets had been withdrawn, and went directly home. For the remaining 2 or 3 days of the job's duration, Bonin and Arnaud reported directly to the work site.

The Trial Examiner found that Respondents violated Section 8(b)(4)-(i)(B) by (1) picketing at the premises of the secondary employer, U.S. Tire, rather than at the office of the primary employer, Plauche, relying on the Washington Coca Cola decision [Brewery and Beverage Drivers and Workers, Local No. 67, 107 N.L.R.B. 299, enforced, 220 F.2d 380], and (2) picketing while the employees of Plauche working on the U.S. Tire job left for lunch and a coffee break, relying on the Moore Drydock decision [92 N.L.R.B. 547].

The Washington Coca Cola decision has heretofore been construed by the Board as imposing a rigid rule that picketing at the common situs is unlawful when the primary employer has a regular place of business in the locality which can be picketed. This rigid rule has been rejected by the courts which have had occasion to pass upon its validity. As stated by the Circuit Court of the District of Columbia in the Sales Drivers case (229 F.2d 514, at 517): "Section 8(b)(4)(A) does not contain a provision which condemns concerted activity of employees with respect to their own employer merely because it occurs at a place where it comes to the attention of and incidentally affects employees of another, even where the activity could be carried on at a place where the primary employer alone does business. The existence of a common site, of such incidental effect, and of another place which can be picketed, are factors to be considered in determining whether or not the section has been violated, but alone are not conclusive. The presence of these factors does not warrant a failure to consider other facts which are relevant and perhaps countervailing. . . . No rigid rule which would make these few factors conclusive is contained in or deducible from the statute. To read it into the statute by implication would unduly invade the application of section 13 which preserves the right to strike 'except as specifically provided' in other provisions of the Act. It is not specifically provided that picketing at a common site, with an incidental effect upon employees of a neutral employer, is unlawful in every case where picketing could also be conducted against the primary employer at another of its places of business." . . .

In the light of such judicial criticism of the Washington Coca Cola rule . . . we shall not adhere to the rule of that case. We shall not automatically find unlawful all picketing at the site where the employees of the primary employer spend practically their entire working day simply because, as in this case, they may report for a few minutes at the beginning and end of each day to the regular place of business of the primary employer.

In thus overruling Washington Coca Cola to the extent it is inconsistent herewith we are not unmindful of the references to that case in the legislative history of the 1959 amendments. In amending Section 8(b)(4) Congress added a proviso to the new 8(b)(4)(B) that "nothing in this clause (B) shall be construed to make unlawful, where not otherwise unlawful, any primary strike or primary picketing." Referring to that proviso, the Conference Report states (H. Rept. 1147, 86th Cong., 1st Sess., p. 38; Vol. I Legislative History of the Labor Management Reporting and Disclosure Act of 1959, p. 942); "This provision does not eliminate, restrict, or modify the limitations on picketing at the site of a primary labor dispute that are in existing law," citing, inter alia, Washington Coca Cola. Senator Goldwater's post-enactment analysis (II Leg. Hist. 1857) contains a similar reference, adding a more explicit statement that "The rules laid down in certain decisions with respect to such picketing are still the law . . ." These references, however, do not preclude our reexamination of Washington Coca Cola as applied to the instant case. In the first place the discussion in the House Conference Report was specifically directed at the proviso holding picketing lawful. Second, Washington Coca Cola, as is established by the cases . . . which cite it, was enforced only because it "rested in considerable part upon additional findings" (Sales Drivers, 229 F.2d at 517); it did not at the time of the 1959 amendments represent the courts' view of "existing law" on the issue involved here. Finally, and most important of all, both the House Conference Report and Senator Goldwater cite Pittsburgh Plate Glass Co., 110 N.L.R.B. 455, with the same approval they give Washington Coca Cola. Yet, on the precise question involved here — whether picketing at a common situs is unlawful when the employees of the primary employer report at their employer's main establishment twice a day — Pittsburgh Plate substantially limits, if it is not in square conflict with, Washington Coca Cola. The legislative history plainly leaves us as free to return to Pittsburgh Plate as to follow Washington Coca Cola.

In overruling Washington Coca Cola we do not, of course, hold that the place of picketing is irrelevant in determining the legality of the picketing. We shall in the future, as we have with court approval in the past, consider the place of picketing as one circumstance among others, in determining an object of the picketing. . . .

In the instant case, we hold that the office of Plauche was not the sole permissible situs for the publicization of the dispute relating to the performance of electrical work by Plauche's employees at the premises of U.S. Tire. Accordingly, we reject the finding of the Trial Examiner that picketing at the U.S. Tire premises was per se unlawful.

Employees of neutrals as well as of the primary employer were working at the U.S. Tire premises. Accordingly, the picketing to be lawful had to accord with the Moore Drydock standards. These standards also are not to be applied on an indiscriminate "per se" basis, but are to be regarded merely as aids in determining the underlying question of statutory violation. Unlike Washington Coca Cola, however, these standards, so applied, have met with consistent judicial approval, and we find they may be properly applied here.

It is not disputed that the picketing at U.S. Tire did accord with these standards with one possible exception: Respondents continued to picket when Plauche's employees took time off for lunch or a coffee break. The Trial Examiner found that because of this circumstance the entire picketing was unlawful. Moore Drydock states that in a mixed situs situation picketing of the premises of a secondary employer is primary if "(b) at the time of the picketing the primary employer is engaged in its normal business at the situs." Manifestly, Plauche's normal business at the common situs did not come to an end merely because his employees temporarily departed under these circumstances. Otherwise every common situs picket line, however otherwise observant of Moore Drydock standards, would be mechanically converted from lawful to unlawful picketing by picketing unsynchronized with lunch, coffee, or other temporary work interruption occasioned by personal need. The standard set forth above is to be applied with common sense. It is not to be interpreted in the absurd manner suggested. We find that the picketing of the U.S. Tire premises was in conformance with the Moore Drydock standards.

Accordingly, we find that by their picketing of Plauche at the U.S. Tire premises Respondents did not violate Section 8(b)(4)(i)(B) of the Act. . . .

[The dissenting opinions of Members Rodgers and Leedom are omitted.]

LOCAL 1976, UNITED BROTHERHOOD OF CARPENTERS v. NLRB
GENERAL DRIVERS UNION AND INTERNATIONAL ASSOCIATION OF MACHINISTS v. NLRB

Supreme Court of the United States, 1958
357 U.S. 93, 78 Sup. Ct. 1011, 2 L. Ed. 2d 1186

MR. JUSTICE FRANKFURTER delivered the opinion of the Court.

These cases involve so-called "hot cargo" provisions in collective bargaining agreements. More particularly, they raise the question whether such a provision is a defense to a charge against a union of an unfair labor practice under §8(b)(4)(A) of the National Labor Relations Act . . .

No. 127 arises out of a labor dispute between carpenter unions and an employer engaged in the building construction trade in Southern California. The Sand Door and Plywood Company is the exclusive distributor in Southern California of doors manufactured by the Paine Lumber Company of Oshkosh, Wisconsin. Watson and Dreps are millwork contractors who purchase doors from Sand. Havstad and Jensen are general contractors who were, at the time of the dispute involved, engaged in the construction of a hospital in Los Angeles. Havstad and Jensen are parties to a master labor agreement negotiated with the United Brotherhood of Carpenters and Joiners of America on behalf of its affiliated district councils and locals including petitioner unions. This agreement comprehensively regulating the labor relations of Havstad and Jensen and its carpenter employees, includes a provision that, "workmen shall not be required to handle non-union material."

In August 1954 doors manufactured by Paine and purchased by Sand were delivered to the hospital construction site by Watson and Dreps. On the morning of August 17, Fleisher, business agent of petitioner Local 1976, came to the construction site and notified Steinert, Havstad and Jensen's foreman, that the doors were nonunion and could not be hung. Steinert therefore ordered employees to cease handling the doors. When Nicholson, Havstad and Jensen's general superintendent, appeared on the job and asked Fleisher why the workers had been prevented from handling the doors, he stated that they had been stopped until it could be determined whether the doors were union or nonunion. Subsequent negotiations between officers of Sand and the union failed to produce an agreement that would permit the doors to be installed.

On the basis of charges filed by Sand and a complaint duly issued, the National Labor Relations Board found that petitioners had induced and encouraged employees to engage in a strike or concerted refusal to handle Paine's doors in order to force Havstad and Jensen and Sand to cease doing business with Paine, all in violation of §8(b)(4)(A). 113 N.L.R.B. 1210. The Court of Appeals for the Ninth Circuit enforced the Board's cease-and-desist order, 241 F.2d 147, and we granted certiorari. 355 U.S. 808 . . . The sole question tendered by the petition for certiorari concerned the relation between the hot cargo provision in the collective bargaining agreement and the charge of an unfair labor practice proscribed by §8(b)(4)(A).[1]

Nos. 273 and 324 arise out of a labor dispute in Oklahoma City in which certain unions are said to have induced the employees of five common carriers to cease handling the goods of another employer in violation of §8(b)(4)(A). American Iron and Machine Works was engaged in a controversy with Local 850 of the International Association of Machinists, the bargaining representative of its production and maintenance employees, and a strike had been called at the company's plants. Picketing at the plants prevented the carriers that normally served American Iron from making pick-up and deliveries, so American Iron hauled freight in its own trucks to the loading platforms of the carriers. The Machinists followed the trucks to the carriers' platforms and picketed them there, without making it clear that their dispute was only with American Iron. In addition, there was evidence that they expressly requested employees of some of the carriers not to handle American Iron freight. Teamsters Union Local 886, representative of the carriers' employees, instructed the employees to cease handling the freight. All the carriers except one expressly ordered their employees to move American Iron freight, but nevertheless they refused to do so. The Teamsters' contract with the carriers contained a provision that, "Members of the Union shall not be allowed to handle or haul freight to or from an unfair company, provided, this is not a violation of the Labor Management Relations Act of 1947."

On the basis of charges filed by American Iron, the Board issued complaints against the unions and found that both the Machinists and Teamsters, by their appeals or instructions to the carriers' employees, had violated §8(b)(4)(A), notwithstanding the hot cargo provision in the collective bargaining agreement. 115 N.L.R.B. 800. The Court of Appeals for the District of Columbia set aside the order as to the Teamsters because of the hot cargo provision (No. 273), but enforced the order against the

[1] We therefore find it unnecessary to consider other contentions now made by petitioners on issues resolved against them by both the Board and the Court of Appeals: (1) Whether Steinert, when he instructed the employees to stop handling the doors, acted as a representative of Havstad and Jensen, the employers, or in his capacity as a member of the union, bound to enforce its rules. (2) Whether there was substantial evidence to support the Board's conclusion that the union conduct was not primary activity outside the scope of §8(b)(4)(A). See Irvine v. People of State of California, 347 U.S. 128, 129-130; Rule 23(c) of the Revised Rules of the Supreme Court of the United States, 28 U.S.C.A.

Machinists (No. 324). 101 U.S. App. D.C. 80, 247 F.2d 71. We granted certiorari in all three cases because of conflicts among the circuits as to the meaning of §(b)(4)(A), as well as because of the importance of the problem raised in the administration of the Labor Management Relations Act, and ordered them consolidated for argument. 355 U.S. 808 . . .[2]

Whatever may have been said in Congress preceding the passage of the Taft-Hartley Act concerning the evil of all forms of "secondary boycotts" and the desirability of outlawing them, it is clear that no such sweeping prohibition was in fact enacted in §8(b)(4)(A). The section does not speak generally of secondary boycotts. It describes and condemns specific union conduct directed to specific objectives. It forbids a union to induce employees to strike against or to refuse to handle goods for their employer when an object is to force him or another person to cease doing business with some third party. Employees must be induced; they must be induced to engage in a strike or concerted refusal; an object must be to force or require their employer or another person to cease doing business with a third person. Thus, much that might argumentatively be found to fall within the broad and somewhat vague concept of secondary boycott is not in terms prohibited. A boycott voluntarily engaged in by a secondary employer for his own business reasons, perhaps because the unionization of other employers will protect his competitive position or because he identifies his own interests with those of his employees and their union, is not covered by the statute. Likewise, a union is free to approach an employer to persuade him to engage in a boycott, so long as it refrains from the specifically prohibited means of coercion through inducement of employees.

From these considerations of what is not prohibited by the statute, the true scope and limits of the legislative purpose emerge. The primary employer, with whom the union is principally at odds, has no absolute assurance that he will be free from the consequences of a secondary boycott. Nor have other employers or persons who deal with either the primary employer or the secondary employer and who may be injuriously affected by the restrictions on commerce that flow from secondary boycotts. Nor has the general public. We do not read the words "other person" in the phrase "forcing or requiring . . . any employer or other person" to extend protection from the effects of a secondary boycott to such other person when the secondary employer himself, the employer of the employees involved, consents to the boycott. When he does consent it

---

[2] Certain contentions of the unions in Nos. 273 and 324 can be quickly disposed of. The controversy was not rendered moot simply because, after the filing of the charges and before the complaint issued, picketing had ceased and the Machinists had entered into a collective bargaining agreement containing a no-strike clause. We cannot say that there was no danger of recurrent violation, see United States v. W. T. Grant Co., 345 U.S. 629, 632-633, and that the Board was not justified in concluding that, under all the circumstances, it was desirable to add the sanction of its order to whatever agreement the parties had reached. The Machinists' contention that their activity was only legitimate primary activity is foreclosed by the Board's contrary finding on the basis of conflicting evidence.

cannot appropriately be said that there is a strike or concerted refusal to handle goods on the part of the employees. Congress has not seen fit to protect these other persons or the general public by any wholesale condemnation of secondary boycotts, since if the secondary employer agrees to the boycott, or it is brought about by means other than those proscribed in §8(b)(4)(A), there is no unfair labor practice. . . .

The question is whether a hot cargo provision, such as is found in the collective bargaining agreements in these cases, can be a defense to a charge of an unfair labor practice under §8(b)(4)(A) when, in the absence of such a provision, the union conduct would unquestionably be a violation. This question has had a checkered career in the decisions of the National Labor Relations Board since it first came before that tribunal some nine years ago. In the Conway's Express case, In re International Brotherhood of Teamsters, 1949, 87 N.L.R.B. 972, affirmed sub nom. Rabouin v. National Labor Relations Board, 2 Cir., 195 F.2d 906, the Board (Members Houston, Murdock, and Gray), found that there was nothing in a hot cargo provision as such repugnant to the policy of the statute, and that the union had not violated §8(b)(4)(A) when, pursuant to the provision, it had instructed employees not to handle goods, and the employers had apparently acquiesced. Chairman Herzog concurred in the finding that §8(b)(4)(A) had not been violated on the facts of the particular case, but was of the opinion that the hot cargo provision did not license the union itself to take action to induce the employees to refuse to handle goods. 87 N.L.R.B. at pages 983, note 33. Member Reynolds dissented on the ground that a hot cargo provision was in conflict with the policy of the statute and could not be invoked as a defense to a charge of a violation of §8(b)(4)(A). In the Pittsburgh Plate Glass case, Chauffeurs Union, 1953, 105 N.L.R.B. 740, where the union had also induced employees not to handle goods and the employers had acquiesced in the enforcement of the hot cargo provisions, the Board without dissent (Members Houston, Murdock, Styles and Peterson; Chairman Herzog took no part) adhered to the Conway decision. Since "the employers in this proceeding consented to the 'unfair goods' provision of the contracts, their employees' failure to handle these goods was not a strike or concerted refusal to work under Section 8(b)(4)(A)." 105 N.L.R.B. at page 744.

In the McAllister case, International Brotherhood of Teamsters, 1954, 110 N.L.R.B. 1769, the Board took a different position. Members Rodgers and Beeson were of the view that §8(b)(4)(A) prohibited all secondary boycotts and had been enacted as much for the protection of the primary employer and the public as the secondary employers, and that a contract between the secondary employers and the union was ineffective to waive the protection granted these other interests. They called for overruling the Conway case and a declaration that a hot cargo provision is no defense to a charge under §8(b)(4)(A). Chairman Farmer concurred in finding a violation of the statute, on the ground that the case was distinguishable from the Conway and Pittsburgh Plate Glass decisions in that the employers had not acquiesced in the employees' failure to handle the goods. He found nothing contrary to the statute in the execution of a hot cargo provision and mutual adherence to it by employer and union, but only in the inducement of employees to refuse to handle goods in the face of express instructions to do so. Members Murdock and Peterson dissented on the ground that since the employers had by the hot cargo provision consented in advance to the boycott, there was no strike or concerted refusal to handle goods within the meaning of the statute, apparently even assuming that the employers had instructed their employees to handle the goods.

Still further mutations in the position of the Board and the views of the individual members took place in the Sand Door case, Local 1976, United Brotherhood of Carpenters, 1955, 113 N.L.R.B. 1210, now here as No. 127. Chairman Farmer and Member Leedom maintained that, although hot cargo clauses are not themselves in conflict with the statute, any direct appeal by a union to the employees of a secondary employer to induce them to refuse to handle goods, and in this manner to assert their rights under the contract, violates §8(b)(4)(A). The importance of the fact that, evidently, the employer in the case before the Board had not acquiesced in the stoppage was not made clear. Member Rodgers concurred in the result on the basis of the principal opinion in the McAllister case and his view that hot cargo clauses as such violate the policy of the statute. Members Murdock and Peterson, dissenting, adhered to the views they had expressed in McAllister. . . .

In the American Iron case, General Drivers Union, 1956, 115 N.L.R.B. 800, now here as Nos. 273 and 324, Members Leedom and Bean relied on the principal opinion in the Sand Door case, making it clear that any direct appeal to the employees was forbidden whether or not the employer acquiesced in the boycott. Member Rodgers concurred on the basis of his previous opinions. Members Murdock and Peterson dissented, noting that since there was a violation of the statute even if the employer acquiesced, the Conway doctrine had at last been clearly repudiated. . . .

In a decision handed down after the granting of certiorari in the cases now before the Court, Truck Drivers Union (Genuine Parts Co.), 1957, 119 N.L.R.B. No. 53, two members of the Board, Chairman Leedom and Member Jenkins, rested on a broader ground than that taken in the principal opinion in the Sand Door and American Iron cases: when the secondary employer is a common carrier subject to the Interstate Commerce Act, 24 Stat. 379, as amended by Act of Aug. 9, 1935, 49 Stat. 543, amended, 49 U.S.C. §§301-327, a hot cargo clause is invalid at its inception and cannot be recognized by the Board as having any force or effect. It is also strongly suggested in the opinion filed by these members that it would be desirable to establish such a rule in respect to all employers, and that the mere existence of a hot cargo clause should be deemed prima facie evidence of inducement in violation of §8(b)(4)(A). Member Rodgers concurred on the basis of his earlier opinions, without considering the implications of the Interstate Commerce Act. Member Bean concurred solely on the basis of the Sand Door case. Member Murdock dissented, objecting particularly to what he conceived to be the extreme suggestion that the mere existence of a hot cargo provision should be deemed prima facie evidence of a violation of §8(b)(4)(A), and pointing out that a majority of the Board appears to have abandoned the theory of the Sand Door and American Iron cases even before this Court could review them.

The argument that a hot cargo clause is a defense to a charge of a violation of §8(b)(4)(A) may be thus stated. The employer has by contract voluntarily agreed that his employees shall not handle the goods. Because of this consent, even if it is sought to be withdrawn at the time of an actual work stoppage and boycott, it cannot be said, in the light of the statutory purpose, either that there is a "strike or a concerted refusal" on the part of the employees, or that there is a "forcing or requiring" of the employer. Only if consideration is confined to the circumstances immediately surrounding the boycott, in disregard of the broader history of the labor relations of the parties, is it possible to say that the employer is coerced into engaging in the boycott. If the purpose of the statute is to protect neutrals from certain union pressures to involve them involuntarily in the labor disputes of others, protection should not extend to an employer who has agreed to a hot cargo provision, for such an employer is not in fact involuntarily involved in the dispute. This must at least be so when the employer takes no steps at the time of the boycott to repudiate the contract and to order his employees to handle the goods. The union does no more than inform the employees of their contractual rights and urge them to take the only action effective to enforce them.

The Board in the present cases has rejected the argument as not comporting with the legislative purpose to be drawn from the statute, projected onto the practical realities of labor relations. We agree, duly heedful of the strength of the argument to the contrary. There is nothing in the legislative history to show that Congress directly considered the relation between hot cargo provisions and the prohibitions of §8(b)(4)-(A). Nevertheless, it seems most probable that the freedom of choice for the employer contemplated by §8(b)(4)(A) is a freedom of choice at the time the question whether to boycott or not arises in a concrete situation calling for the exercise of judgment on a particular matter of labor and business policy. Such a choice, free from the prohibited pressures — whether to refuse to deal with another or to maintain normal business relations on the ground that the labor dispute is no concern of his — must as a matter of federal policy be available to the secondary employer notwithstanding any private agreement entered into between the parties. See National Licorice Co. v. National Labor Relations Board, 309 U.S. 350, 364. This is so because by the employer's intelligent exercise of such a choice under the impact of a concrete situation when judgment is most responsible, and not merely at the time a collective bargaining agreement is drawn up covering a multitude of subjects, often in a general and abstract manner, Congress may rightly be assumed to have hoped that the scope of industrial conflict and the economic effects of the primary dispute might be effectively limited.

Certainly the language of the statute does not counter such an interpretation. The employees' action may be described as a "strike or concerted refusal," and there is a "forcing or requiring" of the employer, even though there is a hot cargo provision. The realities of coercion are not altered simply because it is said that the employer is forced to carry out a prior engagement rather than forced now to cease doing business with another. A more important consideration, and one peculiarly within the cognizance of the Board because of its closeness to and familiarity with the practicalities of the collective bargaining process, is the possibility that the contractual provision itself may well not have been the result of choice on the employer's part free from the kind of coercion Congress has condemned. It may have been forced upon him by strikes that, if used to bring about a boycott when the union is engaged in a dispute with some primary employer, would clearly be prohibited by the Act. Thus, to allow the union to invoke the provision to justify conduct that in the absence of such a provision would be a violation of the statute might give it the means to transmit to the moment of boycott, through the contract, the very pressures from which Congress has determined to relieve secondary employers.

Thus inducements of employees that are prohibited under §8(b)(4)(A) in the absence of a hot cargo provisions are likewise prohibited when there is such a provision. The Board has concluded that a union may not, on the assumption that the employer will respect his contractual obligation, order its members to cease handling goods, and that any direct appeal to the employees to engage in a strike or concerted refusal to handle goods is proscribed. This conclusion was reached only after considerable experience with the difficulty of determining whether an employer has in fact acquiesced in a boycott, whether he did or did not order his employees to handle the goods, and the significance of an employer's silence. Of course if an employer does intend to observe the contract, and does truly sanction and support the boycott, there is no violation of §8(b)(4)(A). A voluntary employer boycott does not become prohibited activity simply because a hot cargo clause exists. But there remains the question whether the employer has in fact truly sanctioned and supported the boycott, and whether he has exercised the choice contemplated by the statute. The potentiality of coercion in a situation where the union is free to approach the employees and induce them to enforce their contractual rights by self help is very great. Faced with a concerted work stoppage already in progress, an employer may find it substantially more difficult than he otherwise would to decide that business should go on as usual and that his employees must handle the goods. His "acquiescence" in the boycott may be anything but free. In order to give effect to the statutory policy, it is not unreasonable to insist, as the Board has done, that even when there is a contractual provision the union must not appeal to the employees or induce them not to handle the goods. Such a rule expresses practical judgment on the effect of union conduct in the framework of actual labor disputes and what is necessary to preserve to the employer the freedom of choice that Congress had decreed. On such a matter the judgment of the Board must be given great weight, and we ought not set against it our estimate of the relevant factors.

There is no occasion to consider the invalidity of hot cargo provisions as such. The sole concern of the Board in the present cases was whether the contractual provision could be used by the unions as a defense to a charge of inducing employees to strike or refuse to handle goods for objectives proscribed by §8(b)(4)(A). As we have said, it cannot be so used. But the Board has no general commission to police collective bargaining agreements and strike down contractual provisions in which there is no element of an unfair labor practice. Certainly the voluntary observance of a hot cargo provision by an employer does not constitute a violation of §8(b)(4)(A), and its mere execution is not, contrary to the suggestion of two members of the Board in the Genuine Parts case, Truck Drivers Union, 119 N.L.R.B. No. 53, prima facie evidence of prohibited inducement of employees. It does not necessarily follow from the fact that the unions cannot invoke the contractual provision in the manner in which they sought to do so in the present cases that it may not, in some totally different context not now before the Court, still have legal radiations affecting the relations between the parties. All we need now say is that the contract cannot be enforced by the means specifically prohibited in §8(b)(4)-(A).

In Nos. 273 and 324, the Board in its brief suggests that we should go further and find that the contract provisions in these cases are invalid as such because the secondary employers are common carriers subject to the Interstate Commerce Act. . . . In the recent Genuine Parts case, already referred to, Truck Drivers Union, 119 N.L.R.B. No. 53, two members of the Board in fact took this position, stating that when common carriers are involved hot cargo clauses are "invalid at their inception and can be given no operative cognizance so far as the administration of this [the Labor Management Relations] Act is concerned." This is true, it is said, because by entering a contract not to handle the goods the carrier violates its obligations under the Interstate Commerce Act to provide nondiscriminatory service and to observe just and reasonable practices. See Act of Aug. 9, 1935, §216, 49 Stat. 558, amended, 49 U.S.C. §316. The carrier's consent to boycott is therefore void, and it follows that it is likewise void for all purposes concerned with the Labor Management Relations Act. Since the Genuine Parts decision was handed down, the Interstate Commerce Commission has in fact ruled, in Galveston Truck Line Corp. v Ada Motor Lines, Inc., 73 M.C.C. 617 (Dec. 16, 1957), that the carriers there involved were not relieved from their obligations under the Interstate Commerce Act by a hot cargo clause.

It is significant to note the limitations that the Commission was careful to draw about its decision in the Galveston case. It was not concerned to determine, as an abstract matter, the legality of hot cargo clauses, but only to enforce whatever duty was imposed on the carriers by the Interstate Commerce Act and their certificates. The Commission recognized that it had no general authority to police such contracts, and its sole concern was to determine whether a hot cargo provision could be a defense to

a charge that the carriers had violated some specific statutory duty. It is
the Commission that in the first instance must determine whether, because of certain compelling considerations, a carrier is relieved of its usual
statutory duty, and necessarily it makes this determination in the context
of the particular situation presented by the case before it. Other agencies
of government, in interpreting and administering the provisions of statutes specifically entrusted to them for enforcement, must be cautious not
to complicate the Commission's administration of its own act by assuming
as a fixed and universal rule what the Commission itself may prefer to
develop in a more cautious and pragmatic manner through case-by-case
adjudication.

But it is said that the Board is not enforcing the Interstate Commerce
Act or interfering with the Commission's administration of that statute,
but simply interpreting the prohibitions of its own statute in a way consistent with the carrier's obligations under the Interstate Commerce Act.
Because of that Act a carrier cannot effectively consent not to handle the
goods of a shipper. Since he cannot effectively consent, there is, under
§8(b)(4)(A), a "strike or concerted refusal," and a "forcing or requiring"
of the carrier to cease handling goods just as much as if no hot cargo
clause existed. But the fact that the carrier's consent is not effective to
relieve him from certain obligations under the Interstate Commerce Act
does not necessarily mean that it is ineffective for all purposes, nor should
a determination under one statute be mechanically carried over in the
interpretation of another statute involving significantly different considerations and legislative purposes. Whether a carrier has without justification failed to provide reasonable and nondiscriminatory service is a
question of defining the carrier's duty in the framework of the national
transportation policy. Whether there is a "strike or concerted refusal," or
a "forcing or requiring" of an employer to cease handling goods is a matter of the federal policy governing labor relations. The Board is not
concerned with whether the carrier has performed its obligations to the
shipper, but whether the union has performed its obligation not to induce employees in the manner proscribed by §8(b)(4)(A). Common
factors may emerge in the adjudication of these questions, but they are,
nevertheless, distinct questions involving independent considerations.
This is made clear by a situation in which the carrier has freely agreed
with the union to engage in a boycott. He may have failed in his obligations under the Interstate Commerce Act, but there clearly is no violation of §8(b)(4)(A); there has been no prohibited inducement of
employees.

The case is not like that in Southern S.S. Co. v. National Labor Relations Board, 316 U.S. 31, where the Board was admonished not to apply
the policies of its statute so single-mindedly as to ignore other equally
important congressional objectives. A specific remedy ordered by the
Board — reinstatement of employees who had engaged in a strike —
worked directly to weaken the effectiveness of a statutory prohibition
against mutiny by members of the crew of a vessel. Presumed illegality
under the mutiny statute was not used to establish a violation of the labor

statute. It was relied on to establish an abuse of discretion in giving a remedy. Much less was there any suggestion that the Board should abandon an independent inquiry into the requirements of its own statute and mechanically accept standards elaborated by another agency under a different statute for wholly different purposes.

The unions in Nos. 273 and 324 violated §8(b)(4)(A) for the reasons set forth in the first part of this opinion, and not as a consequence of prohibitions in the Interstate Commerce Act.

The judgments in Nos. 127 and 324 are affirmed. The judgment in No. 273 is reversed and the cause remanded to the Court of Appeals with instructions to grant enforcement of the order of the Board.

MR. JUSTICE DOUGLAS with whom THE CHIEF JUSTICE and MR. JUSTICE BLACK concur, dissenting.

The Court concedes that the voluntary observance of a hot cargo provision by an employer does not constitute a violation of §8(b)(4)(A) of the National Labor Relations Act . . . I fail to see, therefore, why enforcement of a provision in a collective bargaining agreement outlawing work on nonunion goods violates the Act.

The provision of the collective bargaining agreement in the Carpenters case is typical of those in issue here:

"Workmen shall not be required to handle non-union material."

That provision was bargained for like every other claim in the collective agreement. It was agreed to by the employer. How important it may have been to the parties — how high or low in their scale of values — we do not know. But on these records it was the product of bargaining, not of coercion. The Court concedes that its inclusion in the contracts may not be called "forcing or requiring" the employer to cease handling other products within the meaning of the Act. Enforcing the collective bargaining agreement — standing by its terms — is not one of the coercive practices at which the Act was aimed. Enforcement of these agreements is conducive to peace. Disregard of collective agreements — the flouting of them — is disruptive. That was the philosophy of the Conway's Express decision of the Labor Board, 87 N.L.R.B. 972, affirmed sub nom. Rabouin v. National Labor Relations Board, 2 Cir., 195 F.2d 906, and I think it squares with the Act.

The present decision is capricious. The boycott is lawful if the employer agrees to abide by this collective bargaining agreement. It is unlawful if the employer reneges.

The hostile attitude of labor against patronizing or handling "unfair" goods goes deep into our history. It is not peculiarly American, though it has found expression in various forms in our history from the refusal of Americans to buy British tea, to the refusal of Abolitionists to buy slave-made products, to the refusal of unions to work on convict-made or on other nonunion goods. Unions have adhered to the practice because of their principle of mutual aid and protection. Section 7 of the Act, 29 U.S.C.A. §157, indeed, recognizes that principle in its guarantee that "Employees shall have the right . . . to engage in . . . concerted activities for the purpose of collective bargaining or other mutual aid or protection." We noticed in Apex Hosiery Co. v. Leader, 310 U.S. 469, 503, that the elimination of "competition from non-union made goods" was a legitimate labor objective.

The reason an employer may also agree to that phase of union policies, the reason he may acquiesce in the inclusion of such a clause in a particular collective agreement, may only be surmised. Perhaps he sees eye to eye with the union. Perhaps he receives important concessions in exchange for his assistance to the union.

Certain it is that where he voluntarily agrees to the "unfair" goods clause he is not forced or coerced in the statutory sense. What Judge Clark said in Milk Drivers & Dairy Employees, etc. v. National Labor Relations Board, 2 Cir., 245 F.2d 817, 822, has not yet been answered:

"In the absence of a prior agreement, work to be done by employees is determined unilaterally by the employer; but where a collective agreement specifies the work to be done, that agreement defines the normal work of the employees and a 'strike' or 'refusal' must be a refusal to do that normal work. The employer obviously cannot impose additional work on the employees contrary to the agreement and then charge that their refusal to perform it constitutes an unfair practice. We see no difference in this respect between tasks exempted by the agreement because they are offensive to health or safety and tasks exempted because their performance is contrary to the interests of organized labor and, in this case, the local itself."

We act today more like a Committee of the Congress than the Court. We strain to outlaw bargaining contracts long accepted, long used. Perhaps these particular provisions have evils in them that should be declared contrary to the public interest. They are, however, so much a part of the very fabric of collective bargaining that we should leave this policy-making to Congress and not rush in to undo what a century or more of experience has imbedded into labor-management agreements. I have not found a word of legislative history which even intimates that these "unfair" goods provisions of collective bargaining agreements are unlawful.

ORANGE BELT DISTRICT COUNCIL OF PAINTERS NO. 48 v. NLRB

United States Court of Appeals, District of Columbia Circuit, 1964
328 F.2d 534

J. SKELLY WRIGHT, Circuit Judge.

The central issue before us for decision is whether the unions here, violated Section 8(b)(4)(ii)(B) of the Labor Act by making threats against a general contractor in the construction industry to enforce his union agreement concerning subcontracting. The Board found that the action threatened here was secondary and within the proscription of Section §8(b)(4)(ii)(B). On this record, we are unable to accept the basis given by the Board for its conclusion, and so remand.

I

The agreement between the unions and the general contractor here apparently contained two subcontractor clauses, neither of which is in the record: Paragraph Four presumably limited subcontracting to firms which had signed union contracts, Paragraph Five made the general contractor financially responsible for certain fringe benefits if his subcontractor did not pay them "as provided under the appropriate [union] agreement." In October, 1961, the union sent the general contractor a letter stating he had violated both Paragraphs Four and Five by subcontracting to a firm which had neither signed a union contract nor paid the required fringe benefits. To redress the violation of Paragraph Four's union-signatory clause, the letter threatened a lawsuit. For violation of Paragraph Five's fringe-benefits provision, the letter threatened economic coercion in the form of picketing.

After hearing on an unfair labor practices complaint, the Trial Examiner found that Paragraph Four had been legally enforced solely through the threat of lawsuit, and that Paragraph Five was "a legally unencumbered lawful provision," so that both that clause itself and picketing to enforce it were primary activity, outside the prohibitions of Section 8(e), even without the proviso, and outside Section 8(b)(4)(ii)(B). No mention of a relation between Paragraphs Four and Five was made.

The Board, in overruling its Trial Examiner, held that Paragraph Five was a penalty clause for Paragraph Four, and that the use of threats of picketing to enforce Paragraph Five was intended indirectly to enforce Paragraph Four. It held that this indirect economic enforcement of Paragraph Four had as its object the cessation of business between the general contractor and his non-union subcontractor, thus violating Section 8(b)(4)(ii)(B). The Board chose to rely on this reasoning rather than adopt the General Counsel's contention that economic enforcement of Paragraph Five standing alone was sufficient to violate Section §8(b)(4)(ii)-(B). Thus the Board apparently disagreed with both its Trial Examiner and its General Counsel.

I I

Secondary subcontracting clauses in the construction industry are lawful, under the proviso to Section 8(e), and economic force may be used to obtain them notwithstanding Section 8(b)(4)(A), because Section 8(b)(4)-(A) incorporates that proviso by reference. But under Section 8(b)-(4)(B) such secondary clauses may be enforced only through lawsuits, and not through economic action. Primary subcontracting clauses, on the other hand, fall outside the ambit of Section 8(e),[10] as the Board concedes.

---

[10] "A restriction upon subcontracting which seeks to protect the wages and job opportunities of the employees covered by the contract, by forbidding the employer from having certain kinds of business done outside his own shop, is quite different in purpose and effect from blacklisting specified employers or groups

Moreover, economic enforcement thereof is not proscribed by Section 8(b)(4)(B) since it is not directed at involving neutral employers in a labor dispute "not their own."

The key question presented by subcontracting clauses in union agreements with general contractors is whether they are addressed to the labor relations of the subcontractor, rather than the general contractor. If, so, they are secondary as to the general contractor and may not be enforced against him through economic weapons. Thus, any attempt to enforce, by economic means, a subcontracting clause which blacklists all non-union subcontractors would violate Section 8(b)(4)(ii)(B). But not all subcontracting clauses are so designed. The test as to the "primary" nature of a subcontractor clause in an agreement with a general contractor has been phrased by scholars as whether it "will directly benefit employees covered thereby," [14] and "seeks to protect the wages and job opportunities of the employees covered by the contract." We have phrased the test as whether the clauses are "germane to the economic integrity of the principal work unit," and seek "to protect and preserve the work and standards (the union) has bargained for," or instead "extend beyond the (contracting) employer and are aimed really at the union's difference with another employer." As we said in Retail Clerks, the Board may not rely on "blanket pronouncements in respect to subcontracting clauses. These clauses take many forms. Some prohibit subcontracting under any circumstances; some prohibit it unless there is sufficient work in the shop to keep shop employees busy; some prohibit it except where the subcontractor maintains a wage scale and working conditions commensurate with those of the employer who is party to the collective agreement. On the face of it, these provisions would seem to be legitimate attempts by the union to protect and preserve the work and standards it has bargained for. In the latter supposition, for example, the union may be attempting to remove the economic incentive for contracting out, and thus to preserve the work for the contracting employees." [296 F.2d 368, 373-374.] Similarly, in discussing union-standards subcontracting clauses in District No. 9, International Assn. of Machinists v. N.L.R.B. . . . we indicated that "to limit the work to employers maintaining labor standards commensurate with those required by the Union" was within "the area of a legitimate union claim." [315 F.2d 33, 36.] It is not clear that the Board endorses these principles, but we have been shown no reason to gainsay them.

III

With this background, we may turn to the clauses here involved. Unfortunately, for reasons not disclosed, the text of these clauses is not in the

---

of employers because their products or labor policies are objectionable to the union." Cox, The Landrum-Griffin Amendments to the National Labor Relations Act, 44 Minn. L. Rev. 257, 273 (1959).

[14] Aaron, The Labor-Management Reporting and Disclosure Act of 1959, 73 Harv. L. Rev. 1086, 1119 (1960).

record. Consequently, neither the Board nor this court is in a position to determine precisely what they mean. The union freely admits that Paragraph Four is a union-signatory clause, lawful only because of the proviso to Section 8(e) and unenforceable by economic means. But it points out that its threat of economic action was carefully limited to violations of Paragraph Five, which it claims is a union-standards clause limited to fringe benefits and as such is primary to the general contractor and enforceable against him through economic means.

The union's interpretation of Paragraph Five seems to have been accepted by the Trial Examiner. The General Counsel's contention before the Board was that Paragraph Five, standing alone, is secondary and therefore unenforceable through economic means because it in effect requires at least partial recognition of petitioner unions by any subcontractors with whom the general contractor might deal. The Board, overruling its Trial Examiner and explicitly refusing to rely on the ground advanced by its General Counsel, held that the Paragraph Five fringe-benefits guarantee was a penalty for doing business with a non-union subcontractor in violation of Paragraph Four. The Board's only discussion of this point follows:

"It is . . . apparent that a contractor who failed to comply with Paragraph 4 — admittedly a 'hot cargo' provision — would be required to make the payments called for under Paragraph 5, regardless of the conditions of employment applicable to the subcontractor's employees. Paragraph 5 is thus, in effect, a penalty imposed on the contractor for failure to comply with the provisions of Paragraph 4."

Because the text of the clauses is not before us, we are unable to appraise the relative merits of the various positions taken by the union, the Trial Examiner, the General Counsel, and the Board. Under the circumstances, we shall vacate the Board's order and remand this matter so that the record may be supplemented with the text and details of Paragraphs Four and Five, plus additional evidence concerning "the employees covered by the contract" and the specific facts surrounding any contemplated payments under Paragraph Five, including who will receive them and to whose benefit they are to inure. Based upon the principles here announced, the Board may then determine whether the threatened economic enforcement of Paragraph Five is primary or secondary activity. Jurisdiction will be retained to dispose of the case, when the record is returned. . . .

NOTES

1. The Board had held that economic pressure to obtain an agreement unlawful under Section 8(e) apart from the construction-industry proviso is a violation of Section 8(b)(4)(A) even in the construction industry. It has since abandoned this position in deference to such authority as Construction Laborers Local 383 v. NLRB, 323 F.2d 422 (9th Cir. 1963). However it says that the proviso has no effect on Section 8(b)(4)(B). Northeastern Indiana Building Trades Council and Centlivre Village

Apartments, 148 N.L.R.B. No. 93 (1964). Judicial enforcement of an agreement that is within the proviso is not prohibited by clause (ii) of Section 8(b)(4). Local 48, Sheet Metal Workers v. Hardy Corp., 332 F.2d 682 (5th Cir. 1964).

The construction-industry proviso to Section 8(e) does not exempt an agreement that if materials are prefabricated off-site the work will be done by members of the union, even though such work has traditionally been done at the site. Ohio Valley Carpenters District Council and Cardinal Industries, 136 N.L.R.B. 977 (1962). Hauling concrete in truck-mixers to the site is not on-site construction. Teamsters Local 559 and Connecticut Sand & Stone Corp., 138 N.L.R.B. 532 (1962).

2. The union's attempt to obtain compliance with an agreement that violates Section 8(e) has the purpose of getting the employer to "enter into" such agreement, within the meaning of Section 8(b)(4)(A), as well as serving the purpose of subparagraph (B). Los Angeles Mailers Union No. 9 v. NLRB, 311 F.2d 121 (D.C. Cir. 1962).

3. An agreement that interstate drivers will deliver to city terminals rather than ultimate consignees, and local drivers (represented by the union) will complete the movement, from terminal to consignee, is primary rather than secondary, because such work is "fairly claimable by the bargaining unit." Especially is this the case when the work thus covered is substantially work that, because of increased use of trucks over rails and shifts of plant location, had previously been within the unit. Meat Drivers Local 710 v. NLRB, 335 F.2d 709 (D.C. Cir. 1964). On the other hand, an agreement that in contracting out work preference will be given to employers having contracts with, or approved by, the union conflicts with Section 8(e). District 9, International Assn. of Machinists and Greater St. Louis Automotive Trimmers, 134 N.L.R.B. 1354, enforced, 315 F.2d 33 (D.C. Cir. 1962).

The Board had held invalid a clause that if the employer because of inadequate equipment should contract work out the secondary employer must provide the same or greater wages and other benefits as provided in the agreement with the primary employer. The Court of Appeals, rejecting the argument that this was to aid union members generally rather than members of the unit, held that the object of one party alone is not sufficient to support the conclusion that the contract itself violates Section 8(e). Meat Drivers Local 710 v. NLRB, supra.

4. A provision that it shall not be cause for discharge or discipline "if any employee refuses to perform any service which, but for the existence of a controversy between a labor union and any other person (whether party to this Agreement or not), would be performed by the employees of such person" is invalid. It covers more than work "farmed out" by the struck employer under such circumstances as to make the contracting employer a primary party or "ally" of the struck employer. Truck Drivers Local 413 v. NLRB, 334 F.2d 539 (D.C. Cir. 1964). Under Douds v. Metropolitan Federation of Architects, 75 F. Supp. 672 (S.D.N.Y. 1948), and NLRB v. Business Machine & Office Appliance Mechanics, 228 F.2d 553 (2d Cir. 1955), cert. denied, 351 U.S. 962 (1956), it is required not

only that work be otherwise done by the strikers, but that the contracting employer take it in pursuant to an arrangement with the struck employer. In NLRB v. Amalgamated Lithographers, 309 F.2d 31 (9th Cir. 1962), cert. denied, 372 U.S. 943 (1963), a provision construed to refer to a strike against a noncontracting employer was held to be within the "ally" doctrine, though there was no express requirement of an "arrangement."

A "chain shop" clause, excusing employees from working at any plant if at another plant or at the plant of a corporate subsidiary of the contracting employer the union is on strike, is valid. It is an undertaking with respect to the employer's own work rather than that of another, even if the corporate subsidiary is not within the meaning of the Act an "other" employer. Amalgamated Lithographers case, supra.

A "trade shop" clause, giving the union the option to reopen the entire agreement or any part thereof if any employee is asked to handle work made in any shop not under contract with the union, violates Section 8(e). Amalgamated Lithographers case, supra; Employing Lithographers v. NLRB, 301 F.2d 20 (5th Cir. 1962).

An agreement not to discipline employees for refusal to handle goods is equivalent to agreeing not to handle goods. Dan McKinney Co., 137 N.L.R.B. 649 (1962). But an agreement to excuse refusal to cross a picket line does not have to be limited in the case of other employers to picket lines established in conformity with the proviso to Section 8(b)(4). It is sufficient to escape the ambit of Section 8(e) that the immunity extends only to respecting picketing in support of primary pressure. Truck Drivers Local 413 v. NLRB, 334 F.2d 539 (D.C. Cir. 1964).

When a clause covers conduct both within and without Section 8(e), is a general provision that terms are to be enforced "to the extent legal" sufficient to save its invalidity? Apparently not, in a case of striking to renew a "nonunion condition" exception to the no-strike provision. A nonunion condition means working without a collective bargaining agreement on work "normally performed by employees working under a collective bargaining agreement" with an AFL-CIO building trades union. Essex County Council and Associated Contractors, 141 N.L.R.B. 858 (1963), enforcement denied (following the Local 383 case, supra Note 1), 332 F.2d 636 (3d Cir. 1964).

NLRB v. SERVETTE, INC.

Supreme Court of the United States, 1964
377 U.S. 46, 84 Sup. Ct. 1098, 12 L. Ed. 2d 121

Mr. Justice Brennan delivered the opinion of the Court.

Respondent Servette, Inc., is a wholesale distributor of specialty merchandise stocked by retail food chains in Los Angeles, California. In 1960, during a strike which Local 848 of the Wholesale Delivery Drivers and Salesmen's Union was conducting against Servette, the Local's representatives sought to support the strike by asking managers of supermarkets of the food chains to discontinue handling merchandise supplied by Servette. In most instances the representatives warned that handbills asking the public not to buy named items distributed by Servette would be passed out in front of stores which refused to cooperate, and in a few cases handbills were in fact passed out. [The NLRB dismissed a complaint issued on Servette's charges that this conduct violated Sections 8(b)-(4)(i) and (ii). The NLRB adopted the trial examiner's finding that these managers had authority to determine whether to continue doing business with Servette in the face of threatened or actual handbilling. The NLRB held that as to subsection (i) the effort to enlist the managers' help was not within the meaning of inducing an "individual," and that as to subsection (ii) the publicity proviso protected the handbilling. The Ninth Circuit set aside the order, holding that the managers were "individuals" and the proviso was inapplicable because the products were distributed, not "produced," by Servette.]

The Court of Appeals correctly read the term "individual" in subsection (i) as including the supermarket managers,[4] but it erred in holding that the Local's attempts to enlist the aid of the managers constituted inducement of the managers in violation of the subsection. The 1959 statute amended §8(b)(4)(A) of the Taft-Hartley Act, which made it unlawful to induce or encourage "the employees of any employer" to strike or engage in a "concerted" refusal to work. We defined the central thrust of that statute to be to forbid "a union to induce employees to strike against or to refuse to handle goods for the employer when an object is to force him or another person to cease doing business with some third party." Local 1976, United Brotherhood of Carpenters and Joiners of America, A.F.L. v. Labor Board, 357 U.S. 93, 98. In the instant case, however, the Local, in asking the managers not to handle Servette items, was not attempting to induce or encourage them to cease performing their managerial duties in order to force their employers to cease doing business with Servette. Rather, the managers were asked to make a managerial decision which the Board found was within their authority to make. Such an appeal would not have been a violation of §8(b)(4)(A) before 1959, and we think that the legislative history of the 1959 amendments makes it clear that the amendments were not meant to render such an appeal an unfair labor practice.

The 1959 amendments were designed to close certain loopholes in the application of §8(b)(4)(A) which had been exposed in Board and court decisions. Thus, it had been held that the term "the employees of any employer" limited the application of the statute to those within the statutory definitions of "employees" and "employer." Section 2(2) of the National Labor Relations Act defines "employer" to exclude the federal and state governments and their agencies or subdivisions, nonprofit hospitals,

[4] The Board reached a contrary conclusion on the authority of its decision in Carolina Lumber Co., 130 N.L.R.B. 1438, 1443, which viewed the statute as distinguishing "low level" supervisors from "high level" supervisors, holding that inducement of "low level" supervisors is impermissible but inducement of "high level" supervisors is permitted. We hold today that this is not the distinction drawn by the statute; rather, the question of the applicability of subsection (i) turns upon whether the union's appeal is to cease performing employment services, or is an appeal for the exercise of managerial discretion.

and employers subject to the Railway Labor Act. 29 U.S.C. §152(2). The definition of "employee" in §2(3) excludes agricultural laborers, supervisors, and employees of an employer subject to the Railway Labor Act. 29 U.S.C. §152 (3). Furthermore, since the section proscribed only inducement to engage in a strike or "concerted" refusal to perform services, it had been held that it was violated only if the inducement was directed at two or more employees. To close these loopholes, subsection (i) substituted the phrase "any individual employed by any person" for "the employees of any employer," and deleted the word "concerted." The first change was designed to make the provision applicable to refusals by employees who were not technically "employees" within the statutory definitions, and the second change was intended to make clear that inducement directed to only one individual was proscribed. But these changes did not expand the type of conduct which §8(b)(4)(A) condemned, that is, union pressures calculated to induce the employees of a secondary employer to withhold their services in order to force their employer to cease dealing with the primary employer.

Moreover, the division of §8(b)(4)(A) into subsections (i) and (ii) by the 1959 amendments has direct relevance to the issue presented by this case. It had been held that §8(b)(4)(A) did not reach threats of labor trouble made to the secondary employer himself. Congress decided that such conduct should be made unlawful, but only when it amounted to conduct which "threaten[s], coerce[s] or restrain[s] any person"; hence the addition of subsection (ii). The careful creation of separate standards differentiating the treatment of appeals to the employees of the secondary employer not to perform their employment services, from appeals for other ends which are attended by threats, coercion or restraint, argues conclusively against the interpretation of subsection (i) as reaching the Local's appeals to the supermarket managers in this case. If subsection (i), in addition to prohibiting inducement of employees to withhold employment services, also reaches an appeal that the managers exercise their delegated authority by making a business judgment to cease dealing with the primary employer, subsection (ii) would be almost superfluous. Harmony between (i) and (ii) is best achieved by construing subsection (i) to prohibit inducement of the managers to withhold their services from their employer, and subsection (ii) to condemn an attempt to induce the exercise of discretion only if the inducement would "threaten, coerce or restrain" that exercise.

We turn finally to the question whether the proviso to amended §8(b)(4) protected the Local's handbilling. The Court of Appeals, following its decision in Great Western Broadcasting Co. v. Labor Board, 310 F.2d 591 (C.A. 9th Cir.), held that the proviso did not protect the Local's conduct because, as a distributor, Servette was not directly involved in the physical process of creating the products, and thus "does not produce any products." The Board on the other hand followed its ruling in Lohman Sales Co., 132 N.L.R.B. 901, that products "produced by an employer" included products distributed, as here, by a wholesaler with whom the primary dispute exists. We agree with the Board. The proviso was the outgrowth of a profound Senate concern that the unions' freedom to appeal to the public for support of their case be adequately safeguarded. We elaborated the history of the proviso in National Labor Relations Board v. Fruit & Vegetable Packers, etc., Local 760, 377 U.S. 58. It would fall far short of achieving this basic purpose if the proviso applied only in situations where the union's labor dispute is with the manufacturer or processor. Moreover, a primary target of the 1959 amendments was the secondary boycotts conducted by the Teamsters Union, which ordinarily represents employees not of manufacturers, but of motor carriers. There is nothing in the legislative history which suggests that the protection of the proviso was intended to be any narrower in coverage than the prohibition to which it is an exception, and we see no basis for attributing such an incongruous purpose to Congress.

The term "produced" in other labor laws was not unfamiliar to Congress. Under the Fair Labor Standards Act, the term is defined as "produced, manufactured, mined, handled, or in any other manner worked on . . . ," 29 U.S.C. §203(j), and has always been held to apply to the wholesale distribution of goods. The term "production" in the War Labor Disputes Act has been similarly applied to a general retail department and mail-order business. The Court of Appeals' restrictive reading of "producer" was prompted in part by the language of §8(b)(4)(B), which names as a proscribed object of the conduct defined in subsections (i) and (ii) "forcing or requiring any person to cease . . . dealing in the products of any other *producer, processor*, or *manufacturer*." (Italics supplied.) In its decision in Great Western Broadcasting Corp. v. Labor Board, supra, the Court of Appeals reasoned that since a "processor" and a "manufacturer" are engaged in the physical creation of goods, the word "producer" must be read as limited to one who performs similar functions. On the contrary, we think that "producer" must be given a broader reach, else it is rendered virtually superfluous. . . .

Finally, the warnings that handbills would be distributed in front of noncooperating stores are not prohibited as "threats" within subsection (ii). The statutory protection for the distribution of handbills would be undermined if a threat to engage in protected conduct were not itself protected.

Reversed.

NLRB v. FRUIT AND VEGETABLE PACKERS, LOCAL 760

Supreme Court of the United States, 1964
377 U.S. 58, 84 Sup. Ct. 1063, 12 L. Ed. 2d 129

MR. JUSTICE BRENNAN delivered the opinion of the Court.

. . . The question in this case is whether the respondent unions violated this section when they limited their secondary picketing of retail stores to an appeal to the customers of the stores not to buy the products of certain firms against which one of the respondents was on strike.

Respondent Local 760 called a strike against fruit packers and warehousemen doing business in Yakima, Washington. The struck firms sold

Washington State apples to the Safeway chain of retail stores in and about Seattle, Washington. Local 760, aided by respondent Joint Council, instituted a consumer boycott against the apples in support of the strike. They placed pickets who walked back and forth before the customers' entrances of 46 Safeway stores in Seattle. The pickets — two at each of 45 stores and three at the 46th store — wore placards and distributed handbills which appealed to Safeway customers, and to the public generally, to refrain from buying Washington State apples, which were only one of numerous food products sold in the stores. Before the pickets appeared at any store, a letter was delivered to the store manager informing him that the picketing was only an appeal to his customers not to buy Washington State apples, and that the pickets were being expressly instructed "to patrol peacefully in front of the consumer entrances of the store, to stay away from the delivery entrances and not to interfere with the work of your employees, or with deliveries to or pickups from your store." A copy of written instructions to the pickets — which included the explicit statement that "you are also forbidden to request that the customers not patronize the store" — was enclosed with the letter. Since it was desired to assure Safeway employees that they were not to cease work and to avoid any interference with pickups or deliveries, the pickets appeared after the stores opened for business and departed before the stores closed. At all times during the picketing, the store employees continued to work, and no deliveries or pickups were obstructed. Washington State apples were handled in normal course by both Safeway employees and the employees of other employers involved. Ingress and egress by customers and others was not interfered with in any manner.

[The NLRB heard the case on a stipulation of facts and waiver of proceedings before a trial examiner and held that there was no violation of Section 8(b)(4)(i)(B), but relying upon the publicity proviso to Section 8(b)(4) and "the interpretive gloss placed thereon by its drafters" issued an order under Section 8(b)(4)(ii)(B). The District of Columbia Court of Appeals set it aside and remanded, holding that to satisfy the element of "threaten, coerce, or restrain" there would have to be proof that the retail outlet had suffered or was likely to suffer a substantial economic impact as a result of the union conduct. The NLRB was authorized to reopen the record to receive such evidence.]

The Board's reading of the statute — that the legislative history and the phrase "other than picketing" in the proviso reveal a congressional purpose to outlaw all picketing directed at customers at a secondary site — necessarily rested on the finding that Congress determined that such picketing always threatens, coerces or restrains the secondary employer. We therefore have a special responsibility to examine the legislative history for confirmation that Congress made that determination. Throughout the history of federal regulation of labor relations, Congress has consistently refused to prohibit peaceful picketing except where it is used as a means to achieve specific ends which experience has shown are undesirable. "In the sensitive area of peaceful picketing Congress has dealt explicitly with isolated evils which experience has established flow from such picketing." National Labor Relations Board v. Drivers etc. Local Union, 362 U.S. 274, 284. We have recognized this congressional practice and have not ascribed to Congress a purpose to outlaw peaceful picketing unless "there is the clearest indication in the legislative history," ibid., that Congress intended to do so as regards the particular ends of the picketing under review. Both the congressional policy and our adherence to this principle of interpretation reflect concern that a broad ban against peaceful picketing might collide with the guarantees of the First Amendment.

We have examined the legislative history of the amendments to §8(b)-(4), and conclude that it does not reflect with the requisite clarity a congressional plan to proscribe all peaceful consumer picketing at secondary sites, and, particularly, any concern with peaceful picketing when it is limited, as here, to persuading Safeway customers not to buy Washington State apples when they traded in the Safeway stores. All that the legislative history shows in the way of an "isolated evil" believed to require proscription of peaceful consumer picketing at secondary sites was its use to persuade the customers of the secondary employer to cease trading with him in order to force him to cease dealing with, or to put pressure upon, the primary employer. This narrow focus reflects the difference between such conduct, and peaceful picketing at the secondary site directed only at the struck product. In the latter case, the union's appeal to the public is confined to its dispute with the primary employer, since the public is not asked to withhold its patronage from the secondary employer, but only to boycott the primary employer's goods. On the other hand, a union appeal to the public at the secondary site not to trade at all with the secondary employer goes beyond the goods of the primary employer, and seeks the public's assistance in forcing the secondary employer to cooperate with the union in its primary dispute.[7] This is not to say that this distinction was expressly alluded to in the debates. It is to say, however, that the consumer picketing carried on in this case is not attended by the abuses at which the statute was directed. . . .

. . . We are faithful to our practice of respecting the congressional policy of legislating only against clearly identified abuses of peaceful picketing when we conclude that the Senate neither specified the kind of picket-

---

[7] The distinction between picketing a secondary employer merely to "follow the struck goods," and picketing designed to result in a generalized loss of patronage, was well established in the state cases by 1940. The distinction was sometimes justified on the ground that the secondary employer, who was presumed to receive a competitive benefit from the primary employer's nonunion, and hence lower, wage scales, was in "unity of interest" with the primary employer, Goldfinger v. Feintuch, 276 N.Y. 281, 286, 11 N.E.2d 910; Newark Ladder & Bracket Sales Co. v. Furniture Workers Local 66, 125 N.J. Eq. 99, 4 A.2d 49; Johnson v. Milk Drivers & Dairy Employees Union, Local 854, 195 So. 791 (Ct. App. La. 1940), and sometimes on the ground that picketing restricted to the primary employer's product is "a primary boycott against the merchandise." Chiate v. United Cannery Agricultural Packing and Allied Workers of America, 2 CCH Lab. Cas. 125, 126 (Cal. Sup. Ct.). See I Teller, Labor Disputes and Collective Bargaining §123 (1940).

ing here involved as an abuse, nor indicated any intention of banning all consumer picketing.

The House history is similarly beclouded, but what appears confirms our conclusion. . . .

No Conference Report was before the Senate when it passed the compromise bill, and it had the benefit only of Senator Kennedy's statement of the purpose of the proviso. He said that the proviso preserved "the right to appeal to consumers by methods other than picketing asking them to refrain from buying goods made by nonunion labor *and* to refrain from trading with a retailer who sells such goods. . . . We were not able to persuade the House conferees to permit picketing in front of that secondary shop, but were able to persuade them to agree that the unions shall be free to conduct informational activity short of picketing. In other words, the union can hand out handbills at the shop . . . and can carry on all publicity short of having ambulatory picketing. . . ." (Italics supplied.) This explanation does not compel the conclusion that the Conference Agreement contemplated prohibiting any consumer picketing at a secondary site beyond that which urges the public, in Senator Kennedy's words, to "refrain from trading with a retailer who sells such goods." To read into the Conference Agreement, on the basis of a single statement, an intention to prohibit all consumer picketing at a secondary site would depart from our practice of respecting the congressional policy not to prohibit peaceful picketing except to curb "isolated evils" spelled out by the Congress itself.

Peaceful consumer picketing to shut off all trade with the secondary employer unless he aids the union in its dispute with the primary employer, is poles apart from such picketing which only persuades his customers not to buy the struck products. . . .

This distinction is opposed as "unrealistic" because, it is urged, all picketing automatically provokes the public to stay away from the picketed establishment. The public will, it is said, neither read the signs and handbills, nor note the explicit injunction that "This is not a strike against any store or market." Be that as it may, our holding today simply takes note of the fact that a broad condemnation of peaceful picketing, such as that urged upon us by petitioners, has never been adopted by Congress, and an intention to do so is not revealed with that "clearest indication in the legislative history," which we require. National Labor Relations Board v. Drivers, etc. Local Union, supra.

We come then to the question whether the picketing in this case, confined as it was to persuading customers to cease buying the product of the primary employer, falls within the area of secondary consumer picketing which Congress did clearly indicate its intention to prohibit under §8(b)-(4)(ii). We hold that it did not fall within that area, and therefore did not "threaten, coerce, or restrain" Safeway. While any diminution in Safeway's purchases of apples due to a drop in consumer demand might be said to be a result which causes respondents' picketing to fall literally within the statutory prohibition, "it is a familiar rule that a thing may be within the letter of the statute and yet not within the statute, because not within its spirit nor within the intention of the makers." Holy Trinity Church v. United States, 143 U.S. 457, 459. See United States v. American Trucking Ass'ns, 310 U.S. 534, 543-544. When consumer picketing is employed only to persuade customers not to buy the struck product, the union's appeal is closely confined to the primary dispute. The site of the appeal is expanded to include the premises of the secondary employer, but if the appeal succeeds, the secondary employer's purchases from the struck firms are decreased only because the public has diminished its purchases of the struck product. On the other hand, when consumer picketing is employed to persuade customers not to trade at all with the secondary employer, the latter stops buying the struck product, not because of a falling demand, but in response to pressure designed to inflict injury on his business generally. In such case, the union does more than merely follow the struck product; it creates a separate dispute with the secondary employer. . . .

The Court of Appeals judgment is vacated, and it is directed to enter judgment setting aside the order. . . .

MR. JUSTICE DOUGLAS took no part in the consideration or decision of this case.

MR. JUSTICE BLACK, concurring.

Because of the language of §8(b)(4)(ii)(B) of the National Labor Relations Act and the legislative history set out in the opinions of the Court and of my Brother Harlan, I feel impelled to hold that Congress, in passing this section of the Act, intended to forbid the striking employees of one business to picket the premises of a neutral business where the purpose of the picketing is to persuade customers of the neutral business not to buy goods supplied by the struck employer. Construed in this way, as I agree with Brother Harlan that it must be, I believe, contrary to his view, that the section abridges freedom of speech and press in violation of the First Amendment. . . .

Even assuming that the Federal Government has power to bar or otherwise regulate patrolling by persons on local streets or adjacent to local business premises in the State of Washington, it is difficult to see that the section in question intends to do anything but prevent dissemination of information about the facts of a labor dispute — a right protected by the First Amendment. It would be different (again assuming federal power) if Congress had simply barred or regulated all patrolling of every kind for every purpose in order to keep the streets around interstate businesses open for movement of people and property, Schneider v. State [308 U.S. 160-161]; or to promote the public safety, peace, comfort, or convenience, Cantwell v. Connecticut, 310 U.S. 296, 304; or to protect people from violence and breaches of the peace by those who are patrolling, Thornhill v. Alabama [310 U.S. 88, 105]. Here the section against picketing was not passed for any of these reasons. The statute in no way manifests any government interest against patrolling as such, since the only patrolling it seeks to make unlawful is that which is carried on to advise the public, including consumers, that certain products have been produced by an employer with whom the picketers have a dispute. All who do not patrol to publicize this kind of dispute are, so far as this section of the statute is concerned, left wholly free to patrol. Thus the section is aimed at outlawing free discussion of one side of a certain kind of labor dispute and cannot be sustained as a permissible regulation of patrolling. Cf. Carlson v. California, 310 U.S. 106, 112.

Nor can the section be sustained on the ground that it merely forbids picketers to help carry out an unlawful or criminal undertaking. Compare Giboney v. Empire Storage & Ice Co. [336 U.S. 490]. For the section itself contains a proviso which says that it shall not be construed "to prohibit publicity, other than picketing, for the purpose of truthfully advising the public, including consumers . . . that a product or products are produced by an employer with whom . . . (the picketers have) a primary dispute. . . ." Thus, it is clear that the object of the picketing was to ask Safeway customers to do something which the section itself recognizes as perfectly lawful. Yet, while others are left free to picket for other reasons, those who wish to picket to inform Safeway customers of their labor dispute with the primary employer, are barred from picketing — solely on the ground of the lawful information they want to impart to the customers.

In short, we have neither a case in which picketing is banned because the picketers are asking others to do something unlawful nor a case in which all picketing is, for reasons of public order, banned. Instead, we have a case in which picketing, otherwise lawful, is banned only when the picketers express particular views. The result is an abridgment of the freedom of these picketers to tell a part of the public their side of a labor controversy, a subject the free discussion of which is protected by the First Amendment.

I cannot accept my Brother Harlan's view that the abridgment of speech and press here does not violate the First Amendment because other methods of communication are left open. This reason for abridgment strikes me as being on a par with holding that governmental suppression of a newspaper in a city would not violate the First Amendment because there continue to be radio and television stations. First Amendment freedoms can no more validly be taken away by degrees than by one fell swoop.

For these reasons I concur in the judgment of the Court vacating the judgment of the Court of Appeals and remanding the case with directions to enter judgment setting aside the Board's order.

MR. JUSTICE HARLAN, whom MR. JUSTICE STEWART joins, dissenting. . . .

The Union's activities are plainly within the letter of subdivisions 4(ii)-(B) of §8(b), and indeed the Court's opinion virtually concedes that much. . . .

The difference to which the Court points between a secondary employer merely lowering his purchases of the struck product to the degree of decreased consumer demand and such an employer ceasing to purchase one product because of consumer refusal to buy any products, is surely too refined in the context of reality. It can hardly be supposed that in all, or even most, instances the result of the type of picketing involved here will be simply that suggested by the Court. Because of the very nature of picketing there may be numbers of persons who will refuse to buy at all from a picketed store, either out of economic or social conviction or because they prefer to shop where they need not brave a picket line. Moreover, the public can hardly be expected always to know or ascertain the precise scope of a particular picketing operation. Thus in cases like this, the effect on the secondary employer may not always be limited to a decrease in his sales of the struck product. And even when that is the effect, the employer may, rather than simply reducing purchases from the primary employer, deem it more expedient to turn to another producer whose product is approved by the union.

The distinction drawn by the majority becomes even more tenuous if a picketed retailer depends largely or entirely on sales of the struck product. If, for example, an independent gas station owner sells gasoline purchased from a struck gasoline company, one would not suppose he would feel less threatened, coerced, or restrained by picket signs which said "Do not buy X gasoline" than by signs which said "Do not patronize this gas station." To be sure Safeway is a multiple article seller, but it cannot well be gainsaid that the rule laid down by the Court would be unworkable if its applicability turned on a calculation of the relation between total income of the secondary employer and income from the struck product.

The Court informs us that "Peaceful consumer picketing to shut off all trade with the secondary employer unless he aids the union in its dispute with the primary employer, is poles apart from such picketing which only persuades his customers not to buy the struck product" . . . The difference was, it is stated, "well established in the state cases by 1940" . . . that is before the present federal enactment. In light of these assertions, it is indeed remarkable that the Court not only substantially acknowledges that the statutory language does not itself support this distinction . . . but cites no report of Congress, no statement of a legislator, not even the view of any of the many commentators in the area, in any way casting doubt on the applicability of §8(b)(4)(ii)(B) to picketing of the kind involved here.

[Mr. Justice Harlan then appraised the legislative history of Section 8(b)(4)(ii)(B) as not sustaining the Court's distinction and continued:]

Under my view of the statute the constitutional issue is therefore reached. Since the Court does not discuss it, I am content simply to state in summary form my reasons for believing that the prohibitions of §8(b)-(4)(ii)(B), as applied here, do not run afoul of constitutional limitations. This Court has long recognized that picketing is "inseparably something more (than) and different" from simple communication. Hughes v. Superior Court, 339 U.S. 460, 464; see, e.g., Building Service Employees v. Gazzam, 339 U.S. 532, 537; Bakery Drivers v. Wohl, 315 U.S. 769, 776 (concurring opinion of Douglas, J.). Congress has given careful and continued consideration to the problems of labor-management relations, and its attempts to effect an accommodation between the right of unions to publicize their position and the social desirability of limiting a form of communication likely to have effects caused by something apart from the message communicated, are entitled to great deference. The decision of Congress to prohibit secondary consumer picketing during labor disputes is, I believe, not inconsistent with the protections of the First Amendment, particularly when, as here, other methods of communication are left open.[5]

Contrary to my Brother Black, I think the fact that Congress in prohibiting secondary consumer picketing has acted with a discriminating eye is the very thing that renders this provision invulnerable to constitutional attack. That Congress has permitted other picketing which is likely to have effects beyond those resulting from the "communicative" aspect of picketing does not, of course, in any way lend itself to the conclusion that Congress here has aimed to "prevent dissemination of information about the facts of a labor dispute." . . . Even on the highly dubious assumption that the "non-speech" aspect of picketing is always the same whatever the particular context, the social consequences of the "non-communicative" aspect of picketing may certainly be thought desirable in the case of "primary" picketing and undesirable in the case of "secondary" picketing, a judgment Congress has indeed made in prohibiting secondary but not primary picketing.

I would enforce the Board's order.

NOTES

1. In the cases in this section attention has been directed primarily to determining what constitutes a violation of Section 8(b)(4). It should be emphasized, however, that for a union the consequences of such a violation may be substantially more than the "slap on the wrist" of a NLRB order to cease and desist from such conduct. For example, in International Longshoremen's and Warehousemen's Union v. Juneau Spruce Corp., 342 U.S. 237 (1952), an injured employer was awarded a judgment for $750,000 in a suit brought under Section 303 of the Act for damages caused by conduct violating Section 8(b)(4)(D). Moreover, more than one employer may be injured by the prohibited secondary activities and bring suit under Section 303. As the Juneau Spruce case establishes, the availability of such a suit is not conditioned upon a determination by the NLRB that the union has in fact violated Section 8(b)(4), and aggrieved persons may pursue such a remedy upon their own initiative.

However, as will be seen, there is a question concerning the effect on a Section 303 suit of a NLRB determination in a Section 10(k) proceeding that a union is entitled to work, the assignment of which it attempted to force by secondary pressures otherwise prohibited by Section 8(b)(4)(D).

2. The limited applicability of the federal antitrust laws (including the statutory remedy of treble damages and a reasonable attorney's fee) to

[5] I mean to intimate no view on the constitutionality of the regulation or prohibition of picketing which publicizes something other than a grievance in a labor-management dispute.

secondary union pressure is starkly pointed up in Hunt v. Crumboch, 325 U.S. 821 (1945). There the Teamsters had called a strike to compel all truckers hauling for A & P to join the union. The plaintiff, a trucking partnership, continued hauling for A & P in spite of the strike. Violence occurred, a union member was killed, and one of the partners was tried for murder but acquitted. The Teamsters finally won the closed-shop agreement with A & P but then refused to allow the partners to join and prevented them from hauling for A & P or any other unionized firm. The Court held that although the union's conceded object was to drive the plaintiff out of business by means of a secondary boycott, there was no violation of the Sherman Act.

Consideration of the role of the antitrust laws in governmental regulation of labor management relations will be found infra page 725.

4.　*Work Assignment Disputes*

ENDERBY PROBLEM 7
(*See page 306 supra for Enderby Problem 6*)

I

Suppose that in addition to the federal court action against Local 7, Tilelayers Union, Blair had filed Section 8(b)(4)(B) and (D) charges against it. What disposition would you expect?

I I

Twenty months after the first election, another was held which resulted in Local 417 being certified by the Board as the exclusive bargaining representative of "all production, maintenance and clerical employees, but excluding all tabulating machine operators in the Statistical Department at the Enderby plant . . ." At the same time, Local 1, Business Machine Operators Union, was certified as the collective bargaining representative of the excluded tabulating machine operators.

Tabulating machines process punched IBM cards and produce therefrom printed reports which are then available for further analysis. Twenty machines introduced shortly after the first election each require a highly skilled operator, specially trained by several years of IBM schooling. Local 1 and Enderby had little trouble in reaching agreement and signing a collective bargaining contract.

Negotiations with Local 417, however, dragged along from month to month, the parties accusing each other of not wanting a contract. Then the company began the installation of radically improved tabulating machines requiring little skill on the part of the operator. In fact, several weeks of training would be quite sufficient for the average clerical employee.

Local 417 then modified its outstanding proposals to include a demand that laid-off clerical employees from its membership should have preference to tabulating machine operators represented by Local 1 in working the new tabulating machines.

White said this was one of the more interesting of Curme's recent proposals and could have a good deal of merit as a money saver, but that he couldn't think that the union seriously believed that the company was in any position to go along with any such proposition. He suggested that Local 417 might talk the matter over with Local 1. Curme told White that the company was really demanding a strike over the matter. White replied, "You may have something there, Oliver; but, before you start the merry-go-round this time, why don't you get Dan Cooper's advice? He just might be able to help you."

NLRB v. RADIO AND TELEVISION BROADCAST ENGINEERS UNION

Supreme Court of the United States, 1961
364 U.S. 573, 81 Sup. Ct. 330, 5 L. Ed. 2d 302

MR. JUSTICE BLACK delivered the opinion of the Court.

This case, in which the Court of Appeals refused to enforce a cease-and-desist order of the National Labor Relations Board, grew out of a "jurisdictional dispute" over work assignments between the respondent union composed of television "technicians," and another union, composed of "stage employees." Both of these unions were certified bargaining agents for their respective Columbia Broadcasting System employee members and had collective bargaining agreements in force with that company, but neither the certifications nor the agreements clearly apportioned between the employees represented by the two unions the work of providing electric lighting for television shows. This led to constant disputes, extending over a number of years, as to the proper assignment of this work, disputes that were particularly acrimonious with reference to "remote lighting," that is, lighting for telecasts away from the home studio. Each union repeatedly urged Columbia to amend its bargaining agreement so as specifically to allocate remote lighting to its members rather than to members of the other union. But, as the Board found, Columbia refused to make such an agreement with either union because "the rival locals had failed to agree on the resolution of this jurisdictional dispute over remote lighting." Thus feeling itself caught "between the devil and the deep blue," Columbia chose to divide the disputed work between the two unions according to criteria improvised apparently for the sole purpose of maintaining peace between the two. But, in trying to satisfy both of the unions, Columbia has apparently not succeeded in satisfying either. During recent years, it has been forced to contend with stoppages by each of the two unions when a particular assignment was made in favor of the other.

The precise occasion for the present controversy was the decision of Columbia to assign the lighting work for a major telecast from the Waldorf-Astoria Hotel in New York City to the stage employees. When the technicians' protest of this assignment proved unavailing, they refused to operate the cameras for the program and thus forced its cancellation. This caused Columbia to file the unfair labor practice charge which started these proceedings, claiming a violation of §8(b)(4)(D) of the Taft-Hartley Act. . . . Obviously, if §(b)(4)(D) stood alone, what this union did in the absence of a Board order or certification entitling its members to be assigned to these particular jobs would be enough to support a finding of an unfair labor practice in a normal proceeding under §10(c) of the Act. But when Congress created this new type of unfair labor practice by enacting §8(b)(4)(D) as part of the Taft-Hartley Act in 1947, it also added §10(k) to the Act. Section 10(k) . . . quite plainly emphasizes the belief of Congress that it is more important to industrial peace that jurisdictional disputes be settled permanently than it is that unfair labor practice sanctions for jurisdictional strikes be imposed upon unions. Accordingly, §10(k) offers strong inducements to quarrelling unions to settle their differences by directing dismissal of unfair labor practice charges upon voluntary adjustment of jurisdictional disputes. And even where no voluntary adjustment is made, "the Board is empowered and directed," by §10(k), "to hear and determine the dispute out of which such unfair labor practice shall have arisen," and upon compliance by the disputants with the Board's decision the unfair labor practice charges must be dismissed.

In this case respondent failed to reach a voluntary agreement with the stage employees union so the Board held the §10(k) hearing as required to "determine the dispute." The result of this hearing was a decision that the respondent union was not entitled to have the work assigned to its members because it had no right to it under either an outstanding Board order or certification, as provided in §8(b)(4)(D), or a collective bargaining agreement. The Board refused to consider other criteria, such as the employer's prior practices and the custom of the industry, and also refused to make an affirmative award of the work between the employees represented by the two competing unions. The respondent union refused to comply with this decision, contending that the Board's conception of its duty "to determine the dispute" was too narrow in that this duty is not at all limited, as the Board would have it, to strictly legal considerations growing out of prior Board orders, certifications or collective bargaining agreements. It urged, instead, that the Board's duty was to make a final determination, binding on both unions, as to which of the two union's employees was entitled to do the remote lighting work, basing its determination on factors deemed important in arbitration proceedings, such as the nature of the work, the practices and customs of this and other companies and of these and other unions, and upon other factors deemed relevant by the Board in the light of its experience in the field of labor relations. On the basis of its decision in the §10(k) proceeding and the union's challenge to the validity of that decision, the Board issued an order under §10(c) directing the union to cease and desist from striking to compel Columbia to assign remote lighting work to its members. The

Court of Appeals for the Second Circuit refused to enforce the cease-and-desist order, accepting the respondent's contention that the Board had failed to make the kind of determination that §10(k) requires. . . .

We agree . . . that §10(k) requires the Board to decide jurisdictional disputes on their merits and conclude that in this case that requirement means that the Board should affirmatively have decided whether the technicians or the stage employees were entitled to the disputed work. The language of §10(k), supplementing §8(b)(4)(D) as it does, sets up a method adopted by Congress to try to get jurisdictional disputes settled. The words "hear and determine the dispute" convey not only the idea of hearing but also the idea of deciding a controversy. And the clause "the dispute out of which such unfair labor practice shall have arisen" can have no other meaning except a jurisdictional dispute under §8(b)(4)-(D) which is a dispute between two or more groups of employees over which is entitled to do certain work for an employer. To determine or settle the dispute as between them would normally require a decision that one or the other is entitled to do the work in dispute. Any decision short of that would obviously not be conducive to quieting a quarrel between two groups which, here as in most instances, is of so little interest to the employer that he seems perfectly willing to assign work to either if the other will just let him alone. This language also indicates a congressional purpose to have the Board do something more than merely look at prior Board orders and certifications or a collective bargaining contract to determine whether one or the other union has a clearly defined statutory or contractual right to have the employees it represents perform certain work tasks. For, in the vast majority of cases, such a narrow determination would leave the broader problem of work assignments in the hands of the employer, exactly where it was before the enactment of §10(k) — with the same old basic jurisdictional dispute likely continuing to vex him, and the rival unions, short of striking, would still be free to adopt other forms of pressure upon the employer. The §10(k) hearing would therefore accomplish little but a restoration of the pre-existing situation, a situation already found intolerable by Congress and by all parties concerned. If this newly granted Board power to hear and determine jurisdictional disputes had meant no more than that, Congress certainly would have achieved very little to solve the knotty problem of wasteful work stoppages due to such disputes. . . .

The Board contends, however, that this interpretation of §10(k) should be rejected. . . . In support of this contention, it first points out that §10(k) sets forth no standards to guide it in determining jurisdictional disputes on their merits. From this fact, the Board argues that §8(b)(4)(D) makes the employer's assignment decisive unless he is at the time acting in violation of a Board order or certification and that the proper interpretation of §10(k) must take account of this right of the employer. It is true, of course, that employers normally select and assign their own individual employees according to their best judgment. But here, as in most situations where jurisdictional strikes occur, the employer has contracted with two unions, both of which represent employees capable of doing the particular tasks involved. The result is that the employer has been placed in a situation where he finds it impossible to secure the benefits of stability from either of these contracts, not because he refuses to satisfy the unions, but because the situation is such that he cannot satisfy them. Thus, it is the employer here, probably more than anyone else, who has been and will be damaged by a failure of the Board to make the binding decision that the employer has not been able to make. We therefore are not impressed by the Board's solicitude for the employer's right to do that which he has not, and most likely will not, be able to do. It is true that this forces the Board to exercise under §10(k) powers which are broad and lacking in rigid standards to govern their application. But administrative agencies are frequently given rather loosely defined powers to cope with problems as difficult as those posed by jurisdictional disputes and strikes. It might have been better, as some persuasively argued in Congress, to intrust this matter to arbitrators. But Congress, after discussion and consideration, decided to intrust this decision to the Board. It has had long experience in hearing and disposing of similar labor problems. With this experience and a knowledge of the standards generally used by arbitrators, unions, employers, joint boards, and others in wrestling with this problem, we are confident that the Board need not disclaim the power given it for lack of standards. Experience and common sense will supply the grounds for the performance of this job which Congress has assigned the Board.

The Board also contends that respondent's interpretation of §10(k) should be avoided because that interpretation completely vitiates the purpose of Congress to encourage the private settlement of jurisdictional disputes. This contention proceeds on the assumption that the parties to a dispute will have no incentive to reach a private settlement if they are permitted to adhere to their respective views until the matter is brought before the Board and then given the same opportunity to prevail which they would have had in a private settlement. Respondent disagrees with this contention and attacks the Board's assumption. We find it unnecessary to resolve this controversy for its turns upon the sort of policy determination that must be regarded as implicitly settled by Congress when it chose to enact §10(k). Even if Congress has chosen the wrong way to accomplish its aim, that choice is binding both upon the Board and upon this Court.

The Board's next contention is that respondent's interpretation of §10(k) should be rejected because it is inconsistent with other provisions of the Taft-Hartley Act. The first such inconsistency urged is with §§8(a)(3) and 8(b)(2) of the Act on the ground that the determination of jurisdictional disputes on their merits by the Board might somehow enable unions to compel employers to discriminate in regard to employment in order to encourage union membership. The argument here, which is based upon the fact that §10(k), like §8(b)(4)(D), extends to jurisdictional disputes between unions and unorganized groups as well as to disputes between two or more unions, appears to be that groups represented by unions would almost always prevail over nonunion groups in such a determination because their claim to the work would probably have more basis in custom and tradition than that of unorganized groups. No such danger is present here, however, for both groups of employees are represented by unions. Moreover, we feel entirely confident that the Board, with its many years of experience in guarding against and redressing violations of §§8(a)(3) and 8(b)(2), will devise means of discharging its duties under §10(k) in a manner entirely harmonious with those sections. A second inconsistency is urged with §303(a)(4) of the Act, which authorizes suits for damages suffered because of jurisdictional strikes. The argument here is that since §303(a)(4) does not permit a union to establish, as a defense to an action for damages under that section, that it is entitled to the work struck for on the basis of such factors as practice or custom, a similar result is required here in order to preserve "the substantive symmetry" between §303(a)(4) on the one hand and §§8(b)(4)(D) and 10(k) on the other. This argument ignores the fact that this Court has recognized the separate and distinct nature of these two approaches to the problem of handling jurisdictional strikes. Since we do not require a "substantive symmetry" between the two, we need not and do not decide what effect a decision of the Board under §10(k) might have on actions under §303 (a)(4).

The Board's final contention is that since its construction of §10(k) was adopted shortly after the section was added to the Act and has been consistently adhered to since, that construction has itself become a part of the statute by reason of congressional acquiescence. In support of this contention, the Board points out that Congress has long been aware of its construction and yet has not seen fit to adopt proposed amendments which would have changed it. In the ordinary case, this argument might have some weight. But an administrative construction adhered to in the face of consistent rejection by Courts of Appeals is not such an ordinary case. Moreover, the Board had a regulation on this subject from 1947 to 1958 which the Court of Appeals for the Seventh Circuit thought, with some reason, was wholly inconsistent with the Board's present interpretation. With all this uncertainty surrounding the eventual authoritative interpretation of the existing law, the failure of Congress to enact a new law simply will not support the inference which the Board asks us to make.

We conclude therefore that the Board's interpretation of its duty under §10(k) is wrong and that under that section it is the Board's responsibility and duty to decide which of two or more employee groups claiming the right to perform certain work tasks is right and then specifically to award such tasks in accordance with its decision. Having failed to meet that responsibility in this case, the Board could not properly proceed under §10(c) to adjudicate the unfair labor practice charge. The Court of Appeals was therefore correct in refusing to enforce the order which resulted from that proceeding.

Affirmed.

LOCAL 5, UNITED ASSOCIATION OF JOURNEYMEN
and ARTHUR VENNERI CO.
National Labor Relations Board, 1964
145 N.L.R.B. 1580

[Venneri, a general contractor, was awarded a construction contract to build two airplane hangars at Andrews Air Force Base, Maryland. Venneri then contracted the inside plumbing work to Akron and the outside utilities to Nickles, which had a contract with Local 456 Laborers. After it had been awarded the subcontract Akron entered into a contract with Local 5 Plumbers. This agreement contained a clause which read in part: "32. It shall be a violation of this agreement for any contractor to contract for a job where plumbing work has been withheld from the plumbing contract by either the owner or general contractor for the purpose of being installed by other than journeyman plumbers and their apprentices . . ." Local 5 then learned that Akron had accepted only inside plumbing work. It forthwith reasserted jurisdiction over both the inside and outside plumbing and objected to Akron's acquiescence in the assignment of some of the plumbing work to Nickles, since installation of any plumbing by Nickles would violate clause 32 of the collective bargaining agreement. To further its claim Local 5 refused to refer plumbers to work on the hangar jobs and it induced Akron's employees to refrain from working on these projects, not to move pipe en route to the hangars, nor to fabricate pipe destined for these buildings.

In 137 N.L.R.B. 828, the Board found that these activities violated Sections 8(b)(4)(i) and (ii)(B). A majority rejected contentions that the union's conduct was protected primary activity solely designed to redress Akron's breach of contract and that the pendency of a Section 8(b)(4)(D) charge and proceeding under Section 10(k) required the Board to defer decision on the Section 8(b)(4)(B) complaint. The Court of Appeals enforced the Board's order with minor modification (321 F.2d 366 (D.C. Cir. 1963)). In the present case the Board turned to the jurisdictional dispute proceeding:]

Section 8(b)(4)(D) of the Act, which the charge in this case accuses Respondent Plumbers of having violated, prohibits certain union conduct where "an object thereof" is "forcing or requiring any employer to assign particular work to employees in a particular labor organization or in a particular trade, craft, or class rather than to employees in another labor organization or in another trade, craft, or class. . . ." And in a Section 10(k) proceeding, before making an affirmative award of the work in dispute, the Board is required to find that there is reasonable cause to believe that Section 8(b)(4)(D) has been violated by the respondent union. We so find in this case, notwithstanding the Plumbers' contentions to the contrary.

As detailed above, Respondent admittedly engaged in the type of conduct proscribed in Section 8(b)(4)(i) and (ii), as the Board and the Court of Appeals found. . . . In moving to quash the Section 10(k) notice of hearing, however, Respondent contends, in substance, that the "object" of its conduct was merely to redress Akron's violation of Clause 32 — i.e., by preventing Akron from performing its contract with Venneri — and not to compel any of the several employers involved in the case, least of all Nickles, to "assign" the disputed work to Local 5 Plumbers, as opposed to employees in some other "class." In arguing that no such Section 8(b)(4)(D) objective was present here, Respondent assumes that Venneri did not, any more than Akron, have the disputed work to assign, once it had been contracted out to Nickles. With these two employers eliminated, the argument concludes, only Nickles remains, and the record shows conclusively that Respondent was not trying to get him to hire its members.

We reject the foregoing contentions and deny Respondent's motion to quash the proceeding. For it is clear that the whole purpose of Clause 32, which Respondent was admittedly attempting to enforce in this case, is to insure that Local 5 Plumbers . . . employed by mechanical contractors like Akron will obtain the particular work which, in this instance, was awarded by Venneri to Nickles and his Local 456 Laborers instead. Thus, Respondent's ultimate objective, in attempting to enforce Clause 32 here, was not merely to compel Venneri to cancel his contracts with either or both Akron or Nickles. Rather, it was to force Venneri to transfer Nickles' contract to Akron, or some other employer in compliance with Clause 32, and thereby cause the disputed work to be assigned to Respondent's members (and laborers of its choice) instead of the Local 456 Laborers, employed by Nickles, who were doing it at the time. The Board has held consistently, and we adhere to the view, that Section 8(b)(4)(D) applies to such attempts to force changes in subcontracting arrangements between employers.

In sum, we find that the jurisdictional dispute in this case is properly before the Board for determination under Section 10(k) of the Act.[5] . . .

As to the work in dispute, upon consideration of all pertinent factors appearing in the record in its entirety, we shall assign it to the laborers represented by Local 456. They are as skilled in the performance of the work as the plumbers who compete for it; they have done it numerous times in like situations in the very geographic area of this dispute; their employer's assignment to them conforms with his past practice and with the collective-bargaining agreement then in effect with Local 456; and their efficiency in accomplishing the integrated task of preparing the ditches and laying the pipe in a sequential operation is no less than that demonstrated by the plumbers. Against these direct and convincing considerations the principal arguments for a contrary award advanced by the Plumbers are unpersuasive. . . .

Member Fanning, dissenting:

On June 26, 1962, a majority of the Board found Respondent Local 5

[5] With all deference for our dissenting colleague's thoughtful reiteration of the position he set forth in Venneri, 137 N.L.R.B. 828, 834, we adhere to the view therein expressed by the majority, that Sections 8(b)(4)(B) and 8(b)(4)(D) are not mutually exclusive.

in violation of Section 8(b)(4)(ii)(B) of the Act by encouraging its members to refuse to perform plumbing work with an object of forcing Arthur Venneri, the general contractor, to cease doing business with Nickles Bros., Inc., a subcontractor. That decision was subsequently affirmed by the Court of Appeals for the District of Columbia, 321 F.2d 366. Certiorari was denied by the Supreme Court on November 18, 1963. The Circuit Court's decision is therefore the law of that case. The Board's determination that Local 5 had engaged in an unlawful secondary boycott was made at a time when the instant 10(k) proceeding was pending before the Board. Both proceedings are based on precisely the same facts. It is one and the same dispute with the identical parties involved. I dissented from the Board's procedure in considering the secondary boycott charges before determining whether or not a jurisdictional dispute existed, perceiving no purpose served in dividing the dispute for formalistic procedural reasons, and issuing two decisions more than 6 months apart. . . .

In view of the Board's and the court's decisions that Respondent's conduct against Venneri, the same conduct alleged to be in violation of Section 8(b)(4)(D), is unlawful under Section 8(b)(4)(B), I must accept this conclusion as the law of that case. It follows that such conduct, whether or not in violation of another provision of the Act, cannot, in any event, be justified or protected. Having concluded that the means selected by the Respondent to secure an assignment of work in its favor has been proscribed by the Act in another Section, I must further conclude that such conduct cannot give rise to a justiciable dispute within the meaning of Section 10(k) of the Act. For it is clear to me that Congress intended this Section to take the place of an arbitration award and, with respect to charges properly cognizable as jurisdictional disputes, the alleged unlawful conduct must be enjoined or permitted, depending upon the Board's determination of the dispute. With great reluctance I find that this dispute is not properly before me for determination under Section 10(k) and I would quash the Notice of Hearing.

In reaching this conclusion, however, I would be remiss if I did not restate my view that in the administration of the Act a proper balance must be struck between the sometime conflicting consequences in the settlement of jurisdictional disputes and conduct otherwise prohibited by the Act. Where, as here, but for the court's decision, I would find a true jurisdictional dispute, I would not find Respondent's conduct to be in violation of another Section of the Act. If Respondent were found to be entitled to the work in a 10(k) determination, I would permit it to continue its strike against one of the parties to the dispute. If it were found not to be entitled to the work, it would be forbidden from engaging in such conduct under Section 8(b)(4)(D). I am, of course, aware that Akron, against whom Respondent struck, may properly be regarded as a "secondary" employer under long established Board and court decisions. I point out, however, that the Board's original interpretation of Section 8(b)(4)(B), subsequently approved by the courts, was itself a balancing of Congressional objectives in that Section and Sections 7 and 13 of the Act. Literally interpreted, the former Section would have forbidden conduct protected by the latter. The theory was therefore developed, after long and painstaking effort, that "primary" conduct, regardless of the provisions of Section 8(b)(4)(B), would be permitted, but that "secondary" conduct, regardless of the provisions of Sections 7 and 13, would not be permitted. In my opinion, an entirely different distinction and a different accommodation is required when weighing the efficacy of Sections 10(k) and 8(b)(4)(D) against other Congressional objectives in the Statute. Characterizing Respondent's action as "primary" or "secondary" does not automatically answer the important question whether it should be permitted or forbidden if it is properly cognizable under the unique provisions of Section 10(k). While an employer, such as Akron, may well be a "secondary" employer, it is equally clear that he is one of the parties to a jurisdictional dispute. To hold, as the majority does, that Congress intended the provisions of Section 8(b)(4)(B) to insulate him from the consequences of a jurisdictional dispute emanating, in part, from his own conduct, does not take into account the intervening purposes of Sections 10(k) and 8(b)(4)(D). I do not believe it sufficient to say that Respondent might be permitted to strike for the assignment of work in some other manner. That case is not before us. If, however, I am wrong and the majority is right in its guarantee to employers, such as Akron, then I would hold, as I have in the instant case, that the Respondent cannot use such means to secure a possible determination that it is entitled to the work for which it is striking. Conduct, which is clearly violative of the Statute, reasonably should not be the basis upon which the Board undertakes to arbitrate the justness of Respondent's action. To illustrate this point, assume that in the instant case, Respondent had struck a supplier of Venneri to cause a cessation of business between those two with the object of forcing Venneri to make a work assignment in Respondent's favor. Clearly such a strike would be "secondary." Would it also give rise to a 10(k) determination? Literally, the language of Sections 10(k) and 8(b)(4)(D) is applicable. It is inconceivable to me, however, that the Board would do more than seek an injunction against the Respondent's strike as a violation of Section 8(b)(4)(B). It would be immaterial that Respondent might, in fact, be entitled to the assignment of the work it sought. The means used to achieve that objective would be too remote from the situs of the original dispute and the parties actually involved, whether they be regarded as "primary" or "secondary," to warrant giving the Respondent a hearing under 10(k) and a possible favorable award. Nevertheless, this hypothetical case logically is in the same posture as the instant case, where the Board has found that Respondent's conduct is unlawful under Section 8(b)(4)(B), but insists at the same time that the dispute must be determined under Section 10(k). In my opinion, the majority's interpretation of these provisions of the Act precludes the sort of accommodation I am convinced is necessary and desirable to effectuate Congressional intent. Every strike over the assignment of work need not give rise to a 10(k) hearing. Such conduct should be examined with great care to determine whether the striking union is entitled to the extraordinary procedure of this Section which might result in the Board's stamp of approval, a determination which depends in substantial part on whether the employer against whom the union's pressure is directed is in reality involved in the jurisdictional dispute. Without attempting to delineate further the proper boundaries between jurisdictional strikes giving rise to 10(k) hearings and other strikes, a determination which, in my view, should be developed on a case to case basis, I adhere to my position, with due respect for the Court of Appeals for the District of Columbia, that the Respondent's conduct with respect to Akron should have resulted in the application of Sections 10(k) and 8(b)(4)(D) without the contradictory application of Section 8(b)(4) (B).

NOTES

1. Are you now able to answer the question as to the effect of a decision in a Section 10(k) proceeding favorable to a union upon a suit against it under Section 303 for conduct in violation of Section 8(b)(4)(D)? Are there any circumstances in which such conduct would not also violate Section 8(b)(4)(B)?

2. Suppose that the Board had decided the Venneri Company case in favor of the Plumbers on the merits of the claims of the two groups of employees. Suppose further that the employers refused to comply with the Board's decision. How could the Plumbers obtain compliance with the Board determination?

3. The NLRB's response to the Supreme Court's direction to determine Section 10(k) disputes first appeared in Machinists Union (J. A. Jones Construction Co.), 135 N.L.R.B. 1402 (1962). In that case the Board said, "At this beginning stage in making jurisdictional awards as required by the Court, the Board cannot and will not formulate general rules for making them. Each case will have to be decided on its own facts. The Board will consider all relevant factors in determining who is entitled to the work in dispute, e.g., the skills and work involved, certifications by the Board, company and industry practice, agreements between unions and between employers and unions, awards of arbitrators, joint boards and the AFL-CIO in the same or related cases, the assignment made by the employer, and the efficient operation of the employer's business. This list of factors is not meant to be exclusive, but is by way of illustration. The Board cannot at this time establish the weight to be given the various factors. Every decision will have to be an act of judgment based on common sense and experience rather than on precedent. It may be that later, with more experience in concrete cases, a measure of weight can be accorded the earlier decisions."

Subsequently the Board indicated that, while it would not give conclusive effect to the lower wage rates paid one of the competing groups of employees, it did believe that the element of cost was one of many relevant factors to be considered. Local 46, Lathers Union (Precrete, Inc.), 136 N.L.R.B. 1072 (1962). The Board has also since indicated that in deciding disputes concerning assignments to machines utilizing new and different processes of production, consideration will be given to the fact that one of the competing groups of employees previously performed that work, though utilizing different techniques. Longshoremen's Union (Howard Terminal), 147 N.L.R.B. No. 42 (1964); Typographical Union (Philadelphia Inquirer), 142 N.L.R.B. 36 (1963); but see Typographical Union (E. P. Rivas Co.), 147 N.L.R.B. No. 21 (1964).

4. The current difficulties of assessing the weight which will be given any one factor are well illustrated by a case involving a dispute between the Carpenters Union and the Lathers Union. The National Joint Board for the Settlement of Jurisdictional Disputes, established by agreement between the unions affiliated with the Building Trades Department of the AFL and the Associated General Contractors of America, had previously awarded similar work to Carpenters in about 300 cases. The Carpenters argued that they were entitled to the disputed work upon the basis of these decisions and a specific award made concerning the work in the case before the NLRB. The NLRB concluded, however, that the decisions indicated no more than that the dispute was one of long standing between the unions, and awarded the disputed work to the Lathers upon the basis of training, area practice, and comparative efficiency. Carpenters Union (O. R. Karst), 139 N.L.R.B. 591 (1962). In short, agreements between unions for the settlement of jurisdictional disputes have an uncertain weight in absence of an agreement binding the employer involved to the settlement. Compare Carpenters Union (J. O. Veveto & Son), 146 N.L.R.B. No. 133 (1964), with Local 68, Lathers (Acoustics & Specialties, Inc.), 142 N.L.R.B. 1073 (1963). The same may be said of arbitration awards rendered without participation of one of the claiming unions. Typographical Union (E. P. Rivas Co.), 147 N.L.R.B. No. 21 (1964).

The precedential value of Board determinations in Section 10(k) proceedings is, of course, minimal if no formula is given for determining the relative weight of the various factors considered. It has been charged that the consequence of the fluidity in the NLRB's evaluation of the various factors involved in making the determinations has been a continuance in almost all cases of its former policy of confirming the employer's assignment. O'Donoghue, Jurisdictional Disputes in the Construction Industry Since CBS, 52 Geo. L.J. 314 (1964).

5. In one of the first Section 10(k) cases decided by the NLRB after the CBS decision, a question arose as to the phraseology of the award to be made. Said the NLRB, "We do not agree with [the employer's] contention that our assignment should run to unspecified 'individuals in the employ of the employer' inasmuch as we have found that the disputed work is performed as an incident to work traditionally performed by hod carriers." Operating Engineers Union (Frank P. Badolato & Son), 135 N.L.R.B. 1392 (1962). The award made was to "Employees engaged as hod carriers . . ."

In the first case in which the NLRB decided a Section 10(k) proceeding in favor of the union which did not represent the employees assigned to the work by the employer the Board said, ". . . [W]e are assigning the disputed work to lathers, who are represented by Lathers Local 68, but not to Lathers Local 68 or its members." Local 68 Lathers Union (Acoustics & Specialties, Inc.), 142 N.L.R.B. 1073 (1963). The NLRB has continued to use similar terminology in making its awards.

Do you find any significance in this way of phrasing the award?

6. A Section 10(k) proceeding may properly be brought before the NLRB for determination even though one group of employees claiming work is not represented by a union, since jurisdictional disputes under the Act may be between unions and unorganized groups as well as between two or more unions. Electrical Workers Union (Bendix Corp.), 138 N.L.R.B. 689 (1962).

7. Controversies peripheral to Section 10(k) disputes may arise, presenting questions concerning the appropriate procedures to be followed in bringing about their settlement. For example, according to the NLRB, demands for recognition of one or more unions' claims to represent certain employees, even though presented in the form of a proposed contract provision recognizing the union's "jurisdiction" over certain work and backed by strike action, will not give rise to a Section 10(k) proceeding if the unions seek only to represent the employees performing certain work and do not contest the assignment of work to those employees. Printing Pressmen's Union (Sperry Rand Corp.), 147 N.L.R.B. No. 172 (1964). The same conclusion was reached in a case in which the union caused its members to leave their jobs during contract negotiations in support of a union demand for a "jurisdiction" clause covering work actually performed by an employee whom it did not seek to represent. Typographical Union (Rocky Mountain Bank Note Co.), 145 N.L.R.B. 921 (1964). Presumably such controversies might be settled by the filing of representation petitions, petitions for clarification of existing NLRB certifications, or, if the union has already been certified, by the filing of refusal to bargain charges.

On the other hand, the NLRB will not permit the use of representation proceedings to effect a transfer of work from one group of employees to another. Gas Service Co., 140 N.L.R.B. 445 (1963). In representation cases the NLRB views its function as being that of determining the bargaining representative for an appropriate unit and not that of determining whether employees in the unit are entitled to do any particular type of work or whether the employer has improperly assigned work from employees in the unit to other employees.

Another complication arises from cases in which the union to whose members the employer has assigned certain work does not claim the work, but instead recognizes the jurisdictional claim of a union which has taken strike action to compel the reassignment of the work to its own members. The NLRB has held Section 10(k) inapplicable to such disputes because of the absence of competing employee groups. Lathers Union (Acoustics & Specialties, Inc.), 139 N.L.R.B. 598 (1962); Sheet Metal Workers Union (Valley Sheet Metal Co.), 136 N.L.R.B. 1402 (1962); Highway Truckdrivers & Helpers, Teamsters Union (Safeway Stores, Inc.), 134 N.L.R.B. 1320 (1961).

8. The problems of procedures and remedies available for solution of possible Section 10(k) and peripheral controversies, such as enforcing contract provisions for arbitration, petitioning for clarification of NLRB certifications, or filing refusal to bargain charges, are well illustrated by Carey v. Westinghouse Electric Corp., printed as a principal case, infra page 907.

D. FEDERALISM

GARNER v. TEAMSTERS, CHAUFFEURS & HELPERS LOCAL 776

Supreme Court of the United States, 1953
346 U.S. 485, 74 Sup. Ct. 161, 98 L. Ed. 228

MR. JUSTICE JACKSON delivered the opinion of the Court. . . .

Petitioners were engaged in the trucking business and had twenty-four employees, four of whom were members of respondent union. The trucking operations formed a link to an interstate railroad. No controversy, labor dispute or strike was in progress, and at no time had petitioners objected to their employees joining the union. Respondents, however, placed rotating pickets, two at a time, at petitioners' loading platform. None were employees of petitioners. They carried signs reading "Local 776 Teamsters Union (A.F. of L.) wants Employees of Central Storage & Transfer Co. to join them to gain union wages, hours and working conditions." Picketing was orderly and peaceful, but drivers for other carriers refused to cross this picket line and, as most of petitioners' interchange of freight was with unionized concerns, their business fell off as much as 95%. The [Pennsylvania] courts below found that respondents' purpose in picketing was to coerce petitioners into compelling or influencing their employees to join the union.

The equity court held that respondents' conduct violated the Pennsylvania Labor Relations Act. The Supreme Court of the Commonwealth held, quite correctly, we think, that petitioners' grievance fell within the jurisdiction of the National Labor Relations Board to prevent unfair labor practices. It therefore inferred that state remedies were precluded. . . .

The national Labor Management Relations Act, as we have before pointed out, leaves much to the states, though Congress has refrained from telling us how much. We must spell out from conflicting indications of congressional will the area in which state action is still permissible.

This is not an instance of injurious conduct which the National Labor Relations Board is without express power to prevent and which therefore either is "governable by the State or it is entirely ungoverned." In such cases we have declined to find an implied exclusion of state powers. International Union v. Wisconsin Board, 336 U.S. 245, 254. Nor is this a case of mass picketing, threatening of employees, obstructing streets and highways, or picketing homes. We have held that the state still may exercise "its historic powers over such traditionally local matters as public safety and order and the use of streets and highways." Allen-Bradley Local v. Wisconsin Board, 315 U.S. 740, 749. Nothing suggests that the activity enjoined threatened a probable breach of the state's peace or would call for extraordinary police measures by state or city authority. Nor is there any suggestion that respondents' plea of federal jurisdiction and pre-emption was frivolous and dilatory or that the federal Board would decline to exercise its powers once its jurisdiction was invoked.

Congress has taken in hand this particular type of controversy where it affects interstate commerce. In language almost identical to parts of the Pennsylvania statute, it has forbidden labor unions to exert certain types of coercion on employees through the medium of the employer. It is not necessary or appropriate for us to surmise how the National Labor Relations Board might have decided this controversy had petitioners presented it to that body. The power and duty of primary decision lies with the Board, not with us. But it is clear that the Board was vested with power to entertain petitioners' grievance, to issue its own complaint against respondents and, pending final hearing, to seek from the United States District Court an injunction to prevent irreparable injury to petitioners while their case was being considered. The question then is whether the State, through its courts, may adjudge the same controversy and extend its own form of relief.

Congress did not merely lay down a substantive rule of law to be enforced by any tribunal competent to apply law generally to the parties. It went on to confide primary interpretation and application of its rules to a specific and specially constituted tribunal and prescribed a particular procedure for investigation, complaint and notice, and hearing and decision, including judicial relief pending a final administrative order. Congress evidently considered that centralized administration of specially designed procedures was necessary to obtain uniform application of its substantive rules and to avoid these diversities and conflicts likely to result from a variety of local procedures and attitudes toward labor controversies. Indeed, Pennsylvania passed a statute the same year as its labor relations Act reciting abuses of the injunction in labor litigations attributable more to procedure and usage than to substantive rules. A multiplicity of tribunals and a diversity of procedures are quite as apt to produce incompatible or conflicting adjudications as are different rules of substantive law. The same reasoning which prohibits federal courts from intervening in such cases, except by way of review or on application of the federal Board, precludes state courts from doing so. Cf. Myers v. Bethlehem Shipbuilding Corp., 303 U.S. 41; Amalgamated Utility Workers v. Consolidated Edison Co., 309 U.S. 261. And the reasons for excluding state administrative bodies from assuming control of matters expressly placed within the competence of the federal Board also exclude state courts from like action. Cf. Bethlehem Steel Co. v. New York Board, 330 U.S. 767.

This case would warrant little further discussion except for a persuasively presented argument that the National Labor Relations Board enforces only a public right on behalf of the public interest, while state equity powers are invoked by a private party to protect a private right. The public right, it is said, is so distinct and dissimilar from the private right that federal occupancy of one field does not debar a state from continuing to exercise its conventional equity powers over the other. . . .

Even if we were to assume, with petitioners, that distinctly private rights were enforced by the state authorities, it does not follow that the state and federal authorities may supplement each other in cases of this type. The conflict lies in remedies, not rights. The same picketing may injure both public and private rights. But when two separate remedies are brought to bear on the same activity, a conflict is imminent. It must be remembered that petitioners' state remedy was a suit for an injunction prohibiting the picketing. The federal Board, if it should find a violation of the national Labor Management Relations Act, would issue a cease-and-desist order and perhaps obtain a temporary injunction to preserve the status quo. Or if it found no violation, it would dismiss the complaint, thereby sanctioning the picketing. To avoid facing a conflict between the state and federal remedies, we would have to assume either that both authorities will always agree as to whether the picketing should continue, or that the State's temporary injunction will be dissolved as soon as the federal Board acts. But experience gives no assurance of either alternative, and there is no indication that the statute left it open for such conflicts to arise.

The detailed prescription of a procedure for restraint of specified types of picketing would seem to imply that other picketing is to be free of other methods and sources of restraint. For the policy of the national Labor Management Relations Act is not to condemn all picketing but only that ascertained by its prescribed processes to fall within its prohibitions. Otherwise, it is implicit in the Act that the public interest is served by freedom of labor to use the weapon of picketing. For a state to impinge on the area of labor combat designed to be free is quite as much an obstruction of federal policy as if the state were to declare picketing free for purposes or by methods which the federal Act prohibits.

Whatever purpose a classification of rights as public or private may serve, it is too unsettled and ambiguous to introduce into constitutional law as a dividing line between federal and state power or jurisdiction. . . .

We conclude that when federal power constitutionally is exerted for the protection of public or private interests, or both, it becomes the supreme law of the land and cannot be curtailed, circumvented or extended by a state procedure merely because it will apply some doctrine of private right. To the extent that the private right may conflict with the public one, the former is superseded. To the extent that public interest is found to require official enforcement instead of private initiative, the latter will ordinarily be excluded. Of course, Congress, in enacting such legislation as we have here, can save alternative or supplemental state remedies by express terms, or by some clear implication, if it sees fit.

On the basis of the allegations, the petitioners could have presented this grievance to the National Labor Relations Board. The respondents were subject to being summoned before that body to justify their conduct. We think the grievance was not subject to litigation in the tribunals of the State.

Judgment affirmed.

SAN DIEGO BUILDING TRADES COUNCIL v. GARMON

Supreme Court of the United States, 1959
359 U.S. 236, 79 Sup. Ct. 773, 3 L. Ed. 2d 775

MR. JUSTICE FRANKFURTER delivered the opinion of the Court.

This case is before us for the second time. The present litigation began with a dispute between the petitioning unions and respondents, copartners in the business of selling lumber and other materials in California. Respondents began an action in the Superior Court for the County of San Diego, asking for an injunction and damages. Upon hearing, the trial court found the following facts. In March of 1953 the unions sought from respondents an agreement to retain in their employ only those workers who were already members of the unions, or who applied for membership within thirty days. Respondents refused, claiming that none of their employees had shown a desire to join the union, and that, in any event, they could not accept such an arrangement until one of the unions had been designated by the employees as a collective bargaining agent. The unions began at once peacefully to picket the respondents' place of business, and to exert pressure on customers and suppliers in order to persuade them to stop dealing with respondents. The sole purpose of these pressures was to compel execution of the proposed contract. The unions contested this finding, claiming that the only purpose of their activities was to educate the workers and persuade them to become members. On the basis of its findings, the court enjoined the unions from picketing and from the use of other pressures to force an agreement, until one of them had been properly designated as a collective bargaining agent. The court also awarded $1,000 damages for losses found to have been sustained.

At the time the suit in the state court was started, respondents had begun a representation proceeding before the National Labor Relations Board. The Regional Director declined jurisdiction, presumably because the amount of interstate commerce involved did not meet the Board's monetary standards in taking jurisdiction.

On appeal, the California Supreme Court sustained the judgment of the Superior Court, 45 Cal. 2d 657, 291 P.2d 1, holding that, since the National Labor Relations Board had declined to exercise its jurisdiction, the California courts had power over the dispute. They further decided that the conduct of the union constituted an unfair labor practice under §8(b)(2) of the National Labor Relations Act, 29 U.S.C.A. §158(b)(2), and hence was not privileged under California law. As the California court itself later pointed out this decision did not specify what law, state or federal, was the basis of the relief granted. Both state and federal law played a part but, "(a)ny distinction as between those laws was not thoroughly explored." Garmon v. San Diego Bldg. Trades Council, 49 Cal. 2d 595, 602, 320 P.2d 473, 477.

We granted certiorari, 351 U.S. 923, and decided the case together with Guss v. Utah Labor Relations Board, 353 U.S. 1, and Amalgamated Meat Cutters, etc. v. Fairlawn Meats, Inc., 353 U.S. 20. In those cases, we held that the refusal of the National Labor Relations Board to assert jurisdiction did not leave with the States power over activities they otherwise would be pre-empted from regulating. Both Guss and Fairlawn involved relief of an equitable nature. In vacating and remanding the judgment of the California court in this case, we pointed out that those cases controlled this one, "in its major aspects." 353 U.S. 26, at page 28. However, since it was not clear whether the judgment for damages would be sustained under California law, we remanded to the state court for consideration of that local law issue. The federal question, namely, whether the Labor Management Relations Act, 29 U.S.C.A. §§141 et seq., precluded California from granting an award for damages arising out of the conduct in question, could not be appropriately decided until the antecedent state law question was decided by the state court.

On remand, the California court, in accordance with our decision in Guss, set aside the injunction, but sustained the award of damages. Garmon v. San Diego Building Trades Council, 49 Cal. 2d 595, 320 Cal. P.2d 473 (three judges dissenting). After deciding that California had jurisdiction to award damages for injuries caused by the union's activities, the California court held that those activities constituted a tort based on an unfair labor practice under state law. In so holding the court relied on general tort provisions of the West's Ann. California Civil Code, §§1667, 1708, as well as state enactments dealing specifically with labor relations, West's Ann. Calif. Labor Code, §923 (1937); ibid., §§1115-1118 (1947).

We again granted certiorari, 357 U.S. 925, to determine whether the California court had jurisdiction to award damages arising out of peaceful union activity which it could not enjoin. . . .

The case before us concerns one of the most teasing and frequently litigated areas of industrial relations, the multitude of activities regulated by §§7 and 8 of the Labor Management Relations Act. 61 Stat. 140, 29 U.S.C. §§157, 158. These broad provisions govern both protected "concerted activities" and unfair labor practices. They regulate the vital, economic instruments of the strike and the picket line, and impinge on the clash of the still unsettled claims between employers and labor unions. The extent to which the variegated laws of the several States are displaced by a single, uniform, national rule has been a matter of frequent and recurring concern. . . .

In determining the extent to which state regulation must yield to subordinating federal authority, we have been concerned with delimiting areas of potential conflict; potential conflict of rules of law, of remedy, and of administration. The nature of the judicial process precludes an ad hoc inquiry into the special problems of labor-management relations involved in a particular set of occurrences in order to ascertain the precise nature and degree of federal-state conflict there involved, and more particularly what exact mischief such a conflict would cause. Nor is it our business to attempt this. Such determinations inevitably depend upon judgments on the impact of these particular conflicts on the entire scheme of federal labor policy and administration. Our task is confined to dealing with classes of situations. To the National Labor Relations Board and to Congress must be left those precise and closely limited demarcations that can be adequately fashioned only by legislation and administration. We have necessarily been concerned with the potential conflict of two law-enforcing authorities, with the disharmonies inherent in two systems, one federal the other state, of inconsistent standards of substantive law and differing remedial schemes. But the unifying consideration of our decisions has been regard to the fact that Congress has entrusted administration of the labor policy for the Nation to a centralized administrative agency, armed with its own procedures, and equipped with its specialized knowledge and cumulative experience. . . .

Administration is more than a means of regulation; administration is regulation. We have been concerned with conflict in its broadest sense; conflict with a complex and interrelated federal scheme of law, remedy, and administration. Thus, judicial concern has necessarily focused on the nature of the activities which the States have sought to regulate, rather than on the method of regulation adopted. When the exercise of state power over a particular area of activity threatened interference with the clearly indicated policy of industrial relations, it has been judicially necessary to preclude the States from acting. However, due regard for the presuppositions of our embracing federal system, including the principle of diffusion of power not as a matter of doctrinaire localism but as a promoter of democracy, has required us not to find withdrawal from the States of power to regulate where the activity regulated was a merely peripheral concern of the Labor Management Relations Act. See International Assn. of Machinists v. Gonzales, 356 U.S. 617. Or where the regulated conduct touched interests so deeply rooted in local feeling and responsibility that, in the absence of compelling congressional direction, we could not infer that Congress had deprived the States of the power to act.

When it is clear or may fairly be assumed that the activities which a State purports to regulate are protected by §7 of the Taft-Hartley Act, or constitute an unfair labor practice under §8, due regard for the federal enactment requires that state jurisdiction must yield. To leave the States free to regulate conduct so plainly within the central aim of federal regulation involves too great a danger of conflict between power asserted by Congress and requirements imposed by state law. Nor has it mattered whether the States have acted through laws of broad general application rather than laws specifically directed towards the governance of industrial relations. Regardless of the mode adopted, to allow the States to control conduct which is the subject of national regulation would create potential frustration of national purposes.

At times it has not been clear whether the particular activity regulated by the States was governed by §7 or §8 or was, perhaps, outside both these sections. But courts are not primary tribunals to adjudicate such issues. It is essential to the administration of the Act that these determinations be left in the first instance to the National Labor Relations Board. What is outside the scope of this Court's authority cannot remain within a State's power and state jurisdiction too must yield to the exclusive primary competence of the Board. . . .

The case before us is such a case. The adjudication in California has throughout been based on the assumption that the behavior of the petitioning unions constituted an unfair labor practice. This conclusion was derived by the California courts from the facts as well as from their view of the Act. It is not for us to decide whether the National Labor Relations Board would have, or should have, decided these questions in the same manner. When an activity is arguably subject to §7 or §8 of the Act, the States as well as the federal courts must defer to the exclusive competence of the National Labor Relations Board if the danger of state interference with national policy is to be averted.

To require the States to yield to the primary jurisdiction of the National Board does not ensure Board adjudication of the status of a disputed activity. If the Board decides, subject to appropriate federal judicial review, that conduct is protected by §7, or prohibited by §8, then the matter is at an end, and the States are ousted of all jurisdiction. Or, the Board may decide that an activity is neither protected nor prohibited, and thereby raise the question whether such activity may be regulated by the States. However, the Board may also fail to determine the status of the disputed conduct by declining to assert jurisdiction, or by refusal of the General Counsel to file a charge, or by adopting some other disposition which does not define the nature of the activity with unclouded legal significance. This was the basic problem underlying our decision in Guss v. Utah Labor Relations Board, 353 U.S. 1. In that case we held that the failure of the National Labor Relations Board to assume jurisdiction did not leave the States free to regulate activities they would otherwise be precluded from regulating. It follows that the failure of the Board to define the legal significance under the Act of a particular activity does not give the States the power to act. In the absence of the Board's clear determination that an activity is neither protected nor prohibited or of compelling precedent applied to essentially undisputed facts, it is not for this Court to decide whether such activities are subject to state jurisdiction. The withdrawal of this narrow area from possible state activity follows from our decisions in Weber and Guss. The governing consideration is that to allow the States to control activities that are potentially subject to federal regulation involves too great a danger of conflict with national labor policy.

In the light of these principles the case before us is clear. Since the National Labor Relations Board has not adjudicated the status of the conduct for which the State of California seeks to give a remedy in damages, and since such activity is arguably within the compass of §7 or §8 of the Act, the State's jurisdiction is displaced.

Nor is it significant that California asserted its power to give damages rather than to enjoin what the Board may restrain though it could not compensate. Our concern is with delimiting areas of conduct which must be free from state regulation if national policy is to be left unhampered. Such regulation can be as effectively exerted through an award of damages as through some form of preventive relief. The obligation to pay compensation can be, indeed is designed to be, a potent method of governing conduct and controlling policy. Even the States' salutory effort to redress private wrongs or grant compensation for past harm cannot be exerted to regulate activities that are potentially subject to the exclusive federal regulatory scheme. See Garner v. Teamsters, etc. Union, 346 U.S. 485, 492-497. It may be that an award of damages in a particular situation will not, in fact, conflict with the active assertion of federal authority. The same may be true of the incidence of a particular state injunction. To sanction either involves a conflict with federal policy in that it involves allowing two law-making sources to govern. In fact, since remedies form an ingredient of any integrated scheme of regulation, to allow the State to grant a remedy here which has been withheld from the National Labor Relations Board only accentuates the danger of conflict.

It is true that we have allowed the States to grant compensation for the consequences, as defined by the traditional law of torts, of conduct marked by violence and imminent threats to the public order. International Union, United Automobile, Aircraft and Agricultural Implement Workers, etc. v. Russell, 356 U.S. 634; United Construction Workers, etc. v. Laburnum Const. Corp., 347 U.S. 656. We have also allowed the States to enjoin such conduct. Youngdahl v. Rainfair, Inc., 355 U.S. 131; United Automobile, Aircraft and Agricultural Implement Workers, etc. v. Wisconsin Employment Relations Board, 351 U.S. 266. State jurisdiction has prevailed in these situations because the compelling state interest, in the scheme of our federalism, in the maintenance of domestic peace is not overridden in the absence of clearly expressed congressional direction. We recognize that the opinion in United Construction Workers, etc. v. Laburnum Const. Corp., 347 U.S. 656, found support in the fact that the state remedy had no federal counterpart. But that decision was determined, as is demonstrated by the question to which review was restricted, by the "type of conduct" involved, i.e., "intimidation and threats of violence." In the present case there is no such compelling state interest.

The judgment below is reversed.

MR. JUSTICE HARLAN, whom MR. JUSTICE CLARK, MR. JUSTICE WHITTAKER and MR. JUSTICE STEWART join, concurring.

I concur in the result upon the narrow ground that the Union's activities for which the State has awarded damages may fairly be considered protected under the Taft-Hartley Act, and that therefore state action is precluded until the National Labor Relations Board has made a contrary determination respecting such activities. As the Court points out, it makes no difference that the Board has declined to exercise its jurisdiction. . . .

Were nothing more than this particular case involved, I would be content to rest my concurrence at this point without more. But as today's decision will stand as a landmark in future "pre-emption" cases in the labor field, I feel justified in particularizing why I cannot join the Court's opinion.

If it were clear that the Union's conduct here was unprotected activity under Taft-Hartley, I think that United Construction Workers, etc. v. Laburnum Construction Corp., 347 U.S. 656, and International Union, United Automobile, Aircraft and Agricultural Implement Workers, etc. v. Russell, 356 U.S. 634, would require that the California judgment be sustained, even though such conduct might be deemed to be federally prohibited. In both these cases state tort damage judgments against unions were upheld in respect of conduct which this Court assumed was prohibited activity under the Federal Labor Act. The Court now says, however, that those decisions are not applicable here because they were premised on violence, which the States could also have enjoined, United Automobile, Aircraft and Agricultural Implement Workers, etc. v. Wisconsin Employment Relations Board, 351 U.S. 266, whereas in this case the Union's acts were peaceful. In this I think the Court mistaken.

The threshold question in every labor pre-emption case is whether the conduct with respect to which a State has sought to act is, or may fairly be regarded as, federally protected activity. Because conflict is the touchstone of pre-emption, such activity is obviously beyond the reach of all state power. . . . That threshold question was squarely faced in the Russell case, where the Court, 356 U.S. at page 640, said: "At the outset, we note that the union's activity in this case clearly was not protected by federal law." The same question was, in my view, necessarily faced in Laburnum.

In both cases it was possible to decide that question without prior reference to the National Labor Relations Board because the union conduct involved was violent, and as such was of course not protected by the federal Act. Thus in Laburnum, the pre-emption issue was limited to the "type of conduct" before the Court. 347 U.S at page 658. Similarly in Russell, which was decided on Laburnum principles, the Court stated that the union's activity "clearly was not protected," and immediately went on to say (citing to prior "violence" cases) that "the strike was conducted in such a manner that it could have been enjoined" by the State. 356 U.S. at page 640. In both instances the Court, in reliance on former "violence" cases involving injunctions, might have gone on to hold, as the Court now in effect says it did, that the state police power was not displaced by the federal Act, and thus disposed of the cases on the ground that state damage awards, like state injunctions, based on violent conduct did not conflict with the federal statute. The Court did not do this, however.

Instead the relevance of violence was manifestly deemed confined to rendering the Laburnum and Russell activities federally unprotected. So rendered, they could then only have been classified as prohibited, or "neither protected nor prohibited." If the latter, state jurisdiction was beyond challenge. International Union, United Automobile Workers, etc. v. Wisconsin Employment Relations Board, 336 U.S. 245. Conversely, if the activities could have been considered prohibited, primary decision by the Board would have been necessary, if state damage awards were inconsistent with federal prohibitions. Garner v. Teamsters, etc. Union, 346 U.S. 485. To determine the need for initial reference to the Board, the Court assumed that the activities were unfair labor practices prohibited by the federal Act. Laburnum, supra, 347 U.S. at pages 660-663; Russell, supra, 356 U.S. at page 641. It then considered the possibility of conflict and held that the state damage remedies were not pre-empted because the federal Act afforded no remedy at all for the past conduct involved in Laburnum, and less than full redress for that involved in Russell. The essence of the Court's holding, which made resort to primary jurisdiction unnecessary, is contained in the following passage from the opinion in Laburnum, supra, 347 U.S. at page 665 (also quoted in Russell, supra, 356 U.S. at page 644):

"To the extent that Congress prescribed preventive procedure against unfair labor practices, that case [Garner v. Teamsters Union] recognized that the Act excluded conflicting state procedure to the same end. To the extent, however, that Congress has not prescribed procedure for dealing with the consequences of tortious conduct already committed, there is no ground for concluding that existing criminal penalties or liabilities for tortious conduct have been eliminated. The care we took in the Garner case to demonstrate the existing conflict between state and federal administrative remedies in that case was, itself, a recognition that if no conflict had existed, the state procedure would have survived."

Until today this holding of Laburnum has been recognized by subsequent cases. . . .

The Court's opinion in this case cuts deeply into the ability of States to furnish an effective remedy under their own laws for the redress of past nonviolent tortious conduct which is not federally protected, but which may be deemed to be, or is, federally prohibited. Henceforth the States must withhold access to their courts until the National Labor Relations Board has determined that such unprotected conduct is not an unfair labor practice, a course which, because of unavoidable Board delays, may render state redress ineffective. And in instances in which the Board declines to exercise its jurisdiction, the States are entirely deprived of power to afford any relief. Moreover, since the reparation powers of the Board, as we observed in Russell, are narrowly circumscribed, those injured by nonviolent conduct will often go remediless even when the Board does accept jurisdiction.

I am, further, at loss to understand, and can find no basis on principle or in past decisions for, the Court's intimation that the States may even be powerless to act when the underlying activities are clearly "neither protected nor prohibited" by the federal Act. Surely that suggestion is foreclosed by International Union, United Automobile Workers, etc. v. Wisconsin Employment Relations Board, 336 U.S. 245, supra, as well as by the approach taken to federal pre-emption in such cases as Allen-Bradley Local, etc. v. Wisconsin Employment Relations Board [315 U.S. 740]; Bethlehem Steel Co. v. New York State Labor Relations Board, 330 U.S. 767, 773, and Algoma Plywood and Veneer Co. v. Wisconsin Employment Relations Board, 336 U.S. 301, not to mention Laburnum and Russell and the primary jurisdiction doctrine itself. Should what the Court now intimates ever come to pass, then indeed state power to redress wrongful acts in the labor field will be reduced to the vanishing point.

In determining pre-emption in any given labor case, I would adhere to the Laburnum and Russell distinction between damages and injunctions and to the principle that state power is not precluded where the challenged conduct is neither protected nor prohibited under the federal Act. Solely because it is fairly debatable whether the conduct here is federally protected, I concur in the result of today's decision.

NOTES

1. In United Construction Workers v. Laburnum Construction Corp., 347 U.S. 656 (1954), the union demanded that employees engaged in certain construction work become members and that it be recognized as the bargaining agent for those employees. The company and many of its employees refused these demands. Thereafter the union compelled the company to abandon the construction project by intimidating the company's officers and employees with threats of violence. In a suit brought in a state court for the loss of profits on the abandoned contract, the company obtained a judgment for compensatory damages of approximately $30,000 and punitive damages of $100,000. The United States Supreme Court upheld the jurisdiction of the state court and affirmed the judgment even though it was assumed that the conduct of the union constituted a violation of Section 8(b)(1). The Court found no substantial reason for denying the company compensation or providing the union with an immunity for its tortious conduct, noting that Congress had neither provided nor suggested any substitute for traditional state court procedures for collecting damages for injuries caused by tortious conduct.

In United Auto Workers v. Russell, 356 U.S. 634 (1958), the union prevented Russell and others from working during a strike by force and threats of force. The Alabama courts held that Russell had proved the tort of wrongful interference with a lawful occupation and awarded him a judgment of $10,000, of which approximately $9500 must have been for punitive damages and for mental pain and anguish. Again assuming that the union's conduct constituted a violation of Section 8(b)(1), the United States Supreme Court upheld the jurisdiction of the state court and affirmed the judgment. The back-pay award which the NLRB might have entered was viewed as only a partial alternative to an employee's suit upon his common law rights in state courts.

2. In Local 20, Teamsters Union v. Morton, 377 U.S. 252 (1964), the company sued the union in federal district court for damages for engag-

ing in a secondary boycott in violation of Section 303 of LMRA. The violation was established and compensatory damages were awarded. This decision was upheld by the Supreme Court. But, in addition, the company asked for compensatory and punitive damages under an Ohio law which prohibited direct appeals to a struck employer's customers or suppliers to stop doing business with the struck employer. The union did engage in this conduct. Compensatory damages were awarded, and also there was a judgment for punitive damages under state law in spite of the lack of violence in the conduct of the union. The Supreme Court reversed the judgments, based upon state law, for compensatory and punitive damages. The Court assumed that (p. 258), "at least some of the secondary activity here involved was neither protected nor prohibited" by the NLRA. But the Court said (p. 259): "If the Ohio law of secondary boycott can be applied to proscribe the same type of conduct which Congress focused upon but did not proscribe when it enacted §303, the inevitable result would be to frustrate the congressional determination to leave this weapon of self-help available." The Court also quoted from the last paragraph of the majority opinion in Garmon, supra page 363, which seems to limit Laburnum and Russell to situations where violence is involved. Actually, were the awards of damages in those cases measured to effectuate the state's interest in the maintenance of domestic peace or were they made to vindicate both private and state interests in preventing tortious interference with advantageous relationships? If you conclude that they were made primarily for the latter purpose, is there any reason why Ohio should not be able to vindicate similar interests in the context of Morton? Has Congress struck a balance with respect to the consequences of the use of force comparable to the balance struck with respect to forms of economic pressures?

3. In Retail Clerks International Assn., Local 1625 v. Schermerhorn, 375 U.S. 96 (1963), the Supreme Court upheld the right of a state to enforce its "right-to-work" law, prohibiting the union or agency shop, under Section 14(b) of NLRA. The Court said (p. 102): "Since it is plain that Congress left the States free to legislate in that field, we can only assume that it intended to leave unaffected the power to enforce those laws." The Schermerhorn case appears as a principal case infra page 665, where consideration of union security under NLRA takes place.

LOCAL 100, UNITED ASSN. OF JOURNEYMEN v. BORDEN
Supreme Court of the United States, 1963
373 U.S. 690, 83 Sup. Ct. 1423, 10 L. Ed. 2d 638

MR. JUSTICE HARLAN delivered the opinion of the Court. . . .

I

The respondent, H. N. Borden, who was then a member of the Shreveport, Louisiana, local of the plumbers union, arrived in Dallas, Texas, in September 1953, looking for a job with the Farwell Construction Company on a particular bank construction project. Farwell's hiring on this project was done through union referral, although there was no written agreement to this effect Borden was unable to obtain such a referral from the business agent of the Dallas local of the plumbers union, even after the agent had accepted Borden's clearance card from the Shreveport local and after the Farwell foreman on the construction project had called the business agent and asked to have Borden sent over. According to Borden's testimony, the business agent told him: "You are not going to work down there on the bank job or for Farwell, you have come in here wrong, you have come in here with a job in your pocket." And according to the Farwell foreman, the business agent answered his request by saying: "I am not about to send that old —— down there, he shoved his card down our throat and I am not about to send him to the bank."

Borden never did get the job with Farwell, although he was referred to and accepted several other jobs during the period before the bank construction project was completed.

Subsequently, he brought the present suit against the Dallas local, petitioner here . . . seeking damages under state law for the refusal to refer him to Farwell. He alleged that the actions of the defendants constituted a willful, malicious, and discriminatory interference with his right to contract and to pursue a lawful occupation; that the defendants had breached a promise, implicit in the membership arrangement, not to discriminate unfairly or to deny any member the right to work . . .

At trial, the case was submitted to the jury on special issues and the jury's answers included findings that Borden had been promised a job by a Farwell representative; that the Farwell foreman asked the union business agent to refer Borden; that the business agent "wilfully" refused to let Borden work on the bank project, knowing that Borden was entitled to work on that project under union rules; and that the conduct of the business agent was approved by the officers and members of petitioner. Actual loss of earnings resulting from the refusal to refer Borden to the Farwell job was found to be $1,916; compensation for mental suffering, $1,500; and punitive damages, $5,000. The trial court disallowed recovery for mental anguish and ordered a remittitur of the punitive damages in excess of the amount of actual damages, thus awarding total damages of $3,832. . . .

II

This Court held in San Diego Building Trades Council v. Garmon, 359 U.S. 236, that in the absence of an overriding state interest such as that involved in the maintenance of domestic peace, state courts must defer to the exclusive competence of the National Labor Relations Board in cases in which the activity that is the subject matter of the litigation is arguably subject to the protections of §7 or the prohibitions of §8 of the National Labor Relations Act. This relinquishment of state jurisdiction, the Court stated, is essential "if the danger of state interference with national policy is to be averted," 359 U.S., at 245, and is as necessary in a suit for damages as in a suit seeking equitable relief. Thus the first inquiry, in any case in which a claim of federal preemption is raised, must be whether the conduct called into question may reasonably be asserted to be subject to Labor Board cognizance.

In the present case, respondent contends that no such assertion can be made, but we disagree. The facts as alleged in the complaint, and as found by the jury, are that the Dallas union business agent, with the ultimate approval of the local union itself, refused to refer the respondent to a particular job for which he had been sought, and that this refusal resulted in an inability to obtain the employment. Notwithstanding the state court's contrary view, if it is assumed that the refusal and the resulting inability to obtain employment were in some way based on respondent's actual or believed failure to comply with internal union rules, it is certainly "arguable" that the union's conduct violated §8(b)(1)(A), by restraining or coercing Borden in the exercise of his protected right to refrain from observing those rules, and §8(b)(2), by causing an employer to discriminate against Borden in violation of §8(a)(3). See, e.g., Radio Officers v. Labor Board, 347 U.S. 17; Local 568, Hotel Employees, 141 N.L.R.B. No. 29; International Union of Operating Engineers, Local 624 A-B, 141 N.L.R.B. No. 57. As established in the Radio Officers case, the "membership" referred to in §8(a)(3) and thus incorporated in §8(b)(2) is broad enough to embrace participation in union activities and maintenance of good standing as well as mere adhesion to a labor organization. 347 U.S., at 39-42. And there is a substantial possibility in this case that Borden's failure to live up to the internal rule prohibiting the solicitation of work from any contractor was precisely the reason why clearance was denied. Indeed this may well have been the meaning of the business agent's remark, testified to by Borden himself, that "you have come in here wrong, you have come in here with a job in your pocket."

It may also reasonably contended that after inquiry into the facts, the Board might have found that the union conduct in question was not an unfair labor practice but rather was protected concerted activity within the meaning of §7. This Court has held that hiring-hall practices do not necessarily violate the provisions of federal law, Teamsters Local v. Labor Board, 365 U.S. 667, and the Board's appraisal of the conflicting testimony might have led it to conclude that the refusal to refer was due only to the respondent's efforts to circumvent a lawful hiring-hall arrangement rather than to his engaging in protected activities. The problems inherent in the operation of union hiring halls are difficult and complex, see Rothman, The Development and Current Status of the Law Pertaining to Hiring Hall Arrangements, 48 Va. L. Rev. 871, and point up the importance of limiting initial competence to adjudicate such matters to a single expert federal agency.

We need not and should not consider whether the petitioner's activity in this case was federally protected or prohibited, on any of the theories suggested above or on some different basis. It is sufficient for present purposes to find, as we do, that it is reasonably "arguable" that the matter comes within the Board's jurisdiction.

III

Respondent urges that even if the union's interference with his employment is a matter that the Board could have dealt with, the state courts are still not deprived of jurisdiction in this case under the principles declared in International Assn. of Machinists v. Gonzales, 356 U.S. 617. Gonzales was a suit against a labor union by an individual who claimed that he had been expelled in violation of his contractual rights and who was seeking restoration of membership. He also sought consequential damages flowing from the expulsion, including loss of wages resulting from loss of employment and compensation for physical and mental suffering. It was recognized in that case that restoration of union membership was a remedy that the Board could not afford and indeed that the internal affairs of unions were not in themselves a matter within the Board's competence. The Court then went on to hold that, in the presence of admitted state jurisdiction to order restoration of membership, the State was not without power "to fill out this remedy" by an award of consequential damages, even though these damages might be for conduct that constituted an unfair labor practice under federal law. The Taft-Hartley Act, the Court stated, did not require mutilation of "the comprehensive relief of equity." 356 U.S., at 621.

The Gonzales decision, it is evident, turned on the Court's conclusion that the lawsuit was focused on purely internal union matters, i.e., on relations between the individual plaintiff and the union not having to do directly with matters of employment, and that the principal relief sought was restoration of union membership rights. In this posture, collateral relief in the form of consequential damages for loss of employment was not to be denied.

We need not now determine the extent to which the holding in Garmon, supra, qualified the principles declared in Gonzales with respect to jurisdiction to award consequential damages, for it is clear in any event that the present case does not come within the Gonzales rationale. The suit involved here was focused principally, if not entirely, on the union's actions with respect to Borden's efforts to obtain employment. No specific equitable relief was sought directed to Borden's status in the union, and thus there was no state remedy to "fill out" by permitting the award of consequential damages. The "crux" of the action (Gonzales, 356 U.S., at 618) concerned Borden's employment relations and involved conduct arguably subject to the Board's jurisdiction.

Nor do we regard it as significant that Borden's complaint against the union sounded in contract as well as in tort. It is not the label affixed to the cause of action under state law that controls the determination of the relationship between state and federal jurisdiction. Rather, as stated in Garmon, supra, at 246, "(o)ur concern is with de-limiting *areas of conduct* which must be free from state regulation if national policy is to be left unhampered." (Emphasis added.) In the present case the conduct on which the suit is centered, whether described in terms of tort or contract, is conduct whose lawfulness could initially be judged only by the federal agency vested with exclusive primary jurisdiction to apply federal standards.

Accordingly, we conclude that the judgment of the court below must be reversed.

MR. JUSTICE GOLDBERG took no part in the consideration or decision of this case.

MR. JUSTICE DOUGLAS, with whom MR. JUSTICE CLARK concurs, dissenting.

While I dissented in International Association v. Gonzales, 356 U.S. 617, I fail to see how that case can fairly be distinguished from this one. Both Gonzales and San Diego Building Trades Council v. Garmon, 359 U.S. 236, were written by the same author, who had no difficulty in reconciling them. And they were decided before Congress reentered the labor relations field with the Landrum-Griffin Act of 1959. 73 Stat. 519. Yet, the Court points to no indication that Congress thought Gonzales had incorrectly interpreted the balance it had struck between state and federal jurisdiction over these matters.

The distinction the Court draws between this case and Gonzales — that in Gonzales the lawsuit focused on purely internal union matters — is not one that a court can intelligently apply in the myriad of cases in the field. This lawsuit started with a quarrel between respondent and his union, concerning the scope of membership rights in the union, as did Gonzales; and it is with those rights that this litigation is concerned, as was Gonzales. And, as here, it was conceded in Gonzales that the conduct complained of might well amount to an unfair labor practice within the Labor Board's jurisdiction. Because of these similarities, and because the Court is clearly right in saying "(i)t is not the label affixed to the cause of action under state law that controls the determination of the relationship between state and federal jurisdiction," I am able to find no support for the Court's distinction of Gonzales in the fact that it was primarily an "equitable" case where damages were allowed only to "fill out" the union member's remedy. Cf. Federal Rules of Civil Procedure, Rules 1, 2 and 54(c).

San Diego Building Trades Council v. Garmon, supra, involved a controversy between union and employer in the classical case for National Labor Board jurisdiction. Suits for damages by individual employees against the union or the employer fall in the category of Moore v. Illinois Central R. Co., 312 U.S. 630. As a matter of policy, there is much to be said for allowing the individual employee recourse to conventional litigation in his home town tribunal for redress of grievances. Washington, D.C. and its administrative agencies — and even regional offices — are often distant and remote and expensive to reach. Under today's holding the member who has a real dispute with his union may go without a remedy.[1] See, e.g., San Diego Building Trades Council v. Garmon,

[1] It is by no means clear that the General Counsel, who by §3(d) has "final authority" to investigate charges and to issue complaints, can be made to file a charge on behalf of this individual claimant. See Hourihan v. Labor Board,

supra; Guss v. Utah Labor Board, 353 U.S. 1. When the basic dispute is between a union and an employer, any hiatus that might exist in the jurisdictional balance that has been struck can be filled by resort to economic power. But when the union member has a dispute with his union, he has no power on which to rely. If Gonzales — written in the spirit of Moore — is to survive, this judgment should be affirmed.

NOTES

1. Perko, a foreman and member of the Iron Workers Union, instructed boilermakers with respect to performance of certain phases of work which the ironworkers claimed. Thereafter the local of the Iron Workers Union found him guilty of violating a union rule prohibiting assistance to boilermakers and placed him on probation with a suspended fine. Subsequently, ironworkers refused to take orders from him because he had assisted the boilermakers, and thereafter his employer laid him off because of his dispute with the union. He brought suit in a state court and recovered judgment against the union and certain of its officers.

The United States Supreme Court held that the state court was without jurisdiction to provide such a remedy. Although the NLRA excludes supervisors from the definition of an employee, the NLRB might decide that Perko was entitled to the protection afforded employees because he sometimes worked as a regular ironworker, and hence had a fluctuating supervisory status. Moreover, even if he were solely a supervisor the NLRB might grant relief either upon the theory that union discipline of a supervisor coerces nonsupervisory employees or on the theory that causing his discharge might constitute coercion of his employer in the selection of its representatives for the purpose of adjusting grievances. Because of these possibilities, the subject of the lawsuit arguably came within the NLRB jurisdiction. Iron Workers Union v. Perko, 373 U.S. 701 (1963).

2. In cases in which an employer seeks an injunction in a state court against a strike, picketing, or other union concerted activities the union may challenge the court's jurisdiction upon pre-emption grounds. Suppose, however, that the state court issues a preliminary injunction pending its determination of the jurisdictional question. What remedies are available to the union if it is convinced that the pre-emption doctrine is applicable and that compliance with the temporary injunction will effectively conclude the matter either because it will break the employees' organizational spirit or because, as in the construction industry, resumption of concerted activities at a later date will come too late to have an effect upon the matter in dispute?

In Amalgamated Clothing Workers v. Richman Brothers, 348 U.S. 511 (1955), the Supreme Court held that the union could not collaterally attack the state court's jurisdiction by bringing an action in federal court to

---

201 F.2d 187; Dunn v. Retail Clerks, 299 F.2d 873; Dunn v. Retail Clerks, 307 F.2d 285.

enjoin the state proceeding because of the general prohibition against such suits found in 28 U.S.C. §2283. Subsequently an attorney for a union, believing that an injunction issued ex parte on application of an employer was invalid on grounds of pre-emption, advised the union to contest the order by continuing to picket. After a hearing in which the court refused to hear evidence relating to its jurisdiction to issue the injunction, the attorney was held in contempt for disobeying a lawful order of the court, fined, and sentenced to jail. The state courts denied him relief upon his petition for habeas corpus. The United States Supreme Court reversed, holding that the state court was without power to hold one in contempt for violating an injunction that it had no power to enter by reason of pre-emption, and that it violates due process for a court to convict a person of a contempt of this nature without an opportunity to prove that the state court was acting in a field reserved exclusively for the NLRB. In re Green, 369 U.S. 689 (1962). See also Ex parte George, 371 U.S. 72 (1962). Compare United States v. United Mine Workers, 330 U.S. 258 (1947), holding, in a case which did not involve a question of pre-emption of a field by Congress, that disobedience of a temporary restraining order issued by a court whose claim to jurisdiction was not frivolous may be punished by contempt even if it is determined on appeal that such jurisdiction was lacking.

In Local 438, Construction & Laborers Union v. Curry, 371 U.S. 542, (1963), the employer had sought an injunction in a Georgia court on the ground that the union's picketing was for the purpose of requiring it to hire only union labor in violation of the state right-to-work law. The union contended that the picketing was only for the purpose of publicizing information that the employer was not paying wages conforming to those paid for similar work in the area, and the evidence would have sustained a finding that this was true. The trial court denied the requested temporary injunction without opinion. However the Supreme Court of Georgia concluded that picketing was for the purpose of compelling a violation of the right-to-work law and held that the trial judge had erred in denying an interlocutory injunction. The United States Supreme Court found at least an arguable violation of the NLRA, and thus concluded that the Georgia courts were without jurisdiction to issue the injunction.

Although its appellate jurisdiction under 28 U.S.C. §1257 is limited to the review of final judgments, the United States Supreme Court found it had the power to review the order directing the issuance of the temporary injunction. The judgment of the Georgia court finally and erroneously determined the issue of jurisdiction and that issue was deemed wholly separate from and independent of the merits of the employer's case. Issuance of the temporary injunction might effectively dispose of the union's rights and render illusory his right to review of a final order as well as his right to a hearing before the NLRB. Moreover, the union conceded that it had no further factual or legal issues to litigate in the Georgia trial court and there was nothing more of substance to be decided by the trial court.

Do these decisions evince a determination on the part of the United States Supreme Court to exert control over state courts which are not alerted to or sympathetic with the doctrine of federal pre-emption? If the trial court in Local 438 v. Curry had issued a temporary injunction and the Georgia Supreme Court had denied review of its order upon the ground that it was interlocutory and not final, could the union have obtained review by the United States Supreme Court?

SUMMARY COMMENT ON FEDERAL PRE-EMPTION

In connection with the cases in this section consideration should be given to Smith v. Evening News Assn., infra page 904. As you will see, in that case the United States Supreme Court held that a suit might be brought in a state court under Section 301 of the Labor Management Relations Act for violation of a contract provision that "there shall be no discrimination against any employee because of his membership or activity in the [union]." The alleged conduct of the employer in that case was, not only "arguably" but concededly, an unfair labor practice within the jurisdiction of the NLRB.

From these cases it should be apparent that an accommodation must be made between state and private interests on the one hand and the federal interest in effectuating the policies embodied in federal labor legislation. The starting point, but no sure solution, is found in Article VI, Section 2, of the United States Constitution: "This Constitution, and the Laws of the United States which shall be made in Pursuance thereof . . . shall be the supreme Law of the Land; and the Judges in every State shall be bound thereby, any Thing in the Constitution or Laws of any State to the Contrary notwithstanding." How far and in what areas state government must retreat from a conflict, or possible conflict, with federal law has been one aspect of the problem; how far and in what areas the federal law permits or approves of state action and remedies has been another aspect of the problem.

There are issues at stake beyond a mechanical interest in establishing a federal system, operating smoothly and free of the friction or worse obstructions which might be created by contact or conflict with state legal systems. A pervasive and uniform law governing the relations between management and labor goes far to insure that economic competition between different regions of the country will not be affected by considerations of whether labor laws of a particular area favor either management or labor. If, as recited in the findings and policies of the National Labor Relations Act, inequality of bargaining power between employees and employers burdens the flow of commerce, aggravates business depressions, depresses wages and purchasing power, and prevents stabilization of competitive wage rates and working conditions, and if, as also recited in the findings and policies of the National Labor Relations Act, certain practices of employers and labor organizations burden and obstruct the flow of commerce, the intrusion of state regulation of labor-management relations might upset the federal scheme devised to protect the national interest in the flow of commerce. When consideration is given to the role currently played by the federal government in assuring the economic health of the nation, it becomes apparent that such intrusions cannot be lightly ignored.

On the other hand, the emphasis given the national or federal interest is achieved only at the expense of certain local and private interests. Thus development of the pre-emption doctrine has in many cases deprived employers of access to state courts for protection against what they conceive to be violations of their rights and legitimate interests. Instead, in these cases, they must convince the General Counsel of the NLRB or his agents that there has been a violation of the *public* interests embodied in the NLRA. (In this largely unforeseen and unexpected development from the Taft-Hartley Act we may find the reason why organized labor no longer insists upon outright repeal of that Act.) On the other side, as pointed out by Justice Douglas' dissent in Local 100, United Assn. of Journeymen v. Borden, supra page 371, the pre-emption doctrine may also require an individual workman to seek relief from the NLRB or one of its thirty regional offices upon the basis that there has been a violation of the public interest rather than resorting to a much more conveniently located state trial court for the vindication of his private interests. And, as demonstrated by the cases recognizing state rights to regulate and determine the legal consequences of violent conduct, there are a number of state policies which impinge upon labor problems though they are not properly characterized as state labor policies. Does not the use of the "arguably subject" test prohibit effectuation of state policies without attempt to balance the harm to these state and private interests against the possible harm to the federal labor policies? Is the regulation in the public interest provided by the federal system so comprehensive, so satisfactory, or so important that it may be properly substituted for all private and state remedies against conduct which is "arguably subject" to regulation by the federal law?

Congress has given express recognition to these state and private interests in a few instances. Thus, Section 14(b) of the NLRA provides the exception for state right-to-work laws involved in Retail Clerks International Assn. v. Schermerhorn, infra page 665. In DeVeau v. Braisted, 363 U.S. 144 (1960), the Supreme Court decided that the provisions of Title V of the LMRDA, disqualifying certain ex-convicts from union office, did not pre empt a provision of the New York Waterfront Commission Act, which barred convicted felons from union office unless they have been pardoned or have received parole board good-conduct certificates. In so holding the Court gave controlling weight to the fact that Congress had approved an interstate compact governing certain aspects of waterfront employment, thereby consenting to enactments in furtherance of the compact, among which it was known was the provision of the New York Waterfront Commission Act. Another instance of affirmative approval of state action may be found in the addition made in Section 14(c) of the NLRA by the 1959 LMRDA authorizing state courts and agencies to assert jurisdiction over those cases which affect interstate commerce but over which the NLRB in its discretion has refused to assert its jurisdiction. The Supreme Court's construction of Section 301 as permitting suit in state courts for contract violations which are also unfair labor practices is another instance in which the value of permitting access to a local forum in vindication of private interests has been given unexplained recognition.

As this brief summary indicates, Congress has done little to define and delimit the pre-emption worked in a presumed implementation of its legislative purposes. Indeed, in 1959 when congressional attention was directed to the pre-emption problem, it dealt only with the relatively simple problem of the "no-man's land" created by the decision in Guss v. Utah Labor Relations Board, 353 U.S. 1 (1957). It made the previously mentioned addition to the NLRA found in Section 14(c). By that time the aspects of the pre-emption problem with which the cases in this section have been concerned were already obvious, and the Supreme Court had already commented on the difficulties of determining the pre-empted area, saying, "The statutory implications concerning what has been taken from the States and what has been left to them are of a Delphic nature, to be translated into concreteness by the process of litigating elucidation." International Assn. of Machinists v. Gonzales, 356 U.S. 617, 619 (1958). Do you gain any insights into the process by which law is made, legislatively and judicially, from consideration of congressional inaction in this field?

The problems of federalism and pre-emption have attracted much interest, and there are many excellent discussions to be found in the law reviews. Among them are Cox, Federalism in Labor Law, 67 Harv. L. Rev. 1297 (1954); Gregory, Constitutional Limitations on the Regulation of Union and Employer Conduct, 49 Mich. L. Rev. 191 (1950); McCoid, Notes on a "G" String: A Study of the "No Man's Land" of Labor Law, 44 Minn. L. Rev. 205 (1959); Meltzer, The Supreme Court, Congress and State Jurisdiction over Labor Relations, 59 Colum. L. Rev. 6, 269 (1959); Wollett, State Power to Regulate Labor Relations, 33 Wash. L. Rev. 364 (1958).

E. UNIT STABILITY

AMERICAN SEATING CO.
National Labor Relations Board, 1953
106 N.L.R.B. 250

On September 20, 1949, following an election, the Board certified International Union, United Automobile, Aircraft and Agricultural Implement Workers of America (UAW-CIO), and its Local No. 135, herein called the UAW-CIO, as bargaining representative of the Respondent's production and maintenance employees. On July 1, 1950, the Respondent and the UAW-CIO entered into a 3-year collective-bargaining contract covering all employees in the certified unit. Shortly before the expiration of 2 years from the date of signing of the contract, Pattern Makers'

Association of Grand Rapids, Pattern Makers' League of North America, AFL, herein called the Union, filed a representation petition seeking to sever a craft unit of patternmakers from the existing production and maintenance unit. Both the Respondent and the UAW-CIO opposed the petition, contending that their 3-year contract which would not expire until July 1, 1953, was a bar. In a decision issued on September 4, 1952, the Board rejected this contention. It held that, as the contract had already been in existence for 2 years, and as the contracting parties had failed to establish that contracts for 3-year terms were customary in the seating industry, the contract was not a bar during the third year of its term. Accordingly, the Board directed an election in a unit of patternmakers which the Union won.

On October 6, 1952, the Board certified the Union as bargaining representative of the Respondent's patternmakers. Approximately 10 days later, the Union submitted to the Respondent a proposed collective-bargaining agreement covering terms and conditions of employment for patternmakers to be effective immediately. The Respondent replied that it recognized the Union as bargaining representative of the patternmakers and that it was willing to negotiate or discuss subjects properly open for discussion, but that the existing contract with the UAW-CIO was still in full force and effect and remained binding upon all employees, including patternmakers, until its July 1, 1953, expiration date.

There is no question raised as to the Board's power to direct an election upon its finding that the existing contract between the UAW-CIO and the Respondent was not a bar. The parties differ, however, as to the effect to be given to the new certification resulting from this election. The Respondent contends that the certification of the Pattern Makers merely resulted in the substitution of a new bargaining representative for patternmakers in place of the old representative, with the substantive terms of the contract remaining unchanged.[3] In support of this position, the Respondent argues that the UAW-CIO was the agent of the patternmakers when it entered into the 1950 agreement with that organization, and that the patternmakers, as principals, are bound by that contract to the expiration date thereof, notwithstanding that they have changed their agent. The General Counsel, on the other hand, contends that the certification of the Pattern Makers resulted in making the existing contract with the UAW-CIO inoperative as to the employees in the unit of patternmakers.

The Respondent's principal agent argument assumes that common-law principles of agency control the relationship of exclusive bargaining representative to employees in an appropriate unit. We think that this assumption is unwarranted and overlooks the unique character of that relationship under the National Labor Relations Act.

Under the common law, agency is a consensual relationship. On the

[3] In its brief, the Respondent concedes that the procedural aspects of the existing contract grievance procedure, the number of union stewards, and union security might be required subjects of negotiation with the newly certified bargaining representative.

other hand, the status of exclusive bargaining representative is a special one created and governed by statute, "Representatives designated or selected for the purposes of collective bargaining by the majority of the employees in a unit appropriate for such purposes, shall be the exclusive representative of all the employees in such unit for the purposes of collective bargaining. . . ." A duly selected statutory representative is the representative of a shifting group of employees in an appropriate unit which includes not only those employees who approve such relationship, but also those who disapprove and those who have never had an opportunity to express their choice.[7] Under agency principles, a principal has the power to terminate the authority of his agent at any time. Not so in the case of a statutory bargaining representative. Thus, in its most important aspects the relationship of statutory bargaining representative to employees in an appropriate unit resembles a political rather than a private law relationship. In any event, because of the unique character of the statutory representative, a solution for the problem presented in this case must be sought in the light of that special relationship rather than by the device of pinning labels on the various parties involved and applying without change principles of law evolved to govern entirely different situations.

The National Labor Relations Act provides machinery for the selection and change of exclusive bargaining representatives. If, after the filing of a petition by employees, a labor organization, or an employer, and the holding of a hearing, the Board is convinced that a question of representation exists, it is directed by statute to conduct an election by secret ballot and certify the results thereof. The Act does not list the situations

---

[7] The nature of a statutory representative's constituency is well illustrated by the facts in this case. In the 1949 election to select a bargaining representative for the Respondent's production and maintenance employees, including patternmakers, there were three contending unions: the UAW-CIO, Upholsterers' International Union of North America, AFL, herein called the Upholsterers, and United Furniture Workers of America, CIO, herein called the Furniture Workers. At the first election, of approximately 1,488 eligible voters, 1,293 voted. Of these 569 voted for the UAW-CIO, 238 voted for the Upholsterers, 416 voted for the Furniture Workers, 65 voted against all participating labor organizations, 1 voted under challenge, and 4 cast void ballots. As this election was indecisive, a runoff election was held with only the Furniture Workers and the UAW-CIO on the ballot. In this second election, 594 employees voted for the Furniture Workers and 706 voted for the UAW-CIO. There were also 9 void ballots. As the UAW-CIO received a majority of valid votes cast in the runoff election, it was certified as bargaining representative of all employees in the plantwide unit. It is interesting to observe that before the runoff election was held, the Pattern Makers moved to intervene in order to urge that a separate unit of patternmakers be established. The motion was denied because the Pattern Makers' evidence of interest was procured after the original hearing. The United Boat Service Corporation, 55 N.L.R.B. 671. As the election was secret, it is not known how the handful of patternmakers voted. But the Respondent and the UAW-CIO, when they entered into their bargaining contract in 1950, must have been aware of the patternmakers' interest in their own craft union. It is also significant that this interest was sustained for the 2 years of representation by the UAW-CIO, as evidenced by the fact that in the election held in 1952, all the patternmakers voted for representation by the Pattern Makers.

in which a "question of representation affecting commerce exists." That has been left to the Board to decide. One of the problems in this connection arises from the claim that a collective-bargaining contract of fixed term should bar a new election during the entire term of such contract. In solving this problem, the Board has had to balance two separate interests: The interest of employees and society in the stability that is essential to the effective encouragement of collective bargaining, and the sometimes conflicting interest of employees in being free to change their representatives at will. Reconciling these two interests in the early days of the Act, the Board decided that it would not consider a contract of unreasonable duration a bar to an election to determine a new bargaining representative. The Board further decided that a contract of more than 1 year was of unreasonable duration and that it would direct an election after the first year of the existence of such a contract. In 1947, in the further interest of stability, the Board extended from 1 to 2 years the period during which a valid collective-bargaining contract would be considered a bar to a new determination of representatives. Contracts for periods longer than 2 years may be a bar, if such longer term contracts are customary in the industry, or as more recently stated, if "a substantial part of the industry is covered by contracts of a similar term."

These contract-bar rules have been affirmed many times and have become an established part of the law of labor relations. They received the approval of Congress when it amended the Act in 1947, and have been "as it were, written into the statute." Therefore, when the Respondent and the UAW-CIO entered into their 3-year bargaining contract in 1950, they were on notice that, after the first 2 years of its term, unless it could be shown that longer term contracts were customary in the industry, the contract would not prevent the selection of a new bargaining representative for any group of employees who might constitute an appropriate unit. Neither the Board nor the courts have decided, however, the effect of a new certification has upon an existing, collective-bargaining contract which has been held not a bar to a new determination of representatives because it is of unreasonable duration.

In 1952, the Board decided that the Respondent's patternmakers, who constitute one of the most skilled craft groups, might, after 2 years of experience as part of a plantwide unit of approximately 1,500 employees, if they so desired, constitute a separate appropriate unit. Apparently dissatisfied with their representation by the UAW-CIO, all six patternmakers voted for a separate unit to be represented by the Pattern Makers, which is the labor organization that traditionally represents patternmakers in industry. The Board thereupon certified the Pattern Makers as bargaining representative for those employees. Although the certification of October 6, 1952, gave the Pattern Makers immediate status as exclusive representative for the purposes of collective bargaining "in respect to rates of pay, wages, and hours of employment," the Respondent would qualify the Pattern Makers' authority as to these subjects by adding "after July 1, 1953." If the Respondent's contention is sound, a certified bargaining representative might be deprived of effective statutory power as to the most important subjects of collective bargaining for an unlimited number of years as the result of an agreement negotiated by an unwanted and repudiated bargaining representative. There is no provision in the statute for this kind of emasculated certified bargaining representative. Moreover, the rule urged by the Respondent seems hardly calculated to reduce "industrial strife" by encouraging the "practice and procedure of collective bargaining," the declared purpose of the National Labor Relations Act, as amended.

The purpose of the Board's rule holding a contract of unreasonable duration not a bar to a new determination of representatives is the democratic one of insuring to employees the right at reasonable intervals of reappraising and changing, if they so desire, their union representation. Bargaining representatives are thereby kept responsive to the needs and desires of their constituents; and employees dissatisfied with their representatives know that they will have the opportunity of changing them by peaceful means at an election conducted by an impartial Government agency. Strikes for a change of representatives are thereby reduced and the effects of employee dissatisfaction with their representatives are mitigated. But, if a newly chosen representative is to be hobbled in the way proposed by the Respondent, a great part of the benefit to be derived from the no-bar rule will be dissipated. There is little point in selecting a new bargaining representative which is unable to negotiate new terms and conditions of employment for an extended period of time.

We hold that, for the reasons which led the Board to adopt the rule that a contract of unreasonable duration is not a bar to a new determination of representatives, such contract may not bar full statutory collective bargaining, including the reduction to writing of any agreement reached, as to any group of employees in an appropriate unit covered by such contract, upon the certification of a new collective-bargaining representative for them. Accordingly, we find that by refusing on and after October 16, 1952, to bargain with the Pattern Makers concerning wages, hours, and other working conditions for employees in the unit of pattern makers, the Respondent violated Section 8(a)(5) and (1) of the Act.

BROOKS v. NLRB

Supreme Court of the United States, 1954
348 U.S. 96, 75 Sup. Ct. 176, 99 L. Ed. 125

Mr. Justice Frankfurter delivered the opinion of the Court.

The National Labor Relations Board conducted a representation election in petitioner's Chrysler-Plymouth agency on April 12, 1951. District Lodge No. 727, International Association of Machinists, won by a vote of eight to five, and the Labor Board certified it as the exclusive bargaining representative on April 20. A week after the election and the day before the certification petitioner received a handwritten letter signed by nine of the 13 employees in the bargaining unit stating: "We, the undersigned majority of the employees . . . are not in favor of being represented by Union Local No. 727 as a bargaining agent."

Relying on this letter and the decision of the Court of Appeals for the Sixth Circuit in Labor Board v. Vulcan Forging Co., 188 F.2d 927, petitioner refused to bargain with the union. The Labor Board found, 98 N.L.R.B. 976, that petitioner had thereby committed an unfair labor practice in violation of §§8(a)(1) and 8(a)(5) of the amended National Labor Relations Act, 61 Stat. 140-141, 29 U.S.C. §§158(a)(1), 8(a)(5), and the Court of Appeals for the Ninth Circuit enforced the Board's order to bargain, 204 F.2d 899. In view of the conflict between the Circuits, we granted certiorari, 347 U.S. 916.

The issue before us is the duty of an employer toward a duly certified bargaining agent if, shortly after the election which resulted in the certification, the union has lost, without the employer's fault, a majority of the employees from its membership.

Under the original Wagner Act, the Labor Board was given the power to certify a union as the exclusive representative of the employees in a bargaining unit when it had determined, by election or "any other suitable method," that the union commanded majority support. §9(c), 49 Stat. 453. In exercising this authority the Board evolved a number of working rules, of which the following are relevant to our purpose:

(a) A certification, if based on a Board-conducted election, must be honored for a "reasonable" period, ordinarily "one year," in the absence of "unusual circumstances."

(b) "Unusual circumstances" were found in at least three situations: (1) the certified union dissolved or became defunct; (2) as a result of a schism, substantially all the members and officers of the certified union transferred their affiliation to a new local or international; (3) the size of the bargaining unit fluctuated radically within a short time.

(c) Loss of majority support after the "reasonable" period could be questioned in two ways: (1) employer's refusal to bargain, or (2) petition by a rival union for a new election.

(d) If the initial election resulted in a majority for "no union," the election — unlike a certification — did not bar a second election within a year.

The Board uniformly found an unfair labor practice where, during the so-called "certification year," an employer refused to bargain on the ground that the certified union no longer possessed a majority. While the courts in the main enforced the Board's decisions, they did not commit themselves to one year as the determinate content of reasonableness. The Board and the courts proceeded along this line of reasoning:

(a) In the political and business spheres, the choice of the voters in an election binds them for a fixed time. This promotes a sense of responsibility in the electorate and needed coherence in administration. These considerations are equally relevant to healthy labor relations.

(b) Since an election is a solemn and costly occasion, conducted under safeguards to voluntary choice, revocation of authority should occur by a procedure no less solemn than that of the initial designation. A petition or a public meeting — in which those voting for and against unionism are disclosed to management, and in which the influences of mass psychology are present — is not comparable to the privacy and independence of the voting booth.

(c) A union should be given ample time for carrying out its mandate on behalf of its members, and should not be under exigent pressure to produce hothouse results or be turned out.

(d) It is scarcely conducive to bargaining in good faith for an employer to know that, if he dillydallies or subtly undermines, union strength may erode and thereby relieve him of his statutory duties at any time, while if he works conscientiously toward agreement, the rank and file may, at the last moment, repudiate their agent.

(e) In situations, not wholly rare, where unions are competing, raiding and strife will be minimized if elections are not at the hazard of informal and short-term recall.

Certain aspects of the Labor Board's representation procedures came under scrutiny in the Congress that enacted the Taft-Hartley Act in 1947, 61 Stat. 136. Congress was mindful that once employees had chosen a union they could not vote to revoke its authority and refrain from union activities, while if they voted against having a union in the first place, the union could begin at once to agitate for a new election. The National Labor Relations Act was amended to provide that (a) employees could petition the Board for a decertification election, at which they would have an opportunity to choose no longer to be represented by a union, 61 Stat. 144, 29 U.S.C. §159(c)(1)(A)(ii); (b) an employer, if in doubt as to the majority claimed by a union without formal election or beset by the conflicting claims of rival unions, could likewise petition the Board for an election, 61 Stat. 144, 29 U.S.C. §159(c)(1)(B); (c) after a valid certification or decertification election had been conducted, the Board could not hold a second election in the same bargaining unit until a year had elapsed, 61 Stat. 144, 29 U.S.C. §159(c)(3); (d) Board certification could only be granted as the result of an election, 61 Stat. 144, 29 U.S.C. §159-(c)(1), though an employer would presumably still be under a duty to bargain with an uncertified union that had a clear majority, see Labor Board v. Kobritz, 193 F.2d 8 (C.A. 1st Cir.).

The Board continued to apply its "one year certification" rule after the Taft-Hartley Act came into force, except that even "unusual circumstances" no longer left the Board free to order an election where one had taken place within the preceding 12 months. Conflicting views became manifest in the Courts of Appeals when the Board sought to enforce orders based on refusal to bargain in violation of its rule. Some Circuits sanctioned the Board's position. The Court of Appeals for the Sixth Circuit denied enforcement. The Court of Appeals for the Third Circuit held that a "reasonable" period depended on the facts of the particular case.

The issue is open here. No case touching the problem has directly presented it. In Franks Bros. Co. v. Labor Board, 321 U.S. 702, we held that where a union's majority was dissipated after an employer's unfair labor practice in refusing to bargain, the Board could appropriately find that such conduct had undermined the prestige of the union and require the employer to bargain with it for a reasonable period despite the loss of majority. And in Labor Board v. Mexia Textile Mills, Inc., 339 U.S. 563, we held that a claim of an intervening loss of majority was no defense to a proceeding for enforcement of an order to cease and desist from certain unfair labor practices.

Petitioner contends that whenever an employer is presented with evidence that his employees have deserted their certified union, he may forthwith refuse to bargain. In effect, he seeks to vindicate the rights of his employees to select their bargaining representative. If the employees are dissatisfied with their chosen union, they may submit their own grievance to the Board. If an employer has doubts about his duty to continue bargaining, it is his responsibility to petition the Board for relief, while continuing to bargain in good faith at least until the Board has given some indication that his claim has merit. Although the Board may, if the facts warrant, revoke a certification or agree not to pursue a charge of an unfair labor practice, these are matters for the Board; they do not justify employer self-help or judicial intervention. The underlying purpose of this statute is industrial peace. To allow employers to rely on employees' rights in refusing to bargain with the formally designated union is not conducive to that end, it is inimical to it. Congress has devised a formal mode for selection and rejection of bargaining agents and has fixed the spacing of elections, with a view of furthering industrial stability and with due regard to administrative prudence.

We find wanting the arguments against these controlling considerations. In placing a non-consenting minority under the bargaining responsibility of an agency selected by a majority of the workers, Congress has discarded common-law doctrines of agency. It is contended that since a bargaining agency may be ascertained by methods less formal than a supervised election, informal repudiation should also be sanctioned where decertification by another election is precluded. This is to make situations that are different appear the same. Finally, it is not within the power of this Court to require the Board, as is suggested, to relieve a small employer, like the one involved in this case, of the duty that may be exacted from an enterprise with many employees.

To be sure, what we have said has special pertinence only to the period during which a second election is impossible. But the Board's view that the one-year period should run from the date of certification rather than the date of election seems within the allowable area of the Board's discretion in carrying out congressional policy. See Phelps Dodge Corp. v. Labor Board, 313 U.S. 177, 192-197; Labor Board v. Seven-Up Bottling Co., 344 U.S. 344. Otherwise, encouragement would be given to management or a rival union to delay certification by spurious objections to the conduct of an election and thereby diminish the duration of the duty to bargain. Furthermore, the Board has ruled that one year after certification the employer can ask for an election or, if he has fair doubts about the union's continuing majority, he may refuse to bargain further with it. This, too, is a matter appropriately determined by the Board's administrative authority.

We conclude that the judgment of the Court of Appeals enforcing the Board's order must be affirmed.

COMMENT ON THE CONTRACT BAR DOCTRINE

As the decision in the American Seating Company case states, the NLRB had previously held in a representation proceeding that the existence of an unexpired collective bargaining agreement between the employer and the UAW did not constitute a basis for refusing to hold an election upon the petition filed by the Pattern Makers Association. The contract, which had been in effect for more than two years, was said not to be a bar to the election.

The set of rules under which the NLRB determines whether the existence of an unexpired collective bargaining agreement will, or will not, prevent the holding of an election upon the filing of an otherwise valid representation petition is commonly referred to as the Board's contract bar doctrine. This doctrine is one which the Board developed, without express statutory authority, under the Wagner Act and which it has continued to develop and modify since that time. The doctrine is not stated in the Board's Rules and Regulations, and its details and current status can be determined only by resort to the published Board decisions in representation cases.

The use of a contract bar doctrine first found legislative approval in the Senate-House Conference Report, H.R. Rep. No. 510 (Conference Report), 80th Cong., 1st Sess. (1947), on the Taft-Hartley amendments to the NLRA. (It was at this time that Congress enacted the related prohibition against holding elections in a bargaining unit within which a valid election had been held within the preceding twelve-month period. See Section 9(c)(3).) A more recent legislative approval of a contract bar doctrine may be found in the 1959 amendments, adding the prohibition found in Section 8(b)(7)(A) against organizational and recognitional picketing when the employer has recognized another union and a question of representation may not be raised under Section 9(c). See also the final proviso to Section 8(f), likewise added by the 1959 amendments.

The two major and conflicting policy considerations underlying the contract bar doctrine involve the weight to be given to preserving employee freedom of choice and the weight to be given to preserving the stability of an existing collective bargaining relationship. Other considerations exist. Thus, it is desirable to avoid the unsettling effects that organizational campaigns and pending elections have upon labor relations and actual production in a plant. Administrative convenience as well as speed in processing a caseload of more than 10,000 representation cases a year are served if the rules formulated are simple to apply and do not require extensive factual inquiries in the course of representation hearings.

The rules developed also influence the bargaining strategy of both employers and unions. Thus, while an employer might be willing to make substantial concessions in exchange for the stability and predictability that a four- or five-year contract would give, his willingness to do so will be decreased if he knows that a rival union, which would not be bound by that contract, might be certified and demand bargaining anew before the expiration of the contract term. A union will likewise be unwilling to commit itself to a long-term contract if it sees the possibility that, while it is bound by that contract, a rival might attempt a "raid," making promises of beneficial contract changes. A rival union seeking to replace an incumbent union, of course, times its organizational campaign so that it will be prepared to file a petition when the existing contract is no longer a bar.

Contracts to which the NLRB gives the effect of a bar to elections must be in writing and signed by the parties, they must contain substantial terms and conditions governing the employment relationship, they may not be limited to union members only, and they must cover employees in an appropriate bargaining unit. The union must be recognized as the exclusive bargaining agent for all employees in the unit. Appalachian Shale Products Co., 121 N.L.R.B. 1160 (1958). Contracts terminable at will and contracts of indefinite duration will not constitute bars to elections. Pacific Coast Assn. of Pulp & Paper Manufacturers, 121 N.L.R.B. 990 (1958).

The Board's policy with respect to illegal union security provisions has varied somewhat. At one time the Board held that contracts with union security clauses which were ambiguous or did not clearly comply with the NLRA requirements could nevertheless bar elections if reference to other documents, the practice of the parties, or other evidence established that the clause had not been applied in an illegal manner. O. B. Andrews Co., 86 N.L.R.B. 59 (1949); Humboldt Lumber Handlers Inc., 108 N.L.R.B. 393 (1954). In 1958, the Board changed this policy and held that an agreement would not constitute a bar if it contained a union security clause which did not on its face comply with the NLRA. Keystone Coat, Apron and Supply Co., 121 N.L.R.B. 880 (1958). In 1961, taking a cue from some expressions in a Supreme Court opinion and concluding that experience under the 1958 rule had not been satisfactory, the Board held that a union security clause will not prevent a contract from acting as a bar unless it is unlawful on its face. Paragon Products Corp., 134 N.L.R.B. 662 (1961). Such unlawful provisions include (1) those which expressly require the employer to give preference to union members in hiring, laying off, or seniority, (2) those which specifically withhold the thirty-day statutory grace period for incumbent nonmembers or new employees, and (3) those which expressly require as a condition of employment the payment of sums other than periodic dues and initiation fees uniformly required. Evidence relevant only to the practice of the parties under a contract urged as a bar will not be received in representation proceedings, but a contract with an ambiguous, though not clearly unlawful, union security clause will not bar an election if it has been determined to be illegal in an unfair labor practice proceeding.

On the other hand, the Board has held, overruling an earlier decision, that a collective bargaining agreement may operate as a bar even though it contains a "hot-cargo" clause in violation of Section 8(e). Food Haulers, Inc., 136 N.L.R.B. 394 (1962). The reasoning supporting the current policy is that a "hot-cargo" clause, unlike an illegal union security clause, does not act as a restraint on employee freedom of choice of a bargaining representative. Moreover, the Board thought that denial of effect as a bar would be a more drastic sanction than that provided in Section 8(e), which merely provides that a contract containing such a clause "shall be to such extent unenforcible and void." Since execution of contracts discriminating between employees on the basis of race would be basis for revoking the certification of a union, contracts containing such provisions will not operate as a bar. Pioneer Bus Co., 140 N.L.R.B. 54 (1962).

There have also been changes in the rule as to the length of time for which a contract for a fixed term may operate as a bar. Originally the Board held that contracts could operate as a bar for only one year, but in 1947 it decided to extend the period to two years. Reed Roller Bit Co., 72 N.L.R.B. 927 (1947). Subsequently, it was decided to allow a contract for a term longer than two years to operate as a bar if a substantial portion of the industry was covered by agreements of the same length. General Motors Corp., 102 N.L.R.B. 1140 (1953). In 1958, the Board reversed this policy, and held that a contract for a term in excess of two years could operate as a bar for only two years even though a substantial part of the industry was covered by contracts for a longer term. Pacific Coast Assn. of Pulp and Paper Manufacturers, 121 N.L.R.B. 990 (1958). In 1962, the Board decided to extend the period for which a contract can be a bar to rival union petitions to three years, though a contract for a longer term will bar petitions by either party to the contract for its full term. General Cable Corp., 139 N.L.R.B. 1123 (1962). In doing so, the Board noted a substantially unified stand on the part of management and labor favoring a longer period, the approval of a no-raiding code by the AFL-CIO, the adoption of the Landrum-Griffin Act providing union members with remedies for relief from undemocratic or corrupt union practices, and a continuing trend even after 1958 toward execution of agreements of terms longer than two years.

A contract will not operate as a bar if the union which is a party to the contract has become defunct. Hershey Chocolate Corp., 121 N.L.R.B. 901 (1958). The loss of all members in the union does not render a union defunct if the representative otherwise continues in existence and is willing and able to represent the employees in the unit. The Board may also find that a contract does not bar an election if there has been a schism in the union which is a party to the contract. A schism exists when action has been taken by employees in the bargaining unit, after notice and opportunity to vote, in the context of a basic intra-union conflict over policy at the highest level of an international union. The consequence of the employees' action must have been to create such confusion in the bargaining relationship that stability can be restored only by an election, such as is the case where an employer is faced with demands of two organizations, both claiming with some show of right to be the organization previously chosen by the employees. Hershey Chocolate

Corp., supra. A contract may also cease to be a bar if the work force expands so that the employees hired prior to execution of the contract constitute less than 30 per cent of the total employed or if the job classifications in existence when the contract was executed constitute less than half of the job classifications in effect at the time of the hearing. General Extrusion Co., 121 N.L.R.B. 1165 (1958).

An otherwise valid contract will bar a petition if it has been both executed and made effective, immediately or retroactively, before the filing of the petition. Such a contract will also bar a petition filed on the same day that the contract was executed if the employer has not been informed at the time of execution that a petition has been filed. In such cases the cut-off time is midnight, even though the contract is signed after midnight as the result of continuous bargaining. Deluxe Metal Furniture Co., 121 N.L.R.B. 995 (1958).

A petition filed more than ninety days before the terminal date of a contract valid as a bar will be regarded as premature and dismissed. Leonard Wholesale Meats, Inc., 136 N.L.R.B. 1000 (1962). The purpose of this rule is to limit the period of time during which the parties to the contract will be subject to the disruptions which accompany organizing campaigns. Likewise, a petition filed less than sixty-one days prior to the terminal date of such a contract will be dismissed upon the theory that the parties to the contract should have a sixty-day insulated period during which they may negotiate and execute a new or amended agreement without the intrusion of a rival petition. Leonard Wholesale Meats, Inc., supra; Deluxe Metal Furniture Co., supra. If the existing contract is of unreasonable duration — that is for a term longer than that during which a contract may serve as a bar — the insulated period for negotiation of a new agreement is the last sixty days of the reasonable period during which it serves as a bar. Deluxe Metal Furniture Co., supra. If a contract valid as a bar is prematurely extended by establishing a later termination date, it will not bar a petition filed more than sixty days but less than ninety days before the terminal date of the original contract. The rules governing premature extensions do not apply to contracts extended during the insulated period, after termination of the old contract, or at a time when the old contract would not have served as a bar. Leonard Wholesale Meats, Inc., supra; Deluxe Metal Furniture Co., supra. As with other aspects of the contract bar doctrine, the Board has made a number of changes with respect to the timeliness of filing of petitions, and the rules here stated are no more than the current rules.

As this summary indicates, the Board's contract bar doctrine consists of an intricate and detailed set of rules for determining whether an existing collective bargaining agreement precludes the holding of an election on a representation petition. Indeed, as resort to the Board decisions will reveal, the rules contain a number of intricacies not here stated. You may find it interesting, however, for an understanding of the administrative process, to consider whether draftsmen of the Wagner Act could have anticipated the problems involved in the contract bar doctrine. If you conclude that they could not have done so, do you think that now that the problems have been revealed by Board experience Congress should legislate on the subject? Or do you think that there is still much to be gained in leaving this part of law-making to the administrative process?

It is the Board's view that its contract bar policies are compelled neither by the NLRA nor by judicial decision, but are rather discretionary rules which may be applied or waived as the facts in a given case may require in the interests of effectuating the policies of the Act. Hershey Chocolate Corp., 121 N.L.R.B. 901 (1958).

The NLRB has consistently exercised its powers to change these rules through the adjudication of representation cases, giving its new rules a retroactive effect by making them applicable to all pending cases.[30] As mentioned above, an employer may have made substantial concessions to obtain the stability and predictability of a long-term contract only to find that, because of a change in the rules, he is under an obligation to bargain with a newly certified representative before the expiration of the contract. On the other side, a union may have made a considerable investment of finances and energy in an organizational campaign directed to the filing of a representation petition at the appropriate time only to find that, because of a change in the rules, an election cannot be had. Are you satisfied that these changes in rules should be made in the Board's discretion, uncompelled by judicial decision?

Whether or not one agrees with the NLRB's position, until quite recently it appeared that the Board had an exceptional freedom in changing the rules of the contract bar doctrine because of the limited judicial review applicable to representation cases. Direct review was considered to be precluded because of the statutory scheme for channeling all review of questions which arise in representation cases to the judicial review arising from an employer's refusal to bargain with a newly certified representative. American Federation of Labor v. NLRB, 308 U.S. 401 (1940); cf Switchmen's Union v. National Mediation Board, 320 U.S. 297 (1943) Inland Empire District Council v. Millis, 325 U.S. 697 (1945). This course of action is not open to a union defeated in an election, and thus provides no relief to a defeated incumbent union whose contract has been held not to constitute a bar. If the incumbent union wins the election, it continues to be the bargaining agent and the question becomes moot Thus only employers appeared to be in a position to challenge the Board on contract bar matters. Do you believe that this situation has been changed by the Supreme Court decision in Leedom v. Kyne, supra page 193? See Peck, The Atrophied Rule-Making Powers of the National Labor Relations Board, 70 Yale L.J. 729, 738-743 (1961).

---

[30] An exception was made in Leonard Wholesale Meats, Inc., 136 N.L.R.B. 1000 (1962), in which the Board reduced the period of time during which a petition might be filed prior to the termination date of a contract from 150 days to 90 days. The Board recognized that a retroactive application of the new rule to pending petitions could result in a detriment to parties who had acted in good-faith reliance upon the Board's former rules.

NOTE

Another rule affecting the timing of elections is known as the election bar and is found in Section 9(c)(3) of the Act. It provides: "No election shall be directed in any bargaining unit or any subdivision within which, in the preceding twelve month period, a valid election shall have been held."

The prohibition is applicable only if the election held was a valid election. For example, if the election has been set aside because of conduct of the parties improperly affecting the results, another election may be held even though less than twelve months have elapsed since the holding of the invalid election. See NLRB v. Capital Transit Co., 221 F.2d 864 (D.C. Cir. 1955). The twelve-month period runs from the date of balloting, and not from the date of certification of results. Mallinckrodt Chemical Works, 84 N.L.R.B. 291 (1949). Moreover, where applicable, the prohibition applies only to the holding of the election, so that a petition will be treated as timely if it is filed not more than sixty days prior to the anniversary date of an election in which no union was selected. Vickers, Inc., 124 N.L.R.B. 1051 (1959). A valid election held by a state agency is given the same effect as an election held by the NLRB itself. Olin Mathieson Chemical Corp., 115 N.L.R.B. 1501 (1956).

NLRB v. WEYERHAEUSER CO.

United States Court of Appeals, Seventh Circuit, 1960
276 F.2d 865

[In this case the Board had found Section 8(a)(5) and (1) violations when the employer refused to bargain with the Lithographers Union, which had been certified after a craft severance election.]

HASTINGS, Chief Judge. . . .

Respondent's final challenge to the enforcement of the Board's order is that the Board erred in refusing to consider the defense that Lithographers, in filing its representation petition, violated the "no-raiding" provision of the AFL-CIO constitution to which Lithographers and Paperworkers had subscribed.[3] . . .

The Board contends that respondent cannot now raise this issue since it was neither a party to nor a third party beneficiary of the no-raiding agreement. However, as we have pointed out, this issue was before the Board at every stage of this proceeding. The Board refused to consider or give effect to the alleged violation of the no-raiding agreement as a defense to the refusal to bargain. We think this refusal by the Board is

---

[3] Article III, Sec. 4 of the AFL-CIO Constitution provides that ". . . no affiliate shall raid the established collective bargaining relationship of any other affiliate." In addition it set up a procedure for settling and arbitrating disputes. Lithographers and Paperworkers subscribed to these provisions by approving and joining in the merger of the AFL and the CIO . . .

properly before us for review in this case and should not be rejected on technical procedural grounds.

The Board then argues, in the alternative, that it was not required to give controlling effect to the no-raiding agreement between the two unions in this case and that it properly directed an election to ascertain the desires of the lithographic employees here involved as to separate representation by Lithographers. This is consistent with its established policy against considering such agreements . . .

In United Textile Workers v. Textile Workers Union, 7 Cir., 1958, 258 F.2d 743, we held that Section 301 of the Labor Management Relations Act, 29 U.S.C.A. §185, provides a forum in a federal district court wherein an action may be brought by one of the union signatories to a private no-raiding agreement between unions to compel observance thereof by the other signatory. The complaining union sought equitable relief to enforce the findings of an impartial umpire appointed under the provisions of the AFL-CIO no-raiding agreement. The umpire found the agreement had been violated. This court affirmed an order of the district court directing the violating union to withdraw a representation petition from the Board. The Board had previously rejected the incumbent union's contention regarding the effect of the no-raiding agreement and had directed an election, but such election had not been held. Thereafter, the Board permitted withdrawal of the petition, but stated it did not acquiesce in this court's decision and that it would not, in the future, permit withdrawal unless the Board was made a party to court litigation so that it might express its views. Personal Products Corporation, 122 N.L.R.B. 563 (1958). Our holding in United Textile Workers gives effect to a contract right arising from a no-raiding agreement in a Section 301 proceeding in the district court. It makes apparent that proceedings before the Board and judicial review under Section 10(e) of the Act are no longer the exclusive channel for deciding representation questions. Cf. Leedom v. Kyne, 1958, 358 U.S. 184.

Unlike the situation in United Textile Workers, in the instant case there has been neither a decision by an umpire nor a suit brought in the district court under Section 301. We are concerned here with a judicial review under Section 10(e) of the Act. The Board correctly asserts that respondent and Paperworkers, by their offers of proof, were attempting to litigate the alleged no-raiding violation in a representation hearing and in the subsequent unfair practice hearing. The rights which arise under the AFL-CIO no-raiding agreement give unions a contractual immunity from organizational raids of competing unions. An established union which feels its rights have been violated has a forum in the district court under Section 301. In the case at bar it should be remembered that Lithographers chose to disaffiliate from AFL-CIO. There may be a serious question whether under these circumstances an alleged prior breach of the no-raiding agreement could now be made the subject of a Section 301 action or be asserted as a bar to the representation proceeding. Under the narrow factual situation before us, we hold that the Board did not err in adhering to its policy of refusing to consider an alleged violation of the no-raiding agreement.

The extent to which such inter-union no-raiding agreements shall encroach on the Board's established policy of disregarding them in representation hearings must be worked out in the future on a case-by-case basis. This is in harmony with the mandate of the Supreme Court in Textile Workers Union of America v. Lincoln Mills of Alabama, 1957, 353 U.S. 448.

We do not here give blanket approval to the Board's policy of refusing to recognize no-raiding agreements. The resolution of that broader problem calls into play the balancing of two beneficial, but conflicting, policy goals. The desire for stability in labor relations is in opposition to the right of freedom of choice in bargaining representation. There will also be the need for accommodating the statutory power of the courts to enforce contractual rights on the one hand with the jurisdiction vested in the Labor Board to determine questions as to representation on the other. These matters will be determined in appropriate cases.[31]

[31] For discussion of the general problem, see Aaron, Inter Union Representation Disputes and the NLRB, 36 Texas L. Rev. 846 (1958); Sovern, Section 301 and the Primary Jurisdiction of the NLRB, 76 Harv. L. Rev. 529, 568 (1963). — ED.

PART THREE

Collective Bargaining: Process
and Scope

Collective bargaining is a process for the *private* adjustment of questions and issues concerning the terms and conditions of employment. It must be remembered, however, that there exist, in addition, a substantial number of governmental programs which also impinge upon the employment relation, and that collective bargaining takes place within this framework. These public programs involve such varied subjects as control upon wages and hours, compensation for industrial injury, unemployment insurance, benefits upon retirement, and so forth. There are interrelationships between these public programs and privately negotiated benefits. And, indeed, important problems and policy issues arise for any industrial relations and collective bargaining system, both in the United States and abroad, in determining what matters are best left to private adjustment, and what areas should be subject to public control.

The materials that follow are designed to explore both the nature of the collective bargaining process and the legal framework which surrounds that process.

A. The Statutory Duty to Bargain

ENDERBY PROBLEM 8
(See page 343 supra for Enderby Problem 7)

The Enderby Company and Local 417 are engaged in negotiations over the terms of a new contract. The union, speaking through Curme, the chairman of its negotiating committee, makes the following demands:

1. An across-the-board wage increase of 25 cents an hour.

2. A union security clause which provides that every employee within the bargaining unit must, within thirty days after the agreement is signed (or, in the case of new employees, within thirty days after being hired), be a member of Local 417 in good standing as a condition of employment.

3. An agreement to expand operations of the Miscellaneous Division by (a) instituting production of rubber soles and heels for footwear and (b) ceasing production of all tile except acoustical tile and placing pro-

duction of acoustical tile on a ready-made rather than a made-to-order basis.

The union's last demand is based upon a market survey which was conducted for Local 417 by an independent firm of marketing analysts. According to Curme, who offers to show the report to the company, the survey indicates (a) that there is an increasing demand for light, flexible, all-weather shoes and (b) that none of the tiles produced by Enderby are competitive except its acoustical tile, that this is a superior product, and that Enderby can capture a substantial share of the market for acoustical tile by moving into mass production, coupled with a nationwide promotional campaign.

Curme argues that, by using the secret Enderby formula for fire hose, Enderby can produce rubber soles and heels that will be greatly superior to any competing product. He also argues that the proposed changes in production can be accomplished with very little capital investment and a minimum of employee retraining.

White, speaking for the company, makes the following counterproposals:

1. An across-the-board wage increase of 10 cents an hour.

2. Acceptance of the union's proposal on union security provided (a) that the contract contains a provision fixing initiation fees at $10 and monthly dues at $3, and (b) that Local 417 agrees to provide the company with copies of its constitution and bylaws, all amendments thereto, and periodic reports as to action taken on applications for membership and discipline of members.

3. Rejection of the proposal with respect to expansion of operations in the Miscellaneous Division and a demand that the introductory clause of the management rights provision of the contract be amended to read: "The company shall have sole and exclusive authority to exercise the normal and usual functions, duties, and responsibilities of management, such as scheduling production, including all decisions as to what is produced and how it is produced . . ."

Consider the following alternative situations in terms of the statutory duty of the company and the union to bargain collectively:

1. After fourteen meetings during a period of three weeks, the company and the union dispose of all matters at issue except No. 1. The company has offered 12 cents an hour, but the union is unwilling to accept less than 20 cents an hour. After three more meetings, at which there is no change in the position of either party, the company puts into effect a wage increase of 12 cents an hour.

2. The parties dispose of all matters at issue except No. 2. Local 417 says it will not sign an agreement that does not contain the union security provision it has proposed. The union refuses to discuss the provisos set forth in the company's counterproposal on the ground that they deal with matters that are exclusively union business. The company says it will not sign an agreement containing such a union-shop provision unless it includes those provisos.

3. The company and the union dispose of all matters at issue except

No. 3. The union, through Curme, indicates that it is willing, at least for the time being, to drop its demands with respect to the mass production of acoustical tile, but states that it cannot sign an agreement unless it contains some kind of company commitment either to produce or consider production of rubber soles and heels for footwear. White, speaking for the company, replies: "The question of who decides what this company is to produce and how it is to be produced is not a bargaining matter. Such decisions are part of management's right to manage. The company will not sign any agreement which does not make this clear."

4. Curme states that the union will accept an across-the-board wage increase of 15 cents an hour provided that the company will pay time and a half for all work performed on Saturday and double time for all work performed on Sunday. White says that this wage package is more than the company can afford to pay. Curme counters by asking White to permit a union-paid auditor to check the company's books.

(a) White flatly refuses for two reasons: (1) the company is not required to give the union a look at its books, and (2) other locals of the United Rubber Workers negotiate with Enderby's competitors, and the company is unwilling to run the risk that such confidential data may get into unfriendly hands.

(b) Suppose the company permits the union to inspect its books. The union, on the basis of information thus acquired, asserts that the company is hiding assets by depreciating capital investment at an inordinately high rate and argues that, if the rate of depreciation is set at a reasonable and realistic figure, the company can afford to grant the wage increase the union wants. The company refuses to discuss the matter.

5. The day after the bargaining session during which it becomes apparent that the company and the union are in sharp disagreement on the question of the company's ability to pay the wage increase demanded by the union, O'Doul, plant superintendent, reports to White at the end of the shift that the employees in both the Tire and Miscellaneous Divisions behaved strangely. Substantially all of them were ten minutes late returning from the morning rest period and twenty minutes late returning from lunch. Moreover, there were approximately thirty times more "answers to calls of nature" than is normal. The workers persist in this bizarre behavior for several days.

The company and the union finally settle their differences on the following basis:

1. An across-the-board wage increase of 14 cents an hour coupled with a provision permitting reopening of the contract on the question of "general wage rates," after specified notice and no sooner than one year after execution of the contract. See Article XV of contract in Reference Supplement.

2. Agreement to carry forward unchanged the management rights provision contained in the prior contract. See Article IX.

3. A voluntary checkoff, coupled with a union security provision

which provides that employees who are members of the union on a specified date or who become members after that date must maintain their membership as a condition of employment. See Article I.

4. A provision prohibiting strikes or lockouts. See Article III. (The union stoutly resisted agreement to a no-strike clause, but gave in, in order to get the checkoff and union security provisions described above, when the company agreed that the no-strike clause would be inapplicable to negotiations over general wage rates pursuant to the reopening provisions of the contract and agreed to a more comprehensive seniority clause than had been in the prior agreement.)

1.　*Refusal to Bargain in Good Faith*

NLRB v. REED & PRINCE MANUFACTURING CO.
United States Court of Appeals, First Circuit, 1953
205 F.2d 131, certiorari denied, 346 U.S. 887 (1953)

MAGRUDER, J.

In the petition now before us, the National Labor Relations Board asks us to enforce a Board order entered October 16, 1951, directing Reed & Prince Manufacturing Co., upon request, to bargain collectively with United Steelworkers of America, CIO, as the exclusive representative of all the production and maintenance employees of respondent at its plant at Worcester, Massachusetts. . . .

. . . [T]his is not a simple case where the employer has made a clear refusal to recognize or bargain with the certified representative of its employees. Rather, it is one where the employer engaged in a lengthy series of bargaining conferences, which got nowhere. In such a case the question is whether it is to be inferred from the totality of the employer's conduct that he went through the motions of negotiation as an elaborate pretense with no sincere desire to reach an agreement if possible, or that it bargained in good faith but was unable to arrive at an acceptable agreement with the union. Particularly in this area of mixed fact and law, a court will not lightly disregard the over-all appraisal of the situation by the Labor Board "as one of those agencies presumably equipped or informed by experience to deal with a specialized field of knowledge, whose findings within that field carry the authority of an expertness which courts do not possess and therefore must respect." Universal Camera Corp. v. N.L.R.B., 1951, 340 U.S. 474, 488. . . .

. . . [I]t seems clear that if the Board is not to be blinded by empty talk and by the mere surface motions of collective bargaining, it must take some cognizance of the reasonableness of the positions taken by an employer in the course of bargaining negotiations. See Wilson & Co., Inc. v. N.L.R.B., 8 Cir., 1940, 115 F.2d 759, 763. See also Smith, The Evolution of the "Duty to Bargain" Concept in American Law, 39 Mich. L. Rev. 1065, 1108 (1941). Thus if an employer can find nothing whatever to agree to in an ordinary current-day contract submitted to him, or in some of the union's related minor requests, and if the employer makes not a single serious proposal meeting the union at least part way, then certainly the Board must be able to conclude that this is at least some evidence of bad faith, that is, of a desire not to reach an agreement with the union. In other words, while the Board cannot force an employer to make a "concession" on any specific issue or to adopt any particular position, the employer is obliged to make *some* reasonable effort in *some* direction to compose his differences with the union, if §8(a)(5) is to be read as imposing any substantial obligation at all.

After an attentive examination of the entire record of the bargaining negotiations herein, we are definitely of the opinion that this is a case in which, under the standard laid down in Universal Camera Corp. v. N.L.R.B., supra, we should accept the ultimate finding of the Board that respondent did not participate in the bargaining negotiations with the good faith required of it by law.

As the outcome of a representation proceeding and a subsequent election held on July 12, 1950, the Board on July 20, 1950, certified United Steelworkers of America, CIO, as the exclusive bargaining representative of certain of respondent's employees. There was no dispute at that time, nor is there now, as to the appropriateness of the designated bargaining unit. On or about August 1 following, the chief negotiator for the Union called upon respondent's president with the request for a bargaining conference as soon as convenient. He was informed by the president that because of other commitments no definite date could be set at that time. On or about August 9 the Company sent word to the Union that it would be impossible to arrange a meeting before Labor Day in view of the fact that various members of the Company's negotiating committee were on vacation until that time. After Labor Day it was finally agreed that the initial bargaining session would be held on September 15. In its decision the Board questioned "whether the Respondent would have delayed, for such a relatively long period of time, negotiations for a business contract or a bank loan it was desirous of concluding." The Board went on to say that although "the Respondent's conduct in this respect, standing alone, might be deemed equivocal, appraising it in the context of the Respondent's whole course of conduct we conclude that it was another aspect of the Respondent's calculated effort to avoid reaching an agreement with the Union while preserving the appearance of bargaining."

Meanwhile, on or about August 9, the Union by telephone requested permission to post certain non-controversial notices on the Company bulletin boards. It was told that this request could not be granted at that time but that the matter should be brought up at the first meeting. By letter of August 9 the Union requested respondent to furnish it with wage rates and classifications and the age and length of service of all employees in the bargaining unit, "In order to enable the United Steelworkers of America to bargain intelligently" with the Company. Although the Union made several further requests for this data, the Company did not supply it in full until some time in October. Commenting upon this, the Board observed that "the Respondent's delay in supplying the requested data may be viewed legitimately as a significant part of its entire course of conduct in determining whether or not the Respondent has exercised good faith in its bargaining negotiations with the Union."

On September 15 the first meeting took place as scheduled. Apparently the Union wanted to begin the discussions on a broad base, exploring potential areas of agremeent and disagreement. The Company, however, insisted that the Union submit a written list of its contract proposals, which the Union immediately did.

Subsequently there were twelve further meetings between the parties running from the beginning of October through early in February, 1951. The first five of these conferences were devoted to a discussion of the suggested contract submitted by the Union. The principal Union proposals were (1) a substantial wage increase; (2) some form of union security, either a union shop or a maintenance of membership clause as an alternative; (3) a check-off provision; (4) a grievance procedure with arbitration as the ultimate resort; (5) six paid holidays annually; (6) a seniority provision; and (7) some form of insurance and pensions.

With respect to the matter of wages, the Company offered a general wage increase of ten cents per hour, with the express condition that if the offer were accepted there would be no further negotiations on this subject. The Union, having originally requested fifteen cents, or maybe more, was unwilling to accept the offer on these terms; however, it repeatedly stated that it would regard all the various economic benefits as a single "package," and hence might be able to agree to the ten-cent increase, once the Company's position was made known on certain other demands, e.g., pensions, insurance, and paid holidays.

The Company announced its general opposition on principle to any form of union security and to arbitration.

On the check-off proposal, the Company registered its opposition, mainly on the ground that this was not a proper subject of collective bargaining. In this the Company was mistaken. The Company added that in any event it could not accept a check-off provision because its administration would be too much of a bookkeeping burden. As the Board observed, an employer who takes the erroneous position that a particular subject matter is not bargainable "can hardly approach the discussion of this subject with an open mind and a willingness to reach an agreement."

As to the proposed grievance procedure, the Company took exception to the first step, providing that an employee complaining to his foreman be accompanied by the steward, and to the ultimate provision for arbitration. The Union manifested some willingness to yield on these matters, provided the other terms of the contract could be worked out. But when in response to the Company's request the Union submitted a more detailed proposal with reference to grievance procedure, the Company objected that this was too "complex." Apparently it did not point out any particulars in which the proposal might be simplified, though the

Union claimed that it had submitted a typical grievance clause which worked effectively at other plants.

The Company also rejected the Union's demand for six paid holidays, referring to its current practice of giving year-end bonuses. When the Union urged the Company as an alternative to commit itself in the contract to a continuance of this practice, the Company declined.

The seniority proposal submitted by the Union was found by the Company to be unacceptable in various items, for instance, in the provision allowing seniority to accumulate during absences not exceeding two years on account of lay-offs or disability. Subsequently the Company submitted its own seniority proposal, which was culled from the 1941 contract negotiated between respondent and the labor organization then representing its employees.

Finally, as to pensions and insurance, the Company listened to an exposition by a union expert, but expressed the view that these areas were sufficiently covered by Social Security and Blue Cross, to both of which the Company contributed. It added, however, that it would consider the Union proposals and would offer some of its own, which so far as we can discover the Company never did. The Union submitted certain fairly detailed written proposals on the subject of pensions and insurance; but respondent's vice president, testifying before the trial examiner, conceded on cross-examination that the Company's final position on insurance and pensions was never communicated to the Union.

In addition to the foregoing major issues, there were several lesser items brought into the discussion:

(1) At the first meeting the Union again raised the question of bulletin board space. The Company replied that while it could not comply with this request, it might be able to arrange for posting of Union notices on plant gates. Despite repeated requests by the Union, the Company never took definite action in this matter. The Board observed that the granting of such posting permission is a common industrial practice, and expressed the opinion "that the Respondent's handling of the bulletin board matter, taken in the context of this case, indicates the Respondent's basic unwillingness to accept the principle of collective bargaining and further strengthens our conclusion that the Respondent has not bargained in good faith."

(2) At the end of the recognition clause proposed by the Union, the Company wanted to insert the first proviso of §9(a) of the statute, recognizing the right of individual employees to present grievances directly to the employer. The Union agreed to this on the condition that there also be inserted in the recognition clause the second proviso in §9(a), "That the bargaining representative has been given opportunity to be present at such adjustment." The Company took this countersuggestion under advisement, but presumably ultimately rejected it, since the recognition clause in the proposed contract which the Company submitted to the Union on November 22 contained only the first proviso of §9(a). On this matter the Board stated: "We cannot conceive of a good faith basis for a refusal to incorporate a statutory obligation into a contract in

the very words of the statute. This type of quibbling conduct is consistent only with the conclusion that there was bad, not good, faith bargaining."

(3) The Union suggested a 40-hour workweek with time and one-half on Saturday. The Company was unwilling to accept the latter point, feeling that time and one-half should begin only after an employee had already worked 40 hours during the week. Subsequently the Union came up with a modified proposal to the effect that employees who, in following management schedules, were required to work on Saturday should be paid time and a half, but that time and a half would not apply where an employee had to work on Saturday because he had lost time for personal reasons during the regular workweek. The modified proposal, however, was not accepted by the Company.

(4) Another provision in the proposed Union contract related to leaves of absence to be granted to employees "with the consent of the Union and the Company." The Company squelched this proposal on the ground that it was not its practice to grant such leaves of absence. However, at the hearing before the trial examiner the Board introduced in evidence a Company "Book of Information for Employees" which included this sentence: "This [section relating to employee service credits] does not apply to cases where the Management has granted in writing permission for Leave of Absence."

(5) During the course of the negotiations the Union pointed out that at present employees who were on a piece-work basis received insufficient information to compute their incentive pay. The Union requested the Company so far as possible to supply each employee with a daily record of what he had done on that particular day similar to a method being used by other companies. Respondent rejected this suggestion, claiming that it was impossible for it to make these computations.

By October 31, since no agreement had been reached on even the most minor matters, both sides seemed to feel that the negotiations were at an impasse. Nevertheless, there were seven further meetings. On or about November 10 the Union submitted a final proposed contract which was complete except for a wage clause. On November 22 the Company, in turn, submitted its first and only proposed "contract," to which we shall make further reference subsequently. Neither of these documents served to bring the parties any closer to an agreement.

On December 4 respondent announced to its employees that a Christmas bonus would be paid to them "in recognition of their loyalty during the past year," with the expression of hope "that we shall be able to continue the payment for many years to come." On December 5 respondent posted a notice stating: "Based on certain decisions of the National Labor Relations Board, the Management is now permitted to put into effect immediately the 10¢ an hour increase previously offered to the factory employees in the National Labor Relations Board bargaining unit." This notice the Board regarded as another aspect of respondent's "lack of good faith in the bargaining negotiations with the Union." The Board also went on to add: "[We have] frequently had occasion to point out that the unilateral granting of a wage increase during the course of negotiations with the legally constituted bargaining representative . . . is a violation of the Act. Such action necessarily has the effect of undermining the representative status and prestige of the bargaining agent." While it was recognized that such a unilaterally announced wage increase might legally be made effective once the parties had reached, as a result of good faith bargaining, an impasse in the bargaining negotiations, it was the Board's view that the responsibility for the impasse here must be attributed to respondent's lack of good faith in the prior negotiations with the Union. It further found that "Respondent emphasized this bad faith by announcing the wage increase in such a way that the Union could not and did not in any way share the credit for it."

In the meantime the Union was becoming increasingly disturbed over what it called "the Company's bad faith" and the consequently decreasing likelihood of ever arriving at an agreement. On or about November 14 the Union reported to its membership that the Company was strongly against all the "basic provisions" suggested by the Union and that it appeared "that the Company is just stalling." Shortly thereafter the employees authorized a strike. At the December 27 meeting the Union advised the Company that there would be a strike at the plant effective January 2 "because they were not bargaining in good faith with the union." This strike was called, and was still in progress at the time of the hearing before the trial examiner. . . .

Subsequently the federal and the Massachusetts conciliation services — which had come to play an active part in the negotiations — made several further, but unsuccessful, efforts to get the parties together. The Company told the conciliators that the parties were still bargaining and that it thought more progress could be made by direct negotiations between the Union and the Company, even though at the same time the Company admitted, as indeed it had to in order to sustain the validity of its unilateral announcement on December 5 of a wage increase, that the parties had reached an impasse. The conciliators suggested arbitration of the principal issues of disagreement, which proposal was accepted by the Union but not replied to by the Company. They also proposed various compromises, which the Company refused.

Shortly after the beginning of the strike, the Company initiated several back-to-work efforts. In this it was aided by one Donald Pierce, a Company stock expediter, who was entrusted with a Company car to furnish transportation to returning strikers. One employee testified that Pierce urged him to return to work "because Alden Reed (respondent's treasurer) is never going to sign a contract with the union" and told him that respondent "would rather sell the plant than sign a contract with the union." The admission of this testimony was strenuously objected to by respondent, but since Pierce was acting for the Company in these back-to-work activities, it seems clear that on ordinary agency principles the testimony as to Pierce's remark, which was uncontradicted, was properly let in as an admission by the Company.

Before us, respondent has sought to ascribe the undoubted stalemate to an adamant insistence by the Union upon acceptance of the basic provisions of its standard contract, submitted on a take-it-or-leave-it basis. As evidence of this, respondent relies upon certain expressions in a leaflet circulated by the Union negotiating committee to the employees, purporting to describe the bargaining meeting of November 14. But an examination of the record of the lengthy negotiations between the Company and the Union indicates that the Union's bargaining efforts were marked by a considerable flexibility of approach, for the Union negotiator at many important points submitted modifications of its proposals in an effort to meet Company objections. It even appears that the Union might have been willing to accept a contract with no union security provision or arbitration clause in it if the other provisions could have been worked out acceptably.

The plain fact is that after months of negotiations, as the Board observed, "practically all the Union could report to its membership in the way of progress was the 10-cent wage offer — freely given by the Respondent in an inflationary period of rising wages." Even in minor matters, such as the Union's request for use of the Company bulletin board, and the Union's request that the second proviso of §9(a) of the Act be inserted in the recognition clause, the Company withheld assent. The Company's asserted justification for this is that it was "bargaining technique." But it may be wondered how the Company could in good faith ever expect to arrive at an agreement if the major proposals submitted by the Union are refused on principle and assent on the minor ones is withheld as a matter of bargaining technique.

In sustaining the Board's ultimate conclusion of lack of good faith, as deduced from the record as a whole and from the totality of respondent's conduct in its bargaining relations with the Union, we do not necessarily have to sustain the Board on each and every one of its subsidiary findings of fact. . . .

Nor do we have to agree with the Board as to each and every one of the incidents which it specially emphasized in its decision as indicating a lack of good faith on the Company's part in the conduct of the bargaining negotiations. For instance, we are not inclined to agree with the Board that the Company's insistence, over the Union's strenuous objection, on having a stenotypist present at all the bargaining meetings to take down a verbatim transcript of the proceedings was evidence of the Company's bad faith. On the other hand, we think that the Board might well have lifted out from the record another item for special comment, as indicative of bad faith on the Company's part. We refer to the fact that, after discussion at several meetings of the Union's various proposals of items to be included in the contract, the Company on November 22 submitted its own proposal of a so-called contract. This was a brief two-page document containing a recognition clause which paraphrased the first proviso of §9(a) of the Act but made no reference to the second proviso, and contained a provision as to hours of work substantially copied from its 1941 agreement, but had no provisions as to wages, grievance procedure, or the other major items which the Union had proposed for inclusion in the contract. It is difficult to believe that the Company with a straight face and in good faith could have supposed that this proposal had the slightest chance of acceptance by a self-respecting union, or even that it might advance the negotiations by affording a basis of discussion; rather, it looks more like a stalling tactic by a party bent upon maintaining the pretense of bargaining.

There may be cases where the ultimate finding of an administrative agency rests in part upon findings of subsidiary fact, or inferences therefrom, which a reviewing court deems insupportable, and where, because the court is in substantial doubt whether the administrative agency would have made the same ultimate finding with the erroneous findings or inferences removed from the picture, it may be appropriate for the court to remand the case to the administrative agency for further consideration. But in view of the record in its entirety, we are satisfied that this is not such a case. . . .

A decree will be entered enforcing the order of the Board.

NOTES

1. Cox, The Duty to Bargain in Good Faith, 71 Harv. L. Rev. 1401, 1114-1115 (1958), states:*

"In order to distinguish the real from the sham [the NLRB] established a subjective test making the employer's state of mind the decisive factor. So much is clear. The difficult problem is to identify the state of mind precisely. Such phrases as 'present intention to find a basis for agreement' and 'sincere effort to reach common ground' suggest that willingness to compromise is an essential ingredient of good faith. The inference becomes even stronger when the phrases are read against the background of the old National Labor Relations Board opinions which assert the duty 'to match their proposals, if unacceptable, with counter-proposals, and to make every reasonable effort to reach an agreement.' A man may wish to negotiate an agreement provided that his terms are met but be quite unwilling to compromise; or he may be so anxious to reach an agreement that he is willing to accept whatever terms he can get. Which state of mind — which of all the intermediate states of mind — is necessary to bargain 'in good faith'?"

Consider, in this connection, the analysis of the trial examiner, whose conclusions were adopted by the Board, in Hollywood Brands, Inc., 142 N.L.R.B. 304 (1963):

"From the entire record in this case it is crystal clear that the Respondent entered into negotiations for a new contract with a predetermination to renew the expiring contract in its exact terminology and language, and to make no deviation from that position whatever. Its attorney merely listened to proposals from the Union, and gave them no considera-

---

* This excerpt and the one on p. 446, infra, from the article by Prof. Archibald Cox, now Solicitor General of the United States, is reproduced with the permission of Mr. Cox and the Harvard Law Review. Copyright, ©, 1958, by the Harvard Law Review Association.

tion. Admittedly, his mind was closed to all proposals except his own initially made to renew the expired contract for 1 year under the exact terms and conditions provided therein. . . . Although Respondent recognized the Union as . . . bargaining representative in this case, it made not even a pretense of trying to reach an agreement of any kind. It merely took the unyielding position (not a bargaining position) that the old contract was the only thing it would enter into in the nature of a collective-bargaining agreement. By adopting such a position, I find that the Respondent refused to bargain in good faith with the certified exclusive representative of its employees in violation of Section 8(a)(5) of the Act."

Has the trial examiner correctly answered the question put by Cox? Compare the following floor statement of Senator Ellender, in support of the then-pending amendments to the Act defining the duty to bargain and imposing that duty on unions as well as employers:

"[T]he employees are not compelled to bargain collectively. In some cases, some of them frustrate the duty to bargain collectively, by delivering an ultimatum on a 'take it or leave it' basis. . . . I am sure that Senators remember the steel strike which occurred in 1946, when Mr. Murray gave notice that he would demand that every steel company grant his union a 30- and 40-cent wage increase. Mr. Murray succeeded in getting the United States Steel Co. and the Bethlehem Steel Co. to sign a contract; but after he got those two large concerns to sign a contract, he said, 'We are not going to go back to work now until we get all of the companies to sign a contract.' How did they bargain, Mr. President?

"They simply said, in effect, 'Here is a contract. We want so much pay an hour. We want you to do this, that, and the other. Sign here on the dotted line.' No effort was made to bargain with the smaller companies. . . .

"The same situation existed with respect to General Motors, when the president of the Union dealing with it, Mr. Reuther, presented to General Motors the proposition, 'We want a 30-cent increase in wages, and we will not take "No" for an answer. . . .' That attitude was assumed throughout the collective-bargaining period.

"I say to my colleagues that such action is not collective bargaining. In order to remedy this situation, the pending bill provides that both parties must bargain in good faith. . . ." 93 Cong. Rec. 4135 (Apr. 28, 1947). Did the Senator accurately describe the statute he was voting for? Compare the General Electric case, infra page 423.

2. A union had been recognized by an employer, without a Board election, in an agreement expiring June 1. On June 2, the employer filed a petition for an election, but expressed a willingness to continue to meet with the union in bargaining sessions over renewal of the agreement. When the employer refused to withdraw the petition, the union called a strike. The strikers were replaced, and the strike failed. The strikers sought their jobs back, claiming the status of unfair labor practice strikers entitled to reinstatement on request, on the ground the strike was

caused by an unlawful refusal to bargain. Assume that the NLRB finds that the employer did not doubt that the union had majority support when it filed the petition and when it refused to withdraw it. What result? Cf. Shelly & Anderson Manufacturing Co., Inc., 130 N.L.R.B. 744 (1961).

NLRB v. INSURANCE AGENTS' INTERNATIONAL UNION, AFL-CIO

Supreme Court of the United States, 1960
361 U.S. 477, 80 Sup. Ct. 419, 4 L. Ed. 2d 454

MR. JUSTICE BRENNAN delivered the opinion of the Court.

This case presents an important issue of the scope of the National Labor Relations Board's authority under §8(b)(3) of the National Labor Relations Act, which provides that "It shall be an unfair labor practice for a labor organization or its agents . . . to refuse to bargain collectively with an employer, provided it is the representative of his employees. . . ." The precise question is whether the Board may find that a union, which confers with an employer with the desire of reaching agreement on contract terms, has nevertheless refused to bargain collectively, thus violating that provision, solely and simply because during the negotiations it seeks to put economic pressure on the employer to yield to its bargaining demands by sponsoring on-the-job conduct designed to interfere with the carrying on of the employer's business.

Since 1949 the respondent Insurance Agents' International Union and the Prudential Insurance Company of America have negotiated collective bargaining agreements covering district agents employed by Prudential in 35 States and the District of Columbia. The principal duties of a Prudential district agent are to collect premiums and to solicit new business in an assigned locality known in the trade as his "debit." He has no fixed or regular working hours except that he must report at his district office two mornings a week and remain for two or three hours to deposit his collections, prepare and submit reports, and attend meetings to receive sales and other instructions. He is paid commissions on collections made and on new policies written; his only fixed compensation is a weekly payment of $4.50 intended primarily to cover his expenses.

In January 1956 Prudential and the union began the negotiation of a new contract to replace an agreement expiring in the following March. Bargaining was carried on continuously for six months before the terms of the new contract were agreed upon on July 17, 1956. It is not questioned that, if it stood alone, the record of negotiations would establish that the union conferred in good faith for the purpose and with the desire of reaching agreement with Prudential on a contract.

However, in April 1956, Prudential filed a §8(b)(3) charge of refusal to bargain collectively against the union. The charge was based upon actions of the union and its members outside the conference room, occurring after the old contract expired in March. The union had announced in February that if agreement on the terms of the new contract was not reached when the old contract expired, the union members would then participate in a "Work-Without-Contract" program — which meant that they would engage in certain planned, concerted on-the-job activities designed to harass the company.

A complaint of violation of §8(b)(3) issued on the charge and hearings began before the bargaining was concluded. It was developed in the evidence that the union's harassing tactics involved activities by the member agents such as these: refusal for a time to solicit new business, and refusal (after the writing of new business was resumed) to comply with the company's reporting procedures; refusal to participate in the company's "May Policyholders' Month Campaign"; reporting late at district offices the days the agents were scheduled to attend them, and refusing to perform customary duties at the offices, instead engaging there in "sit-in-mornings," "doing what comes naturally" and leaving at noon as a group; absenting themselves from special business conferences arranged by the company; picketing and distributing leaflets outside the various offices of the company on specified days and hours as directed by the union; distributing leaflets each day to policyholders and others and soliciting policyholders' signatures on petitions directed to the company; and presenting the signed policyholders' petitions to the company at its home office while simultaneously engaging in mass demonstrations there. . . .

[T]he Board . . . entered a cease-and-desist order. 119 N.L.R.B. 768. The Court of Appeals for the District of Columbia Circuit . . . set aside the Board's order. 260 F.2d 736. We granted the Board's petition for certiorari to review the important question presented. 358 U.S. 944.

The hearing examiner found that there was nothing in the record, apart from the mentioned activities of the union during the negotiations, that could be relied upon to support an inference that the union had not fulfilled its statutory duty; in fact nothing else was relied upon by the Board's General Counsel in prosecuting the complaint. The hearing examiner's analysis of the congressional design in enacting the statutory duty to bargain led him to conclude that the Board was not authorized to find that such economically harassing activities constituted a §8(b)(3) violation. The Board's opinion answers flatly "We do not agree" and proceeds to say ". . . the Respondent's reliance upon harassing tactics during the course of negotiations for the avowed purpose of compelling the Company to capitulate to its terms is the antithesis of reasoned discussion it was duty-bound to follow. Indeed, it clearly revealed an unwillingness to submit its demands to the consideration of the bargaining table where argument, persuasion, and the free interchange of views could take place. In such circumstances, the fact that the Respondent continued to confer with the Company and was desirous of concluding an agreement does not *alone* establish that it fulfilled its obligation to bargain in good faith. . . ." 119 N.L.R.B., at 769, 770-771. Thus the Board's view is that irrespective of the union's good faith in conferring with the employer at the bargaining table for the purpose and with the desire of reaching agreement on contract terms, its tactics during the course of the negotiations constituted per se a violation of §8 (b)(3). Accordingly, as is said in the Board's brief, "The issue here . . . comes down to whether the Board is authorized under the Act to hold that such tactics, which the Act does not specifically forbid but Section 7 does not protect, support a finding of a failure to bargain in good faith as required by Section 8(b)(3)." . . .

. . . Obviously there is tension between the principle that the parties need not contract on any specific terms and a practical enforcement of the principle that they are bound to deal with each other in a serious attempt to resolve differences and reach a common ground. And in fact criticism of the Board's application of the "good-faith" test arose from the belief that it was forcing employers to yield to union demands if they were to avoid a successful charge of unfair labor practice. Thus, in 1947 in Congress the fear was expressed that the Board had "gone very far, in the guise of determining whether or not employers had bargained in good faith, in setting itself up as the judge of what concessions an employer must make and of the proposals and counter proposals that he may or may not make." H.R. Rep. No. 245, 80th Cong., 1st Sess., p. 19. Since the Board was not viewed by Congress as an agency which should exercise its powers to arbitrate the parties' substantive solutions of the issues in their bargaining, a check on this apprehended trend was provided by writing the good-faith test of bargaining into §8(d) of the Taft-Hartley Act. . . .

The same problems as to whether positions taken at the bargaining table violate the good-faith test continue to arise under the Act as amended. See Labor Board v. Truitt Mfg. Co., 351 U.S. 149; Labor Board v. Borg-Warner Corp., 356 U.S. 342, 349. But it remains clear that §8(d) was an attempt by Congress to prevent the Board from controlling the settling of the terms of collective bargaining agreements. Labor Board v. American National Ins. Co., 343 U.S. 395, 404.

. . . At the same time as it was statutorily defining the duty to bargain collectively, Congress, by adding §8(b)(3) of the Act through the Taft-Hartley amendments, imposed that duty on labor organizations. Unions obviously are formed for the very purpose of bargaining collectively; but the legislative history makes it plain that Congress was wary of the position of some unions, and wanted to ensure that they would approach the bargaining table with the same attitude of willingness to reach an agreement as had been enjoined on management earlier. It intended to prevent employee representatives from putting forth the same "take it or leave it" attitude that had been condemned in management. 93 Cong. Rec. 4135, 4363, 5005. . . .

We believe that the Board's approach in this case — unless it can be defended, in terms of §8(b)(3), as resting on some unique character of the union tactics involved here — must be taken as proceeding from an erroneous view of collective bargaining. It must be realized that collective bargaining, under a system where the Government does not attempt to control the results of negotiations, cannot be equated with an academic collective search for truth — or even with what might be thought to be the ideal of one. The parties — even granting the modification of views that may come from a realization of economic interdependence — still proceed from contrary, and to an extent antagonistic viewpoints and concepts of self-interest. The system has not reached the ideal of the philosophic notion that perfect understanding among people would lead to perfect agreement among them on values. The presence of economic weapons in reserve, and their actual exercise on occasion by the parties, is part and parcel of the system that the Wagner and Taft-Hartley Acts have recognized. Abstract logical analysis might find inconsistency between the command of the statute to negotiate toward an agreement in good faith and the legitimacy of the use of economic weapons, frequently having the most serious effect upon individual workers and productive enterprises, to induce one party to come to the terms desired by the other. But the truth of the matter is that at the present statutory stage of our national labor relations policy, the two factors — necessity for good-faith bargaining between parties, and the availability of economic pressure devices to each to make the other party incline to agree on one's terms — exist side by side. One writer recognizes this by describing economic force as "a prime motive power for agreements in free collective bargaining." Doubtless one factor influences the other; there may be less need to apply economic pressure if the areas of controversy have been defined through discussion; and at the same time, negotiation positions are apt to be weak or strong in accordance with the degree of economic power the parties possess. . . .

. . . [W]e think the Board's approach involves an intrusion into the substantive aspects of the bargaining process — again, unless there is some specific warrant for its condemnation of the precise tactics involved here. The scope of §8(b)(3) and the limitations on Board power which were the design of §8(d) are exceeded, we hold, by inferring a lack of good faith not from any deficiencies of the union's performance at the bargaining table by reason of its attempted use of economic pressure, but solely and simply because tactics designed to exert economic pressure were employed during the course of the good faith negotiations. Thus the Board in the guise of determining good or bad faith in negotiations could regulate what economic weapons a party might summon to its aid. And if the Board could regulate the choice of economic weapons that may be used as part of collective bargaining, it would be in a position to exercise considerable influence upon the substantive terms on which the parties contract. As the parties' own devices became more limited, the Government might have to enter even more directly into the negotiation of collective agreements. Our labor policy is not presently erected on a foundation of government control of the results of negotiations. See S. Rep. No. 105, 80th Cong., 1st Sess., p. 2. Nor does it contain a charter for the National Labor Relations Board to act at large in equalizing disparities of bargaining power between employer and union.

. . . The use of economic pressure, as we have indicated, is of itself not at all inconsistent with the duty of bargaining in good faith. But in three cases in recent years, the Board has assumed the power to label particular union economic weapons inconsistent with that duty. See the Personal Products case,[15] . . . (Textile Workers Union), 108 N.L.R.B. 743, set aside, 227 F.2d 409; the Boone County case, United Mine Workers, 117 N.L.R.B. 1095, set aside, 257 F.2d 211; and the present case. The Board freely (and we think correctly) conceded here that a "total" strike called by the union would not have subjected it to sanctions under §8(b)(3), at least if it were called after the old contract, with its no-strike clause, had expired. Cf. United Mine Workers, supra. The Board's opinion in the instant case is not so unequivocal as this concession (and therefore perhaps more logical). But in the light of it and the principles we have enunciated, we must evaluate the claim of the Board to power, under §8(b)(3), to distinguish among various economic pressure tactics and brand the ones at bar inconsistent with good-faith collective bargaining. We conclude its claim is without foundation.

(a) The Board contends that the distinction between a total strike and the conduct at bar is that a total strike is a concerted activity protected against employer interference by §§7 and 8(a)(1) of the Act, while the activity at bar is not a protected concerted activity. We may agree, arguendo, with the Board that this Court's decision in the Briggs-Stratton case, Automobile Workers v. Wisconsin Board, 336 U.S. 245, establishes that the employee conduct here was not a protected concerted activity. On this assumption the employer could have discharged or taken other appropriate disciplinary action against the employees participating in these "slow-down," "sit-in," and arguably unprotected disloyal tactics. See Labor Board v. Fansteel Metallurgical Corp., 306 U.S. 240; Labor Board v. Electrical Workers, 346 U.S. 464. But surely that a union activity is not protected against disciplinary action does not mean that it constitutes a refusal to bargain in good faith. The reason why the ordinary economic strike is not evidence of a failure to bargain in good faith is not that it constitutes a protected activity but that, as we have developed, there is simply no inconsistency between the application of economic pressure and good-faith collective bargaining. The Board suggests that since (on the assumption we make) the union members' activities here were unprotected, and they could have been discharged, the activities should also be deemed unfair labor practices, since thus the remedy of a cease-and-desist order, milder than mass discharges of personnel and less disruptive of commerce, would be available. The argument is not persuasive. There is little logic in assuming that because Congress was willing to allow employers to use self-help against union tactics, if they were willing to face the economic consequences of its use, it also impliedly declared these tactics unlawful as a matter of federal law. Our problem remains that of construing §8(b)(3)'s terms, and we

[15] The facts in Personal Products did, in the Board's view, present the case of a union which was using economic pressure against an employer in a bargaining situation without identifying what its bargaining demands were — a matter which can be viewed quite differently in terms of a §8(b)(3) violation from the present case. . . . The Board's decision in Personal Products may have turned on this to some extent, see 108 N.L.R.B., at 746; but its decision in the instant case seems to view Personal Products as turning on the same point as does the present case.

do not see how the availability of self-help to the employer has anything to do with the matter.

(b) The Board contends that because an orthodox "total" strike is "traditional" its use must be taken as being consistent with §8(b)(3); but since the tactics here are not "traditional" or "normal," they need not be so viewed. Further, the Board cites what it conceives to be the public's moral condemnation of the sort of employee tactics involved here. But again we cannot see how these distinctions can be made under a statute which simply enjoins a duty to bargain in good faith. Again, these are relevant arguments when the question is the scope of the concerted activities given affirmative protection by the Act. But as we have developed, the use of economic pressure by the parties to a labor dispute is not a grudging exception to some policy of completely academic discussion enjoined by the Act; it is part and parcel of the process of collective bargaining. On this basis, we fail to see the relevance of whether the practice in question is time-honored or whether its exercise is generally supported by public opinion. It may be that the tactics used here deserve condemnation, but this would not justify attempting to pour that condemnation into a vessel not designed to hold it. The same may be said for the Board's contention that these activities, as opposed to a "normal" strike, are inconsistent with §8(b)(3) because they offer maximum pressure on the employer at minimum economic cost to the union. One may doubt whether this was so here, but the matter does not turn on that. Surely it cannot be said that the only economic weapons consistent with good-faith bargaining are those which minimize the pressure on the other party or maximize the disadvantage to the party using them. The catalog of union and employer weapons that might thus fall under ban would be most extensive.[28]

. . . These distinctions essayed by the Board here, and the lack of relationship to the statutory standard inherent in them, confirm us in our conclusion that the judgment of the Court of Appeals, setting aside the order of the Board, must be affirmed. For they make clear to us that when the Board moves in this area, with only §8(b)(3) for support, it is functioning as an arbiter of the sort of economic weapons the parties can

---

[28] There is a suggestion in the Board's opinion that it regarded the union tactics as a unilateral setting of the terms and conditions of employment and hence also on this basis violative of §8(b)(3), just as an employer's unilateral setting of employment terms during collective bargaining may amount to a breach of its duty to bargain collectively. Labor Board v. Crompton-Highland Mills, Inc., 337 U.S. 217. See 119 N.L.R.B., at 772. Prudential, as amicus curiae here, renews this point though the Board does not make it here. It seems baseless to us. There was no indication that the practices that the union was engaging in were designed to be permanent conditions of work. They were rather means to another end. The question whether union conduct could be treated, analogously to employer conduct, as unilaterally establishing working conditions, in a manner violative of the duty to bargain collectively, might be raised for example by the case of a union, anxious to secure a reduction of the working day from eight to seven hours, which instructed its members, during the negotiation process, to quit work an hour early daily. Cf. Note, 71 Harv. L. Rev. 502, 509. But this situation is not presented here, and we leave the question open.

use in seeking to gain acceptance of their bargaining demands. It has sought to introduce some standard of properly "balanced" bargaining power, or some new distinction of justifiable and unjustifiable, proper and "abusive" economic weapons into the collective bargaining duty imposed by the Act. The Board's assertion of power under §8(b)(3) allows it to sit in judgment upon every economic weapon the parties to a labor contract negotiation employ, judging it on the very general standard of that section, not drafted with reference to specific forms of economic pressure. We have expressed our belief that this amounts to the Board's entrance into the substantive aspects of the bargaining process to an extent Congress has not countenanced. . . .

. . . Where Congress has in the statute given the Board a question to answer, the courts will give respect to that answer; but they must be sure the question has been asked. We see no indication here that Congress has put it to the Board to define through its processes what economic sanctions might be permitted negotiating parties in an "ideal" or "balanced" state of collective bargaining.

It is suggested here that the time has come for a re-evaluation of the basic content of collective bargaining as contemplated by the federal legislation. But that is for Congress. Congress has demonstrated its capacity to adjust the Nation's labor legislation to what, in its legislative judgment, constitutes the statutory pattern appropriate to the developing state of labor relations in the country. Major revisions of the basic statute were enacted in 1947 and 1959. To be sure, then, Congress might be of opinion that greater stress should be put on the role of "pure" negotiation in settling labor disputes, to the extent of eliminating more and more economic weapons from the parties' grasp, and perhaps it might start with the ones involved here; or in consideration of the alternatives, it might shrink from such an undertaking. But Congress' policy has not yet moved to this point, and with only §8(b)(3) to lean on, we do not see how the Board can do so on its own.

Affirmed.

Separate opinion of MR. JUSTICE FRANKFURTER, which MR. JUSTICE HARLAN and MR. JUSTICE WHITTAKER join.

The sweep of the Court's opinion, with its far-reaching implications in a domain of lawmaking of such nationwide importance as that of legal control of collective bargaining, compels a separate statement of my views. . . .

The record presents two different grounds for the Board's action in this case. The Board's own opinion proceeds in terms of an examination of respondent's conduct as it bears upon the genuineness of its bargaining in the negotiation proceedings. From the respondent's conduct the Board drew the inference that respondent's state of mind was inimical to reaching an agreement, and that inference alone supported its conclusion of a refusal to bargain. The Board's position in this Court proceeded in terms of the relation of conduct such as respondent's to the kind of bargaining required by the statute, without regard to the bearing of such conduct on the proof of good faith revealed by the actual bargaining. The Board maintained that it "could appropriately determine that the basic statutory purpose of promoting industrial peace through the collective bargaining process would be defeated by sanctioning resort to this form of industrial warfare as a collective bargaining technique."

The opinion of this Court, like that of the Court of Appeals, disposes of both questions by a single broad stroke. It concludes that conduct designed to exert pressure on the bargaining situation with the aim of achieving favorable results is to be deemed entirely consistent with the duty to bargain in good faith. No evidentiary significance, not even an inference of a lack of good faith, is allowed to be drawn from the conduct in question as part of a total context.

I agree that the position taken by the Board here is not tenable. In enforcing the duty to bargain the Board must find the ultimate fact whether, in the case before it and in the context of all its circumstances, the respondent has engaged in bargaining without the sincere desire to reach agreement which the Act commands. I further agree that the Board's action in this case is not sustainable as resting upon a determination that respondent's apparent bargaining was in fact a sham, because the evidence is insufficient to justify that conclusion even giving the Board, as we must, every benefit of its right to draw on its experience in interpreting the industrial significance of the facts of a record. See Universal Camera Corp. v. Labor Board, 340 U.S. 474. What the Board has in fact done is lay down a rule of law that such conduct as was involved in carrying out the "Work Without a Contract" program necessarily betokens bad faith in the negotiations.

The Court's opinion rests its conclusion on the generalization that "the ordinary economic strike is not evidence of a failure to bargain in good faith . . . because . . . there is simply no inconsistency between the application of economic pressure and good-faith collective bargaining." This large statement is justified solely by reference to §8(b)(3) and to the proposition that inherent in bargaining is room for the play of forces which reveal the strength of one party, or the weakness of the other, in the economic context in which they seek agreement. But in determining the state of mind of a party to collective bargaining negotiations the Board does not deal in terms of abstract "economic pressure." It must proceed in terms of specific conduct which it weighs as a more or less reliable manifestation of the state of mind with which bargaining is conducted. . . .

Moreover, conduct designed to exert and exerting "economic pressure" may not have the shelter of §8(b)(3) even in isolation. Unlawful violence, whether to person or livelihood, to secure acceptance of an offer, is as much a withdrawal of included statutory subjects from bargaining as the "take it or leave it" attitude which the statute clearly condemns. One need not romanticize the community of interest between employers and employees, or be unmindful of the conflict between them, to recognize that utilization of what in one set of circumstances may only signify resort to the traditional weapons of labor may in another and relevant context offend the attitude toward bargaining commanded by the statute. Section 8(b)(3) is not a specific direction, but an expression of a governing viewpoint or policy to which, by the process of specific application, the Board and the courts must give concrete, not doctrinaire content. . . .

. . . For the Court to fashion the rules governing collective bargaining on the assumption that the power and position of labor unions and their solidarity are what they were twenty-five years ago, is to fashion law on the basis of unreality. Accretion of power may carry with it increasing responsibility for the manner of its exercise.

Therefore, in the unfolding of law in this field it should not be the inexorable premise that the process of collective bargaining is by its nature a bellicose process. The broadly phrased terms of the Taft-Hartley Act should be applied to carry out the broadly conceived policies of the Act. At the core of the promotion of collective bargaining, which was the chief means by which the great social purposes of the National Labor Relations Act were sought to be furthered, is a purpose to discourage, more and more, industrial combatants from pressing their demands by all available means to the limits of the justification of self-interest. This calls for appropriate judicial construction of existing legislation. The statute lays its emphasis upon reason and a willingness to employ it as the dominant force in bargaining. That emphasis is respected by declining to take as a postulate of the duty to bargain that the legally impermissible exertions of so-called economic pressure must be restricted to the crudities of brute force. Cf. Labor Board v. Fansteel Metallurgical Corp., 306 U.S. 240.

However, it of course does not follow because the Board may find in tactics short of violence evidence that a party means not to bargain in good faith that every such finding must be sustained. Section 8(b)(3) itself as previously construed by the Board and this Court and as amplified by §8(d), provides a substantial limitation on the Board's becoming, as the Court fears, merely "the arbiter of the sort of economic weapons the parties can use to gain acceptance of their bargaining demands." The Board's function in the enforcement of the duty to bargain does not end when it has properly drawn an inference unfavorable to the respondent from particular conduct. It must weigh that inference as part of the totality of inferences which may appropriately be drawn from the entire conduct of the respondent, particularly its conduct at the bargaining table. The state of mind with which the party charged with a refusal to bargain entered into and participated in the bargaining process is the ultimate issue upon which alone the Board must act in each case, and on the sufficiency of the whole record to justify its decision the courts must pass. Labor Board v. American National Ins. Co., 343 U.S. 395. . . .

Moreover, in undertaking to fashion the law of collective bargaining in this case in accordance with the command of §8(b)(3), the Board has considered §8(b)(3) in isolation, as if it were an independent provision of law, and not a part of a reticulated legislative scheme with interlacing purposes. It is the purposes to be drawn from the statute in its entirety, with due regard to all its interrelated provisions, in relation to which §8(b)(3) is to be applied. Cf. Textile Workers Union v. Lincoln Mills, 353 U.S. 448, 456. . . .

As the last clause of §13 makes plain, the section does not recognize an unqualified right, free of Board interference, to engage in "strikes," as respondent contends. . . . But "limitations and qualifications" do not extinguish the rule. For the Board to proceed, as it apparently claims power to do, against conduct which, but for the bargaining context in which it occurs, would not be within those limitations, it must rely upon the specific grant of power to enforce the duty to bargain which is contained in §8(b)(3). In construing that section the policy of the rule of construction set forth by §13, see Automobile Workers v. Wisconsin Board, 336 U.S. 245, 259, must be taken into account. In the light of that policy there is no justification for divorcing from the total bargaining situation particular tactics which the Board finds undesirable, without regard to the actual conduct of bargaining in the case before it.

The scope of the permission embodied in §13 must be considered by the Board in determining, under a proper rule of law, whether the totality of the respondent's conduct justifies the conclusion that it has violated the "specific" command of §8(b)(3). When the Board emphasizes tactics outside the negotiations themselves as the basis of the conclusion that the color of illegitimacy is imparted to otherwise apparently bona fide negotiations, §13 becomes relevant. A total, peaceful strike in compliance with the requirements of §8(d) would plainly not suffice to sustain the conclusion; prolonged union-sponsored violence directed at the company to secure compliance as plainly would. Here, as in so many legal situations of different gradations, drawing the line between them is not an abstract, speculative enterprise. Where the line ought to be drawn should await the decision of particular cases by the Board. . . .

. . . Apart from any restraint upon its conclusion imposed by §13, a matter which the Board did not consider, no reason is manifest why the respondent's nuisance tactics here should be thought a sufficient basis for the conclusion that all its bargaining was in reality a sham. On this record it does not appear that respondent merely stalled at the bargaining table until its conduct outside the negotiations might force Prudential to capitulate to its demands, nor does any other evidence give the color of pretence to its negotiating procedure. From the conduct of its counsel before the Trial Examiner, and from its opinion, it is apparent that the Board proceeded upon the belief that respondent's tactics were, without more, sufficient evidence of a lack of a sincere desire to reach agreement to make other consideration of its conduct unnecessary. For that reason the case should be remanded to the Board for further opportunity to introduce pertinent evidence, if any there be, of respondent's lack of good faith. . . .

AMERICAN SHIP BUILDING CO. v. NLRB
Supreme Court of the United States, 1965
380 U.S. 300, 85 Sup. Ct. 955, 13 L. Ed. 2d 855

MR. JUSTICE STEWART delivered the opinion of the Court.

The American Ship Building Company seeks review of a decision of the United States Court of Appeals for the District of Columbia enforcing an order of the National Labor Relations Board which found that the company had committed an unfair labor practice under §§8(a)(1) and 8(a)(3) of the National Labor Relations Act. The question presented is that expressly reserved in Labor Board v. Truck Drivers Local Union, 353 U.S. 87, 93; namely, whether an employer commits an unfair labor practice under these sections of the Act when he temporarily lays off or "locks out" his employees during a labor dispute to bring economic pressure in support of his bargaining position. . . .

The American Ship Building Company operates four shipyards on the Great Lakes — at Chicago, at Buffalo, and at Toledo and Lorain, Ohio. The company is primarily engaged in the repairing of ships, a highly seasonal business concentrated in the winter months when the freezing of the Great Lakes renders shipping impossible. What limited business is obtained during the shipping season is frequently such that speed of execution is of the utmost importance to minimize immobilization of the ships.

Since 1952 the employer has engaged in collective bargaining with a group of eight unions. Prior to the negotiations here in question, the employer had contracted with the unions on five occasions, each agreement having been preceded by a strike. The particular chapter of the collective bargaining history with which we are concerned opened shortly before May 1, 1961, when the unions notified the company of their intention to seek modification of the current contract, due to expire on August 1. . . .

[O]n August 9, after extended negotiations, the parties separated without having resolved substantial differences on the central issues dividing them and without having specific plans for further attempts to resolve them — a situation which the trial examiner found was an impasse. Throughout the negotiations, the employer displayed anxiety as to the unions' strike plans, fearing that the unions would call a strike as soon as a ship entered the Chicago yard or delay negotiations into the winter to increase strike leverage. The union negotiator consistently insisted that it was his intention to reach an agreement without calling a strike; however, he did concede incomplete control over the workers — a fact borne out by the occurrence of a wildcat strike in February 1961. Because of the danger of an unauthorized strike and the consistent and deliberate use of strikes in prior negotiations, the employer remained apprehensive of the possibility of a work stoppage.

In light of the failure to reach an agreement and the lack of available work, the employer decided to lay off certain of his workers. On August 11 the employees received a notice which read: "Because of the labor dispute which has been unresolved since August 1, 1961, you are laid off until further notice." The Chicago yard was completely shut down and all but two employees laid off at the Toledo yard. A large force was retained at Lorain to complete a major piece of work there and the employees in the Buffalo yard were gradually laid off as miscellaneous tasks were completed. Negotiations were resumed shortly after these layoffs and continued for the following two months until a two-year contract was agreed upon on October 27. The employees were recalled the following day. . . .

[The trial examiner] found that the employer's primary purpose in locking out his employees was to avert peculiarly harmful economic consequences which would be imposed on him and his customers if a strike were called either while a ship was in the yard during the shipping season or later when the yard was fully occupied. . . .

A three-to-two majority of the Board rejected the trial examiner's conclusion that the employer could reasonably anticipate a strike. Finding the unions' assurances sufficient to dispel any such apprehension, the Board was able to find only one purpose underlying the layoff: a desire to bring economic pressure to secure prompt settlement of the dispute on favorable terms. . . .

The Board concluded that the employer "by curtailing its operations at the South Chicago yard with the consequent layoff of the employees, coerced employees in the exercise of their bargaining rights in violation of Section 8(a)(1) of the Act, and discriminated against its employees within the meaning of Section 8(a)(3) of the Act."

The difference between the Board and the trial examiner is thus a narrow one turning on their differing assessments of the circumstances which the employer claims gave him reason to anticipate a strike. Both the Board and the examiner assumed, within the established pattern of Board analysis, that if the employer had shut down his yard and laid off his workers solely for the purpose of bringing to bear economic pressure to break an impasse and secure more favorable contract terms, an unfair labor practice would be made out. . . .

The Board has, however, exempted certain classes of lockouts from proscription. "Accordingly, it has held that lockouts are permissible to safeguard against loss where there is reasonable ground for believing that a strike was threatened or imminent." Quaker State Oil Refining Co., 121 N.L.R.B. 334, 337. Developing this distinction in its rulings, the Board has approved lockouts designed to prevent seizure of a plant by a sitdown strike, Link Belt Co., 26 N.L.R.B. 227; to forestall repetitive disruptions of an integrated operation by quickie strikes, International Shoe Co., 93 N.L.R.B. 907; to avoid spoilage of materials which would result from a sudden work stoppage, Duluth Bottling Assn., 48 N.L.R.B. 1335; and to avert the immobilization of automobiles brought in for repair, Betts v. Cadillac-Olds, 96 N.L.R.B. 268. In another distinct class of cases the Board has sanctioned the use of the lockout by a multiemployer bargaining unit as a response to a whipsaw strike against one of its members. Labor Board v. Truck Drivers Local Union, 109 N.L.R.B. 447, rev'd. 231 F.2d 110, rev'd, 353 U.S. 87.

In analyzing the status of the bargaining lockout under §§8(a)(1) and 8(a)(3) of the National Labor Relations Act, it is important that the practice with which we are here concerned be distinguished from other forms of temporary separation from employment. No one would deny that an employer is free to shut down his enterprise temporarily for reasons of renovation or lack of profitable work unrelated to his collective bargaining situation. Similarly, we put to one side cases where the Board has concluded on the basis of substantial evidence that the employer has used a lockout as a means to injure a labor organization or to evade his duty to bargain collectively. Hopwood Retinning Co., 4 N.L.R.B. 922; Scott Paper Box Co., 81 N.L.R.B. 535. What we are here concerned with is the use of a temporary layoff of employees solely as a means to bring economic pressure to bear in support of the employer's bargaining position, after an impasse has been reached. This is the only issue before us, and all that we decide.[8] . . .

The Board's position is premised on the view that the lockout interferes with two of the rights guaranteed by §7: the right to bargain collectively and the right to strike. In the Board's view, the use of the lockout "punishes" employees for the presentation of and adherence to demands made by their bargaining representatives and so coerces them in the exercise of their right to bargain collectively. . . . The employer intended to resist the demands made of him in the negotiations and to secure modification of these demands. We cannot see that this intention is in any way inconsistent with the employees' rights to bargain collectively. . . .

Nor is the lockout one of those acts which is demonstrably so destructive of collective bargaining that the Board need not inquire into employer motivation, as might be the case, for example, if an employer permanently discharged his unionized staff and replaced them with employees known to be possessed of a violent antiunion animus. Cf. Labor Board v. Erie Resistor Corp., 373 U.S. 221. The lockout may well dissuade employees from adhering to the position which they initially adopted in the bargaining, but the right to bargain collectively does not entail any "right" to insist on one's position free from economic disadvantage. Proper analysis of the problem demands that the simple intention to support the employer's bargaining position as to compensation and the like be distinguished from a hostility to the process of collective bargaining which could suffice to render a lockout unlawful. See Labor Board v. Brown, 380 U.S. 278.

The Board has taken the complementary view that the lockout interferes with the right to strike protected under §§7 and 13 of the Act in that it allows the employer to pre-empt the possibility of a strike and thus leave the union with "nothing to strike against." Insofar as this means that once employees are locked out, they are deprived of their right to call a strike against the employer because he is already shut down, the argument is wholly specious, for the work stoppage which would have been the object of the strike has in fact occurred. It is true that recognition of the lockout deprives the union of exclusive control of the timing and duration of work stoppages calculated to influence the result of collective bargaining negotiations, but there is nothing in the statute which would imply that the right to strike "carries with it" the right exclusively to determine the timing and duration of all work stoppages. The right

[8] Contrary to the views expressed in a concurring opinion filed in this case, we intimate no view whatever as to the consequences which would follow had the employer replaced his employees with permanent replacements or even temporary help. Cf. Labor Board v. Mackay Radio & Telegraph Co., 304 U.S. 333.

to strike as commonly understood is the right to cease work — nothing more. No doubt a union's bargaining power would be enhanced if it possessed not only the simple right to strike but also the power exclusively to determine when work stoppages shall occur, but the Act's provisions are not indefinitely elastic, content-free forms to be shaped in whatever manner the Board might think best conforms to the proper balance of bargaining power.

Thus, we cannot see that the employer's use of a lockout solely in support of a legitimate bargaining position is in any way inconsistent with the right to bargain collectively or with the right to strike. Accordingly, we conclude that on the basis of the findings made by the Board in this case, there has been no violation of §8(a)(1). . . .

To find a violation of §8(a)(3) . . . the Board must find that the employer acted for a proscribed purpose. Indeed, the Board itself has always recognized that certain "operative" or "economic" purposes would justify a lockout. But the Board has erred in ruling that only these purposes will remove a lockout from the ambit of §8(a)(3), for that section requires an intention to discourage union membership or otherwise discriminate against the union. There was not the slightest evidence and there was no finding, that the employer was actuated by a desire to discourage membership in the union as distinguished from a desire to affect the outcome of the particular negotiations in which he was involved. We recognize that the "union membership" which is not to be discouraged refers to more than the payment of dues and that measures taken to discourage participation in protected union activities may be found to come within the proscription. . . . However, there is nothing in the Act which gives employees the right to insist on their contract demands, free from the sort of economic disadvantage which frequently attends bargaining disputes. Therefore, we conclude that where the intention proven is merely to bring about a settlement of a labor dispute on favorable terms, no violation of §8(a)(3) is shown.

The conclusions which we draw from analysis of §§8(a)(1) and 8(a)(3) are consonant with what little of relevance can be drawn from the balance of the statute and its legislative history. In the original version of the Act, the predecessor of §8(a)(1) declared it an unfair labor practice "[t]o attempt, by interference, influence, restraint, favor, coercion, or lockout, or by any other means, to impair the right of employees guaranteed in section 4." Prominent in the criticism leveled at the bill in the Senate Committee hearings was the charge that it did not accord even-handed treatment to employers and employees because it prohibited the lockout while protecting the strike. In the face of such criticism, the Committee added a provision prohibiting employee interference with employer bargaining activities and deleted the reference to the lockout. A plausible inference to be drawn from this history is that the language was deleted to mollify those who saw in the bill an inequitable denial of resort to the lockout, and to remove any language which might give rise to fears that the lockout was being proscribed per se. It is in any event clear that the Committee was concerned with the status of the lockout and that the bill, as reported and as finally enacted, contained no prohibition on the use of the lockout as such.

Although neither §8(a)(1) nor §8(a)(3) refers specifically to the lockout, various other provisions of the Labor Management Relations Act do refer to the lockout, and these references can be interpreted as a recognition of the legitimacy of the device as a means of applying economic pressure in support of bargaining positions. Thus 29 U.S.C. §158(d)(4) prohibits the use of strike or lockout unless requisite notice procedures have been complied with; 29 U.S.C. §173(c) directs the Federal Mediation and Conciliation Service to seek voluntary resolution of labor disputes without resort to strikes or lockouts; and 29 U.S.C. §§176, 178, authorize procedures whereby the President can institute a board of inquiry to forestall certain strikes or lockouts. The correlative use of the terms "strike" and "lockout" in these sections contemplates that lockouts will be used in the bargaining process in some fashion. This is not to say that these provisions serve to define the permissible scope of a lockout by an employer. That, in the context of the present case, is a question ultimately to be resolved by analysis of §§8(a)(1) and 8(a)(3).

The Board has justified its ruling in this case and its general approach to the legality of lockouts on the basis of its special competence to weigh the competing interests of employers and employees and to accommodate these interests according to its expert judgment. . . . [T]he Board points out that the employer has been given other weapons to counterbalance the employees' power of strike. The employer may permanently replace workers who have gone out on strike, or by stockpiling and subcontracting, maintain his commercial operations while the strikers bear the economic brunt of the work stoppage. Similarly, the employer can institute unilaterally the working conditions which he desires once his contract with the union has expired. Given these economic weapons, it is argued, the employer has been adequately equipped with tools of economic self-help.

There is of course no question that the Board is entitled to the greatest deference in recognition of its special competence in dealing with labor problems. In many areas its evaluation of the competing interests of employer and employee should unquestionably be given conclusive effect in determining the application of §§8(a)(1), (a)(3), and (a)(5). However, we think that the Board construes its functions too expansively when it claims general authority to define national labor policy by balancing the competing interests of labor and management.

While a primary purpose of the National Labor Relations Act was to redress the perceived imbalance of economic power between labor and management, it sought to accomplish that result by conferring certain affirmative rights on employees and by placing certain enumerated restrictions on the activities of employers. . . . Having protected employee organization in countervailance to the employers' bargaining power, and having established a system of collective bargaining whereby the newly coequal adversaries might resolve their disputes, the Act also contemplated resort to economic weapons should more peaceful measures not avail. Sections 8(a)(1) and 8(a)(3) do not give the Board a general authority to assess the relative economic power of the adversaries in the bargaining process and to deny weapons to one party or the other because of its assessment of that party's bargaining power. Labor Board v. Brown, 380 U.S. 278. In this case the Board has, in essence, denied the use of the bargaining lockout to the employer because of its conviction that use of this device would give the employer "too much power." In so doing, the Board has stretched §§8(a)(1) and 8(a)(3) far beyond their functions of protecting the rights of employee organization and collective bargaining. . . .

We are unable to find that any fair construction of the provisions relied on by the Board in this case can support its finding of an unfair labor practice. Indeed, the role assumed by the Board in this area is fundamentally inconsistent with the structure of the Act and the function of the sections relied upon. The deference owed to an expert tribunal cannot be allowed to slip into a judicial inertia which results in the unauthorized assumption by an agency of major policy decisions properly made by Congress. Accordingly, we hold that an employer violates neither §8(a)(1) nor §8(a)(3) when, after a bargaining impasse has been reached, he temporarily shuts down his plant and lays off his employees for the sole purpose of bringing economic pressure to bear in support of his legitimate bargaining position.

Reversed.

MR. JUSTICE GOLDBERG, with whom THE CHIEF JUSTICE joins, concurring in the result.

I concur in the Court's conclusion that the employer's lockout in this case was not a violation of either §8(a)(1) or §8(a)(3) of the National Labor Relations Act, 49 Stat. 453, as amended, 29 U.S.C. §§158(a)(1) and (3), and I therefore join in the judgment reversing the Court of Appeals. I reach this result not for the Court's reasons, but because, from the plain facts revealed by the record, it is crystal clear that the employer's lockout here was justifiable. The very facts recited by the Court in its opinion show that this employer locked out his employees in the face of a threatened strike under circumstances where, had the choice of timing been left solely to the unions, the employer and his customers would have been subject to economic injury over and beyond the loss of business normally incident to a strike upon the termination of the collective bargaining agreement. . . .

The Board overturned the trial examiner's ultimate holding, reaching what, on this record, is a totally unsupportable conclusion — that the employer's fear of a strike was unreasonable. The Board rested its conclusion upon the grounds that "the Unions made every effort to convey to the Respondent their intention not to strike; and they also gave assurances that if a strike were called, any work brought into Respondent's yard before the strike would be completed. The Union's further offered to extend the existing contract [which contained a no-strike provision] for 6 months, or indefinitely, until contract terms were reached . . . ." 142 N.L.R.B., at 1364. Upon analysis it is clear that none of these grounds will support the Board's conclusion that the employer had no reasonable basis to fear a strike.

The Board's finding that "the Unions made every effort to convey to the respondents their intention not to strike" is based upon statements made by union negotiators during the course of the negotiations. The chief negotiator for the unions testified that on the first day of negotiations, "I stated that it was my understanding that in the past there seemed to have been a strike at every — during every negotiation since World War II from information I had received, and it was our sincere hope that we could negotiate this agreement — go through those negotiations and negotiate a new agreement without any strife, that personally I always had a strong dislike to strike and that I thought if two parties sincerely desired to reach an agreement, one could be reached without strike. The Company . . . stated that the Company concurred in those thoughts, that they too disliked strikes, and it was their hope, also, that an agreement could be reached amicably." The negotiators for the unions expressed this same sentiment on several other occasions during the negotiations.

These statements, which one would normally expect a union agent to make during the course of negotiations as a hopeful augury of their outcome rather than as a binding agreement not to strike, scarcely vitiate the reasonableness of the employer's fear of a strike in light of the long history of past strikes by the same unions. Further, they cannot be deemed to render the employer's fear of a strike unreasonable after the negotiations had reached an impasse, particularly in view of the fact that a strike vote had been taken by the union's membership, and the membership rather than the union representatives had final authority to determine whether a strike would take place.

The fact that the assistant business managers of Local 85 and Local 374 of the Boilermakers Union "gave assurances that if a strike were called, any work brought into Respondents' yard before the strike would be completed" likewise cannot be deemed to offset the unions' threat of a strike and its consequences. These men were officials of locals in only one of the eight separate unions involved. At most they could give assurances as to a few of the men at two of the company's four yards. And even had all of the unions joined in these statements, which was not the case, the employer had been subject to wildcat strikes at a time when the unions were bound by a no-strike clause in their contract. Therefore, without impugning the good faith of these union agents, it surely was not unreasonable for the employer, notwithstanding this assurance, to fear that his employees might not complete work on ships when they were not bound by a no-strike clause.

The Board also relies on the fact that the unions offered a six-month extension of the present contract. . . . [T]his would have caused the contract to expire during the employer's busiest season. The employer had a perfect right to reject this stratagem. Had he agreed, the unions would have achieved one of their important objectives without the necessity for striking. By the same token it is clear that the unions would have agreed not to strike had the employer accepted their proposals for increases in wages and benefits. Surely the employer had every right to reject these proposals, and his rejection of them would not show that he was unreasonable in fearing a strike based upon his failure to accede to the union's demands.

Finally, the offer of an indefinite extension of the contract is an equally unsupportable basis for the Board's conclusion. An indefinite extension presumably would mean under traditional contract theory that the unions could strike at any time or after giving brief notice. Surely the employer would be reasonable in fearing that such an arrangement would peculiarly place the timing of the strike in the unions' hands.

The sum of all this is that the record does not supply even a scintilla of, let alone any substantial evidence, to support the conclusion of the Board that the employer's fear of a strike was unreasonable, but, rather, this conclusion appears irrational. Cf. Erie Resistor Corp. v. Labor Board, 373 U.S. 221, at 236. I would therefore hold on this record that the employer's lockout was completely justified. . . .

My view of this case would make it unnecessary to deal with the broad question of whether an employer may lock out his employees solely to bring economic pressure to bear in support of his bargaining position. The question of which types of lockout are compatible with the labor statute is a complex one as this decision and the other cases decided today illustrate. See Textile Workers' Union v. Darlington Mfg. Co., 380 U.S. 263; Labor Board v. Brown, 380 U.S. 278.

The Court not only overlooks the factual diversity among different types of lockout, but its statement of the rules governing unfair labor practices under §§8(a)(1) and (3) does not give recognition to the fact that "[t]he ultimate problem [in this area] is the balancing of the conflicting legitimate interests." Labor Board v. Truck Drivers Union, 353 U.S. 87, 96. The Court states that employer conduct, not actually motivated by antiunion bias, does not violate §§8(a)(1) or (3) unless it is "demonstrably so destructive of collective bargaining," . . . or "so prejudicial to union interests and so devoid of significant economic justification," . . . that no antiunion animus need be shown. This rule departs substantially from both the letter and the spirit of numerous prior decisions of the Court. See, e.g., Labor Board v. Truck Drivers Union, supra, at 96; Republic Aviation Corp. v. Labor Board, 324 U.S. 793; Labor Board v. Babcock & Wilcox Co., 351 U.S. 105; Labor Board v. Burnup & Sims, Inc., 379 U.S. 21.

These decisions demonstrate that the correct test for determining whether §8(a)(1) has been violated in cases not involving an employer antiunion motive is whether the business justification for the employer's action outweighs the interference with §7 rights involved. . . .

In view of the necessity for, and the desirability of, weighing the legitimate conflicting interests in variant lockout situations, there is not and cannot be any simple formula which readily demarks the permissible from the impermissible lockout. This being so, I would not reach out in this case to announce principles which are determinative of the legality of all economically motivated lockouts whether before or after a bargaining impasse has been reached. In my view both the Court and the Board, in reaching their opposite conclusions, have inadvisably and unnecessarily done so here. Rather, I would confine our decision to the simple holding, supported both by the record and the actualities of industrial relations, that the employer's fear of a strike was reasonable, and therefore, under the settled decisions of the Board, which I would approve, the lockout of his employees was justified.

MR. JUSTICE WHITE, concurring in the result.

The Court today holds that the use of economic weapons by an employer for the purpose of improving his bargaining position can never violate the broad provisions of §§8(a)(1) and 8(a)(3) and hence a bargaining lockout of employees in resistance to demands of a union is invariably exempt from the proscriptions of the Act. As my Brother GOLDBERG well points out, the Court applies legal standards that cannot be reconciled with decisions of this Court defining the Board's functions in applying these sections of the Act and does so without pausing to ascertain if the Board's factual premises are supported by substantial evidence. I also think the Court, in the process of establishing the legality of a bargaining lockout, overlooks the uncontradicted facts in this record and the accepted findings of the trial examiner which indicate to me that the employer's closing of the Chicago yard was not a "lockout" for the purpose of bringing economic pressure to break an impasse and to secure more favorable contract terms. . . .

Since the Court does rule on the status of the bargaining lockout under the National Labor Relations Act, I feel constrained to state my views. This Court has long recognized that the Labor Act "did not undertake the impossible task of specifying in precise and unmistakable language each incident which would constitute an unfair labor practice," but "left to the Board the work of applying the Act's general prohibitory language in light of the infinite combinations of events which might be charged as violative of its terms." Republic Aviation Corp. v. Labor Board, 324 U.S. 793, 798. Thus the legal status of the bargaining lockout, as the Court indicated in Labor Board v. Truck Drivers Union, 353 U.S. 87, 96, is to be determined by "the balancing of the conflicting legitimate interests."

The Board has balanced these interests here—the value of the lockout as an economic weapon against its impact on protected concerted activities, including the right to strike, for which the Act has special solicitude, Labor Board v. Erie Resistor Corp., 373 U.S. 221, 234, and has determined that the employer's interest in obtaining a bargaining victory does not outweigh the damaging consequences of the lockout. It determined that to deprive employees of their livelihood because of demands made by their representatives, and in order to compel submission to the employer's demands, coerces employees in their exercise of the right to bargain collectively and discourages resort to that right. And it interferes with the right to strike, sharply reducing the effectiveness of that weapon and denying the union control over the timing of the economic contest. The Court rejects this reasoning on the ground that the lockout is not conduct "demonstrably and so invariably destructive of collective bargaining that the Board need not inquire into motives." . . . Since the employer's true motive is to bring about settlement of the dispute on favorable terms, there can be no substantial discouragement of union membership or interference with concerted activities. And the right to strike is only the right to cease work, which the lockout only encourages rather than displaces.

This tour de force denies the Board's assessment of the impact on employee rights and this truncated definition of the right to strike, no where supported in the Act, is unprecedented. Until today the employer's true motive or sole purpose has not always been determinative of the impact on employee rights. . . .

If the Court means what it says today, an employer may not only lock out after impasse consistent with §§8(a)(1) and 8(a)(3), but replace his locked-out employees with temporary help, cf. Labor Board v. Brown, ante, or perhaps permanent replacements, and also lock out long before an impasse is reached. Maintaining operations during a labor dispute is at least equally important an interest as achieving a bargaining victory, see Labor Board v. Mackay Radio & Telegraph, 304 U.S. 333, and a shutdown during or before negotiations advances an employer's bargaining position as much as a lockout after impasse. And the hiring of replacements is wholly consistent with the employer's intent "to resist demands made of him in the negotiations and to secure modifications of these demands." Ante, at 9. I would also assume that under §§8(a)(1) and 8(a)(3) he may lock out for the sole purpose of resisting the union's assertion of grievances under a collective bargaining contract, absent a no-lockout clause. Given these legitimate business purposes, there is no antiunion motivation, and absent such motivation, a lockout cannot be deemed destructive of employee rights. . . . I think the Board may assess the impact of a bargaining lockout on protected employee rights, without regard to motivation, and think the Court errs in failing to give due consideration to the Board's conclusions in this regard.

[MR. JUSTICE WHITE concurred on the ground that the NLRB had not given sufficient justification in the record for its conclusion that this particular lockout was in violation of the NLRA.]

GENERAL ELECTRIC CO.
National Labor Relations Board, 1964
150 N.L.R.B. No. 36

INTERMEDIATE REPORT OF TRIAL EXAMINER

This case arises out of the 1960 national contract negotiations between the IUE and GE. The negotiations led to an unsuccessful 3-week strike, alleged in the complaint to have been an unfair labor practice strike, before the IUE finally capitulated to GE's prestrike contract terms. The complaint basically alleges that the Respondent during the course of the negotiations failed and refused to bargain in good faith with the

Union and engaged in related conduct in derogation of the Union's status as bargaining agent, all in violation of Section 8(a)(5) and (1) of the Act. As a subordinate issue, the complaint also alleges a violation of Section 8 (a)(1) and (3) based upon an alleged threat to discharge striking employees at the Respondent's Augusta, Georgia, plant and upon the Respondent's failure and refusal to reinstate 20 named employees at that plant who had been replaced during the course of the strike. As to the 8(a)(3) issue, however, all parties are agreed that a finding of unlawful discrimination must stand or fall on the disposition to be made of the complaint's allegation that the strike was caused or prolonged by the Respondent's refusal to bargain.

With respect to the key 8(a)(5) and (1) issue, the complaint as last amended prior to the hearing includes the broad allegation that at all times since June 13, 1960, the date the Union first submitted its contract proposals, Respondent negotiated with the Union in bad faith. As the General Counsel made clear at the prehearing conference, and as his voluminous bill of particulars several times supplemented reflects, the intent of the pleading is to place in issue the Respondent's overall course of conduct, both at and away from the bargaining table, insofar as it bears on the Respondent's bargaining frame of mind during the entire period of the negotiations. Without limiting the generality of the foregoing broad allegation, the complaint also contains a number of more specific allegations. Thus, it alleges in substance that on or about August 30, 1960, the Respondent adopted and thereafter maintained what was in effect a "take-it-or-leave-it" position with respect to a counteroffer the Respondent had submitted that day. The complaint also alleges that "in order to undermine the Union" and "in derogation of the status of the Union as bargaining agent," the Respondent by means of communications and other appeals directed to employees in the bargaining units (a) engaged in a campaign throughout the period of negotiations to discredit and impugn the motives and abilities of the Union's leadership; (b) attempted through direct contact with employees to induce employee acceptance of the Respondent's August 30 counteroffer; and (c) attempted during the latter part of September to induce employees to depart from the Union-prescribed method for conducting a scheduled vote on the Respondent's counteroffer. The complaint further alleges that during October 1960, while national negotiations with the Union were being conducted, the Respondent attempted — further in derogation of the Union's status as national bargaining agent — to bargain directly with employees and/or their local representatives at certain of its plants, and offered at some of them terms and conditions of employment more favorable than those it had theretofore offered the Union in national negotiations. Finally, the complaint alleges that the Respondent failed and refused timely to furnish the Union with certain relevant data the Union had requested in connection with the bargaining. The alleged attempts to bargain directly with employees and the alleged refusal to supply requested information are relied upon by the General

Counsel both as providing additional evidence of bad faith bargaining and as constituting independent violations of Section 8(a)(5) and (1).

GE's present approach to employee and union relations was first conceived in 1947 and developed largely under the guidance of Lemuel R. Boulware, then and for many years later GE's Vice-President-Relations-Service. The approach has often been referred to as "Boulwareism," although GE itself abjures use of that term, claiming it has been misconstrued by outsiders to reflect a concept not actually GE's. It came into being as an aftermath of a lengthy companywide strike which the UE had conducted against GE in 1946. That strike was settled only after GE raised its wage offer from a prestrike 10 cents an hour to a poststrike 18½ cents an hour. As appears from one Company report, GE's management regarded UE's "highly successful strike" as "little short of a debacle." Management had theretofore had a "feeling" of "security in the knowledge that the Company had been a good employer [which] had treated employees fairly, and had pioneered in the voluntary installation of many employee benefit programs." Nevertheless, the strike had been "broadly supported" by employees. The realization that its earlier feeling of security had been a false one was a "somber event" for GE management.

The jolt of the 1946 strike led GE management to take a new look. GE sought to determine why it had failed (as it saw it) to achieve the same high degree of success and effectiveness in its employee relations as it had in other areas of its operations, such as, for example, in product development and marketing. Management concluded, inter alia, that to gain employee job satisfaction, loyalty and support, it was not enough that the Company be a good employer. It was equally if not more important that the Company be *known* to its employees as a good employer. With regard to employee pay, benefits and other terms and conditions of employment, as well as other elements entering into employee job satisfaction, the employees must be made to understand that it was the Company's aim "to do right voluntarily" and to allow its employees all that was fairly warranted, bearing in mind the "balanced best interests" of employees and all others having a stake in the Company's enterprise. Moreover, the employees must also be made to understand that, just as there was no need to drag reluctantly from the Company all that was fairly coming to them, so, too, there could be no profit in a show of force by a labor organization designed to extract more for the employees than the facts — as management evaluated them — justly warranted. This involved essentially a selling problem, or, as the Company termed it, one of "job marketing." If the Company was to achieve ultimately the same success in job marketing that it had accomplished in its highly successful product marketing, it must assimilate to the latter what it had learned in the former about sound product planning and research, market development and merchandising.

Application of this program necessitated a revision of the Company's approach to collective bargaining. The Company had theretofore engaged in the traditional type of bargaining, under which a union initially asks more than it expects to get and an employer offers less than it expects to give, and, through the process of compromise and give-and-take, both sides, if bargaining is successful, eventually arrive at a mutually acceptable middle ground. But that type of bargaining had to go if the Company was to establish its credibility with employees that it was putting into effect *voluntarily* and without need of outside pressures all that was warranted in the way of wage and benefit improvements.

Under GE's present approach to bargaining, as GE states it, the Company itself seeks through extensive year-round research into all pertinent facts to determine what is "right" for employees. Its research includes not only a study of business conditions, competitive factors, economic trends and the like, but the gathering of its own information as to employee needs and desires through independent employee attitude surveys, comments made by employees at informative meetings, direct discussions by supervisors with employees and statements in union publications. When bargaining begins, the Company, as part of its overall research, listens to the presentations made by all the unions with which it deals, and evaluates the unions' demands with the help of all the facts it has on hand, including those supplied by the unions.

On the basis of its study so made, GE makes its own determination of what is "right." GE then makes an offer which — as it declares to the unions and to its employees — includes *everything* it has found to be warranted, without anything held back for later trading or compromising. GE makes precisely the same basic offer to substantially all unions with which it is engaged in negotiations. Contrary to the assertion of the General Counsel, GE does not initially present its offer on an avowed "take-it-or-leave-it" basis. It professes a willingness to make prompt adjustments in its offer whenever (but only when) new information from any source or a significant change in facts indicates that its initial offer fell short of being right. But GE believes — or at least so declares — that if it has done its preliminary research into the facts accurately, no substantial reason for changing its offer should ever exist, save in the event of some new unforeseen development having an impact on the economy as a whole. And GE repeatedly emphasizes, especially to employees, that as a matter of policy it will not make any change it believes to be incorrect because of a strike or threat of strike and that it will "take" a strike of any duration to resist doing what it considers to be "wrong." . . .

All that has been said above is tied to what clearly appears to be the keystone of Respondent's bargaining philosophy — the marketing of management positions directly to employees so that the employees in turn may influence union acceptance. It is a stated policy of the Company to achieve maximum involvement and participation of employees in decisions affecting its business, including specifically though not limited to decisions relating to collective bargaining; to minimize opposition to steps management takes; and to build active employee support for management's goals and objectives. Toward that end GE has fashioned an elaborate employee communications system, making use of plant newspapers, daily news digests, employee bulletins, letters to employees' homes, television and radio broadcasts and other media of mass communication, as well as personal contacts. Supervisors are instructed as to GE's views on controversial subjects and are expected to speak out to employees on such subjects and seek to gain employee confidence in the correctness of company decisions. The direct employee communications — if 1960 may be considered as representative — are utilized on a most extensive scale both before and during negotiations to influence employee attitudes to a favorable reception of the Company's views and rejection of the union's conflicting positions. After the Company's offer is presented to the unions, the flow of communications, directed toward that end, reaches flood proportions. At that time, the Company also discusses the terms of its offer at plant meetings; invites employees to take up individually with their supervisors or managerial officials any questions they may have about the offer; and seeks through direct contact of its supervisors with employees to sound out for its own guidance employee reactions to its offer. The avowed purpose of the communications program is to equip employees to render their own independent judgment on matters commonly affecting their own interests and those of the Company. But, as related to bargaining issues, the record in this case, as will be seen, leaves no doubt that GE's more basic purpose is to compete with the bargaining representative for the allegiance and support of employees.[1]

Another consideration which shapes the Respondent's approach to bargaining is its uniformity policy.

As noted above, GE deals with some 100-odd unions. With regard to wage and benefit improvements, it is GE's policy to see to it that no union gets more favored treatment than any other. GE justifies that policy on the basis of fair play, business realism, and as necessary to avoid whipsawing. In line with that policy, GE prepares and presents to substantially all unions with which it deals the same basic offer with regard to wage adjustments and benefit programs.

Moreover, as further noted above, about half of GE's employees are unrepresented. Representation elections frequently are held among different groups of such employees, and sometimes decertification elections among groups of employees previously represented. Where such elections are held, GE engages in preelection campaigning in which it makes no secret of its opposition to union organization. In urging its employees to vote against union representation, GE emphasizes, inter alia, that a

---

[1] "In addition," as the examiner described General Electric's employee communications program during and immediately prior to the strike, "the Company in its communications and local advertisements repeatedly warned the employees and the communities that a vote against the company offer — which it always referred to as a vote to strike — would jeopardize employee jobs and inflict serious harm upon the communities. The warnings, with few exceptions, were couched in the language of general predictions as to asserted permanent losses of business that would flow from a strike. But the constant repetition of this theme and the manner of its presentation quite clearly reflect a purposeful design to play on employee fears and insecurities." — ED.

union can obtain for them no benefits they would not otherwise receive. It points up the Company's policy to "do right voluntarily" and to put into effect for nonrepresented employees the same pay and benefit program it makes available to represented employees.[7]   In keeping with such assurances, GE applies in the case of its unrepresented employees the same principle of uniformity that it applies to represented groups.   The terms of the basic offer made to unions are also put into effect for nonrepresented employees.   Prior to 1960, GE invariably withheld such action until either the IUE contract had been settled or the anniversary date of the prior IUE contract had expired.

Theoretically, it is possible for company negotiators engaged in negotiations with a given union to improve as to that union the basic offer made by GE to unions generally, even though the offer has already been put into effect for other bargaining units or for unrepresented employees. But the Company witness testifying on that point . . . could recall only one instance where that was ever done. . . .   In one important area, the Company's negotiators have no flexibility whatever. . . .   [T]he Company insists for practical reasons on a single uniform pension plan covering all GE employees, and once an offer has been put in effect for other bargaining units or for nonrepresented employees, the freedom of negotiators to effect changes is foreclosed. . . .

[The examiner found that General Electric had refused to bargain collectively as required by Section 8(a)(5).]

DECISION AND ORDER OF NLRB

. . . In challenging the Trial Examiner's finding that it violated Section 8(a)(5), Respondent argues that an employer cannot be found guilty of having violated its statutory bargaining duty where it is desirous of entering into a collective-bargaining agreement, where it has met and conferred with the bargaining representative on all required subjects of bargaining as prescribed by statute and has not taken unlawful unilateral action, and where it has not demanded the inclusion in the collective-bargaining contract of any illegal clauses or insisted to an impasse upon any nonmandatory bargaining provisions.   Given compliance with the above, Respondent further argues that an employer's technique of bargaining is not subject to approval or disapproval by the Board.

Respondent reads the statutory requirements for bargaining collectively too narrowly.   It is true that an employer does violate Section 8(a)(5) where it enters into bargaining negotiations with a desire not to reach an agreement with the union, or has taken unilateral action with respect to a term or condition of employment, or has adamantly demanded the inclusion of illegal or nonmandatory clauses in the collective-bargaining contract.[2]   But, having refrained from any of the foregoing conduct, an

---

[7] What is said here is not meant to suggest that GE's participation in such election campaigns is illegal.   No GE election has ever been set aside because of improper preelection conduct by the Company.

[2] On unilateral action, and illegal and nonmandatory clauses, see pages 447 and 440 infra. — ED.

employer may still have failed to discharge its statutory obligation to bargain in good faith. As the Supreme Court has said: ". . . the Board is authorized to order the cessation of behavior which is in effect a refusal to negotiate, *or* which directly obstructs or inhibits the actual process of discussion, *or* which reflects a cast of mind against reaching agreement." (Emphasis supplied.)

Thus, a party who enters into bargaining negotiations with a "take-it-or-leave-it" attitude violates its duty to bargain although it goes through the forms of bargaining, does not insist on any illegal or nonmandatory bargaining proposals, and wants to sign an agreement. For good-faith bargaining means more than "going through the motions of negotiating." ". . . [T]he essential thing is rather the serious intent to adjust differences and to reach an acceptable common ground. . . ."

Good-faith bargaining thus involves both a procedure for meeting and negotiating, which may be called the externals of collective bargaining, and a bona fide intention, the presence or absence of which must be discerned from the record. It requires recognition by both parties, not merely formal but real, that "collective bargaining" is a shared process in which each party, labor union and employer, has the right to play an active role. On the part of the employer, it requires at a minimum recognition that the statutory representative is the one with whom it must deal in conducting bargaining negotiations, and that it can no longer bargain directly or indirectly with the employees. It is inconsistent with this obligation for an employer to mount a campaign, as Respondent did, both before and during negotiations, for the purpose of disparaging and discrediting the statutory representative in the eyes of its employee constituents, to seek to persuade the employees to exert pressure on the representative to submit to the will of the employer, and to create the impression that the employer rather than the union is the true protector of the employees' interests. As the Trial Examiner phrased it, the employer's statutory obligation is to deal with the employees through the union, and not with the union through the employees.

We do not rely solely on Respondent's campaign among its employees for our finding that it did not deal in good faith with the Union. Respondent's policy of disparaging the Union by means of the communications campaign as fully detailed in the Trial Examiner's Intermediate Report, was implemented and furthered by its conduct at the bargaining table. Thus, the negotiations themselves, although maintaining the form of "collective bargaining," fell short, in a realistic sense, of the concept of meaningful and fruitful "negotiation" envisaged by the Act. As the record in the case reflects, Respondent regards itself as a sort of administrative body which has the unilateral responsibility for determining wages and working conditions for employees, and it regards the union's role as merely that of a kind of advisor for an interested group — the employees. . . . This "bargaining" approach undoubtedly eliminates the "ask-and-bid" or "auction" form of bargaining, but in the process devitalizes negotiations and collective bargaining and robs them of their commonly accepted meaning. "Collective bargaining" as thus practiced is tantamount to mere formality and serves to transform the role of the statutory representative from a joint participant in the bargaining process to that of an advisor. In practical effect, Respondent's "bargaining" position is akin to that of a party who enters into negotiations "with a predetermined resolve not to budge from an initial position," an attitude inconsistent with good-faith bargaining. In fact Respondent here went even further. It consciously placed itself in a position where it could not give unfettered consideration to the merits of any proposals the Union might offer. Thus, Respondent pointed out to the Union, after Respondent's communications to the employees and its "fair and firm offer" to the Union, that "everything we think we should do is in the proposal and we told our employees that, and we would look ridiculous if we changed now."

In short, both major facets of Respondent's 1960 "bargaining" technique, its campaign among the employees and its conduct at the bargaining table, complementing each other, were calculated to disparage the Union and to impose without substantial alteration Respondent's "fair and firm" proposal, rather than to satisfy the true standards of good-faith collective bargaining required by the statute. A course of conduct whose major purpose is so directed scarcely evinces a sincere desire to resolve differences and reach a common ground. For the above reasons, as well as those elaborated at greater length by the Trial Examiner in his Intermediate Report, we adopt his conclusion that Respondent did not bargain in good faith with the Union, thereby violating Section 8(a)(5) and (1) of the Act.

Our concurring colleague, Member Jenkins, who joins us in finding certain conduct of the Respondent inconsistent with its bargaining obligation under the statute, misreads the majority opinion, and the Trial Examiner's Intermediate Report which we affirm, in asserting that our decision is not based on an assessment of Respondent's conduct, but only on its approach to or techniques in bargaining.

On the contrary our determination is based upon our review of the Respondent's entire course of conduct, its failure to furnish relevant information, its attempts to deal separately with locals and to bypass the national bargaining representative, the manner of its presentation of the accident insurance proposal, the disparagement of the Union as bargaining representative by the communication program, its conduct of the negotiations themselves, and its attitude or approach as revealed by all these factors.

Nothing in our decision bans fact-gathering or any specific methods of formulating proposals. We prescribe no timetable for negotiators. We lay down no rules as to any required substance or content of agreements. Our decision rests rather upon a consideration of the totality of Respondent's conduct.

In one central point of our colleague's comment, with all respect we believe he is in error. His strictures in relation to our interpretation of the law's restraints on "take-it-or-leave-it" bargaining were decisively answered by the Supreme Court in its review of the nature of the bargaining obligation in Insurance Agents: ". . . the legislative history [of

Taft-Hartley] makes it plain that Congress was wary of the position of some unions, and wanted to ensure that they would approach the bargaining table with the same attitude of willingness to reach an agreement as had been enjoined on management earlier. It intended to prevent employee representatives from putting forth the same 'take-it-or-leave-it' attitude that had been condemned in management."

And in Justice Frankfurter's opinion in Truitt [infra page 447, note 3] upon which our colleague relies, the Justice also wrote: ". . . it (good faith) is inconsistent with a predetermined resolve not to budge from an initial position." . . .

[The Board order required the company to "cease and desist from refusing to bargain collectively in good faith' with the union.]

Member Jenkins, concurring:

. . . This Board has repeatedly held that conduct designed to undermine the Union, or to demonstrate to employees the futility of engaging in collective bargaining through a union, fails to meet the standard of good-faith bargaining. If my colleagues had been content to thus ground their finding in the instant case, I would have no reason to disagree. The record clearly supports their findings with respect to (a) the failure of Respondent to furnish certain information requested by the Union during contract negotiations, (b) the attempts to deal separately with locals on matters which were properly the subject of national negotiations, and (c) the Respondent's importuning of locals to abandon or refrain from supporting the strike authorized by the collective-bargaining representative. . . .

. . . Within the context of the facts of this case, were the Board to conclude that the foregoing derelictions justify a broad remedial order, I would be able to join and find no fault with the disposition of the case. However, in view of the fact that the majority has gone beyond conduct and indeed concedes that it is not basing its finding of overall bad faith on conduct but rather is basing that finding on an assessment of the Respondent's approach to its duty to bargain in good faith, I am constrained to disavow their comments concerning the employer's bargaining technique.

In effect I read the majority opinion to hold that the Act so regulates a party's choice of techniques in collective bargaining as to make unlawful an advance decision, and a frank communication of that decision, concerning the position from which a party is unwilling to retreat. The majority would apparently find that it is unlawful for a union to present a contract proposal on a take-it-or-leave-it basis since I assume the majority would not apply different standards to unions than to employers. The bargaining technique often employed by unions in support of "area standards" contracts is not significantly different from the technique described as the "firm fair offer" by an employer. I would not find a lack of good-faith bargaining where either the employer or the union entered the negotiations with a fixed position from which it proposed not to retreat, engaged in hard bargaining to maintain or protect such position, and made no concessions from that position as a result of bargaining. . . . [G]ood faith is not necessarily incompatible with stubbornness or even with what to an outsider may seem unreasonableness.

The majority states frankly that the holding of a predetermined resolve not to budge from an initial position is incompatible with good-faith bargaining. That statement seems to ignore the language in Section 8(d) of the Act which makes it clear in unequivocal words that "such obligation does not compel either party to agree to a proposal or require the making of a concession." The opinion of my colleagues fails to distinguish between two important concepts, viz., the formulation of a settlement position and the techniques employed in reaching a settlement. The Act does not dictate the methods which a party may choose to utilize in formulating its bargaining position. Indeed, many unions and employers use surveys of one sort or another as a fact-gathering device in advance of bargaining. Moreover, both employers and unions are free from statutory regulation under this Act in formulating the kind of proposal or counter proposal which each will communicate to the other. I know of no decision of this Board which has sought to interpret the statute as requiring either unions or employers to follow a prescribed timetable in communicating the various shifts in position which seem desirable as a matter of self interest. Thus, if either an employer or a union for reasons dictated by self interest chooses to include in a proposal trading items which it is willing later to withdraw or conversely chooses to limit its proposal to items which it will never withdraw voluntarily, the choice is its and not the Board's. . . .

Member Leedom, dissenting in part:

. . . Although I agree with the specific violations found, I cannot justify the bad-faith finding with respect to the Respondent's overall bargaining conduct.

On the issue as to Respondent's overall good or bad faith it should be conceded that there are various approaches to, and tactics in, negotiations that are wholly consistent with the bargaining obligation imposed by the Act; and it seems to me that both management and labor should not be discouraged from seeking new techniques in dealing with the constantly evolving problems with which they are faced across the bargaining table. Consequently we should take care not to create the impression that we view with suspicion novel approaches to, and techniques of, collective-bargaining. . . .

No matter how much we may disclaim any intent to compel bargaining to proceed in some set form, the fact that we closely scrutinize what goes on at the bargaining table will necessarily have the effect of directing bargaining into channels which we have in the past approved, for in such channels will lie security in bargaining, if not success.[23]

---

[23] The majority cites the Supreme Court to the effect that to bargain collectively as used in the Act "has been considered to absorb and give statutory approval to the philosophy of bargaining as worked out in the labor movement in the United States." . . . With this statement I certainly agree and, in fact, am arguing here that this process of working out be permitted to continue with a flexibility capable of meeting new problems as they arise. But if only standards

Whether the substitution of our judgment as to the proper forms and content of bargaining be made directly or indirectly is a difference of no consequence insofar as it interferes with free bargaining and tends to discourage innovation both in tactics and proposals which, as I believe, could be of benefit not only to the parties but to the public as well. Consequently, good policy suggests that we leave the parties to their own devices at the bargaining table unless some compelling facts force us into the area of bargaining. . . .

I do not mean to suggest that the issue of good or bad faith has any clear cut answer here. My position is not dictated so much by strong conviction as by uncertainty. I am not persuaded by the reasons that the majority state for their finding of bad-faith bargaining; and the finding itself and the supporting rationale leave me in the dark as to their practical efficacy. But I am particularly disturbed by the treatment accorded Respondent's communications. Surely the Respondent can lawfully communicate with its employees. Yet here, although the communications are held to be some evidence of bad faith, the majority neither in its decision nor in adopting the Trial Examiner's Recommended Order provides the Respondent with any guides by which it can with reasonable certainty determine what it can lawfully say to its employees. In areas such as this bordering on Section 8(c) of the Act and free speech, I believe that the Respondent is entitled to something more by way of clarification than the vague proscription implied in the general bargaining order. But I doubt if the facts and findings indicate what specific limitations can properly be laid down. In any event, the situation with respect to the bad-faith finding is at best ambiguous, and I would, therefore, find that the General Counsel has failed to prove by a preponderance of the evidence that the Respondent did not bargain in good faith during the 1960 negotiations with the Union.

2. *Refusal to Bargain Per Se*

The statutory definition of the duty to bargain collectively in terms obligates employers and unions to "meet at reasonable times and confer in good faith with respect to wages, hours, and other conditions of employment." Section 8(d). This language apparently ratifies the consistent Board view that an employer, although he in good faith accepts the union's representative status and seeks to reach agreement with it, violates Section 8(a)(5) if he refuses to discuss a specific subject falling within the statutory terms. See, e.g., Inland Steel Co. v. NLRB, 170 F.2d 247 (7th Cir. 1948), cert. denied, 336 U.S. 960 (1949) (pensions); NLRB v. J. H. Allison & Co., 165 F.2d 766 (6th Cir.), cert. denied, 335 U.S. 814 (1948) (merit increases).[3] Two broad questions are thereby

---

of conduct approved in the past are to have Board approval now and in the future, as seems to be the majority's position, then change will be difficult if not impossible, and industry and labor will be saddled with archaic rules and procedures for their conduct in negotiations.

[3] For an argument that such a requirement goes beyond the original purpose

raised: (1) What conduct, apart from a literal refusal to discuss a matter, constitutes a breach of this obligation "to meet and confer"? (2) What is the scope of the statutory concept, as to which the duty is imposed, of "wages, hours, and other conditions of employment"?

NLRB v. AMERICAN NATIONAL INSURANCE CO.

Supreme Court of the United States, 1952
343 U.S. 395, 72 Sup. Ct. 824, 96 L. Ed. 1027

MR. CHIEF JUSTICE VINSON delivered the opinion of the Court. . . .

The Office Employees International Union, A.F. of L., Local No. 27, certified by the National Labor Relations Board as the exclusive bargaining representative of respondent's office employees, requested a meeting with respondent for the purpose of negotiating an agreement governing employment relations. At the first meetings, beginning on November 30, 1948, the Union submitted a proposed contract covering wages, hours, promotions, vacations and other provisions commonly found in collective bargaining agreements, including a clause establishing a procedure for settling grievances arising under the contract by successive appeals to management with ultimate resort to an arbitrator.

. . . Following a recess for study of the Union's contract proposals, respondent objected to the provisions calling for unlimited arbitration. To meet this objection, respondent proposed a so-called management functions clause listing matters such as promotions, discipline and work scheduling as the responsibility of management and excluding such matters from arbitration. The Union's representative took the position "as soon as (he) heard (the proposed clause)" that the Union would not agree to such a clause so long as it covered matters subject to the duty to bargain collectively under the Labor Act. [The proposed clause read:]

"The right to select and hire, to promote to a better position, to discharge, demote or discipline for cause, and to maintain discipline and efficiency of employees and to determine the schedules of work is recognized by both union and company as the proper responsibility and prerogative of management to be held and exercised by the company, and while it is agreed that an employee feeling himself to have been aggrieved by any decision of the company in respect to such matters, or the union in his behalf, shall have the right to have such decision reviewed by top management officials of the company under the grievance machinery hereinafter set forth, it is further agreed that the final decision of the company made by such top management officials shall not be further reviewable by arbitration."

At this stage of the negotiations, the National Labor Relations Board filed a complaint against respondent based on the Union's charge that

---

and proper function of the duty to bargain, see Cox and Dunlop, Regulation of Collective Bargaining by the National Labor Relations Board, 63 Harv. L. Rev. 389, 391-401 (1950).

respondent had refused to bargain as required by the Labor Act and was thereby guilty of interfering with the rights of its employees guaranteed by Section 7 of the Act and of unfair labor practices under Sections 8(a)-(1) and 8(a)(5) of the Act. While the proceeding was pending, negotiations between the Union and respondent continued with the management functions clause remaining an obstacle to agreement. During the negotiations, respondent established new night shifts and introduced a new system of lunch hours without consulting the Union.

On May 19, 1949, a Union representative offered a second contract proposal which included a management functions clause containing much of the language found in respondent's second counterproposal, quoted above, with the vital difference that questions arising under the Union's proposed clause would be subject to arbitration as in the case of other grievances. Finally, on January 13, 1950, after the Trial Examiner had issued his report but before decision by the Board, an agreement between the Union and respondent was signed. The agreement contained a management functions clause that rendered nonarbitrable matters of discipline, work schedules and other matters covered by the clause. The subject of promotions and demotions was deleted from the clause and made the subject of a special clause establishing a union-management committee to pass upon promotion matters.

While these negotiations were in progress, the Board's Trial Examiner conducted hearings on the Union's complaint. The Examiner held that respondent had a right to bargain for inclusion of a management functions clause in a contract. However, upon review of the entire negotiations, including respondent's unilateral action in changing working conditions during the bargaining, the Examiner found that from and after November 30, 1948, respondent had refused to bargain in a good faith effort to reach agreement. The Examiner recommended that respondent be ordered in general terms to bargain collectively with the Union.

The Board agreed with the Trial Examiner that respondent had not bargained in a good faith effort to reach an agreement with the Union. But the Board rejected the Examiner's views on an employer's right to bargain for a management functions clause and held that respondent's action in bargaining for inclusion of any such clause "constituted, quite (apart from) Respondent's demonstrated bad faith, per se violations of Section 8(a)(5) and (1)." Accordingly, the Board not only ordered respondent in general terms to bargain collectively with the Union (par. (2)(a)), but also included in its order a paragraph designed to prohibit bargaining for any management functions clause covering a condition of employment. (Par. 1(a)). 89 N.L.R.B. 185. . . .

First. The National Labor Relations Act is designed to promote industrial peace by encouraging the making of voluntary agreements governing relations between unions and employers. The Act does not compel any agreement whatsoever between employees and employers. Nor does the Act regulate the substantive terms governing wages, hours and working conditions which are incorporated in an agreement. The theory of the Act is that the making of voluntary labor agreements is encouraged by protecting employees' rights to organize for collective bargaining and by imposing on labor and management the mutual obligation to bargain collectively.

Enforcement of the obligation to bargain collectively is crucial to the statutory scheme. And, as has long been recognized, performance of the duty to bargain requires more than a willingness to enter upon a sterile discussion of union-management differences. Before the enactment of the National Labor Relations Act, it was held that the duty of an employer to bargain collectively required the employer "to negotiate in good faith with his employees' representatives; to match their proposals, if unacceptable, with counterproposals; and to make every reasonable effort to reach an agreement." The duty to bargain collectively, implicit in the Wagner Act as introduced in Congress, was made express by the insertion of the fifth employer unfair labor practice accompanied by an explanation of the purpose and meaning of the phrase "bargain collectively in a good faith effort to reach an agreement." This understanding of the duty to bargain collectively has been accepted and applied throughout the administration of the Wagner Act by the National Labor Relations Board and the Courts of Appeal.

In 1947, the fear was expressed in Congress that the Board "has gone very far, in the guise of determining whether or not employers had bargained in good faith, in setting itself up as the judge of what concessions an employer must make and of the proposals and counterproposals that he may or may not make." Accordingly, the Hartley Bill, passed by the House, eliminated the good faith test and expressly provided that the duty to bargain collectively did not require submission of counterproposals. As amended in the Senate and passed as the Taft-Hartley Act, the good faith test of bargaining was retained and written into Section 8(d) of the National Labor Relations Act. That Section contains the express provision that the obligation to bargain collectively does not compel either party to agree to a proposal or require the making of a concession.

Thus it is now apparent from the statute itself that the Act does not encourage a party to engage in fruitless marathon discussions at the expense of frank statement and support of his position. And it is equally clear that the Board may not, either directly or indirectly, compel concessions or otherwise sit in judgment upon the substantive terms of collective bargaining agreements.

Second. The Board offers in support of the portion of its order before this Court a theory quite apart from the test of good faith bargaining prescribed in Section 8(d) of the Act, a theory that respondent's bargaining for a management functions clause as a counterproposal to the Union's demand for unlimited arbitration was "per se," a violation of the Act.

Counsel for the Board do not contend that a management functions clause covering some conditions of employment is an illegal contract term. As a matter of fact, a review of typical contract clauses collected for convenience in drafting labor agreements shows that management functions clauses similar in essential detail to the clause proposed by respondent have been included in contracts negotiated by national unions with many employers. The National War Labor Board, empowered during the last war "(t)o decide the dispute, and provide by order the wages and hours and all other terms and conditions (customarily included in collective-bargaining agreements)," ordered management functions clauses included in a number of agreements. Several such clauses ordered by the War Labor Board provided for arbitration in case of union dissatisfaction with the exercise of management functions, while others, as in the clause proposed by respondent in this case, provided that management decisions would be final. Without intimating any opinion as to the form of management functions clause proposed by respondent in this case or the desirability of including any such clause in a labor agreement, it is manifest that bargaining for management functions clauses is common collective bargaining practice.

If the Board is correct, an employer violates the Act by bargaining for a management functions clause touching any condition of employment without regard to the traditions of bargaining in the particular industry or such other evidence of good faith as the fact in this case that respondent's clause was offered as a counterproposal to the Union's demand for unlimited arbitration. The Board's argument is a technical one for it is conceded that respondent would not be guilty of an unfair labor practice if, instead of proposing a clause that removed some matters from arbitration, it simply refused in good faith to agree to the Union proposal for unlimited arbitration. The argument starts with a finding, not challenged by the court below or by respondent, that at least some of the matters covered by the management functions clause proposed by respondent are "conditions of employment" which are appropriate subjects of collective bargaining under Sections 8(a)(5), 8(d) and 9(a) of the Act. The Board considers that employer bargaining for a clause under which management retains initial responsibility for work scheduling, a "condition of employment," for the duration of the contract is an unfair labor practice because it is "in derogation of" employees' statutory rights to bargain collectively as to conditions of employment.

Conceding that there is nothing unlawful in including a management functions clause in a labor agreement, the Board would permit an employer to "propose" such a clause. But the Board would forbid bargaining for any such clause when the Union declines to accept the proposal, even where the clause is offered, as a counterproposal to a Union demand for unlimited arbitration. Ignoring the nature of the Union's demand in this case, the Board takes the position that employers subject to the Act must agree to include in any labor agreement provisions establishing fixed standards for work schedules or any other condition of employment. An employer would be permitted to bargain as to the content of the standard so long as he agrees to freeze a standard into a contract. Bargaining for more flexible treatment of such matters would be denied employers even though the result may be contrary to common collective bargaining practice in the industry. The Board was not empowered so to disrupt collective bargaining practices. On the contrary, the term "bargain collectively" as used in the Act "has been considered to absorb and give statutory approval to the philosophy of bargaining as worked out in the labor movement in the United States." Telegraphers v. Railway Express Agency, 321 U.S. 342, 346 (1944).

Congress provided expressly that the Board should not pass upon the desirability of the substantive terms of labor agreements. Whether a contract should contain a clause fixing standards for such matters as work scheduling or should provide for more flexible treatment of such matters is an issue for determination across the bargaining table, not by the Board. If the latter approach is agreed upon, the extent of union and management participation in the administration of such matters is itself a condition of employment to be settled by bargaining.

Accordingly, we reject the Board's holding that bargaining for the management functions clause proposed by respondent was, per se, an unfair labor practice. Any fears the Board may entertain that use of management functions clauses will lead to evasion of an employer's duty to bargain collectively as to "rates of pay, wages, hours and conditions of employment" do not justify condemning all bargaining for management functions clauses covering any "condition of employment" as per se violations of the Act. The duty to bargain collectively is to be enforced by application of the good faith bargaining standards of Section 8(d) to the facts of each case rather than by prohibiting all employers in every industry from bargaining for management functions clauses altogether. . . .

MR. JUSTICE MINTON, with whom MR. JUSTICE BLACK and MR. JUSTICE DOUGLAS join, dissenting:

I do not see how this case is solved by telling the National Labor Relations Board that since some "management functions" clauses are valid (which the Board freely admits), respondent was not guilty of an unfair labor practice in this case. The record is replete with evidence that respondent insisted on a clause which would classify the control over certain conditions of employment as a management prerogative and that the insistence took the form of a refusal to reach a settlement unless the Union accepted the clause. The Court of Appeals agreed that respondent was "steadfast" in this demand. Therefore, this case is one where the employer came into the bargaining room with a demand that certain topics upon which it had a duty to bargain were to be removed from the agenda — that was the price the Union had to pay to gain a contract. There is all the difference between the hypothetical "management functions" clauses envisioned by the majority and thus "management functions" clause as there is between waiver and coercion. No one suggests that an employer is guilty of an unfair labor practice when it proposes that it be given unilateral control over certain working conditions and the union accepts the proposal in return for various other benefits. But where, as here, the employer tells the union that the only way to obtain a contract as to wages is to agree not to bargain about certain other working conditions, the employer has refused to bargain about those other working conditions. There is more than a semantic difference between a proposal that the union waive certain rights and a demand that the union give up those rights as a condition precedent to enjoying other rights.

I need not and do not take issue with the Court of Appeals' conclusion that there was no absence of good faith. Where there is a refusal to bargain, the Act does not require an inquiry as to whether that refusal was in good faith or bad faith. The duty to bargain about certain subjects is made absolute by the Act. The majority seems to suggest that an employer could be found guilty of bad faith if it used a "management functions" clause to close off bargaining about all topics of discussion. Whether the employer closes off all bargaining or, as in this case, only a certain area of bargaining, he has refused to bargain as to whatever he has closed off, and any discussion of his good faith is pointless.

That portion of §8(d) of the Act which declares that an employer need not agree to a proposal or make concessions does not dispose of this case. Certainly the Board lacks power to compel concessions as to the substantive terms of labor agreements. But the Board in this case was seeking to compel the employer to bargain about subjects properly within the scope of collective bargaining. That the employer has such a duty to bargain and that the Board is empowered to enforce the duty is clear.

An employer may not stake out an area which is a proper subject for bargaining and say, "As to this we will not bargain." To do so is a plain refusal to bargain in violation of §8(a)(5) of the Act. If employees' bargaining rights can be cut away so easily, they are indeed illusory. I would reverse.

NOTES

1. For a vigorous exposition of the view adopted by the Court in the principal case, see Cox and Dunlop, Regulation of Collective Bargaining by the National Labor Relations Board, 63 Harv. L. Rev. 389, 401-432 (1950).

2. Compare White v. NLRB, 255 F.2d 564 (5th Cir. 1958), where the Court of Appeals thus stated the issue before it:

"May the charge of refusal to bargain in good faith be sustained solely by reference to the terms of the employment contract which management finally says it is willing to sign if such proposed contract could fairly be found to be one which would leave the employees in no better state than they were without it. For the purpose of considering this question we may assume that the Board could find that the terms of the contract insisted on by the company requiring the surrender by the employees of their right to strike and their agreeing to leave to management the right to hire and fire and fix wages in return for agreements by the company respecting grievances and security that gave the union little, if any, real voice in these important aspects of employment relations would in fact have left the union in no better position than if it had no contract. It is perfectly apparent that the company representatives approached the bargaining table with a full understanding of their obligations to meet with, and discuss with, representatives of the employees any terms and conditions of employment that either party put forward; that they must at least expose themselves to such argument and persuasion as could be put forward, and that they must try to seek an area of agreement at least as to some of the terms of employment; that if they were able to arrive at such agreement they must be willing to reduce it to writing and sign it. It is of some significance that at the fourth of the six bargaining sessions, when challenged by the employees' bargaining agent the company's managing partner signed the company's proposed complete contract and tendered it to the union, which declined to accept it. The question is: Can the company's insistence on terms overall favorable to it in net result be taken as proof that it did not approach the bargaining table in good faith, but that it approached the bargaining table only to give the outward sign of compliance when it had already excluded the possibility of agreement?"

Relying in substantial part on the principal case, a majority of the court set aside a finding of refusal to bargain, reasoning that if the management clause there "is not per se proof of failure to bargain in good faith then a fortiori insistence on physical examination by the company's own doctor, refusal to include terms of a Christmas bonus, a refusal to grant specified wage increases, refusal to 'freeze' rent and utility charges on company-owned houses and like issues could not either separately or collectively constitute such proof." Is this a sound reading of the American National Insurance case? Cf. Feinsinger, The National Labor Relations Act and Collective Bargaining, in Collective Bargaining and the Law (Univ. of Mich. Law School Summer Institute) 17-20 (1959).

NLRB v. WOOSTER DIVISION OF BORG-WARNER CORP.

Supreme Court of the United States, 1958
356 U.S. 342, 78 Sup. Ct. 718, 2 L. Ed. 2d 823

MR. JUSTICE BURTON delivered the opinion of the Court.

In these cases an employer insisted that its collective-bargaining contract with certain of its employees include: (1) a "ballot" clause calling for a pre-strike secret vote of those employees (union and nonunion) as to the employer's last offer, and (2) a "recognition" clause which excluded, as a party to the contract, the International Union which had been certified by the National Labor Relations Board as the employees' exclusive bargaining agent, and substituted for it the agent's uncertified local affiliate. The Board held that the employer's insistence upon either of such clauses amounted to a refusal to bargain, in violation of

§8(a)(5) of the National Labor Relations Act, as amended. The issue turns on whether either of these clauses comes within the scope of mandatory collective bargaining as defined in §8(d) of the Act. For the reasons hereafter stated, we agree with the Board that neither clause comes within that definition. Therefore, we sustain the Board's order directing the employer to cease insisting upon either clause as a condition precedent to accepting any collective-bargaining contract. . . .

Read together, [Sections 8(a)(5) and 8(d)] establish the obligation of the employer and the representative of its employees to bargain with each other in good faith with respect to "wages, hours, and other terms and conditions of employment. . . ." The duty is limited to those subjects, and within that area neither party is legally obligated to yield. Labor Board v. American Insurance Co., 343 U.S. 395. As to other matters, however, each party is free to bargain or not to bargain, and to agree or not to agree.

The company's good faith has met the requirements of the statute as to the subjects of mandatory bargaining. But that good faith does not license the employer to refuse to enter into agreements on the ground that they do not include some proposal which is not a mandatory subject of bargaining. We agree with the Board that such conduct is, in substance, a refusal to bargain about the subjects that are within the scope of mandatory bargaining. This does not mean that bargaining is to be confined to the statutory subjects. Each of the two controversial clauses is lawful in itself. Each would be enforceable if agreed to by the unions. But it does not follow that, because the company may propose these clauses, it can lawfully insist upon them as a condition to any agreement.

Since it is lawful to insist upon matters within the scope of mandatory bargaining and unlawful to insist upon matters without, the issue here is whether either the "ballot" or the "recognition" clause is a subject within the phrase "wages, hours, and other terms and conditions of employment" which defines mandatory bargaining. The "ballot" clause is not within that definition. It relates only to the procedure to be followed by the employees among themselves before their representative may call a strike or refuse a final offer. It settles no term or condition of employment — it merely calls for an advisory vote of the employees. It is not a partial "no-strike" clause. A "no-strike" clause prohibits the employees from striking during the life of the contract. It regulates the relations between the employer and the employees. See Labor Board v. American Insuarance Co., supra, at 408, n. 22. The "ballot" clause, on the other hand, deals only with relations between the employees and their unions. It substantially modifies the collective-bargaining system provided for in the statute by weakening the independence of the "representative" chosen by the employees. It enables the employer, in effect, to deal with its employees rather than with their statutory representative. Cf. Medo Photo Corp. v. Labor Board, 321 U.S. 678.

The "recognition" clause likewise does not come within the definition of mandatory bargaining. The statute requires the company to bargain with the certified representative of its employees. It is an evasion of that duty to insist that the certified agent not be a party to the collective-bargaining contract. The Act does not prohibit the voluntary addition of a party, but that does not authorize the employer to exclude the certified representative from the contract. . . .

MR. JUSTICE HARLAN, whom MR. JUSTICE CLARK and MR. JUSTICE WHITTAKER join, concurring in part and dissenting in part.

I agree that the company's insistence on the "recognition" clause constituted an unfair labor practice, but reach that conclusion by a different route from that taken by the Court. However, in light of the finding below that the company bargained in "good faith," I dissent from the view that its insistence on the "ballot" clause can support the charge of an unfair labor practice. . . .

The Court considers both the "ballot" and "recognition" clauses to be outside the scope of the mandatory bargaining provisions of §8(d) of the Act, which in connection with §§8(a)(5) and 8(b)(3) imposes an obligation on an employer and a union to ". . . confer in good faith with respect to wages, hours, and other terms and conditions of employment . . ." From this conclusion it is said to follow that although the company was free to "propose" these clauses and "bargain" over them, it could not "insist" on their inclusion in the collective bargaining contract as the price of agreement, and that such insistence was a per se unfair labor practice because it was tantamount to a refusal to bargain on "mandatory" subjects. At the same time the Court accepts the Trial Examiner's unchallenged finding that the company had bargained in "good faith," both with reference to these clauses and all other subjects, and holds that the clauses are lawful in themselves and ". . . would be enforceable if agreed to by the unions."

Preliminarily, I must state that I am unable to grasp a concept of "bargaining" which enables one to "propose" a particular point, but not to "insist" on it as a condition to agreement. The right to bargain becomes illusory if one is not free to press a proposal in good faith to the point of insistence. Surely adoption of so inherently vague and fluid a standard is apt to inhibit the entire bargaining process because of a party's fear that strenuous argument might shade into forbidden insistence and thereby produce a charge of an unfair labor practice. This watered-down notion of "bargaining" which the Court imports into the Act with reference to matters not within the scope of §8(d) appears as foreign to the labor field as it would be to the commercial world. To me all of this adds up to saying that the Act limits *effective* "bargaining" to subjects within the three fields referred to in §8(d), that is "wages, hours, and other terms and conditions of employment," even though the Court expressly disclaims so holding. . . .

At the start, I question the Court's conclusion that the "ballot" clause does not come within the "other terms and conditions of employment" provision of §8(d). The phrase is inherently vague and prior to this decision has been accorded by the Board and courts an expansive rather than a grudging interpretation. Many matters which might have been thought to be the sole concern of management are now dealt with as compulsory bargaining topics. E.g. National Labor Relations Board v. J. H. Allison & Co., 6 Cir., 165 F.2d 766 (merit increases). And since a "no strike" clause is something about which an employer can concededly bargain to the point of insistence, see Shell Oil Co., 77 N.L.R.B. 1306, I find it difficult to understand even under the Court's analysis of this problem why the "ballot" clause should not be considered within the area of bargaining described in §8(d). It affects the employer-employee relationship in much the same way, in that it may determine the timing of strikes or even whether a strike will occur by requiring a vote to ascertain the employees' sentiment prior to the union's decision.

Nonetheless I shall accept the Court's holding that this clause is not a condition of employment, for even though the union would accordingly not be *obliged* under §8(d) to bargain over it, in my view it does not follow that the company was *prohibited* from insisting on its inclusion in the collective bargaining agreement. In other words, I think the clause was a permissible, even if not an obligatory, subject of good faith bargaining.

The legislative history behind the Wagner and Taft-Hartley Acts persuasively indicates that the Board was never intended to have power to prevent good faith bargaining as to any subject not violative of the provisions or policies of those Acts. As a leading proponent for the Wagner Act explained:

"When the employees have chosen their organization, when they have selected their representatives, all the bill proposes to do is to escort them to the door of their employer and say, 'Here they are, the legal representatives of your employees.' What happens behind those doors is not inquired into, and the bill does not seek to inquire into it." 79 Cong. Rec. 7660.

The Wagner Act did not contain the "good faith" qualification now written into the bargaining requirements of §8(d), although this lack was remedied by early judicial interpretation which implied from former §8(5), 49 Stat. 453, the requirement that an employer bargain in good faith. E.g., National Labor Relations Board v. Griswold Mfg. Co., 3 Cir., 106 F.2d 713. But apart from this essential check on the bargaining process, the Board possessed no statutory authority to regulate the *substantive* scope of the bargaining process insofar as lawful demands of the parties were concerned. . . .

The . . . history [of the Taft-Hartley amendments] evinces a clear congressional purpose to assure the parties to a proposed collective bargaining agreement the greatest degree of freedom in their negotiations, and to require the Board to remain as aloof as possible from regulation of the bargaining process in its substantive aspects.

The decision of this Court in 1952 in National Labor Relations Board v. American National Insurance Co., supra, was fully in accord with this legislative background in holding that the Board lacked power to order an employer to cease bargaining over a particular clause because such bargaining under the Board's view, entirely apart from a showing of bad faith, constituted per se an unfair labor practice. . . .

I therefore cannot escape the view that today's decision is deeply inconsistent with legislative intention and this Court's precedents. The Act sought to compel management and labor to meet and bargain in good faith as to certain topics. This is the *affirmative* requirement of §8(d) which the Board is specifically empowered to enforce, but I see no warrant for inferring from it any power in the Board to *prohibit* bargaining in good faith as to lawful matters not included in §8(d). The Court reasons that such conduct on the part of the employer, when carried to the point of insistence, is in substance equivalent to a refusal to bargain as to the statutory subjects, but I cannot understand how this can be said over the Trial Examiner's unequivocal finding that the employer did in fact bargain in "good faith," not only over the disputed clauses but also over the statutory subjects.

It must not be forgotten that the Act requires bargaining, *not* agreement, for the obligation to bargain ". . . does not compel either party to agree to a proposal or require the making of a concession." §8(d). Here the employer concededly bargained but simply refused to *agree* until the union would accept what the Court holds would have been a lawful contract provision. It may be that an employer or union, by adamant insistence in good faith upon a provision which is not a statutory subject under §8(d), does in fact require the other party to bargain over it. But this effect is traceable to the economic power of the employer or union in the circumstances of a given situation and should not affect our construction of the Act. If one thing is clear, it is that the Board was not viewed by Congress as an agency which should exercise its powers to aid a party to collective bargaining which was in an economically disadvantageous position.

The most cursory view of decisions of the board and the circuit courts under the National Labor Relations Act reveals the unsettled and evolving character of collective bargaining agreements. Provisions which two decades ago might have been thought to be the exclusive concern of labor or management are today commonplace in such agreements. The bargaining process should be left fluid, free from intervention of the Board leading to premature crystallization of labor agreements into any one pattern of contract provisions, so that these agreements can be adapted through collective bargaining to the changing needs of our society and to the changing concepts of the responsibilities of labor and management. What the Court does today may impede this evolutionary process. Under the facts of this case, an employer is precluded from attempting to limit the likelihood of a strike. But by the same token it would seem to follow that unions which bargain in good faith would be precluded from insisting upon contract clauses which might not be deemed statutory subjects within §8(d).

As unqualifiedly stated in American National Insurance Co., 78 S. Ct. 727, it is through the "good faith" requirement of §8(d) that the Board is to enforce the bargaining provisions of §8. A determination that a party bargained as to statutory or nonstatutory subjects in good or bad faith must depend upon an evaluation of the total circumstances surrounding any given situation. I do not deny that there may be instances where unyielding insistence on a particular item may be a relevant consideration in the overall picture in determining "good faith," for the demands of a party might in the context of a particular industry be so extreme as to constitute some evidence of an unwillingness to bargain. But no such situation is presented in this instance by the "ballot" clause. "No strike" clauses, and other provisions analogous to the "ballot" clause limiting the right to strike, are hardly novel to labor agreements. And in any event the uncontested finding of "good faith" by the Trial Examiner forecloses that issue here.

Of course an employer or union cannot insist upon a clause which would be illegal under the Act's provisions, Labor Board v. National Maritime Union, 175 F.2d 686, or conduct itself so as to contravene specific requirements of the Act. Medo Photo Supply Corp. v. Labor Board, 321 U.S. 678. But here the Court recognizes, as it must, that the clause is lawful under the Act,[3] and I think it clear that the company's insistence upon it violated no statutory duty to which it was subject. The fact that the employer here *did* bargain with the union over the inclusion of the "ballot" clause in the proposed agreement distinguishes this case from the situation involved in the Medo Photo Supply Corp. case, supra, where an employer, without the sanction of a labor agreement contemplating such action, negotiated *directly* with its employees in reference to wages. . . . The important consideration is that the Act does not purport to define the terms of an agreement but simply secures the representative status of the union for purposes of bargaining. The controlling distinction from Medo Photo is that the employer here has not sought to bargain with anyone else over the terms of the agreement being negotiated. . . .

, The company's insistence on the "recognition" clause, which had the effect of excluding the International Union as a party signatory to agreement and making Local 1239 the sole contracting party on the union side, presents a different problem. In my opinion the company's action in this regard did constitute an unfair labor practice since it contravened specific requirements of the Act.

. . . I think it hardly debatable that this language [of the NLRA] must be read to require the company, if so requested, to sign any agreement reached with the same representative with which it is required to bargain. By conditioning agreement upon a change in signatory from

[3] I find no merit in the union's position that the "ballot" clause is unlawful under the Act since in derogation of the representative status of the union. The statute and its legislative background undermine any such argument, for the Taft-Hartley Act incorporates in two sections (§§203(c), 209(b)) provisions for a pre-strike ballot of employees and earlier drafts of the Act would have made an employee ballot *mandatory* as a condition precedent to all strikes. . . .

the certified exclusive bargaining representative, the company here in effect violated this duty. . . .[4]

NOTES

1. For cogent criticisms of the decision in the principal case, see Cox, Labor Decisions of the Supreme Court at the October Term, 1957, 44 Va. L. Rev. 1057, 1074-1086 (1958); Fleming, The Obligation to Bargain in Good Faith, in Public Policy and Collective Bargaining 67-70 (Shister, Aaron, and Summers, eds. 1962). Does the 1960 Insurance Agents decision, supra page 404, reflect a disavowal of Borg-Warner's approach to the duty to bargain?

2. As the opinions in the principal case suggest, it is a breach of the duty to bargain collectively for a union or employer to seek a contractual provision which is itself a violation of law. Cf. Local 1367, ILA (Galveston Maritime Assn., Inc.), 148 N.L.R.B. No. 44 (1964), holding that a union violates Section 8(b)(3) by a demand for a contract provision inconsistent with its duty of fair representation, owed to the employees.

3. Whitin Machine Works, 108 N.L.R.B. 1537, 1538 (1954): "[T]he authority conferred by Section 9(a) of the Act upon a union representing a majority of the employees in an appropriate unit entitles the union to all wage information essential to the intelligent representation of the employees and . . . when such information is reasonably available only from the employer's records, it is the employer's duty, on request, to accommodate the union. . . . Refusal by an employer to supply such necessary information makes impossible the full development of the collective-bargaining negotiations which the Act is intended to achieve. It therefore constitutes a violation of Section 8(a)(5) of the Act. . . . [I]n these cases it is sufficient that the information sought by the Union is related to the issues involved in collective bargaining, and . . . no specific need as to a particular issue must be shown. . . ."

Cf. Cox, The Duty to Bargain in Good Faith, 71 Harv. L. Rev. 1401, 1427-1428 (1958): "It is now settled that it is an unfair labor practice for an employer to refuse to furnish the bargaining representative with information concerning individual earnings, job rates and classifications, merit increases, pension data, time-study data, incentive earnings, piece rates, and the operation of the incentive system. Although many of the cases use the language of bad faith, proof of the denial of the information is sufficient standing alone to make out the violation of Section 8(a)(5). . . . A union cannot participate in the award of merit increases to individual employees whose wage history and rates of pay the employer insists upon keeping secret. Nor can there be joint discussion of job standards or an incentive system until their method of operation is disclosed. In some of the cases the employer avowedly challenged the bargainability of the subject upon which information was

---

[4] Justice Frankfurter's opinion, essentially agreeing with the position of Justice Harlan, is omitted. — ED.

withheld. In others he was obviously seeking to avoid negotiations upon the issue. In virtually all the cases, except those involving financial data, there could be no negotiation on the subject, in any sense of the term, until the information was supplied to the union. And since there was no bargaining on a statutory subject the NLRB was not required to review . . . the employer's state of mind. . . ."

Why does Cox except financial data? The Supreme Court, in NLRB v. Truitt Manufacturing Co., 351 U.S. 149 (1956), upheld the view that an employer who resists a union demand on the ground of an asserted inability to pay must provide the union with financial data on request. The Court, per Black, J., reasoned (p. 152):

"Good-faith bargaining necessarily requires that claims made by either bargainer should be honest claims. This is true about an asserted inability to pay an increase in wages. If such an argument is important enough to present in the give and take of bargaining, it is important enough to require some sort of proof of its accuracy. And it would certainly not be farfetched for a trier of fact to reach the conclusion that bargaining lacks good faith when an employer mechanically repeats a claim of inability to pay without making the slightest effort to substantiate the claim. . . . We agree with the Board that a refusal to attempt to substantiate a claim of inability to pay increased wages may support a finding of a failure to bargain in good faith.

"The Board concluded that under the facts and circumstances of this case the respondent was guilty of an unfair labor practice in failing to bargain in good faith. We see no reason to disturb the findings of the Board. We do not hold, however, that in every case in which economic inability is raised as an argument against increased wages it automatically follows that the employees are entitled to substantiating evidence. Each case must turn upon its particular facts. The inquiry must always be whether or not under the circumstances of the particular case the statutory obligation to bargain in good faith has been met."

Despite the Court's use of the language of over-all good faith, it is clear that the Board regarded the obligation as unconditional, so long as the employer had put ability to pay in issue, and the form of the union's demand did not unduly burden the company. See Justice Frankfurter's separate opinion, 351 U.S. at 154. The Board has continued to apply the doctrine as a per se rule. See, e.g., NLRB, 22nd Ann. Rep. 82 (1958). On what approach to the duty to bargain can such a position be justified? Cf. Cox, supra, at 1433-1435; Summers, in Collective Bargaining and the Law 52-53 (Univ. of Mich. Law School Summer Institute 1959).

NLRB v. KATZ

Supreme Court of the United States, 1962
369 U.S. 736, 82 Sup. Ct. 1107, 8 L. Ed. 2d 230

MR. JUSTICE BRENNAN delivered the opinion of the Court.

Is it a violation of the duty "to bargain collectively" imposed by

§8(a)(5) of the National Labor Relations Act for an employer, without first consulting a union with which it is carrying on bona fide contract negotiations, to institute changes regarding matters which are subjects of mandatory bargaining under §8(d) and which are in fact under discussion? The National Labor Relations Board answered the question affirmatively in this case, in a decision which expressly disclaimed any finding that the totality of the respondents' conduct manifested bad faith in the pending negotiations. 126 N.L.R.B. 288. A divided panel of the Court of Appeals for the Second Circuit denied enforcement of the Board's cease-and-desist order, finding in our decision in Labor Board v. Insurance Agents' Union, 361 U.S. 477, a broad rule that the statutory duty to bargain cannot be held to be violated, when bargaining is in fact being carried on, without a finding of the respondent's subjective bad faith in negotiating. 289 F.2d 700. . . . We granted certiorari, 368 U.S. 811, in order to consider whether the Board's decision and order were contrary to Insurance Agents. We find nothing in the Board's decision inconsistent with Insurance Agents and hold that the Court of Appeals erred in refusing to enforce the Board's order. . . .

[Between July, 1956, and May, 1957, the union and the company were engaged in negotiations over renewal of their agreement. Included in the union's list of proposed subjects for discussion were merit increases, general wage increases, and a sick-leave proposal.] As amended and amplified at the hearing and construed by the Board, the complaint's charge of unfair labor practices particularly referred to three acts by the company; unilaterally granting numerous merit increases in October 1956 and January 1957; unilaterally announcing a change in sick-leave policy in March 1957; and unilaterally instituting a new system of automatic wage increases during April 1957. As the ensuing litigation has developed, the company has defended against the charges along two fronts: First, it asserts that the unilateral changes occurred after a bargaining impasse had developed through the union's fault in adopting obstructive tactics. According to the Board, however, "the evidence is clear that the Respondent undertook its unilateral actions before negotiations were discontinued in May 1957, or before, as we find on the record, the existence of any possible impasse." 126 N.L.R.B., at 289-290. . . .

The second line of defense was that the Board could not hinge a conclusion that §8(a)(5) had been violated on unilateral actions alone, without making a finding of the employer's subjective bad faith at the bargaining table; and that the unilateral actions were merely evidence relevant to the issue of subjective good faith. . . .

The duty "to bargain collectively" enjoined by §8(a)(5) is defined by §8(d) as the duty to "meet . . . and confer in good faith with respect to wages, hours, and other terms and conditions of employment." Clearly, the duty thus defined may be violated without a general failure of subjective good faith; for there is no occasion to consider the issue of good faith if a party has refused even to negotiate in fact — "to meet . . . and confer" — about any of the mandatory subjects. A refusal to negotiate in fact as to any subject which is within §8(d), and about which the union seeks to negotiate, violates §8(a)(5) though the employer has every desire to reach agreement with the union upon an overall collective agreement and earnestly and in all good faith bargains to that end. We hold that an employer's unilateral change in conditions of employment under negotiation is similarly a violation of §8(a)(5), for it is a circumvention of the duty to negotiate which frustrates the objectives of §8(a)(5) much as does a flat refusal.[11]

The unilateral actions of the respondent illustrate the policy and practical considerations which support our conclusion.

We consider first the matter of sick leave. A sick-leave plan had been in effect since May 1956, under which employees were allowed ten paid sick-leave days annually and could accumulate half the unused days, or up to five days each year. Changes in the plan were sought and proposals and counterproposals had come up at three bargaining conferences. In March 1957, the company, without first notifying or consulting the union, announced changes in the plan, which reduced from ten to five the number of paid sick-leave days per year, but allowed accumulation of twice the unused days, thus increasing to ten the number of days which might be carried over. This action plainly frustrated the statutory objective of establishing working conditions through bargaining. Some employees might view the change to be a diminution of benefits. Others, more interested in accumulating sick-leave days, might regard the change as an improvement. If one view or the other clearly prevailed among the employees, the unilateral action might well mean that the employer had either uselessly dissipated trading material or aggravated the sick-leave issue. On the other hand, if the employees were more evenly divided on the merits of the company's changes, the union negotiators, beset by conflicting factions, might be led to adopt a protective vagueness on the issue of sick leave, which also would inhibit the useful discussion contemplated by Congress in imposing the specific obligation to bargain collectively.

Other considerations appear from consideration of the respondents'

---

[11] Compare Medo Corp. v. Labor Board, 321 U.S. 678; May Department Stores v. Labor Board, 326 U.S. 376; Labor Board v. Crompton-Highland Mills, 337 U.S. 217.

In Medo, the Court held that the employer interfered with his employees' right to bargain collectively through a chosen representative, in violation of §8(1), 49 Stat. 452 (now §8(a)(1)), when it treated directly with employees and granted them a wage increase in return for their promise to repudiate the union they had designated as their representative. It further held that the employer violated the statutory duty to bargain when he refused to negotiate with the union after the employees had carried out their promise.

May held that the employer violated §8(1) when, after having unequivocally refused to bargain with a certified union on the ground that the unit was inappropriate, it announced that it had applied to the War Labor Board for permission to grant a wage increase to all its employees except those whose wages had been fixed by "closed shop agreements."

Crompton-Highland Mills sustained the Board's conclusion that the employer's unilateral grant of a wage increase substantially greater than any it had offered to the union during negotiations which had ended in impasse clearly manifested bad faith and violated the employer's duty to bargain.

unilateral action in increasing wages. At the April 4, 1957, meeting the employers offered, and the union rejected, a three-year contract with an immediate across-the-board increase of $7.50 per week, to be followed at the end of the first year and again at the end of the second by further increases of $5 for employees earning less than $90 at those times. Shortly thereafter, without having advised or consulted with the union, the company announced a new system of automatic wage increases whereby there would be an increase of $5 every three months up to $74.99 per week; an increase of $5 every six months between $75 and $90 per week; and a merit review every six months for employees earning over $90 per week. It is clear at a glance that the automatic wage increase system which was instituted unilaterally was considerably more generous than that which had shortly theretofore been offered to and rejected by the union. Such action conclusively manifested bad faith in the negotiations, Labor Board v. Crompton-Highland Mills, 337 U.S. 217, and so would have violated §8(a)(5) even on the Court of Appeals' interpretation, though no additional evidence of bad faith appeared. An employer is not required to lead with his best offer; he is free to bargain. But even after an impasse is reached he has no license to grant wage increases greater than any he has ever offered the union at the bargaining table, for such action is necessarily inconsistent with a sincere desire to conclude an agreement with the union.[12]

The respondents' third unilateral action related to merit increases, which are also a subject of mandatory bargaining. Labor Board v. Allison & Co., 165 F.2d 766. The matter of merit increases had been raised at three of the conferences during 1956 but no final understanding had been reached. In January 1957, the company, without notice to the union, granted merit increases to 20 employees out of the approximately 50 in the unit, the increases ranging between $2 and $10. This action too must be viewed as tantamount to an outright refusal to negotiate on that subject, and therefore as a violation of §8(a)(5), unless the fact that the January raises were in line with the company's long-standing practice of granting quarterly or semiannual merit reviews — in effect, were a mere continuation of the status quo — differentiates them from the wage increases and the changes in the sick-leave plan. We do not think it does. Whatever might be the case as to so-called "merit raises" which are in fact simply automatic increases to which the employer has already committed himself, the raises here in question were in no sense automatic, but were informed by a large measure of discretion. There simply is no way in such case for a union to know whether or not there has been a substantial departure from past practice, and therefore the union may properly insist that the company negotiate as to the procedures and criteria for determining such increases.[14]

---

[12] Of course, there is no resemblance between this situation and one wherein an employer, after notice and consultation, "unilaterally" institutes a wage increase identical with one which the union has rejected as too low. . . .

[14] . . . Compare the isolated individual wage adjustments held not to be unfair labor practices in Labor Board v. Superior Fireproof Door & Sash Co., 289 F.2d 713, 720, and White v. Labor Board, 255 F.2d 564, 565.

It is apparent from what we have said why we see nothing in Insurance Agents contrary to the Board's decision. The union in that case had not in any way whatever foreclosed discussion of any issue, by unilateral actions or otherwise. The conduct complained of consisted of partial-strike tactics designed to put pressure on the employer to come to terms with the union negotiators. We held that Congress had not, in §8(b)-(3), the counterpart of §8(a)(5), empowered the Board to pass judgment on the legitimacy of any particular economic weapon used in support of genuine negotiations. But the Board *is* authorized to order the cessation of behavior which is in effect a refusal to negotiate, or which directly obstructs or inhibits the actual process of discussion, or which reflects a cast of mind against reaching agreement. Unilateral action by an employer without prior discussion with the union does amount to a refusal to negotiate about the affected conditions of employment under negotiation, and must of necessity obstruct bargaining, contrary to the congressional policy. It will often disclose an unwillingness to agree with the union. It will rarely be justified by any reason of substance. It follows that the Board may hold such unilateral action to be an unfair labor practice in violation of §8(a)(5), without also finding the employer guilty of over-all subjective bad faith. While we do not foreclose the possibility that there might be circumstances which the Board could or should accept as excusing or justifying unilateral action, no such case is presented here. . . .

Mr. Justice Frankfurter and Mr. Justice White took no part in the decision of this case.

FIBREBOARD PAPER PRODUCTS CORP. v. NLRB
Supreme Court of the United States, 1964
379 U.S. 203, 85 Sup. Ct. 398, 13 L. Ed. 2d 233

Mr. Chief Justice Warren delivered the opinion of the Court. . . .

Petitioner, Fibreboard Paper Products Corporation (the Company), has a manufacturing plant in Emeryville, California. Since 1937 the East Bay Union Machinists, Local 1304, United Steelworkers of America, AFL-CIO (the Union) has been the exclusive bargaining representative for a unit of the Company's maintenance employees. In September 1958, the Union and the Company entered the latest of a series of collective bargaining agreements which was to expire on July 31, 1959. . . . On May 26, 1959, the Union gave timely notice of its desire to modify the contract and sought to arrange a bargaining session with Company representatives. . . . Efforts by the Union to schedule a bargaining session met with no success until July 27, four days before the expiration of the contract, when the Company notified the Union of its desire to meet.

The Company, concerned with the high cost of its maintenance operation, had undertaken a study of the possibility of effecting cost savings by engaging an independent contractor to do the maintenance work. At the July 27 meeting, the Company informed the Union that it had determined that substantial savings could be effected by contracting out the work upon expiration of its collective bargaining agreements with the various labor organizations representing its maintenance employees. The Company delivered to the Union representatives a letter which stated in pertinent part:

"For some time we have been seriously considering the question of letting out our Emeryville maintenance work to an independent contractor, and have now reached a definite decision to do so effective August 1, 1959.

"In these circumstances, we are sure you will realize that negotiation of a new contract would be pointless. However, if you have any questions, we will be glad to discuss them with you."

After some discussion of the Company's right to enter a contract with a third party to do the work then being performed by employees in the bargaining unit, the meeting concluded with the understanding that the parties would meet again on July 30.

By July 30, the Company had selected Fluor Maintenance, Inc., to do the maintenance work. Fluor had assured the Company that maintenance costs could be curtailed by reducing the work force, decreasing fringe benefits and overtime payments, and by preplanning and scheduling the services to be performed. . . .

At the July 30 meeting, the Company's representative, in explaining the decision to contract out the maintenance work, remarked that during bargaining negotiations in previous years the Company had endeavored to point out through the use of charts and statistical information "just how expensive and costly our maintenance work was and how it was creating quite a terrific burden upon the Emeryville plant." He further stated that unions representing other Company employees "had joined hands with management in an effort to bring about an economical and efficient operation," but "we had not been able to attain that in our discussions with this particular Local." The Company also distributed a letter stating that "since we will have no employees in the bargaining unit covered by our present Agreement, negotiation of a new or renewed Agreement would appear to us to be pointless." On July 31, the employment of the maintenance employees represented by the Union was terminated and Fluor employees took over. That evening the Union established a picket line at the Company's plant.

The Union filed unfair labor practice charges against the Company, alleging violations of §§8(a)(1), 8(a)(3) and 8(a)(5). After hearings were held upon a complaint issued by the National Labor Relations Board's Regional Director, the Trial Examiner filed an Intermediate Report recommending dismissal of the complaint. The Board accepted the recommendation and dismissed the complaint. 130 N.L.R.B. 1558.

Petitions for reconsideration, filed by the General Counsel and the Union, were granted. Upon reconsideration, the Board adhered to the Trial Examiner's finding that the Company's motive in contracting out its maintenance work was economic rather than anti-union but found nevertheless that the Company's "failure to negotiate with . . . [the Union] concerning its decision to subcontract its maintenance work constituted a violation of Section 8(a)(5) of the Act." This ruling was based upon the doctrine established in Town & Country Mfg. Co., 136 N.L.R.B. 1022, 1027, enforcement granted, 316 F.2d 846 (C.A. 5th Cir. 1963), that contracting out work, "albeit for economic reasons, is a matter within the statutory phrase 'other terms and conditions of employment' and is a mandatory subject of collective bargaining within the meaning of Section 8(a)(5) of the Act."

The Board ordered the Company to reinstitute the maintenance operation previously performed by the employees represented by the Union, to reinstate the employees to their former or substantially equivalent positions with back pay computed from the date of the Board's supplemental decision, and to fulfill its statutory obligation to bargain.

On appeal, the Court of Appeals for the District of Columbia Circuit granted the Board's petition for enforcement. 322 F.2d 411. Because of the importance of the issues and because of an alleged conflict among the courts of appeals, we granted certiorari limited to a consideration of the following questions:

1. Was Petitioner required by the National Labor Relations Act to bargain with a union representing some of its employees about whether to let to an independent contractor for legitimate business reasons the performance of certain operations in which those employees had been engaged?

2. Was the Board, in a case involving only a refusal to bargain, empowered to order the resumption of operations which had been discontinued for legitimate business reasons and reinstatement with back pay of the individuals formerly employed therein? . . .

I

. . . Because of the limited grant of certiorari, we are concerned here only with whether the subject upon which the employer allegedly refused to bargain — contracting out of plant maintenance work previously performed by employees in the bargaining unit, which the employees were capable of continuing to perform — is covered by the phrase "terms and conditions of employment" within the meaning of §8(d).

The subject matter of the present dispute is well within the literal meaning of the phrase "terms and conditions of employment." See Order of Railroad Telegraphers v. Chicago & N.W.R. Co., 362 U.S. 330. A stipulation with respect to the contracting out of work performed by members of the bargaining unit might appropriately be called a "condition of employment." The words even more plainly cover termination of employment which, as the facts of this case indicate, necessarily results from the contracting out of work performed by members of the established bargaining unit.

The inclusion of "contracting out" within the statutory scope of collective bargaining also seems well designed to effectuate the purposes of the National Labor Relations Act. One of the primary purposes of the

Act is to promote the peaceful settlement of industrial disputes by subjecting labor-management controversies to the mediatory influence of negotiation. The Act was framed with an awareness that refusals to confer and negotiate had been one of the most prolific causes of industrial strife. Labor Board v. Jones & Laughlin Steel Corp., 301 U.S. 1, 42-43. To hold, as the Board has done, that contracting out is a mandatory subject of collective bargaining would promote the fundamental purpose of the Act by bringing a problem of vital concern to labor and management within the framework established by Congress as most conducive to industrial peace.

The conclusion that "contracting out" is a statutory subject of collective bargaining is further reinforced by industrial practices in this country. While not determinative, it is appropriate to look to industrial bargaining practices in appraising the propriety of including a particular subject within the scope of mandatory bargaining. Labor Board v. American Nat'l Ins. Co., 343 U.S. 395, 408. Industrial experience is not only reflective of the interests of labor and management in the subject matter but is also indicative of the amenability of such subjects to the collective bargaining process. Experience illustrates that contracting out in one form or another has been brought, widely and successfully, within the collective bargaining framework.[6] Provisions relating to contracting out exist in numerous collective bargaining agreements,[7] and "contracting out work is the basis of many grievances; and that type of claim is grist in the mills of the arbitrators." United Steelworkers v. Warrior & Gulf Nav. Co., 363 U.S. 574, 584.

The situation here is not unlike that presented in Local 24, Teamsters Union v. Oliver, 358 U.S. 283, where we held that conditions imposed upon contracting out work to prevent possible curtailment of jobs and the undermining of conditions of employment for members of the bargaining unit constituted a statutory subject of collective bargaining. The issue in that case was whether state antitrust laws could be applied to a provision of a collective bargaining agreement which fixed the minimum rental to be paid by the employer motor carrier who leased vehicles to be driven by their owners rather than the carrier's employees. We held that the agreement was upon a subject matter as to which federal law directed the parties to bargain and hence that state antitrust laws could not be applied to prevent the effectuation of the agreement. . . .

The facts of the present case illustrate the propriety of submitting the dispute to collective negotiation. The Company's decision to contract out the maintenance work did not alter the Company's basic operation. The maintenance work still had to be performed in the plant. No capital investment was contemplated; the Company merely replaced ex-

---

[6] See Lunden, Subcontracting Clauses in Major Contracts, 84 Monthly Lab. Rev. 579, 715 (1961).

[7] A Department of Labor study analyzed 1,687 collective bargaining agreements, which applied to approximately 7,500,000 workers (about one-half of the estimated work force covered by collective bargaining agreements). Among the agreements studied, approximately one-fourth (378) contained some form of a limitation on subcontracting. Lunden, supra, at 581.

isting employees with those of an independent contractor to do the same work under similar conditions of employment. Therefore, to require the employer to bargain about the matter would not significantly abridge his freedom to manage the business.

The Company was concerned with the high cost of its maintenance operation. It was induced to contract out the work by assurances from independent contractors that economies could be derived by reducing the work force, decreasing fringe benefits, and eliminating overtime payments. These have long been regarded as matters peculiarly suitable for resolution within the collective bargaining framework, and industrial experience demonstrates that collective negotiation has been highly successful in achieving peaceful accommodation of the conflicting interests. Yet, it is contended that when an employer can effect cost savings in these respects by contracting the work out, there is no need to attempt to achieve similar economies through negotiation with existing employees or to provide them with an opportunity to negotiate a mutually acceptable alternative. The short answer is that, although it is not possible to say whether a satisfactory solution could be reached, national labor policy is founded upon the congressional determination that the chances are good enough to warrant subjecting such issues to the process of collective negotiation.

The appropriateness of the collective bargaining process for resolving such issues was apparently recognized by the Company. In explaining its decision to contract out the maintenance work, the Company pointed out that in the same plant other unions "had joined hands with management in an effort to bring about an economical and efficient operation," but "we had not been able to attain that in our discussions with this particular Local." Accordingly, based on past bargaining experience with this union, the Company unilaterally contracted out the work. While "the Act does not encourage a party to engage in fruitless marathon discussions at the expense of frank statement and support of his position," Labor Board v. American Nat'l Ins. Co., 343 U.S. 395, 404, it at least demands that the issue be submitted to the mediatory influence of collective negotiations. As the Court of Appeals pointed out, "it is not necessary that it be likely or probable that the union will yield or supply a feasible solution but rather that the union be afforded an opportunity to meet management's legitimate complaints that its maintenance was unduly costly."

We are thus not expanding the scope of mandatory bargaining to hold, as we do now, that the type of "contracting out" involved in this case — the replacement of employees in the existing bargaining unit with those of an independent contractor to do the same work under similar conditions of employment — is a statutory subject of collective bargaining under §8(d). Our decision need not and does not encompass other forms of "contracting out" or "subcontracting" which arise daily in our complex economy.[8]

[8] As the Solicitor General points out, the terms "contracting out" and "subcontracting" have no precise meaning. They are used to describe a variety of business arrangements altogether different from that involved in this case. . . .

I I

The only question remaining is whether, upon a finding that the Company had refused to bargain about a matter which is a statutory subject of collective bargaining, the Board was empowered to order the resumption of maintenance operations and reinstatement with back pay. We believe that it was so empowered.

Section 10(c) . . . "charges the Board with the task of devising remedies to effectuate the policies of the Act." Labor Board v. Seven-Up Bottling Co., 344 U.S. 344, 346. The Board's power is a broad discretionary one, subject to limited judicial review. Ibid. "[T]he relation of remedy to policy is peculiarly a matter for administrative competence. . . ." Phelps Dodge Corp. v. Labor Board, 313 U.S. 177, 194. "In fashioning remedies to undo the effects of violations of the Act, the Board must draw on enlightenment gained from experience." Labor Board v. Seven-Up Bottling Co., 344 U.S. 344, 346. The Board's order will not be disturbed "unless it can be shown that the order is a patent attempt to achieve ends other than those which can fairly be said to effectuate the policies of the Act." Virginia Elec. & Power Co. v. Labor Board, 319 U.S. 533, 540. Such a showing has not been made in this case.

There has been no showing that the Board's order restoring the status quo ante to insure meaningful bargaining is not well designed to promote the policies of the Act. Nor is there evidence which would justify disturbing the Board's conclusion that the order would not impose an undue or unfair burden on the Company.[10]

It is argued, nonetheless, that the award exceeds the Board's powers under §10(c) in that it infringes the provision that "no order of the Board shall require the reinstatement of any individual as an employee who has been suspended or discharged, or the payment to him of any back pay, if such individual was suspended or discharged for cause. . . ." The legislative history of that provision indicates that it was designed to preclude the Board from reinstating an individual who had been discharged because of misconduct. There is no indication, however, that it was designed to curtail the Board's power in fashioning remedies when the loss of employment stems directly from an unfair labor practice as in the case at hand.

Affirmed.

Mr. Justice Goldberg took no part in the consideration or decision of this case.

Mr. Justice Stewart, with whom Mr. Justice Douglas and Mr. Justice Harlan join, concurring.

---

[10] The Board stated: "We do not believe that requirement [restoring the status quo ante] imposes an undue or unfair burden on Respondent. The record shows that the maintenance operation is still being performed in much the same manner as it was prior to the subcontracting arrangement. Respondent has a continuing need for the services of maintenance employees; and Respondent's subcontract is terminable at any time upon 60 days' notice." 138 N.L.R.B., at 555, n. 19.

Viewed broadly, the question before us stirs large issues. The Court purports to limit its decision to "the facts of this case." But the Court's opinion radiates implications of such disturbing breadth that I am persuaded to file this separate statement of my own views. . . .

The basic question is whether the employer failed to "confer in good faith with respect to . . . terms and conditions of employment" in unilaterally deciding to subcontract this work. This question goes to the scope of the employer's duty in the absence of a collective bargaining agreement.[2] It is true, as the Court's opinion points out, that industrial experience may be useful in determining the proper scope of the duty to bargain. See Labor Board v. American Nat'l Ins. Co., 343 U.S. 395, 408. But data showing that many labor contracts refer to subcontracting or that subcontracting grievances are frequently referred to arbitrators under collective bargaining agreements, while not wholly irrelevant, do not have much real bearing, for such data may indicate no more than that the parties have often considered it mutually advantageous to bargain over these issues on a permissive basis. In any event, the ultimate question is the scope of the duty to bargain defined by the statutory language.

It is important to note that the words of the statute are words of limitation. The National Labor Relations Act does not say that the employer and employees are bound to confer upon any subject which interests either of them; the specification of wages, hours, and other terms and conditions of employment defines a limited category of issues subject to compulsory bargaining. . . .

The phrase "conditions of employment" is no doubt susceptible of diverse interpretations. At the extreme, the phrase could be construed to apply to any subject which is insisted upon as a prerequisite for continued employment. Such an interpretation, which would in effect place the compulsion of the Board behind any and all bargaining demands, would be contrary to the intent of Congress, as reflected in this legislative history. Yet there are passages in the Court's opinion today which suggest just such an expansive interpretation, for the Court's opinion seems to imply that any issue which may reasonably divide an employer and his employees must be the subject of compulsory collective bargaining.[6]

Only a narrower concept of "conditions of employment" will serve the statutory purpose of delineating a limited category of issues which are

[2] There was a time when one might have taken the view that the National Labor Relations Act gave the Board and the courts no power to determine the subjects about which the parties must bargain — a view expressed by Senator Walsh when he said that public concern ends at the bargaining room door. 79 Cong. Rec. 7659 (1939). See Cox and Dunlop, Regulation of Collective Bargaining by the NLRB, 63 Harv. L. Rev. 389. But too much law has been built upon a contrary assumption for this view any longer to prevail, and I question neither the power of the Court to decide this issue nor the propriety of its doing so.

[6] The opinion of the Court seems to assume that the only alternative to compulsory collective bargaining is unremitting economic warfare. But to exclude subjects from the ambit of compulsory collective bargaining does not preclude the parties from seeking negotiations about them on a permissive basis. And there are limitations upon the use of economic force to compel concession upon subjects which are only permissively bargainable. Labor Board v. Wooster Div. of Borg-Warner Corp., 356 U.S. 342.

subject to the duty to bargain collectively. . . . In common parlance, the conditions of a person's employment are most obviously the various physical dimensions of his working environment. What one's hours are to be, what amount of work is expected during those hours, what periods of relief are available, what safety practices are observed, would all seem conditions of one's employment. There are other less tangible but no less important characteristics of a person's employment which might also be deemed "conditions" — most prominently the characteristic involved in this case, the security of one's employment. On one view of the matter, it can be argued that the question whether there is to be a job is not a condition of employment; the question is not one of imposing conditions on employment, but the more fundamental question whether there is to be employment at all. However, it is clear that the Board and the courts have on numerous occasions recognized that union demands for provisions limiting an employer's power to discharge employees are mandatorily bargainable. Thus, freedom from discriminatory discharge, seniority rights, the imposition of a compulsory retirement age, have been recognized as subjects upon which an employer must bargain, although all of these concern the very existence of the employment itself.

While employment security has thus properly been recognized in various circumstances as a condition of employment, it surely does not follow that every decision which may affect job security is a subject of compulsory collective bargaining. Many decisions made by management affect the job security of employees. Decisions concerning the volume and kind of advertising expenditures, product design, the manner of financing, and of sales, all may bear upon the security of the workers' jobs. Yet it is hardly conceivable that such decisions so involve "conditions of employment" that they must be negotiated with the employees' bargaining representative.

In many of these areas the impact of a particular management decision upon job security may be extremely indirect and uncertain, and this alone may be sufficient reason to conclude that such decisions are not "with respect to . . . conditions of employment." Yet there are other areas where decisions by management may quite clearly imperil job security, or indeed terminate employment entirely. An enterprise may decide to invest in labor-saving machinery. Another may resolve to liquidate its assets and go out of business. Nothing the Court holds today should be understood as imposing a duty to bargain collectively regarding such managerial decisions, which lie at the core of entrepreneurial control. Decisions concerning the commitment of investment capital and the basic scope of the enterprise are not in themselves primarily about conditions of employment, though the effect of the decision may be necessarily to terminate employment. If, as I think clear, the purpose of §8(d) is to describe a limited area subject to the duty of collective bargaining, those management decisions which are fundamental to the basic direction of a corporate enterprise or which impinge only indirectly upon employment security should be excluded from that area.

Applying these concepts to the case at hand, I do not believe that an employer's subcontracting practices are, as a general matter, in themselves conditions of employment.   Upon any definition of the statutory terms short of the most expansive, such practices are not conditions — tangible or intangible — of any person's employment.   The question remains whether this particular kind of subcontracting decision comes within the employer's duty to bargain.   On the facts of this case, I join the Court's judgment, because all that is involved is the substitution of one group of workers for another to perform the same task in the same plant under the ultimate control of the same employer.   The question whether the employer may discharge one group of workers and substitute another for them is closely analogous to many other situations within the traditional framework of collective bargaining.   Compulsory retirement, layoffs according to seniority, assignment of work among potentially eligible groups within the plant — all involve similar questions of discharge and work assignment, and all have been recognized as subjects of compulsory collective bargaining.

Analytically, this case is not far from that which would be presented if the employer had merely discharged all his employees and replaced them with other workers willing to work on the same job in the same plant without the various fringe benefits so costly to the company. . . . Similarly, had the employer in this case chosen to bargain with the union about the proposed subcontract, negotiations would have inevitably turned to the underlying questions of cost, which prompted the subcontracting.   Insofar as the employer frustrated collective bargaining with respect to these concededly bargaining issues by its unilateral act of subcontracting this work, it can properly be found to have violated its statutory duty under §8(a)(5).

This kind of subcontracting falls short of such larger entrepreneurial questions as what shall be produced, how capital shall be invested in fixed assets, or what the basic scope of the enterprise shall be.   In my view, the Court's decision in this case has nothing to do with whether any aspects of those larger issues could under any circumstances be considered subjects of compulsory collective bargaining under the present law. . . .

NOTES

1. On the issue of the subjects which must be bargained about see also Inland Steel Co. v. NLRB, infra page 611.

2. For the kinds of circumstances which have heretofore led the NLRB to find limits on the scope of mandatory bargaining, compare NLRB v. Borg-Warner, supra page 440, and Detroit Resilient Floor Decorators Union (Mill Floor Covering, Inc.), 136 N.L.R.B. 769 (1962), enforcement granted, 317 F.2d 269 (6th Cir. 1963), raising the question whether a union can compel bargaining over a demand that the employer contribute to a fund established to promote the floor covering industry:

"An industry promotion fund seems to us to be outside of the employment relationship.   It concerns itself rather with the relationship of employers to one another or, like advertising, with the relationship of an employer to the consuming public.

"The ability of an employer or an industry to meet changing conditions may, as the Respondent argues, affect employees' opportunities in the long run, and labor organizations are understandably concerned with the future of the industries from which their members derive their livelihood. Such long-range prospects may also be affected by conditions and events of even more general applicability, such as developments on the economic or political scene, legislation, taxation, and foreign competition. Nothing prevents an employer and a union from joining voluntarily in a mutual effort to attempt to influence their industry's course of development, provided, of course, that other legislative enactments do not prohibit such activities. To hold, however, under this Act, that one party must bargain at the behest of another on any matter which might conceivably enhance the prospects of the industry would transform bargaining over the compensation, hours, and employment conditions of employees into a debate over policy objectives."

The Board has consistently held that the giving of a performance or indemnity bond or other security, whether by employer or union, is not a mandatory subject, regardless of the financial responsibility of the party or the reasonableness of the demanding party's fears of a breach. A recent reaffirmation of this view produced two dissenting votes, however. Carpenters' District Council (Excello Dry Wall Co.), 145 N.L.R.B. 663 (1963).

3. If, during a strike, an employer decides permanently to subcontract out work formerly done by his striking employees, does the duty to bargain, which continues during a strike, require him to notify the union in advance of the implementation of this decision? In Hawaii Meat Co., Ltd. v. NLRB, 321 F.2d 397 (9th Cir. 1963), the Court of Appeals reversed an affirmative Board answer to this question, saying (p. 399):

"We think that when an employer is confronted with a strike, his legal position is, in some respects, different from that which exists when no strike is expected or occurs. No case holds that a struck employer may not try to keep his business operating; on the contrary, it is quite clear that he has the right to do so. He may not use the strike as an excuse for committing unfair labor practices. . . . But it does not follow that what this employer did to meet the strike was an unfair labor practice, even though it might have been one in the absence of a strike. . . .

"We think it no more proper for the Board to intrude upon the decision of the employer, in a strike situation, to keep going by subcontracting, than to intrude upon a decision to replace, permanently, individual strikers. . . ."

4. What is the appropriate remedy for unlawful unilateral discontinuance of an operation? In the Town & Country decision, 136 N.L.R.B. 1022, cited in the principal case, the Board reasoned (p. 1030):

"It would be an exercise in futility to attempt to remedy this type of violation if an employer's decision to subcontract were to stand. No genuine bargaining over a decision to terminate a phase of operations can be conducted where that decision has already been made and implemented. . . . (T)he remedy must be 'adapted to the situation which calls for redress,' and (we will) require an employer to restore the status quo ante by abrogating its subcontract and fulfilling its statutory obligation to bargain. Of course, where that obligation has been satisfied after the resumption of bargaining, an employer may lawfully subcontract unit work."

Does the decision in the principal case suggest that the NLRB may order resumption of operations in any unilateral-action case? The Board has not done so as a matter of course. Cf. Winn-Dixie Stores, Inc., 147 N.L.R.B. No. 89 (1964). The trial examiner found a violation of Section 8(a)(5) of the Act in the employer's failure to notify, consult with, or bargain with the union about the elimination of the cheese packaging operation, but limited his recommended order to a requirement that the respondent bargain about the effects on its employees of its unilateral action. In rejecting the recommendation as too limited, the Board said:

"In framing his recommended remedial order, the Trial Examiner relied on Renton News Record (136 N.L.R.B. 1294 (1962)) where the order was similarly limited. But that case involved special circumstances of a compelling nature not present in the instant case. There the employer was confronted with a situation where the change unilaterally effected was unavoidable because of pressing economic necessity. . . .

"This case is different. Here we have an employer who by its past conduct has given evidence of its opposition to the policies of the Act. There are no intervening outside interests that would suffer serious injury if the action taken were undone. Nor can it be said here that the action taken was compelled by pressing economic necessity. . . . In sum, we find in this case no mitigating circumstances of a kind which might have excused the Respondent *then* from fully complying with its bargaining obligation, or which would justify us *now* in fashioning an order that would fall short of the remedial measures appropriate to meet the violation we have found . . .

"The nature of the violation would justify us in directing the Respondent to restore the status quo ante by reestablishing the discontinued operation. However, we believe that our remedy should also be tempered by practical considerations. Reviewing the nature of the Respondent's general business operations, the likelihood that the affected employees are suitable for employment elsewhere in the Respondent's organization, and the possibility that the discontinued operation may now be outmoded, we are of the opinion that such reestablishment is not essential in this case to the moulding of a meaningful remedy suited to the practical needs of the situation before us. We shall therefore not impose any such requirement.

"Effectuation of the policies of the Act does require, however, if the unilaterally discontinued operation is not restored, that the Respondent undo the specific violation found, by offering now to bargain with the Union, not only about the effects on the employees of the discontinued operation, but also about the resumption of such operation. Our order will so provide. . . .

". . . [W]e shall further order that the Respondent shall make the discharged employees whole for any loss of pay they may have suffered as a result of the Respondent's unfair labor practice. The liability for such backpay shall cease upon the occurrence of any of the following conditions: (1) reaching mutual agreement with the Union relating to the subjects which Respondent is herein required to bargain about; (2) bargaining to a bona fide impasse; (3) the failure of the Union to commence negotiations within 5 days of the receipt of the Respondent's notice of its desire to bargain with the Union; or (4) the failure of the Union to bargain thereafter in good faith. Of course, if the Respondent decides to resume its cheese packaging operations and offers to reinstate its former employees to their same or substantially equivalent positions, its liability will cease as of that date. . . ."

3. Effect of an Existing Agreement

JACOBS MANUFACTURING CO.
National Labor Relations Board, 1951
94 N.L.R.B. 1214

. . . In July 1948, the Respondent and the Union executed a 2-year bargaining contract which, by its terms, could be reopened 1 year after its execution date for discussion of "wage rates." In July 1949 the Union invoked the reopening clause of the 1948 contract, and thereafter gave the Respondent written notice of its "wage demands." In addition to a request for a wage increase, these demands included a request that the Respondent undertake the entire cost of an existing group insurance program, and another request for the establishment of a pension plan for the Respondent's employees. When the parties met thereafter to consider the Union's demands, the Respondent refused to discuss the Union's pension and insurance requests on the ground that they were not appropriate items of discussion under the reopening clause of the 1948 contract.

The group insurance program to which the Union alluded in its demands was established by the Respondent before 1948. It was underwritten by an insurance company, and provided life, accident, health, surgical, and hospital protection. All the Respondent's employees were eligible to participate in the program, and the employees shared its costs with the Respondent. When the 1948 contract was being negotiated, the Respondent and the Union had discussed changes in this *insurance program,* and had agreed to increase certain of the benefits as well as the costs. However, neither the changes thereby effected, nor the insurance program itself, was mentioned in the 1948 contract.

As indicated by the Union's request, there was no pension plan for the Respondent's employees in existence in 1949. The subject of *pensions* moreover, had not been discussed during the 1948 negotiations; and, like insurance, that subject is not mentioned in the 1948 contract. . . .

We are satisfied . . . that the 1948 contract did not in itself impose on the Respondent any obligation to discuss pensions or insurance. The reopening clause of that contract refers to *wage rates,* and thus its intention appears to have been narrowly limited to matters directly related to the amount and manner of compensation for work. For that reason, a requirement to discuss pensions or insurance cannot be predicated on the language of the contract.

On the other hand, a majority of the Board believes that, regardless of the character of the reopening clause, the Act itself imposed upon the Respondent the duty to discuss *pensions* with the Union during the period in question. [Member Murdock found that the question whether the reopening clause required the company to bargain over pensions or insurance was the only issue raised by the union demand.]

It is now established as a principle of law that the matter of pensions is a subject which falls within the area where the statute requires bargaining. . . . The issue raised, therefore, is whether the Respondent was absolved of the obligation to discuss pensions because of the limitation contained in Section 8(d) of the amended Act dealing with the duty to discuss or agree to the modification of an existing bargaining contract. . . .

. . . The crucial point at issue here, as in the earlier cases, is the construction to be given the phrase "terms and conditions *contained in a* contract." (Emphasis supplied.) The Board, in the Tide Water case (85 N.L.R.B. 1096), concluded that the pertinent portion of Section 8(d) "*refers to terms and conditions which have been integrated and embodied into a writing.* Conversely it does not have reference to matters relating to 'wages, hours and other terms and conditions of employment,' which have not been reduced to writing. As to the written terms of the contract either party may refuse to bargain further about them, under the limitations set forth in the paragraph, without committing an unfair labor practice. With respect to unwritten terms dealing with wages, hours and other terms and conditions of employment,' the obligation remains on both parties to bargain continuously."

Members Houston and Styles have carefully reexamined the Board's construction of Section 8(d) in the Tide Water case, and are persuaded that the view the Board adopted in the Tide Water case best effectuates the declared policy of the Act. Chairman Herzog, while joining in the result with respect to the obligation to bargain here concerning pensions — never previously discussed by the parties — joins in the rationale herein *only* to the extent that it is consistent with his views separately recited below, concerning the insurance program.

By making mandatory the discussion of bargainable subjects not already covered by a contract, the parties to the contract are encouraged to arrive at joint decisions with respect to bargainable matters, that, at least to the party requesting discussion, appear at the time to be of some importance. The Act's policy of "encouraging the practice and procedure of collective bargaining" is consequently furthered. A different construction of Section 8(d) in the circumstances — one that would permit a party to a bargaining contract to avoid discussion when it was sought on subject matters not contained in the contract — would serve, at its best, only to dissipate whatever the good will that had been engendered by the previous bargaining negotiations that led to the execution of a bargaining contract; at its worst, it could bring about the industrial strife and the production interruptions that the policy of the Act also seeks to avert.

The significance of this point cannot be overemphasized. It goes to the heart of our disagreement with our dissenting colleague, Member Reynolds. His dissent stresses the need for "contract stability," and asserts that the furtherance of sound collective bargaining requires that the collective bargaining agreement be viewed as fixing, for the term of the contract, all aspects of the employer-employee relationship, and as absolving either party of the obligation to discuss, during that term, even those matters which had never been raised, or discussed in the past. We could hardly take issue with the virtue of "contract stability," at least in the abstract, and we would certainly agree that everyone is better off when, in negotiating an agreement, the parties have been able to foresee what all the future problems may be, to discuss those problems, and either to embody a resolution of them in the contract, or to provide that they may not be raised again during the contract. But we are here concerned with the kind of case in which, for one reason or another, this has *not* been done, and the question is what best effectuates the policies of the Act in *such* a case.

In this connection we cannot ignore the fact that to say that a party to an agreement is absolved by Section 8(d) of an obligation to discuss a subject not contained in a contract does not mean that the other party is prohibited from taking economic action to compel bargaining on that subject. The portion of Section 8(d) we are here considering does no more than provide a *defense* to a charge of a refusal to bargain under Section 8(a)(5) or 8(b)(3) of the Act. It does not render unlawful economic action aimed at securing lawful objectives.[10] That being so, the view urged by Member Reynolds achieves "contract stability" but only at the price of industrial strife, and that is a result which now more than ever we must avoid. The basic policy of this Act to further collective bargaining is founded on the proposition — amply demonstrated by experience — that collective bargaining provides an escape valve for the

10 We must note, however, contrary to the assertion of Member Reynolds, that nothing in this decision is to be construed as a determination of the issue of whether a union may strike to compel bargaining on a modification of a contract which seeks to add a matter not contained in the contract without complying with the procedural requirements of Section 8(d). Our decision here is limited to a construction of the language "modification of the terms and conditions *contained in* a contract." The issue raised by our dissenting colleague is not before us in this case, and we in no way pass upon it. [What is the impact of the Borg-Warner decision, supra page 440, on the lawfulness of such a strike? — ED.]

pressures which otherwise result in industrial strife. With this policy in mind, we are loath to narrow the area of mandatory bargaining, except where the amended statute, in the clearest terms, requires that we do so.

The construction of Section 8(d) adopted by the Board in the Tide Water case serves also to simplify, and thus to speed, the bargaining process. It eliminates the pressure upon the parties at the time when a contract is being negotiated to raise those subjects that may not then be of controlling importance, but which might in the future assume a more significant status. It also assures to both unions and employers that, if future conditions require some agreement as to matters about which the parties have not sought, or have not been able to obtain agreement, then some discussion of those matters will be forthcoming when necessary.

We cannot believe that Congress was unaware of the foregoing considerations when it amended the Act by inserting Section 8(d), or that it sought, by the provision in question, to freeze the bargaining relationship by eliminating any mandatory discussion that might lead to the addition of new subject matter to an existing contract.[11] What Section 8(d) does do is to reject the pronouncements contained in some pre-1947 Board and court decisions — sometimes dicta, sometimes necessary to the holding — to the effect that the duty to bargain continues even as to those matters upon which the parties have reached agreement and which are set forth in the terms of a written contract. But we believe it does no more. Those bargainable issues which have never been discussed by the parties, and which are in no way treated in the contract, remain matters which both the union and the employer are obliged to discuss at any time.

In so holding, we emphasize that under this rule, no less than in any

[11] Unlike Member Reynolds we find little in the legislative history that sheds any real light on the meaning of that portion of Section 8(d) involved in this case. Even were we to assume, as our dissenting colleague asserts, that the provision in question had its origin in the House bill, it is significant that the provision in the House bill referred broadly to "modifications of an agreement," and did not contain the language finally enacted, i.e. "modification of the terms and conditions *contained in* a contract." In that posture we find no basis for our dissenting colleague's reliance on the House report, which correctly notes that the House bill language did "not require bargaining *on any matter* during the term of a collective bargaining contract."

The most pertinent reference to the relevant portion of Section 8(d) as enacted is the following statement by Senator Taft:

"The amendment to this sub-section prividing that the duty to bargain collectively should not be construed as requiring either party to discuss or agree to any modification of the terms of a contract if such modification is to become effective before the contract may be reopened has been construed on the floor to mean "Parties will be bound by contract without an opportunity for further collective bargaining." The provision has no such effect. It merely provides that either party to a contract may refuse to change its terms or discuss such a change to take effect during the life thereof without being guilty of an unfair labor practice. Parties may meet and discuss the meaning of the terms of their contract and may agree to modification on change of circumstances, but it is not mandatory that they do so." 93 Cong. Rec. 7002; Legislative History of the Labor Management Relations Act, 1947, U.S. Government Printing Office, p. 1625.

other circumstance, the duty to bargain implies only an obligation to *discuss* the matter in question in good faith with a sincere purpose of reaching some agreement. It does not require that either side agree, or make concessions. And if the parties originally desire to avoid later discussion with respect to matters not specifically covered in the terms of an executed contract, they need only so specify in the terms of the contract itself. Nothing in our construction of Section 8(d) precludes such an agreement, entered into in good faith, from foreclosing future discussion of matters not contained in the agreement.[13] . . .

Chairman Herzog, concurring in part:

I believe that this Respondent was *not* under a duty to discuss the Union's *group insurance* demand. The individual views which lead me, by a different road, to the result reached on this issue by Members Reynolds and Murdock, are as follows:

Unlike the issue of pensions, concerning which the contract is silent and the parties did not negotiate at all in 1948, the subject of group insurance was fully discussed while the Respondent and the Union were negotiating the agreement. True, that agreement is silent on the subject, so it cannot literally be said that there is a term "contained in" the 1948 contract relating to the group insurance program. The fact remains that during the negotiations which preceded its execution, the issue was consciously explored. The record reveals that the Union expressly requested that the preexisting program be changed so that the Respondent would assume its entire cost, the very proposal that was again made as part of the 1949 midterm demand which gave rise to this case. The Respondent rejected the basic proposal on this first occasion, but agreement was then reached — although outside the written contract — to increase certain benefits under the group insurance program.

In my opinion, it is only reasonable to assume that rejection of the Union's basic proposal, coupled in this particular instance with enhancement of the substantive benefits, constituted a part of the contemporaneous "bargain" which the parties made when they negotiated the entire 1948 contract. In the face of this record as to what the parties discussed and did, I believe that it would be an abuse of this Board's mandate to throw the weight of Government sanction behind the Union's

---

[13] For an example of a contract in which such a provision was incorporated, see the contract between United Automobile Workers of America and General Motors Corporation, set forth in Labor Relations Manual (BNA), Vol. 26, p. 63, 91, which states:

"The parties acknowledge that during the negotiations which resulted in this agreement, each had the unlimited right and opportunity to make demands and proposals with respect to any subject or matter not removed by law from the area of collective bargaining, and that the understandings and agreements arrived at by the parties after the exercise of that right and opportunity are set forth in this agreement. Therefore, the Corporation and the Union, for the life of this agreement, each voluntarily and unqualifiedly waives the right, and each agrees that the other shall not be obligated, to bargain collectively with respect to any subject or matter not specifically referred to or covered in this agreement, even though such subjects or matter may not have been within the knowledge or contemplation of either or both of the parties at the time that they negotiated or signed this agreement."

attempt to disturb, in midterm, a bargain sealed when the original agreement was reached.

To hold otherwise would encourage a labor organization — or, in a Section 8(b)(3) case, an employer — to come back, time without number, during the term of a contract, to demand resumed discussion of issues which, although perhaps not always incorporated in the written agreement, the other party had every good reason to believe were put at rest for a definite period. I do not think that the doctrine of the Tide Water case was ever intended to go so far as to extend to facts like these, or that it should be so extended. Without regard to the niceties of construing the words of Section 8(d) of the amended Act, I am satisfied that it would be both inequitable and unwise to impose a statutory obligation to bargain in situations of this sort. That would serve only to stimulate uncertainty and evasion of commitments at a time when stability should be the order of the day.

Member Reynolds, concurring separately and dissenting in part: . . .

. . . [T]he relevant language of the Section 8(d) proviso appears to have had its genesis in the original House bill, and . . . the report accompanying that bill explained the language as not requiring "bargaining on any matter during the term of a collective bargaining agreement, except as the express terms of the agreement permit." There is nothing in the Conference Report which indicates that such a construction would not be a reasonable construction with respect to the language of Section 8(d) in question. Indeed a statement by Senator Taft during debate on the Conference Agreement supports the conclusion that this is the proper construction. Senator Morse, after a lengthy analysis of Section 8(d), stated "the parties will be bound by the contract, without an opportunity for further collective bargaining in regard to it." Senator Taft noting that the relevant language of Section 8(d) had "been construed on the floor to mean parties will be bound by contract without an opportunity for further collective bargaining," explained that "the provision has no such effect. It merely provides that either party to a contract *may refuse* to change its terms or discuss such a change to take effect during the life thereof without being guilty of an unfair labor practice. Parties may meet and discuss the terms of their contract and may agree to modifications on change of circumstances, but *it is not mandatory* that they do so."

Thus Senator Taft clearly interpreted Section 8(d) as stating that the parties are not bound to discuss changes to take place during the life of the contract.

On the basis of the foregoing, it is my opinion that Section 8(d) imposes no obligation on either party to a contract to bargain on any matter during the term of the contract except as the express provisions of the contract may demand. This is a result reasonably compatible with the particular Section 8 (d) language involved, as well as with Section 8(d) as a whole. Moreover, not only does the result accord stability and dignity to collective bargaining agreements, but it also gives substance to the practice and procedure of collective bargaining. . . .

That a collective bargaining agreement stabilizes all rights and conditions of employment is consonant with the generally accepted concept of the nature of such an agreement. The basic terms and conditions of employment existing at the time the collective bargaining agreement is executed, and which are not specifically altered by, or mentioned in, the agreement, are part of the status quo which the parties, by implication, consider as being adopted as an essential element of the agreement. This view is termed "reasonable and logical," and its widespread endorsement as sound industrial relations practice makes it a general rule followed in the arbitration of disputes arising during the term of a contract. The reasonableness of the approach is apparent upon an understanding of collective bargaining techniques. Many items are not mentioned in a collective bargaining agreement either because of concessions at the bargaining table or because one of the parties may have considered it propitious to forego raising one subject in the hope of securing a more advantageous deal on another. Subjects traded off or foregone should, under these circumstances, be as irrevocably settled as those specifically covered and settled by the agreement. To require bargaining on such subjects during midterm debases initial contract negotiations.[5] . . .

BEACON PIECE DYEING AND FINISHING CO., INC.
National Labor Relations Board, 1958
121 N.L.R.B. 953

The Respondent and the Union have had several collective-bargaining agreements since the Union was certified as bargaining representative in 1952. Their current contract runs from January 1, 1956, to December 31, 1958. This agreement, as well as all previous agreements, makes no reference to workloads or the number of machines an employee shall be required to operate, and sets forth only minimum or starting rates of pay.

The testimony on both sides is that in the negotiations on the initial contract in 1952 the Union proposed a contract provision limiting the number of machines (jigs and dye boxes) to be operated by an operator, the proposal was discussed, and the proposal was rejected by the Respondent. . . .

On August 13, 1956, the Respondent ordered all "jig" operators in the wet department to operate 3 jigs on a regular basis, where formerly 2 jigs were normally operated on a regular basis. A few days later the Respondent granted a wage increase therefor of 16 cents per hour to the jig operators retroactive to August 13, a sum never offered to, or even discussed with, the Union for such an increased workload. It is undisputed that this action taken by the Respondent was taken unilaterally and without any notice to the Union, and the Trial Examiner so found.

On or about August 27, 1956, the Union met with the Respondent con-

---

[5] For an analysis of the competing policy considerations, essentially supporting the Reynolds position, see Cox and Dunlop, The Duty to Bargain Collectively During the Term of an Existing Agreement, 63 Harv. L. Rev. 1097, 1110-1116 (1950). — ED.

cerning the action taken by the Respondent. According to the credited testimony of the Respondent, the Respondent told the Union that the Respondent was willing to discuss the matter with the Union to see what could be done, and if no agreement resulted the Union could take the matter to arbitration under the contract; the Union said that it would see about it. The Union's decision was to file the charge herein.

The Trial Examiner found no violation of Sections 8(a)(5), primarily on the grounds that: (1) Respondent was free to increase the workload since there was no workload clause in the contract, and the subject of workload had been "bargained for" in all bargaining sessions and then dropped in exchange for concessions by Respondent on other proposals by the Union; and (2) Respondent also was free to grant unilateral wage increases above the minimum and starting rates in the contract, because Respondent, with the Union's acquiescence, had always granted individual wage increases above the minimum. Thus, the Trial Examiner found in effect that the Union had "waived" or "bargained away" its statutory rights to bargaining on both increased workloads and general wage increases therefor. He found further that the complaint should be dismissed because of the grievance procedure, including compulsory arbitration, in the parties' contract.

The Board has consistently held that an employer's action in changing the wage rates or other working conditions of its employees without notice to, or consultation with, the labor organization which they have chosen to represent them is in derogation of its duty to bargain and is violative of Section 8(a)(5).[6] Moreover, although the Board has also held repeatedly that statutory rights may be "waived" by collective bargaining,[7] it has also said that such a waiver "will not readily be inferred" and there must be "a clear and unmistakable showing" that the waiver occurred. The primary issue in this case, therefore, is whether the Union "clearly and unmistakably" waived or "bargained away" its statutory rights to bargaining on an increased workload and a general wage increase therefor.

With respect to workload, whatever may have happened relating to waiver in negotiations on prior contracts, it is clear that the Union, by demanding a workload clause in the negotiations on the current contract, came into such negotiations with no intent to waive its bargaining rights on workload. Indeed, the Union made it clear that it intended to exercise its bargaining rights on workload. Moreover, it is also clear that there was no such waiver thereafter in the negotiations. . . . [A]t the negotiations on the current contract the Respondent stated that "it would be impossible to discuss anything about workloads," and further stated, "Before we go into any negotiations of any kind I won't discuss

---

[6] To what extent does the rationale of NLRB v. Katz, supra page 447, upholding this "per se" doctrine, apply to action taken during a contract term, outside a context of renewal negotiations? — ED.

[7] See the contract provision quoted in footnote 13 of the Jacobs opinion, supra page 466. Cf. Leroy Machine Co., 147 N.L.R.B. No. 140 (1964) (waiver through scope of the management-functions clause). — ED.

anything about workloads"; and upon the basis of this testimony, and the entire testimony of the Respondent in this connection, we find that in the negotiations on the current contract the Respondent did not bargain or negotiate on the Union's workload demand but rather refused to even discuss the matter. Accordingly, we find further that this complete absence of any bargaining but refusal instead by the Respondent to even discuss workload could not possibly be construed as a waiver by the Union of its bargaining rights on workload. The Union was rather an unwilling victim of a complete removal of this subject from the bargaining table by the Respondent. . . .

We disagree with our dissenting colleague's contention that the decision in Speidel Corporation, 120 N.L.R.B. 733, is controlling here. That was a situation where with each payment in the past of an employer-instituted bonus the employer had reminded its employees that the bonus was "voluntary" and was not to be construed as establishing a precedent, and the employer had a reasonable basis for believing that its employees, and the union as well, concurred in this position that it had taken in the past that the payment of bonuses was a matter within its own prerogative, and was not a matter concerning which the union, or anyone else, claimed dominion; and then at the latest contract negotiations the employer rejected a union-proposed broad "Maintenance of privileges" provision for the stated reason of avoiding a contractual obligation on bonuses, thereby reiterating in effect its previous position in substance that bonuses were a subject of "management prerogative," and the union by its complete silence acquiesced in this position.

In the instant case, even assuming that the Respondent did bargain on workload at negotiations on the current contract, as so strongly insisted upon by our dissenting colleague, the Speidel decision still remains clearly distinguishable. The first important distinction is that here, unlike Speidel, there is no evidence that in past years the Respondent ever stated either to the employees or the Union in any way, either in or outside of contract negotiations, that the Respondent considered workload to be a matter of "management prerogative" on which it reserved the right to take unilateral action, or that either the employees or the Union concurred in any such nonexistent position. On the contrary, the evidence clearly shows that the Respondent, as well as the Union, has always considered workload to be a bargainable matter. Thus, the Respondent's credited testimony shows that at negotiations on each of the past contracts, the Union made a workload demand, the Respondent bargained on such demand, and the Union ultimately gave up such demand for other concessions; and there is no evidence that the Respondent ever took any manner of "management prerogative" position on these workload demands. Moreover, the record shows further that outside of contract negotiations the Respondent bargained extensively with the Union with respect to workload over a period of several years. Accordingly, there is no background of any concurrence by either the Union or the employees in any position of "management prerogative" on workload, but rather a background of clear recognition by the Respondent that workload was a bargaining matter. The second important distinction is that here, unlike Speidel, the evidence will not support a finding that even in the negotiations on the current contract did the Respondent take a position that workload was a matter of "management prerogative" on which it reserved the right to take unilateral action. Thus, all that the Respondent did say at these negotiations was that its refusal to discuss anything about workloads was based on the fact that the Union had negotiated contracts with similar concerns in the area which did not contain workload provisions. This adds up simply to a position by the Respondent that it did not wish to give the Union any more than the Union had been able to obtain from similar companies in the area. . . . Moreover, subsequently, during the term of the current contract, the Respondent and the Union again engaged in extra-contract negotiations on workload, which not only shows a continuing recognition that workload was still a bargainable matter, but also provides further proof that the antecedent contract negotiations were not intended to give the Respondent the right of unilateral action on workload. The last important distinction is that here, unlike Speidel, the Union cannot be said to have acquiesced in any "management prerogative" position on workload so as to "hand over" to the Respondent the Union's statutory bargaining rights on workload. In the first place, as shown above, the Respondent took no such position for the Union to acquiesce in. In the second place, the Union was simply trading off one demand in return for concessions on another, which is an everyday occurrence in collective bargaining having no relation whatsoever to an asserted "management prerogative" position by an employer and the union's acquiescence therein.[11]

In our opinion, the basic fallacy in our dissenting colleague's position is that he has lost sight of the crucial fact that more often than not, as here, an employer will resist inclusion of a certain provision in a contract simply because he is opposed to the provision *on its merits,* and not because he is seeking the right to act unilaterally on the subject as a matter of "management prerogative"; and the union, as here, also with no thought in mind that a possible relinquishment of its statutory bargaining rights on the subject are involved, will trade off its demands on the subject in return for concessions on other demands as a part of the normal and everyday collective-bargaining process. Is our dissenting colleague prepared to say that the Board should find a "waiver" of statutory bargaining rights in this common "give and take" bargaining situation? To read into such an essential and basic part of the collective-bargaining process, as our dissenting colleague would do, an *implied* "management prerogative" position by the employer, an *implied* agreement

---

[11] Cf. Speidel, where the union simply remained acquiescently silent to the employer's position that bonuses were a matter of "management prerogative." [See also Press Co., Inc., 121 N.L.R.B. 976 (1958), where the union expressed disagreement with the employer's position that commission rates were a "management prerogative," but declared that it would not press the matter in view of the employer's statement that it had no present plans to change the rate.]

thereon by the union, and a resulting *implied* waiver of the union's statutory bargaining rights on the subject, would . . . encourage employers to firmly resist inclusion in contracts of as many subjects as possible, with a view to such resistance giving them a right of unilateral action thereafter on all subjects excluded from the contract, thereby impeding the collective-bargaining process and creating an atmosphere which inevitably would lead to more strikes; and . . . would discourage unions from presenting *any* subject in negotiations, for a simple refusal by the employer to agree to the demand on the subject would leave the union in the unhappy dilemma of either giving up the demand and thereby losing its bargaining rights on the subject, or striking in support of the demand — this too would seriously impede the collective-bargaining process and lead to more strikes. . . .

With respect to wages, we cannot agree with the Trial Examiner that the Union's apparent waiver of its right to bargain on individual merit wage increases should be construed as a waiver also of its right to bargain on a general wage increase, particularly where the general wage increase was given not on a merit basis but in return for an increased workload. In our opinion, the subject matter of the apparent waiver and the subject matter of the unilateral action are so patently different as to require no extended discussion to support our conclusion that the apparent waiver of one was not a waiver of the other. . . .

As indicated above, the Trial Examiner gave as a further reason for dismissing the complaint the fact that the parties had a grievance procedure including compulsory arbitration in their contract which covered not only contract matters but matters "germane to" the contract. . . . Presumably, the implied rationale for this finding is that the subject matter of the unilateral action was covered by the grievance procedure, that therefore the Union's only remedy was through the grievance procedure, and accordingly that the Board has no jurisdiction over the instant subject matter. However, the Board has consistently held that the collective-bargaining requirement of the Act is not satisfied by a substitution of the grievance procedure of a contract, unless the grievance provisions of the contract contain a waiver of the statutory right "expressed in clear and unmistakable terms." And the Board has held further that there is no such unequivocal waiver where, as here, the grievance provisions make no mention of such a waiver. We therefore find, contrary to the Trial Examiner, that the existence of the grievance procedure in the contract constitutes no basis for dismissing the complaint. . . .

[Member Bean's dissenting opinion is omitted.]

NOTE

The Board's treatment of the employer's reliance on the existence of the grievance and arbitration processes is no longer authoritative, see Timken Roller Bearing Co. v. NLRB, infra page 788, and the question of the effect of a grievance procedure on the duty to bargain has recently begun to produce substantial litigation and controversy. E.g.,

Square D Co. v. NLRB, 332 F.2d 360 (9th Cir. 1964); Sinclair Refining Co. v. NLRB, 306 F.2d 569 (5th Cir. 1962); Hercules Motor Corp., 136 N.L.R.B. 1648 (1962).

NLRB v. LION OIL CO.
Supreme Court of the United States, 1957
352 U.S. 282, 77 Sup. Ct. 330, 1 L. Ed. 2d 331

Mr. CHIEF JUSTICE WARREN delivered the opinion of the Court.

In this case we are called upon . . . to interpret §8(d) of the National Labor Relations Act, as amended. . . . The sole question presented by the petition for certiorari is:

"Whether the requirement of this Section is satisfied where a contract provides for negotiation and adoption of modifications at an intermediate date during its term, and a strike in support of modification demands occurs after the date on which such modifications may become effective — and after the 60-day notice period has elapsed — but prior to the terminal date of the contract."

We are told by the Solicitor General that the question is of major importance in the negotiation and administration of hundreds of collective bargaining agreements throughout the country; that there is a decided trend among unions and employers to execute contracts of longer duration than formerly and to include provisions for reopening to negotiate changes during the contract term. Because of the importance of the question, we granted certiorari, 350 U.S. 986, to review a decision of the Court of Appeals for the Eighth Circuit to the effect that §8(d)(4) bans strikes to obtain modifications of a contract until the contract by its terms or by the action of the parties has terminated.

[The collective agreement, dated October 23, 1950, provided that it should run for one year and then continue in force indefinitely until canceled in the manner it prescribed. It then provided that if either party desired to amend the agreement, that party should serve notice on the other. During the sixty days after this notice the parties should attempt to agree on the amendments. If no accord was reached, either party could terminate the agreement upon the giving of a sixty-day notice of termination.

On August 24, 1951, the union served notice on the employer of its desire to amend the agreement and sent copies to the Federal Mediation and Conciliation Service and the State Labor Commissioner in compliance with Section 8(d)(2) of the NLRA. Negotiations continued until April 30, 1952, when the union struck. However, it had not given any notice of termination, so that the collective agreement was at all times in effect. The strike continued until August 3, when a new contract was made.

The union charged the employer with numerous unfair labor practices during the strike, including refusal to bargain and wrongful refusal to reinstate strikers. The company defended on the ground that the strike was in violation of Section 8(d)(4), and therefore not protected by the Act, because it occurred while the contract was in effect.]

. . . A majority of the Board rejected this defense, holding that "The term 'expiration date' as used in Section 8(d)(4) . . . has a twofold meaning; it connotes not only the terminal date of a bargaining contract, but also an agreed date in the course of its existence when the parties can effect changes in its provisions."

The Board held that since, under the contract in dispute, October 23, 1951, was such an "agreed date," the notice given August 24 followed by a wait of more than 60 days satisfied the statute. The company was ordered to cease and desist and, affirmatively, to make whole employees found to have been discriminated against. 109 N.L.R.B. 680, 683. . . .

That §8(d)(4) is susceptible of various interpretations is apparent when §8(d) is read as a whole. Its ambiguity was recognized by the Joint Committee of Congress created by the very act of which §8(d) was a part to study the operation of the federal labor laws. Members of the National Labor Relations Board, the agency specially charged by Congress with effectuating the purposes of the national labor legislation, have expressed divergent views on the proper construction of §8(d)(4); none of them has taken the position adopted by the court below.[6] In the face of this ambiguity it will not do simply to say Congress could have made itself clearer and automatically equate the phrase "expiration date" only with the date when a contract comes to an end. . . . [Such a result] would discourage the development of long-term bargaining relationships. Unions would be wary of entering into long-term contracts with machinery for reopening them for modification from time to time, if they thought the right to strike would be denied them for the entire term of such a contract, though they imposed no such limitations on themselves. . . .

. . . We conceive that a notice of desired modification would typically be served in advance of the date when the contract by its own terms was subject to modification. Notice of desired termination would ordinarily precede the date when the contract would come to an end by its terms or would be automatically renewed in the absence of notice to terminate. Therefore we conclude that Congress meant by "expiration date" in §8(d)(1) to encompass both situations, and the same phrase in §8(d)(4) must carry the same meaning. "Expiration" has no such fixed and settled meaning as to make this an unduly strained reading.

Our conclusion is buttressed by a provision of §8(d) which was added by the Conference Committee.

"[T]he duties . . . imposed [by subsections (2), (3) and (4)] shall not be construed as requiring either party to discuss or agree to any modification of the terms and conditions contained in a contract for a fixed period, if such modification is to become effective before such terms and conditions can be reopened under the provisions of the contract."

---

[6] The Board's original view in Wilson & Co., 89 N.L.R.B. 310, was that §8(d) permitted strikes in support of contract changes any time after 60 days' notice. Member Peterson, concurring specially in the present case, adhered to that view. Member Murdock dissented on the same ground on which he had concurred specially in Wilson & Co., namely, that §8(d) applies only during the period around the termination of a contract.

The negative implication seems clear: Congress recognized a duty to bargain over modifications when the contract itself contemplates such bargaining. It would be anomalous for Congress to recognize such a duty and at the same time deprive the union of the strike threat which, together with "the occasional strike itself, is the force depended upon to facilitate arriving at satisfactory settlements." . . .

The contemporary legislative history manifests no real recognition of the problem before us. A reading of the committee reports and the floor debates alone could well lead to the conclusion that both the sponsors and the opponents of the bill saw in §8(d)(4) no more than a means for preventing "quickie" strikes by requiring a "cooling-off" period which would not in any circumstances exceed 60 days. But the language used in the statute goes beyond this limited purpose. Significance must be given to the clause, "or until the expiration date of such contract, whichever occurs later." We believe our construction gives meaning to the congressional language which accords with the general purpose of the Act. . . .

Nor can we accept respondents' alternative contention that, even apart from §8(d), the strike was in breach of contract and the strikers were for that reason not entitled to relief at the hand of the Board. Respondents rely upon Labor Board v. Sands Mfg. Co., 306 U.S. 332. In Sands, as in this case, the contract did not contain an express no-strike clause. Employees there refused in the course of the contract to continue work "in accordance with their contract." Id., at 344. The refusal occurred midway in a fixed-term contract which did not provide for modifications during its term. This Court sustained the propriety of the employer's action in discharging the employees. Here the strike occurred at a time when the parties were bargaining over modifications after notice and in accordance with the terms of the contract. Where there has been no express waiver of the right to strike, a waiver of the right during such a period is not to be inferred. We do not believe that the two-phase provision for terminating this contract means that it was not within the contemplation of the parties that economic weapons might be used to support demands for modification before the notice to terminate was given.

The judgment below is reversed and the case remanded for proceedings in conformity with this opinion.

[The opinions of Justices Frankfurter and Harlan, concurring in the construction given Section 8(d), but urging remand of the breach-of-contract issue for initial consideration below, are omitted.]

MASTRO PLASTICS CORP. v. NLRB

Supreme Court of the United States, 1956
350 U.S. 270, 76 Sup. Ct. 349, 100 L. Ed. 309

[The employer had a collective agreement with Carpenters Local 3127, which had a termination date of November 30, 1950. In the months preceding the termination of the contract, the employer attempted to compel its employees to shift their membership to Local 318 of the Pulp Workers, but they refused to do so. On September 29, the Carpenters served a sixty-day notice of desire to modify the contract. On November 10, the employer discharged one of the leaders of the Carpenters. This discriminatory discharge, culminating a series of unfair labor practices by the employer, precipitated a strike which lasted four months. At the end of that time the strikers made an unconditional offer to return to work, but they were denied reinstatement and were discharged. The employer was charged with violation of Sections 8(a)(1), (2), and (3).]

MR. JUSTICE BURTON delivered the opinion of the Court.

. . . Does §8(d) of the National Labor Relations Act, as amended, deprive individuals of their status as employees if, within the waiting period prescribed by §8(d)(4), they engage in a strike solely against unfair labor practices of their employers? . . . [T]he background is the dual purpose of the Act (1) to protect the right of employees to be free to take concerted action as provided in §§7 and 8(a), and (2) to substitute collective bargaining for economic warfare in securing satisfactory wages, hours of work and employment conditions. Section 8(d) seeks to bring about the termination and modification of collective-bargaining agreements without interrupting the flow of commerce or the production of goods, while §§7 and 8(a) seek to insure freedom of concerted action by employees at all times. . . .

. . . Since the Board expressly found that the instant strike was not to terminate or modify the contract, but was designed instead to protest the unfair labor practices of petitioners, the loss-of-status provision of §8(d) is not applicable. We sustain that interpretation. Petitioners' construction would produce incongruous results. It concedes that prior to the 60-day negotiating period, employees have a right to strike against unfair labor practices designed to oust the employees' bargaining representative, yet petitioners' interpretation of §8(d) means that if the employees give the 60-day notice of their desire to modify the contract, they are penalized for exercising that right to strike. This would deprive them of their most effective weapon at a time when their need for it is obvious. Although the employees' request to modify the contract would demonstrate their need for the services of their freely chosen representative, petitioners' interpretation would have the incongruous effect of cutting off the employees' freedom to strike against unfair labor practices aimed at that representative. This would relegate the employees to filing charges under a procedure too slow to be effective. The result would unduly favor the employers and handicap the employees during negotiation periods contrary to the purpose of the Act. There also is inherent inequity in any interpretation that penalizes one party to a contract for conduct induced solely by the unlawful conduct of the other, thus giving advantage to the wrongdoer.

Petitioners contend that, unless the loss-of-status clause is applicable to unfair labor practice strikes, as well as to economic strikes, it adds nothing to the existing law relating to loss of status. Assuming that to be so, the clause is justifiable as a clarification of the law and as a warning to employees against engaging in economic strikes during the statutory waiting period. Moreover, in the face of the affirmative emphasis that is placed by the Act upon freedom of concerted action and freedom of choice of representatives, any limitation on the employees' right to strike against violations of §§7 and 8(a) protecting those freedoms, must be more explicit and clear than it is here in order to restrict them at the very time they may be most needed. . . .

MR. JUSTICE FRANKFURTER, whom MR. JUSTICE MINTON and MR. JUSTICE HARLAN join, dissenting.

. . . Section 8 of the Wagner Act was amended [by the Taft-Hartley Act] and duties were placed upon unions. Collective action which violates any of these duties is of course activity unprotected by §7. See Cox, The Right to Engage in Concerted Activities, 26 Ind. L.J. 319, 325-333 (1951). One of these new union duties, and an important one, is contained in §8(d): unions may not strike to enforce their demands during the 60-day "cooling-off" period.

By reason of this new enactment, participating workers would not be engaged in a protected activity under §7 by striking for the most legitimate economic reasons during the 60-day period. The strike would be in violation of the provision of that section which says that during the period there shall be no resort to a strike. The employer could discharge such strikers without violating §8. This would be so if §8 were without the loss-of-status provision. The Board would be powerless to order reinstatement under §10. The loss-of-status provision in §8(d) does not curtail the Board's power, since it did not have power to order reinstatement where a strike is resorted to for economic reasons before the 60-day period has expired. In such a situation the striker has no rights under §§8 and 10. Yet the Board would have us construe the loss-of-status provision as applicable only to the economic striker and qualifying a power which the Board does not have.

It is with respect to the unfair-labor-practice striker that the provision serves a purpose. This becomes clear if we assume that there were no such provision and examine the consequences of its absence. On such an assumption, a strike based on an unfair labor practice by the employer during the 60-day period may or may not be a protected activity under §7. If it is, obviously discharged strikers would be entitled to reinstatement. The strike would not be a §7 activity, however, if, for example, it were in breach of a no-strike clause in the contract which extends to a work stoppage provoked by an employer unfair labor practice, cf. Labor Board v. Sands Mfg. Co., 306 U.S. 332, 344, or if the no-strike clause in §8(d)(4) (not to be confused with the loss-of-status provision) extends to such a work stoppage. However, even if the strike is not a §7 activity, the Board in the unfair-labor-practice strike situation as distinguished from the economic strike situation, may in its discretion order the discharged participants reinstated. This is so because of the antecedent employer unfair practice which caused the strike, and which gave employees rights under §8. If the Board finds that reinstatement of such strikers is a remedy that would effectuate the policies of the Act, it has the power under §10 (c) to issue the necessary order.

This would not be the case, however, if the loss-of-status provision were held applicable to unfair-labor-practice strikes, because participating workers would lose their rights as "employees" for the purposes of §§8 and 10. Under the Act only "employees" are eligible for reinstatement. The unfair-labor-practice strike, then, is the one situation where loss of status for the purposes of §§8 and 10 is of significance. At any rate, we have not been advised of any other situation to which the provision would apply.

We are therefore confronted with the demonstrable fact that if the provision stripping strikers of their status as employees during the 60-day period is to have any usefulness at all and not be an idle collection of words, the fact that a strike during that period is induced by the employer's unfair labor practice is immaterial. Even though this might on first impression seem an undesirable result, it is so only by rejecting the important considerations in promoting peaceful industrial relations which might well have determined the action of Congress. In the first place, the Congress may have set a very high value on peaceful adjustments, i.e., the absence of strikes. One may take judicial notice of the fact that this consideration was at the very forefront of the thinking and feeling of the Eightieth Congress. And there is another consideration not unrelated to this. While in a particular case the cause of a strike may be clear, and in a particular case there may be no controversy regarding the circumstances which prove that an employer committed an unfair labor practice, as a matter of experience that is not always true, indeed often it is not true. One of the sharpest controversies, one of the issues most difficult of determination, is the very question of what precipitated a work stoppage. This is especially true where a new contract is being negotiated. It is not at all unreasonable, therefore, to find a congressional desire to preclude litigation over what all too often is a contentious subject and to deter all strikes during the crucial period of negotiation.

We need not agree with a legislative judgment in order to obey a legislative command. It is enough for us that Congress did not legislate idly, but did intend the loss-of-status provision to have an effect. . . . Since the loss-of-status provision has an effect only in an unfair-labor-practice strike, the judgment of the Court of Appeals should be reversed.

NOTES

1. A second defense urged by the company in the principal case was that the strike was in breach of a contract clause committing the union "to refrain from engaging in any strike or work stoppage during the term of this agreement," and was therefore unprotected under the Act. While recognizing that the right to strike could be waived by contract, the Court unanimously held that a standard "no-strike" provision such as the quoted clause would be construed to apply only to the "economic relationship" between the parties, and that "compelling expression" of a broader intent was needed before a waiver of the right to strike in protest against unfair labor practices would be inferred. 350 U.S. 270, 281, 283

(1956). This interpretation of no-strike clauses was vigorously criticized in Cox, The Legal Nature of Collective Bargaining Agreements, 57 Mich. L. Rev. 1, 16-19 (1958); and in Arlan's Dept. Store, Inc., 133 N.L.R.B. 802 (1961), a majority of the Board construed Mastro to protect only strikes against "flagrant" or "serious" unfair labor practices, i.e., those "destructive of the foundation on which collective bargaining must rest." 133 N.L.R.B. at 808, quoting 350 U.S. at 281. A strike over the discriminatory discharge of a single employee, in a context suggesting no warning to employees generally regarding their choice of a bargaining representative, was held not protected under Mastro.

2. A union proposes certain modifications of an agreement. The company opposes these, and suggests modification of its own. The union abandons its demands, and expresses a willingness to renew the expiring agreement without any change. When the company insists on its proposals, the union strikes. Is the strike within Section 8(d)? Would it make any difference if the company had accepted the union's proposed changes? See Fort Smith Chair Co., 143 N.L.R.B. 514 (1963).

3. Is a strike to compel an employer to agree not to subcontract certain work within Section 8(d)? The issue might arise in several contexts: (a) the union claims, and the company denies, that the subcontract violates an express or implied term of the agreement; (b) the union has filed a grievance over the proposed subcontract, and an arbitrator has ruled in the company's favor; (c) the union, conceding that there is no existing contractual restriction on subcontracting, seeks to induce the company to agree to its inclusion. See Local 9735, United Mine Workers v. NLRB, 258 F.2d 146 (D.C. Cir. 1958); cf. Jacobs Manufacturing Co., supra page 462. To what extent are the issues dealt with in Jacobs relevant here?

B. THE SUBJECTS OF COLLECTIVE BARGAINING AND THEIR STATUTORY AND ECONOMIC CONTEXT

1. *Wages and Hours*

a. REGULATION OF WAGES AND HOURS

UNITED STATES v. DARBY
Supreme Court of the United States, 1941
312 U.S. 100, 657, 61 Sup. Ct. 451, 85 L. Ed. 609

Mr. Justice Stone delivered the opinion of the Court.

The two principal questions raised by the record in this case are, first, whether Congress has constitutional power to prohibit the shipment in interstate commerce of lumber manufactured by employees whose wages are less than a prescribed minimum or whose weekly hours of labor at that wage are greater than a prescribed maximum, and, second, whether it has power to prohibit the employment of workmen in the production of goods "for interstate commerce" at other than prescribed wages and hours. A subsidiary question is whether in connection with such prohibitions Congress can require the employer subject to them to keep records showing the hours worked each day and week by each of his employees including those engaged "in the production and manufacture of goods to wit, lumber, for 'interstate commerce.' " . . .

The Fair Labor Standards Act set up a comprehensive legislative scheme for preventing the shipment in interstate commerce of certain products and commodities produced in the United States under labor conditions as respects wages and hours which fail to conform to standards set up by the Act. Its purpose . . . is to exclude from interstate commerce goods produced for the commerce and to prevent their production for interstate commerce, under conditions detrimental to the maintenance of the minimum standards of living necessary for health and general well-being; and to prevent the use of interstate commerce as the means of competition in the distribution of goods so produced, and as the means of spreading and perpetuating such substandard labor conditions among the workers of the several states. . . .

Section 15 of the statute prohibits certain specified acts and §16(a) punishes willful violation of it by a fine of not more than $10,000 and punishes each conviction after the first by imprisonment of not more than six months or by the specified fine or both. Section 15(a)(1) makes unlawful the shipment in interstate commerce of any goods "in the production of which any employee was employed in violation of section 6[206] or section 7[207]," which provide, among other things, that during the first year of operation of the Act a minimum wage of 25 cents per hour shall be paid to employees "engaged in (interstate) commerce or in the production of goods for (interstate) commerce," §6, and that the maximum hours of employment for employees "engaged in commerce or in the production of goods for commerce" without increased compensation for overtime, shall be forty-four hours a week. §7.

Section 15(a)(2) makes it unlawful to violate the provisions of §§6 and 7 including the minimum wage and maximum hour requirements just mentioned for employees engaged in production of goods for commerce. Section 15(a)(5) makes it unlawful for an employer subject to the Act to violate §11(c) which requires him to keep such records of the persons employed by him and of their wages and hours of employment as the administrator shall prescribe by regulation or order.

The indictment charges that appellee is engaged, in the state of Georgia, in the business of acquiring raw materials, which he manufactures into finished lumber with the intent, when manufactured, to ship it in interstate commerce to customers outside the state, and that he does in fact so ship a large part of the lumber so produced. There are numerous counts charging appellee with the shipment in interstate commerce from Georgia to points outside the state of lumber in the production of which, for interstate commerce, appellee has employed workmen at less than the prescribed minimum wage or more than the prescribed maximum hours without payment to them of any wage for overtime. Other counts charge the employment by appellee of workmen in the production of lumber for interstate commerce at wages of less than 25 cents an hour or for more than the maximum hours per week without payment to them of the prescribed overtime wage. Still another count charges appellee with failure to keep records showing the hours worked each day a week by each of his employees as required by §11(c) and the regulation of the administrator, Title 29, Ch. 5, Code of Federal Regulations, Part 516, and also that appellee unlawfully failed to keep such records of employees engaged "in the production and manufacture of goods, to-wit lumber, for interstate commerce."

The demurrer, so far as now relevant to the appeal, challenged the validity of the Fair Labor Standards Act under the Commerce Clause, Art. 1, §8, cl. 3, and the Fifth and Tenth Amendments. The district court quashed the indictment in its entirety upon the broad grounds that the Act, which it interpreted as a regulation of manufacture within the states, is unconstitutional. . . .

The prohibition of shipment of the proscribed goods in interstate commerce. Section 15(a)(1) prohibits, and the indictment charges, the shipment in interstate commerce, of goods produced for interstate commerce by employees whose wages and hours of employment do not conform to the requirements of the Act. Since this section is not violated unless the commodity shipped has been produced under labor conditions prohibited by §6 and §7, the only question arising under the commerce clause with respect to such shipments is whether Congress has the constitutional power to prohibit them.

While manufacture is not of itself interstate commerce the shipment of manufactured goods interstate is such commerce and the prohibition of such shipment by Congress is indubitably a regulation of the commerce. The power to regulate commerce is the power "to prescribe the rule by which commerce is to be governed." Gibbons v. Ogden, 9 Wheat. 1, 196, 6 L. Ed. 23. It extends not only to those regulations which aid, foster and protect the commerce, but embraces those which prohibit it. . . . It is conceded that the power of Congress to prohibit transportation in interstate commerce includes noxious articles . . . stolen articles . . . kidnapped persons . . . and articles such as intoxicating liquor or convict made goods, traffic in which is forbidden or restricted by the laws of the state of destination. . . .

The power of Congress over interstate commerce "is complete in itself, may be exercised to its utmost extent, and acknowledges no limitations, other than are prescribed by the constitution." Gibbons v. Ogden, 9 Wheat. 196. That power can neither be enlarged nor diminished by the exercise or non-exercise of state power. . . . Congress, following its own conception of public policy concerning the restrictions which may appropriately be imposed on interstate commerce, is free to exclude from the commerce articles whose use in the states for which they are destined it may conceive to be injurious to the public health, morals or welfare, even though the state has not sought to regulate their use. . . .

Such regulation is not a forbidden invasion of state power merely because either its motive or its consequence is to restrict the use of articles of commerce within the states of destination and is not prohibited unless by other Constitutional provisions. It is no objection to the assertion of the power to regulate interstate commerce that its exercise is attended by the same incidents which attend the exercise of the police power of the states. . . .

The motive and purpose of the present regulation is plainly to make effective the Congressional conception of public policy that interstate commerce should not be made the instrument of competition in the distribution of goods produced under substandard labor conditions, which competition is injurious to the commerce and to the states from and to which the commerce flows.

. . . [W]e conclude that the prohibition of the shipment interstate of goods produced under the forbidden substandard labor conditions is within the constitutional authority of Congress.

In the more than a century which has elapsed since the decision of Gibbons v. Ogden, these principles of constitutional interpretation have been so long and repeatedly recognized by this Court as applicable to the Commerce Clause, that there would be little occasion for repeating them now were it not for the decision of this Court twenty-two years ago in Hammer v. Dagenhart, 247 U.S. 251. In that case it was held by a bare majority of the Court over the powerful and now classic dissent of Mr. Justice Holmes setting forth the fundamental issues involved, that Congress was without power to exclude the products of child labor from interstate commerce. The reasoning and conclusion of the Court's opinion there cannot be reconciled with the conclusion which we have reached, that the power of Congress under the Commerce Clause is plenary to exclude any article from interstate commerce subject only to the specific prohibitions of the Constitution.

Hammer v. Dagenhart has not been followed. The distinction on which the decision was rested that Congressional power to prohibit interstate commerce is limited to articles which in themselves have some harmful or deleterious property — a distinction which was novel when made and unsupported by any provision of the Constitution — has long since been abandoned. . . . The thesis of the opinion that the motive of the prohibition or its effect to control in some measure the use or production within the states of the article thus excluded from the commerce can operate to deprive the regulation of its constitutional authority has long since ceased to have force. . . . And finally we have declared "The authority of the Federal Government over interstate commerce does not differ in extent or character from that retained by the states over intrastate commerce." United States v. Rock Royal Co-Operative, Inc., 307 U.S. 533, 569.

The conclusion is inescapable that Hammer v. Dagenhart, was a departure from the principles which have prevailed in the interpretation of the commerce clause both before and since the decision and that such vitality, as a precedent, as it then had has long since been exhausted. It should be and now is overruled.

Validity of the wage and hour requirements. Section 15(a)(2) and §§6 and 7 require employers to conform to the wage and hour provisions with respect to all employees engaged in the production of goods for interstate commerce. As appellee's employees are not alleged to be "engaged in interstate commerce" the validity of the prohibitions turns on the question whether the employment, under other than the prescribed labor standards, of employees engaged in the production of goods for interstate commerce is so related to the commerce and so affects it as to be within the reach of the power of Congress to regulate it.

To answer this question we must at the outset determine whether the particular acts charged in the counts which are laid under §15(a)(2) as they were construed below, constitute "production for commerce" within the meaning of the statute. As the Government seeks to apply the statute in the indictment, and as the court below construed the phrase "produced for interstate commerce," it embraces at least the case where an employer engaged, as are appellees, in the manufacture and shipment of goods in filling orders of extrastate customers, manufactures his product with the intent or expectation that according to the normal course of his business all or some part of it will be selected for shipment to those customers.

Without attempting to define the precise limits of the phrase, we think the acts alleged in the indictment are within the sweep of the statute. The obvious purpose of the Act was not only to prevent the interstate transportation of the proscribed product, but to stop the initial step toward transportation, production with the purpose of so transporting it. Congress was not unaware that most manufacturing business shipping their product in interstate commerce make it in their shops without reference to its ultimate destination and then after manufacture select some of it for shipment interstate and some intrastate according to the daily demands of their business, and that it would be practically impossible, without disrupting manufacturing businesses, to restrict the prohibited kind of production to the particular pieces of lumber, cloth, furniture or the like which later move in interstate rather than intrastate commerce. . . .

There remains the question whether such restriction on the production of goods for commerce is a permissible exercise of the commerce power. The power of Congress over interstate commerce is not confined to the regulation of commerce among the states. It extends to those activities intrastate which so affect interstate commerce or the exercise of the power of Congress over it as to make regulation of them appropriate means to the attainment of a legitimate end, the exercise of the granted power of Congress to regulate interstate commerce. See McCulloch v. Maryland, 4 Wheat. 316, 421. Cf. United States v. Ferger, 250 U.S. 199.

While this Court has many times found state regulation of interstate commerce, when uniformity of its regulation is of national concern, to be incompatible with the Commerce Clause even though Congress has not legislated on the subject, the Court has never implied such restraint on state control over matters intrastate not deemed to be regulations of interstate commerce or its instrumentalities even though they affect the commerce. . . .

But it does not follow that Congress may not by appropriate legislation regulate intrastate activities where they have a substantial effect on interstate commerce. See Santa Cruz Fruit Packing Co. v. National Labor Relations Board, 303 U.S. 453, 466. A recent example is the National Labor Relations Act, 29 U.S.C.A. §§151 et seq., for the regulation of employer and employee relations in industries in which strikes, induced by unfair labor practices named in the Act, tend to disturb or obstruct interstate commerce. See National Labor Relations Board v. Jones & Laughlin Steel Corp., 301 U.S. 1, 38, 40; National Labor Relations Board v. Fainblatt, 306 U.S. 601, 604, and cases cited. But long before the adoption of the National Labor Relations Act, this Court had many times held that the power of Congress to regulate interstate commerce extends to the regulation through legislative action of activities intrastate which have a substantial effect on the commerce or the exercise of the Congressional power over it.

In such legislation Congress has sometimes left it to the courts to determine whether the intrastate activities have the prohibited effect on the commerce, as in the Sherman Act, 15 U.S.C.A. §§1-7, 15 note. It has sometimes left it to an administrative board or agency to determine whether the activities sought to be regulated or prohibited have such effect, as in the case of the Interstate Commerce Act, 49 U.S.C.A. §§1 et seq., and the National Labor Relations Act or whether they come within the statutory definition of the prohibited Act as in the Federal Trade Commission Act, 15 U.S.C.A. §§41 et seq. And sometimes Congress itself has said that a particular activity affects the commerce as it did in the present act, the Safety Appliance Act, 15 U.S.C.A. §§1 et seq., and the Railway Labor Act, 45 U.S.C.A. §§181 et seq. In passing on the validity of legislation of the class last mentioned the only function of courts is to determine whether the particular activity regulated or prohibited is within the reach of the federal power. . . .

Congress, having by the present Act adopted the policy of excluding from interstate commerce all goods produced for the commerce which do not conform to the specified labor standards, it may choose the means reasonably adapted to the attainment of the permitted end, even though they involve control of intrastate activities. Such legislation has often been sustained with respect to powers, other than the commerce power granted to the national government, when the means chosen, although not themselves within the granted power, were nevertheless deemed appropriate aids to the accomplishment of some purpose within an admitted power of the national government. . . .

We think also that §15(a)(2), now under consideration, is sustainable independently of §15(a)(1), which prohibits shipment or transportation of the proscribed goods. As we have said the evils aimed at by the Act are the spread of substandard labor conditions through the use of the facilities of interstate commerce for competition by the goods so produced with those produced under the prescribed or better labor conditions; and the consequent dislocation of the commerce itself caused by the impairment or destruction of local businesses by competition made effective through interstate commerce. The Act is thus directed at the suppression of a method or kind of competition in interstate commerce which it has in effect condemned as "unfair," as the Clayton Act, 38 Stat. 730, has condemned other "unfair methods of competition" made effective through interstate commerce. . . .

The Sherman Act and the National Labor Relations Act are familiar examples of the exertion of the commerce power to prohibit or control activities wholly intrastate because of their effect on interstate commerce.

The means adopted by §15(a)(2) for the protection of interstate commerce by the suppression of the production of the condemned goods for interstate commerce is so related to the commerce and so affects it as to be within the reach of the commerce power. . . . Congress, to attain its objective in the suppression of nationwide competition in interstate commerce by goods produced under substandard labor conditions, has made no distinction as to the volume or amount of shipments in the commerce or of production for commerce by any particular shipper or producer. It recognized that in present day industry, competition by a small part may affect the whole and that the total effect of the competition of many small producers may be great. See H. Rept. No. 2182, 75th Cong. 1st Sess., p. 7. . . .

Validity of the requirement of records of wages and hours. §15(a)(5) and §11(c). These requirements are incidental to those for the prescribed wages and hours, and hence validity of the former turns on validity of the latter. Since, as we have held, Congress may require production for interstate commerce to conform to those conditions, it may require the employer, as a means of enforcing the valid law, to keep a record showing whether he has in fact complied with it. The requirement for records even of the intrastate transaction is an appropriate means to the legitimate end. . . .

Validity of the wage and hour provisions under the Fifth Amendment. Both provisions are minimum wage requirements compelling the payment of a minimum standard wage with a prescribed increased wage for overtime of "not less than one and one-half times the regular rate" at which the worker is employed. Since our decision in West Coast Hotel Co. v. Parrish, 300 U.S. 379, it is no longer open to question that the fixing of a minimum wage is within the legislative power and that the bare fact of its exercise is not a denial of due process under the Fifth more than under the Fourteenth Amendment. Nor is it any longer open to question that it is within the legislative power to fix maximum hours. Holden v. Hardy, 169 U.S. 366 . . .

Reversed.

NOTES

1. In 1949, the FLSA was amended to narrow the coverage of the statute somewhat. The inclusion of occupations "necessary" to the production of goods for commerce was narrowed to "closely related" occupations "directly essential" to such production. §3(j). The House Managers of the Conference Committee then proceeded to detail specifi-

cally which cases holding coverage were meant to be overruled by this change in wording. This interesting device to accomplish a specific change in the statute by general wording was successful. A similar broadening of the general exemption of "retail and service establishments" also was accomplished at the same time. §13(a)(2, 3, 4).

In 1961, an entirely new concept of coverage under the statute was superimposed upon the already existing standards of coverage. Coverage was extended to business enterprises which in general do $1,000,000 gross annual business and to all establishments of those enterprises which do $250,000 gross business per year. §3(s). This new standard of coverage eliminated the retail exemption for businesses meeting these standards of size except for certain businesses still exempted by specific provision, e.g., hotels, restaurants, motion picture theaters, hospitals. §13(a)(2) (ii, iii). There are other detailed and partial exemptions from the enterprise coverage. One of the significant aspects of the extension of coverage to enterprises, as defined, was to provide for the coverage by the Act of all of the employees of the enterprise regardless of their particular duties. This is a fundamental change from the earlier coverage provisions which base coverage upon the activities of each employee. Kirschbaum v. Walling, 316 U.S. 517 (1942).

2. The FLSA now provides for a minimum wage of $1.25 per hour with a requirement of payment of time-and-a-half for all hours over forty worked in a week. The wage and hour provisions are independent in that if an employee is being paid well above the minimum his time-and-a-half pay will be based upon his hourly rate, not the statutory minimum of $1.25. Thus, any employee regularly paid $2.60 per hour must be paid an additional $1.30 per hour for each hour over forty he works in a given week.

Consider the implications upon collective bargaining and the role of unions if the unions prevail in their demand of 1965 that the minimum wage be raised to $2.00 per hour and the maximum hours be set at thirty-five per week.

3. Experience of the states with wage and hour legislation formed a useful background for federal action and the Fair Labor Standards Act. But the enactment of the latter did not preclude further state action or render it unnecessary. The federal Act expressly provides that higher state standards shall prevail. §18. Limitations of the coverage and exemptions specified in the federal statute leave a substantial part of the total labor force with no statutory protection of wage and hour standards but that provided by state laws. It should be noted, however, that many exempt or uncovered employees are actually paid at or above the federal minimum, either as a result of labor market pressures or because of requirements in collective bargaining agreements.

All states have some wage and hour laws. They are, however, widely varied in the standards they impose and the degree or type of control. All states, territories, and the District of Columbia restrict hours of work of young minors. Comprehensive state programs contain minimum wage and maximum hour regulations limited largely to the protection of female workers and minors. Laws covering time off to vote, control of industrial homework, limits on deductions from wages, requirements of call-in pay, prohibitions against discrimination in wages on the basis of sex, and other regulations have also been enacted. In 1963 the Fair Labor Standards Act was amended to include an equal pay for women provision. §6(d).

State minimum wage laws originally extended only to women and minors, and most laws are still so limited. The laws in some jurisdictions, however, also cover adult males either through broadening the statutory definition of employee or by prohibiting employment of men in specified occupations at wages lower than those fixed in applicable wage orders for female workers. Minimum wages are prescribed usually in terms of hourly rates. A few states, however, have enacted legislation making employers guarantee their permanent employees a full weekly wage for work approximating a full week.

State minimum wage laws are principally significant in service and mercantile industries — retail trade, laundry and dry cleaning, personal service, and hotels and restaurants — where many female workers are unskilled and remain unorganized. A majority of the state minimum wage orders issued in the past decade cover these employees. In these and other industries, wage boards, in addition to fixing minimum rates, have intervened to prevent the undermining of such rates by employers through charges and deductions from the employees' wages for services provided to them at the place of work. Prices for meals, lodging, and laundry services have been strictly regulated and great strides have been made in preventing unjustified deductions from the employee's wage. In spite of all these efforts the minimum wage rates ordered by the boards continue to be substantially below the minimum fixed by the federal statute. The advantages of statutory fixing are uniformity and breadth of coverage. The arguments for delegating this function to wage boards are that such agencies are apt to be more flexible in adjusting to changing economic conditions and more familiar with conditions prevailing in various industries. Wage boards have not always made full use of these advantages, however, and in many instances wage orders have been permitted to continue unchanged during long periods of rising prices.

State laws regulating hours of work have been more widely adopted than minimum wage laws. As indicated above, all states, the District of Columbia, and Puerto Rico regulate hours of work of young minors. The regulation of hours of women is almost as widely prevalent, and is effected through limits on the number of hours which may be worked, control of night work, provisions for a day of rest, requirements of meal and rest periods, or provisions for premium pay for overtime. A number of states prohibit the employment of women in specified classifications of work. Occupations to which most of the prohibitory laws for adult women apply are mining and work in establishments serving liquor. In a number of states maximum hour provisions, days of rest, and meal periods also apply to adult males.

TENNESSEE COAL, IRON & R. CO. v. MUSCODA LOCAL NO. 123

Supreme Court of the United States, 1944
321 U.S. 590, 64 Sup. Ct. 698, 88 L. Ed. 949

Mr. JUSTICE MURPHY delivered the opinion of the Court.

We are confronted here with the problem of determining in part what constitutes work or employment in underground iron ore mines within the meaning of the Fair Labor Standards Act, 52 Stat. 1060, 29 U.S.C. §§201, et seq. This question, which is one of first impression, arises out of conflicting claims based upon the actual activities pursued and upon prior custom and contract in the iron ore mines. Such an issue can be resolved only by discarding formalities and adopting a realistic attitude, recognizing that we are dealing with human beings and with a statute that is intended to secure to them the fruits of their toil and exertion.

Three iron ore mining companies, petitioners herein, filed declaratory judgment actions to determine whether time spent by iron ore miners in traveling underground in mines to and from the "working face" [2] constitutes work or employment for which compensation must be paid under the Act. The respondent labor unions and their officials, representing petitioners' employees, were named as defendants and the Administrator of the Wage and Hour Division of the Department of Labor was allowed to intervene. . . . It is conceded that if underground travel constitutes employment, the miners worked more than the statutory maximum workweek and are entitled to be paid one and one-half times the regular rate for the excess hours. But if the travel time is excluded from the workweek, thus limiting it to the time spent at the working face, no overtime payments are due.

After extended hearings, the District Court found that the travel time "bears in a substantial degree every indicia of worktime: supervision by the employer, physical and mental exertion, activity necessary to be performed for the employers' benefit, and conditions peculiar to the occupation of mining." (40 F. Supp. 4, 10.) The court accordingly ruled that the travel time, as well as the time spent at the surface obtaining and returning tools, lamps and carbide and checking in and out, was included within the workweek. 40 F. Supp. 4. The Circuit Court of Appeals affirmed as to the travel time, holding that the District Court's findings on that matter were supported by substantial evidence. The judgment was modified by the Circuit Court, however, by excluding from the workweek the time spent in the activities at the surface. 5 Cir., 135

---

[2] The "working face" is the place in the mine where the miners actually drill and load ore. The "face to face" basis of compensation, advocated by petitioners, includes only the time spent at the working face. The "portal to portal" basis, proposed by respondents, includes time spent in traveling between the portal or entrance to the mine and the working face and back again, as well as the time spent at the working face.

F.2d 320, rehearing denied 5 Cir., 137 F.2d 176. The importance of the problem as to the travel time led us to grant certiorari.[4]

. . . The record shows that petitioners own and operate twelve underground iron ore mines in Jefferson County, Alabama, and that the general pattern of facts underlying the findings of the courts below is essentially the same in each of these mines.

The miners begin their day by arriving on the company property at a scheduled hour and going to the bath house, where they change into working clothes. They then walk to the tally house near the mine entrance or portal; there they check in and hang up individual brass checks, furnished by petitioners, on a tally or check-in board. This enables the foreman and other officials to tell at a glance those individuals who have reported for work and those production and service crews that are incomplete and in need of substitutes. Vacancies are filled and the head miners and crews receive any necessary instructions. In addition, each miner either rents a battery lamp for the day or buys a can of carbide each day or two for underground illumination purposes. And at some of the mines, many miners stop at a tool box or tool house on the surface to pick up other small supplies and tools necessary for their work. These activities consume but a few minutes.

The miners thereupon are required to report at the loading platform at the mine portal and await their turn to ride down the inclined shafts of the mines. Originally the miners could reach the working faces entirely by foot, but as the shafts increased in length petitioners provided transportation down the main shafts. The miners accordingly ride part of the way to the working faces in ore skips[9] or regular man trips,[10] which operate on narrow gauge tracks by means of cables or hoisting ropes. The operation of the skips and man trips is under the strict control and supervision of the petitioners at all times and they refuse to permit the miners to walk rather than ride. Regular schedules are fixed; loading and unloading are supervised; the speed of the trips is regulated; and the conduct of the miners during the rides is prescribed.

About three to six trips are made, depending on the size of the mine and the number of miners. Ten men sit on each man trip car, while from 30 to 40 are crowded into an ore skip. They are forced to jump several feet into the skip from the loading platform, which not infrequently causes injuries to ankles, feet and hands. The skips are usually overcrowded and the men stand tightly pressed together. The heads of

---

[4] No review has been sought of the exclusion from the workweek of the activities at the surface. We therefore do not discuss that issue in this case. . . .

[9] An ore skip is an ordinary four-wheeled ore box car made of steel. It is normally used for transporting ore and its floor is often covered with muck from such haulings. When men are riding in the car it is known as a "man skip trip." It is used for such purposes in the mines of the Tennessee Company and the Republic Company.

[10] A regular man trip is a specially constructed series of cars. Each car is about eight feet long and resembles a stairway. Five men sit on either side of the car facing outwards, back to back with five men on the other side. . . .

most of them are a foot or more above the top of the skips. But since the skips usually clear the low mine ceilings by only a few inches, the miners are compelled to bend over. They thus ride in a close "spoon-fashion," with bodies contorted and heads drawn below the level of the skip top. Broken ribs, injured arms and legs, and bloody heads often result; even fatalities are not unknown.

The length of the rides in the dark, moist, malodorous shafts varies in the different mines from 3,000 feet to 12,000 feet. The miners then climb out of the skips and man trips at the underground man-loading platforms or "hoodlums" and continue their journeys on foot for distances up to two miles. These subterranean walks are filled with discomforts and hidden perils. The surroundings are dark and dank. The air is increasingly warm and humid, the ventilation poor. Odors of human sewage, resulting from a complete absence of sanitary facilities, permeate the atmosphere. Rotting mine timbers add to the befouling of the air. Many of the passages are level, but others take the form of tunnels and steep grades. Water, muck and stray pieces of ore often make the footing uncertain. Low ceilings must be ducked and moving ore skips must be avoided. Overhead, a maze of water and air pipe lines, telephone wires, and exposed high voltage electric cables and wires present ever-dangerous obstacles, especially to those transporting tools. At all times the miners are subject to the hazards of falling rocks.

Moreover, most of the working equipment, except drills and heavy supplies, is kept near the "hoodlums." This equipment is carried each day by foot by the crews through these perilous paths from the "hoodlums" to the working faces. Included are such items as fifty-pound sacks of dynamite, dynamite caps, fuses, gallon cans of oil and servicemen's supplies. Actual drilling and loading of the ore begin on arrival at the working faces, interrupted only by a thirty minute lunch period spent at or near the faces. The service and maintenance men, of course, work wherever they are needed.

At the end of the day's duties at the working faces, the miners lay down their drills, pick up their other equipment and retrace their steps back to the "hoodlums." They wait there until an ore skip or man trip is available to transport them back to the portal. After arriving on the surface, they return their small tools and lamps, pick up their brass checks at the tally house, and proceed to bathe and change their clothes at the bath house. Finally they leave petitioners' property and return to their homes.

In determining whether this underground travel constitutes compensable work or employment within the meaning of the Fair Labor Standards Act, we are not guided by any precise statutory definition of work or employment. Section 7(a) merely provides that no one, who is engaged in commerce or in the production of goods for commerce, shall be employed for a workweek longer than the prescribed hours unless compensation is paid for the excess hours at a rate not less than one and one-half times the regular rate. Section 3(g) defines the word "employ" to include "to suffer or permit to work." . . .

But these provisions, like the other portions of the Fair Labor Standards Act, are remedial and humanitarian in purpose. We are not here dealing with mere chattels or articles of trade but with the rights of those who toil, of those who sacrifice a full measure of their freedom and talents to the use and profit of others. Those are the rights that Congress has specially legislated to protect. Such a statute must not be interpreted or applied in a narrow, grudging manner. Accordingly we view Sections 7(a), 3(g) and 3(j) of the Act as necessarily indicative of a Congressional intention to guarantee either regular or overtime compensation for all actual work or employment. To hold that an employer may validly compensate his employees for only a fraction of the time consumed in actual labor would be inconsistent with the very purpose and structure of those sections of the Act. It is vital, of course, to determine first the extent of the actual workweek. Only after this is done can the minimum wage and maximum hour requirements of the Act be effectively applied. And, in the absence of a contrary legislative expression, we cannot assume that Congress here was referring to work or employment other than as those words are commonly used — as meaning physical or mental exertion (whether burdensome or not) controlled or required by the employer and pursued necessarily and primarily for the benefit of the employer and his business.

Viewing the facts of this case as found by both courts below in the light of the foregoing considerations, we are unwilling to conclude that the underground travel in petitioners' iron ore mines cannot be construed as work or employment within the meaning of the Act. The exacting and dangerous conditions in the mine shafts stand as mute, unanswerable proof that the journey from and to the portal involves continuous physical and mental exertion as well as hazards to life and limb. And this compulsory travel occurs entirely on petitioners' property and is at all times under their strict control and supervision.

Such travel, furthermore, is not primarily undertaken for the convenience of the miners and bears no relation whatever to their needs or to the distance between their homes and the mines. Rather the travel time is spent for the benefit of petitioners and their iron ore mining operations. The extraction of ore from these mines by its very nature necessitates dangerous travel in petitioners' underground shafts in order to reach the working faces, where production actually occurs. Such hazardous travel is thus essential to petitioners' production. It matters not that such travel is, in a strict sense, a non-productive benefit. Nothing in the statute or in reason demands that every moment of an employee's time devoted to the service of his employer shall be directly productive. Section 3(j) of the Act expressly provides that it is sufficient if an employee is engaged in a process or occupation necessary to production. Hence employees engaged in such necessary but not directly productive activities as watching and guarding a building, waiting for work, and standing by on call have been held to be engaged in work necessary to production and entitled to the benefits of the Act. Iron ore miners travelling underground are no less engaged in a "process or occupation" necessary to actual production. . . . Theirs is a fossorial activity bearing all the indicia of hard labor.

The conclusion that underground travel in iron ore mines is work has also been reached by the Administrator of the Wage and Hour Division. . . . [S]tatutes of several important metal mining states provide that the eight-hour per day limitation upon work includes travel underground.

Petitioners, however, rely mainly upon the alleged "immemorial custom and agreements arrived at by the practice of collective bargaining" which are said to establish "the 'face to face' method as the standard and measure for computing working time in the iron ore industry." They further claim that since the Fair Labor Standards Act contains no specific provision regarding underground travel in mines, Congress must be presumed to have intended to perpetuate existing customs or to leave the matter to be worked out through the process of collective bargaining.

The short answer is that the District Court was unable to find from the evidence that any such "immemorial" custom or collective bargaining agreements existed. That court, in making its findings, properly directed its attention solely to the evidence concerning petitioners' iron ore mines and disregarded the customs and contracts in the coal mining industry. There was ample evidence that prior to the crucial date of the enactment of the statute, the provisions in petitioners' contracts with their employees relating to a forty hour workweek "at the usual working place" bore no relation to the amount of time actually worked or the compensation received. Instead, working time and payment appear to have been related to the amount of iron ore mined each day. Hence such contract provisions defining the workweek are of little if any value in determining the workweek and compensation under a statute which requires that they be directly related to the actual work performed.

Likewise there was substantial, if not conclusive, evidence that prior to 1938 petitioners recognized no independent labor unions and engaged in no bona fide collective bargaining with an eye toward reaching agreements on the workweek. Contracts with company-dominated unions and discriminatory actions toward the independent unions are poor substitutes for "contracts fairly arrived at through the process of collective bargaining." The wage payments and work on a tonnage basis, as well as the contract provisions as to the workweek, were all dictated by petitioners. The futile efforts by the miners to secure at least partial compensation for their travel time and their dissatisfaction with existing arrangements, moreover, negative the conclusion that there was any real custom as to the workweek and compensation therefor. A valid custom cannot be based on so turbulent and discordant a history; it requires something more than unilateral and arbitrary imposition of working conditions. . . .

But in any event it is immaterial that there may have been a prior custom or contract not to consider certain work within the compass of the workweek or not to compensate employees for certain portions of their work. The Fair Labor Standards Act was not designed to codify or perpetuate those customs and contracts which allow an employer to claim all of an employee's time while compensating him for only a part of it. Congress intended, instead, to achieve a uniform national policy of guaranteeing compensation for all work or employment engaged in by employees covered by the Act.[18] Any custom or contract falling short of that basic policy, like an agreement to pay less than the minimum wage requirements, cannot be utilized to deprive employees of their statutory rights. . . .

This does not foreclose, of course, reasonable provisions of contract or custom governing the computation of work hours where precisely accurate computation is difficult or impossible. Nor are we concerned here with the effect that custom and contract may have in borderline cases where the other facts give rise to serious doubts as to whether certain activity or non-activity constitutes work or employment. It is sufficient in this case that the facts relating to underground travel in iron ore mines leave no uncertainty as to its character as work. The Act thus requires that appropriate compensation be paid for such work. Any other conclusion would deprive the iron ore miners of the just remuneration guaranteed them by the Act for contributing their time, liberty and strength primarily for the benefit of others.

The judgment of the court below is accordingly affirmed.

[The separate concurring opinions of Justice Frankfurter and Justice Jackson are omitted.]

MR. JUSTICE ROBERTS, dissenting. . . .

The record presents no dispute as to the facts. Some are matters of public notoriety susceptible of judicial notice; others are contained in offers of evidence which the District Court excluded as irrelevant; others are exposed in the proofs.

Conditions of labor in iron mines and in coal mines are similar. In both, as the workings become deeper, the men have farther to go to reach the places at which they labor. The time thus consumed by individual workmen varies in the same mine, and in different mines. The conditions in the channels of approach to the places of work are somewhat better in iron mines than in coal mines. The custom in coal mines is, therefore, persuasive, since some of the petitioners maintain coal and iron mines in close proximity, and since the practice in the two has been the same for many years.

In the public arbitration proceedings at Birmingham, Alabama, in 1903, the testimony showed that a miner's day was reckoned "from the

---

[18] Congress was not unaware of the effect that collective bargaining contracts might have on overtime pay. It expressly decided to give effect to two kinds of collective agreements, as specified in Section 7(b)(1) and (2) of the Act. [Providing for leveling off overtime over a period of weeks pursuant to collective agreements when certain limitations are met.] It thus did not intend that other collective agreements should relieve employers from paying for overtime in excess of an actual workweek of 40 hours, regardless of the provisions of such contracts.

time [he] gets to the face of the coal until he leaves the face of the coal," and that the eight hour day was so measured. That arbitration resulted in a wage agreement on the "face to face" basis; that is, on a wage fixed according to the time the miners worked at the face of the coal.

In 1917 a public board of arbitration, whose award was approved by the United States Fuel Administrator, found:

"An eight hour day means eight hours work at the usual working places of all classes of employees. This shall be exclusive of the time required in reaching such working places in the morning and departing from the same at night."

In 1920 the report and award of the Bituminous Coal Commission, which was made the basis of agreement between operators and union miners, employed the language just quoted.

In 1933 the Code of Fair Competition for the Bituminous Coal Industry promulgated by the President under the National Industrial Recovery Act, 48 Stat. 195, provided:

"Seven hours of labor shall constitute a day's work and this means seven hours work at the usual working places for all classes of labor, exclusive of the lunch period, whether they be paid on the day or tonnage or other piece work basis."

In 1933 the Appalachian Agreement, approved by the President, provided:

"Eight hours of labor shall constitute a day's work. The eight hour day means eight hours' work in the mines at the usual working places for all classes of labor exclusive of the lunch period."

Prior to 1938, the petitioner Tennessee Coal, Iron & Railroad Company paid its miners either on a piece work basis or upon a shift basis, as did the petitioners Sloss-Sheffield, and Republic Steel. But the common understanding of men and management was that, at first, ten hours and, later, eight hours constituted a working day. This is shown by the proofs and there is no evidence to the contrary.

On numerous occasions the men working in these mines claimed, through their unions, that they ought to be paid for travel time consumed in the mines in going to or from the face where they worked. Their demands for pay for travel time are eloquent proof that they understood the basis on which their pay was reckoned and that it did not include travel time as working time. No agreement to pay for travel time was made and no practice to pay for it was adopted.

In 1934 Tennessee made an agreement with the Union representing its employes, which was renewed in 1935, and again in 1936. It is undisputed that all of these agreements excluded payment for travel time. On October 6, 1938, before the Fair Labor Standards Act was in effect, a collective bargaining agreement was made between the International Union, affiliated with the CIO, and the Tennessee Company. In this agreement it was provided: . . .

"The eight (8) hour day means eight hours of work in or about the mines at the usual working places for all classes of labor, exclusive of the lunch period, whether they be paid by the day or be paid on the tonnage basis."

This agreement remained in effect until May 5, 1941, when the provisions in question were abrogated pursuant to an opinion promulgated by the Wage and Hour Administrator. . . .

The circumstances are not materially different with respect to Sloss-Sheffield. . . .

Republic Steel has had no formal written agreement with its employes, but it has bargained with their union. As early as 1933 the union suggested that an arrangement be made whereby the men enter the mine on their own time and come out on company time, but the matter was not pressed. It came up again in 1934. After a strike, negotiations resulted in a return of the men to work on the face to face plan of payment. In 1935 the union proposed that the employes should enter on their own time and come out on company time, but in negotiations the matter was dropped. In 1936 the union wrote the company respecting an agreement and, in its proposal, said: "The eight hour day means eight hours in or about the mines at the usual working places for all classes of work." In 1939 the union proposed an agreement containing a like provision. In that year the union preferred charges before the National Labor Relations Board but these did not involve the face to face basis of wage computation. The complaint was settled by stipulation. The company continued to pay for a day's work on the face to face basis until May 1, 1941.

The Fair Labor Standards Act became effective October 24, 1938. At that time coal and iron miners were being paid on the basis of their time spent at their working places in the mine. The miners fully understood this basis.

On July 9, 1940, the director of the legal department of the United Mine Workers of America, in a letter to the Administrator of the Act, requested that he accept the definition of working time contained in the Appalachian agreement, which the letter said embodied "the custom and traditions of the bituminous mining industry." That definition was the same as that quoted from the Tennessee agreement, supra. The letter further said, respecting the face to face method:

"This method of measuring the working time at the place of work has been the standard provision in the basic wage agreements for almost fifty years and is the result of collective bargaining in its complete sense." and further said: "As mines grow older, the working places move farther and farther away from the portal or opening of the mine, and as such conditions develop, it becomes necessary for provision to be made for transportation of the men over long distances to their working places." and added that adjustment of wage rates to any new measurement "would create so much confusion in the bituminous industry as to result in complete chaos, and would probably result in a complete stoppage of work at practically all of the coal mines in the United States."

On the footing of that letter the Administrator issued a release stating that the face to face basis in the bituminous industry would not be unreasonable.

On March 23, 1941, the Administrator announced a modified portal to portal wage hour opinion in which he defined the work day in underground metal mining as starting when the miner reports at the collar of the mine, ends when he returns to the collar, and includes the time spent on the surface in obtaining and returning lamps, carbide, and tools and in checking in and out. Realizing that this was a complete change of opinion, the Administrator announced that he would not seek to compel payment of restitution from mine owners operating on a face to face basis but that he could not interfere with the right of employes or their representatives to sue for past overtime and penalties under §16(b) of the Act. Thereupon the unions representing miners demanded payment of overtime for all travel time since the effective date of the Act, and invoked the penalties specified therein.

. . . It is significant that the District Court avoided any finding as to whether the employers had ever paid travel time or as to the understanding of the parties that the employers were not paying for such travel time. And it is even more significant that the court made no finding whatever about the formal collective bargaining agreements entered into by the respondents with the petitioners in which both parties clearly signified their understanding of what was work in iron mines. And the court could not, under the proofs in this case, have found that these collective bargaining agreements were contrary to the accepted practice in iron and coal mines throughout the country prior to 1941. . . .

Reliance is placed on the trial court's finding that the evidence discloses no custom to exclude travel time from the workweek. But that very reliance exposes the fallacy of the lower court's and this court's position. Unless the statute gave the courts authority to make contracts for the parties, which the statute did not make, a court could not support such a contract by finding that there was no custom with respect to travel time. It would be necessary for it to find that there was a custom to pay for such time, which the District Court failed to do, for the obvious reason that there was no evidence of such custom. . . .

. . . [T]he decision of the case by both courts below turns on the view of a court as to what ought to be considered work and what not, irrespective of the understanding of the parties. Suppose that the parties had agreed that travel time was working time and to be included and paid for in the workweek? Would the courts be at liberty to find the contrary and deprive respondents of the benefit of the agreement. I think not.

I cannot better characterize the result in this case than by quoting from what Judge Sibley said in his dissenting opinion below [135 F.2d 324, 325]:

"If it would be better to include travel time in work time, it ought to be done by a new bargain in which rates of pay are also reviewed. If the change is to be by a special statute (some western States have such statutes), it will operate justly in futuro, and not by unexpected penalty, as here.

"There is nothing in the Act to outlaw agreements that travel time in getting to or from the agreed place of work is not work time. This is true though the employer may organize a means of transportation and make rules for its use. The agreements here that work time includes only time at the face of the ore bed are not illegal. Digging out the ore is what the miners agree to do, and for that they are paid. Getting their tools together and riding or walking to the agreed place of work is not, by force of any law, work done for the mine owner. No one, I suppose, would say that if a group of miners who had spent an hour riding to work decided of their own will not to dig any ore and spent another hour riding back, they had done any work for which they should be paid by force of the Act.

"It is now proposed to assess against these appellants as back pay for overtime an estimated quarter of a million dollars, to be doubled by way of penalty, to compensate the miners for their time in going to and from their place of work, in the face of their agreements that this time was not in their work time. They are to get three times as much per hour for riding and walking to and from the work they were hired to do, as they get for doing the work itself. The injustice of it to me is shocking."

I would reverse the judgment.

[Chief Justice Stone concurred in the dissenting opinion.]

NOTES

1. Is the position of the majority of the Court valid in tending to ignore the role of collective bargaining? To what extent should collective bargaining play a role in the application of a statute such as the FLSA?

2. The principal case and a later case, Anderson v. Mt. Clemens Pottery Co., 328 U.S. 680 (1946) (holding walking time from the company parking lot to an employee's work station could be work time if not de minimis), resulted in claims being filed for well over six billion dollars for additional overtime compensation based upon an amazing variety of walking, clothes changing, washup time, and the like being asserted as work time. This situation resulted in the enactment of the Portal-to-Portal Act of 1947, designed to wipe out most of these claims retroactively and prospectively. 61 Stat. 84, 29 U.S.C. §251. Since the passage of that Act, walking or riding to the place of "performance of the principal activity" of the employee or any activities "preliminary or postliminary" to such principal activities are noncompensable unless there is an express provision in a contract between employee and employer or between an exclusive bargaining representative and an employer making such activities compensable, or unless a custom is clearly established making such activities compensable so long as not in conflict with a contract or collective bargaining agreement. §4(a,b). See also

Section 3(o) of the FLSA providing for the exclusion of clothes changing or washing from work time if excluded by contract or collective bargaining agreement.

In Steiner v. Mitchell, 350 U.S. 247 (1956), the Supreme Court held that the time spent by workers in a battery factory changing clothes in the morning and taking a shower and changing clothes in the evening was principal activity because of the caustic and toxic materials which they handled. The time thus occupied, approximately thirty minutes per day, was work time even though there was no contract or custom establishing it as work time. In a companion case, Mitchell v. King Packing Co., 350 U.S. 260 (1956), the Court held that butchers in a meat packing plant were engaged in compensable work within the meaning of the statute while engaged in sharpening their knives. The company supplied a work room for the purpose of knife sharpening but required that they be sharpened during scheduled lunch hour or before or after scheduled starting or quitting times. There was no contract or custom making this time work time.

WALLING v. HARNISCHFEGER CORP.

Supreme Court of the United States, 1945
325 U.S. 427, 433, 65 Sup. Ct. 1246, 1250, 89 L. Ed. 1711

MR. JUSTICE MURPHY delivered the opinion of the Court. . . .

Respondent is a Wisconsin corporation engaged in producing electrical products for interstate commerce. About one-half of respondent's production employees, called incentive or piece workers, are involved in this case.

As a result of collective bargaining by their union, these employees entered into a collective agreement with respondent whereby they are each paid a basic hourly rate plus an "incentive bonus" or "piecework earnings." The various jobs performed by these incentive workers are "time studied" by the management. The time which the job is shown to consume is multiplied by a "standard earning rate" [2] per unit of time. The amount so obtained is known as the "price" placed on that job. When an employee is given work on a job that has been so priced, he receives a job card bearing the price.

The worker is paid his agreed base or hourly rate (ranging from 55 cents to $1.05 per hour) for the time which he takes to perform the job. If the job price exceeds this base pay, he ultimately receives the difference between the two amounts. The excess of the job price over the hourly earnings is known as an "incentive bonus" or "piecework earnings." Thus the sooner a job is completed the greater will be this incentive bonus. When the job price is smaller than the hourly earnings the employee receives only the hourly rate for the time worked, being as-

---

[2] The "standard earning rate" is the hourly rate of pay which workers in the Milwaukee, Wisconsin, district receive for that type of work. This "standard earning rate" is not the base rate of any worker in respondent's plant, nor is it the average hourly earned rate of any worker.

sured of that rate regardless of his efficiency or speed. About 98.5% of the incentive workers, however, work with sufficient efficiency and speed to earn compensation over and above their base pay. These incentive bonuses were found by the District Court to form about 22% of the total compensation received each pay day by these workers, exclusive of overtime payments, although respondent claims that the bonuses vary from 5% to 29% of each payroll.

On many jobs which have not been "time studied" the respondent has agreed to pay, and does pay, each incentive worker an hourly rate at least 20% higher than his basic hourly rate. And when an incentive worker is temporarily assigned to "non-incentive" work he is paid at least 20% more than his basic hourly rate. Moreover, vacation pay is based on an employee's average hourly straight time earnings over a three-month period and not on his base rate.

These incentive workers frequently work in excess of the statutory maximum workweek. For these extra hours they receive a premium of 50% of the basic hourly rate, which does not reflect the incentive bonuses received. Likewise, when incentive workers are working on jobs that have not been "time-studied" or are temporarily doing "non-incentive" work they receive overtime pay on the basis of their basic hourly rates rather than on the 20% higher hourly rates actually paid them during the non-overtime hours.

The Administrator of the Wage and Hour Division of the Department of Labor brought this action[8] to compel the respondent to comply with the provisions of Section 7(a) of the Act. In defense, respondent pointed to the provision in the collective contract to the effect that "the parties agree that, for all purposes, the regular rate of pay at which each employee who participates in an incentive plan is employed, is the base rate of each such employee." The District Court held that the respondent was violating the Act by excluding from the computation of overtime the piece rates actually paid. 54 F. Supp. 326. The Seventh Circuit Court of Appeals reversed that judgment by a divided vote. 145 F.2d 589. . . .

It is evident that all the incentive workers receive a guaranteed basic hourly pay as a minimum. As to those who receive no regular additional payments during their non-overtime hours the respondent complies fully with Section 7(a) by paying them one and one-half time the basic hourly rate for all overtime hours. But the vast majority of the employees do receive regular though fluctuating amounts for work done during their non-overtime hours in addition to their basic hourly pay.

(1) Those who receive hourly rates at least 20% higher than their guaranteed base rates clearly are paid a regular rate identical with the higher rate and the failure of respondent to pay them for overtime labor on the basis of such a rate is a plain violation of the terms and spirit of Section 7(a). No contract designation of the base rate as the "regular rate" can negative the fact that these employees do in fact regularly re-

---

[8] Such suits are now brought by the Secretary of Labor under 1950 Reorganization Plan No. 6. See 5 U.S.C. §611, note. — ED.

ceive the higher rate. To compute overtime compensation from the lower and unreceived rate is not only unrealistic but is destructive of the legislative intent. A full 50% increase in labor costs and a full 50% wage premium, which were meant to flow from the operation of Section 7(a), are impossible of achievement under such a computation.

(2) Those who receive incentive bonuses in addition to their guaranteed base pay clearly receive a greater regular rate than the minimum base rate.[3] If they received only piece work wages it is indisputable that the regular rate would be the equivalent of the translation of those wages into an hourly rate. . . . It follows that piece work wages forming only a part of the normal weekly income must also be an ingredient of the statutory regular rate. Piece work wages do not escape the force of Section 7(a) merely because they are paid in addition to a minimum hourly pay guaranteed by contract. Indeed, from another viewpoint, the incentive employees so compensated are in fact paid entirely on a piece work basis with a minimum hourly guaranty.[4] The conclusion that only the minimum hourly rate constitutes the regular rate opens an easy path for evading the plain design of Section 7(a). We cannot sanction such a patent disregard of statutory duties.

In this instance 98.5% of the incentive employees receive incentive bonuses in addition to their guaranteed hourly wages, demonstrating that such bonuses are a normal and regular part of their income. Once the parties agree that these employees should receive such piece work wages, those wages automatically enter into the computation of the regular rate for purposes of Section 7(a) regardless of any contract provision to the contrary. Moreover, where the facts do not permit it, we cannot arbitrarily divide bonuses or piece work wages into regular and overtime segments, thereby creating an artificial compliance with Section 7(a).

It matters not how significant the basic hourly rates may be in determining the compensation in situations where incentive bonuses are not paid. When employees do earn more than the basic hourly rates because of the operation of the incentive bonus plan the basic rates lose their significance in determining the actual rate of compensation. Nor is it of controlling importance that the respondent now pays a premium for overtime employment so as to make the overtime rate somewhat above

[3] This is shown by the following example. An incentive worker is assigned a basic rate of $1 an hour and works 50 hours a week on 15 "time studied" jobs that have each been given a "price" of $5. He completes the 15 jobs in the 50 hours. He receives $50 basic pay plus $25 incentive pay (the difference between the base pay and 15 job prices). In addition, the worker receives $5 extra for the 10 overtime hours. This is computed on the basis of 50% of the $1 base rate, or 50 cents an hour premium. Actually, however, this worker receives compensation during the week at the actual rate of $1.50 an hour ($75 divided by 50 hours) and the overtime premium should be computed on that basis, giving the worker a premium of 75 cents an hour or $7.50 for the 10 overtime hours.

[4] Thus, in the example given in footnote 3, the worker earns $75 during the week exclusive of the overtime premium. This $75 may be considered either (1) the amount received for completing the 15 "priced" jobs with a $50 minimum guaranty or (2) the sum of the $50 hourly pay and the $25 piece work pay.

the piece work earnings per hour.[5] Until that premium is 50% of the actual hourly rate received from all regular sources Section 7(a) has not been satisfied. . . .

Reversed.

[The concurring opinion of Justice Frankfurter and the dissenting opinion of Chief Justice Stone are omitted.]

NOTES

1. In further consideration of the relationship between collective bargaining and wage and hour legislation, Bay Ridge Operating Co. Inc. v. Aaron, 334 U.S. 446 (1948), should be mentioned. This case involved a collective agreement which, in providing for premium pay for holiday and off-shift work, set premiums at time-and-a-half basic hourly rates. The company contended that these amounts actually were a form of overtime and to treat them as part of the regular rate for calculating overtime was awarding "overtime on overtime." The Court disagreed and held such premiums part of the regular rate.

This case and cases like the principal case led to clarifying (and in the Bay Ridge case to some extent reversing) amendments in 1949. §7(d). There are specific provisions covering gifts, show-up pay, holiday pay, etc., as well as more complicated provisions for bonus, profit-sharing, and pension contributions. Concerning the Bay Ridge case, amendments to the same section provided that time-and-a-half premiums for holiday and off-shift work would not be counted in the regular rate so long as certain requirements were met. One of the requirements as to off-shift or shift premium payments is that they must be pursuant to a bona fide contract or collective bargaining agreement.

2. Another significant facet of governmental wage and hour control is that involved in statutes regulating working conditions of employees of government contractors. The most far-reaching federal statute concerning such employees is the Walsh-Healey (Public Contracts) Act, 49 Stat. 2036 (1936), as amended, 41 U.S.C. §35, covering contracts exceeding $10,000 for supplies and equipment. The Walsh-Healey Act requires that such contracts include undertakings by the contractor to pay the applicable minimum wage and overtime compensation for more than eight hours' work daily or forty weekly, whichever is greater, to employ no child or convict labor, and to provide safe and sanitary working conditions. Since the enactment of FLSA, the chief economic importance of Walsh-Healey is as a minimum wage measure under which the government is enabled to maintain wage standards in advance of FLSA, which may also cover the same employees.

In contrast to FLSA, Walsh-Healey provides that employees shall be paid minimum wages "determined by the Secretary of Labor to be the prevailing minimum wages for persons employed on similar work or in the particular or similar industries . . . operating in the locality" where

---

[5] The overtime rate now paid amounts to about one and one-third or one and one-fourth the regular hourly rate of actual earnings.

the goods contracted for are to be made or furnished. §1(b). Lacking a prevailing minimum wage determination by the Secretary, the minimum wage stipulation in the government's contract does not apply.

"Locality" is not defined in the Act. The Secretary considered that a restrictive interpretation of the term would give maximum effect to regional wage differentials and afford a competitive advantage to bidders for government contracts from low-wage areas. From the beginning, therefore, the Secretary interpreted the term "locality" broadly, and in most prevailing minimum wage determinations the "locality" has comprised the entire United States.

The Secretary's interpretation was challenged in Perkins v. Lukens Steel Co., 310 U.S. 113 (1940), but the Supreme Court held that the management of government purchasing is an executive function and therefore the interpretation of the Secretary of Labor was not reviewable at the instance of a prospective bidder.

Similarly immune from judicial review was the Secretary's interpretation that the exemption from the Act of purchases of such goods "as may usually be bought in the open market" (§9) refers to purchases which the government may make without advertising for bids and not to standard items obtainable on the market.

Opposition to these determinations led to an amendment in 1952, 66 Stat. 308, 41 U.S.C. §43a, which provides that the Administrative Procedure Act, 60 Stat. 237 (1946), 5 U.S.C. §1001, shall apply in the administration of the Walsh-Healey Act. It also provides for judicial review of wage determinations and of interpretations and gives standing to sue to prospective bidders.

A prevailing minimum wage determination of the Secretary of Labor for a branch of the textile industry, effective February 21, 1953, on a national basis, was challenged under the 1952 Amendment on the ground, among others, that the term "locality" was too broad. Summary judgment was awarded to all the plaintiffs, and the Secretary was permanently enjoined from putting the determination into effect as to any of them. Covington Mills v. Mitchell, 129 F. Supp. 740 (D.D.C. 1955). On appeal, however, the decision of the lower court was reversed, 229 F.2d 506 (D.C. Cir. 1955), cert. denied, 350 U.S. 1002 (1956). The appellate court upheld the right of the Secretary to fix a minimum rate applicable to all employers in a particular industry where, because competition in the particular industry is industry wide, only an industry-wide minimum will effectuate the purposes and the policies of the Act. The use of the word "locality" in the statutory wage-fixing authority, the court held, does not require that separate minima be established on the basis of wages prevailing in each separate region or community in which employers in the industry are located.

The Davis-Bacon Act, 46 Stat. 1494 (1931), as amended, 40 U.S.C. §276a, requires mechanics and laborers under federal building and construction contracts for more than $2000 to be paid minimum wages determined by the Secretary of Labor to be prevailing on similar projects in the community. This statute is designed to maintain labor standards in the locality, thus minimizing labor troubles and unrest on federal projects; it seeks to deny competitive advantage on bids for government contracts to contractors who are willing to cut wages below prevailing rates or to import cheaper labor. The Act's purpose is to protect employees and not contractors. But by requiring a predetermination by the Secretary of the prevailing wage, it was considered that contractors bidding for federal contracts might be enabled to ascertain in advance what their approximate labor costs would be. Contractors, however, are not protected against the possibility of being required to pay higher wages than those incorporated in contract specifications.

To cope with a practice of undercutting standards through the exaction from employees of rebates from prevailing wages paid, Congress passed the Anti-Kickback Act, 48 Stat. 948 (1934), 18 U.S.C. §874, which complements the Davis-Bacon Act by making it a crime to exact rebates from employees on projects financed wholly or partly by the United States.

Federal labor standards regulations affecting specific industries or occupations include Part I of the Interstate Commerce Act, 34 Stat. 1415 (1907), as amended, 45 U.S.C. §61 (limiting hours of service of employees of interstate railroads); Merchant Marine Eight Hour Act, 38 Stat. 1164 (1915), as amended, 46 U.S.C. §§673, 690 (limiting hours of work on certain merchant vessels of the United States); Motor Carriers Act, 49 Stat. 544 (1935), as amended, 49 U.S.C. §304(a)(3) (empowering the Interstate Commerce Commission to establish maximum hours of service for certain employees of interstate motor carriers); Civil Aeronautics Act of 1938, 52 Stat. 987, 49 U.S.C. §1421(a)(5) (relating to hours of employees engaged in interstate air transportation); and Sugar Act of 1947, 61 Stat. 929, 7 U.S.C. §1131 (regulating child labor and wages of workers on farms producing sugar beets or sugar cane).

It should be added, finally, that during World War II three departments of the Federal Government established cooperatively the policy of including by negotiation in government contracts for the procurement of foreign materials needed for the war, clauses requiring the producer to "comply with all local laws and regulations affecting labor relations, hours of work, wages . . ." and to "pay wages no less than those paid in any other comparable operations now or hereafter carried on by the Seller in the Republic of . . . . nor less than those paid by other persons for comparable work in the Republic of . . . . , whichever is higher." Several hundred contracts containing these or similar terms were entered into. For a description of this program see Mathews, Labor Standards Provisions in Government Foreign Procurement Contracts, 42 Ill. L. Rev. 141 (1947).

b. BARGAINING THE WAGE ISSUE

ENDERBY PROBLEM 9
(*See page 392 supra for Enderby Problem 8*)

The current Enderby contract designates May 10 as its automatic renewal date. On March 8, Curme, president of Local 417, wrote to O'Doul, plant superintendent of the Enderby Company, advising him that "Local 417 hereby gives notice that it is terminating the current contract on May 10th, and this constitutes the 60-day notice of termination required by the current agreement and Section 8(d)(1) of the National Labor Relations Act, as amended."

On March 11, O'Doul replied: "We have received your notice of March 8. Since you are terminating a contract which is satisfactory to us, it is our position that your notice of termination should also have included your demands for change in the contract. We shall expect your proposals for change at once since the federal law contemplates a full 60-day period of negotiations."

There was another letter from Curme to O'Doul on March 13. Its tone was not friendly. Curme protested that O'Doul's "legalistic attempt to avoid bargaining or at least to delay it so as to save a few pennies has caused much bad feeling in the plant." Curme's letter went on to say that "although it had been hoped to seek a common ground for negotiations, and to avoid 'demands,' your letter leaves no alternative. We hereby demand a general wage increase of 25 cents per hour, effective as of May 10; an additional 10 cents per hour per employee to be paid into the Savings and Stock Bonus Plan fund; an increase in the shift premiums to bring them all up to 10 cents per hour; and a revision of the piecework rates and standards on the following jobs: [listing thirty-six jobs, the piecework rates for which had been the subject of dispute during the preceding twelve months]."

Arrangements were made for a negotiating conference to be held on March 17. A long series of conferences followed. It became clear in the course of these meetings that the union's real demand was for a general increase in the neighborhood of 15 cents an hour. It also developed that the company was willing to grant some increase, but only in terms of percentages rather than of so many cents across the board; and that it would probably go along on an adjustment of about 3 per cent in all hourly and base rates.

It became apparent, too, as the negotiations developed, that the union would not press its Savings and Stock Bonus demand, but that it was going to insist upon either an adjustment in the shift premiums or a substantial change in a number of the thirty-six disputed piece rates. At one session, White, the industrial relations manager, declared: "Some of those thirty-six rates are on the low side, but we'll never do anything about them until you agree to changes in some others we all know are too high."

The arguments relied upon by the union in defending its general wage increase (in terms of cents across the board) included the following:

1. That the cost of living in Chicago had increased 12 per cent in the past year; that it would take a 19-cent general increase in hourly rates to neutralize this change in living costs; that the cost of living could be expected to rise at least another 5 per cent in the coming year, and that the wage increase should therefore be 26 or 27 cents an hour.

2. That general wage increases of 11 cents, 12 cents, 16 cents, and 19 cents had been granted the employees of the "Big Four" rubber com-

panies (U.S. Rubber, Goodyear, Goodrich, and Firestone) in the past year.

3. That a 15-cent increase had recently been granted by the big meat-packing companies (three of which have plants within five miles of the Enderby plant); and that this represented "a higher percentage increase in the average rate in the meat-packing plants than Local 417 is seeking here."

4. That employees at the Enderby plant in Tulsa, Oklahoma, had received a wage increase averaging 16 cents per hour in January; that the Chicago plant rates had been 20 cents an hour above the Tulsa plant rates a year ago, but were, after the increase at the Tulsa plant, only 8 cents above those rates (there having been some other adjustments in the past year).

5. That the net profits of the Enderby Company for the past year had been, after taxes, $9,300,000; that the company's statement showed that at least 33 per cent of these earnings were allocable to the Chicago plant's operations; that the comparable earnings figure for the first quarter of the current year would be roughly $3,000,000; that the 25 cents per hour general increase would cost the company only $600,000 a year and that the employees were more entitled to this than the shareholders.

6. That there was no justification for a percentage increase because this would mean the largest increases to those who needed it least.

7. That any increase agreed upon should go into the base rates of all incentive workers.

In conclusion the union stated that there "will be a strike on May 11 unless this whole thing is cleared up."

The company's position was based on the following arguments:

1. That any increases in the cost of living in the past year had been substantially matched by increases in the take-home pay of Enderby employees, many of whom had been upgraded and almost all of whom had been working considerable amounts of overtime during recent months; that the average rate at the Enderby plant (in Chicago) had risen in the past ten years 100 per cent, compared with an increase in the cost of living of only 80 per cent.

2. That the increases in the Big Four plants had no bearing on the Enderby wage negotiations; that Enderby wage rates had historically been lower and that "they must be if Enderby is to remain competitive, in view of the economies which the bigger companies' larger-scale operations permit"; that the Big Four plants are (with one or two small exceptions) not located in the Chicago labor market area.

3. That the percentage increase in the meat-packing plants was irrelevant; that the relevant point was that the Enderby present average rate was 30 cents higher than the meat-packing rate even after the recent increases; that, furthermore, the Enderby rates "are, on the average, 4 cents higher than those paid by comparable companies for comparable jobs in the Chicago area, a fact reflected in the unusually low turnover rate at the Enderby plant."

4. That the rates paid at the Enderby plant in Tulsa have nothing

to do with the Chicago rates; that the 16-cent increase in January was the result of another union's just being recognized there; that the Tulsa rates were still 8 cents below the Chicago rates and that a 34-cent differential would be ridiculous.

5. That profits have no place in the discussion of wage rates; that the union is in no position to evaluate the significance of the "earnings" figure; that dividend payments to stockholders had increased less than wage payments to employees, regardless of the years of comparison; that most of the corporate earnings had been earmarked for an expansion of the Chicago plant and that this would mean creating 600 new jobs in five years; that the union "cannot argue ability to pay unless it is willing to agree to take wage cuts when profits go down."

6. That a percentage increase is the only fair way of recognizing skill differences, and that the spread between the common labor rate and the highest skilled rates had already been compressed unduly (past contract increases having been in cents per hour across the board).

7. That increases to incentive workers, if any, should be added to their earnings figures and could not be put in their base rates without discriminating against hourly workers.

On April 6, Curme, on behalf of the union, notified the Federal Mediation and Conciliation Service and the Illinois Department of Labor of the bargaining dispute and the fact that no new agreement had been reached. Shortly thereafter, a mediator from the FMCS showed up and spent two days talking to the parties together and separately, without any progress. After these meetings, he left. Sporadic meetings continued during the rest of April with no real accomplishment. On May 6, the FMCS mediator returned. He found no change in the position of the parties. By meeting with company and union representatives separately and then having them meet together, he finally got the union representatives to agree to either (a) a 13-cent general increase, a 3-cent increase in all shift premiums, and arbitration of the thirty-six disputed piecework rates; or (b) a 16-cent general increase in all hourly and base rates.

The company turned down this alternate offer and instead offered a flat 5 per cent increase in all hourly and base rates. It refused any arbitration of the disputed piecework rates.

The mediator kept the parties in session all day on May 10, and into the night. At midnight, the union proposed that both parties submit the entire dispute to arbitration. The company quickly rejected this course as "a clear intrusion upon the company's right to manage."

On May 11, the plant was struck.

1. What factors, other than those enumerated in the above statement probably entered into the consideration of this problem by the respective parties?

2. What should the mediator assigned to this dispute have said to each of the parties (privately) with respect to the various points enumerated above?

3. How would you, as an arbitrator, have resolved this issue if it had

been submitted to you? What disposition would you have made of the enumerated points? What account would you have taken of any factors not enumerated?

4. How would you, as counsel for Local 417, have advised the union regarding its right to strike?

(1) The Lawyer's Role

Although the issue of wages arises more frequently and attracts more public attention than any other in the negotiation of collective agreements, and raises problems of infinite complexity, lawyers do not usually participate actively in its solution. So far as a general wage increase is concerned, whether based on percentage or cents per hour, the critical question is how much; the drafting problems are negligible.

The typical "wage package" today, however, contains much more than an increase in wage rates or salaries. Increasingly, it includes a greater variety of so-called fringe benefits: paid vacations and holidays, call-in pay, severance pay, pensions, health and welfare benefits, and the like. Many of these provisions have been included in collective agreements for years. While a number of them suffer from poor draftmanship, most parties learn from experience how to put in writing what they mean. Drafting a pension trust agreement, however, is as technical and exacting a task as most lawyers are likely to encounter. Here the need for expertise is paramount.

Despite the limited role of the lawyer in wage negotiations, he should acquaint himself generally with how various aspects of the wage issue are customarily handled. What follows is little more than an introduction and a glossary of terms.

(2) Arbitration of the General Wage Issue

In some industries it is fairly common to submit the general wage issue to arbitration by a single arbitrator or board when the parties reach an impasse in their negotiations. This occurs most commonly in those industries heavily weighted with "public interest," such as gas, water, and light utilities, and urban transportation systems. Arbitration of wages has also been fairly common in the printing industry, and is occasionally resorted to in a variety of others.

Awards of arbitrators resolving these bargaining disputes are exceedingly complex. The factors which might enter into the establishment of a wage rate are painstakingly evaluated. Perhaps it can be said that the four factors to which arbitrators usually attach the greatest weight are: (1) the cost of living, (2) the industry wage pattern, (3) the wage pattern of the locality, and (4) the financial condition of the company. But it should be stressed that they rely upon a number of other factors as well.

Good examples of wage arbitration awards, showing the thorough weighing of factors by the arbitrators, are Mohawk Carpet Mills, 26

L.A. 651 (1956); Twin City Rapid Transit Co., 16 L.A. 749 (1951); Mason Contractors' Assn. of Detroit, 12 L.A. 909 (1949); and R. H. Macy & Co., 11 L.A. 450 (1948).

On the setting of wages by the arbitration process see, in general, Backman, Economic Data Utilized in Wage Arbitration (1952); Bernstein, Arbitration of Wages (1954); Kuhn, Arbitration in Transit: An Evaluation of Wage Criteria (1952); Taylor and Pierson, New Concepts in Wage Determination (1957), particularly the chapter by Ross entitled The External Wage Structure, at 173.

(3)   Additional Economic Benefits

Incentive pay.   A great many industrial workers operate under some system of piecework pay which enables them to increase their wages as they become more efficient.   The typical pattern is the establishment of a base rate of pay on a time basis, with piecework pay added to the base rate for all production over established norms.   Many disputes can arise out of the establishment, application, and alteration of these incentive rates.   Since these disputes arise under an existing collective contract they are in the nature of grievances and, if not resolved by the parties ultimately are settled through arbitration as the terminal step in the grievance procedure.

Incentive pay provisions in collective agreements usually restrict the employer's right to establish new incentive rates or to alter an incentive rate once it is established.   (See the Enderby contract, Art. XI, Secs. 8 11, in Reference Supplement.)   If this were not so, the employer could undermine the negotiated wage level through the device of lowering incentive pay scales.

Cost-of-living adjustment and annual improvement factor.   Many collective agreements today provide for automatic readjustment of wages usually every three months, based upon the fluctuation of the Bureau o Labor Statistics' Consumer Price Index.[9]   Such provisions, known a "escalator clauses," require a fixed cents-per-hour increase for each specified increase in the index.   Usually, the contract provision does not allow reduction of wages beyond those established at the beginning of the contract term.

In addition to the cost-of-living factor, which has resulted in a steady increase in wages in important sectors of industry, collective agreement are increasingly found to include an "annual improvement factor."   This factor is designed to recognize a continuing improvement in managerial efficiency based upon technological progress, better tools, methods, processes, and equipment.   As the 1958 Ford Motor Company contract said "To produce more with the same amount of human effort is a sound economic and social objective."   This annual increment typically provide for an automatic wage increase of a specified amount every six months o every year.   In the Ford contract this amount was 6 cents per hour on yearly basis.

[9] See the description of the Consumer Price Index in 3 CCH Lab. L. Rep. ¶7775.

Profit-sharing, guaranteed annual wage, and supplementary unemployment benefits. In this country, profit-sharing provisions are uncommon in the collective bargaining agreement. Those companies that do have profit-sharing plans are usually unorganized. The union prefers to rely upon more direct guarantees of compensation through cost-of-living adjustments, annual improvement factors, guaranteed wages, and the like. One means by which employees in organized plants engage in a measure of profit-sharing is through bargained stock purchase plans which give employees ownership of part of the business, and they indirectly share in the profits through this means. But even these stock purchase plans are not very common in collective agreements and often have their origins in plans instituted before collective bargaining was established.

In a significant break with tradition, American Motors and the United Automobile Workers concluded an agreement which went into effect on October 1, 1961, providing for profit-sharing by workers. After a 10 per cent deduction for shareholders, 15 per cent of net profits before taxes are set aside for employees. One third of this amount is earmarked for stock purchases to be held by a trustee. The remaining two thirds is used to finance insurance and pension plans, S.U.B., and general economic well-being of the workers, in that order. The text of the agreement will be found in 48 L.R.R.M. 18 (1961). This plan should be contrasted with the Kaiser Steel contract, which is not a profit-sharing plan.

A part of the Kaiser Steel settlement in 1959 was the setting up of a tripartite committee which was given a broad charge to recommend a plan for the future economic progress of the company, including that of the workers. The plan was made public in December, 1962. In attempting to avoid future strikes over wage issues, a formula is created for continuing wage revision based upon increased productivity and all savings in the use of material. This formula is not based on profit-sharing. Further, the plan contains a guarantee to employees against loss of income resulting from automation. The text of the agreement will be found in 51 L.R.R.M. 10 (1962).

Most of the widely publicized and critical labor disputes since the steel strike of 1959 have in significant measure involved issues of automation and the displacement of workers. The troublesome issue of the size and composition of work crews, which was a major stumbling block in the settlement of the prolonged East Coast longshoremen's dispute of 1962, was resolved by an agreement to submit the work crew issue to the Department of Labor for a thorough and impartial study. 52 L.R.R. 81 (1963).

The Progress Report of the Armour Automation Committee, published June 19, 1961, 48 L.R.R. 239 (1961), is an excellent consideration of the automation problem discussed in the context of a particular industry. See also the report of the President's Advisory Committee on Labor-Management Policy, 50 L.R.R.M. 11 (1962).

In recent years much interest in collective bargaining has revolved around the guaranteed annual wage (GAW) and supplementary unemployment benefits (SUB). At one time GAW was felt to be a major objective of unions; ultimately, this may still be the case. However, in the last few years the drive for GAW has been somewhat sidetracked by the development of SUB. While GAW and SUB are different, they fulfill at least in part the same function: they both guard against the temporary layoff which plagues employees in much of American industry.

Health, welfare, and pension plans. There are almost as many kinds of these plans in collective contracts as there are kinds of insurance and annuities. They commonly fulfill the following functions: (1) supplement social security benefits upon retirement, combined with life insurance in case of death or disability before retirement age; (2) pay the costs of medical and hospital treatment; (3) pay for loss of income in case of illness or disability after sick leave benefits provided for in the collective agreement have been exhausted; and (4) supplement regular workmen's compensation benefits in case of accidental injury.

2.   *Industrial Safety and Accidents*

a.   STATE SAFETY LEGISLATION

State industrial safety legislation falls into two distinct periods. The pivotal date which divides these periods is about 1920. Prior to that year, the states generally had enacted a multitude of detailed factory safety laws. These were almost never directly enforced. Practically speaking, enforcement was almost wholly through personal injury suits based upon industrial injury and brought by the servant against the master. The role of the state factory safety laws was simply this: violations of their provisions constituted negligence per se in such suits. Some states went even further and, by legislation, made violations of some of these statutes the grounds for absolute liability. The law reports, prior to 1920, are replete with such cases.

After 1920 these cases largely disappear from the reports. The reason for this was the enactment of the workmen's compensation laws, which substituted an exclusive statutory remedy for the common law tort remedy in cases where the worker was covered by the statute and the injury was compensable thereunder. Negligence of the employer was no longer relevant under those laws; thus negligence per se also became irrelevant. The result was that if states were to continue to enforce factory safety statutes, a new tack had to be taken. Hence we find the development of state administrative boards to enforce these statutes through factory inspection, and in some states, to make detailed rules for factory safety as well. In contrast to the years prior to 1920, these modern state factory controls stimulate practically no litigation in the appellate courts.

A most active and robust appendage of the pre-1920 body of master-and-servant litigation enforcing factory safety regulations still exists in the Federal Safety Appliance and Boiler Inspection Acts, which are the subject of consideration infra page 512. The short answer to explain this is the fact that the railroad workers recover for personal injury under the Federal Employers' Liability Act, which is not a workmen's compensation law but requires proof of employer negligence.

In the states, only a smattering of the enforcement of factory safety legislation by servant-master personal injury suit remains. These are the cases which fall outside the coverage of the workmen's compensation statutes. Agricultural employment, typically, is not covered by workmen's compensation. Governmental employment is not covered, and in situations where the state or its subdivision allows injured employees to sue, the factory safety statutes operate to establish negligence per se. E.g., Scalia v. State, 147 Misc. 622, 264 N.Y. Supp. 327 (N.Y. Ct. Cl. 1933) (prisoner in state prison workshop). There have been attempts to hold employers responsible for diseases contracted by employees, diseases which are not covered by occupational disease provisions of the compensation laws. These attempts are rarely successful because of the difficulty of proving negligence and causation.

Two examples of attempts to establish negligence per se in such situations by using violations of factory safety laws are to be found in Hartman v. Otis Elevator Co., 260 N.Y. 640, 184 N.E. 126 (1932), and Cool v. Curtis-Wright, Inc., 362 Pa. 60, 66 A.2d 287 (1949). In the Hartman case, the employee claimed that failure to place a guard around a large flywheel set up drafts created by the revolving flywheel and these, in turn, caused pneumonia and pleurisy. The court denied recovery, holding that statutes requiring the guarding of machinery were designed to protect employees only from physical contact with the moving machine. In the Cool case, an employee claimed damages for deafness allegedly caused by continuous noise in an airplane propeller factory. In denying recovery, the court gave the same reason as in the Hartman case: the factory safety Acts were meant to protect against physical contact with machinery.

On the theory that a safety statute is designed to protect the workman against his inability, because of unequal bargaining power, to protect himself, it is generally held that assumption of risk is not a defense to a negligence action brought under a factory Act. Similarly, on the ground that a factory Act is designed to protect the particular class of plaintiffs, namely, workmen, against the consequences of their own negligence, contributory negligence is generally held not to be a defense to such an action.

State safety legislation aims largely at the correction or prevention of unsafe working conditions, *e.g.*, hazardous plant layout or unguarded machinery. However, it may also deal with the other major cause of industrial accidents — the commission of unsafe acts by workers.

Statutes which set up apprenticeship programs, limit the hours of work per day or per week, or require rest periods may also be classified as forms of safety legislation because of the effect they may have on the prevention of industrial accidents.

It has been widely believed that workmen's compensation statutes have also been responsible for preventing industrial accidents. It has been argued that merit rating, additional penalties for failure to observe safety measures, and accident reporting — all devices developed under compensation systems—have helped substantially to further the program of accident prevention.

b. FEDERAL LAWS ON RAILROAD AND MINE SAFETY

The Federal Employers' Liability Act, 45 U.S.C. §51, is the general statute affording a remedy for work-incurred injury to railroad employees. It is not a compulsory insurance scheme affording recovery for such injuries regardless of fault as are the workmen's compensation laws. Employer negligence must be proved. But the traditional common law defenses of the fellow servant rule and the assumption of risk are specifically withdrawn from availability to the employer defendant. The third traditional common law defense, contributory negligence, is modified. No longer will such negligence defeat recovery, but it can be shown in mitigation of damages.

Suits under the FELA are brought in court; there is no administrative body involved in the hearing as is typical in workmen's compensation. Trial is usually with a jury. There has been a running controversy for a number of years in the United States Supreme Court over the extent to which courts should be free to overturn jury verdicts granting recovery because of a lack of sufficient evidence to uphold the verdict. For one such series of cases and a thorough discussion of the issue in opinions see Rogers v. Missouri Pacific R.R. Co., 352 U.S. 500 (1957). See also Harris v. Pennsylvania RR. Co., 361 U.S. 15 (1959), which contains a concurring opinion by Justice Douglas cataloguing and giving a statistical analysis of such cases. In the last few terms of the Court the number of these cases has lessened as lower courts have been forced to accept the Supreme Court's insistence that jury verdicts must be upheld as long as there is at least some slight quantum of evidence in the record which can by inference uphold a recovery. See in general Symposia, 17 Ohio St. L.J. 356 (1956); 25 Tenn. L. Rev. 123 (1958); Miller, Federal Employers' Liability Act Revisited, 6 Catholic U.L. Rev. 158 (1957); Comment, Supreme Court Certiorari Policy and the Federal Employers' Liability Act, 43 Cornell L.Q. 451 (1958).

Under the Federal Safety Appliance Act, 45 U.S.C. §1, if any item of safety equipment therein required breaks, there is liability for injury resulting regardless of any fault on the part of the railroad. In O'Donnell v. Elgin, Joliet & Eastern Ry., 338 U.S. 384 (1949), a coupling broke. Without any showing of negligence on the part of the railroad, recovery was allowed, the Court holding that the jury must be separately charged when such a claim is made that the mere failure of the equipment resulting in injury is enough to establish liability. Carrying the same principle of liability without fault is the Federal Boiler Inspection Act, 45 U.S.C. §22, which applies to locomotive safety.

The present federal program for coal mine safety begins with the Federal Coal Mine Inspection Act of 1941. This law, as now amended, is to be found in 30 U.S.C. §451. It is limited to mine inspection and the required filing of reports.

In 1952, the Federal Coal Mine Safety Act, 66 Stat. 692, 30 U.S.C. §471, was passed. It provides that the Director of the Bureau of Mines shall inspect all coal mines, and he is given the power to forbid the approach of employees to any area which he determines to be dangerous in and around a mine. Exceptions are made to cover employees specifically assigned to alleviate the danger, and owners and union representatives. These orders are appealable to the Federal Coal Mine Safety Board of Review and then to the courts. Section 479 of the statute contains detailed rules concerning coal mine safety which cover roof support, ventilation, coal and rock dust, electrical equipment, fire protection, and other matters. Congress rejected a Senate Committee proposal which would have given the Bureau full rule-making authority to design and alter safety codes and regulations. See Somers and Somers, Workmen's Compensation 212 (1954).

C. THE PROTECTION OF HEALTH AND SAFETY THROUGH COLLECTIVE BARGAINING

RUBENSTEIN and WOLK, SAFETY PROVISIONS IN UNION AGREEMENTS
71 Monthly Labor Review 342 (1950)

Clauses dealing with employee safety were included in 51 percent of the 2,411 current labor-management contracts recently examined by the Bureau of Labor Statistics. These "safety clauses" — provisions designed to help reduce the risks of occupational hazards — covered more than 2¼ million workers in 20 major manufacturing industries and 10 nonmanufacturing groups.

Fifty-six percent of the agreements covering firms engaged in manufacturing and 40 percent of the agreements of nonmanufacturing firms included safety provisions. Among manufacturing industries such clauses were most common in petroleum and coal products and transportation equipment agreements. In each of these major industry groups slightly over 80 percent of the contracts included in the survey had safety clauses.

In nonmanufacturing industries safety clauses were concentrated among contracts of two major industry groups. These were electric and gas utilities in which 86 percent of the contracts contained such clauses; and mining and crude petroleum with 79 percent of the agreements containing safety clauses.

Types of Safety Clauses[10]

Provisions dealing with the problem of occupational hazards were incorporated in various types of clauses of the collective bargaining agreements studied. Labor-management committees to promote safe operations in the plant were established in 28 percent of the 1,232 agreements with safety provisions, a general pledge by management and labor jointly — or, by management solely — to further the safety of workers on the job. Others listed responsibilities and rights of management; and,

[10] See the safety provisions in the Enderby Contract, Reference Supplement, page 11. — ED.

those of unions and of employees in maintaining safe working conditions.

A number of contracts combined several methods of dealing with the problem of workers' safety. For example, it was not uncommon for contracts to provide joint labor-management committees while also listing management responsibilities.

Joint Committees — Prevalence

In the rubber industry 65 percent of the contracts with safety clauses provided for the establishment of safety committees. (Most of these covered plants of the four largest rubber companies.) More than half of the contracts with safety clauses in mining and crude petroleum production, and in primary metals industries called for joint committees; as did about 45 percent of such agreements in the chemicals, and stone, clay, and glass products industries. Approximately 30 percent of the agreements in the petroleum and coal products, lumber and timber basic products, and machinery (except electrical) industries also provided for such committees. . . .

Functions of the safety committee stipulated in the agreements analyzed were predominantly of an advisory character. Under certain provisions the committees were instructed to consider and make recommendations on any or all plant health and safety problems such as the promotion of health and safety. Under other provisions the committees were required to inspect plants for safety conditions and sanitary facilities; investigate accidents and analyze their causes; and make recommendations on safety devices to be installed, etc. . . .

Less frequently, the committees' functions were of an executive type. The following clause, for example, made all recommendations of the safety committee mandatory.

"The Employer shall adopt all recommendations agreed upon by a majority of the safety committee.

"If the safety committee is unable to reach a majority decision on any question of safety, the question shall be referred to the person or persons selected by the majority of the committee to decide the issue. The decision of such person or persons shall be carried out by the employer."

Among the contracts analyzed, as in the following illustration, the committee was authorized to order employees off the job when the tasks performed were considered abnormally hazardous:

"The Safety and Health Committee shall have authority, by a majority of four (4) votes, to order employees off jobs when abnormal hazards are present. In the event that the committee should be equally divided, the matter shall be referred immediately to a special safety and health arbitrator for disposition . . ."

A few agreements vested in the joint committee power to settle disputes between employers and employees involving safety matters. . . .

Other Safety Provisions

. . .

The general type of safety provision is usually a simple statement of the intent of management or management and union to eliminate health-safety hazards insofar as possible. One such clause stated:

"The union will cooperate with the company in the objectives of eliminating accidents and reducing health hazards as far as is practical."

The following is illustrative of a general clause in which the company stated its intention of complying with safety legislation:

"The company shall make reasonable provisions for the safety and health of its employees in the plant during the hours of employment in accordance with the statutes of the State of Pennsylvania and the regulations of the Department of Labor."

The most frequent type of provision dealing with rights and responsibilities of employers required the employer to install or furnish safety devices, such as guards on machines, fire fighting equipment, etc.

[Other clauses found in collective bargaining agreements require the employer to maintain satisfactory sanitary facilities, to keep on hand first-aid equipment and personnel, and to provide employees with wearing apparel and equipment when necessary to protect them from injury. Others require the union to cooperate with the employer in obtaining employee observance of safety and health rules, privilege employees to refuse to work under conditions that create hazards in excess of those normally incident to the work, and provide for preferred handling of grievances involving issues of safety or health.]

d. WORKMEN'S COMPENSATION

Today every state has a workmen's compensation statute, Mississippi completing the list in 1948. In addition there are compensation laws in Puerto Rico and the District of Columbia, the Federal Employees' Compensation Act, 39 Stat. 742 (1916), as amended, 5 U.S.C. §751, and the Longshoremen's and Harbor Workers' Compensation Act, 44 Stat. 1424 (1927), as amended, 33 U.S.C. §901.

The theory of workmen's compensation was expressed in the slogan attributed to David Lloyd George: "The cost of the product should bear the blood of the workman." [11] Some courts have found this convincing. Thus, in Phil Hollenbach Co. v. Hollenbach, 181 Ky. 262, 273-274, 204 S.W. 152, 157 (1918), the court observed:

"The purpose intended to be accomplished by this recent legislation is a fair and just distribution of the burdens or losses which result from accident to an employee while regularly engaged in an effort to produce

---

[11] Prosser, Torts 383 (2d ed. 1955); Bohlen, A Problem in the Drafting of Workman's Compensation Acts, 25 Harv. L. Rev. 328, 401, 517 (1912). See also Stertz v. Industrial Insurance Commission, 91 Wash. 588, 590, 158 Pac. 256, 258 (1916): 'All agreed that the blood of the workman was a cost of production, that the industry should bear the charge."

something which will serve a purpose or fill a demand. The workman who is disabled through accident arising out of his employment is, so far as the final result to the community is concerned, much in the same attitude as a disabled machine in the same shop, and the loss and misfortune in each case are and should be charged to and absorbed by the business. If it takes a man and a machine a given time to produce a given number of pairs of shoes, and the machine becomes broken or disabled and new parts must be purchased to repair those broken or worn out, the cost of the repairs is charged to the business as one of the elements entering into the cost of production, just as the price of a day's labor, or the price of material, is charged as part of the cost of production, and the whole is distributed to and borne by the ultimate consumer. This is eminently fair and just. If that be granted, is the man who operates the machine, and who, while in the regular course of his employment, is disabled through accident which arises from the nature of the business, entitled to be treated with less consideration or generosity? An editorial writer in the Outlook illustrates the principle well by the following: 'When a machine is injured in the course of its use, the owner of the machine bears the cost of the injury and charges it to the expense of production, for which he receives payment as he sells his goods. When, however, a workman is injured in the course of his employment, the cost of the injury comes upon him, who can ill afford to bear it; and if his injury is serious, resulting in long incapacity for work, or in death, his family is drafted into that great army of dependents that is a reproach to our civilization. There is no reason that common sense can accept why the cost in human efficiency and human life of the production of the things that people need should not be charged to the account of that production, just as it is charged the cost of injury to machinery.' "

Edwin E. Witte, however, thought this explanation inaccurate. He pointed out that "workmen's compensation does not place the *entire* cost of accident on industry. The most liberal of our compensation laws allow the injured workman two-thirds of his wage loss, and even these laws limit the period during which compensation is payable and prescribe a maximum wage for purposes of computing compensation." [12] Moreover, the concept that workmen's compensation is added to the cost of production and shifted to the consumer does not, Witte explained, agree with the known facts. "It is probable that a part of the costs are normally shifted; but all employers, with their greatly varying costs, certainly do not escape painless. . . .

"Workmen's compensation does not place the cost of accidents upon industry, but provides for a sharing of the resulting economic loss between employers and employees on a predetermined basis, without reference to fault, under a plan designed to insure prompt and certain recovery, at minimum expense. Its justification is, not that the consumers in the end pay the bill, but that workmen's compensation reduces the eco-

[12] The Theory of Workmen's Compensation, 20 Am. Lab. Leg. Rev. 411, 412 (1930).

nomic loss resulting from industrial accidents to a minimum. This is the principle of the 'least social cost.' " [13]

WIEDA v. AMERICAN BOX BOARD CO.
Supreme Court, Michigan, 1955
343 Mich. 182, 72 N.W.2d 13

CARR, C. J. It does not appear that any material facts in this case are in dispute. On February 15, 1952, and for several years prior thereto, plaintiff was employed by defendant as a turbine operator. He was on said date 39 years of age. His employment was concerned with the operation of a steam turbine which generated electricity for the use of defendant's plant. Said turbine was located on two floors, or levels, of the building in which it was placed, separated by a set of metal stairs comprising 26 steps. He was required each hour to make a tour of inspection of the equipment to ascertain if it was operating properly, such tour requiring approximately five minutes. Otherwise he observed certain gauges and meters in the furtherance of the same general purpose.

In connection with his work plaintiff was furnished a list of specific instructions as to what should be done in case of a power shortage. It appears from his testimony that one such shortage had occurred when he was on duty prior to February 15, 1952. The employer had also caused drills to be carried out by employees connected with the operation of the turbine, the purpose being to prepare each one concerned with reference to the course to be followed in event of the occurrence of a power shortage.

On the date mentioned plaintiff began work at 10 o'clock in the evening. Approximately an hour later, while in the washroom, he heard a noise that caused him to hurry up the stairs to the second floor. He then discovered that the voltage was out of control. From then on it appears that he followed the instructions that had been given to him, taking each step as directed and without any uncertainty on his part as to what it was necessary to do. In the course of his operations another employee, who was plaintiff's superior in the plant, came to his aid. They finally succeeded in getting the equipment working and were advised by another employee that they might turn on an auxiliary switch, which operation resulted in the receipt of electric current from the Consumers Power Company. The turbine was then started. The entire operation consumed approximately 45 minutes.

In endeavoring to restore the turbine to its normal functioning plaintiff hurried, or ran as he testified, up and down the stairs referred to at least six times. His instructions did not specifically require him to run, but apparently he was anxious to restore the equipment under his supervision to its normal operation as soon as possible. At one time during the 45-minute period referred to he experienced a dizzy feeling, which he testified passed away as the result of his shaking his head. After the

[13] Id. at 414.

situation had been corrected, however, he again experienced dizziness, and he was taken to the first aid room of the plant and then to a hospital where he remained for approximately 10 hours. Thereafter he returned to his home and remained in bed for a period of about three weeks. . . .

The physician who attended plaintiff on the occasion in question was called as a witness in his behalf, testifying that plaintiff had suffered a heart attack referred to as a coronary infarction or coronary occlusion. . . .

. . . [T]here was testimony before the deputy commissioner indicating that there was a pre-existing heart condition apparently unknown to plaintiff. Undoubtedly his activity during the 45-minute period following the power failure aggravated this condition and brought about the heart attack.

Plaintiff . . . urged, in substance, that the power failure was a fortuitous event, that it resulted in plaintiff's disability, and that the compensation commission was in error in declining to award him compensation. . . . It is apparent that the failure of the turbine to function properly was not the result of an accident in the ordinary acceptance of that term. Such failure had occurred on prior occasions and once, at least, when plaintiff was on duty. The conducting of drills in order to prepare defendant's employees concerned in the operation of the turbine for any such occurrence, and the giving of specific instructions as to each step to be followed in remedying the situation, must be regarded as indicating that power shortages were anticipated by the employer and said employees. The loss of power on the occasion in question may not be regarded as accidental or fortuitous.

It must be borne in mind also that plaintiff's disability did not result directly from the power shortage or from any accidental occurrence in the course of or arising out of his employment. Rather, his unfortunate condition was brought about by his own acts during the 45-minute period following the development of the power shortage. His running up and down the stairs was actuated by his own desire to restore the operation of the turbine as soon as possible. A conclusion that there was an accidental occurrence bringing about the heart attack may not be predicated, under the facts here involved, on the fact that his exertions in conjunction with the pre-existing heart condition brought about the result. In Robbins v. Original Gas Engine Co., 191 Mich. 122, 128, 157 N.W. 437, 439, it was said in referring to the distinction to be observed between the means by which an injury is produced and the result of the producing cause or causes:

"It is not sufficient that there be an unusual and unanticipated result; the means must be accidental — involuntary and unintended. There must, too, be some proximate connection between accidental means and the injurious result." . . .

In the instant case . . . there was nothing in the occurrence preceding plaintiff's acts that resulted in his disability that was unforeseen or unexpected. On the contrary, power shortages were anticipated and arrangements made to deal with them in a proper and methodical manner when they occurred. An unfortunate result may not be given the retroactive effect of making a particular event or happening accidental in nature which was not of such character when it took place.

This Court has repeatedly considered cases involving situations analogous to that in the case at bar. In Hagopian v. City of Highland Park, 313 Mich. 608, 22 N.W.2d 116, it was held that an employee engaged in lifting cans containing rubbish and who suffered an acute heart ailment was not entitled to compensation, said ailment being an ordinary disease of life to which the public generally is exposed and from which plaintiff had suffered prior to the attack on which his claim was based. As in the case at bar, it was not argued that the heart condition was an occupational disease. Likewise, as here, there was no accident. In O'Neil v. W. R. Spencer Grocer Co., 316 Mich. 320, 25 N.W.2d 213, 214, dependents of an employee of the defendant company sought to recover compensation because of his death which was claimed to have resulted from undue exertion on his part in operating his automobile in heavy snow. There was no showing of an accident in which the employee was involved. . . .

In Kasarewski v. Hupp Motor Car Corp., 315 Mich. 225, 232, 23 N.W.2d 689, it was held that the aggravation of a previously existing non-occupational disease is not compensable under part 2 of the workmen's compensation law unless the aggravating injury is accidental in character. . . .

In May v. A. H. Powell Lumber Co., 335 Mich. 420, 56 N.W.2d 242, the claim for compensation was presented by dependents of Victor May who was an employee of the Powell Lumber Company. On the day prior to his death he operated a bulldozer which did not function properly. In consequence fumes and smoke resulted from oil splashed over the motor. This caused the employee to cough and gag, and apparently such effects of inhaling the fumes persisted during the evening and night. The next morning at approximately 4 o'clock his death occurred from a heart condition. Medical testimony disclosed that he was in fact suffering from an advanced coronary condition of a serious nature of which he apparently had no knowledge. It was held that the death of the employee had not been brought about by accidental means aggravating the existing ailment, and that, in consequence, the provisions of part 2 of the workmen's compensation law, under which the claim was filed, could not be construed as authorizing compensation. . . .

The order from which the appeal has been taken is affirmed, with costs to appellee.

SMITH, J. (dissenting). . . .

What is the meaning of the word "accident" as employed in the workmen's compensation act? Our Court has frequently and recently divided on the question. Much of our present difficulty traces back to language employed by Mr. Justice Stone in Adams v. Acme White Lead & Color Works, 1914, 182 Mich. 157, 148 N.W. 485, L.R.A.1916A, 283. For that reason alone I will examine it in some detail. The case involved lead poisoning, an ailment which we would today class as an occupational disease and, in fact, it was so classified by the then Industrial Accident Board (P. 158). The claim was made on behalf of the injured workman that our act, in granting compensation for "a personal injury arising out of and in the course of his employment," was broad enough to cover occupational diseases. The court held not. It held that the act required an accidental injury. As to what was an accident, it cited and quoted from Hensey v. White, (1900) 1 Q.B. 481, the following language, which in essence is found in our cases up to the present time:

" 'I think the idea of something fortuitous and unexpected is involved in both words, "peril" or "accident." ' "

The Hensey case . . . was a case in which a workman was injured (ruptured) while "doing his ordinary work in the ordinary way," there being nothing fortuitous in what happened. For this reason it was held that he had not suffered an accident and recovery was denied.

There are two difficulties with this English decision. The first is that such construction of the word "accident" does violence to our language. Words in a statute should receive their ordinary meanings, unless the context forces some subtle use. In our usual speech, when a man goes to his work and breaks his leg, or ruptures himself in the performance of such work, even though it was merely his ordinary work done in the ordinary way, he has suffered an accident at his work. It is no less an accident, of course, if something falls from the ceiling and hurts him. That, too, is an "accident." The idea of the unexpected is predominant, and it is present in both uses of the word. The difference in the uses, putting it very roughly, is that the one use refers to a cause and the other to an effect. But both uses are permissible and both form a part of our constant, daily speech.

Not only did the construction of the English court in the Hensey case do violence to the language, but also to the plain purpose, of the act. The statute, as well as the employer, takes human beings as it finds them. Not all are stalwart and able. The weak and the stumbling must also work, and, if they are injured in their work, even though one stronger might not have been, they are equally protected. Hills v. Oval Wood Dish Co., 191 Mich. 411, 158 N.W. 214. There are some who complain that this means opening wide the flood gates, turning a workmen's compensation act into general insurance for the sick and needy. Not so. The claimant still must prove a direct causal connection between work and injury. This is the essential link. Lacking it, the act does not speak. But if the injury comes from the work, compensation should be paid, even though one of more robust physique would not have suffered therefrom.

Not surprising is it, then, to find that the Hensey case was overruled . . . in Fenton v. J. Thorley & Co., Ltd., (1903) A.C. 443 . . .

. . . [I]n Watson v. Publix Riviera Theatre, 255 Mich. 115, 237 N.W. 541, the plaintiff was an actor who turned somersaults. On one of them "plaintiff's leg gave way and he fell." The Court held that his injuries were the result of an accident. As recently as Nichols v. Central Crate & Box Co., 340 Mich. 232, 65 N.W.2d 706, we interpreted this case as involving a truly accidental occurrence. It involved, we said, "The sudden giving way of a member and consequent falling." Yet in the case at bar we have the sudden giving way of the heart and it is held no accident. I cannot reconcile the two cases. . . .

. . . [W]e have been attempting the impossible, the differentiation of the accidental means from the accidental result, a differentiation easy to hypothesize but impossible to make in practice. Thus a man is at work. He is straightening a bent piece of material. He does it every day. On this occasion he exerts too much pressure. If the material breaks, we say he broke it by accident. If his abdominal wall breaks, we say it is no accident. Or is it? We commence our laborious search. Is this his ordinary work? Or does his ordinary work involve less stubborn material? How will we define the strength of material which causes him to pass the border enclosing ordinary work? Did his work involve over-exertion? What is standard exertion for the work? . . .

The act contemplates no such appraisal of degrees of exertion. It takes the workman as it finds him. What is overexertion for one is underexertion for another. What is stress and strain for one is relative peace and quiet for a third. Humans differ in all of these character-istics. . . .

The question we have been forced to answer, then, upon our interpre-tation of the meaning of the act, is this: Is the injury the unexpected result of ordinary work or is it the ordinary result of unexpected work? This question is nothing more or less than a verbal puzzle. As long as compensation is made to turn on it we will have constant litigation and distinctions will multiply beyond all hope of reconciliation. Mr. Justice Cardozo's concern in his dissent in Landress v. Phoenix Mutual Life In-surance Co., 291 U.S. 491, comes forcibly to mind:

"The attempted distinction between accidental results and accidental means will plunge this branch of the law into a Serbonian Bog." . . .

It is my opinion, then, that the word "accident" as employed in the act comprehends the unexpected result, as well as the unexpected cause, that we should now so hold, and that we should overrule those cases in-consistent therewith. . . .

The defendant . . . points out that the remedial steps to be under-taken in event of power failure had often been rehearsed, hence it argues that it could not be said that the incident was unexpected, though, of course, the results (the physical injuries and death) were. . . .

If I were called upon to base this decision upon whether or not there was an "accident," in the sense of an extraneous, fortuitous occurrence as distinguished from ordinary work, I would feel no hesitation in saying that there was. The emergency confronting the plaintiff was serious in the extreme. The plant was threatened with the "disintegration," according to the record, of a revolving turbine. The fact that careful foresight makes plans for rapid and efficient remedial measures in case of an accident makes the accident nonetheless a threatening emergency when and if it occurs. . . .

But I do not place my decision on this ground, valid though I believe it to be. I place it on the ground that the word "accident" includes both the unexpected cause and the unexpected result, that the claimant suffered an accident, an injury from a single event or series thereof which arose out of and in the course of his employment.

SHEPPARD v. MICHIGAN NATIONAL BANK
Supreme Court, Michigan, 1957
348 Mich. 577, 83 N.W.2d 614

BLACK, J. Eula Sheppard was awarded compensation on strength of facts appellants have stated with commendable brevity in their brief. I quote:

"In her work as an I.B.M. operator the plaintiff, Eula Sheppard, lifted and handled 6 or 8 trays of I.B.M. cards each day. Each tray of cards weighed approximately 25 pounds. On December 14, 1953, the plaintiff leaned over to pick up a tray of cards from a tub file. The tray stuck, and then the plaintiff yanked on it, and when she yanked, the 'pains flew all over' her back. . . ."

Thus we have before us another "strain case" arising under the workmen's compensation act. Ere end of the year this case, along with others to come, may lift us from the abominable morass into which the decade since Hagopian v. City of Highland Park, 313 Mich. 608, has thrust this Court and our imprecation-muttering legal profession. The compensation act was proclaimed upon enactment as a welfare-promoting means toward certain and inexpensive determination of right to "compensation of workmen for industrial injuries upon the basis of trade risks relating to the industry, to be charged against it as part of the cost" (quotation from Mackin v. Detroit-Timkin Axle Co., 187 Mich. 8, 14), yet our Kilkenny decisions in strain cases have fought each other from Sam Hagopian's injury through Donald Brazauskis' death to the point where there is nothing left so far as certainty is concerned excepting the well-chewed tails thereof.

Brazauskis (Brazauskis v. Muskegon County Board of Road Commissioners, 345 Mich. 480), the 4 to 4 deadlock of April 2d last, and now the misshapen 3-2-2 monster known as Beltinck's Case (Beltinck v. Mt. Pleasant State Home and Training School, 346 Mich. 494), unitedly prove the parable. . . .

Happily, the end of all this legal teratology is near, as forecast in Wieda's dissent last year (Wieda v. American Box Board Co., 343 Mich. 182, 191). Two of my Brothers, having refused to sign Mr. Justice Smith's exhaustive dissent in Wieda, now accept in Beltinck the tried and sound linchpins of such dissent. . . . Four members of the present Court are thus on record in support of the proposition that the word "accident," as employed in the workmen's compensation act, means "an unexpected result attending the operation or performance of a usual or necessary act or event." Why, in these circumstances, should we continue to wander aimlessly from case to case as the legal world gazes curiously on our strange paralysis? . . .

. . . I move then, this 5th day of September in the year 1956, that cases of industrial strain be governed henceforth by Justice Smith's unerring postulate in Wieda, that the word "accident" includes both the unexpected cause and the unexpected result, and that we advise the profession of steadfast intention to follow Fenton's guide, quoted as follows from Wieda, in pending and future cases (p. 196):

"If a man, in lifting a weight or trying to move something not easily moved, were to strain a muscle or rick his back, or rupture himself, the mishap in ordinary parlance would be described as an accident.   Anybody would say that the man had met with an accident in lifting a weight, or trying to move something too heavy for him."

Whether we adopt Fenton's rule forthrightly at this time, or whether we do it later with or without aid of the 1937 and 1943 amendments of the workmen's compensation act, makes but little difference save only to the countless victims of continued purblindness.   Justice Smith's lone and majority-ignored spadework in Wieda has inexorably and righteously headed this Court toward the light of Fenton, of Larson, of Pound, and now the Florida supreme court (Gray v. Employers Mutual Liability Ins. Co., 64 So.2d 650 [Fla.]).

Eula Sheppard, having suffered an accidentally disabling and hence compensable rick of the back, is entitled to affirmance of the award below, with costs.

ADDENDUM (June 10, 1957).

This case was duly assigned to the writer, preceding submission during our June term last year.   In pursuance of such assignment the foregoing dated opinion was prepared and distributed for consideration of my Brothers more than 9 months ago.   Since then Justices Carr, Edwards, Dethmers, Smith, and Kelly have written in the case and our personnel has partially changed.   Five present members of the Court declare now their devotion to that which Mr. Justice Smith originally urged upon the Court in Wieda.   This is progress.   That the profession be enabled to count and identify us with convenience, I am today signing Mr. Justice Smith's opinion in this case of Eula Sheppard.

SMITH, J. (concurring).   We continue to pursue our melancholy way in these compensation cases, the Court dividing and re-dividing with monotonous regularity as the egregious errors of the past continue to war with the humanitarian objectives of the act we must construe.   Our "eminence" in these cases, as Dean Pound so cogently observed (see Mr. Justice Black in Mack v. Reo Motors, Inc., 345 Mich. 268, 281), is bad indeed.   It will remain bad, and our people will continue to know a sorrow and distress peculiar to them alone, until our Court forsakes its "stubborn" (I borrow the word from the Chief Justice) refusal to correct its judge-made errors.   Our Court, commendably quick to correct the errors of others, must be equally quick to correct its own.   Since my dissent in Wieda v. American Box Board Co., pointing out Florida's reversal of its former erroneous construction of the word "accident," Arkansas has likewise acted.   In the case of Bryant Stave & Heading Co. v.

White, 227 Ark. 147 (296 S.W.2d 436), after commenting upon the controversy and litigation over the meaning of the word "accident," the court said: "We agree that litigants, lawyers and members of the commission are entitled to a definite and unequivocal settlement of the legal question here posed. In undertaking to do so, we see no valid reason for not aligning Arkansas with the decided weight of authority on the subject." The court then concludes:

"Notwithstanding anything we may have said in prior cases, we hold that an accidental injury arises out of the employment when the required exertion producing the injury is too great for the person undertaking the work, whatever the degree of exertion or the condition of his health, provided the exertion is either the sole or a contributory cause of the injury. In short, that an injury is accidental when either the cause or result is unexpected or accidental, although the work being done is usual or ordinary. The judgment of the circuit court affirming the award is accordingly affirmed."

Thus in one State after another a rule of reason consonant with the purpose of the act replaces arbitrary judicial fiat. Neither Arkansas, it will be noted, nor Florida acted under the whip of legislative compulsion. Each was secure in the knowledge that a court has inherent power to purge itself of its own errors. Failing in this duty, the day inevitably approaches when a court will stand alone, while the stream of life flows by, avoiding, but not being impeded by, the curious derelict in its path.

Our problems are multiplied, not simplified, by the current outpourings of opinion. It is now sought to perpetuate, with respect to our rulings concerning this simple term, accident, the spurious distinction between the ill and the healthy, between the weak and the strong, between those suffering to some degree from the ordinary diseases of life (who doesn't?) and those with no ailments or defects antedating the accident. This is clear from Croff v. Lakey Foundry & Machine Co., 320 Mich. 581, 585, heavily relied upon this date. It is pointed out in Croff "it can hardly be said that the 1943 amendment broadens the act to allow an award in a case of aggravation of a pre-existing disease without an accident or fortuitous event." But, it is concluded, the disabilities of one without pre-existing disease or condition ("as distinguished from disabilities resulting from the aggravation of pre-existing disease or condition") are compensable without proof of accident or fortuitous event.

Thus mankind is placed in 2 categories as respects recovery for accidental injuries: those with a pre-existing "disease or condition" and those not so handicapped. This classification we completely reject. Nothing is better settled in compensation law than that the act takes the workmen as they arrive at the plant gate. Some are weak and some are strong. Some, particularly as age advances, have a pre-existing "disease or condition" and some have not. No matter. All must work. They share equally the hazards of the press and their families the stringencies of want, and they all, in our opinion, share equally in the protection of the act in event of accident, regardless of their prior condition of health. See 18 NACCA Law Journal 90-92, and cases there cited. . . .

These conclusions, it will be observed, are fully consistent with the underlying purpose of the act, to require industry to bear the burden of the injuries, rather than have them fall with crushing force on the workman himself. If lifting a garbage can (Hagopian v. City of Highland Park, 313 Mich. 608, compensation denied) or a gun barrel (Anderson v. General Motors Corporation, 313 Mich. 630, compensation granted) actually disables the workman, his inability to work is an industrial casualty for which compensation is payable under our act (particularly as amended). He is equally disabled, of course, if the garbage can accidently rolls off the truck and hurts him, but in either event we note that the result is the same (disability) and the cause actually arises out of the work. It will be observed that in neither of these instances have we even mentioned the pre-existing health of the injured workman. Given the injury in fact and the causal connection (neither of which is questioned in Eula Sheppard's case) the state of the workman's pre-existing health is immaterial. . . .

. . . As Horovitz so well puts it in his treatise on Workmen's Compensation (p. 8):

"(The workmen's compensation law) was a revolt from the old common law and the creation of a complete substitute therefor, and not a mere improvement thereon. It meant to make liability dependent on a relationship to the job, in a liberal, humane fashion, with litigation reduced to a minimum."

It is high time that we of the Court lifted our eyes from the intricacies of spelling and punctuation and looked to the beneficent purposes of the legislation. It is not our function to deny by a grudging construction of the law what our people have seen fit to grant.

In this connection we reject, without qualification, the asserted "general rule of interpretation" quoted to us this date, to the effect that "the workmen's compensation law, being in derogation of the common law, must be strictly construed." The substitution, for thought, of this legal cliche has rarely had more lamentable result than in this area, depriving for years, as it has, the casualties of industry of the benefits awarded by a compassionate people. No one denies that statutes in derogation of the common law are to be strictly construed. But the maxim is not a corpus juris. Nor does it, like one of the Ten Commandments, contain within its limited borders either an unalterable moral principle or an inflexible command. It has, in truth, a companion, from which it cannot be separated, save by the feckless or the reckless: that statutes must be interpreted to accomplish their legislative purpose. The proper statement, then, runs something like this: "The rule that statutes in derogation of the common law are to be strictly construed does not require such an adherence to the letter as would defeat an obvious legislative purpose or lessen the scope plainly intended to be given to the measure." Jamison v. Encarnacion, 281 U.S. 635, 640. . . .

Eula Sheppard should recover. The act authorizes compensation for accidents suffered at work, and the word "accident," after the 1943 amendments, *comprehending a personal injury due to a single event, includes both the unexpected cause and the unexpected result.* Her prior physical condition, whether in good health or poor, is completely immaterial to the recovery sought by her. There is no legislative impediment now, nor has there ever been, to our own correction of our own errors.

This case was submitted to us some time back. In the intervening period, as drafts of opinions, and conferences, have come and gone the Court has lost one cherished Brother and gained another. Under these circumstances, Mr. Justice Voelker has deemed it proper to authorize our statement that, although he cannot participate, he is in full accord with the reasoning expressed in this opinion, and the result reached.

Affirmed. Costs to appellee.

ADDENDUM.

Since writing the above opinion, the various opinions in the case of Coombe v. Penegor, 348 Mich. 635, have been circulated to the Court. It has been decided, apparently, that the Sheppard opinion is not to be published independently of Coombe, but concurrently therewith, and, also, that discussion of the result of the Coombe Case is pertinent as well to the Sheppard opinion. This being the case, we will, in the interests of clarity, now make certain observations respecting the Coombe Case in its relation to the case (Sheppard) primarily before us. For it is to be hoped that today's pair of compensation cases, Sheppard-Coombe, will not be as prolific of disagreement, controversy, and unsound distinctions as that prior ill-starred pair, Hagopian-Anderson, both decided March 4, 1946.

We had pointed out to us in considerable detail in Eula Sheppard's case the importance of distinguishing between the workman with a pre-existing illness and him not so afflicted. Such cases were to be separately ruled, for precedents in the one case were not precedents in the other. Why? It was simple: one involved a pre-existing defect and the other did not. This distinction was both mischievous and unwarranted but nevertheless insisted upon, with citation of cases assertedly in support thereof. A majority has now affirmed Eula Sheppard's award. She had no pre-existing disease or condition.

A majority is also affirming Ewart Coombe's award. Did he have a pre-existing ailment? His attending doctor says he "must" have had. The appeal board says he "may" have had. The defendants say he did have. Notwithstanding, it is proposed that his award of compensation under part 2 be affirmed. Authority? Eula Sheppard's case. Apparently it is no longer critical whether there was a pre-existing "disease or condition" or not. We agree. It never was. But what has become of stare decisis, which, so recently as Eula Sheppard, confronted us? What of certainty in the law?

Error is thus to be quietly interred. The embarrassment of explicit overruling by name of prior inconsistent decisions will be avoided. But despite the tortuous paths trod, particularly this date, despite the gusts of words, despite the forays of relentless logic that have started on the broad highway of reason and ended in a cornfield of confusion — despite all this, one fact stands out: It is now agreed by others than the signers of this opinion that one suffering a personal injury due to a single event may receive award under part 2 without fortuitous cause and without regard to the claimant's pre-existing health.

Wisdom, we agree, should never be rejected merely because it comes late. (Cf., United States v. Union Pacific R. Co., 91 U.S. 72.) But let future scholars make no mistake over the position of those signing this opinion. Eula Sheppard and Ewart Coombe are each entitled to compensation, not because we "eliminate" accident from the act, not because of the presence or lack of pre-existing ailment (we will not speculate on which, if either, may in the future, consistent with certain of today's opinions, be required) but *simply because each suffered an unexpected mishap (an accident, in our everyday speech) while doing his ordinary work in his ordinary way.* See Wieda v. American Box Board Co., 343 Mich. 182, dissent, p. 191.

BLACK, J., concurred with SMITH, J.

[The concurring opinions of Justices Edwards and Kelly and of Chief Justice Dethmers, and the dissenting opinion of Justice Carr, are omitted.]

NOTES

1. In Coombe v. Penegor, 348 Mich. 635, 83 N.W.2d 603 (1957), the claimant suffered a stroke from heavy exertion while engaged in his usual job duties.

2. The most recent approach to the heart attack problem seems to be the awarding of compensation if the attack followed very shortly upon the usual exertion of the work or followed in a reasonable period of time from unusual exertion on the job so that it can be considered as traceable to the work. See, in general, 1 Larson, Workmen's Compensation §§38.61-38.81 (1952).

BAILEY v. AMERICAN GENERAL INSURANCE CO.

Supreme Court, Texas, 1955
154 Tex. 430, 279 S.W.2d 315

SMITH, Justice.

This is a workmen's compensation suit. The case was submitted to a jury upon special issues, resulting in a verdict and judgment for petitioner for 50% partial disability. That judgment has been reversed and rendered by the Court of Civil Appeals. 268 S.W.2d 528.

The petitioner and another workman, while in the course of their employment were at opposite ends of a movable scaffold which was supported by cables from the roof of a building. The end of the scaffold opposite that on which petitioner stood gave way, and the other work-man fell to his death on the roof of another building eight stores below. Petitioner saw his co-worker strike the roof below and thought he him-self was about to fall and be killed, but was caught in the cable in such manner that he did not fall. The wind was blowing and the scaffold swung away from the wall, but as it swung back petitioner was released and was able to jump to the roof of another building which was about the same height as the scaffold. Petitioner suffered a bruise on his leg and cable burn, but such injuries were minor in nature, were completely healed within a short time after the incident, and did not cause or con-tribute to any disability on his part. Petitioner contends that the trau-matic effect of the accident upon his nervous system directly resulted in a disabling neurosis, termed an "anxiety reaction" or "anxiety state" by both medical experts heard in the trial court, which has rendered it im-possible for claimant to engage in the field of employment for which he is trained and upon which he depends for his livelihood. The majority of the Court of Civil Appeals sustained respondent's contention that the petitioner's disability is not due to an injury within the meaning of the statutory definition of injury. With this conclusion we do not agree.

The question here is: Has Emery Eugene Bailey suffered damage or harm to the physical structure of his body? Petitioner, as a young man, became an iron worker, took an apprenticeship, graduated fairly promptly to a journeyman's scale in journeyman's work, and the evidence shows that at all times prior to the date of this unfortunate accident pe-titioner was able to perform capably duties as an iron worker: that he was considered one of the better iron workers and that he was not suf-fering from any nervous disorder and was as steady as the average indi-vidual. The testimony in the trial shows that when petitioner tried to resume his work as an iron worker he was tense, nervous, jumpy and af-fected with an overpowering terror and fear of impending disaster. His faculties for alertness, concentration and ability to think and act under the normal stress and strain of his employment have been definitely im-paired to such an extent that he is no longer qualified as a structural steel and iron worker. He has become moody and irritable; he has periods of "blanking out"; he is unable to rest at the end of a working day and is affected with constant, recurring nightmares evidenced by quivering, jumping and crying out in his sleep. The record shows that on one occasion petitioner "froze," literally paralyzed, while attempt-ing to work at a considerable height following his accident. Tests per-formed by the two neurosurgeons prior to the trial showed that pe-titioner's blood pressure was 140/92; that he was hypersensitive to pain, and that there was tremor of his closed eyelids and that his reflexes were underactive. . . .

No issue is raised concerning the causal relationship between the acci-dent and the psychic and psychosomatic injury described above. All parties agree that the experience of seeing a fellow workman plunge to his death and narrowly escape death himself, directly produced the in-jury which has disabled this petitioner.

In determining the meaning of the definition of injury contained in the Workmen's Compensation Statute, Vernon's Ann. Civ. St. art. 8306 et seq., the Court should be guided by the often announced rule of construction in reference to this statute, that since it is "remedial," "if there be any reasonable doubt which may arise in a particular case as to the right of the injured employee to compensation, same should be solved in favor of such right."   Jones v. Texas Indemnity Ins. Co., Tex. Civ. App. 1949, 223 S.W.2d 286, 288, writ refused.

The following definition is contained in Section 1, Article 8309, Subsection 5, Workmen's Compensation Law: "The terms 'injury' or 'personal injury' shall be construed to mean *damage* or *harm* to the *physical structure of the body* and such diseases or infection as naturally result therefrom." (Emphasis added.)   There are two ways to construe the words "physical structure of the body."   The respondent considers "physical structure" to imply a grouping of individual, but connected, parts — as bones, tissues, nerves, blood vessels, etc.   Then, so the reasoning proceeds, the statutory definition requires a lesion or actual gross alteration of one or more of these individual parts in order to qualify as an "injury."   We do not agree with this interpretation.   A liberal construction of the statute, as outlined below, is the more desirable and proper interpretation.

The phrase "physical structure of the body," as it is used in the statute, must refer to the *entire* body, not simply to the skeletal structure or to the circulatory system or to the digestive system.   It refers to the *whole,* to the complex of perfectly integrated and interdependent bones, tissues and organs which function together by means of electrical, chemical and mechanical processes in a living, breathing, functioning individual.   To determine what is meant by "physical structure of the body," the structure should be considered that of a living person — not as a static, inanimate thing.

Now the question arises, has there been "damage or harm" to the "physical structure" of claimant's body?   Recall the description of plaintiff's symptoms set out earlier.   What was the verdict or estimation of the various witnesses concerning these symptoms?   Mr. Kirk, claimant's foreman or pusher, said, "he is just out of luck."   Dr. Brown stated that plaintiff had suffered a severe "psychic trauma" and by that he meant "injury or damage to the individual so that he is not functioning properly."   In answer to a question by plaintiff's attorney, Dr. Brown affirmed that such an injury was "calculated to be just as real and disabling . . . as damage to *any other* part of the usable body of a man." (Emphasis added.)

The substance of all of the testimony shows agreement that plaintiff's body no longer functions properly.   Now, can we say that, as a matter of law, even though a "physical structure" no longer functions properly, it has suffered no "harm"?   What meaning can the word "harm" to the body have if not that, as a result of the event or condition in question, the body has ceased to function properly?   "Harm" with reference to a living, active structure — as the body is — in fact means essentially that the structure no longer functions as it should.   It is a natural construction of the word "harm" with reference to the "physical structure" of a living person, to look to the effect of the event or condition in question upon the effective functioning of that structure.

We feel that it is not without significance that the words "damage or harm" were used by the Legislature in the definition of injury. We cannot assume that either the word "damage" or "harm" is extraneous. Some difference must have been intended. The ordinary as well as legal connotation of "harm" is that it is of broader import than "damage." Damage embraces direct physical injury to a cell, tissue, organ or organ system; "harm" to the physical structure of the body embraces also impairment of use or control of physical structures, directly caused by the accident. This interference with use or control in an organism whose good health depends upon unified action and balanced synthesis can be productive of the same disabling signs and symptoms as direct physical injury to the cells, tissues, organs or organ systems. This conclusion is supported by the medical testimony in this case. . . .

Another compelling reason to hold that the type of injury sustained by petitioner comes within the definition of "injury" as contained in the statute is the fact that the Workmen's Compensation Act eliminates the right of an employee to bring an action for damages against an employer subject to the Act, except for gross negligence. . . . We do not believe that the Legislature intended that such an injury as sustained by petitioner would be compensable at common law, but not under the Compensation Act. To hold otherwise would place the employer in the position of being required to defend an action at common law even though such employer had exercised the foresight to qualify under the terms of the Act and procured compensation insurance for the protection of both the employer and employee. Further, the employer, in order to provide for himself adequate protection, would be forced to provide for insurance against liability at common law or assume the risk of becoming individually responsible for the payment of any judgment which might be obtained against him as the result of such common-law action, while at the same time he was paying compensation insurance premiums for the protection of his employees under the Workmen's Compensation Act. . . .

Therefore this cause is reversed and remanded to the Court of Civil Appeals for further proceedings consistent with this opinion.

[The dissenting opinion of Justice Walker is omitted.]

CARTER v. GENERAL MOTORS CORP.

Supreme Court, Michigan, 1960
361 Mich. 577, 106 N.W.2d 105

SOURIS, Justice.

Ordinarily, compensation under our workmen's compensation act is awarded for incapacity to work because of the crushing of a hand or foot, the inhalation of silicotic dust, or other similar injury arising out of and in the course of employment.   Benefits are not awarded for the injury as such, but rather for the loss of earning capacity.   Hence, even this Michigan Court, years ago, recognized the right of a claimant under the act to compensation for loss of such earning capacity caused by a mental or emotional disability resulting from a physical injury to claimant or even resulting from observing a physical injury to a fellow employee of claimant.   In due course we shall examine the authorities so holding, including decisions of this Court made venerable by age and by the compelling logic of their reasoning, for it is upon those past decisions of this Court that our decision in this case is firmly planted.   Our decision is that workmen's compensation benefits are payable for incapacity to work because of a claimant's paranoid schizophrenia arising out of and in the course of employment.

Plaintiff had worked as a machine operator for defendant, General Motors Corporation, with intermittent layoffs, since 1953.   On October 8, 1956 he was recalled to work after a 5-month layoff and worked for 4 days on a "brace job" and then was transferred on October 12th to a "hub job."   This operation required him to take a hub assembly (consisting of a case and cover) from a nearby fellow employee's table to his own workbench, remove burrs with a file and grind out holes in the assembly with a drill, and place the assembly on a conveyor belt.   Plaintiff was unable to keep up with the pace of the job unless he took 2 assemblies at a time to his workbench, and he feared another layoff should he prove unable satisfactorily to do the work.   He was instructed repeatedly by his foreman not to take 2 assemblies at a time because the assembly parts became mixed up on the conveyor belt when he did so.   However, plaintiff continued having trouble "getting on to the job" as it was supposed to be performed.   Thus, when he took only 1 hub assembly at a time, he fell behind; when he fell behind, he took 2 assemblies; but, when he took 2 assemblies, he got the assemblies mixed up and was berated by the foreman.

We are told that the dilemma in which plaintiff found himself resulted on October 24, 1956 in an emotional collapse variously described as paranoid schizophrenia and schizophrenic reaction residual type.   He was subsequently hospitalized for a period of 1 month, during which time he received shock therapy.   In July of 1957, he filed an application for hearing and adjustment of claim for compensation under the workmen's compensation act.

It should be noted that there is not involved in this case a psychosis resulting from a single fortuitous event nor is there involved a psychosis resulting from a direct physical blow to plaintiff's body.   Instead, there is involved a psychosis claimed to be the result of emotional pressures encountered by plaintiff daily in the performance of his work.

The referee entered an award of workmen's compensation for a disability described as "traumatic neurosis, traumatic psychosis, functional disability and sequelae thereof."   The workmen's compensation appeal board, by a divided vote affirmed the award for total disability from October 24, 1956 until January 7, 1957, plus reimbursement for medical and hospital care. The appeal board, in addition, allowed to plaintiff continuing compensation from and after January 7, 1957. . . .

However, in order to uphold the board's decision awarding *any* compensation, this Court must be satisfied, first, that there is competent evidence to uphold the finding of causal connection made by a majority of the board, and second, that plaintiff suffered a disability which is compensable under the act.

As to the first point, the only medical testimony offered is that of the treating physician. He testified as follows: . . .

". . . I think that he has had the personality predisposition towards the development of this illness for a number of years. This is what usually happens, but then this is the straw that breaks the camel's back, and they develop the actual psychosis in which they are out of touch with reality. Now, we have no reason to believe that he was before out of touch with reality."

This was competent expert opinion testimony, upon which the board could and did base a finding of causal connection. . . .

The second point, whether or not plaintiff suffered a disability compensable under the act, presents a more difficult question. This Court has previously held that emotional disabilities are compensable under the act. Klein v. Len H. Darling Co., 217 Mich. 485, 187 N.W. 400; Karwacki v. General Motors Corp., 293 Mich. 355, 292 N.W. 328; Hayes v. Detroit Steel Casting Co., 328 Mich. 609, 44 N.W.2d 190; and Redfern v. Sparks-Withington Co. [353 Mich. 286, 91 N.W.2d 516]. Whether the cause of such emotional disability is a direct physical injury (Redfern v. Sparks-Withington Co.) or a mental shock (Klein v. Len H. Darling Co.), we have held the disability compensable. What distinguishes the case at bar from our other decisions which recognize the compensability of such disabilities is that this plaintiff's disability was caused by neither a single *physical* injury to plaintiff nor by a single mental shock to him. Instead, his disability was caused by emotional pressures produced by production line employment not shown by him to be unusual in any respect, — that is, not shown by him to be any different from the emotional pressures encountered by his fellow workers in similar employment. As noted above, the finding of causal relationship between plaintiff's disability and the pressures of his employment was supported by the evidence. The question then becomes, must industry, under our laws bear the economic burden of such disability? Implicit in the question as stated is the further question: Is a worker unable to work because of a mental injury caused by his employment to be treated differently from a worker unable to work because of a physical injury caused by his employment? . . .

Appellant contends that there was no single event which precipitated plaintiff's psychotic breakdown and that, therefore, there can be no award of compensation under part 2 of the act. Appellant recognizes that for an award under part 2, no longer is it necessary to find an "accident" or a fortuitous event, citing Sheppard v. Michigan National

Bank [348 Mich. 577, 83 N.W.2d 614], and Coombe v. Penegor [348 Mich. 635, 83 N.W.2d 603], but appellant further states that it appears from these cases that part 2 applies only to single event injuries. However, it does *not* appear from the Sheppard and Coombe cases that injuries not attributable to a single event are not covered by part 2. . . .

The case at bar involves a series of mental stimuli or events — (the pressure of his job and the pressure of his foreman) — which caused an injury or disability under the act, causal connection in fact having been found by the board, supported by competent evidence. We find further that Mr. Carter's disabling psychosis resulting from emotional pressures encountered by him daily in his work is compensable under part 2 of the act. Such conclusion renders unnecessary any discussion of the applicability of part 7 to the facts of this case. . . .

[The dissenting opinion of Justice Kelly is omitted.]

STATE EMPLOYEES' RETIREMENT SYSTEM v. INDUSTRIAL ACCIDENT COMMISSION
Court of Appeals, California, 1950
97 Cal. App. 2d 380, 217 P.2d 992

SPARKS, J. pro tem.

This is a proceeding upon writ of review of a death benefit award made by the Industrial Accident Commission in favor of the widow and three minor children of Karl Lund, deceased. Petitioner State Employees' Retirement System seeks an annulment of the award, on the grounds that respondent commission had acted without and in excess of its powers and that the evidence was insufficient to justify the findings of fact.

The decedent, Karl Lund, was employed as a game warden by the Department of Natural Resources. As such officer his duties were to enforce the provisions of the Fish and Game Code, and in so doing he had no regular or prescribed hours of duty. At times he was required to go on night patrol and to station himself in isolated areas where infractions of the Fish and Game Code might occur. An automobile equipped with a two-way radio was furnished him by his employer. The car was also so equipped that it might be converted into a bed, and it was permissible for him, while on night patrol, to sleep in the car.

On June 13, 1948, the deceased went on duty at 10 o'clock in the morning According to the entries in his diary he went on patrol to "Napa State Hospital, Soscal, thence to Cuttings Wharf, Brown's Valley to Oakville night patrol Trinity Road." At 2:58 P.M. on the 13th Lund reported by radio to the sheriff's office that he was in service. No further reports were received from him. On the 14th, Lund not having returned or checked in by radio, a search was made for him. At a point 16 or 18 miles from Napa, the car furnished Lund by the state was found. It was parked about 20 feet off a side road, facing into a hill. This side road was a slight distance from the Oakville-Trinity Mountain road. It was in "wild" country and where, according to Lund's superior officer, apprehensions were made of violators hunting deer at night with spotlights. About 12 feet to the rear of the state car there was another automobile parked. Investigation revealed that the interior of the state car had been converted into a bed, and on this bed were found the dead bodies of Karl Lund and of a woman, Chelsea Miami. The bodies were clad respectively only in shorts and panties and were partially covered by a blanket. The ignition switch, radio and heater of the car were all turned on and the gasoline tank was empty. All of the doors and windows were closed with the exception of one side wing-window which was slightly open. Lund's clothes, boots and gun were in the back of the car and under the seat. The deaths were attributed by the coroner to carbon monoxide poisoning, the vapor of which apparently had infiltrated into the car from the running motor and had been inhaled while the deceased were lying on the bed. Approximate time of death was fixed as between 1 and 3 A.M. of June 14th. Herminia Miami, the sister of Chelsea, testified that Chelsea had received a telephone call at their home from Lund shortly before 9 P.M.; that he had asked Chelsea to meet him, and within a few minutes after receiving the call Chelsea had changed to slacks and left in her own car.

There was no rule or regulation of the department by whom Lund was employed which prohibited any of the game wardens, while on duty, from having company. . . .

From this and other facts and circumstances in the record, we cannot say there was not substantial evidence to support the findings of the commission, or that the findings were irrational. In doing so we are well aware of the contrary inferences which might have been drawn from the same set of facts. The secluded spot in a remote area could have been selected by Lund for its advantages as a rendezvous in which to conduct an illicit love affair. The manner in which the cars were parked, the state of partial dishabille in which the bodies were found, the fact that Lund had divested himself of his uniform and placed his gun and boots underneath the seat all are circumstances from which the trier of facts might have reasonably concluded that he had either abandoned or deviated from his duty. However, as stated above, it is not our province to resolve these facts or to substitute our own views for those of the commission. Lund, while acting in the scope of his employment, was permitted to drive to isolated spots where game violators might be found. It was a matter of discretion with him whether or not at such times he converted the car into a bed and slept. In so doing he was acting within the course of his employment. (California C. I. Exchange v. Industrial Acc. Com., 5 Cal. 2d 185 [53 P.2d 758].) There was no rule which forbade him from having company while on duty, and the presence of a woman in the car with him does not necessarily compel a conclusion that he had thereby either abandoned his employment or deviated therefrom.

There being a choice between two inferences reasonably deducible from the evidence, we cannot say that the commission acted without or in excess of its powers or that its findings of fact were unreasonable.

The award is affirmed.

NOTES

1. For general information concerning workmen's compensation, the following should be consulted: U. S. Chamber of Commerce, Analysis of Workmen's Compensation Laws (1960); U. S. Dept of Labor, Bureau of Labor Standards, State Workmen's Compensation Laws, Bull. No. 161 (1964). See also Governmental Responsibility in Workmen's Compensation Programs, 81 Mo. Lab. Rev. 631 (1958); Katz, Workmen's Compensation in the United States, 9 Lab. L.J. 866 (1958); Keefe, Changes in the Workmen's Compensation and Occupational Diseases Act, 47 Ill. B.J. 52 (1958).

2. On the problem of statutory exclusions from coverage, consult U. S. Dept. of Labor, Bureau of Labor Standards, State Workmen's Compensation Laws, Bull. No. 161, pp. 14-18 (1964). Pages 15-16 of this bulletin provide a tabular summary of workmen's compensation coverage for farm workers.

3. On the subject of psychoneurotic reactions see Bonin, Comments on Recent Important Workmen's Compensation Cases, 23 NACCA L.J. 157 (1959), 24 id. 134; Page, Comments on Recent Important Workmen's Compensation Cases, 25 id. 201 (1960); Note, Recovery for Mental Disability in Absence of Any Physical Impact or Injury, 46 Iowa L. Rev. 939 (1961); Note, Schizophrenia Stemming from Mental Causes Is Noncompensable, 35 Notre Dame Law. 471 (1960); Note, Compensable Injury — Paranoid Schizophrenia Caused by Emotional Pressures Is Compensable, 38 U. Det. L.J. 496 (1961); Workmen's Compensation Awards for Psychoneurotic Reactions, 70 Yale L.J. 1129 (1961).

4. With reference to occupational disease see Fleming and Alonzo, Modern Occupational Medicine (2d ed. 1960); Johnstone and Miller, Occupational Diseases and Industrial Medicine (1960); Sears and Groves, Worker Protection Under Occupational Disease Disability Statutes, 31 Rocky Mt. L. Rev. 462 (1959).

5. A problem of increasing concern is that posed by radiation hazards in the atomic energy industry. For a general treatment see Stason, Estey, and Pierce, Atoms and the Law 781-846 (1959). Two bills on the subject were introduced in the 87th Congress, 1st Session, H.R. 1267 and H.R. 2731 (1961). See also Hearings Before the Subcommittee on Research and Development of the Joint Committee on Atomic Energy, 86th Cong., 1st Sess. (1959), Employee Radiation Hazards and Workmen's Compensation; Joint Committee on Atomic Energy, Joint Committee Print, Selected Materials on Employee Radiation Hazards and Workmen's Compensation (1959); Note, Radiation Injury Amendment, 58 Mich. L. Rev. 302 (1959).

6. For a modern evaluation of workmen's compensation law see Brodie, Adequacy of Workmen's Compensation as Social Insurance: A Review of Developments and Proposals, 1964 Wis. L. Rev. 57. Professor Brodie points out, inter alia, the lack of coverage of many workers, e.g., agricultural, which is contrary to the usual pattern of broad coverage of so-

cial insurance. He also mentions the possibility of a federal workmen's compensation law to eliminate the grossly inadequate benefits in some jurisdictions, and the hodgepodge of differences in laws and interpretations.

3. *Economic Security and Welfare*

a. SECURITY AND TENURE OF EMPLOYMENT

(1) Seniority

SLICHTER, HEALY, AND LIVERNASH, THE IMPACT OF COLLECTIVE BARGAINING ON MANAGEMENT *
104-115 (1960)

It is doubtful whether any concept has been as influential, pervasive, and troublesome in collective bargaining as that of seniority. For our purposes, seniority will be defined simply as an employee's length of service with the company for which he works. In any given collective bargaining relationship, however, the word acquires special meanings through the language of the agreement, through practices followed in the daily administration of the contract, and not uncommonly through arbitration decisions.

It is the purpose of this chapter to develop an understanding of the growth in the use of seniority and of the more basic ground-rules that have been developed in applying the seniority principle. This will be done under the following headings: (1) The importance of seniority in labor relations, (2) General principles in the application of the seniority criterion, (3) Legal aspects of seniority, and (4) General implications of the use of seniority. . . .

IMPORTANCE OF SENIORITY

For a number of reasons, seniority has become progressively more important during the past twenty years. First, there has been a growing belief among both managements and employees that for many purposes the long-service workers are entitled to greater security and superior benefits as a matter of equity. This is indicated by the increasing willingness of companies to make many concessions to protect the senior employees at a time of layoff.

Second, as a "basic regulatory mechanism" this criterion has the merit of objectivity. Therefore, it often prevails over subjective criteria that might be considered appropriate. From the union standpoint, its objectivity is compatible with internal political considerations, and it frees the union from the uncomfortable and unpopular judgments required by use of less tangible criteria. Management, too, either by

---

* This selection, consisting of a portion of Chapter 5, is reproduced with the permission of the publisher, The Brookings Institution.

default or by deliberate, rational policy, is insisting less on a high weighting of nonseniority factors.

Third, the last two decades have witnessed a dramatic rise in the number and types of benefit programs. Almost without exception, entitlement to these new benefits has been geared to seniority. In fact, this was occasionally a part of bargaining strategy; the new benefit was made more palatable cost-wise to management by limiting it to employees with long service. Subsequent negotiations often led to a reduction in the seniority requirement or, in the case of a few benefits, its complete elimination. It was not uncommon in the first contracts providing for payment for unworked holidays to limit payment to those with at least one, two, or even more years of service. This seniority requirement has now largely disappeared. However, because of the nature of nearly all new benefit programs, the element of seniority service still plays an important integral part.

Fourth, seniority has acquired added influence through the decisions of arbitrators. Oftentimes the discharge of an employee with long service has been set aside for this extenuating reason alone. In such cases the arbitrator would freely admit that the stated "cause" for discharge would have been a "just cause" if an individual with less seniority had been involved. Arbitrators sometimes have interpreted contract language so as to increase the influence of seniority.

Fifth, the enactment of certain laws, especially the Selective Service Act, has given added importance to seniority, as have the decisions of certain government agencies. There is no question that the decisions of the War Labor Board of World War II and, to a lesser extent, of the Wage Stabilization Board during the Korean War gave impetus to the extension of seniority arrangements. These wartime boards encouraged deferred-payment benefit plans in an effort to curb pressures for immediate wage increases . . . They also extended the seniority criterion to such areas as shift preference and vacation preference.

The importance of seniority in labor relations today can perhaps best be shown by listing the areas in which it may affect an employee's status. . . .

The list is undoubtedly incomplete. Its length and variety suggest that many other such arrangements may exist in practice or by contract. The listing is divided into two groups. The first includes those categories for which length of service determines an employee's status in relation to other employees. It is a criterion that helps resolve what might be a source of competition among employees. For example, employees vie with one another for promotional opportunities, for the limited jobs available at a time of work reduction, for desirable parking spaces, and the like. It will be convenient to identify this as "competitive status seniority."

The second category involves those benefits, rights, or privileges to which a man is entitled either explicitly, as in the case of severance pay, or implicitly, as in the case of partial protection from discharge, just because he has attained a certain number of years of service. The competitive aspect of seniority is of limited importance in this group. This will be identified as "benefit seniority."

Applications of Competitive Status Seniority

LAYOFFS AND RECALLS. It is in this area that the principle of seniority was first introduced and has been most widely extended. The general principles that the last person hired should be the first person laid off and that recalls from layoff should be in inverse order of layoff are expressed in nearly every current collective bargaining agreement in the manufacturing and transportation industries. Even in many highly seasonal industries, such as building construction and the needle trades, where the policy of equal distribution of work is more prevalent, the agreements sometimes adopt seniority as the guide in making permanent displacements.

PROMOTIONS. Within the past twenty years seniority has come to play an increasingly more important part in deciding who among several competing employees is entitled to fill a promotional vacancy. Unions have succeeded in establishing as a minimum the principle that where ability is relatively equal, seniority shall govern. In many cases they have been able to assign even greater weight to the seniority criterion.

TRANSFERS. Sometimes the lateral, upward, or downward movements of employees on a temporary, day-to-day basis are governed, in part at least, by seniority. These are transfers occasioned by the absence of the regular job incumbents because of illness, vacation, leaves of absence, or other reasons; or they may be required by temporary production needs. While the seniority arrangements for such transfers vary greatly, where they do exist, they usually give the senior employee the preference for the available work and at the same time give him the privilege of rejecting the transfer; thus, the obligation of accepting transfer often falls on the least senior person. Generally, however, seniority plays a less important role in temporary transfers than in permanent transfers.

JOB OR WORK ASSIGNMENT. Claims to specific job assignments on the basis of seniority are closely related to layoffs, promotions, and transfers. Where seniority governs the distribution of work, serious problems may be created for management. The opportunity to match individual skills to the assignments involved becomes limited. The senior, more skilled employees may select only the easy work, leaving the less well-trained, junior employees to handle the difficult assignments. Or where there is an incentive system, the senior men may select only those assignments that allow the greatest opportunity for earnings. . . .

A variant of this problem, which is more of an irritant than a serious cost matter to management, is "machine seniority." A senior worker may be given his choice of machine in a bank of identical or similar machines. In the winter he might select a machine which is in a warm part of the room; in the summer he might select that machine nearest to open windows or doors. Or he might select the machine nearest to the locker room, time clock, cafeteria, or rest room.

SHIFT PREFERENCE. Although evidence on this subject is limited, it is safe to conclude that there is increasing use of seniority as a basis for shift preference. Complications may arise over such questions as (1) the frequency with which applications for choice of shift may be made; (2) the scope of interchange, that is, the type of jobs to which workers may move when changing shifts; (3) the length of time a worker must remain on his shift before he may move after applying to do so; and (4) the length of time before shift preference balance must be restored following a layoff that disrupts preferences. . . .

SELECTION OF DAYS OFF. Related to shift preference is the use of seniority in a few contracts to determine the assignment of days off each week. For example, an agreement between a large news service organization and the Commercial Telegraphers' Union provides that employees shall have the right to choose days off on the basis of seniority, subject only to the requirement that the days selected be among those available as days off on the schedule prepared by the company.

OVERTIME DISTRIBUTION. The principle of equal distribution of overtime is probably more firmly established than is that of allocation of overtime opportunities on the basis of seniority. However, a few agreements provide for the distribution of overtime by seniority without any attempt at equalization. Sometimes, as in the case of transfers, the senior man is given preference for overtime, but he also has the right (denied to the least senior man) to refuse to work overtime. Some companies in the steel industry that have adopted the "local practice" clause in their contracts with the United Steelworkers have through practice committed themselves to this. To illustrate, if two or more employees have been doing the same work on a shift and a chance to "double over" on the next shift arises, it has been the practice and is obligatory under the contract to offer the overtime to the one with the longest service in the seniority unit.

VACATION PRIVILEGES. The status of an employee on the seniority roster may determine whether he will be granted vacation at the time of his choice. A typical clause is the following: "Vacations will, as far as practicable, be granted for the period selected by the employee, but final allocation of vacation periods is left to the company in order to assure orderly operation of the plant. In the choice of vacation dates, departmental seniority shall prevail." In some contracts, employees with long service are allowed to accumulate vacation credits beyond one year.

PARKING PRIVILEGES. The growing parking problem at many industrial plants has been handled in part by the use of seniority. One company assigned each employee a space according to his length of service, the most senior men having the most convenient spots. Because of the union's refusal to allow a time interval between the end of one shift and the start of the next, at any one shift two-thirds of the spots were vacant. The company estimated that seniority had tripled its necessary investment in parking space.[1]

[1] As a final illustration of "competitive status seniority" there should be mentioned the company in which senior employees had the right to punch out first at the time clock. Junior employees went to the end of the line.

Applications of Benefit Seniority

VACATIONS. The amount of vacation to which an employee is entitled is normally related to his length of service. The phrase "one-for-one and two-for-five" (that is, one week of vacation for one year of service and two weeks of vacation after five years' service), which was the War Labor Board vacation formula, illustrates the tie-in between vacation benefit and seniority. . . .

PENSIONS. Service credits play an important part in the operation of pension plans throughout American industry. Seniority determines eligibility for pension plan coverage, the right to disability retirement, the creation of vested rights, and, in many instances, the amount of the pension benefit to be received. Very often it has been necessary to adjust existing seniority arrangements to meet the needs of pension plans. . . .

SEVERANCE PAY. The eligibility for and the amount of payment made under formal or ad hoc severance pay plans are correlated directly with service credits. . . .

HOLIDAYS. As stated above, many provisions for payment for unworked holidays formerly included a service requirement. Although this is less frequently the case today, many clauses limit payment to regular or so-called seniority employees and exclude part-time, temporary, or probationary employees.

SICK LEAVE PROVISIONS. Where paid sick leave is provided, it is customary to relate the eligibility and the amount of such payment to length of service. One such clause in an agreement between an aircraft engine company and its UAW local for salaried employees provides: "Sick leave allowances within each calendar year . . . are contingent on the length of time during which an employee has been continuously within the Employer's employ as of the last day worked prior to absence.

Continuous Employment	*Allowances*
Less than one month	5 days
One month but less than six months	10 days
Six months but less than one year	15 days
One year or more	20 days

GROUP LIFE AND HOSPITALIZATION INSURANCE, HEALTH, AND WELFARE PLANS. The coverage of these plans is normally extended only to those persons who have completed a certain minimum period of service with the company. The service requirement is not necessarily the same as the probationary period designated in the agreement. . . .

PROFIT SHARING. Eligibility for and often the allocation of employee shares under profit-sharing plans are determined by length of service. Particularly, deferred types of profit sharing, comparable to pensions, use the seniority factor in allocating profits to individuals.

SUPPLEMENTARY UNEMPLOYMENT BENEFIT, EMPLOYMENT SECURITY, AND GUARANTEED ANNUAL WAGE PLANS. These plans . . . rely upon the seniority criterion in several ways. For example, minimum service of one year is required for coverage under the SUB plans of the automobile industry. In others, such as the plans negotiated initially by the large car companies, three years' service is required to establish eligibility. In addition, under the automobile plans the rate of accrual of credits is related to seniority, as is the rate of cancellation of credits when benefits are drawn. Low-seniority workers surrender more accrued credits per benefit payment than do high-seniority employees. . . .

LENGTH-OF-SERVICE WAGE ADJUSTMENTS. In a very limited number of cases, special wage adjustments are given to long-service employees, thus creating personal rates for them rather than the established job rate. In one company, for example, as soon as an employee attains his fifth year of service he receives nine cents over and above the job rate; when he reaches eight years of service, he is given an additional four cents. Men doing the same work on single-rated jobs, therefore, get varying wage rates. Adjustments of this type are not always a heritage from pre-union days. In the case cited the practice originated in 1951, long after the company was unionized.

AUTOMATIC PROMOTION. In some instances the movement from one job classification to another is based entirely upon length of service. Admittedly, this arrangement is very similar to automatic progression within a rate range since the so-called classifications have little or no meaning in terms of job content. For example, one company promotes a man from a Second Class Laborer B job to a Second Class A job at the end of 4 months' service; from a Second Class A to a First Class B at the end of 8 months; and from a First Class B to a First Class A at the end of 12 months. But it is significant that, after the one year of service, this same company must automatically advance the Class A laborer to a still higher classification, or if it prefers to avoid an actual transfer, it must pay the laborer the higher rate or the rate of a process helper rather than the rate of any of the labor classes.

BONUSES. The payment of special bonuses, such as Christmas or "service anniversary" bonuses, is directly related to service with respect both to eligibility and to the amount of payment. For example, under the agreement between a large paper company and its union, the company is obligated to give a Christmas "gift" in the amount of $10 to those with six months to one year's mill seniority and $15 to those with one year's mill seniority.

LONG-SERVICE REWARDS. Long before unionization, companies had developed the practice of giving special recognition to long-service employees. While the service pin, service club, service watch, and other similar ceremonial or token gestures are well known, there are other less publicized policies that are more interesting, especially when their observance is continued by practice in a collective bargaining framework. Some companies unilaterally provide that employees upon attainment of a certain service level will no longer be required to punch a time clock. One company for many years before unionization and for a number of years after unionization automatically converted 25-year service employees from an hourly pay basis to a salary. Another company gives its employees one share of stock at the completion of each five years of service.

With collective bargaining, the wisdom of some of these long-service benefits is being reviewed anew. First, even though the labor agreement is silent on the subject of these benefits, there is a question whether the company may not have forfeited the right to discontinue such practices at its discretion. Extensive reliance by arbitrators on past practice means that what started as a unilateral grant may become a fixed obligation. This could be a serious problem since the number of high-service people in most long-established plants is rising steadily.

Second, the practices themselves often raise problems that affect the administration of the labor agreement or the collective bargaining demands. Excessive tardiness on the part of a long-service employee who does not have to punch a time clock, if tolerated, may be cited as proof of discrimination in a grievance involving discipline of another employee for tardiness. The salary method of payment gives rise to disparate treatment of employees when absences occur. A one-day absence due to illness would mean loss of pay to a less senior worker but not to a long-service employee on salary. Other similar consequences could be cited. The net effect in a unionized situation would be to make the company vulnerable to a demand for the extension of the "most favored employee treatment" to all employees or to those with a lower level of service.

PROTECTION FROM LOSS OF SENIORITY. . . . [T]he level of seniority itself may determine the loss of the seniority property right during periods of sustained absence from the job, because of either an extended layoff or a protracted illness. To illustrate, an agreement between a farm equipment company and the UAW provides that an employee will lose his seniority if he has been laid off by the company for a period of time equal to his seniority prior to layoff or for a period of three years, whichever is greater.

PROTECTION FROM DISCIPLINARY ACTION. It has already been observed that length of service may be a mitigating factor in determining the penalty for wrongdoing. Companies may recognize this in administering a disciplinary program, or they may be persuaded to this view by union arguments in the grievance procedure. The concept is given stature by numerous arbitration decisions, particularly when the discipline involves the loss of seniority and with it the many benefits and rights described above. . . . [C]onsideration of length of service in administering discipline often makes the adoption of fixed penalties for stated rule violations unrealistic and untenable.

The foregoing list of areas in which competitive status seniority and benefit seniority apply, shows why seniority has become such an important consideration in the relations between unions and managements.

Parties to collective bargaining have not always made the sharp distinction suggested by these two categories. However, some contracts are careful to distinguish between the two uses of seniority, both in terminology and in application. For example, an electrical manufacturing company agreement with its union speaks of "job seniority" and "benefit seniority." The former applies to layoff, recall, transfer, and promotion and is carried by a worker only if he moves to a division of the company that is treated as part of the job seniority unit. "Benefit seniority," however, accompanies him wherever he may move within the company. Usually benefit seniority has the widest possible application and is unimpaired by movements of the employee within the company. This is often true even when an employee moves to another plant of the same company which is represented by a different bargaining unit. "Competitive status seniority" is less easily moved from one location to another within a company. This is understandable because the latter involves the rights of one employee vis-à-vis the rights of another employee. Many agreements purposely use the term "service" or "credited service" to describe the basis for benefit payments, as contrasted with "seniority," which is the criterion involved in relative ranking of employees for layoff, promotion, transfer, and recall purposes.

Given the substantial body of rights and benefits that flow from length of service, it is easy to understand why seniority has become a very valuable property right of the employee. It is deceptive because to the layman it appears to be a simple concept. It is anything but simple. In the negotiation and administration of the labor agreement there have been few issues as troublesome to the parties concerned. If one were to generalize on the trends in labor relations over the past twenty years, these conclusions on seniority would be reasonable:

(1) The basic principles and general ground rules of seniority have been resolved satisfactorily to both parties. Seldom are they a cause of serious bargaining difficulties or of grievances during the life of the contract.

(2) The question of which elements of the employment relationship shall be affected entirely or partially by the seniority factor is still a matter of some contention in many companies. It arises either as a bargaining issue or as a grievance involving deviation from past practice. Such elements as transfers, overtime preference, shift preference, job assignment (including machine seniority), and vacation preference have yielded more and more to the seniority influence. But its acceptance in all of these areas is by no means widespread. On the other hand, the use of the seniority principle to some degree for layoffs, recalls, and promotions and the use of the service factor for various benefit plans are no longer a point of contention.

(3) The *degree* to which seniority is to serve as a regulatory mechanism is also a source of continuing controversy, although . . . it is less and less a cause of grievances and seldom is considered a strike issue. . . .

NOTE

The purpose of the consideration of the seniority principle at this point in the materials is to relate seniority to the job security aspects of modern industrial employment. Extensive consideration of the problems of enforcement of seniority in the collective bargaining relationship will be found infra page 912.

(2)   The United States Employment Service

CHASE, THE JOB-FINDING MACHINE: HOW TO CRANK IT UP*

Harper's 31-36 (July, 1964)

Lots of jobs go empty while millions are unemployed — largely because the service which is supposed to bring the two together isn't working right.

On at least one vital front the war against poverty in the 1960s is being fought with tragically obsolete weapons. A crucial part of the battle consists in finding jobs for people who now don't have them, and the only nationwide mechanism designed to do this is the United States Employment Service.

Although a heroic effort is now under way to improve it, the agency — as of this writing — is still pitifully unequal to its mammoth responsibility. Indeed USES does not even know, on a national basis, where the job openings exist or are likely to occur, or the location, and skills or lack of them, of the unemployed men and women who might fill those vacancies. This is a major cause of that baffling phenomenon of our time — the existence of some four million unemployed workers while hundreds of thousands of jobs go begging. . . .

USES was established in 1933 at the depth of the depression and was quickly overwhelmed by the task of referring millions of destitute men and women to public relief projects. With the advent of unemployment insurance later in the 'thirties it was swamped with unemployment claims. This task quickly took priority over job placement. Ever since, USES has been widely considered, and often called, "the unemployment office." Skilled workers, white-collar or blue, have seldom looked to it as a likely source of good leads for jobs. Though housewives and restaurant operators may phone in for casual help, personnel offices of most companies use other recruiting methods.

About 20 per cent of all USES non-farm job placements today are in domestic service, although household work accounts for only about 3 per cent of all non-farm jobs generally. The well-advertised concern of USES for parolees, Indians, disabled vets, school dropouts, and others at the bottom of the labor market has helped reinforce its reputation as a kind of welfare service for the unfortunate.

The two thousand local offices of USES are financed out of the fed-

* *Edward T. Chase, who has written extensively on technology and manpower problems, is currently consultant both for a Ford Foundation-sponsored national conference on unemployment, and for the New York City Planning Commission. He is also writing the official report on Mobilization for Youth and is active on the Board of the Henry Street Settlement. This article is reproduced with the permission of the author, and the publisher, Harper's Magazine.*

eral payroll tax. But they are run by the individual states as neighborhood facilities. This local orientation is peculiarly frustrating at a time when the job market is increasingly regional and national. For instance, I know a conscientious young USES interviewer in a Brooklyn office who was recently confronted with several unemployed welders. There were no known local openings to offer them. Quite by chance, the interviewer had heard that welders were being sought right then in Connecticut. Now to match the applicants with the jobs through official channels would involve a cumbersome mailing process called interstate clearance. Since time is of the essence in getting a job, he urged the welders to go after the Connecticut jobs on their own.

This is not a step a man broke and out of work for many weeks can take; nor is it a satisfactory way for a national public employment service to function. Yet few interviewers can give even this much sensible advice. Most of them have had little contact with the world of business and industry, and few of them go calling at offices or factories.

As a result, even in their own hometowns, USES offices have only meager data about local job openings. And there is virtually no incentive for employers to make their needs known to USES, despite the urgency of the present manpower crisis. The whole operation has a voluntary character like that of a travel agency — while over four million Americans are jobless and triple that number will be out of work for varying intervals in the year ahead. Obviously, pinpointing the job opportunity is more than half the battle in placing a man. Dr. Arthur Burns, who was chairman of President Eisenhower's Council of Economic Advisers, has called the lack of national job-vacancy statistics a "vital missing link in our entire system of economic intelligence."

Is Its Goal Sinister?

Against great odds USES has been trying, within the past several years, to transform itself from a down-at-the-heels social-welfare relic of the New Deal — absorbed with unemployment compensation and the placement of domestics — into a national manpower agency responsible for the most efficient use of our total labor resources. This new self-assertive spirit has triggered a savage assault on the agency. The attackers are private employment agencies, defending the sacred right to make a commissionable buck. Ironically, their self-serving militancy may, in the end, boomerang by arousing an indifferent public to sympathetic support of the vital mission of USES.

Within the past year, the attack was pressed right into the halls of Congress and even into a Presidential press conference, where USES was accused of competing with private enterprise both in the business community and on the campus, and of the further sin of soliciting jobs for people who already are employed. President Kennedy promised to look into the matter.

Not long ago, I talked with the affable spokesman for the private employment agencies. He is John Willetts, a Dartmouth man from

Milwaukee, who assured me that I'd perform a needed public service if I could somehow uncover what USES was *really* up to.

Its sinister goal is the monopolistic control of all manpower and this "could lead to eventual control of the nation's means of production and distribution of goods," according to Harold Nelson, an Akron agency man, who testified before a Senate subcommittee. Nelson distributes sample letters for the like-minded to copy and send to their Congressmen to alert them to the expected USES coup. In his Senate testimony Nelson compared USES practices with the Russians', the Third Reich's, Red China's, and Castro Cuba's.

The National Employment Association, headquartered in Detroit, which represents 4,300 agencies, is raising $75,000 for its current "Operation Freedom" campaign. It depicts USES as bent on destroying the private agencies, indifferent to the unemployed, and determined to control the entire labor market. The NEA has a voluble and thoroughly alarmed freedom fighter in the person of Representative Frank Bow, a Republican Congressman from Ohio, who ceaselessly guards the ramparts for the private agencies. "Never before, not even in the dramatic and devastating days of the New Deal and the Fair Deal, has the strangulation of private enterprise been so imminent," Bow told the recent NEA annual convention. The convention was reassured that his excessive agitation would not distract the Congressman from his mission. "I repeat you are not alone, or rather *we* are not alone, for I take a great and genuine pride in carrying a musket in your ranks in this battle. But this battle is not over; it is certain to be a continuing one in a long war — provided, as I have emphasized before, that *we* stand up and fight and fight hard. Each of you in the private employment industry has more than just this issue at stake. I say to you without hesitation that your very survival in business is at stake today. Even more significantly, your very rights and freedoms as Americans are threatened as never before in your lifetime or in the history of this nation."

Such accusations might be dismissed as ludicrously exaggerated — and relatively harmless — manifestations of private greed or lunatic conservatism, were not our current need for an effective federal employment service so critical. Under these conditions, this kind of sniping could cripple the effort just beginning to remedy the inadequacies of USES.

To assess the gap between what we need and what we now have, it is instructive to look at a successful national employment service in operation — Sweden's for instance.

To be sure, as defenders of the status quo love to point out, Sweden is a small nation with a homogeneous population and is therefore not comparable to the United States. Yet these particular characteristics lessen the smaller country's need for an effective national employment service. Sweden does not have to cope with our demographic variety, racial discrimination, and complex industrial development now racked by automation — all factors which complicate the adjustment of manpower supply and demand in this huge country.

ONE SERVICE THAT WORKS

The Swedes swear by their employment service. They credit it not only with mastering the employment process, but also with contributing to productivity and growth. The biggest difference, however, between their service and USES is the enthusiastic support it gets from the population generally and Swedish businessmen in particular.

Swedish employers *use* their service. They make their job vacancies known without any formal mandate. They also volunteer detailed advance notice of any important changes they contemplate that will affect the labor market. The Swedish government then helps workers to move as needed. It provides travel allowances which include the cost of sending the man's wife along when he is interviewed for the job so that she may satisfy herself on housing and schooling in the new locality. Prefabricated houses are provided while the relocated worker looks for a permanent home and he gets an adequate family subsistence allowance and training and retraining as needed.

Employees of the Swedish service are mostly well-educated professionals. They are well paid and there are enough of them for the time-consuming task of keeping in touch with employers. A leading Swedish employment service officer, Nils Kelgren, after observing the American system over many weeks commented, "Not on one single occasion in the United States did I hear an employer himself calling an officer [of USES], presenting the vacancy and his wishes."

Gunnar Myrdal has pointed out that Sweden's employment service, unlike ours, spends more to *prevent* unemployment than it ever did for unemployment relief. "This policy is an investment in higher productivity," he says. "The state is seen to be rendering a service to expanding businesses as well as to the workers threatened by unemployment. *For this the business community is grateful.*" (Italics mine.)

"ANOTHER FIRST"

Immediately after his inauguration, President Kennedy enjoined the Secretary of Labor to reform USES to cope with the already disturbing rise in the number of jobless. The then Secretary of Labor, now Supreme Court Justice, Arthur Goldberg, and his successor, Willard Wirtz, are both intellectuals intensely concerned with the dynamics of the labor market, and they have instructed USES to become a "manpower service." President Johnson is equally emphatic. Appropriations have been increased, and there have been implementing directives and legislation. But the chief product until quite recently has been a welter of self-congratulatory literature about the "new" USES mission. . . .

MORE MONEY, NEW ROLES

. . . In the decade from 1947 to 1957, the USES budget and staff dwindled by 23 per cent and its job placements declined proportionately. With increased appropriations in 1961 and 1962, the reverse happened. What can be accomplished was demonstrated in 1962 in a test conducted in Muncie, Indiana. In that typical small-city office, five interviewers and a clerk were added, bringing the total staff to thirty-five. They were then able to call on every employer in Muncie. The office doubled its newspaper advertising, and mailed resumés of its applicants to 2,200 local employers. As a result, overall job placements increased by two-thirds, and among the semi-skilled by 350 per cent.

This kind of service must be made available all over the country if we are to have any hope of halting the creeping menace of long-term structural unemployment. The average twenty-year-old today can anticipate six different careers in his lifetime, and at least one per cent of workers now employed will have to be retrained annually if they are to find jobs. This means 700,000 workers a year — nearly seven times as many as were trained last year under the pioneering Manpower Development and Training Act, which got under way in 1962.

USES is the agency which must set up retraining programs, interview employers in systematic surveys of regional job prospects, and work closely with local vocational school systems if the program is to work. Moving into this area has proved an eye-opening experience for USES. In the past year 112,000 unemployed or underemployed men and women took retraining courses or have been approved for retraining. About 70 per cent of the "graduates" got jobs. Eighteen-year-old draftees who flunk preinduction tests are now being referred to USES offices for counseling, training under MDTA, or job placement. To encourage this salvage operation, President Johnson announced in May that a personal letter from him urging young men to seek the help of their local employment offices will be enclosed with future draft rejection notices. USES counselors are discovering that many of those flunking the tests are from broken homes. Skilled referrals to social and psychiatric services are required. This is a novel but appropriate role for USES.

Amendments to the Manpower Development and Training Act passed last year permit programs for overcoming illiteracy as well as teaching vocational skills. This should make it possible for the training programs to reach those most in need of help. To date, this has not been the case. . . .

Amendments to federal statutes on vocational education also will require (1) a closer working rapport between USES and vocational education, which — as a result of legislation passed in 1963 — is scheduled for a steep increase in federal financing, and (2) a new flexibility permitting more emphasis on office jobs and less on farm training. These reforms should help make USES more effective.

Better integration of interstate USES operations is also in prospect. It has set up a new Professional Office Network with separate offices in 160 cities which use special phone and mail channels — chiefly to place engineers, teachers, accountants, and nurses. In a pilot program, nine such offices in California have been linked via teletype. USES is also exploring the use of electronic data-processing in an attempt to cut through the elephantine paper work now involved in matching man with job. Some day perhaps a meaningful file on an applicant will be stored on tape and made instantly usable through computers.

At the same time USES is struggling to rise above being "the unemployment office." In forty-four large metropolitan centers the employment service and unemployment offices are physically separated. Unfortunately both services are still under one head in most states and where offices are short-handed, the same people must hand out unemployment checks and act as job counselors. As a result, vital counseling, testing, and interviewing are skimped.

These functions also suffer because of the present need to justify an annual appropriation before Congress. Long-range planning, counseling, and testing services are less impressive at budget hearings than a high score on job placements. The fact that many of these jobs are temporary does not show up in the statistics. Actually, however, last year one third of all USES placements were for less than three days. Though such achievements help raise the score, they have little bearing on a positive manpower policy.

GETTING BUSINESS TO USE IT

For the real role of an effective national employment service is — though few Americans realize this — actually to create employment. It does this through a battery of services which together perform the complicated job of matching labor supply with labor demand. The basic steps are to provide information on employment trends, to interview, counsel, test, and classify job applicants and refer them to prospective employers. Training and retraining as well as relocation may be necessary. Workers must be given early warning of technological or other trends which may result in unemployment. Many employers also need help in anticipating their manpower needs and in recruiting and testing applicants — a function USES has brought to a high level of proficiency.

To perform in this fashion USES needs more than increased funds, better personnel, modern equipment and operating methods. It must have increased public support — above all, from business and industry. If such cooperation is not forthcoming voluntarily, conceivably it will have to be achieved by law. Organized labor has been pressing for mandatory listing of all job vacancies with USES. This has been done before but only in wartime. If unemployment grows worse, a federal executive order might well be issued requiring all government contractors to list their job openings with USES. The rationale would be that a worker shouldn't have to pay a fee to a private agency to get employment deriving from government business.

Eventually all industries may be persuaded to list their job vacancies by carrot-and-stick methods. For example, unemployment-insurance tax rates might be lowered for employers who offer job-vacancy data. But however it is brought about, a national employment service can never be really useful if it does not have full information on jobs and, as a consequence, patronage by most of the qualified workers rather than just the ill-equipped. Otherwise it remains only a peripheral operation.

There are small signs on the horizon that industry is beginning to get the point. For example, the New Jersey Manufacturers Association has persuaded its members to list their hard-to-fill job vacancies with USES. In the first year, over two thousand job openings were listed by some two hundred companies and USES was able to fill a great many of them.

A substantial dollar saving is involved when the service can cut down the interval between jobs. Last year USES made 6.7 million job placements. If the time each of these workers spent looking for work was reduced by one week and his average weekly wage was $60, a total of $402 million was saved. That is a conservative estimate, yet the sum about equals the current annual appropriations for USES and the administration of unemployment insurance combined. And the $402 million is only the dollar wage income produced — it does not include the savings in relief costs or unemployment compensation nor the value of goods and services added to the gross national product by the employment.

FOR HOW LONG?

The real significance of speeding up the employment process is manifest when one considers that long-term unemployment (six months or more) has been on a relentless increase in the United States regardless of boom or slump. In mid-1953 the very-long-term unemployed were 58,000, or 3.7 per cent of the unemployed. In mid-1957 they numbered 260,000, or 9.6 per cent of the unemployed. By mid-1960 they had grown to 411,000, or 11.9 per cent, and in mid-1963 they numbered 643,000, or *15.8 per cent* of all the unemployed.

Half the rise in unemployment over the past decade is attributable to the longer duration of joblessness, rather than new unemployment. This is an ominous and entirely new experience for the United States. Against this dismal background, and the prospect of accelerating automation plus an explosively expanding labor force, USES can be properly seen as an indispensable agency. Clearly, a vastly strengthened USES is a necessary first step in any serious war on poverty.

(3)   Unemployment Insurance

(i) PURPOSE AND NATURE OF THE PROGRAM [14]

U.S. BUREAU OF EMPLOYMENT SECURITY, UNEMPLOYMENT INSURANCE: PURPOSES AND PRINCIPLES
(*Mimeo, December, 1950*)

Unemployment insurance is a program of short-term insurance for the payment of benefits to workers as a matter of right during unemployment which is beyond their control.   The program is designed to provide protection only to workers who are ordinarily employed, who are currently unemployed due to lack of suitable work, and who are ready, willing, and able to accept such work.   The primary objective of benefit payments is to replace enough of the current wage loss of unemployed workers who meet the program's requirements so that most such workers need not turn to other programs for aid, under normal and recession conditions. The program is designed also to facilitate the speedy reabsorption of workers into the right jobs by maintaining constant contact between unemployed workers who are entitled to benefits and the State employment services.   It thereby provides a basis for more effective Nation-wide organization of the labor market than would otherwise exist.

Unemployment insurance provides an orderly way of meeting the cost of unemployment to the individual and the community.   Properly financed, such a system of insurance makes it possible to accumulate reserves during good years to meet the drains of poor years so that the full cost of unemployment need not be met when business and the community are least able to meet it.   Because it has [largely] replaced, by a system of insurance, . . . devices for relieving unemployment distress . . . based on need, the program gives the individual worker greater security and freedom from the fear of unemployment.   The protection provided sustains the morale and conserves the skills and standards of living of those who become unemployed by enabling them to meet their essential expenses for a reasonable period until they are able to obtain suitable work.   By facilitating effective organization of the labor market, the program helps preserve individual skills and earning power, promote maximum utilization of the labor force, and maintain national productivity.   By maintaining essential consumer purchasing power, on which production plans are based, the program provides a brake on

---

[14] For an account of the early history of the unemployment insurance program, see Witte, Development of Unemployment Compensation, 55 Yale L.J. 21 (1954); Perkins, The Roosevelt I Knew, c. 23 (1946); Wyatt and Wandel, The Social Security Act in Operation, c. 12 (1937).   For a detailed summary of current state laws, see U.S. Dept. of Labor, Bureau of Employment Security, Comparison of State Unemployment Insurance Laws as of January 1, 1964 (BES No. U-141, 1964). This publication is revised at two-year intervals.   An interim supplement also is available. — ED.

downturns in business activity, helps to stabilize employment, and lessens the momentum of deflation during periods of recession. It thereby serves the further purpose of helping to sustain the confidence of the community and the general level of economic activity.

Unemployment insurance must, however, be regarded as only one phase of a broad program to promote full employment. In addition to assuring prompt and adequate payment of benefits to the eligible unemployed, unemployment insurance plans should be designed to fit in with other plans to promote maximum utilization of the labor force and to stabilize employment.

U.S. SOCIAL SECURITY ADMINISTRATION, SOCIAL SECURITY IN THE UNITED STATES
26-30 (1952)

The Federal Unemployment Tax Act, which is now part of the Internal Revenue Code, lays a tax on employers at the rate of [3.35] per cent of workers' pay in covered jobs, not counting anything over $3,000 paid to a worker in a year. The employer can offset against as much as 90 per cent of this tax the amount he has paid under an approved State unemployment insurance law or from which he has been excused under the State law. States originally had to require covered employers to pay as much as they could offset — 2.7 per cent of the wages subject to contribution. Now all States reduce the contribution rates of employers whose workers have little unemployment; some excuse an employer from making any contribution at all in a particular year. In [1957] the average contribution rate of employers under State laws was [1.3] per cent of their covered payroll [in 1962 the average rate had risen to 2.4 per cent].

The remaining [portion] of the Federal tax — [0.4] per cent of covered payroll — is collected by the Treasury and goes into general Federal revenues. In return, Congress appropriates money for grants to States for State administration of the program. In the fiscal year [1962] such grants totaled [almost $449 million], including amounts for administration of public employment services. The Bureau of Employment Security in the United States Department of Labor is responsible for [determining] each year whether the State program still meets Federal requirements for these grants and the tax offset and for recommending the amounts of the grants. The Secretary of Labor certifies his determination of the facts to the Treasury.

FEDERAL REQUIREMENTS

All contributions collected under the State laws must be deposited in the unemployment trust fund in the United States Treasury. The fund is invested as a whole, but each State has a separate account to which its deposits and its share of interest on investments are credited. The

State may withdraw money from the account at any time but only to pay benefits.

Benefits must be paid through public employment offices or other federally approved agencies. The State must have methods of adminis-tration that will ensure full payment of benefits when due. Workers must have a right to appeal a decision of the State agency concerning their claims. Benefits cannot be denied to a claimant because he re-fuses to accept a job under certain conditions designed to protect the established standards as to prevailing wages, working conditions, and union affiliation.

These and some other requirements of Federal law are intended to assure that a State participating in the program has a sound and genu-ine unemployment insurance system, fairly administered. The State it-self decides what workers it will cover, how workers will qualify for benefits, how much they receive a week and for how long if they con-tinue to be unemployed. The State decides what the employers' con-tribution rates will be. The State unemployment insurance agency makes rules for payment of benefits and handles and decides claims of unemployed workers.

State Unemployment Insurance Programs

Unemployment insurance differs from State to State and only the gen-eral pattern of the State programs can be outlined here.

Qualifying for Benefits

In general, an unemployed worker can receive benefits if he meets the following conditions:

1. He must register for work at a public employment office and enter his claim.
2. He must have been employed in a job covered by the State law. Generally, this must be a job in private industry or commerce, such as jobs in factories, stores, mines, offices and so on. [About half the States require this job to have been with a firm that had at least four employees in twenty weeks of the year, but more than twenty States cover firms with one or more employees.]
3. He must have earned a certain amount of "wage credits" in covered jobs. That is, he must have had a certain amount of pay or worked for a certain time in a period set by the law before he lost his job.
4. He must be able to work and available for work and ready to take a suitable job if one is offered him.

In general, a worker cannot get unemployment benefits if he is sick or unable to work for any other reason. A few States pay unemploy-ment benefits to a worker who becomes sick after he loses his job, and they continue to pay the benefits for which the worker qualifies so long as there is no suitable job to offer him. Three States have separate provisions to pay disability benefits to workers insured under their unemployment insurance laws when the worker's unemployment is due to sickness or other disability; in a fourth State the temporary disability insurance program is administered by the State workmen's compensation agency but covers substantially the same workers as are covered by unemployment insurance.

NOTE

The most significant developments in the unemployment insurance program during recent years have been a substantial increase in the coverage of the program (the average monthly number of covered workers has grown from about 23 million in 1940 to about 43 million in 1964), and the adoption of a number of special supplementary or temporary programs.

In 1954 only three states included government services in their definitions of "employment," and only about 115,000 state government workers were protected. By 1964, however, thirty-three states were providing coverage for some of their own employees or for local governmental employees. Ten had provisions covering state employees on a compulsory basis, and one, Hawaii, had mandatory local government employee coverage as well. In the remaining jurisdictions coverage varied, commonly being elective at the local level.

For civilian employees of the Federal Government, unemployment insurance protection began in January, 1955, under a program paying benefits in accordance with state law provisions and financed by the Federal Government. In October, 1958, coverage was extended to members of the armed forces.

In connection with the financing of state unemployment benefits, the Employment Security Administrative Financing Act of 1954 (also known as the Reed Act) authorized advances on an interest-free basis to states with depleted unemployment reserves, as indicated by the ratio of funds available to benefits paid. If this multiple was reduced lower than one, i.e., when a state's reserve had shrunk to less than the amount expended in unemployment insurance benefits over the period of twelve months preceding, that state became eligible for a loan. On June 30, 1958, the cash balance in the Federal Unemployment Account was over $208,000,000, but as a result of the 1957-1958 recession, some very large advances (loans) had to be made to hard-hit states. After $113 million went to Michigan and over $112 million to Pennsylvania, and less to Oregon and Alaska, the Account was practically exhausted.

In 1958 Congress enacted the Temporary Unemployment Compensation Act, which provided that additional unemployment insurance could be paid on a temporary basis to jobless workers who exhausted their regular unemployment insurance benefit rights after June 30, 1957, or some later date selected by the participating state. In effect, this provided a 50 per cent increase in the duration of benefits, for example, from thirty to forty-five weeks in Pennsylvania. The Act was effective

June 19, 1958, and eventually terminated as of June 30, 1959. The TUC "advances" (or "loans") had to be repaid by participating states prior to December 1, 1963. If not then repaid, the debtor states (then owing about $446 million) were subject to reductions in the federal tax offset, i.e., scheduled increases in the federal payroll tax provided for automatic collection of these advances.

Only seventeen states took advantage of the TUC advance provisions and a few states also adopted so-called state extended benefit provisions applicable in periods of high unemployment. When the 1961-1962 recession struck, Congress took a different approach. Under the Temporary Extended Unemployment Compensation Act of 1961[15] the Federal Government still bore the initial burden of state extended benefit costs, but the 50 per cent extra entitlement provisions in the TEUC Act provided for no more than thirty-nine weeks of regular plus extended benefits. To repay the Federal Government the TEUC Act provided for a flat $\frac{4}{10}$ per cent increase in the federal payroll tax for the years 1962 and 1963. All states adopted TEUC programs. States like Michigan, Ohio, and Pennsylvania paid out more in TEUC benefits than their federally taxable employers were liable for in TEUC-mandated tax increases, but in other cases low-unemployment states paid more than they actually spent for TEUC benefits.[16] In all, TEUC benefit payments totaled more than $700 million.

Unquestionably the Federal Government and the states took strong measures to alleviate some of the human costs of two recessions. It is also true that repaying the costs of TUC and other extended benefit legislation will continue until 1967 or later.[17]

BENEFIT PAYMENTS

States differ in the weekly amount of the benefits they pay to unemployed workers with similar wage credits and in the length of time a worker can continue to get payments if he cannot find a suitable new job.

In general, the weekly amount is intended to be about half the worker's previous weekly pay except that there are minimum and maximum amounts on the payment. Eleven states increase the amount for workers who have dependents. In January, 1965 the maximum weekly benefit for a worker without dependents ranges among the states from $30 to $55 a week. The minimum weekly amount for any worker who qualifies ranges from $3 to $25, the majority clustering around the $10-$12 level. All states pay partial benefits for partial unemployment. All but three

[15] Public Law 87-6, March 24, 1961, effective April 8, 1961. No new TEUC claims were accepted after April 1, 1962, and TEUC benefits were terminated as of June 30, 1962.

[16] The federal TEUC tax ultimately was reduced from $\frac{4}{10}$ per cent to $\frac{25}{100}$ per cent for 1963. See Public Law 88-31, May 29, 1963, the so-called Mills-Byrne Law.

[17] Public Law 88-173, November 7, 1963, in effect gave the states a stretchout for sums owing under the Reed Act and froze the extra TUC tax at a $\frac{3}{10}$ per cent maximum.

states also require a waiting period, usually a week, after a worker becomes unemployed before his benefits can begin.

In most states, a worker's past earnings or employment under the law determine the length of time he can continue to receive benefits if he continues to be unemployed. In some, it may be as short as six weeks; in some, as long as thirty-nine weeks. Ten states have a "uniform duration" for benefits to any qualified worker. Uniform duration ranges among these states from twelve weeks to thirty weeks.

DISQUALIFICATIONS

A claimant may be disqualified from benefits even if he has the wage credits he needs to be insured. He is generally disqualified if:

1. He has quit his job voluntarily without good cause. (Some state laws say without good cause "attributable to the employer" or "connected with the work.")
2. He was discharged for misconduct in connection with his work.
3. He has refused or has failed, without good cause, to apply for or accept suitable work.
4. He is unemployed because of a stoppage of work as the result of a labor dispute.

In some states, disqualification means that a worker must serve a longer waiting period before he can get benefits. Other states not only postpone the benefits otherwise due him, but also reduce them. A few states may cancel all the benefit rights of a disqualified worker; then he cannot receive anything under the system until he has again had enough covered employment to build up the necessary wage credits.

The amount of "base period wages," i.e., the employment necessary to qualify for benefits, has been increasing. All the formulas in use aim to benefit only workers genuinely in the labor market. They show a good deal of legislative ingenuity. A number of states require qualifying earnings equal to $1\frac{1}{2}$ times high-quarter earnings. Some (Washington and West Virginia, for example) specify a flat sum — $800, $700, etc. Others, like New York and Vermont, require a specified number of weeks with at least a specific weekly wage, i.e., twenty weeks employment at $20 or more. Also much used are eligibility formulas wherein qualifying wages must be "X" times the weekly benefit amount (as in Arkansas, whose statute calls for wages of thirty times the "wba"). And of course combinations of these (and other) formulas are in use.

No definite trend has been established with reference to legislative changes in the disqualification provisions of the various state laws. For example, seventeen states modified the voluntary quit disqualification between 1955 and 1960, and of these, nine increased and seven decreased the severity of the provision. There appears to have been no significant shift in the terms of the other disqualification provisions.

The importance as well as the deficiencies of the unemployment compensation system, fiscally, socially, and politically, are not open to question. The figures in the following table give some perspective on program operations over the years.

TABLE I.   SUMMARY DATA ON STATE UNEMPLOYMENT
INSURANCE ACTIVITIES

Selected Years 1940-1962[1]

Data	1940	1950	1960	1962
Total number of beneficiaries[2]	5,220	5,212	6,753	6,074
Number of claimants exhausting benefits[2]	2,590	1,853	1,603	1,638
Average weekly benefit (total unemployment)	$10.56	$20.76	$32.87	$34.56
Average benefit duration (weeks)	9.8	13.0	12.7	13.1
UC taxes collected (millions of dollars)	$854	$1,191	$2,289	$2,952
Benefits paid (millions of dollars)	$519	$1,373	$2,727	$2,675

[1] Source: Social Security Bulletin, Annual Statistical Supplement, 1962, Table 13, p. 12.
[2] 000's omitted.

(ii) UNEMPLOYMENT BENEFITS

PROBLEM: THE STORMY VOYAGE OF REGAL YACHT
CORPORATION

The Regal Yacht Corporation employs approximately 100 people in the construction of small pleasure craft. The main plant is located on the east bank of the Royal River, about five miles upstream from the business section of the city of Metropolis. The company has two smaller plants, one known as Factory A, located on the west bank of the river about one mile downstream, and the other, Factory B, located in the town of Little Grove, 200 miles away in an adjoining state.

On January 5, the painting crew in the main plant was laid off because of the seasonal slump. Tom Grogan, the foreman of this crew, returned to his home town of Hickoryville at the end of the second week, after he was told by the management that the outlook for rehiring before the end of February was not good. Grogan was sixty years old and had started working at Regal during World War II. He was getting tired of his small room in the city and felt that he could not afford to stay there anyway without a steady income. Accordingly, he returned to Hickoryville and filed a claim for unemployment insurance at the state employment office there. He told the clerk that he was a handy man as well as a painter, but that his back was getting weak and that he could not take work involving heavy lifting or long periods on a high ladder. Hickoryville is a town of 4000 people; it has a large resort hotel, a small box factory, and a furniture factory. The clerk at the employment office told Grogan that there were no unfilled work orders for painters or handy men at that time. Grogan made no independent effort to find a job and was still out of work when Regal recalled its painters early in April. He was offered a job at Metropolis as foreman on the night shift, a job which he refused because he could not sleep during the day and did not want to go back to live in the big city. Hickoryville was two hours by bus from Metropolis, with no other public transportation available, and the first bus out of Metropolis to Hickoryville in the morning was at 10 A.M. Grogan did not own an automobile. Upon refusal to return to Regal, the company filed a protest against the payment to him of any further unemployment benefits.

In the meantime, on February 25, one of the company's master carpenters, John McGregor, injured his right hand while operating a band saw in the cutting department of the main plant. He was working at a special assignment at the time of his injury, for which he was paid his regular rate of $2.85 per hour. His doctor advised him that the injury would incapacitate him for any work for two weeks, after which he might be able to do light work not requiring excessive use of his right hand. However, the doctor forbade his return to his regular job or the use of the tools of his trade for at least six weeks.

McGregor filed a claim for unemployment benefits the day after he was injured. At the end of two weeks Regal offered him a job operating a heavy cutter in the metal shop of Factory A, at the rate of $2.10 per hour, the going rate for cutting machine operators. McGregor refused the job for the following reasons: (1) it would take him at least twenty minutes longer to drive from his home on the east side of the river to Factory A; (2) the pay was too low, considering that the union scale for a master carpenter was $2.85 per hour; and (3) as a result of his experience with the band saw, he had developed a fear of fast-moving machinery and was concerned about the possibility of sustaining further injury. The company immediately filed a protest against McGregor's claim. It offered no other jobs to McGregor, who began to look for work elsewhere, indicating that he would take any job that paid a minimum of $2.50 per hour. At the end of six weeks, Regal wrote to McGregor, offering him his old job back; but he was still angry about the company's attitude and did not bother to reply. By this time McGregor had ceased making the rounds of other plants, since none of them was hiring new employees. He continued, however, to report each week to the state employment office in downtown Metropolis. After two more weeks, Regal wrote to McGregor again; receiving no reply within one week, the company hired another master carpenter and notified the state unemployment compensation commission that McGregor had voluntarily quit his job without good cause.

On Friday, May 13, three inches of rain fell in the Metropolis area within a period of twenty-four hours, and by noon the next day the Royal was overflowing. The main plant was flooded with six feet of water. The company immediately announced that it would shut down operations for a period of at least four weeks, and notified all production workers that they were laid off until further notice.

Mary Moore in the sail division was one of the girls laid off. She had been operating a heavy sewing machine used to stitch sailcloth, at the rate of $1.70 per hour. When Mary filed her claim for unemployment benefits on the Monday following the flood, the state employment office offered her three different jobs. The first was a riveter's job at a boiler works located in a tough section of town called the Flats. The pay for this job was $1.95 per hour, but it was on the night shift. Mary explained that she had mentioned her three weeks as a riveter in an aircraft plant in 1942 only because the interviewer had asked her where she had been employed prior to her enlistment in the Waves. She declared that she did not like riveting and refused to accept the job, pointing out that she would have to walk four blocks on Skid Row and past eight bars in order to get from the bus stop to the main entrance of the boiler works. The second job was that of sewing machine operator in the canvas cover department of Titan Trucks, Inc., manufacturers of bodies of dump trucks. The rate of pay was $1.40 per hour. Mary refused this offer on the ground that the rate of pay was too low. She explained that the regional chief of the Wage and Hour Division had stated in a talk at a union meeting just a few days previously that the prevailing wage for sewing machine operators in that area was $1.55 per hour. The third available job was that of flour girl at the Van Dragen Bakery, at the rate of $1.50 per hour. Mary recalled that the workers at the bakery had been on strike for six weeks and were then picketing the plant; she therefore refused the job, stating that she had never crossed a picket line in her life and did not intend to do so now.

During the next several days Mary inquired among her friends concerning jobs that might be available for four or five weeks until Regal resumed operations and recalled her. She telephoned one former employer to inquire if he had a pick-up job, and she watched the want ads every night during the first ten days of her unemployment for likely temporary work, but none of these sources was productive. The state employment office had no further positions to offer when she reported the second and third times.

At the end of the third week, Regal's personnel director telephoned one of Mary's fellow workers, June Mason, and offered her a job as office girl at Factory B, which she could take on either a temporary or permanent basis. The starting salary would be $60 per week, with an opportunity for advancement. After thinking it over, June declined the offer. She mentioned the fact that she was only twenty years old and had never before been away from home. She added that she was disturbed about rumors among the women workers of Factory B concerning the plant manager.

Phil Carlson, the operator of Regal's gasoline pump at the main plant, accepted a transfer to Factory A, and after the flood damage had been repaired, he was recalled to the main plant. Carlson quit his job at

Factory A immediately, but when he reported for work at the main plant on the following Monday, he was advised that his recall had been premature and that it would be three more weeks before the pump was restored to working order. In the meantime Factory A had hired a replacement, and Carlson was given a separation slip stating that he had voluntarily left his job at Factory A without good cause. Carlson then went to the main plant and demanded an explanation. There he was told that for hiring purposes the two plants operated independently as separate employers. Carlson lost his temper and told the manager just what he thought of the company. Following this outburst, he received a separation notice from the main plant marked "discharge for misconduct — insubordination."

During the summer Regal's operations got back to normal and the company seemed to be well on its way to catching up with its backlog of orders, when lumber shipments to the main plant began to slow down. By August 22, the supply was so low that the main plant was forced to suspend operations, and all of the production workers at that plant were laid off. On September 3, one truck load of new lumber arrived, but there was still no assurance of a steady supply, so the decision to issue recalls was delayed. On September 6, the contract between the union and the company expired at Factory B, and operations there also ceased when the workers refused to return to their jobs pending the outcome of negotiations for a new contract. The contract at Factory A, which was represented by a different local of the same international union, still had a year to run, as did the contract of the main plant, which was represented by an affiliate of a different international union, but it was a fixed policy of the company to give any gains at one plant to the employees of the other two.

Factory A continued to produce engines until its supply of special parts, furnished by Factory B, ran out; then Factory A also closed down on September 15. By October 9, the lumber supply was back to normal and there were engines enough on hand to keep the main plant going for at least two weeks, but the company decided not to open the main plant until the strike was settled so there would be some assurance that once production started, it would not be interrupted again. When no settlement had been reached at Factory B by October 24, however, the company officials decided upon a new strategy. They sent out recall notices to all of the employees of the main plant and started hiring new workers for Factory B.

By October 31, Factory B was back in operation with the new workers recruited by the company, and operations continued until November 11 without serious difficulty, although a picket line was established on November 7 and was maintained for the remainder of that week. The employees of Factory A held a meeting, however, and decided to picket the main plant, commencing October 26. As a result, none of the main plant workers would return, for threats of violence had been made and several workers had been removed bodily from their cars while approaching the plant. The company therefore abandoned its plan on November

12 and filed protest against all unemployment claims made after September 6. A new contract with Factory B was finally executed on November 23, and all three plants resumed operations on November 28.

With the help of the following materials, determine whether any of the above-mentioned employees is entitled to unemployment benefits and also whether any or all employees idled during the period between August 22 and November 28 are similarly entitled.

NOTES

1. Reger v. Administrator, 132 Conn. 647, 46 A.2d 844 (1946). The plaintiff, a married woman thirty-one years of age, with no children, was employed as a bookkeeper by a wholesale grocery firm in New Haven from March, 1943, until January, 1944. She then voluntarily left that employment to go to Ozark, Alabama, where she joined her husband, who, as a member of the United States Army, was stationed at Camp Rucker nearby. She expected to remain in that locality about a year. Ozark has a population of forty-five hundred and its principal industries are textiles, lumber, and the manufacture of peanut and cottonseed oils. Dothan, the largest town in that region, is twenty-eight miles away and has twenty-five thousand inhabitants. Its principal industries are transportation as carried on in the general offices of a railroad, wholesale distribution, peanut and cottonseed oil processing, textiles and lumber. In both places retail trade is at a very high level, but in Ozark the other work is on a seasonal basis which starts about September 1. The plaintiff filed claims for unemployment benefits covering the period from April 30 to July 16, 1944. Throughout this time she was physically and mentally able to work and was classified as a general office clerk, but would accept any office employment for which she could qualify, starting at $15 per week, and was willing to work any hours of the day and to travel thirty miles to her work. Many employers in Ozark and Dothan would not employ servicemen's wives because of the uncertainty of the length of time they would remain in that area. Five of the two hundred and nine placements made by the United States employment office at Dothan in May, 1944, were of office workers. The plaintiff refused no referrals by the employment office. She independently applied for a position as clerk-typist with the civil service commission at Camp Rucker but was advised that there were no jobs available. She also applied for a position with the U.S.O. in Ozark but was not hired because she was unable to take dictation, a requirement of the job.

Held: Benefits awarded. 1. There is a labor market for her skills in the community. 2. Plaintiff is available for work even though there is difficulty in getting employment because local businessmen are reluctant to hire servicemen's wives.

2. Fannon v. Federal Cartridge Corp., 219 Minn. 306, 18 N.W.2d 249 (1945). When the claimant commenced working at the Twin Cities Ordnance Plant in 1942, she was in perfect health. After working as a

visual inspector for eight months, she was transferred to the incendiary bullet department, where she was required to work with gunpowder, and this seriously affected her physical condition. Her face, hands, and feet began to swell and her skin turned a greenish shade. After she had consulted a doctor the foreman transferred her to a job as "move woman," which involved the pushing of heavy iron trucks loaded with shells in a temperature of 132 degrees. In May, 1943, the claimant collapsed. She went to the hospital and her doctor advised her not to return to the Twin Cities Ordnance Plant, indicating that she would not be able to recover as long as she worked there. As a result, she quit her job with this company. The claimant was in bed until September, 1943, and was almost blind during this period. In September she recovered sufficiently to go back to work, although she was physically unable to handle the duties of a "move woman." She worked for short periods for two other companies, being laid off from her second job on January 13, 1944, because of a material shortage.

Held: Benefits awarded. 1. There is good cause "attributable to the employer" for her quitting. Attributable to employer does not mean employer misconduct but actually means good cause "in connection with employment" (as the statutes of some states read). 2. No disqualification for failure to accept suitable work.

3. Bowman v. Troy Launderers & Cleaners, Inc., 215 Minn. 226, 9 N.W.2d 506 (1943). Claimant was employed by the employer as a steam cleaner in the dry-cleaning department for about five years prior to December 6, 1941. On November 28, 1941, he received a notification by letter from the employer that one week from that date it would not be able to provide him with work in that department until resumption of "better dry cleaning volume." In the same letter the employer advised claimant that it had made arrangements to give him work such as he previously had during off seasons and asked him to report the next week "for this change over to another department." On December 3 claimant conferred with an officer of the employer and was informed that his work for the off season would consist of light garage work, stock work, and some truck driving. His wage at his regular work approximated $24 per 40-hour week. The off-season work offered him would have netted him $20 for a 48-hour week. Claimant is not experienced or trained as a mechanic, nor is he licensed as a truck driver. He is a member of the Laundry Workers and Cleaners International Union, but is not affiliated with any mechanics' or drivers' unions. Before giving his employer a definite answer whether or not he would accept the work offered, claimant sought the counsel of the business representative of the union to which he belonged. He was advised that if he accepted the work and engaged himself as a mechanic or truck driver he would be violating an agreement between his union and other craft unions in the city, and that he might be liable to expulsion from his union for so doing. He then reported to his employer that he would not accept the offered job.

Claimant admitted that during the off seasons of other years he had worked in other departments at different rates of pay; that the off season is usually about two and one-half or three months long; and that each time when the dry-cleaning business again accelerated he was put back into his position as a steam cleaner.

Held: Benefits awarded. No disqualification for failure to accept suitable work.

4. Boynton Cab Co. v. Neubeck, 237 Wis. 249, 296 N.W. 636 (1941). About two weeks after he was hired, Neubeck overcharged a passenger in the amount of 15 cents and put the money in his own pocket. When the passenger complained, the company made Neubeck pay back the 15 cents and warned him against such practices. A month later, Neubeck was involved in a series of three minor accidents within a period of twelve days. He failed to report the first accident, which did not result in any material damage. In reporting the second accident, he failed to mention a slight personal injury to one of the people involved, but later said that he did not know anyone had been hurt. When his car skidded on some ice on the ramp in the company's garage and collided with another car as he reached the street, he was discharged. Company apparently had accepted Neubeck's explanation of the overcharge and of his lack of knowledge of the slight injury in the second accident.

Held: Benefits awarded. Misconduct as a disqualification under the statute must be willful or wanton. Mere inefficiency, inability, incapacity, and ordinary negligence in isolated instances are not misconduct within the statutory meaning.

5. Sherbert v. Verner, 374 U.S. 398 (1963). Claimant, a member of the Seventh-day Adventist Church, was discharged by her employer, a textile mill, because she would not work on Saturday. She was unable to obtain other employment because of her conscientious scruples.

Held: South Carolina disqualification from benefits violates the freedom of religion of the First and Fourteenth Amendments.

6. In the Matter of Tyson, S.S. #237-46-2399, 253 N.C. 662, 117 S.E.2d 854 (1961). In the spring of 1959, Swift & Co., meat-packing company, closed its Rocky Mount, N.C., plant because it had built a new and larger plant at Wilson. Claimants were fourteen employees permanently terminated from the Rocky Mount plant. Under a collective bargaining agreement with the United Packinghouse Workers, when claimants were terminated they received severance pay ranging from $249.60 (equivalent of three weeks' wages) to $1407.60 (equivalent of eighteen weeks' wages). They also received vacation pay the equivalent of one to four weeks' wages. These payments were calculated under the formula provided for in the collective agreement.

Held: Benefits denied. These sums are "wages" prorated on the weekly basis upon which they were calculated. Swift is required to pay social security taxes on these sums as wages. If they are wages for the tax law they are wages for the benefit law also.

7. Townsend v. Employment Security Dept., 54 Wash. 2d 532, 341

P.2d 877 (1959). Claimant was not willing to accept a job which paid less than $18 a day, which was the wage rate he earned as a miner. No mining jobs were available in the vicinity.

Held: Benefits denied. Claimant has withdrawn himself from the labor market by his setting of the inflexible condition concerning the wage he will accept.

8. In re Buffelen Lumber & Manufacturing Co., 32 Wash. 2d 205, 201 P.2d 194 (1948). The union which was the exclusive bargaining representative of the employees concluded a collective agreement with the employer providing for paid vacations for employees who had been employed a certain period of time. The agreement gave the employer the option of staggering the vacations or closing down the plant. He chose the latter alternative. Employees who were ineligible for paid vacations claimed unemployment compensation.

Held: Benefits denied. Unemployment is voluntary.

9. On the various facets of unemployment compensation see the following symposium issues of law reviews, devoted entirely to the law: 55 Yale L.J. 1 (1945), 10 Ohio St. L.J. 117 (1949), 8 Vand. L. Rev. 179 (1955).

(iii) UNEMPLOYMENT INSURANCE AND LABOR DISPUTES

DALLAS FUEL CO. v. HORNE
Supreme Court, Iowa, 1941
230 Iowa 1148, 300 N.W. 303

WENNERSTRUM, J. . . .

The individuals involved in this appeal were, prior to the time for which they claim unemployment benefits, employed by the Dallas Fuel Company. They were all members of the United Mine Workers of America and were under the particular jurisdiction of District No. 13 (Iowa), of that organization. During the spring of 1937, District No. 13 (Iowa), United Mine Workers of America, through its officers entered into a contract with the Iowa Coal Operator's Association, which contract made provision for the wage scale, working conditions, and hours under which coal would be produced in mines owned by companies that belonged to the Iowa Coal Operator's Association for the two year period beginning with April 1, 1937, and ending on March 31, 1939. Contracts of a similar nature between these two groups had been entered into for two year periods for a number of years. These contracts, and their terms as to working conditions, wages, and hours were substantially the same as the agreements which were negotiated biannually in the Appalachian coal fields, where a large proportion of the coal of the United States is mined. In years past no agreement had been negotiated between the miners' organization, representing the miners of District No.

13, and the Iowa Coal Operator's Association until the basic Appalachian agreement had been concluded. During a part of March, 1939, and for a month or more thereafter, negotiations were carried on in New York City for the purpose of concluding an Appalachian agreement. At these conferences representatives of District No. 13 were present. Representatives of the Iowa Coal Operator's Association have participated in these negotiations in the past, but the record does not disclose there was a representative of the Iowa Coal Operator's Association present during the 1939 deliberation.

On March 27, 1939, District No. 13 of the United Mine Workers of America and the Iowa Coal Operator's Association, through their respective officials, entered into a work pending agreement which provided that the mines should continue to be operated after April 1, 1939, under the scale of wages and working conditions incorporated in their agreement for the period of 1937-1939, pending the conclusion of the Appalachian Joint Basic Contract, then being negotiated. It was agreed that this work pending agreement could be cancelled on fifteen (15) days' notice from either party to the agreement. Similar agreements had been entered into in other parts of the country between the various union district organizations and operators. These work pending agreements were made with the approval of the national officials and the negotiating committees of the miners' union.

On April 19, 1939, John L. Lewis, President of the United Mine Workers of America, sent a communication from New York City, where negotiations were in progress regarding the Appalachian agreement, to the President of District No. 13 of the United Mine Workers of America, which, as shown by the record, was in part as follows:

"Negotiations have reached a point that necessitates the consolidation of the strength of our union. You are therefore directed on receipt of this telegram to file fifteen day notices of cancellation of all work pending agreements, as well as agreements with individual companies. Please file such notice by telegram confirmed in writing, and subordinate all district activities to the execution of this policy. Written confirmation of this message will follow. This action is taken under the authority vested in the Appalachian negotiating committee by international policy committee. Please confirm receipt.

"Very truly yours,
"JOHN L. LEWIS."

Pursuant to the above communication the President of District No. 13 gave notice to the President of the Iowa Coal Operator's Association that the work pending agreement would be cancelled in fifteen days. No employees of the Dallas Fuel Company reported for work on May 4, 1939, although on May 3, 1939, as shown by the record, the employees were directed by notice on the blackboard maintained at the mine, to "report tomorrow."

The record further shows that the negotiations in regard to the Appalachian Joint Basic Contract started March 14, 1939, and continued until May 11, 1939 when an agreement was reached. Thereafter the representatives of District No. 13 of the United Mine Workers of America and of the Iowa Coal Operator's Association concluded negotiations as to the conditions and terms under which miners would be employed in District No. 13 for the biannual period. The claimants, who had worked in the Dallas Fuel Company mine, filed a claim for unemployment compensation benefits covering the period that they were not employed, and upon hearing, the commission's deputy allowed their claims. Upon appeal by the Dallas Fuel Company, the Iowa Employment Security Commission ordered the matter of the appeal to be referred to it for immediate consideration. Upon a final hearing the findings and holdings of the deputy were affirmed by a two to one vote of the commission. There was a majority opinion and decision filed and a minority opinion was also filed by one of the commissioners. As previously stated the Dallas Fuel Company thereafter applied for and secured a temporary injunction in the District Court of Dallas County, Iowa, enjoining the payment of unemployment benefits to the claimants, and upon the submission of the entire issue the district court reversed the commission and found that the claimants were disqualified to receive benefits because their unemployment was due to a stoppage of work caused, as held by that court, by a "labor dispute." The temporary injunction as to the payment of unemployment benefits was made permanent. The claimants have appealed to this court. . . .

The particular portion of the statute which necessitates our . . . consideration is section 5 and 5(d) of chapter 102 of the Laws of the 47th General Assembly which is in part as follows:

"Sec. 5. An individual shall be disqualified for benefits: . . .

"Sec. 5(d). For any week with respect to which the commission finds that his total or partial unemployment is due to a stoppage of work which exists because of a labor dispute at the factory, establishment, or other premises at which he is or was last employed . . ."

The commission found that there was not a labor dispute between the plaintiff and the claimants at the time of the termination of the work pending agreement. The district court held there was not sufficient competent evidence to warrant the making of the order and decision of the commission. It is our conclusion that the court was correct in its ruling.

Under the National Labor Relations Act, Title 29, Sec. 152(9), U.S.C.A., the term "labor dispute" is defined as follows: "The term 'labor dispute' includes any controversy concerning terms, tenure or conditions of employment, or concerning the association or representation of persons in negotiating, fixing, maintaining, changing, or seeking to arrange terms or conditions of employment regardless of whether the disputants stand in the proximate relation of employer and employee." With this definition as a guide it is the conclusion of this court that the facts undeniably show that the union officials, national and district acting for the members of the union under the jurisdiction of District No. 13, were a factor in the negotiations pertaining to the conclusion of the Appalachian Joint Basic Contract. The facts also undeniably show that the United Mine Workers of America is a national organization and that District No. 13 terminated its "pending work agreement" at the direction of the president of the national organization because "negotiations have reached a point that necessitates the consolidation of the strength of our union." Even though the members of District No. 13, United Mine Workers of America, were not directly participating in the labor dispute in the Appalachian field, yet by reason of the apparent authority exercised over them by their district officials and the officials of the national organization and its policy committee these members became involved in a labor dispute. It is true that the above definition is found in a federal statute which relates to certain labor relations over which the federal government has jurisdiction. However, we are of the opinion that the provisions of this definition are applicable to our present problem.

It is contended in the majority opinion of the commission that if the claimants had continued in employment they would have lost their membership in their union organization and that because of the benefits which they received from this organization in the way of relief in various forms they were justified in following the directions of their officials and that their unemployment was thereby occasioned by "good cause." There is no question in the mind of this court but what the coal miners of this state have benefitted economically and socially by reason of the past activities of their organization but the benefits received by claimants from their organization and their continuation of membership do not in our opinion justify us in holding that the unemployment involved in this appeal was for "good cause," when there is an unquestioned labor dispute as is found in the record in this case.

It is our conclusion that where action is taken by either a labor organization or employer that has a bearing upon a controversy as to wages, or conditions of employment, a labor dispute has developed. As stated in the definition (Title 29, supra) this is true "regardless of whether the disputants stand in the proximate relation of employer and employee." The "work pending agreement" was terminated by District No. 13 because, as stated in the Lewis communication, negotiations had "reached a point that necessitates a consolidation of the strength of our union." In following the direction of the union officials, who terminated the "work pending agreement" the claimants became involved in a labor dispute. The fact that they were unable to work because of the termination of the temporary agreement did not prevent their unemployment from being the result of a labor dispute.

It is the contention of the claimants that a labor dispute did not exist. It is their claim that their unemployment was due to a lack of a contract. It is our judgment and conclusion that the failure to negotiate and enter into a contract was due to a labor dispute. Holdings to this same effect are found in Barnes v. Hall, 285 Ky. 160, 146 S.W.2d 929; Block Coal & Coke Co. v. United Mine Workers of America, Tenn. Sup., 148 S.W.2d 364. . . .

Upon a full consideration of the record before us and the question submitted to us for consideration, we hold that the trial court was correct in its decision and that it should be affirmed. . . .

NOTES

1. Was there a labor dispute at Factory B of the Regal Yacht Corporation? For a definition of the term similar to that in Dallas Fuel Co. v. Horne, see Miners in General Group v. Hix, 123 W. Va. 637, 17 S.E.2d 810 (1941); Sandoval v. Industrial Commission, 110 Colo. 108, 130 P.2d 930 (1942). The Alabama law contains an express definition to this effect. Ala. Code Ann., tit. 26, §214A (1940). If a state court has applied a different definition for another purpose, which definition would you consider applicable for unemployment insurance purposes? Compare La France Electrical Construction & Supply Co. v. International Brotherhood of Electrical Workers, 108 Ohio St. 61, 140 N.E. 899 (1923), with Baker v. Powhatan Mining Co., 146 Ohio St. 600, 67 N.E.2d 714 (1946). See Comment, Labor Dispute Disqualification Under the Ohio Unemployment Compensation Act, 10 Ohio St. L.J. 238, 240 (1949).

In Ablondi v. Board of Review, 8 N.J. Super. 71, 73 A.2d 262 (1950), the court said:

"Definition of the term 'labor dispute' is found in other labor enactments but not in the Unemployment Compensation Law. Cf. R.S. 2:29-77.8; Kohn v. Local No. 195, 132 N.J. Eq. 512 (Ch. 1942). However, courts have given weight to such legislative definition and have held that the term broadly includes any controversy concerning terms or conditions of employment or arising out of the respective interests of employer and employee. See Miners in General Group v. Hicks [Hix] . . . ; Adkins v. Indiana Employment Security Division, 117 Ind. App. 132, 70 N.E.2d 31 (1946). Lockouts as well as strikes have been included. In re North River Logging Co., 15 Wash. 2d 204, 130 P.2d 64 (Sup. Ct. 1942); Adkins v. Indiana Employment Security Division, supra; Fierst and Spector . . . [Unemployment Compensation in Labor Disputes, 49 Yale L.J. 461 (1940)] at p. 479. Cf. R.S. 43:21-5 (c)(2)(a)."

2. Suppose the employer's work was seasonal and the negotiations broke down after the seasonal layoff. Would the labor dispute disqualification still be applicable? See Unemployment Compensation Commission of Alaska v. Aragon, 329 U.S. 143 (1946).

3. Suppose a strike had been called at Regal's main plant on September 6. In your opinion would the workers at that plant have been disqualified for the week ending September 10? Explain. If your answer is in the negative, at what point, if at all, would you say that the labor dispute disqualification became applicable? See Muncie Foundry Division of Borg-Warner Corp. v. Review Board, 114 Ind. App. 475, 51 N.E.2d 891 (1943); Clapp v. Unemployment Compensation Commission, 325 Mich. 212, 38 N.W.2d 325 (1949); Abbott v. Unemployment Compensation Commission, 323 Mich. 32, 34 N.W.2d 542 (1948). On the question of when unemployment is "due" to a labor dispute, compare

the situation of the Alaska Salmon Company with that of the other two employers in Unemployment Compensation Commission of Alaska v. Aragon, supra.

4. On the labor dispute disqualification in general, see Lesser, Labor Disputes and Unemployment Compensation, 55 Yale L.J. 167 (1945); Lewis, The Law of Unemployment Compensation in Labor Disputes, 13 Lab. L.J. 174 (1962); Williams, The Labor Dispute Disqualification — A Primer and Some Problems, 8 Vand. L. Rev. 338 (1955).

LAWRENCE BAKING CO. v. MICHIGAN UNEMPLOYMENT
COMPENSATION COMMISSION
Supreme Court, Michigan, 1944
308 Mich. 198, 13 N.W.2d 260, 154 A.L.R. 660,
cert. denied, 323 U.S. 738 (1944)

STARR, J.

Plaintiff appeals from a circuit court judgment affirming an award of unemployment compensation benefits by the appeal board of defendant commission.

The facts are stipulated. Plaintiff, a Michigan Corporation, is engaged in the wholesale baking business in the city of Lansing. Prior to July 1, 1941, the United Bakery & Confectioners Workers, affiliated with the United Retail & Wholesale Workers of America, C.I.O., attempted to organize the employees of plaintiff company into a union. The union representatives and plaintiff's officials conferred on several occasions regarding a collective bargaining agreement as to hours of work, wages, seniority, and other conditions of employment. Such negotiations failed, and on July 1, 1941, 16 union members of plaintiff's 98 employees stopped work and went on strike. Such strike interrupted plaintiff's baking operations for a period of only about 15 minutes. It immediately hired new employees, and after July 1st there was no further interruption or stoppage of its work and operations. On July 2d it notified each of the 16 striking employees, by letter, that "due to your participation in the strike it has been necessary to replace you with a new employee." The Union established a picket line at plaintiff's plant and continued such picketing until about September 16th.

Eleven of the 16 striking employees filed claims with defendant commission for unemployment compensation benefits for the period from July 8 to July 22, 1941. The commission issued its determination allowing such claims, and plaintiff appealed to the referee, who affirmed the allowance. The appeal board of the commission affirmed the referee's decision, and, upon review by certiorari, the circuit court entered judgment affirming the appeal board. Plaintiff appeals from such judgment. . . .

. . . Prior to the 1941 amendment . . . section 29(c) of the 1936 act, as then last amended by Act No. 324, Pub. Acts 1939, and designated herein as section 29(d), provided in part:

"An individual shall be disqualified for benefits: . . .

"(d) For any week with respect to which his total or partial unemployment is due to a labor dispute which is actively in progress in the establishment in which he is or was last employed."

The 1941 act amended said section 29 to read in part as follows:

"An individual shall be disqualified for benefits: . . .

"(c) For any week with respect to which his total or partial unemployment is due to a *stoppage of work* existing because of a labor dispute in the establishment in which he is or was last employed."

To summarize, section 29(c) of the 1936 act disqualified an employee for benefits if his unemployment was *"due to a labor dispute . . .* actively in progress *in the establishment."* The 1941 amendment of said section disqualified an employee for benefits if his unemployment is *"due to a stoppage of work* existing because of a labor dispute *in the establishment."* Plaintiff contends that the phrase of the amendment, "stoppage of work," means the work or employment of the individual employee. Under such contention plaintiff argues that by stopping their work and going on strike, the claimants disqualified themselves for benefits. Defendant contends, as held by the circuit court, that such phrase means the stoppage of the operations or work of the employer establishment. . . .

In said 1941 amendment of section 29(c) the legislature adopted the identical provision used in the unemployment statutes of many other states to impose disqualification for unemployment benefits. See Social Security Yearbook 1940, p. 64 et seq. . . .

In the present case, in holding that the claimants were not disqualified from receiving benefits, the circuit court said in part:

"Under the present form of the statute, the disqualification to receive benefits is not imposed on the employee unless a stoppage of work results from the labor dispute. On behalf of plaintiff it is contended that the language used in the amended act should be construed as having reference to the status of the employee. However, such interpretation would make the phrase 'stoppage of work' practically synonymous with 'unemployment' as used in the same sentence. Furthermore such interpretation would, as a practical proposition, leave the amendment without significance. The decisions dealing with this matter, both in England and in this country, uniformly support the construction accepted by the appeal board. It must be assumed that the legislature made the amendment of 1941, using the language quoted, in the light of prior judicial and administrative interpretation."

We cannot agree with plaintiff's argument that the circuit court's construction of section 29(c), as amended, is in conflict with the declaration of public policy stated in section 2 of the 1936 act. Said section provide in part:

"Declaration of policy. The legislature acting in the exercise of the police power of the state declares that the public policy of the state i as follows: . . . The systematic accumulation of funds during period of employment to provide benefits for periods of unemployment by set ting aside of unemployment reserves to be used for the benefit of person *unemployed through no fault of their own,* thus maintaining purchasing power and limiting the serious social consequences of relief assistance, is for the public good, and the general welfare of the people of this state."

Plaintiff's argument is based upon the assumptions that the claimants were wrongfully on strike; were not justified in striking; that the strike was their own fault; and that they were unemployed because of their own fault. As stated in said section 2, the basic purpose of the unemployment compensation law is to afford protection against the hazard of unemployment. The payment of unemployment benefits is not dependent upon the merits of a labor controversy, and we cannot establish a rule that in all instances an employee on strike is unemployed necessarily because of his own fault. The amendment of section 29(c) is not, we believe, in conflict with the policy of the act. Furthermore, the legislature had the power to adopt the amendment and, if a conflict with said section 2 resulted, the amendment must control. . . .

We are convinced that by the 1941 amendment of section 29(c) the legislature intended to disqualify an employee for benefits only when his unemployment resulted from a stoppage or substantial curtailment of the work and operations of the employer establishment because of a labor dispute. The phrase "stoppage of work" refers to the work and operations of the employer establishment and not to the work of the individual employee.

Plaintiff relies upon the case of Board of Review v. Mid-Continent Petroleum Corp., Okl. Sup., 141 P.2d 69, 72. . . . In considering a provision of the Oklahoma unemployment compensation law similar to the 1941 amendment of section 29(c), the court said:

"Had the Legislature intended to refer to the shut-down of the plant and not to the cessation of work by the employee, the term 'stoppage of operation' would have been far more appropriate. It seems to us that the word 'work' ordinarily refers to or comprehends the activities of the workman, not the operation of a factory. That portion of the Act . . . which disqualified a workman for benefits 'for any week in which . . . his total or partial unemployment is due to a stoppage of work which exists because of a labor dispute at the factory' refers, with respect to the workman, to his unemployment and to his stoppage of work. A strike in the labor sense is generally defined as a stoppage of work by common agreement of workingmen. 15 C.J.S., Conspiracy, p. 1008, Sec. 11. That was the definition evidently in the mind of the Legislature; the term 'stoppage of work' was considered as synonymous with 'strike.' "

We call attention to the dissenting opinion in the above Oklahoma case which states, in substance, that benefits should be paid to the employees if there was no stoppage of the employer's work or production. Such dissent states in part:

"In 1941 the Legislature again decided to change its policy. It provided disqualification for benefits 'For any week with respect to which the commission finds that his unemployment is due to a stoppage of work which exists at the factory, establishment or other premises at which he is or was last employed, because of a labor dispute . . .' All the parties herein virtually admit that a striking employee could recover under that act if the employee were not otherwise disqualified and there was no stoppage of production."

The majority opinion of the Oklahoma court is based upon its interpretation of the phrase "stoppage of work" as being synonymous with the word "strike." We cannot agree with such interpretation which is contrary to the clear meaning and import of the words used. Plaintiff also cites Miners in General Group v. Hix, 123 W. Va. 637, 17 S.E.2d 810, which involved a statute similar to the 1941 amendment of section 29(c). However, the factual situation presented in that case distinguishes it from the case at hand. Furthermore, such case did not involve the question as to whether or not claimant employees should be disqualified for benefits when there was no stoppage of the employer's work or production. The case of Bodinson Mfg. Co. v. California Employment Comm., Calif. App., 101 P.2d 165, affirmed 17 Cal. 2d 321 [109 P.2d 935], cited by the plaintiff and also cited in the Mid-Continent Petroleum Corporation case, supra, involved an entirely dissimilar statute which did not contain the phrase "stoppage of work." Our decision in Chrysler Corp. v. Smith, 297 Mich. 438, 298 N.W. 87, 135 A.L.R. 900, did not involve the interpretation of the 1941 amendment of section 29(c).

Plaintiff further contends that the circuit court's construction of the 1941 amendment, which construction we have hereinbefore affirmed, renders said amendment unconstitutional as denying plaintiff employer due process and equal protection of law. Under such contention plaintiff argues that the circuit court's construction results in arbitrary discrimination between employers by classifying them on the basis of (1) those who elect to stop work and close down and (2) those who do not elect to stop work or close down during a strike. The amendment, as construed, does not so classify employers. All employers who are similarly affected "because of a labor dispute" are treated alike. Under the amendment, as construed, employees are disqualified if the labor dispute does not result in such stoppage. This is a reasonable means of determining qualification for benefits and does not result in arbitrary or unjust discrimination between employers. . . .

We are satisfied that the 1941 amendment of section 29(c), as construed by the circuit court, does not result in an arbitrary or unjust classification of, or in discrimination between, employers involved in a labor dispute.

Under its contention of unconstitutionality, plaintiff further argues that, because the employer's contribution to the unemployment compensation fund is determined upon a variable tax rate based upon the employer's experience record, Act No. 1, Sec. 19, Pub. Acts 1936, Ex. Sess. as last amended by Act No. 364, Pub. Acts 1941, Comp. Laws Suppl. 1942 Sec. 8485-59 Stat. Ann. 1942 Cum. Supp. Sec. 17.520, the payment of unemployment benefits to employees on strike, without a judicial determination of the merits of the labor controversy, constitutes an arbitrary intervention by the State in aid of one party to the controversy. In other words, plaintiff claims that the 1941 amendment of section 29(c), a construed, is unconstitutional because it does not base disqualification for benefits upon a determination of the merits of the labor dispute resulting in unemployment, and because it imposes a penalty against the employer, which constitutes an intervention by the State in behalf of the employees in the labor dispute.   In Chrysler Corp. v. Smith, supra, Mr. Justice Wiest approved the following statement by the appeal board, pages 446, 447 of 297 Mich., at page 90 of 298 N.W., 135 A.L.R. 900:

"All interested parties who are involved in a claim for unemployment compensation . . . must be dealt with on an impartial basis.   The unemployment compensation fund should never be used to finance claimants who are directly involved in a labor dispute, nor should it ever be denied to claimants who are legally entitled to receive benefits. . . . None of the money accumulated in this fund should ever be disbursed for the purpose of financing a labor dispute nor should it be illegally withheld for the purpose of enabling an employer to break a strike. The State of Michigan, in so far as this Act is concerned, must remain neutral in all industrial controversies."

Plaintiff's argument is based upon the premise that the payment of compensation to employees on strike is a penalty upon the employer, because its rate of contribution to the unemployment fund will thereby be increased.   The public purpose of the unemployment compensation law is to alleviate the distress of unemployment, and the payment of benefits is not conditioned upon the merits of the labor dispute causing unemployment.   Likewise, the required contribution of the employer to the unemployment compensation fund is not determined upon the basis of the merits of the dispute.   The increase in the amount of the employer's contribution to the fund because of its experience record of payments to employees is not in any sense a penalty.   By the unemployment compensation act, the legislature provided a method of determining the employer's contribution to the compensation fund, and it did not see fit to base the amount of such contribution upon the merits of a labor dispute or upon the right or wrongdoing of the employer in connection with such dispute.   Such legislative enactment is presumed to be constitutional unless the contrary clearly appears. . . .

We conclude that in the present case the payment of unemployment benefits to claimant employees would not result in a penalty against plaintiff and would not constitute an intervention by the State on behalf of the employees in the pending labor dispute.   The payment of such benefits is not dependent upon a determination of the merits of the dispute.   The 1941 amendment of section 29(c), as construed, does not deny plaintiff due process or equal protection of law, and we hold such amendment to be constitutional.

Much of plaintiff's brief is devoted to arguing the wisdom of the 1941 amendment.   As it is not within our province to consider or to determine the wisdom or policy of legislative enactment such arguments might better have been addressed to the legislature.

The judgment of the circuit court is affirmed.   Public questions being involved no costs are allowed. . . .

BOYLES, J. (dissenting).

Under Section 29 of the unemployment compensation act, as amended by Act No. 364, Publ. Acts 1941 (Stat. Ann. 1941 Cum. Supp. Sec. 17.531), the law is stated to be as follows:

"An individual shall be disqualified for benefits: . . .

"(c) For any week with respect to which his total or partial unemployment is due to a stoppage of work existing because of a labor dispute in the establishment in which he is or was last employed: Provided, however, That no individual shall be disqualified under this section if he shall establish that he is not directly involved in such dispute. For the purpose of this section, no individual shall be deemed to be directly involved in a labor dispute, unless it is established:

"(1) That, at the time or in the course of a labor dispute in the establishment in which he was then employed, he shall in concert with one or more other employees have voluntarily stopped working other than at the direction of his employer, or . . ."

I think it is plain, from the context of (c) above, that it was the legislative intent to refer to "a labor dispute in the establishment," and not to "stoppage of work" in the establishment. The language is plain. It says "his . . . unemployment is due to a stoppage of work existing because of a labor dispute in the establishment."

An individual is disqualified from receiving unemployment compensation benefits for any week with respect to which his unemployment is due to a stoppage of work because of a labor dispute, unless he proves that he is not directly involved in such labor dispute; and he is not deemed to be directly involved in the labor dispute *unless it is established* that at the time of the labor dispute he *voluntarily stopped working,* in concert with one or more other employees. The corollary of this statement is that if an employee, in concert with one or more others, voluntarily stops working, at the time of a labor dispute, he is deemed to be directly involved in the labor dispute and disqualified from receiving compensation for any week with respect to which his unemployment was due to such stoppage of work (unless he otherwise establishes that he was not directly involved in such dispute).

In the instant case it is conceded that these claimants voluntarily quit work in concert, at the time of the labor dispute. They must establish the fact that they were not directly involved in the dispute. That they were directly involved is conceded. I think it was the legislative intent that they be disqualified from receiving unemployment compensation during the time their unemployment was due to their voluntary stoppage of work. Any other construction of the act would result in compelling an employer to indirectly pay an employee after he voluntarily quit work, through the indirect method of compelling the employer to contribute to the unemployment compensation fund out of which the employee received compensation. Such was not the legislative intent, and for that reason the award should be set aside, but without costs, a public question being involved.

WEIST, J. (dissenting).

I do not join in the opinion of Mr. Justice Starr. The gist of his opinion appears in his approval of the following quotation from the decision of the circuit judge:

" 'The legislature has seen fit to make the actual stoppage of work in the establishment concerned the controlling feature in determining whether the employee is disqualified from demanding and receiving unemployment compensation.' "

The term "stoppage of work," read in connection with disqualifications of an employee for compensation, relates to him as an individual and not to cessation of work in the factory. . . .

If the unemployment was by reason of voluntary cessation of work by the employee on account of his joinder in a strike there can be no compensation awarded, whether there is stoppage or continuance of plant operation.

In Board of Review et al. v. Mid-Continent Petroleum Corp., Okl. Sup., 141 P.2d 69, 76, the claimant urged that he was entitled to compensation unless stoppage of work at the plant caused a substantial shutdown where the strike took place. The court held that "stoppage of work," as used in the act, refers to the individual work of the employee. One of the justices in a concurring opinion aptly said:

"The thing which must exist at the factory is the labor dispute, not the stoppage of work. When a labor dispute at a factory results in a stoppage of work by the individual he is disqualified to receive benefits if he is a participant in the dispute and is not working by reason of his own voluntary desire, regardless of whether the factory stops or does not stop operating."

The claimant voluntarily stopped work and joined with several others in a strike, and the statute of the State bars granting him compensation.

The award in the circuit court should be reversed, with costs against claimant. . . .

NOTES

1. Under a state law containing the "stoppage of work" clause, would the regular workers at Factory B of the Regal Yacht Corporation be entitled to benefits for the period October 31 to November 11? Would your answer be different in states which omit the "stoppage of work" language? In addition to the Lawrence Baking Co. case, see Sakrison v. Pierce, 66 Ariz. 162, 185 P.2d 528 (1947); Robert S. Abbott Publishing Co. v. Annunzio, 414 Ill. 559, 112 N.E.2d 101 (1953). Compare Board of Review v. Mid-Continent Petroleum Corp., 193 Okla. 36, 141 P.2d 69 (1943); Chrysler Corp. v. Review Board, 120 Ind. App. 425, 92 N.E.2d 565 (1950).

2. How much of a curtailment is necessary to constitute a work stoppage? Suppose Factory B was successful in returning to only 50 per cent of normal production. Would the disqualification be applicable in the "stoppage of work" states? See Magner v. Kinney, 141 Neb. 122, 2 N.W.2d 689 (1942).

3. The leading case on the causal relationship required by the statu-

tory phrase, "unemployment due to a stoppage of work," is Mark Hopkins, Inc. v. California Employment Commission, 24 Cal. 2d 744, 151 P.2d 229 (1944). A portion of the court's opinion follows:

"In 1937 fifty-five San Francisco hotels entered into collective bargaining agreements with the San Francisco Local Joint Executive Board of the Hotel and Restaurant Employees International Alliance and Bar Tenders League of America. On July 1, 1941, these agreements expired by virtue of a notice given by the Local Joint Board, but were extended until August 30, 1941, pending negotiations for a new contract. Twenty-eight of the hotels were members of the Hotel Employers' Association of San Francisco, which represented them for collective bargaining purposes, and negotiations for an agreement with respect to these hotels were conducted by the association with the union. When no new agreement was reached upon the expiration of the extension of the old agreement, the union established picket lines at four of the hotels, and subsequently took strike action against various other hotels that were members of the association until eighteen of them were struck and their premises picketed.

"During this period the union sought to provide the striking employees with other work in hotels unaffected by the strike and in restaurants. The thirty-four claimants involved in this proceeding obtained such employment but for various reasons became unemployed again before the termination of the strike and applied for unemployment insurance benefits. They admittedly left their original work voluntarily because of a trade dispute, but contend that their original disqualification under section 56(a) of the Unemployment Insurance Act was terminated by their subsequent employment. . . .

"Section 56(a) of the California Unemployment Insurance Act, under which claimants were originally disqualified, provides that 'An individual is not eligible for benefits for unemployment, and no such benefit shall be payable to him . . . (a) If he left his work because of a trade dispute and for the period during which he continues out of work by reason of the fact that the trade dispute is still in active progress in the establishment in which he was employed.' (Stats. 1939, ch. 7, §4; Deering's Gen. Laws, 1939 Supp., Act 8780d, §56(a)). A claimant is thus ineligible for benefits if the trade dispute is the direct cause of his continuing out of work. If a claimant who leaves his work because of a trade dispute subsequently obtains a permanent full-time job, however, he is no longer out of work and the continuity of his unemployment is broken. If he loses his new job for reasons unrelated to the dispute, he is unemployed by reason, not of the trade dispute, but of the loss of the new employment . . . The trade dispute that caused him to leave his original employment is not the cause of his subsequent unemployment, and he would no more be disqualified from receiving benefits for such unemployment than if he had not been previously employed in the struck establishment.

"The termination of a claimant's disqualification by subsequent employment thus depends on whether it breaks the continuity of the

claimant's unemployment and the causal connection between his unemployment and the trade dispute. Such employment must be bona fide
and not a device to circumvent the statute. . . . It must sever completely the relation between the striking employee and his former employer. The strike itself simply suspends the employer-employee relationship but does not terminate it. . . . Mere temporary or casual work
does not sever this relationship, for it does not effectively replace the
former employment. The worker expects its termination and does not
look forward to that continuity of work and income that characterizes
permanent employment. . . . Similarly, part-time employment of a
claimant does not break the causal relation between the trade dispute
and his unemployment. . . . Only permanent full-time employment can
terminate the disqualification. If bona fide, it completely replaces the
claimant's former employment, terminating whatever relation existed
between the claimant and his former employer. It must be judged prospectively rather than retrospectively, with regard to the character of the
employment, how it was obtained, and whether it was in the regular
course of the employer's business and the customary occupation of the
claimant. . . . In the absence of special circumstances, employment of a
short duration admits of an inference that it was not entered into in
good faith with the intent that it be permanent."

FORD MOTOR CO. v. NEW JERSEY
DEPARTMENT OF LABOR AND INDUSTRY
Supreme Court, New Jersey, 1950
5 N.J. 494, 76 A.2d 256

HEHER, J.

The issue here is whether certain employees of the Ford Motor Company at its New Jersey assembly plants in Edgewater and Metuchen are
by force of R.S. 43:21-5(d) disqualified for unemployment compensation
for the period from May 11, 1949 to and including June 7, 1949, when
the New Jersey plants were shut down; and this, in turn, depends
upon whether the work stoppage resulted from a labor dispute at the
"factory, establishment, or other premises at which" the workmen were
"last employed," for there is such disqualification in that event unless the
workmen come within the provisions of subdivisions (1) and (2) of
that section.

The Appellate Division of the Superior Court sustained an allowance
of benefits to the respondent John Kiernan, an employee of Ford at its
Edgewater plant at the time in question, and the respondent George Bo-
hacs, then employed at its Metuchen plant; and on Ford's motion this
court certified the cause for appeal. Some 4,000 of Ford's New Jersey employees are in the same category.

The essential inquiry concerns the meaning of the phrase "factory,
establishment, or other premises." By the cited section of the statute,
the individual is disqualified for benefits:

"(d) For any week with respect to which it is found that his unemployment is due to a stoppage of work which exists because of a labor dispute at the factory, establishment, or other premises at which he is or was last employed; provided, that this subsection shall not apply if it is shown that: (1) He is not participating in or financing or directly interested in the labor dispute which caused the stoppage of work; and (2) He does not belong to a grade or class of workers of which, immediately before the commencement of the stoppage, there were members employed at the premises at which the stoppage occurs, any of whom are participating in or financing or directly interested in the dispute; provided, that if in any case in which (1) or (2) above applies separate branches of work which are commonly conducted as separate businesses in separate premises are conducted in separate departments of the same premises, each such department shall, for the purpose of this subsection, be deemed to be a separate factory, establishment, or other premises."

Ford is a Delaware corporation engaged in the manufacture and sale of Ford, Mercury and Lincoln automobiles. Its principal office and manufacturing plant are located at Dearborn, Michigan. There, it manufactures the "major parts" which are assembled into automobiles at its various assembly plants; and there it also maintains a central department for the purchase of parts which it does not itself manufacture, 60% of the whole, which are first shipped to Michigan and thence to the assembly plants. These assembly plants, it is said, are maintained to secure the benefit of the more favorable freight rates for the shipment of parts as compared with shipping charges for the completed unit. The Metuchen plant is used exclusively for the assembling of parts shipped from Dearborn into automobiles; the Edgewater plant is devoted to the same use, but there trucks are also boxed for export and a stock of parts and accessories is kept for dealers.

The Company also has factories and assembly plants abroad. Its operative units are grouped into seven "divisions." Two divisions are primarily concerned with the assembly process; one division operates a depot for automobile parts and accessories; another division manages the Company's business in foreign countries; and three divisions fabricate, manufacture and ship automobile parts to the assembly plants. The Metuchen plant is one of four plants comprising the Lincoln-Mercury Division; the Edgewater plant is one of fifteen plants constituting the Ford Assembly Division. The General Production Division includes the "Rouge," a term applied to Ford's multiple plant at Dearborn. . . .

All New Jersey employees of Ford, with minor exceptions, are members of the local union of International Union, United Automobile, Aircraft and Agricultural Implement Workers of America, CIO, known as UAWCIO, No. 906 at Edgewater and No. 980 at Metuchen, pursuant to closed-shop provisions of the master labor contract with the Union. Membership in the local union constitutes membership in International. Loss of union membership requires discharge from employment. With some exceptions, International is the exclusive bargaining agent for all these employees; and its negotiations in their behalf are usually on a company-wide basis with Ford's representatives at Dearborn. International's constitution conditions the local union's right to strike upon approval of International's executive board; but a local strike may be called only by the local union itself, after that course of action has been sanctioned by two-thirds of the membership voting on the question by secret ballot. International is empowered only to call a general strike within the industry after approving action is taken "by a referendum vote of the membership." International has more than 900 autonomous locals throughout the United States, representing not only employees of Ford but of many other employers as well. . . .

. . . On May 8, 1949 a strike was declared at the Rouge and the Detroit Lincoln plants, and the result was a cessation of all operations at those plants until June 2nd ensuing. The strike at these plants was authorized by the local unions and approved by the executive board of International. Neither of the New Jersey locals took a strike vote and neither authorized or approved the strike at the Michigan plants, or participated therein directly or indirectly. Indeed, the workers at these plants continued in service until laid off for want of material. Ford concedes that "As a result of this strike, the New Jersey plants were unable to receive further supplies or materials from Michigan and thus were forced to discontinue operations some six days later." The contention of respondents is that the Michigan strike and the underlying dispute were purely local and involved only the members of the Michigan locals. But Ford maintains that the basic issue of operational speed "was not local but company-wide involving the master contract provision applicable to all employees at all locations"; and that the subsequent arbitral settlement of the controversy operated to the advantage of the workers at all of Ford's assembly plants in the United States. Reference is here made to the refusal of International to "localize" the strike by confining it to Building "B" in Dearborn, and thus to permit "the recall of 72,000 members in Detroit, and 25,000 Ford employees in assembly plants throughout the country." International's response to this proposal was that the Ford workers "are equally conscious of the strength their solidarity gives them and of the economic pressure it is bringing to bear on the Company"; that they "recognize also that while only the "B" Building and the Lincoln workers are involved in the immediate dispute they are all directly affected by the basic principle." It was conceded below that the settlement was in terms made applicable only to the Michigan plants directly involved in the strike.

Each local union pays a per capita tax to the International, part of which, five cents per month, is set aside as International's "strike fund, to be drawn upon to aid Local Unions engaged in authorized strikes and in cases of lockout"; but it seems to be conceded that no part of this fund was used to finance the Michigan strike. It is said merely that "the fund was available for such purpose."

It is the insistence of Ford that the New Jersey assembly plants "are so functionally integrated and synchronized with the Michigan plants as to constitute a single establishment" within the intendment of R.S. 43: 21-5(d), and therefore the stoppage of work at these plants was due to a disqualifying labor dispute. The reasoning is that each plant is "an essential part" of Ford's manufacturing and distribution facilities; that without the plant at Dearborn, "the assembly plants would have no existence and would have no functions to perform"; and that the New Jersey assembly plants "have substantially but one function to perform, namely, that of assembling into complete motor vehicles the parts shipped" from Dearborn, and they "are in reality as much a part of the Ford establishment as the assembly plant located at Dearborn and perform the same functions," and so these plants, "functionally integrated with, completely dependent upon, and fully managed and controlled as part of the main plant in Michigan, together constitute an establishment within the purview of the Act."

The standard of "functional integration" is not to be found in the legislative expression. The statutory sense of the term "establishment" is not embracive of the whole of Ford's far-flung enterprise as a single industrial unit. It has reference to a distinct physical place of business. Such is its normal usage in business and in government. Phillips v. Walling, 324 U.S. 490 (1945). "Establishment" is defined as the "place where one is permanently fixed for residence or business"; also, "an institution or place of business." Webster's New International Dictionary, 2nd ed. . . .

If "establishment" be given the broad significance urged by Ford, then the words "factory" and "other premises" would have no meaning whatever. . . . The phrase " 'factory, establishment or other premises' takes color, not from 'establishment' as the plaintiff would have it, but rather from the word 'factory.' In common parlance the latter ordinarily means a single industrial plant. No one, for instance, would speak of the many units of General Motors Corporation, scattered as they are throughout several states, as a factory. . . . By embodying in the phrase the word 'establishment,' the legislative intent was to broaden the field of operation and extend the beneficence of the act to those employed in places other than factories," such as banks, theaters, hotels, mercantile houses and other places not of the factorial class. General Motors Corporation v. Mulquin, 134 Conn. 118, 55 Atl.(2d) 732 (1947). In common acceptation, "factory" is a "place" where material is fashioned, by human labor and machinery, for use in a different form. Red Hook Cold Storage Co. v. Department of Labor, 295 N.Y. 1, 64 N.E.(2d) 265 (1945).

In the absence of an explicit indication of a special meaning, words are to be given their common usage. Even where by amendment of a similar provision, the word "establishment" alone was used to define the statutory class, it was held that the change in terminology did not enlarge or diminish the group, and the determinative inquiry is whether "the unit under consideration is a separate establishment from the standpoint of employment and not whether it is a single enterprise from the standpoint of management or for the more efficient production of goods." Nordling v. Ford Motor Company, 231 Minn. 68, 42 N.W.(2d) 576 (1950). This case involved a stoppage of work at Ford's plant in St. Paul, Minnesota, as a result of the same labor dispute in Michigan involved in this proceeding; and the holding was that, while the St. Paul branch "is highly integrated with other units of the company for purposes of efficient management and operation," it is "separate insofar as the employees are concerned for the purpose of employment," and that "Employment under the act relates to services performed within the state or localized here." And in Tucker v. American Smelting & Refining Co., 189 Md. 250, 55 Atl.(2d) 692 (1947), the Court of Appeals of Maryland ruled that a copper smelter in Utah and a Baltimore refinery, which with sixteen other plants (mines, smelters and refineries) had a common ownership and management, were not one "establishment" within the purview of the statutory provision here under review, and so a stoppage of work at the Baltimore refinery due solely to a failure of copper supply from the strike-bound Utah smelter, did not serve to disqualify the unemployed workers at Baltimore for benefits. There, also, the local unions were members of an "international" C.I.O. union, under the same general relationship to the employer and to one another as exists here.

Appellant cites in support of the contrary interpretation Chrysler Corporation v. Smith, 297 Mich. 438, 298 N.W. 87 (1941); Chrysler Corporation v. Appeal Board of Michigan Unemployment Compensation Commission, 301 Mich. 351, 3 N.W.(2d) 302 (1942), certiorari denied 317 U.S. 635 (1942), and Spielmann v. Industrial Commission, 236 Wis. 240, 295 N.W. 1 (1940). But the cases are not in point. There, "establishment" alone was used to define the statutory class; and there were geographical proximity and other factors which in the judgment of the court made the totality of members one "establishment," so that a labor dispute at one plant would include all as a unitary whole.

Here, geographical separation and the nature of the function combine to make the New Jersey plants distinct establishments within the intendment of the statutory provision under consideration. Parts are there assembled into automobiles ready for regional market distribution. This localization of the plants is an essential part of Ford's own economy. The plants constitute separate factories or establishments. While integrated with the central plant, there is a physical and functional separation, for this purpose, which gives the local plants the status of a factory or an establishment in the statutory sense.

The view contra is not a realistic appraisal of the statutory policy of relief against involuntary unemployment, in the interest of general social and economic security. Protection against the hazards of economic insecurity is afforded by the compulsive setting aside of unemployment reserves for the benefit of persons unemployed after qualifying periods of employment, though able and available for work. R.S. 43:21-2. Contributions to New Jersey's unemployment reserves are made only for Ford's employees at the local plants; and only those of Ford's employees are eligible for benefits from the fund thus created. R.S. 43:21-7; 43:21-9. The spirit of a statute gives character and meaning to particular terms. Valenti v. Board of Review of Unemployment Compensation Commission, 4 N.J. 287, 72 Atl.(2d) 516 (1950). The statutory concept is an employment unit within the State, and compensation where the unemployment is involuntary. There is disqualification for benefits under the particular clause only where the unemployment is the result of a labor dispute at the factory, establishment, or other premises where the claimant "is or was last employed," and not then if individual nonparticipation is shown as provided in the statute. Physical place is the major element in this definition. . . . And in R.S. 43:20(g), which defines the term "employing unit," it is provided that "all individuals performing services within this State for any employing unit which maintains two or more separate establishments within this State shall be deemed to be employed by a single employing unit for all the purposes of this chapter." This provision would be entirely unnecessary if the word "establishment" had the broad connotation now ascribed to it by Ford. It is a contextual refutation of the thesis that "establishment" in section 21:5(d) embraces as a single unit all plants in a vast enterprise like Ford's merely because of "functional integrality" and "synchronization" with the central plant.

There was no participation in the strike here by the local unions or the individual claimants, such as constitutes a bar to relief under the statute. International's failure to "localize" the strike, however that was to be accomplished, is not attributable to the New Jersey locals or to the claimant members; and it is not a relevant circumstance in this inquiry that the standards set by the arbitral award were eventually extended to the New Jersey plants.

The judgment is accordingly affirmed.

NOTES

1. Were the workers at Factory A of the Regal Yacht Corporation entitled to unemployment benefits after September 15? If so, for how long? Compare with the principal case Ford Motor Co. v. Abercrombie, 207 Ga. 464, 62 S.E.2d 209 (1950). On the question of the difference, if any, where the term "establishment" alone is used, compare the Spielman and Chrysler cases cited in the principal case with Tennessee Coal, Iron & R. Co. v. Martin, 251 Ala. 153, 36 So.2d 535, 547 (1948). Would the provision concerning interest in the dispute have any bearing on the eligibility of the workers (a) in Factory A, or (b) in the main plant? In general, see the annotation to the Nordling case, 231 Minn. 68, 42 N.W.2d 576 (1950), quoted in the principal case, in 28 A.L.R.2d 287 (1953).

See also the following recent "establishment" cases, among others: Park v. Employment Security Board, 355 Mich. 103, 94 N.W.2d 407 (1959); Easthagen v. Naugle-Leck, Inc., 109 N.W.2d 556 (Minn. 1961); Weiss v. Klein Super Markets, Inc., 108 N.W.2d 4 (Minn. 1961); Capra v. Carpenter Paper Co., 104 N.W.2d 532 (Minn. 1960); In re Gilmartin, 10 N.Y.2d 16, 176 N.E.2d 51 (1961); In re Curatalo, 10 N.Y.2d 10, 176 N.E.2d 48 (1961); In re Ferrara, 10 N.Y.2d 1, 176 N.E.2d 43 (1961).

2. An amendment to the various state laws, sponsored by the Ford Motor Company and designed to reverse the holding in the principal case and similar holdings in a number of other states, added after the words

"factory, establishment, or other premises at which he is or was last employed" (see the statute supra page 566) the following words: "or because of a labor dispute at another place, either within or without this State, which is owned or operated by the same employing unit which owns or operates the premises at which he is or was last employed, and supplies materials or services necessary to the continued and usual operation of the premises at which he is or was last employed . . ." For this amendment, as enacted in Texas in 1955, see Tex. Civ. Stat., art. 5221b-3(d)(ii) (Vernon, 1955).

3. Would the office workers at the main plant be disqualified after October 9? See Outboard Marine & Manufacturing Co. v. Gordon, 403 Ill. 523, 87 N.E.2d 610 (1949). How about the janitor at the main plant? See Kieckhefer Container Co. v. Unemployment Compensation Commission, 125 N.J.L. 55, 13 A.2d 648 (1940). Consider the situation of the patternmakers at the main plant, supposing that they were independently organized with a separate contract of their own. See Caterpillar Tractor Co. v. Durkin, 380 Ill. 11, 42 N.E.2d 541 (1942).

4. If not already disqualified for some reason previously considered, what is the effect of the picketing activities of Factory A workers at the main plant? See Tucker v. American Smelting & Refining Co., 189 Md. 250, 55 A.2d 692 (1947).

See also Bowen v. Florida Industrial Commission, 117 So.2d 220 (Fla. Dist. Ct. App. 1959).

5. What effect, if any, did the refusal of main plant workers to cross the picket lines have? See Kalamazoo Tank & Silo Co. v. Unemployment Compensation Commission, 324 Mich. 101, 36 N.W.2d 226 (1949). Compare Local Union No. 222 v. Gordon, 406 Ill. 145, 92 N.E.2d 739 (1950).

The general rule is that in the absence of violence or threats thereof failure to cross a picket line disqualifies the applicant. See Pledger v. Department of Industrial Relations, 40 Ala. App. 127, 108 So.2d 697 (1959); Soricelli v. Board of Review, 46 N.J. Super. 299, 134 A.2d 723 (1957). As to whether violence constitutes a valid excuse for not crossing a picket line, compare Achenbach v. Board of Review, 179 N.E.2d 873 (Ind. 1962), with Deere Manufacturing Co. v. Iowa Employment Security Commission, 249 Iowa 1066, 90 N.W.2d 750 (1958).

6. In the principal case the court did not discuss the proviso in the disqualification section of the statute relating to employees not "directly interested" in the labor dispute. That issue lay at the heart of the case of Local No. 658 v. Brown Shoe Co., 403 Ill. 484, 87 N.E.2d 625 (1949). A portion of the court's opinion follows:

"Differences between the company and the union had arisen in January, 1946, over the question of repairing or correcting imperfectly manufactured parts of shoes and the pay for this work. It had previously been done by designated individuals in the department in which the defective operation had occurred. The company wanted each individual in a department to repair his own defective work. An increased rate of pay for this was proposed for a 30- to 90-day trial period, after which it was to be the subject of revision by negotiation. On the day this plan was instituted by the company, with the consent of the union, eighteen workers in the lasting department walked off the job when appointed by the employer as a 'team' to perform the work in their department under the new plan.   The resulting bottleneck, or gap, in the production line made it necessary for the rest of the line to come to a halt as soon as it was cleared of shoes in various stages of completion.   All other production and maintenance workers, including twenty-seven employees in the lasting department, other than the eighteen designated to work on the faulty shoes, remained at work.   The evidence shows that the union may have been actively urging the eighteen workers in the lasting department to stay on the job, and to return to work pending further negotiations, after they had stopped work. It was found as a fact that the union had not authorized the eighteen men to walk off the job. . . .

"In the present case it seems that in the first part of the proviso of section 7(d) the words 'participating in,' 'financing,' and 'directly interested in' have a different meaning, one from the other, and that the third expression is not superfluous as being included within the first.   Each of these expressions . . . refers not to the stoppage of work but to the labor dispute which causes the stoppage of work.   Appellees argue, however, that all of the production workers, except the eighteen, by continuing work until the plant was forced to shut down, had then no dispute of any kind or character with their employer.   This argument obscures or overlooks the distinction between labor dispute and resultant stoppage of work.   All the production workers on the one hand initially had a dispute with their employer and were engaged in the settlement thereof through their representative.   A labor dispute remains such until finally settled.   The plan agreed to was acceptable to the union, it may be presumed, because the wages thereby changed were to be the subject of renegotiation after a trial period.   The degree of acceptability of this plan to the individual union members, which might vary all the way from wholehearted acceptance to intense opposition to the plan, is of no moment in determining whether a work stoppage by a part of the union production workers immediately thereafter threw out of work all of the present claimants; the question is, did the ultimate stoppage trace back to the dispute as a matter of effect and cause.   When thus analyzed, all the facts show that it did.   If all production workers were interested directly in the dispute initially, the character of their interest remained direct until the dispute ceased to be a dispute.

"The bargaining agent of the union is given power to negotiate with the employer for the benefit of every employee, and to use the economic pressure of the entire group in obtaining satisfactory settlements of labor disputes.   Were it otherwise the bargaining agent of a union could subordinate the interests of the whole collective group to those of a part thereof.   The proof that appellees had a direct interest in the labor dispute in this case lies in the fact that the employer is subjected to the joint economic pressure of the whole group without power to negotiate with the dissatisfied few, although they constituted an essential link in a continuous joint operation of all of the employees.   When a labor dispute, which concerns a part or all employees, causes, as a direct result, a stoppage of work, it is one in which, under section 7(d), every employee hereby put out of employment is directly interested." 403 Ill. at 486-491, 87 N.E.2d at 627-628.

This is probably the most extreme holding on what constitutes being "directly interested" in a labor dispute. However, this case and others like it, e.g., Nobes v. Michigan Unemployment Commission, 313 Mich. 472, 21 N.W.2d 820 (1946), are widely accepted today. See Shadur, Unemployment Benefits and the "Labor Dispute" Disqualification, 17 U. Chi. L. Rev. 294, 329 (1950); Fierst and Spector, Unemployment Compensation in Labor Disputes, 49 Yale L.J. 461, 487 (1940).

The following recent cases deal with the "directly interested" problem: Chrysler Corp. v. California Unemployment Insurance Appeal Board, 18 Cal. Rptr. 843 (Dist. Ct. App. 1962); Unemployment Insurance Commission v. Louisville Builders Supply Co., 351 S.W.2d 157 (Ky. App. 1961); Henzel v. Commissioner, 365 P.2d 498 (Ore. 1961); Lepper v. Board of Review, 188 Pa. Super. 158, 146 A.2d 337 (1958); United Steelworkers, Local 5486 v. Board of Review, 12 Utah 2d 136, 363 P.2d 1116 (1961).

(iv) PRIVATE UNEMPLOYMENT BENEFIT PLANS

Private unemployment benefit plans have a long history but until a decade ago they never were widely adopted;[18] indeed, the introduction of the public unemployment compensation (UC) system in the 1930's and the return to full employment during the war years and the 1940's seemed almost to herald the demise of such plans.[19] The developments in the 1950's demonstrated that this was not to be the case. Several guaranteed annual wage plans continued in existence and a few others were adopted.[20] In 1955 the United Automobile Workers and the United Steelworkers of America negotiated the first supplemental unemployment benefit (SUB) plans and other unions in other industries followed suit. Various shutdown and severance pay plans also were developed.[21]

There were good reasons for these developments. The United Steelworkers of America had proposed a guaranteed annual wage (GAW) to the steel industry as early as 1943. Although the National War Labor

---

[18] Stewart, Unemployment Benefits in the United States (1930), provides the best historical summary of such plans, bringing the story down to the eve of the Great Depression.

[19] The Hormel & Company plan (meat-packing) was adopted in 1931 and the Nunn-Bush Company (shoes) plan was created in 1935.

[20] The 1961 contract between the Telegraphers and the Southern Pacific Railroad in effect guaranteed almost all telegraphers jobs until retirement. Annual guarantees can be found in some sugar refining contracts.

[21] The shutdown pay provisions in the meat-packing industry and various ILGWU contracts, the severance pay provisons involving General Electric and Westinghouse employees, and the reliance on early retirement clauses in pension plans illustrate three other possible approaches. Note also should be made of the individually vested security plans negotiated in the flat glass industry and by Local 3, International Brotherhood of Electrical Workers. In effect these enable workers to draw on individual thrift or savings funds when unemployed.

Board then had turned down the proposal, subsequent Board and presidential action had led to the appointment of a commission and the publication of an influential report [22] suggesting supplementation of UC benefits through private schemes as inherently more promising than wage guarantees. The 1949-1950 and 1954-1955 recessions showed that brimful employment would not last indefinitely. Technological advance in the automobile and steel industries was beginning to show up in reduced labor requirements. Also, postwar successes in bargaining for fringe or non-wage benefits stimulated union regard for private benefit programs. Pensions and insurance out of the way, there was new interest in protection against the most searing and depressing of all economic hazards — unemployment.

The 1955 steel and auto contracts provided no annual guarantee of wages but called instead for the creation of employer-financed trust funds out of which supplemental unemployment benefits would be paid to men who had been separated or laid off. Calling for employer contributions of from $.03 to $.05 per man hour worked, they paid weekly benefits of up to $25 a week for twenty-six weeks (fifty-two weeks in the steel industry). Eligibility was heavily dependent on seniority and benefits were integrated with UC benefits, i.e., if the SUB plan called for benefits of 50 per cent of wages and if a laid-off worker formerly earning $100 a week drew $30 per week in state UC benefits, the SUB plan would pay him an additional $20 per week. Comparable plans were also negotiated in the rubber and plastics, agricultural implement, and other industries.

The years since 1955 have been substantial liberalizations in the original SUB plans. Maximum benefit payments have been increased (to as much as $50 or $60 weekly plus allowances of $1.50 per week for up to four dependents), weekly wage guarantees (so-called "short work-week" benefits) of from 50 to 75 per cent of pay have been added, and benefit durations have gone up (a maximum of fifty-two weeks now is typical of most plans). The employer contributions also have been increased, often to as much as 10 cents an hour.

The experience under SUB plans generally has been favorable. Although contract negotiations almost invariably result in more benefits and higher employer contributions, the employer's maximum liability nevertheless is fixed and in some companies contributions have been for less than the maximum. Supplemental private benefits have played an important role in enhancing employee welfare; the SUB experience, particularly in autos and steel during the 1957-1958 and 1960-1961 recessions, is strong evidence of this. Clearly the SUB plans have not triggered a mad rush to liberalize state unemployment compensation benefits, thereby reducing the cost of private benefits. Neither, as the summary below shows, have they spread (like private pension plans and private health and welfare plans) to cover 25 to 40 million workers; in fact they have grown very little. On the other hand, continuing liberalization of SUB schemes in time well may lead to a guaranteed annual wage, or at least to something very near it. The United Steelworkers' slogan "total

[22] Latimer, Guaranteed Wages, Report to the President by the Advisory Board, Office of War Mobilization and Conversion (Jan. 31, 1947).

job security," the Steelworkers' January, 1965, contract with the Alan Wood Steel Company (providing (1) SUB payments plus state UC (benefits totaling 85 per cent of weekly base pay, (2) a minimum two-year benefit duration plus (3) a guaranteed annual income and a guaranteed 38-hour week) and intraunion political rivalry together suggest that a guaranteed period of employment after hiring, plus long periods of high (public *plus* private) unemployment benefits after layoff or separation, is a likely possibility for the steel industry and, possibly, other industries as well.

U.S. DEPT. OF HEALTH, EDUCATION AND WELFARE, THE COVERAGE OF SUPPLEMENTAL UNEMPLOYMENT BENEFIT PLANS, 1962*

In the mid-1950's unions and managements in some mass-production industries negotiated contracts inaugurating a new private employee benefit plan — supplemental unemployment benefits (SUB). Designed to aid workers during periods of unemployment, these new plans paid benefits to workers that supplemented a state's unemployment compensation payment. Workers had no vested interest in the contributions made by employers to most plans, and only the unemployed were entitled to benefits. Employer contributions for some plans, however, were credited and payable to an individual member or his heirs when he terminated employment, as well as when he became unemployed. The former plans were typically termed "pooled plans"; the latter, "individual accounts." [1] . . .

. . . Benchmark estimates, which are presented and analyzed [here] . . . confirm the view that "the coverage of supplemental unemployment benefit plans has changed little since their inception in the mid-1950's." [2] Moreover, they are concentrated among negotiated plans in industries whose employment is not likely to increase and may even decrease during the 1960's. Unless SUB plans are adopted in other industries, it seems likely that their coverage will not increase significantly and may even decrease during the remainder of the decade.

As indicated in Table 1, the coverage of SUB plans in 1962 was about 1.8 million, almost all of whom were members of negotiated plans. Nonnegotiated plans covered only 77,000 employees, and many of these plans covered the salaried employees of companies that had negotiated SUB plans covering production workers.

Since SUB plans are concentrated among negotiated plans, coverage

---

* U.S. Department of Health, Education and Welfare, Social Security Administration, Division of Research and Statistics, Research and Statistics Note No. 13 — 1964. Prepared by Joseph Krislov, now a member of the faculty of the University of Kentucky.

[1] For a brief discussion of the details of SUB plans, see Valdemar Carlson, Economic Security in the United States, New York, 1962, pp. 154-58. For a description of their operating experience, see John W. McConnell, Initial Experience in Operation of Supplemental Unemployment Benefit Plans in Harold W. Davey (Editor), New Dimensions in Collective Bargaining, New York, 1959, pp. 73-90.

[2] Krislov, Employee-Benefit plans, 1954-62 Social Security Bulletin, April 1964, p. 7.

tends to be concentrated among production workers. About two-thirds of the coverage was among plans whose membership was confined to production workers.[3] There is, however, some coverage of salaried employees. Plans whose membership included all the company's employees covered approximately one-half million, and those whose membership was limited to only salaried employees, 53,000.

SUB coverage is not only concentrated among negotiated plans, it is also concentrated among two large unions — the United Auto Workers (UAW) and the United Steelworkers of America (USA). Combined, these two unions accounted for about three-fourths of the SUB coverage in 1962, and they, as well as the Rubber Workers, have each succeeded in covering roughly 70 per cent of their memberships under SUB plans. . . . SUB coverage in 1962, which follows below, reflects the jurisdictions of these unions. . . .

Contributions to plans negotiated by the UAW in 1962 represented over half the total contributions ($158 million), while contributions to Steelworkers' plans constituted about one-third. The pattern of benefit payments in 1962 was practically the reverse. Benefits from plans negotiated by the Steelworkers accounted for about one-half, while benefits from plans negotiated by the UAW accounted for one-third of the total benefits paid in 1962 ($108 million).

Practically all workers were members of funded plans. Pooled funds predominated in 1962, with only 57,000 workers covered by individual account plans. Assets in 1962 totaled $372 million, excluding the contingent liability assumed by employers under the steelworkers' plans. Almost all of the assets were held by negotiated plans. About two-thirds of

Table 1. — Coverage, contributions and benefits of supplemental unemployment benefit plans by union representation, 1962

Union represented	Workers covered[1] (thousands)	Contributions (millions of dollars)	Benefits (millions of dollars)
All plans	1,849	$158.3	$107.5
Negotiated plans	1,772	156.9	103.7
Auto workers	779	85.3	36.5
Steelworkers	611	52.5	53.1
Rubber workers	107	3.0	1.8
Other unions[2]	276	16.2	12.2
Nonnegotiated plans . .	77	1.4	3.9

[1] Includes some workers not in bargaining unit.

[2] Includes such major unions as United Cement, Lime and Gypsum Workers; International Union of Electrical Workers; National Maritime Union; Retail Clerks' International Union; and United Glass and Ceramic Workers.

[3] Included among these plans are many negotiated by the United Steelworkers of America with a coverage provision that was not amenable to classification by type of employee covered because they typically specified that covered employees were "those in a group of employees of the company who are designated for such coverage."

all reserves were held by the trustees of plans negotiated by the UAW, largely because most of the reserves under the steel plans are in the form of the contingent liability.

NOTE

The first SUB plans posed a number of legal questions. Were SUB benefits "income" or "wages" disqualifying beneficiaries for state (public) UC benefits? Were employer contributions to SUB funds part of the "regular rate of pay" for computing overtime due under the Fair Labor Standards Act and the Walsh Healey Public Contracts Act? How were employer contributions to be treated for income tax purposes? Were SUB benefits "wages" subject to withholding and did they constitute taxable income to the employee? Article X of the 1955 SUB agreement between the United Auto Workers and the Ford Motor Company contained several saving clauses providing that "the Plan shall not become effective, and no Company contribution shall be made . . ." until favorable rulings on these questions had been received. Agreements between Ford Motor Company and the UAW-CIO, 36 L.R.R.M. 73 (1955).

Rulings generally favorable to SUB plans were in fact soon forthcoming. As of January 1, 1965, every state in the union but one — Virginia — authorized the receipt of supplemental unemployment benefits without affecting UC rights and benefits. Most jurisdictions relied on interpretative rulings by the attorney general or the state administrative agency. One (Maine) authorized supplementation as a result of a court decision while eight others (including California, Indiana, and Ohio) amended their UC laws. In 1955 the Wage-Hour Administrator also issued a favorable ruling, agreeing that employer contributions to negotiated SUB funds were "contributions irrevocably made by an employer to a trustee or third person . . ." and therefore properly excludable from regular rate calculations. Opinion Letter of Newell Brown, Administrator of the Wage and Hour and Public Contracts Divisions, to Joseph O. O'Reilly, Office of the General Counsel, Ford Motor Company, September 7, 1955. In 1956 the Internal Revenue Service took similar action. Employer contributions to SUB funds are an "ordinary and necessary business expense" and therefore deductible from gross income. Rev. Rul. 102, 1956-1, Cum. Bull. 91. Likewise, while SUB benefits constitute taxable income when received, they are not deemed to be "wages" for withholding tax purposes. Rev. Rul. 219, 1956 1, Cum Bull. 488.

The SUB plans not of the pooled-fund-no-vested interest variety are treated a little differently. In plans of the Libbey-Owens-Ford type, where X cents per hour goes into an individual employees "account," where the employee's interest is vested, and where he can draw benefits not only when he is laid off, but also if he is sick or permanently separated, different logics apply. While contributions are a proper employer "expense" and while they are not wages for "regular rate" calculations, they are "wages" for all withholding tax purposes, i.e., federal income tax, social security, and unemployment insurance.

b. RETIREMENT BENEFITS

(1) Old Age and Survivor's Insurance

At the end of 1949, an average male retired and drawing old-age benefits got $26.50 a month. A year later, at the end of 1950, retired men were getting an average of $44.60. Why? Collectively bargained pension plans always have constituted both a protest against, and a response to, meager social security benefits. Also some private pension plan developments have contributed directly to liberalizations of the Social Security Act. The Steel Board's Report (1949) and some related developments illustrate these interactions.

In the summer of 1949 President Truman appointed a Steel Industry Fact-Finding Board to head off a threatened national stoppage. Its report (part of which is printed below) came in September, 1949. The steel companies refused to accept the report as a basis for bargaining and a strike followed. In the meantime (on September 28, 1949, effective March 16, 1950) the UAW (CIO) had concluded a new contract with the Ford Motor Company which provided, among other things, for company pensions of $100 per month less primary old age insurance (social security) benefits for workers aged sixty-five with thirty years of company service. The Ford agreement, substantially similar to the recommendations of the Steel Board, was a landmark. When the Bethlehem Steel Company accepted the Board's proposals, the other steel companies followed suit and a seven-week strike in the industry was over.

During the summer of 1949 Congress had been leisurely considering changes in the social security program. Now a new force — some large corporations — came out in favor of higher OASI benefits. Ernest Breech of the Ford Motor Company and other industrial spokesmen testified that OASI benefits were too low. On October 5, 1949, the House adopted H.R. 6000, a bill to amend and liberalize the Social Security Act, by a vote of 333 to 14. The Senate followed suit (on June 20, 1950) by a vote of 81 to 2. After agreement had been reached on a Conference Bill, both houses passed it and Public Law 734 was signed by the President on August 28, 1950. Additional changes followed:[23]

1. In 1950 OASI was a system providing protection against the economic costs of two hazards: (1) old age and (2) premature death of a breadwinner. Now OASI is a three-hazard program. Since 1957 cash benefits also have been provided for persons permanently and totally dis-

---

[23] The best source of data on the OASDI system is the Social Security Bulletin, a monthly publication edited by the Social Security Adminstration, U.S. Dept. of Health, Education and Welfare. For sale by the Superintendent of Documents, a twelve-month subscription costs $2.75. Also to be noted is the Social Security Handbook on Old-Age, Survivors, and Disability Insurance (Second Edition) (U.S. Dept. of Health, Education and Welfare, Social Security Administration, Washington: USGPO, Jan. 1963), available from the Superintendent of Documents for $1.25.

abled.   Appropriately the measure now is known as the Old Age, Survivors and *Disability* Insurance (OASDI) program.

2. There have been extensive changes in coverage.   Many new groups have been covered on a compulsory basis (including farmers, additional farm workers and domestic employees, members of the armed forces, the self-employed members of all but one of the major professions and federal employees not under some federal staff retirement program).   Since 1950 coverage has been extended on an elective or voluntary agreement basis to members of state and local governmental retirement systems, to employees of nonprofit organizations, and to ministers and members of certain religious orders.   In 1964 self-employed physicians, federal employees in federal staff retirement programs, and state and local government employees comprised the main groups not in the system.   Better than nine workers out of ten now are under OASDI.

3. The total annual earnings on which taxes are levied and on which benefits are based have been increased twice — to $4200 beginning January 1, 1955, and to $4800 starting January 1, 1959.   There also have been changes in the tax rates.   In late 1964 current and projected OASDI tax rates were as follows:

TABLE II

Tax Rate for

Year	Employee	Employer	Self-Employed
1963-1965	3.625	3.625	5.4
1966-1967	4.125	4.125	6.2
1968 and after	4.625	4.625	6.9

4. Changes in the eligibility rules have added many new beneficiaries to the rolls.   New definitions of quarters of insured coverage and a reduction in the retirement age — from age sixty-five to age sixty-two — are two of the liberalizing mechanisms which have been used.   In May, 1964, over 19 million beneficiaries were on the OASDI rolls — about 15 million of them persons aged sixty-two or over.

5. The OASDI benefit formulas have been liberalized, thus increasing the size of monthly benefit payments.   The minimum monthly family benefit now is $40 and the maximum is $254, or 80 per cent of the wage earner's average monthly wage (but not less than 150 per cent of his "primary insurance amount"), whichever is smaller.   In 1950 the average monthly benefit going to retired workers was about $44.00; in May, 1964, it was about $77.00.

6. Reflecting changing labor market conditions, the increased size and political power of the beneficiary group, and shrinkages in non-OASDI-covered employment, the so-called "retirement test" has been extensively liberalized.   Where beneficiaries once could earn only up to $14.99 per month and stay on the benefit rolls, the earnings ceiling now has been raised to $1200 per year.   In addition, for every $2 of earnings from $1201

to $1700 benefits are reduced $1. Only after earnings exceed $1700 are OASDI benefits reduced on a dollar of benefits per dollar of earnings basis.

7. Congress has chosen to fund the OASDI system neither on a full reserve basis nor on a pay-as-you-go basis. Instead, the system's two reserve funds (the OASI trust fund and the DI trust fund) can best be described as "contingency reserves." In May, 1964, the OASI Trust Fund held over $19 billion in U.S. government obligations while the Disability Insurance Trust Fund disposed of more than $2 billion.

8. After many years of being blocked in the House Ways and Means Committee, the administration's "Medicare" bill was reported out and then passed by the House of Representatives on April 8, 1965, by a vote of 313-115. It appears almost certain that the Senate will also pass the measure. The Senate passed a similar bill as a rider to a Social Security law in 1964, but the House refused to accept it. While all the details of the program in its final form are not yet set because Senate passage has not occurred as of the manuscript deadline, the basic and controversial feature is seemingly settled. This feature is the setting up of a compulsory medical and hospital care insurance program for persons over 65 to be paid out of Social Security and to be financed by an increased payroll tax under Social Security.

A rival measure, called "Eldercare," strongly backed by the American Medical Association, would have provided benefits through present private programs such as Blue-Cross and Blue-Shield. There would have been federal subsidies out of general revenue to aid in keeping such a program solvent. Participation by elderly people would have been voluntary and would have required, in non-charity situations, contributions by covered persons to pay part of the costs.

9. Scores of cases have been decided concerning eligibility for disability benefits under the new disability provisions of the Act. To qualify, it is necessary to show that physical or mental impairments have made it impossible for the claimant to engage in "any substantial gainful activity," considering his age, education, work experience, and training.

The word "any" as used in this provision, it has been said, must be read in the light of what is reasonably possible, and not what is conceivable. Roop v. Flemming, 190 F. Supp. 820 (W.D. Va. 1960). The term must be considered in relation to the industrial complex in which the claimant resides. Sobel v. Flemming, 178 F. Supp. 891 (E.D. Pa. 1959).

The test, it has been held, must be subjective, Aaron v. Flemming, 168 F. Supp. 291 (M.D. Ala. 1958), and not concerned with a standard man of ordinary or customary ability, but with the particular person claiming benefits and the effect of the impairment on that person, Dunn v. Folsom, 166 F. Supp. 44 (W.D. Ark. 1958). The claimant is not required to show that he has exhausted every possible outlet in his attempt to obtain employment where he lacks experience for any other kind of work. Parfenuk v. Flemming, 182 F. Supp. 532 (D. Mass. 1960). Abstract speculation as to the possible attainment of employment does not constitute "evidence" sufficient to defeat a claim. Corn v. Flemming, 184 F. Supp. 490 (S.D. Fla. 1960).

The severity of the claimant's condition, it has been held, must be proved by medical evidence. Crooks v. Folsom, 156 F. Supp. 631 (E.D.N.Y. 1957). If there is a conflict in the medical evidence, weight will be given to that which is substantiated by clinical or laboratory findings. Butler v. Folsom, 167 F. Supp. 684 (W.D. Ark. 1958).

FLEMMING v. NESTOR

Supreme Court of the United States, 1960
363 U.S. 603, 80 Sup. Ct. 1367, 4 L. Ed. 2d 1435

MR. JUSTICE HARLAN delivered the opinion of the Court.

From a decision of the District Court for the District of Columbia holding §202(n) of the Social Security Act (68 Stat. 1083, as amended, 42 U.S.C. §402(n)) unconstitutional, the Secretary of Health, Education, and Welfare takes this direct appeal pursuant to 28 U.S.C. §1252. The challenged section, set forth in full in the margin,[1] provides for the termination of old-age, survivor, and disability insurance benefits payable to, or in certain cases in respect of, an alien individual who, after September 1, 1954 (the date of enactment of the section), is deported

[1] Section 202(n) provides as follows:

"(n)(1) If any individual is (after the date of enactment of this subsection) deported under paragraph (1), (2), (4), (5), (6), (7), (10), (11), (12), (14), (15), (16), (17), or (18) of section 241(a) of the Immigration and Nationality Act, then, notwithstanding any other provisions of this title —

"(A) no monthly benefit under this section or section 223 [42 U.S.C. §423, relating to "disability insurance benefits"] shall be paid to such individual, on the basis of his wages and self-employment income, for any month occurring (i) after the month in which the Secretary is notified by the Attorney General that such individual has been so deported, and (ii) before the month in which such individual is thereafter lawfully admitted to the United States for permanent residence,

"(B) if no benefit could be paid to such individual (or if no benefit could be paid to him if he were alive) for any month by reason of subparagraph (A), no monthly benefit under this section shall be paid, on the basis of his wages and self-employment income, for such month to any other person who is not a citizen of the United States and is outside the United States for any part of such month, and

"(C) no lump-sum death payment shall be made on the basis of such individual's wages and self-employment income if he dies (i) in or after the month in which such notice is received, and (ii) before the month in which he is thereafter lawfully admitted to the United States for permanent residence.

"Section 203(b) and (c) of this Act shall not apply with respect to any such individual for any month for which no monthly benefit may be paid to him by reason of this paragraph.

"(2) As soon as practicable after the deportation of any individual under any of the paragraphs of section 241(a) of the Immigration and Nationality Act enumerated in paragraph (1) in this subsection, the Attorney General shall notify the Secretary of such deportation."

The provisions of §241(a) of the Immigration and Nationality Act are summarized in notes 10, 13, post. . . .

under §241(a) of the Immigration and Nationality Act (8 U.S.C. §1251(a)) on any one of certain grounds specified in 202(n.)

Appellee, an alien, immigrated to this country from Bulgaria in 1913, and became eligible for old-age benefits in November 1955. In July 1956 he was deported pursuant to §241(a)(6)(c)(i) of the Immigration and Nationality Act for having been a member of the Communist Party from 1933 to 1939. This being one of the benefit-termination deportation grounds specified in §202(n), appellee's benefits were terminated soon thereafter, and notice of the termination was given to his wife, who had remained in this country. Upon his failure to obtain administrative reversal of the decision, appellee commenced this action in the District Court, pursuant to §205(g) of the Social Security Act (53 Stat. 1370, as amended, 42 U.S.C. §405(g)), to secure judicial review. On cross-motions for summary judgment, the District Court ruled for appellee, holding §202(n) unconstitutional under the Due Process Clause of the Fifth Amendment in that it deprived appellee of an accrued property right. 169 F. Supp. 922. The Secretary prosecuted an appeal to this Court, and, subject to a jurisdictional question hereinafter discussed, we set the case down for plenary hearing. 360 U.S. 915. . . .

I

We think that the District Court erred in holding that §202 (n) deprived appellee of an "accrued property right." 169 F. Supp., at 934. Appellee's right to Social Security benefits cannot properly be considered to have been of that order. . . .

The Social Security system may be accurately described as a form of social insurance, enacted pursuant to Congress' power to "spend money in aid of the 'general welfare,'" Helvering v. Davis [301 U.S. 619 (1937)] at 640, whereby persons gainfully employed, and those who employ them, are taxed to permit the payment of benefits to the retired and disabled, and their dependents. Plainly the expectation is that many members of the present productive work force will in turn become beneficiaries rather than supporters of the program. But each worker's benefits, though flowing from the contributions he made to the national economy while actively employed are not dependent on the degree to which he was called upon to support the system by taxation. It is apparent that the noncontractual interest of an employee covered by the Act cannot be soundly analogized to that of the holder of an annuity, whose right to benefits is bottomed on his contractual premium payments.

It is hardly profitable to engage in conceptualizations regarding "earned rights" and "gratuities." . . .

To engraft upon the Social Security system a concept of "accrued property rights" would deprive it of the flexibility and boldness in adjustment to ever-changing conditions which it demands. See Wollenberg, Vested Rights in Social-Security Benefits, 37 Ore. L. Rev. 299, 359. It was doubtless out of an awareness of the need for such flexibility that Congress included in the original Act, and has since retained, a clause expressly reserving to it "[t]he right to alter, amend, or repeal any provision" of the Act. §1104, 49 Stat. 648, 42 U.S.C. §1304. That provision makes express what is implicit in the institutional needs of the program. . . . It was pursuant to that provision that §202(n) was enacted.

We must conclude that a person covered by the Act has not such a right in benefit payments as would make every defeasance of "accrued" interests violative of the Due Process Clause of the Fifth Amendment.

I I

This is not to say, however, that Congress may exercise its power to modify the statutory scheme free of all constitutional restraint. The interest of a covered employee under the Act is of sufficient substance to fall within the protection from arbitrary governmental action afforded by the Due Process Clause. In judging the permissibility of the cut-off provisions of §202(n) from this standpoint, it is not within our authority to determine whether the Congressional judgment expressed in that section is sound or equitable, or whether it comports well or ill with the purposes of the Act. . . . Particularly when we deal with a withholding of a non-contractual benefit under a social welfare program such as this, we must recognize that the Due Process Clause can be thought to interpose a bar only if the statute manifests a patently arbitrary classification, utterly lacking in rational justification.

Such is not the case here. The fact of a beneficiary's residence abroad — in the case of a deportee, a presumably permanent residence — can be of obvious relevance to the question of eligibility. One benefit which may be thought to accrue to the economy from the Social Security system is the increased over-all national purchasing power resulting from taxation of productive elements of the economy to provide payments to the retired and disabled, who might otherwise be destitute or nearly so, and who would generally spend a comparatively large percentage of their benefit payments. This advantage would be lost as to payments made to one residing abroad. For these purposes, it is, of course, constitutionally irrelevant whether this reasoning in fact underlay the legislative decision, as it is irrelevant that the section does not extend to all whom the postulated rationale might in logic apply.[5] See United States v. Petrillo, 332 U.S. 1, 8-9; Steward Machine Co. v. Davis, 301 U.S. 548, 584-585; cf. Carmichael v. Southern Coal Co., 301 U.S. 495, 510-513. Nor, apart from this, can it be deemed irrational for Congress to have concluded that the public purse should not be utilized to contribute to the support of those deported on the grounds specified in the statute.

---

[5] The Act does not provide for the termination of benefits of nonresident citizens, or of some aliens who leave the country voluntarily — although many nonresident aliens do lose their eligibility by virtue of the provisions of §202(t), 70 Stat. 835, as amended, 42 U.S.C. §402(t) — or of aliens deported pursuant to paragraphs 3, 8, 9, or 13 of the 18 paragraphs of §241(a) of the Immigration and Nationality Act. See note 13, post.

We need go no further to find support for our conclusion that this provision of the Act cannot be condemned as so lacking in rational justification as to offend due process.

III

The remaining, and most insistently pressed, constitutional objections rest upon Art. I, §9 cl. 3, and Art. III, §2, cl. 3, of the Constitution, and the Sixth Amendment. It is said that the termination of appellee's benefits amounts to punishing him without a judicial trial, see Wong Wing v. United States, 163 U.S. 228; that the termination of benefits constitutes the imposition of punishment by legislative act, rendering §202(n) a bill of attainder, see United States v. Lovett, 328 U.S. 303; Cummings v. Missouri, 4 Wall. 277; and that the punishment exacted is imposed for past conduct not unlawful when engaged in, thereby violating the constitutional prohibition on ex post facto laws, see Ex parte Garland, 4 Wall. 333. Essential to the success of each of these contentions is the validity of characterizing as "punishment" in the constitutional sense the termination of benefits under §202(n). . . .

. . . [A]ppellee cannot successfully contend that the language and structure of §202(n), or the nature of the deprivation, requires us to recognize a punitive design. Cf. Wong Wing v. United States, supra (imprisonment, at hard labor up to one year, of person found to be unlawfully in the country). Here the sanction is the mere denial of a noncontractual governmental benefit. No affirmative disability or restraint is imposed, and certainly nothing approaching the "infamous punishment" of imprisonment, as in Wong Wing, on which great reliance is mistakenly placed. Moreover, for reasons already given (ante, pp. 611-612), it cannot be said, as was said of the statute in Cummings v. Missouri, supra, at 319; see Dent v. West Virginia, 129 U.S. 114, 126, that the disqualification of certain deportees from receipt of Social Security benefits while they are not lawfully in this country bears no rational connection to the purposes of the legislation of which it is a part, and must without more therefore be taken as evidencing a Congressional desire to punish. Appellee argues, however, that the history and scope of §202(n) prove that no such postulated purpose can be thought to have motivated the legislature, and that they persuasively show that a punitive purpose in fact lay behind the statute. We do not agree. . . .

Section 202(n) was enacted as a small part of an extensive revision of the Social Security program. The provision originated in the House of Representatives. H.R. 9366, 83d Cong., 2d Sess., §108. The discussion in the House Committee Report, H.R. Rep. No. 1698, 83d Cong., 2d Sess., pp. 5, 25, 77, does not express the purpose of the statute. However, it does say that the termination of benefits would apply to those persons who were "deported from the United States because of illegal entry, conviction of a crime, or subversive activity. . . ." Id., at 25. It was evidently the thought that such was the scope of the statute resulting from its application to deportation under the 14 named paragraphs of §241(a) of the Immigration and Nationality Act. Id., at 77.[10]

The Senate Committee rejected the proposal, for the stated reason that it had "not had an opportunity to give sufficient study to all the possible implications of this provision, which involves termination of benefit rights under the contributory program of old-age and survivors insurance. . . ." S. Rep. No. 1987, 83d Cong., 2d Sess., p. 23; see also id., at 76. However, in Conference, the proposal was restored in modified form,[11] and as modified was enacted as §202(n). See H.R. Conf. Rep. No. 2679, 83d Cong., 2d Sess., p. 18.

Appellee argues that this history demonstrates that Congress was not concerned with the *fact* of a beneficiary's deportation — which it is claimed alone would justify this legislation as being pursuant to a policy relevant to regulation of the Social Security system — but that it sought to reach certain *grounds* for deportation, thus evidencing a punitive intent.[12] It is impossible to find in this meagre history the unmistakable evidence of punitive intent which, under principles already discussed, are required before a Congressional enactment of this kind may be struck down. Even were that history to be taken as evidencing Congress' concern with the grounds, rather than the fact, of deportation, we do not think that this, standing alone, would suffice to establish a punitive purpose. . . . The legislative record, however, falls short of any persuasive showing that Congress was in fact concerned alone with the grounds of deportation. To be sure Congress did not apply the termination provision to all deportees. However, it is evident that neither did it rest the operation of the statute on the occurrence of the underlying act. The

---

[10] Paragraphs (1), (2), and (10) of §241(a) relate to unlawful entry, or entry not complying with certain conditions; paragraphs (6) and (7) apply to "subversive" and related activities; the remainder of the included paragraphs are concerned with convictions of designated crimes, or the commission of acts related to them, such as narcotics addiction or prostitution.

[11] For example, under the House version termination of benefits of a deportee would also have terminated benefits paid to secondary beneficiaries based on the earning records of the deportee. The Conference proposal limited this effect to secondary beneficiaries who were nonresident aliens. . . .

[12] Appellee also relies on the juxtaposition of the proposed §108 and certain other provisions, some of which were enacted and some of which were not. This argument is too conjectural to warrant discussion. In addition, reliance is placed on a letter written to the Senate Finance Committee by appellant's predecessor in office, opposing the enactment of what is now §202(u) of the Act, 70 Stat. 838, 42 U.S.C. §402(u), on the ground that the section was "in the nature of a penalty and based on considerations foreign to the objectives" of the program. Social Security Amendments of 1955, Hearings before the Senate Committee on Finance, 84th Cong., 2d Sess., p. 1319. The Secretary went on to say that "present law recognizes only three narrowly limited exceptions [of which §202(n) is one] to the basic principle that benefits are paid without regard to the attitudes, opinions, behavior, or personal characteristics of the individual. . . ." It should be observed, however, that the Secretary did not speak of §202(n) as a penalty, as he did of the proposed §202(u). The latter provision is concededly penal, and applies only pursuant to a judgment of a court in a criminal case.

fact of deportation itself remained an essential condition for loss of benefits, and even if a beneficiary were saved from deportation only through discretionary suspension by the Attorney General under §244 of the Immigration and Nationality Act (66 Stat. 214, 8 U.S.C. §1254), §202(n) would not reach him.

Moreover, the grounds for deportation referred to in the Committee Report embrace the great majority of those deported, as is evident from an examination of the four omitted grounds, summarized in the margin.[13] Inferences drawn from the omission of those grounds cannot establish, to the degree of certainty required, that Congressional concern was wholly with the acts leading to deportation, and not with the fact of deportation.[14] . . .

The same answer must be made to arguments drawn from the failure of Congress to apply §202(n) to beneficiaries voluntarily residing abroad. But cf. §202(t), ante, note 5. Congress may have failed to consider such persons; or it may have thought their number too slight, or the permanence of their voluntary residence abroad too uncertain, to warrant application of the statute to them, with its attendant administrative problems of supervision and enforcement. Again, we cannot with confidence reject all those alternatives which imaginativeness can bring to mind, save that one which might require the invalidation of the statute.

Reversed.

[The dissenting opinions of Justices Black, Douglas, and Brennan are omitted.]

NOTE

The Old Age, Survivors and Disability Insurance (OASDI) program is administered entirely by the U.S. government, except for the exercise of certain responsibilities for disability determination by the states. Major administrative functions include the collection of the social security taxes, the maintenance of wage records, eligibility determination, and the payment of benefits.

Tax collections are the responsibility of the Internal Revenue Service under the Federal Insurance Contributions Act (Subtitle C, c. 21, of the Internal Revenue Code of 1954) and under Sections 1401 and 1402 of the Code, which govern the payroll taxes on self-employment income. Each

---

[13] They are: (1) persons institutionalized at public expense within five years after entry because of "mental disease, defect, or deficiency" not shown to have arisen subsequent to admission (§241(a)(3)): (2) persons becoming a public charge within five years after entry from causes not shown to have arisen subsequent to admission (§241(a)(8)); (3) persons admitted as nonimmigrants (see §101(a)(15), 66 Stat. 167, 8 U.S.C. §1101(a)(15)) who fail to maintain, or comply with the conditions of, such status (§241(a)(9)); (4) persons knowingly and for gain inducing or aiding, prior to or within five years after entry, any other alien to enter or attempt to enter unlawfully (§241(a)(13)).

[14] Were we to engage in speculation, it would not be difficult to conjecture that Congress may have been led to exclude these four grounds of deportation out of compassionate or de minimis considerations.

covered employer must file a quarterly return, and forward his tax payment, together with taxes withheld from the wages of his employees, to the local District Director of Internal Revenue. His tax return must be accompanied by a report listing the name, social security number, and wages of each individual employed during the quarter. Individuals receiving covered self-employment income file annual returns and pay the social security tax with their regular federal income tax returns. Funds thus collected are appropriated in full to two trust funds, the Federal Old Age and Survivors Trust Fund and the Disability Insurance Trust Fund. Benefit payments and all administrative costs of the program, including those incurred by the Internal Revenue Service, are charged against these funds.

The remaining administrative functions involved in the OASDI program are performed by the Social Security Administration, an agency of the U.S. Department of Health, Education and Welfare, chiefly within the Administration's Bureau of Old Age, Survivors and Disability Insurance. The Bureau maintains a central administrative staff in Washington; a central accounting establishment in Baltimore for the maintenance of wage records; a number of area offices; and some 600 district offices (plus itinerant stations in over 3000 other communities) to provide direct contact with claimants, employers, and the public.

The record-keeping operations involved in the OASDI program are staggering. Earnings reports received from the Internal Revenue Service are processed and earnings records maintained for each covered individual; new benefit claims are processed; and regular monthly payments to beneficiaries are certified to the Treasury. During the fiscal year ending June 30, 1962, the Bureau of Old Age, Survivors and Disability Insurance received about 265 million earnings items from employers and the self-employed, for posting to 75 million individual accounts. During the same year the Bureau received over 4 million applications and claims while paying out $13.7 billion in benefits. At the end of June, 1964, about 19.5 beneficiaries were on the OASDI rolls, 15.2 million of them persons aged sixty-two or over.

Specific application has to be made for the benefits provided by the OASDI program. One of the major responsibilities of the local field offices is to receive such applications and to advise and assist claimants in their preparation. Upon receipt of a claim, the local field office obtains wage records from the central accounting establishment of the Bureau and makes an initial determination with respect to the eligibility of the claimant and the amount of benefit payable. If the award to the claimant is approved by the area office, certification for monthly benefit payments is made by that office to the Treasury. If a claim is disallowed, the claimant may petition the local office for reconsideration, which will be granted at the local and area level. If the reconsideration procedure fails to produce a determination satisfactory to the claimant, he may file an appeal for a hearing before a referee, may appeal the referee's decision to the Appeals Council of the Social Security Administration in Washington, and, in the last instance, may file a civil action in the United States

District Court for a review of the final decision of the Social Security Administration.

Despite the magnitude of the operations involved, in 1962 the total costs of administration, including the costs of social security tax collection incurred by the Internal Revenue Service, came to around $270 million, approximately 2 per cent of tax collections totaling about $12.5 billion. Employed were around 33 thousand people.

SOCIAL SECURITY BOARD v. NIEROTKO
Supreme Court of the United States, 1946
327 U.S. 358, 66 Sup. Ct. 637, 90 L. Ed. 718

MR. JUSTICE REED delivered the opinion of the Court.

A problem as to whether "back pay," which is granted to an employee under the National Labor Relations Act, shall be treated as "wages" under the Social Security Act comes before us on this record. If such "back pay" is a wage payment, there is also at issue the proper allocation of such sums to the quarters of coverage for which the "back pay" was allowed.

The respondent, Joseph Nierotko, was found by the National Labor Relations Board to have been wrongfully discharged for union activity by his employer, the Ford Motor Company, and was reinstated by that Board in his employment with directions for "back pay" for the period February 2, 1937, to September 25, 1939. The "back pay" was paid by the employer on July 18, 1941. Thereafter Nierotko requested the Social Security Board to credit him in the sum of the "back pay" on his Old Age and Survivor's Insurance account with the Board. In conformity with its minute of formal general action of March 27, 1942, the Board refused to credit Nierotko's "back pay" as wages. On review of the Board's decision, the District Court upheld the Board. The Circuit Court of Appeals reversed. 149 F.2d 273. . . . We granted certiorari.[4]

During the period for which "back pay" was awarded respondent the Federal Old Age Benefits were governed by Title II of the Social Security Act of 1935. . . . As Title II of the Social Security Act Amendments of 1939 became effective January 1, 1940, the actual payment of the "back wages" occurred thereafter. In our view the governing provisions which determined whether this "back pay" is wages are those of the earlier enactment.[5]

Wages are the basis for the administration of Federal Old Age Benefits. . . . Only those who earn wages are eligible for benefits. The periods of time during which wages were earned are important and may be crucial on eligibility under either the original act or the Amendments of

[4] The briefs of the Government advise us that more than thirty thousand individual employees were allowed "back pay" in "closed" cases by the National Labor Relations Board under Sec. 10(c), 49 Stat. 454, in the period 1939-1945. The aggregate in money exceeded $7,700,000 in the fiscal years 1939 to 1944 as shown by the reports of the N.L.R.B. for those years.

[5] By the foregoing statement it is not intended to imply that the variations in the definitions of wages between the two enactments are significant on the issues herein considered. . . .

1939. . . .   Obviously a sharply defined line between payments to employees which are wages and which are not is essential to proper administration.   Under the National Labor Relations Act an employee is described as "any individual whose work has ceased . . . because of any unfair labor practice."   Sec. 2(3), 49 Stat. 450, 29 U.S.C.A. Sec. 152(3).

The purpose of the "back pay" allowance is to effectuate the policies of the Labor Act for the preservation of industrial peace. . . .   While the legislative history of the Social Security Act and its amendments or the language of the enactments themselves do not specifically deal with whether or not "back pay" under the Labor Act is to be treated as wages under the Social Security Act, we think it plain that an individual, who is an employee under the Labor Act and who receives "back pay" for a period of time during which he was wrongfully separated from his job, is entitled to have that award of back pay treated as wages under the Social Security Act definitions which define wages as "remuneration for employment" and employment as "any service . . . performed . . . by an employee for his employer . . ."

Surely the "back pay" is remuneration.   Under Section 10(c) of the Labor Act, the Labor Board acts for the public to vindicate the prohibitions of the Labor Act against unfair labor practices . . . and to protect the right of employees to self-organization which is declared by Section 7, 29 U.S.C.A. Sec. 157.   It is also true that in requiring reparation to the employee through "back pay" that reparation is based upon the loss of wages which the employee has suffered from the employer's wrong. "Back pay" is not a fine or penalty imposed upon the employer by the Board.   Reinstatement and "back pay" are for the "protection of the employees and the redress of their grievances" to make them "whole."   Republic Steel Corp. v. Labor Board, 311 U.S. 7, 11, 12. . . .

Since Nierotko remained an employee under the definition of the Labor Act, although his employer had attempted to terminate the relationship, he had "employment" under that act and we need further only consider whether under the Social Security Act its definition of employment, as "any service . . . performed . . . by an employee for his employer," covers what Nierotko did for the Ford Motor Company.   The petitioner urges that Nierotko did not perform any service.   It points out that Congress in considering the Social Security Act thought of benefits as related to "wages earned" for "work done."   We are unable, however, to follow the Social Security Board in such a limited circumscription of the word "service."   The very words "any service . . . performed . . . for his employer," with the purpose of the Social Security Act in mind import breadth of coverage.   They admonish us against holding that "service" can be only productive activity.   We think that "service" as used by Congress in this definitive phrase means not only work actually done but the entire employer-employee relationship for which compensation is paid to the employee by the employer[17] . . .

[17] For example the Social Security Board's Regulations No. 3 in considering "wages" treats vacation allowances as wages.   26 CFR, 1940 Supp., 402.227(b). . . .
    Treasury Department Regulations No. 91 relating to the Employees' Tax and

. . . Congress might have declared that "back pay" awards under the Labor Act should or should not be treated as wages. Congress might have delegated to the Social Security Board to determine what compensation paid by employers to employees should be treated as wages. Except as such interpretive power may be included in the agencies' administrative functions, Congress did neither. . . . Congress used a well-understood word — "wages" — to indicate the receipts which were to govern taxes and benefits under the Social Security Act. There may be borderline payments to employees on which courts would follow administrative determination as to whether such payments were or were not wages under the act.

We conclude, that the Board's interpretation of this statute to exclude back pay goes . . . beyond the permissible limits of administrative interpretation.

Petitioner further questions the validity of the decision of the Circuit Court of Appeals on the ground that it must be inferred from the opinion that the "back pay" must be allocated as wages by the Board to the "calendar quarters" of the year in which the money would have been earned, if the employee had not been wrongfully discharged.

If, as we have held above, "back pay" is to be treated as wages, we have no doubt that it should be allocated to the periods when the regular wages were not paid as usual. Admittedly there are accounting difficulties which the Board will be called upon to solve but we do not believe they are insuperable.

Affirmed.

NOTES

1. "Wages" means remuneration paid for employment, and includes the cash value of remuneration paid in any medium other than cash. There is a monetary limitation of $4800 a year, and any remuneration above this amount is not counted. Retirement, sickness, and hospital benefit payments are excluded under certain circumstances specified in the definition.

In Ringling Bros.-Barnum & Bailey Combined Shows, Inc. v. Higgins, CCH Unemp. Ins. Serv., Fed., ¶9407 (S.D.N.Y. 1950), aff'd, 189 F.2d 865 (2d Cir. 1951), the issue was whether the cash value of the board and lodging furnished to the plaintiff's employees constituted "wages" within the meaning of the Act. The court held that it did, saying in part:

"It should be noted that the statute defined 'wages' to include *all* remuneration for employment and made no exception. Treasury Regulation 90 provides that 'facilities or privileges' offered by the employer are

---

the Employer's Tax under Title VIII of the Social Security Act, 1936, Art. 16, classifies dismissal pay, vacation allowances or sick pay, as wages. Regulations 106 under the Federal Insurance Contributions Act, 1940, pp. 48, 51, continues to consider vacation allowances as wages. It differentiates voluntary dismissal pay. . . .

not remuneration for services *if* such facilities or privileges are offered or furnished *merely* as a convenience to the employer or as a means of promoting the health, good will, contentment, or efficiency of his employees . . .

"However, it is clear that the board and lodging were furnished to the employees not merely for the convenience of the plaintiff but were remuneration for services and therefore constituted wages within the meaning of the applicable statute. Pacific American Fisheries, Inc. v. United States, 138 F.2d 464 (9th Cir. 1943). The board and lodging were a substantial part of the consideration for the performance of services by the employees. If the furnishing of the board and lodging were not remuneration for services, the plaintiff could have charged its employees for them.

"According to the testimony, the average wage received by an ordinary workingman with the circus was $60 a month plus board and lodging. It is quite doubtful if they could have procured board and lodging for $60 a month while constantly traveling, or that they would have been willing to work for $60 a month were they not furnished board and lodging or if they had to pay the plaintiff for these services out of the $60 a month. . . ."

2. In MacPherson v. Ewing, 107 F. Supp. 666 (N.D. Cal. 1952), the issue was whether eight monthly payments of $300 each, paid by the employer to the deceased during a period of the latter's illness, were "wages." The Administrator had found that these amounts were "generosity pay" and not within the definition, although not made pursuant to any benefit plan or system. In the words of the court:

"Whatever may have been the motives of the employer, whether prompted by generosity or selfishness, they are immaterial in determining the nature of the payments. The record, without dispute, shows that the relation of employer and employee existed. To permit the Administrator to rest decision upon the *motives* of the employer or upon the *effectiveness* or *adequacy* of the employee's services or labor, absent any element of fraud or deceit, would be to entrust to him a power far beyond that statutorily conferred upon him."

3. For a brief general discussion of this problem as it arises under statutes, see Annotation, 14 A.L.R.2d 634 (1950).

(2)   Responsibilities of Government and of Industry

REPORT AND RECOMMENDATIONS OF
STEEL INDUSTRY FACT-FINDING BOARD
SEPTEMBER 10, 1949
13 L.A. 46, 86-91, 97-98 (1949)

There was a time of unenlightened social opinion in this country when it was felt that the need of workers for insurance against the insecurities of modern economic life was the concern of nobody but the worker himself — or of charity. In some way he was supposed to be thrifty enough to put aside from his limited wages sufficient to take care of the "rainy day"

— loss of wages through illness and accident, expenses for doctors and hospitals, loss of income because of unemployment — and also to buy insurance for his family in case of his death. At the end of his years of working usefulness, he was supposed also to have saved enough to take care of him and his wife in his old age. Those who were not able to do all this were considered improvident, and were supposed to live on the bounty of their children or relatives — or in the county poorhouse.

In this generation, that philosophy has been rejected by overwhelming public opinion — and by most of industry itself. Today, it has generally been accepted that the worker is entitled to insurance against at least some of these hazards. . . .

Insurance against the other hazards of modern industrial and economic life — death, accident, disease, hospitalization — has not yet been provided at all by the Federal Government in any amount, and a bare beginning has been made in only four States. Apparently, the date of passage of such measures by the Congress is still far off.

There might be advantages to the economy as a whole if the Government were itself to extend the field of security to cover all these other hazards. It would certainly be more just to those millions of workers who have been and will be unable to secure these advantages either around the table of collective bargaining or through their own personal efforts. Social insurance, at least in its minimal form, should be founded on a universal base for all workers in the United States, as it now is with respect to old-age pensions and unemployment insurance. That could be done only by Government itself in a Nation-wide, compulsory program. But even if Government should decide to enact such insurance, there would still probably be the same inadequacy of amount that there is now in the field of old-age pensions. . . .

It is of some significance that of three great basic industries — steel, coal and railroads — steel alone has made no industry-wide move toward social security for its wage earners. This is all the more noteworthy because the larger fully integrated steel companies are partially in the coal mining and railroad business, and in dealing with many of their employees in such activities they are operating under such programs.

The money spent by employers in providing social insurance and pensions is a legitimate normal business expense. It should be the concern of management to see to it that the workers in a plant have adequate protection against insecurity. In this highly industrialized era, the insurance against these hazards should be considered an operational cost the same as insurance against occupational accident. So far as the effect on the worker and on the general economy is concerned, it makes little difference whether a crippling accident took place in the plant or outside the plant.

In many ways the cost of pensions and insurance is much akin to the cost of providing for maintenance and depreciation of plant and machinery, and for insurance against destruction and loss of tools and machines.

One of the reasons assigned by many of the companies for their inability to meet the demand for higher wage rates or the costs of plans for insurance and pensions and also for their inability to pay higher dividends was that they have adopted the definite policy of plowing back into modernization and replacement of plant, machinery, and equipment, all the earnings which they have accumulated during the recent years of substantial profits.

The evidence before us indicated that, since the end of the war, many steel companies have been engaged in large programs for such purposes, and that many have commitments of this nature for several years ahead. These programs have been financed largely through the use of undistributed profits, since depreciation reserves have been found to be inadequate.

The desirability of plant rehabiliation and modernization in the postwar years is obvious. . . .

No matter what the source is of modernization and expansion funds, however, the steel companies have, with some exceptions, overlooked the fact that the machines and plant on which the industry has prospered, and on which it must depend in the future, are not all made of metal or brick and mortar. They are also made of flesh and blood. And the human machines, like the inanimate machines, have a definite rate of depreciation. Of all our natural and national resources, our human resources are the most precious and useful, and should be most carefully hoarded and protected. These human machines need the same kind of treatment for depreciation and disability that the other machines are getting. Earnings are being used for rebuilding, replacing, and for maintaining the efficiency of plant; a part of these earnings should be used to take care of wear and tear and maintenance of the human machines in the industry — the workers.

What does that mean in terms of steelworkers? It should mean the use of earnings to insure against the full depreciation of the human body — say at age 65 — in the form of a pension or retirement allowance. It means insurance to take care of maintenance and provide against breakdowns in the human body caused by accident or disease. When a machine is laid up, it must still be provided for. Human machines that are laid up have to continue to eat and pay rent. Taking care of the human machine means also that when the worker dies, his widow and dependent minor children must be given a chance to avoid becoming immediate objects of charity. Above all we must remember that the human being has the dignity of man which he has a right to have preserved — he should not be cast aside when laid up temporarily or when used up permanently by a lifetime of labor. . . .

We are recommending . . . that in general the system . . . established by the parties should be noncontributory. We have come to this conclusion for the following reasons:

1. The general . . . substantial trend during the last year [is] toward the noncontributory form . . .

The Bureau of Internal Revenue, to which pension plans are submitted for approval for tax purposes, reports that through August 31, 1946, some 6,862 pension and profit-sharing plans covering 3,290,608 employees had been approved. The majority of the plans and the majority of the workers covered were in the noncontributory class. . . . The contributory plans seemed to predominate only in plants with smaller numbers of employees.

2. Such noncontributory plans will cover all the workers in a plant instead of making the individual employee elect, subject to individual temptation, to remain out of the plan in order not to forego any part of his current spendable income.

3. There will be no reduction in the present take-home pay of workers.

4. Stability will be promoted because costs can be better integrated into the labor cost structure.

5. Taxwise, more insurance [and pensions] can be bought for a given number of dollars than if the employee contributed from his own earnings after he had paid a tax on them himself.

The companies urged that making pensions noncontributory would tend to discourage the hiring of other than younger men. The union did not concede this; but it is apparently convinced that, in any event, other advantages outweigh this consideration. Moreover, the existence of a pension plan would be of benefit to the employers in that workers would be less apt to quit their jobs, having a stake in the pension plan, and the resulting drop in labor turn-over would to a degree result in reducing the expense of training replacements.

We have carefully considered and discussed the arguments on the other side. The claim was made that the contributory system is more calculated to preserve the dignity and self-reliance and incentive of the worker. There is no evidence, however, that workers in industries where the employer pays all are any less dignified or self-reliant than other workers, or that their employers are more paternalistic. So long as the cost of the plan is integrated into the labor cost structure and has a bearing on the rates set in wage negotiations the worker will know that he is in fact paying for his own insurance. Therefore, he will be just as careful about abuses and malingering as if he were contributing to the insurance fund directly. It is true that Government insurance is predominantly contributory, except with respect to unemployment insurance. But in private industry the general trend in collective bargaining is the other way. . . .

It seems to us that a similar study on pensions and retirement plans is even more necessary than was that on insurance [which the union and United States Steel Corporation jointly undertook in 1947]. The subject is much more involved, the basic principles much less defined, and the commitments are much more serious in both time and money. An insurance program runs from year to year, but a pension plan approaches permanency. . . .

A few guideposts are recommended. While the level of benefits may be changed by agreement of the parties from time to time, the basic features must be fixed at the outset. For the reasons already mentioned, the plan should be noncontributory. We believe that the retirement benefits recommended herein should be added to amounts available under title II of the Social Security Law.

The questions as to whether the payments should be a uniform flat one or should vary with the years of service and the rate of earnings, and whether there should be a minimum number of years to qualify for a pension, and what that minimum should be — all these questions should, we recommend, be left to collective bargaining after a full study has been made of all these factors.

(3) Private Pension Plans

For more than two decades the pressures inherent in an aging society, federal tax policy, and the collective bargaining push for retirement benefits have combined to focus considerable public attention on private pension plans.[24] Many of these plans have been developed through collective bargaining, although most have been unilaterally created by the employers, although now legally subject to collective bargaining. In all, there were probably more than 60,000 private pension plans in operation, many of them quite small. The great majority of them have been created since 1940.[25] In mid-1964 almost one out of every two employees in the nonagricultural labor force had some pension protection under a private program.

[24] For a detailed analysis of the experience up to 1932 with private pension plans and an exposition of actuarial and financial principles, see Latimer, Industrial Pension Systems in the United States and Canada (1932). The problems of establishing and administering pension plans are discussed in Bureau of National Affairs, Pensions and Profit Sharing (3d ed. 1964). Probably the best texts on pensions and pension plans are: Hamilton and Bronson, Pensions (1958); McGill, Fundamentals of Private Pensions (2d ed. 1964). Very useful also are three other books: Patterson, Legal Protection of Private Pension Expectations (1960); Aaron, Legal Status of Employee Benefit Rights Under Private Pension Plans (1961); McGill, Fulfilling Pension Expectations (1962). The last four of the above are Pension Research Council (Wharton School of Finance and Commerce, University of Pennsylvania) publications. Last and most recent is Bernstein, The Future of Private Pensions (1964).

See also Dean, Accounting for the Cost of Pensions — A Lien on Production, 28 Harv. Bus. Rev. 25 (July, 1950), 102 (Sept. 1950); Rowe and Paine, Pension Plans Under Collective Bargaining Agreements, 76 Mo. Lab. Rev. 237, 484, 714 (1953); Comment, Employee Pensions in Collective Bargaining, 59 Yale L.J. 678 (1950).

For a broad survey of government and private arrangements on income maintenance for the aged and future problems of an aging society, see Corson and McConnell, Economic Needs of Older People (1956); Joint Committee Print, 82d Cong., 2d Sess., Pensions in the United States (1952), part of which is abstracted infra page 625. See Senate Committee on Labor and Public Welfare, S. Rep. No. 1734, 84th Cong., 2d Sess., Welfare and Pension Plans Investigation (1956), for the results of a study and investigation of private pension plans established under collective bargaining.

[25] No one knows with certainty how many U.S. private pension plans are in existence. Figures from the U.S. Internal Revenue Service indicated there were about 92,000 qualified pension, profit-sharing, and stock bonus plans in existence at the end of 1963. Since many profit-sharing plans do not call for deferred benefits, most of more than 30,000 profit-sharing plans technically cannot be counted as pension plans. There were over 47,000 insured pension plans in force at the end of 1963, but some of these really were created for owners rather than employees.

Actually private pension plans are no innovation in American industry. Functioning mostly as instruments of management policy, the first private pension plans date from the late nineteenth century. They were viewed, variously, as means to induce long service and achieve reductions in employee turnover, to reduce payrolls by retiring high-paid older employees and replacing them with lower-paid younger workers, to increase efficiency, to assure employee loyalty, or to discourage unionism.

Railroads and allied carriers (the American Express Company's plan was created in 1875) were among the first to adopt pension programs. They were followed by some of the public utilities (like Consolidated Gas Company of New York, 1892) and a few banks and insurance companies. Pension plans in manufacturing industries generally developed later, the Carnegie Steel Company (1901) and the Standard Oil Company of New Jersey (1903) being among the earliest to adopt them. This is not to say that the needs of superannuated employees of these last industries were less urgent, only that the legal, economic, and institutional characteristics of the transportation, public utility, banking and insurance industry probably provided somewhat more incentive to adopt retirement plans. Business units of considerable size appeared early and the effect of pension outlays upon competitive position were probably less significant, where competition was limited by law and expenditures for pensions could be passed on to consumers. In railroading the hazardous nature of some employments and the risks of operating with superannuated employees also were important factors.

A half-century ago organized labor often was hostile or indifferent to pension plans. Pensions were considered paternalistic, or as economic and disciplinary weapons in the hands of employers, especially when pensions were considered as gratuities to which employees had no legally enforceable rights.[26] Many of the early pension plans were on a cash disbursement or pay-as-you-go basis and employees were dependent on the survival and continued prosperity of the enterprise long after retirement from active service.[27] Experience during the depression years, especially with the railroad plans, strengthened some of the opposition to employer-sponsored pension plans.[28] Also a number of international unions developed their own insurance or annuity programs. With the expansion of labor organization in the 1930's there was little new union pressure for pensions. This was primarily a reflection of first, weakness, and later, after the Wagner Act, of an overwhelming primary concern with organization.

Several factors encouraged the spread of employee retirement plans in the late 1930's and early 1940's, at the same time combining to change

[26] See Note, Legal Status of Private Industrial Pension Plans, 53 Harv. L. Rev. 1375 (1940); Note, Contractual Aspects of Pension Plan Modification, 56 Colum. L. Rev. 251 (1956).

[27] For example, when a merger took Morris and Company, the Chicago meatpacking firm, out of business in 1923, pensions to retirants soon were discontinued, even though the plan had called for a 3 per cent employee contribution.

[28] S. Rep. No. 6, 83d Cong., 1st Sess., Retirement Policies and the Railroad Retirement System, pt. 1, pp. 28, 57 (1953).

their characteristics. Insurance companies strongly promoted the sale of the group annuity plans first developed in the 1920's. The financial weakness of many pay-as-you-go systems had been revealed. Enactment of the Social Security Act in 1935 encouraged the adoption of supplementary plans, especially for employees whose salaries exceeded the social security maximum (then $3000 per year). Most important were the wartime developments.

For many years the Federal Internal Revenue Code had provided some fairly strong incentives for the establishment of employer retirement plans. Deductions from gross income were permitted employers for contributions to qualified pension trusts. The earnings of qualified trusts were exempted from federal taxes. Employees were not taxed on employer contributions to such pension plans or trusts. Even though contributions were fully vested, they were exempt from taxation until actually received by employees — in the form of retirement benefits. Mounting wartime individual income tax rates stimulated employer interest in plans deferring compensation to later years. (It also greatly stimulated executive interest in such plans.) The enactment of wartime corporation taxes, including the excess profits tax, had the effect of reducing the net or actual expenditures for pensions for some employers to about 20 per cent of the amount actually contributed.[29]

Perhaps as influential as tax incentives, however, were wartime wage stabilization policies. While manpower shortages and competition for labor were making it often difficult to attract and hold employees, cash wage increases were drastically restricted. Fringe benefits, particularly pension and insurance benefits not seen as inflationary, were not so limited. The Stabilization Act of October 2, 1964, c. 578, §10, 56 Stat. 768, empowered the President to limit wage increases, but excluded "insurance and pension benefits in a reasonable amount" from such limitations. Whereas changes in wage rates were subject to approval by the National War Labor Board,[30] in contrast the Economic Stabilization Director was authorized to define the excluded pension and insurance benefits.[31] He adopted the criterion, so far as pension plan contributions were concerned, of compliance with the requirements of Section 165(a) of the Internal Revenue Code, 32 C.F.R. §400.1(h)(1) (1944).

The net result was greatly sharpened interest, by both employers and unions, in fringe benefits. Although few pension plans were negotiated during the wartime period (most negotiated programs were for insurance), many employers established pension plans on a unilateral basis. Between 1940 and 1945 more than 5000 retirement plans were created, covering about 2 million employees. Unquestionably the wartime ex-

[29] Concerned lest pension plans become a medium for substantial tax avoidance, Congress adopted a number of amendments in 1942. See Hearings on Revenue Revision of 1942 Before House Committee on Ways and Means, 77th Cong. 2d Sess.; H.R. Rep. No. 2333, 77th Cong., 2d Sess., and Revenue Act of 1942, 56 Stat. 862.

[30] Exec. Order No. 9250, 7 Fed. Reg. 7871 (1942), as amended by Exec. Order No. 9381, 8 Fed. Reg. 13083 (1943).

[31] Exec. Order No. 9250, supra note 30, Title III, §2.

perience with fringe benefits in lieu of direct wage increases directly influenced postwar labor relations policies.[32]

In the postwar years negotiations by the United Mine Workers securing collective agreements for old age pensions,[33] the decision of the National Labor Relations Board that pensions were a subject upon which collective bargaining could be required,[34] and the 1949 recommendations of the President's Fact-Finding Board that the steel industry provide noncontributory pensions,[35] ushered in a period in which the major demands of the large industrial unions were for pension plans. In the subsequent fifteen-year period another 15 million employees have obtained some kind of pension coverage.

The pension plans developed in recent years, especially those established through collective bargaining, differ in many ways from earlier, unilaterally adopted plans. The latter generally have related benefits to levels of earnings and length of active service, usually by taking a percentage of earnings and multiplying the resultant figure by years of service. Some of the negotiated plans, on the other hand, provide the same level of benefits to all workers, regardless of wages in active service. Although many do relate benefits to earnings, bargained plans rely heavily on length of service in benefit calculations.[36] Before World War II the private pension programs often called for employee contributions, but war and rising taxes have changed this. Today's pensions are overwhelmingly financed by employer contributions, in a national ratio of $6 or $7 to every $1 from employees. Provision for compulsory retirement at a prescribed age is a characteristic of many unilateral systems. Unions, by contrast, generally have opposed compulsory retirement, and under negotiated plans provisions are often made for active employment beyond the normal retirement age.

The labor's push for pension plans was an important force behind the Social Security Act Amendments of 1950, the first major changes since 1939. A number of the private pension plans adopted before mid-1950 used benefit formulas in which the OASI primary benefit was *included* in calculating retirement benefits. Hence increases in statutory (OASI) benefits did not necessarily increase benefits to employees; they simply reduced amounts due from the private plans. One consequence, therefore, was enlarged employer support for OASI benefit liberalization. As a second consequence, many unions and employers renegotiated pensions

[32] Latimer, Social Security in Collective Bargaining, N.Y.U. 1st Annual Conf. on Labor Law 6, 7 (1948).

[33] See United States v. United Mine Workers, 330 U.S. 258, 286 (1947).

[34] Inland Steel Co. v. NLRB, 170 F.2d 247 (7th Cir. 1948), cert. denied, 336 U.S. 960 (1949).

[35] Report to the President on the Labor Dispute in the Basic Steel Industry by the Steel Industry Board Appointed July 15, 1949, p. 9 (1949).

[36] For example, the 1964 contracts negotiated by the United Automobile Workers and the major auto companies generally provided for pensions of $4.25 per month per year of credited service. Thus a forty-year man would get $170 a month and a twenty-year man $85 a month.

to provide benefits *exclusive* of, instead of inclusive of, benefits already provided by law.[37]

Establishing a pension plan involves financial, economic, and legal problems. Compliance with requirements of the Internal Revenue Code of 1954, §§401(a), 404, 501(a), is a condition to exemption from income taxation of the earnings of any fund created for the payment of pensions, and may likewise be a condition to the employer's right to deduct from gross income the full amount of his contribution. If the employer's contributions are to a fund established by a union, the Labor Management Relations Act, 1947, 61 Stat. 1957, §302(c)(5), 29 U.S.C. §186(c)(5), must be followed. State corporation, banking, insurance, and trust laws may also apply.

Congressional concern with the administration of pension and other welfare plans was reflected in 1958 in the enactment of the Welfare and Pension Plans Disclosure Act (70 Stat. 997, 29 U.S.C. §§301-309). This statute was strengthened in 1962. It requires disclosure of the description and operation of covered plans to beneficiaries and to the Secretary of Labor, and provides administrative, civil, and criminal remedies for its enforcement.

At the end of 1963, more than 23 million individuals had some pension plan coverage, more than 2 million beneficiaries were drawing benefits from these plans, their benefits in 1962 totaling over $2.1 billion.[38]

INLAND STEEL CO. v. NLRB

United States Court of Appeals, Seventh Circuit, 1948
170 F.2d 247, certiorari denied, 336 U.S. 960 (1949)

MAJOR, J. . . .

In the beginning, it seems appropriate to set forth that portion of the Board's order which gives rise to the questions here in controversy. The order requires the Company to

"Cease and desist from:

"(a) Refusing to bargain collectively with Local Unions Nos. 1010 and 64, United Steelworkers of America (CIO), with respect to its pension and retirement policies . . ."

. . . It follows that the issue for decision is, as the Board asserts, whether pension and retirement plans are part of the subject matter of compulsory collective bargaining within the meaning of the Act . . .

Briefly, the plan as originally initiated on January 1, 1936, provided for the establishment of a contributory plan for the payment of retirement annuities pursuant to a contract between the Company and the Equitable Life Assurance Society. Only employees with earnings of $250.00 or more per month were eligible to participate. Effective December 31, 1943, the

---

[37] For a good summary, see Stanley, Pension Plans Negotiated by the UAW-CIO, 77 Mo. Lab. Rev. 13 (1954).

[38] Krislov, Employee-Benefit Plans, 1954-1962, U.S. Social Security Bulletin 16 Apr. 1964).

plan was extended to cover all employees regardless of the amount of their earnings, provided they had attained the age of 30 and had five years of service. The plan from the beginning was optional with the employees, who could drop out at any time, with rights upon retirement fixed as of that date. . . .

An integral and it is asserted an essential part of the plan from the beginning was that employees be compulsorily retired at the age of 65. (There are some exceptions to this requirement which are not material here.)

The Company's plan had been in effect for five and one-half years when, because of the increased demands for production and with a shortage of manpower occasioned by the war, it was compelled to suspend the retirement of its employees as provided by its established program. In consequence there were no retirements for age at either of the plants involved in the instant proceeding from August 26, 1941 to April 1, 1946. This temporary suspension of the compulsory retirement rule was abrogated, and it was determined by the Company that no retirements should be deferred beyond June 30, 1946. By April 1, 1946, all of the Company's employees, some 224 in number, who had reached the age of 65, had been retired. Thereupon, the Union file with the company a grievance protesting its action in the automatic retirement of employees at the age of 65. The Company refused to discuss this grievance with the Union, taking the position that it was not required under the Act to do so or to bargain concerning its retirement and pension plan, and particularly concerning the compulsory retirement feature thereof. Whereupon, the instant proceeding was instituted before the Board, with the result already noted. . . .

The Supreme Court in National Licorice Co. v. N.L.R.B., 309 U.S. 350, 360, held that collective bargaining extends to matters involving discharge actions and . . . the Company in its contract with the Union has so recognized. We are unable to differentiate between the conceded right of a Union to bargain concerning a discharge, and particularly a nondiscriminatory discharge, of an employee and its right to bargain concerning the age at which he is compelled to retire. In either case, the employee loses his job at the command of the employer; in either case, the effect upon the "conditions" of the person's employment is that the employment is terminated, and we think, in either case, the affected employee is entitled under the Act to bargain collectively through his duly selected representatives concerning such termination. . . . The Company's position that the age of retirement is not a matter for bargaining leads to the incongruous result that a proper bargaining matter is presented if an employee is suddenly discharged on the day before he reaches the age of 65, but that the next day, when he is subject to compulsory retirement, his Union is without right to bargain concerning such retirement. . . .

The Company also concedes that seniority is a proper matter for collective bargaining and, as already noted, has so recognized by its contract with the Union. It states in its brief that seniority is "the very heart of conditions of employment." Among the purposes which seniority serves is the protection of employees against arbitrary management conduct in connection with hire, promotion, demotion, transfer and discharge, and the creation of job security for older workers. A unilateral retirement and pension plan has as its main objective not job security for older workers but their retirement at an age predetermined by the Company, and we think the latter is as much included in "conditions of employment" as the former. What would be the purpose of protecting senior employees against lay-off when an employer could arbitrarily and unilaterally place the compulsory retirement age at any level which might suit its purpose? . . .

The Company in its brief as to seniority rights states that it "affects the employee's status every day." In contrast, the plain implication to be drawn from its argument is that an employee is a stranger to a retirement and pension plan during all the days of his employment and that it affects him in no manner until he arrives at the retirement age. We think such reasoning is without logic. . . . It surely cannot be seriously disputed but that such a pledge on the part of the Company forms a part of the consideration for work performed, and we see no reason why an employee entitled to the benefit of the plan could not upon the refusal of the Company to pay, sue and recover such benefits. In this view, the pension thus promised would appear to be as much a part of his "wages" as the money paid him at the time of the rendition of his services. . . .

The Board cites a number of authorities wherein the term "wages" in other fields of law has been broadly construed in support of its conclusion in the instant case that the term includes retirement and pension benefits for the purpose of collective bargaining. . . . For instance, the Board has been sustained in a number of cases where it has treated for the purpose of remedying the effects of discriminatory discharges, in violation of Sec. 8(3) of the Act, pension and other "beneficial insurance rights of employees as part of the employees' real wages and, in accordance with its authority under Sec. 10(c), to order reinstatement of employees with . . . back pay," and has required the employer to restore such benefits to employees discriminated against. See Butler Bros., et al. v. N.L.R.B., 7 Cir., 134 F.(2d) 981, 985; General Motors Corp. v. N.L.R.B., 3 Cir., 150 F.(2d) 201, and N.L.R.B. v. Stackpole Carbon Co., 3 Cir., 128 F.(2d) 188. In the latter case, the court stated (128 F.(2d) at page 191) that the Board's conclusion "seems to us to be in line with the purposes of the Act for the insurance rights in substance were part of the employee's wages."

In the Social Security Act, 49 Stat. 642, Sec. 907, 42 U.S.C.A. sec. 1107, the same Congress which enacted the National Labor Relations Act defined taxable "wages" as embracing "all remuneration . . . [for services performed by an employee for his employer], including the cash value of all remuneration paid in any medium other than cash . . ." This definition has been construed, as the Supreme Court noted, in Social Security Board v. Nierotko, 327 U.S. 358, 365, as including "vacation allowances," "sick pay," and "dismissal pay."

In the field of taxation, pension and retirement allowances have been deemed to be income of the recipients within the Internal Revenue Act definition of wages as "compensation for personal services." 26 U.S.C.A. Int. Rev. Code Sec 22(a). Thus, in Hooker v. Hoey, D.C., 27 F. Supp. 489, 490, affirmed, 2 Cir., 107 F.(2d) 1016, the court said: "It cannot be doubted that pensions or retiring allowances paid because of past services are one form of compensation for personal service and constitute taxable income . . ."

It is our view, therefore, and we so hold that the order of the Board, insofar as it requires the Company to bargain with respect to retirement and pension matters, is valid, and the petition to review, filed by the Company in No. 9612, is denied.

NOTES

1. In W. W. Cross & Co. v. NLRB, 174 F.2d 875 (1st Cir. 1949), the court, in reliance on the Inland Steel case, enforced an order of the Board that the employer bargain with the union on a group health and accident insurance program which the employer had unilaterally initiated.

2. In Weyerhaeuser Timber Co., 87 N.L.R.B. 672 (1949), the NLRB held that the price of meals served at the place of employment where there is no public eating place available is a subject of compulsory bargaining. The Board took a similar position with respect to leases on company homes in Elgin Standard Brick Manufacturing Co., 90 N.L.R.B. 1467 (1950). Compare NLRB v. Bemis Bros. Bag Co., 206 F.2d 33 (5th Cir. 1953), where the employer was not required to negotiate over the rental of company-owned houses because the rent was not under market price and the employees were not required to live in the company houses.

3. Suppose the employer in the Inland Steel case had countered the union's demand by proposing inclusion in the contract of a provision placing decisions with respect to pensions and retirement in the exclusive control of management. See the American National Insurance Co. case, supra page 434.

KOLODRUBETZ, CHARACTERISTICS OF THE PRIVATE PENSION STRUCTURE
87 Monthly Labor Review 774 (1964)

The private pension structure represents a major element in the promise of security in retirement for millions of the Nation's workers and their dependents. Although private plans cannot be expected to achieve the same status as the universal social security system, with its broad protection and coverage, their place as a permanent fixture in the country's overall security structure is assured. The coverage of private plans doubled during the period 1950-60, and is expected to double again by 1980. . . .

Scope and Method

A private pension plan, as defined for this study, is a plan established unilaterally by an employer or a union, or jointly by both, that provides a cash income for life to qualified workers upon retirement. . . .

The chief source of data for this study were the reports and documents filed with the Department's Office of Labor-Management and Welfare-Pension Reports, pursuant to the law, by private pension plans covering more than 25 workers. . . .

Growth

About 16,000 private pension plans, as defined for this study, covering more than 15.8 million active workers and paying benefits to about 1.2 million retired workers, filed financial reports with the Department of Labor for 1960. About two-thirds of the plans for which the date of establishment was known, accounting for half of the coverage, were established since 1949. . . .

Size of Plans

The plans studied ranged in size from 26 active and retired workers (the smallest plan required to file reports in 1960) to approximately 370,-000 active workers. The number of persons currently drawing benefits from the plans ranged from none to over 10,000 per plan and totaled about 1.2 million.

Although most private pension plans are small-scale undertakings, over 60 percent of the covered workers were in plans with 5,000 workers or more. . . . The 15 largest plans — 7 multiemployer, 7 single employer, and 1 union-operated — each with over 100,000 active workers altogether had over a sixth of the worker coverage. Nearly 14,000 plans with fewer than 1,000 members each accounted for almost 90 percent of the plans, but only 15 percent of worker coverage. Over 60 percent of the plans had fewer than 200 active members each and less than 5 percent of the coverage.

Industry and Type of Employer. . . .

In general, multiemployer plans were predominant in industries that are marked by multiemployer bargaining patterns. Such plans represent, roughly, three-fifths of the coverage of all multiemployer bargaining agreements (excluding railroads).[39] Single employer plans predominate in industries in which the bargaining relationship is on an establishment or company basis, as well as in industries where collective bargaining is uncommon.

Collective Bargaining and Financing

Reports for slightly more than 1 out of 3 plans, covering about 2 out of 3 workers, indicated that the plan was mentioned in a collective bargaining agreement. . . .

Employers financed the entire cost of retirement benefits (noncontributory plans) of about 3 out of 4 plans covering about the same proportion of workers. . . . A fourth of the plans, with about a fourth of the workers, were financed by joint employer-employee contributions (contributory plans), while in a small number of union-sponsored and -operated

[39] Railroad workers are covered by the Railroad Retirement Act, 45 U.S.C. §228. Many railroad companies, however, have supplementary plans. — ED.

plans (110), accounting for about a quarter million workers, the workers alone financed the plans. Most multiemployer plans were noncontributory, while 30 percent of the single employer plans with about the same proportion of the workers required the employees to contribute. Moreover, a higher proportion of plans not "mentioned" in collective bargaining than those "mentioned" were contributory.

The pattern of financing the plans reflected the industrial pattern of bargaining; industries mostly with negotiated plans had mostly noncontributory plans, and vice versa. Noncontributory plans, therefore, were common in the manufacturing industries (such as apparel, and printing and publishing) which had a heavy concentration of negotiated, multiemployer plans and in the highly unionized metal working industries. On the other hand, nonmanufacturing industries (such as finance) and some industries in manufacturing (such as chemicals, petroleum, and textiles), where single employer plans not under bargaining predominated, had a significant number of jointly financed plans.

Included in the jointly financed plans were 489 plans, covering almost 600,000 workers, in which an employee might elect to make contributions in order to build up larger benefits than were offered by a noncontributory plan alone. Under these plans, the contributions were optional, commonly based on earnings in excess of a specified amount, with benefits usually determined on the same basis. . . .

Type of Worker and Administration

A fourth of the private plans studied, covering 10 percent of the workers, were restricted to salaried workers. . . . Almost a third of the plans with over 45 percent of the coverage were plans for blue-collar workers, while the remaining plans, covering 40 percent of the workers, included both production and salaried workers. Many of these all-employee plans were originally limited to white-collar groups and later were broadened to include production workers.

The salaried workers' plans (with about a third of their coverage) more frequently required employee contributions than the plans covering production workers only (with less than a tenth of their coverage). In plans covering both worker groups, roughly a third of the plans with about the same proportion of workers were contributory, apparently reflecting the influence of inclusion of salaried workers within the plan. . . .

The administration of benefits — i.e., the determination of eligibility, handling of appeals, and final decision — was the sole responsibility of the employer in over 4 out of 5 plans covering 3 out of 5 workers. Bipartite or tripartite boards determined benefits in about an eighth of the plans with over a third of the workers. Over half of these boards served in multiemployer situations. The grievance procedure of the collective bargaining agreement could be utilized in about 1,000 plans — mostly those negotiated by the Steelworkers — covering roughly a half million workers. In a small number of plans — union-operated plans — the union administered benefit determination.

(4) The Multiple-Eligibility Issue

As social insurance programs (like OASDI and Unemployment Compensation) enlarge their coverage and expand the hazards (or risks) to which they apply, and as private benefit plans likewise expand, horizontally to cover more workers and more hazards, and vertically to provide more benefits, multiple-eligibility cases (where a single employee may be eligible for benefits under two or more programs) are bound to proliferate. A badly disabled employee, hypothetically, might draw benefits under three or more programs to which he and/or his employer had contributed — a state workmen's compensation program, the Federal Disability Insurance program, and a private pension plan providing permanent and total disability benefits; and he might be eligible for veterans' benefits as well. The cases which follow are illustrative of some of these so-called "overlap" or "duplication" problems.

Underlying the decisions are some important, unresolved philosophical questions, two of which merit brief notice. (1) Are public and private benefits to be paid as a matter of right and irrespective of income, or are benefit "rights" conditional and subject to cancellation or reduction when income attains a certain level? (2) How does the society reconcile conflicting purposes among different programs? For example, *if* the major purpose of private pension plans is to encourage retirement and withdrawal from the labor market, it is easy to support a blanket policy denying unemployment benefits to pensioners. But the OASDI retirement test (which is as much a compromise as a policy) explicitly authorizes *some* post-retirement earnings (currently up to $1200 without benefit reduction). Also, where retirement is compulsory the pensioner may have withdrawn from the labor market involuntarily, with every intention of seeking other work after retirement.

HURD v. ILLINOIS BELL TELEPHONE CO.
United States Court of Appeals, Seventh Circuit, 1956
234 F.2d 942

LINDLEY, J. . . .
Each appeal involves the validity of defendants' interpretation and administration of the company sponsored retirement benefits plan commonly known as the Bell System Pension Plan. In 1913, each defendant executed and put into effect a retirement pension plan for its employees. The three plans involved are identical and are hereinafter referred to as the Bell plan or the pension plan, without distinction. This plan is a unilateral arrangement whereby each defendant undertook to provide retirement benefits to its employees, and, for this purpose, to allocate a determinable sum annually to a fund set aside for that purpose. No employee contribution is required. Each defendant has deposited sums allocated to its plan with defendant Bankers Trust Company under separate trust agreements whereby the latter company has undertaken to dis-

burse the funds in accord with the orders of the respective settlors. No question of breach of trust by Bankers is presented; it is a nominal defendant only, and is not included in the generic term defendants when used herein.

The plan provided for the payment of pensions to each employee retiring after specified periods of employment, in an amount to be computed upon the basis of a percentage of such employee's average wage multiplied by the number of the years of his employment. In 1914, in apparent anticipation of public pensions or benefits to aged persons, the plan was amended by the addition of a provision in the following language, which now appears as Section 8(27):

"In case any benefit or pension shall become payable under the laws now in force or hereafter enacted of any State or Country to any employee of the Company or his beneficiaries under such laws, the excess only, if any, of the amount prescribed in these Regulations above the amount of such benefit or pension prescribed by law shall be the benefit or pension payable under these Regulations . . ."

With the advent of the Social Security Act, 42 U.S.C. §§301, et seq., defendants amended the plan in 1940 by inserting therein a new paragraph, Section 8(28), which provided that, upon the date when any pensioner becomes "entitled" to receive Old Age and Survivors Insurance benefits under the Act, "the amount of his monthly service pension otherwise payable under this Plan shall be reduced by one-half of said 'primary insurance benefit' (OASI) . . ." This provision was not modified in any material detail until 1952 when the section was amended in certain respects which will be discussed subsequently.

Plaintiffs as retired employees, are beneficiaries under the plan by reason of their employment for the requisite number of years. Each of those who retired within the decade from 1940 to 1950, since retirement, has received monthly pension payments in accord with defendants' interpretation and application of the plan, i.e., in an amount computed consistently with the basic arithmetical formula prescribed in the plan, less one-half of the monthly OASI benefit to which the employee was "entitled" at the date when the monthly pension check was payable. In other words, upon retirement, the amount of an employee's monthly gross pension is finally fixed by application of the formula, but the deduction therefrom on account of OASI entitlement is scaled upward as Congress increases the primary OASI benefits and the net pension payment from the fund is commensurately scaled downward. Until 1952, Section 8(28) was amended in form, but not in substance, to comport with amendments of the Social Security Act.

Plaintiffs in each case set out these facts; each asked for judgment in the aggregate amount by which the pension payments received by him since retirement have been reduced by deductions on account of OASI benefits. The theory of each cause rests upon basic contentions, first, that the pension plan, and, specifically, Section 8(27) did not contemplate deduction of OASI benefits from private pension payments, and, second, that interpretation of the plan to permit the deduction of a private industry pension because of the entitlement to, or receipt of, OASI benefits is a violation of the Social Security Act, specifically Section 207 thereof, 42 U.S.C. §407. A number of contentions are asserted by plaintiffs, but all are parts or variations of those major premises. . . .

The pension plan is a unilateral contract which creates a vested right in those employees who accept the offer it contains by continuing in employment for the requisite number of years. The first major contention of plaintiffs largely depends upon just what the right is which vests in an employee upon his retirement in accord with the plan. Such an employee receives only a right to receive a monthly pension, not in a specified amount, but in an amount computed in accord with the provisions and conditions of the whole contract.

One such condition arises out of the provisions of Section 8(27) which requires the deduction from gross pension under the plan of any public benefits to which a pensioner is entitled under federal or state statutes. We agree with the trial court that this provision is broad enough to comprehend OASI benefits. Juristic niceties of distinction between such terms as "pension," "benefit" and "insurance" as applied to this question must give way before the manifest intention of the parties as shown by their writing. We think there can be no doubt that Section 8(27), when read in conjunction with the contract as a whole, was intended to encompass all public payments of old age benefits by whatever name they may be called. And we agree with the determination that OASI is within the category of benefits to which the section applies.

We agree, also, that the policy which was written into the plan requiring the deduction of one-half of OASI benefits from the private payments violates neither the letter nor the spirit of the Social Security Act. The reported opinion has supplied us with a detailed analysis of both the proscription against transfers contained in Section 207 of the Act and the Congressional policy embodied in the enactment. We need add little; we merely observe that if defendants do receive an economic benefit from OASI by the reduction of payments from the private pension funds, that benefit is largely theoretical. In part, at least, the deduction of one-half of OASI entitlement represents a writing-off or balancing of a superadded liability, inasmuch as the federal OASI tax would otherwise impose upon defendants a greater economic burden than that which they voluntarily assumed when they adopted the private plan. It can be as legitimately said that the deduction complained of is a device to maintain in balance the assumed burden of contribution to pension funds generally, as to say that it represents a "reaching" for an economic benefit. In any event, we think this poses a problem within the realm of moral evaluation, not legal.

Our remarks may be concluded with a brief consideration of the validity of the trial court's conclusion as to the effect of the 1952 amendment to Section 8(28) of the plan. In 1952, Congress so amended the Social Security Act as to increase the primary OASI benefit which would have required a further reduction of the private pension payments to retired employees. In response to this amendment, however, Section 8(28) of the plan was amended to provide that deductions from pension payments of employees retired prior to 1952 would be scaled to the primary OASI benefit under the 1950 Act, while payment to employees retired after 1952 would be reduced by an amount equal to one-half of the OASI benefit to which such employees would be entitled under the statute in force at the time of retirement. This provision is challenged as discriminatory.

We cannot agree. The effect of that amendment upon plaintiffs was to remove the uncertainty of the superseded section, which had conditioned the determination of the amount of pension payments upon subsequent amendments of the Social Security Act and to fix a final condition subsequent which would establish once and for all time, the amount of their monthly pension checks. As to employees, active in 1952, the revised section represents a new basic procedure for determining the amount of OASI deductions and, in this respect, a new unilateral contract which they could accept by continuing in employment for the requisite number of years. In other words, the 1952 amendment represents two separate contracts in one, closing the group who had accepted the offer upon retirement prior to 1952, and opening a new group composed of the then active employees who ultimately might qualify thereafter.

Plaintiffs have no cause for complaint if their net pension entitlement was computed by application of the provisions of the contract as it existed at the time of their retirement, irrespective of whether successor employees might receive enhanced benefits from a new contractual undertaking. We believe that plaintiffs have received the full measure of their rights under the plan.

The following language from Hurd v. Illinois, 136 F. Supp. at 156, adequately sums up the correct disposition of these appeals:

"The decision is in no way a judgment of the merits of the offset device. The court has concluded only that the Bell Plan authorized the deduction of Social Security benefits in the manner followed and that no rule of law, including the Social Security Act, makes unlawful a pension system which takes advantage of governmental benefits to which employees subsequently become entitled. Whether the integration of a private pension plan with Social Security to produce the results found in this case is good policy or unfair and misleading to the employees is a question which the court cannot decide for the parties in this action."

The judgments are affirmed.

CAMPBELL SOUP CO. v. BOARD OF REVIEW
Supreme Court, New Jersey, 1953
13 N.J. 431, 100 A.2d 287

BRENNAN, J.

The primary question here is whether a worker retired on pension at age 65 as required by a collective bargaining agreement has "left work voluntarily without good cause" so as to be disqualified for unemployment compensation under R.S. 43:21-5(a) providing that an individual shall be disqualified for benefits "for the week in which he has left work voluntarily without good cause, and for each week thereafter until he has earned in employment . . . at least four times his weekly benefit rate . . ."

These consolidated cases arise from claims filed by a number of former employees of Campbell Soup Company who were retired on pension by the company as each attained age 65. Retirement at that age is made compulsory by the terms of a collective bargaining agreement dated March 22, 1950 between the company and Food, Agricultural and Allied Workers Union of America, Local 80. The contract plan supplanted a retirement policy initiated unilaterally by the company in 1938. Pensions at company expense are provided for such retired employees as have had at least five years of service with the company.

The Appellate Division, 24 N.J. Super. 311, 94 A.2d 514, 518 (1953), held that the claimants were disqualified for benefits, concluding that the contract made for the claimants by the union is the claimants' contract and that, "having called for retirement by the company at age 65, the employees made the matter compulsory as to the company and removed it from the realm of involuntariness as to the employees" who are therefore to be considered as having "voluntarily terminated" their employment. . . .

If the inquiry is isolated to the time of termination, plainly none of the claimants left voluntarily in the sense that on his own he willed and intended at the time to leave his job. On the contrary, each claimant resisted his termination and left against his will only upon his employer's insistence that the contract obligation gave neither of them any alternative but to sever the relationship. . . .

The act is designed to provide unemployment compensation for workers who ordinarily have been workers and would be workers now but for their inability to find suitable jobs. Krauss v. A. & M. Karagheusian, Inc., 13 N.J. 447 (1953). . . . The Legislature plainly intended that the reach of the subsection [5(a)] was to be limited to separations where the decision whether to go or to stay lay at the time with the worker alone and, even then, to bar him only if he left his work without good cause. The claimants here did not choose of their own volition to leave the employ of Campbell Soup Company when they were separated. They left because they had no alternative but to submit to the employer's retirement policy, however that policy as presently constituted was originated. Their leaving in compliance with the policy was therefore involuntary for the purposes of the statute.

The fact, given controlling effect by the Appellate Division, that the claimants through their agent, the union, voluntarily subscribed to the contract is made unimportant by this interpretation of subsection 5(a), manifestly required in order to limit its operation within the apparent intention of the Legislature, having in mind also that the act is to be liberally construed to further its remedial and beneficent purposes, . . .

. . . R.S. 43:21-15, provid[es] that "Any agreement by an individual to waive, release, or commute his rights to benefits or any other rights under this chapter shall be void." While the treating as voluntary of a worker's leaving at the appointed time pursuant to the contract may not bring the contract within section 15, yet in practical effect the contract operates as an advance surrender of benefits, and an interpretation of subsection 5(a) to embrace such leaving is clearly inconsistent with the attainment of the statutory objectives. If an understanding as to the duration of employment were to have that effect, countless claimants would be disqualified for benefits. Applicants for work very frequently must take jobs which the employers tell them at the time will engage their services for only a stipulated period. It would not be suggested that voluntary acceptance of such work, knowing in advance of its fixed duration, constitutes the leaving of it at the agreed time a voluntary leaving for the purposes of subsection 5(a). The agreement by which the claimants were to leave the employ of Campbell Soup Company at age 65 is equally ineffective for that purpose.

Nor is the result different because the termination agreement also provides a pension for the worker. The statutory scheme for compensating unemployed workers for wage losses makes no provision for an inquiry as to individual financial need. An unemployed individual otherwise entitled to benefits is entitled to them however large or small his means may be. In passing it should be noted that the instant contract provides pensions only for the terminated employees who have had five years of service with the company and that the record discloses that some employees retired under the contract did not meet that requirement and are not receiving pensions. . . .

Reversed.

NOTES

1. In the Krauss case, cited by Judge Brennan, the claimant had left his employment at the age of sixty-eight under an option contained in the collective agreement whereby at that age he might elect to retire and procure a pension of $10.90 a month. Judge Brennan, speaking for a unanimous court, held that the claimant "left work voluntary without good cause and is disqualified for benefits." Krauss v. Karagheusian, Inc., 13 N.J. 447, 100 A.2d 277 (1953).

2. Under many unemployment compensation Acts a person is not eligible for benefits during any week in which he has received remuneration in the form of wages or "any payment by way of compensation for loss of wages." After his involuntary retirement a worker applied for benefits and was confronted by a refusal based upon the fact that he was receiving a pension from his former employer. Holding the pension not to be wages, a Connecticut court characterized it as "closely akin to wages in at least three particulars. It consists of payments made by or provided by an employer. Although it is not paid in direct compensation for services rendered currently, it is paid in consideration of services rendered in the past. . . . It serves the same purpose as wages to a recipient in that it helps him meet the expense of living. . . . It is a substitute for the wages

which the employee has lost by reason of the loss of his job." His claim was therefore denied. Kneeland v. Administrator, 138 Conn. 630, 632-633, 88 A.2d 376, 377-378 (1952). Compare Case No. 6, Matter of Tyson, supra page 563.

3. A number of states have enacted statutes concerning the relation of payments under an industrial retirement system to unemployment compensation benefits. Not all provide for complete disqualification. One example is Wis. Stat. §108.04 (1955):

"(15) *Retirement Payments.* If an employe claims benefits based on his past work for a covered employer, but such employer duly notifies the commission pursuant to subsection (13), and the commission determines, that the employe is receiving or has claimed and will receive retirement payments, as to any week covered by his benefit claim, under a group retirement system to whose financing any employer has substantially contributed or under a government retirement (or old-age insurance) system or under both, then the benefits thus claimed:

"(a) Shall be denied for any such week, from the account of such employer, if the employe left his employment with that employer to retire before he reached the compulsory retirement age used by that employer.

"(b) Shall not be denied for any such week, from the account of such employer, if the employe is otherwise eligible and left or lost his employment with that (or any other) employer because he had reached the compulsory retirement age used by the employer in question.

"(c) Shall, if payable, be determined for any such week by treating as if it were wages:

"1. That amount of the employe's weekly rate of retirement payments which has been financed by his employer or others (and not by the employe's own contributions) under any retirement system where such amount is separately calculated, or can be estimated with reasonable accuracy, provided acceptable evidence as to such amount is furnished the commission.

"2. All but $5 of the employe's weekly rate of retirement payments under one or more other retirement systems."

BROMBERG v. WHELAN STORES CORP.
New York Supreme Court, Special Term, 1951
27 L.R.R.M. 2480

BREITEL, J.

Plaintiff, employed by defendant for over twenty-two years, seeks specific performance by defendant of provisions of its "retirement policy." The "retirement policy" consists of three "organization notices," each subsequent one amending the earlier in some particular. These notices were unilaterally propounded and published by defendant to its employees between the period 1946 to 1948. The latest notice has remained extant since.

The retirement plan provides for graduated lump sum payments to employees upon retirement for age, ranging between the equivalent of one month's salary to eighteen months' salary depending upon the length of prior employment. In addition, the plan provides that upon retirement defendant will cause the employee's group life insurance policy to be converted into ordinary life insurance and that defendant will pay the premiums thereon for the balance of the retired employee's life.

The plan also provided that: "Employees who have had five (5) or more years of continuous service with the Company, and whose retirement has been recommended by the Company's Medical Staff, for reasons of ill health, will also receive the benefits of this plan, regardless of age."

Plaintiff on February 1, 1948, reached for a one-pound can of tobacco, and sustained a cardiac attack. Since then he has been intermittently hospitalized, and under the continuous treatment of a physician. His condition is diagnosed as a progressive irreversible degenerative cardiac condition. His expectancy is precariously slight, and he is described as incapable of doing any work. . . .

After the February 1, 1948, incident plaintiff made claim for workmen's compensation. It was determined by the appropriate tribunals that he had suffered an "industrial accident" and that he was entitled to compensation benefits including medical expenses. Plaintiff has since been receiving such benefits. Plaintiff has also been receiving hospitalization benefits, the premiums of which are paid by plaintiff at the rate of $1.60 per month and which are available only to continuing employees of defendant.

Plaintiff was not retirable for "ill health" within the meaning of the provision of the plan above quoted. That provision to make any sense must be deemed to refer to ill health not compensable under the Workmen's Compensation Law. Otherwise there is a duplication of benefits. Moreover, an employee who ceases to work because of compensable disability is restorable to employment once the disability is removed. It is immaterial that in the instant case plaintiff's disability is most unlikely to be ever removed. An employee retired under the plan, whether for age or ill health, is permanently retired. Plaintiff has never been so retired. In addition, plaintiff has shown that he so views it, too, by continuing to receive benefits as a continuing employee on leave, paying hospitalization premiums and receiving hospitalization benefits available only to employees.

As a matter of fact plaintiff is in a better position considered as an employee receiving hospitalization benefits on top of the substantial workmen's compensation benefits he has received. Together these exceed vastly the amounts involved in this suit.

Accordingly, the court finds that plaintiff is not entitled to the relief sought, namely, a lump sum payment equivalent to twelve months' salary which the court finds was $2,084.92 or to a conversion of the group life insurance policy to an ordinary life insurance policy with premiums payable by the defendant.

Defendant's motions are granted, without costs of the action. Plaintiff's motion is denied.

Settle judgment.

NOTES

1. Provisions for the deduction of workmen's compensation benefits are common in pension plans which provide for retirement for disability. Can pensions payable in a case of occupational disability be credited by the employer against workmen's compensation? See Nichols v. Colonial Beacon Oil Co., 284 App. Div. 581, 132 N.Y.S.2d 72 (3d Dept. 1954).

2. As has been seen in the section on regulation of wages and hours of work, supra page 479, Section 7(a) of FLSA provides for overtime pay for a covered employee "at a rate not less than one and one-half times the regular rate at which he is employed." Section 7(d) defines "regular rate" and includes "all remuneration" paid for employment, but expressly excepts "contributions to a trustee or third person pursuant to a bona fide plan for providing old-age, retirement, life, accident or health or similar benefits for employees."

3. The Massachusetts Fair Labor Practices Act, as amended in 1950, makes it an unlawful employment practice for an employer, because of the age of any individual between forty-five and sixty-five years "to refuse to hire or employ or to bar or to discharge from employment such individuals or to discriminate against such individual in compensation or in terms, conditions or privileges of employment, unless based upon a bona fide occupational qualification." Mass. Ann. Laws, c. 151B, §§1(8), 4(1). Under this statute the Massachusetts Commission Against Discrimination has ruled that compulsory retirement for age between forty-five and sixty-five years is unlawful and that the terms of any retirement plan which so provides are ineffective. 30 L.R.R.M. 124 (1952).

The Pennsylvania Fair Employment Practice Act of 1955, which makes it an unlawful employment practice for any employer to discriminate in employment because of the age of any person between forty and sixty-two years, inclusive, does "not apply, to (1) termination of employment because of the terms or conditions of any bona fide retirement or pension plan, (2) operation of the terms or conditions of any bona fide retirement or pension plan which have the effect of a minimum service requirement . . ." Pa. Stat., tit. 43, §955, as amended by Act No. 428, approved March 28, 1956.

(5)   Policy Questions

BALL, PENSIONS IN THE UNITED STATES: A SUMMARY *
Joint Committee on the Economic Report, 82d Cong., 2d Sess. (1952)

Several major questions of public policy need more research and consideration before intelligent action can be taken. . . .   In some areas action should be taken immediately. . . .

* Excerpt from the summary section of a report prepared under the auspices of the National Planning Association for the Joint Committee on the Economic Report. Material in brackets has been interpolated to cover developments since

Private Plans and the Basic Public Program

Since pension plans in private industry and the nonprofit area are designed to supplement OASDI, their character is greatly influenced by the nature of that system.

OASDI is geared not to a budget concept of minimum subsistence, as is the British system, but rather to individual circumstances. It pays to many of those under the system only part-time less than public assistance would pay; to the earner of minimum or near-minimum wages who is under the system full-time, it aims to pay amounts that make assistance unnecessary except in special need; to the worker with higher wages, it will pay benefits somewhat above the assistance level in most States.

How reasonable is it to pay benefits below subsistence to many who spend only part of their working lives under the program? People spend less than full time under OASDI for varied reasons. It seems reasonable that women who leave covered employment because they do not work after marriage and workers who shift to noncovered employment should get lower retirement benefits than full-time workers in covered employment who contribute most of their working lives. The present formula [however] is . . . harsh on the worker with involuntary unemployment; a solution would be to pay full-rate benefits to those in the system 30 out of the possible 45 working years between age 20 and 65, with reductions only for those with less than 30 years. A worker might then be able to get maximum benefits even if he were out of the system for part of his working life.

There is little quarrel with the idea of paying the minimum wage worker an amount at least equal to a low subsistence level if he is under the program full time. Labor, management and experts also agree that benefits should vary with wages and that those who earn more than minimum wages should receive more. But how much more? Should the second step in the benefit formula remain at 15 per cent . . . ? [Subsequent amendments have raised the second-step percentage to 20 per cent in the 1954 Act and to 21.4 per cent in the 1958 Act.] Should only the first $3600 [now $4800] of annual earnings be counted as at present, or should the maximum amount be raised? Should the weighted part of the formula be applied to more of the average monthly wage? It is unlikely that benefits for workers with above-minimum wages would be high enough to be considered sufficient retirement income for themselves. The issue that concerns the relationship of OASDI and the private supplementary plans is therefore one of degree.

Decisions on such points regarding OASDI will affect substantially the character of the job the private-pension movement is to do. If OASDI is improved for workers with above-minimum wages, the stand-

---

1952. This report was written by Robert M. Ball, who was long an official in the Bureau of Old Age, Survivors and Disability Insurance. He is now (fall 1964) Commissioner of Social Security.

ards for total retirement income will be raised and the goals of joint OASDI and private supplementary plans enlarged. Eventually, too, private-plan sponsors may want to put less money into pensions and more into disability benefits or health protection if the public pension program is improved and arrangements for health and disability are inadequate.

Pensions provided may be too high, of course, when considered in the light of many other things people want to do with their money. Coverage is usually mandatory. The necessity of setting aside funds for pensions limits the amount the individual has to spend as he wishes. In a free economy such limitations should be approached with caution. The task is to leave as high a proportion of income as is compatible with adequate social protection to the individual's free choice.

The dynamic character of the pension problem resulting from price, wage, and standard-of-living changes is also an important factor in determining the relationship between OASDI and the other programs. If OASDI benefits are raised as wages rise, then the need to adjust for economic changes is much reduced for private plans.

Private-plan protection should be extended and improved; nevertheless, the OASDI benefit must be set in recognition of the fact that in the foreseeable future it will be the only form of regular retirement pay for most retired workers, their wives, and aged widows. . . .

Private Plans and Government Regulation

The growth of private pension plans has led to concern about their security. Can they continue in less favorable conditions? If not, will Government be under pressure to assume the obligations of some of them to protect the workers' expectations?

The private plan's continued existence docs depend on its sponsor's financial position. Plans adopted in prosperity and under favorable tax conditions may be discontinued under less favorable circumstances. Even in good times, some plans are dropped. Individual businesses are continually being replaced, and whole industries become outmoded.

It is likely that the inability of any big collective-bargaining plan to continue would result in pressure from Government to assume the plan's liabilities. Some argue, therefore, that it would be desirable to require strict funding of private plans as a Federal tax-offset condition. Others hold that Government should offer to operate supplementary plans by allowing employers and employees to buy additional protection under the Government system on an actuarial basis and with all rights vested in the individual so that he would get some protection despite the failure of an individual business or the discontinuance of a plan.

Both suggestions require thorough study and discussion. Additional regulation of funding by Government would be complicated administratively. Criteria are hard to establish, and real control would involve the Government in a determination of the most likely assumptions for cost estimating. Protection supplementary to OASDI, if sold by the Government, would follow the worker from job to job. Employers can, however, now buy such protection for their employees from insurance companies if they wish. The cost is high, but it would also be high if operated by the Government. No clear need for Government operation in this area has been shown.

Because of the interest in vesting provisions, it has sometimes been proposed that a certain minimum vesting be required as a condition of plan approval for tax offset. This type of regulation should be approached with caution. In general, private-plan provisions should be left to individual decision and collective bargaining. Only by leaving individuals and groups free to experiment and to deviate from what is now considered desirable can the private plans pioneer in new fields and solve some of the problems raised in this report.

c.   HEALTH CARE

KIRKLAND, NEGOTIATION AND ADMINISTRATION OF HEALTH AND WELFARE PROGRAMS *
80 Monthly Labor Review 576-579 (1957)

Scope and Operation

A very distorted picture of health and welfare programs has developed in the public mind. In that picture, the typical health and welfare plan is regarded as a large fund of money, controlled and administered in a more or less discretionary fashion by a union officer — with perhaps a meek and thoroughly intimidated employer representative around in a rubber-stamp capacity.

This is, of course, almost exactly the reverse of the situation that most often exists in actual fact. The most common type of plan is one in which: (a) there is no "fund," and (b) the union has nothing to do with the business administration of the plan nor with the handling of the moneys involved. . . .

[The objective for health and welfare plans] as defined in a resolution adopted by the first convention of the AFL-CIO, is as follows:

". . . to reduce operating expenses and nonbenefit costs to the minimum consistent with the safety and security of the program, and to make available to the members the maximum in terms of actual prepaid health services (as distinguished from cash payments covering an unpredictable portion of actual medical bills) obtainable within the limits of the revenue of the fund."

The first line of distinction that might be noted, as among the various types of plans, lies in the manner in which the cost to the employer is determined (or left undetermined) in the collective bargaining agree-

* This article, by Lane Kirkland, Department of Social Security, AFL-CIO, is excerpted from a paper delivered by him at the Conference on Negotiation and Administration of Health and Welfare Programs conducted by the Industrial Union Department of the AFL-CIO in Washington, March 27, 1957.

ment. Two broad categories exist: (1) level-of-benefit plans, and (2) fixed contribution plans.

Level-of-Benefit Plans

Under the former, the agreement stipulates that the employer shall provide certain benefits, which may be expressed in either cash indemnity terms, or in terms of a medical service program. No stipulation is made as to how much the employer shall pay for those benefits. The agreement does, however, frequently specify how much the employee shall pay, in the form of sums withheld from his wages by the employer, toward the cost of the benefits.

While, in theory at least, the employer might establish a fund for the receipt of contributions and the disbursement of benefits or premiums, this is seldom done. Most commonly, the employer simply conveys the price of the plan to an outside carrier, either a commercial insurance company or a so-called "service" plan.

This is not to say that costs, as such, are not an important factor in the negotiation of such plans, or do not influence the terms of the bargain. Nor does it mean that the employees and their union have no legitimate interest in the actual cost of the plan to the employer, the efficiency and honesty with which it is administered, or the nature and identity of the outside agency or carrier employed.

On the contrary, the cost of the plan is an ever-present party at the bargaining table. Its influence is felt not only upon the scope and adequacy of the benefits, but upon the cash wage settlement as well. As one ingredient in the finite economic package that emerges from negotiations, it subtracts, in greater or lesser measure, from what is available for all of the other — including the cash — ingredients.

Consequently, the interests of all employees suffer when a settlement is made upon the understanding that the employer is bearing a substantial share of the cost of the plan, but where the employer subsequently pockets dividends which reduce or eliminate any element of expense to him while employee contributions remain fixed at a higher level than experience warrants. Likewise, those interests suffer where the employer has ties of a compromising nature with particular outside agencies or carriers whose costs might be higher and benefit services inferior to others equally available.

Fixed Contribution Plans

In the case of fixed contribution plans, the agreement simply defines the amount that the employer shall pay for health and welfare purposes on a cents-per-hour, a percent-of-payroll, or, in some cases, a royalty basis. While the benefits envisaged may enter into negotiations on a more or less tentative or exploratory basis, they are not spelled out in the agreement, but are left to the determination of those responsible for the administration of the plan.

The operation of such a program requires the establishment of a trust fund for the receipt of employer contributions and the disbursement of benefits to employees or premium payments to outside insurance carriers or providers of benefits. Usually, the full cost of these programs is borne by employer payments and there are no direct additional contributions by employees, the employer payments being properly regarded as a form of wages.

One of the characteristics common to many, if not most, of these funds is their conservatism. The level of benefits maintained tends to be appreciably less than the revenues can support, resulting in the accumulation of substantial reserves. While the need for some reserves as a safeguard against employment fluctuations and to carry members over jobless periods is apparent, in view of the nature of the industries involved, there can be little doubt that, in many cases, they go well beyond the requirements of caution. Often, they are sufficient to maintain the current benefit structure for several years, even if all further contributions were to cease.

On the other hand, much of the criticism that has been directed against this accumulation has failed to take account of the fact that it is, or should be, to a large extent, a temporary phenomenon, peculiar to the early years of a program — and most funds are in their early years. After the point of maximum buildup is reached, such plans can make a more efficient use of current revenues — paying out 100 percent, or more if necessary, in benefits — with complete safety, than can programs which are not backed by large reserves. Furthermore, the existence of reserves facilitates the saving of costs by a shift to a self-insurance basis, since — from the economic standpoint — a commercial insurance carrier is so much superfluous baggage to a fund whose internal resources are more than ample. It should also be noted that these reserve funds can also, potentially at least, provide the resources needed for the development of better methods and facilities for meeting the medical-care needs of working people.

Choice of Plans

I do not mean to suggest that most unions have a free and clear choice as to whether they should proceed on a level-of-benefit or a fixed contribution basis. In most cases, the decision is made for them, being inherent in the nature of the industry, the pattern of collective bargaining, or the influence of past and prevailing practice.

Any discussion of the level-of-benefit approach is, of course, strictly academic to unions which bargain on a multiemployer basis, where the labor force is casualized and the union is the main, or only, unifying factor. The establishment of a central fund on a fixed contribution basis is the only feasible way to preserve uniformity of labor charges, provide continuity of coverage, and permit the inclusion of small units as well as large. It is, therefore, typical of the building, trucking, apparel, maritime, entertainment, and service trades.

In manufacturing, public utilities, and other industries where bargaining is more often on a single-employer basis, the level-of-benefit ap proach prevails. Some unions, for reasons of their own, have preferred this approach. Others, while preferring the fixed contribution approach, found that the line of least resistance lay in the direction of agreement on benefits and proceeded accordingly. Since level-of-benefit plans leave a wider area of discretion in the hands of management, they are preferred by industrial employers, which is why they offer the line of least resistance in company or plantwide negotiations.

Administrative Control of Plans

Closely related to the basis upon which contributions are made is the question of administrative control. Where a fixed employer contribution is made to a plan established through union auspices, the administration of the plan must be — since the Taft-Hartley Act at least — the joint responsibility of employers and the union, with provision for a neutral umpire. The law further requires the establishment of a formal trust fund, an annual audit of the fund and the public posting of the results of the audit. Such plans are already, therefore, the most closely regulated of any form of health and welfare plan.

Level-of-benefit plans, on the other hand, are usually administered unilaterally by the employer, with union participation limited to the policing of the benefit agreement through grievance channels.

According to estimates set forth in the final report of the Douglas Subcommittee, of all workers covered by some form of health and welfare plan, about 92 percent are under plans administered solely by the employer; about 7.5 percent are under jointly administered plans; and about one-half of 1 percent are covered by union-administered plans. In the latter category are some that were established prior to the Taft-Hartley Act as well as those financed entirely from membership dues and assessments. . . .

Participation by Community Groups

Turning to another aspect of the subject, geography has a definite bearing upon the ability of health and welfare plans to perform their intended function in the most effective manner. The function of health insurance is to help the members and their families to meet their health-care needs. In the last analysis, those needs must be met at the level of the local community, where the members live and where they must find the doctors, hospitals, and other medical facilities necessary to the provision of adequate medical services.

As they have gained experience with the problems and deficiencies inherent in prepayment plans offered by the most common types of outside agencies, many unions have reached the conclusion that their plans cannot function efficiently unless new and better facilities and methods of controlling the cost and improving the quality of medical services are developed locally. This has led them to take an active leadership role in the promotion of new patterns of prepaid health care.

One outstanding example is the multiunion Medical Service Plan of Philadelphia. Here 29 local unions, of different international affiliations, have joined together to develop a program based upon the principle of the group practice of medicine, providing services through the medium of a labor health center. The conspicuous success of this program has stimulated widespread interest in the possibilities and advantages of the local multiunion approach on the part of labor groups in other cities.

Another example with great potential significance is the communitywide program that is now in the developmental stage in the city of Detroit. Through the leadership of the United Auto Workers, a Community Health Association has been formed in that city with the object of establishing a genuinely comprehensive prepaid medical-service plan, open not only to union members but to all groups in the community.

One of the obstacles in the way of broader local union participation in community programs of this type is the fact that many locals are tied to a centralized plan established on a national or regional basis. Such plans usually grow out of the pattern of collective bargaining that prevails in the particular trade or industry, as, for example, where a uniform standard contract is negotiated with a multiplant interstate corporation, or where national or regional agreements are negotiated with an association of employers.

In other cases, however, the health and welfare plan has been deliberately established through a central national fund by unions in which collective bargaining is usually carried out on a local or company-by-company basis. One of the main purposes, in such cases, is to enhance the position of the plan in negotiations with commercial insurance carriers, so as to realize the economies of volume and to make possible the purchase of more insurance at a lower cost than would otherwise be possible.

However, unless some means is provided that will permit local groups to participate with other unions in plans which — from the medical-service standpoint — more nearly meet the objectives of labor, in communities where they are available, the effort to achieve efficiency along conventional lines through centralization may serve as a barrier to local progress in the promotion of better health programs.

One solution to this problem is the incorporation of the "local option" principle in the national or regional plan. This is now a feature of the Auto Workers' agreements with the large automobile companies. While those agreements set up a uniform national standard of health benefits along Blue Cross lines, they provide that locals in cities where satisfactory comprehensive medical-service plans are available may offer their members the alternative of enrolling in such plans. Through this option, it has become possible for UAW members to join such plans as HIP [Health Insurance Plan] in New York and the Kaiser Foundation on the West Coast. . . .

NOTES

1. Consider the implications upon collectively bargained programs of the continually increasing costs of medical and health care. Health care

costs (and expenditures) are climbing, both absolutely and relatively. In 1928-1929 our public and private expenditures for health and medical care totaled $3.6 billion, about 3.6 per cent of gross national product. Of this total, $415 million (about 14 per cent) came out of public funds, the lion's share ($3.1 billion) coming from private sources. Thirty-five years later, in 1963-1964, not only had *total* U.S. health and medical care expenditures increased by almost 900 per cent, to $35.4 billion, but expenditures in relation to GNP also had climbed — to 5.9 per cent, a jump of 66 per cent in thirty-five years.

2. Consider also the long-term trend toward greater public expenditure for health and medical care. Tax dollars now finance a little more than a quarter of all our health outlays; thirty-five years ago they financed about 15 per cent of them. Many of the extra tax dollars go for more and better services to sick people, for example in state mental hospitals, in the Carville (La.) Leprosarium or in New York City's municipal hospitals. Other taxes are spent for services provided by local health departments, many of them preventive services. More dollars go for overhead, staff, and research purposes — $661 million worth of Public Health Service awards and research grants during the 1963 fiscal year, to cite one example. To the extent that research grants widen the frontiers of medical knowledge, or finance construction costs or research facilities in medical schools, the public doubtless gains. But the coin of health progress also has its tarnished side. Research grants attract physicians and health technicians but lure some out of private medical practice. Likewise, when rising hospital utilization and rising hospital costs are the major causes in the health care cost spiral, 146 million federal tax dollars for hospital construction help local hospitals but they also do their bit to increase costs, for a hospital bed once built and available generates a unique magnetism to keep itself occupied.

3. Finally, the obvious implications of present proposals for "medicare" for the aged, financed through social security, and constant broader proposals for compulsory national health insurance are relevant to any developing private health and medical care programs. Will developments turn labor unions away from private plans to political activities toward a governmental take-over, as in the British National Health Service, for example?

4.   *Union Security*

a.   VARIETIES OF CONTRACTUAL ARRANGEMENTS

A union is a social institution, and like all other institutions it is subject to growth and decline. Since its vitality and continued existence depend, in large part, upon its ability to meet the specific needs of its members, the union itself needs to be strong. It therefore seeks to achieve sovereignty and to obtain rights for itself as an organization. In this way it is better able to protect and to implement rights gained for the workers.

Threats to the welfare of organized workers come from three principal sources: employers, other unions, and the workers themselves. Employer opposition to the growth of labor organization is not entirely a matter of history, and even where it is, that history is still vivid in the minds of union leaders and their members, and the basic feeling of insecurity of most unions has yet to be completely dispelled. Rival unionism and jurisdictional disputes are outstanding characteristics of the American labor movement; many unions have successfully met the challenge of employers, only to succumb to attacks by their more powerful competitors within the "house of labor." Finally, union standards have constantly been undermined by the tendency of individual workers to compete against each other; this has been true particularly in periods of economic depression.

The most important means by which unions attempt to establish their own strength with respect to employers, other unions, and workers are the so-called "union security provisions" frequently included in collective bargaining agreements. These provisions generally fall into the following categories:

The closed shop. Under closed-shop agreements, the employer contracts not to hire anyone except members of the appropriate union, and to discharge any employee who does not remain a union member in good standing throughout the life of the agreement. Most of the closed-shop agreements require employers to hire through the union unless the latter is unable to furnish suitable persons within a given period; in such cases the persons hired elsewhere must join the union before starting to work.

Example. "The Company hereby agrees to employ only members in good standing of Local No. 114; . . . all positions to be supplied through the employment office of said Local unless within 48 hours the Local is unable to provide a suitable employee."

The union shop. Under union-shop agreements, employers are permitted to hire workers on the open market, but all new employees must join the union within a specified period and must continue their membership in good standing throughout the life of the agreement. Failure to do so results automatically in discharge by the employer.

Example. "It shall be a condition of employment that all employees of the Employer covered by this agreement who are members of the Union in good standing on the effective date of this agreement shall remain members in good standing; that those who are not members on the effective date of this agreement shall, on or before the thirtieth day following the effective date of this agreement, become and remain members of the Union; and that all employees hired on or after the effective date shall, on or before the thirtieth day following the beginning of such employment, become and remain members in good standing in the Union."

The preferential shop. Some agreements provide that preference in employment shall be given to union members. Under such agreement the employer is free to hire workers on the open market only if no suitable union members are supplied within a specified period of time. A preferential-hiring provision is frequently incorporated as a supplement to a union-shop agreement. In that event, the union security provision as a whole has practically the same effect as a closed shop.

Example. "It is agreed that in hiring new employees the employer shall give preference to union members but in the event union members are not available, new members may be hired from any source."

Maintenance of membership. In order to avoid the compulsory aspects of the closed and the union shop, some employers and unions have agreed upon maintenance of membership as a compromise. The National War Labor Board employed this means of adjustment during World War II. Under this arrangement, membership in the union is not required of new employees; they may join or not, as they prefer. Once they do join, however, they are obligated to maintain their union membership in good standing for the life of the collective agreement as a condition of employment. Some maintenance-of-membership provisions specify an "escape period," usually at the end of the contract term, during which time members may withdraw from the union with impunity. For an example of a typical maintenance-of-membership clause, see the Enderby Agreement, Art. I, Sec. 4, in the Reference Supplement, page 4.

The agency shop. In recent years there has come into use a clause relating exclusively to the payment to the union by nonunion employees of a sum of money equal to that paid by union members, as initiation fees and dues. Membership in the union is expressly made noncompulsory, but the payment of these sums is made a condition of continued employment by management.

Example. "All employees shall, as a condition of continued employment, pay to the Union, the employee's exclusive bargaining representative, an amount of money equal to that paid by other employees in the bargaining unit who are members of the Union, which shall be limited to an amount of money equal to the Union's regular and usual initiation fees, and its regular and usual dues and its general and uniform assessments."

The checkoff. The checkoff is also a form of union security. It is a device whereby employers aid unions by insuring the collection of dues and initiation fees (and sometimes fines and assessments) with a minimum of trouble to the union. The employer makes a deduction from the paychecks of those employees who have dues obligations and transmits the amounts so deducted to the union. The deduction can be automatic and compulsory, or it can be made only upon the consent of the individual employee. Such consent can be written or oral, revocable or irrevocable. Section 302(c)(4) of the LMRA restricts the permissible form of the checkoff.

It is significant that the issue of union security is confined largely to the United States. American workers have been more difficult to organize and to keep organized than European workers. In European industrial relations the union shop has never become a major issue. There are a number of reasons why this is so. In Europe, the higher degree of unionization, the homogeneity of the working classes, and the relative lack of opportunities for the wage earner to progress up the economic scale have made for a stronger feeling of solidarity among the workers. In the United States, however, the presence of great numbers of immigrants, the relatively frequent opportunities for wage earners to rise out of the ranks of labor, as well as other economic and social factors have retarded the development of a spirit of class solidarity. The American worker has traditionally been individualistic rather than class-conscious; the knowledge that he might some day be a "boss" has tended to spur his ambition and to make him less amenable to discipline and control.

This tradition has been largely responsible for the emphasis which American labor unions have placed upon union security. Threatened on the one hand by those workers who were willing to accept low wages and long hours, in the belief that their position as wage earners was only temporary, and on the other hand by immigrant workers with lower standards of living, most American unions have come to regard the closed or union shop as their only real protection. Thus, in the early 1800's American craftsmen refused to work with nonunionists, and by the time of the Civil War virtually all unions favored excluding nonunionists from employment. The principle of the closed shop was officially adopted by the American Federation of Labor, and the beginning of the twentieth century saw the closed shop firmly established as a keystone of union bargaining policy.

The principle of union security, and indeed of unionism itself, was strongly attacked by organized American industry, which favored the open (i.e., nonunion) shop. The industry program was launched on a broad scale in the first decade of the 1900's by the National Association of Manufacturers. This antiunion campaign was partially effective but union membership and strength increased tremendously during World War I. Industry's second organized attempt to retard the growth of unionism, begun in 1919, met with considerably more success. By 1922, militant unionism in the United States had been largely suppressed, and the open shop, or "American Plan" as it was then called, prevailed generally. The moral which American unions drew from this defeat was that real collective bargaining was possible only if they could secure the closed or union shop.

During the years that have elapsed since the passage of the NLRA in 1935, the principle of collective bargaining has become firmly established in American industry. A union which is the certified representative of a majority of employees within an appropriate bargaining unit is authorized to bargain exclusively for all employees in that unit, regardless of their union affiliation. The issue of the degree of union security to which the employer should agree, however, is still unresolved in a major part of American industry.

(b)   THE TAFT-HARTLEY UNION SHOP

NATIONAL LABOR RELATIONS BOARD v.
GENERAL MOTORS CORP.

Supreme Court of the United States, 1963
373 U.S. 734, 83 Sup. Ct. 1453, 10 L. Ed. 2d 670

MR. JUSTICE WHITE delivered the opinion of the Court.

The issue here is whether an employer commits an unfair labor practice, National Labor Relations Act §8(a)(5), when it refuses to bargain with a certified union over the union's proposal for the adoption of the "agency shop." More narrowly, since the employer is not obliged to bargain over a proposal that he commit an unfair labor practice, the question is whether the agency shop is an unfair labor practice under §8(a)(3) of the Act or else is exempted from the prohibitions of that section by the proviso thereto. We have concluded that this type of arrangement does not constitute an unfair labor practice and that it is not prohibited by §8.

Respondent's employees are represented by the United Automobile, Aerospace and Agricultural Implement Workers of America, UAW, in a single, multiplant, company-wide unit. . . .

The union . . . sent respondent a letter proposing the negotiation of a contractual provision covering Indiana plants "generally similar to that set forth" in the Meade case [Meade Elec. Co. v. Hagberg, 129 Ind. App. 631, 159 N.E.2d 408 (1959)]. Continued employment in the Indiana plants would be conditioned upon the payment of sums equal to the initiation fee and regular monthly dues paid by the union members. The intent of the proposal, the National Labor Relations Board concluded, was not to require membership but to make membership available at the employees' option and on nondiscriminatory terms. Employees choosing not to join would make the required payments and, in accordance with union custom, would share in union expenditures for strike benefits, educational and retired member benefits, and union publications and promotional activities, but they would not be entitled to attend union meetings, vote upon ratification of agreements negotiated by the union, or have a voice in the internal affairs of the union. The respondent made no counterproposal, but replied to the union's letter that the proposed agreement would violate the National Labor Relations Act and that respondent must therefore "respectfully decline to comply with your request for a meeting" to bargain over the proposal.

The union thereupon filed a complaint with the National Labor Relations Board against respondent for its alleged refusal to bargain in good faith. . . . [T]he Board ruled that respondents had committed an unfair labor practice by refusing to bargain in good faith with the certified bargaining representative of its employees, and it ordered respondent to bargain with the union over the proposed arrangement; no back-pay award is involved in this case. 133 N.L.R.B. 451. . . .

[The Court first considered the legislative history of the Section 8(a)(3) proviso. On the basis of its consideration, it concluded:]

We find nothing in the legislative history of the Act indicating that Congress intended the amended proviso to §8(a)(3) to validate only the union shop and simultaneously to abolish, in addition to the closed shop, all other union-security arrangements permissible under state law. There is much to be said for the Board's view that, if Congress desired in the Wagner Act to permit a closed or union shop and in the Taft-Hartley Act the union shop, then it also intended to preserve the status of less vigorous, less compulsory contracts which demanded less adherence to the union.

Respondent, however, relies upon the express words of the proviso which allow employment to be conditioned upon "membership": since the union's proposal here does not require actual membership but demands only initiation fees and monthly dues it is not saved by the proviso. This position, of course, would reject administrative decisions concerning the scope of §8(3) of the Wagner Act, . . . Moreover, the 1947 amendments not only abolished the closed shop but also made significant alterations in the meaning of "membership" for the purposes of union security contracts. Under the second proviso to §8(a)(3), the burdens of membership upon which employment may be conditioned are expressly limited to the payment of initiation fees and monthly dues. It is permissible to condition employment upon membership, but membership, insofar as it has significance to employment rights, may in turn be conditioned only upon payment of fees and dues. "Membership" as a condition of employment is whittled down to its financial core. This Court has said as much before in Radio Officers Union v. Labor Board, 347 U.S. 17, 41:

"This legislative history clearly indicates that Congress intended to prevent utilization of union security agreements for any purpose other than to compel payment of union dues and fees. Thus Congress recognized the validity of unions' concern about 'free riders,' i.e., employees who received the benefits of union representation but are unwilling to contribute their fair share of financial support to such union, and gave the unions the power to contract to meet that problem while withholding from unions the power to cause the discharge of employees for any other reason. . . ."

We are therefore confident that the proposal made by the union here conditioned employment upon the practical equivalent of union "membership," as Congress used that term in the proviso to §8(a)(3). The proposal for requiring the payment of dues and fees imposes no burdens not imposed by a permissible union shop contract and compels the performance of only those duties of membership which are enforceable by discharge under a union shop arrangement. If an employee in a union shop unit refuses to respect any union-imposed obligations other than the duty to pay dues and fees, and membership in the union is therefore denied or terminated, the condition of "membership" for §8(a)(3) purposes is nevertheless satisfied and the employee may not be discharged for nonmembership even though he is not a formal member. Of course, if the union chooses to extend membership even though the employee will meet only the minimum financial burden, and refuses to support or "join" the union in any other affirmative way, the employee may have to become a "member" under a union shop contract, in the sense that the union may be able to place him on its rolls. The agency shop arrangement proposed here removes that choice from the union and places the option of membership in the employee while still requiring the same monetary support as does the union shop. Such a difference between the union and agency shop may be of great importance in some contexts, but for present purposes it is more formal than real. To the extent that it has any significance at all it serves, rather than violates, the desire of Congress to reduce the evils of compulsory unionism while allowing financial support for the bargaining agent.[12]

In short, the employer categorically refused to bargain with the union over a proposal for an agreement within the proviso to §8(a)(3) and as such lawful for the purposes of this case. By the same token, §7, and derivatively §8(a)(1), cannot be deemed to forbid the employer to enter such agreements, since it too is expressly limited by the §8(a)(3) proviso. We hold that the employer was not excused from his duty to bargain over the proposal on the theory that his acceding to it would necessarily involve him in an unfair labor practice. Whether a different result obtains in States which have declared such arrangements unlawful is an issue still to be resolved in Retail Clerks Union v. Schermerhorn, 373 U.S. 746 [see page 665 infra] . . . and one which is of no relevance here because Indiana law does not forbid the present contract proposal. In the context of this case, then, the employer cannot justify his refusal to bargain. He violated §8(a)(5), and the Board properly ordered him to return to the bargaining table.

Reversed and remanded.

MR. JUSTICE GOLDBERG took no part in the consideration or decision of this case.

NOTE

The conditions of the lawfulness of a union security clause in an agreement are expressed in the first proviso to Section 8(a)(3). The requirement of an unassisted majority in a representative segment of the

---

[12] Also wide of the mark is respondent's further suggestion that Congress contemplated the obligation to pay fees and dues to be imposed only in connection with actual membership in the union, so as to insure the enjoyment of all union benefits and rights by those from whom money is extracted. Congress, it is said, had no desire to open the door to compulsory contracts which extract money but exclude the contributing employees from union membership. But, as analyzed by the Board and as the case comes to us, there is no closed-union aspect to the present proposal by the union. Membership remains optional with the employee and the significance of desired, but unavailable, union membership, or the benefits of membership, in terms of permissible §8(a)(3) security contracts, we leave for another case. In view of the legislative history of the Taft-Hartley amendments to §8(a)(3) and of their purposes, we cannot say that optional membership, which is neither compulsory nor unavailable membership, vitiates an otherwise valid union-security arrangement.

employer's work force, see Guy F. Atkinson Co., 90 N.L.R.B. 143 (1950), proved unduly restrictive in the building and construction industry, where employees are hired anew for each job, and jobs are typically of short duration. The enactment in 1959 of Section 8(f)(1) permitted "pre-hire" agreements, made prior to the hiring of employees, in that industry. In addition to majority status, the Act originally required a special "authorization" election and an affirmative vote of a majority of all employees in the bargaining unit (whether voting or not) before a union shop could be negotiated. The percentage of union victories was so high that by 1951 "both sides of the aisle seem[ed] to agree that the union-shop elections serve no purpose but entail a heavy drain upon the limited resources of the NLRB" (97 Cong. Rec. 10464 (1951), remarks of Sen. Humphrey), and the requirement was repealed in favor of the present "de-authorization" procedure set forth in clause (ii) of the first proviso.

The second major limitation contained in the first proviso is the ban on a requirement of pre-existing union membership, i.e., on the closed shop. Again, the special problems of the construction industry led in 1959 to a shortening, in Section 8 (f)(2), of the period after which membership could lawfully be compelled. For the rest of industry, however, the 30-day minimum remains. In Argo Steel Construction Co., 122 N.L.R.B. 1077 (1959), the contract required new employees to sign a statement of intention to join the union within thirty days of their employment. The Board held such a requirement invalid: "There is nothing in the Act which sanctions such a provision. The Act legalizes, as a maximum, union-security provisions which require employees to join unions on or after the thirtieth day following the beginning of their employment. The instant provisions enlarge upon the maximum sanctioned by the Act. Under them, persons who may be unwilling to signify an advance intent to join the union cannot be employed. The Act requires no such signification of advance intent; it gives employees 30 days of *employment* before they can be compelled to make a choice." Id. at 1082. Absent evidence that the clause was designed to prevent the hiring of nonunion men (there was such evidence in Argo), is the matter so clear? Why might the employer desire such a clause? Why did Congress give employees "30 days of employment"?

UNION STARCH & REFINING CO.
National Labor Relations Board, 1949
87 N.L.R.B. 779

The major issue in this case arises from the discharges of employees John Ralph, Nelly Ralph, and Mary Rawlings. The facts pertinent to these discharges may be briefly summarized. The Respondent Union threatened a work stoppage if, pursuant to a valid union-shop contract, the Respondent Company failed to discharge certain employees for "failure to pay dues and initiation fees." Knowing that several of the individuals named in the request had been supporters of a rival union prior to the representation election, the Respondent Company undertook to investigate the facts and circumstances surrounding the Respondent Union's demands, in order to ascertain whether or not membership was available to these employees on the same terms and conditions generally applicable to all other nonmembers.

In the course of this investigation, the Respondent Company learned that all of the employees whose discharge was requested *had* tendered the amount of the dues and initiation fees uniformly required to the Respondent Union's business agent, who had refused the tender, saying that payment could not be accepted until after they had become members. The business agent told them that, in order to qualify for membership, any nonmember must (1) attend the next regular union meeting, at which applicants would be voted upon and accepted, (2) take the obligation to the Union, and (3) then pay the initiation fee and prepay 2 months' dues. After the Company had completed this inquiry, the Respondent Union repeated its request for the discharge of certain employees, for "non-membership" in the Respondent Union, and listed the terms it uniformly imposed upon the acquisition of membership. Thereupon the Respondent Company gave the designated employees approximately 20 hours in which to fill out a questionnaire concerning their willingness to comply with the three conditions which the Union imposed. All but the three employees named above indicated their willingness to comply. These three did not and were then discharged. Each of these employees had stated to the Union's business representative the grounds for their unwillingness to comply with other of the conditions imposed. In the case of the two Ralphs, these grounds were religious in character and were matters of moral scruple. [Mary Rawlings refused to tender her dues at a meeting, although she had done so at the union office. Her reason was not disclosed.]

On these facts the issue before us is whether an employee who tenders to a union holding a valid union-shop contract an amount equal to the initiation fees and accrued dues thereby brings himself within the protection from discharge contained in the provisos of Section 8(a)(3) and in Section 8(b)(2) of the amended Act. . . .

The Trial Examiner found that the Respondent Company was justified, under the duly-authorized union-shop contract, in honoring the Respondent Union's demand for the discharge of three nonmembers; although the Respondent Company knew that these nonmembers *had* tendered "initiation fees and dues" to the Respondent Union without being accorded membership in the Union. He found that proviso (*A*) of Section 8(a)(3) was not violated, on the ground that before making the discharges, the Company had ascertained that membership was available to any employee on the same terms and conditions applicable to any other nonmember and applied to all new members admitted since January 6, 1948, when the Union was certified as bargaining representative. The Trial Examiner found that proviso (B) of Section 8(a)(3) was not relevant in this case despite the fact that the Respondent Union had, as the Company knew, refused to accept the initiation fees and dues tendered by the dischargees, for the following reasons: ". . . each of them failed and refused to do anything toward becoming a member other than to offer to pay a sum of money equal to the initiation fee and dues which members were currently paying. *Membership in the Respondent Union was never denied them, but, on the contrary, the three employees were assured that they would be accepted as members if they complied with the terms and conditions of membership generally applicable to all members in the bargaining unit,* that is if they (1) attended the meeting at which they were to be voted upon, (2) took the obligation of membership, and (3) paid the initiation fees and dues." [Emphasis supplied.]

Having found no violation of 8(a)(3), the Trial Examiner found no violation of 8 (b)(2) in the Union's demands for the discharge of nonmembers.

We agree with the Trial Examiner's conclusion insofar as he found that proviso (A) of Section 8(a)(3) was not violated. Unlike the Trial Examiner, however, we find the discharges violative of proviso (B) of Section 8(a)(3) and of Section 8(b)(2).

As we read the statutory language, the provisos to Section 8(a)(3) spell out two separate and distinct limitations on the use of the type of union-security agreements permitted by the Act. Proviso (A) protects from discharge for nonmembership in the contracting union any employee to whom membership is not available for some discriminatory reason; i.e., any reason which is not generally applicable. Proviso (B) protects employees who have tendered the requisite amount of dues and initiation fees and been denied membership for *any other reason, even though* that reason be nondiscriminatory.

At first blush the provisos appear to involve duplication. Indeed, the Respondent Company argues that such a reading of the statute, when applied to employees who have never been members of the contracting union, renders meaningless proviso (A), contending that any discriminatory reason for denying an employee membership would always be a reason other than his failure to pay dues or initiation fees. More careful analysis, however, readily discloses that provisos (A) and (B) have ample independent scope, and the elementary principle of statutory construction which favors giving some meaning to each part of a statute is thereby satisfied. Thus, for example, it is clear that proviso (B) requires a tender of dues and fees, whereas proviso (A) protects any employee discriminatorily excluded from membership whether or not such tender is made.

We therefore read proviso (B) as extending protection to any employee who tenders periodic dues and initiation fees without being accorded membership. If the union imposes any other qualifications and conditions for membership with which he is unwilling to comply, such an employee may not be entitled to membership, but he is entitled to keep his job. Throughout the amendment to the Act, Congress evinced a strong concern for protecting the individual employee in a right to refrain from union activity[12] and to keep his job even in a union shop. Congress carefully limited the sphere of permissible union security, and even in that limited sphere accorded the union no power to effect the discharge of nonmembers except to protect itself against "free rides."

We cannot say, as did the Trial Examiner, that by refusing to comply with the Union's requests the employees had demonstrated that they "were entirely unwilling to become members" and therefore that "membership" had not been "denied" to them. The employees *were* willing to comply with the only term or condition for membership which we think can, under the provisos, legally be enforced by discharge — the tender of the periodic dues and the initiation fees uniformly required. . . .

Nor does the legislative history which Respondent Company urges upon us call for a different result. Quite the contrary. Although the legislative history does establish that Congress wanted to protect from discharge an employee "unreasonably" denied membership, Congress specified what it regarded as reasonable the failure of the employee to tender the dues and initiation fees. The statements of Senator Taft . . . establish that he thought the bill in its final form successfully and constitutionally protected not only the union from "free riders" but also protected those employees willing to pay for their ride. . . .

Finally, we note that the Trial Examiner also sought to buttress his conclusion by pointing out that a construction such as we place upon the provisos to Section 8(a)(3) "would tend to destroy all union security," because employees could "choose to remain outside the union" and thereby lessen the union's effectiveness in representing the employees. The very argument the Trial Examiner advances was unsuccessfully urged upon the Congress which enacted the proviso. That decision is binding upon us, whether or not we think it wise, practical, or fair.

Moreover, viewing the situation realistically, we believe that the Trial Examiner has overstated the case. It appears highly improbable that employees would be encouraged by our interpretation of the statute merely to tender dues and refrain from actual participation in the union. As a general rule, rather than refraining, employees are likely to insist upon participating in the affairs of a union to whose treasury they are required to contribute. . . .

Members Houston and Reynolds, dissenting:

. . . [I]f all our colleagues had decided was that, on the facts of this case, the three discharged employees had been denied membership after having demonstrated a willingness to become *members* of the union, in

---

[12] Section 7. This section protects employees in their negative right not to join or assist labor organizations, except to the extent that that section is modified by the provisions of Section 8(a)(3). Section 8(3) is therefore an exception to Section 7. As Section 7 expresses the legislative policy, the exceptions made in Section 8(a)(3) must, under general rules of statutory construction, be strictly construed, to remove from the purview of Section 7 only those "subjects expressly . . . freed from the operation of the statute." 2 Sutherland, Statutory Construction (3rd ed.) §4933; 59 C.J. 1089.

the full sense of that term, i.e. a willingness to do *more* than pay the dues and fees, then we might do no more than take issue with the inference they draw from the evidence before us.[34] But their decision goes far beyond the facts of this particular case. It postulates, as a rule of law, that within the meaning of the provisos to Section 8(a)(3) employees seek "membership" when they do no more than tender the dues and fees, and are "denied" membership if those dues and fees are not accepted. Thus, even in the situation in which employees openly admitted that they wished to have nothing to do with the union, were unwilling to participate in any of its activities or bear any allegiance to it, and were willing *only* to pay dues and fees for the right to work under the union-shop contract, the refusal of the union to accept these employees on those terms would, under the majority decision, be a denial of membership within the meaning of the provisos to Section 8(a)(3). It is from this particular aspect of our colleagues' decision that we most vigorously dissent.

Congress clearly recognized that unions operating under union-shop agreements usually impose certain "terms and conditions" for acquiring membership. In fact, in proviso (A) of Section 8(a)(3), Congress required that these "terms and conditions" must be nondiscriminatory. Our colleagues, however, say, in substance, that in the very next sentence, in proviso (B), Congress prescribed that such unions may impose *no* "terms or conditions" on acquiring membership — whether or not they are discriminatory — other than the tender of dues or fees. This is a forced construction containing the most obvious inconsistencies, and one we believe wholly unnecessary. For us it seems far more reasonable to construe the provisos, insofar as they apply to employees who must join the union, as follows: Proviso (A) permits unions to prescribe "terms and conditions" for acquiring membership in the union so long as they are nondiscriminatory, i.e. so long as all applicants are required to comply with them. Proviso (B) requires that *once these nondiscriminatory "terms and conditions" have been met,* by the employee seeking membership in the union, he cannot be denied membership for any other reason than failure to tender the dues and fees. In other words, under proviso (B), an employee has not been "denied" membership if he is unwilling to comply with the nondiscriminatory "terms or conditions" permitted under proviso (A). He is protected against discharge, under proviso (A), if the "terms and conditions" imposed are discriminatory. He is protected, under proviso (B), if, despite his willingness to comply with nondiscriminatory "terms and conditions" and his tender of the required dues and fees, he is not accepted as a member. So viewed, on the facts of the instant case, we would conclude that the discharged employees,

[34] We are persuaded, on the record as a whole, that in fact the three employees were unwilling to do more than pay dues. In reaching this conclusion, we are impressed with their failure to attend the union meeting at which their names were to be presented. If the Ralphs, for example, were really willing to do everything asked of them by the union except take an oath, it would appear reasonable for them to have come to the meeting, explained their religious scruples, and asked for a waiver of the requirement in their case.

having failed to comply with the union's nondiscriminatory "terms and conditions" for acquiring membership, were not "denied" membership within the meaning of proviso (B) and this discharge was protected under the valid union-shop contract. . . .

As we read the pertinent legislative history, one fact stands out: Congress carefully considered the possibility of outlawing all forms of union-security agreements, and despite vigorous efforts made to do just that, decided to permit the union shop with certain limitations. But those limitations had a very specific purpose. That purpose was expressed by Senator Taft in these terms: ". . . we have to have an open shop or an open union. The committee decreed an open union. I believe that will permit the continuation of existing relationships, and will not violently tear apart a great many long-existing relationships and make trouble in the labor movement; and yet at the same time it will meet the abuses which exist." The limitations contained in provisos (A) and (B) of Section 8(a)(3) were thus designed to assure that a union holding a union-shop contract shall be an "open" union. From the examples to which repeated references are made in the debates, it becomes abundantly clear that by an "open" union Congress meant a union which does not deny membership on some *arbitrary,* or *unreasonable basis.* Union shops are permitted, but the union cannot deny membership to employees who seek it, and who are willing to comply with reasonable nondiscriminatory terms and conditions, for some arbitrary or discriminatory reason. The construction we place upon the provisos to Section 8(a)(3) would fully accomplish what Congress sought to achieve. We find no evidence of an intent to distort union-shop agreements into mere devices by which unions can insure that all employees *pay* for the right to work. Yet that is the clear effect of the majority decision. . . .

NOTES

1. An employee was an officer of the respondent union, but supported a rival union's effort to displace the respondent. He refused to execute a non-Communist affidavit in order to prevent (under Section 9(h) of the Act as it then provided) the respondent union from appearing on the ballot. For this act, he was expelled from the union and discharged pursuant to a lawful union-shop agreement. Both union and company were held to have violated the Act. The ground for termination of union membership, the Board said, "however understandable and laudable standing by itself, remains one *other* than that failure to tender dues which Congress has specifically provided shall be the *sole* defense under the amended statute." Kingston Cake Co., Inc., 97 N.L.R.B. 1445, 1448 (1952). Cf. Sen. Minority Report No. 105, 80th Cong., 1st Sess. 9 (1947):

"Even under a union-security contract which this bill permits, an employee could with impunity completely defy the union. He could defame it, he could betray confidential union information, he could seek to wreck it, attempt to bring it into disrepute, act as a spy or stool-pigeon or strikebreaker, be a racketeer or a grafter, and yet the union would have no effective sanction against him. If he pays or offers to pay his dues and initiation fees, the employer need not fire him and any attempt by the union to persuade the employer to do so would be an unfair labor practice on the part of the union. The union would be completely shorn of effective power to discipline its members for good cause."

Why might Congress have imposed such a rule? Compare an editorial in the New York Times of November 27, 1961, entitled "Firmness Pays Off": "The swift termination of a crippling strike at a Nevada nuclear test site indicates that resolute action by union leaders who are willing to lead is a dependable safeguard against rank-and-file irresponsibility. The national heads of the A.F.L.-C.I.O. construction unions closed ranks behind Secretary of Labor Goldberg in his demand that their balky members at the base comply with the no-strike pledge labor gave last spring to stop inexcusable interference with the top-priority missile and space programs. Once it became clear that union cards and future jobs would be imperiled by continued defiance, the dissidents submitted their row to arbitration. This victory for orderly procedure is in refreshing contrast to the indecisiveness many union officials are exhibiting these days in restraining demagogues and hotheads from pushing their members into needless strikes or unrealistic bargaining positions." Is the Times applauding a flagrant violation of Section 8(b)(2)?

2. Does the right to refrain from union activities impose any restrictions on a union's capacity to fine, suspend, or expel a member, where his job is not sought to be affected? See the proviso to Section 8(b)(1)(A); Local 283, UAW (Wisconsin Motor Corp.), 145 N.L.R.B. 1097 (1964) (fine for violation of bylaw limiting the amount of incentive pay an employee may earn).

3. Demands for discharge have given rise to difficult questions even when they are based on loss of union membership for nonpayment of dues. Consider these problems:

(a) The union bylaws provide: "Monthly dues shall be $4.00. One dollar refund of dues collected for attendance at monthly meeting." An employee tenders $3.00, but the tender is refused as insufficient. If expelled from the union for nonpayment of dues, may he be discharged? See Leece-Neville Co., 140 N.L.R.B. 56 (1962), modified, 330 F.2d 242 (6th Cir. 1964).

(b) If an employee is expelled from a union for delinquency in his dues, and his discharge is demanded, what is the legal effect of a subsequent tender, prior to discharge, of all back dues? See General Motors Corp., 134 N.L.R.B. 1107 (1961), overruling Aluminum Workers International Union (Metal Ware Corp.), 112 N.L.R.B. 619 (1955); cf. Leece-Neville, supra, 140 N.L.R.B. at 59-62.

(c) International Union of Electrical Workers v. NLRB, 307 F.2d 679 (D.C. Cir. 1962): "We hold the Union may not refuse a good faith tender of dues made within a reasonable time after the employee has learned or reasonably should have learned that he must join the Union in order to keep his job. . . . Snyder was not forever barred from Union membership when he failed by January 19th to offer an application for membership along with the necessary monies, inasmuch as the record supports a view that he was not apprised of the necessity of membership before February 26. His technically belated tender, on February 27, 1959, of more than the necessary sums for membership, was received by the Union within a reasonable time after he was informed of this necessity. The Union's rejection of this tender was therefore improper, unless the tender itself was improperly made. [Snyder then owed a $5 initiation fee and $6 in dues, and sent a money order for $15 without explanation.] We hold it was properly made.

"A union may not treat as adversaries either its members or those potential members whose continued employment is dependent upon union membership. The Union's failure to inform Snyder of what he needed to do to protect his rights made it impossible for him to make a proper tender sooner than he did. The Union is bound by law to represent all employees in the bargaining unit. . . . The Union's assertion of improper tender, based on Snyder's failure specifically to allocate the $15 to dues and the initiation fee respectively, must be viewed by the Board and the court in the context provided by the statutory concept of fair play. We think a minimum of fair treatment would have included at least some notice to Snyder that his tender was excessive and that he should have indicated the manner in which he wished the money applied. Out-of-hand rejection of the money order, without a word of explanation, amounts in our view to an arbitrary failure on the Union's part to meet its obligations and peculiar responsibilities under the Act. As we agree that Snyder made the tender in good faith, the Board was clearly correct in asserting that the Union 'was under an obligation to explain the mechanics of reinstatement to Snyder and give him the opportunity to direct allocation of his tender in the manner required by the Union's rules for reinstatement.' " Pp. 683-684. See also NLRB v. Hotel Employees Union, 320 F.2d 254 (3d Cir. 1963).

(d) Note the prohibition in Section 8(b)(5) of any requirement that employees subject to a union-shop agreement pay "excessive or discriminatory" membership fees. See NLRB v. Television Broadcasting Studio Employees, 315 F.2d 398 (3d Cir. 1963) (use of substantial increase in initiation fee to discourage hiring of part-time employees).

4. To what extent are the Union Starch case and the cases discussed in these Notes explainable as a reflection of Board hostility to union security clauses? The Supreme Court has criticized the policy of strict construction of the proviso to Section 8(a)(3), expressed in footnote 12 to the principal case, supra page 643. "[I]t is the entire Act, and not merely one portion of it, which embodies 'the definitive statement of national policy.' It is well known, and the legislative history of the 1947 Taft-Hartley amendments plainly shows, that §8(a)(3) — including its proviso — represented the Congressional response to the competing demands of employee freedom of choice and union security. Had Congress thought one or the other overriding, it would doubtless have found words adequate to express that judgment. It did not do so; it accommodated both interests, doubtless in a manner unsatisfactory to the ex-

treme partisans of each, by drawing a line it thought reasonable. It is not for the administrators of the Congressional mandate to approach either side of that line grudgingly." Local 1424, International Assn. of Machinists v. NLRB, 362 U.S. 411, 417 n.7 (1960).

5. Compare the approach to the union security problem taken by the Massachusetts Labor Relations Act with that manifested in Section 8(a)(3) of the NLRA. Union-shop and closed-shop agreements are there permitted, except as applied to employees ineligible for "full membership and voting rights" in the union (Mass. Ann. Laws, c. 150A, §4(3)), but employees threatened with discharge pursuant to such agreements may appeal to the State Labor Relations Commission. Section 6A of the Act provides:

"If upon all the evidence the commission shall determine that the employee was unfairly denied admission to membership in such organization, or that such discipline —

"(1) Was imposed by the labor organization in violation of its constitution and by-laws; or

" (2) Was imposed without a fair trial, including an adequate hearing and opportunity to defend; or

"(3) Was not warranted by the offense, if any, committed by the employee against the labor organization; or

"(4) Is not consistent with the established public policy of the commonwealth; then the commission shall state its determinations and shall issue and cause to be served on the labor organization an order requiring it, in its discretion, either to admit or restore the employee to membership in good standing together with full voting rights, or else to refrain from seeking to bring about any discrimination against him in his employment because he is not a member in good standing, and to return to him such union dues and assessments as may have been collected from him during the period of his suspension or expulsion from the union. If the commission shall not make such a determination after hearing, it shall enter an order dismissing the charge filed by the employee."

See Cox, Some Aspects of the Labor Management Relations Act, 1947, 61 Harv. L. Rev. 1, 274, 291-299 (1948), for an analysis generally favoring the Massachusetts approach.

COMMENT ON UNION SECURITY IN FOREIGN COUNTRIES

Union security policies in other countries cover the spectrum from compulsory unionism by force of law, as in New Zealand and Ghana, to an absolute prohibition against union security arrangements, as in Denmark and Belgium. Between these polarities one may find permissive policies, as in Great Britain, Sweden, and Norway, as well as systems which attempt both to solve the "free rider" problem and to avoid interference with the right to refrain from membership — the "negative" right of association. Formal arrangements tell only part of the story. Even in the absence of union security clauses, the 100 per cent union shop commonly exists in Great Britain, Norway, Sweden, Denmark, Finland, West Germany, and Austria.

WESTERN EUROPE

"The dominant pattern in western democratic countries is a union shop without specific contract provisions. Trade-unions enforce this by a variety of methods, including the strike, boycott, refusal to work with nonunionists, and social pressure on unorganized workers. Jointly managed hiring systems, or halls, are sometimes set up, thus in effect assuring the preferential employment of members of the participating unions." Flexner, Union-Security Safeguards in Foreign Countries, 75 Mo. Lab. Rev. 134, 136 (1952).

Austria. The following 1930 enactment is still in effect today: "Provisions in collective bargaining contracts between employers and employees are null and void if they are intended (1) to ensure that no persons other than members of a particular union are employed in the shop, or (2) to keep from employment in the shop persons who are members of a particular union."

Unionists secured a modification of this basic law in 1954 to allow a dues checkoff arrangement between an individual employee and the employer. Lenhoff, The Problem of Compulsory Unionism in Europe, 5 Am. J. Comp. L. 18, 29 nn.49, 50 (1956). "In many industries there is a de facto union shop, and since most workers who have refused to join unions are former Nazis, no one is much concerned about their right to abstain. . . . In Austria, as in Scandinavia, the power of the union is so pervasive that membership is simply taken for granted." Galenson, Trade Union Democracy in Western Europe 28-29 (1961).

Western Germany. A general principle of freedom of association is established in Article 9 of the Basic Law of Bonn. Whether it was meant to include the right to refrain from joining unions has not yet been resolved by Germany's highest court, the Reichsgericht. At least one appellate court and several commentators find compulsory unionism contrary to the federal constitution. As a practical matter, union security clauses occasionally are included in collective agreements. See Brickman, Freedom of Association in Eight European Countries, 86 Mo. Lab. Rev. 1020, 1024 (1963); Lenhoff, supra, 30-35.

France. In France a strong individualistic tradition operates against union security, and the law is also adverse, as the following provision indicates: "No employer shall take account of trade union membership or the pursuit of union activities in reaching any decision on such matters as recruitment, the management and allocation of work, vocational training, promotion, remuneration, the award of social benefits, disciplinary action and dismissal.

"No employer shall deduct trade union dues from the wages of his employees or pay such dues on their behalf.

"No head of an undertaking or any of his representatives shall exert any form of pressure either for or against any trade union organization whatsoever.

"Any action taken by an employer in contravention of the preceding paragraphs shall be deemed to be an abusive practice and shall give rise to compensation for damages.

"The foregoing provisions shall render any agreement to the contrary null and void."

In practice, however, the union shop has been established in several industries, including publishing, marine trades, and building trades.

Switzerland. The 1956 Swiss Code of Obligations provides that "Any clause of an agreement or arrangement between the parties to compel employers or employees to join a contracting association shall be null and void." An important alternative approach to union security has developed from Parliament's 1956 approval of the principle of "loyalty to the contract." Similar to our "agency shop," this arrangement requires nonmembers to pay a "solidarity levy" to the union. Payment is insured by requiring the employer to employ only those workers "loyal to the contract." This concept gained judicial approval and in 1956, at the same time Parliament enacted the above quoted prohibitory language, it provided a detailed framework for application of the loyalty clause. A distinguishing feature is that levies or deposits must always be less than members' dues — contrary to the practice under the agency shop. Note also that the amounts of payments or deposits are subject to judicial determination; levied funds may be used only to defray costs of executing and applying the collective agreement or for purposes beneficial to all workers in the unit or trade. Members of rival unions cannot be compelled to contribute unless their union has had an opportunity to join the contract.

Denmark. A broad agreement negotiated by organized employers and workers in 1899 is still the basis for the Danish system of labor relations. This compact, known as the September Agreement, has been interpreted as a renunciation by unions of their right to demand closed or union shop provisions in collective agreements. Even use of hiring halls to apportion work is said to be prohibited. However, the national Labor Court has ruled that closed shop clauses in agreements with nonassociation employers operate as a bar to collective agreements with rival unions. This ruling may prove of great significance in the future since only about 40 per cent of Danish unionists were employed by the Employers' Association at last count. Brickman, supra, at 1022. Moreover, even though members of this association are prohibited from entering into agreements containing security clauses, "many employers, including those who belong to the employers' associations, follow closed- or union shop procedure as a matter of policy." Galenson, supra, at 78.

Norway. There is no legislation protecting the rank-and-file's right to refrain from joining unions. But nongovernmental bodies have offered some protection against infringement of associational rights. The Norwegian Federation of Labor adopted a "bill of rights" in 1934 which prohibits some forms of compulsory unionism. The aim of this bill of rights was to allow rival unionism. The National Employers Association in 1907 resolved that union shop agreements were "incompatible with the principle of freedom to work, and may not be concluded by members of the Employers Association." Galenson, Labor in Norway 205 (1949). As a result, the Labor Federation includes union security clauses in agreements only with independent employers. With over 90 per cent of the work force organized, however, a closed shop system in fact prevails.

Sweden. Specific guarantees of the right of association have existed since the passage of the Collective Bargaining Act of 1936. However, the Act has not been construed to give employees the right to refrain from membership, but only the positive right to join. Again, the Employers' Association forbids its members to be parties to a union security clause, but the success of the unions in Sweden has resulted in the closed shop in fact.

GREAT BRITAIN AND CANADA

As a result of the Trade Union Act of 1871, the Trade Disputes Act of 1906, and the cases interpreting these statutes, "it can be said that to-day the closed shop objective may be pursued by customary trade union methods without giving rise to actionable consequences. The reaching of a closed shop agreement, excluding non-members of specified unions, either on a post-entry or pre-entry basis, is neither a statutory or common law crime, nor a ground for action under statute or common law. Any man may refuse to work with another who is not a member of a specified trade union, and may persuade others to do likewise. Any man, or group of men, may threaten to strike if non-members are not removed." McCarthy, The Closed Shop in Britain 214 (1964). The quoted statement appears no longer to be true. In Rookes v. Barnard, [1964] 2 Weekly L.R. 269, 1 All E.R. 367, the House of Lords affirmed a finding of liability against defendants, members of a union who had urged a strike against British Overseas Airways Corporation, in breach of a no-strike commitment, unless BOAC discharged an employee who had withdrawn from the union. The effect of this decision on the future application of the Trade Disputes Act, 1906, 6 Edw. 7, c. 47, is discussed in Wedderburn, Intimidation and the Right to Strike, 27 Modern L. Rev. 257 (1964).

McCarthy, quoted above, uses the following definition of "closed shop" in his study: a "situation in which employees come to realize that a particular job is only to be obtained and retained if they become and remain members of one of a specified number of trade unions." He has determined that one out of every six workers is employed in a closed shop, and concludes that "in several skilled trades the entire craft is more or less comprehensively closed to the non-unionist, and among some semi-skilled and unskilled groups a number of rather specialized occupations are widely affected. . . . There is also a tendency for the closed shop to rise, to a greater extent, among employees of the larger firms and among skilled craftsmen generally. . . .

"About a fifth of workers in closed shops are in some sort of pre-entry shop and are subject to various forms of entry control. About half are in formally recognized closed shops, or are employed in industries where the great majority of employers will co-operate in its implementation. Outside mining, few are affected by the check off, and there is little membership choice." McCarthy, supra, at 78-79.

In most countries where the closed or union shop exists by law or in fact, there has arisen a movement to control the union's power to refuse admission or to expel members. See the excellent discussion of current British proposals in McCarthy at 231-255.

Canadian law permits all forms of union security clauses. "Nevertheless, 18 percent of the collective agreements in manufacturing industries covering 22 percent of the workers . . . analyzed in the most recent governmental survey, contained only the so-called Rand formula, In re Ford Motor Co. of Canada and UAW-CIO, 1 L.A. 439 (1946), under which workers are not required to join the contracting union but the employer deducts dues from non-members as well as from members." Dudra, Approaches to Union Security in Switzerland, Canada, and Colombia, 86 Mo. Lab. Rev. 136, 138 (1963).

Australia and New Zealand

Union security provisions, whether enacted by the several parliaments, awarded by industrial tribunals, or included in collective agreements, are of either of two types. The first is the preferential; the second is denominated "compulsory unionism." Both may be further subdivided: the former into absolute and qualified preference; the latter into closed (pre-entry) and union shops. See Martin, Legal Enforcement of Union Security in Australia, 13 Ind. & Lab. Rel. Rev. 227 (1960).

Colombia

Colombia, like other Latin American countries, guarantees and sanctions the rights both to join and to refrain from joining unions. Employers and unions are prohibited from interfering with the workers' freedom of association, and clauses which condition employment on union membership are made unlawful. An important recent amendment to the Labor Code provides that "unorganized workers who wish to benefit from a collective agreement shall pay to the union during the life of the agreement an amount equal to 50 percent of union dues," and that "the employer shall deduct from the wages of such workers corresponding amounts." Dudra, supra, at 137. An interesting feature of this arrangement is that employers are required to collect these amounts from the wages of nonmembers, but have no obligation to collect dues from union members.

(c) EMPLOYER DISCRIMINATION ENCOURAGING
UNION MEMBERSHIP

Except as its provisos permit, Section 8(a)(3) forbids an employer "by discrimination to encourage union membership," and a union is required by Section 8(b)(2) not "to cause or attempt to cause" an employer violation. The Supreme Court first considered the scope of these restrictions in Radio Officers Union v. NLRB, 347 U.S. 17 (1954). Three cases were argued together: in Teamsters, the employer had agreed to a union-sponsored reduction of the seniority of Frank Boston for delinquency in union dues payment (the agreement did not contain a union-shop clause); Radio Officers involved a union request to suspend William Fowler for seeking employment with the company, thereby "bumping" another employee, without attempting to obtain clearance from the union as required by the union's rules; Gaynor News arose out of a company decision not to extend the benefits of a wage increase negotiated with the union to nonmembers, on the ground that it was not affirmatively obliged to do so by the contract and, "in its business judgment," chose not to do so.

Three words in the statutory terminology called for construction: "discrimination," "encourage," and "membership." In an opinion by Justice Reed, the Court adopted a broad construction of each. "Discrimination is not contested in these cases: involuntary reduction of seniority, refusal to hire for an available job, and disparate wage treatment are clearly discriminatory." 347 U.S. at 39. Union "membership" was held to encompass any "participation in union activities" within the protection of Section 7: "The policy of the Act is to insulate employees' jobs from their organizational rights. Thus §§8(a)(3) and 8(b)(2) were designed to allow employees to freely exercise their right to join unions, be good, bad, or indifferent members, or abstain from joining any union without imperiling their livelihood. The only limitation Congress has chosen to impose on this right is specified in the proviso to §8(a)(3). . . ." Id. at 40. Finally, "encouragement" was held satisfied by an inference of a "tendency to encourage"; ". . . subjective evidence of employee response . . . is not required where encouragement or discouragement can be reasonably inferred from the nature of the discrimination." Id. at 51. The Court asserted: "Obviously, it would be gross inconsistency to hold that an inherent effect of certain discrimination is encouragement of union membership, but that the Board may not reasonably infer such encouragement. . . . [A] natural result of the disparate wage treatment in Gaynor was encouragement of union membership; thus it would be unreasonable to draw any inference other than that encouragement would result from such action. . . . The circumstances in Radio Officers and Teamsters are nearly identical. In each case the employer discriminated upon the instigation of the union. The purposes of the unions in causing such discrimination clearly were to encourage members to perform obligations or supposed obligations of membership.   Obviously, the unions would not have invoked such a sanction had they not considered it an effective method of coercing compliance with union obligations or practices."   Id. at 51-52.

The Court did not hold, however, that any disparate or unfavorable treatment of an employee which was likely to make employees want to support union policies or programs violated Section 8(a)(3).   Noting that the section prohibited neither all encouragement, nor all discrimination, but "only such discrimination as encourages or discourages membership in a labor organization," the Court emphasized the factor of motive:

"The relevance of the motivation of the employer in such discrimination has been consistently recognized under both §8(a)(3) and its predecessor. . . .

"But it is also clear that specific evidence of intent to encourage or discourage is not an indispensable element of proof of violation of §8(a)(3). . . .   Both the Board and the courts have recognized that proof of certain types of discrimination satisfies the intent requirement. This recognition that specific proof of intent is unnecessary where employer conduct inherently encourages or discourages union membership is but an application of the common-law rule that a man is held to intend the foreseeable consequences of his conduct. . . .   Thus an employer's protestation that he did not intend to encourage or discourage must be unavailing where a natural consequence of his action was such encouragement or discouragement.   Concluding that encouragement or discouragement will result, it is presumed that he intended such consequence.   In such circumstances intent to encourage is sufficiently established. . . .

"In Gaynor it was conceded that the sole criterion for extra payments was union membership. . . .   We express no opinion as to the legality of disparate payments where the union is not exclusive bargaining agent, since that case is not before us.   We do hold that in the circumstances of this case, the union being exclusive bargaining agent for both member and nonmember employees, the employer could not, without violating §8(a)(3), discriminate in wages solely on the basis of such membership even though it had executed a contract with the union prescribing such action. . . .   Such discriminatory contracts are illegal and provide no defense to an action under §8(a)(3).   See Steele v. Louisville & Nashville R. Co., 323 U.S. 192; Wallace Corp. v. Labor Board, 323 U.S. 248. . . ."[40]   Id. at 43-48.

Does the Court hold that foreseeability of encouragement, which suffices to establish "encouragement" within the meaning of Section 8(a)(3), likewise warrants an inference of intent or motive to encourage?   If so, does the requirement of proof of discriminatory motive add anything of substance?   To what extent is the *union's* motive significant in explain-

---

[40] The Steele and Wallace cases established that the exclusive representative owed a duty of "fair representation" to all employees in the bargaining unit, whether union members or not. — ED.

ing these cases? Would it violate Section 8(a)(3), as construed in Radio Officers, for a company to discharge several employees at the request of the union for refusing to abide by a resolution adopted at a union meeting, pledging that employees would not purchase automobiles manufactured by the employer's competitors? Cf. Studebaker Corp., 110 N.L.R.B. 1307, 1322-1327 (1954).

LOCAL 357, INTERNATIONAL BROTHERHOOD OF TEAMSTERS v. NLRB

Supreme Court of the United States, 1961
365 U.S. 667, 81 Sup. Ct. 835, 6 L. Ed. 2d 11

MR. JUSTICE DOUGLAS delivered the opinion of the Court.

Petitioner union (along with the International Brotherhood of Teamsters and a number of other affiliated local unions) executed a three-year collective bargaining agreement with California Trucking Associations, which represented a group of motor truck operators in California. The provisions of the contract relating to hiring of casual or temporary employees were as follows:

"Casual employees shall, wherever the Union maintains a dispatching service, be employed only on a seniority basis in the Industry whenever such senior employees are available. An available list with seniority status will be kept by the Unions, and employees requested will be dispatched upon call to any employer who is a party to this Agreement. Seniority rating of such employees shall begin with a minimum of three months service in the Industry, *irrespective of whether such employee is or is not a member of the Union.*

"Discharge of any employee by any employer shall be grounds for removal of any employee from seniority status. No casual employee shall be employed by any employer who is a party to this Agreement in violation of seniority status if such employees are available and if the dispatching service for such employees is available. The employer shall first call the Union or the dispatching hall designated by the Union for such help. In the event the employer is notified that such help is not available, or in the event the employees called for do not appear for work at the time designated by the employer, the employer may hire from any other available source." (Emphasis added.)

Accordingly the union maintained a hiring hall for casual employees. One Slater was a member of the union and had customarily used the hiring hall. But in August 1955 he obtained casual employment with an employer who was party to the hiring-hall agreement without being dispatched by the union. He worked until sometime in November of that year, when he was discharged by the employer on complaint of the union that he had not been referred through the hiring-hall arrangement.

Slater made charges against the union and the employer. Though, as plain from the terms of the contract, there was an express provision that employees would not be discriminated against because they were or were not union members, the Board found that the hiring-hall provision was unlawful per se and that the discharge of Slater on the union's request constituted a violation by the employer of §8(a)(1) and §8(a)(3) and a violation by the union of §8(b)(2) and §8(b)(1)(A) of the National Labor Relations Act, as amended by the Taft-Hartley Act. . . . The . . . Board's ruling in Mountain Pacific Chapter, 119 N.L.R.B. 883 . . . rendered in 1958, departed from earlier rulings and held, Abe Murdock dissenting, that the hiring-hall agreement, despite the inclusion of a nondiscrimination clause, was illegal per se.

[The following excerpts from the Mountain Pacific opinion state the Board's reasoning:

"The Respondents do not, nor could they, argue that this contract does not make employment conditional upon union approval, for a more complete and outright surrender of the normal management hiring prerogative to a union could hardly be phrased in contract language. . . .

"From the standpoint of the working force generally — those who, for all practical purposes, can obtain jobs only through the grace of the Union or its officials — it is difficult to conceive of anything that would encourage their subservience to union activity, whatever its form, more than this kind of hiring-hall arrangement. Faced with this hiring-hall contract, applicants for employment may not ask themselves what skills, experiences, or virtues are likely to win them jobs at the hands of AGC contracting companies. Instead their concern is, and must be: What, about themselves, will probably please the Unions or their agents? How can they conduct themselves best to conform with such rules and policies as Unions are likely to enforce? In short, how to ingratiate themselves with the Union, regardless of what the Employer's desires or needs might be. . . .

"Here the very grant of work at all depends solely upon union sponsorship, and it is reasonable to infer that the arrangement displays and enhances the Union's power and control over the employment status. Here all that appears is unilateral union determination and subservient employer action with no above-board explanation as to the reason for it, and it is reasonable to infer that the Union will be guided in its concession by an eye towards winning compliance with a membership obligation or union fealty in some other respect. The Employers here have surrendered all hiring authority to the Union and have given advance notice via the established hiring hall to the world at large that the Union is arbitrary master and is contractually guaranteed to remain so. From the final authority over hiring vested in the Respondent Union by the three AGC chapters, the inference of encouragement of union membership is inescapable." 119 N.L.R.B. at 894-896.]

The Board went on to say that a hiring-hall arrangement to be lawful must contain protective provisions. Its views were stated as follows:

"We believe, however, that the inherent and unlawful encouragement of union membership that stems from unfettered union control over the hiring process would be negated, and we would find an agreement to be nondiscriminatory on its face, only if the agreement explicitly provided that:

"(1) Selection of applicants for referral to jobs shall be on a nondiscriminatory basis and shall not be based on, or in any way affected by, union membership, bylaws, rules, regulations, constitutional provisions, or any other aspect or obligation of union membership policies, or requirements.

"(2) The employer retains the right to reject any job applicant referred by the union.

"(3) The parties to the agreement post in places where notices to employees and applicants for employment are customarily posted, all provisions relating to the functioning of the hiring arrangement, including the safeguards that we deem essential to the legality of an exclusive hiring agreement." Id., 897.

The Board recognizes that the hiring hall came into being "to eliminate wasteful, time-consuming, and repetitive scouting for jobs by individual workmen and haphazard uneconomical searches by employers." Id. 896, N. 8. The hiring hall at times has been a useful adjunct to the closed shop. But Congress may have thought that it need not serve that cause, that in fact it has served well both labor and management — particularly in the maritime field and in the building and construction industry. In the latter the contractor who frequently is a stranger to the area where the work is done requires a "central source" for his employment needs; and a man looking for a job finds in the hiring hall "at least a minimum guarantee of continued employment."

Congress has not outlawed the hiring hall, though it has outlawed the closed shop except within the limits prescribed in the provisos to §8(a)(3). Senator Taft made clear his views that hiring halls are useful, that they are not illegal per se, that unions should be able to operate them so long as they are not used to create a closed shop:

"In order to make clear the real intention of Congress, it should be clearly stated that the hiring hall is not necessarily illegal. The employer should be able to make a contract with the union as an employment agency. The union frequently is the best employment agency. The employer should be able to give notice of vacancies, and in the normal course of events to accept men sent to him by the hiring hall. He should not be able to bind himself, however, to reject nonunion men if they apply to him; nor should he be able to contract to accept men on a rotary-hiring basis. . . .

". . . The National Labor Relations Board and the courts [in early decisions] did not find hiring halls as such illegal, but merely certain practices under them. The Board and the court found that the manner in which the hiring halls operated created in effect a closed shop in violation of the law. Neither the law nor these decisions forbid hiring halls, even hiring halls operated by the unions as long as they are not so operated as to create a closed shop with all of the abuses possible under such an arrangement, including discrimination against employees, prospective employees, members of union minority groups, and operation of closed union." S. Rep. No. 1827, 81st Cong., 2d Sess., pp. 13, 14.[41]

There being no express ban of hiring halls in any provisions of the Act, those who add one, whether it be the Board or the courts, engage in a legislative act. The Act deals with discrimination either by the employers or unions that encourages or discourages union membership. . . .

But surely discrimination cannot be inferred from the face of the instrument when the instrument specifically provides that there will be no discrimination against "casual employees" because of the presence or absence of union membership. The only complaint in the case was by Slater, a union member, who sought to circumvent the hiring-hall agreement. When an employer and the union enforce the agreement against union members, we cannot say without more that either indulges in the kind of discrimination to which the Act is addressed.

It may be that the very existence of the hiring hall encourages union membership. We may assume that it does. The very existence of the union has the same influence. When a union engages in collective bargaining and obtains increased wages and improved working conditions, its prestige doubtless rises and, one may assume, more workers are drawn to it. When a union negotiates collective bargaining agreements that include arbitration clauses and supervises the functioning of those provisions so as to get equitable adjustments of grievances, union membership may also be encouraged. The truth is that the union is a service agency that probably encourages membership whenever it does its job well. But . . . the only encouragement or discouragement of union membership banned by the Act is that which is "accomplished by discrimination."

Nothing is inferrable from the present hiring-hall provision except that employer and union alike sought to route "casual employees" through the union hiring hall and required a union member who circumvented it to adhere to it.

It may be that hiring halls need more regulation than the Act presently affords. As we have seen, the Act aims at every practice, act, source or institution which in fact is used to encourage and discourage union membership by discrimination in regard to hire or tenure, term or condition of employment. Perhaps the conditions which the Board attaches to hiring-hall arrangements will in time appeal to the Congress. Yet, where Congress has adopted a selective system for dealing with evils, the Board is confined to that system. . . . Where, as here, Congress has aimed its sanctions only at specific discriminatory practices, the Board cannot go further and establish a broader, more pervasive regulatory scheme. . . .

The present agreement for a union hiring hall has a protective clause in it, as we have said; and there is no evidence that it was in fact used unlawfully. We cannot assume that a union conducts its operations in

[41] What is the significance of the fact that this statement was made in 1949? — ED.

violation of law or that the parties to this contract did not intend to adhere to its express language. Yet we would have to make those assumptions to agree with the Board that it is reasonable to infer the union will act discriminatorily. . . .

Reversed.

MR. JUSTICE FRANKFURTER took no part in the consideration or decision of this case.

MR. JUSTICE HARLAN, whom MR. JUSTICE STEWART joins, concurring.

I join the Court's opinion upon considerations which, though doubtless implicit in what my Brother Douglas has written, in my view deserve explicit articulation.

The Board's condemnation of these union "hiring hall" procedures as violative of §§8(a)(1), 8(a)(3), 8(b)(1), and 8(b)(2) of the National Labor Relations Act, as amended by the Taft-Hartley Act, ultimately rests on a now well-established line of circuit court cases to the effect that a clause in a collective bargaining agreement may, without more, constitute forbidden discrimination. See, e.g., Red Star Express Lines v. Labor Board, 196 F.2d 78. While seeming to recognize the validity of the proposition that contract terms which are equivocal on their face should ordinarily await an independent evaluation of their actual meaning and effect before being deemed to give rise to an unfair labor practice, such cases have justified short-circuiting that course upon these considerations: The mere existence of a clause that on its face appears to declare preferential rights for union members encourages union membership among employees or job applicants, persons not privy to the undisclosed intent of the parties, yet affected by the apparent meaning of the contract. Hence the mere possibility that such a clause may actually turn out not to have been administered by the parties so as to favor union members is not enough to save it from condemnation as an unlawful discrimination.

I think this rationale may have validity under certain circumstances, but that it does not carry the day for the Board in these cases. . . .

What in my view is wrong with the Board's position in these cases is that a mere showing of foreseeable encouragement of union status is not a sufficient basis for a finding of violation of the statute. It has long been recognized that an employer can make reasonable business decisions, unmotivated by an intent to discourage union membership or protected concerted activities, although the foreseeable effect of these decisions may be to discourage what the act protects. For example, an employer may discharge an employee because he is not performing his work adequately, whether or not the employee happens to be a union organizer. See Labor Board v. Universal Camera Corp., 190 F.2d 429. Yet a court could hardly reverse a Board finding that such firing would foreseeably tend to discourage union activity. Again, an employer can properly make the existence or amount of a year-end bonus depend upon the productivity of a unit of the plant, although this will foreseeably tend to discourage the protected activity of striking. Pittsburgh-Des Moines Steel Co. v. Labor Board, 284 F.2d 74. A union, too, is privileged to make decisions which are reasonably calculated to further the welfare of all the employees it represents, nonunion as well as union, even though a foreseeable result of the decision may be to encourage union membership.

. . . We must determine whether the Board's action is consistent with the balance struck by the Wagner and Taft-Hartley Acts between protection of employee freedom with respect to union activity and the privilege of employer and union to make such nondiscriminatory decisions as seem to them to satisfy best the needs of the business and the employees.

The legislative background to §8(a)(3) of the Act is quite clear in its indications of where this balance was to be struck. The Senate Report on this section of the original Wagner Act states:

"The fourth unfair labor practice [then Section 8(3)] is a corollary of the first unfair labor practice. An employer, of course, need not hire an incompetent man and is free to discharge an employee who lacks skill or ability. But if the right to join or not to join a labor organization is to have any real meaning for an employee, the employer ought not to be free to discharge an employee *merely* because he joins an organization or to refuse to hire him *merely* because of his membership in an organization. Nor should an employer be free to pay a man a higher or lower wage *solely* because of his membership or nonmembership in a labor organization. The language of the bill creates safeguards against these possible dangers." S. Rep. No. 1184 on S. 2926, 73d Cong., 2d Sess. 6. (Emphasis added.)

[Other excerpts from the legislative history, quoted by Mr. Justice Harlan, are omitted]. Considered in this light, I do not think we can sustain the Board's holding that the "hiring hall" clause is forbidden by the Taft-Hartley Act. The Board has not found that this clause was without substantial justification in terms of legitimate employer or union purposes. . . . Whether or not such a finding would have been supported by the record is not for us now to decide. The Board has not, in my view, made the type of showing of an actual motive of encouraging union membership that is required by Universal Camera v. Labor Board, supra. All it has shown is that the clause will tend to encourage union membership, and that without substantial difficulty the parties to the agreement could have taken additional steps to isolate the valid employer or union purposes from the discriminatory effects of the clause. I do not think that these two elements alone can justify a Board holding of an unfair labor practice unless we are to approve a broad expansion of the power of the Board to supervise nondiscriminatory decisions made by employer or union. Whether or not such an expansion would be desirable, it does not seem to me consistent with the balance the labor acts have struck between freedom of choice of management and union ends by the parties to a collective bargaining agreement and the freedom of employees from restraint or coercion in their exercise of rights granted by §7 of the Act.

I therefore agree with the Court that the Board holding that the clause in question is invalid cannot be sustained.

MR. JUSTICE CLARK, dissenting.

I cannot agree with the casual treatment the Court gives to the "casual employee" who is either unable to get employment or is fired therefrom because he has not been cleared by a union hiring hall. Inasmuch as the record, and the image of a hiring hall which it presents, are neglected by the Court, a short résumé of the facts is appropriate.

Lester Slater, the complainant, became a "casual employee" in the truck freight business in 1953 or early 1954. He approached an employer but was referred to the union hiring hall. There the dispatcher told him to see Barney Volkoff, an official of the union, whose office in the union headquarters building was some three miles away. Describing his visit to Volkoff, Slater stated that "(I) just give him (Volkoff) the money to send back East to pay up my dues back there for the withdrawal card, . . . and I went right to the (hiring) hall and went to work." However, this was but the beginning of Slater's trouble with the hall. After some difficulty with one of his temporary employers (Pacific Intermountain Express), the hall refused to refer Slater to other employers. In order to keep employed despite the union hall's failure to dispatch him, Slater relied on a letter from John Annand, an International Representative of the union, stating that "you may seek work wherever you can find it in the freight industry without working through the hiring hall." It was this letter that obtained Slater his employment with Los Angeles-Seattle Motor Express, where he was characterized by its dock foreman as being "a good worker." After a few months employment, the Business Agent of the union (Victor Karaty) called on the Los Angeles-Seattle Motor Express, advising that it could not hire Slater "any longer here without a referral card"; that the company would "have to get rid of Slater, and if (it) . . . didn't, that he was going to tie the place up in a knot, (that he) would pull the men off." Los Angeles-Seattle Motor Express fired Slater, telling him that "(We) . . . can't use you now until you get this straightened out with the union. Then come back; we will put you to work." He then went to the union, and was again referred to Volkoff who advised, "I can't do anything for this job." Upon being shown the Annand letter, Volkoff declared "I am the union." On later occasions when Slater attempted to get clearance from Volkoff he was asked "How come you weren't out on that — didn't go out on the picket line?" (Apparently the Union had been on a strike.) Slater testified, "I told him that nobody asked me to. I was out a week. I thought the strike was on. The hall was closed. The guys told me there weren't no work." The landlady of Slater also approached Volkoff in an effort to get him cleared and she testified that "I asked Mr. Barney Volkoff what he had against Lester Slater and why he was doing this to him." And she quoted him as saying: "For a few reasons, one is about the P.I.E. (Pacific Intermountain Express) . . . (a)nother thing, he is an illiterate." She further testified that "he (Volkoff) didn't like the way he dressed. And he (Volkoff) fussed around and fussed around." He therefore refused to "route," as the Court calls it, Slater through the union hiring hall.

I do not doubt for a moment that men hired through hiring halls are saved the expense and delay of making the rounds of prospective employers on their own. Nor do I doubt their utility to employers with varying employee demands. And I accept the fact that Congress has outlawed only closed shops and allowed hiring halls to remain in operation. But just as those observations are not, in the final analysis, relied upon by the Court today in reaching its decision, my acquiescence in them is only a prologue to my dissent from the remaining considerations upon which its decision actually rests. These considerations are dependent upon the construction given §8(a)(3) and I therefore . . . turn to that section.

The word "discrimination" in the section, as the Board points out and I agree, includes not only distinctions contingent upon "the presence or absence of union membership," but all differences in treatment regardless of their basis. This is the "cause" portion of the section. But §8(a)(3) also includes an "effect" clause which provides that the intended or inherent effect of the discrimination must be "to encourage or discourage [union] membership." The section has, therefore, a divided structure. Not all discriminations violate the section, but only those the effect of which is encouragement or discouragement of union membership. . . . Each being a requirement of the section, both must be present before an unfair labor practice exists. On the other hand, the union here contends, and the Court agrees, that there can be no "discrimination" within the section *unless it is based on* union membership, i.e., members treated one way, nonmembers another, with further distinctions, among members, based on good standing. Through this too superficial interpretation, the Court abuses the language of the Congress and unduly restricts the scope of the proscription so that it forbids only the most obvious "hard-sell" techniques of influencing employee exercise of §7 rights.

Even if we could draw no support from prior cases, the plain and accepted meaning of the word means to distinguish or differentiate. Without good reason, we should not limit the word to mean to distinguish in a particular manner (i.e., on the basis of union membership or activity) so that a finding that the hall dispatched employees without regard to union membership or activity bars a finding of violation. The mere fact that the section *might* be read in the manner suggested by the union does not license such a distortion of the clear intent of the Congress, i.e., to prohibit all auxiliaries to the closed shop, and all pressures on employee free choice, however subtly they are established or applied. . . .

Given that interpretation of the word "discrimination," it becomes necessary to determine the class of employee involved, and then whether *any* differences in treatment within that class are present. The Board found the class affected by the union hiring hall to be that group which was qualified, in the sense of ability, to do the work required by the employer and who had applied for work through the hiring hall. Obviously, not all of those who apply receive like treatment. Not all applicants receive referral cards. Clearly, then, the class applying to the hiring hall is itself divided into two groups treated differently — those cleared by the union and those who were not. The next question is whether the contract requiring and endorsing that discrimination or differentiation is designed to, or inherently tends to, encourage union membership. If it does, then §8(a)(3) has been violated. . . .

I would hold that there is not only a reasonable likelihood, but that it must inescapably be concluded under this record, that, without the safeguards at issue, a contract conditioning employment *solely upon union referral* encourages membership in the union by that very distinction itself. . . .

MR. JUSTICE WHITTAKER joins in . . . this dissent.

NOTES

1. Are there any circumstances under which the Board can now find an exclusive hiring hall provision to violate Section 8(a)(3) or 8(b)(2)? Could the Board, after this decision, take the position that exclusive hiring hall agreements, even if not discriminatory within the meaning of Sections 8(a)(3) and 8(b)(2), nevertheless violate Sections 8(a)(1) and 8(b)(1)(A)? See Note, Unilateral Union Control of Hiring Halls: The Wrong and the Remedy, 70 Yale L.J. 661 (1961). What is the effect of the Court's construction of Section 8(a)(3) on the permissible scope of Section 8(a)(1)?

2. Mountain Pacific was a response to the fact that hiring halls are often operated as closed shops, and that adjudications of individual acts of discrimination are at best effective to redress and deter isolated violations only. See also United Assn. of Journeymen Plumbers (Brown-Olds Plumbing & Heating Corp.), 115 N.L.R.B. 594 (1956), where the Board held that it would order the parties to an unlawful union security agreement to reimburse all employees in the bargaining unit for all dues and assessments paid for the period beginning six months prior to the filing of the charge. The Supreme Court held such a reimbursement order to be outside the Board's remedial powers. Local 60, United Brotherhood of Carpenters v. NLRB, 365 U.S. 651 (1961). Cf. J. J. Hagerty, Inc., 139 N.L.R.B. 633 (1962), in which the union hiring hall had been repeatedly found to have violated the Act in its referral practices. The Board ordered the union, "in conjunction with the Regional Director of the Board and subject to his supervision and approval, to set up a nondiscriminatory hiring and referral system"; to keep permanent records, available for the Regional Director's inspection, of its hiring and referral operation; and to submit to the Regional Director four quarterly reports about the application, referral, and employment records of the charging parties. The Regional Director was directed, at his discretion, to conduct spot checks during the year of the union's hiring and referral system. Id. at 638-639. The Court of Appeals gave this order a quick burial: "Although the Board has broad power to fashion remedies appropriate to the needs of each case . . . it may not require a union to set up a hiring hall. . . . We

have granted enforcement of the Board's order prohibiting discrimination in the operation of the hiring hall, and this we think is as far as the Board may go. Representatives of the Board should not be injected into the procedures by which the union, in conjunction with employers, establishes a referral system. Therefore, we deny enforcement of the provision requiring that the union set up a hiring hall. In view of the pattern of continuing discrimination in the operation of its hiring hall, however, we think that the Board was justified in directing the union to keep full records of its operations and make them available to the Board and its representative." Local 138, International Union of Operating Engineers v. NLRB, 321 F.2d 130, 137-138 (2d Cir. 1963). Is this all that deserves to be said? In what ways does Hagerty represent a more responsible attempt than Mountain Pacific or Brown-Olds to cope with a vexing problem?

3. Consider Summers, A Summary Evaluation of the Taft-Hartley Act, 11 Ind. & Lab. Rel. Rev. 405, 409-410 (1958):

"The real failure of the law is that it has not been obeyed. The closed shop and hiring hall are still standard practice in the construction industry and are only thinly disguised in printing, longshore, and maritime. In the building trades the established practice of the unions and employers is to ignore the law, pay any claims filed, and keep away from the courts. The very industries in which the abuses were most severe have not changed their ways.

"The moral here again is that it is difficult to legislate against union-management cooperation, but the problem runs much deeper. The closed shop, closed union, and hiring hall — an inseparable trilogy — persist because of practical needs of both unions and employers. In industries where employment is short-term, seniority structures are impossible. Those workers who are established in the industry seek priority of job rights by requiring that new entrants wait until established workers are employed. The auto worker, the steel worker, and even the office worker has his seniority clause which gives him job priority. In these industries there is no 'free labor market;' a man cannot get a job where he wants it. For the hodcarrier, the bricklayer, or the carpenter, the closed shop trilogy provides his substitute for seniority. The statute attempted to wipe out all this and substituted nothing in its place. This desperate need for job priority cannot thus be wished away with a wand of words. The employer's need is nearly as compelling. In these industries the employer needs a pool of labor on which to draw on short notice; he cannot advertise or even maintain an adequate personnel department. The hiring hall is a practical and proven solution.

"The Taft-Hartley Act gave no recognition to these stubborn economic facts. Where there were genuine economic needs of the parties, it attempted to create a vacuum. It blandly assumed that, if the union were prohibited from having a closed shop, the employers would protect the individuals. The signal lesson of the Taft-Hartley Act is that when the union's needs are acute, and when the employer's needs or desires for cooperation are strong, legal measures must be carefully constructed to permit the creating of new institutions to meet the genuine needs."

(d) STATE "RIGHT-TO-WORK" LAWS AND SECTION 14(b)

"The term 'right-to-work' is normally used to describe statutes or constitutional provisions that prohibit the requirement of union membership as a condition of employment. Twenty states have such laws. . . . The constitutionality of such laws was upheld in Plumbers Union v. Graham, 345 U.S. 192 (1953). [See also Lincoln Federal Labor Union v. Northwestern Iron and Metal Co., 335 U.S. 525 (1949).] Right-to-work laws differ widely, however, with respect to scope and remedies. Some consist simply of a constitutional amendment to the effect that the right of persons to work shall not be denied or abridged on account of membership or nonmembership in any labor organization. . . . Most laws declare agreements in conflict with that policy unlawful. . . . In addition, some laws prohibit: (1) 'combinations' or 'conspiracies' to deprive persons of employment because of non-membership . . . (2) strikes or picketing for the purpose of inducing an illegal agreement . . . (3) denial of employment to any persons because of membership or nonmembership . . . (4) conspiracy to cause the discharge or denial of employment to an individual by inducing other persons to refuse to work with him because he is a non-member. . . . With respect to remedies, most laws provide for damages to persons injured by a violation . . . many provide for injunctions . . . and some make violation a misdemeanor subject to criminal penalties. . . . Many right-to-work laws appear to go beyond a prohibition against making union membership or non-membership a condition of employment. . . . [S]ome laws proscribe requirements of membership in or 'affiliation with' a labor organization as a condition of employment. . . . Many expressly prohibit a requirement that an individual pay 'dues, fees, or other charges of any kind to a union as a condition of employment.' . . . Several contain a prohibition against compelling a person to join a union or strike against his will by threatened or actual interference with his person, family, or property. . . . Even further afield, some laws appear to sanction individual bargaining in the face of collective bargaining. . . . In addition to the right-to-work states, some states have laws regulating union security agreements more restrictively than does federal law, without prohibiting them. . . ." Grodin and Beeson, State Right-to-Work Laws and Federal Labor Policy, 52 Calif. L. Rev. 95, 96 n.6 (1964).

RETAIL CLERKS INTERNATIONAL ASSN. v. SCHERMERHORN

Supreme Court of the United States, 1963
373 U.S. 746, 83 Sup. Ct. 1461, 10 L. Ed. 2d 678

[The question was whether Florida had power to invalidate an agency-shop agreement between an employer and petitioner, the certified bargaining representative of the employer's employees. The agreement required nonmembers of the union, as a condition of employment, to pay a "service fee" equal to the initiation fee and dues, "for the purpose of aiding the Union in defraying costs in connection with its legal obligations and responsibilities as the exclusive bargaining agent of the employees in the appropriate bargaining unit." In NLRB v. General Motors Corp., 373 U.S. 734 (1963), see page 637 supra, decided the same day as the principal case, the Court rejected the view that, because an agency-shop agreement was not one requiring "membership" in a union, it did not fall within the permission to engage in discrimination encouraging union membership contained in the first proviso to Section 8(a)(3). The Court relied on long-standing Board and court interpretations of the proviso as setting merely the outer limit on permissible union security arrangements, and read the Taft-Hartley amendment to the first proviso as designed only to contract that outer limit to exclude the closed shop. In response to the company's reliance on the statute's express reference to "membership," the Court noted that by virtue of the second proviso " 'membership' as a condition of employment is whittled down to its financial core." Id. at 742.]

MR JUSTICE WHITE delivered the opinion of the Court. . . .

The connection between the §8(a)(3) proviso and §14(b) is clear. Whether they are perfectly coincident, we need not now decide, but unquestionably they overlap to some extent. At the very least, the agreements requiring "membership" in a labor union which are expressly permitted by the proviso are the same "membership" agreements expressly placed within the reach of state law by §14(b). It follows that the General Motors case rules this one, for we there held that the "agency shop" arrangement involved here — which imposes on employees the only membership obligation enforceable under §8(a)(3) by discharge, namely, the obligation to pay initiation fees and regular dues — is the "practical equivalent" of an "agreement requiring membership in a labor organization as a condition of employment." Whatever may be the status of less stringent union-security arrangements, the agency shop is within §14(b). At least to that extent did Congress intend §8(a)(3) and §14(b) to coincide.

Petitioners, belatedly, would now distinguish the contract involved here from the agency shop contract dealt with in the General Motors case on the basis of allegedly distinctive features which are said to require a different result. Article 19 provides for nonmember payments to the union "for the purpose of aiding the Union in defraying costs in connection with its legal obligations and responsibilities as the exclusive bargaining agent of the employees in the appropriate bargaining unit," a provision which petitioners say confines the use of nonmember payments to collective bargaining purposes alone and forbids their use by the union for institutional purposes unrelated to its exclusive agency functions, all in sharp contrast, it is argued, to the General Motors situation where the nonmember contributions are available to the union without restriction.

We are wholly unpersuaded. . . . There is no ironclad restriction imposed upon the use of nonmember fees, for the clause merely describes the payments as being for "the purpose of aiding the Union" in meeting collective bargaining expenses.   The alleged restriction would not be breached if the service fee was used for both collective bargaining and other expenses, for the union would be "aided" in meeting its agency obligations, not only by the part spent for bargaining purposes but also by the part spent for institutional items, since an equivalent amount of other union income would thereby be freed to pay the costs of bargaining agency functions.

But even if all collections from nonmembers must be directly committed to paying bargaining costs, this fact is of bookkeeping significance only rather than a matter of real substance.   It must be remembered that the service fee is admittedly the exact equal of membership initiation fees and monthly dues, . . . and that, as the union says in its brief, dues collected from members may be used for a "variety of purposes, in addition to meeting the union's costs of collective bargaining."   Unions "rather typically" use their membership dues "to do those things which the members authorize the union to do in their interest and on their behalf."   If the union's total budget is divided between collective bargaining and institutional expenses and if nonmember payments, equal to those of a member, go entirely for collective bargaining costs, the nonmember will pay more of these expenses than his pro rata share.   The member will pay less and to that extent a portion of his fees and dues is available to pay institutional expenses.   The union's budget is balanced.   By paying a larger share of collective bargaining costs the nonmember subsidizes the union's institutional activities.   In over-all effect, economically, and we think for the purposes of §14(b), the contract here is the same as the General Motors agency shop arrangement.   Petitioners' argument, if accepted, would lead to the anomalous result of permitting Florida to invalidate the agency shop but forbidding it to ban the present service fee arrangement under which collective bargaining services cost the nonmember more than the member. . . .

MR. JUSTICE GOLDBERG took no part in the consideration or decision of this case.

NOTES

1. Does Section 14(b) permit a state to apply its "right-to-work" law, as in Kaiser v. Price-Fewell, Inc., 235 Ark. 295, 359 S.W.2d 449 (1962), to prohibit an agreement for exclusive employer use of a union-operated hiring hall?   Cf. Houston Chapter, Associated General Contractors, 143 N.L.R.B. 409 (1963).   Does it permit a state to construe its law, as in Piegts v. Amalgamated Meat Cutters, 228 La. 131, 81 So.2d 835 (1955), to outlaw an exclusive recognition clause in a collective bargaining agreement with a majority union?

2. Some states do not prohibit the union shop, but impose conditions on its legality going beyond those contained in the first proviso to Section 8(a)(3).   E.g., Colo. Rev. Stat. Ann. §80-5-6(1)(C), prohibiting a union shop agreement unless 75 per cent of the employees have by secret ballot authorized it.   The NLRB has suggested that Section 14(b) authorizes states

to "prohibit," but not to "regulate," union security, and that such statutes are therefore overridden by the federal Act. See Cyclone Sales, Inc., 115 N.L.R.B. 431 (1956); Northland Greyhound Lines, Inc., 80 N.L.R.B. 288 (1948). The Supreme Court seems to have rejected this view in Algoma Plywood Co. v. Wisconsin Employment Relations Board, 336 U.S. 301, 314 (1949): "[I]f there could be any doubt that the Act shall not be construed to authorize any 'application' of a union-security contract, such as discharging an employee, which under the circumstances 'is prohibited' by the State, the legislative history of the section would dispel it."

3. Unlike the NLRA, Section 2, Eleventh, of the Railway Labor Act permits union shop agreements in the railroad and airline industries "notwithstanding any other provisions of . . . any other statute or law . . . of any State. . . ." See Railway Employees Department v. Hanson, 351 U.S. 225 (1956).

RETAIL CLERKS INTERNATIONAL ASSN. v. SCHERMERHORN

Supreme Court of the United States, 1963
375 U.S. 96, 84 Sup. Ct. 219, 11 L. Ed. 2d 179

MR. JUSTICE DOUGLAS delivered the opinion of the Court.

The sole question in the case is the one we set down for reargument in 373 U.S. 746, 747-748: "whether the Florida courts, rather than solely the National Labor Relations Board, are tribunals with jurisdiction to enforce the State's prohibition" against an "agency shop" clause in a collective bargaining agreement. . . .

We start from the premise that, while Congress could preempt as much or as little of this interstate field as it chose, it would be odd to construe §14(b) as permitting a State to prohibit the agency clause but barring it from implementing its own law with sanctions of the kind involved here.

Section 14(b) came into the law in 1947, some years after the Wagner Act. The latter did not bar as a matter of federal law an agency-shop agreement. Section 8(a)(3) of the Taft-Hartley Act also allowed it, saying that "nothing in this Act, or in any other statute of the United States, shall preclude" one.

By the time §14(b) was written into the Act, twelve States had statutes or constitutional provisions outlawing or restricting the closed shop and related devices — a state power which we sustained in Lincoln Union v. Northwestern Co., 335 U.S. 525. These laws — about which Congress seems to have been well informed during the 1947 debates — had a wide variety of sanctions, including injunctions, damage suits, and criminal penalties. In 1947 Congress did not outlaw union-security agreements per se; but it did add new conditions, which, as presently provided in §8(a)(3), require that there be a 30-day waiting period before any employee is forced into a union, that the union in question is the appropriate representative of the employees, and that an employer not discriminate against an employee if he has reasonable grounds for believing that membership in the union was not available to the employee on a nondiscriminatory basis or that the employee's membership was denied or terminated for reasons other than failure to meet union-shop requirements as to dues and fees. In other words, Congress undertook pervasive regulation of union-security agreements, raising in the minds of many whether it thereby preempted the field under the decision in Hill v. Florida, 325 U.S. 538, and put such agreements beyond state control. That is one reason why a section, which later became §14(b), appeared in the House bill — a provision described in the House Report as making clear and unambiguous the purpose of Congress not to preempt the field. That purpose was restated by the House Conference Report in explaining §14(b). Senator Taft in the Senate debates stated that §14(b) was to continue the policy of the Wagner Act and avoid federal interference with state laws in this field. As to the Wagner Act he stated, "But that did not in any way prohibit *the enforcement of State laws* which already prohibited closed shops." (Italics added.) He went on to say, "That has been the law ever since that time. It was the law of the Senate bill; and in putting in this express provision from the House bill, (§14(b)) we in no way change the bill as passed by the Senate of the United States."

In light of the wording of §14(b) and this legislative history, we conclude that Congress in 1947 did not deprive the States of any and all power to enforce their laws restricting the execution and enforcement of union-security agreements. Since it is plain that Congress left the States free to legislate in that field, we can only assume that it intended to leave unaffected the power to enforce those laws. Otherwise, the reservation which Senator Taft felt to be so critical would become empty and largely meaningless.

As already noted, under §8(a)(3) a union-security agreement is permissible, for example, if the union represents the employees as provided in §9(a) (subject to rescission of the authority to make the agreement as provided in §8(a)(3)). Those are federal standards entrusted by Congress to the Labor Board. Yet even if the union-security agreement clears all federal hurdles, the States by reason of §14(b) have the final say and may outlaw it. There is thus conflict between state and federal law; but it is a conflict sanctioned by Congress with directions to give the right of way to state laws barring the execution and enforcement of union-security agreements. It is argued that if there is a violation of a state union-security law authorized by §14(b), it is a federal unfair labor practice and that the federal remedy is the exclusive one. It is urged that that course is necessary, if uniformity is to be achieved. But §14(b) gives the States power to outlaw even a union-security agreement that passes muster by federal standards. Where Congress gives state policy that degree of overriding authority, we are reluctant to conclude that it is nonetheless enforceable by the federal agency in Washington.

This result on its face may seem to be at war with San Diego Council v. Garmon, 359 U.S. 236, decided in 1959, and holding that where action is "arguably subject to §7 or §8 of the Act, the States as well as the federal courts must defer to the exclusive competence of the National Labor Relations Board." Id., at 245. In Garmon a state court was held precluded by the Taft-Hartley Act from awarding damages under state law for eco nomic injuries resulting from peaceful picketing of a plant by labor un·

ions that had not been selected by a majority of the employees as their bargaining agents.

Garmon, however, does not state a constitutional principle; it merely rationalizes the problems of coexistence between federal and state regulatory schemes in the field of labor relations; and it did not present the problems posed by §14(b), viz., whether the Congress had precluded state enforcement of select state laws adopted pursuant to its authority. The purpose of Congress is the ultimate touchstone. Congress under the Commerce Clause may displace state power . . . or it may even by silence indicate a purpose to let state regulation be imposed on the federal regime.

Congress . . . chose to abandon any search for uniformity in dealing with the problems of state laws barring the execution and application of agreements authorized by §14(b) and decided to suffer a medley of attitudes and philosophies on the subject.

As a result of §14(b), there will arise a wide variety of situations presenting problems of the accommodation of state and federal jurisdiction in the union-security field. . . . Algoma Plywood Co. v. Wisconsin Board [336 U.S. 301], upheld the right of a State to reinstate with back pay an employee discharged in violation of a state union-security law. On the other hand, picketing in order to get an employer to execute an agreement to hire all-union labor in violation of a state union-security statute lies exclusively in the federal domain (Local Union 429 v. Farnsworth & Chambers Co., 353 U.S. 969, and Local No. 438 v. Curry, 371 U.S. 542), because state power, recognized by §14(b), begins *only with actual negotiation and execution of the type of agreement described by §14(b)*. Absent such an agreement, conduct arguably an unfair labor practice would be a matter for the National Labor Relations Board under Garmon.

We held in Plumbers' Union v. Borden, 373 U.S. 690, and in Iron Workers v. Perko, 373 U.S. 701, that Garmon preempted the field where employees were suing unions for damages arising out of practices that arguably were unfair labor practices subject to regulation by the National Labor Relations Board. Those cases, however, did not present for decision any problem under §14(b), though the question was tendered in the Borden case but not passed on either by the state tribunal or by us. 373 U.S., at 692, n. 2.

The relief prayed for below is within the ambit of Algoma Plywood Co. v. Wisconsin Board, supra, and the regulatory scheme that Congress designed when it adopted §14(b).

Affirmed.

MR. JUSTICE GOLDBERG took no part in the consideration or decision of this case.

NOTES

1. The Court was first presented with the problem of the application of the pre-emption doctrine in the context of injunctions against concerted activities based on state "right-to-work" laws in Local 429, IBEW v.

Farnsworth & Chambers Co., Inc., 353 U.S. 969 (1957). Without argument or opinion, the Court reversed a Tennessee injunction, simply citing two pre-emption cases which did not involve union security or state "right-to-work" laws. In Local 438, Construction Union v. Curry, 371 U.S. 542 (1963), the Court settled the question in as few words as possible: "Nor is the jurisdiction of the Georgia courts sustainable . . . by reason of the Georgia right-to-work law and by §14(b) of the National Labor Relations Act. . . . This precise contention has been previously considered and rejected by this Court [citing Farnsworth]." Id. at 547-548. The principal case, holding that enforcement of a union-shop agreement may be enjoined or otherwise made actionable in a state court, but that picketing to obtain such an agreement "lies exclusively in the federal domain," for the first time supplied a rationale for the application of Section 14(b) to the pre-emption issue. What basis is there in the underlying purposes of the pre-emption doctrine for drawing the line the Court has drawn?

2. "State right-to-work laws have frequently been invoked in such cases [as] the discriminatory operation of a hiring hall, the discharge of an employee because of his union membership or nonmembership when no agreement is involved, picketing to force the discharge of non-union employees and the hiring of union members, and other actions which the Board would find to violate the [National] Act. Discrimination of this kind, indeed, is more prevalent than the enforcement of a closed shop contract, for few employers and unions enter into such obviously illegal agreements." Grodin and Beeson, State Right-to-Work Laws and Federal Labor Policy, 52 Calif. L. Rev. 95, 107 (1964). Does Schermerhorn II apply in these cases, giving the state courts jurisdiction concurrent with that of the NLRB?

C. COLLECTIVE BARGAINING AND THE PUBLIC INTEREST

1. *The Benefits and Burdens of Technological Advances*

OPERA ON TOUR v. WEBER
Court of Appeals, New York, 1941
285 N.Y. 348, 34 N.E.2d 349

FINCH, J.

The question presented for decision is far reaching and of vital importance to the best interests of unions of employees, of employers and of the general public. The only issue is whether the leaders of the defendant unions were engaged in promoting a lawful labor objective when the Musicians' Union induced the Stagehands' Union to join in a combination to destroy an enterprise solely because of the use of machinery in the production of music in place of the employment of live musicians. . . .

After a trial at Special Term, it was found upon sufficient evidence that plaintiff was engaged in the business of rendering performances of grand opera with an orchestral accompaniment of music mechanically reproduced from records instead of by an orchestra of live musicians. The purpose was to make grand opera available in those cities and towns of the United States which could not afford otherwise this form of entertainment because of the prohibitive cost of transporting a grand opera orchestra. Each of the two defendants is a labor union.

It was found that the members of the defendant unions had no other grievance of any kind, nor did there exist any controversy except this demand to discard machinery, between plaintiff and the defendant unions. The defendant Musicians' Union threatened to and did put plaintiff out of business solely because of the use of recorded music. The defendant Musicians' Union induced the defendant Stagehands' Union to order its members to cease rendering any service to plaintiff, which order had to be obeyed by the members of the defendant Stagehands' Union since over ninety-five per cent of the theatres and auditoria in the United States are closed shop, and without membership in the defendant Stagehands' Union the latter find it practically impossible to obtain employment. In addition, the defendant Musicians' Union ordered that no member of that union render services to plaintiff, and caused the American Guild of Musical Artists to order its members not to render services to plaintiff, and members of the Stagehands' Union not to accept employment from plaintiff. If they had not been so ordered, the members of the defendant Stagehands' Union would have continued to render services to plaintiff. As a result of this conspiracy between the two defendant unions, plaintiff was unable to fulfill its bookings and its contracts which had already been made and was prevented from entering into further engagements for the presentation of opera, and in consequence thereof this entire enterprise was forced to come to a complete stop. . . .

Does this demand of these defendant unions, that plaintiff discard machinery in the interest of the immediate employment of a few individuals, constitute a lawful labor objective? . . .

To make impossible the continuance of a business and thus to prevent the employment of a full complement of actors, singers, and stagehands merely because a machine is not discarded and in place thereof live musicians employed, is not a lawful labor objective. In Hopkins v. Oxley Stave Co., 8 Cir., 83 F. 912, the labor objective sought was to abandon certain machines for hooping barrels which materially lessened the cost of making the same. The introduction of the machine actually resulted in the dismissal of certain employees, and the court held the labor objective unlawful.

In Haverhill Strand Theatre v. Gillen, 229 Mass. 413, 118 N.E. 671, the owner of a motion picture theatre used an organ played by hand during the presentation of its pictures. A union sought to compel the use of an orchestra of five pieces. The Supreme Court of Massachusetts held that defendants were guilty of an unlawful labor objective. . . .

In essence the case at bar is the same as if a labor union should demand of a printing plant that all machinery for typesetting be discarded because it would furnish more employment if the typesetting were done by hand. . . .

Since the endeavor to prevent the use of a mechanical device bears no reasonable relation to wages, hours of employment, health, safety, the right of collective bargaining, or any other condition of employment or for the protection of labor from abuses, there is no labor dispute within either the letter or the spirit of the Civil Practice Act. Civil Practice Act, §876-a, subd. 10; Thompson v. Boekhout, 273 N.Y. 390, 7 N.E.2d 674; Luft v. Flove, 270 N.Y. 640, 1 N.E.2d 369. In other words, there is involved in the case at bar solely the demand that a new enterprise shall not make use of machinery in order to create places for live musicians. Neither in the previous judicial decisions of this court has it been held, nor in any statute enacted, that a dispute is a labor dispute which has no connection with or relation to terms or conditions of employment, collective bargaining, protection from abuses, or respective interests of employer and employee. In the case at bar there is no actual employment at all. There is the use of a machine in place of a human relationship between one individual and another. Section 876-a, subd. 10, par. c, defines a labor dispute as any controversy concerning terms or conditions of employment, or concerning representation in arranging terms and conditions of employment, or any controversy arising out of the respective interests of employer and employee whether they stand in such relationship or not. All these words assume the existence of a human relationship. The words of this statute eo nomine relate to terms or conditions of employment, the right of representation for purposes of collective bargaining concerning such terms and conditions of employment, and the respective interests of employer and employee. Such respective interests of employer and employee must be interests that grow out of or have some relationship to employment. Advantage not connected with employment is not the interest referred to in the statute. . . .

LEHMAN, Chief Justice, dissenting. . . .

Here the objective sought is to compel producers of stage performances to abandon the use of mechanical devices which take the place of human labor. I agree with the statement in the opinion of Judge Finch that "in essence the case at bar is the same as if a labor union should demand of a printing plant that all machinery for typesetting be discarded because it would furnish more employment if the typesetting were done by hand." As in the case suggested the union is asserting a right "to insist that machinery be discarded in order that manual labor may take its place and thus secure additional opportunity of employment," and though in the suggested case the injury to the public would perhaps outweigh more overwhelmingly possible benefit to labor, the difference is one of degree, not of principle, and if the courts are free to weigh the interest of the public against the self-interest of the union members, then argument not without force may be made to sustain the decision of the court at Special Term.

I assume argumentatively that the unions have no dispute with the employer concerning the wages, hours of employment, health, safety, right of bargaining, or other incident of the employment of any member of the Stagehands' Union or any other person presently in the employ of the plaintiff, and that the objective of the strike is not to improve the conditions of such employment, but to compel the employment of more musicians by stopping the use of musical devices "operated," as Judge Finch points out, "in place of the employment of live musicians." That the use of machines which displace men causes unemployment among those displaced is obvious; though at times the resultant saving of labor cost may so increase sales of the product that loss of employment by one set of workers may be offset by increased employment of other workmen or benefit to the public may, in the minds of reasonable men, far outweigh the harm caused by loss of employment in the group displaced by the labor-saving machine. In this case it was shown that the number of professional musicians employed in public performances has been enormously reduced by the use of talking machines, radio, or other devices for reproduction of music. Is it unlawful now for musicians and members of affiliated unions, likewise employed in stage productions, to combine to organize strikes with the objective of compelling employers to abandon the use of such devices, and thus stop further inroads and to regain the loss of employment already suffered?

Heretofore this court has unequivocally affirmed the right of workmen to combine for similar objectives. Here is an economic conflict between workers and producers. The workers seek to compel the producers to employ more men than the producers desire to employ, or than are required for the conduct of their business in a manner which is acceptable to the public and which will produce greatest profit to the producers. The labor-saving machine displaces labor and reduces costs. That is its purpose. By displacing labor it causes unemployment in some places; by reducing costs it may make it possible to conduct at a profit a business which would otherwise be doomed to failure. A combination to compel the abandonment of cost-reducing devices may thus be a threat of ruin to a business already upon a precarious economic footing. Here it is such a threat to the plaintiff. Almost every strike indeed involves threat of ruin to the employer unless the employer accepts the demands of the strikers, for ordinarily strikes are successful only where the employer concludes that to run his business he must make terms with the strikers. None the less a strike to achieve a legitimate economic purpose cannot be outlawed because if successful some employers will no longer be able to conduct business at a profit; nor is a combination unlawful because it includes all the workers within a trade and thus no employer can find workers who know that trade and are willing to accept employment unless the employer reaches an agreement with the members of the combination. . . .

The court's command to the unions to cancel their strike order is not only contrary to the policy of the State as established by an unbroken line of judicial decisions, but it disregards a direct and clear legislative mandate that such a strike is not unlawful and may not be enjoined.

No court may under the statute directly or indirectly prohibit a strike, conducted peacefully and in orderly fashion "in any case involving or growing out of a labor dispute." The statute defines a labor dispute as follows: "The term 'labor dispute' includes any controversy concerning terms or conditions of employment, or concerning the association or representation of persons in negotiating, fixing, maintaining, changing or seeking to arrange terms or conditions of employment, or concerning employment relations, or any other controversy arising out of the respective interests of employer and employee, *regardless of whether or not the disputants stand in the relation of employer and employee*." (Civ. Prac. Act, §876-a, subd. 10, par. c.) The validity of the statute is not now challenged. It could hardly be since this court has in careful and comprehensive opinions sustained and applied the statute. . . .

We are told, however, that the statute does not apply here because there is no labor dispute. Why there is no "labor dispute" here remains a mystery to me. Reliance is placed upon Thompson v. Boekhout (273 N.Y. 390), where this court held that there can be no labor dispute where there is no relation of employer and employee and that a strike called to compel the owner of a business to hire employees though he desires to run his business alone is unlawful. Here, however, there was relation of employer and employee, between the plaintiff and the members of the Stagehands' Union, and, therefore, the case of Thompson v. Boekhout does not apply. . . . Judge Finch in May's Furs & Ready-to-Wear, Inc., v. Bauer (282 N.Y. 331, 339) has pointed out that the statute in explicit terms "provides that if the other requisites are present then a labor dispute shall be found to exist 'regardless of whether or not the disputants stand in the relation of employer and employee.' (Subd. 10-c.) It is undisputably clear that the existence or nonexistence of the employer-employee relation cannot be the factor by which to determine the presence or absence of a labor dispute." It follows that the controversy here is no less a labor dispute because the strike of the plaintiff's employees is primarily to assist members of an affiliated union in the same industry in an economic conflict for the purpose of procuring employment. That is a dispute "concerning employment relations" and under the express terms of the statute is clearly a labor dispute. The unambiguous language of the statute and what was said and decided in May's Furs & Ready-to-Wear, Inc. v. Bauer (supra) leaves, I think, no room for doubt on that point. . . .

The judgment should be affirmed.

NOTES

1. In Harper v. Hoecherl, 153 Fla. 29, 14 So.2d 179 (1943), the employer sought to enjoin the Painters Union from enforcing its rule prohibiting the use of spray guns. Although the employer was building army barracks during time of war and had been asked by the army to rush the work, the court refused to issue an injunction. In Bayer v. Brotherhood of Painters, 108 N.J. Eq. 257, 154 Atl. 759 (1931), a con-

tractor who owned stock in a corporation loaned it money to buy a paint-spraying machine. The Painters Union ordered its members not to work for the contractor on any of its projects, and the court refused to issue an injunction.

In United States v. Carrozzo, 37 F. Supp. 191 (N.D. Ill. 1941), aff'd sub nom. United States v. International Hod Carriers, 313 U.S. 539 (1941), the Hod Carriers struck to prevent the use of cement mixers unless the contractor would guarantee no reduction in employment. This was found to be no violation of the antitrust laws. See also United States v. American Federation of Musicians, 47 F. Supp. 304 (N.D. Ill. 1942), where the Musicians' bar on recordings was held not to be a violation of the antitrust laws.

2. The insecurity of employment may induce unions to engage in "featherbedding" practices also. This making of work by requiring employers to hire unnecessary employees has been held by some courts to be an unlawful objective. In LaFayette Dramatic Productions Inc. v. Ferentz, 305 Mich. 193, 9 N.W.2d 57 (1943), the court voided a contract to employ six musicians for a theatrical production. The Musicians Union two hours before curtain time threatened to call a strike of the stagehands if the musicians were not hired. See also Folsom Engraving Co. v. McNeil, 235 Mass. 269, 126 N.E. 479 (1920); Moreland Theatres v. Portland Moving Picture Machine Operators, 140 Ore. 35, 12 P.2d 333 (1932). But for decisions finding this to be a lawful objective, see Scott-Stafford Opera House Co. v. Minneapolis Musicians Assn., 118 Minn. 410, 136 N.W. 1092 (1912); Empire Theatre Co. v. Cloke, 53 Mont. 183, 163 Pac. 107 (1917).

The legislatures have been as undecided as the courts in determining the legality of this objective. Many states, at the prodding of the railroad brotherhoods, have passed "full crew" laws which ostensibly have been for safety purposes but strongly motivated by the desire to preserve jobs. On the other hand, some state legislatures have made illegal union efforts to require the hiring of stand-ins, to restrict production, or to prevent changes in business methods. See Note, Legislative Shackles on Featherbedding Practices, 34 Cornell L.Q. 255 (1948).

In 1946, Congress sought to outlaw the Musicians' practices of requiring stand-ins when "canned music" was used in broadcasting. The Lea Act made it a crime to compel an employer to employ "any person or persons in excess of the number of employees needed." 60 Stat. 89, 47 U.S.C. §506(a)(1) (1958). Petrillo, the president of the Musicians, was indicted for threatening to strike a station unless it hired three extra musicians. The court allowed an expert to testify that these three were "needed" to satisfy the public demand for "live" music, and to fulfill the station's duty to promote the public interest by providing employment for musicians. The court found there was nothing but evidence of a good faith attempt to obtain honest employment for additional musicians and dismissed the indictment. United States v. Petrillo, 75 F. Supp. 176 (N.D. Ill. 1948).

AMERICAN NEWSPAPER PUBLISHERS ASSN. v. NLRB
Supreme Court of the United States, 1953
345 U.S. 100, 73 Sup. Ct. 552, 97 L. Ed. 852

MR. JUSTICE BURTON delivered the opinion of the Court.

The question here is whether a labor organization engages in an unfair labor practice, within the meaning of §8(b)(6) of the National Labor Relations Act, as amended by the Labor Management Relations Act, 1947, when it insists that newspaper publishers pay printers for reproducing advertising matter for which the publishers ordinarily have no use. For the reasons hereafter stated, we hold that it does not. . . .

Printers in newspaper composing rooms have long sought to retain the opportunity to set up in type as much as possible of whatever is printed by their respective publishers. In 1872, when printers were paid on a piecework basis, each diversion of composition was at once reflected by a loss in their income. Accordingly, ITU, which had been formed in 1852 from local typographical societies, began its long battle to retain as much typesetting work for printers as possible.

With the introduction of the linotype machine in 1890, the problem took on a new aspect. When a newspaper advertisement was set up in type, it was impressed on a cardboard matrix, or "mat." These mats were used by their makers and also were reproduced and distributed, at little or no cost, to other publishers who used them as molds for metal castings from which to print the same advertisement. This procedure by-passed all compositors except those who made up the original form. Facing this loss of work, ITU secured the agreement of newspaper publishers to permit their respective compositors, at convenient times, to set up duplicate forms for all local advertisements in precisely the same manner as though the mat had not been used. For this reproduction work the printers received their regular pay. The doing of this "made work" came to be known in the trade as "setting bogus." It was a wasteful procedure. Nevertheless, it has become a recognized idiosyncrasy of the trade and a customary feature of the wage structure and work schedule of newspaper printers.

By fitting the "bogus" work into slack periods, the practice interferes little with "live" work. The publishers who set up the original compositions find it advantageous because it burdens their competitors with costs of mat making comparable to their own. Approximate time limits for setting "bogus" usually have been fixed by agreement at from four days to three weeks. On rare occasions the reproduced compositions are used to print the advertisements when rerun, but, ordinarily, they are promptly consigned to the "hell box" and melted down. Live matter has priority over reproduction work but the latter usually takes from 2 to 5% of the printers' time. By 1947, detailed regulations for reproduction work were included in the "General Laws" of ITU. They thus became a standard part of all employment contracts signed by its local unions. The locals were allowed to negotiate as to foreign language publications, time limits for setting "bogus" and exemptions of mats received from commercial compositors or for national advertisements.

Before the enactment of §8(b)(6), the legality and enforceability of payment for setting "bogus," agreed to by the publisher, was recognized. Even now the issue before us is not what policy should be adopted by the Nation toward the continuance of this and other forms of featherbedding. The issue here is solely one of statutory interpretation: Has Congress made setting "bogus" an unfair labor practice? . . .

. . . [T]he court below concluded that the insistence by ITU upon securing payment of wages to printers for setting "bogus" was not an unfair labor practice. It found that the practice called for payment only for work which actually was done by employees of the publishers in the course of their employment as distinguished from payment "for services which are not performed or not to be performed." Setting "bogus" was held to be service performed and it remained for the parties to determine its worth to the employer. The Board here contends also that the insistence of ITU and its agents has not been "in the nature of an exaction" and did not "cause or attempt to cause an employer" to pay anything "in the nature of an exaction." Agreement with the position taken by the court below makes it unnecessary to consider the additional contentions of the Board. . . .

. . . [T]he Taft-Hartley bill, H.R. 3020, when it passed the House, April 17, 1947, contained in §§2(17) and 12(a)(3)(B) an explicit condemnation of featherbedding. Its definition of featherbedding was based upon that in the Lea Act. For example, it condemned practices which required an employer to employ "persons in excess of the number of employees reasonably required by such employer to perform actual services," as well as practices which required an employer to pay "for services . . . which are not to be performed." [9] The substitution of

[9] H.R. 3020 as it passed the House provided that:

"Sec. 2. When used in this Act — . . .

"(17) The term 'featherbedding practice' means a practice which has as its purpose or effect requiring an employer —

"(A) to employ or agree to employ any person or persons in excess of the number of employees reasonably required by such employer to perform actual services; or

"(B) to pay or give or agree to pay or give any money or other thing of value in lieu of employing, or on account of failure to employ, any person or persons, in connection with the conduct of the business of an employer, in excess of the number of employees reasonably required by such employer to perform actual services; or

"(C) to pay or agree to pay more than once for services performed; or

"(D) to pay or give or agree to pay or give any money or other thing of value for services, in connection with the conduct of a business, which are not to be performed; or

"(E) to pay or agree to pay any tax or exaction for the privilege of, or on account of, producing, preparing, manufacturing, selling, buying, renting, operating, using, or maintaining any article, machine, equipment, or materials; or to accede to or impose any restriction upon the production, preparation, manufacture, sale, purchase, rental, operation, use, or maintenance of the same, if such restric-

the present §8(b)(6) for that definition compels the conclusion that §8(b)(6) means what the court below has said it means.   The Act now limits its condemnation to instances where a labor organization or its agents exact pay from an employer in return for services not performed or not to be performed.   Thus, where work is done by an employee, with the employer's consent, a labor organization's demand that the employee be compensated for time spent in doing the disputed work does not become an unfair labor practice.   The transaction simply does not fall within the kind of featherbedding defined in the statute.   In the absence of proof to the contrary, the employee's compensation reflects his entire relationship with his employer. . . .

. . . Section 8(b)(6) leaves to collective bargaining the determination of what, if any, work, including bona fide "made work," shall be included as compensable services and what rate of compensation shall be paid for it.

Accordingly, the judgment of the Court of Appeals sustaining dismissal of the complaint, insofar as it was based upon §8(b)(6), is affirmed.

MR. JUSTICE DOUGLAS, dissenting.

I fail to see how the reproduction of advertising matter which is never used by a newspaper but which indeed is set up only to be thrown away is a service performed for the newspaper.   The practice of "setting bogus" is old and deeply engrained in trade union practice.   But so are other types of "feather-bedding."   Congress, to be sure, did not outlaw all "feather-bedding" by the Taft-Hartley Act.   That Act leaves unaffected the situation where two men are employed to do one man's work. . . .

But the situation in this case is to me quite different.   Here the typesetters, while setting the "bogus," are making no contribution whatsoever to the enterprise.   Their "work" is not only unwanted, it is indeed wholly useless.   It does not add directly or indirectly to the publication of the newspaper nor to its contents.   It does not even add an "unwanted" page or paragraph.   In no sense that I can conceive is it a "service" to the employer.   To be sure, the employer has agreed to pay for it.   But the agreement was under compulsion. . . .   No matter how time-honored the practice, it should be struck down if it is not a service performed for an employer.

The outlawry of this practice under §8(b)(6) of the Taft-Hartley Act might be so disruptive of established practices as to be against the

---

tion is for the purpose of preventing or limiting the use of such article, machine, equipment, or materials. . . .

"Sec. 12. (a) The following activities, when affecting commerce, shall be unlawful concerted activities: . . .

"(3) Calling, authorizing, engaging in, or assisting — . . .

"(B) any strike or other concerted interference with an employer's operations, an object of which is to compel an employer to accede to featherbedding practices; . . ." 1 Legislative History of the Labor Management Relations Act, 1947, 160, 170-171, 204, 205.

public interest. But the place to obtain relief against the new oppression is in the Congress, not here.

MR. JUSTICE CLARK, with whom THE CHIEF JUSTICE [VINSON] joins, dissenting.

Today's decision twists the law by the tail. If the employees had received pay for staying home, conserving their energies and the publisher's material, the Court concedes, as it must, that §8(b)(6) of the National Labor Relations Act would squarely apply. Yet in the Court's view these printers' peculiar "services" snatch the transaction from the reach of the law. Those "services," no more and no less, consist of setting "bogus" type, then proofread and reset for corrections, only to be immediately discarded and never used. Instead, this type is consigned as waste to a "hell box" which feeds the "melting pot"; that, in turn, oozes fresh lead then molded into "pigs" which retravel the same Sisyphean journey. The Court thus holds that an "anti-featherbedding" statute designed to hit wasteful labor practices in fact sanctions additional waste in futile use of labor, lead, machines, proofreading, "hell-boxing," etc. Anomalously, the more wasteful the practice the less effectual the statute is.

Section 8(b)(6) declares it an unfair labor practice for a labor organization or its agents *"to cause or attempt to cause* an employer to pay or deliver or agree to pay or deliver any money or other thing of value, *in the nature of an exaction,* for *services* which are not performed or not to be performed."* But "to cause or attempt to cause" can refer equally to the ordinary give-and-take of the collective bargaining process or the unleashing of the ultimate weapons in a union's armory. Likewise, "in the nature of an exaction" may imply that a union's pay demands must be tantamount to extortion to bring §8(b)(6) into play; on the other hand, the phrase may merely describe payments "for services which are not performed or not to be performed." Again, "services" may designate employees' conduct ranging from shadow boxing on or off the plant to productive effort deemed beneficial to the employer in his judgment alone.

The Court solves these complex interpretive problems by simply scrapping the statute. A broadside finding that "bogus" is "work," making analysis of all other statutory criteria superfluous, automatically takes the case out of §8(b)(6). And the printers' doing solely that which then must be undone passes for "work." An imaginative labor organization need not strain far to invent such "work." With that lethal definition to stifle §8(b)(6), this Court's first decision on "featherbedding" may well be the last. . . .

. . . [W]e would read the statute's test of "services" as more than a hollow phrase. Recognizing the administrative difficulties in deciding how many employees are too many for a particular job, Congress perhaps spared the National Labor Relations Board from that. But the Board should certainly not need efficiency engineers to determine that printers setting "bogus" indulge in frivolous make-work exercise. An interpretation of "services" in §8(b)(6) to exclude contrived and patently useless job operations not to the employer's benefit could effectuate the legislative purpose. . . . And the Labor Board should not so modestly disclaim its oft-recognized expertise which assures full qualifications for administering this task.

It may well be that union featherbedding practices reflect no more than labor's fears of unstable employment and sensitivity to displacement by technological change. But in a full-employment economy Congress may have deemed this form of union security an unjustifiable drain on the national manpower pool. In any event, that judgment was for the legislature. Under our system of separation of powers the Court ought not so blithely mangle the congressional effort.

NOTES

1. On the same day, the Court decided NLRB v. Gamble Enterprises, 345 U.S. 117 (1953). In this case, a local of the American Federation of Musicians demanded, as a condition of allowing traveling orchestras to appear on a local theater's programs, that a local orchestra also be hired to (a) play overtures and intermissions, or (b) play for vaudeville acts, or (c) play at half the total number of stage shows each year. The Court, speaking through Justice Burton, held that the union was demanding actual employment for its members and not "stand-by" payments, and thus was not in violation of the LMRA. Chief Justice Vinson and Justice Clark dissented. Justice Jackson also dissented even though he had concurred with the majority in the American Newspaper Publishers case. He distinguished that case on the ground that the "bogus work" practice was an old custom developed with the consent of the industry and thus could be viewed as a fair adjustment of the working conditions in the industry. In contrast, the demand involved in the Gamble case was a new demand, designed to get around the clear condemnation of "stand-by" payments.

On the other hand, it should be noted that Justice Douglas, who had dissented in the Publishers case, was with the majority in the Gamble case. His distinction between the two cases, stated in an omitted portion of his dissent printed above, was that in the Gamble case, whether wasteful or not, the employer would be getting services from the orchestra. In the Publishers case, as he saw it, the employer received no benefit whatsoever.

2. United States v. Green, 350 U.S. 415 (1956), involved a union representative and his union, indicted for violation of the Hobbs Act, 62 Stat. 793 (1948), 18 U.S.C. §1951 (1958). This Act prohibits extortion in interstate commerce by threats of violence. The Court held sufficient an indictment which charged Green and his union with threatening violence to compel the employer to hire workers he did not need and to pay wages for fictitious services. The Court distinguished the Publishers and Gamble cases on the ground that here the demands were being en-

forced by threats of violence. Justice Douglas, joined by Chief Justice Warren and Justice Black, dissented on the ground that the case was not a proper one for direct appeal from the Federal District Court.

3. For discussion of the LMRA antifeatherbedding provisions see Cox, Some Aspects of the Labor Management Relations Act, 1947, 61 Harv. L. Rev. 274, 288 (1948); Note, Featherbedding and Taft-Hartley, 52 Colum. L. Rev. 1020 (1952). Consider also the following suggestion: "If featherbedding is not to be freed from all governmental restraints, it would seem preferable to permit the widest latitude of experimentation in what Holmes described as the 'insulated chambers afforded by the several states.' Such a policy would undoubtedly result in considerable confusion and much bad law, but the evil effects would be limited in scope and the experience might prove salutory." Aaron, Governmental Restraints on Featherbedding, 5 Stan. L. Rev. 680, 718 (1953). This article is a thorough study of the whole area of attempts to control featherbedding by law.

4. What is the pre-emptive effect of the NLRA on state power to regulate union efforts to prevent the use of laborsaving machinery or to force an employer to hire or retain employees whom it reasonably regards as unnecessary? See Cox and Seidman, Federalism and Labor Relations, 64 Harv. L. Rev. 211, 237-238 (1950).

ORDER OF RAILROAD TELEGRAPHERS v. CHICAGO AND NORTH WESTERN RAILROAD CO.

Supreme Court of the United States, 1960
362 U.S. 330, 80 Sup. Ct. 761, 4 L. Ed. 2d 774

MR. JUSTICE BLACK delivered the opinion of the Court.

According to the verified complaint filed in a United States District Court in Illinois by the respondent, Chicago & North Western Railway Company, against the petitioner, the Order of Railroad Telegraphers and its labor union officials, "This is an action for injunction to restrain and enjoin the calling and carrying out of a wrongful and unlawful strike or work stoppage on plaintiff's railroad." Section 4 of the Norris-LaGuardia Act provides, however, that "No court of the United States shall have jurisdiction to issue any restraining order or temporary or permanent injunction in any case involving or growing out of *any labor dispute* to prohibit any person or persons . . . from . . . (a) Ceasing or refusing to perform any work or to remain in any relation of employment; . . ." The main question in this case . . . is, whether this prohibition of the Norris-LaGuardia Act bars an injunction in the circumstances of this case.

Respondent railroad, owning and operating a rail system of over 9,000 miles in the States of Illinois, Wisconsin, Iowa, Minnesota, Michigan, Nebraska, South Dakota, North Dakota, and Wyoming, is an integral part of the nationwide railway system important to the transportation of passengers and freight in interstate commerce. When the railroad began operations, about 100 years ago, traffic was such that railroad stations were established about 7 to 10 miles apart. Trucks, automobiles, air-planes, barges, pipelines and modern roads have reduced the amount of railroad traffic so that the work now performed at many of these stations by agents is less than one hour during a normal eight-hour day. Main-tenance of so many agencies where company employees do so little work, the complaint alleges, is wasteful and consequently in 1957 the railroad filed petitions with the public utility commissions in four of the nine States in which it operated asking permission to institute a "Central Agency Plan whereby certain stations would be made central agencies . . ." and others abolished. The plan would necessarily result in loss of jobs for some of the station agents and telegraphers, members of the petitioner union. A few weeks after the state proceedings were filed and before any decision had been made, the petitioner union . . . notified the railroad under §6 of the Railway Labor Act, 45 U.S.C. §156, that it wanted to negotiate with the railroad to amend the current bargaining agreement by adding the following rule: "No position in existence on December 3, 1957, will be abolished or discontinued except by agreement between the carrier and the organization." The railroad took the posi-tion, according to its complaint, that this request did not constitute a "labor dispute under the Railway Labor Act," that it did not raise a bargainable issue, and that the union had no right to protest or to seek relief except by appearing before the state public utility commissions which had power to determine whether station agencies could be discon-tinued, a power which private parties could not thwart by entering into a bargaining agreement. The respondent added that maintenance of the unnecessary agencies was offensive to the national transportation policy Congress adopted in the Interstate Commerce Act, 49 U.S.C. §§1-27, and that the duties that Act imposed on railroads could not be contracted away.

The union contended that the District Court was without jurisdiction to grant injunctive relief under the provisions of the Norris-LaGuardia Act because this case involved a labor dispute, and that the railroad had refused to negotiate in good faith on the proposed change in the agree-ment in violation of §2, First, of the Railway Labor Act, 45 U.S.C. §152, First, which requires the railroad to exert every reasonable effort to make and maintain agreements concerning rates of pay, rules and working conditions. Therefore, the union argued, an injunction in federal court is barred if for no other reason because of §8 of the Norris-LaGuardia Act which provides: "No restraining order or injunctive re-lief shall be granted to any complainant who has failed to comply with any obligation imposed by law which is involved in the labor dispute in question, or who has failed to make every reasonable effort to settle such dispute either by negotiation or with the aid of any available govern-mental machinery of mediation or voluntary arbitration." 29 U.S.C. §108. See Brotherhood of Railroad Trainmen v. Toledo, P. & W.R.R., 321 U.S. 50.

After hearings, the District Court found, so far as is relevant here, . . . that "The dispute giving rise to the proposed strike is a major dispute and not a minor grievance under the Railway Labor Act, and no issue involved therein is properly referable to the National Railroad Adjustment Board"; and that the contract change proposed in the §6 notice, related to "rates of pay, rules and working conditions," and was therefore a bargainable issue under the Railway Labor Act. On its findings and conclusions of law, the District Court granted temporary relief but declined to grant a permanent injunction on the ground that it was without jurisdiction to do so.

On appeal the Court of Appeals did grant a permanent injunction. . . . It held that the Norris-LaGuardia Act did not apply to bar an injunction against this strike and we granted certiorari. . . .

We hold, with the District Court, that this case involves or grows out of a labor dispute within the meaning of the Norris-LaGuardia Act and that the District Court was without jurisdiction permanently to enjoin the strike.

Section 4 of the Norris-LaGuardia Act specifically withdraws jurisdiction from a District Court to prohibit any person or persons from "ceasing or refusing to perform any work or to remain in any relation of employment" "in any case involving or growing out of any labor dispute" as "herein defined." Section 13(c) of the Act defines a labor dispute as including, "any controversy concerning terms or conditions of employment, or concerning the association or representation of persons in negotiating, fixing, maintaining, changing, or seeking to arrange terms or conditions of employment, regardless of whether or not the disputants stand in the proximate relation of employer and employee." Unless the literal language of this definition is to be ignored, it squarely covers this controversy. Congress made the definition broad because it wanted it to be broad. . . . The hearings and committee reports reveal that Congress attempted to write its bill in unmistakable language because it believed previous measures looking toward the same policy against nonjudicial intervention in labor disputes had been given unduly limited constructions by the courts.

Plainly the controversy here relates to an effort on the part of the union to change the "terms" of an existing collective bargaining agreement. The change desired just as plainly referred to "conditions of employment" of the railroad's employees who are represented by the union. The employment of many of these station agents inescapably hangs on the number of railroad stations that will either be completely abandoned or consolidated with other stations. And, in the collective bargaining world today, there is nothing strange about agreements that affect the permanency of employment. The District Court's finding that "collective bargaining as to the length or term of employment is commonplace," is not challenged.

We cannot agree with the Court of Appeals that the union's efforts to negotiate about the job security of its members "represents an attempt to usurp legitimate managerial prerogative in the exercise of business judgment with respect to the most economical and efficient conduct of its operations." The Railway Labor Act and the Interstate Commerce Act recognize that stable and fair terms and conditions of railroad employment are essential to a well-functioning national transportation system. . . .

In 1942 this Court held that when a railroad abandons a portion of its lines, the Interstate Commerce Commission has power to include conditions for the protection of displaced workers in deciding what "the public convenience and necessity may require." We so construed the Interstate Commerce Act specifically on the basis that imposition of such conditions "might strengthen the national system through their effect on the morale and stability of railway workers generally." Interstate Commerce Comm. v. Railway Labor Exec. Ass'n, 315 U.S. 373, 375, citing United States v. Lowden, 308 U.S. 225. The brief for the Railroad associations there called our attention to testimony previously given to Congress that as early as 1936 railroads representing 85% of the mileage of the country had made collective bargaining agreements with their employees to provide a schedule of benefits for workers who might be displaced or adversely affected by coordinations or mergers. In an effort to prevent a disruption and stoppage of interstate commerce, the trend of legislation affecting railroads and railroad employees has been to broaden, not narrow, the scope of subjects about which workers and railroads may or must negotiate and bargain collectively. Furthermore, the whole idea of what is bargainable has been greatly affected by the practices and customs of the railroads and their employees themselves. It is too late now to argue that employees can have no collective voice to influence railroads to act in a way that will preserve the interests of the employees as well as the interests of the railroad and the public at large.

The railroad has argued throughout the proceedings that the union's strike here may be enjoined, regardless of Norris-LaGuardia, because its effort to bargain about the consolidation and abandonment of railroad stations is unlawful. It is true that in a series of cases where collective bargaining agents stepped outside their legal duties and violated the Act which called them into being, we held that they could be enjoined. None of these cases, however, enjoined conduct which the Norris-LaGuardia Act withdrew from the injunctive power of the federal courts except the Chicago River case which held that a strike could be enjoined to prevent a plain violation of a basic command of the Railway Labor Act "adopted as a part of a pattern of labor legislation." 353 U.S. 30, 42. The Court there regarded as inapposite those cases in which it was held that the Norris-LaGuardia Act's ban on federal injunctions is not lifted because the conduct of the union is unlawful under some other, nonlabor statute. Here, far from violating the Railway Labor Act, the union's effort to negotiate its controversy with the railroad was in obedience to the Act's command that employees as well as railroads exert every reasonable effort to settle all disputes "concerning rates of pay, rules, and working conditions." 45 U.S.C. §152, First. Moreover, neither the respondent nor anyone else points to any other specific legal command that the union violated here by attempting to bring about a change in its collective bargaining agreement. It would stretch credulity too far to say that the Railway Labor Act, designed to protect railroad workers, was somehow violated by the union acting precisely in accordance with that Act's purpose to obtain stability and permanence in employment for workers. There is no express provision of law, and certainly we can infer none from the Interstate Commerce Act, making it unlawful for unions to want to discuss with railroads actions that may vitally and adversely affect the security, seniority and stability of railroad jobs. And for a number of reasons the state public utility proceedings, invoked by the railroad to obtain approval of consolidation or abandonment of stations, could not stamp illegality on the union's effort to negotiate this whole question with the railroad. The union merely asked for a contractual right to bargain with the railroad about any voluntary steps it might take to abandon stations or to seek permission to abandon stations and thus abolish jobs. Nothing the union requested would require the railroad to violate any valid law or the valid order of any public agency. There is no testimony and there are no findings that this union has set itself up in defiance of any state mandatory order. In fact, there was no state order of any kind at the time the union first asked to negotiate about the proposed contractual change. . . .

In concluding that the injunction ordered by the Court of Appeals is forbidden by the Norris-LaGuardia Act, we have taken due account of the railroad's argument that the operation of unnecessary stations, services and lines is wasteful and thus runs counter to the congressional policy, expressed in the Interstate Commerce Act, to foster an efficient national railroad system. In other legislation, however, like the Railway Labor and Norris-LaGuardia Acts, Congress has acted on the assumption that collective bargaining by employees will also foster an efficient national railroad service. It passed such Acts with knowledge that collective bargaining might sometimes increase the expense of railroad operations because of increased wages and better working conditions. It goes without saying, therefore, that added railroad expenditures for employess cannot always be classified as "wasteful." It may be, as some people think, that Congress was unwise in curtailing the jurisdiction of federal courts in railroad disputes as it did in the Norris-LaGuardia Act. Arguments have even been presented here pointing to the financial debilitation of the respondent Chicago & North Western Railroad and to the absolute necessity for the abandonment of railroad stations. These arguments, however, are addressed to the wrong forum. If the scope of the Norris-LaGuardia Act is to be cut down in order to prevent "waste" by the railroads, Congress should be the body to do so. Such action is beyond the judicial province and we decline to take it. . . .

The judgment of the Court of Appeals is reversed and that of the District Court is affirmed insofar as it held that the court was without jurisdiction under the Norris-LaGuardia Act to enter the injunction. . . .

MR. JUSTICE WHITTAKER, with whom MR. JUSTICE FRANKFURTER, MR. JUSTICE CLARK and MR. JUSTICE STEWART join, dissenting.

By Part 1 of the Interstate Commerce Act, Congress has provided a pervasive scheme of regulation of all common carriers engaged in transportation by railroad in interstate commerce. The declared policy of that Act was to promote economical and efficient transportation services at reasonable charges and, as this Court has said, "It is a primary aim of that policy to secure the avoidance of waste. That avoidance, as well as the maintenance of service, is viewed as a direct concern of the public." State of Texas v. United States, 292 U.S. 522, 530. "Congress has long made the maintenance and development of an economical and efficient railroad system a matter of primary national concern. Its legislation must be read with this purpose in mind." Seaboard Air Line R. Co. v. Daniel, 333 U.S. 118, 124-125.

To aid in effectuating that policy, Congress has contemplated the abandonment of railroad lines, stations, depots and other facilities and services when found by designated public regulatory bodies to be burdensome and no longer required to serve the public convenience and necessity. To this end, it has empowered the Interstate Commerce Commission, upon application and after notice and public hearing, to issue a certificate authorizing the abandonment of "all or any portion of a line of railroad," it has provided that "[f]rom and after issuance of such certificate . . . the carrier by railroad may, without securing approval other than such certificate . . . proceed with the . . . abandonment covered thereby." And in the Transportation Act of 1958 (72 Stat. 568), Congress has empowered the Commission, under stated conditions, to authorize the abandonment of "any train or ferry." However, Congress has not sought completely to accomplish its abandonment policies through the Commission. Rather, it has sought to make use of state regulatory commissions, as additional instruments for the effectuation of its policies, in respect to the abandonment of some railroad facilities and services. Among others, it has long left to state regulatory commissions abandonments of railroad stations and station agency service; and, in 1958, after extensive review of that subject in the process of enacting the Transportation Act of 1958, it deliberately reaffirmed that policy. Moreover, in its report on S. 3778, which culminated in the Transportation Act of 1958, the Senate Subcommittee on Interstate and Foreign Commerce critically attributed a major part of the financial plight of the railroads to their failure to apply to regulatory bodies for permission to abandon burdensome and needless services in accordance with congressional policy, and strongly advocated that such be done.

For the fair and firm effectuation of these policies, Congress has provided that issues respecting the propriety of an abandonment shall be determined by a public regulatory body. It has contemplated that the carrier shall propose to the proper regulatory body the abandonment of particular facilities or services and that, after notice and hearing — at which all persons affected, including employees and their union representatives, may appear and be heard — the public regulatory body shall determine whether the proposal is in the public interest, and its order, unless reversed on judicial review, is binding upon all persons. These procedures plainly exclude any right or power of a carrier, at its will alone, to effectuate, or of a labor union representing its employees to veto, any proposed abandonment. Although both may be heard, neither of them, nor the two in agreement, even if their agreement be evidenced by an express contract, may usurp the Commission's decisional function by dictating the result or thwarting its effect. It is obvious that any abandonment, authorized by a proper regulatory body, will result in abolishment of the jobs that were involved in the abandoned service. And inasmuch as the maintenance of these jobs constituted at least a part of the wasteful burden that necessitated the abandonment, it is equally obvious that Congress intended their abolishment. Yet, here, the union has demanded, and threatens to force by a strike, acceptance by the carrier of a covenant that no job in existence on December 3, 1957, will be abolished without its consent. Certainly that demand runs in the teeth of the recited provisions and policies of the Interstate Commerce Act. It plainly would destroy the public regulation of abandonments, provided and contemplated by Congress in the public interest, and render them subject to the Union's will alone. A demand for such a contractual power surely is an unlawful demand. . . .

There is no dispute in the record that the carrier sought to bargain and agree with the Union upon matters in mitigation of hardships to employees displaced by the station abandonments. It offered to bargain about (1) transferring the agents affected to productive jobs, (2) limiting the job abolishments to an agreed number per year, and (3) paying supplemental unemployment benefits to the employees affected. Short of foregoing the station abandonments, this is all it lawfully could do. It is not suggested that it should have done more in this respect. Indeed, the Union refused even to discuss these proposals. Instead, as its president testified at the trial, the only "alternative" the Union "offered the North Western Railroad was to comply with this rule or strike."

This also answers the Court's argument that there is nothing in the Interstate Commerce Act "making it unlawful for unions to want to discuss with railroads actions that may vitally and adversely affect the security, seniority, and stability of railroad jobs." The quoted statement is literally true. But the further truth is that the carrier offered to bargain and agree with the Union about those matters, but the Union refused even to discuss them. Ibid. The Union's demand was not for a right "to discuss" such matters with the carrier, but was, rather, that the carrier agree that no jobs in existence on December 3, 1957, be abolished without the Union's consent. And the only "alternative" it offered was: "Comply with this rule or strike." Ibid. The foregoing likewise answers the Court's argument that the Union "merely asked for a contractual right to bargain with the railroad about any voluntary steps it might take to abandon stations . . . and thus abolish jobs." Plainly the Union's demand was not for a right "to bargain with" the carrier about "abolish[ing] jobs," but was for a unilateral right to prohibit the abolishment of any job without its consent. . . .

. . . Here, as has been shown, the Union's demand was in derogation of the provisions and policies of the Interstate Commerce Act. It could not therefore be a lawfully bargainable subject within the purview of §2, First, of the Railway Labor Act. The carrier could not lawfully accept it, and hence a strike to force its acceptance would be one to force a violation of the law . . .

Nor does the Norris-LaGuardia Act render federal courts impotent to enjoin unlawful conduct or strikes to force acceptance of unlawful demands. That Act, in terms, permits federal courts to enjoin "unlawful acts [that] have been threatened and will be committed unless restrained." This Court has consistently held that the Norris-LaGuardia Act does not prevent a federal court from enjoining an unlawful abuse of power conferred upon a labor union by the Railway Labor Act or a threatened strike to force acceptance of an unlawful demand.

In Brotherhood of Railway Trainmen v. Chicago River & Indiana R. Co., 353 U.S. 30, a union threatened a strike to force a carrier to accept demands which Congress had placed within the exclusive jurisdiction of the Railroad Adjustment Board. Holding that the demands were in derogation of that Act of Congress and therefore illegal, a federal court enjoined the threatened strike to enforce them. The union contended here that the Court was without jurisdiction to issue the injunction because "the Norris-LaGuardia Act has withdrawn the power of federal courts to issue injunctions in labor disputes [and that the] limitation . . . applies with full force to all railway labor disputes." 353 U.S. at pages 39-40. In rejecting that contention, this Court said: "We hold that the Norris-LaGuardia Act cannot be read alone in matters dealing with railway labor disputes. There must be an accommodation of that statute and the Railway Labor Act so that the obvious purpose in the enactment of each is preserved. We think that the purposes of these Acts are reconcilable." 353 U.S. at page 40. And finding that the union's demands violated the provisions of the Railway Labor Act, this Court held "that the specific provisions of the Railway Labor Act, take precedence over the more general provisions of the Norris-LaGuardia Act," and, reaffirming its decision in Brotherhood of Railroad Trainmen v. Howard, 343 U.S. at page 768, it further held " 'that the District Court [had] jurisdiction and power [to enjoin the threatened strike] notwithstanding the provisions of the Norris-LaGuardia Act.' "

There, as here, the union's demand was in derogation of the specific provisions of an Act of Congress, and here, as there, those specific provisions must "take precedence over the more general provisions of the Norris-LaGuardia Act." . . .

NOTE

For a survey of the impact of automation, see page 101 supra.

2.   *The National Emergency Labor Dispute*

UNITED STEELWORKERS OF AMERICA v. UNITED STATES

Supreme Court of the United States, 1959
361 U.S. 39, 80 Sup. Ct. 1, 177, 4 L. Ed. 2d 12, 169

[The following statement of facts appears in the joint concurring opinion of Justices Frankfurter and Harlan:

"This action by the United States for an injunction under §208 of the Labor Management Relations Act of 1947 (61 Stat. 155, 29 U.S.C. §178) was commenced by the Attorney General at the direction of the President of the United States in the District Court for the Western District of Pennsylvania on October 20, 1959. The strike which was the concern of the action arose out of a labor dispute between petitioner, the collective bargaining agent of the workers, and the steel companies, and was nationwide in scope. The strike began on July 15, 1959, fifteen days after the contracts between the steel companies and petitioner expired. On October 9, 1959, the President created the Board of Inquiry provided by §§206 and 207 of the Act, 29 U.S.C.A. §§176, 177, to inquire into the issues involved in the dispute. The President deemed the strike to affect a 'substantial part of . . . an industry,' and concluded that, if allowed to continue, it would imperil the national 'health and safety.' On October 19 the Board submitted its report, which concluded: '[T]he parties have failed to reach an agreement and we see no prospect for an early cessation of the strike. The Board cannot point to any single issue of consequence whatsoever upon which the parties are in agreement.' The President filed the report with the Federal Mediation and Conciliation Service and made its contents public, in accordance with §206, and ordered the Attorney General to commence this action, reiterating his former pronouncements that the continuance of the strike constituted a threat to the national health and safety.

"Pursuant to stipulations of the parties, the District Court heard the case on affidavits. On October 21 it granted the injunction. Its order was stayed by the Court of Appeals for the Third Circuit, pending that court's final determination of petitioner's appeal. On October 27 it affirmed the decision of the District Court (one judge dissenting) and granted an additional stay to enable petitioner to seek relief here. On October 28 this Court denied the motion of the United States to modify the stay. On October 30 we granted certiorari, set the argument down for November 2, and extended the stay pending final disposition. . . .

"The injunction was challenged on three grounds: (1) the lower courts were not entitled to find that the national emergency, upon which the District Court's jurisdiction is dependent under §208, existed; (2) even if the emergency existed, the District Court failed to exercise the discretion, claimed to be open to it under §208, whether or not to grant the relief sought by the United States; (3) even if the injunction was otherwise unassailable it should have been denied because §208 seeks to charge the District Courts with a duty outside the scope of 'judicial power' exercisable under Art. III, §2, of the Constitution."

The decision of the Court was handed down on November 7, 1959.]

PER CURIAM. . . .

The arguments of the parties here and in the lower courts have addressed themselves in considerable part to the propriety of the District Court's exercising its equitable jurisdiction to enjoin the strike in question . . . These arguments have ranged widely into broad issues of national labor policy, the availability of other remedies to the executive, the effect of a labor injunction on the collective bargaining process, consideration of the conduct of the parties to the labor dispute in their negotiations, and conjecture as to the course of those negotiations in the future. We do not believe that Congress in passing the statute intended that the issuance of injunctions should depend upon judicial inquiries of this nature. Congress was not concerned with the merits of the parties' positions or the conduct of their negotiations. Its basic purpose seems to have been to see that vital production should be resumed or continued for a time while further efforts were made to settle the dispute. To carry out its purposes, Congress carefully surrounded the injunction proceedings with detailed procedural devices and limitations. The public report of a board of inquiry, the exercise of political and executive responsibility personally by the President in directing the commencement of injunction proceedings, the statutory provisions looking toward an adjustment of the dispute during the injunction's pendency, and the limited duration of the injunction, represent a congressional determination of policy factors involved in the difficult problem of national emergency strikes. This congressional determination of the policy factors is of course binding on the courts.

The statute imposes upon the courts the duty of finding, upon the evidence adduced, whether a strike or lockout meets the statutory conditions of breadth of involvement and peril to the national health or safety. We have accordingly reviewed the concurrent findings of the two lower courts. Petitioner here contests the findings that the continuation of the strike would imperil the national health and safety. The parties dispute the meaning of the statutory term "national health"; the Government insists that the term comprehends the country's general well-being, its economic health; petitioner urges that simply the physical health of the citizenry is meant. We need not resolve this question, for we think the judgment below is amply supported on the ground that the strike imperils the national safety. Here we rely upon the evidence of the strike's effect on specific defense projects; we need not pass on the Government's contention that "national safety" in this context should be given a broader construction and application.

The petitioner suggests that a selective reopening of some of the steel mills would suffice to fulfill specific defense needs. The statute was designed to provide a public remedy in times of emergency; we cannot construe it to require that the United States either formulate a reorganization of the affected industry to satisfy its defense needs without the complete reopening of closed facilities, or demonstrate in court the unfeasibility of such a reorganization. There is no room in the statute for this requirement which the petitioner seeks to impose on the Government.

We are of opinion that the provision in question as applied here is not violative of the constitutional limitation prohibiting courts from exercising powers of a legislative or executive nature, powers not capable of being conferred upon a court exercising solely "the judicial power of the United States." Keller v. Potomac Elec. Power Co., 261 U.S. 428; Federal Radio Comm. v. General Elec. Co., 281 U.S. 464. Petitioner contends that the statute is constitutionally invalid because it does not set up any standard of lawful or unlawful conduct on the part of labor or management. But the statute does recognize certain rights in the public to have unimpeded for a time production in industries vital to the national health or safety. It makes the United States the guardian of these rights in litigation. Cf. United States v. American Bell Tel. Co., 128 U.S. 315, 370; Sanitary District of Chicago v. United States, 266 U.S. 405. The availability of relief, in the common judicial form of an injunction, depends on findings of fact, to be judicially made. Of the matters decided judicially, there is no review by other agencies of the Government. Cf. Gordon v. United States, 2 Wall. 561, 117 U.S. 697. We conclude that the statute entrusts the courts only with the determination of a "case or controversy," on which the judicial power can operate, not containing any element capable of only legislative or executive determination. We do not find that the termination of the injunction after a specified time, or the machinery established in an attempt to obtain a peaceful settlement of the underlying dispute during the injunction's pendency, detracts from this conclusion.

The result is that the judgment of the Court of Appeals for the Third Circuit, affirming that of the District Court, is affirmed. Our mandate shall issue forthwith.

It is so ordered.

Separate opinion of MR. JUSTICE FRANKFURTER and MR. JUSTICE HARLAN, concurring in the opinion of the Court. . . .

In its findings of fact No. 15, the District Court described four instances of serious impediment to national defense programs as a result of existing and prospective procurement problems due to the strike. The programs affected included the missile, nuclear submarine and naval shipbuilding, and space programs. Each of these findings had, as the Court of Appeals found, ample support in the affidavits submitted by the United States. According to the affidavit of Thomas S. Gates, Jr., Acting Secretary of Defense, delays in delivery of materials critical to the creation of the Atlas, Titan and Polaris missile systems had become so severe that each additional day of the strike would result in an equal delay in project completion; and a "significant portion of the steel specified in procurement contracts is of a composition not common to commercial usage nor available from existing civilian inventories by exercise of allocation or eminent domain powers of the Government. . . . [T]hese programs in many cases require special sizes and shapes, many of which can be fabricated only by firms having a long experience in their production and the necessary special facilities therefor. . . ."

The affidavit of Hugh L. Dryden, Deputy Administrator of the Aeronautics and Space Administration, stated, in some detail, that space projects including tracking centers, rocket engine test stands, and other critical facilities were, at the time of the hearing in the District Court, already subjected to delays of as much as seven weeks, with longer delays anticipated from the continuation of the strike. The affidavit of A. R. Luedecke, the General Manager of the Atomic Energy Commission, stated that minor delays in projects had, at the time of its making, already been experienced in critical programs of the Atomic Energy Commission, and that if the strike should continue into 1960 "there would be an appreciable effect upon the weapons program."

In view of such demonstrated unavailability of defense materials it is irrelevant that, as petitioner contended and the United States conceded, somewhat in excess of 15% of the steel industry remained unaffected by the stoppage, and that only about 1% of the gross steel product is ordinarily allocated to defense production. . . .

Moreover, under §208 the trier of these facts was called upon to make a judgment already twice made by the President of the United States: once when he convened the Board of Inquiry; and once when he directed the Attorney General to commence this action. His reasoned judgment was based upon the affidavits we have summarized, and it is not for us to set aside findings consistent with them. The President's judgment is not controlling; §208 makes it the court's duty to "find" the requisite jurisdictional fact for itself. But in the discharge of its duty a District Court would disregard reason not to give due weight to determinations previously made by the President, who is, after all, the ultimate constitutional executive repository for assuring the safety of the Nation, and upon whose judgment the invocation of the emergency provisions depends. . . .

. . . Petitioner claimed that as a matter of fact the procurement embarrassments found by the courts below were the result not of the entire steel stoppage or even of a substantial part of it, but only of the closing of a "handful" of the hundreds of plants affected; and that therefore the entire industry-wide strike should not have been enjoined under either construction of §208 which it asserted.

In the first place, the requisite fact was found against petitioner's contention. The Court of Appeals found that "[t]he steel industry is too vast and too complicated to be segmented" so as to alleviate the existing and foreseeable peril to the national defense by the mere reopening of a few plants. . . .

Nor was it a refutation of the finding of the Court of Appeals to suggest, as petitioner did here, that "needed" facilities might be opened for all purposes. The problem is self-evidently one of programming months in advance every specialized commodity needed for defense purposes, a project which itself must require months of effort and the delays such effort would entail. Other obvious difficulties are not less formidable. Upon what basis would the plants to be reopened be chosen, assuming the number of plants needed could be determined? According to what standard would the production of particular complexes of plants be regulated? What of problems of cost and overhead, and the cost of and time required for intra-company planning to determine the practicality of partially restricting the operation of giant complexes such as those of the major producers?

No doubt a District Court is normally charged with the duty of independently shaping the details of a decree when sitting in equity in controversies that involve simple and relatively few factors; factors, that is, far less in number, less complicated and less interrelated than in the case before us. But a court is not qualified to devise schemes for the conduct of an industry so as to assure the securing of necessary defense materials. It is not competent to sit in judgment on the existing distribution of factors in the conduct of an integrated industry to ascertain whether it can be segmented with a view to its reorganization for the supply exclusively, or even primarily, of government-needed materials. Nor is it able to readjust or adequately to reweigh the forces of economic competition within the industry or to appraise the relevance of such forces in carrying out a defense program for the Government. Against all such assumptions of competence, the finding of the Court of Appeals was amply supported by the record. . . .

The legislative history confirms what the provisions themselves amply reveal, that this portion of the Taft-Hartley Act contains a dual purpose, on the one hand to alleviate, at least temporarily, a threat to the national health or safety; and on the other to promote settlement of the underlying dispute of industry-wide effect. The former purpose is to be accomplished by the injunction, and by whatever additional remedies the President may seek and the Congress grant in pursuance of the command of §210 of the Act, 29 U.S.C.A. §180, that the matter be returned to Congress by the President with full report in the event of a failure of settlement within the injunction period. The latter purpose is to be accomplished by the command of §209, 29 U.S.C.A. §179, that the parties to the dispute "make every effort to adjust . . . their differences"; by the secret ballot of employees provided by §209 with reference to the last offer of the companies; and finally by further action by the President and Congress pursuant to §210. To hold, as petitioner alternatively urged, that a District Court may enjoin only that part of the total stoppage which is shown to be the cause in fact of the peril, would at best serve only the purpose of alleviating the peril, while stultifying the provisions designed to effect settlement of the underlying dispute. . . .

. . . [T]he evidentiary burdens upon the Government which would have resulted from the adoption of either of the constructions urged by petitioner would tend to cripple the designed effectiveness of the Act. It is extremely doubtful whether in strikes of national proportion information would be available to the United States within a reasonable time to enable it to show that particular critical orders were placed with particular facilities no longer available; or whether the United States could within such time, effect a theoretical reorganization of its procurement program so as to demonstrate to a court that it cannot successfully be conducted without the reopening of particular facilities. . . .

Having decided that the strike was one which created a national emergency within the terms of the statute, the next question is whether upon that finding alone, the "eighty-day" injunction for which the Government prayed should have issued, or whether the District Court was to exercise the conventional discretionary function of equity in balancing conveniences as a preliminary to issuing an injunction. . . . We con clude that under the national emergency provisions of the Labor Management Relations Act it is not for the judiciary to exercise conventional "discretion" to withhold an "eighty-day" injunction upon a balancing of conveniences.

"Discretionary" jurisdiction is exercised when a given injunctive remedy is not commanded as a matter of policy by Congress, but is, as a presupposition of judge-made law, left to judicial discretion. Such is not the case under this statute. The purpose of Congress expressed by the scheme of this statute precludes ordinary equitable discretion. In this respect we think the role of the District Courts under this statute is like the role of the Courts of Appeals under provisions for review by them of the orders of various administrative agencies, such as the National Labor Relations Board. 29 U.S.C. §160(e). This Court has held that if the Board's findings are sustained, the remedy it thought appropriate must be enforced. National Labor Relations Board v. Bradford Dyeing Ass'n, 310 U.S. 318.

In the national emergency provisions of the Labor Management Relations Act Congress has with particularity described the duration of the injunction to be granted and the nature of specific collateral administrative procedures which are to be set in motion upon its issuance. We think the conclusion compelling that Congress has thereby manifested that a District Court is not to indulge its own judgment regarding the wisdom of the relief Congress has designed. Congress expressed its own judgment and did not leave it to a District Court. The statute embodies a legislative determination that the particular relief described is appropriate to the emergency, when one is found to exist. Moreover, it is a primary purpose of the Act to stop the national emergency at least for eighty days, which would be defeated if a court were left with discretion to withhold an injunction and thereby permit an emergency it has found to exist to continue. The hope is that within the period of the injunction voluntary settlement of the labor dispute will be reached, and to that end the statute compels bargaining between the parties during that time. If no voluntary settlement is concluded within the period of the injunction the President is to report to Congress so that that body may further draw upon its constitutional legislative powers. How else can these specific directions be viewed but that the procedures provided are, in the view of Congress, the way to meet the emergencies which come within the statute? It is not for the judiciary to negative the direction of Congress because of its own confident prophecy that the "eighty-day" injunction and the administrative procedures which follow upon it will not induce voluntary settlement of the dispute, or are too drastic a way of dealing with it. . . .

MR. JUSTICE DOUGLAS, dissenting.

Great cases, like this one, are so charged with importance and feeling that, as Mr. Justice Holmes once remarked (Northern Securities Co. v. United States, 193 U.S. 197, 400-401, dissenting opinion), they are apt to generate bad law. We need, therefore, to stick closely to the letter of the law we enforce to keep this controversy from being shaped by the intense interest which the public rightfully has in it. The statute, which Congress had authority to pass, speaks in narrow and guarded terms. . . . The President in appointing the board of inquiry in this case stated:

"The strike has closed 85 percent of the nation's steel mills, shutting off practically all new supplies of steel. Over 500,000 steel workers and about 200,000 workers in related industries, together with their families, have been deprived of their usual means of support. Present steel supplies are low and the resumption of full-scale production will require some weeks. If production is not quickly resumed, severe effects upon the economy will endanger the economic health of the nation."

It is plain that the President construed the word "health" to include the material well-being or public welfare of the nation. When the Attorney General moved under §208 for an injunction in the District Court based on the opinion of the President and the conclusions of the board of inquiry, the union challenged the conclusion that "the national health or safety" was imperiled, as those words are used in the Act. The District Court found otherwise, stating five ways in which a continuance of the strike would, if permitted to continue, imperil "the national health and safety." . . .

Here again it is obvious that "national health" was construed to include the economic well-being or general welfare of the country. The Court of Appeals, in sustaining the injunction, was apparently of the same view. This seems to me to be an assumption that is unwarranted. I think that Congress when it used the words "national health" was safeguarding the heating of homes, the delivery of milk, the protection of hospitals, and the like. The coal industry, closely identified with physical health of people, was the industry paramount in the debates on this measure. The coal industry is indeed cited on the Senate side in illustration of the need for the measure. S. Rep. No. 105, 80th Cong., 1st Sess., p. 14. There were those on the Senate who wanted to go so far as to outlaw strikes "in utilities and key nation-wide industries" in order to protect the "public welfare," 93 Cong. Rec. A1035. Reference was, indeed, made to strikes in industries "like coal or steel" among those to be barred in "the public interest." Ibid. But the Senate did not go that far. The Senate bill reached only situations where there was peril to the "national health or safety." The House bill went further and included cases where there was peril to "the public health, safety, or interest." The Senate view prevailed, that version being adopted by the Conference. Some light is thrown on the wide difference between those two standards — if words are to be taken in their usual sense — by the following colloquy on the floor of the House:

"Mr. Kennedy. I believe that this country should certainly be in a position to combat a strike that affects the health and safety of the people. Therefore, I feel that the President must have the power to step in and stop those strikes. I am not in the position of opposing everything in this bill, but there are certain things in the bill that are wrong. I do not see how the President is going to have the power to stop strikes that will affect the health and safety of the people under the procedure listed in section 203. I think he must have that power.

"I agree with you that any bill providing for an injunction should carefully consider the position of the striking union and make sure that their rights are protected. I think that in those cases Federal seizure until the dispute is settled would perhaps equalize the burden in the fairest possible manner.

"MR. OWENS. Will not the gentlemen admit that we have a third word in there? It is 'interest.' Could we not better use the word 'welfare' instead of 'interest,' because the word 'welfare' occurs in the Constitution? It is just as broad as the word 'interest' and more practical.

"MR. KENNEDY. The proposal embraces two separate things, health, and safety. Because the remedy is drastic these two, in my opinion, are sufficient. I believe we should apply this remedy when the strike affects health or safety, but not the welfare and interest, which may mean anything. I would not interfere in an automobile strike because while perhaps that affects national interest, it does not affect health and safety.

"MR. OWENS. Does not the gentleman agree that 'welfare' is the stronger and in line with the President's idea?

"MR. KENNEDY. No. Both 'welfare' and 'interest' are too indefinite. They could cover anything. I would not have the law apply except in cases where the strike affected health and safety."

To read "welfare" into "health" gives that word such a vast reach that we should do it only under the most compelling necessity. . . .

It is a fact of which we can take judicial notice that steel production in its broadest reach may have a great impact on "national health." Machinery for processing food is needed; hospitals require surgical instruments; refrigeration is dependent on steel; and so on. Whether there are such shortages that imperil the "national health" is not shown by this record. But unless these particularized findings are made no case can be made out for founding the injunction on impending peril to the "national health."

Nor can this broad injunction be sustained when it is rested solely on "national safety." The heart of the District Court's finding on this phase of the case is in its statement, "Certain items of steel required in top priority military missile programs are not made by any mill now operating, nor available from any inventory or from imports." Its other findings, already quoted, are also generalized. One cannot find in the record the type or quantity of the steel needed for defense, the name of the plants at which those products are produced, or the number or the names of the plants that will have to be reopened to fill the military need. We do know that for one and a half years ending in mid-1959 the shipments of steel for defense purposes accounted for less than 1% of all the shipments from all the steel mills. If 1,000 men, or 5,000 men, or 10,000 men can produce the critical amount the defense departments need, what authority is there to send 500,000 men back to work?

There can be no doubt that the steel strike affects a "substantial" portion of the industry. Hence the first requirement of §208(a) of the

Act is satisfied. But we do know that only a fraction of the production of the struck industry goes to defense needs. We do not know, however, what fraction of the industry is necessary to produce that portion. Without that knowledge the District Court is incapable of fashioning a decree that will safeguard the national "safety," and still protect the rights of labor. Will a selective reopening of a few mills be adequate to meet defense needs? Which mills are these? Would it be practical to reopen them solely for defense purposes or would they have to be reopened for all civilian purposes as well? This seems to me to be the type of inquiry that is necessary before a decree can be entered that will safeguard the rights of all the parties. Section 208(a) gives the District Court "jurisdiction to enjoin" the strike. There is no command that it *shall* enjoin 100% of the strikers when only 1% or 5% or 10% of them are engaged in acts that imperil the national "safety." We are dealing here with equity practice which has several hundred years of history behind it. We cannot lightly assume that Congress intended to make the federal judiciary a rubber stamp for the President. His findings are entitled to great weight; and I along with my Brethren accept them insofar as national "safety" is concerned. But it is the court, not the President, that is entrusted by Article III of the Constitution to shape and fashion the decree. If a federal court is to do it, it must act in its traditional manner, not as a military commander ordering people to work willy-nilly, nor as the President's Administrative Assistant. If the federal court is to be merely an automaton stamping the papers an Attorney General presents, the judicial function rises to no higher level than an IBM machine. Those who grew up with equity and know its great history should never tolerate that mechanical conception.

An appeal to the equity jurisdiction of the Federal District Court is an appeal to its sound discretion. One historic feature of equity is the molding of decrees to fit the requirements of particular cases. Equity decrees are not like the packaged goods this machine age produces. They are uniform only in that they seek to do equity in a given case. We should hesitate long before we conclude that Congress intended an injunction to issue against 500,000 workers when the inactivity of only 5,000 or 10,000 of the total imperils the national "safety." That would be too sharp a break with traditional equity practice for us to accept, unless the statutory mandate were clear and unambiguous. . . .

Plainly there is authority in the District Court to protect the national "safety" by issuance of an injunction. But there is nothing in this record to sustain the conclusion that it is necessary to send 500,000 men back to work to give the defense department all it needs for the nation's "safety." If more men are sent back to work than are necessary to fill the defense needs of the country, other objectives are being served than those specified in the statute. What are these other objectives? What right do courts have in serving them? What authority do we have to place the great weight of this injunction on the backs of labor, when the great bulk of them affected by it have nothing to do with production of goods necessary for the nation's "safety" in the military sense of that word? . . .

. . . Collective bargaining and mediation are today the norm, except for the period of time in which an injunction is in force. By the terms of §209, however, any injunction rendered may not continue longer than 80 days. The Act thus permits an injunction restricted in duration and narrowly confined by the requirements of the "national health or safety." When we uphold this injunction we force men back to work when their inactivity has no relation to "national health or safety." Those whose inactivity produces the peril to "national health or safety" which the Act guards against and only those should be covered in the injunction. The rest — who are the vast majority of the 500,000 on strike — should be treated like the employers are treated. They should continue under the regime of collective bargaining and mediation until they settle their differences or until Congress provides different or broader remedies. When we assume that all the steelworkers are producing steel for defense when in truth only a fraction of them are, we are fulfilling the dreams of those who sponsored the House bill and failed in their efforts to have Congress legislate so broadly.

Though unlikely, it is possible that, had the District Court given the problem the consideration that it deserves, it could have found that the only way to remove the peril to national safety caused by the strike was to issue the broad, blanket injunction. It may be that it would be found impractical to send only part of the steelworkers back to work. The record in this case, however, is completely devoid of evidence to sustain that position. Furthermore, there is no indication that the District Court ever even considered such a possibility. I am unwilling to take judicial notice that it requires 100% of the workers to produce the steel needed for national defense when 99% of the output is devoted to purposes entirely unconnected with defense projects.

I would reverse this decree and remand the cause to the District Court for particularized findings as to how the steel strike imperils the "national health" and what plants need to be reopened to produce the small quantity of steel now needed for the national "safety." There would also be open for inquiry and findings any questions pertaining to "national health" in the narrow sense in which the Act uses those page 724.)

NOTES

1. The labor dispute out of which the principal case grew was settled, before the eighty-day injunction expired, on January 4, 1960. The Federal Government, through the active offices of Vice President Nixon and Secretary of Labor Mitchell, was deeply involved in its final resolution.

[42] For two views of the problem presented by the 1959 steel strike, see Cox, Strikes and the Public Interest: A Proposal for New Legislation, 205 Atlantic Monthly 48 (1960), and Davis, Should Labor Be Coerced? 189 Nation 371 (1959). — ED.

Impartial observers agreed that the settlement, quite favorable to the union and unfavorable to the companies, was brought about in large measure because of a fear that Congress would either step in and resolve this particular dispute by legislation or would pass far more restrictive general legislation to deal with emergency disputes.

2. As of January, 1965, the "national emergency" provisions of the Taft-Hartley Act have been invoked by the President on twenty-three occasions. In only nineteen of them, however, was the injunction provided for in the statute sought and obtained. In eight of the nineteen instances where injunctions were issued, the full eighty days ran their course, the injunction was dissolved, and the strike resumed (Atomic Workers, in 1948 and 1954; West Coast Longshoremen, in 1948; East Coast Longshoremen, in 1948, 1953, 1957, 1962, and 1964). In the other eleven instances, settlement took place during the eighty-day period. However, three of those eleven instances involved matters extraneous to the supposed "cooling-off" function of the injunction. In the coal dispute of 1948 the settlement was reached during the period of the injunction because the core of the dispute, which was over the union welfare fund, was resolved by a court decision at that time. In the coal dispute of 1950, settlement came about because President Truman threatened to go to Congress to get legislation authorizing seizure of the coal mines. In the nonferrous metals dispute of 1951, settlement had been reached with the major producer before the eighty-day injunction period began. Settlement with smaller producers took place during the eighty-day period along the lines of the pattern established.

There have been ten instances of the so-called last offer vote. In every case the last offer of the employer has been overwhelmingly turned down by the voters. In one instance, the West Coast Longshoremen's dispute of 1948, the union boycotted the last offer election and not a single vote was cast.

The government has engaged in litigation with the United Mine Workers and John L. Lewis under the eighty-day injunction provisions of the law. In each case the government charged that the union and Lewis were acting in contempt of the injunction. In the 1948 dispute, the government was successful in a prosecution for contempt. The union was fined $1,400,000 and Lewis, $20,000. United States v. United Mine Workers, 77 F. Supp. 563 (D.D.C. 1948), aff'd, 177 F.2d 29 (D.C. Cir. 1949). In the dispute of 1950 the same claim was made by the government but Lewis and the union were acquitted. United States v. United Mine Workers, 89 F. Supp. 179 (D.D.C. 1950). See the revealing narrative description of this latter coal dispute in Wirtz, The "Choice of Procedures" Approach to National Emergency Disputes, in Emergency Disputes and National Policy 149, 152 (Bernstein, Enarson, and Fleming eds. 1955).

3. Brief work stoppages at missile sites have been much in the news the last year or two. A Missile Sites Labor Commission was created by Executive Order of the President on May 26, 1961 (No. 10946, 26 Fed. Reg 4629). Senator McClellan introduced a bill to outlaw strikes at missile

sites and other defense facilities, S. 288, 88th Cong., 1st Sess. (1963). See Van de Water, *Applications of Labor Law to Construction and Equipping of United States Missile Bases,* 12 Lab. L.J. 1003 (1961).

4. In general, the criticisms of current provisions of the law for handling national emergency disputes are:

(a) The fact-finding process usually operates pro forma simply for the purpose of obtaining the injunction, which is the opposite of the deliberation needed. The way the statute is designed, the injunction cannot be obtained until the appointed board has made some findings of fact.

(b) The board of inquiry is not authorized to make recommendations. Since it is accepted by many that recommendations by a fact-finding board are the ultimate goal of the process, this lack of power in a Taft-Hartley board constitutes a limitation upon the usefulness of the process itself.

(c) The concept of "national emergency" is too loosely defined.

(d) The last offer vote has been tried and found wanting. It simply serves as a means of solidifying the disputing employees against the employer's position.

(e) Experience has indicated that the process of collective bargaining is usually not carried on effectively during the eighty-day period of the injunction. Where settlements have taken place during this period, often they have come from outside pressures, as in the 1959 steel dispute, rather than from collective bargaining. Further, in case the dispute is not settled during the eighty-day period, the parties are right back where they started, and there is no further process immediately available to the government to avert an emergency work stoppage.

(f) The terms of the statute are too definite. The parties know just exactly what can happen to them. Thus, there is no threat hanging over their heads of some alternative processes which may be applied to them if they do not settle their dispute without a work stoppage. This criticism is made by those who favor the "choice of procedures" approach to emergency disputes. (See the discussion in the following Comment, page 724.)

(g) The apparent purpose of the Taft-Hartley provisions is to allow time for the public to react to the demands of the parties and thus to bring about a settlement through the medium of public pressure. There is substantial doubt that public opinion actually makes much difference in the settlement of such disputes, especially when no recommendations for settlement may be made.

(h) Allowing a strike to be carried on for a time and then stopping it by the eighty-day injunction applies economic pressure unevenly to the parties, usually unfavorably to the union. Thus, in the steel dispute of 1959, there was a work stoppage for 116 days. The strikers, without pay checks, were under serious economic pressure during all this period. Yet the companies, because of anticipatory stockpiling, were not under serious pressure until just before the Taft-Hartley provisions were invoked. It was not until the dwindling stockpile created a "national emergency" that the companies also began to feel heavy economic pressure.

For critical evaluations of the current law see Pierson, An Evaluation of the National Emergency Provisions, in Emergency Disputes and National Policy 129 (Bernstein, Enarson, and Fleming, eds. 1955); McDermott, Ten Years of the National Emergency Procedure, 9 Lab. L.J. 227 (1958); Rehmus, Operation of the National Emergency Provisions of Taft-Hartley, 62 Yale L.J. 1047 (1953); Warren, National Emergency Provisions, 4 Lab. L.J. 130 (1953).

In its report of May 1, 1962, 50 L.R.R.M. 11 (1962), the President's Advisory Committee on Labor-Management Policy recommended the following changes in the emergency provisions of the Taft-Hartley Act: (1) The Director of the Federal Mediation and Conciliation Service would recommend to the President the establishment of an Emergency Dispute Board which would have a mediating function. (2) The President would be authorized to direct the Board to hold a hearing on the question of whether a strike threatens the national health or safety. Upon the receipt of the Board's report, the President would be authorized to determine whether such a threat existed and, if so, he would be empowered to direct the parties to continue or resume operations either in whole or in part. His declaration of an emergency would be subject to court review. (3) Upon the declaration of an emergency, the Board would be empowered to continue mediation, but also to make fact-findings and recommendations for settlement of the dispute. (4) The last offer ballot would be eliminated. (5) If the attempts to settle the dispute failed over the eighty-day period, the President would refer the matter to Congress with his recommendation.

5. The United States and possibly Canada are the only two countries of the free world that have a continuing problem of the "national emergency" strike. Since World War II, the other free nations have developed the means, if they did not have them before, of handling labor relations in such a way that the "national emergency" work stoppage has not been a problem unless the strike is in the nature of a "general strike" to engage in some sort of political protest. The pattern of development has been strikingly similar in these countries. The marked characteristic of the bargaining systems in England, Norway, the Netherlands, France, West Germany, and Italy is the concept of nationwide bargaining. See page 164 supra. A nationwide employer organization, somewhat comparable to our National Association of Manufacturers, bargains directly with a nationwide organization of trade-unions, somewhat comparable to our AFL-CIO organization.

Because of the obvious monopolistic power of these two organizations in bargaining to set the basic wage throughout the country, and for all industries — something that would be wholly unacceptable under our antitrust laws — close and detailed governmental control of the bargains reached is recognized as necessary to protect the public. Thus, in all the countries named, except England, the government retains the right to approve or disapprove of the bargain made. The net effect of this is that the ultimate authority to set the basic wage pattern lies in the government. In England the same power is lodged in the government, but the difference is that it lies in the government because of a voluntary agreement made in 1951 by the employer and trade-union associations to submit the basic wage bargain to a government agency. This agency is entitled to intervene in the bargaining session without the request of either party.

The procedures briefly described above are detailed in Sturmthal, Contemporary Collective Bargaining in Seven Countries (1957). In addition, for the situation in Great Britain, see Teller, British Versus American Labor Laws and Practices: A Study in Contrasts, in Proceedings, A.B.A., Section of Labor Relations Law 30 (1957).

The system of compulsory arbitration used for well over half a century in Australia and New Zealand is clearly designed to provide for the ultimate resolution of labor disputes by the government itself. See the various books by Foenander, particularly Towards Industrial Peace in Australia (1937), Solving Labour Problems in Australia (1941), Industrial Regulation in Australia (1947), and Studies in Australian Labour Law and Relations (1952); Walker, Australia, in Comparative Labor Movements 173 (Galenson ed. 1952); Evatt, Control of Labor Relations in the Commonwealth of Australia, 6 U. Chi. L. Rev. 529 (1939); Merrifield, Wage Determination Under Compulsory Arbitration: The Basic Wage in Australia, 24 Geo. Wash. L. Rev. 157 (1955); Williams, The Compulsory Settlement of Contract Negotiation Labor Disputes, 27 Texas L. Rev. 587, 591 (1949).

6. Political strikes called to bring pressure on the government have not been common in this country, but it is generally accepted that such strikes are illegal. In NLRB v. Bretz Fuel Co., 210 F.2d 392 (4th Cir. 1954), the court held the mining company justified in discharging an employee who led a work stoppage for the purpose of protesting the passage of a bill pending in the state legislature. The bill, called the Fire Boss Bill, was directly related to the miners' work situation, since it had to do with authorizing supervisory personnel to act as fire bosses, i.e., the safety inspectors who enter the mines first to see if they are safe for work. The court held that a work stoppage to protest pending legislation was not "concerted activity" protected by the NLRA.

As a result of widespread publicity about racketeering on the waterfront in the New York port, New York and New Jersey entered into a compact creating a Waterfront Commission. The compact required the Commission to establish a register of longshoremen eligible to work in the Port of New York and to maintain "Employment Information Centers." The compact further required that "No person shall directly or indirectly, hire any person for work as a longshoreman or port watchman within the port of New York district except through such employment centers . . ." The purpose and effect of this were to eliminate the "shape-up" method of hiring which had been used as an instrument of control and corruption.

The ILA sought to discredit and embarrass the Waterfront Commission by a series of stoppages. The avowed purpose of the union was to compel the governors of both states to sit down with the union and discuss its grievances against the Commission. Upon petition of the employers' association, an injunction was issued against further stoppages for the purpose of interfering with the Commission. Stoppages continued and the culmination was the call of a general strike of all ports on the Atlantic and Gulf Coasts. Contempt proceedings were brought against the union officers. In New York Shipping Assn. v. International Longshoremen's Assn., 154 N.Y.S.2d 360, 376, 378 (Sup. Ct. 1956), the court said: "From first to last the strike had nothing to do with contract clauses or any other labor-management controversy. Simply stated, the strike was not waged against the [Employers] Association or its members, but against the Waterfront Commission and the Waterfront Compact. Its calculated purpose was political, not economic; to force government officials to adopt a course of action desired by the union . . . However liberally the [anti-injunction] statute be interpreted, it is nevertheless clear that a controversy between a union and a government regulatory agency does not qualify as a labor dispute." The court also rejected the claim that the state had no power to act, on the ground that the union's activity was "neither protected nor proscribed" under the Taft-Hartley Act.

The non-Communist affidavit provision in Section 9(h) of the Taft-Hartley Act (repealed by the Labor-Management Reporting and Disclosure Act of 1959) was presumably based in part on the belief that Communists sought to control unions in order to call strikes for political purposes. In upholding that provision the Supreme Court relied heavily on this objective, saying: "There can be no doubt that Congress may, under its constitutional power to regulate commerce among the several states, attempt to prevent political strikes and other kinds of direct action designed to burden and interrupt the free flow of commerce." American Communications Assn., CIO v. Douds, 339 U.S. 382, 390 (1950). Section 504(a) of the LMRDA, in prohibiting Communist Party members, or ex-members for a period of five years, from serving as union officers, would also seem to be based in part upon the fear of political strikes.

AMALGAMATED ASSN. OF STREET, ELECTRIC RAILWAY & MOTOR COACH EMPLOYEES v. MISSOURI

Supreme Court of the United States, 1963
374 U.S. 74, 83 Sup. Ct. 1657, 10 L. Ed. 2d 763

Opinion of the Court by MR. JUSTICE STEWART, announced by MR. JUSTICE WHITE.

The appellant union is the certified representative of a majority of the employees of Kansas City Transit, Inc., a Missouri corporation which operates a public transit business in Kansas and Missouri. A collective bargaining agreement between the appellant and the company was due to expire on October 31, 1961, and in August of that year, after appropriate notices, the parties commenced the negotiation of an amended agreement.   An impasse in these negotiations was reached, and in early November the appellant's members voted to strike.   The strike was called on November 13.

The same day the Governor of Missouri, acting under the authority of a state law known as the King-Thompson Act,[1] issued a proclamation that the public interest, health and welfare were jeopardized by the threatened interruption of the company's operations, and by an executive order purported to take possession "of the plants, equipment, and all facilities of the Kansas City Transit, Inc., located in the State of Missouri, for the use and operation by the State of Missouri in the public interest."   A second executive order provided in part that "All rules and regulations . . . governing the internal management and organization of the company, and its duties and responsibilities, shall remain in force and effect throughout the term of operation by the State of Missouri."

Pursuant to a provision of the Act which makes unlawful any strike or concerted refusal to work as a means of enforcing demands against the utility or the State after possession has been taken by the State, the State petitioned the Circuit Court of Jackson County for an injunction on November 15, 1961.[2]   A temporary restraining order was issued on that day, and the strike and picketing were discontinued that evening.   After a two-day trial, the order was continued in effect, and the Circuit Court later entered a permanent injunction barring the continuation of the strike "against the State of Missouri."

On appeal to the Supreme Court of Missouri, the appellants argued that the King-Thompson Act is in conflict with and is pre-empted by federal labor legislation, and that it abridges rights guaranteed by the First, Thirteenth, and Fourteenth Amendments.   Reaffirming its earlier decisions in cases arising under the Act, the Supreme Court of Missouri rejected these arguments and affirmed the issuance of the injunction.   361 S.W.2d 33.   We noted probable jurisdiction. . . .

The King-Thompson Act defines certain public utilities as "life essentials of the people" and declares it to be the policy of the State that "the possibility of labor strife in utilities operating under governmental franchise or permit or under governmental ownership and control is a threat to the welfare and health of the people."   The Act imposes requirements in connection with the duration and renewal of collective bargaining agreements, and creates a State Board of Mediation and pub-

---

[1] The King-Thompson Act is Chapter 295 of the Revised Statutes of Missouri, 1959.   The section of the statute authorizing seizure is Mo. Rev. Stat., 1959, §295.180.

[2] Missouri Rev. Stat., 1959, §295.200, par. 1, provides:
"It shall be unlawful for any person, employee, or representative as defined in this chapter to call, incite, support or participate in any strike or concerted refusal to work for any utility or for the state after any plant, equipment or facility has been taken over by the state under this chapter, as means of enforcing any demands against the utility or against the state."
Section 295.200, par. 6, provides:
"The courts of this state shall have power to enforce by injunction or other legal or equitable remedies any provision of this chapter or any rule or regulation prescribed by the governor hereunder."

lic hearing panels whose services are to be invoked whenever the parties cannot themselves agree upon the terms to be included in a new agreement. And where, as here, the recommendations of these agencies are not accepted, and the continued operation of the utility is threatened as a result, the Governor is empowered to "take immediate possession of" the utility "for the use and operation by the state of Missouri in the public interest."

In Bus Employees v. Wisconsin Board, 340 U.S. 383, this Court held that the Wisconsin Public Utility Anti-Strike Law, which made it a misdemeanor for public utility employees to engage in a strike which would cause an interruption of an essential public utility service, conflicted with the National Labor Relations Act and was therefore invalid under the Supremacy Clause of the Constitution. The Supreme Court of Missouri in the present case rejected the appellants' argument that the Wisconsin Board decision was determinative of the unconstitutionality of the Missouri statute here in issue. The court held that the provisions of the King-Thompson Act dealing with the mediation board and public hearing panels were severable from the remainder of the statute, and refused to pass on any but those provisions which authorize the seizure and the issuance of injunctions against strikes taking place after seizure has been imposed. These provisions, the court ruled, do not — as in the Wisconsin Board case — provide a comprehensive labor code conflicting with federal legislation, but rather represent "strictly emergency legislation" designed solely to authorize use of the State's police power to protect the public from threatened breakdowns in vital community services. Emphasizing that the company was not a party to the injunction suit, the court concluded that, although the State did not actively participate in the management of the utility's operations, the Governor's executive order had been sufficient to convert the strike into one against the State, and that an injunction barring such a strike is therefore not barred by the provisions of federal labor legislation. 361 S.W.2d, at 44, 46, 48-52.

We disagree. None of the distinctions drawn by the Missouri court between the King-Thompson Act and the legislation involved in Wisconsin Board seem to us to be apposite. First, whatever the status of the title to the properties of Kansas City Transit, Inc., acquired by the State as a result of the Governor's executive order, the record shows that the State's involvement fell far short of creating a state-owned and operated utility whose labor relations are by definition excluded from the coverage of the National Labor Relations Act. The employees of the company did not become employees of Missouri. Missouri did not pay their wages, and did not direct or supervise their duties. No property of the company was actually conveyed, transferred, or otherwise turned over to the State. Missouri did not participate in any way in the actual management of the company, and there was no change of any kind in the conduct of the company's business. As summed up by the Chairman of the State Mediation Board: "So far as I know the company is operating now just as it was two weeks ago before the strike."

Secondly, the Wisconsin Board case decisively rejected the proposition that a state enactment affecting a public utility operating in interstate commerce could be saved from a challenge based upon a demonstrated conflict with the standards embodied in federal law simply by designating it as "emergency legislation." There the Court said that where "the state seeks to deny entirely a federally guaranteed right which Congress itself restricted only to a limited extent in case of national emergencies, however serious, it is manifest that the state legislation is in conflict with federal law." 340 U.S., at 394.

The short of the matter is that Missouri, through the fiction of "seizure" by the State, has made a peaceful strike against a public utility unlawful, in direct conflict with federal legislation which guarantees the right to strike against a public utility, as against any employer engaged in interstate commerce.[9] In forbidding a strike against an employer covered by the National Labor Relations Act, Missouri has forbidden the exercise of rights explicitly protected by §7 of that Act. Collective bargaining, with the right to strike at its core, is the essence of the federal scheme. As in Wisconsin Board, a state law which denies that right cannot stand under the Supremacy Clause of the Constitution.

It is hardly necessary to add that nothing we have said even remotely affects the right of a State to own or operate a public utility or any other business, nor the right or duty of the chief executive or legislature of a State to deal with emergency conditions of public danger, violence, or disaster under appropriate provisions of the State's organic or statutory law.

Reversed.

NOTES

1. In Society of New York Hospital v. Hanson, 185 Misc. 937, 59 N.Y.S.2d 91 (Sup. Ct. 1945), aff'd, 272 App. Div. 998, 73 N.Y.S.2d 835 (1st Dept. 1947), an injunction was sought by the privately owned hospital to stop a strike of its maintenance employees. The strike was for higher wages and was peaceful. In granting the injunction, Judge Pecora said, 185 Misc. at 942, N.Y.S.2d at 96:

"The right to strike has proven to be of such proper potency to labor in our industrial history that this court would not curtail it in any respect except for the most compelling of reasons. But there are some contravening considerations which can be of even greater importance to the public interests as a whole. It is difficult to conceive of a public service of greater value than the maintenance of hospitals for the care of the sick and the injured. It is almost impossible to conceive of such

---

[9] In enacting the Taft-Hartley Act, Congress expressly rejected the suggestion that public utilities be treated differently from other employers. As explained by Senator Taft, "If we begin with public utilities, it will be said that coal and steel are just as important as public utilities. I do not know where we could draw the line. So far as the bill is concerned, we have proceeded on the theory that there is a right to strike and that labor peace must be based on free collective bargaining." 93 Cong. Rec. 3835.

hospitals functioning properly if they are subject to interference with their activities by strikes or otherwise. Obviously ministration to the sick cannot be delayed. Surgical operations, as well as the routine care of those requiring medical attention, must be permitted to proceed at all times. The effective strength of medicines and serums must be preserved continuously under scientific conditions. The frantic immediacy which is required for the treatment of emergency cases, cannot be suspended while awaiting the outcome of parleys between the hospital management and its employees over terms of labor. These elements imperatively command that the generally broad right to strike be enjoined or otherwise limited in such cases.

"A strike by its employees which injuriously affects the essential functions of a hospital, must therefore be held to be improper and inimical to public interest. The public cannot brook any interference with the activities of an institution on which it relies for the treatment of the sick and hurt. A stoppage of electric current, a delay in deliveries of vital supplies or any number of readily conceivable difficulties created by a strike might result in loss of life. The necessity of avoiding such tragic consequences to the public clearly outweighs the sound general policy favoring the protection of labor's right to strike. Hence this court explicitly rules that no strike productive of such results can be permitted against a hospital which is supported by the public through voluntary contributions as well as through contributions made by the local government, and which is maintained for the benefit of the entire public, including those who cannot pay either in whole or in part the cost of their care and medical attention. . . .

"An injunction will, therefore, issue permanently restraining the defendants from striking and from organizing for the purpose of striking or inducing others to strike against the plaintiff or the hospital operated by the plaintiff."

2. Suppose a strike is threatened which would shut off all electric power in a city of one million people. Would this be a threat of a *national* emergency? If not, what remedy is available to the city in the face of this strike threat which locally is as critical as any national emergency might be?

KAUFMAN, THE RAILROAD LABOR DISPUTE: A MARATHON OF MANEUVER AND IMPROVISATION *

18 Industrial and Labor Relations Review 196-212 (1965)

> We thank with brief thanksgiving
> Whatever gods may be . . .
> That even the weariest river
> Winds somewhere safe to sea.

These four lines from Swinburne were quoted by the Secretary of Labor, W. Willard Wirtz, in an address before the National Academy of Arbitrators, after referring to the long-drawn-out proceedings in the air-

* These excerpts of the article by Jacob J. Kaufman are reproduced with the permission of the publisher, the Industrial and Labor Relations Review.

line industry and East Coast longshoremen disputes.[1] . . . The procedures followed in attempting to settle the railroad work rules dispute can be similarly characterized.

The railroad labor dispute over work rules was initiated on November 2, 1959 when the railroads submitted a series of proposals to the five railroad operating labor organizations. The proposals were concerned with the use of firemen on diesels, the basis of pay, the assignment of employees, and the consist of crews. On November 2, 1963, a special railroad arbitration board completed hearings on two issues — the firemen and crew consist questions — and issued its award on November 26, 1963.[5] The remaining issues, including proposals of the railroad labor organizations, were tentatively settled on April 22, 1964, subject to ratification procedures of the unions, by mediation under the supervision of the office of the President of the United States.[6] The award of the special arbitration board, which was challenged in the courts by the labor organizations, was upheld by the federal courts, the Supreme Court denying certiorari on April 27, 1964.[7]

"MANEUVER" AND "IMPROVISATION"

Since the inception of the dispute in November 1959, a number of procedures have been followed, some of which have been pursuant to the procedures of the Railway Labor Act, as amended, and others which have been "ad hoc" and outside of the provisions of the law.

It is unnecessary to describe in detail the procedures followed pursuant to law. These included, in the early phases of the dispute, the filing of notices by the railroad on November 2, 1959, and the filing of notices by the employee organizations on September 7, 1960. The usual conferences, as required by law, were held on the individual properties of the carriers as well as on a national basis. On October 17, 1960 the parties entered into an agreement which provided for the establishment of a Presidential Railroad Commission and which was subsequently created by executive order of the President of the United States. . . .

. . . [A]fter the issuance of the Presidential Railroad Commission Report, the National Mediation Board entered into the dispute. Subsequently, the President of the United States created a statutory emergency board which issued its report on May 13, 1963. The formal, statutory intervention by the government took place despite the fact that the parties had agreed that "the proceedings of the [Presidential] Commission, including its mediatory efforts and its report, shall be considered and accepted as in lieu of the mediation and emergency board procedures provided by Sections 5 and 10 of the Railroad Labor Act."

[1] W. Willard Wirtz, "The Challenge to Free Collective Bargaining," in Mark L. Kahn, ed., Labor Arbitration and Industrial Change, Proceedings of the Sixteenth Annual Meeting, National Academy of Arbitrators (Washington: BNA, 1963), p. 302.

[5] See Railroads v. Operating Brotherhoods, 41 L.A. 673.

[6] New York Times, April 23, 1964.

[7] Brotherhood of Locomotive Firemen and Enginemen, et al. v. Certain Carriers, et al., April 27, 1964, 84 S. Ct. (1964), p. 1181.

During the period between the issuance of the Report of the Presidential Railroad Commission and the report of the emergency board, the parties were involved in court litigation. The labor organizations sought to enjoin the carriers from promulgating changes in the work rules. After considerable legal maneuvering and litigation, the United States Supreme Court ruled "that the Railway Labor Act procedures had been exhausted" and therefore the proposed changes were "proper." [43] It is important to note that the Supreme Court did not pass on the merits of the dispute nor did it question the good faith of the parties.

Subsequent to issuance of the report of the emergency board, conferences were resumed between the parties. On June 1, 1963, the Secretary of Labor was advised by the parties of their inability to resolve the dispute, whereupon the Secretary of Labor, along with the National Mediation Board, intervened.

For over a month, from June 4 to July 10, 1963, according to a statement by the railroads, about one-hundred meetings were held under these auspices. During this period a variety of events took place. On or about June 15, 1963, the President was advised by the Secretary of Labor that there was "no progress," whereupon the President obtained an agreement from the parties to maintain the status quo until July 10, during which time further bargaining was to take place. Various proposals were put forth during this period by the Secretary for the settlement of the dispute, without results. On July 3, 1963, the carriers announced that the revised work rules would be put into effect at 12:01 A.M. on Thursday, July 11. Again the Secretary, without success, made additional proposals for settlement. On July 9, 1963 — one day prior to the deadline — the President of the United States proposed that the parties "agree to submit all issues in dispute between them for final settlement to Associate Justice of the Supreme Court Arthur J. Goldberg." The carriers accepted but the unions rejected the proposal. On July 10, 1963, on the eve of the deadline, the President created a special subcommittee of six persons, selected from his Labor-Management Advisory Committee, "to undertake, immediately, in full consultation with the parties, a comprehensive review and report limited to the facts and issues in this case and the respective positions of the parties." At the same time, the parties agreed to maintain the status quo until July 29, 1963.

The special committee issued its unanimous report on July 19, 1963.[18] The committee, which consisted of two union representatives, two management representatives, and the Secretaries of Commerce and Labor, set forth the facts and positions of the parties with respect to eight issues.

On July 22, 1963 — seven days before the next deadline — the President of the United States transmitted a special message to the Congress, in

---

[43] Brotherhood of Locomotive Engineers v. Baltimore and Ohio R.R. Co., 372 U.S. 248 (1963). — ED.

[18] Report of the President on the Railroad Rules Dispute, by the Special Subcommittee of the President's Advisory Committee on Labor-Management Policy, Washington, D.C., 1963, reprinted in Senate Hearings on Railroad Work Rules Dispute, pp. 15-19.

which he set forth the background of the dispute and made recommendations to Congress for legislation to dispose of the dispute.[19]   There were extensive hearings by the Senate Committee on Commerce and the House Committee on Interstate and Foreign Commerce. While these were in progress (1) the carriers were urged (and eventually agreed) to withdraw their promulgation of the revised work rules until August 29; and (2) further negotiations and mediation took place, without success.   The Congress, therefore, on August 28, 1963, approved a joint resolution which, in effect, called for the arbitration of two of the eight issues and for the further negotiation of the remaining six issues.[20]   The award of the arbitration board on two issues — the fireman and the crew consist questions — was challenged in the courts, and negotiations were carried on by the parties on the remaining six basic issues, with little success until the President of the United States intervened again and, with the assistance of two private mediators, brought about a settlement of the issues.

In this recital of events we observe that the Presidential Railroad Commission, after 96 days of hearings, a record of 15,306 pages of transcript, a total of 319 exhibits aggregating 20,319 pages, the presentation of many visual exhibits, the preparation of 22 technical monographs by members of the Commission's staff as well as by outside consultants, and a large number of field inspection trips, failed to dispose of the dispute.

Similarly, the Presidential Emergency Board, which functioned primarily as a mediatory body, failed to produce a settlement.   In fact, there appeared to be some disagreement among the members of the emergency board itself.   The letter of transmittal states that two members (out of three) of the board "note their realization that there may be some differences of opinion as to the exact scope of the terminal procedures contained in Section 6 of the Report, but express their confidence that procedures for the resolving of any such differences can be developed in the course of the negotiation period." [22]   Although this statement is relatively mild, it might be noted that it has significance, considering the delicacy of the entire matter.

Again, the extensive and intensive intervention of the Secretary of Labor also failed to produce any results, despite an illusory ray of hope when the Secretary of Labor announced on August 16, 1963 that "the carrier parties to the dispute accepted and the organization parties to the dispute accepted *with certain reservations* the Secretary of Labor's suggestion that the Firemen (Helper) and Crew Consist issues be resolved by binding arbitration. . . ." [23]   This agreement to arbitrate the dispute collapsed when the parties did not agree on the specific terms of the arbitration agreement.

Further, the extensive hearings by both committees of Congress, in addi-

[19] This message appears in Senate Hearings on Railroad Work Rules Dispute, pp. 4-13.

[20] Public Law 88-108, 88th Cong., 1st sess., S.V. Res. 102.   For a full discussion of the bill, see the Congressional Record of August 26, 27, and 28, 1963.

[22] Emergency Board Report No. 154, p. i.

[23] This appears in the preamble to Public Law 88-108. . . .   Report No. 459, p. 9.   Italics added.

tion to informal efforts by congressional leaders,[24] also failed to produce results. In addition, the intensive efforts of President Kennedy and the White House Staff were also unsuccessful. The award of the arbitration board has been unsuccessfuly challenged in the courts. Eventually, the intervention of President Johnson produced a settlement.

Why did all these measures, except for the final Presidential intervention, fail? Why was the intervention of President Johnson successful? . . .

THE 1963 INTERVENTION OF THE EXECUTIVE BRANCH

. . .

It is evident that the resolution of the conflict was not possible under the conditions which prevailed during the mediatory efforts. From the time the Presidential Railroad Commission Report was issued there had been frequent statements made by the Administration that "a nationwide railroad strike would be 'unthinkable.' " [48] Apparently, this attitude on the part of the Administration did not contribute to a negotiated settlement. Frequent references to the fact that a strike will not be tolerated by the government are not conducive to settlement, particularly if one of the parties to the dispute has consistently sought compulsory arbitration as the end of the collective bargaining process.

The fact is that the railroads have for many years supported the principle of compulsory arbitration. In 1950, the railroads supported the so-called Donnell bill which in effect would have outlawed strikes in the railroad industry.[49] As late as July 23, 1963, the railroads inserted a newspaper advertisement in the New York Times urging the compulsory arbitration of the current dispute. In testifying in support of a bill to impose compulsory arbitration in the maritime industry, a railroad spokesman stated in 1963: "We support the bill because it exemplifies a principle that we are convinced should apply to the ultimate disposition of major labor disputes in *our own industry*, namely, that there should be a final and binding resolution of them that would preclude the occurrence of strikes and stoppages." [50]

One hypothesis as to why the railroads sought the establishment of the principle of compulsory arbitration in the railroad industry is that they have, over the years, faced threats of strikes. Such threats, even if not eventually fulfilled, tend to divert traffic from the railroads to other forms

[24] See Congressional Record, August 26, 1963, p. 15050.

[48] Senate Hearings on Railroad Work Rules Dispute, p. 552.

[49] Hearings before the Subcommittee on Railway Labor Act Amendments of the Committee on Labor and Public Welfare, To Prohibit Strikes and to Provide for Compulsory Arbitration in the Railroad Industry, 81st Cong., 2nd Sess., on S. 3463, 1950, p. 146 ff.

[50] Statement of Daniel P. Loomis, president, Association of American Railroads, Hearings before the Committee on Merchant Marine and Fisheries, House of Representatives, 88th Cong., 1st sess., on H.R. 1897, H.R. 2004, H.R. 2331, Maritime Labor Legislation, 1963, part 2, p. 1033, italics added.

of transportation.   A ban on strikes would eliminate such threats and diversions of traffic.

The point was made frequently by union witnesses before the Senate Committee in 1963 that the goal of compulsory arbitration removed the railroads' incentive to bargain.[51]   At one stage of the hearings, the Acting Chairman of the Committee inquired as to how "Management's incentive to run out the clock [could] be removed"?   He asked: "How can we do that?" [52]   On the next day it became apparent to the committee members that this was a significant issue because several senators began commenting that the decision of the committee was uncertain.   The Acting Chairman asserted: "It is not a foregone conclusion one way or another." [53] These comments and assertions can be interpreted as an attempt to restore an element of uncertainty since the Secretary of Labor had indicated to the committee that he was reopening discussions between the parties.[54] This attempt to introduce the element of uncertainty was somewhat unrealistic in view of the fact that one member of the committee stated, in the hearing of the previous day, that he believed "from discussions I have heard, the bill will probably pass the Congress. . . ." [55]

The evidence is clear that intensive intervention on the part of the Administration failed to settle the dispute, and that eventually the issue was to be placed in the hands of Congress for disposition.   It must be noted, however, that the intervention of the Secretary of Labor did produce a situation in which the issues were clarified in the sense that they emerged as questions of broad principle rather than of detail.   In fact, the subcommittee of the Labor-Management Advisory Committee was able to summarize the entire dispute into eight general issues.[56]   It was this report which gave impetus to the idea that, if the firemen and crew consist issues could be settled, the other issues might well lend themselves to easier resolution.   The 1964 agreement might appear to support this hypothesis.

THE INTERVENTION OF THE LEGISLATIVE BRANCH

On July 22, 1963, seven days before the July 29 deadline for the promulgation of the revised work rules by the carriers, the President of the United States transmitted a message to Congress, which was accompanied by a proposed joint resolution designed to handle the dispute.[58]   The

[51] Senate Hearings on Railroad Work Rules Dispute, pp. 448.
[52] Ibid., p. 452.
[53] Ibid., p. 517.
[54] Ibid., p. 474.
[55] Ibid., p. 463.
[56] See reference at n. 18.
[58] Reprinted in Senate Hearings on Railroad Work Rules Dispute, pp. 4-15. During the hearings, the carriers agreed to postpone the promulgation of the revised work rules at the insistent request of the congressional committees.   See ibid., pp. 88-90, 416.   The carriers agreed to a postponement until August 24, 1963.

President found that a strike was "clearly intolerable" and that there was adequate "precedent for congressional intervention of this type." [59]   The latter comment was in reference to congressional action in establishing an eight-hour work day in the railroad industry in 1916 to forestall a strike. He recommended that interim work rules changes, which cannot be agreed upon by the parties, be submitted to the Interstate Commerce Commission for disposition.   Under the proposal the parties could at any time resolve the dispute between themselves and the ruling, if necessary, would apply for two years.   The President stated in his message: "Unlike compulsory arbitration, this method would preserve and prefer collective bargaining and give precedence to its solutions." [60]   It is not intended to discuss the details of the proposal in this article, but it is proposed to examine its underlying philosophy and its eventual disposition by Congress.

One basic question arises: Was the proposal "compulsory arbitration"? The President replied in the negative.   The Secretary of Labor supported this position by stating that the proposal "does preserve collective bargaining as the preferred method of resolving issues between labor and management." [61]   Under questioning the Secretary did, however, admit that during the interim period, if the parties do not agree, the ICC's decision is binding and that, therefore, there would be "no difference" between the temporary order and compulsory arbitration.[62]   It was his judgment that the proposed legislation in no way favored either party, since the unions were prevented from striking and the railroads were prevented from putting the proposed work rules into effect pending a determination by the ICC.[63]   To his repeated assertions that the proposed procedures were not compulsory arbitration, several Senators indicated some doubt about this conclusion.[64]

The proposal received the support of the railroads.   Their spokesman supported the position of the Secretary of Labor that the bill was not compulsory arbitration and that it would enhance the collective bargaining process.[65]   Needless to say, the five labor organizations were unanimously opposed to the legislation, all being convinced that the proposal was basically compulsory arbitration, and all indicating that a decision of a third party which imposed an order on the parties, without consent, even for a limited period, came under such description.   All were unanimous in their opposition to turning over the decision-making process to the ICC.

The congressional hearings reveal the extreme reluctance on the part of Congress to handle such type of legislation and a constant urging by

[59] Ibid., pp. 7-8.
[60] Ibid., p. 10.
[61] Ibid., p. 40.
[62] Ibid., p. 51.
[63] Ibid., pp. 60-61.
[64] See, for example, Senator Hartke's comments, ibid., p. 79.   Another reaction appears on p. 395.   See also House Hearings on Railroad Work Rules Dispute, pp. 69-70.
[65] Ibid., passim, and particularly pp. 370-371.

members of Congress that the parties solve their dispute by collective bargaining. But if the many boards and commissions and the intensive intervention by the Executive Branch failed to produce this result, it is inconceivable that exhortation would be successful. Pleas of this type reveal the utter lack of understanding of the collective bargaining process; namely, that there must be certain forces operating to induce the parties to bargain. Similarly, the attempt to cover up compulsory arbitration with the argument that the parties were free to settle the dispute between themselves also reveals either a lack of sophistication in labor relations or an attempt to cover up a politically unpalatable decision by the Administration. What inducement was there for the railroads to settle when they realized the opportunity was at hand to establish the principle of compulsory arbitration in the railroad industry? . . .

. . . [T]he Congress passed, and the President signed, a law several hours before the railroads' deadline. During the three days of congressional debate the proposed legislation was amended and revised repeatedly, with a high degree of coordination between the two houses of Congress in order to avoid any delay caused by the necessity of a conference to iron out any differences between the legislation passed by both houses of Congress.[71]

The law provided for the arbitration, by a seven-man board (two selected by management, two by the unions, and three public members by the President of the United States), of the fireman and crew consist issues. Emphasis was given to the August 2, 1963 proposal of the Secretary of Labor who was directed to present to the board the extent to which there was agreement, tentative agreement, and disagreement on the August 2, 1963 proposals. The parties were directed, by law, to resume collective bargaining on all other issues, with no mention in the law of what would happen if these additional matters were not resolved.

The law, in an effort to maintain the fiction of "non-compulsion," provided for a two-year limitation to the award of the board. Presumably, the two issues can be "wide open" after two years. . . .

The award of the board provided, in effect, for the eventual elimination of the firemen by the process of attrition, although the two-year limitation on the effectiveness of the award will probably have limited effect on the number of firemen eliminated. With respect to the crew consist issue, the board established the principle of a three-man crew in the road service but opened up the standard-sized crew of three workers in the yard service for negotiation and eventual arbitration.[76]

After the issuance of the award, the labor organizations attacked it in the courts on two grounds: first, that the law itself was unconstitutional and, second, that the award was subject to impeachment because it failed to conform to the procedural requirements of the law. These questions were disposed of by the Supreme Court of the United States on April 27, 1964, when it denied the unions' petition for a writ of certiorari.[44]

[71] Congressional Record, August 26, 27, and 28, 1963, passim.
[76] See 41 L.A. 673 ff.
[44] 377 U.S. 918 (1964). — ED.

To what extent did the arbitration board dispose of the two issues in the dispute? The award called for the discharge of a number of recently hired firemen, the elimination by attrition of additional numbers, and the provision of certain financial protective devices for certain groups of firemen. On the basic question of whether the issue was disposed of, it should be reiterated that the award lapses on May 7, 1966, at which time, according to a statement by the President of the Brotherhood of Locomotive Firemen and Engineermen, the union "will insist that the status quo be restored" and that all firemen laid off under the terms of the Arbitration Award be restored to duty.[78] Although it is not anticipated that the impact of the award on yard brakemen will be as heavy, it is not unreasonable to assume that when the Arbitration Award expires on February 25, 1966, the affected unions will seek a restoration of the status quo for this group of workers. Thus, on the two allegedly major issues in the dispute we have only a temporary solution.

THE 1964 INTERVENTION OF THE EXECUTIVE BRANCH

The settlement of the remaining issues by the intervention of President Johnson reveals that the railroads failed to achieve any significant revision of (1) the wage structure (actually yard *rates* were increased, and road *rates* cannot contribute to any further increasing disparity between yard and road earnings); (2) the contract rules governing road and yard assignments which, with certain minor exceptions, remain substantially unchanged; (3) the interdivisional rule, which is to be submitted to a study commission consisting of union and management representatives and two neutrals, without any binding authority.[79]

The net effect of this agreement, which provided for certain improvements in the working conditions of the employees, is a virtual capitulation by the railroads on the so-called "secondary" issues. How does one explain this phenomenon after years of turmoil and disagreement? There are four possible explanations, which are not necessarily contradictory. Rather, they are re-enforcing.

First, it is quite clear that the railroads received assurances from the President that they will receive continuing support and understanding of their desires for certain interpretations by the Internal Revenue Service, and the easing of certain regulations by the Interstate Commerce Commission.[80]

Second, the railroads were confronted with a set of mediation proposals which were accepted by the unions. A rejection by the railroads would have placed the burden of a strike on their shoulders. This must be considered in the light of the railroads' consistent public position that they have always accepted the recommendations of the neutrals. It is

---

[78] Labor, May 9, 1964.

[79] For a detailed discussion of the settlement and the diary of the Presidential intervention, see The New York Times, April 27, 1964.

[80] Ibid. See also Report of the Committee on Interstate and Foreign Commerce on H.R. 9903, Transportation Amendments of 1964, House Report No. 1144, Feb. 18, 1964.

difficult to discard the gnawing idea that the recommendations, so favorable to the unions, represented a political decision of the President.

Third, on the assumption that the Supreme Court of the United States does follow the newspapers, the acceptance of the proposed mediation settlement by the railroads made it difficult for the Supreme Court to reopen the firemen and crew consist issues, which were of great importance to the railroads. The entire dispute would have been reopened if the Supreme Court had granted certiorari and had eventually supported the position of the unions. The acceptance by the railroads of the proposals of the mediators perhaps helped to avoid the possibility of an unfavorable ruling by the Court.

Fourth, the recommendations of the mediators could not favor the railroads because the demands of the railroads were *politically* unacceptable to the leadership of the labor organizations. The union leadership must be more responsive to its constituency than the management of the railroads to its constituency of stockholders. This "political" factor must have played a significant role in directing the recommendations of the mediators.

Does this settlement represent a victory for the free collective bargaining process, as claimed by the President? Does it represent a turning point in the collective bargaining relationships between labor and management in the railroad industry? The answer to both questions is in the negative.

Free collective bargaining means a process by which either party has the power to impose economic damage on the other party through the strike. It means that either party accepts or rejects certain proposals freely, on the basis of balancing the costs of accepting or rejecting these proposals. The decisions are made by the parties without any coercive *third* force. These conditions did not prevail during the thirteen-day period from April 10 to April 27, 1964.

As to the future of collective bargaining in the railroad industry, the fact remains that the fireman and crew consist issues will be reopened in 1966, unless there is a prior agreement between the parties. One can visualize a substantial amount of conflict during the two-year period.[81] In addition, there is little, if any, evidence that the fundamental conflict between management's drive for efficiency and the unions' objective of job security has in any way been resolved. It is this conflict which has had, and will continue to have, an important impact on collective bargaining in the railroad industry.

CONCLUSION

The labor dispute in the railroad industry, after a good deal of maneuvering and improvisation, apparently has been disposed of. It has taken about four and one-half years of judicial, legislative, and executive

[81] New York Times of May 6, 1964 reports possibilities of wildcat strikes by firemen who are "intensely bitter over the way some railroads intended to apply the award." Reports of awards of arbitrators who are interpreting the arbitration award indicate extreme dissatisfaction by the unions.

intervention to dispose of it. But we are still confronted with certain basic questions: (1) What will occur, with respect to the fireman and crew consist issues, in 1966 when the Arbitration Award expires? (2) How can free collective bargaining, with the right to strike as an inherent part of that process, be restored in the railroad industry? Or is this freedom to be subordinated to an elusive concept of the so-called "public interest"? (3) How can a free and democratic society resolve the basic conflict between management's drive for efficiency and the unions' demand for job security in an era of substantial technological change and of high levels of unemployment? It would seem that the demands of the parties have temporarily been tabled but that the basic dispute remains.

The failure of the various procedures to resolve the basic issues is quite evident. It is clear that all of these procedures, without the essential ingredient of the right to strike, will not lead to a resolution of the conflict between the railroads and the labor organizations. The role of the right to strike in the settlement of railroad labor disputes is clearly revealed in several situations involving the non-operating unions and the railroads. For example, over the years — and even recently — there have been many agreements entered into between the parties involving changes in contracts on individual railroads, where the strike threat has been present. In recent years, for example, the Order of Railroad Telegraphers has signed a number of agreements on individual railroads concerning job security.

This approach provides a clue to the possible solution of many of the vexing problems on the railroads; namely, to leave the issues to bargaining on the individual railroads and to remove them from national negotiations, thereby avoiding the impact of a national strike. On individual railroads, the right to strike can exist and can continue to be the motivating force in the resolution of disputes.[83] The improved utilization of noncoercive third-party intervention might also contribute toward an effective solution to many of these problems. It is essential that the collective bargaining process be re-established in the railroad industry, possibly with the aid of neutrals, not with power to make binding decisions, but with the purpose of creating an environment in which the parties can negotiate successfully. In such an environment, the conflicting objectives of management for efficiency and of unions for job security can be better reconciled by the parties themselves, without the imposition of a binding decision of a third party.

NOTE

Compare Williams, Settlement of Labor Disputes in Industries Affected with a National Interest, 49 A.B.A.J. 862, 865 (1963): "Pragmatically, there is no right to strike all the nation's railroads at the same time. Such strike action is not forbidden by law, but it simply cannot be tolerated, as

---

[83] The potential for the "whipsaw" tactic by the unions is limited by the facts that the railroads, to a large extent, do not compete with each other and that the alternative forms of transportation bargain with other labor organizations.

some past experiences show. A work stoppage for a few days might be allowed, but the right to strike for a few days is not a right to strike effectively. In the coal and steel industries, the right to strike is directly related to the size of the stockpile. If there is a large stockpile, there is a right to strike. If there is no stockpile, then a strike simply cannot be tolerated. A demonstration of this principle was given in 1959 when the steel production stoppage was permitted to continue for 116 days because of the stockpile. As soon as the stockpile was gone, the national emergency occurred, and the Taft-Hartley injunction was invoked to force the employees back to work. . . .

"In spite of the extent to which the efficacy of collective bargaining is undermined, it is necessary that governmental intervention be accepted in these disputes. Without something to take the place of the right to strike, the union would be forced into the position of trying to bargain without bargaining strength. Insistence upon bargaining under these conditions would surely lead to a complete loss of faith in bargaining and a demand by workers for drastic governmental controls.

"The question, then, is as to the nature of the governmental intervention. Here there should be no opposition to the basic proposition that governmental intrusion should be kept to a minimum needed to prevent strikes which cannot be tolerated."

COMMENT ON PROPOSED MEANS OF DEALING WITH EMERGENCY LABOR DISPUTES

Fact-finding and recommendation of terms of settlement. As noted earlier, the present Taft-Hartley "national emergency" provisions are criticized by many persons because the fact-finding board is forbidden to make recommendations for settlement of the labor dispute it is considering. A number of impartial observers believe that if these critical disputes were submitted to a fact-finding process which included recommendations for settlement announced by the board, the process would be much more effective than it now is. The belief is that reasonable terms of settlement, widely publicized, would tend to force the disputants to settle along the lines of the recommendation.

President Truman, who made no secret of his dislike of the national emergency provisions of Taft-Hartley (although he invoked them several times), used the device of fact-finding with recommendations in the 1949 steel dispute. The United Steelworkers' demands at that time included a request for employer-paid health and welfare plans. The steel companies resisted and a strike was called. The President did not invoke the Taft-Hartley Act, but convened a special board of inquiry to hold hearings and make recommendations. The report of this board, in the main, supported the union's demands as fair and not unduly inflationary. Shortly after the report was issued the strike was settled on terms substantially equivalent to the board's recommendations. The board's report, Basic Steel Industry and United Steelworkers of America, is found in 13 L.A. 46 (1949).

Under the Railway Labor Act, the use of a fact-finding board which recommends settlement is a regular order of procedure. These boards are Emergency Boards appointed by the President under the provisions of Section 10 of the statute. The reports of these ad hoc boards include recommendations concerning most of the typical clauses in collective contracts, such as paid vacations, seniority, overtime pay, the scheduling of shifts, health and welfare plans, and the like. As examples of typical omnibus recommendations by Emergency Boards, including a basic wage recommendation as well as others, see Albany Port District R.R. and Various Cooperating Railway Labor Organizations (Nonoperating), 25 L.A. 506 (1955); Akron, Barbarton Belt Ry. and Brotherhood of Railroad Trainmen, 28 L.A. 110 (1957). On the handling of labor disputes under the Railway Labor Act, see Lecht, Experience Under Railway Labor Legislation (1955); Kaufman, Emergency Boards Under the Railway Labor Act, 9 Lab. L.J. 910 (1958).

Compulsory arbitration. As noted at page 702 supra, some form of compulsory settlement by government of critical labor disputes has become the norm in most of the free countries of the world. This process may or may not take the form of arbitration, but the significant fact is that the government does have the final authority to promulgate a settlement which must be accepted by the disputants. In Australia and New Zealand this use of governmental power has a long tradition, and the free European countries have come to it as well, though in less specific and detailed form.

There have been some earlier experiments in the United States with the compulsory arbitration of emergency labor disputes. The theory behind them is that there are certain industries where strikes cannot be tolerated. The purpose, then, is to force the parties to submit their dispute to an impartial board of arbitration whose award will be binding upon them. This was the established means of dealing with labor disputes during World War II under the War Labor Disputes Act, 57 Stat. 163 (1943), 50 U.S.C. App. §1501 (1946). See Boudin, The Authority of the National War Labor Board over Labor Disputes, 43 Mich. L. Rev. 329 (1944).

A number of state statutes have attempted to provide compulsory arbitration for disputes in public utilities. However, such statutes have met numerous obstacles in the courts. The Wisconsin law was held unconstitutional as conflicting with the federal policy of protecting the right to strike in industries affecting interstate commerce. Amalgamated Assn. of Street Railway Employees v. WERB, 340 U.S. 383 (1951).

The New Jersey statute was held unconstitutional before amendment because no standards were provided to guide the arbitration board in reaching its decision. State v. Traffic Telephone Workers, 2 N.J. 335, 66 A.2d 616 (1949). The Michigan law was invalidated because the delegation of power to the circuit judges to act as arbitrators violated the principle of separation of powers. Local 170, Transport Workers, CIO v. Gadola, 322 Mich. 332, 34 N.W.2d 71 (1948). Earlier, the United States Supreme Court had declared that a Kansas compulsory arbitration law took property without due process of law when applied to meat packing, but hinted that it might be valid as applied to public utilities. Wolff Packing Co. v. Kansas Court of Industrial Relations, 262 U.S. 522 (1923). This constitutional obstacle probably no longer remains, in view of the Court's present application of the due process clause. See Williams, The Compulsory Settlement of Contract Negotiation Labor Disputes, 27 Texas L. Rev. 587, 625 (1949). For a discussion of some of the problems faced under the state arbitration statutes, see Cushman, Compulsory Arbitration in Action — The New Jersey Telephone Case, 2 Syracuse L. Rev. 251 (1951); Updegraff, Compulsory Settlement of Public Utility Disputes, 36 Iowa L. Rev. 61 (1950).

Governor Meyner of New Jersey appointed a special committee, with David L. Cole as chairman, to study the operation of the New Jersey compulsory arbitration statute. The committee recommended that the Public Utility Labor Disputes Act of New Jersey be repealed and that the "choice of procedures" approach, discussed below, be used in future emergency disputes. The report is reprinted in full in 8 Ind. & Lab. Rel. Rev. 408 (1955). See also the Princeton study, Compulsory Arbitration in New Jersey, Princeton University Industrial Relations Section (1951). For the Pennsylvania experience under a similar statute see Syme, Should the Government Intervene in Public Utility Disputes? 27 Pa. B.A.Q. 248 (1956).

Government seizure. During World War II, government seizure was used to end strikes in critical industries. In most cases the army or navy took possession, operating the plant through the regular management but with the terms of employment fixed by the government. This device was almost exclusively a wartime expedient for enforcing decisions of the National War Labor Board. See Teller, Government Seizures in Labor Disputes, 60 Harv. L. Rev. 1017 (1947); Willcox and Landis, Government Seizures in Labor Disputes, 34 Cornell L.Q. 155 (1948). See, generally, Securing Compliance with Board Orders, 1 NWLB, Termination Report 415.

In the fall of 1951, the Steelworkers notified the steel companies that when their contract expired on the last day of the year, substantial wage increases would be demanded. Because this was during the Korean War, the President referred the ensuing dispute to the Wage Stabilization Board, which was charged with the responsibility of carrying out the wage stabilization program then in effect. After extensive hearings and efforts at mediation, the Board issued its report on March 20, 1952. The report recommended a substantial wage increase which the Board insisted was, nevertheless, within the wage stabilization pattern. The Board also recommended that the union be granted some form of union shop.

The companies refused to accept the Board's recommendations. The union set April 9 as a strike deadline. A few hours before the deadline, President Truman issued an Executive Order directing the Secretary of Commerce to take possession of the steel mills and operate them. The President justified not using the Taft-Hartley national emergency provisions on the ground that the dispute had already been submitted to the fact-finding process through the wage stabilization procedures applicable at that time and that the Steelworkers had already delayed their strike for ninety-nine days while that fact-finding process was carried on.

Congress debated the seizure with great heat but took no action. There was strong congressional sentiment that the President should have invoked the emergency provisions of Taft-Hartley. In the meantime the battle had moved to the courts. The steel companies brought proceedings in the Federal District Court to enjoin the seizure as unconstitutional. On April 30 the District Court enjoined the seizure and the union immediately called a strike. This strike call was canceled the same day when the Court of Appeals stayed the District Court's injunction pending appeal. The Supreme Court granted certiorari and ordered immediate argument of the case. From the time of the seizure until the Supreme Court's decision on June 2, no serious collective bargaining took place.

In Youngstown Sheet & Tube Co. v. Sawyer, 343 U.S. 579, 587 (1952), the Supreme Court held the seizure unconstitutional. Justice Black, delivering the opinion of the Court, held that in the absence of any statute granting him the power, the President had no constitutional power to order the seizure of the industry. He did not have the power as Commander in Chief "to take possession of private property in order to keep labor disputes from stopping production. This is a job for the Nation's lawmakers, not for its military authorities." Nor was this power inherent in his position as chief executive. "In the framework of our constitution, the President's power to see that the laws are faithfully executed refutes the idea that he is to be a lawmaker. The Constitution limits his function in the law-making process to the recommending of laws he thinks wise and the vetoing of laws he thinks bad. The Constitution is neither silent nor equivocal about who shall make the laws which the President shall execute." Justice Black reasoned further that there was not only an absence of congressional authority for seizure but an implied denial of that power. In passing the Taft-Hartley Act, Congress had rejected provisions for seizure and had adopted instead the device of temporary injunctions to permit cooling-off periods.

Justices Jackson, Burton, Clark, Douglas, and Frankfurter each wrote concurring opinions spelling out in more detail the various aspects briefly mentioned by Justice Black. Justice Clark argued that although the President had power to act to meet an emergency for which Congress had not provided, Congress had provided procedures for meeting this particular kind of emergency. The Taft-Hartley Act provided for an eighty-day delay, and the Selective Service Act provided for seizure of plants which failed to produce goods required by the armed forces. The President had not exhausted either of these procedures and therefore could not act on any independent power. Justice Frankfurter, as an appendix to his opinion, set forth in chart form all legislation authorizing seizure of industrial property and all instances of seizure of industrial property by the President.

Chief Justice Vinson, in a dissenting opinion joined by Justices Reed and Minton, argued that the President did not act in defiance of Congress but in aid of Congress by preserving the status quo until Congress had time to take steps to meet the crisis. This was within the President's power as chief executive in seeing that the laws were enforced. The Chief Justice further argued that the Defense Production Act, by giving the Wage Stabilization Board power to deal with labor disputes, provided a procedure which was an alternative to the Taft-Hartley Act. Referral to the Board was an exercise of this alternative and excluded the use of Taft-Hartley emergency strike procedures.

After the mills were returned to the owners, the workers struck. The dispute was finally settled, with the personal intervention of President Truman in the negotiations, seven weeks after the strike began. See Westin, The Anatomy of a Constitutional Case (1958), which is devoted entirely to the Youngstown case; Corwin, The Steel Seizure Case: A Judicial Brick Without Straw, 53 Colum. L. Rev. 53 (1953); Kauper, The Steel Seizure Case: Congress, the President and the Supreme Court, 51 Mich. L. Rev. 141 (1952); Williams, The Steel Seizure: A Legal Analysis of a Political Controversy, 2 J. Pub. L. 29 (1953).

The kind of seizure involved in enforcement of the orders of the War Labor Disputes Act during World War II and the steel dispute which culminated in the Youngstown case must be distinguished from seizure of a business to prevent an "emergency" strike when the seizure is viewed as an end in itself. In the former situations, seizure is simply an enforcing device designed to pressure the parties into acceptance of a settlement which comes from some other source. Under the War Labor Disputes Act it was the War Labor Board. In the steel controversy, it was the Wage Stabilization Board. Seizure for its own sake without any other provision of law designed to establish a recommended or compelled settlement is sometimes advocated as a device to be used in emergency situations. It should be noted, however, that the result of seizure in such circumstances is that the workers are simply ordered by the seizure not to strike, but then are left to continue the process of collective bargaining. This means that the workers are forced to bargain with their bargaining strength emasculated.

For an article considering the use of seizure as a device for handling emergency labor disputes see Cox, Seizure in Emergency Disputes, in Emergency Disputes and National Policy 224 (Bernstein, Enarson, and Fleming, eds. 1955).

The "nonstoppage strike." There have been several proposals for a system imposing financial penalties upon both the company and the employees in an emergency labor dispute should a work stoppage take place. The theory is that through the imposition of substantial financial loss the parties will be forced to reach agreement, and the public will not suffer from a work stoppage in a critical industry. For example, the proposal by Professor Goble is that the company deposit weekly in a special government fund an amount equal to its average weekly net profits for the taxable year immediately preceding the dispute, together with 25 per cent of the salaries of specified officers and executives of the company. At the same time the employees would be required to submit to a weekly deduction of 25 per cent of their wages. If the parties settled their dispute within ninety days, all amounts paid into this fund would be returned. If they failed to reach an agreement within ninety days, the entire deposit would be forfeited to the United States Government. The same procedure would then be repeated for the next ninety days, and so on until the parties reached an agreement. See Goble, The Nonstoppage Strike, 2 Lab. L.J. 105 (1951); Goble, An Alternative to the Strike, 6 id. 83 (1955). See also Marshall and Marshall, Nonstoppage Strikes and National Labor Policy — A Critique, 7 id. 299 (1956).

The choice-of-procedures approach. One criticism of the present national emergency provisions of the Taft-Hartley Act is that they are so definite that the parties know exactly what will happen to them, once the procedures are invoked. The report of the committee appointed by Governor Meyner of New Jersey to study that state's handling of emergency labor disputes concluded that the most effective device is to have a number of possible courses of action available in order to keep the parties in doubt as to what may happen if they do not resolve the dispute on their own. This approach to emergency labor disputes has been advocated by a number of authorities in the field. One state, Massachusetts, has adopted it. This is the Slichter Law (taking its name from the late Professor Sumner H. Slichter, who headed a committee appointed by Governor Bradford to investigate and make recommendations upon this problem) which was passed in 1947 and amended in 1954. Mass. Ann. Laws, c. 150B (1957). Under this law, the governor is given four alternative procedures which he may invoke in such a situation: First, the company and union representatives may be required to appear before a moderator appointed by the governor to show cause why they should not submit the dispute to arbitration. No change in conditions of employment, unless mutually agreeable, and no strikes are permitted during the moderator's inquiry. The moderator is also empowered to act as a mediator in the dispute. Second, the governor may request the parties voluntarily to submit their dispute to an emergency board empowered to recommend terms for settlement. Again no changes in conditions of employment and no strike are permitted. Third, the governor may enter into "arrangements with either or both parties for continuing such part of their production or distribution of goods or services as may be necessary to the public health and safety." Fourth, the governor may also seize and operate the plant. He is empowered during seizure to put into effect the recommendations previously made by an emergency board, or if there has been no emergency board, he may appoint one and have it submit recommendations. The seizure ends only when the parties notify the governor that the dispute has been settled. For careful consideration of this approach to emergency disputes see Wirtz, The "Choice of Procedures" Approach to National Emergency Disputes, in Emergency Disputes and National Policy 149 (Bernstein, Enarson, and Fleming, eds. 1955); Shultz, The Massachusetts

Choice-of-Procedures Approach to Emergency Disputes, 10 Ind. & Lab. Rel. Rev. 358 (1957).

3.   *The Antitrust Laws as Protecting the Public Interest*

HILDEBRAND, COLLECTIVE BARGAINING AND THE ANTITRUST LAWS *

Public Policy and Collective Bargaining 152-171 (Shister, Aaron, and Summers, eds. 1962)

The passage of the Sherman Act in 1890 symbolized a certain continuity in the Anglo-American tradition. Within the common law, there was the well-established principle that contracts in restraint of trade were not enforceable. Coupled to it was the native American doctrine of economic egalitarianism, exalting the free man and making competition "the servo-mechanism of economic life." [1] The doctrine means that every man has the right of access to a market, and that combinations of private power do not conform to the natural competitive order; hence they are forever suspect. The Sherman law put the federal government behind these ideas, providing a means of public prosecution against transgressors. But who were they?

The activities of unions in the labor market have never fitted comfortably with competitive precepts. Yet they accorded well with the economic egalitarianism of that day. It was then a case of the little man against the trusts. Unionism gave the worker a means to cope with the rapidly growing power of capital, and so commanded popular appeal. However, the remedy it afforded required combination — combination to eliminate competition among workingmen in dealing with their employers. To exert this power, the union must attain monopoly in the labor market.

As the Webbs pointed out in *Industrial Democracy* over half a century ago, to make its monopoly fully effective, the union cannot limit itself to a single employer alone but must extend its power to embrace all of the employers in the industry. Thus its goal is really a double one: to end competition among workers at the level of the firm, and to "take wages out of competition" as among competing firms in a common industry or trade. Accordingly, control of the labor market implies indirect control of the product market as well.

So arises a paradox: While the union expresses the egalitarian tradition, it practices monopoly. To practice monopoly effectively, it must seek privileges and immunities under law, although these stand condemned by the tradition itself. In consequence, the partisans of unionism and collective bargaining were driven from the outset to proclaim a

---

* The excerpts of this chapter by George H. Hildebrand, Professor of Economics and of Industrial and Labor Relations, Cornell University, are reproduced with the permission of the publisher, Harper & Row.

[1] Louis B. Schwartz, Free Enterprise and Economic Organization: Legal and Related Materials, 2nd ed., Brooklyn: Foundation Press, 1959, p. 3.

dual standard: monopoly in the labor market stands on a different footing from monopoly in the product market.[2] . . .

DOMINANCE OF THE COMPETITIVE VIEW, 1890-1932

Before the Clayton Act of 1914

The Sherman law makes no references to unions and is most elastic in its coverage of proscribed activities. Hence it was an obvious threat from its inception. Section 1 outlaws *"Every* contract, combination in the form of trust *or otherwise,* or conspiracy, in restraint of trade or commerce" (emphasis supplied). Section 2 makes it a misdemeanor to monopolize, to attempt to monopolize, or to "combine or conspire" with others for such ends. Did this language apply to labor unions? . . .

[In answering "yes" to this question, the author details the history of the application of the antitrust laws to labor union activity which is more briefly recounted supra page 35. He concludes with this observation:]

Although it is dangerous to look for rigorous logic in the history of the law, there is a thread of consistency running through the decisions of the Supreme Court during this lengthy period. Trade unionism was still very much a minority movement in industrial life, commanding in the minds of most of the justices neither much sympathy nor understanding of its purposes and its methods. On the one hand, the court acknowledged the legality of the union as an institution, including those national bodies that had long since begun to concert their local activities in industry-wide programs. On the other, the court's sympathies were undoubtedly allied to the consumer-oriented and competitive spirit of the Sherman Act. From this point of view, it looked askance at the monopolizing efforts of industry-wide unions, in particular attempts through boycotts and sympathetic strikes to drive competing non-union goods off the market. A "legitimate" labor dispute, notwithstanding the broad scope of Section 20, was one limited to an employer and his own employees. Beyond this, fraternity had to yield to liberty. Boycotts and sympathetic strikes improperly widened what Brandeis had called "the allowable area of economic conflict," because they introduced outsiders who had no lawful interest at stake. Where used, they converted a labor

---

[2] The supporting arguments are various, partly inconsistent, and diverse in quality of reasoning: (1) the economic impacts of unionism are negligible; (2) unions can achieve a more "just" distribution of income, in favor of all wage-earners at the expense not of consumers but of property-owners; (3) unions have no intent to injure consumers; (4) unions do injure consumers, but workers have separate interests as workers, and the consumers' welfare optimum should not be the exclusive standard for policy or appraisal; (5) unions overcome the bargaining handicaps of the isolated worker; (6) unions provide countervailing power against the ubiquitous monopsony advantages of employers. All but one of these contentions are discussed by Donald Dewey, Monopoly in Economics and Law, Chicago: Rand McNally, 1959, pp. 265-269. The most thoroughgoing economic analysis of these and related arguments is in Fritz Machlup, The Political Economy of Monopoly: Business, Labor and Government Policies, Baltimore: The Johns Hopkins Press, 1952, pp. 339-417.

dispute into an illegal restraint of trade, depriving the union of statutory protection. So far as industry-wide unionism was concerned, it could legally exist, but under this construction of the law its freedom of action was narrowly circumscribed.

THE TRIUMPH OF THE DOCTRINE OF LICIT MONOPOLY IN LABOR MARKETS, 1932-1941

The Norris-LaGuardia Act

Between 1932 and 1941, the legal status of unionism and collective bargaining in the United States underwent a sea-change. On the union side, restraint by the judiciary gave way to liberation by statute, in the Norris-LaGuardia and Wagner Acts, passed in 1932 and 1935. Then in 1940 and 1941 the Supreme Court, perhaps following Mr. Dooley, turned liberator itself, largely freeing the unions from the incubus of the antitrust laws by major decisions in the Apex and Hutcheson cases. These events marked the abandonment of the antitrust approach to the labor market in favor of the doctrine of licit monopoly.[15] . . .

[In Norris-LaGuardia, by adopting its] broad conception of a lawful labor dispute Congress rendered immune from injunction the use of "strangers" in the prosecution of the issue, particularly on the union side, so long as they could be shown to have a tangible economic interest in the outcome. By implication, at least, the exemption covered organizational and sympathetic strikes, primary and secondary boycotts, stranger picketing, and related formerly judicially-circumscribed techniques of self-help and self-defense. By opening up the field, the law gave expression to a notion akin to a syndicalist or cartel version of affected economic interests — still well short of class conflict, but nonetheless a realistic version of the doctrine of bargaining struggle in American unionism. Having cleared the field of conflict from enjoinder by the federal courts, Congress introduced a peculiar version of laissez faire for the labor market. However, it was organizational laissez faire, not the atomistic competitive individualism of classical economics. Because it was organizational, it rested upon a form of preclusive monopoly, the very foundation of free collective bargaining. And for the same reason, the social-economic system implied for the labor market, and now in the process of formation, lacked the precise balancing and equilibrating mechanism inherent to traditional competition. Examination of the relevant provisions of the Wagner Act will make this more apparent. . . .

. . . Section 9(b) gave the Board power to designate the unit "appropriate" to collective bargaining, allowing it latitude to choose among plant, company, and craft units, or subdivisions of these. The administrative authority so conferred had much to do with the rapid growth of industrial unionism in the later thirties. But the main point is a differ-

---

[15] The word "monopoly" is used throughout in its descriptive sense, to refer to exclusive control of supply by sellers in order to fix price — in this case combinations of workmen in unions to control wages. That is all.

ent one: the law contained no bar either to industry-wide unions or to employer-representation associations.

So long as a given national union could win representation elections or gain voluntary recognition, it could enlarge the scope of its bargaining power to encompass an entire industry. There was precedent for such expansion in the long history of national unions, and it found early expression in the printing, building, and railroad industries. It also has its inherent logic: for labor monopoly to be fully effective, the union must extend its range of organizational control in the labor market to match the competitive span of the product market — in other words, it must gain indirect control of the product market as well. In any case, the law permitted the rapid advance of industry-wide unionism in a host of new fields. Further, employers in the same trade or industry were also left free to organize themselves for collective representation, so long as they stayed within the law — an equally logical tactic for meeting common pressure. Thus the act also permitted the rise of industry-wide bargaining.[18] Both the industry-wide union and the multiple-employer association were eventually to become targets for those who were to propose later the re-application of the antitrust laws to the labor field.

Omission from the act of any prohibitions against comprehensive organization by unions and employers for purposes of collective bargaining illustrates well the dual standard under antitrust. There is no doubt that the exclusion was intentional, in deference to the already long-established institution of national unionism. Acting as a kind of cartel, the national union can expand to embrace most, if not all, of the employers serving a common product market.[19] But while the market occupancy ratio of such a union could reach even 100 percent of the relevant labor market, and extend into others besides — with obvious implications for costs and prices in the allied product market — no business enterprise could attempt or achieve similar dominance in its product market without running afoul of antitrust. Nor could any group of business competitors, through trust, cartel, or organized collusion, escape a similar fate. This is the heart, if not the whole, of the problem of labor monopoly today.

Judicial Emancipation of Organized Labor from Antitrust: The Apex and Hutcheson Cases

Although Norris-LaGuardia made the federal labor injunction largely a nullity, both criminal and damage suits under antitrust remained a real threat where . . . a union called an organizational strike or re-

---

[18] Industry-wide, or employer-association, bargaining may be local, regional, or national, usually according to the geographic reach of product competition. Although it may accompany product-market wide unionism, the two are not identical, although they are often confused.

[19] This, of course, was true long before the Wagner law, so long as the means used were compatible with a narrow judicial view of antitrust. As they did with Section 20 in 1914, the lawmakers took the national union for granted as a natural institutional development under a regime of organizational laissez faire.

sorted to a boycott to end competition from non-union products. With the Apex and Hutcheson decisions in 1940 and 1941, the court virtually removed the Sherman Act from the union scene, save in cases of outright collusion with employers to fix commodity prices.[20]

On May 4, 1937, the Hosiery Workers struck Apex, turning it into a sit-down strike two days later. Organized violence and damage were committed. During the almost seven weeks' occupation of the plant, the employer was forceably prevented from shipping his product. He sued under the Sherman Act, and the issue before the Supreme Court was whether the strikers had committed an illegal restraint of trade. The majority thought that they had not, while conceding the tortious and criminal character of their acts.

According to Justice Stone, the Sherman law was not conceived as a measure for policing interstate shipments. Its purpose, or so he thought, was to prevent suppression of commercial competition. The intent of the Apex union was not such a restraint, but to organize the firm, of which the blockade of shipments, while probably a violation of local law, was a necessary consequence. There was no effect upon hosiery prices, nor was such intended. Indeed, union activities may restrict the competitive freedom of employers in the product market, but this does not make them illegal. A successful product-market wide union inevitably reduces competition from non-union goods, but this is essential and "has not been considered . . . the kind of curtailment of price competition prohibited by the Sherman Act." [21]

If one thinks that the Sherman Act should not be employed to establish labor policy through judicial interpretations of lawful means and lawful purposes, then the Apex decision was a great step forward. Yet, as Cox points out, it left some troublesome questions: (1) could the Teamsters lawfully encourage retail employees not to handle the products of a supplier with whom the union has a dispute? (2) Is the question of intent still decisive where a union makes preclusive agreements requiring that machinery may only be installed by contractors also having agreements with it? (3) If product price is adversely affected by the union's acts, do the latter become illegal trade restraints? [22]

The Hutcheson case involved a jurisdictional dispute between the carpenters and the machinists over construction work at the Anheuser-Busch brewery in St. Louis. Despite a prior agreement to arbitrate, President Hutcheson and three other officials called a strike against the company and its contractor, also promulgating a boycott against Budweiser beer. The government then obtained an indictment under the Sherman Act, charging a criminal combination and conspiracy in restraint of trade.

[20] Apex Hosiery Co. v. Leader, 310 U.S. 469 (1940); United States v. Hutcheson, 312 U.S. 219 (1941).

[21] Justice Stone was indulging in fiction here. . . . As Gregory suggests, Stone was trying to salvage consistency with the past while facing up to the times. Gregory [Labor and the Law], p. 265.

[22] Archibald Cox, "Labor and the antitrust laws — a preliminary analysis," University of Pennsylvania Law Review, 104:2 (November 1953), pp. 263-264.

Speaking for the majority, Justice Frankfurter began by asking whether the acts complained of were prohibited by the "three interlacing statutes" — Sherman, Clayton, and Norris-LaGuardia. Nothing in Section 20 precluded a jurisdictional strike, or picketing in its behalf, or a boycott in its support. All three were protected acts in self-defense, lawful under Clayton. The fact that outsiders shared in the conduct — a decisive point in the Duplex case — did not remove this protection. Under Norris-LaGuardia, a legitimate labor dispute was confined no longer to those who "stand in the proximate relation of employer and employee." Admittedly, Norris-LaGuardia was directed at injunctions, not criminal proceedings, but to contend that Duplex still survives for the latter "is to say that that which on the equity side of the court is allowable conduct may in a criminal proceeding become the road to prison." The statute was the legislature's answer to judicial doctrine in the Duplex and Bedford cases, hence the means of effectuating its original purpose in enacting Section 20.

There is a certain disingenuousness about this opinion that was not lost on Justice Robérts, who submitted a scathing dissent. As with Apex, however, the virtue, or lack of it, of the Hutcheson decision depends upon one's view of the use of the antitrust laws to regulate the labor-market activities of unions. What this verdict did was to make them immune from the doctrine of illegal trade restraints. Consistent with the very premise of the dual standard, the law regarding the coercive weapons of unionism was now completely divorced from the restrictions of the Sherman Act. . . .

[Additional portions of this article appear infra page 737.]

ALLEN BRADLEY CO. v. LOCAL 3, INTERNATIONAL BROTHERHOOD OF ELECTRICAL WORKERS

Supreme Court of the United States, 1945
325 U.S. 797, 65 Sup. Ct. 1533, 89 L. Ed. 1939

MR. JUSTICE BLACK delivered the opinion of the Court.

The question presented is whether it is a violation of the Sherman Anti-trust Act for labor unions and their members, prompted by a desire to get and hold jobs for themselves at good wages and under high working standards, to combine with employers and with manufacturers of goods to restrain competition in, and to monopolize the marketing of, such goods.

Upon the complaint of petitioners and after a lengthy hearing the District Court held that such a combination did violate the Sherman Act, entered a declaratory judgment to that effect, and entered an injunction restraining respondents from engaging in a wide range of specified activities. 41 F. Supp. 727, 51 F. Supp. 36. The Circuit Court of Appeals reversed the decision and dismissed the cause, holding that combinations of unions and business men which restrained trade and tended to monopoly were not in violation of the Act where the bona fide purpose of the unions was to raise wages, provide better working conditions, and bring about better conditions of employment for their members.   145 F.2d 215.   The Ninth Circuit Court of Appeals having reached a contrary conclusion in a similar case, 144 F.2d 546, we granted certiorari in both cases. . . .

Petitioners are manufacturers of electrical equipment.   Their places of manufacture are outside of New York City, and most of them are outside of New York State as well.   They have brought this action because of their desire to sell their products in New York City, a market area that has been closed to them through the activities of respondents and others.

Respondents are a labor union, its officials and its members.   The union, Local No. 3 of the International Brotherhood of Electrical Workers, has jurisdiction only over the metropolitan area of New York City. It is therefore impossible for the union to enter into a collective bargaining agreement with petitioners.   Some of petitioners do have collective bargaining agreements with other unions, and in some cases even with other locals of the I.B.E.W.

Some of the members of respondent union work for manufacturers who produce electrical equipment similar to that made by petitioners; other members of respondent union are employed by contractors and work on the installation of electrical equipment, rather than in its production.

The union's consistent aim for many years has been to expand its membership, to obtain shorter hours and increased wages, and to enlarge employment opportunities for its members.   To achieve this latter goal — that is, to make more work for its own members — the union realized that local manufacturers, employers of the local members, must have the widest possible outlets for their product.   The union therefore waged aggressive campaigns to obtain closed-shop agreements with all local electrical equipment manufacturers and contractors.   Using conventional labor union methods, such as strikes and boycotts, it gradually obtained more and more closed-shop agreements in the New York City area.   Under these agreements, contractors were obligated to purchase equipment from none but local manufacturers who also had closed-shop agreements with Local No. 3; manufacturers obligated themselves to confine their New York City sales to contractors employing the Local's members.   In the course of time, this type of individual employer-employee agreement expanded into industry-wide understandings, looking not merely to terms and conditions of employment but also to price and market control.   Agencies were set up composed of representatives of all three groups to boycott recalcitrant local contractors and manufacturers and to bar from the area equipment manufactured outside its boundaries.   The combination among the three groups, union, contractors, and manufacturers, became highly successful from the standpoint of all of them.   The business of New York City manufacturers had a phenomenal growth, thereby multiplying the jobs available for the Local's members.   Wages went up, hours were shortened, and the New York electrical equipment prices soared, to the decided financial profit of local contractors and manufacturers.   The success is illustrated by the fact that some New York manufacturers sold their goods in the protected city market at one price and sold identical goods outside of New York at a far lower price. All of this took place, as the Circuit Court of Appeals declared, "through the stifling of competition," and because the three groups, in combination as "co-partners," achieved "a complete monopoly which they used to boycott the equipment manufactured by the plaintiffs." Interstate sale of various types of electrical equipment has, by this powerful combination, been wholly suppressed.

Quite obviously, this combination of business men has violated both §§1 and 2 of the Sherman Act, unless its conduct is immunized by the participation of the union. For it intended to and did restrain trade in and monopolize the supply of electrical equipment in the New York City area to the exclusion of equipment manufactured in and shipped from other states, and did also control its price and discriminate between its would-be customers. Apex Hosiery Co. v. Leader, 310 U.S. 469, 512-513. Our problem in this case is therefore a very narrow one — do labor unions violate the Sherman Act when, in order to further their own interests as wage earners, they aid and abet business men to do the precise things which that Act prohibits? . . .

. . . [W]e have two declared congressional policies which it is our responsibility to try to reconcile. The one seeks to preserve a competitive business economy; the other to preserve the rights of labor to organize to better its conditions through the agency of collective bargaining. We must determine here how far Congress intended activities under one of these policies to neutralize the results envisioned by the other.

Aside from the fact that the labor union here acted in combination with the contractors and manufacturers, the means it adopted to contribute to the combination's purpose fall squarely within the "specified acts" declared by §20 not to be violations of federal law. For the union's contribution to the trade boycott was accomplished through threats that unless their employers bought their goods from local manufacturers the union laborers would terminate the "relation of employment" with them and cease to perform "work or labor" for them; and through their "recommending, advising, or persuading others by peaceful and lawful means" not to "patronize" sellers of the boycotted electrical equipment. Consequently, under our holdings in the Hutcheson case and other cases which followed it, had there been no union-contractor-manufacturer combination the union's actions here, coming as they did within the exemptions of the Clayton and Norris-LaGuardia Acts, would not have been violations of the Sherman Act. We pass to the question of whether unions can with impunity aid and abet business men who are violating the Act.

On two occasions this Court has held that the Sherman Act was violated by a combination of labor unions and business men to restrain trade. In neither of them was the Court's attention sharply called to the crucial questions here presented. Furthermore, both were decided before the passage of the Norris-LaGuardia Act and prior to our holding in the Hutcheson case. It is correctly argued by respondents that these factors greatly detract from the weight which the two cases might otherwise have in the instant case. See United States v. Hutcheson, supra, 236. Without regard to these cases, however, we think Congress never intended that unions could, consistently with the Sherman Act, aid non-labor groups to create business monopolies and to control the marketing of goods and services.

Section 6 of the Clayton Act declares that the Sherman Act must not be so construed as to forbid the "existence and operation of labor, agricultural, or horticultural organizations, instituted for the purposes of mutual help . . ." But "the purpose of mutual help" can hardly be thought to cover activities for the purpose of "employer-help" in controlling markets and prices. And in an analogous situation where an agricultural association joined with other groups to control the agricultural market, we said:

"The right of these agricultural producers thus to unite in preparing for market and in marketing their products, and to make the contracts which are necessary for that collaboration, cannot be deemed to authorize any combination or conspiracy *with other persons* in restraint of trade that these producers may see fit to devise." United States v. Borden Co., 308 U.S. 188, 204-205. (Italics supplied.)

We have been pointed to no language in any act of Congress or in its reports or debates, nor have we found any, which indicates that it was ever suggested, considered, or legislatively determined that labor unions should be granted an immunity such as is sought in the present case. It has been argued that this immunity can be inferred from a union's right to make bargaining agreements with its employer. Since union members can without violating the Sherman Act strike to enforce a union boycott of goods, it is said they may settle the strike by getting their employers to agree to refuse to buy the goods. Employers and the union did here make bargaining agreements in which the employers agreed not to buy goods manufactured by companies which did not employ the members of Local No. 3. We may assume that such an agreement standing alone would not have violated the Sherman Act. But it did not stand alone. It was but one element in a far larger program in which contractors and manufacturers united with one another to monopolize all the business in New York City, to bar all other business men from that area, and to charge the public prices above a competitive level. It is true that victory of the union in its disputes, even had the union acted alone, might have added to the cost of goods, or might have resulted in individual refusals of all of their employers to buy electrical equipment not made by Local No. 3. So far as the union might have achieved this result acting alone, it would have been the natural consequence of labor union activities exempted by the Clayton Act from the coverage of the Sherman Act. Apex Hosiery Co. v. Leader, supra, 503. But when the unions participated with a combination of business men who had complete power to eliminate all competition among themselves and to prevent all competition from others, a situation was created not included within the exemptions of the Clayton and Norris-LaGuardia Acts.

It must be remembered that the exemptions granted the unions were special exceptions to a general legislative plan. The primary objective of all the Anti-trust legislation has been to preserve business competition and to proscribe business monopoly. It would be a surprising thing if Congress, in order to prevent a misapplication of that legislation to labor unions, had bestowed upon such unions complete and unreviewable authority to aid business groups to frustrate its primary objective. For if business groups, by combining with labor unions, can fix prices and divide up markets, it was little more than a futile gesture for Congress to prohibit price fixing by business groups themselves. Seldom, if ever, has it been claimed before, that by permitting labor unions to carry on their own activities, Congress intended completely to abdicate its constitutional power to regulate interstate commerce and to empower interested business groups to shift our society from a competitive to a monopolistic economy. Finding no purpose of Congress to immunize labor unions who aid and abet manufacturers and traders in violating the Sherman Act, we hold that the district court correctly concluded that the respondents had violated the Act.

Our holding means that the same labor union activities may or may not be in violation of the Sherman Act, dependent upon whether the union acts alone or in combination with business groups. This, it is argued, brings about a wholly undesirable result — one which leaves labor unions free to engage in conduct which restrains trade. But the desirability of such an exemption of labor unions is a question for the determination of Congress. Apex Hosiery Co. v. Leader, supra. It is true that many labor union activities do substantially interrupt the course of trade and that these activities, lifted out of the prohibitions of the Sherman Act, include substantially all, if not all, of the normal peaceful activities of labor unions. It is also true that the Sherman Act "draws no distinction between the restraints effected by violence and those achieved by peaceful . . . means," Apex Hosiery Co. v. Leader, supra, 513, and that a union's exemption from the Sherman Act is not to be determined by a judicial "judgment regarding the wisdom or unwisdom, the rightness of wrongness, the selfishness or unselfishness of the end of which the particular union activities are the means." United States v. Hutcheson, supra, 232. Thus, these congressionally permitted union activities may restrain trade in and of themselves. There is no denying the fact that many of them do so, both directly and indirectly. Congress evidently concluded, however, that the chief objective of Anti-trust legislation, preservation of business competition, could be accomplished by applying the legislation primarily only to those business groups which are directly interested in destroying competition. The difficulty of drawing legislation primarily aimed at trusts and monopolies so that it could also be applied to labor organizations without impairing the collective bargaining and related rights of those organizations has been emphasized both by congressional and judicial attempts to draw lines between permissible and prohibited union activities. There is, however, one line which we can draw with assurance that we follow the congressional purpose. We know that Congress feared the concentrated power of business organizations to dominate markets and prices. It intended to outlaw business monopolies. A business monopoly is no less such because a union participates, and such participation is a violation of the Act. . . .

Respondents objected to the form of the injunction and specifically requested that it be amended so as to enjoin only those prohibited activities in which the union engaged in combination "with any person, firm or corporation which is a non-labor group . . ." Without such a limitation, the injunction as issued runs directly counter to the Clayton and the Norris-LaGuardia Acts. The district court's refusal so to limit it was error.

The judgment of the Circuit Court of Appeals ordering the action dismissed is accordingly reversed and the cause is remanded to the district court for modification and clarification of the judgment and injunction, consistent with this opinion.

Reversed.

MR. JUSTICE ROBERTS.

While I should reverse the judgment, I am unable to concur in the court's opinion. I think it conveys an incorrect impression of the genesis and character of the conspiracy charged in the complaint, and misapplies recent decisions of the court. . . .

There can be no question of the purpose of the union. It was to exclude from use in the City of New York articles of commerce made outside the city and offered for sale to users within the city; it was completely to monopolize the manufacture and sale of all electrical equipment and devices within New York, and to exclude from use in the area every such article manufactured outside the city, whether in a closed union shop or not. The results of this programme are obvious. Interstate commerce between New York City and manufacturers having establishments outside the city was completely broken off, and the monopoly created raised, standardized and fixed the prices of merchandise and apparatus.

As I understand the opinion of the court, such a programme, and such a result, is wholly within the law provided only that employers do not jointly agree to comply with the union's demands. Unless I misread the opinion, the union is at liberty to impose every term and condition as shown by the record in this case and to enforce those conditions and procure an agreement from each employer to such conditions by calling strikes, by lockout, and boycott, provided only such employer agrees for himself alone and not in concert with any other.

I point out again, as respects certain employers here concerned, that that is the situation, whereas, with respect to the building construction employers, there was mutual agreement with the union. But the opinion takes no note of the distinction in fact. It seems to me that the law as announced by the court creates an impossible situation such as Congress never contemplated and leaves commerce paralyzed beyond escape. . . .

. . . [T]wo branches of the industry, the manufacturers and employers, one by one, succumbed to union pressure and entered into agreements. Was not such an action, in each instance, a conspiracy? Are more than two parties required to conspire, and did not each of those conspiracies, to some extent, hinder and restrain interstate commerce and affect the market and the competitive price situation? As each agreement was consummated the market was, to that extent, closed and the boycott against out-of-the-city manufactures tightened.

But more. The union did not conduct its campaign in a corner. Albeit the findings are that manufacturers and repairers of electrical appliances violently resisted the unionization of their businesses, they, one by one, surrendered and signed. In doing so, many must have had knowledge of what others were doing or had done. And, as the coverage became complete, each one was enabled to stifle out-of-town competition and to raise prices. In any action against them and the union charging conspiracy, it would be urged that a conspiracy need not consist of a written or verbal agreement but might be inferred from similarity of action. And it would be little protection to the employers concerned that, in each instance, a separate agreement was signed between union and employer.

The course of decision in this court has now created a situation in which, by concerted action, unions may set up a wall around a municipality of millions of inhabitants against importation of any goods if the union is careful to make separate contracts with each employer, and if union and employers are able to convince the court that, while all employers have such agreements, each acted independently in making them, — this notwithstanding the avowed purpose to exclude goods not made in that city by the members of the union; notwithstanding the fact that the purpose and inevitable result is the stifling of competition in interstate trade and the creation of a monopoly.

The only answer I find in the opinion of the court is that Congress has so provided. I think it has not provided any such thing and that the figmentary difference between employers negotiating jointly with the only union with which they can deal, — which imposes like conditions on all employers — and each employer dealing separately with the same union is unrealistic and unworkable. And the language of §20 of the Clayton Act makes no such distinction. . . .

I would not limit the injunction as the opinion directs.

MR. JUSTICE MURPHY, dissenting.

My disagreement with the Court rests not so much with the legal principles announced as with the application of those principles to the facts of the case.

If the union in this instance had acted alone in its self-interest, resulting in a restraint of interstate trade, the Sherman Act concededly would be inapplicable. But if the union had aided and abetted manufacturers or traders in violating the Act, the union's statutory immunity would disappear. I cannot agree, however, that the circumstances of this case demand the invocation of the latter rule.

The union here has not in any true sense "aided" or "abetted" a primary violation of the Act by the employers. In the words of the union, it has been "the dynamic force which has driven the employer-group to enter into agreements" whereby trade has been affected. The fact that the union has expressed its self-interest with the aid of others rather than solely by its own activities should not be decisive of statutory liability. What is legal if done alone should not become illegal if done with the assistance of others and with the same purpose in mind. Otherwise a premium of unlawfulness is placed on collective bargaining.

Had the employers embarked upon a course of unreasonable trade restraints and had they sought to immunize themselves from the Sherman Act by using the union as a shield for their nefarious practices, we would have quite a different case. The union then could not be said to be acting in its self-interest in combining with the employers to carry out trade restraints primarily for the employers' interests, even though incidental benefits might accrue to the union. Under such conditions the union fairly could be said to be aiding and abetting a violation of the Act and its immunity would be lost. The facts of this case, however, do not allow such conclusions to be drawn.

I would therefore affirm the judgment of the court below.

HILDEBRAND, COLLECTIVE BARGAINING AND THE ANTITRUST LAWS *

Public Policy and Collective Bargaining 152, 171-179 (Shister, Aaron, and Summers, eds. 1962)

PROPOSALS TO RENEW APPLICATION OF ANTITRUST TO REGULATION OF THE LABOR MARKET

Since the end of World War II, many proposals have arisen for revitalizing antitrust as a means for remaking national labor policy. Some of these hardly go beyond incantation, and amount to little more than an indiscriminate attack on a whole range of admittedly difficult problems — corruption, coercion, big unionism, national strikes, and even collective bargaining itself. What this line of thinking involves is far more than a return to antitrust. In reality, it intends a complete reconstruction of national labor policy, a subject beyond the scope of this paper.

The more carefully framed proposals to resurrect antitrust either aim to correct specific abuses, such as make-work rules, or to reduce the economic impacts of collective bargaining. Some of them would have the courts again distinguish the licit from the illicit without precise statutory guidance — an act of supreme folly in view of past experience. Yet some of the problems with which they purport to deal are serious. They give every indication of becoming even more acute in the sixties, where the now-permanent combination of cold war and intense foreign

---

* This is a continuation of the chapter by George H. Hildebrand, see page 725 supra, reproduced with the permission of the publisher, Harper & Row.

competition has made uninterrupted and more efficient production a national imperative.

These proposals would renew antitrust to cope with four major problems: national-emergency strikes, make-work policies, direct efforts to control the product market, and the effects of collective bargaining upon wages.

Regarding the first, the argument runs that the dual standard now allows national unions to do what no group of producers could do on their own: close down almost an entire industry by use of concentrated organizational power. This, it is said, is restraint of trade in its most extreme form. It should no longer be permitted.

So stated, the argument is really mostly about industry-wide unionism, and will be discussed later under that head. However, the short answer is that strikes are essential to collective bargaining, while collective bargaining continues to be national policy. The Taft-Hartley law already recognizes that some stoppages may unreasonably impose upon third parties; hence it contains a special procedure for national emergencies. In certain respects, it has proved defective. Correction lies either in legislation to improve the technique of intervention, or possibly to provide return to strict non-intervention, although the latter obviously would be unacceptable to those who demand strike control. Either way, antitrust supplies no solution. What it would do is to resurrect the old judicial concept that obstruction of production and transit is a restraint of trade, which would outlaw many strikes unqualifiedly. . . .

The second area — make-work policies — covers a host of complex and vexing problems. Here the short answer is that the issues are too technical for the courts to handle with informed discretion, while to call this group of policies attempted trade retraints would not only go far off the mark but would threaten the whole bargaining system.

The problems in this field range widely: refusal to work with new materials, prefabricated products, tools, and machines; manning requirements, regulation of equipment speeds, and output controls; job and work jurisdictions, and full-crew regulations. Not all such devices are intended to "make work" — often their rationale is safety or reasonable working speeds, arrived at by bargaining. But odious cases of make-work are not hard to find, usually in craft-ridden industries such as construction, railroads, and entertainment. They may arise because the union has created unemployment by monopolistic wage-fixing, or because the industry is in attrition and the union resorts to crude methods of job protection. However, work rules are not inevitably a trade restraint, even under a broad conception of the term. A manning rule, for example, does not qualify, even if costly enough to affect product price. By contrast, a refusal of carpenters to work on pre-glazed sash is a deliberate trade restraint, denying such producers access to a market.

Work rules lie at the heart of the collective agreement. Their origins are diverse and their nature complex. Good and bad alike, they express equities established by bargaining, as part of the web of rules by which the parties govern themselves. Wise men do not lightly tear this fabric apart. Thus to make work rules subject to antitrust would be far too sweeping. It would assign to the courts the impossible technical burden of segregating licit from illicit strikes and supportive union activities, in a field in which the judiciary is notoriously inexpert. Neither jurists nor lawmakers are competent to prescribe in detail the appropriate contents of a collective agreement. The whole approach rests upon a major premise that is simpliste: that all work rules are suspect and most of them economically and morally wrong; that collective bargaining should restrain the employer only in the area of wages and hours; that in all else his demands are proper, and the verdict of a court the last word.

It would seem more prudent to consider less risky alternatives. One of these would be a carefully drafted statute to get at concerted refusals to work with new materials, products, tools, or machines, all of which are union tactics to control product markets. However, even this interdiction might be easy for a union to evade, simply by translating the issue into one involving wages appropriate to a change in job content. Another line of attack, suggested by Gomberg, is to establish a technically qualified equity court to undertake "valuation proceedings" for hampering work rules, handing down awards under which the employer could "buy out" a particular rule for a decreed sum to be paid the union — an approach akin to eminent domain. In itself, this is a major departure, free neither of difficulties nor of objections. Short of it, there is the current proposal to give voluntary methods another chance, through extended mediation and bargaining, using "adopted" neutrals and study committees, on the premise that conventional bargaining can still yield constructive results in this difficult field if its procedures and resources are strengthened.

The third area of renewed antitrust embraces direct efforts by unions, through strikes and collective agreements, to control the product market. In part, the Allen Bradley decision dealt with this problem, by outlawing collusive agreements between the union and *groups* of employers in which control of market price was the larger explicit design. However, the majority opinion in that case suggested both that the union might still negotiate *separate* agreements lawfully excluding outside products for the benefit of its members and a preferred group of employers, and that, since the purpose was improved wages and conditions, such a demand could still give rise to a valid "labor dispute" within the meaning of Norris-LaGuardia. Beyond this, the construction trades are replete with devices to restrict the market to certain contractors, to fix bid prices, and to limit market access.[26]

Here, at least, there is a measure of agreement that the consumer interest is predominant, that antitrust can be applied consistently under the dual standard. As Cox suggests, the task is to guide the courts with precision, by an explicit statutory declaration carefully separating protected union activity from efforts to rig the product market. Agreements with employers to fix prices, limit production, or close off access to a market would become illegal, and strikes, boycotts, and other concerted acts to

[26] Cox, op. cit., pp. 266-267. [P. 729, supra]

compel such agreements would also be illicit. However, Cox would exempt exclusion of an employer from the market incidental to disputes over representation or wages and working conditions, even if "strangers" participate. In its sole proposal affecting labor policy, the Attorney General's National Committee recommended a similar approach, but with a more comprehensive definition of proscribed activities and without the exemption noted.[27]

The fourth target for revived antitrust is reduction of the monopoly power of unions in the labor market itself. What must be abolished are multi-product or multi-industry unions such as the Teamsters, and along with them industry-wide unions as well. To the extent that its spread is economically motivated, the multi-industry union attempts to end competition *among* industries, such as railroads, water shipping, and trucking. The industry-wide union would end competition *among* firms in the same industry — a lesser type of indirect control over the product market.

Both must go, it is argued, because the only tenable economic case for labor monopoly is at the local level, to correct employer monopsony. Multi-industry and industry-wide unionism yield extra monopoly gains by reducing indirect competition among substitutes — through the elimination of non-union products and the establishment of uniform wages and conditions. The consequences have been adverse to the economy in three ways: major distortions in relative wages and reduced national income; sustained inflationary pressures from wage costs; and damaging large-scale strikes. Growth, full employment, and price stability have thus become incompatible ends for policy. The remedy is to break the monopoly power of multi-employer unions, by limiting labor organizations to the plant or company level, by prohibiting collusion among them, and by outlawing employer-bargaining associations.[28]

There is rather a radically utopian quality in this limitist approach. To conserve a competitive system it would undertake a major reconstruction of unionism, bargaining institutions, and the entire body of labor law, breaking decisively with the past. . . .

Considered on its own terms, localized or "enterprise" unionism poses serious questions and difficulties. One is that the stabilizing role of the national union would be destroyed. Usually the locals produce the hotheads and put forward the most extreme demands, while the national office exerts restraint because it must take a wider view of the employment effects of the wage bargain.

Closely allied is the question whether rival enterprise unions in the same industry would reduce or increase wage pressure. In cases where sellers are few, wage and price leadership by the strongest firm seems likely to continue. An aggressive local union could use the claim of

---

[27] Ibid., pp. 283-284; Report of the Attorney General's National Committee to Study the Antitrust Laws, Washington: Government Printing Office, 1955, pp. 304-305.

[28] See . . . Cox, op. cit., pp. 275-279; and H. Gregg Lewis, "The labor-monopoly problem: A positive program," Journal of Political Economy, LIX:4 (August 1951), pp. 277-287.

"ability to pay" with moral fervor and with no less force than now. Armed with the standards won in such a settlement, the other local bodies would still have both incentive and opportunity to follow along without overt collusion, while the employers could no longer unite against them.   Furthermore, it is difficult to see why the threat of added unemployment would be any more effective than it is now among workers in weaker concerns, or why such firms would be better able or more willing to stand out than they do now against industry-wide unionism. In consequence, enterprise unionism in concentrated industries offers no assurance of improved wage behavior, and some prospect of worse.   To better the results and to provide even-handed justice to the workers involved, it would be necessary to break up the firms as well.

For highly atomistic industries, equally difficult problems emerge. In very small firms, local unions could hardly survive, or if they could they would lack the financial resources and technical skills required for effective bargaining and contract administration.   Beyond this, the proposal would make incomplete organization of an industry a powerful threat against any effective bargaining.   In addition, the hard-won standards of unions in the casual trades would necessarily disintegrate.   Indeed, the built-in weakness of local unionism in atomistic industries would have precluded most, if not all, of the undeniable achievements of centrally-directed national unions in the areas of private social security, work rules, and industrial jurisprudence.   Finally, atomization would probably serve the objective of more flexible, market-responsive wages in highly diffuse industries, but it is doubtful that interfirm differentials or internal wage structures would be cured of monopsonistic — in contrast to monopolistic — distortions.

To sum up, the difficulties with the limitist approach derive not from its sound technical critique of multi-employer unionism, nor from its proper concern about the adverse economic consequences of present collective bargaining, but with the cure itself.   While the statistical evidence for wage distortion is not yet conclusive, there is little doubt that unions in industries such as steel, construction, railroads, and coal have pushed wages far beyond competitive levels.   The grounds are even stronger for attributing part of the creeping inflation of recent years to union-imposed cost pressures and the price policies they invoke.[29]

However, the cure may prove worse than the disease.   Politically, the attempt to achieve enterprise unionism would unleash a costly and divisive struggle, for men do not lightly yield up institutions they have dedicated a century in building.   Nor is this all.   Dissolution of national unions seems certain to destroy the present balance of political power.   At the same time, it implies new and comprehensive areas for government intervention — in "divestiture proceedings" against national unions and

[29] Robert Ozanne, "Impact of unions on wage levels and income distribution," Quarterly Journal of Economics, LXXIII:2 (May 1959), pp. 177-196; W. Fellner, M. Gilbert, B. Hansen, R. Kahn, F. Lutz, and P. de Wolff, The Problem of Rising Prices, a study for the OEEC (1961); and Frank C. Pierson, "The economic influence of big unions," Annals of the American Academy of Political and Social Science, vol. 333 (January 1961), pp. 96-107.

in enforcement of non-collusory behavior. This would be an odd kind of limitism indeed, for it would merely substitute one kind of concentrated power for another — public for private. And because it would greatly weaken, if not destroy, collective bargaining, it would divert the functions performed by bargaining to government instead, promising even further expansion of political intervention into the labor-management field. The situation is not yet so desperate that it requires so Draconian a measure.

Conclusion

. . .

Our experiment with relatively unhampered national unionism in the labor market has yielded some undeniable benefits and some unquestionable costs. The benefits require no elaboration. Among the costs are some upward push on wages and prices, some distortion of wage structure, some wage-induced unemployment, some great strikes, and some sobering revelations of corruption and abuses of power involving certain union leaders. It was proper that unions again would come under critical scrutiny, and inevitable that they would be blamed beyond fair warrant for the economic difficulties of recent times. Public criticism is a vital ingredient of a free society, for it is the one reliable means to well-conceived reforms.

Granting the problems, what promise does a return to antitrust actually hold? The answer is: relatively little for the problems at hand. What renewed antitrust really means is a return to judicial appraisal of the means and ends of union policy. Unless the courts are carefully circumscribed by statute, the outcome could only be chaos and uncertainty. If they are confined by measures to deal with specific abuses such as make-work or exclusion from the product market, antitrust could yield some modest benefits. But this approach would not cure the problems of corruption, of great strikes, or of the arrogant use of power. If antitrust were applied as the limitists propose, it would not only bring in the courts again with a vengeance, but would require government intervention so extensive that the whole bargaining system would be disrupted, if not destroyed. The price is too high for the quite speculative benefits such a change would bring. Labor-management relations today are not that desperate, nor are they lacking potential for constructive development on a voluntaristic basis. Legislative reforms are also needed. To be sound, they must derive from careful study and well-drafted statutes. To this end, antitrust has little to contribute but confusion.

D. Public Employees and Collective Bargaining

Collective bargaining by organized labor is universally accepted in the industrial world, but in the field of public employment its very right to exist has been challenged, and it has been the subject of discordant and contradictory judicial decisions. See, e.g., Cornell, Collective Bargaining by Public Employee Groups, 107 U. Pa. L. Rev. 43 (1958).

The purpose and function of a collective bargaining agreement must be kept in mind. Its purpose and function are to limit and restrict the control and direction of the working force by the employer. These rights are commonly known as management's prerogatives. In industry, there can be no doubt of the right of an employer to limit his prerogatives by means of contract. However, where some governmental unit is the employer, legal doubts arise. A number of cases have held that public employers cannot bargain away their continuing "legislative" discretion, and that for this reason public employers are not authorized to enter into collective bargaining agreements with public employee unions.

NUTTER v. CITY OF SANTA MONICA

District Court of Appeal, Second District
Division 3, California, 1946
74 Cal. App. 2d 292, 168 P.2d 741

SHINN, Justice.

The City of Santa Monica operates a local and intercity motor coach line, serving the public in the City of Santa Monica, with one branch extending into the westerly section of the City of Los Angeles. The city employs 63 bus operators, 62 of them being members of Lodge No. 22 of the Brotherhood of Railroad Trainmen; they have designated the Brotherhood as their collective bargaining agent. Plaintiffs are members and representatives of the Brotherhood and they brought this action as such, and in behalf of the members of the Brotherhood and of Lodge No. 22 against the City of Santa Monica and defendants Freeman, Millikan and Murray, as commissioners and members of the City Council. Defendant Freeman is the commissioner in charge of the city's transportation lines. . . .

The sole purpose of this action is to obtain a mandatory injunction requiring defendants to recognize the Brotherhood and the individual plaintiffs, as members of the Brotherhood, as the bargaining agents of the bus operators and requiring defendants to bargain collectively with the plaintiffs and the Brotherhood, to the end that a voluntary agreement may be reached. After a trial a decree was entered, reading as follows: ". . . [The] defendants are ordered to recognize the plaintiffs and the Brotherhood of Railroad Trainmen as the duly selected bargaining agents of the bus operator employees of the City of Santa Monica and to bargain collectively in good faith with plaintiffs as said representatives of the said employees of the defendants."

Notwithstanding the indirect approach to the objective of the Brotherhood, which is to secure a contract with the city, the judgment, which enjoins defendants from refusing to recognize the Brotherhood as bargaining agent "to the end that a voluntary agreement may be reached," amounts to a declaration that the city and the defendant commissioners are under a legal duty to enter into a contract with the Brotherhood, as representatives of the bus operators, if the terms can be agreed upon, and they are commanded to negotiate with plaintiffs for that sole purpose.

The theory of plaintiffs is that such legal duty exists by virtue of certain sections of the Labor Code and that the court may, under its general equity powers, compel the defendants to perform that duty. The defendants maintain that the Labor Code sections have no application to municipal corporations, they deny that those sections impose upon employers a legal duty to enter into labor contracts, or to bargain collectively for the purpose of negotiating the terms of labor contracts . . .

. . . Section 923 reads as follows:

"In the interpretation and application of this chapter, the public policy of this State is declared as follows: Negotiation of terms and conditions of labor should result from voluntary agreement between employer and employees. Governmental authority has permitted and encouraged employers to organize in the corporate and other forms of capital control. In dealing with such employers, the individual unorganized worker is helpless to exercise actual liberty of contract and to protect his freedom of labor, and thereby to obtain acceptable terms and conditions of employment. Therefore it is necessary that the individual workman have full freedom of association, self-organization, and designation of representatives of his own choosing, to negotiate the terms and conditions of his employment, and that he shall be free from the interference, restraint, or coercion of employers of labor, or their agents, in the designation of such representatives or in self-organization or in other concerted activities for the purpose of collective bargaining or other mutual aid or protection."

. . . Defendants criticize the judgment as judicial legislation, and in other respects. Whatever our views may be as to the authority of the courts, dependent upon these sections, to compel affirmative action on the part of either employers or employees in private industry, it would be inappropriate to state them here, since we have reached the conclusion that it was not the purpose of the Legislature, in the enactment of section 923, to inaugurate a state policy with reference to labor relations which would be applicable to the state or its political subdivisions. . . .

The several sections relate to the field of industry in which employer-employee relationships are fixed by contract. This is essentially the field of private industry. . . . The Legislature recognized that there has been, and is, oppression of labor in the field of private industry, where there has not been freedom of contract. The incentive of personal gain which is reflected in large profits and the expansion of business inheres in private ownership, but there is no intimation in the Labor Code sections that that incentive and its attendant evils are found in public employment. The text of section 923 indicates that the Legislature has not discerned in public employment the existence of the conflicts between labor and capital that exist in private industry. The reason for the silences of the Legislature upon that subject is not obscure. In Mugford v. Mayor and Council of Baltimore, 1944, Circuit Court No. 2 of Baltimore City, Maryland, 9 Mun. Law Journal 46, the court expressed it in the following appropriate language:

"The distinction between private employment and public service is an important one. Private employers if not restrained by law, are free to adopt any policy toward their employes which they believe calculated to promote the success of their enterprises, without regard to its effect upon the welfare of the employes; and it is therefore proper to restrain this freedom to some degree, and to safeguard the right of the workers to combine with each other, and to use the strength of this union in bargaining in the matter of wages, hours, terms and conditions of employment, and to strike if need be.

"In the field of public employment, on the other hand, altogether different conditions prevail. Public officers do not have the same incentive to oppress the worker; and fair treatment sought to be coerced by collective bargaining in the field of private employment, is in the public field, to a large extent, compelled by law. Public officers, therefore, do not have the same freedom of action which private employers enjoy. Their authority is confided to them by public law, and by that law is limited. That authority may not be delegated or surrendered to others, since it is public property. And so it has been almost uniformly held that governmental authority may not discriminate in favor of union labor." . . .

The principle espoused by section 923 is essentially the same as that fostered by the National Labor Relations Act, 29 U.S.C.A. §§151 et seq., namely, the right of workmen to enjoy free collective bargaining over terms and conditions of employment. In adopting that act Congress did not recognize the existence of the right of collective bargaining in public employment and did not consider it necessary to adopt a national policy which would extend into the field of public employment. Section 2(2) of the act expressly excepts from the definition of the term "employer" the United States and any state or political subdivision thereof.

. . . The City of Santa Monica adopted a personnel system in 1937, which provides an exclusive method for the employment, suspension, demotion and dismissal of employees. So far as the state, municipalities and other political subdivisions are concerned, the policy of the state in the matter of public employment is reflected in its Constitution and laws and in the charters of counties and cities. It has been a progressive policy, developed through many years, and by means of considered legislation. We find nothing in the legislative history which would suggest, even remotely, that the Legislature would make a general surrender of its duty and responsibility to maintain public employment at a high level of desirability and efficiency. . . .

There is also the fact that the elaborate system of laws which constitute the policy of the state in the domain of public employment would be largely nullified if the legislation should be construed as applicable to public employment, to the full extent that it is applicable to private employment. Government by law would then have to give way to government by contract, and this without action by the Legislature which expressed an intention to establish an entirely new system in the field of public employment.

It was argued to the learned trial judge, apparently with success, that the Legislature intended to require the state and municipalities to contract for terms and conditions of employment at least as to matters not covered by the laws of the state or the charters or ordinances of counties and cities.   If there is any such undefined territory, the Legislature has made no attempt to identify it, and we cannot.   If section 923 should be construed to mean merely that terms and conditions of employment must be fixed by contract in all respects in which they are not fixed by law, it would be illogical and meaningless, for the state and the municipalities would retain the power to cover the entire field of employment by broadening the base of legislation governing the same so as to leave none of the terms and conditions of employment unprovided for.   So construed, the legislation manifestly would not affect sovereign powers or interfere with the capacity to perform governmental functions but we cannot subscribe to this construction.   An endeavor by the courts to define some limited field for the contract system would be an attempt at judicial legislation. . . .

It is also argued that terms and conditions of employment should be fixed by contract in all activities of the state or municipalities conducted in a proprietary capacity, if not in a governmental capacity.   Much has been said in the briefs as to the capacity in which the city operates the bus lines, but that question, we think, is beside the point.   If the courts were to say that the legislation relates to public employment in the exercise of proprietary functions, but not governmental functions, that would be judicial legislation.   The distinction between employment in one field and the other would be wholly without legislative foundation. If any such distinction is to be drawn it must be by the Legislature.   We are not aware of any rule of law which would furnish a basis for applying the provisions of section 923 to one group of public employees to the exclusion of all others. . . .

It appears to us that the defendants have a proper conception of their duties.   They have given and expect to give respectful consideration to complaints registered by the bus drivers or their representatives.   It is not claimed that they have ever turned a deaf ear to the requests of the employees with respect to the improvement of working conditions.   As we stated in the beginning, the demand which the plaintiffs have made upon defendants, and which is in dispute, is not for different conditions of employment; it is a demand for union recognition.   Defendants have no desire to deal with the bus drivers as individuals or to refuse to deal with their representatives.   There is no reason to believe that they would refuse any requests or demand of the employees, in the absence of a labor contract, which they would be willing to incorporate in a contract. They do not refuse to consider making changes in terms and conditions of employment insofar as they are subject to arrangement; they only refuse to take the preliminary steps toward entering into a contract with the Brotherhood.

The word "negotiate" as used in section 923, and as used by the parties, means to confer regarding terms and conditions governing the employment of the bus operators, which, so far as agreed upon, would be incorporated in a contract between the city and the Brotherhood. The command of the decree that defendants "bargain collectively" with the Brotherhood has a like meaning. We think the Legislature has not imposed that duty upon municipalities.

In our opinion, the complaint stated no ground for relief, and the demurrer of the defendants should have been sustained.

The judgment is reversed.

NOTE

The court in Nutter indicates that a municipality does not have a duty to bargain with an organization of its employees. Implicit in this, perhaps, is the idea that organization itself is not desirable in terms of the public welfare. Should this approach be applicable in all areas of government employment, such as police, firemen, teachers, or public utilities?

NORWALK TEACHERS' ASSN. v. BOARD OF EDUCATION OF CITY OF NORWALK

Supreme Court of Errors of Connecticut, 1951
138 Conn. 269, 83 A.2d 482

JENNINGS, Justice.

This is a suit between the Norwalk Teachers' Association as plaintiff and the Norwalk board of education as defendant for a declaratory judgment, reserved on the admitted allegations of the complaint for the advice of this court.

The complaint may be summarized as follows: The plaintiff is a voluntary association and an independent labor union to which all but two of the teaching personnel of approximately 300 in the Norwalk school system belong. In April, 1946, there was a dispute between the parties over salary rates. The board of estimate and taxation was also involved. After long negotiations, 230 members of the association rejected the individual contracts of employment tendered them and refused to return to their teaching duties. After further negotiations, in which the governor and the state board of education took part, a contract was entered into between the plaintiff and the defendant, and the teachers returned to their duties. . . . From September, 1946, to the present and particularly with reference to the contract for 1950-1951, much doubt and uncertainty have arisen concerning the rights and duties of the respective parties, the interpretation of the contract and the construction of the state statutes relating to schools, education and boards of education. . . .

The parties agreed that the contract for the school year 1949-1950 would govern their relations for the school year 1950-1951, that they would join in this action, and "that whatever contractual obligations exist will be forthwith modified so soon as they shall have received from the Court judgments and orders declaring their respective rights, privileges, duties and immunities." [The plaintiff sought the adjudication of the following questions, among others:

"(a) Is it permitted to the plaintiff under our laws to organize itself as a labor union for the purpose of demanding and receiving recognition and collective bargaining?

"(b) Is it permitted to the plaintiff organized as a labor union to demand recognition as such and collective bargaining?

" (c) Is it permissible under Connecticut law for the defendant to recognize the plaintiff for the purpose of collective bargaining?

"(d) Is collective bargaining to establish salaries and working conditions permissible between the plaintiff and the defendant?

"(e) May the plaintiff engage in concerted action such as strike, work stoppage, or collective refusal to enter upon duties? . . ."

The discussion of plaintiff's questions concerning arbitration and mediation is omitted.]

Under our system, the government is established by and run for all of the people, not for the benefit of any person or group. The profit motive, inherent in the principle of free enterprise, is absent. It should be the aim of every employee of the government to do his or her part to make it function as efficiently and economically as possible. The drastic remedy of the organized strike to enforce the demands of unions of government employees is in direct contravention of this principle. It has been so regarded by the heads of the executive departments of the states and the nation. . . .

The commentators, generally, subscribe to this proposition. . . .

Few cases involving the right of unions of government employees to strike to enforce their demands have reached courts of last resort. That right has usually been tested by an application for an injunction forbidding the strike. The right of the governmental body to this relief has been uniformly upheld. It has been put on various grounds: public policy; interference with governmental function; illegal discrimination against the right of any citizen to apply for government employment (where the union sought a closed shop). . . .

The plaintiff, recognizing the unreasonableness of its claims in the case of such employees as the militia and the judiciary, seeks to place teachers in a class with employees employed by the municipality in its proprietary capacity. No authority is cited in support of this proposition. "A town board of education is an agency of the state in charge of education in the town. . . ." Board of Education of Stamford v. Board of Finance, 127 Conn. 345, 349, 16 A.2d 601, 603. In fulfilling its duties as such an agency, it is acting in a governmental, not a proprietary, capacity. . . .

In the American system, sovereignty is inherent in the people. They can delegate it to a government which they create and operate by law. They can give to that government the power and authority to perform certain duties and furnish certain services. The government so created and empowered must employ people to carry on its task. Those people are agents of the government. They exercise some part of the sovereignty entrusted to it. They occupy a status entirely different from those who carry on a private enterprise. They serve the public welfare and not a private purpose. To say that they can strike is the equivalent of saying that they can deny the authority of government and contravene the public welfare. The answer to question (e) is "No."

Questions (a) and (b) relate to the right of the plaintiff to organize itself as a labor union and to demand recognition and collective bargaining. The right to organize is sometimes accorded by statute or ordinance. . . . The right to organize has also been forbidden by statute or regulation. Perez v. Board of Police Commissioners, 78 Cal. App. 2d 638, 178 P.2d 537. In Connecticut the statutes are silent on the subject. Union organization in industry is now the rule rather than the exception. In the absence of prohibitory statute or regulation, no good reason appears why public employees should not organize as a labor union. Springfield v. Clouse, 356 Mo. 1239, 1246, 206 S.W.2d 539. It is the second part of the question (a) that causes difficulty. . . . The question is phrased in a very peremptory form. The common method of enforcing recognition and collective bargaining is the strike. It appears that this method has already been used by the plaintiff and that the threat of its use again is one of the reasons for the present suit. As has been said, the strike is not a permissible method of enforcing the plaintiff's demands. . . . There is no objection to the organization of the plaintiff as a labor union, but if its organization is for the purpose of "demanding" recognition and collective bargaining the demands must be kept within legal bounds. What we have said does not mean that the plaintiff has the right to organize for all of the purposes for which employees in private enterprise may unite, as those are defined in §7391 of the General Statutes. Nor does it mean that, having organized, it is necessarily protected against unfair labor practices as specified in §7392 or that it shall be the exclusive bargaining agent for all employees of the unit, as provided in §7393. It means nothing more than that the plaintiff may organize and bargain collectively for the pay and working conditions which it may be in the power of the board of education to grant. . . .

No costs will be taxed in this court to either party.

In this opinion the other judges concurred.

NOTES

1. As indicated in the Norwalk Teachers case, the judiciary, for the most part, has not hesitated to enjoin strikes and picketing by government employees. The reasons stated for this rigid rule have varied, but

"public policy" considerations have played an important part. These "policy" considerations have even prevented on occasion the *organization* of employees of certain private nonprofit enterprises.

In St. Luke's Hospital v. Industrial Commission of Colorado, 142 Colo. 28, 349 P.2d 995 (1960), the court determined whether ". . . a charitable private hospital is amenable to the collective bargaining provisions of The Colorado Labor Peace Act." The Building Service Employees' Union sought to organize and represent employees of the hospital in the engineering and maintenance, housekeeping, laundry, and dietary departments. The pertinent provisions of the Act read, ". . . (2) The term 'employer' means a person who regularly engages the services of eight or more employees other than persons within the classes expressly exempted under the terms of subsection (3) of this section . . . (3) The term 'employee' shall include any person, other than an independent contractor, domestic servants employed in and about private homes and farm and ranch labor, working for another for hire in the state of Colorado in a non-executive or non-supervisory capacity . . ." Colo. Rev. Stat. Ann. §80-5-2 (1953).

The majority of the court, holding that the employees did not have the right to organize and bargain collectively under the Act, stated the question to be whether a hospital comes within the sweep of the chapter in the light of its declared underlying and predominant aim, not whether it is expressly exempted. The hospital was found to be a public charity, not a commercial enterprise, and thus it did not come within the ambit of the Act. To bolster this reasoning, the court found that the nonprofessional employees had legal duties owing to the patients, which could not be performed in the event of a strike. Although recognizing that the question was not before it, the court said that if the Labor Peace Act applies to a hospital and its employees it applies fully, including the right to strike with all its attendant ramifications. In the view of the court, the legal duties owed the patients would make such activity intolerable. In conclusion the opinion stated, ". . . [I]f it is necessary to determine the primacy of policies, the public policy of The Labor Peace Act must yield to the public policy that its employees may not in concert take any action detrimental or inimical to the welfare of patients of a hospital." 142 Colo. at 38, 349 P.2d at 1000.

The dissent, after analyzing the provisions of the Act, stated that there was no exemption in favor of the charitable corporation and such an association could not be considered a subdivision of the state. "The true basis for the majority opinion . . . is its belief that charitable hospitals ought to be exempted even if they are not. The majority proceeds from this premise to the conclusion that the Legislature intended to exempt this type of activity but failed to do so expressly and under such circumstances an implied exemption ought to be read into the statute. . . ." 142 Colo. at 42, 349 P.2d, at 1002. Compare Society of New York Hospital v. Hanson, supra page 707, and also the approach used by the court in Utah Labor Relations Board v. Utah Valley Hospital, 120 Utah 463, 235 P.2d 520 (1951).

2. The court in Norwalk Teachers' Assn. v. Board of Education of City of Norwalk stated that it should be the aim of every employee of the government to do his or her part to make it function as efficiently as possible. In Nutter v. City of Santa Monica it was pointed out that public officers do not have the same incentive to oppress the worker as do private employers. What more could any employee ask? As illustrated by the following quotation, however, the individual public employee has sometimes had to go to extreme lengths to promote efficiency and has not always been able to achieve, through individual bargaining, the most advantageous terms of employment.

"I promise to take a vital interest in all phases of Sunday-school work, donating of my time, service, and money without stint for the benefit and uplift of the community.

"I promise to abstain from dancing, immodest dressing, and any other conduct unbecoming a teacher and a lady.

"I promise not to go out with any young men except insofar as it may be necessary to stimulate Sunday-school work. [*Sic!*]

"I promise not to fall in love, to become engaged or secretly married.

"I promise to remain in the dormitory or on the school grounds when not actively engaged in school or church work elsewhere.

"I promise not to encourage or tolerate the least familiarity on the part of any of my boy pupils . . ."

The above, taken from a teacher's contract in a North Carolina town, is set forth in Odegard, The American Public Mind 83 (1930).

3. In his book, Collective Bargaining in the Federal Civil Service (1961), Wilson R. Hart has concluded that a sovereign employer can bargain collectively so long as there is not an irrevocable surrender to the bargaining agent of the employees of the power to make governmental rules and regulations. The author asserts that the bargaining agent can initiate, but he cannot be given the exclusive authority to make decisions for the executive. Management must retain the right and power to repudiate any collective bargaining agreement at any time and for any reason.

A general survey of the status of the public employee and unions is found in Sullivan, Labor Problems in Public Employment, 41 Ill. B.J. 432 (1953), in which the author argues that there is no valid reason to deny to public employees the right to join labor unions and to bargain collectively with the public agency for which they work. See also Kaplan, The Law of Civil Service (1958); Rhyne, Labor Unions and Municipal Employee Law (1946); Ziskind, One Thousand Strikes of Government Employees (1941); Cohen, Legal Aspects of Unionization Among Public Employees, 30 Temple L.Q. 187 (1957); Goldberg, Constructive Employee Relations in Government, 8 Lab. L.J. 551 (1957); Krislov, The Union Quest for Recognition in Government Service, 9 id. 421 (1958); Note, Union Organization and Activities of Public Employees, 31 A.L.R.2d 1142 (1953). Where a business purpose of the governmental unit can be found, courts may permit the employees to use some of the usual techniques in labor disputes.

LOCAL 266, INTERNATIONAL BROTHERHOOD
OF ELECTRICAL WORKERS v. SALT RIVER
PROJECT AGRICULTURAL IMPROVEMENT AND
POWER DISTRICT

Supreme Court, Arizona, 1954
78 Ariz. 30, 275 P.2d 393

La Prade, Justice.
This appeal presents two questions:

1. Can an agricultural improvement district of the State of Arizona,
organized by virtue of and pursuant to the provisions of Article 7 of
Chapter 75, A.C.A. 1939, as amended, legally enter into collective bargaining agreements with its employees regarding wages, hours, and
other conditions of employment?

2. May the employees of such a District, by concerted action, strike to
enforce the execution of such an agreement?

The appellant, Local 266, International Brotherhood of Electrical
Workers, A.F.L., is a labor organization whose membership is com-
prised exclusively of the employees of the appellee District and Salt
River Valley Water Users' Association. . . .

The Salt River Project Agricultural Improvement and Power District
is engaged in the manufacture and development of electric power
through hydroelectric power installations located along the Salt River,
and is engaged in the distribution of electric power to consumers, principally in the city of Mesa, Arizona . . .

For some years prior to November 1, 1949, there existed between the
parties hereto (or their predecessors in interest) a collective bargaining
agreement which expired on that date. Upon its expiration appellee refused to enter into any agreement covering the terms and conditions
of employment . . . on the ground that as a political subdivision of the
State of Arizona, with the rights, privileges, and immunities of a municipal corporation, it could not lawfully so do. Upon the District's refusal
to recede from this position, the Union called a strike and placed the
usual picket line about the several business establishments of the District.

The District filed its complaint against the Union and caused a temporary restraining order to issue, enjoining the Union from picketing,
striking, or causing a slow down. After various court proceedings the
parties stipulated all the material facts which they deemed essential to a
proper determination of the issues presented by the pleadings, whereupon the superior court granted a judgment and made its temporary
restraining order permanent. This appeal followed.

The appellants claim error "for the reason that the acts and conduct of
appellants, which the injunction restrained, were but the lawful exercise
of lawful rights for a lawful objective granted to and confirmed to the
appellants by the Constitution, statutes and court decisions of the State
of Arizona."

In support of this assignment appellants assert (1) that the District is engaged in a purely proprietary business for the benefit of a restricted class of citizens, and is governed generally by the same rules that govern private individuals and corporations engaged in similar business, and (2) that the law under which the District is organized vests in the District full power and authority to negotiate and execute collective bargaining agreements affecting terms and conditions of their employment in the District's business.

Any discussion of the legal status of the District must begin with Section 7 of Article 13 of the Constitution of the State of Arizona, which provides as follows:

"(Improvement districts political subdivisions) — Irrigation, power, electrical, agricultural improvement, drainage, and flood control districts, and tax levying public improvement districts, now or hereafter organized pursuant to law, shall be political subdivisions of the state, and vested with all the rights, privileges and benefits, and entitled to the immunities and exemptions granted municipalities and political subdivisions under this Constitution or any law of the state or of the United States; . . ."

Appellants contend that the foregoing amendment to the Arizona Constitution did nothing more than to grant the District immunity from taxation. . . . A review of all of the decisions of this court since the adoption of the foregoing constitutional provision establishes that the court has consistently recognized improvement districts . . . to be political subdivisions of the state, vested with the rights, privileges, and immunities granted municipalities and political subdivisions of the state. . . . Appellants' contention is incorrect.

As a municipal corporation the District asserts the following consequences. The first is that the District, as a political subdivision of the state, is powerless to enter into collective bargaining negotiations with its employees. They state the reason to be that, "The process of collective bargaining calls upon the governmental agency to delegate to a private agency the authority to operate and control the activities of the governmental agency itself."

The second contention of the District is that since it is powerless to enter into a collective bargaining agreement, a strike by its employees for this purpose should be permanently enjoined as illegal.

To support the assertion that it is powerless to enter into a collective bargaining agreement the District cites us cases from other jurisdictions. The first of these is Mugford v. Mayor and City Council of Baltimore, 1946, 185 Md. 266, 44 A.2d 745, 747. There a taxpayer enjoined the City of Baltimore and the Municipal Chauffeurs and Garage Employees Union from entering into a collective bargaining agreement. The lower court held that the city was denied the power to do so by the terms of its charter. . . .

The District refers us to comments made by that court on the findings of the lower court which had not been appealed. The case constitutes no precedent. In its dicta the Maryland court stated, "[t]o the extent that these matters are covered by the provisions of the City Charter, creating a budgetary system and a civil service, those provisions of law are controlling." Statutory regulation of employment negates the view that such would be open for contractual negotiations between the employer and employees. If a civil service scheme provides for the regulation of matters normally contained in a collective bargaining agreement the conflicting terms of both could not exist concurrently. The inconsistency would be resolved in favor of the statute. Under these circumstances the power to enter into a collective bargaining agreement would be properly denied as an attempt to subvert legislative direction. A statute must be given effect. Buggeln v. Cameron, 1907, 11 Ariz. 200, 90 P. 324.

In the case before this court we have no legislative expression of public policy to control the terms of employment by a District as existed in the Mugford case, supra.

The District cites us next to City of Springfield v. Clouse, 1947, 356 Mo. 1239, 206 S.W.2d 539, 546. There a declaratory judgment was requested to determine whether the city was empowered to enter into collective bargaining with its employees. The Union argued that the Missouri Constitution, section 29, Article 1, V.A.M.S., which granted employees the right to organize and bargain collectively, applied. The City asserted that this provision was intended to apply only to private employers. An argument not before this court.

The court in the Springfield case found this provision of the constitution not applicable to governmental employees. The court then considered whether the city had the *power* to enter into collective bargaining negotiations with the union, even if not so required by the constitution. The court ruled that while these public employees may organize they may not demand the right to bargain collectively. The court specified the manner in which such a collective bargaining agreement would conflict with the laws of Missouri. Under Missouri Stats. 6678-6688, V.A.M.S., §§75.620 to 75.710, all the city officers and employees were covered by civil service. The court indicated the breadth of this personnel system in the following language: "Thus the General Assembly has provided a single complete all inclusive scheme for selection, tenure, transfer, promotion and removal, which applies to all city officers and employees under civil service. . . ." An agreement which conflicted with the regulatory power of the city under its civil service system would constitute bargaining away of legislative discretion, as the court there stated, 206 S.W.2d at page 543:

". . . legislative discretion cannot be lawfully bargained away and no citizen or group of citizens have any right to a contract for any legislation or to prevent legislation."

As we have pointed out the case at bar does not present the issue of the compatibility of a collective bargaining agreement with provisions of a civil service or other statutory scheme of employment. We reserve judgment on this question . . .

The District cites . . . State of California v. Brotherhood of Railway

Trainmen, 1951, 37 Cal. 2d 412, 232 P.2d 857. In this case the question was whether the employees of a state-owned railway were under the provisions of the Federal Railway Labor Act, 45 U.S.C.A. §§151, 152, in which case the employees would have had the right to enter into collective bargaining agreements with their employer, or whether such employees of the state were exempt from that Act and subject to the authority of the state civil service commission, in which case the authority of the commission could not be avoided by contract. It was held that the employees were not subject to the federal Act and their employment was to be regulated by civil service. This case, as those previously discussed, is not in point. At bar there is neither a dispute between federal or state authority nor have we an analogous personnel system present in the above cases. . . .

. . . [W]e fail to find support for the District's contention that it is powerless to enter into a collective bargaining agreement with its employees. Moreover, the powers of this District are less to be determined by case law from other jurisdictions than by the legislative pronouncement which enabled such Districts to exist. . . .

That the District is not specifically given the power to make employment contracts, with the exception of an engineer, tells us little. The authorization to do business in itself implies the necessity of hiring labor. . . .

If the board of this District finds that an agreement with its employees is a "necessary contract," "proper for the interest of the district or to carry out or accomplish any of the purposes authorized or permitted by the provisions of this article . . ." [statutory wording] then from this language it has the power to make such agreements. The grant of express powers to exist and operate carries with it all the implied powers necessary to effectuate those expressly given. . . .

The sections of the statute quoted above expressly give the District the power to make necessary contracts. No more necessary contract than that for personal services would appear conceivable, but that is a matter for the Board. For the court to read into these limitations upon the type contracts which the District may find to be necessary would be judicial legislation which we may not do. . . .

We hold that the District herein is not denied the power to enter into collective bargaining agreements with its employees. Norwalk Teachers Ass'n v. Board of Education, [138 Conn. 269, 83 A.2d 482 (1951)]. . . .

The next question presented by this appeal is whether the employees of the District may engage in strikes. The District asserts that they may not because:

"Employees in governmental service have an obligation to serve the whole people, whereas, a strike manifests nothing but an intent to prevent the operations of government until the strike demands are satisfied; the fulfillment of strike action would be an abdication of governmental authority to private individuals and private agencies and, therefore, deprive the people of the sovereignty of government which is inherent in only themselves."

This question is closely connected to that of the power of the District to execute a collective bargaining agreement previously discussed. If the power to enter a collective bargaining agreement is denied to a municipal corporation, a strike by its employees for such purpose would be illegal as contrary to the policy of the law. Here we have found no such statutory restriction on the District's powers. Consequently the question is this: though the purpose, a collective bargaining agreement, is legal, may it be said that the strike, as a method of obtaining such an agreement, is denied to these employees?

The District cites us the case of City of Los Angeles v. Los Angeles Bldg. & Const. Trades Council, 1949, 94 Cal. App.2d 36, 210 P.2d 305, 311. There the city undertook to expand the water and electric facilities serving its inhabitants. To do so the city negotiated with contractors to perform some of the work. Many employees of such contractors were members of the Trade Council. The city also assigned some of its civil service employees on the expansion project. The Trade Council requested that such city employees either become members of the Trade Council or be withdrawn from the job. The city, in substance, refused and a strike ensued. The court ruled that this strike was for an illegal purpose and enjoined the Trade Council. The illegality of this strike was found in the civil service status of the employees involved, and the court stated:

"From what has already been said, we think it is self-evident that defendants may not, consistently with the public policy expressed in the Los Angeles City Charter, lawfully either strike or picket for the purpose of enforcing demands as to conditions of employment in respect to which neither the city nor the Department of Water and Power is obligated to bargain collectively."

The statute does not deprive the District of the power to enter into collective bargaining agreements and we find no grounds to imply a public policy against peaceful striking and picketing for this legal purpose. . . .

. . . [M]ay these employees be denied the right to strike on the general grounds of public necessity? The District refers us to a letter written by the late President [Franklin D.] Roosevelt to the president of the National Federation of Federal Employees which seems to indicate that public employees should be denied the right to strike due to the vital necessity of the continuity in governmental operations to the people of the country. As quoted in Rhyne, Labor Unions and Municipal Employee Law (1946), at page 192, the letter reads in part:

"Upon employees in the federal service rests the obligation to serve the whole people, whose interests and welfare require orderliness and continuity in the conduct of government activities. . . . Such action looking toward the paralysis of government by those who have sworn to support it is unthinkable and intolerable."

The court, in Norwalk Teachers Ass'n v. Board of Education, supra [138 Conn. 269, 83 A.2d 485], in denying the employees the right to strike, termed them, "Those people are agents of the government. They exercise some part of the sovereignty entrusted to it." Even assuming that this court could enunciate the public policy of Arizona in the absence of statutory direction, can it be said that the employees of this District are the type of persons to whom this language refers? These employees cannot be characterized as "agents of the government," nor can they be said to have "sworn to support" the District. The nature of the District's operations and purposes are not designed to "serve the whole people" as we commonly conceive the role of government. . . .

As to the nature and functions of the District an examination of its organization is necessary to understand its purposes. The District here is organized pursuant to sections 75-701 to 75-748, A.C.A. 1939. Section 75-701 provides that five or more agricultural landowners whose lands may be improved by irrigation and drainage works may propose the organization of such a district. The purpose of these Districts is varied, they may secure, store or distribute irrigation waters. They may also provide electric power for the ". . . use of the owners or occupants of such land . . ." or they may sell such power or surplus water to the general public to ". . . reduce the cost of irrigation, drainage and power to the owners of the lands in said district . . ."

This court has had occasion to discuss the nature of such Districts both before and after the Constitutional Amendment, supra, which designated them political subdivisions of the state. In Day v. Buckeye Water etc. District, 1925, 28 Ariz. 466, 237 P. 636, at page 638, we stated:

"On the other hand, irrigation districts and similar public corporations, while in some senses subdivisions of the state, are in a very different class. Their function is purely business and economic, and not political and governmental. They are formed in each case by the direct act of those whose business and property will be affected, and for the express purpose of engaging in some form of business, and not of government."

Following the constitutional amendment in which the status of the District became fixed, we again were presented with an opportunity to discuss the nature of such organizations. In Taylor v. Roosevelt Irrigation District, supra, we said, 226 P.2d at page 156:

"We are of the opinion that the primary functions of these irrigation districts have not been changed by the Constitutional Amendment, supra, and in the conduct of their ordinary business, they are not exercising governmental or political prerogatives as they are not operated for the direct benefit of the general public but only of those inhabitants of the district itself. . . ."

Yet another distinction between the District and other municipal corporations is to be noted. Most municipal corporations are owned by the public and managed by public officials. It might be said that a strike by the employees of such municipal corporations would constitute a strike against the public. Such is not the case here. Public employment means employment by some branch of government or body politic specially serving the needs of the general public. It cannot be said that the District's employees are paid from the public treasury as are employees of the public. The public does not own the District. A governmental entity such as a city or town does not manage or benefit from the profits of this District. Instead the owners are private landholders. The profits from the sale of electricity are used to defray the expense in irrigating these private lands for personal profit. The public interest is merely that of consumers of its product, for which they pay. In view of this additional factual distinction between the usual municipal corporation and the District it cannot be said that a strike here is a strike against the public. The District does not function to "serve the whole people" but rather the District operates for the benefit of these "inhabitants of the district" who are private owners. . . .

The business purpose of this District implies possible competitors in the economy over which the District would be given a discriminatory advantage if its employees may not use all usual techniques in labor disputes. We have expressed our reluctance to allow discrimination to occur. Sumid v. City of Prescott, 1929, 27 Ariz. 111, 230 P. 1103.

We find no indication from either the cases or statutes which indicate that the employees of this District may not engage in a peaceful strike. This is not to imply that such social friction is desirable, only that the District, as a business entity, is subject to the hazards of the economy as are its possible competitors.

Our judgment extends only to this governmental unit. We make no decision as to the status and rights of other municipal corporations.

The two questions presented at the outset of this opinion are answered in the affirmative.

The judgment of the lower court is reversed, with instructions to make and enter an order dismissing the complaint and dissolving the permanent injunction theretofore granted.

AMERICAN BAR ASSOCIATION, SECTION OF LABOR RELATIONS LAW, REPORT OF THE COMMITTEE ON LAW OF GOVERNMENT EMPLOYEE RELATIONS *
188 (1960)

. . . This area of employee relations, while very much at large as a matter of general law, has continued to assume increasing importance with the growth of organization among public employees, with the emerging role of government as an employer, and, consequently, with the compelling need to serve the public interest by devising realistic means to meet the challenges presented. While some governmental entities are still adhering to past restrictive and paternalistic attitudes, the general trend is unmistakably in the direction of seeking gradually to close the gap, at least in basic concepts, between public and private employment. . . .

* This portion of the full report is reprinted with the permission of the American Bar Association, Section of Labor Relations Law.

ORGANIZATION AND RECOGNITION: LEGISLATIVE DEVELOPMENTS
The Grant of Incidental Privileges

A characteristic of the slow and restricted development of an affirmative labor relations policy in the public service has been the peculiar technique for handling the grant of the checkoff privilege. While that privilege is normally the product of the collective bargaining process in private employment, it has usually been accorded unilaterally as a matter of sovereign largesse in the public service. Looked upon as being essentially in the nature of a wage assignment for the convenience of the employees, much the same as are contributions to charitable and fraternal associations, the deduction of labor organization dues from employee wages has been permitted in jurisdictions where the recognition of labor organizations is virtually outlawed. Consequently, unions in government are in the anomolous position of enjoying the benefits of the dues checkoff while having no collective bargaining rights. Indeed, by now, unions have come to expect the unilateral grant of the checkoff as an early perquisite of their relations with government. On the other hand, the privilege has been denied in some areas as a unilateral governmental practice, for reasons of public policy against wage assignments. . . .

Prohibition of Concerted Activity Against A Municipality

A number of states and the federal government have declared expressly by legislation a policy against strikes by their respective employees. Some jurisdictions have imposed severe penalties for violation of the prohibition. However, peaceful picketing for a lawful purpose, unrelated to a strike and not actually tantamount to a strike, has not been condemned under federal law. Nor has it been generally outlawed by the states. Hence, it has been available to government employees as a technique for achieving stated objectives through appeals to the public, the third party most directly concerned with the quality of the services involved and, thus, with the character of the relationship between their government and its employees.

On March 29, 1960, in an unusual step, the City of Birmingham, Alabama, acting as a municipality, adopted a local ordinance declaring its own sweeping policy banning both strikes and picketing against the City as an employer.

Thus, any city employee who engages in a strike or a concerted stoppage or slowdown of work is subject to immediate discharge and is disqualified for reemployment for a period of one year.

The ban on picketing calls for closer analysis in view of its broad scope and the express justification for its enactment: The ordinance declares that picketing the City "as a result of determinations" as to the terms of employment of its employees "would necessarily involve more than communication of thought or idea, and would cause interruption of operations of said City of Birmingham." Accordingly, it is made unlawful for "any person, group of persons, association, corporation or union" "to picket or to cause, aid, abet or participate in picketing" of the City of Birmingham or any of its governmental buildings or locations for any of these all-inclusive purposes: (1) to aid in a strike or concerted stoppage or slowdown, (2) to induce any person to cease work for the City or to refrain from such work, (3) to coerce the City to grant any demand or request as to grievances or terms or conditions of employment of any of its present or former employees, (4) to notify the public that a "labor dispute" exists or that the City or its governing body or any of its officers is "unfair," (5) to accomplish any objective in relation to any past or present or future employee of the City or in relation to terms of employment with the City. To complete the pattern of total inhibition, the ordinance contains a general injunction against the use by any person toward another of "abusive or opprobrious words" or against the performance of any "act, word, gesture or otherwise" to threaten or cause injury to another "in order to prevent or discourage the rendition of service" by anyone to or for the City.

It is plain that this unusual piece of legislation raises serious constitutional questions. Principal among these is: The extent to which government, when acting as an employer, may deny to its own employees and their organizations fundamental guarantees of freedom of speech and assembly and of the right to petition for the redress of grievances available to other classes of employees and persons. . . .

THE RIGHT OF PUBLIC EMPLOYEES TO ORGANIZE: OPINIONS OF ATTORNEYS GENERAL

Opinions issued by state officials during the past year on whether public employees may join a union show how reliance on different concepts of the role of the sovereign as an employer and of the character of government employment will produce different results.

New Mexico:

The Attorney General of New Mexico was asked by the Town of Gallup for an opinion as to whether its employees could (1) join a union and (2) engage in collective bargaining, picketing, striking "and other activities generally regarded as union rights." In reply, the Attorney General, on July 31, 1959, advised the Town that, while the employees could probably "belong informally" to a labor union, "such membership could properly be made grounds for their dismissal, should the municipal authorities so rule." In any event, he ruled, the Town would not have to recognize the union and the employees could not engage in collective bargaining, picketing or striking. . . .

Oklahoma:

A more reasonable, yet realistic and responsible, position was taken by the Attorney General of Oklahoma. On April 2, 1960, he ruled that, while state employees may not strike because they are engaged in a governmental function, there is nothing to prohibit them from joining labor unions. . . .

WOLLETT, THE PUBLIC EMPLOYEE AT THE BARGAINING TABLE: PROMISE OR ILLUSION? *
15 Labor Law Journal 8 (1964)

The organization of public employees into trade unions and other associations for the purpose of gaining a share in the process of decision making fixing the terms and conditions of employment is not new.   However, it has grown apace in recent years. . . .

I shall now proceed to examine in depth the principal characteristics of public employment which cause the shapes and forms of collective bargaining to fit badly. . . .

One of the essentials of bargaining in private industry is that management have power to make binding commitments in respect to economic and other matters affecting the terms and conditions of employment, and, having made such commitments, the ability to make them good.

The management of governmental enterprise frequently lacks such authority.   Its financial resources are determined by some other organ of government, and, since it is not marketing a service or producing a product the price of which it may adjust in order to increase revenues, bargaining over many matters may be an illusory exercise. . . .

Failure to recognize this fundamental characteristic . . . may result in destructive consequences. . . .

Nor are resource restrictions the only limitations on the authority of governmental management.   For examples, the following matters may be erased from the bargaining table by law: (a) recruitment and promotions because they are governed by civil service regulations; (b) retirement and pension programs because, for financial and actuarial reasons, they have been fixed by state law; (c) job security which in the case of teachers has overtones of academic freedom and may, therefore, be protected by a statewide tenure system instead of being left to the vagaries and diversities of local negotiations. . . .

Thus, bargaining between governmental management and the organizational representative of its employees is typically limited to the following matters:

(1) Terms and conditions which have no direct fiscal implications and which are within managerial discretion;

(2) Allocation of resources within prescribed budgetary limitations;

(3) Joint recommendations to be made to the governmental agency or

* Donald H. Wollett, Chairman, ABA Committee on Law of Government Employee Relations, and attorney, Kaye, Scholer, Fierman, Hayes & Handler, New York.   This selection is reproduced with the permission of the publisher, Commerce Clearing House, Inc.   The article is the text of an address by the author presented at the Joint Annual Meeting of the Association of State Mediation Agencies and the National Association of State Labor Relations Agencies.

organ which has authority to act on a matter which is fixed by law, regulation or directive. . . .

Public Enterprise and Private Interests

The management of governmental enterprise, whether it be a board, commission, or a single administrator — elected or appointed — is responsible, directly or indirectly, to the body politic for the performance of the enterprise which has been entrusted to it. Generally, within such statutory and budgetary limitations as those described above, public management has authority commensurate with this responsibility. The question posed by collective bargaining is: Can governmental management, responsible to the general public, delegate or share its derivative authority with private groups who are responsive to narrow, particularized interests?

The problem arises in an acute form in bargaining over the allocation of budgeted revenue. This is so because the decision to spend more money in one area necessarily reduces expenditures in some other area. . . .

The Determinant of Public Policy: Economic Muscle or Reasoned Accommodation?

. . .

I would . . . state categorically that strikes are impermissible in any governmental bargaining system. I do not mean to say that strikes will not occasionally occur or even evoke sympathy, particularly if there is no other means whereby public employees can "make their interests and point of view visible to the community." I do mean to say, however, that strikes cannot and should not function as the determinant of substantive policies in governmental enterprises. . . .

Most labor relations practitioners agree that the *threat* to strike is a more effective weapon than the strike itself. . . .

It is, therefore, a tempting tactic for a union of public employees to threaten to strike, thereby instilling fear in the community and mobilizing pressure on the management of the enterprise (and the politicians who hold the purse strings) to "cop out" in order to avoid "disaster." At the eleventh hour, having squeezed every penny, the union settles without having had to test its weapon. . . .

In sum, it remains doubtful that either strikes or strike threats, even with all their accompanying sound and fury, are genuinely effective. . . .

Constructive Bilateral Decision Making in Public Enterprise

[The author offers the following opinions and suggestions pertaining to a future collective bargaining system:]

(1) The range and type of decisions subject to bilateral determination, the scope of the bargaining unit, and the nature of procedures for dispute settlement should depend upon the extent to which the employee

commonly identify with the quality of the service or product provided or produced by the enterprise.

(2) The extent of identification will usually turn on the range of skills and competence, the breadth of interests, and the tradition and psychology of the employees and the trade or occupation of which they are a part.

(3) Monolithic rules or doctrines as to what is bargainable and what is managerial prerogative, unit delineations, and methods of dispute settlement are impracticable.   Transit authorities, law enforcement agencies, school systems, and other functionally distinct enterprises should be treated differently. . . .

(4) A supervisor should not be excluded from participation in the process unless there is an immediate real and demonstrable conflict between his responsibilities as an employee and his responsibilities toward the organization.

(5) All public employee organizations should —

(a) Recognize the inherent limitations of the bargaining table and educate their members accordingly;

(b) Build and implement legislative and political programs. . . .

(c) Bargain by reasoned argument supported by pertinent data, thus laying the background, in the event of failure at the bargaining table, to make the case persuasively in the political arena.

You will note that I have said nothing about the role of state laws and state agencies in implementing these suggestions and guidelines.   My silence on this point reflects my feeling that extensive and formalized legislation is premature. . . .

AMERICAN BAR ASSOCIATION, SECTION OF LABOR RELATIONS LAW, REPORT OF THE COMMITTEE ON LAW OF GOVERNMENT EMPLOYEE RELATIONS *
133-135, 139-141 (1963)

[Under Section 305 of LMRA, strikes by federal employees are not permitted.   Yet in recent years there has been an expansion of the concept of employee organization in the federal service.   This was brought about mainly by the signing of Executive Order No. 10988 by President Kennedy in January, 1962.   See Reference Supplement, page 92.   This order, dealing with employee-management cooperation, was the result of extensive investigation by the Presidential Task Force, appointed in 1961 to study the existing situation and to recommend appropriate action.

In Executive Order 10988: An Experiment In Employee-Management Cooperation In The Federal Service, 52 Geo. L.J. 420 (1964), David S.

* The full report of this committee will be found in the second part of the 1963 Proceedings of the Section of Labor Relations Law at 126-162.   The above excerpts are reprinted with the permission of the American Bar Association, Section of Labor Relations Law.

Barr presents an excellent analysis of the Order and the reasons for its promulgation. The Task Force found that many federal agencies had no stated labor relations policy, and that where labor-management arrangements did exist there was no uniformity among the agencies. In an effort to remedy the situation, the Order directed federal agencies to grant three levels of recognition to qualifying labor organizations. Recognition ranges from listening to views on matters of concern to the members of the organization to negotiating a formal written agreement. The level of recognition granted is dependent upon the number of employees in the organization and whether it can demonstrate that it has been authorized to act as an exclusive representative by a majority of the employees in the unit involved. It was the conclusion of the Task Force that employee organizations could contribute more to the effective conduct of public business, and for this reason the Order was recommended.]

By April 15, 1963, less than one year after the July 1 deadline for agency implementation of [Executive Order 10988], more than 93,000 Federal employees were included in 147 appropriate units represented by 41 different organizations. These totals do not include employees in 24 Interior Department units which existed before the Executive Order was issued; nor do they include almost 500,000 employees in Post Office craft units. . . .

Section 11 of the Order provides the only formal, centralized "review" procedure for agency determinations. The review is limited to unit and election problems. . . .

The largest classifiable group of . . . cases has resulted from the tendency of some agencies to favor the largest possible unit, generally an entire installation. This preference, which appears in regulations governing unit structure, has uniformly been resisted by craft organizations and others whose traditional jurisdictions have been limited to particular kinds or classes of employees, such as classified (white collar), wage board (blue collar), craft or technical or professional. Other resistance has come from groups, such as the International Association of Machinists, which may organize on industrial, craft or occupational lines, but which find their pattern of representation at a particular establishment inconsistent with the agency's determination.

The single most important cluster of cases now pending before arbitrators has resulted from Navy Department determinations at seven shipyards: Norfolk, Boston, New York (Brooklyn), Portsmouth (New Hampshire), Long Beach, Puget Sound (Bremerton), and Philadelphia.

In all of these the Navy Department determined that the entire installation was the appropriate unit. Appeals were received in each case from one or more of the following groups: Patternmakers (craft); American Federation of Government Employees (white collar); American Federation of Technical Engineers (occupational); and a Metal Trades Council (blue collar). There is some overlap between the unit claims of AFGE, AFTE and Metal Trades at several of the yards; by and large their claims have dove-tailed and they support each other's positions.

Other pending cases result from roughly similar considerations. Installation-wide unit determinations which have blocked severance of craft, occupational or other narrower groups are involved in five other Navy Department cases, and have been disposed of in two of the three completed cases. Cases now pending with the Air Force, the Veterans Administration, General Services Administration, and the Smithsonian Institute all present the same general issue.

A characteristic of most of the cases posing the "installation-wide" problem is that, as a general rule, no organization has sought such a unit at locations where it has become an issue. Normally, only the agency itself feels that the broad unit is appropriate.

Of the five arbitral recommendations received so far, only one has resulted in a finding that a unit sought only by the agency was appropriate. In this case the arbitrator rejected claims based primarily on distinctions between different methods of pay (wage board as compared with classified, or salaried workers) and found a broad community of interest among all employees at the installation.

In another case an arbitrator agreed with an agency and one of two competing organizations that the entire agency constituted an appropriate unit.

Three other cases, however, have resulted in craft or occupational severance: one machine shop, one unit of inspectors, and one technical unit. . . .

When the Task Force study was made, the Post Office Department was the largest single employer in the United States. More than 580,000 employees worked for the Department, and of these almost 490,000 belonged to one of the postal unions. Although the tradition of union membership was more deeply rooted among Post Office workers than among those of any other agency, testimony before the Task Force suggested that many postal workers were totally dissatisfied with the Department's labor relations.

In little more than a year the Post Office Department has completely overhauled its labor relations. The Department has run the nation's largest single representation election, has certified exclusive representatives of more employees in more units than any other American employer, and has negotiated a national Basic Agreement with six craft unions which fixes important working conditions for these record numbers of employees and units, and has embarked on local negotiations in over 20,000 post offices across the land.

Bargaining Units

The Post Office has established bargaining units along craft lines. Because of its great size, and the similarity of its operations from post office to post office, the Department concluded that meaningful negotiations could be held on many important aspects of postal work only at the national level. To accomplish this end the Department instituted national level bargaining on those matters which affect all members of a craft wherever located.

Although national negotiations are essential for a number of major problems, many of the most pressing employee-management relations questions faced by the Post Office require local settlement by local negotiation between a postmaster and a local union representative. Accordingly, postal units are established on the regional and post office, as well as the national, level. Organizations which won a majority of the votes in a local craft group received exclusive recognition for that group within the local post office, although their votes were also counted in regional and national level tabulations.

Over 22,000 exclusive, local craft units resulted from the election. Exclusive recognition at the post office has frequently been given to a different organization than the national level exclusive representative. Thus in New York City the National Postal Union is exclusive representative for the Clerks and Maintenance Custodial Employees, although these crafts are represented exclusively at the national level by a different organization. In Brooklyn, on the other hand, where National Postal Union won among the clerks and the National Association of Letter Carriers among the carriers, three organizations (NPU, NALC, and Mail Handlers), share formal recognition for mail handlers.

Still a third level of recognition exists for other purposes at the fifteen postal regions, and with different patterns of recognition. While contract negotiations do not occur at the regional level, one step of the grievance procedure may be handled there. A postal employee may therefore have one exclusive representative at the post office, a formal representative at the region, and a different exclusive representative at the national level.

The possibilities for ludicrous results are reduced by three things: informal recognition, whereby minority representatives may be heard even as to problems affecting a unit of employees exclusively represented by another union; the exclusive representative's right to be present at grievance or other discussions involving employees it represents; and the individual employee's right to choose his own representative.[45]

It remains to be seen whether these checks will suffice to protect all interests which may be at stake in contract negotiations. Many issues appropriate for discussions at the national level may affect interests having great local importance. With the existence in many places of two representatives, the possibilities for divergent views, whipsawing, and competition between rivals seem endless.

NOTES

1. The Lloyd-La Follette Act, 37 Stat. 555 (1912), 5 U.S.C. §652(c), provides that membership in an organization of postal employees shall not be cause for reduction in rank or compensation or removal from

[45] See Executive Order No. 10988, §§4, 6(b), 3(c)(1). — ED.

the service if the organization is not affiliated with any outside organization imposing a duty to strike, or proposing to assist a strike, against the United States. A later statute, 69 Stat. 624-625 (1955), 5 U.S.C. §118p, condemns as a felony the holding of federal office or employment by a member of an organization that asserts the right to strike against the Federal Government. See Hart, Collective Bargaining in the Federal Civil Service (1961). It is reported that in the Department of the Interior, bargaining units range from less than 50 to almost 1000, "encompassing a single plant, project, area, or region, as well as a series of craft units, or a combination of those two." Terry, Collective Bargaining in the U.S. Department of Interior, 22 Pub. Admin. Rev. 19, 23 (1962).

On the right of public school teachers to organize and bargain, in addition to page 747 supra consider Seitz, Rights of School Teachers to Engage in Labor Organizational Activities, 44 Marq. L. Rev. 36 (1960), stressing the value of voluntary negotiations for exposing vital problems in school administration. Contrast the executive determination as the result of which the United Federation of Teachers, AFL-CIO, was certified in 1961 as representing a unit of 40,000 classroom teachers in New York City. 2 A.B.A., Section of Labor Relations Law Proceedings 144 (1963). Other New York City developments are discussed in Klaus, Collective Bargaining by Government Employees, N.Y.U., 12th Annual Conf. on Labor Law 21, 30-37 (1959). Frequently, however, rules against public employee membership in any labor organization have been sustained in the courts. Cornell, Collective Bargaining by Public Employee Groups, 107 U. Pa. L. Rev. 43 (1958); Holt, Labor Rights of Public Employees, 2 Sw. L.J. 226 (1948).

2. The British nationalized industries, coal, transport, gas, and civil aviation, use the corporate structure, headed by boards appointed by the relevant minister. Although this corporation is unequivocally public, its autonomy in management is greater than such an organization as the Tennessee Valley Authority or the Federal Deposit Insurance Corporation. On the other hand, its labor relations are complicated by Whitley council arrangements for collective bargaining and consultation. In coal the hierarchy of joint industrial councils runs from the pit to the district to the nation. This system is subdivided into three distinct segments, for miners, for supervisors, and for managerial employees. The three categories in electricity are manual, clerical, and technical. In rails there is also a three-tiered structure (local, sectional, and national). At the national level, four of the employee members are chosen by the industrial union and two each from two craft unions that represent engine service and salaried workers. See Spero, Labor Relations in British Nationalized Industry (1955).

3. The exclusion of governmental employers in NLRA §2(2) is not paralleled by the Railway Labor Act. As explained in California v. Taylor, 353 U.S. 553, 566-567 (1957), concerning a common carrier in interstate commerce owned and operated by the state:

"The fact that the Act's application will supersede state civil service laws which conflict with its policy of promoting collective bargaining does not detract from the conclusion that Congress intended it to apply to any common carrier by railroad engaged in interstate transportation, whether or not operated by a State. The principal unions in the railroad industry are national in scope, and their officials are intimately acquainted with the problems, traditions and conditions of the railroad industry. Bargaining collectively with these officials has often taken on a national flavor, and agreements are uniformly negotiated for an entire railroad system."

PART FOUR

Administration of the Labor Agreement
Including the Duty of Fair
Representation

ENDERBY PROBLEM 10

(See page 503 supra for Enderby Problem 9)

While White, the company's industrial relations manager, was having lunch in the plant cafeteria one bleak winter day, Curme, president of the local, approached his table and remarked that some of the people back in the warehouse were pretty upset. It had been a severe winter and the space heaters on some days couldn't get the warehouse temperature above freezing. One of the towmotors had been broken down for more than a year, and the men had to lift bundles much more than usual. Whenever anyone complained, the foreman swore a blue streak and refused to discuss the matter. White agreed that it had been a tough winter but said there wasn't much he could do about it, and he didn't think the contract covered any of these complaints. Curme pointed out that the warehouse wouldn't be so cold if the space heaters worked properly, that the towmotor had not worked last summer either, and that the men didn't have to put up with the foreman's abusive language.

The following day the steward for the warehouse filed three grievances with the foreman, each signed by a different employee and each covering one of the three matters raised by Curme. The foreman's face turned pink, then red, and finally purple as he reached each of the grievances in turn. Without a word he tore them into bits, carefully piled the scraps in the center of the large ash tray on his desk, and lit them with the gold-plated cigarette lighter which he had received that morning for twenty-five years of faithful service. Lefty O'Leary, who had signed the grievance about the towmotor and extra lifting, was then ordered to move one of the large, 1000-pound crates by hand dolly without assistance. When he refused on the basis that two men had always handled loads of this size and on the basis that his previous back injury had not entirely healed, he was fired on the spot for insubordination. When the foreman came upon Joe Constanzo, who had signed the grievance about abusive language, he let loose with a string of epithets juicier than usual. When Joe replied in a similar vein, adding a few choice epithets of his own, he received a three-day disciplinary suspension. These developments resulted in the filing of two additional grievances.

O'Doul, the plant superintendent, denied all five grievances at the second step of the grievance procedure and White did the same at the third step. In the meantime, O'Leary decided to file an unfair practice charge on his own with the Regional Office of the NLRB.

Thereafter, in due course, an arbitrator was chosen from a list submitted by the Federal Mediation and Conciliation Service, in the manner specified by Article II, Section 5, of the Enderby Contract. The hearing was held in the conference room at the plant, with Attorney Blair representing the company and Layton, the International Representative, appearing for Local 417.

At the outset Blair announced that none of the grievances could properly be considered by the arbitrator. The first three, he said, clearly were not arbitrable since they involved matters not covered by the terms of the agreement. Since O'Leary had filed an unfair practice charge with the NLRB based on his discharge, Blair pointed out, this matter was now before that agency and obviously could not be settled by the arbitrator. The appeal to White at the third step on the second Constanzo grievance, Blair said, was not filed until the third day after O'Doul had given his answer at the second step, and therefore was untimely and should be dismissed.

Layton replied that the first three grievances clearly involved working conditions, which are inherently covered by any collective bargaining agreement. O'Leary's decision to go to the NLRB, he argued, had no bearing on the employee's rights under the Enderby Contract, and O'Leary was entitled to a decision by the arbitrator and back pay for all time lost if the discharge action was found to be unjust and improper. In passing, Layton remarked that O'Leary went to the NLRB without consulting the union and he doubted that any action would be taken by the Regional Office, although he understood the circumstances were still under investigation. On the last grievance, Layton said that O'Doul had gone to Florida for some deep-sea fishing shortly after the grievance meeting at the second step and did not issue his answer on Constanzo until the tenth day after the meeting. Moreover, he pointed out, White's answer was not given to the committee until the third day after the third step meeting. Nothing had been said about timeliness, he concluded, until now.

The arbitrator listened to the evidence and more detailed argument on all of the procedural matters and then indicated that he would take this phase of each matter under advisement. In the meantime, he explained, he was prepared to go forward on the merits and would only get to this part of each problem if he found that it was arbitrable and properly before him. Blair objected to this and said that since the company was not prepared to go forward on the merits at this time, they would take no part in any further proceedings. Layton said the arbitrator was right, that this was normal procedure, and that he was prepared to present his evidence. When the arbitrator said he would hear the union, Blair and the company representatives politely excused themselves and left the conference room. The union's evidence was then presented.

When word of the company's action in the oral hearing before the arbitrator reached the plant, several of the men in the mixing department were reminded that six or eight of the grievances they filed two weeks before had gone to the second step but had not yet been answered by O'Doul. One grievance involved the subcontracting of the cleaning and maintenance work in the plant to an outside firm, which had resulted in the layoff of two cleaners, one painter, and three general maintenance repairmen. Another grievance concerned a claim by one of the mixers that he and a few others had been given a week of their vacation during hunting season for the past nine years without question, but this year the new foreman had said they were too busy and the requests were not granted. Bo Yost had grieved about an overtime assignment made to one employee with less seniority and to another employee with more seniority, but also a greater number of overtime hours credited at the time of the particular assignment, while he sat home and was not called by the foreman. A fourth grievance had been filed when a new automatic mixer was installed and only the operator was retained out of a crew of five, four helpers having been laid off and such of their duties as remained having been assigned to the operator or handled by the foreman himself. The other grievances related to broken safety equipment and overtime pay.

When O'Doul said he needed more time and would issue his answers when he was ready, Herb Moss and Carl Marcz passed this word throughout the plant and a walkout resulted, shutting down production completely. Curme was on his coffee break when the walkout started. Although he instructed his stewards to get the men back, it was too late so he also went home. The leaders of the walkout said the men would return when the pending grievances were either granted by the company or referred to arbitration. White announced that no further action on any of the grievances would be taken until the men were back and the plant in production. Cooper, the union's attorney, filed unfair practice charges against the company on behalf of Local 417, and Blair filed a suit in federal court against the union and its leaders for breach of contract and damages resulting from canceled orders and loss of production.

When peace was finally restored, the company fired Moss and Marcz, along with ten other men selected at random by the company as an example to the others, and Curme for not having done more to prevent the walkout and eventually leaving the plant himself. Grievances protesting this action are filed immediately.

Consider the issues raised by these facts in the light of the materials which follow and the provisions of the Enderby Contract. Do you agree with the advice and actions of counsel for each party? How do you feel the procedural questions should be settled and the grievances themselves should be decided? Consider any alternatives that may be available as to the course of action to be followed by either side.

A. The Nature of the Collective Agreement

The exact nature as well as the legal consequences of collective bargaining agreements have been subject to considerable doubt. The ordinary legal mind, including the judicial mind, is likely to be conditioned in its thinking about "contracts" in a manner which hardly serves to suggest a solution. It is important to understand the basic nature of these labor agreements in terms of their purpose, if this confusion and uncertainty are to be avoided.

One consequence of the failure to analyze the nature of labor-management relations has been the development of a rather large assortment of legal theories concerning the nature and effect of collective bargaining agreements.[1] These theories may be grouped into two general categories.

Agreement Without Legal Effect

The usage theory. The oldest theory concerning the nature of collective agreements in the United States and England is the "usage theory," which developed in cases between individual employees and their employers involving collective agreements. The courts refused to look upon the collective agreement as a contract but did regard it as a "usage" that the individual parties to the employment relationship incorporated into their employment agreement.[2] The collective agreement had legal significance only to the extent that the usage theory was deemed applicable.

The moral obligation theory. In a few cases the collective agreement is held to be a "moral obligation," not enforceable but influential in determining whether equitable relief shall be given.[3]

Agreement With Legal Effect

The agency theory. A few courts, holding that the collective agreement was not enforceable because negotiated by or between unincorporated associations, which lacked juristic personality, nevertheless gave it effect in actions between individual employees and employers on the theory that the negotiators were agents of the individual members of the unions (or employers' group) so that the collective agreement was the members' contract.[4]

The third party beneficiary theory. Another theory, invoked in actions

---

[1] See Fuchs, Collective Labor Agreements in American Law, 10 St. Louis L. Rev. 1 (1925); Lenhoff, The Present Status of Collective Contracts in the American Legal System, 39 Mich. L. Rev. 1109 (1941); Rice, Collective Labor Agreements in American Law, 44 Harv. L. Rev. 572 (1931); Witmer, Trade Union Liability, 51 Yale L.J. 40 (1941); Witmer, Collective Labor Agreements in the Courts, 48 id. 195 (1938).

[2] The leading case is Hudson v. Cincinnati, N.O. & T.P.R.R., 152 Ky. 711, 154 S.W. 47 (1913). This and other cases are discussed in Fuchs, supra note 1, at 3-7. See also Rice, supra note 1, at 581-593.

[3] Both the principle and the cases are discussed by Fuchs, supra note 1, at 7-12.

[4] The leading case is Barnes & Co. v. Berry, 169 Fed. 225 (6th Cir. 1909).

between individuals involving collective agreements, was the "third party beneficiary theory." This held that the collective agreement itself was valid and enforceable, and that an individual could obtain relief pursuant to the terms of the collective agreement because the contracting parties so intended.[5]

The contract theory. A substantial body of case law, both in this country and abroad, has dealt with collective agreements according to the traditional pattern of contract litigation. In many instances American courts held agreements unenforceable because negotiated by unincorporated associations which, lacking legal personality, had no standing to sue or be sued.[6] In others they examined the agreements, found numerous promises on the part of employers but no express undertakings on the part of the unions, and declared them to be invalid for lack of consideration.[7] Still other courts denied specific enforcement in terms of the rule against compelling the performance of personal services, or in converse situations, because of the lack of mutuality of remedy.[8] But courts in many American states and many foreign countries, proceeding along traditional lines of contract law, held them to be enforceable.

In a number of comparatively early American cases, employers obtained injunctions against strikes, the courts basing their action on the ground that the contracts contained no-strike clauses.[9] More numerous, however, are suits instituted by unions. Schlesinger v. Quinto, 201 App. Div. 487, 194 N.Y. Supp. 401 (1st Dept. 1922), is generally regarded as the fountainhead of this line of cases. The court enjoined the employers from reducing the wages and increasing the hours contrary to the collective agreement. The allegation that this constituted an order of specific performance of a contract for personal services was rejected, the court taking the position that this was an agreement between two responsible organizations. There have been innumerable subsequent holdings of the same kind in New York, and the same position has been taken in many other states. The opinion of the Texas Court of Civil Appeals in Harper v. Local 520, International Brotherhood of Electrical Workers, 48 S.W.2d 1033 (Tex. Civ. App. 1932), contains an illuminating discussion of the issue and of the developing precedent. The Mississippi court in 1931

---

[5] The doctrine is discussed in Rice, supra note 1, at 595-597. Some earlier cases decided on this theory are Hall v. St. Louis-San Francisco Ry., 224 Mo. App. 431, 28 S.W.2d 687 (1930); Blum & Co. v. Landau, 23 Ohio App. 426, 155 N.E. 154 (1926); Gulla v. Barton, 164 App. Div. 293, 149 N.Y. Supp. 952 (3d Dept. 1914). The principle was more recently invoked in the case of In re Norwalk Tire & Rubber Co., 100 F. Supp. 706 (D. Conn. 1951).

[6] See generally Witmer, Trade Union Liability, 51 Yale L.J. 40 (1941); and for a comparatively recent case see Hallman v. Wood, Wire and Metal Lathers Int. Union, 219 N.C. 798, 15 S.E.2d 361 (1941). See also Comment, Unions as Juridical Persons, 66 Yale L.J. 712 (1957).

[7] See Witmer, Collective Labor Agreements in the Courts, 48 Yale L.J. 195, 203 (1938).

[8] Ibid.

[9] E.g., Nederlandsch Amerikaansche Stoomvaart Maatschappij v. Stevedores' & Longshoremen's Benev. Soc., 265 Fed. 397 (E.D. La. 1920); Burgess v. Georgia F. & A. Ry., 148 Ga. 417, 96 S.E. 865 (1918); Gilchrist Co. v. Metal Polishers Union, 113 Atl. 320 (N.J. Eq. 1919).

noted this trend and commented: "The time has at last arrived when, under patriotic and intelligent leadership [the labor unions'] place has become secure in the confidence of the country, and their contracts are no longer construed with hesitancy or strictures, but are accorded the same liberality, and receive the same benefits of the application of the principles of modern law, bestowed upon other agreements which pertain to the important affairs of life." [10]   A minority of state courts still maintains the contrary position.[11]

Departure from traditional concepts. Justice Jackson, in the majority opinion in J. I. Case Co. v. NLRB, 321 U.S. 332 (1944), see page 70 supra, described collective bargaining agreements in the following terms (pp. 334-335):

"Contract in labor law is a term the implications of which must be determined from the connection in which it appears.   Collective bargaining between employer and the representatives of a unit, usually a union, results in an accord as to terms which will govern hiring and work and pay in that unit.   The result is not, however, a contract of employment except in rare cases; no one has a job by reason of it and no obligation to any individual ordinarily comes into existence from it alone.   The negotiations between union and management result in what has often been called a trade agreement, rather than in a contract of employment. Without pushing the analogy too far, the agreement may be likened to the tariffs established by a carrier, to standard provisions prescribed by supervising authorities for insurance policies, or to utility schedules of rates and rules for service, which do not of themselves establish any relationships but which do govern the terms of the shipper or insurer or customer relationship whenever and with whomever it may be established.   Indeed, in some European countries, contrary to American practice, the terms of a collectively negotiated trade agreement are submitted to a government department and if approved become a governmental regulation ruling employment in the unit."

Justice Brennan of the United States Supreme Court, while still a member of the New Jersey Supreme Court, examined the question at length in his opinion in Kennedy v. Westinghouse Electric Corp., 16 N.J. 280, 108 A.2d 409 (1954).   After reviewing the various theories discussed supra, he adverted to the suggestion that a new legal category for collective agreements might be required.   However, Archibald Cox has warned of the danger that those who are knowledgeable about collective bargaining may demand that all precepts of contract law be discarded — a step he considers both unfeasible and unwise.[12]

W. Willard Wirtz has referred to these collective agreements as more than orthodox contracts and makes the following observations:[13]

[10] Yazoo & M.V.R.R. v. Sideboard, 161 Miss. 4, 13, 133 So. 669, 671 (1931).

[11] See, e.g., Swart v. Huston, 154 Kan. 182, 117 P.2d 576 (1941).

[12] Cox, The Legal Nature of Collective Bargaining Agreements, 57 Mich. L. Rev. 1, 14-15 (1958).

[13] Wirtz, Collective Bargaining: Lawyers' Role in Negotiations and Arbitrations, 34 A.B.A.J. 547, 548 (1948).   The excerpt from this article is printed with the permission of the American Bar Association Journal.

"Our first and probably most basic difficulty has been in appreciating the differences between collective bargaining agreements and ordinary commercial contracts. The fact that they are called 'contracts' has led us to try to fit them into the familiar molds of Willistonian concepts. The result, in England and Canada, has been that the Courts, finding more duress than consideration in the origin of these 'agreements,' have refused to enforce them. Our own Courts have fortunately taken a more flexible approach. After several decades of vain attempt to fit these square pegs into the familiar round holes of the 'usage' and 'agency' and 'third party beneficiary' theories, the American Courts have concluded that these are not ordinary contracts at all, being rather in the nature of 'treaties' or 'tariff schedules.' This makes them, of course, no less enforceable than if they were orthodox 'contracts.' The nature of these 'laws by agreement' is still more exactly reflected in the language of the agreements themselves, wherein the parties refer to them as representing an exercise of the 'legislative function.'

"For practical purposes, the biggest difference between collective bargaining agreements and ordinary commercial contracts is that these agreements *cover only a part of the relationship between the parties to them.* A buyer and a seller, or a licensor and a licensee, are bound together only as the terms of their agreement bind them. Yet no collective bargaining agreement even purports to cover everything that is important to the employment relationship. The employees can be just as much affected by management's action with respect to matters left within its discretion (e.g., production schedules) as by the application of the 'seniority' clause. The basically important issue of productive effort is rarely covered, except indirectly, in the terms of these agreements."

COX AND DUNLOP, THE DUTY TO BARGAIN COLLECTIVELY DURING THE TERM OF AN EXISTING AGREEMENT*
63 Harvard Law Review 1097, 1116-1120 (1950)

A collective bargaining agreement should be deemed, unless a contrary intention is manifest, to carry forward for its term the major terms and conditions of employment, not covered by the agreement, which prevailed when the agreement was executed.

During the term of a collective bargaining agreement controversies occasionally arise concerning a condition of employment which the agreement does not "cover." Few collective bargaining contracts deal either expressly or by necessary implication with every term and condition of employment. Potentially important items are often omitted because they have been overlooked, because both parties are satisfied with existing conditions, or because it seems tactically undesirable to raise the issue.

* This excerpt from The Duty to Bargain Collectively During the Term of an Existing Agreement by Archibald Cox and John T. Dunlop is reprinted by permission of the Harvard Law Review. Copyright 1950 by the Harvard Law Review Association. — ED.

For example, when two New England textile mills were permanently shut down in 1949, TWUA demanded severance pay for the workers. Although both mills were parties to comprehensive collective bargaining agreements, neither contract contained a provision relating to severance pay. A similar issue was raised in the summer of 1949 when the United Steelworkers requested the establishment of noncontributory pension plans during the term of unexpired collective bargaining agreements which contained no provision with respect to pensions and which did not expressly reserve the right to raise this issue before the contract expired. The disposition of such controversies depends upon the implications of a collective bargaining agreement for matters not covered thereby. Few problems have invoked more contrariety of opinion, but it is possible to identify three basically different points of view.

(1) Many spokesmen for management look upon a labor contract as a document by which the union and employees secure a limited number of defined rights in derogation of the management's once-absolute prerogatives.[58] The powers which management does not surrender by the contract, it is asserted, management necessarily retains and may exercise unilaterally. Under this view, an employer would be free to establish a pension plan during the term of a collective bargaining agreement without consulting the union; if there was an existing plan, not covered by the agreement, he might modify or terminate it at will.

(2) At the opposite pole are those who argue that all terms and conditions of employment are subject to renegotiation at any time. At present Section 8(d) [of the NLRA] makes this position untenable with respect to matters expressly dealt with in the contract, but as to all others the union would be free to present new demands and, under a broad arbitration clause, to have the arbitrator pass upon their merit without regard to the practices prevailing when the contract was signed. In the pension dispute of 1949 the Steel Industry Board partially acquiesced in this view under pressure of NLRB rulings.

(3) The third view, which we advocate, lies between these extremes. It holds that the parties to a comprehensive collective bargaining agreement, in the absence of contrary evidence, are to be presumed to have executed the agreement upon the understanding that major conditions of employment not covered by the agreement would continue "as they were" unless changed by mutual agreement. Thus, if a union were to protest a company's unilateral discontinuance of a hospitalization plan which the company had voluntarily maintained for a considerable period, an arbitrator, hearing the case under a broad-form arbitration clause, should sustain the union's grievance even though the plan was not men-

---

[58] Hill and Hook, Management at the Bargaining Table 74 (1945). The same view is sometimes expressed in arbitration awards, but in many of those cases the award in the company's favor could equally have been grounded either upon limitations on the arbitrator's jurisdiction or upon an implied commitment to adhere to existing procedure as suggested in the third view outlined above. E.g., Warren City Mfg. Co., Award of Byron R. Abernathy, Feb. 28, 1947 (affirming right of management to select employees for merit increases during term of agreement).

tioned in the collective agreement.   If the matter were not arbitrable, the unilateral action would be an unfair labor practice remedial by the NLRB.

The proposition that existing arrangements are carried forward except as changed by the collective agreement, does not imply that all existing *substantive* conditions of employment should be regarded as frozen.   In any large business, adjustments are constantly being made in piece rates or incentive systems, job content and job evaluation, merit ratings, work loads, etc.   Other terms and conditions of employment, such as basic wages, seniority, and pensions, are more enduring.   Altering them is not a day-to-day adjustment but a fundamental revision.   Thus, at any given time the status quo is made up of (a) the modes of procedure followed in making decisions concerning matters subject to continuous review and (b) the basic substantive terms and conditions of employment which are changed only upon annual or biennial review.   Where the collective bargaining agreement is silent, the pre-existing arrangement — whether it is a procedure for making continuous changes or an existing substantive term — should be deemed to be carried forward.

Nor does the proposition state a rigid rule.   The principle rests on the distinction between the legislative process of negotiating basic employment terms and the administrative or quasi-judicial function of applying an existing agreement.   New laws should be written at periodic legislative sessions.   In the intervals the problems are those of administering rules already formulated.   But the distinction is only one of degree and the processes shade into one another.   Even when a collective agreement covers a problem, the problem cannot be solved until the meaning of the contract is determined by particularizing its policy as well as its words.   On other occasions, where the contract is wholly silent, decisions under the grievance procedure must be drawn from the "common law" of the plant — customs and unwritten understandings, established practices, and sound industrial relations standards.[61]   But while this is "making law," it differs from the legislative process of negotiating a basic agreement in the same sense that the work of the courts differs from that of the legislature.

It would be an obvious mistake to force every collective bargaining relationship into the suggested mold.   Any of the three views may be written into the collective agreement.   Some agreements explicitly reserve subjects for continued negotiation.   Others are so obviously incomplete as to show that neither party intended to foreclose discussion of additional subjects.   Such contracts adopt the second view.   Occasionally, the extreme management view is wholly or partly incorporated into a collective bargaining agreement.   The intermediate position advocated in this paper has also been written into important labor contracts.[62]   Moreover, it

---

[61] To illustrate the creative character of the process, compare Bethlehem Steel Co., 5 BNA Lab. Arb. Rep. 649 (1946), with Novelty Shawl Co., 4 BNA Lab. Arb. Rep. 655 (1946).

[62] E.g., Agreement between Carnegie-Illinois Steel Corp. and United Steelworkers of Am., CIO, dated April 22, 1947, §2(B).

must also be kept in mind that the relationship between employees, union, and management in any industrial establishment is the product of different personalities, unique history, and peculiar local needs. All sorts of understandings, explicit or tacit, have been worked out for dealing with terms and conditions of employment not covered by the collective bargaining agreement. Any wise philosophy of grievance arbitration, like any sound government regulation, must take such variations into account. Our attempt is simply to state what we believe to be the normal, albeit inarticulate, understanding of the parties as well as the soundest relation for them to achieve.

WOLLETT, THE DUTY TO BARGAIN OVER THE "UNWRITTEN" TERMS AND CONDITIONS OF EMPLOYMENT*

36 Texas Law Review 863, 876-877 (1958)

The question of the dimensions and obligations of the duty to bargain during the life of a contract over matters not covered by it, i.e., the "unwritten" terms and conditions of employment, is a problem, not only of statutory construction but also of striking a balance between the desirability of contract stability and the desirability of continuous collective bargaining as an escape hatch for pressures which develop and seek immediate release.

Prior to the enactment of section 8(d) the latter consideration was underlined and the former consideration largely ignored by a series of Board decisions which apparently meant that all terms and conditions of employment were subject to renegotiation at any time. Section 8(d) placed contract stability on the scales, but its weight was substantially reduced by the Board's decisions in the Allied Mills and Tide Water Oil cases.

The doctrine of the Jacobs case brought about a balance which perhaps conforms more closely to congressional understanding of what section 8(d) would accomplish and probably conforms more closely to the usual understanding of the parties when they execute a comprehensive collective bargaining. Furthermore, the willingness of the Board to give effect to waiver provisions makes it possible for the parties, by agreement, to achieve a high degree of contract stability.

However, there would seem to be sufficient warrant in the statute and ample reason, both policy-wise and in terms of ease of administration, to justify at least the regret that the Board did not adopt the view that, when the parties execute a comprehensive contract, there is a presumption that they do so on the basis of an understanding that all major terms and conditions of employment, "written" or "unwritten," will remain in statu quo during the life of the contract, unless changed by mutual consent.

Such a doctrine would have at least two salutary effects. First, it

* This excerpt from The Duty to Bargain Over the "Unwritten" Terms and Conditions of Employment by Donald H. Wollett is reprinted with the permission of the editors of the Texas Law Review. — ED.

would further limit involvement of the Board in the business of resolving issues of contract interpretation and enforcement. The party who proposed a change and claimed that the other party was obligated to bargain about it would be asserting a *contractual,* rather than a *statutory,* right. Whether such a duty existed would be an issue which ordinarily the parties would have placed by agreement in another forum. It would not usually be NLRB business.

Second, it would prohibit strikes (or lockouts) to compel agreement to changes during the life of the contract. The same result can largely be accomplished by holding, as the Board has, that economic action in violation of the agreement is a refusal to bargain. The principal objection to this position is that it involves the NLRB in the business of specifically enforcing no-strike promises, a job which Congress entrusted to the courts. Furthermore, it involves the Board in something of an inconsistency. In cases of unilateral action where the question is whether the contract permitted or prohibited the conduct, the Board has wisely kept it hands off the dispute. "The Board is not the proper forum for parties seeking to remedy an alleged breach of contract or to obtain specific enforcement of its terms." [65] It is difficult to see why the same policy should not obtain in the case of a strike which allegedly violates the agreement.

NOTE

Suppose it has been a custom for many years at a particular plant to give five-year employees three-week paid vacations. Nothing about vacations appears in the collective agreement. Then, suppose one year the employer announces that he cannot afford the past vacation arrangements and says that only eight-year employees will get three-week paid vacations. Under a typical management prerogative contract provision, may he do this? If it is concluded that the contract does not speak to this issue, then must he bargain about it under the Jacobs case rule, see supra page 462.

Suppose that the employer unilaterally decides to start charging employees for "buy, sell or swap" notices which he has previously allowed to be posted free on a bulletin board in the company lunchroom. If the contract is silent, may he do so?

Suppose the employees arrive at the plant one Monday morning to find 10¢ pay locks installed on the toilets in the employees' rest room. Can the employer do this because the contract says nothing about it?

B. PRIVATE ADMINISTRATION OF THE COLLECTIVE AGREEMENT

1. *Grievance Procedure*

a. NATURE OF THE PROCESS

The application and enforcement of the collective bargaining agreement are carried out typically through an administrative process referred to as the grievance procedure. Virtually all collective agreements con-

[65] United Tel. Co. of the West, 112 N.L.R.B. 779, 782 (1955).

tain clauses, sections, or entire articles which refer to grievance handling and establish the procedure for the parties' day-to-day working relationship. These provisions, taken as a whole across the country, represent one of the most significant developments in the jurisprudence of the twentieth century. The daily dispositions of private disputes thereunder are undoubtedly greater in number than the cases being handled in all the state and federal courts in the country.

The grievance procedure under the Enderby Contract is to be found in Article II thereof and should be consulted at this point. See Reference Supplement, page 5.

KATZ, MINIMIZING DISPUTES THROUGH THE ADJUSTMENT OF GRIEVANCES *
12 Law and Contemporary Problems 249, 257-259 (1947)

The grievance channel must be deeply dug to receive all complaints.

Grievances are complex reactions by workers to the interplay of psychological, social, and economic forces. A proper grievance procedure will be so designed that it will carry all grievances. Yet, in the early stages of the collective relation, management's bargainers tend to be concerned with preventing the adjustment of all but a restricted class of grievances. The grievances they would consider are only those which involve the interpretation and application of the terms of the agreement. This limitation misses the entire point of the grievance procedure and its office in the collective relation. The error derives from failure to appreciate the multi-faceted nature of the collectively bargained agreement.

The collective bargaining agreement is at once a business compact, a code of relations and a treaty of peace. As an economic accord it sets forth the terms which will govern hiring, work and pay. Normally it is not a contract of employment. As a peace pact it assures against strikes and lockouts. As a code of relations it seeks to create a *system of government* through the processes of which grievances are resolved, understanding achieved, a line of communication opened between management and employees, and a self-disciplining labor force secured.

The collective agreement is thus a different kind of document from the commercial agreement. The ordinary contract does not partake of the nature of governmental systems; the adjustment clause sometimes incorporated in it serves merely to provide a substitute for a court to resolve disputes over interpretations of the other contract terms which define with care the boundaries of a limited relation between the parties. Thus it is merely ancillary to the other terms of the contract. In the collective agreement, on the other hand, the grievance procedure is a "system of government" which exists independently of the other clauses of the agreement.[14]

* The excerpt from this statement by Isadore Katz, then General Counsel to the Textile Workers Union of America (CIO), is reproduced with the permission of the editors of Law and Contemporary Problems.

[14] Syme, Arbitrability of Labor Disputes, 5 Rutgers L. Rev. 455, 472 (1951), emphasizes the contrast as follows: "A parallel has been drawn between com-

The narrow view that a complaint need not be considered unless it involves the interpretation or application of the provisions of the agreement is the least desirable approach to the objective of adjusting grievances. It is not only at odds with the ultimate goal of developing a harmonious and amicable relation in which each worker feels that he is a vital and worthy part, but it proceeds on the erroneous assumption that the relation is capable of precise definition in the contract. It predicates a static relationship in which every point of contact between the contracting parties can be fully reflected in words. Though this may be true of commercial relationships in which the only interest one party has in the other is the article bought or sold, the premises leased or sold, or the money earned or lent, it is not true of the dynamic relation between management and labor. Here the relationship is a multifarious web made up of economic, social and psychological strands inextricably interwoven yet continuously changing in pattern. This community is affected by changes in population, outside competitive forces, outside community activities, changes in production techniques, scientific discoveries, market conditions, internal group relations, and a host of other unpredictable events necessitating quick accommodations — in short, it is a dynamic field of adversary and co-operative group relations. The contingencies in such a relationship can no more be set forth in a contract than can the contingencies of the marital relation. Both defy definition. . . .

The grievance procedure furnishes a means of orderly life in the mill. . . . It serves as an outlet for the aggrieved worker and at the same time keeps management in close touch with the tone and temper of the relationships in the plant. It reveals to management the reactions of the individuals and the code of behavior of the group of which they are a part. The knowledge thus gained is of utmost importance to the policy makers on both sides. To block up this index of plant morale is not the way to minimize labor disputes but rather the way to remain ignorant of their physiology.

FAIRWEATHER and SHAW, MINIMIZING DISPUTES IN LABOR CONTRACT NEGOTIATIONS *

12 Law and Contemporary Problems 297, 307-309, 315-316 (1947)

A labor contract is a statement of policy which is established through negotiations and which is to remain in effect for a fixed period of time. If it is a policy to control the relationship between the parties, it must

---

mercial and labor arbitration. The two are entirely dissimilar. Their origin is different, their purposes are disparate and their functioning is antithetic. *Commercial arbitration evolved as a substitute for litigation.* The parties either litigated or arbitrated. They invoked the use of either one type of tribunal or the other. *Labor arbitration is not a substitute for litigation. Labor arbitration is a substitute for the strike."* — ED.

* The excerpts from this statement by Owen Fairweather and Lee C. Shaw are reproduced with the permission of the editors of Law and Contemporary Problems.

clearly set forth the rights and obligations of the parties so that they can properly perform their respective functions. . . .

Management's prime function is to manage — that is, to plan the work and to direct the working forces. Management is a group of individuals trained, at great expense, in industrial "know-how." If management does not do its job properly, the plant will not be as efficient as it would otherwise be. Management must have the right under the contract to manage the plant efficiently if the efficiency principle considered above is to be followed.

Management is charged with carrying out many policies. One of these policies is contained in the contract with the union. Therefore, it becomes management's job to manage the plant under this contractual policy. The management is always the "acting" party; there is no basis for the idea that, because a labor contract exists, the union shares jointly the obligation to manage the plant efficiently. That is solely management's obligation. . . .

Since efficient operation is necessarily a management function, the provisions of a labor contract should make it clear that management has the rights which are necessary to the performance of this function. It is interesting to note how this functional concept of management's rights has been reflected in the War Labor Board's decisions and in arbitration awards, which together are the only source of "common law" on rights of unions and managements under labor contracts. . . .

During the life of the contract the union's concern is to see that management, in its everyday operation of the plant, does not violate the contractual policy. The union's function can properly be considered to be that of "watch dog," in contrast to the management's function, which is to carry the responsibility as the "acting" party for efficient operations.

If being the watch dog is the union's function, then the union must have the right under the contract to perform this function. The grievance procedure established by the contract provides the method by which the union challenges management on the ground that it has not followed the contract. . . .

The purpose of the grievance procedure is simply to provide a method whereby the union can obtain compliance with the contract itself. It should not be a method by which the union questions all of management's decisions, nor should it be written so that the union can force management to place questions of managerial judgment before outside arbitrators who bear none of the responsibility for mistakes of judgment. A "grievance" should be considered simply as an allegation that management has not properly followed a given provision of the agreed policy.

PLATT, INTERIM REPORT ON GRIEVANCE PROBLEMS *

Since both parties have a stake in industrial peace, both have the responsibility of keeping the grievance channels unclogged and of making the grievance system work. An overloaded grievance system is an ineffec-

* This interim report by Harry H. Platt of Detroit, Michigan, a widely known and respected labor arbitrator, resulted from a study requested jointly by the

tive, demoralizing, practically worthless system.   The overload may stem not merely from an excessive grievance production rate but from misuse of the grievance machinery and failure to settle grievances promptly.   To be effective a grievance procedure must deal with grievances promptly. While exact figures are yet lacking, the indications are that in the present overloaded condition of the grievance procedure it would take between four and five years to process a grievance through all of its steps.   This hardly makes it an effective procedure.   And the real sufferers are of course the employees who have legitimate grievances, not those who have bad or weak ones.   For it makes less difference to the latter than to the former how long it takes for a grievance to be processed while settlement or even a grant of a good grievance long delayed can be a denial of justice.

Promptness in grievance settlement is of course best assured when those who have intimate knowledge of the facts of a complaint and authority to remedy it undertake to deal with it at the start.   Refusal or failure of some employees to take their complaints directly to Supervision as a first step and a tendency by some Supervisors to treat employee complaints lightly when they are brought to them, minimizes the opportunity for achieving prompt grievance settlements and increases tension between Supervision and employees.   Early and effective disposition of grievances contribute to better relations; neither party should resort to delaying tactics in grievance handling and settlement. . . .

A common complaint has been that foremen are unwilling to hear and discuss oral claims and that they in fact invite written grievances.   Similarly, it is charged that second step grievances are not seriously considered by some departmental Superintendents who refer them instead to their labor relations representatives for an answer without themselves making any attempt to settle them. . . .

Another complaint is that Management's alleged rigidity and excessive formalism in the grievance procedure causes unreasonable delays in grievance processing and helps to clog the procedure. . . .

There is ample evidence that the parties' grievance system is overfilled with insignificant, improperly filed, and unmeritorious grievances.   To be effective, a grievance procedure must not be overloaded with large numbers of inconsequential claims and grievances which have no contractual basis and which are predestined to be withdrawn or denied at a later time.   That kind of grievance handling only results in slowing down the grievance process — which is something the Union does not wish to have happen and strongly protests.

Successful grievance handling requires exercise of sound judgment by

---

union and the employer after a tremendous backlog of unsettled grievances had accumulated.   The scope of the backlog by 1964 was comparable to the civil court dockets in some of our big cities.   The selections from this unpublished report, which was issued on September 24, 1964, contain some of the most significant observations of the author and have been reproduced with the permission of the parties for whom the study was made.   Mr. Platt submitted a set of recommendations which were to be given a trial during the balance of 1964.   A final report was contemplated at the completion of the study. — ED.

Union representatives. They should know that through grievance dis-position there is gradual development of "a system of law" which affects plant relationships and hence the more "bad" grievances there are in the procedure the greater is the chance of "bad" principles instead of "good" principles developing. It surely cannot benefit a Committeeman if he permits himself to be pressured into filing grievances which are of slight importance or as to which a final denial would establish a principle un-favorable to the Union and to the employees as a group. In deciding whether to process a grievance he should weigh the interest of the bar-gaining unit in the effectiveness of a grievance procedure against the in-terest of an individual grievant asking payment for a real or fancied per-sonal wrong. There is no need for nor obligation upon a Committeeman to accept unmeritorious grievances the effect of which would be to over-burden and weaken the grievance procedure.

From all indications, a high grievance volume is appealing to some Grievance Committeemen. Some in fact appear to be deliberately build-ing up a backlog in the higher steps perhaps in order to avoid withdraw-ing grievances or in the interest of horse-trading. This, of course, is a subversion of the grievance procedure as well as the arbitration process. It should be remembered that the grievance procedure is an important union and worker bulwark. It should not be subverted from a grievance system to a means of harassing Management or the Union. Indis-criminate grievance filing and stubborn insistence upon processing them through all the steps of the procedure, regardless of merit, can hardly have any other purpose than to harass and create hostility.

The grievance procedure should not be employed for political purposes or for political advantage. The duty of a Committeeman to assist em-ployees with their shop problems does not carry an obligation with it to process questionable grievances for them. Experience teaches that repre-sentatives who find it impossible to resist pressure to file large numbers of questionable grievances or who file them because of a desire to demon-strate their militancy succeed only in overloading and weakening the grievance procedure and seldom achieve lasting favor with their constit-uents. All Committeemen should tell an employee or spokesman for any work group that a grievance is weak or wholly without merit and should withdraw or cause such grievances to be withdrawn if already filed. It goes without saying that they should also be willing to settle grievances in the early stages of the procedure. Currently, there appears to be little effort by Committeemen to clarify the facts or issues in the lower stages so that the representatives at the higher levels will be in a better position to consider the merits of a grievance. It should be plain to all Committeemen that if they relieve themselves of handling trivial or spurious grievances they would have more time for fact-gathering and for expediting the processing and settlement of vital and legitimate cases. . . .

Certainly there should be a union review or screening procedure to insure that unmeritorious grievances are not routinely appealed to the progressively higher steps of the procedure. Such screening should be done at all stages of the grievance procedure, including the fourth and fifth steps. Indeed, marginal paragraph 44(a) of the Agreement commands that no grievance shall be permitted to progress into the fourth step without review by the District Union Executive. What the parties doubtless had in mind in so providing was that a union official who is not subject to political pressure, who is detached from the emotions and partisanship of the original incidents involved, and who may be expected to judge issues in the context of the total employment relationship would review the appealed grievances from step three and not permit any unmeritorious ones to progress beyond it. Failure of such official to carry out his screening duties and knowingly to appeal unmeritorious ones is as much a failure of responsibility as the failure of the representatives at the lower levels to exercise their authority and discretion to withdraw bad grievances. . . .

The disadvantages of an overloaded arbitration step are many. It not only means delay in presenting and deciding cases but discontent among workers and uncertainty and indecisiveness in supervisors while they wait for grievances to be finally resolved. As a practical matter, a case long delayed at the lower levels becomes much more difficult to present properly in arbitration; large accumulations of potential back pay awards make settlements short of arbitration also difficult and often impossible; minor issues, becoming magnified in importance by reason of their age, grow into big disputes; workers with weak grievances are encouraged to live in false hopes of winning; arbitrating stale and potentially worthless claims is costly and burdensome for any local treasury. . . .

In connection with the time taken to decide cases in the above period (I am informed by the parties that the elapsed average time for deciding cases was about the same for the 3-year period preceding January 1, 1963), it should be pointed out: (1) discharge cases and relatively uncomplicated cases were decided in far less time than the average indicated above; (2) some of the time was consumed in waiting for transcripts and sometimes for additional data and briefs; (3) many of the cases involved novel, technical, and complex issues, e.g. incentive and job class issues. Even so, it is understandable that an average of seven months for deciding arbitration cases is thought by some grievance repesentatives as too long. However, for them to take an average of $11\frac{1}{2}$ to $19\frac{1}{2}$ months to process a case in the 5th step before it is submitted to the Board is also too long. Thus, as may be seen, it would take several years and several arbitrators to hear and decide all the cases now pending in the arbitration step. Considering the past results in arbitration and the parties' present needs, I cannot believe that either party would seriously consider it advantageous to have a large backlog of arbitration cases.

b. TYPICAL GRIEVANCE PROVISIONS

In contrast with the provisions in Article II, Section 5, of the Enderby Contract, the following are grievance provisions from collective bargaining agreements recently in force in some of the major American industries.

(1) From a contract between a small rubber company and the United Rubber Workers:

"Any employee or group of employees having a complaint in connection with his or their work shall first present such complaint to his foreman, either directly or in company with his appropriate Union representative.

"If a satisfactory settlement is not reached, the employee or group of employees involved in the complaint shall have seventy-two (72) hours within which to reduce their complaint to writing and present the same to the Factory Manager or his designated representative for disposition. . . ."

The factory manager is given seventy-two hours to issue his written answer and the next step (to the general manager) must be taken within five working days. Discharge or layoff grievances must be presented in writing within two working days from the date the union is notified of such action.

(2) From an agreement between a small aluminum and brass foundry in the Midwest and the United Automobile Workers:

"Step 1. Any employee having a grievance, or one designated member of a group having a grievance, should first take the grievance up with the foreman who will attempt to adjust it; or

"Any employee may request the foreman to call the Steward to handle a grievance with the foreman. The foreman will send for the appropriate Union representative without undue delay and without further discussion of the grievance. The foreman shall answer the grievance within two (2) days of its presentation.

"Step 2. If the grievance is not adjusted by the foreman, it shall be reduced to writing and signed by the employee involved and one copy shall be given to the foreman. The Bargaining Committeeman may then take the grievance up with the Personnel Manager. If the grievance is not presented to the Personnel Manager within three (3) days of the foreman's answer, it shall be assumed settled on the basis of the foreman's answer. The Personnel Manager will give his answer, in writing, within three (3) days following the meeting in Step 2."

Two other steps are specified: to the plant manager and plant bargaining committee within three days after the personnel manager's answer, and to arbitration within twenty days after receipt of the company's answer in Step 3, in accordance with the rules of the American Arbitration Association.

(3) From an agreement between one of the corporations in basic steel and the United Steelworkers:

"Should any difference arise between the Company and the Union or any employee and the Company as to the meaning or application of or compliance with sections of this Agreement, or as to any question relative to rates of pay, hours of work and conditions of employment, there shall be no interruption or impeding of the work, work stoppages, strikes or lockouts on account of such differences, but an earnest effort shall be made to settle such differences . . ."

A five-step procedure follows, starting with discussion with the foreman, then a written grievance containing certain specified information to be filed with the department superintendent, and culminating in an appeal to arbitration within ten days after receipt of the fourth step answer. Grievances must be filed "promptly after the occurrence thereof."

NOTE

Grievance procedures exist in other countries, but the provisions for the disposition of such disputes vary considerably.

Grievance procedures are provided and utilized in England, but there is a reluctance to use the arbitration step. It is said that the English tend to feel that arbitration is an instrument more appropriate for the settlement of questions of interest and basic contract terms than of disputes concerning rights and duties under existing contracts. Gratch, Grievance Settlement Machinery in England, 12 Lab. L.J. 861 (1961). The author goes on to point out that the English preference seems to rest, in part, on two factors. First, while most English generally oppose third party decisions in the labor-management field, they realize that economic warfare is highly wasteful. Since most collective bargaining in England is industry-wide, with associations of unions and employers negotiating basic wage and hour terms, strikes and lockouts here would invariably be as widespread. In order to avoid such consequences, the parties, in a comparatively large number of cases, are willing to arbitrate those basic contract issues which they cannot settle. Local labor grievance disputes usually do not create such necessity, and hence the parties do not as readily agree to arbitrate in this sphere; rather, the risks of economic battle here are not thought of as so threatening. A second factor seems to be that both labor and management officials feel that grievances, which usually are of local significance, can be handled adequately only by persons who are closely involved with the particular industrial situation in question. Basic wage and hour questions, on the other hand, are seen as problems of general significance which can be understood by outsiders.

In Canada, the Federal Industrial Relations and Disputes Investigation Act, which extends to about 5 per cent of the Canadian nonagricultural labor force, and seven of the ten provincial statutes require that collective agreements contain clauses providing for the final and binding arbitration of rights disputes (involving the interpretation of existing contracts) during the life of the agreement without stoppage of work. Craig, Arbitration of Labor-Management Disputes in Canada, 12 Lab. L.J. 1053 (1961).

In Australia, grievance procedures as found in the United States are practically unknown. This can be explained, it is said, by the Australian system of compulsory arbitration and by the prevailing concept of the employment contract. No grievance needs to be filed to obtain compliance with the usual commissioner's award — deviations are subject to legal action. Disciplinary actions, even discharge, are considered management's responsibility, and seniority is used as a basis for promotion or retention only as the employer chooses. De Vyver, 12 Lab. L.J. 933, 942-943 (1961).

In Sweden a Labor Court has been created with jurisdiction to decide disputes as to the meaning and application of collective agreements. This court has developed a substantial body of law defining the relative rights of the individual and the organization under the collective agreement. Summers, Collective Power and Individual Rights in the Collective Agreement — A Comparison of Swedish and American Law, 72 Yale L.J. 421, 435-436 (1963). See also McPherson, Labor Courts in Western Europe, 18 Ill. Bus. Rev. 6 (1961).

C.   RELATION OF GRIEVANCE PROCEDURE TO DUTY

TO BARGAIN

TIMKEN ROLLER BEARING CO. v. NLRB
United States Court of Appeals, Sixth Circuit, 1947
161 F.2d 949 (1947)

[The company, an Ohio corporation, entered into a collective bargaining agreement, dated February 19, 1943, with the United Steelworkers of America covering all production and maintenance employees in the company's bearing, steel, and tube plants in Canton and Gabrinus, and its bearing plants at Columbus. The agreement contained a standard no-strike clause and a grievance procedure which read, in part, as follows:

"Should differences arise between the Company and the Union as to the meaning and application of the provisions of this agreement or should any local trouble of any kind arise in the plant, there shall be no suspension of work on account of such differences, but an earnest effort shall be made to settle such differences promptly in the manner hereinafter outlined."

On October 15, 1945, the union commenced a general strike in the Canton and Gabrinus plants of the company. The strike was primarily in response to disciplinary action taken against employees of the 10″ mill who had left their jobs because of a shortage in the work crew, and because of certain work schedules placed in effect for maintenance employees of the Canton plant. As soon as the strike was called, the company stopped bargaining on two grievances then in process, and refused to participate in any grievance proceedings relating to the causes of the strike until the men returned to work. No grievances had been initiated by the union over the causes of the strike prior to the time that the strike was called. Several days after the strike had begun, the union demanded a meeting between representatives of the company and its grievance committee. The company replied that the strike was a breach of the collective agreement, but that its representatives would meet with the grievance committee under the grievance procedure of the agreement, after the union had permitted employees to return to work and had called off the strike, and after grievances had been filed in respect to any matter concerning which any employees had a complaint. On November 4, while the strike was still in progress, the company indicated its willingness to modify the grievance procedure so as to waive the preliminary steps, and to proceed with grievances relating to the alleged causes of the strike in combined Steps 3 and 4 of the grievance procedure. It also suggested that any grievances not resolved could be submitted to arbitration in accordance with the terms of the agreement. The union did not reply to this offer, but on November 16 it called off the strike, and the employees returned to work on November 19, on which date grievances were filed and handled in accordance with the company's suggestion.

Thereafter, charges were filed by the union, and a complaint issued by the NLRB, against the company for allegedly refusing to bargain with the union. The trial examiner's finding that the company had unlawfully refused to bargain concerning a lack of sufficient employees in the 10″ mill and with respect to the working schedules of maintenance employees, and had thus violated Section 8(5) of the Act, was upheld by the Board. 70 N.L.R.B. 500 (1946). In its opinion the Board stated (p. 504 n.9):

"We also concur with the Trial Examiner's conclusion that the existence of a strike allegedly in violation of a no-strike clause does not impair the obligation to bargain. It is the declared policy of the Act to mitigate and eliminate obstructions to the free flow of commerce by encouraging the practice and procedure of collective bargaining. A no-strike clause is designed to keep disputes from interrupting the respondent's operations but, as the case under consideration amply demonstrates it constitutes no guarantee that such interruptions will not occur. Unless the statutory duty to bargain collectively is held to remain in force even after a labor contract previously made has been broken, the purpose of the Act to promote industrial peace through collective bargaining will be attained only in small measure. Consequently, the refusal of the respondent to bargain with the Union after the strike is a violation of Section 8(5) of the Act."

The company then sought to have the Board's order set aside, and the Board petitioned for its enforcement.]

SIMONS, J. . . .

The petitioner's position is that it is not an unfair labor practice for an employer with a bargaining agreement with his employees containing a no-strike clause, and provisions for adjustment of grievances, to stand upon the terms of the bargain and demand that a strike be terminated and grievances handled within the framework of the contract, and that it is not an unfair labor practice for an employer to present his view as to the coverage of the contract in respect to subcontracts when the terms of the contract provided that differences as to the meaning and application of the provisions of the agreement should be settled in the manner therein provided. The Board's all-enveloping response to this is, as we interpret it, a contention that under the National Labor Relations Act there is a continuous statutory obligation to bargain which exists independently of all contractual obligations, and that a breach of contract on the part of the union does not relieve the employer from this obligation. As its counsel fervently urged in argument, the company must bargain and again bargain and yet again bargain without regard to breaches of contract by the union. It is this contention that we must now examine, and it is not without its difficulties.

Our first consideration must be the status and effect of an agreement in the statutory scheme for equalizing the economic position of management and labor in bargaining as to conditions of employment. An analysis of the terms of the Act, its declaration of policy, the reports of the committees submitting the draft to the Congress and the interpretations put upon the law by the courts, makes it abundantly clear that the bargaining duty imposed upon employers by the law had, for its end and purpose, the negotiating and concluding of a binding agreement. This must be so for it would be mere futility to bargain without such objective. So §1 of the Act declares that one of its purposes is the negotiation of terms and conditions of employment, and the report of the House Committee (H.R. 1147, p. 20, 74th Congress, 1st Session) declares the purpose of the bill to be "to encourage collective bargaining and the making of agreements." In Consolidated Edison Co. v. N.L.R.B., 305 U.S. 197, the Supreme Court said, "The Act contemplates the making of contracts with labor organizations. That is the manifest objective in providing for collective bargaining." Indeed, so important is an agreement to the bargaining process that when it is reached the Act requires a permanent memorial of its terms to avoid frustrating the bargaining process. An authentic record of its terms must be provided which could be exhibited to employees as evidence of the good faith of the employer, and so avoid fruitful sources of dissatisfaction and disagreement. H. J. Heinz Co. v. N.L.R.B., 311 U.S. 514, 523, 524, affirming our decision in 110 Fed. (2d) 843. There the court said,

". . . the signed agreement has been regarded as the effective instrument of stabilizing labor relations and preventing, through collective bargaining, strikes, and industrial strife. . . . Congress, in thus incorporating in the new legislation the collective bargaining requirement of the earlier statutes included as a part of it, the signed agreement long recognized under the earlier acts as the final step in the bargaining process."

This repeated asseveration of the importance of a written and signed agreement as the culminating step in the bargaining process so as to avoid industrial strife, does not contemplate and can by no process of reasoning be conceived as contemplating a unilateral undertaking by the employer binding upon him but devoid of controls on the bargaining agent or those for whom it speaks. Certainly, it is not without its disciplines over both of the parties to it, within the reasonable scope of its terms and conditions. The observation by the Second Circuit Court of Appeals in N.L.R.B. v. Remington Rand, Inc., 94 Fed. (2d) 862, "though the union may have misconducted itself, it has a locus poenitentiae," is in reference to misconduct outside the scope of an agreement and has no application to any issue here involved.

As we view the controversy, we have no problem in respect to the enforcement of the agreement. When employees undertake a strike in breach of a covenant not to do so, there is no power in the Labor Board nor in this court to compel them to work. We may not restrain them in the exercise of lawful activities, normally incident to the prosecution of a strike. Our sole problem is to determine whether there was refusal to bargain, in view of the terms of the contract and in the light of undisputed facts. In careful endeavor to isolate the precise issue calling for decision we face no obligation to determine whether, by breach of a no-strike agreement, the union surrendered bargaining rights preserved for it by the Act, even though the Labor Board has, upon occasion, itself come to that conclusion. In re Scullin Steel Co., 65 N.L.R.B. No. 219; In re Joseph Dyson and Sons, Inc., 72 N.L.R.B. No. 82, in respect to violations of §8(1) on the one hand, and violations of §8(3) on the other. Moreover, we give consideration to the rule proclaimed by the Labor Board in In re Consolidated Aircraft Corp., 47 N.L.R.B. 694, that it has no power under the Act to police collective bargaining contracts between employers and labor organizations, and to the view expressed in Terminal Railroad Association of St. Louis v. Brotherhood of Railroad Trainmen, 318 U.S. 1, 6, where Mr. Justice Jackson, speaking for a unanimous court, said,

"The Railway Labor Act, like the National Labor Relations Act, does not undertake governmental regulations of wages, hours or working conditions. . . . So far as the Act itself is concerned these conditions may be as bad as the employees will tolerate or be made as good as they can bargain for. The Act does not fix and does not authorize anyone to fix generally applicable standards for working conditions."

Had the contract here involved contained no procedures for the adjustment of grievances, we would have a different case and one which need not here be adjudicated. Adjustment of grievances by conferences between grievance representatives of management and grievance committees of the union and leading, in the event of failure, to arbitration, is itself a bargaining process, and we know of no mandate of the law that bargaining must be undertaken and pursued in a particularized manner, excluding every other. The only standard of compliance we are aware of is that bargaining shall be undertaken and pursued in good faith. No provision of the Act, either expressly or by reasonable implication, limits the right of employer and employees to agree upon the mode in which bargaining is done. Nor is there denial of the right of a collective bargaining agent to seek, or the obligation of an employer to consider a request to amend an existing contract. That is not this case. Nowhere in the record is there evidence that the union sought to change its contract with the company. The contention that a request to negotiate in respect to the causes of the strike or other grievances outside the grievance procedures of the contract is impliedly a demand upon the company to negotiate a change in the contract, only begs the question, for if every grievance, however important or unimportant, is a request to change the contract, then the parties are back where they started, and the written agreement with its detailed procedures for adjusting grievances, is truly but a "scrap of paper."

Having thus narrowed the issue to the question whether in the circumstances disclosed, and in the light of contractual terms, the company refused to bargain by its several inter-party communications, we come to consider more particularly the precise circumstances upon which the Board relied. They relate to the position of the company in respect to the causes of the strike, to the grievances initiated prior to the strike, and to the question of subcontracting.

It must be remembered in considering the causes of the strike, that no grievances had been filed in accordance with the terms of the contract. The record discloses no categorical refusal to bargain. The company's position was that it would negotiate in respect to the causes of the strike if the breach of contract were repaired, the men put back to work and grievances filed in accordance with the grievance procedures. Indeed, the company went further, — it offered to eliminate certain steps in the procedure which might have delayed adjustment, and to pass at once to the final steps provided. This was an offer reasonably in pursuit of the bargaining process. To construe it as refusal to bargain can be justified only by the fact that the offer was not made in good faith. Not only is there no finding by the Labor Board that the proposal of the company was made in bad faith in pursuit of a purpose to avoid bargaining, but there is not a scintilla of evidence that would support such a finding if made, and its earlier and subsequent bargaining history repels any inference in that respect. The same is true of the failure to complete an adjustment of grievances in process through the grievance procedures of the contract when the strike was called. The strike was in breach of the agreement and the company proposed to carry on within its terms when the men went back to work, — a proposal again within the normal processes of collective bargaining. . . .

Our conclusion is that the petitioner did not commit any unfair labor practice; that its effort to channel collective bargaining within the provisions of a contract with the union, was not a refusal to bargain; that there is no finding and no evidence that would sustain a finding that its efforts so to do was in the exercise of bad faith; that the controlling question is one of law and not of fact and so within the competence of this Court to decide; Wherefore,

The petition to set aside the Labor Board's order is granted and the petition by the Labor Board for its enforcement is denied.

KNIGHT MORLEY CORP.
National Labor Relations Board, 1956
116 N.L.R.B. 140

[The company operates a manufacturing plant at Richmond, Michigan, engaged in the production of rear view mirrors and other automobile accessories. On October 20, 1950, the company entered into a collective agreement with a local of the United Auto Workers (CIO). The agreement contained a five-step grievance procedure and a no-strike clause. The following additional facts are taken from the opinion of the appellate court, whose decision is quoted infra page 799.

"Under Mich. Stat. Ann., Sections 17.26 and 17.36 to 17.39, respondent was required to provide in its buffing room exhaust fans for the purpose of carrying off dust from emery wheels and grinders and dust-creating machinery. Sections 17.36 and 17.37 read together require that blowers and hoods be provided to protect the persons using buffing wheels from dust produced thereby and to catch and dispose of the dust thrown off by centrifugal force.

"The initial difficulty in the immediate case arose out of the breakdown of respondent's blower system in its buffing room. Beginning Friday, August 21, 1953, the blower, which when in operation properly sucked up much of the dirt, dust, lint and abrasives thrown off in the buffing process, was out of order on various occasions. Serious trouble arose on August 28 when a fire destroyed the switchbox which controlled the blower. On Saturday, August 29, a new switchbox was installed but in this operation the wires of the motor were reversed. This caused the fan to turn in reverse so that there was not enough suction in the blower system to draw off the waste material resulting from the polishing and buffing. On Monday, August 31, because of this situation, the morning shift of buffers was sent home after two hours work. The blower pipes were immediately cleaned, but in the afternoon of August 31 the blower still blew dirt, grit and abrasives into the men's faces, irritating eyes, ears and throats. On this day the temperature was from 96° to 98° in the shade and the atmosphere was very humid. A thermometer inside the buffing room showed the temperature there to be 110°. The buffers complained through their union steward and the union president to their foreman and to management. Respondent's president, Morley, made a cursory examination, putting his hand near the wheels of some of the buffing machines. He testified that the blower sucked in smoke from his cigar. Morley concluded that the blower was operating properly and rejected a suggestion from an experienced employee that the wires should be reversed. It was shown by the great weight of the testimony that the blower system on this day did not dispose of much of the dirt. The buffers, through their union steward and president, asked permission to stop working, but were told that they must continue and that anyone who left the plant would be discharged. All 17 of the afternoon buffers walked out of the plant at 5:15 P.M. Several of them testified at the hearing that they believed it would be injurious to their health to work under the conditions of the heat and dust.

"On the morning of September 1 there was no improvement in the operation and the rest of the men threatened to leave if the blower was not fixed. One buffer, Herbert Fox, was told to quit if he wanted to lose his job and he immediately quit. Thereafter Morley had the wires changed to the proper position. The blower then operated normally.

When the afternoon buffers returned to work September 1 they learned that they had been discharged.

"At the time the union was in process of negotiating a new contract with respondent, the original contract being due to expire on September 25, 1953. The union protested discharge of the 17 buffers and, in accordance with its collective bargaining contract which established a detailed grievance procedure, it submitted a formal written grievance with reference to the matter. As to this grievance, the first four steps of the grievance procedure were followed by the parties, but neither party receded from its position, respondent asserting that the buffers had been discharged for violation of proper management orders. Under step 5 of the grievance procedure it was optional with the parties to proceed to arbitrate. Neither party pursued arbitration to settlement of the particular controversy. Upon the ground that the grievance procedure should have been followed to its ultimate conclusion, respondent refused to bargain on matters relating to the buffers' discharge in connection with negotiations for a new collective bargaining contract.

"No meeting was held with respondent after September 25 and on September 30 two-thirds of the employees walked out on strike, although Morley sent them word and also told them personally that they would be discharged if they ceased work. Respondent then notified all strikers to return to the plant by October 5 and, as to those who did not return, cancelled group insurance and treated their employment as terminated."

In its opinion the Board stated, in part, as follows:]

The broad issue posed by these facts is whether the walkout by the buffers was protected concerted activity so as to render their discharge unlawful, or whether it was a strike in violation of the no-strike clause of the contract and therefore unprotected activity so as to render their discharge lawful.

Section 501 of the Act defines a "strike" under the Act. Section 502 of the Act, which is captioned "Saving Provision," provides: ". . . nor shall the quitting of labor by an employee or employees in good faith because of abnormally dangerous conditions for work at the place of employment of such employee or employees be deemed a strike under this Act." The General Counsel contends in substance that the walkout was a "quitting of labor" within the meaning of Section 502, and was therefore not a "strike" in violation of the no-strike clause in the contract; and consequently that the walkout was protected concerted activity, and the discharge of the buffers was unlawful. The Respondent contends in substance that the working conditions of the buffers were not "abnormally dangerous" and such was not the "good faith" reason for the walkout, and in any event that Section 502 did not protect the walkout; and the walkout was therefore unprotected because it was a violation of the no-strike clause of the contract, and consequently the discharge of the buffers was lawful.

Upon the basis of the credited testimony . . . we find that this danger of "heat disease" and the physical ailments which the "dust" would and did cause constituted "abnormally dangerous conditions for work" within the meaning of Section 502. While there is no evidence that any "heat disease" actually occurred, we note, as the Trial Examiner did, that the buffers worked only 1¾ hours and therefore may have escaped such illness by quitting work when they did. We also note, as the Trial Examiner did, that one of the morning buffers went so far as to quit the next morning because of the dust, which lends corroboration to the bad dust conditions when the 17 buffers walked out the previous afternoon. . . .

We also agree with the Trial Examiner's finding that since the walkout was a "quitting of labor by employees in good faith because of abnormally dangerous conditions for work," and therefore was not a "strike" under Section 502 of the Act, the buffers were engaged in protected concerted activity under Section 7 of the Act,[9] and therefore their discharge was unlawful. Although not spelled out, the Trial Examiner's rationale in making this finding, with which we agree, would appear to be that Section 502 gives employees a right to walk out because of abnormally dangerous working conditions and be protected, even in the face of a no-strike clause in their contract with an employer. There appears to be no legislative history on Section 502 to explain the purpose of that section. However, as argued by the General Counsel, it is logical to assume that such was the purpose of Section 502, in view of: (1) The decisions of the Board and the courts under the Wagner Act holding that certain "strikes," including strikes in violation of no-strike clauses, were unprotected; and (2) the fact that the amended Act renders certain "strikes" unprotected under Section 8(d). Accordingly, we believe that a walkout because of abnormally dangerous working conditions was declared by Congress not to be a "strike" in order to give protection to such a walkout, without regard to limitations on strikes such as those imposed by "no-strike" clauses or by Section 8(d). We can conceive of no other reasonable purpose. The Respondent argues that: (1) Since such a walkout is not a "strike" under Section 502, "it more logically follows" that it is *not* protected concerted activity; and (2) Section 502 has no bearing at all on whether the walkout was protected or unprotected. In our opinion, these arguments are not only illogical and unreasonable, but if accepted would render Section 502 meaningless and a nullity. Congress surely had some purpose in mind other than to simply declare that such a walkout is not a "strike." And the most reasonable purpose, in our view, was to protect the right of employees to quit their labor without penalty in order to protect their health and their lives. The Respondent also cites two cases which it contends "are directly in point and involve situations almost identical with that which exists in the present case." In the first of these cases, the Board held that a walkout because of "hazardous" working conditions was protected, but the Court of Appeals for the Fifth Circuit reversed the Board;[10] however, the

---

[9] The walkout was, of course, a concerted activity "for the purpose of [the buffers'] mutual aid or protection" under Section 7.

[10] N.L.R.B. v. American Mfg. Co. of Texas, 203 F.2d 212 (C.A. 5), reversing 98 N.L.R.B. 226.

grounds for the reversal, neither of which is present here, were that the walkout was inconsistent with the understanding between the bargaining agent and the employer on the grievance, and with the terms of the safety provision of the collective-bargaining agreement which called for "corrective measures [to be taken by the employer] *within a reasonable time*"; and thus there were extenuating circumstances for not applying the protection of Section 502 to the employees. In the second of these cases,[11] both the Board and the Seventh Circuit held that a walkout because of the shutting off of a "blower system" was not protected, but rested their decisions on findings that the walkout was an "intermittent work stoppage";[12] and thus the inherently unlawful nature of the walkout deprived the employees of the protection of Section 502. In the instant case, the buffers did report for work the next day, but there is no evidence which indicates that if allowed to work, which they were not, they would walk out again before completing their shift; and thus there is insufficient evidence of a "partial strike."

In view of the foregoing, the Board finds that the walkout of the buffers was protected concerted activity by virtue of Section 502 of the Act, despite the no-strike clause in the contract, and that their discharge was therefore unlawful. As we have found that the discharge of the buffers was an unfair labor practice, we also adopt the Trial Examiner's rejection of the Respondent's contention that the Board has not or should not assert jurisdiction with respect to the discharge of the buffers because the grievance procedure of the contract had not been exhausted.[14] . . .

At several meetings prior to September 25, 1953, Respondent and the Union had not only discussed a new contract, but several grievances as well, including the discharge of the buffers. However, at a meeting on September 25, the Respondent stated that when the contract expired at midnight that day the possibility of further discussions on the grievances ended with the expiration of the contract, and that henceforth it was willing to bargain on a new contract but unwilling to discuss further the grievances on which it had already given unfavorable replies to the Union. At that time there were 8 grievances pending, including the discharge of the buffers; and although not followed to the letter, the Union had in substance gone through the first 4 steps of the grievance procedure in the contract on these grievances,[20] and there remained only the fifth step of "permissive" arbitration.[21] Neither the Respondent nor the

[11] N.L.R.B. v. Kohler Co., 220 F.2d 3 (C.A. 7), enfg. 108 N.L.R.B. 207.

[12] Thus, the employees indicated that they intended to continue working but to quit when they felt like it and not to complete any shift until the employer yielded to their demands. See Auto Workers v. Wisconsin Board, 336 U.S. 245.

[14] See N.L.R.B. v. Walt Disney Products, 146 F.2d 44 (C.A. 9); N.L.R.B. v. Wagner Iron Works, 220 F.2d 126 (C.A. 7).

[20] Five of the eight grievances had been presented and answered in writing in accordance with step 4; and although the other three had been presented and answered only orally, the record shows that oral grievances were sometimes considered and disposed of at step 4, i.e., with "Plant Management."

[21] Step 5 provides that "If the grievance remains unsettled, the Union or the Company *may* present it to an arbitrator mutually agreed upon by the Company and the Union, if no arbitrator is agreed upon, then an arbitration Panel con-

Union made any request for arbitration of the grievances at the September 25 meeting. However, both parties had attempted to arrange for arbitration of the grievance on the discharge of the buffers at a September 14 meeting, but this was unsuccessful because they were unable to agree on an arbitrator. At a meeting on October 14, Respondent again took the position that it had no legal obligation to discuss the grievances, and would discuss only a new contract; and took the further position that any new contract would apply only to nonstrikers and not to the strikers. At a meeting on October 29, the Respondent again refused to discuss the grievances, on the ground that they were dead issues since the contract had expired under which those grievances had arisen. . . .

The Trial Examiner agrees with Respondent's contention, and finds that Respondent's refusal to bargain on the grievances after the contract expired was not a violation of Section 8(a)(5). In support of his finding, the Trial Examiner relies on a line of cases which hold, in substance, that where an employer has satisfied its "channelized" bargaining duty under the grievance procedure of a contract, there is no further bargaining duty under the Act.[22]   However, as pointed out by the General Counsel and the Union, these were all cases involving the duty of an employer to discuss grievances during the life of a contract when the grievance procedure was still in effect to be utilized; whereas in the instant case the contract had expired and the grievance procedure was no longer in effect to be utilized;[23] and therefore the grievances could be processed further only through the "general" bargaining process provided for by the Act. Accordingly, this line of cases is distinguishable, and not dispositive of the issue in the instant case. In our opinion, these cases stand only for the principle that a contractual grievance procedure is the "channel" for the collective-bargaining duty on grievances which *may* be disposed of under such procedure, or are *finally disposed* of under such procedure. If that "channel" of bargaining is no longer available for grievances remaining *unsettled* under it, it follows that the general duty to bargain on grievances under the Act is once again operative. Such grievances do not "expire" with the contract simply because they arose under it, but are rather returned to the area of general bargaining under the Act in the absence of any "channelization" of bargaining. And this is certainly so where, as here, the contract does not provide for any such "expiration."   Accordingly, the question in the instant

---

sisting of three members; one member to be chosen by the Company and one member to be chosen by the Union. These two members shall choose the third member. . . ." [Emphasis supplied.]

[22] Textron Puerto Rico, 107 N.L.R.B. 583; McDonnell Aircraft Corporation, 109 N.L.R.B. 930; Timken Roller Bearing Company v. N.L.R.B., 161 F.2d 949 (C.A. 6); Crown Zellerbach Corp., 95 N.L.R.B. 753.

[23] The no-strike clause of the contract provides: "It is agreed between the Union and the Company that *during the term of this agreement,* there shall be no strike, slowdown or other stoppage of work, and in the event the Union and the Company are unable to settle a particular grievance, it shall be settled by arbitration pursuant to [step 5 of the grievance procedure] at the request of either party in writing." [Emphasis supplied.]

case is whether the grievances in issue were "finally disposed of" under the grievance procedure, or whether they were still "unsettled" at the expiration of the contract; if finally disposed of under the grievance procedure there was no further duty to bargain on them under the "general" statutory duty to bargain, but if still unsettled there was a further general statutory duty to bargain on them.

The Respondent points to the fact that, although arbitration procedure was available, the Union did not request arbitration on September 25; and suggests that this therefore was "final disposition" of the grievances under the grievance procedure. However, there was no time limit on invoking any of the steps in the grievance procedure, which would mean that a "reasonable" time was permitted. Only 11 days prior to September 25 the Union had unsuccessfully attempted to present the buffer grievance to "an arbitrator mutually agreed upon" under the first step of the arbitration provision. In the absence of any time limit on invoking the next step of selecting an "arbitration panel," [24] we do not believe that the Union's failure to invoke this next step within 11 days was "unreasonable" or violative of the arbitration provision of the contract. We find, therefore, that the buffer grievance at least was still "unsettled" at the expiration of the contract, and consequently that the Respondent's refusal to bargain on the buffer grievance after the expiration of the contract was a violation of Section 8(a)(5) of the Act.[25]

The General Counsel excepts to the Trial Examiner's failure to find that the Respondent also violated Section 8(a)(5) by taking the position at the October 14 bargaining meeting that any new contract would apply to nonstrikers and not to the strikers. As recently stated by the Board, Board and court precedent hold that a refusal to bargain with a certified bargaining representative during a strike is a violation of Section 8(a)(5).[26] The rationale behind this doctrine is that strikers retain their "employee" status under the Act; the representative thus remains the statutory representative of the "employees"; and therefore the representative is entitled to bargain on behalf of such "employees" even though they are on strike.[27] In the instant case, the Respondent did not completely refuse to bargain with the certified bargaining representative during the strike, but only refused to bargain with respect to the strikers. However, the same rationale is applicable, viz, that the Union was entitled to bargain with respect to the striker "employees" as well as the nonstriker "employees," and therefore Respondent's refusal to bargain with respect to the strikers was unlawful.[28] Indeed, it might be argued

---

[24] See footnote 20, supra.

[25] As the General Counsel apparently does not seek a finding that Respondent's refusal to bargain on the other seven grievances was unlawful, we shall not consider that issue. In any event, such a finding would not affect our Order herein. Chairman Leedom would not reach any part of the grievance issue on the ground the Order is not affected thereby.

[26] See R. J. Oil & Refining Co., Inc., 108 N.L.R.B. 641, and cases cited therein.

[27] See N.L.R.B. v. Reed & Prince Mfg. Co., 118 F.2d 874, 885 (C.A. 1).

[28] There is of course no question as to whether the strikers were still "employees," in view of the fact that they were unfair labor practice strikers who could not lawfully be replaced.

that this is a more aggravated and even stronger case than a complete refusal to bargain during a strike, because of the "discriminatory" position taken by the Respondent that it would bargain only with respect to the nonstrikers and not with respect to the strikers. We find, therefore, that the Respondent's position taken at the October 14 meeting, that any new contract would apply only to nonstrikers and not to the strikers, was a violation of Section 8(a)(5).

As we have found that the Respondent has also engaged in unfair labor practices in violation of Section 8(a)(5) of the Act, we shall . . . order the Respondent to cease and desist therefrom, and to bargain collectively upon request with the Union as the exclusive bargaining representative of all employees in the bargaining unit described herein with respect to wages, rates of pay, hours of employment, or other conditions of employment, and, if an understanding is reached, embody such understanding in a signed agreement.

NLRB v. KNIGHT MORLEY CORP.
United States Court of Appeals, Sixth Circuit, 1957
251 F.2d 753

ALLEN, J.

This case arises on petition for enforcement of a decision and order of the National Labor Relations Board which held that respondent had violated Section 8(a)(1)(3) and (5) of the Labor Management Relations Act, 1947 . . . and ordered reinstatement with back pay of certain employees whom it found to have been improperly discharged. . . .

Respondent also attacks the Board's conclusion that respondent's insistence that the grievance concerning the buffers' discharge should be handled through grievance proceedings rather than as a part of the negotiation for a new contract violates Section 8(a)(5) and constitutes refusal to bargain. The trial examiner found to the contrary, basing his conclusion largely upon the decision of this court in Timken Roller Bearing Company v. National Labor Relations Board, 161 Fed. (2d) 949, 955. The Board endeavors to distinguish the instant case from the Timken case, supra, upon the ground that the grievance as to the buffers' discharge had not been disposed of when the contract expired. While there were some factual differences between the Timken case and the instant controversy, the grievance there involved, as here, had not been settled and, this court held, the employer's effort to channel the grievances into agreed grievance procedures was not a refusal to bargain. This court approved and follows that case in National Labor Relations Board v. Standard Oil Company, 196 Fed. (2d) 892, 895. Here, as there, the duty to bargain could be directed by the parties through contractual agreement and such a contract had been executed. See also Textile Workers Union of America v. Lincoln Mills of Alabama, 353 U.S. 448, in which the Supreme Court reversed a judgment of the Court of Appeals and affirmed a judgment of the District Court which held that, when a grievance arose from the operation of the collective bargaining agreement and while it was in effect, the expiration of the bargaining agreement did not relieve respondent of its contractual obligation to arbitrate. We think the Board erred in deciding that respondent violated Section 8(a)(5) of the Act in dealing with the grievance.

However, this conclusion does not require that the order be modified, for the Board also found that respondent on October 14 refused to bargain with the union as the representative of the striking employees, in violation of Section 8(a)(5) of the Act. The strike of September 30 was clearly an unfair labor practice strike. The strikers retained their employee status and their bargaining representative was entitled to recognition in their behalf. National Labor Relations Board v. Deena Artware, Inc., 198 Fed. (2d) 645, 651 (C.A. 6), certiorari denied 345 U.S. 906; National Labor Relations Board v. Pecheur Lozenge Co., 209 Fed. (2d) 393, 403 (C.A. 2), certiorari denied 347 U.S. 953.

It is ordered that a decree shall issue enforcing the Board's order as prayed in the petition.

NOTE

The Knight Morley case was noted in 43 Va. L. Rev. 263 (1957) and in 55 Mich. L. Rev. 882 (1957). The latter note pointed out that previous to Knight Morley, the Sixth Circuit had held that spontaneous walkouts and temporary work stoppages prompted by health reasons were protected concerted activities under Section 7 of the amended Act. NLRB v. Southern Silk Mills, Inc., 209 F.2d 155 (6th Cir. 1953). In that case, however, a no-strike clause was not involved. When such a clause is incorporated in an agreement, state and federal courts have generally held that a work stoppage constitutes a violation. NLRB v. Kaiser Aluminum & Chemical Corp., 217 F.2d 366 (9th Cir. 1954); General Electric Co. v. United Auto Workers, 93 Ohio App. 139, 108 N.E.2d 211 (1952); NLRB v. Fruin-Colnon Construction Co., 330 F.2d 885 (8th Cir. 1964). In the latter case it was held that Section 502 of the LMRA does not automatically sanction, as protected concerted activity, work stoppages resulting from a good faith belief that dangerous work conditions exist. The crew had been working on a ledge to widen a vertical shaft running from the top of a mountain to connect with a horizontal shaft several hundred feet below. The men considered the footing uncertain because of wetness and an updraft in the shaft and refused to go down on the day in question, but had worked under somewhat similar conditions the previous day. The court found that the work was "hazardous" but not "abnormally dangerous," and ruled that if the proof of the physical facts fails to support the employees' belief, they run the risk of discharge for engaging in the unprotected activity of striking for the purpose of dictating to management their own terms and conditions of employment. The court said that Knight Morley was factually distinguishable and that the court's pronouncement in that case implied a construction of Section 502 to which the Eighth Circuit did not subscribe. The contract contained a no-strike clause. The order of the

NLRB directing reinstatement was held unenforceable.   See page 273 supra.

Mastro Plastics Corp. v. NLRB, 350 U.S. 270 (1956), is a leading case in making an exception for stoppages called to protest an employer's unfair labor practices.   See page 475 supra.

2. *Arbitration*

a.   NATURE OF THE PROCESS

HEPBURN and LOISEAUX, THE NATURE OF THE ARBITRATION PROCESS *
10 Vanderbilt Law Review 657, 659-665 (1957)

In the past twenty-five years the use of arbitration in the labor-management field has grown to an extraordinary degree and there is every reason today to believe that this growth will continue.   Reasons for this growth can be summarized in a phrase — convenient necessity.   To the parties, arbitration offers solutions to vexing and frequently explosive problems.   Without such a decision-making process the parties might be forced into economic warfare or litigation.   Neither is desirable.   Arbitration offers speed, relative economy, and flexibility.   Litigation is unsatisfactory to the parties because of great expense, undesired technicality and delay.   The public interest would suffer if courts were required to decide many thousands of disputes between management and labor, which would impede the traditional work of courts.   Moreover, the regular courts are not equipped to handle a large proportion of cases that now go to arbitration.   Economic warfare, the other alternative in addition to litigation available to parties who do not agree to arbitrate their unsolved problems, is in almost every case unsatisfactory and in general productive only of tragic economic waste and personal hardship.   Equally important in considering alternatives is the nature of the result sought.   In litigation the parties are compelled to fit their frequently unique questions into established legal doctrine.   A suit for breach of contract between labor and management must fit traditional patterns, parties must play their proper doctrinal parts, and the court is limited in the type and scope of remedy which it can award.   This economically and socially sensitive continuing relationship could not stand the strain if it were necessary to use our historical legal processes to solve every dispute.

Thus, today, because of necessity and convenience, labor and management have by agreement established a procedure for settling disputes which includes their own forum and their own private judges, or arbitrators.   How do the parties find these private judges?   Obviously it is necessary to choose someone upon whom the parties can agree.   What are the formal qualifications for this work?   The only essential qualifica-

---

* This selection from the article by William M. Hepburn and Pierre R. Loiseaux is reproduced with the permission of the editors of the Vanderbilt Law Review.

tion is an ability to understand the dispute and to make a "fair," rational and dispassionate decision. For this task parties have selected businessmen, lawyers, ministers, engineers, sociologists, economists, and, in particular controversies, persons from almost every walk of life. University professors with training in law, business, economics or sociology are very frequently appointed. All people are judges in various ways — decision making is a part of life from which few escape. However, as the number of labor arbitrations has increased many persons who have proved satisfactory as arbitrators have been frequently reappointed. Some of these have become professional arbitrators and have given up other vocations to devote all of their time to the arbitration process. At the present time there are doubtlessly more persons serving as arbitrators on an occasional basis than there are permanent arbitrators.

The parties select the arbitrator by agreement, or accept one appointed by some agreed-upon third party. The third party may be a state or federal agency, the American Arbitration Association, or some other organization or person. Occasionally the contract will provide that a federal judge, the governor of the state, or the president of a university shall select the arbitrator, but such provisions are usually in new contracts and the parties soon change to one of the established sources of appointment. An appointing agency does not ordinarily name the arbitrator individually, unless requested specifically to do so. A list of qualified persons is submitted by the agency to both sides, and the parties strike names which are unacceptable and number the remaining names in order of preference. The agency then names the individual with the lowest total as arbitrator. Permanent umpires in major industries are well known, but even in such permanent appointments few are full-time professional arbitrators.

In the broadest sense, what both parties want from their private judge is a fair and practical decision. Frequently the arbitrator is sore pressed to know exactly what and how much he is to decide. At times the parties are not fully aware of the basis of their dispute, and the arbitrator must initially decide that issue. Some contracts provide for this. However, the arbitrator must make a decision even if it is only that he cannot make a decision on the substantive question. What does the arbitrator bring with him to the arbitration hearing? Unlike the judge in legal procedures, often the arbitrator does not know the nature of the dispute he will be called upon to determine. If he has knowledge of industrial techniques and personnel policies he will be better able to accomplish the initial task of learning.

By what process does an arbitrator reach a decision? Probably no two follow identical rules. Often the same individual varies his method. That judges follow no definite formula seems evident. The methods of philosophy, history, tradition, sociology which Cardozo discussed are not foreign to the arbitrator; nor is precedent or reliance upon the subconscious. He quoted Munroe Smith that:

"The rules and principles of case law have never been treated as final truths, but as working hypotheses, continually retested in the great laboratories of the law, the courts of justice. Every new case is an experiment; and if the accepted rule which seems applicable yields a result which is felt to be unjust, the rule is reconsidered.[9]

Probably, the first thing a judge or arbitrator does is to obtain as complete an understanding of the facts as he can from the parties' opening statements, testimony, summations and briefs; then he sets up tentative questions and thinks in terms of possible answers, in terms of the collective bargaining agreement, practical knowledge, sense of justice. He must allocate various pieces of information to different sides of the formulated questions and assign some relative value to each. The final step usually involves a choice between two or more alternatives, but this is not always so. There are cases, for example, where the facts and the contract are so clear that only one answer is possible. For at times, both management and labor arbitrate cases which are clearly without merit, and the arbitrator's function, and it is a useful one to the parties, is to serve as whipping boy. But when the arbitrator must choose between alternatives, quite often a subjective element on a narrow point may lead him to his decision.

What are the arbitrator's tools? His authority comes from the collective bargaining agreement, plus the submission or stipulation, if there is one. Frequently the grievance is submitted, and the question is: What disposition shall be made of it under the contract? Very often the terms of the contract do not give a ready answer to the question or dispute that has been brought to the arbitrator. If there were a ready answer in the contract the case would usually have been settled during the grievance steps.

In making a decision what criteria are available to the arbitrator, what criteria does he use, and what criteria does he say he uses? The theme of this paper is that grievance arbitration in general follows the "law" and that the arbitrator functions principally as a judge.[10] . . .

[9] Cardozo, The Nature of the Judicial Process 23 (1921), quoting Smith, Jurisprudence 21 (1909).

[10] ". . . arbitration, except as provided by statute, is solely a creature of the parties. If the parties prefer an arbitrator to function as a 'mutual friend,' as a labor relations psychiatrist, or as a father-confessor, they are privileged to seek out an arbitrator who can fulfill such a role. If they prefer an arbitrator to adhere strictly to the traditional quasi-judicial approach, this can be made clear. It is important to the success of the relationship that the parties understand and agree upon the type of arbitration they want and that they make this clear to the arbitrator. Personally, I continue to hold the view that in grievance arbitration the arbitrator's function is properly a quasi-judicial one." Davey, Labor Arbitration: A Current Appraisal, 9 Ind. & Lab. Rel. Rev. 85, 88 (1955). See also Taylor, The Voluntary Arbitration of Labor Disputes, 49 Mich. L. Rev. 787 (1951); Warren and Bernstein, A Profile of Labor Arbitration, 4 Ind. & Lab. Rel. Rev. 200 (1950); Braden, The Function of the Arbitrator in Labor-Management Disputes, 4 Arb. J. (n.s.) 35 (1949); Singer, Labor Arbitration: Should It Be Formal or Informal? 2 Lab. L.J. 89 (1951); Hoebrecx, In Defense of Judicial Arbitration, 3 Lab. L.J. 487 (1952); Code of Ethics and Procedural Standards for Labor-Management Arbitration, Part 1, §1 (AAA 1950).

[In Australia, arbitration is required by statute, both as to the terms of the collective agreement and disputes arising thereunder. The process, although

It is not uncommon to make a record of the hearing in cases of importance. In many disputes the parties file briefs after the hearing. This post-hearing document smacks of both a closing argument and an appellate brief. It contains argument about the facts presented and their weight and applications such as is usual in closing argument, but it also contains extensive argument about the major premise under which these facts are to be placed. This argument of principles involves at times extensive use of legal sources, industrial statistics, other arbitration proceedings, state and federal statutes, practice and custom in industry or in a particular industry, and sometimes an element of emotion.

In making his decision the arbitrator then has a record of the hearing and written argument. He usually writes an opinion to accompany his award, and the parties expect this. An arbitration award is not merely the settlement of a dispute. Often it forms a rule or interpretation for the parties' future conduct, and they must live with it. . . .

There are no pleadings in an arbitration proceeding, although the grievance and the company's answer may be analogous to pleadings when no submission is executed. . . .

b.   PROCEDURAL PROBLEMS IN ARBITRATION

AARON, SOME PROCEDURAL PROBLEMS IN ARBITRATION *
10 Vanderbilt Law Review 733, 734-745 (1957)

FRAMING THE ISSUE

The typical collective bargaining agreement outlines the steps of the grievance procedure that must be followed before the dispute can be appealed to arbitration. Ideally, the movement of the grievance through the successive steps specified in the agreement is similar, in at least one respect, to the movement of a law suit from the trial court to the highest appellate tribunal; that is, the issue initially submitted is stripped of irrelevancies and reduced to its barest essentials in the course of this refining process. Some points are settled by adjustment along the way, others are dropped. Facts are clarified and are frequently stipulated. Thus, by the time the grievance finally reaches arbitration, the parties have sharply defined their points of difference, and have reduced to a minimum their disagreement with respect to "the facts."

---

judicial in form, is legislative in effect, and it is possible for the terms of collective agreements and awards in disputes to become a "common rule" binding on all employers and employees in the industry concerned. See O'Connell, Australian Compulsory Arbitration System, 35 Notre Dame Law. 640 (1960). For a history of the development of the arbitration process in Australia and a comparative evaluation, see Brissenden, Arbitration in Australia and the United States, 11 Lab. L.J. 493 (1960).]

* This selection from the article by Benjamin Aaron is reproduced with the permission of the editors of the Vanderbilt Law Review.

Alas, what an immeasurable distance there is between this Heaven of theoretical perfection and the Hell of actual practice! An attorney called in to represent one of the parties in arbitration will discover, frequently if not typically, that the issue to be submitted is only distantly related to the original grievance and was cast in its present form during informal discussions following the last step of the grievance procedure; or that the initial complaint has grown in amplitude and ambiguity at each step of the grievance procedure, instead of undergoing the prescribed reducing treatment; or, worst of all, that the parties now cannot agree as to what issue or issues are in dispute and should be submitted to arbitration. In short, the neat little controversy that he anticipated, with its well-ordered facts and carefully delineated boundaries, all too often turns out to be a sprawling, shifting free-for-all, a jumble of conflicting claims, arguments, and objectives.

A case in the condition just described obviously must be confined within some kind of procedural framework before being submitted to an arbitrator for decision. The most commonly used instrument for that purpose is the submission agreement, a document setting forth, among other things, the issue or issues to be determined by the arbitrator. The submission agreement properly should serve two principal purposes: first, to tell the arbitrator, as precisely as possible, the questions he must resolve, and second, to place such limitations upon his discretion as the parties agree are necessary and desirable.

Any well-trained lawyer should be able to draft a submission agreement that will state the issue clearly, briefly, and simply. Unfortunately, the attorney we have in mind is handicapped by his training and experience in purely adversary proceedings; his automatic reaction is to protect his client's interests by winning the case, if possible, before the matter is even heard by the arbitrator. Frequently, therefore, the lawyer who has had little or no collective bargaining experience tries to draft a submission agreement on a "heads-I-win-tails-you-lose" basis. Such tactics are to be deplored because they defeat the very purpose the arbitration process is intended to serve: the peaceful, cooperative solution of a problem affecting both parties to the collective agreement.

Another impulse that the inexperienced attorney has difficulty suppressing is to insist that the submission agreement set forth the exact provision of the agreement relied upon by the other side. Suppose the union has grieved over the transfer of an employee, against his will, from the day to the night shift. The company will naturally inquire what article and section of the agreement it has allegedly violated. Let us say that the union representative cites section B (transfers) of the seniority article and that this claim is duly set forth in the submission agreement. So far so good; but now suppose that during the arbitration it becomes apparent that the issue really involves the interpretation and application of section D (shift preference) rather than section B. Our hypothetical lawyer may be inclined to insist that the arbitrator refuse to hear any argument relating to section D, on the ground that this provision was not specified in the submission agreement. Again, we must reject such an approach, not only because it smacks of sharp practice, but because it is contrary to the best interests of both parties. The point that must never be lost sight of is that arbitration is intended to settle problems, not to evade them. . . .

One rule to which all arbitrators give lip service, but which is more honored in the breach than in the observance, is that no issue should go to arbitration until it has been thoroughly worked over in the grievance procedure. Since this rule is so manifestly sensible, why should it not be scrupulously observed? The reason can be found in the nature of ad hoc arbitration. An arbitrator chosen for the particular case only is usually a stranger to one or both parties and knows little or nothing about the way the grievance procedure functions. Charges by one party that the other has raised a new issue or argument at the hearing will invariably be met by outraged denials and the assertion that the point was emphasized time and again at earlier stages of the case. What is the arbitrator to do? If the party professing to be surprised can demonstrate that it will require more time to prepare evidence and argument to meet the new issue, the arbitrator may decide to grant a postponement. Such a situation occurs relatively infrequently, however, because in most cases each side has anticipated all the arguments of the other. Moreover, having gone through the time-consuming and troublesome procedure of selecting the arbitrator, both parties are inclined to finish up the case without further delay. What usually happens, therefore, even in cases in which there has been a quite obvious failure to "exhaust" the grievance procedure, is that the parties complain bitterly to the arbitrator about each other's lack of good faith and then go on with the hearing.

The standing umpire or impartial chairman can deal with this type of problem much more effectively. He knows the parties intimately, is thoroughly familiar with the functioning of the grievance procedure, and is thus able to discern whether he is being confronted by an isolated instance or a chronic condition. His continuing relationship with the parties makes it much more feasible for him to refer a case back to the grievance procedure, and many an umpire does exactly that when he feels that the parties are tending to postpone all purposeful collective bargaining on disputes until the final stage of arbitration.

Many collective agreements expressly exclude from arbitration grievances dealing with particular matters, such as the fixing of wage rates for new jobs or the introduction of new methods or processes. If the exclusion is clear, the arbitrator must observe it; this is one case in which the problem raised, however serious or urgent it may be, is beyond his power to resolve. Lawyers new to arbitration, however, are sometimes prone to look for restrictions on the arbitrator's authority that are not expressly set forth in the agreement. Such a practice is dangerous and ought to be undertaken only with great caution. For one thing, arbitration, as has been so frequently observed, is a substitute for a strike or lockout, and most agreements permit employees to strike and employers to lock out over issues not subject to arbitration. Convincing an arbitrator that he lacks jurisdiction over a particular grievance may thus prove to be a Pyrrhic victory. Moreover, the nature of a collective bargaining relationship can often change rapidly and quite unexpectedly; last year's argument, or even last week's, may sometimes turn out to be inappropriate, if not downright embarrassing, in today's case. It therefore behooves the representatives of both parties to use very sparingly the argument that the arbitrator lacks jurisdiction over the grievance. . . .

PRESENTING THE CASE

Many of the so-called problems encountered in presenting a case in ad hoc arbitration are, even more than those involved in framing the issue, purely synthetic. Several of the difficulties referred to in the preceding section arose out of the nature of the grievance or the language of the collective bargaining agreement. By contrast, most of those dealt with below, as we shall see, are entirely man-made. Regrettably, one must report that these problems are often fabricated by lawyers whose experience in trial work handicaps their effectiveness in arbitration cases. This seeming paradox is actually easily explained. The trial of a law suit is an adversary proceeding in which the principal aim is to win by any legitimate means. Procedural technicalities are of the utmost importance, and interim rulings on such matters as burden of proof, admissibility of evidence, scope of cross-examination, and the like, may decisively affect the outcome. Indeed, as every lawyer knows, the line between procedural and substantive questions is frequently a shadowy one. The trial attorney is thus conditioned to take full advantage of all the exclusionary rules of evidence, to exploit the elements of surprise and suspense, and, especially in jury trials, to attempt to sway the emotions when the chances of persuading the intellect seem dim.

In contrast to the trial of a law suit, an arbitration hearing is, or should be, a cooperative effort by the parties and the arbitrator to bring out all facts and arguments relevant to the dispute. True, the proceeding retains something of an adversary character: in terms of the language of the award, one side usually "wins." On the other hand, since the relationship between the parties is a continuing one, each usually realize that it is better to "lose" a case than to "win" it at the cost of a permanent impairment of the collective bargaining process. Consequently, many of the tactics commonly used in the trial of a law suit are regarded as bad form, or even as indications of bad faith, in an arbitration proceeding.

The contrast between the objectives and procedures of an arbitration hearing and those of a law suit has been so generally noticed by arbitrators, lawyers, and laymen that one is puzzled by the ubiquity of certain procedural arguments in arbitration. Of these, surely the most senseless is the dispute over which side should proceed first. An insistence that the other side has the burden of going forward implies a plaintiff-defendant relationship in which the former must set up a prima facie case before the latter is obligated to respond. But this concept is plainly inapplicable to an arbitration proceeding. As an extension of the grievance procedure, an arbitration hearing serves many purposes, not the least of which is to give the grievant the satisfaction of knowing that the other party has been compelled to account for its conduct before an impartial third person. Again, the hearing may serve to educate a union committee, or a group of foremen, on the manner in which their respective actions may subsequently be reviewed and questioned. Even when it is apparent to an arbitrator, therefore, after the complaining party has presented its case, that the grievance lacks merit, he will almost never grant a request by the opposing party for an immediate ruling in its favor. . . .

By far the greatest number of procedural problems arising in ad hoc labor arbitration concern the introduction of evidence and the examination of witnesses. These are the problems, too, which seem to bring out in some attorneys those irritating qualities that comprise the average layman's stereotype of the lawyer. A few of the more unpleasant of these traits may be mentioned in passing. First, by a wide margin, is the use of legal mumbo-jumbo: the monotonous objection to the introduction of evidence on grounds that it is "incompetent, irrelevant, and immaterial," or "not part of the res gestae." A close second is the eat-'em-alive method of cross-examination: the interrogation of each witness as if he were a Jack the Ripper finally brought to the bar of justice. Last, but scarcely least, there is the affectation of what may be called advanced documentship: throwing an exhibit at one's opponent across the table, as if contamination would result if it were handed over in the normal way, or contemptuously referring to the opponent's exhibits as "pieces of paper that purport to be," and so forth. These tactics may be well suited to stage or cinema portrayals of the district-attorney-with-a-mind-like-a-steel-trap or the foxy defense counsel at work, but they are wholly out of place in an arbitration proceeding. Moreover, they can be counted upon almost invariably to exacerbate the feelings of those on the other side and to initiate bitter and time-consuming arguments between the parties. . . .

Despite the generally accepted principle that arbitration procedures are necessarily more informal than those of a court of law, objections to evidence on such grounds as that it is hearsay, not the best evidence, or contrary to the parol evidence rule, are still frequently raised in ad hoc arbitration. To the extent that these and similar objections are intended to exclude the proffered evidence, they generally fail. The arbitrator is interested in getting all the relevant facts he can; his principal objective is to render a viable decision, and any information that adds to his knowledge of the total situation will almost always be admitted.

This is not to say, however, that the arbitrator will evaluate all the evidence on an equal basis. Even non-lawyers learn by experience that many of the legal rules of evidence are founded on common sense and fairness. Thus arbitrators, when interpreting a specific provision of a collective bargaining agreement, commonly give weight to evidence of alternative provisions offered and rejected during previous negotiations. Yet nothing will build a healthier respect for the wisdom of the parol evidence rule than a dispute between the parties over the meaning of a contract provision, in which one side adduces testimony purporting to show that the negotiators intended something different from what they wrote. Such testimony, invariably contradicted by the other side, serves only to confuse the arbitrator and to convince him that, for better or for worse, he must apply the disputed language as it is written.

Similarly, a competent arbitrator may be depended upon substantially to discount some kinds of hearsay evidence that he has admitted over objection. He will do so selectively, however, and not on the assumption that hearsay evidence, as such, is not to be credited. If, for example, a newly appointed personnel manager, or a recently elected business agent, offers a letter to his predecessor from a third party, the arbitrator is likely to ignore the fact that the evidence is hearsay; if satisfied that the document is genuine, he will give it such weight as its relevancy dictates. On the other hand, hearsay testimony about statements allegedly made by "the boys in the shop" or by executives in the "front office," though perhaps not excluded from the record by the arbitrator, probably will have no effect on his decision. . . .

In the matter of examining and cross-examining witnesses the rules and practices of the law courts are again, unfortunately, apt to be more of a hindrance than a help. The lawyer new to arbitration sometimes has difficulty understanding that the principal purpose of interrogating a witness is to develop, as quickly as possible, *all* the relevant facts, not merely a judicious selection of his own. To his dismay, the arbitrator may intervene at any time to bring out, through his own questions, the very points that counsel has been at great pains to avoid. Similarly, cross-examination is seldom restricted to matters covered on direct. The practice of cutting off a witness in mid-sentence with a curt "That's all" is definitely not observed, and some arbitrators make a point of asking the witness, at the conclusion of his examination, whether he has anything else he wants to say. They do so, not in the hope of developing more pertinent evidence, but simply in order to let the witness have his say, to "tell the arbitrator all about it." The practice has its drawbacks, particularly since arbitration seems to turn up a high percentage of witnesses suffering from the ability of total recall. Nevertheless, it directs attention once again to the fact that arbitration is part of the grievance procedure and, as such, serves more than one purpose. In addition to providing a forum for the final disposition of unresolved disputes, it permits the participants to blow off steam, to experience a catharsis that relaxes tempers and eases tensions.

NOTES

1. Consider the following cases where the question of arbitrability was raised before the arbitrator:

(a) In Trubitz Hardware & Electric Co., Inc. and United Mechanics, Local 150, 32 L.A. 930 (1959), the employee sought indemnification from the employer for legal costs resulting from an altercation which occurred while the employee was delivering a letter for the employer. It was ruled that the question was arbitrable under contract language pro-

viding that any matters in dispute between the parties, whether arising
from or outside of the agreement, shall be referred to arbitration.

(b) Where the agreement contained a provision barring discrimination against union stewards for performing their duties, it was ruled that
a complaint about a foreman's abusive language addressed to a steward
was arbitrable. Nationl Steel & Shipbuilding Co. and Iron Workers,
Shopmen's Local 627, 40 L.A. 125 (1963). What if the same language
had been addressed to a union committeeman?

(c) In John Deere Tractor Co. and Farm Equipment Workers, Local
241, 9 L.A. 73 (1947), the union sought to require the company to reinstate an employee who had been discharged for alleged incompetence
while he was still a probationary employee. The contract provided that
"nothing contained herein shall be construed so as to limit in any manner the right of the company to terminate finally and without recourse
to the Grievance Procedure the employment of any probationary employee for failure satisfactorily to meet job performance requirements."
The arbitrator ruled that the grievance was not arbitrable. If it could
be shown that the foreman had made periodic written reports to the personnel office stating that the employee's work had been either good or
satisfactory, and the discharge had occurred immediately after the employee had questioned the safety of a particular job assignment, would
the result be the same?

2. In Mosaic Tile Co. and Glass Workers, Local 79, 14 L.A. 953
(1950), the arbitrator found that the union's complaint over the operation of a particular incentive plan was a grievance under the collective
bargaining agreement. But he ruled the issue was not arbitrable because it fell within a provision of the contract expressly stating that the
arbitrator had "no authority over wage rates established by this agreement." His opinion stated in part (p. 960):

"Let it be said in closing that this arbitrator views with extreme reluctance an award of non-arbitrability. The function of a collective
agreement is essentially that of industrial self-government, and the grievance procedure with its culminating step of arbitration is the administrative mechanism which the parties have themselves set up to resolve all
their differences as to the meaning or application of that agreement.
Their contract should, wherever consistent with its language, be viewed
as a flexible body of principles capable of governing all relations between the company and the members of the bargaining unit for which
it was negotiated. . . . Where, however, the parties have expressly excluded from arbitration certain enumerated issues, an award of arbitrability of such issues would expose the arbitrator to the just criticism that
he was in fact writing into the contract a term the parties had agreed to
exclude."

3. Where the matter is one of meeting time limits within which a grievance must be filed or taken to the succeeding steps of the grievance
procedure, or some other procedural requirement written into the agreement, it is referred to as a question of procedural arbitrability. The following rulings will furnish some idea of the scope of this problem.

(a) In Olin Mathieson Chemical Corp. and Steelworkers, 37 L.A.

588 (1961), the agreement provided that a written grievance shall be given to the supervisor within two working days after the employee receives his initial oral answer. The employee was given a three-day disciplinary suspension on November 21; he protested at that time, and was told that the action would stand. He had been scheduled to work November 22 and 23, but a written grievance was not filed until November 25, November 24 being Thanksgiving. The arbitrator dismissed the grievance as being untimely. Compare Trinity Alps Lumber Co. and Sawmill Workers, Local 2608, 36 L.A. 1241 (1961), where the agreement provided that a grievance was to be "conclusively presumed waived" if not brought to the attention of the department head within three days or submitted in writing within one week from the time such grievance arose. The grievant was laid off for lack of work on June 30, the plant was shut down (but the office was open) from July 1 to July 10, and a written grievance protesting that the layoff was not in accordance with his seniority was filed July 11. The arbitrator ruled that the grievance was timely since the department head was off bear hunting from July 1 to July 4 and the plant shutdown effectively blocked the grievant from exercising his rights.

(b) Where the agreement specified only that all grievances should be filed within a reasonable time so that they may be promptly settled, a grievance protesting deprivation of seniority rights, which was filed almost seven months after the union was notified of the company's action, was found not subject to arbitration in the absence of extenuating circumstances. Walter Kidde & Co., Inc. and UAW, Local 146, 16 L.A. 369 (1951). Compare Carnegie-Illinois Steel Corp. and Steelworkers, 16 L.A. 794 (1951), ruling that under a provision requiring the prompt filing of written grievances, a delay of approximately seven months in filing a grievance respecting severance pay for displaced employees did not require the grievance to be dismissed as untimely where local representatives of both the union and the company were unfamiliar with the severance pay provision. If the agreement contains no reference to the time within which a grievance must be filed or appealed, should there be any limit?

(c) A grievance will not be considered untimely if the alleged violation is a continuing one. ACF Industries and IAM, Local Lodge 794, 38 L.A. 14 (1962).

C.   ILLUSTRATIVE ISSUES

(1)   Discipline and Discharge

BETHLEHEM STEEL CO. and STEELWORKERS, LOCAL 2601

41 L.A. 1152 (1963)

PORTER, Arbitrator:

This grievance protests a one-day penalty imposed upon X —, a Repairman in the Blast Furnace Mechanical Department, for his failure to wear safety glasses during a portion of the 7 to 3 turn, June 22, 1962. The Union contends the penalty was unjust, because of mitigating circumstances which, in its view, warranted X —'s decision to remove his glasses at the time in question.

The Union stresses at the outset its complete support for the Safety Program, including the safety glasses requirement involved here. It contends, however, that there must be exceptions to every rule and that X —'s case represents one of the permissible exceptions. The extenuating circumstances which, in its view, place this case in the exceptional category were as follows: X — and 2 or 3 other employees were assigned on this particular turn to replace a coke-carrying belt at No. 30 Gallery. This job entailed removing the old belt, pulling the new belt into position, clamping the ends of the new belt to pull the belt tight, cutting the ends of the belt squarely to permit proper splicing and then splicing the ends together. After the new belt had been pulled into position and clamped, it was X —'s job to make the cut using a razor-sharp tool designed for this purpose. X — testifies that when he began to make the cut his glasses were fogged and he could not see well enough to be sure of cutting along the line marked on the belt. He states further that even after he had taken off the glasses and cleaned them, the fogging still persisted and that he therefore decided to remove them while making the cut. This was necessary, according to the Union, in order to insure a straight cut and prevent X — from possibly cutting himself with the sharp tool.

The Union advances three primary arguments on the grievant's behalf. First, it contends that the atmosphere in #30 Gallery was particularly warm and humid on the turn in question. Secondly, it claims that X — is a special case because he perspires more easily than most employees. Thirdly, it argues that employees must be permitted to exercise their own discretion in some situations and that, here, X —'s exercise of discretion must be deemed reasonable because there was nothing in the immediate area where he was working which could have caused an eye injury.

In the Umpire's judgment none of the reasons cited by the Union can be accepted herein. With regard to the temperature and humidity conditions, the evidence shows that on June 22 the temperature in Buffalo ranged from 58°F to 81°F with an average of 70°F for the day, while the humidity ranged from 40 to 80 with a median of 60. The incident occurred at 10:30 A.M., well before the normal peak temperature of the day, and in an area which is reasonably well ventilated and free of artificial heat or humidity-producing processes. The Umpire cannot, therefore, accept the Union's claim that atmospheric conditions were, in part, responsible for the grievant's decision to remove his safety glasses.

As for the grievant's alleged proneness to perspire freely, the Umpire finds that this protest comes too late to be accepted. The record shows that the Company provides sweat bands and an anti-fogging solution to prevent the kind of condition the grievant maintains to be a chronic problem for him. Yet the grievant has never sought to use either of these devices to minimize his alleged tendency toward profuse perspiration. In these circumstances, his claim cannot be accepted at face value.

Last but not least, the Umpire cannot sustain the Union's plea for the exercise of individual employee discretion. Obviously, a safety program based upon permitting thousands of employees to decide when they may safely remove their glasses would be doomed to fail from the outset. True, Supervision in the Blast Furnace Mechanical Department has told the employees that there must be room for employees to use their heads in this matter. But it has also made clear that consent from Supervision must be obtained before an employee may undertake to remove his glasses.

Beyond these general considerations, the record shows the following further facts tending to support the imposition of a 1-day suspension: 1) that the safety glasses requirement was first instituted in this department in May 1961; 2) that it encountered considerable employee resistance in the first year; 3) that repeated warnings by Supervision, including at least one prior warning to grievant X —, proved ineffective in overcoming this resistance; 4) that Supervision thereupon announced that henceforth violators of the rule would be given time off; and 5) that, on the very morning on which X — was found working without his glasses, Supervision held a safety meeting for the express purpose of stressing, again, the importance of strict employee adherence to the safety glasses program. In the light of these facts, the Umpire finds that Supervision was fully justified in giving the grievant a day off for the infraction in question.

AWARD

The grievance is denied.

ACME INDUSTRIAL CO. and UNITED AUTOMOBILE, ETC., WORKERS, LOCAL 310

41 L.A. 1176 (1964)

[According to the company's report of the incident, the grievant was persistently whistling loudly in his department and had been cautioned about this on May 8, 1963. On May 13, the supervisor told the grievant to stop whistling and reminded him of the earlier warning. The grievant then began to sing in a loud voice. When taken to the industrial relations office, the grievant reportedly became argumentative and insolent. He was thereupon discharged. The discipline clause of the agreement provided as follows: "The Company's right to issue warning notices, demote, suspend, or discharge may only be exercised for just cause. The Company is committed to the principle of corrective discipline. Any disciplinary action, cause of which has not been repeated within a nine (9) month period, shall be erased from the employee's record."]

UPDEGRAFF, Arbitrator. . . .

When it is observed that this entire matter originated over the usually unimportant but sometimes objectionable habit of whistling while at work the entire incident at first impression appears to be wholly unimportant.   It is to be recalled, however, while ordinary whistling itself is usually disregarded, it and many other acts in disobedience to a clear, reasonable direction of a supervisor may assume very substantial importance.   Much depends upon where, how, and why certain conduct is being carried on and also upon the circumstances and the manner in which a direction of a management representative is rejected by an employee.

A fairly lengthy and detailed hearing was held on the matter at hand.   Impressions from the same lead to the conclusions that X — apparently returned to work after a recent strike with some deep resentment that the same had taken place and had lasted a considerable time, in fact some seven months.   From descriptions given at the hearing he whistled very loudly and very close to the desk of the foreman. He was asked to curb or to stop this extraordinary whistling.   He defiantly stated that he would not do so and called the foreman in the presence of numerous other employees "a nobody."   X —'s whistling, contrary to arguments of his counsel, appears to have been unusually shrill and loud.   The foreman testified that, after several informal verbal warnings a more formal verbal warning was given X — and a written "Incident Report" was handed him, as quoted above.   This was corroborated by Mr. Frank Larr, another management witness.   Despite this he continued to whistle with unusual loudness to the obvious annoyance of his supervisor and in defiance of directions.   The Industrial Relations Manager Mr. T. J. Bellush went to the floor where X — worked to discuss the matter with him on May 9 and he agreed to stop it, but the unfortunate disturbance was soon resumed thereafter.

In the office of Mr. Bellush on May 13, X — was told that he would have to discontinue his loud whistling and singing to the annoyance of his supervisor and apparently to the disturbance of some other coworkers.   He became loudly and openly defiant and as a result management representatives felt there was no alternate but to discharge him for insubordination to his foreman and to the Industrial Relations Manager.

It would have been suitable conduct under the circumstances for X — to discontinue whistling and singing while at work and to file a grievance indicating that his Foreman, Harold Larson, was unreasonably denying him the privilege to whistle and to sing while at work in such manner as might reasonably be carried on.   This he chose not to do but rather adopted a hostile, defiant and uncooperative attitude.

The company urged that a discharge in a case like this should not he thought of as a termination of employment for merely whistling. Ordinary whistling in and of itself would certainly furnish no basis for discharge if a reasonable direction to curb the same was respected and obeyed.   On the other hand, a stubborn, unswerving insistence upon loudly whistling or singing to the known and intended disturbance or distraction of other employees or of a supervisor, constituted an interference with efficiency and an obstruction to production just as much as would certain types of physical misconduct involved in disobedience.

There can be no doubt that while the dignity of the individual worker and his right to human, courteous and intelligent treatment are today assured and while he is entitled to have his working conditions and compensations collectively bargained by able representatives of his own choosing, it still remains a fact that an employee while at work is obligated to obey all reasonable directions from managerial representatives. The conduct of X — in persisting to whistle to the annoyance of his supervisor after having been told not to do so is misconduct. There is no doubt that X — was obligated as an employee of the company to take reasonable directions from his foreman in respect to personal conduct while at work. It was untrue and highly improper for him to say, as the evidence indicates he did say to the foreman, "Who do you think you are? You're just a nobody," and to assert that he did not, "Have to take orders from anybody."

Despite the fact that X — was in grievous error in these matters it does appear that a discharge under the circumstances may well be termed "unjust" because of its extremely severe nature. Had the company imposed a disciplinary suspension and found thereafter that X — still persisted in his attitude, discharge would then seem to have been mature and proper. Moreover, the grievance procedure set forth in Article IV of the agreement had not been followed, probably because the strike had resulted in some union officers not yet having returned to work.

In view of the foregoing the arbitrator believes that the employee should have an opportunity to adapt himself to the rules and regulations of the employer if he desires to do so and to show that he can adopt an attitude of respect and obedience to his Supervisor. There seems to be a good reason to believe that despite the incidents discussed herein, X — may change his attitude and develop into a desirable employee.

AWARD

It is awarded that X — is reinstated to his employment with seniority but without back pay. It is further awarded that the entire period said X — has been off the pay roll shall be regarded as a period of well-deserved disciplinary suspension.

BUICK YOUNGSTOWN CO. and INTERNATIONAL ASSN. OF MACHINISTS, LODGE 1519
41 L.A. 570 (1963)

[The portion of the arbitrator's opinion dealing with the effect of an NLRB ruling on an unfair labor practice charge filed by the grievant himself has been omitted.]

DWORKIN, Arbitrator. . . .

On Friday, August 24, at the end of the grievant's shift, while cleaning up in the washroom, he observed a smoldering blaze adjacent to the body shop. He completely ignored the hazardous condition and made no effort to extinguish the fire, or to notify his foreman. The fire was close to debris and volatile liquids, and other combustible material. The condition was simultaneously observed by other employees, and was extinguished before it could gain headway. The condition is described by the company as being imminently dangerous. It could have resulted in an explosion and a general conflagration, if left unchecked. Following an investigation of the incident, the company concluded that the grievant was grossly negligent, and indifferent to his responsibilities, resulting in a disciplinary discharge on Monday, August 27.

The company's investigation showed that the grievant discovered the fire a few minutes before quitting time, but refused to render any assistance in eliminating the danger. He proceeded to sign out his time card, and left the premises. The fire was in close proximity to an old wooden shack which abuts to the body shop, in which are stored acetyline and oxygen tanks, and paint supplies.

No damage actually resulted due to the prompt action of other employees. However, the potential damage could have been the destruction of the property, and the loss of the company's facilities, which would have resulted in extensive loss of time to many employees.

The company determined that discharge was warranted by reason of the seriousness of the incident, and the grievant's complete lack of loyalty to his job, and his indifference to the welfare of his fellow employees. The company states that the fact that the grievant was a shop steward had no bearing upon its decision to discharge.

The union protests the discharge on the ground that just cause was lacking, and in any event, the penalty was too severe. The union concedes that the grievant discovered the blaze outside the shop window, and left the premises without taking any precautionary measures. However, he was aware that other employees had observed the condition, and had promptly put out the fire, thereby eliminating the danger. Three fellow employees extinguished the fire with the use of hand fire extinguishers. They also reported the condition to the foreman.

The grievant himself testified that he did nothing concerning the hazard, and accounted for his indifference in several ways. He remarked at one point, "Firemen get paid for putting out fires, not me." He stated at the hearing, "I wasn't going out to the fire near an old gas tank and risk my life putting out a fire."

The grievant attributes his discharge to the hostility of the foreman resulting from the grievant's activities as a union steward. He represents that he has been an aggressive and militant union officer and had made persistent demands for wage adjustments for body shop employees. These claims are advanced by way of proof that the company was ulteriorly motivated in its decision to terminate his employment with the company.

Finally, the union urges that the discharge was the result of a misunderstanding as regards the fire incident, which was aggravated by an incorrect and distorted description of the events on the part of fellow employees.   In view of all the circumstances, the discharge is inconsistent with the contract, and fails to conform to the concept of just cause.

There is no question but that the grievant's conduct was highly objectionable, and warranted corrective discipline.   His calloused and indifferent attitude in face of the imminent danger was wholly inconsistent with his duties and responsibilities as an employee.   These obligations extend beyond performing the duties of his job.   His refusal to render assistance in putting out the fire constituted a breach of the obligations implied in the employment relationship.   The fact that other employees responded to the situation, thereby preventing potential loss, does not excuse the grievant's disregard for the elemental principles inherent in the employment relationship.   These standards of behavior need not be spelled out in the employee's job description, or in the contract.   The grievant's conduct constituted gross carelessness, wholly at variance with common sense standards.   His attitude is best summed up in his own words, "fire extinguishing is not part of my job description."   His attitude reflects complete disloyalty towards the employer's interests.   His refusal to aid in extinguishing the smoldering blaze was due to his arbitrary indifference to the consequences which directly affected his own security, the jobs of his fellow employees, and the company's property, and ability to stay in business.   His attitude and behavior were directly contrary to his position of leadership as a union steward.

The Chairman concludes that the grievant's conduct presented just cause for termination of employment.   He proved himself to be unconcerned and demonstrably hostile to the employer's legitimate interests. In face of a potentially dangerous situation, he cavalierly chose to do nothing whatsoever to eliminate the danger.   He failed to act as a reasonably prudent employee, and defaulted in maintaining the normal standards of the employee relationship.

Finally, there is no factual basis supporting the charge that the company was motivated by anti-union bias, or that its action was due to the grievant's activities as a union steward.   The relationship between the union and the company has been excellent, as indicated by the fact that the instant case presents the only grievance filed by any employee.   In view of all the circumstances, just cause existed, and the grievance will be denied.

Award

1. The dismissal of the unfair practice complaint by the NLRB does not operate to preclude the processing of a grievance by the employee or the union based upon the same subject matter; the NLRB proceedings do not constitute a bar to the consideration of the grievance arising under the terms of the collective bargaining agreement, nor do such proceedings affect the jurisdiction of the Board of Arbitration as set forth in the contract.

2. The discharge of the grievant is supported by just cause as contemplated by the contract; the grievant's conduct was grossly irresponsible and failed to conform to the obligations which are inherent in the employment relationship.

NOTES

1. According to most surveys, discipline and discharge cases still make up by far the largest segment of grievances filed and cases appealed to arbitration. All manner of situations arise, reflecting the myriad facets of human nature as they come to the surface in the everyday course of human relations in the plant.

If an employee vents his feelings by hitting a foreman, there is not much doubt about the outcome. See National Castings Co. and UAW, Local 350, 41 L.A. 442 (1963), where the discharge was sustained for striking a foreman and then throwing a casting at him as he retreated. Of course, if the foreman struck the grievant first, the situation might be substantially different. Other aspects involve even-handed treatment of the employees, fair warning for relatively minor infractions, and compliance with any prescribed disciplinary procedure. The following decisions illustrate a few of these situations:

Rockwell-Standard Corp. and Allied Industrial Workers, Local 109, 41 L.A. 345 (1963), in which discharge was considered too severe for sleeping on the job where the employee had no prior infractions and a lesser penalty had been imposed in prior sleeping incidents involving other employees.

Butler County Mushroom Farms and Mushroom Growers, Local 21954, 41 L.A. 568 (1963), involving horseplay which resulted in injury to a fellow employee. Since this was the employee's first infraction, it was ruled that discharge was too severe.

Babcock & Wilcox Co. and Steelworkers, Local 3059, 41 L.A. 862 (1963), in which the plant rules prescribed progressive penalties and notice of intent to discharge at the time of a disciplinary suspension. It was held that discharge was improper in the absence of such a notice.

2. Discipline problems are handled by various methods in other countries. See Symposium on Comparative Labor Law, Part Two: Settlement of Disputes Concerning the Exercise of Employer Disciplinary Power, 18 Rutgers L. Rev. 407 (1964). Under the Italian legal system, an employer's disciplinary power is regulated primarily by the collective contract, which frequently provides for a fine as one of the sanctions for an employee's misbehavior. The fine, paid through the employer's retention of the employee's pay check, is assigned to a social institution. Italian Report, 18 Rutgers L. Rev. 458, 460 (1964). On the other hand, disciplinary power in Hungary is governed by the Labor Code, which specifies the persons entitled to exercise jurisdiction over discipline, the acts and omissions that are considered disciplinary offenses (including violation of the rules of socialist coexistence), and the disciplinary sanctions and procedures. Hungarian law does not permit the levy of a

fine. Hungarian Report, 18 Rutgers L. Rev. 467-470 (1964). In Russia labor discipline problems, such as lateness or absenteeism, may come before Comrades' Courts. These nonjudicial courts in business enterprises may order the offender to make a public apology, or administer a warning or reprimand, or recommend transfer to a lower-paying job. The Comrades' Court may not impose a fine for violation of labor discipline. See Berman and Spindler, Soviet Comrades' Courts, 38 Wash. L. Rev. 842 (1963).

(2)   Assignment of Overtime

BABCOCK & WILCOX CO. and STEELWORKERS, LOCAL 3059
32 L.A. 830 (1959)

DUFF, Arbitrator. . . .

On the dates involved the Company scheduled one Electrician and one Millwright to work, and the three Grievants (who are Electricians) claim that they should have been scheduled to perform the work. The Company's written statement of overtime policy issued on September 26, 1958, by G. W. Kross, Jr., Plant Superintendent, states in part, as follows:

"When overtime is required on any job to which a man is regularly assigned, the man regularly assigned shall be eligible for the overtime assignment . . ."

On November 15, 1958, eight hours of work, principally on cranes was jointly performed by the scheduled Electrician and Millwright. On November 22, 1958 three and one half hours of repair work on cranes was performed by the Electrician and Millwright. On November 28, 1958, both the Electrician and the Millwright jointly performed work for two hours on an overhead Heater. During the remaining portion of the eight hour shift on each of the two days, the Electrician and Millwright performed entirely separate duties. The focal point of the present dispute is the claim that the Company assigned a Millwright to perform work which should have been performed by an Electrician.

The Union claims that work on the crane should not have been performed by a Millwright on November 15th and November 22nd and that the Millwright should not have performed any work on the overhead heating equipment on November 28th. In each case the Union claims that a second Electrician should have performed the work. Therefore, the Union requests that each of the three Grievants (Electricians) be compensated for one day's work at the appropriate rate.

The Company contends that its manner of scheduling work was proper and that no provision of the Contract, past practice or provision of any job description prohibits the work assignments which were made on the days involved.

This case cannot be resolved by a simple interpretation of the Contract. Even in an industrial union, where hard and fast craft lines are not observed with the rigidity that they are in some other unions, the competitive urge between employees in the various job classifications to assert their claims to available extra work is entirely understandable. However, for its exclusive convenience, the Company cannot deprive one group of employees of available work and assign that work to another group without reference to the job classification regularly assigned to the work involved. The Company's written statement dated September 26, 1958, clearly states its position: when overtime work is required, it will be awarded to the man regularly assigned to that work.

It is necessary to examine carefully the precise facts of the present case. The Job Description and Classification Manual of January 1, 1958, contains (page 38) the following provision:

"8. The inherent nature of assigned maintenance work is such that the job content requirements of assigned maintenance jobs may vary from day to day within any given assigned area and as between areas: and, to achieve maximum productivity in any given area, employees engaged therein are called upon to perform varying duties in discharging the responsibilities of their assignments. Therefore:"

On its job description form the Company, following the steel industry pattern, sets forth at the bottom of each job description the following:

"The above statement reflects the general details considered necessary to describe the principal functions of the job identified, and shall not be construed as a detailed description of all of the work requirements that may be inherent in the job."

Under the Millwright job descriptions (Union Exhibits 5 and 6), a Millwright is entrusted with prime responsibility for all maintenance and repair work of a general mechanical nature. Union Exhibits 3 and 4 state that an Electrician is responsible for maintenance jobs of a general electrical repair nature.

The Union asserts that the Electricians and Millwrights work together in normal shifts only when an emergency arises. The Company insists that their cooperative effort extends to other jobs that are of a non-emergency nature. On a regular shift either two Electricians and two Millwrights or three Electricians and three Millwrights are assigned to maintenance work; and from the evidence produced at the Hearing, it is clear to us that there is an inevitable overlapping of duties of Millwrights and Electricians on such items as cranes and similar electrical equipment that could be in need of mechanical or electrical repairs.

Millwrights are responsible for the regular inspection, maintenance, and repair of all the machinery and equipment in the plant. The job description for Electricians clearly includes crane repair work as a responsibility of Electricians, and although the Millwrights job description does not specifically name cranes, the description is broad enough to include cranes, particularly, when we consider the provision that job descriptions "shall not be construed as a detailed description of all of the work requirements."

The Union admits this, in part, because where welding or burning is involved, only the Millwright performs the work, even though it occurs on a crane. Wiring and work on motors, switches, and other strictly electrical components unquestionably belong to employees in the Electrician classification. The "border line" work of replacing or repairing wheels, shafts, bearings, etc., on cranes, while basically mechanical work, very frequently has been performed by Electricians.

The job descriptions and other evidence presented at the Hearing as to the working practices at this Plant, require us to find as a fact that on such borderline work neither classification had exclusive jurisdiction. Electricians frequently perform the work because a crane is basically an electrical apparatus. However, the Millwrights have prime responsibility for mechanical work on all equipment in the Plant. Such fringe duties as placing spacers in a bridge trailer wheel, changing trolley drive wheels, or the installation of a new bushing, while performed on the crane, do not belong exclusively to either classification.

It is understandable that employees in each job classification desire to obtain all available work, particularly premium pay work and work during curtailed-production periods when they have not been scheduled to work for a full week. However, in deciding disputes such as the present one, it is appropriate to recall at least one of the underlying reasons for establishing industrial-type unions in the steel industry. The realization that some craft unions, with rigid classifications of skills, could generate production-disrupting jurisdictional disputes, convinced many that the industrial-type union was better adapted to the realities of production in the steel industry where a close blending of one job duty into another not infrequently creates areas in which no classification has exclusive jurisdiction. Traditionally, industrial unions, while not completely eliminating job classes (because to do so would, among other things, destroy negotiated pay differentials) have seldom insisted upon rigid and inflexible adherence to job classifications and duties.

It is necessary for us to observe the circumstances in which the present case arose. On the days involved a very limited production crew was working. The normal complement of men on production work would have been approximately one hundred, but this complement had been reduced to three production employees who operated the Draw Bench. Maintenance work varies on a day to day basis and consequently the Company was not able to forecast accurately what repairs would be necessary.

With such a fractional production crew, the Company's action in scheduling one Electrician and one Millwright appears equitable to both classifications. If a full complement of production workers had been present, either two or three employees in each of the Electrician and Millwright classifications would have been on duty. Thus the ratio of maintenance workers to production workers on the days involved was extremely high when compared with normal production days. Under such conditions of extremely limited production, the required cooperation between Electrician and Millwright could be expected to be rather close. If the Company had scheduled two Electricians to work on the days involved, there would not have been work for more than one of them.

We find in this case that the nature of the work performed was not within the exclusive jurisdiction of Electricians but that the duties were on the borderline between that classification and the Millwright classification. Under all the circumstances present on the three days involved, the Company was justified in assigning the work to either job classification.

AWARD

Having heard and considered all the evidence submitted at the Hearing and the arguments of both parties, we hereby award as follows:
1. The three Grievances are dismissed.

TORRINGTON MANUFACTURING CO. and UAW, LOCAL 507
33 L.A. 592 (1959)

[This case was submitted to the Connecticut State Board of Mediation and Arbitration.]

DONNELLY and GALLAGHER, Arbitrators:

[The issue is:] Was the assignment of the employees in the Wheel Department between the hours of 12:15 and 5:15 on Saturday, March 21, 1959, in accord with the provisions of the Agreement?

Contract Clauses Involved:

ARTICLE IV — MANAGEMENT

"The Management of the Company has the sole right to manage its business, including, but not limited to, the right to decide the machine and tool equipment, the products to be manufactured, the method of manufacturing, the schedules of production, the processes of manufacture and assembly, the location of plants, to determine the extent and manner in which the plant shall be operated; to maintain order and efficiency in its plants and operations; to hire, lay-off, assign, transfer, recall and to suspend and discharge for proper cause, subject only to the specific agreements and conditions herein provided."

ARTICLE VII — HOURS, OVERTIME AND PREMIUM PAY

"Section 5. The Company agrees to effectuate an impartial distribution of working time within the same departmental occupational group and to reasonably equalize working time among the members of such groups over each three (3) month period commencing with the date of Contract."

On March 21, it was necessary to schedule overtime work for setup men in the Wheel Department. The Company scheduled six men from the first shift to work from 7:00 to 12:00, and four men from the second shift to work from 12:15 to 5:15. One of the four who worked during the second five hours had worked the first five hours also, but he had experience on a particular machine and, for that reason was needed by the Company. A second was a regular second-shift setup man. Th other two setup men who worked the second five hours are from the Fan Department, but who at one time had worked in the Wheel Department as setup men.

The Union states that the Company violated provisions of Article VII, Section 5, when it distributed overtime hours to employees of the Fan Department. The Agreement states specifically that these hours are to be divided equally among "the same departmental occupational group" and, accordingly, this work should have been given to setup men of the Wheel Department who were available for assignment.

The Company states that all available setup men were given the opportunity to work either five hours in the morning or five hours in the afternoon of March 21. Five hours of work were assigned on each of the two shifts. When the Superintendent of Assembly came in Saturday morning, he learned that one setup man of the second shift had gone home sick the day before and would not be in for the second five hours. When he learned that the amount of work to be done would now demand two additional setup men, he called two second-shift men from the Fan Department.

The Company states that the Management Clause gives the Company the right to assign and transfer employees except as otherwise provided in the Agreement. Article VII, Section 5, obliges the Company only to an impartial distribution of overtime, which means that the Company must not discriminate in the manner in which overtime is distributed. It also obliges the Company to a reasonably equal distribution of overtime, and the Company claims that there is no evidence that the Company has failed to equalize overtime hours.

There is no evidence that the Company has not attempted to equalize the distribution of overtime as provided in Article VII, Section 5. But here that is not the question. The question is whether or not the Company has the right to assign overtime hours of the Wheel Department to employees of the Fan Department.

Article VII, Section 5, does provide for an "impartial distribution" of overtime hours and for a reasonable equalization of these hours. However, a substantive provision of Article VII, Section 5, is the provision that this "working time" will be distributed "within the same departmental, occupational group." Clearly, this means that overtime setup work of the Wheel Department must be distributed among setup men of the Wheel Department if they are available and capable of doing the necessary work. The Union testified without contradiction that aside from this instance this has always been the policy of the Company under this clause of the Agreement.

In the instant case the Superintendent testified he did not offer this work to the setup men of the Wheel Department. Some of the setup men of the Wheel Department were in the plant and available. Yet, instead of offering them the overtime work, the Company called in two employees from outside the Wheel Department. In doing so, the Company failed its obligation in Article VII, Section 5, to distribute working time within a department "within the same departmental occupational group." There is no evidence here of any circumstance which would justify the Company departing from its clear obligation under the Agreement.

AWARD

The assignment of employees in the Wheel Department between the hours of 12:15 and 5:15 on Saturday, March 21, 1959, was not in accord with the provisions of the Agreement.

McDONOUGH, Arbitrator, dissenting:

I disagree with the majority decision because it is based on an improper interpretation of Section 5 of Article VII.

The decision ascribes a duty to the Employer of distributing all working time of each departmental group to that group only, to the exclusion of any other employee.

Section 5 of Article VII requires the Employer to see to it that whatever work is assigned to the same departmental occupational group is impartially distributed. This is the only requirement. This article is entitled "Hours' Overtime and Premium Pay" and that is what it should apply to, not to any claimed job or occupational right. For these reasons I believe the award should have affirmed the action of the Company in assigning these employees as part of their right to manage.

NOTE

Gorton-Pew Fisheries and Longshoremen, 16 L.A. 365 (1951), and Lockheed Aircraft Corp. and IAM, District Lodge 33, 31 L.A. 659 (1958), involved overtime grievances. In each, the arbitrator's award was based upon an earlier award. Between the earlier award and the current case new agreements had been negotiated without any change in the provisions on which the earlier awards were based. When similar grievances arose under the new agreements, the arbitrators deferred to the earlier rulings.

These decisions afford a good basis for understanding the principle of stare decisis as it arises in arbitration. Both arbitrators pointed out that they might have decided otherwise if it were not for the earlier awards. Generally speaking, arbitrators are not considered bound by earlier awards. But in these cases where the union failed to obtain any change in the prior rule during intervening negotiations, the arbitrators felt that for them to change the rule would be to give the union a result it could not achieve in collective bargaining.

(3)   Management Rights

BROUGHTON'S FARM DAIRY and TEAMSTERS, LOCAL 175
41 L.A. 1189 (1963)

[X had been a retail milk route salesman for the company for approximately ten years. At the end of June, 1963, his employment was terminated and the route which he had serviced was "sold" to him under an oral arrangement referred to as "bobtailing." At the same time he signed a conditional sales contract to buy the company truck he had been driving for $3100, title to the truck remaining in the company. He also signed a promissory note for the total amount of accounts receivable on his route. The union grieved, claiming that the company's action was a violation of the collective bargaining agreement between the parties and demanding that X and his route be returned to previous status.]

TEPLE, Arbitrator. . . .

Subcontracting is one of the most difficult, and at the same time one of the most frequent, subjects to come before courts and arbitrators in the course of interpreting collective bargaining agreements. The Arbitrator is well aware of the complexities involved and the many diverse opinions upon this broad subject, having had occasion to render decisions in a rather wide variety of situations involving subcontracting of one sort or another . . .

On the first question presented in this case, that of arbitrability, there is little, if any, doubt about the correct answer.

In this Agreement, a grievance is defined as "any controversy, complaint, misunderstanding, or dispute," and any unsettled grievance may be appealed to arbitration (Article X). That a dispute exists between the parties in this case, concerning the Company's right to bobtail the route in question, cannot seriously be denied. Neither can it be correctly said that the dispute is not one of substance. The Arbitrator has no authority to limit the effect of the broad language the parties themselves have used.

Even under a more limited definition, the better view, in the Arbitrator's opinion, is that a challenge of the employer's right to subcontract work is an arbitrable issue. This has been the almost unanimous view of arbitrators. See the learned discussion in Celanese Corp. of America, 33 L.A. 925; also Pacific Laundry & Dry Cleaning Co., Ltd., 39 L.A. 676, and Pittsburgh Steel Co., 61-3 ARB, par. 8656, at p. 5995, cited by the Company in another connection. The courts have been divided. See, Black-Clawson Co., 34 L.A. 215, 218, as well as Celanese Corp., and Pacific Laundry, supra. But the judicial view is more settled since the decision of the United States Supreme Court in Warrior & Gulf, 363 U.S. 574.

In the Arbitrator's opinion, the question raised in this case is clearly arbitrable.

The situation in this case illustrates quite well the inconsistent position which parties frequently take respecting the implications to be drawn from their collective bargaining agreement. The contract between these parties contains neither a management rights clause nor any express prohibition against subcontracting. The Company argues that certain inherent rights to manage the business must nevertheless be recognized, while at the same time urging that it would be highly improper to suggest any limitation upon such rights unless the Agreement specifically so provides. The Union, on the other hand, wants to impose an unwritten limitation while denying the Company the right to turn a finger unless the Agreement specifically grants the right to do so.

In the Arbitrator's view, any collective bargaining agreement must carry with it certain basic implications. One of these is the basic assumption that the employer has the right to run the business in the most efficient way possible. A management rights clause may affirm this basic assumption, and may be of assistance in detailing some of the powers which this right embraces, but the absence thereof cannot take away the very reason for the employer's existence.

By the same token, when a collective bargaining agreement is executed, the parties must be considered to have agreed upon the scope of the bargaining unit and the basic integrity thereof. Numerous decisions have recognized this principle, both in the course of upholding the employer's right to subcontract and in denying that right under the circumstances of the particular case. . . . In National Electric Coil [62-2 ARB, par. 8360], it was pointed out that the janitor services there involved were at most an adjunct of the employer's primary function, and that the basic integrity of the bargaining unit had not been adversely affected. From this Arbitrator's examination of the cases, it is both the overwhelming and the correct view that some limitation upon the employer's right to send work outside of the bargaining unit must be recognized. One of the arbitrators cited with approval by the Company said: "The one principle that does stand out in the study of subcontracting cases is that few, if any, arbitrators will take the position that in the absence of a subcontracting provision in the agreement, the Company's right to contract out is absolute and unlimited." Olin Mathieson Chemical Corp., 61-3 ARB, par. 8653, at p. 5984.

This Arbitrator has followed the view expressed and applied by most arbitrators that subcontracting may be utilized in proper cases. Although some arbitrators have professed to detect a change in the trend of opinion in subcontracting cases, a recent re-examination of the subject supported a denial of any such basic change of viewpoint. The decision of the Court of Appeals in UAW v. Webster Electric Co., 299 F.2d 195, has failed to influence arbitral opinion. In this connection, see Allis Chalmers Mfg. Co., 39 L.A. 1213, 1217. [Cases taking both sides in the subcontracting issue published since the arbitrator's award in Square D Co., 37 L.A. 892, are here listed.]

A review of these decisions, like those outlined in previous opinions already cited, lends weight to the conclusion that it has been largely the adjunct type of service where the subcontracting has been upheld, such as repairs and maintenance of an intermittent or so-called "one shot" nature, janitorial service, cafeteria service provided for the convenience of the employees, hauling (where that is not one of the primary functions of the business), snow removal or special clean-up work, the operations of repair of special rented equipment, and the like. It is clearer than ever to this Arbitrator that the most consistent thread running through the decisions upholding the employer's action is the conclusion that the bargaining unit will not be jeopardized by the action taken, either in principle or in fact.

As noted in the earlier opinions, it has frequently been suggested that good faith is the test.   There has also been an interesting and recurring reference to the reasonableness of the employer's action.   An early and excellent expression of this as a test is to be found in National Tube Co., 17 L.A. 790.   In the opinion in that case, the Arbitrator clearly pointed out that there is an implied condition of the agreement that the employer will not arbitrarily reduce the scope of the bargaining unit by contracting out work normally performed by employees within the unit.   The question in each case, it was said, must be determined on the basis of whether the employer acted reasonably.   Since the parties had failed to consider the issue on this basis in the course of the grievance procedure, the particular dispute was referred back to the parties for further negotiations. The work in that case involved window washing and slag removal.

In a much more recent decision, the Arbitrator pointed out that the employer's affirmative case for any particular decision to subcontract work must be weighed against the impact that decision has upon the integrity of the collective bargaining agreement.   Arranging on an ad hoc basis for an outside contractor to cut particular needed pipe and to machine a piece of laboratory equipment, it was ruled, was not a violation of the agreement in that case since it was safely within the limits of reasonableness.   KVP Sutherland Paper Co., 40 L.A. 737. . . .

Without suggesting that there is any clear line of consistency in the great mass of arbitral decisions, in many of the awards in which the subcontracting was found to be a violation of the agreement the work was considered to be more of an integral part of the employer's business.   In Vulcan Rivet & Bolt Corp., 36 L.A. 871, the nutting of T-head bolts was considered to be production work which had not been subcontracted previously and which was sent out of the plant at a time when the bargaining unit employee who normally did such work was on layoff.   In Gaslight Club, 34 L.A. 14, it was specifically found that the porter's work in question was an integral part of the restaurant operation there under consideration.   The hauling work involved in Dow Metal Products Co., 40 L.A. 27, was in the plant and closely related to the production process.   Likewise, the drilling work subcontracted in Niagara Weldments Inc., 63-1 ARB, par. 8062, which had been done by the Company in the past and could have been accomplished on machinery which the Company owned. . . .

In Pet Milk Co., 33 L.A. 278, it was ruled that the employer had violated the agreement by subcontracting for the shipment of its ice cream mix from plant to customers by truck since over-the-road hauling of the product was work with respect to which the parties negotiated and which the employees, therefore, had the exclusive right to perform.   The nature of the work was the basic test, it was said.   The parties bargain for certain work, and the underlying assumption which forms the basis for the entire agreement, according to this well known arbitrator, is that the work involved is to be performed by the employees.

Another recent illustration can be found in Pacific Laundry & Dry Cleaning Co., Ltd., 39 L.A. 676, where the Company had unilaterally discontinued the night shift and subcontracted the work thereof to a closely affiliated subsidiary which rehired the laid off employees at non-Union wages and under non-Union conditions. The Arbitrator found a violation of the Agreement, the employer having failed, it was said, to meet the tests of reasonableness and good faith.

There have been a few decisions specifically involving situations where employees were transferred to contractor status. In Journal Publishing Co., 22 L.A. 108, a newspaper publisher accepted the resignations of a number of district managers and dealermen who were included within the bargaining unit, and then entered into individual buyer-seller agreements with them whereby they were said to have become independent contractors. The Arbitrator found that such unilateral action violated the agreement since the effect thereof was to remove jobs from the bargaining unit and thus to create a change in the parties' relationship which could properly be made only after negotiation and agreement with the Union. On the other hand, in Washington Post Co., 23 L.A. 728, it was found that the publisher did not violate the agreement by entering into individual dealer agreements with persons who had been circulation managers within the bargaining unit, thereby changing their status from employees to independent contractors, the Arbitrator concluding that the action was not designed to weaken the Union.

In Chupka v. Lorenz-Schneider Co., 51 L.R.R.M. 2376, 39 L.A. 576, the New York Court of Appeals held that driver-salesmen to whom the employer had transferred sales routes were not deprived of property rights without due process where the state court had confirmed an arbitration award holding that the transfer of the routes violated the collective bargaining agreement and directed their return to the Union bargaining unit. In Sloan v. Journal Publishing Co., 42 L.R.R.M. 2490, 30 L.A. 884, the Oregon Supreme Court reached a different result in a case where the Union chose to picket and threaten a strike in an effort to force the employer to comply with the award, and this was enjoined.

A somewhat different situation was involved in Remington Rand, 39 L.A. 552, quoted at some length by the Company, where a dealer-agency was set up to handle sales and service work previously done by the employees of a district office, in accordance with the employer's practice over a period of many years. Independent agencies, somewhat like auto dealerships, already existed in many parts of the country. In this instance, the Company's action was upheld. The dealership was an entirely separate organization, incorporated under state law and not composed of employees from the discontinued district office.

In the Adams Dairy case, 54 L.R.R.M. 3171, recently decided by the 8th Circuit Court of Appeals, it was held that the decision of a dairy company on economic grounds to terminate the distribution of its products through driver-salesmen, and to accomplish this distribution through others, was not a required subject of collective bargaining under Section 8(a)(5) of the Labor Management Relations Act. The court was chiefly concerned with the question of the employer's intent, and held that an unfair labor practice could not properly be found without first finding some illegal motivation. It is also noted that according to the Court's statement of the facts, the Company had been accomplishing its sales to retail outlets through independent distributors in many of the areas which it served prior to the change of method for the balance of its routes. That a finding in an unfair practice case may be neither controlling nor persuasive in a case concerned with the interpretation of the collective bargaining agreement is well illustrated in Penick & Ford Ltd., 38 L.A. 869, another decision cited by the Company, where the situation was reversed and the Arbitrator upheld the subcontracting of the work there involved despite an NLRB finding of an unfair labor practice arising out of the same circumstances.

The fact that the Union in this case sought to obtain a specific and rather detailed prohibition on the subject of subcontracting, as a part of a proposed redraft of the entire agreement, in the Arbitrator's opinion is not as important a factor as the Company suggests. It is well known that collective bargaining agreements frequently need clarification or elucidation, and the parties may endeavor to strengthen their position on either side of the table by language which is designed to explain, clarify or specifically reaffirm a point notwithstanding the proposing party's conviction that it is already covered by general terms, necessary implication, or an understanding based upon past practice. Where the subject is as fundamental as the one here involved, such attempts cannot furnish a sound basis for changing a result which otherwise would have been reached. Efforts to obtain a management prerogative clause, or to strengthen the terms thereof, in the Arbitrator's opinion, would involve the application of the same view. It works both ways, as the parties should recognize.

Some arbitrators and courts have adopted a contrary view and hold that whatever is unsuccessfully sought must be presumed to have been nonexistent. Such a view hardly recognizes the practical side of the collective bargaining process. While such a presumption may clearly be justified in some situations, any such rule must be judiciously applied, even where it is merely a supporting point to bolster a conclusion reached primarily by other means, as often has been the case. A broad and careless statement of such a view is hardly calculated to preserve a healthy atmosphere for frank and open bargaining. This risk of foreclosing the subject completely would be too high a price to pay for attempted clarifications or improvements. In the broad areas of management rights and subcontracting, any such view does not appear sound. For support of this position, see Celanese Corp. of America, 33 L.A. 925. . . .

Having thus settled the principles upon which the parties have argued so vigorously and at such length, it remains to apply them to the facts as they appear in the record.

This is not an adjunct type of service which is only loosely or indirectly related to the Company's primary function. Milk companies like those party to this Agreement have customarily and historically distributed their own product through wholesale and retail delivery routes which are either owned or controlled by the companies themselves. This delivery service is, and has for many years been, an integral part of their business. This undoubtedly accounts for the fact that many of them have entered into collective bargaining agreements with the Teamsters. The work of these routemen certainly was a basic part of what these parties were bargaining about.

What is more, the route drivers account for approximately one-half of the unit here involved. There are as many delivery men as there are production employees. If this work can be subcontracted and removed from the unit, a major part of the unit will be in jeopardy. If the Company's action with respect to the X — route is upheld, on principle there would be nothing to distinguish similar action on all of the remaining routes. As the record indicates, there has already been frank discussion of bobtailing several of the Charleston routes. If this program were carried to its ultimate conclusion, the bargaining unit would be decimated.

Under these circumstances, it is the Arbitrator's conclusion that the integrity of this bargaining unit is clearly threatened. The work involved is an integral part of the Company's business, and the action which has been taken is quite likely to have a major impact upon the bargaining unit. Such action, unilaterally taken, violates one of the basic assumptions upon which the agreement is founded and therefore amounts to a breach thereof.

There is the further circumstance in this case that the Company has effectively maintained its control over the route while avoiding its obligations under the Agreement with respect to the driver who is still serving the Company's customers. . . .

On its facts, this case is entirely different from the ordinary case of contracting out. In most contracting cases, the contractor is already independently established in his own business and serves, at least in the great majority of instances reflected in the published opinions, other similar business establishments. . . .

Except in the name by which the Company and X — have chosen to describe their relationship, the operation of the route has gone forward essentially as it had before the route was bobtailed. According to X — himself, a substantial number of the customers (approximately 25%) were still unaware of any change at the time of the hearing. The greatest part of the savings realized by the Company are the result of the elimination of fringe benefits such as vacation relief, pension deductions, and overnight expense, due under the Agreement.

Realistically, therefore, there is a substantial basis for seriously questioning whether an independent relationship has in fact been created. Under such circumstances, there is an adequate basis for finding that the provisions respecting method of payment as well as those respecting vacations, pension contributions, and other fringe benefits, are in fact being avoided. . . .

For all the reasons given, it is the Arbitrator's carefully considered conclusion that the Company's action in bobtailing this route and removing it from the applicable provisions of the Agreement, is indeed a violation thereof. The grievance is therefore sustained.

For the period which has already elapsed, and for any future period if the Company continues to sell its milk along this route, it is the Arbitrator's award that the provisions of the Agreement shall be complied with in all respects. This will involve steps to cancel the bobtailing arrangement with X — retroactively to July 1, 1963, crediting him with whatever fringe benefits are due for this period, paying the union dues which should have been checked off, reporting his earnings in the manner required for employees, and restoring Route 44 to the bargaining unit. . . .

(4)   Job Evaluation and Work Erosion

Questions involving wages may arise in connection with many kinds of disputes such as those over the appropriate rate of pay under a job evaluation plan, over incentive plans, over vacation and holiday pay, etc.   Job evaluation is used to measure the relative value of a job to determine the base rate of pay.

Consider the following elementary problems in light of the succeeding excerpts from the article on job evaluation:

1. Under a job evaluation plan established by a company and accepted by the union representing its employees, a truck driver job is classified by the company in 1962 in Job Class 7. The only rate of pay for Job Class 7 is $2.50 an hour. In 1965 the incumbent of this job and the union claim that an error was made in classifying the job in 1962, and that it should have been classified at Job Class 8. There has been no change in the duties of the job during the intervening period of time. Should the ratings on the skill, effort, and responsibility factors for this job be open for re-evaluation in the absence of any change in the duties? Should the judgment employed in the original evaluation of a job be open to attack at any time? For all jobs? What weight should be given to the concept of stability in the administration of a job evaluation plan?

2. A boiler house operator on a new job in one part of a plant claims that he should receive the same base rate of pay as a boiler house operator in another part of the same plant, or in another plant of the same company, or in a plant of a different company in the same industry. What comparisons are appropriate for determining the base rate of pay?

3. A jackhammer and shovel used by an equipment operator to remove dirt are replaced by a bulldozer to achieve the same purpose. No job of bulldozer operator previously existed at the plant. Has the company created a new job of bulldozer operator, or has it changed the job of equipment operator? What difference does it make for the purpose of job evaluation?

4. A craft job of bricklayer has been in existence for a long time at a plant. The job was classified on the basis of all duties that a bricklayer might perform, although it was recognized that an incumbent of the job might not be called upon to perform the full scope of these duties. One of the original duties of the bricklayer job was to lay wood blocks. Subsequently, the company establishes what it describes as a new job of wood blocker to lay wood blocks. This job is classified by the company at a lower job class (with a lower rate of pay) than that for a bricklayer.

What is the underlying issue? The right of the company to create a new job? Or whether in fact it has created a new job?

SHERMAN, ARBITRATOR'S ANALYSIS OF JOB EVALUATION DISPUTES *
43 Personnel Journal 365 (1964)

Job evaluation has been defined as a tool to establish or measure the relative value of jobs, its primary purpose being to eliminate wage rate inequities — different rates for what are essentially the same jobs. . . .

General Nature of the Job Evaluation Program. To arbitrate a job evaluation dispute, the arbitrator obviously should know something about the general nature of the program used by the parties. Do the parties use a point system, a factor rating plan, or some kind of a combination system? Is it specially tailored to one industry or one company? It is helpful to the arbitrator if the parties submit a copy of their job evaluation manual to him prior to the hearing date. This procedure permits the arbitrator to become familiar with the general nature of the program before the parties become embroiled in the specifics of the dispute at the hearing.

The arbitrator may wish to know whether the job evaluation program was developed and installed as a result of joint participation by the company and union, or whether the company developed and installed the program unilaterally. The answer to this question does not provide answers to specific questions on which the arbitrator must make rulings, but it helps the arbitrator to understand the atmosphere surrounding the dispute. Where the union has not been a joint participant in the development of the program, it is more likely to adopt the role of a critic.

Since the arbitrator may be required to make rulings with respect to a specific job, or a specific group of jobs, he will want to know whether there are special principles for certain groups of jobs. In the general structure of the job evaluation program, have craft jobs been treated differently from position rated jobs? Have special rules been developed for clerical and technical jobs? Are there special formulas for group-leaders, gangleaders, head men, straw bosses, and working foremen? Are salaried bargaining unit jobs covered by the program as well as hourly rated jobs?

In considering the general nature of the program, the arbitrator will want to know further whether there is a range of rates for a disputed job or whether there is just one rate of pay for the job. If there is more than one rate for a job, the arbitrator may be called upon to slot an employee into the proper level. He may also be called upon to apply criteria for advancement within the range of rates for the job.

Still another general question of interest to the arbitrator is the age of

* This excerpt from the article by Herbert L. Sherman, Jr., is reproduced with the permission of the editors of Personnel Journal. For a discussion of the history and nature of a particular job evaluation program, see Sherman, Arbitration of the Steel Wage Structure 3-5 (1961).

the job evaluation program. If the program was installed many years ago, he will want to know whether any changes have been made in the program to reflect changes in technology and other developments over the intervening years. . . . Where a job evaluation program has been in effect for many years and no changes have been made in the program to give recognition to automation and other intervening developments, it may be difficult for the parties and for the arbitrator to apply the program to a current problem.

Specific Issues. If there has been no change in the content of a job originally classified many years ago, may a present claim of error in the original classification be raised? Many collective bargaining agreements answer this question in the negative. Under such agreements, a valid job evaluation grievance must claim that a new job has been created or that there have been changes in the content of an existing job. Sometimes a claim that a job has been changed is a legal disguise for a claim that there was error in the original classification. This kind of issue may be raised where a current change in a long established job is very minor and insignificant. It should also be noted that a claim that part of an established job should have been classified originally as a separate job may be nothing more than another type of claim of error in the original classification.

Where the classification of a job may properly be raised as an issue, the arbitrator will want to know the content of the job. If there is a job description for the disputed job, he will want a copy of it. He will want to know whether such job description is mutually approved by the parties. If there is no job description, or no mutually approved job description, the arbitrator will want to know whether there is any substantial dispute concerning the content of the job whose classification is disputed.

If the job is to be classified by rating certain factors, the arbitrator must ascertain whether the factors in dispute have been specified in the submission to him, and whether the parties have made their positions clear as to their proposed ratings on these factors. There may be a contract provision which requires the parties to be very specific on these issues.

In determining the proper codings for the disputed factors, the arbitrator must be fully cognizant of the specific premises which underlie the program being applied. If it is clear, for example, that each factor is rated independently of all other factors, that it is the job that is being rated and not the individual, or that workload has no effect on the rating of the skills of a job, the parties will want to make sure that these specific principles are understood by the arbitrator.

If job comparisons are to be made to determine the proper classification of a disputed job, the arbitrator will want to know what kinds of comparisons may properly be made. Where the job evaluation manual establishes certain key jobs or benchmark jobs, there may, nevertheless, be differences of opinion as to the propriety of the comparisons that may be made to establish the proper classification of a new job. . . .

Although there may be differing opinions concerning the propriety of the job comparisons that may be made by the arbitrator, the parties will often have developed a practice which will aid the arbitrator in resolving this question. And, of course, there may be an unambiguous contract provision which controls disposition of this question.

Where the arbitrator is limited in his deliberations to a consideration of a relatively small number of benchmark jobs, it is interesting to compare the information available to him with the information available to the parties when they decide what classification should be assigned to a new job. In actual practice the parties have numerous non-benchmark jobs available as comparisons, as well as the benchmark jobs. Hence, it should be noted that where this procedure prevails, the arbitrator is asked to agree with classifications which are proposed on the basis of comparisons which are denied to the arbitrator.

New Job Versus Changed Job. It often is significant for the arbitrator to know whether a job classification dispute concerns a new job or a changed job. Although the distinction may be of no significance, some job evaluation programs establish special rules for changed jobs. There may be a provision in the program which, in the case of a changed job, permits consideration of only that part of the job affected by the change. Under such a provision the rest of the job is deemed to have been classified correctly. There may be a provision requiring a certain degree of change in order to qualify the job for a different rate of pay.

If there are such special rules for changed jobs, the distinction between a changed job and a new job becomes important. Yet most contracts simply state the consequences of the distinction without providing much guidance as to how the arbitrator is to decide the underlying question. Fortunately for the arbitrator, the parties often agree on whether they are disputing the classification of a changed job or a new job.

If there is a dispute as to whether a new job has been created by the company as a result of certain changes, the arbitrator must scrutinize the evidence carefully. Relevant considerations would be the nature of the changes and the magnitude of the changes. A comparison of the kinds of skills required before and after the changes is in order, and a comparison of the kinds of equipment utilized before and after the changes is in order. Of course, other considerations are also relevant. . . .

Borderline cases are not easy to resolve. But at least it should be understood that the mere word labels, new job or changed job, as the case may be, are not controlling. The real question is what does the evidence show, if the parties are not in agreement?

In this connection, it is also important for the arbitrator, as well as the parties, to make a distinction between the right of a company to create a new job and the question as to whether it, in fact, has created a new job. It is likewise important that a distinction be drawn between the right of a company to change or terminate a job, and the question as to whether the company, in fact, has changed or terminated the job under consideration. Such distinctions are not always recognized in the arguments made to the arbitrator.

The question as to what is the real nature of a job may also be involved when an employee seeks a higher rate of pay for the period of time that he performs spellhand duties. If he has always performed the additional spellhand duties — even when his job was originally classified, and if the original classification may be deemed to embrace the performance of such spellhand duties — then it may properly be concluded that the performance of such duties is part of *his job* and he is not being assigned to *another job* calling for a higher rate of pay. On the other hand, where incumbents of a job have never performed spellhand duties in the past and such duties, requiring higher skills, are assigned to these employees at a later time, it may be concluded that the employees are being assigned to another job calling for a higher rate of pay.

The interesting point here is that most contracts do not provide satisfactory definitions of a job for the purpose of resolving such questions. They simply state the consequences which flow from the answer to the underlying question. Hence the arbitrator must ascertain the content of the employee's basic job, from job descriptions if they exist, past practices, and all other relevant evidence, before he can resolve the rate of pay question.

One final note concerns the limits of an arbitrator's authority in a job evaluation dispute. If the arbitrator believes that an error exists in the job evaluation program, what may the arbitrator do about it? . . .

Of course, the arbitrator may point out to the parties that they are free to revise their benchmarks. He may point out that they can engage in an over-all review of their job evaluation program to correct alleged errors. But he may find that the parties have sharply curtailed his power to dispense his brand of industrial justice.

NOTE

Elimination of duties and other forms of work erosion may affect not only the rates of pay for existing jobs but they may also raise issues concerning established crew sizes. Although it has been held that established crew sizes may be protected by local working conditions provisions of a collective bargaining agreement in the absence of any change in underlying conditions, it has been held that cumulative changes in underlying working conditions over a period of years may justify reductions in established crew sizes. American Chain and Cable Co. and Steelworkers, Local 1391, 33 L.A. 362 (1959); United States Steel Corp. and Steelworkers, Local 1408, 34 L.A. 556 (1960).

(5) Authority to Award Damages and Back Pay

INTERNATIONAL HARVESTER CO. and UNITED FARM EQUIPMENT WORKERS, LOCAL 104
9 L.A. 894 (1947)

[The contract in this case required that when an employee was assigned to a different piecework job, he should be informed in advance of the applicable rate. The arbitrator ruled that pieceworkers who were thus transferred but, through company negligence, were not informed of the rate until almost the end of the shift, were entitled to be compensated at the average earnings rate then applicable on the jobs involved. The arbitrator awarded the difference in each instance between the amount actually received from the company and the higher amount determined on the basis of the average piecework rate at that time. There was no showing that the failure to supply the requisite information had actually caused an impairment of the operators' earnings, but it was shown that in the past situations of this kind had been dealt with by the parties themselves and settled on the basis of payment of average earnings for the time covered by the delay. The company contended, however, that the provision in question established only a "good faith" guide to company action and that it created no contractual obligation. It was argued, in this same connection, that since the contract included no specific "damages" provision, no damages could be awarded here by the arbitrator, the company urging that the arbitrator could not grant the request of the union because to do so would be to "add to the contract" in violation of the clause restricting the arbitrator's jurisdiction.]

WIRTZ, Arbitrator. . . .

There is similarly no substantial basis for the contention made by the Company that Section 10 establishes only a "good faith" guide to Company action and creates no real contractual obligation. This contention is unsupportable either in terms of general contract construction, as applied to collective bargaining agreements, or in terms of the parties' previous construction of this particular clause. The Company contention is that no "money award" is permissible in these cases because the contract "did not provide a penalty for a violation of (this) section." (C.B. p. 54.) This is similarly true of any number of other provisions in the Agreement, including those in which the Union assumes certain obligations. (See Art. II and Art. X.)

The conclusion that no money arbitration award is proper in the case of violations of contract provisions which do not specifically provide for damages would have two effects. The first would be the substitution of some other method of settlement in the place of arbitration. The second would be the cluttering up of the contract with a lot of "liquidated damage" provisions which would invite more trouble than they could ever be expected to prevent. It will be unfortunate if collective bargaining agreements develop along the lines of the revenue laws, with provision necessarily being made for every little hairline question which may arise between adverse parties pressing conflicting interests. They will lose their effectiveness when they become so involved that laymen cannot follow or understand them. It would contribute dangerously to that tendency if it were required that every contract clause had to include a damages provision. This is the kind of thing which it must be assumed the parties intended would be handled in the light of the applicability of a particular clause to the particular problems that might arise under it.

As far as the application of Section 10 itself is concerned, the Company's contention regarding its unenforceability is weakened by two specific considerations. The first of these is that the parties have themselves, in their past practice, taken a very different view of the matter from that which is advanced here. Section 10 was taken over in the 1946 Agreement, without change, from the previous contract. The Union introduced several other grievance records which showed a disposition of Section 10 issues by payment of what Company counsel identifies here as "money damages." Some of these cases arose under the 1942 contract. Two of them arose and were settled under the 1946 Agreement here in question and after the *four grievances presented here had been processed.* Counsel for the Company explained these other grievances as being atypical and as representing nothing more than instances of Management's willingness to make payments over and beyond those required of it. No evidence whatsoever is presented, however, of a single instance wherein any different settlement was made. There is greater support for the Union contention that the cases presented here are the ones which represent possible departures from the norm.

The other point of significance here is that the Company position as to non-enforceability was presented for the first time at the arbitration hearing and is, furthermore, inconsistent with the position which is implicit in the Company's answer at the earlier steps in the handling of some of these particular grievances.

Thus in the second step answer in Grievance No. 588 A, the Company denial of the grievance request is expressed solely in terms of the fact that notice was given before the end of the shift. The statement is made that "we understand that *it is our obligation* to notify the operator within the working hours of the shift." The phrase which has here been italicized suggests that the Company did not, prior to the arbitration hearing, deny any obligation but that it has, in these grievances, contested only the time as of which its obligation is created. The possibility of construing this language as referring to some merely moral obligation is removed by additional language which appears in the Company's answer in Grievance No. 633 A. Here it is stated that the fact of notification before the end of the shift is what supports the contention that "no *penalty payment* is to be made."

It is clear in the light of the practice of the parties in other similar cases and in their handling of these particular cases, as well as against the background of broader principles of contract construction, that Section 10 creates a contractual obligation and is not simply a testimonial of good faith and intentions.

These cases present two further questions, both involving what lawyers refer to as the "measure of damages." There is first the question of whether the employees involved in these cases are entitled to reparation on the basis of a showing that Section 10 was violated, or whether it must also be shown that this violation was actually the cause of an impairment in their earnings. The Union's proof in these cases is limited to a description of the general types of injury which *may* result from a lack of the required notice. The theory upon which recovery is sought is that Section 10 requires no showing of specific injury and that the interests involved are such that they will be prejudiced unless it is *uniformly* adhered to.

It is not shown in any of the four cases that the failure to supply the requisite information actually caused an impairment of the particular operator's earnings. The related question is as to whether the average piecework earning rate is the proper basis for computing the reparation payment which is due if the requisite degree of damage is shown.

These questions would present real difficulty if they were presented as novel issues. They are not so presented. They have arisen before and have been dealt with by the parties themselves under both this 1946 Agreement and the 1942 contract. The record of those other settlements shows affirmatively in each case (a) that the fact of undue delay in supplying the price information was itself considered by both parties to be the controlling factor, and (b) that where there was this delay, the operator involved received average earnings payments for the time covered by the delay. The Company implied at the hearing that there may have been other facts in those cases. If so, they should have been pointed out, for a careful scrutiny of the record does not reveal them.

There is a strong insistence by the Company in this group of cases that an award upholding the "damages" claims presented would constitute an assumption by the Arbitrator of an authority not given him by the contract. It would much more accurately be said that a decision by the Arbitrator to substitute his own rule of "damages" for that adopted by the parties would, in the absence of any contract basis, constitute a violation of his carefully prescribed duties. Counsel for the Company himself expressed the view that the question presented here should be considered in the light of "the construction of (the contract provisions) by the parties over the period of years." If a new rule regarding this point was to have been established, it should have been done at the time the parties had before them the question of whether or not to include Section 10 in the new contract in its old form. . . .

NOTE

Accord: Phillips Chemical Co. and Oil Workers, Local 463, 17 L.A. 721 (1951); Mississippi Aluminum Co. and Aluminum Workers, Local 245, 27 L.A. 625 (1956). See Note 4, infra page 873, for judicial rulings on the power of an arbitrator to fashion a remedy.

Canada has recognized the right of an arbitrator to grant damages for breach of a collective agreement. In Re Polymer Corp. and Oil, Chemical & Atomic Workers International Union, 26 D.L.R.2d 609 (1961), aff'd, 28 D.L.R.2d 81 (1961), the Ontario Court of Appeal upheld the right of an arbitrator to award damages to an employer for a union's breach of a no-strike clause — even though such power was not expressly stated in the agreement.

C.   THE NATIONAL LABOR RELATIONS BOARD
AND ARBITRATION

INTERNATIONAL HARVESTER CO.
National Labor Relations Board, 1962
138 N.L.R.B. 923

. . . The Trial Examiner found, in substance, that the Respondent Local Union 98 and its agent, Barnard, violated Section 8(b)(2) and (1)(A) of the Act by pursuing a grievance to arbitration to compel the Respondent Company to fulfill its contractual obligation to discharge employee Ramsey for failing to pay his union membership dues during the term of a valid union-security agreement, and by insisting that the Company put into effect a rendered arbitration award which subsequently resulted in Ramsey's layoff in an economic reduction in force. The Trial Examiner further found that the Respondent Company violated Section 8(a)(3) and (1) of the Act by reducing Ramsey's seniority in compliance with the arbitration award and thereafter laying him off. Without passing upon the merits of the alleged unfair labor practices, we find that the Trial Examiner erred in not honoring the arbitration award and dismissing the complaint herein. . . .

There is no question that the Board is not precluded from adjudicating unfair labor practice charges even though they might have been the subject of an arbitration proceeding and award. Section 10(a) of the Act expressly makes this plain, and the courts have uniformly so held. However, it is equally well established that the Board has considerable discretion to respect an arbitration award and decline to exercise its authority over alleged unfair labor practices if to do so will serve the fundamental aims of the Act.

The Act, as has repeatedly been stated, is primarily designed to promote industrial peace and stability by encouraging the practice and procedure of collective bargaining. Experience has demonstrated that collective-bargaining agreements that provide for final and binding arbitration of grievance and disputes arising thereunder, "as a substitute for industrial strife," contribute significantly to the attainment of this statutory objective. Approval of the arbitral technique, which has become an effective and expeditious means of resolving labor disputes, finds expression in Section 203(d) of the Labor Management Relations Act, 1947. . . .

[The Board then discussed the Supreme Court's decisions in Lincoln Mills and the 1960 "trilogy." See pages 848, 855 infra.]

If complete effectuation of the Federal policy is to be achieved, we firmly believe that the Board, which is entrusted with the administration of one of the many facets of national labor policy, should give hospitable acceptance to the arbitral process as "part and parcel of the collective bargaining process itself," and voluntarily withhold its undoubted authority to adjudicate alleged unfair labor practice charges involving the same subject matter, unless it clearly appears that the arbitration proceedings were tainted by fraud, collusion, unfairness, or serious procedural irregularities or that the award was clearly repugnant to the purposes and policies of the Act. As the Court has reminded the Board in another context but in language equally applicable to the situation here presented:

". . . that the Board has not been commissioned to effectuate the policies of the Labor Relations Act so single-mindedly that it may wholly ignore other and equally important Congressional objectives. Frequently the entire scope of Congressional purpose calls for careful accommodation of one statutory scheme to another, and it is not too much to demand of an administrative body that it undertake this accommodation without excessive emphasis upon its immediate task." Consistent with this reminder, and aware of the underlying objectives of the Act, the Board in the appropriate case has not permitted parties to bypass their specially devised grievance — arbitration machinery for resolving their disputes and where an arbitration award had already been rendered has held them to it.

From what has been said previously, it is quite clear that, in pursuing its grievance to arbitration, the Union in the present case was simply exercising a contractual right to have that tribunal vindicate its claim that the Company breached its obligation by refusing to enforce their concededly valid union-shop agreement to discharge Ramsey for failing to pay his regular membership dues. The Company did not challenge the Union's right to resort to arbitration and properly so, for this was the very procedure which the parties had agreed in their contract was "adequate to provide a fair and final determination of all grievances arising under the terms of this Contract," and which justified the Union's no-strike commitment. Furthermore, it is apparent that the parties' submission of their controversy was not only required by their agreement, but also, under established law, was mandatory and survived the contract term.

The record is clear that the issue of the Company's contractual obligation to comply with the Union's demand for Ramsey's discharge was fully and fairly litigated before an impartial arbitrator. In a well-reasoned and informed decision, the arbitrator sustained the Union's grievance. There is certainly not the slightest suggestion — nor is such a contention even urged — of fraud, collusion, or other irregularity on the part of any party to "railroad" Ramsey out of his job. Admittedly, Ramsey was in default in his dues payments which, under the contract at least, made him vulnerable to discharge. Although Ramsey was not given notice of the arbitration hearing, his interests were vigorously defended there by the Company, which had at all times supported Ramsey's position that he was not legally required to maintain his union membership and stubbornly resisted the Union's efforts to secure his removal from his job. For these reasons, we find no serious procedural infirmities in the arbitration proceedings which warrant disregarding the arbitrator's award. After all is said and done, "procedural regularity [is] not . . . an end in itself, but [is] . . . a means of defending substantive interests."

Members Rodgers and Fanning dissented.

NOTES

1. In Spielberg Manufacturing Co., 112 N.L.R.B. 1080, 1082 (1955), the Board, in dismissing a complaint, stated: "In summary, the proceedings appear to have been fair and regular, all parties had agreed to be bound, and the decision of the arbitration panel is not clearly repugnant to the purposes and policies of the Act. In these circumstances we believe that the desirable objective of encouraging the voluntary settlement of labor disputes will best be served by our recognition of the arbitrators' award."

2. The International Harvester decision was affirmed by the Court of Appeals, sub nom. Ramsey v. NLRB, 327 F.2d 784 (7th Cir. 1964). The court's opinion included the following (p. 787): "Thus, the Supreme Court has held that the Board has the discretion to defer to the decision of an arbitrator. Our function in reviewing such cases is to determine whether the Board abused its discretion in so deferring. . . .

"Petitioner contends, inter alia, that his rights were denied since he was not given notice of the arbitration hearing and did not appear there. We disagree. There is no statutory or constitutional right of an employee to be present at an arbitration hearing. It appears that the company fully and adequately defended petitioner's position at the hearing.

"Petitioner does not contend that any other procedural irregularity, fraud or collusion entered into the arbitrator's decision. . . .

"We hold that the Board did not abuse its discretion in deferring to the decision of the arbitrator."

3. In Raytheon Co., 140 N.L.R.B. 883 (1963), the arbitrator's authority was limited solely to the contractual issue litigated before him and therefore he did not pass upon whether the discharges were for protected concerted activity or whether the asserted reasons for the discharges were spurious. Noting that these are issues which must be decided if employees are to be afforded their statutory protection, the Board declined to honor the arbitrator's award. In Gateway Transportation Co., 137 N.L.R.B. 1763 (1962), the Board refused to give effect to an award when the grievant had been forced to a hearing with only forty-eight hours' notice, the union counsel refused to represent grievant at the hearing, and grievant's request for a continuance to enable him to prepare his case and call witnesses was denied. For an extensive consideration of the rights of individual employees in the grievance procedure and arbitration, see page 933 infra.

4. An arbitrator held that a contract with a certain union covered certain employees. A representation petition was filed with the Board by a second union, not a party to the arbitration proceeding, which asserted that the employees were not covered by the contract. The Board accepted the arbitrator's interpretation of the contract and dismissed the petition. "While it is true that International Harvester, as well as other cases in which the Board honored arbitration awards, involved unfair labor practice proceedings, we believe that the same considerations which moved the Board to honor arbitration awards in unfair labor practice

cases are equally persuasive to a similar acceptance of the arbitral process in a representation proceeding such as the instant one. Thus where, as here, a question of contract interpretation is in issue, and the parties thereto have set up in their agreement arbitration machinery for the settlement of disputes arising under the contract, and an award has already been rendered which meets Board requirements applicable to arbitration awards, we think that it would further the underlying objectives of the Act to promote industrial peace and stability to give effect thereto. It is true, of course, that under Section 9 of the Act the Board is empowered to decide questions concerning representation. However, this authority to decide questions concerning representation does not preclude the Board in a proper case from considering an arbitration award in determining whether such a question exists." Raley's Inc., 143 N.L.R.B. 256, 258 (1963).

5. On the definition of the bargaining unit by arbitration, see page 907 infra.

ADAMS DAIRY CO.
National Labor Relations Board, 1964
147 N.L.R.B. No. 133

. . . The Trial Examiner found that although Respondent might have violated Section 8(a)(5) by changing the working conditions of some of its drivers [by subcontracting] without notifying or consulting with the Union in advance, the complaint should be dismissed because the Union had not resorted to the arbitration provisions of the existing contract. We do not agree.

The contract subjects to its arbitration procedures only such disputes as concern "the interpretation or application of the terms of this Agreement." But in the instant case, the precise Union claim, which is the subject of the complaint before us, does not relate to the meaning of any established term or condition of the contract, or to any asserted misapplication thereof by Respondent. It is directed instead at Respondent's denial to it of a statutory right guaranteed by Section 8(d) of the Act, namely, the right to be notified and consulted in advance, and to be given an opportunity to bargain, about substantial changes in the working conditions of unit employees in respects *not covered by the contract*. As the particular dispute between the Union and Respondent now before us thus involves basically a disagreement over statutory rather than contractual obligations, the disposition of the controversy is quite clearly within the competency of the Board, and not of an arbitrator who would be without authority to grant the Union the particular redress it seeks and for which we provide below in our remedial order. . . .

We are not unmindful of the fact that the resolution of the unfair labor practice issue in this case has required our consideration, as a subsidiary issue, of Respondent's claim that it was impliedly authorized under the contract to take unilateral action on the matters complained of — a claim we have rejected as without merit. We may assume that this claim gave rise to a difference over the meaning of contractual provisions that might have been submitted for consideration under the contract's arbitration procedures. Nevertheless, we do not consider that reason enough for us to refuse either to entertain the instant unfair labor practice proceeding, or to provide the necessary redress for the violation found. It is quite clear that the Board is not precluded from resolving an unfair labor practice issue, which may call for appropriate relief under the Act, simply because as an incident to such violation it may be necessary to construe the scope of a contract which an arbitrator is also empowered to contrue. Section 10(a) of the Act expressly provides with respect to the Board's power to prevent unfair labor practices that "[t]his power shall not be affected by any other means or adjustment or prevention that has been or may be established by agreement, law, or otherwise."

Nor in our view is the situation presented by this case such as to move us in the exercise of our discretion to withhold our own remedial processes in deference to the arbitration processes the parties have agreed upon for the settlement of contract disputes. None of the considerations that have impelled us to do so in other cases is present here. In the instant case, it does not appear that there is already in existence an arbitration award passing on matters that bear on the ultimate issue we must decide, and to which we are asked to give weight or effect. Indeed, it affirmatively appears that neither party has even so much as sought to invoke arbitration.

Nor is this a case involving an alleged unfair labor practice, the existence of which turns primarily on an interpretation of specific contractual provisions, unquestionably encompassed by the contract's arbitration provisions, and coming to us in a context that makes it reasonably probable that arbitration settlement of the contract dispute would also put at rest the unfair labor practice controversy in a manner sufficient to effectuate the policies of the Act. On the contrary, it is highly conjectural that arbitration in this case, even if resorted to by the Union could have effectively disposed of the basic issue in this case — whether Respondent acted lawfully in engaging in the unilateral actions to which the instant complaint is addressed.

Under all the circumstances, therefore, we are unable to agree with the conclusion of the Trial Examiner that even though Respondent's unilateral action provides a statutory basis for doing so, the Board ought not in this case exercise its power to remedy Respondent's unfair labor practice. Rather, we believe that for us to dismiss this complaint on the ground he states would be an unwarranted abuse of our statutory responsibilities.

Member Brown, concurring: . . .

Cases coming before the Board, where the Board is urged to defer to arbitration may be divided into two broad classes, those where an award has already been rendered and those where arbitration either had not been invoked or has been invoked but no award has yet been rendered. In the former class of cases the Board has long given hospitable acceptance to the arbitral process by refusing to second guess the arbitrator, but limiting the scope of the Board's inquiry to determining whether the procedures were fair and the results not repugnant to the Act. Our deferral to arbitration within these limits has been noted with approval by the Supreme Court, and in my opinion has satisfactorily protected rights guaranteed by the Act while giving full play to the arbitral process.

In those cases where there is no award but where, as here, it is contended that the Board should refuse to process an unfair labor practice complaint but require the parties to settle their dispute under the provisions of the collective-bargaining agreement, the problem is much more difficult. . . .

While it is possible that a party may concurrently pursue both the arbitration and the unfair labor practice routes, I believe that it is inconsistent with the statutory policy favoring arbitration for the Board to resolve disputes which, while cast as unfair labor practices, essentially involve a dispute with respect to the interpretation or application of the collective-bargaining agreement.

. . . We should not, in my opinion, automatically dismiss a case merely because the dispute is arguably subject to arbitration. Such action would be contrary to the principles of Spielberg [see page 841 supra], which although limiting the scope of Board inquiry, nevertheless, establishes the principle that the Board has the duty where a statutory right is involved to examine the fairness of the arbitration proceedings and determine whether the results are repugnant to the Act. Since we cannot predict whether a yet to be held arbitration proceeding will comply with Spielberg standards we should withhold our action pending the arbitrator's award.

If, after an award has been rendered there is a request for Board action, our consideration of the case would be controlled by Spielberg. Wherever the record establishes that the parties to the dispute as part of their collective-bargaining relationship consciously, by contract, bargaining history or past practice have waived statutory rights, bargained such rights away, or bargained to agreement with respect to the subject matter of the dispute, I believe we should leave to the arbitrator the question of the nature of their bargain and the respective rights and obligations of each party.

Where, however, the parties have not by practice, bargaining history or contract resolved their respective rights and obligations with respect to the subject matter of the dispute, we should not defer action on the unfair labor practice case even though the dispute may be generally subject to the arbitration provisions of the collective-bargaining agreement. Since an arbitrator can only enforce the provisions of the contract, to defer to arbitration in such cases would in effect imply a waiver of statutory rights where the only evidence that a waiver was intended would be the silence of the agreement.

The existence of an arbitration clause alone might result in the denial or delay in the exercise of all statutory rights not guaranteed by the contract. Such a result would clearly be contrary to the policies of the Act as it would tend to increase the likelihood of industrial strife by reducing the number of disputes which could be peacefully resolved through either arbitration or an unfair labor practice proceeding. Moreover, such a result may have an adverse effect on the use of arbitration itself since the attractiveness of arbitration clauses may be seriously diminished if they have the effect of cutting off all statutory rights which are arguably comprehended within the meaning of an arbitrable dispute but are neither waived nor guaranteed by the contract.

While it is true that an interpretation of the contractual relationship of the parties is inescapable in order to resolve cases of the kind under consideration here, such contract interpretation is necessarily encompassed within the Board's function. Otherwise, we would have no rational predicate for deciding whether to defer to arbitration or to process the unfair labor practice case. This would leave us with an arbitrary choice between refusing to process any case where the contract contained an arbitration clause or completely disregarding the availability of arbitration and asserting our statutory jurisdiction in every case. I do not believe that the policies of the Act would be effectuated by our resort to that kind of mechanical approach to this problem. . . .

I realize, of course, that our duty to protect the public interest may in special cases require that we do not defer to private agreements to arbitrate, even where arbitration is available and where the subject matter of the dispute appears to be regulated by the terms of the agreement. However, the fact that such cases may arise does not in my opinion detract from the desirability of formulating guidelines for a coherent Board policy toward arbitration, leaving to "the process of litigating elucidation" the development of legal principles to be applied to special problems.

In the instant case, I find nothing in the record which would establish that the parties either by agreement, practice or bargaining history have established their mutual rights and obligations with respect to the subject of subcontracting. I agree, therefore, that the presence of an arbitration clause alone in the contract is no basis for our dismissing the complaint.

NOTES

1. In Dubo Manufacturing Corp., 142 N.L.R.B. 431 (1963), the Board deferred action on discriminatory discharge allegations pending completion of arbitration of grievances filed concerning the discharges.

2. Where a union requests information to process a grievance and the employer refuses to comply on the basis of contract language, the union may decide to go to arbitration or to file Section 8(a)(5) charges with the Board. In Sinclair Refining Co. v. NLRB, 306 F.2d 569 (5th Cir. 1962), the union went to the Board. But the Fifth Circuit reversed the Board's order to supply the information on the ground that the Board's order in this case required determination of the initial substantive issue of the grievance itself. Compare Timken Roller Bearing Co. v. NLRB, 325 F.2d 746 (6th Cir. 1963), where the court upheld the Board's order to bargain after finding that the union's demand did not constitute a

grievance under the arbitration section of the contract. The court referred to the Sinclair Refining decision (p. 754), as follows: "The Court held that the Board proceeding could not be used to secure data for use in a grievance proceeding where determination of relevance and pertinency required determination of the critical substantive issue of the grievance itself, which issue was under the bargaining agreement for the arbitrator, not the Board or the Court. This is but another example of the now established law that where a dispute or 'difference' is subject to grievance procedure and arbitration by reason of the provisions of the bargaining agreement, that procedure is exclusive and will be enforced." Is the last statement sound?

3. The Chairman of the NLRB has stated: ". . . [O]ur agency's accommodation to arbitration also significantly involves the policies for case-handling in the regional offices under the direction of the General Counsel. He and our regional staffs are of course bound by the same Congressional policies and by the Board's interpretation of them. Accordingly, many cases you do not see in the reports are dismissals or withdrawals where in the careful judgment of the General Counsel Spielberg standards are met by arbitrator's awards. The processing of others may be held up to give a pending arbitration the first chance and then to evaluate the award. The variant fact patterns in which these issues arise give the General Counsel many close questions to decide in carrying out his duties under the law. As with so much of the NLRB's other work, therefore, the Board's decisions here too constitute a minor part of our modus operandi with arbitration." McCulloch, The Arbitration Issue in NLRB Decisions, 19 Arb. J. (n.s.) 134, 147 (1964). See also McCulloch, Arbitration and/or the NLRB, in Labor Arbitration and Industrial Change 175 (Kahn ed. 1963); NLRB, 28th Ann. Rep. 38 (1963).

D.   JUDICIAL ENFORCEMENT OF THE COLLECTIVE AGREEMENT

1.   *Agreements to Arbitrate*

a.   THE COMMON LAW

At common law, promises to arbitrate future disputes were not specifically enforceable; nor could substantial damages be predicated on a failure to perform such a promise.[15] Therefore, they could be revoked by either party without legal penalty. Various reasons have been asserted in explanation or support of this result. They include: (1) that the arbitrator was an agent whose authority could be revoked; (2) that equity could not compel the arbitrator to perform; (3) that it was contrary to public policy to allow the parties to oust the court of jurisdiction.[16]

---

[15] Sturges, Commercial Arbitrations and Awards 82-84 (1930).

[16] Gregory and Orlikoff, The Enforcement of Labor Arbitration Agreements, 17 U. Chi. L. Rev. 233 (1950); Sayre, Development of Commercial Arbitration Law, 37 Yale L.J. 595 (1928).

Once an arbitration had been completed, the common law was more hospitable toward an arbitration award. There could be an action on the award, and courts would enforce it, limiting their review to questions going to the fairness of the proceedings, the power of the arbitrator, the finality of the award, and the impact of public policy.[17]

These common law rules were developed in an era before arbitration agreements became a fixture in labor-management relations, but the courts assumed that they were applicable to labor arbitration without studied comparison between the problems of commercial and labor arbitration.[18] When, in 1956, a trial judge in Mississippi attempted to distinguish labor arbitration from commercial arbitration, and to enforce a promise to arbitrate in a labor agreement under the common law, he was promptly reversed by the state supreme court, which held that any such change in the common law rule was for the legislature.[19]

Against this background, legislation specifically dealing with arbitration has been passed in many states.[20] The student should consult local materials for depth evaluation of local problems. All that can be suggested here is the general statutory pattern and certain core problems that seem to arise in most jurisdictions.

b.   STATE AND FEDERAL STATUTES

Arbitration statutes may be considered as performing two functions. They alter the substance of the common law rule and they provide procedures for enforcement of the promise to arbitrate.

The state Acts tend to declare that promises to arbitrate existing or future disputes are valid and enforceable save upon any grounds that would provide a defense in an action on a simple contract.[21] This reverses the common law rule. However, some statutes are limited in scope and do not cover all types of agreements. The statutes of Arizona, Louisiana, and Oregon by their terms do not apply to collective bargaining agreements.[22] The United States Arbitration Act, which applies to "any maritime transaction or a contract evidencing a transaction involving commerce . . ." by its terms does not apply to "contracts of employment." Similarly the California statute did not apply to "contracts for

---

[17] Sturges, supra note 15, at 787-806; Updegraff and McCoy, Arbitration of Labor Disputes 215-217 (2d ed. 1961).

[18] Comment, Arbitration of Labor Disputes, 43 Ill. L. Rev. 678 (1949).

[19] Prairie Local Lodge 1538, IAM v. Machine Products Co., 27 L.A. 285 (Miss. Ch. Ct. 1956), rev'd and remanded, 94 So.2d 344 (Miss. 1957).

[20] General arbitration statutes are cited in 12 Arb. J.(n.s.) 38 (1957). Labor arbitration statutes are collected, along with other state statutory material, in State Labor Laws, a loose-leaf service of the Bureau of National Affairs, and in 4 and 4A CCH Lab. L. Rep. (4th ed.), a loose-leaf service of Commerce Clearing House, Inc. See Cox, Current Problems in the Law of Grievance Arbitration, 30 Rocky Mt. L. Rev. 247 (1958); Feldman, Arbitration Law in California: Private Tribunals for Private Government, 30 So. Cal. L. Rev. 375 (1957); Note, Labor Arbitration in New Jersey, 14 Rutgers L. Rev. 143 (1959).

[21] See, e.g., N.J. Rev. Stat. §2A:24-1 (1951).

[22] Ariz. Rev. Stat. §12-1517 (Supp. 1963); La. Rev. Stat., tit. 9, §4216 (1948); Ore. Rev. Stat., tit. 3, §33.210 (1961).

labor" prior to 1961.[23] Such statutory language simply reintroduces the difficult conceptual problem of the juridical nature of the labor agreement. The California statute was construed as extending to collective bargaining agreements on the theory that they are not contracts for labor.[24] The United States Arbitration Act has never been definitively construed, and the Courts of Appeal have divided on the question of whether the "contracts of employment" exclusion covered the collective bargaining agreement.[25] This debate has become irrelevant in the wake of the Lincoln Mills decision holding that the promise to arbitrate in the collective bargaining agreement is specifically enforceable under Section 301 of the Taft-Hartley Act.

The state acts provide for an action to compel or stay arbitration proceedings which have not yet taken place, in which the issue is whether an agreement to arbitrate has been made, and if so, whether it has been breached. They tend to provide a mechanism for appointment of an arbitrator if the parties have not so provided. They also make provision for a stay of any lawsuit based on a matter subject to arbitration. The New York statute makes the agreement incontestable unless the party resisting arbitration moves promptly into court after receiving notice of intention to arbitrate a particular dispute.[26]

The Acts also provide for an action to confirm or vacate an award once rendered, and usually set forth the grounds upon which the courts may proceed. These grounds relate to the fairness of the proceedings and the jurisdiction of the arbitrator.[27] The Acts may provide a procedure for resubmission of an issue to an arbitrator under certain circumstances.

C. SECTION 301 OF THE LABOR MANAGEMENT RELATIONS ACT

TEXTILE WORKERS UNION OF AMERICA v. LINCOLN MILLS OF ALABAMA

Supreme Court of the United States, 1957
353 U.S. 448, 77 Sup. Ct. 912, 1 L. Ed. 2d 972

MR. JUSTICE DOUGLAS delivered the opinion of the Court.

Petitioner-union entered into a collective bargaining agreement in 1953 with respondent-employer, the agreement to run one year and from year to year thereafter, unless terminated on specified notices. The agreement provided that there would be no strikes or work stoppages

---

[23] Cal. Code Civ. Proc. §1280 (Deering, 1953), repealed by Stats. 1961, c. 461, p. 1540, §1. See Cal. Code Civ. Proc. §1281 (West Supp. 1963).

[24] Levy v. Superior Court, Los Angeles County, 15 Cal. 2d 692, 104 P.2d 770 (1940).

[25] Compare Motor Coach Employees v. Greyhound Lines, 192 F.2d 310 (3d Cir. 1951), with Local 205, United Electrical Workers v. General Electric Co., 233 F.2d 85 (1st Cir. 1956), aff'd on other grounds, 353 U.S. 547 (1957). See Annotation, 64 A.L.R.2d 1332 (1959).

[26] N.Y. Civil Practice Act §1458.

[27] See, e.g., N.Y. Civil Practice Act §1462.

and that grievances would be handled pursuant to a specified procedure. The last step in the grievance procedure — a step that could be taken by either party — was arbitration.

This controversy involves several grievances that concern work loads and work assignments. The grievances were processed through the various steps in the grievance procedure and were finally denied by the employer. The union requested arbitration, and the employer refused. Thereupon the union brought this suit in the District Court to compel arbitration.

The District Court concluded that it had jurisdiction and ordered the employer to comply with the grievance arbitration provisions of the collective bargaining agreement. The Court of Appeals reversed by a divided vote. 230 F.2d 81. It held that, although the District Court had jurisdiction to entertain the suit, the court had no authority founded either in federal or state law to grant the relief. The case is here on a petition for a writ of certiorari which we granted because of the importance of the problem and the contrariety of views in the courts.

The starting point of our inquiry is §301 of the Labor Management Relations Act of 1947, 61 Stat. 156, 29 U.S.C. §185. . . .

There has been considerable litigation involving §301 and courts have construed it differently. There is one view that §301(a) merely gives federal district courts jurisdiction in controversies that involve labor organizations in industries affecting commerce, without regard to diversity of citizenship or the amount in controversy. Under that view §301(a) would not be the source of substantive law; it would neither supply federal law to resolve these controversies nor turn the federal judges to state law for answers to the questions. Other courts—the overwhelming number of them — hold that §301(a) is more than jurisdictional — that it authorizes federal courts to fashion a body of federal law for the enforcement of these collective bargaining agreements and includes within that federal law specific performance of promises to arbitrate grievances under collective bargaining agreements. Perhaps the leading decision representing that point of view is the one rendered by Judge Wyzanski in Textile Workers Union v. American Thread Co., 113 F. Supp. 137. That is our construction of §301(a), which means that the agreement to arbitrate grievance disputes, contained in this collective bargaining agreement, should be specifically enforced.

From the face of the Act it is apparent that §301(a) and §301(b) supplement one another. Section 301(b) makes it possible for a labor organization, representing employees in an industry affecting commerce, to sue and be sued as an entity in the federal courts. Section 301(b) in other words provides the procedural remedy lacking at common law. Section 301(a) certainly does something more than that. Plainly, it supplies the basis upon which the federal district courts may take jurisdiction and apply the procedural rule of §301(b). The question is whether §301(a) is more than jurisdictional.

The legislative history of §301 is somewhat cloudy and confusing. But there are a few shafts of light that illuminate our problem.

The bills, as they passed the House and the Senate, contained provisions which would have made the failure to abide by an agreement to arbitrate an unfair labor practice. S. Rep. No. 105, 80th Cong., 1st Sess., pp. 20-21, 23; H.R. Rep. No. 245, 80th Cong., 1st Sess., p. 21. This feature of the law was dropped in Conference. As the Conference Report stated, "Once parties have made a collective bargaining contract the enforcement of that contract should be left to the usual processes of the law and not to the National Labor Relations Board." H.R. Conf. Rep. No. 510, 80th Cong., 1st Sess., p. 42.

Both the Senate and the House took pains to provide for "the usual processes of the law" by provisions which were the substantial equivalent of §301(a) in its present form. Both the Senate Report and the House Report indicate a primary concern that unions as well as employees should be bound to collective bargaining contracts. But there was also a broader concern — a concern with a procedure for making such agreements enforceable in the courts by either party. At one point the Senate Report, supra, p. 15, states, "We feel that the aggrieved party should also have a right of action in the Federal courts. Such a policy is completely in accord with the purpose of the Wagner Act which the Supreme Court declared was 'to compel employers to bargain collectively with their employees to the end that an employment contract, binding on both parties, should be made. . . .'"

Congress was also interested in promoting collective bargaining that ended with agreements not to strike. The Senate Report, supra, p. 16 states:

"If unions can break agreements with relative impunity, then such agreements do not tend to stabilize industrial relations. The execution of an agreement does not by itself promote industrial peace. The chief advantage which an employer can reasonably expect from a collective labor agreement is assurance of uninterrupted operation during the term of the agreement. Without some effective method of assuring freedom from economic warfare for the term of the agreement, there is little reason why an employer would desire to sign such a contract.

"Consequently, to encourage the making of agreements and to promote industrial peace through faithful performance by the parties, collective agreements affecting interstate commerce should be enforceable in the Federal courts. Our amendment would provide for suits by unions as legal entities and against unions as legal entities in the Federal courts in disputes affecting commerce."

Thus collective bargaining contracts were made "equally binding and enforceable on both parties." Id., at p. 15. As stated in the House Report, supra, p. 6, the new provision "makes labor organizations equally responsible with employers for contract violations and provides for suit by either against the other in the United States district courts." To repeat, the Senate Report, supra, p. 17, summed up the philosophy of §301 as follows: "Statutory recognition of the collective agreement as a valid, binding, and enforceable contract is a logical and necessary step. It will promote a higher degree of responsibility upon the parties to such agreements, and will thereby promote industrial peace."

Plainly the agreement to arbitrate grievance disputes is the quid pro quo for an agreement not to strike. Viewed in this light, the legislation does more than confer jurisdiction in the federal courts over labor organizations. It expresses a federal policy that federal courts should enforce these agreements on behalf of or against labor organizations and that industrial peace can be best obtained only in that way.

To be sure, there is a great medley of ideas reflected in the hearings, reports, and debates on this Act. Yet, to repeat, the entire tenor of the history indicates that the agreement to arbitrate grievance disputes was considered as quid pro quo of a no-strike agreement. And when in the House the debate narrowed to the question whether §301 was more than jurisdictional, it became abundantly clear that the purpose of the section was to provide the necessary legal remedies. Section 302 of the House Bill,[5] the substantial equivalent of the present §301, was being described by Mr. Hartley, the sponsor of the bill in the House:

"MR. BARDEN. Mr. Chairman, I take this time for the purpose of asking the Chairman a question, and in asking the question I want it understood that it is intended to make a part of the record that may hereafter be referred to as history of the legislation.

"It is my understanding that section 302, the section dealing with equal responsibility under collective bargaining contracts in strike actions and proceedings in district courts contemplates not only the ordinary lawsuits for damages but also such other remedial proceedings, both legal and equitable, as might be appropriate in the circumstances; in other words, proceedings could, for example, be brought by the employers, the labor organizations, or interested individual employees under the Declaratory Judgments Act in order to secure declarations from the Court of legal rights under the contract.

"MR. HARTLEY. The interpretation the gentleman has given of that section is absolutely correct." 93 Cong. Rec. 3656-3657.

It seems, therefore, clear to us that Congress adopted a policy which placed sanctions behind agreements to arbitrate grievance disputes,[6] by implication rejecting the common-law rule, discussed in Red Cross Line v. Atlantic Fruit Co., 264 U.S. 109, against enforcement of executory

---

[5] Section 302(a) as it passed the House read as follows:

"Any action for or proceeding involving a violation of an agreement between an employer and a labor organization or other representative of employees may be brought by either party in any district court of the United States having jurisdiction of the parties, without regard to the amount in controversy, if such agreement affects commerce, or the court otherwise has jurisdiction of the cause."

[6] Assn. of Westinghouse Employees v. Westinghouse Electric Corp., 348 U.S. 437, is quite a different case. There the union sued to recover unpaid wages on behalf of some 4,000 employees. The basic question concerned the standing of the union to sue and recover on those individual employment contracts. The question here concerns the right of the union to enforce the agreement to arbitrate which it has made with the employer.

agreements to arbitrate. We would undercut the Act and defeat its policy if we read §301 narrowly as only conferring jurisdiction over labor organizations.

The question then is, what is the substantive law to be applied in suits under §301(a)? We conclude that the substantive law to apply in suits under §301(a) is federal law, which the courts must fashion from the policy of our national labor laws. See Mendelsohn, Enforceability of Arbitration Agreements Under Taft-Hartley Section 301, 66 Yale L.J. 167. The Labor Management Relations Act expressly furnishes some substantive law. It points out what the parties may or may not do in certain situations. Other problems will lie in the penumbra of express statutory mandates. Some will lack express statutory sanction but will be solved by looking at the policy of the legislation and fashioning a remedy that will effectuate that policy. The range of judicial inventiveness will be determined by the nature of the problem. See Board of Commissioners v. United States, 308 U.S. 343, 351. Federal interpretation of the federal law will govern, not state law. Cf. Jerome v. United States, 318 U.S. 101, 104. But state law, if compatible with the purpose of §301, may be resorted to in order to find the rule that will best effectuate the federal policy. See Board of Commissioners v. United States, supra, at 351-352. Any state law applied, however, will be absorbed as federal law and will not be an independent source of private rights.

It is not uncommon for federal courts to fashion federal law where federal rights are concerned. See Clearfield Trust Co. v. United States, 318 U.S. 363, 366-367; National Metropolitan Bank v. United States, 323 U.S. 454. Congress has indicated by §301(a) the purpose to follow that course here. There is no constitutional difficulty. Article III, §2, extends the judicial power to cases "arising under . . . the Laws of the United States. . . ." The power of Congress to regulate these labor-management controversies under the Commerce Clause is plain. Houston & Texas R. Co. v. United States, 234 U.S. 342; Labor Board v. Jones & Laughlin Corp., 301 U.S. 1. A case or controversy arising under §301(a) is, therefore, one within the purview of judicial power as defined in Article III.

The question remains whether jurisdiction to compel arbitration of grievance disputes is withdrawn by the Norris-LaGuardia Act, 47 Stat. 70, 29 U.S.C. §101. Section 7 of that Act prescribes stiff procedural requirements for issuing an injunction in a labor dispute. The kinds of acts which had given rise to abuse of the power to enjoin are listed in §4. The failure to arbitrate was not a part and parcel of the abuses against which the Act was aimed. Section 8 of the Norris-LaGuardia Act does, indeed, indicate a congressional policy toward settlement of labor disputes by arbitration, for it denies injunctive relief to any person who has failed to make "every reasonable effort" to settle the dispute by negotiation, mediation, or "voluntary arbitration." Though a literal reading might bring the dispute within the terms of the Act (see Cox, Grievance Arbitration in the Federal Courts, 67 Harv. L. Rev. 591, 602-604), we see no justification in policy for restricting §301(a) to damage suits, leaving specific performance of a contract to arbitrate grievance disputes to the inapposite procedural requirements of that Act. Moreover, we held in Virginian R. Co. v. System Federation, 300 U.S. 515, and in Graham v. Brotherhood of Firemen, 338 U.S. 232, 237, that the Norris-LaGuardia Act does not deprive federal courts of jurisdiction to compel compliance with the mandates of the Railway Labor Act. The mandates there involved concerned racial discrimination. Yet those decisions were not based on any peculiarities of the Railway Labor Act. We followed the same course in Syres v. Oil Workers International Union, 350 U.S. 892, which was governed by the National Labor Relations Act. There an injunction was sought against racial discrimination in application of a collective bargaining agreement; and we allowed the injunction to issue. The congressional policy in favor of the enforcement of agreements to arbitrate grievance disputes being clear, there is no reason to submit them to the requirements of §7 of the Norris-LaGuardia Act.

A question of mootness was raised on oral argument. It appears that since the date of the decision in the Court of Appeals respondent has terminated its operations and has contracted to sell its mill properties. All work in the mill ceased in March, 1957. Some of the grievances, however, ask for back pay for increased workloads; and the collective bargaining agreement provides that "the Board of Arbitration shall have the right to adjust compensation retroactive to the date of the change." Insofar as the grievances sought restoration of workloads and job assignments, the case is, of course, moot. But to the extent that they sought a monetary award, the case is a continuing controversy.

The judgment of the Court of Appeals is reversed and the cause is remanded to that court for proceedings in conformity with this opinion.

Mr. Justice Black took no part in the consideration or decision of this case.

Mr. Justice Burton, whom Mr. Justice Harlan joins, concurring in the result.

. . . The District Court had jurisdiction over the action since it involved an obligation running to a union — a union controversy — and not uniquely personal rights of employees sought to be enforced by a union. . . . Having jurisdiction over the suit, the court was not powerless to fashion an appropriate federal remedy. The power to decree specific performance of a collectively bargained agreement to arbitrate finds its source in §301 itself, and in a Federal District Court's inherent equitable powers, nurtured by a congressional policy to encourage and enforce labor arbitration in industries affecting commerce.

I do not subscribe to the conclusion of the Court that the substantive law to be applied in a suit under §301 is federal law. At the same time, I agree with Judge Magruder in International Brotherhood v. W. L. Mead, Inc., 230 F.2d 576, that some federal rights may necessarily be involved in a §301 case, and hence that the constitutionality of §301 can be upheld as a congressional grant to Federal District Courts of what has been called "protective jurisdiction."

Mr. Justice Frankfurter, dissenting.

The Court has avoided the difficult problems raised by §301 of the Taft-Hartley Act, 61 Stat. 156, 29 U.S.C. §185, by attributing to the section an occult content. This plainly procedural section is transmuted into a mandate to the federal courts to fashion a whole body of substantive federal law appropriate for the complicated and touchy problems raised by collective bargaining. . . . This is more than can be fairly asked even from the alchemy of construction. . . .[28]

NOTES

1. In a companion case the Supreme Court held that the order of the District Court directing arbitration was final and therefore appealable under 28 U.S.C. §1291. Goodall-Sanford, Inc. v. United Textile Workers, Local 1802, 353 U.S. 550 (1957). This case was later distinguished by the Second Circuit in denying the appealability of an order staying an employer's action for an injunction against arbitration and a declaratory judgment that it was excused from any obligation to arbitrate. The court held that the stay order was interlocutory and not a final decision under 28 U.S.C. §1291. Armstrong-Norwalk Corp. v. Rubber Workers, 269 F.2d 618 (2d Cir. 1959).

Why should the appealability of an order granting or denying arbitration depend upon whether it was issued in an action to compel arbitration or in an action to prevent it? Cf. Drake Bakeries, Inc. v. Local 50, American Bakery Workers, AFL-CIO, 370 U.S. 254 (1962), where the Supreme Court held that a Section 301 action by an employer for damages for breach of a no-strike clause should be stayed pending arbitration.

2. In the second companion case to Lincoln Mills, General Electric Co. v. Local 205, United Electrical Workers, 353 U.S. 547 (1957), the Court affirmed the judgment of the Court of Appeals, 233 F.2d 85 (1st Cir. 1956), which had held the arbitration agreement enforceable by combining Section 301 with the provisions of the United States Arbitration Act, 61 Stat. 669 (1947), 9 U.S.C. §1. Justice Douglas wrote (p. 548): "We follow in part a different path than the Court of Appeals, though we reach the same result. . . ." Thus the Supreme Court sep-

---

[28] The Lincoln Mills decision has led to an extensive literature which includes: Aaron, On First Looking into the Lincoln Mills Decision, in Arbitration and the Law 1 (McKelvey ed. 1959); Bickel and Wellington, Legislative Purpose and the Judicial Process: The Lincoln Mills Case, 71 Harv. L. Rev. 1 (1957); Bunn, Lincoln Mills and the Jurisdiction to Enforce Collective Bargaining Agreements, 43 Va. L. Rev. 1217 (1957); Cox, Reflections on Labor Arbitration, 72 Harv. L. Rev. 1482 (1959); Cox, The Legal Nature of the Collective Bargaining Agreement, 57 Mich. L. Rev. 1 (1958); Feinsinger, Enforcement of Labor Agreements, 43 Va. L. Rev. 1261 (1957); Gregory, The Law of the Collective Agreement, 57 Mich. L. Rev. 635 (1959); Jenkins, The Impact of Lincoln Mills on the National Labor Relations Board, 6 U.C.L.A.L. Rev. 355 (1959); Kramer, In the Wake of Lincoln Mills, 9 Lab. L.J. 835 (1958); Comment, 11 Vand. L. Rev. 243 (1957); Notes, 59 Colum. L. Rev. 153 (1959), 57 id. 1123 (1957), 42 Minn. L. Rev. 1139 (1958), 30 Rocky Mt. L. Rev. 62 (1957). — Ed.

arated the enforcement of arbitration provisions in the labor agreement under Section 301 from the provisions of the Arbitration Act.

3. Retail Clerks International Assn. v. Lion Dry Goods, Inc., 369 U.S. 17 (1962), involved the scope of Section 301(a). A long dispute over representation rights was resolved in a strike settlement agreement which recognized that the union was not a representative of a majority of the employees. The settlement agreement contained a provision for arbitration of differences arising under it. Two such grievances had been decided in favor of the union and employees, but the employers had refused to abide by the awards. The union sought enforcement under Section 301. The employers contended that the term "contract" in Section 301 (a) referred only to collective bargaining agreements negotiated between employers and unions which represented the majority of the employees. The Supreme Court rejected this contention, holding (1) that the strike settlement agreement was a "contract" enforceable under Section 301, and (2) that the section could be invoked by a union even though it was not the statutory representative of the employees for whom it sued.

UNITED STEELWORKERS OF AMERICA v. AMERICAN MANUFACTURING CO.

Supreme Court of the United States, 1960
363 U.S. 564, 80 Sup. Ct. 1343, 4 L. Ed. 2d 1403

MR. JUSTICE DOUGLAS delivered the opinion of the Court.

This suit was brought by petitioner union in the District Court to compel arbitration of a "grievance" that petitioner, acting for one Sparks, a union member, had filed with the respondent, Sparks' employer. The employer defended on the ground (1) that Sparks is estopped from making his claim because he had a few days previously settled a workmen's compensation claim against the company on the basis that he was permanently partially disabled, (2) that Sparks is not physically able to do the work, and (3) that this type of dispute is not arbitrable under the collective bargaining agreement in question.

The agreement provided that during its term there would be "no strike," unless the employer refused to abide by a decision of the arbitrator. The agreement sets out a detailed grievance procedure with a provision for arbitration (regarded as the standard form) of all disputes between the parties "as to the meaning, interpretation and application of the provisions of this agreement." [1]

---

[1] The relevant arbitration provisions read as follows:

"Any disputes, misunderstandings, differences or grievances arising between the parties as to the meaning, interpretation and application of the provisions of this agreement, which are not adjusted as herein provided, may be submitted to the Board of Arbitration for decision. . . .

"The arbitrator may interpret this agreement and apply it to the particular case under consideration but shall, however, have no authority to add to, subtract from, or modify the terms of the agreement. Disputes relating to discharges or such matters as might involve a loss of pay for employees may carry an award of

The agreement reserves to the management power to suspend or discharge any employee "for cause." [2] It also contains a provision that the employer will employ and promote employees on the principle of seniority "where ability and efficiency are equal." Sparks left his work due to an injury and while off work brought an action for compensation benefits. The case was settled, Sparks' physician expressing the opinion that the injury had made him 25% "permanently partially disabled." That was on September 9. Two weeks later the union filed a grievance which charged that Sparks was entitled to return to his job by virtue of the seniority provision of the collective bargaining agreement. Respondent refused to arbitrate and this action was brought. The District Court held that Sparks, having accepted the settlement on the basis of permanent partial disability, was estopped to claim any seniority or employment rights and granted the motion for summary judgment. The Court of Appeals affirmed, 264 F.2d 624, for different reasons. After reviewing the evidence it held that the grievance is "a frivolous, patently baseless one, not subject to arbitration under the collective bargaining agreement." Id., at 628. The case is here on a writ of certiorari, 361 U.S. 881.

Section 203(d) of the Labor Management Relations Act, 1947, 61 Stat. 154, 29 U.S.C. §173(d), states, "Final adjustment by a method agreed upon by the parties is hereby declared to be the desirable method for settlement of grievance disputes arising over the application or interpretation of an existing collective-bargaining agreement. . . ." That policy can be effectuated only if the means chosen by the parties for settlement of their differences under a collective bargaining agreement is given full play.

A state decision that held to the contrary announced a principle that could only have a crippling effect on grievance arbitration. The case was International Assn. of Machinists v. Cutler-Hammer, Inc., 271 App. Div. 917, 67 N.Y.S.2d 317, aff'd 297 N.Y. 519, 74 N.E.2d 464. It held that "If the meaning of the provision of the contract sought to be arbitrated is beyond dispute, there cannot be anything to arbitrate and the contract cannot be said to provide for arbitration." 271 App. Div., at 918, 67 N.Y.S.2d, at 318. The lower courts in the instant case had a like preoccupation with ordinary contract law. The collective agreement requires arbitration of claims that courts might be unwilling to entertain. In the context of the plant or industry the grievance may assume proportions of which judges are ignorant. Yet, the agreement is to submit all griev-

---

back pay in whole or in part as may be determined by the Board of Arbitration.

"The decision of the Board of Arbitration shall be final and conclusively binding upon both parties, and the parties agree to observe and abide by same. . . ."

[2] "The Management of the works, the direction of the working force, plant layout and routine of work, including the right to hire, suspend, transfer, discharge or otherwise discipline any employee for cause, such cause being: infraction of company rules, inefficiency, insubordination, contagious disease harmful to others, and any other ground or reason that would tend to reduce or impair the efficiency of plant operation; and to lay off employees because of lack of work, is reserved to the Company, provided it does not conflict with this agreement. . . ."

ances to arbitration, not merely those that a court may deem to be meritorious. There is no exception in the "no strike" clause and none therefore should be read into the grievance clause, since one is the quid pro quo for the other. The question is not whether in the mind of the court there is equity in the claim. Arbitration is a stabilizing influence only as it serves as a vehicle for handling any and all disputes that arise under the agreement.

The collective agreement calls for the submision of grievances in the categories which it describes, irrespective of whether a court may deem them to be meritorious. In our role of developing a meaningful body of law to govern the interpretation and enforcement of collective bargaining agreements, we think special heed should be given to the context in which collective bargaining agreements are negotiated and the purpose which they are intended to serve. See Lewis v. Benedict Coal Corp., 361 U.S. 459, 468. The function of the court is very limited when the parties have agreed to submit all questions of contract interpretation to the arbitrator. It is confined to ascertaining whether the party seeking arbitration is making a claim which on its face is governed by the contract. Whether the moving party is right or wrong is a question of contract interpretation for the arbitrator. In these circumstances the moving party should not be deprived of the arbitrator's judgment, when it was his judgment and all that it connotes that was bargained for.

The courts, therefore, have no business weighing the merits of the grievance, considering whether there is equity in a particular claim, or determining whether there is particular language in the written instrument which will support the claim. The agreement is to submit all grievances to arbitration, not merely those which the court will deem meritorious. The processing of even frivolous claims may have therapeutic values of which those who are not a part of the plant environment may be quite unaware.

The union claimed in this case that the company had violated a specific provision of the contract. The company took the position that it had not violated that clause. There was, therefore, a dispute between the parties as to "the meaning, interpretation and application" of the collective bargaining agreement. Arbitration should have been ordered. When the judiciary undertakes to determine the merits of a grievance under the guise of interpreting the grievance procedure of collective bargaining agreements, it usurps a function which under that regime is entrusted to the arbitration tribunal.

Reversed.

MR. JUSTICE FRANKFURTER concurs in the result.

MR. JUSTICE WHITTAKER, believing that the District Court lacked jurisdiction to determine the merits of the claim which the parties had validly agreed to submit to the exclusive jurisdiction of a Board of Arbitrators (Textile Workers v. Lincoln Mills, 353 U.S. 448), concurs in the result of this opinion.

MR. JUSTICE BLACK took no part in the consideration or decision of this case.

NOTES

1. The Cutler-Hammer doctrine, rejected by the Court in the principal case, has also been rejected in New York by amendment to the Civil Practice Act. The statute now provides: ". . . [T]he court or judge shall not consider whether the claim with respect to which arbitration is sought is tenable, or otherwise pass on the merits of the dispute." N.Y. Civil Practice Act §1448(a) (1962).

2. Under the Revised Statutes of Canada the collective agreement must provide a method for resolving disputes. Section 19 of the Industrial Relations and Disputes Investigation Act provides in relevant part that "Every collective agreement . . . shall contain a provision for final settlement without stoppage of work, by arbitration or otherwise, of all differences between the parties . . . concerning its meaning or violation." R.S.C. 1952, c. 152.

UNITED STEELWORKERS OF AMERICA v. WARRIOR AND GULF NAVIGATION CO.

Supreme Court of the United States, 1960
363 U.S. 574, 80 Sup. Ct. 1347, 4 L. Ed. 2d 1409

MR. JUSTICE DOUGLAS delivered the opinion of the Court.

Respondent transports steel and steel products by barge and maintains a terminal at Chickasaw, Alabama, where it performs maintenance and repair work on its barges. The employees at that terminal constitute a bargaining unit covered by a collective bargaining agreement negotiated by petitioner union. Respondent between 1956 and 1958 laid off some employees, reducing the bargaining unit from 42 to 23 men. This reduction was due in part to respondent contracting maintenance work, previously done by its employees, to other companies. The latter used respondent's supervisors to lay out the work and hired some of the laid-off employees of respondent (at reduced wages). Some were in fact assigned to work on respondent's barges. A number of employees signed a grievance which petitioner presented to respondent, the grievance reading:

"We are hereby protesting the Company's actions, of arbitrarily and unreasonably contracting out work to other concerns, that could and previously has been performed by Company employees.

"This practice becomes unreasonable, unjust and discriminatory in lieu (sic) of the fact that at present there are a number of employees that have been laid off for about 1 and ½ years or more for allegedly lack of work.

"Confronted with these facts we charge that the Company is in violation of the contract by inducing a partial lock-out, of a number of the employees who would otherwise be working were it not for this unfair practice."

The collective agreement had both a "no strike" and a "no lockout" provision. It also had a grievance procedure which provided in relevant part as follows:

"Issues which conflict with any Federal statute in its application of established by Court procedure or matters which are strictly a function of management shall not be subject to arbitration under this section.

"Should differences arise between the Company and the Union or its members employed by the Company as to the meaning and application of the provisions of this Agreement, or should any local trouble of any kind arise, there shall be no suspension of work on account of such differences but an earnest effort shall be made to settle such differences immediately in the following manner:

"A. For Maintenance Employees:

"First, between the aggrieved employees, and the Foreman involved;

"Second, between a member or members of the Grievance Committee designated by the Union, and the Foreman and Master Mechanic. . . .

"Fifth, if agreement has not been reached the matter shall be referred to an impartial umpire for decision. The parties shall meet to decide on an umpire acceptable to both. If no agreement on selection of an umpire is reached, the parties shall jointly petition the United States Conciliation Service for suggestion of a list of umpires from which selection will be made. The decision of the umpire shall be final."

Settlement of this grievance was not had and respondent refused arbitration. This suit was then commenced by the union to compel it.

The District Court granted respondent's motion to dismiss the complaint. 168 F. Supp. 702. It held after hearing evidence, much of which went to the merits of the grievance, that the agreement did not "confide in an arbitrator the right to review the defendant's business judgment in contracting out work." Id., at 705. It further held that "the contracting out of repair and maintenance work, as well as construction work, is strictly a function of management not limited in any respect by the labor agreement involved here." Ibid. The Court of Appeals affirmed by a divided vote, 269 F.2d 633, the majority holding that the collective agreement had withdrawn from the grievance procedure "matters which are strictly a function of management" and that contracting out fell in that exception. . . .

We held in Textile Workers v. Lincoln Mills, 353 U.S. 448, that a grievance arbitration provision in a collective agreement could be enforced by reason of §301(a) of the Labor Management Relations Act and that the policy to be applied in enforcing this type of arbitration was that reflected in our national labor laws. Id., at 456-457. The present federal policy is to promote industrial stabilization through the collective bargaining agreement. Id., at 453-454. A major factor in achieving industrial peace is the inclusion of a provision for arbitration of grievances in the collective bargaining agreement.

Thus the run of arbitration cases, illustrated by Wilko v. Swan, 346 U.S. 427, becomes irrelevant to our problem. There the choice is between the adjudication of cases or controversies in courts with established procedures or even special statutory safeguards on the one hand and the settlement of them in the more informal arbitration tribunal on the other. In the commercial case, arbitration is the substitute for litigation. Here arbitration is the substitute for industrial strife. Since arbitration of labor disputes has quite different functions from arbitration under an ordinary commercial agreement, the hostility evinced by courts toward arbitration of commercial agreements has no place here. For arbitration of labor disputes under collective bargaining agreements is part and parcel of the collective bargaining process itself.

The collective bargaining agreement states the rights and duties of the parties. It is more than a contract; it is a generalized code to govern a myriad of cases which the draftsmen cannot wholly anticipate. See Shulman, Reason, Contract, and Law in Labor Relations, 68 Harv. L. Rev. 999, 1004-1005. The collective agreement covers the whole employment relationship. It calls into being a new common law — the common law of a particular industry or of a particular plant. As one observer has put it:[6]

". . . (I)t is not unqualifiedly true that a collective-bargaining agreement is simply a document by which the union and employees have imposed upon management limited, express restrictions of its otherwise absolute right to manage the enterprise, so that an employee's claim must fail unless he can point to a specific contract provision upon which the claim is founded. There are too many people, too many problems, too many unforeseeable contingencies to make the words of the contract the exclusive source of rights and duties. One cannot reduce all the rules governing a community like an industrial plant to fifteen or even fifty pages. Within the sphere of collective bargaining, the institutional characteristics and the governmental nature of the collective-bargaining process demand a common law of the shop which implements and furnishes the context of the agreement. We must assume that intelligent negotiators acknowledged so plain a need unless they stated a contrary rule in plain words."

A collective bargaining agreement is an effort to erect a system of industrial self-government. When most parties enter into contractual relationship they do so voluntarily, in the sense that there is no real compulsion to deal with one another, as opposed to dealing with other parties. This is not true of the labor agreement. The choice is generally not between entering or refusing to enter into a relationship, for that in all probability pre-exists the negotiations. Rather it is between having that relationship governed by an agreed-upon rule of law or leaving each and every matter subject to a temporary resolution dependent solely upon the relative strength, at any given moment, of the contending forces. The mature labor agreement may attempt to regulate all aspects of the complicated relationship, from the most crucial to the most minute over an extended period of time. Because of the compulsion to reach agreement and the breadth of the matters covered, as well as the need for a fairly

[6] Cox, Reflections upon Labor Arbitration, 72 Harv. L. Rev. 1482, 1498-1499 (1959).

concise and readable instrument, the product of negotiations (the written document) is, in the words of the late Dean Shulman, "a compilation of diverse provisions: some provide objective criteria almost automatically applicable; some provide more or less specific standards which require reason and judgment in their application; and some do little more than leave problems to future consideration with an expression of hope and good faith." Shulman, supra, at 1005. Gaps may be left to be filled in by reference to the practices of the particular industry and of the various shops covered by the agreement. Many of the specific practices which underlie the agreement may be unknown, except in hazy form, even to the negotiators. Courts and arbitration in the context of most commercial contracts are resorted to because there has been a breakdown in the working relationship of the parties; such resort is the unwanted exception. But the grievance machinery under a collective bargaining agreement is at the very heart of the system of industrial self-government. Arbitration is the means of solving the unforeseeable by molding a system of private law for all the problems which may arise and to provide for their solution in a way which will generally accord with the variant needs and desires of the parties. The processing of disputes through the grievance machinery is actually a vehicle by which meaning and content are given to the collective bargaining agreement.

Apart from matters that the parties specifically exclude, all of the questions on which the parties disagree must therefore come within the scope of the grievance and arbitration provisions of the collective agreement. The grievance procedure is, in other words, a part of the continuous collective bargaining process. It, rather than a strike, is the terminal point of a disagreement.

The labor arbitrator performs functions which are not normal to the courts; the considerations which help him fashion judgments may indeed be foreign to the competence of courts.

"A proper conception of the arbitrator's function is basic. He is not a public tribunal imposed upon the parties by superior authority which the parties are obliged to accept. He has no general charter to administer justice for a community which transcends the parties. He is rather part of a system of self-government created by and confined to the parties. . . ." Shulman, supra, at 1016.

The labor arbitrator's source of law is not confined to the express provisions of the contract, as the industrial common law — the practices of the industry and the shop — is equally a part of the collective bargaining agreement although not expressed in it. The labor arbitrator is usually chosen because of the parties' confidence in his knowledge of the common law of the shop and their trust in his personal judgment to bring to bear considerations which are not expressed in the contract as criteria for judgment. The parties expect that his judgment of a particular grievance will reflect not only what the contract says but, insofar as the collective bargaining agreement permits, such factors as the effect upon productivity of a particular result, its consequence to the morale of the shop, his judgment whether tensions will be heightened or diminished. For the parties' objective in using the arbitration process is primarily to further their common goal of uninterrupted production under the agreement, to make the agreement serve their specialized needs. The ablest judge cannot be expected to bring the same experience and competence to bear upon the determination of a grievance, because he cannot be similarly informed.

The Congress, however, has by §301 of the Labor Management Relations Act, assigned the courts the duty of determining whether the reluctant party has breached his promise to arbitrate. For arbitration is a matter of contract and a party cannot be required to submit to arbitration any dispute which he has not agreed so to submit. Yet, to be consistent with congressional policy in favor of settlement of disputes by the parties through the machinery of arbitration, the judicial inquiry under §301 must be strictly confined to the question whether the reluctant party did agree to arbitrate the grievance or did agree to give the arbitrator power to make the award he made. An order to arbitrate the particular grievance should not be denied unless it may be said with positive assurance that the arbitration clause is not susceptible of an interpretation that covers the asserted dispute. Doubts should be resolved in favor of coverage.

We do not agree with the lower courts that contracting-out grievances were necessarily excepted from the grievance procedure of this agreement. To be sure, the agreement provides that "matters which are strictly a functon of management shall not be subject to arbitration." But it goes on to say that if "differences" arise or if "any local trouble of any kind" arises, the grievance procedure shall be applicable.

Collective bargaining agreements regulate or restrict the exercise of management functions; they do not oust management from the performance of them. Management hires and fires, pays and promotes, supervises and plans. All these are part of its function, and absent a collective bargaining, it may be exercised freely except as limited by public law and by the willingness of employees to work under the particular, unilaterally imposed conditions. A collective bargaining agreement may treat only with certain specific practices, leaving the rest to management but subject to the possibility of work stoppages. When, however, an absolute no-strike clause is included in the agreement, then in a very real sense everything that management does is subject to the agreement, for either management is prohibited or limited in the action it takes, or if not, it is protected from interference by strikes. This comprehensive reach of the collective bargaining agreement does not mean, however, that the language, "strictly a function of management," has no meaning.

"Strictly a function of management" might be thought to refer to any practice of management in which, under particular circumstances prescribed by the agreement, it is permitted to indulge. But if courts, in order to determine arbitrability, were allowed to determine what is permitted and what is not, the arbitration clause would be swallowed up by the exception. Every grievance in a sense involves a claim that management has violated some provision of the agreement.

Accordingly, "strictly a function of management" must be interpreted as referring only to that over which the contract gives management complete control and unfettered discretion. Respondent claims that the contracting out of work falls within this category. Contracting out work is the basis of many grievances; and that type of claim is grist in the mills of the arbitrators. A specific collective bargaining agreement may exclude contracting out from the grievance procedure. Or a written collateral agreement may make clear that contracting out was not a matter for arbitration. In such a case a grievance based solely on contracting out would not be arbitrable. Here, however, there is no such provision. Nor is there any showing that the parties designed the phrase "strictly a function of management" to encompass any and all forms of contracting out. In the absence of any express provision excluding a particular grievance from arbitration, we think only the most forceful evidence of a purpose to exclude the claim from arbitration can prevail, particularly where, as here, the exclusion clause is vague and the arbitration clause quite broad. Since any attempt by a court to infer such a purpose necessarily comprehends the merits, the court should view with suspicion an attempt to persuade it to become entangled in the construction of the substantive provisions of a labor agreement, even through the back door of interpreting the arbitration clause, when the alternative is to utilize the services of an arbitrator.

The grievance alleged that the contracting out was a violation of the collective bargaining agreement. There was, therefore, a dispute "as to the meaning and application of the provisions of this Agreement" which the parties had agreed would be determined by arbitration.

The judiciary sits in these cases to bring into operation an arbitral process which substitutes a regime of peaceful settlement for the older regime of industrial conflict. Whether contracting out in the present case violated the agreement is the question. It is a question for the arbiter, not for the courts.

Reversed.

MR. JUSTICE FRANKFURTER concurs in the result.

MR. JUSTICE BLACK took no part in the consideration or decision of this case.

[Mr. Justice Whittaker dissented.]

MR. JUSTICE BRENNAN, with whom MR. JUSTICE HARLAN joins, concurring.

In each of these two cases [American Manufacturing and Warrior and Gulf] the issue concerns the enforcement of but one promise — the promise to arbitrate in the context of an agreement dealing with a particular subject matter, the industrial relations between employers and employees. Other promises contained in the collective bargaining agreements are beside the point unless, by the very terms of the arbitration promise, they are made relevant to its interpretation. And I emphasize this, for the arbitration promise is itself a contract. The parties are free to make that promise as broad or as narrow as they wish, for there is no compulsion in law requiring them to include any such promises in their agreement. The meaning of the arbitration promise is not to be found simply by reference to the dictionary definitions of the words the parties use, or by reference to the interpretation of commercial arbitration clauses. Words in a collective bargaining agreement, rightly viewed by the Court to be the charter instrument of a system of industrial self-government, like words in a statute, are to be understood only by reference to the background which gave rise to their inclusion. The Court therefore avoids the prescription of inflexible rules for the enforcement of arbitration promises. Guidance is given by identifying the various considerations which a court should take into account when construing a particular clause — considerations of the milieu in which the clause is negotiated and of the national labor policy. It is particularly underscored that the arbitral process in collective bargaining presupposes that the parties wanted the informed judgment of an arbitrator, precisely for the reason that judges cannot provide it. Therefore, a court asked to enforce a promise to arbitrate should ordinarily refrain from involving itself in the interpretation of the substantive provisions of the contract.

To be sure, since arbitration is a creature of contract, a court must always inquire, when a party seeks to invoke its aid to force a reluctant party to the arbitration table, whether the parties have agreed to arbitrate the particular dispute. In this sense, the question of whether a dispute is "arbitrable" is inescapably for the court.

On examining the arbitration clause, the court may conclude that it commits to arbitration any "dispute, difference, disagreement, or controversy of any nature or character." With that finding the court will have exhausted its function, except to order the reluctant party to arbitration. Similarly, although the arbitrator may be empowered only to interpret and apply the contract, the parties may have provided that any dispute as to whether a particular claim is within the arbitration clause is itself for the arbitrator. Again the court, without more, must send any dispute to the arbitrator, for the parties have agreed that the construction of the arbitration promise itself is for the arbitrator, and the reluctant party has breached his promise by refusing to submit the dispute to arbitration.

In American [United Steelworkers of America v. American Manufacturing Co., 363 U.S. 364], the Court deals with a request to enforce the "standard" form of arbitration clause, one that provides for the arbitration of "(a)ny disputes, misunderstandings, differences or grievances arising between the parties as to the meaning, interpretation and application of this agreement. . . ." Since the arbitration clause itself is part of the agreement, it might be argued that a dispute as to the meaning of that clause is for the arbitrator. But the Court rejects this position, saying that the threshold question, the meaning of the arbitration clause itself, is for the judge unless the parties clearly state to the contrary. However, the Court finds that the meaning of that "standard" clause is simply that the parties have agreed to arbitrate any dispute which the moving party asserts to involve construction of the substantive provisions of the contract, because such a dispute necessarily does involve such a construction.

The issue in the Warrior case is essentially no different from that in American, that is, it is whether the company agreed to arbitrate a particular grievance. In contrast to American, however, the arbitration promise here excludes a particular area from arbitration — "matters which are strictly a function of management." Because the arbitration promise is different, the scope of the court's inquiry may be broader. Here, a court may be required to examine the substantive provisions of the contract to ascertain whether the parties have provided that contracting out shall be a "function of management." If a court may delve into the merits to the extent of inquiring whether the parties have expressly agreed whether or not contracting out was a "function of management," why was it error for the lower court here to evaluate the evidence of bargaining history for the same purpose? Neat logical distinctions do not provide the answer. The Court rightly concludes that appropriate regard for the national labor policy and the special factors relevant to the labor arbitral process, admonish that judicial inquiry into the merits of this grievance should be limited to the search for an explicit provision which brings the grievance under the cover of the exclusion clause since "the exclusion clause is vague and arbitration clause quite broad." The hazard of going further into the merits is amply demonstrated by what the courts below did. On the basis of inconclusive evidence, those courts found that Warrior was in no way limited by any implied covenants of good faith and fair dealing from contracting out as it pleased — which would necessarily mean that Warrior was free completely to destroy the collective bargaining agreement by contracting out all the work.

The very ambiguity of the Warrior exclusion clause suggests that the parties were generally more concerned with having an arbitrator render decisions as to the meaning of the contract than they were in restricting the arbitrator's jurisdiction. The case might of course be otherwise were the arbitration clause very narrow, or the exclusion clause quite specific, for the inference might then be permissible that the parties had manifested a greater interest in confining the arbitrator; the presumption of arbitrability would then not have the same force and the Court would be somewhat freer to examine into the merits.

The Court makes reference to an arbitration clause being the quid pro quo for a no-strike clause. I do not understand the Court to mean that the application of the principles announced today depends upon the presence of a no-strike clause in the agreement.

MR. JUSTICE FRANKFURTER joins these observations.

NOTES

1. On July 29, 1964, Congressman Goodell (R., N.Y.) introduced in the House a bill (H.R. 12127) which embodied a resolution previously adopted by the House of Delegates of the American Bar Association, 56 L.R.R. 363 (1964). If adopted, it would amend Section 301 by adding the following subparagraph:

"(f) Where suit is brought under this section to compel the performance of an agreement to arbitrate contained in a collective bargaining agreement, the court will direct arbitration only if the court is convinced that the dispute sought to be arbitrated is one which the language of the collective bargaining agreement clearly makes arbitrable, and, in any order directing arbitration, will specify the issue or issues which are appropriate for arbitration under the language of the collective bargaining agreement; and, where suit is brought under this section to enforce the award of an arbitrator, the court will grant enforcement only if, and to the extent that, the arbitrator has conformed to the jurisdictional area permissible under the controlling collective bargaining agreement."

2. Following the Warrior decision there have been many cases in which arbitration has been ordered. It has been held that a union is entitled to arbitrate the refusal of an employer to pay a "customary" Christmas bonus which is not specifically referred to in the collective agreement, Harris v. United Steelworkers, 298 F.2d 363 (3d Cir. 1962), cert. denied, 369 U.S. 851 (1962); that arbitration should be ordered concerning the discharge of an employee, even though the company relied on its contract with the Federal Government and a government contracting officer had required the discharge, International Assn. of Machinists v. Hayes Corp., 296 F.2d 238 (5th Cir. 1961); and that arbitration should even be ordered for a grievance filed after expiration of the contract under which relief is sought, General Tire Co. v. Rubber Workers, 191 F. Supp. 911 (D.R.I. 1961), aff'd per curiam, 294 F.2d 957 (1st Cir. 1961). In Deaton Truck Line v. Local 612, Teamsters, 314 F.2d 418 (5th Cir. 1962), the court rejected a claim that a contract covering "lessor-drivers" was a commercial contract outside the scope of Section 301(a). It held that a provision that disputes "may" be submitted to arbitration meant that either party had the option of requiring arbitration, and that the federal district court may provide that it will appoint an arbitrator if the parties do not agree on an arbitrator under the method provided in their contract.

3. Many collective bargaining argreements establish, in the grievance procedure, certain conditions precedent to arbitration, which include the requirement that the grievance be processed in accordance with a time schedule. If the union fails to process the grievance in accordance with these procedures, is the employer required by Section 301 to submit the grievance to arbitration? Is the interpretation of the provisions of the contract which deal with procedure prior to arbitration a matter for the arbitrator?

In John Wiley & Sons v. Livingston, 376 U.S. 543 (1964), it was held that while the courts have the task of determining substantive arbitrability (whether the parties are obligated to submit the subject matter to arbitration), procedural questions which grow out of the dispute and bear on its final disposition should be left to the arbitrator. In this case the Court held that the disappearance by merger of a corporate employer which has entered into a collective bargaining agreement does not automatically terminate all rights of the employees covered by the agreement. In appropriate circumstances, the Court observed, the successor employer may be required to arbitrate with the union under the agreement. Although the Court recognized that principles of law governing ordinary contracts would not bind to a contract an unconsenting successor to a contracting party, it pointed out that a collective bargaining agreement is not an ordinary contract and that it is not in any real sense the simple product of a consensual relationship. Hence, in holding that the arbitration provisions of the collective bargaining agreement survived the merger so as to be operative against the successor employer on such matters as seniority rights, job security, severance pay, and vacation pay, the Court found that the fact that the successor employer had not signed the contract was not controlling.

4. The Steelworkers cases define the duty of the District Court in connection with the issue of arbitrability. What of the duty of the arbitrator? If the contention is made before the arbitrator that a matter submitted to him is not within his jurisdiction, is he required to apply the standards established in the Steelworkers cases in deciding this issue? If the District Court has ordered arbitration under the doctrine of the Steelworkers cases, may the arbitrator thereafter determine that he does not have jurisdiction? Or has the District Court's decision become the "law of the case"?

The result of the Warrior decision was an arbitration which is reported in Warrior and Gulf Navigation Co., 61-2 ARB, par. 8401 (1961). The arbitrator examined de novo all the contentions as to arbitrability and concluded that he did have jurisdiction. On the merits, he concluded that the company had engaged in certain improper subcontracting. The only relief he granted was to advance by two years the layoff dates of employees who had been deprived of work by subcontracting.

2. *Arbitration Awards*

UNITED STEELWORKERS OF AMERICA v. ENTERPRISE WHEEL AND CAR CORP.

Supreme Court of the United States, 1960
363 U.S. 593, 80 Sup. Ct. 1358, 4 L. Ed. 2d 1424

MR. JUSTICE DOUGLAS delivered the opinion of the Court.

Petitioner union and respondent during the period relevant here had a collective bargaining agreement which provided that any differences "as to the meaning and application" of the agreement should be submitted to arbitration and that the arbitrator's decision "shall be final and binding on the parties." Special provisions were included concerning the suspension and discharge of employees. The agreement stated:

"Should it be determined by the Company or by an arbitrator in accordance with the grievance procedure that the employee has been suspended unjustly or discharged in violation of the provisions of this Agreement, the Company shall reinstate the employee and pay full compensation at the employee's regular rate of pay for the time lost."

The agreement also provided:

". . . It is understood and agreed that neither party will institute *civil suits or legal proceedings* against the other for alleged violation of any of the provisions of this labor contract; instead all disputes will be settled in the manner outlined in this Article III — Adjustment of Grievances."

A group of employees left their jobs in protest against the discharge of one employee. A union official advised them at once to return to work. An official of respondent at their request gave them permission and then rescinded it. The next day they were told they did not have a job any more "until this thing was settled one way or the other."

A grievance was filed; and when respondent finally refused to arbitrate, this suit was brought for specific enforcement of the arbitration provisions of the agreement. The District Court ordered arbitration. The arbitrator found that the discharge of the men was not justified, though their conduct, he said, was improper. In his view the facts warranted at most a suspension of the men for 10 days each. After their discharge and before the arbitration award the collective bargaining agreement had expired. The union, however, continued to represent the workers at the plant. The arbitrator rejected the contention that expiration of the agreement barred reinstatement of the employees. He held that the provision of the agreement above quoted imposed an unconditional obligation on the employer. He awarded reinstatement with back pay, minus pay for a 10-day suspension and such sums as these employees received from other employment.

Respondent refused to comply with the award. Petitioner moved the District Court for enforcement. The District Court directed respondent to comply. 168 F. Supp. 308. The Court of Appeals, while agreeing that the District Court had jurisdiction to enforce an arbitration award under a collective bargaining agreement, held that the failure of the award to specify the amounts to be deducted from the back pay rendered the award unenforceable. That defect, it agreed, could be remedied by requiring the parties to complete the arbitration. It went on to hold, however, that an award for back pay subsequent to the date of termination of the collective bargaining agreement could not be enforced. It also held that the requirement for reinstatement of the discharged employees was likewise unenforceable because the collective bargaining agreement had expired. 269 F.2d 327. . . .

The refusal of courts to review the merits of an arbitration award is the proper approach to arbitration under collective bargaining agreements. The federal policy of settling labor disputes by arbitration would be undermined if courts had the final say on the merits of the awards. As we stated in United Steelworkers of America v. Warrior & Gulf Navigation Co. [363 U.S. 574], decided this day, the arbitrators under these collective agreements are indispensable agencies in a continuous collective bargaining process. They sit to settle disputes at the plant level — disputes that require for their solution knowledge of the custom and practices of a particular factory or of a particular industry as reflected in particular agreements.

When an arbitrator is commissioned to interpret and apply the collective bargaining agreement, he is to bring his informed judgment to bear in order to reach a fair solution of a problem. This is especially true when it comes to formulating remedies.   There the need is for flexibility in meeting a wide variety of situations.   The draftsmen may never have thought of what specific remedy should be awarded to meet a particular contingency.   Nevertheless, an arbitrator is confined to interpretation and application of the collective bargaining agreement; he does not sit to dispense his own brand of industrial justice.   He may of course look for guidance from many sources, yet his award is legitimate only so long as it draws its essence from the collective bargaining agreement.   When the arbitrator's words manifest an infidelity to this obligation, courts have no choice but to refuse enforcement of the award.

The opinion of the arbitrator in this case, as it bears upon the award of back pay beyond the date of the agreement's expiration and reinstatement, is ambiguous.   It may be read as based solely upon the arbitrator's view of the requirements of enacted legislation, which would mean that he exceeded the scope of the submission.   Or it may be read as embodying a construction of the agreement itself, perhaps with the arbitrator looking to "the law" for help in determining the sense of the agreement.   A mere ambiguity in the opinion accompanying an award, which permits the inference that the arbitrator may have exceeded his authority, is not a reason for refusing to enforce the award.   Arbitrators have no obligation to the court to give their reasons for an award.   To require opinions free of ambiguity may lead arbitrators to play it safe by writing no supporting opinions.   This would be undesirable for a well-reasoned opinion tends to engender confidence in the integrity of the process and aids in clarifying the underlying agreement.   Moreover, we see no reason to assume that this arbitrator has abused the trust the parties confided in him and has not stayed within the areas marked out for his consideration.   It is not apparent that he went beyond the submission.   The Court of Appeals' opinion refusing to enforce the reinstatement and partial back pay portions of the award was not based upon any finding that the arbitrator did not premise his award on his construction of the contract.   It merely disagreed with the arbitrator's construction of it.

The collective bargaining agreement could have provided that if any of the employees were wrongfully discharged, the remedy would be reinstatement and back pay up to the date they were returned to work.   Respondent's major argument seems to be that by applying correct principles of law to the interpretation of the collective bargaining agreement it can be determined that the agreement did not so provide, and that therefore the arbitrator's decision was not based upon the contract.   The acceptance of this view would require courts, even under the standard arbitration clause, to review the merits of every construction of the contract.   This plenary review by a court of the merits would make meaningless the provisions that the arbitrator's decision is final, for in reality it would almost never be final.   This underlines the fundamental error which we have alluded to in United Steelworkers of America v. American Manufacturing Co. [363 U.S. 564], decided this day.   As we there emphasized, the question of interpretation of the collective bargaining agreement is a question for the arbitrator.   It is the arbitrator's construction which was bargained for; and so far as the arbitrator's decision concerns construction of the contract, the courts have no business overruling him because their interpretation of the contract is different from his.

We agree with the Court of Appeals that the judgment of the District Court should be modified so that the amounts due the employees may be definitely determined by arbitration. In all other respects we think the judgment of the District Court should be affirmed. Accordingly, we reverse the judgment of the Court of Appeals, except for that modification, and remand the case to the District Court for proceedings in conformity with this opinion.

MR. JUSTICE FRANKFURTER concurs in the result.

MR. JUSTICE BLACK took no part in the consideration or decision of this case.

MR. JUSTICE WHITTAKER, dissenting. . . .

It is conceded, too, that the collective agreement expired by its terms on April 4, 1957, and was never extended or renewed.

The sole question here is whether the arbitrator exceeded the submission and his powers in awarding reinstatement and back pay for any period after expiration of the collective agreements. Like the Court of Appeals, I think he did. I find nothing in the collective agreement that purports to so authorize. Nor does the Court point to anything in the agreement that purports to do so. Indeed, the union does not contend that there is any such covenant in the contract. Doubtless all rights that accrued to the employees under the collective agreement during its term, and that were made arbitrable by its provisions, could be awarded to them by the arbitrator, even though the period of the agreement had ended. But surely no rights *accrued* to the employees under the agreement after it had expired. Save for the provisions of the collective agreement, and in the absence, as here, of any applicable rule of law or contrary covenant between the employer and the employees, the employer had the legal right to discharge the employees at will. The collective agreement, however, protected them against discharge, for specified reasons, during its continuation. But when that agreement expired, it did not continue to afford rights *in futuro* to the employees — as though still effective and governing. After the agreement expired, the employment status of these 11 employees was terminable at the will of the employer, as the Court of Appeals quite properly held, 269 F.2d, at 331, and see Meadows v. Radio Industries, 222 F.2d 347, 349 (C.A. 7th Cir.); Atchison, T. & S.F.R. Co. v. Andrews, 211 F.2d 264, 265 (C.A. 10th Cir.); Warden v. Hinds, 163 F. 201 (C.A. 4th Cir.), and the announced discharge of these 11 employees then became lawfully effective.

Once the contract expired, no rights continued to accrue under it to the employees. Thereafter they had no contractual right to demand that the employer continue to employ them, and *a fortiori* the arbitrator did not have power to order the employer to do so; nor did the arbitrator have power to order the employer to pay wages to them after the date of termination of the contract, which was also the effective date of their discharges.

The judgment of the Court of Appeals, affirming so much of the award as required reinstatement of the 11 employees to employment status and payment of their wages until expiration of the contract, but not thereafter, seems to me to be indubitably correct, and I would affirm it.

NOTES

1. May a court refuse to enforce an award on the ground that it is against public policy?

Mrs. Doris Walker was a law school graduate, member of Phi Beta Kappa, and editor of the California Law Review. She was admitted to the bar and practiced for four years. In 1946 she went to work in a canning factory and became an organizer for the Food, Tobacco and Agricultural Workers. She then obtained employment with Cutter Laboratories. In her application she concealed her legal training and experience and falsified her previous employment. She did this because of her belief that if the company knew the facts she would not be hired.

Mrs. Walker became active in the union, held several responsible positions, and became president of her local. During contract negotiations in 1949, the company discharged her, and the union carried her case to arbitration. In the arbitration hearing, the company justified her dismissal on two grounds: (1) the omissions and falsifications in her application, and (2) her membership in the Communist Party. The Arbitration Board found these facts to be true, but also found that the company had known these facts for two years and had given no adequate reason for the delay in acting. The Board found that the real reason for the discharge was her union activity, and therefore the discharge was in violation of the collective agreement. The employer refused to comply with the award granting reinstatement with back pay. The union brought proceedings to confirm the award, and the company countermoved to vacate the award.

The trial court ordered enforcement of the award. On appeal, the Supreme Court of California reversed. It stated:

"As ground for reversal the company contends . . . that an arbitration award which directs that a member of the Communist Party who is dedicated to that party's program of 'sabotage, force, violence and the like' be reinstated to employment in a plant which produces antibiotics used by both the military and civilians is against public policy, as expressed in both federal and state laws. . . . With this contention we agree." Black v. Cutter Laboratories, 43 Cal. 2d 788, 798, 278 P.2d 905, 911 (1955). The court held that the type of activity engaged in by Mrs. Walker — membership and participation in the Communist Party — is an activity which, as a matter of public policy, the company should not be held to have waived by its failure to discharge her earlier than it did. The court asserted that parties cannot be estopped from relying on defenses based on considerations of public policy, and that Mrs. Walker's continued membership in the Communist Party, even at the time of the arbitration hearing, was a continuing ground for discharge. Justice Traynor in dissent observed that the majority holding meant that an employer who was indifferent to the fact that an employee was a Communist can nevertheless violate a collective bargaining agreement by discharging the employee for lawful union activity.

On appeal the majority of the Supreme Court of the United States held that the decision involved only California's construction of a local contract under local law, and that no substantial federal question was presented. Justice Douglas, with whom the Chief Justice and Justice Black concurred, dissented. Justice Douglas found that "the blunt truth is that Doris Walker is not discharged for misconduct but either because of her legitimate labor union activities or because of her political ideology or belief. Belief cannot be penalized consistently with the First Amendment." Black v. Cutter Laboratories, 351 U.S. 292, 304 (1956). This case is discussed in Notes, 11 Rutgers L. Rev. 745 (1957), and 68 Harv. L. Rev. 1285 (1955). See also Roberts, Arbitration and Security Risk Disputes, 10 Arb. J.(n.s.) 13 (1955); Annotation, Discharge from private employment on grounds of political views or conduct, 51 A.L.R.2d 742 (1957).

Suppose that the evidence showed that the company knew for two years before Mrs. Walker's discharge that she was active in the Communist Party, that the company knew, before she was discharged, she had quit the party, but that the company decided to discharge her for her past membership and activities. Could it properly be held that the company had condoned her prior conduct for purposes of industrial discipline, even if her conduct was against public policy? What weight should be given to her continued membership and activity in the Communist Party?

2. The Commissioners on Uniform State Laws adopted, and the American Bar Association House of Delegates approved, a Uniform Arbitration Act in 1955. Section 12(a) of the Act dealing with the power of the court to vacate an award provided: "Upon application of a party, the court shall vacate an award where: . . . (3) The Arbitrators exceeded their powers or rendered an award contrary to public policy; . . .", 24 L.A. 886 (1955).

Because of repercussions from the decision in the Cutter Laboratories case, the proposed Act was amended by striking the clause dealing with awards contrary to public policy. See 27 L.A. 910 (1957), and Panel Discussion, The Proposed Uniform Arbitration Act, in Critical Issues in Labor Arbitration 112 (McKelvey ed. 1957).

The Uniform Act has been adopted in five states: Ariz. Rev. Stats. §12-1501; Ill. Ann., c. 10, §101 (Smith-Hurd); Mass. Gen. Laws Ann., c. 251, §1; Minn. Stats. Ann. §572.08; Wyo. Stats. §1-1048.1. See Persig, Minnesota Uniform Arbitration Act and the Lincoln Mills Case, 42 Minn. L. Rev. 333 (1958). Does the amended Uniform Act avoid the problem in the Cutter Laboratories case? Compare Section 13 of the draft United States Labor Arbitration Act proposed by the National Academy of Arbitrators, which provides in part: "The fact that the award orders relief of a kind which might not be granted by a court of law or equity is not ground for vacating the award." 34 L.A. 3, 8 (1960).

3. In Local 543, International Union of Electrical Workers v. Otis Ele-

vator Co., 314 F.2d 25 (2d Cir. 1963), the court refused to find that public policy precluded enforcement of an arbitration award which reinstated an employee who was fired after being convicted of running a "numbers" operation on his employer's premises. The employee was fined under the New York Penal Code, and the arbitrator denied him seven months' back pay. Affirming the award, the court concluded that there was no federal policy that required a greater vindication of public condemnation of gambling. See Blumrosen, Public Policy Considerations in Labor Arbitration Cases, 14 Rutgers L. Rev. 217 (1960); Cox, The Place of Law in Labor Arbitration, in The Profession of Labor Arbitration 76 (McKelvey ed. 1957); Jones, The Nature of the Court's "Jurisdiction" in Statutory Arbitration Post-Award Motions, 46 Calif. L. Rev. 411 (1958); Meiners, Arbitration Awards and Public Policy, 17 Arb. J.(n.s.) 145 (1962); Summers, Judicial Review of Labor Arbitration, 2 Buffalo L. Rev. 1 (1952).

4. Does an arbitrator have power to fashion a remedy if such power is not spelled out in the agreement? In Textile Union v. American Thread Co., 291 F.2d 894 (4th Cir. 1961), the court held that the arbitrator had no power to reduce a discharge to a suspension under a contract which allowed discharge for "just cause," contained a management prerogatives clause, and provided that the arbitrator should not modify or add to the agreement. The issue was again raised in Lodge 12, District 37, International Assn. of Machinists v. Cameron Iron Works, 292 F.2d 112 (5th Cir. 1961), cert. denied, 368 U.S. 926 (1961). The District Court had ordered arbitration of the discharge of fifteen employees. The court held that the arbitrators could award reinstatement but not back pay, because the contract did not so provide. The Court of Appeals found that the language of the contract in question, "the terms and conditions of settlement shall be within the sole discretion of the Board," permitted the arbitrators to conclude that the agreement allowed them to award back pay.

5. An award of a joint labor-management committee settling a grievance may be enforced under Section 301 if the committee is the final step in the grievance procedure and its awards are final and binding. It is not necessary that the parties use the word "arbitration" in the agreement. General Drivers v. Riss and Co., 372 U.S. 517 (1963).

3.   No-Strike Clauses

LOCAL 174, TEAMSTERS v. LUCAS FLOUR CO.
Supreme Court of the United States, 1962
369 U.S. 95, 82 Sup. Ct. 571, 7 L. Ed. 2d 593

[In May, 1958, an employee named Welsch was discharged for "unsatisfactory work" after he ran a new fork lift truck off a loading platform onto some railroad tracks, damaging it. The union struck to force the employer to reinstate him. After a strike of eight days, Welsch's discharge was submitted to arbitration under the collective bargaining contract in effect at the time, which provided that:

"ARTICLE II. The Employer reserves the right to discharge any man in his employ if his work is not satisfactory.

"ARTICLE XIV. Should any difference as to the true interpretation of this agreement arise, same shall be submitted to a Board of Arbitration. . . . [T]he decision of the said Board of Arbitration shall be binding. It is further agreed by both parties hereto that during such arbitration, there shall be no suspension of work.

"Should any difference arise between the employer and the employee, same shall be submitted to arbitration by both parties. Failing to agree, they shall mutually appoint a third person whose decision shall be final and binding."

The Arbitration Board sustained the discharge of Welsch. Meanwhile, the employer sued the union in the Superior Court of Washington for business losses sustained during the strike. A judgment in favor of the employer for $6501.20 was affirmed by Department One of the Supreme Court of Washington, which held (1) that Section 301 neither pre-empted state jurisdiction nor foreclosed application of state substantive law, and (2) that applying the principles of state law, the strike violated the contract because it attempted to coerce the employer to forego his contractual right to discharge for unsatisfactory work.

Justice Stewart, delivering the opinion of the Court, found that the state court had jurisdiction over the litigation even though it was within the purview of Section 301(a), but that federal law should have been applied rather than state law. Nevertheless, he went on to find that application of principles of federal labor law resulted in affirmance of the judgment below.]

Whether, as a matter of federal law, the strike which the union called was a violation of the collective bargaining contract is thus the ultimate issue which this case presents. It is argued that there could be no violation in the absence of a no-strike clause in the contract explicitly covering the subject of the dispute over which the strike was called. We disagree.

The collective bargaining contract expressly imposed upon both parties the duty of submitting the dispute in question to final and binding arbitration. In a consistent course of decisions the Courts of Appeals of at least five Federal Circuits have held that a strike to settle a dispute which a collective bargaining agreement provides shall be settled exclusively and finally by compulsory arbitration constitutes a violation of the agreement.[13] The National Labor Relations Board has reached the same conclusion. W. L. Mead, Inc., 113 N.L.R.B. 1040. We approve that doctrine. To hold otherwise would obviously do violence to accepted principles of traditional contract law. Even more in point, a contrary view would be completely at odds with the basic policy of national labor legislation to promote the arbitral process as a substitute for economic warfare. See United Steelworkers v. Warrior & Gulf Nav. Co., 363 U.S. 574.

What has been said is not to suggest that a no-strike agreement is to be

[13] See International Brotherhood of Teamsters, etc., Union, Local 25 v. W. L. Mead, Inc., 230 F.2d 576, 583-584 (C.A. 1st Cir.) . . .

implied beyond the area which it has been agreed will be exclusively covered by compulsory terminal arbitration. Nor is it to suggest that there may not arise problems in specific cases as to whether compulsory and binding arbitration has been agreed upon, and, if so, as to what disputes have been made arbitrable. But no such problems are present in this case. The grievance over which the union struck was, as it concedes, one which it had expressly agreed to settle by submission to final and binding arbitration proceedings. The strike which it called was a violation of that contractual obligation.

Affirmed.

MR. JUSTICE BLACK, dissenting. . . .

The Court now finds — out of clear air, so far as I can see — that the union, without saying so in the agreement, not only agreed to arbitrate such differences, but also promised that there would be no strike while arbitration of a dispute was pending under this provision. And on the basis of its "discovery" of this additional unwritten promise by the union, the Court upholds a judgment awarding the company substantial damages for a strike in breach of contract.

. . . In view of the fact that [one] provision contains an explicit promise by the union "that during such arbitration, there shall be no suspension of work," it seems to me plain that the parties to this contract, knowing how to write a provision binding a union not to strike, deliberately included a no-strike clause with regard to disputes over broad questions of contractual interpretation and deliberately excluded such a clause with regard to the essentially factual disputes arising out of the application of the contract in particular instances. And there is not a word anywhere else in this agreement which indicates that this perfectly sensible contractual framework for handling these two different kinds of disputes was not intended to operate in the precise manner dictated by the express language of the two arbitration provisions. . . .

. . . The implication found by the Court thus flows neither from the contract itself, nor so far as this record shows, from the intention of the parties. In my judgment, an "implication" of that nature would better be described as a rigid rule of law that an agreement to arbitrate has precisely the same effect as an agreement not to strike — a rule of law which introduces revolutionary doctrine into the field of collective bargaining. . . .

NOTE

In Charles Dowd Box Co. v. Courtney, 368 U.S. 502 (1962), the Supreme Court held that Section 301(a) does not divest a state court of jurisdiction over a suit by a union for violation of a contract between an employer and the union. To the argument that the rationale of Lincoln Mills would be frustrated if state courts were allowed to exercise concurrent jurisdiction over suits within the purview of Section 301(a), the Court replied that there was nothing in the legislative history of that section to indicate that Congress intended to deprive a party to a collective bargaining agreement of the right to seek redress for its violation in an appropriate state tribunal.

ATKINSON v. SINCLAIR REFINING CO.
Supreme Court of the United States, 1962
370 U.S. 238, 82 Sup. Ct. 1318, 8 L. Ed. 2d 462

[The respondent, Sinclair Refining Company, employed 1700 men at its East Chicago Refinery, who were represented by the Oil, Chemical and Atomic Workers and its local. In February, 1959, the company docked three employees a total of $2.19. As a result, alleged the company, a thousand employees struck for two days. The company instituted a three-count action for injunction and damages in the Federal District Court. Count I sought $12,500 damages for breach of a no-strike clause against the international and the local under Section 301. Count II, invoking diversity jurisdiction, sought damages against twenty-four union committeemen, who "contrary to their duty to plaintiff to abide by such contract, and maliciously confederating and conspiring together to cause the plaintiff expense and damage, and to induce breaches of said contract, and to interfere with performance thereof by the said labor organizations, and the affected employees, and to cause breaches thereof, individually and as officers, committeemen and as agents of said labor organizations, fomented, assisted and participated in a strike or work stoppage. . . ." Count III sought injunctive relief, and was decided in a separate opinion in Sinclair Refining Co. v. Atkinson [370 U.S. 195], infra page 882.

The defendants moved to dismiss and stay the proceedings on the grounds that the issues raised were referable to arbitration under the collective agreement, and that some issues were involved in grievances which had been filed and were in arbitration. The District Court refused to dismiss or stay Count I and Count II, but was reversed by the Court of Appeals. The Supreme Court granted certiorari.]

MR. JUSTICE WHITE delivered the opinion of the Court. . . .

I

We have concluded that Count I should not be dismissed or stayed. Count I properly states a cause of action under §301 and is to be governed by federal law. Local 174 v. Lucas Flour Co., 369 U.S. 95, 102-104; Textile Workers Union v. Lincoln Mills, 353 U.S. 448. Under our decisions, whether or not the company was bound to arbitrate, as well as what issues it must arbitrate, is a matter to be determined by the Court on the basis of the contract entered into by the parties. . . . We think it unquestionably clear that the contract here involved is not susceptible to a construction that the company was bound to arbitrate its claim for damages against the union for breach of the undertaking not to strike.

While it is quite obvious from other provisions of the contract that the parties did not intend to commit all of their possible disputes and the whole scope of their relationship to the grievance and arbitration procedures established in Article XXVI, that article itself is determinative of the issue in this case since it precludes arbitration boards from considering any matters other than employee grievances.[3] After defining a grievance as "any difference regarding wages, hours or working conditions between the parties hereto or between the Employer and an employee covered by this working agreement," Article XXVI provides that the parties desire to settle employee grievances fairly and quickly and that therefore a stated procedure "must be followed." The individual employee is required to present his grievance to his foreman, and if not satisfied there, he may take his grievance to the plant superintendent who is to render a written decision. There is also provision for so-called Workmen's Committees to present grievances to the local management. If the local superintendent's decision is not acceptable, the matter is to be referred for discussion between the President of the International and the Director of Industrial Relations for the company (or their representatives), and for decision by the Director alone. If the Director's decision is disputed, then "upon request of the President or any District Director" of the international, a local arbitration board may be convened and the matter finally decided by this board.

Article XXVI then imposes the critical limitation. It is provided that local arbitration boards "shall consider only individual or local employee or local committee grievances arising under the application of the currently existing agreement." There is not a word in the grievance and arbitration article providing for the submission of grievances by the company. Instead, there is the express, flat limitation that arbitration boards should consider only employee grievances. Furthermore, the article expressly provides that arbitration may be invoked only at the option of the union. At no place in the contract does the union agree to arbitrate at the behest of the company. The company is to take its claims elsewhere, which it has now done.

The union makes a further argument for a stay. Following the strike, and both before and after the company filed its suit, 14 of the 24 individual defendants filed grievances claiming reimbursement for pay withheld by the employer. The union argues that even though the company need

[3] We do not need to reach, therefore, the question of whether, under the contract involved here, breaches of the no-strike clause are "grievances," i.e., "difference[s] regarding wages, hours or working conditions," or are "grievances" in the more general sense of the term. See Hoover Express Co. v. Teamsters Local, No. 327, 217 F.2d 49 (C.A. 6th Cir.). The present decision does not approve or disapprove the doctrine of the Hoover case or the Sixth Circuit cases following it (e.g., Vulcan-Cincinnati, Inc. v. United Steelworkers, 289 F.2d 103; United Auto Workers v. Benton Harbor Indus., 242 F.2d 536). See also cases collected in Yale & Towne Mfg. Co. v. Local Lodge No. 1717, 299 F.2d 882, 883-884 n.5, 6 (C.A. 3d Cir.). In Drake Bakeries, Inc. v. Local 50 [370 U.S. 254], decided this day, the question of arbitrability of a damages claim for breach of a no-strike clause is considered and resolved in favor of arbitration in the presence of an agreement to arbitrate "all complaints, disputes or grievances arising between them [i.e., the parties] involving . . . any act or conduct or relation between the parties."

not arbitrate its claim for damages, it is bound to arbitrate these grievances; and the arbitrator, in the process of determining the grievants'
right to reimbursement, will consider and determine issues which also
underlie the company's claim for damages. Therefore, it is said that a
stay of the court action is appropriate.

We are not satisfied from the record now before us, however, that any
significant issue in the damage suit will be presented to and decided by
an arbitrator. The grievances filed simply claimed reimbursement for
pay due employees for time spent at regular work or processing grievances. . . .

The District Court must decide whether the company is entitled to
damages from the union for breach of contract. The arbitrator, if arbitration occurs, must award or deny reimbursement in whole or in part to
all or some of the 14 employees. His award, standing alone, obviously
would determine no issue in the damage suit. If he awarded reimbursement to the employees and if it could be ascertained with any assurance
that one of his subsidiary findings was that the 14 men had not participated in a forbidden work stoppage — the critical issue according to the
union's brief — the company would nevertheless not be foreclosed in court
since, even if it were bound by such a subsidiary finding made by the
arbitrator, it would be free to prove its case in court through the conduct
of other agents of the union. In this state of the record, the union has not
made out its case for a stay.

For the foregoing reasons, the lower courts properly denied the union's
motion to dismiss Count I or stay it pending arbitration of the employer's
damage claim.

I I

We turn now to Count II of the complaint, which charged 24 individual officers and agents of the union with breach of the collective bargaining contract and tortious interference with contractual relations. The
District Court held that under §301 union officers or members cannot be
held personally liable for union actions, and that therefore "suits of the
nature alleged in Count II are no longer cognizable in state or federal
courts." The Court of Appeals reversed, however, ruling that "Count II
stated a cause of action cognizable in the courts of Indiana and, by diversity, maintainable in the District Court."

We are unable to agree with the Court of Appeals, for we are convinced
that Count II is controlled by federal law and that it must be dismissed
on the merits for failure to state a claim upon which relief can be granted.

Under §301 a suit for violation of the collective bargaining contract in
either a federal or state court is governed by federal law . . . and Count
II on its face charges the individual defendants with a violation of the no-
strike clause. . . .

It is universally accepted that the no-strike clause in a collective agreement at the very least establishes a rule of conduct or condition of employment the violation of which by employees justifies discipline or dis-

charge. . . . The conduct charged in Count II is therefore within the scope of a "violation" of the collective agreement.

As well as charging a violation of the no-strike clause by the individual defendants, Count II necessarily charges a violation of the clause by the union itself. The work stoppage alleged is the identical work stoppage for which the union is sued under Count I and the same damage is alleged as is alleged in Count I. Count II states that the individual defendants acted "as officers, committeemen and agents of the said labor organizations" in breaching and inducing others to breach the collective bargaining contract. Count I charges the principal, and Count II charges the agents for acting on behalf of the principal. . . . Count II, like Count I, is thus a suit based on the union's breach of its collective bargaining contract with the employer, and therefore comes within §301(a). When a union breach of contract is alleged, that the plaintiff seeks to hold the agents liable instead of the principal does not bring the action outside the scope of §301.

Under any theory, therefore, the company's action is governed by the national labor relations law which Congress commanded this Court to fashion under §301(a). We hold that this law requires the dismissal of Count II for failure to state a claim for which relief can be granted — whether the contract violation charged is that of the union or that of the union plus the union officers and agents.

When Congress passed §301, it declared its view that only the union was to be made to respond for union wrongs, and that the union members were not to be subject to levy. Section 301(b) has three clauses. One makes unions suable in the courts of the United States. Another makes unions bound by the acts of their agents according to conventional principles of agency law (cf. §301(e)). At the same time, however, the remaining clause exempts agents and members from personal liability for judgments against the union (apparently even when the union is without assets to pay the judgment). The legislative history of §301(b) makes it clear that this third clause was a deeply felt congressional reaction against the Danbury Hatters case (Loewe v. Lawlor, 208 U.S. 274; Lawlor v. Loewe, 235 U.S. 522), and an expression of legislative determination that the aftermath (Loewe v. Savings Bank of Danbury, 236 F. 444 (C.A.2d Cir.)) of that decision was not to be permitted to recur. In that case, an antitrust treble damage action was brought against a large number of union members, including union officers and agents, to recover from them the employer's losses in a nationwide, union-directed boycott of his hats. The union was not named as a party, nor was judgment entered against it. A large money judgment was entered, instead, against the individual defendants for participating in the plan "emanating from headquarters" (235 U.S., at 534), by knowingly authorizing and delegating authority to the union officers to do the acts involved. In the debates, Senator Ball, one of the Act's sponsors, declared that §301, "by providing that the union may sue and be sued as a legal entity, for a violation of contract, and that liability for damages will lie against union assets only, will prevent a repetition of the Danbury Hatters case, in which many members lost their homes" (93 Cong. Rec. 5014). See also 93 Cong. Rec. 3839, 6283; S. Rep. No. 105, 80th Cong., 1st Sess. 16.

Consequently, in discharging the duty Congress imposed on us to formulate the federal law to govern §301(a) suits, we are strongly guided by and do not give a niggardly reading to §301(b). "We would undercut the Act and defeat its policy if we read §301 narrowly" (Lincoln Mills, 353 U.S., at 456). We have already said in another context that §301(b) at least evidences "a congressional intention that the union as an entity, like a corporation, should in the absence of agreement be the sole source of recovery for injury inflicted by it" (Lewis v. Benedict Coal Corp., 361 U.S. 459, 470). This policy cannot be evaded or truncated by the simple device of suing union agents or members, whether in contract or tort, or both, in a separate count or in a separate action for damages for violation of a collective bargaining contract for which damages the union itself is liable. The national labor policy requires and we hold that when a union is liable for damages for violation of the no-strike clause, its officers and members are not liable for these damages Here, Count II, as we have said, necessarily alleges union liability but prays for damages from the union agents. Where the union has inflicted the injury it alone must pay. Count II must be dismissed.

The case is remanded to the District Court for further proceedings not inconsistent with this opinion.

MR. JUSTICE FRANKFURTER took no part in the consideration or decision of this case.

NOTES

1. In Drake Bakeries, Inc. v. Local 50, American Bakery Workers, AFL-CIO, 370 U.S. 254 (1962), the Court held that the Section 301 action by an employer for damages for breach of a no-strike clause should be stayed pending arbitration. See Justice White's statement of the holding in this case in his footnote 3 in the principal case, supra page 877. The opinion, by Justice White, contrasted the language of the Drake contract with that in the Atkinson case (pp. 257-258): "Under Article V of the contract: 'The parties agree that they will promptly attempt to adjust all complaints, disputes or grievances arising between them involving questions of interpretation or application of any cause or matter covered by this contract or any act or conduct or relation between the parties hereto, directly or indirectly.'

"This is broad language, indeed, and the procedure thereafter provided in Article V does not, as it did in Atkinson, exclude claims or complaints of the employer. . . . Article V on its face easily reaches the employer's claim against the union for damages caused by an alleged strike in violation of the contract. . . ."

At page 264 the Court continued: "We could enforce only the no-strike clause by refusing a stay·in the suit for damages in the District Court. We can enforce both the no-strike clause and the agreement to arbitrate by granting a stay until the claim for damages is arbitrated. This we prefer to do. . . . We do not decide in this case that in no circumstances would a strike in violation of the no-strike clause contained in this or other contracts entitle the employer to rescind or abandon the entire contract or to declare its promise to arbitrate forever discharged or to refuse to arbitrate its damage claims against the union. We do decide and hold that Article V of this contract obligates the company to arbitrate its claims for damages from forbidden strikes by the union and that there are no circumstances in this record which justify relieving the company of its duty to arbitrate the consequences of this one-day strike, intertwined as it is with the union's denials that there was any strike or any breach of contract at all.

"If the union did strike in violation of the contract, the company is entitled to its damages; by staying this action, pending arbitration, we have no intention of depriving it of those damages. We simply remit the company to the forum it agreed to use for processing its strike damage claims. That forum, it is true, may be very different from a courtroom, but we are not persuaded that the remedy there will be inadequate. . . . The dispute which this record presents appears to us to be one particularly suited for arbitration, if the parties have agreed to arbitrate. We hold that they did so agree and will hold the company to its bargain."

2. Following the reasoning of the Drake Bakeries case, the Supreme Court held in Local 721, United Packinghouse Workers v. Needham Packing Co., 376 U.S. 247 (1964), that the union's alleged breach of a no-strike clause did not release the employer from his duty to arbitrate two discharge grievances under a broad arbitration clause.

In this case the discharge of an employee caused a work stoppage. Subsequently grievances were filed, protesting the discharge of this employee and also the discharge of those who participated in the work stoppage. To the union's suit to compel arbitration of these grievances, Needham filed a counter-claim for damages for an alleged breach of the no-strike clause.

The Supreme Court held that the employer's duty to arbitrate was, if anything, clearer than it was in the Drake Bakeries case, since there was no question that the union's claim of a wrongful discharge was a claim which Needham had agreed to arbitrate. The Court further held that the fact that the collective bargaining agreement did not require Needham to submit its claim for damages to arbitration, as the employer was required to do in Drake Bakeries, did not indicate a different result. Nor did the Court believe that this case could be distinguished from Drake Bakeries on the ground that the latter case involved only a one-day strike.

In holding that Needham was not precluded from prosecuting its claim for damages in the Iowa courts for the alleged breach of the no-strike clause, the Supreme Court left open the question as to what effect, if any, factual or legal determinations made by an arbitrator would have on the related action in the courts. The Court also made the observation that the principal case, in which the provision for arbitration was similarly limited to employees grievances, was of no relevance to the Needham case, since the question in Atkinson was whether the employer's action for breach of the no-strike clause should be submitted to arbitration.

SINCLAIR REFINING CO. v. ATKINSON
Supreme Court of the United States, 1962
370 *U.S. 195, 82 Sup. Ct. 1328, 8 L. Ed. 2d 440*

MR. JUSTICE BLACK delivered the opinion of the Court.

The question this case presents is whether §301 of the Taft-Hartley Act, in giving federal courts jurisdiction of suits between employers and unions for breach of collective bargaining agreements, impliedly repealed §4 of the pre-existing Norris-LaGuardia Act, which, with certain exceptions not here material, barred federal courts from issuing injunctions "in any case involving or growing out of any labor dispute."

The complaint here was filed by the petitioner Sinclair Refining Company against the Oil, Chemical and Atomic Workers International Union and Local 7-210 of that union and alleged: that the International Union, acting by and with the authority of the Local Union and its members, signed a written collective bargaining contract with Sinclair which provided for compulsory, final and binding arbitration of "any difference regarding wages, hours or working conditions between the parties hereto or between the Employer and an employee covered by this working agreement which might arise within any plant or within any region of operations"; that this contract also included express provisions by which the unions agreed that "there shall be no slowdowns for any reason whatsoever" and "no strikes or work stoppages . . . [f]or any cause which is or may be the subject of a grievance"; and that notwithstanding these promises in the collective bargaining contract the members of Local 7-210 had, over a period of some 19 months, engaged in work stoppages and strikes on nine separate occasions, each of which, the complaint charged, grew out of a grievance which could have been submitted to arbitration under the contract and therefore fell squarely within the unions' promises not to strike. This pattern of repeated, deliberate violations of the contract, Sinclair alleged, indicated a complete disregard on the part of the unions for their obligations under the contract and a probability that they would continue to "subvert the provisions of the contract" forbidding strikes over grievances in the future unless they were enjoined from doing so. In this situation, Sinclair claimed, there was no adequate remedy at law which would protect its contractual rights and the court should therefore enter orders enjoining the unions and their agents "preliminarily at first, and thereafter permanently, from aiding, abetting, fomenting, advising, participating in, ratifying, or condoning any strike, stoppage of work, slowdown or any other disruption of, or interference with normal employment or normal operation or production by any employee within the bargaining unit at plaintiff's East Chicago, Indiana refinery covered by the contract between the parties dated August 8, 1957, in support of, or because of, any matter or thing which is, or could be, the subject of a grievance under the grievance procedure of the said contract, or any extension thereof, or any other contract between the parties which shall contain like or similar provisions."

The unions moved to dismiss this complaint on the ground that it sought injunctive relief which United States courts, by virtue of the Norris-LaGuardia Act, have no jurisdiction to give. . . . [T]he District Court reasoned that the controversy between Sinclair and the unions was unquestionably a "labor dispute" within the meaning of the Norris-LaGuardia Act and that the complaint therefore came within the proscription of §4 of that Act which "withdraws jurisdiction from the federal courts to issue injunctions to prohibit the refusal 'to perform work or remain in any relation of employment' in cases involving *any* labor dispute." The Court of Appeals for the Seventh Circuit affirmed the order of dismissal for the same reasons. Because this decision presented a conflict with the decision on this same important question by the Court of Appeals for the Tenth Circuit,[7] we granted certiorari.

We agree with the courts below that this case does involve a "labor dispute" within the meaning of the Norris-LaGuardia Act. Section 13 of that Act expressly defines a labor dispute as including "any controversy concerning terms or conditions of employment, or concerning the association or representation of persons in negotiating, fixing, maintaining, changing, or seeking to arrange terms or conditions of employment, regardless of whether or not the disputants stand in the proximate relation of employer and employee." Sinclair's own complaint shows quite plainly that each of the alleged nine work stoppages and strikes arose out of a controversy which was unquestionably well within this definition.

Nor does the circumstance that the alleged work stoppages and strikes may have constituted a breach of a collective bargaining agreement alter the plain fact that a "labor dispute" within the meaning of the Norris-LaGuardia Act is involved. Arguments to the contrary proceed from the premise that §2 of that Act, which expresses the public policy upon which the specific anti-injunction provisions of the Act were based, contains language indicating that one primary concern of Congress was to insure workers the right "to exercise actual liberty of contract" and to protect "concerted activities for the purpose of collective bargaining." From that premise, Sinclair argues that an interpretation of the term "labor dispute" so as to include a dispute arising out of a union's refusal to abide by the terms of a collective agreement to which it freely acceded is to apply the Norris-LaGuardia Act in a way that defeats one of the purposes for which it was enacted. But this argument, though forcefully urged both here and in much current commentary on this question,[12] rests more

[7] Chauffeurs, Teamsters & Helpers Local No. 795 v. Yellow Transit Freight Lines, 282 F.2d 345. Both the First and the Second Circuits have also considered this question and both have taken the same position as that taken below. See W. L. Mead, Inc. v. Teamsters Local No. 25, 217 F.2d 6; Alcoa S.S. Co. v. McMahon, 173 F.2d 567; In re Third Ave. Transit Corp., 192 F.2d 971; A. H. Bull Steamship Co. v. Seafarers' International Union, 250 F.2d 326.

[12] One of the most forthright arguments for judicial re-evaluation of the wisdom of the anti-injunction provisions of the Norris-LaGuardia Act and judicial

upon considerations of what many commentators think would be the more desirable industrial and labor policy in view of their understanding as to the prevailing circumstances of contemporary labor-management relations than upon what is a correct judicial interpretation of the language of the Act as it was written by Congress.

In the first place, even the general policy declarations of §2 of the Norris-LaGuardia Act, which are the foundation of this whole argument, do not support the conclusion urged. That section does not purport to limit the Act to the protection of collective bargaining but, instead, expressly recognizes the need of the anti-injunction provisions to insure the right of workers to engage in "concerted activities for the purpose of collective bargaining *or other mutual aid or protection.*" Moreover, the language of the specific provisions of the Act is so broad and inclusive that it leaves not the slightest opening for reading in any exceptions beyond those clearly written into it by Congress itself. We cannot ignore the plain import of a congressional enactment, particularly one which, as we have repeatedly said, was deliberately drafted in the broadest of terms in order to avoid the danger that it would be narrowed by judicial construction.

Since we hold that the present case does grow out of a "labor dispute," the injunction sought here runs squarely counter to the proscription of injunctions against strikes contained in §4(a) of the Norris-LaGuardia Act, to the proscription of injunctions against peaceful picketing contained in §4(e) and to the proscription of injunctions prohibiting the advising of such activities contained in §4(i). . . .

The language of §301 itself seems to us almost if not entirely conclusive of this question. It is especially significant that the section contains no language that could by any stretch of the imagination be interpreted to constitute an explicit repeal of the anti-injunction provisions of the Norris-LaGuardia Act in view of the fact that the section does expressly repeal another provision of the Norris-LaGuardia Act dealing with union responsibility for the acts of agents.[17] If Congress had intended that §301 suits should also not be subject to the anti-injunction provisions of the Norris-LaGuardia Act, it certainly seems likely that it would have made its intent known in this same express manner. That is indeed precisely

---

rather than congressional revision of the meaning and scope of these provisions as applied to conduct in breach of a collective bargaining agreement is presented in Gregory, The Law of the Collective Agreement, 57 Mich. L. Rev. 635. That author, in urging that a strike in breach of a collective agreement should not now be held to involve or grow out of a "labor dispute" within the meaning of the Norris-LaGuardia Act, states: "After all, 1932 was a long time ago and conditions have changed drastically. Judges who still confuse violations of collective agreements with §13 labor disputes and §4 conduct have, in my opinion, lost contact with reality. The passage of time has operated as a function of many other types of judicial output at the highest level. I do not see why it should not do so in this instance, as well." Id., at 645-646, n.39. See also Stewart, No-Strike Clauses in the Federal Courts, 59 Mich. L. Rev. 673, especially at 683; Rice, A Paradox of Our National Labor Law, 34 Marq. L. Rev. 233.

[17] Section 301(e) of the Act, 61 Stat. 156, 29 U.S.C. §185(e) . . . This, of course, was designed to and did repeal for purposes of suits under §301 the previously controlling provisions of §6 of the Norris-LaGuardia Act.

what Congress did do in §101, amending §10(h) of the National Labor Relations Act, and §208(b) of the Taft-Hartley Act, by permitting injunctions to be obtained, not by private litigants, but only at the instance of the National Labor Relations Board and the Attorney General, and in §302(e), by permitting private litigants to obtain injunctions in order to protect the integrity of employees' collective bargaining representatives in carrying out their responsibilities. Thus the failure of Congress to include a provision in §301 expressly repealing the anti-injunction provisions of the Norris-LaGuardia Act must be evaluated in the context of a statutory pattern that indicates not only that Congress was completely familiar with those provisions but also that it regarded an express declaration of inapplicability as the normal and proper manner of repealing them in situations where such repeal seemed desirable.

When the inquiry is carried beyond the language of §301 into its legislative history, whatever small doubts as to the congressional purpose could have survived consideration of the bare language of the section should be wholly dissipated. For the legislative history of §301 shows that Congress actually considered the advisability of repealing the Norris-LaGuardia Act insofar as suits based upon breach of collective bargaining agreements are concerned and deliberately chose not to do so. . . .

We cannot accept the startling argument made here that even though Congress did not itself want to repeal the Norris-LaGuardia Act, it was willing to confer a power upon the courts to "accommodate" that Act out of existence whenever they might find it expedient to do so in furtherance of some policy they had fashioned under §301. . . .

Moreover, we think that the idea that §301 sanctions piecemeal judicial repeal of the Norris-LaGuardia Act requires acceptance of a wholly unrealistic view of the manner in which Congress handles its business. The question of whether existing statutes should be continued in force or repealed is, under our system of government, one which is wholly within the domain of Congress. When the repeal of a highly significant law is urged upon that body and that repeal is rejected after careful consideration and discussion, the normal expectation is that courts will be faithful to their trust and abide by that decision. This is especially so where the fact of the controversy over repeal and the resolution of that controversy in Congress plainly appears in the formal legislative history of its proceedings.[28] Indeed, not a single instance has been called to our attention in which a carefully considered and rejected proposal for repeal

[28] The legislative history of the Taft-Hartley Act shows that Congress actually considered and relied upon this normal functioning of the judicial power as insuring that no unintended repeal of the anti-injunction provisions of the Norris-LaGuardia Act would be declared. Thus Senator Taft, when pressed by Senator Morse with regard to the possibility that a provision inserted in §303(a) declaring secondary boycotts unlawful might be held to justify an injunction previously forbidden by the Norris-LaGuardia Act, stated: "Let me say in reply to the Senator or anyone else who makes the same argument, that that is not the intention of the author of the amendment. It is not his belief as to the effect of it. It is not the advice of counsel to the committee. Under those circumstances, I do not believe that any court would construe the amendment along the lines suggested by the Senator from Oregon." 93 Cong. Rec. 4872, II Leg. Hist. 1396.

has been revived and adopted by this Court under the guise of "accommodation" or any other pseudonym.

Nor have we found anything else in the previous decisions of this Court that would indicate that we should disregard all this overwhelming evidence of a congressional intent to retain completely intact the anti-injunction prohibitions of the Norris-LaGuardia Act in suits brought under §301. Brotherhood of Railroad Trainmen v. Chicago River & Indiana R. Co. [353 U.S. 30], upon which Sinclair places its primary reliance, is distinguishable on several grounds. There we were dealing with a strike called by the union in defiance of an affirmative duty, imposed upon the union by the Railway Labor Act itself, compelling unions to settle disputes as to the interpretation of an existing collective bargaining agreement, not by collective union pressures on the railroad but by submitting them to the Railroad Adjustment Board as the exclusive means of final determination of such "minor" disputes.[30] Here, on the other hand, we are dealing with a suit under a quite different law which does not itself compel a particular, exclusive method for settling disputes nor impose any requirement, either upon unions or employers, or upon the courts, that is in any way inconsistent with a continuation of the Norris-LaGuardia Act's proscription of federal labor injunctions against strikes and peaceful picketing. In addition, in Chicago River we were dealing with a statute that had a far different legislative history than the one now before us. Thus there was no indication in the legislative history of the Railway Labor Act, as there is in the history of §301, that Congress had, after full debate and careful consideration by both Houses and in Joint Conference, specifically rejected proposals to make the prohibitions of the Norris-LaGuardia Act inapplicable. Indeed, the Court was able to conclude in Chicago River "that there was general understanding between both the supporters and the opponents of the 1934 amendment that the provisions dealing with the Adjustment Board were to be considered as compulsory arbitration in this limited field." And certainly no one could contend that §301 was intended to set up any such system of "compulsory arbitration" as the exclusive method for settling grievances under the Taft-Hartley Act. . . .

Nor can we agree with the argument made in this Court that the decision in Lincoln Mills, as implemented by the subsequent decisions in United Steelworkers v. American Manufacturing Co. [363 U.S. 564], United Steelworkers v. Warrior & Gulf Navigation Co. [363 U.S. 574], and United Steelworkers v. Enterprise Wheel & Car Corp. [363 U.S. 593], requires us to reconsider and overrule the action of Congress in refusing to repeal or modify the controlling commands of the Norris-LaGuardia Act. To the extent that those cases relied upon the proposition that the arbitration process is "a kingpin of federal labor policy," we think that

---

[30] The Court in Chicago River expressly recognized and rested its decision upon the differences between provisions for the settlement of disputes under the Railway Labor Act and the Taft-Hartley Act. Id., at 31-32, n.2. See also Order of Railroad Telegraphers v. Chicago & North Western R. Co. [362 U.S.] 330, 338-340.

proposition was founded not upon the policy predilections of this Court but upon what Congress said and did when it enacted §301. . . .

The plain fact is that §301, as passed by Congress, presents no conflict at all with the anti-injunction provisions of the Norris-LaGuardia Act. Obedience to the congressional commands of the Norris-LaGuardia Act does not directly affect the "congressional policy in favor of the enforcement of agreements to arbitrate grievance disputes" [38] at all for it does not impair the right of an employer to obtain an order compelling arbitration of any dispute that may have been made arbitrable by the provisions of an effective collective bargaining agreement. At the most, what is involved is the question of whether the employer is to be allowed to enjoy the benefits of an injunction along with the right which Congress gave him in §301 to sue for breach of a collective agreement. And as we have already pointed out, Congress was not willing to insure that enjoyment to an employer at the cost of putting the federal courts back into the business of enjoining strikes and other related peaceful union activities.

It is doubtless true, as argued, that the right to sue which §301 gives employers would be worth more to them if they could also get a federal court injunction to bar a breach of their collective bargaining agreements. Strong arguments are made to us that it is highly desirable that the Norris-LaGuardia Act be changed in the public interest. If that is so, Congress itself might see fit to change that law and repeal the anti-injunction provisions of the Act insofar as suits for violation of collective agreements are concerned, as the House bill under consideration originally provided. It might, on the other hand, decide that if injunctions are necessary, the whole idea of enforcement of these agreements by private suits should be discarded in favor of enforcement through the administrative machinery of the Labor Board, as Senator Taft provided in his Senate bill. Or it might decide that neither of these methods is entirely satisfactory and turn instead to a completely new approach. The question of what change, if any, should be made in the existing law is one of legislative policy properly within the exclusive domain of Congress — it is a question for lawmakers, not law interpreters. Our task is the more limited one of interpreting the law as it now stands. In dealing with problems of interpretation and application of federal statutes, we have no power to change deliberate choices of legislative policy that Congress has made within its constitutional powers. Where congressional intent is discernible — and here it seems crystal clear — we must give effect to that intent. . . .

Affirmed.

MR. JUSTICE FRANKFURTER took no part in the consideration or decision of this case.

MR. JUSTICE BRENNAN, with whom MR. JUSTICE DOUGLAS and MR. JUSTICE HARLAN join, dissenting.

I believe that the Court has reached the wrong result because it has answered only the first of the questions which must be answered to decide this case. Of course §301 of the Taft-Hartley Act did not, for purposes of

[38] Textile Workers Union v. Lincoln Mills, 353 U.S. 448. at 458-459.

actions brought under it, "repeal" §4 of the Norris-LaGuardia Act. But the two provisions do coexist, and it is clear beyond dispute that they apply to the case before us in apparently conflicting senses. Our duty, therefore, is to seek out that accommodation of the two which will give the fullest possible effect to the central purposes of both. Since such accommodation is possible, the Court's failure to follow that path leads it to a result — not justified by either the language or history of §301 — which is wholly at odds with our earlier handling of directly analogous situations and which cannot be woven intelligibly into the broader fabric of related decisions. . . .

NOTES

1. The House of Delegates of the American Bar Association has adopted the following resolution:
". . . [T]he American Bar Association recommends that the Congress enact a modification to Section 4 of the Norris-LaGuardia Act to permit the issuance of a restraining order, temporary or permanent injunction by a court of the United States in any action brought therein pursuant to Section 301 of the Labor Management Relations Act of 1947, as amended, for the purpose of filling the inequitable gap which exists in the law relating to the mutual enforcement of collective bargaining agreements as provided by the Congress under Section 301 of the Labor Management Relations Act of 1947, as amended, provided that such modification shall require that no injunction against the strike shall be permissible in the absence of notice and hearing." 55 L.R.R. 184 (1964).

2. The Sinclair case did not decide whether state courts may enjoin strikes in breach of contract. With respect to this question see McCarroll v. Los Angeles County District Council of Carpenters, 49 Cal. 2d 45, 315 P.2d 322 (1957), cert. denied, 355 U.S. 932 (1958), where the plaintiffs brought an action in a state court for damages and injunctive relief against a strike allegedly called by the union in violation of a no-strike clause in the collective agreement between the parties. The trial court's issuance of an injunction was affirmed on appeal. After ruling that the strike was not an unfair labor practice under the NLRA, the California Supreme Court declared that it had concurrent jurisdiction with the federal courts over suits arising under Section 301 of the LMRA. Conceding that federal law must be applied, the court pointed out that nothing in the LMRA itself prohibits the granting of an injunction in suits for breach of collective agreements, and that the Norris-LaGuardia Act, which limits the power of federal courts to grant injunctions in labor disputes, is not applicable to state courts. There being no general rule that state courts, in enforcing federal law, are restricted to the remedies available in federal courts, the California court concluded that injunctive relief was a proper and permissible remedy in this case.

3. Nor did the Sinclair case decide whether a state court action to enjoin breach of a no-strike clause could be removed to a federal district court. In American Dredging Co. v. Local 25, Operating Engineers, 338

F.2d 837 (3d Cir. 1964), the court held that a suit brought in a state court, based solely on state created rights, to enjoin a union's violation of the no-strike provisions of a collective bargaining agreement, is not removable to a federal district court. The court held that the Sinclair case did not limit the jurisdiction of state courts to enjoin strikes in breach of contract. In his dissent Judge Hastie argued that under Lucas Flour, supra page 873, federal labor law supersedes local law in a case of this type, and that under federal labor law, as set forth in the Sinclair case, a no-strike clause cannot be enforced by injunction.

For a discussion of the question of removal of Section 301 cases filed in state courts, see Aaron, Strikes in Breach of Collective Agreements: Some Unanswered Questions, 63 Colum. L. Rev. 1027, 1040-1051 (1963).

4. Finally, another question not answered by Sinclair is whether an arbitrator has the power to issue an order against a strike, which may then be enforced by the judiciary. In Ruppert v. Egelhofer, 3 N.Y.2d 576, 148 N.E.2d 129 (1958), the New York Court of Appeals affirmed a lower court's order denying a motion to vacate and confirming an arbitration award enjoining the continuation of union slowdowns in violation of a collective bargaining agreement. The appellate court held that the restrictions on the issuance of injunctions in the state anti-injunction act were not applicable, even though the lower court had, by confirming the award, in effect ordered the injunction. In this case, the court reasoned, the parties had voluntarily established in their collective agreement a specific procedure for disposing of alleged violations of the no-strike clause — a procedure that contemplated the issuance of an injunction by the arbitrator.

4.　*Other Clauses*

INTERNATIONAL UNION, UNITED AUTOMOBILE WORKERS, LOCAL 391 v. WEBSTER ELECTRIC CO.
United States Court of Appeals, Seventh Circuit, 1962
299 F.2d 195

SCHNACKENBERG, Circuit Judge.

Defendant Webster Electric Company, a corporation, appeals from a declaratory judgment of the district court in favor of International Union, United Automobile, Aircraft and Agricultural Implement Workers of America, Local 391, plaintiff. . . .

In June, 1958, defendant contracted with the Racine Police Protective Association, an independent contractor, for the performance of defendant's office janitorial work which theretofore had always been performed by employees of the defendant within the bargaining unit. Defendant thereupon laid off three employees who had formerly performed the janitorial services, all of whom were covered by the union contract. The action was taken without the consent of plaintiff.

The individuals who have performed the janitorial work after June,

1958, are not employees of defendant, but are employees of the Association. They are not members of plaintiff union and are not covered by the provisions of the collective bargaining agreement.

Plaintiff has complied with all grievance provisions of the agreement with reference to these events, but defendant has refused to grant the relief requested. Defendant refused to reinstate the three laid-off employees. This action followed.

By article I of the collective bargaining agreement, defendant agreed to recognize plaintiff as the sole bargaining agency for all its employees, and it was stipulated that the agreement is to cover all persons employed at the Racine plants of defendant, with certain exclusions not here relevant.

By article II defendant agreed that there would be no lockout of the employees and plaintiff agreed that there would be no strike until all prescribed bargaining procedure had been exhausted.

By article IV seniority was recognized, while article XI provided for a union shop.

Plaintiff asked the district court to declare by its judgment that defendant does not have the right to "subcontract" work ordinarily and customarily performed on its premises in the Racine plant by its employees, members of and represented by, the defendant union.

Plaintiff makes the assertion, which is not denied, that there is no clause in the collective bargaining agreement specifically reserving this right to defendant, nor is there any "management prerogatives clause" in said agreement. . . .

1. . . . Steelworkers [United Steelworkers v. Warrior and Gulf Navigation Co., 363 U.S. 574, supra page 858] *did not* decide the question of substantive law, i.e., whether an employer does have a unilateral right to contract out work, where there is no express controlling provision in the existing collective bargaining agreement.

Steelworkers *did* decide, 363 U.S. at 585, that whether contracting out violates an existing bargaining agreement is a question which is for the arbiter and not for the courts, if there be an arbitration clause in the agreement.

Steelworkers recognizes that the judiciary sits to bring into operation an arbitral process which, in that case, was provided for by the bargaining agreement.

Lacking an arbitration clause in the case at bar, the question of whether contracting out violated the agreement is a question for the judiciary.

2. These teachings which we get from Steelworkers leave us without any suggestion as to how to decide the substantive question now before us: Has the right of defendant to contract out work, concededly recognized (except for the unfounded reliance of plaintiff on Steelworkers), been modified or abrogated by the provisions, express or implicit, of the bargaining agreement?

Plaintiff and defendant have an agreement which, while it is in effect, fixes the rights of each against the other. Any right not effectually asserted by either in negotiations leading to the execution of the agreement cannot now be insisted upon during the stated life of the agreement if it be inconsistent with the purpose and scope of that document. There is no express prohibition of contracting out to be found in the agreement. But for the agreement, defendant would have that right, as an incident of management. However, there *is* an agreement providing for a union shop. The employees covered by that agreement are described as *all* defendant's employees, with certain irrelevant exceptions. This classification includes the office janitorial employees. Thus they are required to be members of plaintiff union. If they were to be excluded the agreement should have said so. By including them, the contracting parties in effect negatived any intention to treat them differently from other employees. The fact that they are but three in number does not distinguish their job rights from those of their more numerous union brothers. If this small group can be thus replaced, then other groups could meet the same fate, and eventually it would be possible to deplete a major part of the "protected" union shop force. We hold it would be inconsistent with the basic purpose of the agreement to approve the contracting out of the janitorial jobs here involved.

3. The district court in conclusion of law 5 stated that defendant breached the agreement with plaintiff when it laid off the three employees, and in conclusion of law 6 stated that defendant "does not have the right, without consent of the plaintiff, to subcontract the office janitorial work, to be performed by employees not covered by the bargaining unit, on defendant's premises."

We find no error in this action.

4. We believe that the district court erred in its conclusion of law 4 holding, under the circumstances here, that defendant locked out the three employees. There was no coercion or economic pressure exerted by defendant in this action. There was no lockout. . . . We therefore conclude that paragraph 3 of the judgment order from which this appeal has been taken, reading as follows, "That the defendant Company, by laying off the three employees performing office janitorial work on Company premises, members of the Union, did lock out said employees, contrary to the provisions of Article II, Section 6 of the contract," must be reversed.

For the reasons expressed herein, paragraph 3 of said judgment is reversed and said judgment is in all other respects affirmed.

Judgment partly reversed and partly affirmed.

KNOCH, Circuit Judge (dissenting). . . .

It seems to me that the majority have given consideration to an element which is concededly not an issue in the case before us: the good faith of management. There is no charge of dual unionism or unfair labor practice. The Union presumes that the action was based on economic reasons. The District Court's opinion asserts that "no showing has been made that the subcontracting was done . . . to bring pressure on the Union or its members. . . ." Had there been evidence to support a reasonable fear of the kind of threat which the majority apparently foresee, their conclusion would merit serious consideration.

The agreement between the Union and management was the result of collective bargaining. A long line of cases provided that management had the right to contract out work unless that right were expressly limited by the terms of the agreement. The majority hold that these cases have not been reversed by the ruling in Warrior. Yet the majority would give the Union the benefit of provisions which it may, or may not, have sought, but which, in any event, it did not secure. Management, on the other hand, reasonably relying on that same long line of cases, has been misled to its damage, through no fault of its own.

I do not subscribe to the erosion of the existing rights held by labor or management through the judicial process. Such changes should come about only through agreement, legislation, or voluntary surrender. . . .

ZDANOK v. GLIDDEN CO.

United States Court of Appeals, Second Circuit, 1961
288 F.2d 99

MADDEN, Judge.

The plaintiffs sued in the District Court for the Southern District of New York for damages for alleged breach by the defendant of a contract made for their benefit by a labor union. The District Court had jurisdiction because of diversity of citizenship. The Court decided that they were not entitled to recover, 185 F. Supp. 441, and they have appealed.

From 1929 until November 30, 1957, the defendant operated a plant at Elmhurst, New York, known as its Durkee Famous Foods Division. The plaintiffs are members of General Warehousemen's Union, Local 852, which is affiliated with the Teamsters' Union. The defendant and Local 852 had had collective bargaining agreements since December 1, 1949, each agreement covering a two-year period. The last agreement covered the period December 1, 1955 to November 30, 1957.

Each agreement contained a provision establishing a system of seniority which required that in case of a curtailment of production, employees were to be laid off in the reverse order of seniority. If, at the time he was laid off, an employee had had five or more years of continuous employment, his seniority would entitle him to be reemployed if an opening for reemployment for one having his seniority occurred within three years after his lay-off. If he had had less than five years of employment before his lay-off, he would be entitled to reemployment if an opening for one with his seniority occurred within two years after his lay-off. The contract between the union and the employer contained a non-contributory pension plan, with normal retirement on pension at age 65, early retirement at 55 if the employee had had 15 years of service, and other types of pensions under specified conditions. The contract also included hospital, medical and surgical insurance, life insurance and accidental death insurance to be paid for by the employer.

On September 16, 1957, the defendant gave written notice to the union that it would terminate the collective bargaining contract at its expiration date, November 30, 1957. After September 16 it began to reduce production at Elmhurst, and to remove its machinery and equipment from Elmhurst to a newly established plant at Bethlehem, Pennsylvania. The employment of four of the five plaintiffs was terminated on November 1, and that of the fifth one on November 18. The ages of the five plaintiffs, at the time of their discharge, ranged from 43 to 61 years, and their periods of employment with the defendant ranged from 10 to 25 years.

The defendant removed a considerable part of its machinery from its Elmhurst plant to the new Bethlehem plant, and manufactured there a number of the same products. The Bethlehem plant was more modern and efficient, and apparently had a considerable number of new machines, in addition to the ones moved from Elmhurst. Some of the products formerly made at Elmhurst were, after the closing of that plant, made at the defendant's Louisville plant.

There was work at the Bethlehem plant similar to that done at Elmhurst by three of the plaintiffs. As to the other two plaintiffs, who were men, aged 43 and 49, their work at Elmhurst was to check merchandise that was loaded or unloaded from trucks leaving or entering that plant. At the Bethlehem plant such duties have been incorporated into other job classifications which specify the employee to load and unload the trucks and to operate an electric walking type lift truck to stack the merchandise in the storage area as well as to check the incoming and outgoing merchandise that the employee loads and unloads. This different Bethlehem work would not seem to have required any skill that could not have been acquired in a short time.

The defendant offered to give fair consideration to applications for employment at its Bethlehem plant, to its former employees at Elmhurst, only if they would come to Bethlehem and make application there on the same basis as new applicants who might seek employment there. Two Elmhurst employees, not plaintiffs herein, made such applications, and their applications were accepted. Only one of them actually went to work. He has been considered as a new employee at Bethlehem, with no seniority carried over from Elmhurst.

The plaintiffs contend that they were, as beneficiaries of the contract between their union and the defendant, entitled to the jobs which were created by the opening of the plant at Bethlehem. They say that they were laid off because of the removal of the machinery and the cessation of operations at Elmhurst, and that as work was opened up at Bethlehem they were entitled, by reason of their seniority and the contract provisions relating to it, to go to work at Bethlehem with the seniority which they had acquired at Elmhurst. . . .

[The defendant argued that the matter was res judicata, and the individual employees lacked standing to litigate the loss of seniority rights. The res judicata argument was based on previous litigation in which the union had sought to arbitrate the instant dispute. The defendant employer had successfully moved in the New York Supreme Court to stay the arbitration. Matter of General Warehousemen's Union, 10 Misc. 2d 700, 172 N.Y.S.2d 678 (Sup. Ct. 1958). The Court of Appeals ruled that the New York Supreme Court had held only that the dispute was not arbitrable under contract language allowing arbitration of "any question, grievance or dispute arising out of and involving the interpretation and application of the *specific terms* of this agreement. . . ." Thus the prior decision did not reach the merits of the plaintiff's case and the res judicata argument failed.

The standing to sue argument was based upon Parker v. Borock, 5 N.Y.2d 156, 156 N.E.2d 297 (1959), which held that while the employees were "direct beneficiaries" of the collective bargaining agreement, they had entrusted the enforcement of their rights to the union, which could implement them through the arbitration process. Therefore, they could not proceed against the employer in an action at law. If the union failed to protect their claims by seeking arbitration, the employee had a remedy against it, but could not proceed against the employer for damages. The Court of Appeals held the Parker case inapplicable because the matter in dispute was not subject to arbitration, and concluded that the employees were entitled to assert their rights under the agreement as direct beneficiaries.]

As to the merits of the plaintiffs' claims, the defendant takes the bold position that the collective bargaining contract conferred upon the employees no rights which survived the contract. It says, at page 27 of its memorandum:

"Even if the Elmhurst operations had continued but the collective bargaining agreement had expired, the seniority status of plaintiffs would not have survived the termination of that agreement. For it is only by reason of existing provisions in the agreement that provisions relating to the seniority have any application. When such provisions no longer exist, seniority no longer exists." . . .

We think the defendant's language, quoted above, is not supportable. Suppose an employee had completed five years of service in October, 1957. Under the seniority provision of the collective bargaining agreement, he thinks that he has earned, and acquired, by continuous service, valuable insurance against unemployment; that by reason of having worked continuously for this company longer than many of his fellow workmen, he could not be laid off unless the lay-off cut deep into the working force; that even if he should be reached in a lay-off, he would be sure to be reemployed if at any time within three years after the lay-off his name should be reached on the seniority list, for reemployment. As we have seen, the defendant's position is that the employee had not acquired any such rights.

Rights embodied in a collective bargaining contract negotiated by a union "inure to the direct benefit of employees and may be the subject of a cause of action." Parker v. Borock, 5 N.Y.2d 156, 182 N.Y.S.2d 577, 156 N.E.2d 297-298, citing Barth v. Addie Co. 271 N.Y. 31, 2 N.E.2d 34, and other New York cases. If one has in October a right to demand performance of the corresponding obligation at any relevant time within a period of three years, it would be strange if the other contracting party could unilaterally terminate the right at the end of three weeks. Of course the employee owning the right, or his authorized union agent, could bargain away the employee's right. Nothing of that kind occurred in the instant case.

At the time the Elmhurst employees were discharged, those who had reached the age of 65 and had otherwise satisfied the conditions prescribed in the collective bargaining agreement for receiving retired pay, were placed on the defendant's retired list and have been and are currently receiving their retired pay. Similarly, those who had reached the age of 55, or who had become permanently disabled in the service of the defendant, and had had 15 years of employment with the defendant, are receiving their retired pay. Those who had 15 years of service and had reached the age of 45 at the time of their discharge were advised by the defendant that they had vested rights to retirement benefits and would begin to receive payments when they reached the age of 65.

These rights to retired pay, though their realization will extend far into the future, and though they arise solely and only out of the terms of the union agreement with the defendant, have been treated as "vested" rights and are being voluntarily honored by the defendant. This was, we suppose, because the employees had earned these rights by compliance with the terms of the contract, and the fact that the contract was not renewed, and that other workmen in the future might not have the opportunity to earn similar rights, was irrelevant. We think the plaintiff employees had, by the same token, "earned" their valuable unemployment insurance, and that their rights in it were "vested" and could not be unilaterally annulled.

We think, then, that if the plaintiff had continued to operate the Elmhurst plant, without a renewal of the union contract, or had reopened it after it had been closed for a time, the employees would have been entitled to reemployment, with seniority. This brings us to the issue which Judge Palmieri in the District Court, found to be the critical issue, i.e., whether the unit to which the employees' rights attached "extended beyond the Elmhurst plant." (185 F. Supp. 447.) He held that the rights were not enforceable except in the Elmhurst plant, and therefore denied recovery. With deference, we disagree with this conclusion.

The union contract, in its preamble, recited that it was made by the defendant company "for and on behalf of its plant facilities located at Corona Avenue and 94th Street, Elmhurst, Long Island, New York." If this narrow geographical description is treated as setting fixed boundaries upon the scope of the contract, difficulties immediately arise. If the plant moved from 94th Street to 93d Street in Elmhurst, an entire structure of valuable legal rights would tumble down. A fortiori if the plant moved to a site a few miles or a good many miles away, the consequence would be the same. But one would be obliged to wonder why so catastrophic a consequence should follow a mere change in physical location. And it would be hard to conjure up a reason why it should. Rather it would seem that the recital in the contract would be analogous to the descriptio personae familiar to the law in various situations.

A rational construction of the contract would seem to require that the statement of location was nothing more than a reference to the then existing situation, and had none of the vital significance which the defendant would attach to it. . . .

In the instant case the plant was, of course, not moved from 94th Street to 93d Street in Elmhurst, nor from Elmhurst to another town within commuting distance of the then residences of the employees. It was moved to a city in another state. That fact does not seem to us to be decisive. It would, of course, have confronted the employees with troublesome problems. They would have had to decide whether the advantages of continued employment with this employer, the right to which they had earned in Elmhurst, were sufficient to induce them to make so considerable a move. It is probable that many of them would not have made the move. Those to whom the defendant had offered employment in Bethlehem, who did not accept the offer, would have, in effect, resigned their seniority and the rights that accompanied continued employment.

We can see no expense or embarrassment to the defendant which would have resulted from its adopting the more rational, not to say humane, construction of its contract. The plaintiffs were, so far as appears, competent and satisfactory employees. They had long since completed the period of probation prescribed in the union contract. It would seem that they would have been at least as useful employees as newly hired applicants. The defendant's Bethlehem plant was a new plant. There could not have been an existing union representative or a collective bargaining agreement there, at the time the plant was opened.

In the circumstances, no detriment to the defendant would have resulted from a recognition by the defendant of rights in its employees corresponding with their reasonable expectations. In that situation, a construction of the contract which would disappoint those expectations would be irrational and destructive.

It follows from what we have said that the plaintiffs were entitled to be employed at the defendant's Bethlehem plant, with the seniority and reemployment rights which they had acquired at the Elmhurst plant. The refusal of the defendant to recognize that entitlement was a breach of contract, and the plaintiffs are entitled to recover the damages which that breach has caused them.

The plaintiffs allege in their complaint that they have been "deprived of employment by the defendant," as a result of the defendant's conduct recited above. That is an adequate allegation that they would have accepted employment at Bethlehem if it had been offered to them on the terms to which they were entitled. Proof of this allegation may well fall short of complete conviction, but the trier of fact will not penalize the plaintiffs on account of the uncertainty which has been caused by the defendant's conduct.

Whatever pension rights would have been earned by employment at Bethlehem, if it had been accepted, must be recognized by the defendant.

Since the case will be remanded, we leave to the District Court consideration of the right of recovery, if any, in connection with the welfare plan and the group insurance plan which were included in the union agreement. . . .

Reversed and remanded.

LUMBARD, Chief Judge (dissenting).

For the reasons persuasively set forth in Judge Palmieri's careful and thorough opinion, reported at 185 F. Supp. 441, I would affirm.

It is immaterial to the resolution of the question before us that the employment of competent and satisfactory employees is suddenly terminated, or even that the employer has acted ungenerously, as indeed it has. We are called upon to construe the contract upon which the parties agreed and not to substitute for it one with more humane or less destructive terms. . . .

The federal cases hold that seniority is not inherent in the employment relationship but arises out of the contract. E.g., Elder v. New York Central R.R., 6 Cir., 1945, 152 F.2d 361, 364; see Note, 54 Nw. U.L. Rev. 646, 649-50 (1959). If rights are to persist beyond the term of the collective-bargaining agreement, the agreement must so provide or be susceptible of such construction. See United Steelworkers v. Enterprise Wheel & Car Corp., 1960, 363 U.S. 593.

The agreement we are here called upon to interpret did not expressly provide for any retention of seniority rights beyond the termination of the collective-bargaining agreement. . . . Relocation of an employer's plant does not, of course, automatically terminate all rights under a collective-bargaining agreement; whether such rights continue depends on the terms of the contract. See Metal Polishers, Buffers, Platers, and Helpers Intern. Union, Local 44 A.F.L.-C.I.O. v. Viking Equipment Co., 3 Cir., 1960, 278 F.2d 142. The issue here is whether this collective-bargaining agreement gave the employees the right to "follow the work" to the new site. I would hold that it did not.

The closing of the Elmhurst plant and the removal of the defendant's operations to a new location were concededly done in good faith and were not wholly unforeseeable. As Judge Palmieri points out, it is not uncommon for the parties to extend beyond a single plant the area in which seniority rights are to apply. Surely unions are now fully of age and are able to protect themselves and their members at the bargaining table. The consequences of dismissing the plaintiffs' case might indeed be unfortunate and even "catastrophic" from their point of view, but it is hardly "irrational and destructive" for a court to leave the parties as they are if they have never seen fit to provide otherwise.

NOTES

1. After the Glidden case was remanded to the district court for a determination of damages, the United States Supreme Court held, in Smith v. Evening News Assn., 371 U.S. 195 (1962), see page 904 infra, that an individual employee may have a cause of action under Section 301 for breach of a collective bargaining agreement. In view of that holding, was the Glidden case within the jurisdiction of the federal courts under Section 301? If so, would application of federal law call for a different result as suggested by the dissent?

In a subsequent appeal the original ruling of the majority of the Court of Appeals was reaffirmed. Zdanok v. Glidden Co., 327 F.2d 944 (2d Cir. 1964). Although the court felt that its initial decision was binding as "the law of the case," it expressed doubt as to whether it would follow the Glidden decision in a future case. Judge Lumbard, in a concurring opinion, pointed out that the Glidden decision now represents the views of only one judge of the Second Circuit.

2. In Oddie v. Ross Gear & Tool Co., 305 F.2d 143 (6th Cir. 1962), cert. denied, 371 U.S. 941 (1962), the court held that employees' seniority rights under a contract which confined recognition of their union to the company's plants "located within the city limits of Detroit" did not require the company to offer jobs in Tennessee to such employees when their plant was moved to Tennessee. The court distinguished the Glidden case on the basis of contract language and bargaining history.

Although it has been held that certain monetary benefits (severance pay, vacation rights) survive expiration of a collective bargaining agreement, should non-monetary benefits, such as seniority rights, survive at a relocated plant? Is there a valid distinction between the two kinds of benefits?

3. Does the right to arbitrate a grievance survive expiration of the contract? In Independent Union v. Procter & Gamble, 312 F.2d 181 (2d Cir. 1962), the court held that grievances arising after the expiration of an old contract and before execution of a new contract are not arbitrable. Although the employees continued to work during the interim, there was no express agreement to extend the old contract. To the union argument that the Glidden case supported its claim, the court replied that although the Glidden principle might apply to hold that grievances arising prior to expiration of the contract are arbitrable even after the contract expires, the principle does not apply to grievances arising after the contract expires.

4. When a union protests a company's proposed transfer of its plant or part of its operation to another state and demands that the issue be arbitrated, may the union secure an injunction against the transfer until the issue has been resolved in arbitration? In Local Division 1098, Amalgamated Assn. of Street, Electric Railway and Motor Coach Employees v. Eastern Greyhound Lines, 225 F. Supp. 28 (D.D.C. 1963), the union claimed that certain provisions of the collective bargaining agreement precluded the company's proposed transfer of its repair and maintenance operations from Washington, D.C., to Chicago. The union sought a preliminary injunction against the transfer until the completion of an arbitration proceeding to determine whether the company had the right under the terms of the collective bargaining agreement to carry out its plan. Deciding that it must proceed in accordance with basic principles of equity, the court concluded that the balance of convenience weighed heavily in favor of the union. The preliminary injunction was granted. The court reasoned that since it has power to order specific performance of a covenant to arbitrate grievances, it has collateral power to take steps that would prevent rendering the result of the arbitration futile and ineffective. The court found that the Norris-LaGuardia Act did not apply

to the union's attempt to make the arbitration clause in the agreement effective.

Compare International Union of United Automobile Workers v. Seagrave Division, F.W.D. Corp., 56 L.R.R.M. 2874 (E.D. Ohio, 1964), where the court employed similar language and reasoning. It agreed with the union that it had jurisdiction to issue a preliminary injunction to restrain the company from moving its operations from Columbus, Ohio, to Clintonville, Wisconsin, until the union's protest could be resolved in arbitration. But the court said that the "balance of convenience" favored the company in view of the substantial monetary losses that the company would suffer if the injunction were issued. The court therefore denied the injunction if the company was willing to post a $400,000 bond to protect the employees' rights in the event that the arbitrator should find in favor of the union.

VALLEJO v. AMERICAN RAILROAD CO. OF PORTO RICO
United States Court of Appeals, First Circuit, 1951
188 F.2d 513

HARTIGAN, J. . . .

The main question in this appeal is whether or not the appellants were entitled to a pension upon the termination of their employment, having already qualified as to age and length of service with the company.

The district court in its "Findings of fact, conclusions of law and opinion" filed November 29, 1949, stated in part:

"X I

"The Court is going to find according to the terms of the original Pension Plan dated April 11, 1923, that the pension system therein provided for constituted a privilege or gratuity which might be withdrawn either individually or collectively at any time the company saw fit. However, in 1944 after the Collective Bargaining Agreement was entered into between the American Railroad Company and the Union de los Obreros Unidos de las Ferrovias de Puerto Rico, the pension system or plan of the American Railroad Company was changed by Mr. Emilio S. Jimenez, the General Manager of the American Railroad Company, insofar as it affected non-union employees of the railroad company. Under the Pension Plan as changed by Mr. Jimenez, the pension system was made obligatory as to all employees of the Company whether they belonged to the Union or not, and Mr. Jimenez advised the Assistant Manager, Mr. Etienne Totti, and other department heads, that the pension system would be obligatory to the company and extend to all employees of the company.

"X I I

"That the American Railroad Company having changed the original pension system from an optional pension system to an obligatory pension plan, covering all employees, it accepted the consequences of said act regardless of the economic conditions.

"Thus the claimants may be separated into three classes, to wit:

"(a) those claimants who had retired and were receiving the pension at the time of the filing of the reorganization proceedings and prior to the appointment of the Trustee;

"(b) those claimants who resigned on August 6, 1947 immediately after the Trustee had been appointed; and,

"(c) claimants who were dismissed by the Trustee on August 16 and 18, 1947.

"During the course of the hearings upon these pension claims, the main question arose as to whether or not the Pension Plan was a gratuity or was obligatory. This question has been decided by the Court in its findings. This, however, does not finally dispose of the question as no comment has been made by counsel on either side in connection with several other provisions which are contained in the Pension Plan, to wit, Circular of the Directors No. 379 of April 11, 1923, and the Court will ask counsel to comment and submit whatever authorities they desire to submit upon the effect of the following provisions of said Circular which are as follows:

" 'It is well to clarify that such persons as may have resigned, or abandoned their employment in the past, or who shall resign or abandon their employment voluntarily in the future, shall, of course, be taken as having resigned also the privilege of the pension and shall have no right thereto. If such employees should return to the employment of the company, their term of employment shall begin to count from the date of their employment.'

" 'Nothing herein contained shall be construed to limit in any way or manner the right that the company has to dismiss its employees at any time when the interest of the company shall so require, and the employees so dismissed from their employments shall have no right to the pension privilege, unless they are dismissed for pension purposes.'

" 'The company shall have the right at any time to reduce the pension payments proportionately, to discontinue them or to make such alterations and establish such limitations as it may deem convenient and timely.'

"There is not much question in the Court's mind as to the first class of claimants, that is, those claimants who had already retired and were receiving the pensions at the time of the appointment of the Trustee. The Court has not concluded, however, as to the rights of the claimants who fall in the last two categories, particularly in view of the above mentioned provisions of the Pension Plan and it is upon this particular phase of the matter that the Court desires counsel's advice.

"In short, the Court desires to know what effect, if any, is to be given the above mentioned provisions of the Pension Circular by the Court, insofar as they affect the claims of the claimants who fall in the last two categories."

In its later opinion and order of April 26, 1950, the district court concluded, however, that though some of the pension claims were good yet the claims of the appellants were to be denied because they were dismissed by the trustee for reasons of economy or because they voluntarily resigned and their resignations were accepted also for reasons of economy.

The court said in its "Additional and supplementary findings of fact, conclusions of law, opinion and order" filed April 26, 1950:

"I hold, however, that this change in policy did not take away from the company the right expressly reserved in the pension circular to refuse to pay a pension to any employee or employees who although qualifying as to age and years of service, should resign or abandon their employment voluntarily, or who should be dismissed at any time when the interests of the company should so require, unless the latter should have been dismissed for pension purposes.

"The wording of the pension circular is too clear to that effect to admit any other interpretation.

"As to those employees who were so dismissed, or whose resignations were tendered and accepted, I find that although they qualified as to age and period of service, they did not qualify for pension since they had not complied with all the terms of the pension plan as those terms are expressly contained in the pension circular.

"Should I hold otherwise, I would be holding that, upon the change in policy effected by the management in 1944, all the conditions of the pension circular were abrogated and rendered inoperative, and that thereafter all employees who should attain a certain age and who should have rendered services for a certain period of years would be unqualifiedly entitled to receive a pension. If I should do so, I would, by judicial determination, be rendering inoperative the express provisions of the pension circular which, because they are not inconsistent with the obligatory feature of the pension plan, must be interpreted to mean exactly what they say.

"I also find that in no case was the right to receive a pension made a part of the contract of employment of those claimants who were either dismissed by the Trustee or who resigned their respective employments. Neither did any of said claimants receive payment of their pensions from the company or from the Trustee at any time. I, therefore, find that said claimants have no vested right to receive a pension, and that the Trustee was fully justified in refusing to pay a pension to them."

In attempting to justify this holding of the district court, the appellees argue in their brief that the collective bargaining agreements merely obligated the company *"to maintain a system of retirement with pension for its employees within certain qualifications, all of whom would receive, after being retired,* certain pension benefits."

This argument seems to us to be unrealistic and ignores the ordinary meaning of the word "obligatory."

After the collective bargaining agreements were executed, obligating the company to maintain a system of retirement with pension for certain qualified employees, the company could not on its own accord or by its unilateral act deprive an employee, qualifying as to age and service, of his pension. In short, the obligatory feature of the new pension system superseded the non-obligatory feature of the pension system set up by the company in Circular No. 379, April 11, 1923.

The appellants did everything they could to qualify for the plan. It merely remained for the company to pay them their pensions.

The pension plan being obligatory, as the district court held it to be, the obligation must run to someone. It is only consistent to hold that the obligation runs to each employee who qualifies through age and service and not that the company was obliged merely to maintain a pension system and no more. Under appellees' view, one is not a beneficiary unless he has the status of being discharged for pension purposes. This status is established, according to that view, by the unilateral act of the company. This contention cannot be accepted if we regard the pension plan as obligatory.

To give meaning to this obligatory pension system, the appellants must be considered qualified and entitled to pensions upon satisfying the requirement as to age and service. See Sigman v. Rudolph Wurlitzer Co., 57 Ohio App. 4, 11 N.E.2d 878; Willoughby Camera Stores v. Com'r of Internal Rev., 2 Cir., 125 F.2d 607.

This holding applies to all appellants who qualified through age and service and it is immaterial if some resigned and others were discharged.

The collective bargaining agreement of 1945 states: ". . . that any employee who shall have complied with the requirements for retirement with a pension, may continue to work for the company should he so elect and the company deem it convenient . . ."

This surely is indicative of the fact that the requirements for pension were merely of age and service set out in the collective bargaining agreement. Upon meeting these requirements an employee's pension rights had matured with the further proviso, favorable to the employee, that he might continue as an employee with the consent of the company.

The so-called resignations here can hardly be called voluntary so as to amount to forfeiture of pension rights. If not actively sought by the trustee they were speedily accepted. In any event each of the so-called letters of resignation were conditioned on the claim for a pension. . . . The petition to dismiss the appeal is denied.

The district court's judgment disallowing the claims of the appellants is reversed and the case is remanded to that court for further proceedings in accordance with this opinion; the appellants recover costs on appeal.

NOTES

1. May a union, which represents employees who have complied with all requirements of a negotiated pension plan, bargain away any of their vested rights if the employees elect to continue working for the employer? May the employer and union lawfully agree to do what the employer is forbidden to do unilaterally? Are pension benefits similar to seniority rights? (The latter may be affected by collective bargaining negotiations

without violation of the union's duty to represent fairly all employees in the bargaining unit.)   Or should an individual's pension benefits be regarded as a personal interest, distinct from that of the group?   The answers to these questions are not clear under the present state of the law. See Aaron, Legal Status of Employee Benefit Rights Under Private Pension Plans 61-63 (1961).   On the establishment of private pension plans, see page 607 supra.

2. One theory holds that unilaterally established plans are mere gratuities, creating no rights enforceable by the beneficiary.   Hughes v. Encyclopaedia Britannica, 108 F. Supp. 303 (N.D. Ill. 1952); Dolan v. Heller Bros. Co., 30 N.J. Super. 440, 104 A.2d 860 (1954).   There is judicial authority, however, to support employee claims under such plans on theories of promissory estoppel and unilateral contract (employee accepts employer's offer by remaining on the job), or by viewing pensions as deferred wages.   These theories are explained and analyzed in Chapter 2 of Aaron, supra Note 1.

Aaron continues in Chapters 3 and 4 with the following observations. With the growth of collective bargaining there has been a substantial increase in the number of negotiated pension plans.   Employee rights under the typical negotiated plan are governed by the terms of the plan. Disputes over the interpretation and application of these terms may be settled by rulings of arbitrators or by judicial decisions.   An employee's ability to enforce his claim to a pension may be affected by an act of his own, an act of his employer, or an act of his collective bargaining representative.   Examples of such occasions are voluntary retirement or quit, layoff, compulsory retirement, discharge for cause, termination because of disability, expulsion from the union or disqualification from receipt of collective bargaining benefits, death prior to retirement, or prolonged absence caused by military service or other reasons.   Other circumstances which obviously may affect an employee's rights are bankruptcy of his employer, merger of the business, sale without merger, dissolution of the company, repudiation by the employer of his obligation under the pension plan, and delinquency of the employer in making payments required by the plan.   The status of the plan and employee rights under the plan may also be controlled by statutory provisions, such as those found in the Internal Revenue Code, the Bankruptcy Act, and the Taft-Hartley Act. See, for example, Section 302 of the Taft-Hartley Act.

3. Does an employer have a right to retire an employee against his will? In United Protective Workers of America v. Ford Motor Co., 223 F.2d 49 (7th Cir. 1954), an employee who was retired at age sixty-five against his will was found to have been discharged without just cause in violation of the collective agreement.   Although the employee had received an annuity certificate stating that it was subject to the terms of a group annuity contract which the company had entered with an insurance carrier, neither the union nor the employee had been advised that the group annuity contract contained a provision for compulsory retirement.

Compare United States Steel Corp. v. Nichols, 229 F.2d 396 (6th Cir. 1956), cert. denied, 351 U.S. 950 (1956), where an employee retired under his employer's compulsory retirement policy sought damages on the ground that his employment had been terminated without cause in violation of the collective agreement. The employer's compulsory retirement policy antedated the collective bargaining agreement, which made no mention of it, and the employer had several times in collective bargaining negotiations tried to get agreement for its policy. The court held that the plaintiff's rights had not been violated. And in Bakery & Confectionery Workers v. National Biscuit Co., 177 F.2d 634 (3d Cir. 1949), the court affirmed dismissal of the union's suit for alleged breach of the collective agreement when several employees were retired against their will at age sixty-five. In collective bargaining negotiations the union had unsuccessfully demanded terms covering the employer's retirement policy.

5. *Effect of the Role of the National Labor Relations Board*

SMITH v. EVENING NEWS ASSN.

Supreme Court of the United States, 1962
371 U.S. 195, 83 Sup. Ct. 267, 9 L. Ed. 2d 246

Mr. Justice White delivered the opinion of the Court.

Petitioner is a building maintenance employee of respondent Evening News Association, a newspaper publisher engaged in interstate commerce, and is a member of the Newspaper Guild of Detroit, a labor organization having a collective bargaining contract with respondent. Petitioner, individually and as assignee of 49 other similar employees who were also Guild members, sued respondent for breach of contract in the Circuit Court of Wayne County, Michigan.[1] The complaint stated that in December 1955 and January 1956 other employees of respondent, belonging to another union, were on strike and respondent did not permit petitioner and his assignors to report to their regular shifts, although they were ready, able and available for work. During the same period, however, employees of the editorial, advertising and business departments, not covered by collective bargaining agreements, were permitted to report for work and were paid full wages even though there was no work available. Respondent's refusal to pay full wages to petitioner and his assignors while paying the nonunion employees, the complaint asserted, violated a clause in the contract providing that "there shall be no discrimination against any employee because of his membership or activity in the Guild."

The trial court sustained respondent's motion to dismiss for want of jurisdiction on the ground that the allegations, if true, would make out an unfair labor practice under the National Labor Relations Act and hence the subject matter was within the exclusive jurisdiction of the

---

[1] There was no grievance arbitration procedure in this contract which had to be exhausted before recourse could be had to the courts. Compare Atkinson v. Sinclair Refining Co., 370 U.S. 238; Drake Bakeries Inc. v. Local 50, American Bakery Workers, 370 U.S. 254.

National Labor Relations Board. The Michigan Supreme Court affirmed. . . .

Lucas Flour [365 U.S. 95] and Dowd Box [368 U.S. 502], as well as the later Atkinson v. Sinclair Refining Co., 370 U.S. 238, were suits upon collective bargaining contracts brought or held to arise under §301 of the Labor Management Relations Act and in these cases the jurisdiction of the courts was sustained although it was seriously urged that the conduct involved was arguably protected or prohibited by the National Labor Relations Act and therefore within the exclusive jurisdiction of the National Labor Relations Board. In Lucas Flour as well as in Atkinson the Court expressly refused to apply the pre-emption doctrine of the Garmon case; and we likewise reject that doctrine here where the alleged conduct of the employer, not only arguably, but concededly, is an unfair labor practice within the jurisdiction of the National Labor Relations Board. The authority of the Board to deal with an unfair labor practice which also violates a collective bargaining contract is not displaced by §301, but it is not exclusive and does not destroy the jurisdiction of the courts in suits under §301. If, as respondent strongly urges, there are situations in which serious problems will arise from both the courts and the Board having jurisdiction over acts which amount to an unfair labor practice, we shall face those cases when they arise. This is not one of them, in our view, and the National Labor Relations Board is in accord.

We are left with respondent's claim that the predicate for escaping the Garmon rule is not present here because this action by an employee to collect wages in the form of damages is not among those "suits for violation of contracts between an employer and a labor organization . . . ," as provided in §301. There is support for respondent's position in decisions of the Courts of Appeals, and in Association of Westinghouse Salaried Employees v. Westinghouse Corp., 348 U.S. 437, a majority of the Court in three separate opinions concluded that §301 did not give the federal courts jurisdiction over a suit brought by a union to enforce employee rights which were variously characterized as "peculiar in the individual benefit which is their subject matter," "uniquely personal" and arising "from separate hiring contracts between the employer and each employee." Id., at 460, 461, 464.

However, subsequent decisions here have removed the underpinnings of Westinghouse and its holding is no longer authoritative as a precedent. Three of the Justices in that case were driven to their conclusion because in their view §301 was procedural only, not substantive, and therefore grave constitutional questions would be raised if §301 was held to extend to the controversy there involved. However, the same three Justices observed that if, contrary to their belief, "Congress has itself defined the law or authorized the federal courts to fashion the judicial rules governing this question, it would be self-defeating to limit the scope of the power of the federal courts to less than is necessary to accomplish this congressional aim." Id., at 442. Textile Workers v. Lincoln Mills, 353 U.S 448, of course, has long since settled that §301 has substantive content and that Congress has directed the courts to formulate and apply federal law to suits for violation of collective bargaining contracts. There is no constitutional difficulty and §301 is not to be given a narrow reading. Id., at 456, 457. Section 301 has been applied to suits to compel arbitration of such individual grievances as rates of pay, hours of work and wrongful discharge, Textile Workers v. Lincoln Mills, supra; General Electric Co. v. Local 205, UEW, 353 U.S. 547; to obtain specific enforcement of an arbitrator's award ordering reinstatement and back pay to individual employees, United Steelworkers v. Enterprise Wheel & Car Corp., 363 U.S. 593; to recover wage increases in a contest over the validity of the collective bargaining contract, Dowd Box Co. v. Courtney, supra; and to suits against individual union members for violation of a no-strike clause contained in a collective bargaining agreement. Atkinson v. Sinclair Refining Co., supra.

The concept that all suits to vindicate individual employee rights arising from a collective bargaining contract should be excluded from the coverage of §301 has thus not survived. The rights of individual employees concerning rates of pay and conditions of employment are a major focus of the negotiation and administration of collective bargaining contracts. Individual claims lie at the heart of the grievance and arbitration machinery, are to a large degree inevitably intertwined with union interests and many times precipitate grave questions concerning the interpretation and enforceability of the collective bargaining contract on which they are based. To exclude these claims from the ambit of §301 would stultify the congressional policy of having the administration of collective bargaining contracts accomplished under a uniform body of federal substantive law. This we are unwilling to do.

The same considerations foreclose respondent's reading of §301 to exclude all suits brought by employees instead of unions. The word "between," it suggests, refers to "suits," not "contracts," and therefore only suits between unions and employers are within the purview of §301. According to this view, suits by employees for breach of a collective bargaining contract would not arise under §301 and would be governed by state law, if not preempted by Garmon, as this one would be, whereas a suit by a union for the same breach of the same contract would be a §301 suit ruled by federal law. Neither the language and structure of §301 nor its legislative history requires or persuasively supports this restrictive interpretation, which would frustrate rather than serve the congressional policy expressed in that section. "The possibility that individual contract terms might have different meanings under state and federal law would inevitably exert a disruptive influence upon both the negotiation and administration of collective agreements." Local 174, Teamsters v. Lucas Flour Co., supra, at 103.

We conclude that petitioner's action arises under §301 and is not preempted under the Garmon rule.[9] The judgment of the Supreme Court

_____

[9] The only part of the collective bargaining contract set out in this record is the no-discrimination clause. Respondent does not argue here and we need not consider the question of federal law of whether petitioner, under this contract, has standing to sue for breach of the no-discrimination clause nor do we deal with the standing of other employees to sue upon other clauses in other contracts.

of Michigan is reversed and the cause remanded for further proceedings not inconsistent with this opinion.

Reversed. . . .

MR. JUSTICE BLACK, dissenting. . . .

One example is enough to show how Congress' policy of confining controversies over unfair labor practices to the Labor Board might well be frustrated by permitting unfair labor practice claimants to choose whether they will seek relief in the courts or before the Board. Section 10(b) of the Act provides that "no complaint shall issue based upon any unfair labor practice occurring more than six months prior to the filing of the charge with the Board. . . ." In contrast, the statute of limitations in Michigan governing breach of contract suits like this is six years. The Court's holding thus opens up a way to defeat the congressional plan, adopted over vigorous minority objection, to expedite industrial peace by requiring that both the complaining party and the Board act promptly in the initiation of unfair labor practice proceedings. Instead, by permitting suits like this one to be filed, it is now not only possible but highly probable that unfair labor practice disputes will hang on like festering sores that grow worse and worse with the years. Of course this Court could later, by another major statutory surgical operation, apply the six-months Labor Board statute of limitations to actions for breach of collective bargaining contracts under §301. But if such drastic changes are to be wrought in the Act that Congress passed, it seems important to me that this Court should wait for Congress to perform that operation.

There is another reason why I cannot agree with the Court's disposition of this case. . . . [T]he Court studiously refrains from saying when, for what kinds of breach, or under what circumstances an individual employee can bring a §301 action and when he must step aside for the union to prosecute his claim. Nor does the Court decide whether the suit brought in this case is one of the types which an individual can bring. This puzzles me. This Court usually refrains from deciding important questions of federal law such as are involved in this case without first satisfying itself that the party raising those questions is entitled (has standing) to prosecute the case. It seems to me to be at least a slight deviation from the Court's normal practice to determine the law that would be applicable in a particular lawsuit while leaving open the question of whether such a lawsuit has even been brought in the particular case the court is deciding. This Court has not heretofore thought itself authorized to render advisory opinions. . . .

CAREY v. WESTINGHOUSE ELECTRIC CORP.

Supreme Court of the United States, 1964
375 U.S. 261, 84 Sup. Ct. 401, 11 L. Ed. 2d 320

[The IUE, representing the production and maintenance employees at the plant where the dispute arose, filed a grievance in which it asserted that technical employees who were represented by another union were performing production and maintenance work. The IUE's agreement with the company contained a grievance procedure leading to arbitration.

Westinghouse refused to arbitrate the grievance on the ground that the controversy presented a representation matter for the NLRB. The IUE's petition to the state courts of New York for an order compelling arbitration was denied. The Court of Appeals held that the matter was within the exclusive jurisdiction of the NLRB since it involved a definition of bargaining units.]

MR. JUSTICE DOUGLAS delivered the opinion of the Court. . . .

We have here a so-called "jurisdictional" dispute involving two unions and the employer. But the term "jurisdictional" is not a word of a single meaning. In the setting of the present case this "jurisdictional" dispute could be one of two different, though related, species: either — (1) a controversy as to whether certain work should be performed by workers in one bargaining unit or those in another; or (2) a controversy as to which union should represent the employees doing a particular work. If this controversy is considered to be the former, the National Labor Relations Act (61 Stat. 136, 73 Stat. 519, 29 U.S.C. §151 et seq.) does not purport to cover all phases and stages of it. While §8(b)(4)(D) makes it an unfair labor practice for a union to strike to get an employer to assign work to a particular group of employees rather than to another, the Act does not deal with the controversy anterior to a strike nor provide any machinery for resolving such a dispute absent a strike. The Act and its remedies for "jurisdictional" controversies of that nature come into play only by a strike or a threat of a strike. Such conduct gives the Board authority under §10(k) to resolve the dispute.

Are we to assume that the regulatory scheme contains an hiatus, allowing no recourse to arbitration over work assignments between two unions but forcing the controversy into the strike stage before a remedy before the Board is available? The Board, as admonished by §10(k), has often given effect to private agreements to settle disputes of this character; and that is in accord with the purpose as stated even by the minority spokesman in Congress — "that full opportunity is given the parties to reach a voluntary accommodation without governmental intervention if they so desire." 93 Cong. Rec. 4035; 2 Leg. Hist. L.M.R.A. (1947) 1046. And see Labor Board v. Radio Engineers, 364 U.S. 573, 577.

As Judge Fuld, dissenting below said: "The underlying objective of the national labor laws is to promote collective bargaining agreements and to help give substance to such agreements through the arbitration process." 11 N.Y.2d 452, 458, 230 N.Y.S.2d 703, 706.

Grievance arbitration is one method of settling disputes over work assignments; and it is commonly used, we are told. To be sure, only one of the two unions involved in the controversy has moved the state courts to compel arbitration. So unless the other union intervenes, an adjudication of the arbiter might not put an end to the dispute. Yet the arbitration may as a practical matter end the controversy or put into movement forces that will resolve it. The case in its present posture is analogous to Whitehouse v. Illinois Central R. Co., 349 U.S. 366, where a railroad and two unions were disputing a jurisdictional matter, when the National Railroad Adjustment Board served notice on the railroad and one union of its assumption of jurisdiction. The railroad, not being able to have notice served on the other union, sued in the courts for relief. We adopted a hands-off policy, saying, "Railroad's resort to the courts had preceded any award, and one may be rendered which could occasion no possible injury to it." Id., at 373.

Since §10(k) not only tolerates but actively encourages voluntary settlements of work assignment controversies between unions, we conclude that grievance procedures pursued to arbitration further the policies of the Act.

What we have said so far treats the case as if the grievance involves only a work assignment dispute. If, however, the controversy be a representational one, involving the duty of an employer to bargain collectively with the representative of the employees as provided in §8(a)(5), further considerations are necessary. Such a charge, made by a union against the employer, would, if proved, be an unfair labor practice, as §8(a)(5) expressly states. Or the unions instead of filing such a charge might petition the Board under §9(c)(1) to obtain a clarification of the certificates they already have from the Board; and the employer might do the same. . . .

If this is truly a representation case, either IUE or Westinghouse can move to have the certificate clarified. But the existence of a remedy before the Board for an unfair labor practice does not bar individual employees from seeking damages for breach of a collective bargaining agreement in a state court, as we held in Smith v. Evening News Assn., 371 U.S. 195. We think the same policy considerations are applicable here; and that a suit either in the federal courts, as provided by §301(a) of the Labor Management Relations Act of 1947 (61 Stat. 156, 29 U.S.C. §185(a); Textile Workers v. Lincoln Mills, 353 U.S. 448), or before such state tribunals as are authorized to act (Charles Dowd Box Co. v. Courtney, 368 U.S. 502; Teamsters Local v. Lucas Flour Co., 369 U.S. 95) is proper, even though an alternative remedy before the Board is available, which, if invoked by the employer, will protect him.

The policy considerations behind Smith v. Evening News Assn., supra, are highlighted here by reason of the blurred line that often exists between work assignment disputes and controversies over which of two or more unions is the appropriate bargaining unit. It may be claimed that A and B, to whom work is assigned as "technical" employees, are in fact "production and maintenance" employees; and if that charge is made and sustained the Board, under the decisions already noted, clarifies the certificate. But IUE may claim that when the work was assigned to A and B, the collective agreement was violated because "production and maintenance" employees, not "technical" employees, were entitled to it. As noted, the Board clarifies certificates where a certified union seeks to represent additional employees; but it will not entertain a motion to clarify a certificate where the union merely seeks additional work for employees already within its unit. . . .

As the Board's decisions indicate, disputes are often difficult to classify. In the present case the Solicitor General, who appears amicus, believes the controversy is essentially a representational one. So does Westing-

house. IUE on the other hand claims it is a work assignment dispute.
Even if it is in form a representation problem, in substance it may involve problems of seniority when layoffs occur (see Sovern, Section 301
and the Primary Jurisdiction of the NLRB, 76 Harv. L. Rev. 529, 574-575
(1963)) or other aspects of work assignment disputes. If that is true,
there is work for the arbiter whatever the Board may decide.

If by the time the dispute reaches the Board, arbitration has already
taken place, the Board shows deference to the arbitral award, provided
the procedure was a fair one and the results not repugnant to the
Act. . . .

Should the Board disagree with the arbiter, by ruling, for example, that
the employees involved in the controversy are members of one bargaining
unit or another, the Board's ruling would, of course, take precedence; and
if the employer's action had been in accord with that ruling, it would not
be liable for damages under §301. But that is not peculiar to the present
type of controversy. Arbitral awards construing a seniority provision
(Carey v. General Electric Co., 315 F.2d 499, 509-510), or awards concerning unfair labor practices, may later end up in conflict with Board rulings. See International Association of Machinists, 116 N.L.R.B. 645;
Monsanto Chemical Co., supra. Yet, as we held in Smith v. Evening
News Assn., supra, the possibility of conflict is no barrier to resort to a
tribunal other than the Board.

However the dispute be considered — whether one involving work assignment or one concerning representation — we see no barrier to use of
the arbitration procedure. If it is a work assignment dispute, arbitration
conveniently fills a gap and avoids the necessity of a strike to bring the
matter to the Board. If it is a representation matter, resort to arbitration
may have a pervasive, curative effect even though one union is not a
party.

By allowing the dispute to go to arbitration its fragmentation is
avoided to a substantial extent; and those conciliatory measures which
Congress deemed vital to "industrial peace" (Textile Workers v. Lincoln
Mills, supra, at 455) and which may be dispositive of the entire dispute,
are encouraged. The superior authority of the Board may be invoked at
anytime. Meanwhile the therapy of arbitration is brought to bear in a
complicated and troubled area.

Reversed.

MR. JUSTICE GOLDBERG took no part in the consideration or decision of
this case.

MR. JUSTICE HARLAN, concurring.

I join the Court's opinion with a brief comment. As is recognized by
all, neither position in this case is without its difficulties. Lacking a clear-
cut command in the statute itself, the choice in substance lies between a
course which would altogether preclude any attempt at resolving disputes
of this kind of arbitration, and one which at worst will expose those
concerned to the hazard of duplicative proceedings. The undesirable
consequences of the first alternative are inevitable, those of the second
conjectural. As between the two, I think the Court at this early stage of
experience in this area rightly chooses the latter.

MR. JUSTICE BLACK, with whom MR. JUSTICE CLARK joins, dissenting. . . .

I agree with the New York court and would affirm its judgment. Stripped of obscurantist arguments, this controversy is a plain, garden-variety jurisdictional dispute between two unions. The Court today holds, however, that the National Labor Relations Act not only permits but compels Westinghouse to arbitrate the dispute with only one of the two warring unions. Such an arbitration could not, of course, bring about the "final and binding arbitration of grievances and disputes" that the Court says contributes to the congressional objectives in passing the Labor Act. Unless all the salutary safeguards of due process of law are to be dissipated and obliterated to further the cause of arbitration, the rights of employees belonging to the Federation should not, for "policy considerations," be sacrificed by an arbitration award in proceedings between IUE and Westinghouse alone. Although I do not find the Court's opinion so clear on the point as I would like, I infer that it is not holding that this misnamed "award" would be completely final and binding on the Federation and its members. What the Court does plainly hold, however — that "the weight of the arbitration award is likely to be considerable, if the Board is later required to rule on phases of the same dispute" — seems only a trifle less offensive to established due process concepts. And this means, I suppose, that this same award, ex parte as to Federation, must be given that same or greater weight in any judicial review of the Board's final order involving the same "phases of the same dispute."

Moreover, the Court holds that suits for damages can be filed against the employer in state courts or federal courts under §301 of the Taft-Hartley Act, 29 U.S.C. §185, for the "unfair labor practice" of failing to bargain with the right union when two unions are engaged in a jurisdictional dispute. The employer, caught in that jurisdictional dispute, is ordinarily in a helpless position. He is trapped in a cross-fire between two unions. All he can do is guess as to which union's members he will be required by an arbitrator, the Labor Board, or a court to assign to the disputed jobs. If he happens to guess wrong, he is liable to be mulcted in damages. I assume it would be equally difficult for him to prophesy what award an arbitrator, the Labor Board, or a judge will make as to guess how big a verdict a court or a jury would give against him. It must be remembered that the employer cannot make a choice which will be binding on either an arbitrator, the Board, or a court. The Court's holding, thus subjecting an employer to damages when he has done nothing wrong, seems to me contrary to the National Labor Relations Act as well as to the basic principles of common everyday justice.

The result of all this is that the National Labor Relations Board, the agency created by Congress finally to settle labor disputes in the interest of industrial peace, is to be supplanted in part by so-called arbitration which in its very nature cannot achieve a final adjustment of those disputes. One of the main evils it had been hoped the Labor Act would abate was jurisdictional disputes between unions over which union members would do certain work. The Board can make final settlements of such disputes. Arbitration between some but not all the parties cannot.

I fear that the Court's recently announced leanings to treat arbitration as an almost sure and certain solvent of all labor troubles has been carried so far in this case as unnecessarily to bring about great confusion and to delay final and binding settlements of jurisdictional disputes by the Labor Board, the agency which I think Congress intended to do that very job.

I would affirm.

NOTE

Although the majority of the Court in Carey v. Westinghouse Electric Corp. noted the tendency of the Board to defer to arbitration awards, a Board majority refused to follow an arbitration award in a jurisdictional dispute in New Orleans Typographical Union, 147 N.L.R.B. No. 21 (1964). The Board assigned disputed typesetter work to employees represented by the Lithographers Union (ALA), even though an arbitrator had ruled that the disputed work was covered by the employer's agreement with the Typographical Union (ITU). In a footnote the Board simply stated that: "As the ALA was not a party to the arbitration proceeding and the award did not purport to bind the ALA, we have admitted the arbitration award into evidence for the limited purpose of including in the record the arbitrator's interpretation of the ITU contract as reserving the disputed work for ITU members."

An arbitrator may be able to resolve a jurisdictional dispute by inducing the two unions and the company to engage in trilateral arbitration. See Jones, Autobiography of a Decision: The Function of Innovation in Labor Arbitration, and the National Steel Orders of Joinder and Interpleader, 10 U.C.L.A.L. Rev. 987 (1963); Jones, An Arbitral Answer to a Judicial Dilemma: The Carey Decision and Trilateral Arbitration of Jurisdictional Disputes, 11 id. 327 (1964).

E.   The Individual and the Collective Agreement

1.   *The Union's Duty of Fair Representation*

a.   DISCRIMINATION ON THE BASIS OF SENIORITY

The Selective Training and Service Act of 1940, 54 Stat. 890, entitled after amendment in 1948 the Selective Service Act, 62 Stat. 604, has been known since 1951 as the Universal Military Training and Service Act, 65 Stat. 75, 50 U.S.C. §451. Since 1940 the statute has extended reemployment rights to military personnel returning to civilian life. The principal sections are noted below.[29] The Secretary of Labor, through the

---

[29] "Section 9. . . .

"(b) In the case of any such person who, in order to perform such training and service, has left or leaves a position (other than a temporary position) in the employ of any employer and who (1) receives such certificate, and (2) makes application for reemployment within ninety days after he is relieved from such training

Bureau of Veterans' Reemployment Rights, assists ex-servicemen in asserting their statutory rights, and United States Attorneys are directed by statute to represent them in legal proceedings.

The statute has been a prolific source of litigation, much of which has centered on questions of seniority. From the beginning the Court read the statute as incorporating an "escalator" principle. "Thus he does not step back on the seniority escalator at the point he stepped off. He steps back on at the precise point he would have occupied had he kept his position continuously during the war." Fishgold v. Sullivan Drydock & Repair Corp., 328 U.S. 275, 284 (1946). This principle was later codified by Congress. See Section 9(c)(2).

Some cases have involved unilateral employer action alleged to be contrary to the veteran's statutory rights. Thus, in Tilton v. Missouri Pacific Ry. Co., 376 U.S. 169 (1964), plaintiffs completed part of their apprenticeship training for carmen prior to induction, and the rest after discharge from military service. The employer dated their seniority as carmen as of the completion of the apprenticeship. The Court held that plaintiffs were entitled to have their seniority dated as of the time they would have completed their apprenticeship if they had not entered the service. On the other hand, where a promotion claimed by a veteran was not solely a function of seniority, but turned partially on questions of

---

and service or from hospitalization continuing after discharge for a period of not more than one year — . . .

(B) if such position was in the employ of a private employer, such person shall —

(i) if still qualified to perform the duties of such position, be restored by such employer or his successor in interest to such position or to a position of like seniority, status, and pay; or

(ii) if not qualified to perform the duties of such position by reason of disability sustained during such service but qualified to perform the duties of any other position in the employ of such employer or his successor in interest, be restored by such employer or his successor in interest to such other position the duties of which he is qualified to perform as will provide him like seniority, status, and pay, or the nearest approximation thereof consistent with the circumstances in his case,

unless the employer's circumstances have so changed as to make it impossible or unreasonable to do so; . . .

"(c)(1) Any person who is restored to a position in accordance with the provisions of paragraph (A) or (B) of subsection (b) shall be considered as having been on furlough or leave of absence during his period of training and service in the armed forces, shall be so restored without loss of seniority, shall be entitled to participate in insurance or other benefits offered by the employer pursuant to established rules and practices relating to employees on furlough or leave of absence in effect with the employer at the time such person was inducted into such forces, and shall not be discharged from such position without cause within one year after such restoration.

"(2) It is hereby declared to be the sense of the Congress that any person who is restored to a position in accordance with the provisions of paragraph (A) or (B) of subsection (b) should be so restored in such manner as to give him such status in his employment as he would have enjoyed if he had continued in such employment continuously from the time of his entering the armed forces until the time of his restoration to such employment."

fitness and ability involving management discretion, no violation by the employer was found in failing to make the promotion on the veteran's return. McKinney v. Missouri-Kansas-Texas R.R., 357 U.S. 265 (1958). The rights of veterans under various types of seniority clauses are discussed in Sherman, Seniority and Promotion Rights of Re-employed Veterans, 17 U. Pitt. L. Rev. 20 (1955).

Other cases have raised the question whether the veteran's statutory rights were denied by the provisions of a collective bargaining agreement. It has been held consistently that the seniority which is protected by the statute is not immune from the normal processes of collective bargaining. Fishgold v. Sullivan Drydock & Repair Corp., supra; Trailmobile Co. v. Whirls, 331 U.S. 40 (1947). In Aeronautical Industrial District Lodge 727 v. Campbell, 337 U.S. 521, 526 (1949), the Court, noting that the statute does not define seniority, stated: "It is thus apparent that Congress was not creating a system of seniority but recognizing its operation as part of the process of collective bargaining. We must therefore look to the conventional uses of the seniority system in the process of collective bargaining in order to determine the rights of seniority which the Selective Service Act guaranteed the veteran. Barring legislation not here involved, seniority rights derive their scope and significance from union contracts, confined as they almost exclusively are to unionized industry." Pointing out the many variations in the basis and use of seniority, the Court upheld a contract provision which gave top seniority to union chairmen regardless of length of service, and thus resulted in the layoff of veterans with greater length of service. The Court noted that its result presupposed that the provision "expresses honest desires for the protection of the interests of all members of the union and is not a skillful device of hostility to veterans." 337 U.S. at 529.

The duty of fair representation has been raised with respect to contract provisions relating to seniority claims by veterans. In Trailmobile Co. v. Whirls, supra, a consolidation between Trailer and Highland, its wholly-owned subsidiary, resulted in the formation of Trailmobile on January 1, 1944. After consolidation, an election was held in which Trailer employees outnumbered Highland employees ten to one. After certification, the union negotiated an agreement under which former Trailer employees received seniority dating from their original employment with Trailer, but former Highland employees received seniority as of the date of the consolidation, thus losing all seniority earned under Highland. Whirls, a Highland employee from 1935 to 1942, when he entered military service, returned to work with Highland in May, 1943. The Court held that the collective agreement did not violate Whirls' statutory rights as a veteran, but it did not consider the question of fair representation. Justices Frankfurter and Jackson, however, stated: "The record indicates that [his seniority rights] have never been terminated or modified by good faith collective bargaining in the interests of the craft. It raises the suspicion that they were simply misappropriated to the benefit of the majority group which was under a duty to represent his interests as well as its own." 331 U.S. at 69. The question of fair representation was raised in a subsequent suit. In upholding the union, the court stated: "Whatever we might think of the fairness of the differentiation, the discrimination was in pursuance of the bargaining process and not without some basis, forestalled a strike and was therefore not invalid. . . . Britt v. Trailmobile Co., 179 F.2d 569, 573 (6th Cir. 1950), cert. denied, 340 U.S. 820 (1950).

The leading Supreme Court decision on fair representation with respect to seniority rights of veterans is Ford Motor Co. v. Huffman, 345 U.S. 330 (1953). In this case the contract provision gave seniority credit for military service prior to employment by the company. The effect was to give higher seniority to employees who were employed after Huffman was, thus reducing his seniority relatively. After holding that the provision did not interfere with Huffman's statutory rights as a veteran, the Court considered whether the union had violated its duty of fair representation.

"A wide range of reasonableness must be allowed a statutory bargaining representative in serving the unit it represents, subject always to complete good faith and honesty of purpose in the exercise of its discretion.

"Compromises on a temporary basis, with a view to long-range advantages, are natural incidents of negotiation. Differences in wages, hours and conditions of employment reflect countless variables. Seniority rules governing promotions, transfers, layoffs and similar matters may, in the first instance, revolve around length of competent service. Variations acceptable in the discretion of bargaining representatives, however, may well include differences based upon such matters as the unit within which seniority is to be computed, the privileges to which it shall relate, the nature of the work, the time at which it is done, the fitness, ability or age of the employees, their family responsibilities, injuries received in course of service, and time or labor devoted to related public service, whether civil or military, voluntary or involuntary. See, e.g., Hartley v. Brotherhood of Clerks, 283 Mich. 201, 277 N.W. 885; and see also, Williamson & Harris, Trends in Collective Bargaining (1945), 100-103. . . .

". . . It is not necessary to define here the limits to which a collective-bargaining representative may go in accepting proposals to promote the long-range social or economic welfare of those it represents. . . .

"The provisions before us are within reasonable bounds of relevancy." 345 U.S. at 338, 341.

NLRB v. MIRANDA FUEL CO., INC.
United States Court of Appeals, Second Circuit, 1963
326 F.2d 172

[The contract between company and union contained the following provision: "Section 8. It is further understood and agreed upon that during the dull season of the year, preference shall be given to the fuel oil chauffeurs on the seniority list, and that the Shop Steward shall be the No. 1 fuel oil chauffeur on the list.

"During the slack season, April 15 to October 15, any employee who according to seniority would not have steady employment shall be entitled to a leave of absence and maintain his full seniority rights during that period. Any man so described must report to the Shop Steward not later than 8:00 A.M. on October 15 and sign the seniority roster in order to protect his seniority, and the Employer agrees to accept the certification of said Shop Steward as to the availability of such men when called by the Employer. If October 15 falls on Saturday or Sunday, the reporting day shall be the next working day. Any man failing to report as above specified shall forfeit all seniority rights."

Lopuch was a truck driver whose seniority was eleventh on a list of twenty-one. In early April, Lopuch obtained company permission to leave at the close of business on Friday, April 12, 1957, to spend the summer in Ohio on family business. He told the company he would return by October 12, but due to illness, did not return to work until October 30. Shortly after his return, the union demanded that Lopuch be reduced to the bottom of the seniority list for late return. On learning of his illness, the union abandoned this basis and instead demanded his reduction in seniority because of early departure. The company acquiesced in this demand.

The Board originally held that vesting in the union exclusive control over the seniority status of the drivers constituted per se violations of Sections 8(b)(2) and 8(a)(3). 125 N.L.R.B. 454 (1959). This position was rejected by the Court of Appeals. 284 F.2d 861 (2d Cir. 1960). After the Supreme Court's decision in Local 357, International Brotherhood of Teamsters v. NLRB, 365 U.S. 667 (1961), the Miranda case was remanded to the Board for further proceedings. Without taking additional evidence, the Board made a new decision on the basis of the old record.]

MEDINA, Circuit Judge.

. . . Merely because the Union first relied upon Lopuch's late return, and then, after it was established that the late return was due to illness, placed its request for demotion upon Lopuch's early leaving, with the employer's consent, we are told by the Board that the demotion was due to "whim or caprice," that it constituted action by the Union, acquiesced in by the Company, that was "hostile" and for "irrelevant, unfair or invidious reasons," and that it consequently was a breach of the duty of the Union to act fairly and impartially in its representative capacity under Section 9 of the Act. From this so-called "unlawful discrimination" it is supposed to follow that Lopuch's rights under Section 7 were infringed. On the basis of this reasoning the Board concluded that the Union and the Company were respectively guilty of violations of Section 8(b)(1)(A) and (2) and Section 8 (a) (1) and (3). The remedy applied was to restore Lopuch to his former position on the drivers' seniority roster, with back pay.

Thus the law question, lying at the heart of the case, is whether any sort of discrimination against an employee, affecting the terms and conditions of his employment, can consitute an unfair labor practice under Section 8, even if wholly unrelated to any union considerations. . . .

As the various ways to discriminate against a person, or to be unfair or unjust to him, are legion, it would seem at first blush that the bearing of Sections 7 and 8 . . . is intended to affect only union considerations. Another way of stating the same thing is to say that, to constitute an unfair labor practice under Section 8, the union or the employer must have committed some act the natural and foreseeable consequence of which is to be beneficial or detrimental to the union. The classic way of describing such effect in the typical case is to say that the act in question "encouraged union membership as such."

But here the placing of Lopuch at the bottom of the seniority list, even if done through sheer whim or caprice, and even if arbitrary, unjust and "invidious," whatever that may mean in the context of the facts of this case, could not conceivably have been thought to encourage union membership, because his demotion affected union and nonunion men alike. Indeed, the foreseeable effect, in the context of this case and the terms of Section 8 of the collective bargaining agreement, could only be "to encourage timely return and continuous work until the annual layoff, the identical objective which prompted the contract provision," as pointed out by the dissenting members of the Board.

Thus the Board on reconsideration of the case pursuant to the mandate of the Supreme Court conceived the ingenious, but as we think wholly erroneous theory that any sort of discrimination, unfairness or injustice to an employee, by the Union and acquiesced in by the employer, constituted a breach by the Union of the fiduciary duty implicit in Section 9 to represent the employee fairly, and an unfair labor practice by both the Union and the employer under Sections 8(a)(3), 8(a)(1), 8(b)(2), and 8(b)(1)(A). Accordingly, the single narrow question of law in the case boils down to whether it was the intent of the Congress to read into Section 7 and Section 8 the duty of fair representation implicit in Section 9.

We pause to observe that, against the background of the present nationwide interest in discrimination for reasons of race, nationality, color or religion, and the natural tendency of human beings to attribute their lack of success to discrimination of one kind or another against them, it seems inevitable that the Board would be inundated with charges of this character, were we to sustain the ruling of the Board in this case. The briefs of the NAACP and the Civil Liberties Union, as amici curiae, appear to assume that it is in the public interest to have such controversies channeled into the Board, where the remedy of reinstatement with back pay may be afforded, rather than leave them for decision by the courts. We are not so sure of this. . . . In any event, such matters of policy must be settled and determined by the Congress. In this case our task is not to fix policy but to interpret the statute and say what we think the Congress intended it to mean.

The decision of the Board in this case is the first and only one holding that discrimination, by way of unfair representation arising out of Section 9, constitutes a series of unfair labor practices under Section 8. . . .

The Board . . . was not interested in getting at the real reasons and motives of the parties in connection with Lopuch's demotion and the interpretation given by the parties to Section 8 of the collective bargaining contract. It *was* interested in establishing some sort of per se violations in this type of case. That is how the Board came up with the novel, if not quite revolutionary, theory that any "hostile" action by a union against one of its members "for irrelevant, unfair or invidious reasons," in which action the employer acquiesces, and which "adversely affects (the) terms and conditions of employment," constitutes a breach of the statutory duty of the union to be a fair and impartial representative, also "restrains and coerces the affected employees in the exercise of their guaranteed Section 7 right to bargain collectively through their chosen agent" and thus violates Section 8(b)(1)(A) and Section 8(a)(1). Further ramifications of the theory need not be described. This is the gist of it. Were we to support the doctrine thus propounded the power and jurisdiction of the Board would be vastly extended and increased; and it would seem that such jurisdiction would be primary and the courts would be entirely excluded from the adjudication of such cases. That is what makes the case so interesting and important.

I

Petitioner, in support of its order, relies upon numerous decisions stating in general terms the proposition that a union, as representative of a certain class or craft of workers owes those whom it represents a duty of fair representation. Most of these cases arose under the Railway Labor Act, 45 U.S.C. §§151 et seq., as amended, and, consequently, could not and did not hold that a mere failure on the part of a union fairly to represent the workers constituted an unfair labor practice within the meaning of the National Labor Relations Act, in the absence of discrimination that encourages or discourages membership in a labor organization. Moreover, in the cases thus relied upon by the Board, the violation of the duty of fair representation was held to give rise to a remedy enforceable by the courts, specifically stated to be by way of injunctive relief or an award of damages. . . .

Two textwriters give some support to petitioner's view. Professor Archibald Cox, now Solicitor General, expressed views in 1957, The Duty of Fair Representation, 2 Villanova L. Rev. 151, that seem to do little more than bring the pros and cons of the question to the attention of those interested in the subject, so the issue might not "go by default unless pressed more vigorously upon an early occasion." Professor Michael I. Sovern, in The National Labor Relations Act and Racial Discrimination, 1962, 62 Colum. L. Rev. 563, reasons to the effect that where the union causes the discharge of a non-union employee because he is a Negro "the Negro workers are likely to assume that if they could only join the union, they would be allowed to work," at page 570. See also pp. 587-9, 590-4, 608-13. Moreover, even if the principles supported in these Law Review articles were articulated in the same form as those expressed by petitioner in its decision in this case, they are contrary to the holdings of the adjudicated cases discussed below.

The Legislative History of the NLRA is not particularly illuminating on the issue before us. . . .

We conclude that the authorities relied on by petitioner give little support for the novel principle sought to be established. The case against petitioner, however, is, we think, impressive and all but compelling.

I I

To begin with, this case seems to be controlled by our recent decision in N.L.R.B. v. Local 294, International Brotherhood of Teamsters, 2 Cir., 1963, 317 F.2d 746, in which after examining the authorities, we concluded that: . . .

"These authorities establish the principle that a union does not violate Section 8(b)(2) unless the discrimination which the union seeks would constitute a violation of Section 8(a)(3) if the employer acted without union suggestion of compulsion.   Section 8(b)(2) is violated only by causing or attempting to cause 'an employer to discriminate against an employee in violation of [Section 8(a)(3)].'   An employer who discriminates among employees does not violate Section 8(a)(3) unless the discrimination is based upon union membership or other union-connected activities.   It is obvious, for example, that the employer's promotion or the demotion of an employee who is a union official is not a violation of the Act unless the discrimination for or against him is based on his union activity.   It seems to us to be equally obvious that the union's seeking such a promotion or demotion would not constitute an unfair labor practice if the union's action was based upon the employee's merit or demerit and was unconnected with his union membership or activity. . . .

"The conclusion of the Board that an employer commits an unfair labor practice if he changes an employee's conditions of employment at the instance of the union, is not only contrary to the letter and spirit of the Act and to the precedents, but is based on a view of labor-management policy which is certain to have untoward consequences.   There are countless situations in which the very concept of collective action demands that unions have the power to influence the employer to make changes in the job status of individual employees.   To hold that unions cannot properly press upon an employer their demands for an employee's advancement or demotion would be to weaken greatly the union's effectiveness in representing all the employees in a unit.   The policy of the Board is all the more mistaken if it is based upon disapproval of the union's motives in the instant case.   Not only is the Board without authority to pass upon the wisdom or the desirability of a union's actions as long as those actions are not forbidden by the Act, but the principle applied by the Board would be equally applicable to actions which are clearly beneficial to the majority of employees. . . ."   We agree with the reasoning of the opinion just quoted.

Indeed, we do not see how any other view is compatible with the reasoning of the Supreme Court in Local 357, International Brotherhood of Teamsters, Chauffeurs, Warehousemen and Helpers of America v.

N.L.R.B., 1961, 365 U.S. 667, the case that led to the remand of Miranda to the Board for further proceedings. In effect the court there held that practically everything a union does encourages union membership, and that it is necessary in a particular case to show that the acts complained of were done with the unlawful intent and purpose of encouraging employees to join the union. It is not enough merely to show that the employer discriminated among employees at the behest of the union. An unfair labor practice has been committed only if the discrimination was deliberately designed to encourage membership in the union. . . .

Enforcement denied.

[Judge Lumbard concurred in Judge Medina's view on the Section 8(b)(2) and 8(a)(3) holdings; he thought, however, that it was not necessary to decide whether Section 7 incorporates the duty of fair representation since the facts showed no breach of that duty. Judge Friendly took no position on the Section 7 point; he would have enforced the Board's Section 8(b)(2) and 8(a)(3) holdings, since he believed the evidence supported findings of discrimination and encouragement of union membership.]

HUMPHREY v. MOORE

Supreme Court of the United States, 1964
375 U.S. 335, 84 Sup. Ct. 363, 11 L. Ed. 2d 370

[When Dealers Transport Company absorbed the Southern operations of the E & L Transport Company, a Joint Conference Committee, consisting of employer and union representatives, decided that the seniority of the affected employees should be dovetailed. The employees of both companies were represented by the same local union, the president of which was Paul Priddy. Moore, one of Dealers employees, sought an injunction in the state courts of Kentucky against implementation of the decision of the Committee. He claimed that the Committee exceeded its power under the existing collective bargaining agreement in making the decision to dovetail the seniority lists, and that the decision of the Committee was brought about by dishonest union conduct in breach of its duty of fair representation. The Kentucky Court of Appeals enjoined the implementation of the Committee's decision. The majority of the Supreme Court agreed with the Kentucky court's observation that Moore's action was in the nature of an action to enforce a collective bargaining agreement.]

Mr. Justice White delivered the opinion of the Court.

. . . [T]his action is one arising under §301 of the Labor Management Relations Act and is a case controlled by federal law, Textile Workers Union v. Lincoln Mills, 353 U.S. 448, even though brought in the state court. Local 174 Teamsters v. Lucas Flour Co., 369 U.S. 95; Smith v. Evening News Assn., 371 U.S. 195. Although there are differing views on whether a violation of the duty of fair representation is an unfair labor practice under the Labor Management Relations Act, it is not necessary for us to resolve that difference here. Even if it is, or arguably may be, an unfair labor practice, the complaint here alleged that Moore's discharge would violate the contract and was therefore within the cognizance of federal and state courts, Smith v. Evening News Assn., supra, subject of course, to the applicable federal law. . . .

The power of the Joint Conference Committee over seniority gave it power over jobs. It was entitled under §5 [of the agreement] to integrate the seniority lists upon some rational basis, and its decision to integrate lists upon the basis of length of service at either company was neither unique nor arbitrary. On the contrary, it is a familiar and frequently equitable solution to the inevitably conflicting interests which arise in the wake of a merger or an absorption such as occurred here. The Joint Conference Committee's decision to dovetail seniority lists was a decision which §5 empowered the committee to make.

Neither do we find adequate support in this record for the complaint's attack upon the integrity of the union and of the procedures which led to the decision. Although the union at first advised the Dealers drivers that they had nothing to worry about but later supported the E & L employees before the Joint Conference Committee, there is no substantial evidence of fraud, deceitful action or dishonest conduct. Priddy's early assurances to Dealers employees were not well founded, it is true; but Priddy was acting upon information then available to him, information received from the company which led him to think there was no trade or exchange involved, no "absorption" which might bring §5 into play. Other sections of the contract, he thought, would protect the jobs of Moore, and his fellow drivers. Consistent with this view, he also advised E & L employees that the situation appeared unfavorable for them. However, when he learned of the pending acquisition by Dealers of E & L operating authority in Louisville and of the involvement of other locations in the transaction, he considered the matter to be one for the Joint Committee. Ultimately he took the view that an absorption was involved, that §5 did apply and that dovetailing seniority lists was the most equitable solution for all concerned. We find in this evidence insufficient proof of dishonesty or intentional misleading on the part of the union. And we do not understand the court below to have found otherwise.

The Kentucky court, however, made much of the antagonistic interests of the E & L and Dealers drivers, both groups being represented by the same union, whose president supported one group and opposed the other at the hearing before the Joint Conference Committee. But we are not ready to find a breach of the collective bargaining agent's duty of fair representation in taking a good faith position contrary to that of some individuals whom it represents nor in supporting the position of one group of employees against that of another. . . . Just as a union must be free to sift out wholly frivolous grievances which would only clog the grievance process, so it must be free to take a position on the not so frivolous disputes. Nor should it be neutralized when the issue is chiefly between two sets of employees. Conflict between employees represented by the same union is a recurring fact. To remove or gag the union in these cases would surely weaken the collective bargaining and grievance processes.

As far as this record shows the union took its position honestly, in good faith and without hostility or arbitrary discrimination. After Dealers absorbed the Louisville business of E & L there were fewer jobs at Dealers than there were Dealers and E & L drivers. One group or the other was going to suffer. If any E & L drivers were to be hired at Dealers either they or the Dealers drivers would not have the seniority which they had previously enjoyed. Inevitably the absorption would hurt someone. By choosing to integrate seniority lists based upon length of service at either company, the union acted upon wholly relevant considerations, not upon capricious or arbitrary factors. The evidence shows no breach by the union of its duty of fair representation.

There is a remaining contention. Even though the union acted in good faith and was entitled to take the position it did, were the Dealers employees, if the union was going to oppose them, deprived of a fair hearing by having inadequate representation at the hearing? Dealers employees had notice of the hearing, they were obviously aware that they were locked in a struggle for jobs and seniority with the E & L drivers, and three stewards representing them went to the hearing at union expense and were given every opportunity to state their position. Thus the issue is in reality a narrow one. There was no substantial dispute about the facts concerning the nature of the transaction between the two companies. It was for the Joint Conference Committee initially to decide whether there was an "absorption" within the meaning of §5 and, if so, whether seniority lists were to be integrated and the older employees of E & L given jobs at Dealers. The Dealers employees made no request to continue the hearing until they could secure further representation and have not suggested what they could have added to the hearing by way of facts or theory if they had been differently represented. The trial court found it "idle speculation to assume that the result would have been different had the matter been differently presented." We agree.

Moore has not, therefore, proved his case. Neither the parties nor the Joint Committee exceeded their power under the contract and there was no fraud or breach of duty by the exclusive bargaining agent. The decision of the committee, reached after proceedings adequate under the agreement, is final and binding upon the parties, just as the contract says it is. Drivers Union v. Riss & Co., 372 U.S. 517.

The decision below is reversed and the case remanded for further proceedings not inconsistent with this opinion.

MR. JUSTICE GOLDBERG, with whom MR. JUSTICE BRENNAN joins, concurring in the result.

I concur in the judgment and in the holding of the Court that since "Moore has not . . . proved his case . . ." the decision below must be reversed. I do not, however, agree that Moore stated a cause of action arising under §301(a) of the Labor Management Relations Act, 61 Stat. 156, 29 U.S.C. §185(a). It is my view rather that Moore's claim must be treated as an individual employee's action for a union's breach of its duty of fair representation — a duty derived not from the collective bargaining contract but from the National Labor Relations Act as amended. . . .

MR. JUSTICE HARLAN, concurring in part and dissenting in part.

. . . I would reverse the judgment of the state court to the extent that it rests upon a holding that the Joint Conference Committee acted beyond the scope of its authority, set the case for reargument on the unfair representation issue, and invite the National Labor Relations Board to present its views by brief and oral argument on the preemption question. Cf. Retail Clerks International Assn. v. Schermerhorn, 373 U.S. 746, 757, 375 U.S. 96.

b. DISCRIMINATION ON THE BASIS OF RACE

Steele v. Louisville & Nashville R.R., 323 U.S. 192 (1944), supra page 74, held that the Railway Labor Act required a union which was a bargaining representative of a majority of employees to represent all the employees in the bargaining unit without racial discrimination. The statute was so interpreted to avoid constitutional questions. This case was the first in a series of cases in which courts have been faced with the problem of dealing with racial discrimination by the union representing employees in a bargaining unit, either with or without the aid or agreement of the employer.

In Brotherhood of Railroad Trainmen v. Howard, 343 U.S. 768 (1952), the union, which was all white, obtained an agreement that certain work which had in the past been done by porters should in the future be performed by trainmen. The effect of this was to cause the discharge of Negro porters in favor of white trainmen. The union contended that the Steele doctrine was not applicable because the union represented only the craft of trainmen and did not represent the craft of porters; therefore, it had not discriminated against anyone within its bargaining unit. The Court, however, rejected this argument, saying (p. 774): "The Federal Act thus prohibits bargaining agents it authorizes from using their position and power to destroy colored workers' jobs in order to bestow them on white workers." Justice Minton, joined by Chief Justice Vinson and Justice Reed, dissented. "The majority reaches out to invalidate the contract, not because the train porters are brakemen entitled to fair representation by the Brotherhood, but because they are Negroes who were discriminated against by the carrier at the behest of the Brotherhood. I do not understand that private parties such as the carrier and the Brotherhood may not discriminate on the ground of race. Neither a state government nor the Federal Government may do so, but I know of no applicable federal law which says that private parties may not. That is the whole problem underlying the proposed Federal Fair Employment Practices Code. Of course, this Court by sheer power can say this case is Steele, or even lay down a code of fair employment practices. But sheer power is not a substitute for legality. I do not have to agree with the discrimination here indulged in to question the legality of today's decision."

Syres v. Oil Workers International Union, 223 F.2d 739 (5th Cir. 1955), rev'd and remanded per curiam, 350 U.S. 892 (1956), involved a situation where two unions were certified by the NLRB as joint representatives of a certain unit. Thereafter they amalgamated, and it was agreed at that time, among members and officers of the two unions, that a negotiating committee would be elected and in the forthcoming contract would establish a single line of seniority. In fact, however, they established two lines, one for Negroes and one for whites. Certain Negro union members brought suit in a federal court for declaratory judgment that this agreement was void.

The District Court dismissed the suit for lack of jurisdiction. A majority of the Court of Appeals affirmed, concluding (p. 744) that no federal question was involved, but merely a violation of a "private contract voluntarily made between the two groups of employees." In a dissenting opinion, Judge Rives stated (p. 746) that since the bargaining unit had been determined by the Labor Board and it had supervised the election and certified the representative as exclusive bargaining agent, the federal law "very clearly and definitely entered into the making of this collective bargaining contract." He further said (p. 747) that the Negro members were "constrained to accept racial discrimination because of the duties imposed" by Section 8(d) of the NLRA. Thus did federal law "provide automatic sanctions" for enforcement of the contract. The Supreme Court's per curiam reversal cited the Steele, Tunstall, and Howard decisions. See Blumrosen, The Worker and Three Phases of Unionism: Administrative and Judicial Control of the Worker-Union Relationship, 61 Mich. L. Rev. 1435 (1963), and Sovern, The NLRA and Racial Discrimination, 62 Colum. L. Rev. 563 (1962).

In Conley v. Gibson, 355 U.S. 41 (1957), the Negro petitioners alleged that their bargaining representative, the Brotherhood of Railway and Steamship Clerks, had done nothing to protect them against discriminatory discharges and seniority reductions imposed by the employer, Texas and New Orleans Railroad, and had refused to give them protection comparable to that given white employees. The lower courts dismissed the action on the ground that the Railroad Adjustment Board had exclusive jurisdiction. In reversing, the Supreme Court stated (pp. 45-47): ". . . [W]e hold that under the general principles laid down in the Steele, Graham, and Howard cases the complaint adequately set forth a claim upon which relief could be granted. . . . This Court squarely held in Steele and subsequent cases that discrimination in representation because of race is prohibited by the Railway Labor Act. The bargaining representative's duty not to draw 'irrelevant and invidious' distinctions among those it represents does not come to an abrupt end, as the respondents seem to contend, with the making of an agreement between union and employer. Collective bargaining is a continuing process. Among other things, it involves day-to-day adjustments in the contract and other working rules, resolution of new problems not covered by existing agreements, and the protection of employee rights already secured by contract. The bargaining representative can no more unfairly discriminate in carrying out these functions than it can in negotiating a collective agreement. A contract may be fair and impartial on its face yet administered in such a way, with the active or tacit consent of the union, as to be flagrantly discriminatory against some members of the bargaining unit.

"The respondents point to the fact that under the Railway Labor Act aggrieved employees can file their own grievances with the Adjustment Board or sue the employer for breach of contract. Granting this, it still furnishes no sanction for the union's alleged discrimination in refusing to represent petitioners."

It should be noticed that the Supreme Court in Steele and later cases did not deny the right of the union to exclude the Negro firemen from membership. Such exclusion arguably is the most extreme form of discrimination. But in Oliphant v. Locomotive Brotherhood, 262 F.2d 359 (6th Cir. 1958), the court held that neither the Federal Constitution nor the Railway Labor Act confers upon employees represented by a union the right to participate in the activities of the union. But under the Civil Rights Act of 1964, the law is now different. See the Oliphant case, infra page 999, and the application of the Civil Rights Act, infra page 1004. For a discussion of a theory accommodating this statute and the union's duty of fair representation, see Sherman, Union's Duty of Fair Representation and the Civil Rights Act, 49 Minn. L. Rev. 771 (1965).

Brief mention should be made of remedies which may be available for breach of the union's duty of fair representation. Examples are injunctive relief, revocation of the union's certification, relief granted pursuant to a finding of an unfair labor practice, and refusal to apply the contract bar rule.

In Hughes Tool Co., 104 N.L.R.B. 318 (1953), the Board held that the duty of fair representation imposed by Section 9(a) of the NLRA included the duty to accept and process, impartially and without discrimination, all grievances placed in its hands by the employees it represented. The union's requirement that nonmembers pay $15 for each grievance and $400 for each arbitration handled by the union was found to be a violation of the union's duty and was sufficient ground for the Board to revoke the union's certification as bargaining representative.

In NLRB v. Die & Toolmakers Lodge 113, 231 F.2d 298 (7th Cir. 1956), cert. denied, 352 U.S. 833 (1956), the union threatened that it would not process grievances for employees who refused to pay a strike fund assessment. Upholding the Board's decision that the union had thus violated Section 8(b)(1)(A), the court stated (p. 302): "Section 7 gives employees the right to engage in concerted activities for their mutual aid or protection, and the right to refrain from such activities. The employees of Peerless, therefore, had the right to refrain from paying the 'donation.' Threatening to stop processing grievances for employees who did not pay the proper 'donation' was coercive within the meaning of Section 8(b)(1)(A). It was not simply internal administration of Union affairs because as the certified bargaining representative, the Union is required by the Act to represent and bargain for *all* of the employees in the plant."

Pioneer Bus Co., 140 N.L.R.B. 54 (1962), held that a contract which discriminated against Negroes was not within the protection of the contract bar rules.

HUGHES TOOL CO.

National Labor Relations Board, 1964
147 N.L.R.B. No. 166

[In October, 1961, Locals 1 and 2 of the Independent Metal Workers Union were certified as joint bargaining representative. At this time the unions and the company were operating under a two-year contract negotiated in 1959. This contract provided for Group I jobs open only to white employees, and Group II jobs open only to Negroes, with separate lines of progression and demotion that prevented transfer from one group to the other. After the 1961 certification, the two locals met and agreed on most of the matters to be presented to the company in negotiating a new contract. Local 2 wanted a proposal that would eliminate racial discrimination in job opportunities, but no agreement was reached. In December, 1961, the company and Local 1 executed a document "amending and extending" the 1959 contract. Local 2 objected, but the agreement was put into effect over its protest. Also in December the company and Local 1 agreed to create new apprenticeships in the plant, and in February, 1962, they were posted for bids. Davis, a Negro employed since 1942 and treasurer of Local 2, bid for an apprenticeship. The company refused to include his name on the list of applicants, notwithstanding protest by Local 2's grievance committee. Davis' request to Local 1 to intercede for him was ignored. A charge was filed upon which complaint issued charging violation of Section 8(b)-(1)(A). Local 2 also filed a motion to rescind the 1961 certification. The two cases were consolidated.]

Report of the Trial Examiner. . . .

General Counsel's basic contention is that Local 1's failure to process Davis' grievance constituted restraint and coercion in the exercise of Section 7 rights. Reliance is placed on such cases as Peerless Tool and Engineering Co., 111 N.L.R.B. 853, 858, enforced 231 F.2d 298 (C.A. 7), cert. den. 352 U.S. 833, and M. Eskin & Son, 135 N.L.R.B. 666, enforced as to the union respondent [312 F.2d 108] (C.A. 2, January 7, 1963).

In those cases the unions involved conditioned the processing of grievances on the employees' engaging in a certain activity which the unions demanded of them. Although the cases stand for the well-settled proposition that the bargaining representative has the duty of accepting and processing grievances on which its aid is requested by an employee it represents (see also Conley v. Gibson, 355 U.S. 41, 45-46), their applicability here is considerably diminished by the fact that in those cases the Section 7 right involved was the right to refrain from union activity.

No such right is involved here. What is involved here, instead, is Davis' right under Section 7 to have the bargaining agent represent him.

If a labor organization which is the exclusive bargaining representative declines to process the grievance of a member of the unit, it has to that extent refused to represent him, and hence it has restrained or coerced him in his exercise of his right to be represented. In essence this is the analysis of the Board majority in Miranda Fuel Company, 140 N.L.R.B. No. 7. . . .

In my opinion, Local 1's refusal to process Davis' grievance also violated Section 8(b)(3) of the Act. That section requires the statutory bargaining representative to bargain collectively with an employer. The processing of grievances is, of course, a part of the bargaining function. Conley v. Gibson, supra. A refusal to process a grievance is, therefore, a refusal to bargain. This does not mean, of course, that the bargaining representative must fight every grievance to the bitter end. As noted above, Local 1 might reasonably have found, after brief investigation, that the grievance was unmeritorious because other applicants were better qualified. But the record is clear that Local 1 did not make even this much inquiry into the matter, and refused to handle Davis' grievance for reasons unrelated to his qualifications for the job.

It may be argued that the duty to bargain prescribed by Section 8(b)-(3) is a duty the union owes to employers, not to employees in the unit. But nothing in the statutory language requires such a limitation on the union's duty; certainly the employer's corresponding duty runs both to the union and to the employee in the unit. See Louisville Refining Co., 4 N.L.R.B. 844-860-1, enforced 102 F.2d 678 (C.A. 6). If, for example, a union which represents a majority, should seek to make a "members only" contract, it would appear to be violating its duty to bargain on behalf of all. In that example, it would be dealing with an employer, and hence plainly violating Section 8(b)(3). In the instant case it is, in effect, acting on behalf of "members only" when it refuses to deal with the employer concerning Davis' grievance, and its inaction is as much, if not more, of a refusal to bargain than would be its action on behalf of a minority. Cf. Cox, "The Duty of Fair Representation," 2 Villanova L. Rev. 151, 172-174. Since, as is well settled, the majority union has a statutory obligation to represent all employees in the unit fairly in collective bargaining, I find that a breach of that duty is a breach of the duty to bargain. . . .

Finally, the majority of the Board held in Miranda Fuel Co., 140 N.L.R.B. No. 7, that a labor organization violates Section 8(b)(2) when "for arbitrary or irrelevant reasons or upon the basis of an unfair classification the union attempts to cause or does cause an employer to derogate the employment status of an employee," and that "union membership is encouraged or discouraged whenever a union causes an employer to affect an individual's employment status." What is said in Miranda with respect to union *action* would appear equally applicable to *inaction* which was founded upon "arbitrary or irrelevant reasons or upon the basis of an unfair classification."

Decision of the Board.

With respect to the unfair labor practice case, we agree with the Trial

Examiner for the reasons stated by him that Local No. 1, by its failure to entertain in any fashion or to consider the grievance filed by an employee in the bargaining unit, Ivory Davis, and by its outright rejection of Davis' grievance for reasons of race, violated Section 8(b)(1)(A), 8(b)(2), and 8(b)(3) of the Act.

We further agree with the Trial Examiner, contrary to the Charging Party's contention, that the validity of the racially discriminatory contracts between Local No. 1 and the Company was not placed in issue by the complaint in the unfair labor practice case. Similarly, racial segregation in union membership was not placed in issue in *that* case. This conclusion is not to be construed, however, as a disagreement on our part with the contentions of the Charging Party that the negotiation of racially discriminatory terms or conditions of employment by a statutory bargaining representative violates Section 8(b) of the Act and that racial segregation in membership, when engaged in by such a representative, cannot be countenanced by a Federal Agency and may violate Section 8(b).

We would be content to terminate our discussion of the unfair labor practice case at this point and to rely, as we do, upon the Trial Examiner's treatment of the issues, but the separate opinion of Chairman McCulloch and Member Fanning, in which they disagree with us at length, necessitates additional comments in this majority opinion.

With respect to the Section 8(b)(1)(A) violation, the separate opinion relies upon cases which were advanced by the General Counsel for consideration by the Trial Examiner. The latter's discussion of the subject in his Intermediate Report casts much doubt upon the applicability of the cases. Moreover, as we understand the separate opinion, our colleagues would find an 8(b)(1)(A) violation only because the Negro employee, Ivory Davis, who is a member of the Negro local of Independent Metal Workers Union, is not a member of Local No. 1, the Respondent.

In other words, our colleagues appear to say that, in another factual context, when a statutory bargaining representative does not practice segregation or other racial restrictions in membership, such representative may refuse, on racial grounds as distinguished from nonmembership grounds, to consider a meritorious grievance of a Negro in the bargaining unit, seeking by such refusal to keep Negro employees in inferior jobs, and that such refusal does not violate Section 8(b)(1)(A). We cannot concur in our colleagues' view of the law. We rely instead upon the Trial Examiner's reasoning in finding a violation of Section 8(b)(1)(A).

The separate opinion utilizes this case as an opportunity to reiterate and enlarge the dissenters' views in Miranda Fuel Co., Inc., 140 N.L.R.B. 181. We need not detail the bases of our disagreement. We note only a few facts. When the Supreme Court enunciated the duty of fair representation in Steele [323 U.S. 192] and Tunstall, [323 U.S. 210] which were Railway Labor Act cases, the Court emphasized in each case the lack of an administrative remedy as a reason for holding that Federal courts constitute a forum for relief from breaches of the duty.

In this connection, it should be noted that provisions of the Railway Labor Act which are substantially identical to certain unfair labor practice provisions of the National Labor Relations Act are enforceable by the Federal courts, not by an administrative agency. When the Labor Board, in recognition of the Steele and Tunstall doctrines, held that under the Wagner Act statutory bargaining representatives owe to their constituents a duty to represent fairly, the Board's holding necessarily was confined to representation proceedings because the Board had no power to issue an order against a labor organization. After enactment of the Taft-Hartley Act, however, an administrative remedy became available in our view and in the view of various legal scholars . . . as well as in briefs amici in this case and before the Court of Appeals in N.L.R.B. v. Miranda Fuel Co., Inc., 326 F.2d 172 (C.A. 2). Moreover, a majority of the panel of the Court which decided that case expressly refrained from determining whether a breach of the duty of fair representation violates Section 8(b)(1)(A), and the Supreme Court said recently that the question is open, Humphrey v. Moore, 375 U.S. 335, 344, as indeed our dissenting colleagues concede. . . .

Turning to the representation case, we join the separate opinion of our colleagues in holding that the Pioneer Bus doctrine requires that the certification issued jointly to Locals Nos. 1 and 2 on October 18, 1961, be rescinded because the certified organizations executed contracts based on race and administered the contracts so as to perpetuate racial discrimination in employment. The separate opinion fails, however, to treat two issues which are of crucial importance today. First, the separate opinion disregards certain constitutional limitations upon the Board's powers. Second, the separate opinion fails to join in overturning an outmoded and fallacious doctrine which the Board established long ago.

Specifically, we hold that the Board cannot validly render aid under Section 9 of the Act to a labor organization which discriminates racially when acting as a statutory bargaining representative. Cf. Shelley v. Kraemer, 334 U.S. 1; Hurd v. Hodge, 334 U.S. 24; Bolling v. Sharpe, 347 U.S. 497.

We hold too, in agreement with the Trial Examiner, that the certification should be rescinded because Locals Nos. 1 and 2 discriminated on the basis of race in determining eligibility for full and equal membership and segregated their members on the basis of race. In the light of the Supreme Court decisions cited herein and others to which the Board adverted in Pioneer Bus, we hereby expressly overrule such cases as Atlanta Oak Flooring Co., 62 N.L.R.B. 973; Larus & Brother Co., 62 N.L.R.B. 1075; and other cases epitomized by the language of the Board's Tenth Annual Report, . . . insofar as such cases hold that unions which exclude employees from membership on racial grounds, or which classify or segregate members on racial grounds, may obtain or retain certified status under the Act.

We are not confronted at this time, as we were in Pioneer Bus, with a new petition for certification, and thus we have no present occasion for prescribing a notice such as that recommended by the Trial Examiner as a condition for certification.[30]   We intimate no disapproval of that recommendation, however, and we shall entertain it if occasion to do so should arise.   We also commend it to the consideration of the Regional Director in the event that he should be called upon to issue a certification of representatives at this plant.

Chairman McCulloch and Member Fanning concurring in part and dissenting in part.

We join with the majority members in adopting the Trial Examiner's recommendation for the rescission of the certification.   However, we do so because of the discriminatory contract negotiated by the certified unions and the employer.   We find it unnecessary at this time to pass on the other grounds relied upon by the Trial Examiner in making his recommendation.

We also join with the majority in holding that Respondent violated Section 8(b)(1)(A), but we rest this conclusion on a ground different from that of the majority.   We do not agree with the majority that Respondent violated Section 8(b)(2) and (3). . . .

One of the allegations of the complaint is that Respondent refused to process Ivory Davis' grievance because he was not a member of Respondent Local 1.   In its answer, Respondent admits that it refused to process the grievance and a reason for its refusal was Davis' nonmembership in Local 1.   This refusal to represent him in a grievance matter because of his nonmembership was to this extent predicated upon a consideration specifically condemned by the Act, and therefore prima facie restrained or coerced him in violation of Section 8(b)(1)(A).

Respondent urges three grounds to justify its refusal to press Davis' grievance.   They are: (1) the grievance had no merit because of contractual provisions; (2) a clause in the constitution of the Independent, which was not waived by Local 2, precluded it from handling the grievance; and (3) in the past the Company had refused to process grievances presented by a joint grievance committee unless the grievance pertained to members of both Locals.   We find all these defenses to be without merit. . . .

Accordingly, we find that Respondent Local 1 restrained and coerced Ivory Davis in violation of Section 8(b)(1)(A) of the Act.

In making this finding we do not rely, as does the majority, on a violation of the duty of fair representation.   Our reasons are as follows: . . . Neither Section 7 nor Section 8(b)(1)(A) mentions a duty of fair repre-

---

[30] The Trial Examiner's recommended notice read: "Notice to all Employees: This labor organization has been certified by the National Labor Relations Board as the bargaining representative of the employees in the unit described below. The certification is conditioned upon our not discriminating against any employee because of his race or color, both with respect to membership in this labor organization on terms fully equal to those afforded any member and with respect to terms and conditions of employment and opportunities for advancement under any contract we may negotiate with management.   Any person who believes that this labor organization is not observing a policy of nondiscrimination should bring the matter to the attention of the National Labor Relations Board, Washington 25, D.C., or the Board's Regional Office in Houston." — Ed.

sentation. The majority in the Miranda case, reaffirmed here, found a right to fair representation implied in Section 7 on the basis of the bargaining representative's implied duty of fair representation derived from its status as bargaining representative under Section 9.

There are a number of reasons why this conclusion based on verbal logic does not, in our opinion, represent the intent of Congress, which is after all the goal of statutory construction. Section 7 was part of the Wagner Act which in its unfair labor practice section was aimed only at employer conduct. The Wagner Act also contained the present Section 9(a). It hardly seems reasonable to infer, in these circumstances, that Section 7 contained a protected implied right to fair representation against the bargaining representative, when the entire Wagner Act did not make any conduct by a labor organization unlawful. Section 7 was continued substantially unchanged in the Taft-Hartley Act except for the addition of the "right to refrain" clause, which is not material to our problem. Although the Taft-Hartley Act added union unfair labor practices to the list of prohibited conduct, neither the Act nor the legislative history contains any mention of the duty of fair representation, despite the fact that the Steele and Wallace decisions were well known, having issued 3 years previously. Again, although in the interval between the dates of the Taft-Hartley and Landrum-Griffin Acts, there were additional court decisions and articles by learned commentators in the law journals dealing with the legal problems of fair representation, Congress made no change in the wording of Section 7, and ignored the problem completely in adding a "Bill of Rights" section to the existing statute. If Congress had really intended that violation of the duty of fair representation should be an unfair labor practice, it would seem that the 1959 revision afforded it an opportunity to clear up the uncertainty. Instead it remained silent. We do not believe that realistically this silence can be interpreted as in any way favorable to the contention that the right to fair representation is a protected Section 7 right. There are practical reasons for believing that, if there had been any contemporary understanding that the Act had made it an unfair labor practice for a union to fail in its duty of fair representation, the opposition would have been both strong and loud.

There is another and more important reason why the Board should not undertake to police a union's administration of its duties without a clear mandate from Congress. The purpose of the Act is primarily to protect the organizational rights of employees. But apart from the obligation to bargain in good faith, "Congress intended that the parties would have wide latitude in their negotiations, unrestricted by any governmental power to regulate the substantive solution of their differences." Before Miranda, it was assumed that contract or grievance decisions by employers and unions were immune from examination by the Board unless they were influenced by union considerations. But, under the underlying reasoning of the Miranda majority and that of the present decision, the Board is now constituted a tribunal to which every employee who feels aggrieved by a bargaining representative's action, whether in contract negotiations or in grievance handling, may appeal, regardless of whether the decision has been influenced in whole or in part by considerations of union membership, loyalty, or activity.

The Board must determine on such appeal, without statutory standards, whether the representative's decision was motivated by "unfair or irrelevant or invidious" considerations and therefore to be set aside, or was within the "wide range of reasonableness . . . allowed a statutory representative in serving the unit it represents . . . ," and to be sustained. Inevitably, the Board will have to sit in judgment on the substantive matters of collective bargaining, the very thing the Supreme Court has said the Board must not do, and in which it has no special experience or competence. This is not exaggeration. The duty of fair representation covers more than racial discrimination. Miranda itself did not involve a race issue and since Miranda, the Board has had to decide a number of other cases where allegations of violation of the duty of fair representation rested on other than racial grounds, with many more such cases disposed of at the regional level. . . .

What we are confronted with is an important question of policy which should be resolved not by logomachy, but by a careful weighing of alternatives in the light of the ends to be achieved. Where specific statutory rights or prohibitions are not involved, should enforcement of the duty of fair representation be left to the courts, to the Board, or both? In such circumstances, should cases of breach of this duty insofar as they involve race discrimination be treated differently from breaches involving non-racial factors? If a separate agency is created to handle the task of eliminating employment discrimination by unions and employers based on race, should the Board have a duty in this field? If so, what should it be? To ask these questions is to appreciate that the problem with which we are presented is legislative to be resolved by the Congress and not by an administrative body whose duty it is only to administer the law which Congress has written.

Accordingly, we would rest our finding of a violation of 8(b)(1)(A) not on non-performance of the duty of fair representation, but on those other considerations present in this case which Congress brought within the unfair labor practice ambit of the statute. . . .

In our dissent in Miranda, we expressed the view that 8(b)(2) outlaws only discrimination related to "union membership, loyalty, the acknowledgment of union authority or the performance of union obligations." This position was endorsed by a majority holding of the Court of Appeals in reversing the Board decision in Miranda. We adhere to that view. . . .

The majority has adopted the Trial Examiner's finding that Respondent Union's refusal to process Ivory Davis' grievance also violated Section 8(b)(3). It seems to us that Section 8(b)(3) prescribes a duty owed by a union to employers and not to employees. . . .

The legislative history of Section 8(b)(3) shows conclusively that this Section was intended to be a counterpart of Section 8(a)(5), and under the latter the bargaining duty is owed entirely to the union. Thus the House Report on the proposal which became 8(b)(3) said: "The standards and definitions which have been discussed in relation to Section 2(11) apply in the case of unions, as well as in the case of employers. The duty to bargain now becomes mutual. This, the committee believes, will promote equality and responsibility in bargaining." Similarly, the House Conference Report commenting on 8(b)(3) said: "This provision . . . imposed upon labor organizations the same duty which under Section 8(a)(5) . . . was imposed on employers." The same understanding is reflected by the Supreme Court. . . .

C. DISCRIMINATION ON THE BASIS OF SEX

The Equal Pay Act of 1963, 77 Stat. 56, 29 U.S.C. §206(d), see pages 94, 487 supra, requires equal pay for equal work, regardless of sex. Questions concerning the duty of fair representation by unions are raised by this statute. Thus, it expressly excepts wage differentials based on (1) a seniority system, (2) a merit system, (3) a system which measures earnings by quantity or quality of production, or (4) any factor other than sex. In addition to the equal pay requirements which run against employers, the Equal Pay Law prohibits labor unions from causing or attempting to cause an employer to discriminate against an employee in violation of the equal pay requirements. Recall that, under Section 703 of the Civil Rights Act of 1964, sex is one of the prohibited bases of discrimination, and that the employment discrimination prohibited specifically includes compensation. Although in fact many collective agreements contain provisions relating to equal pay, presumably a union could violate its duty of fair representation by discriminating against women in respect to compensation. Such discrimination therefore violates three separate federal statutes, the Equal Pay Act, the Civil Rights Act, and LMRA, each providing different sanctions or remedies, and each with its own enforcing authority and method of enforcement. What problems are created by this state of affairs? What light does it shed upon the legislative process in Congress?

2. *Individual's Rights in the Grievance Procedure and in Arbitration*

REPORT OF THE COMMITTEE ON LABOR ARBITRATION, AMERICAN BAR ASSOCIATION, SECTION OF LABOR RELATIONS LAW *
(1964)

Much has been written on the subject of individual rights under collective bargaining agreements, including several American Bar Association Committee reports.[1] The present Committee has no desire to explore

* Bernard Dunau, Robben W. Fleming, and Robert Levitt, Co-Chairmen. The above selection is reprinted with the permission of the American Bar Association, Section of Labor Relations Law.

[1] Report of the Comm. on Development of Law under NLRA, A.B.A. Sect. of Lab. Rel. Law, 1963 Proceedings 16, 70; Report of the Comm. on State Labor

further that broad general area, but there are recent developments related to the grievance aspect of the problem which warrant consideration.

A brief word of background is necessary before the current materials are examined. Individual complaints about the grievance procedure tend to fall into two broad categories. The first encompasses those cases in which the union refuses to process the individual's grievance at all, and the second relates to situations in which a settlement is reached which is not satisfactory to the individual. That settlement may, of course, simply be a settlement by default in the sense that the union refuses to take the case to arbitration. Within these broad categories there are many variations. The union may refuse to process the grievance because the individual is not a member, because he has engaged in hostile activity on behalf of another union, because he is a member of the political opposition, or because it is an obviously spurious claim. By the same token, a settlement which is unsatisfactory to the individual may be the result of a "trade" for a more meritorious grievance, a judgment that the claim of the individual is inferior to that of another employee who has a conflicting interest, a reprisal for past behavior which has been obnoxious to the union leadership, or a good faith conclusion that the grievance is without merit. No one doubts that in the overwhelming number of cases in either of the two broad categories a fair solution is reached and no problem is raised. Because the potential for invidious treatment exists in all human organizations one must face the question of what remedies, if any, are to be provided in that situation.

As to those cases in which the union refuses to process the grievance, Professor Aaron has pointed out that there are at least three identifiable points of view as to what should be done about it.

"Some argue that inasmuch as the union's principal reason for being is to improve the economic and social position of its members, the individual member should have a vested right to use the grievance and arbitration provisions of the applicable collective agreement.[2] Others believe that the union must be given a free hand to evaluate the individual's claim in terms of the collective interest and therefore must be allowed to refuse to process the grievance, so long as it acts in good faith.[3] A third position is that the individual employee should be permitted to compel the union to process meritorious grievances involving only the 'critical job interests' of discharge, compensation, and seniority." [4]

Insofar as the union has been willing to handle grievances, the courts

---

Legislation, A.B.A. Sect. of Lab. Rel. Law, 1963 Proceedings, 158, 164; Report of the Comm. on Improvement of Administration of Union-Employer Contracts, A.B.A. Sect. of Lab. Rel. Law, 1954 Proceedings, 33.

[2] E.g., Report of the Comm. on Improvement of Administration of Union Employer Contracts, supra note 1.

[3] E.g., Cox, Rights Under a Labor Agreement, 69 Harv. L. Rev. 601 (1956).

[4] Aaron, The Individual's Legal Rights as an Employee, 86 Mo. Lab. Rev. 666, 671-72 (1963). The "critical job interests" theory is from Blumrosen, Legal Protection for Critical Job Interests: Union-Management Activity Versus Employee Autonomy. 13 Rutgers L. Rev. 631 (1959).

have been reluctant to interfere with settlements, on the ground that the law does not guarantee employees more than the right to participate in and reject settlements made without their consent.[5] . . .

COX, RIGHTS UNDER A LABOR AGREEMENT *
69 Harvard Law Review 601, 618-619, 625-627 (1956)

In my opinion the needs of the industrial community would be served best by leaving management and union free to determine by the terms of their collective bargaining agreement what shall be the respective rights of the union and the individual in its administration. The law could fill any gap resulting from the parties' failure to manifest a reasonably clear intention by formulating presumptions based upon considerations of fairness and convenience mixed with an informed hunch as to the "intent" of the transaction. If this approach is sound, it should embrace three propositions.

(1) The employer and bargaining representative are free to determine by contract in the collective agreement who shall have the right to enforce and settle claims arising out of the employer's failure to observe the agreed conditions of employment. In other words, the power to compromise claims, the right to sue for breach of contract, and the necessity of exhausting a grievance procedure shall be determined by asking what character of rights the parties intended to create when they negotiated the agreement.

(2) Unless a contrary intention is manifest, the employer's obligations under a collective bargaining agreement which contains a grievance procedure controlled by the union shall be deemed to run solely to the union as the bargaining representative, to be administered by the union in accordance with its fiduciary duties to employees in the bargaining unit. The representative can enforce the claim. It can make reasonable, binding compromises. It is liable for breaches of trust in a suit by the employee beneficiaries.

(3) Unless a contrary intention is manifest, a collective agreement which contains no grievance procedure shall be deemed a bilateral contract between the employer and union which contemplates the execution of further bilateral contracts of employment between the employer and individual workers incorporating the wage scale and other conditions of employment set forth in the collective agreement. The union may sue on the collective agreement to enforce the closed shop, check off, and similar provisions inuring to its benefit as an organization, but only individuals may prosecute or settle claims based upon failure to observe the stipulated conditions of employment. . . .

Collective Bargaining Policies. — Apart from statute there are strong reasons for concluding that the bargaining representative ought to have power under a broad industrial agreement to control the prosecution of

[5] Aaron, supra note 4.
* Archibald Cox. These excerpts are reprinted by permission of the Harvard Law Review, copyright 1956 by the Harvard Law Review Association.

claims for breach of contract, whether by pressing grievances, invoking arbitration, or instituting legal proceedings.

(1) The union is sometimes the only party qualified to prosecute the claim, either because its participation is necessary to implement the promise as in the case of the proposed job evaluation study, or because the violation has not injured an identifiable individual, as in some cases of subcontracting. The group interest is often involved to an equal degree when there is past damage to an identifiable individual.

(2) Many grievances result from failure to foresee a problem at the time of contract negotiations. When the contingency arises and conflicting views are asserted, the issue is nominally framed by the past but the truly important question may be, "What rule shall hereafter govern our conduct in these circumstances?" The group may be affected by the future implications of the ruling to an extent that far outweighs the individual claims to damages. . . . The union is the natural spokesman for future implications. Nor can adjudication of past rights be separated from rule making for the future. Both pertain to the interstices of the contract. The parties — and when they fail, an arbitrator — can successfully project general standards upon specific occasions because they are required to make their determinations within a given framework. The process works precisely because the same decision must be both an adjudication of the past and a rule for the future. To separate the two would either take the rule-making function out of the framework of the contract or else produce the unacceptable incongruity of two interpretations upon the same set of facts.

(3) Many claims of contract violation affect employees other than those who were directly damaged by nonperformance. . . .

(4) Vesting the union with control of all grievances increases the likelihood of uniformity and therefore reduces "a potential source of competitions and discriminations that could be destructive of the entire structure of labor relations in the plant." . . .

(5) Competition between rival groups of employees can be troublesome to an employer not only because of the resulting unrest in the plant but also because it deters the bargaining representative from taking what the employer may consider a "responsible position." Public officials and arbitrators no less than employers constantly remind union officials that they have a duty to discountenance disruptive and frivolous claims.

(6) When the interests of several groups conflict, or future needs run contrary to present desires, or when the individual's claim endangers group interests, the union's function is to resolve the competition by reaching an accommodation or striking a balance. The process is political. It involves a melange of power, numerical strength, mutual aid, reason, prejudice, and emotion. Limits must be placed on the authority of the group, but within the zone of fairness and rationality this method of self-government probably works better than the edicts of any outside arbiter. A large part of the daily grist of union business is resolving differences among employees poorly camouflaged as disputes with the employer.

REPORT OF THE COMMITTEE ON IMPROVEMENT OF ADMINISTRATION OF UNION-EMPLOYER CONTRACTS, AMERICAN BAR ASSOCIATION, SECTION OF LABOR RELATIONS LAW *

49-50, 69-71 (1954)

The courts have given clear recognition to two basic rights of the individual within the collective bargaining structure — the right to fair and equal treatment by the majority union, and the right to enjoy the benefits provided for him by the agreement.   However, the legal remedies fall far short of full protection.   Unfairness, especially in the handling of grievances, is difficult to prove except in the most flagrant cases.   Suits for breach of contract stumble on rules of exhaustion, and provide an inadequate remedy of money damages.

The Function of Individual Grievances

With this background it is now appropriate to set forth more explicitly the function of individual grievances, and to fit them within the framework of collective bargaining.   In doing so, it is necessary to distinguish between two classes of grievances; those which claim that a term of the collective agreement has been violated, and those which seek to obtain some benefit not provided in the collective agreement.

The great majority of all individual grievances, those which claim violation of the agreement are essentially the assertions of rights previously granted, whether by explicit terms in the agreement, past practice, or implied understandings.   These rights belong to the individual and are legally enforceable.   The individual grievance in this area does not encroach upon the union's power to bargain for contract terms but is a part of the enforcement process of individual rights created by the contract.   Its greatest potential value is to serve as a substitute for suit.   It provides a method of discussion between the parties in a setting appropriate for the dispute and unencumbered by rigid legalisms.   It is to the individual right what the union grievance procedure is to the collective rights.   If it is carried to arbitration, it is subjected to the same pattern of adjudication as the union grievance.   The remedy provided either by settlement or arbitration will be that commonly accepted in industrial practice, including reinstatement and a declaration of status.

Although the individual grievance may fail to avoid litigation, it helps protect the individual's legal action.   First, it helps him to avoid the pitfall of Elgin, Joliet that he has assented to the union's settlement.   The union may condition its handling of the grievance on the explicit grant of authority to settle, or the courts may find a usage or acquiescence arising out of filing the grievance through the union which binds the in-

---

* Clyde W. Summers, Chairman.   The above selection is reprinted with the permission of the American Bar Association, Section of Labor Relations Law. The full text may be found in 50 Nw. U.L. Rev. 143 (1955), and portions of it in Reynard, ed., Readings on Labor Law 204 (1955).

dividual to the union's settlement. Second, the individual by processing his own grievance can exercise more control in laying the groundwork for legal action, in case it becomes necessary. This is particularly important where the issue is essentially factual, and the collection of the evidence and its presentation in the most favorable light is critical. Third, the prejudicial effect of an unfavorable settlement is escaped. If the union processes the grievance and settles it, even though the individual is not bound, the courts will be extremely reluctant to find otherwise. The settlement will, in the court's mind, tend to carry a prima facie validity which will be overturned only if clearly arbitrary. The individual's protection will then be little more than that provided by the Steele doctrine.

The few individual grievances which involve matters not covered by the collective agreement present entirely different problems. Here the individual grievance does not seek to enforce acquired rights but seeks to bargain for additional rights. It is a form of individual bargaining. A further distinction must be recognized between grievances arising in those areas in which the union has surrendered its right to compel bargaining and grievances arising in those areas in which the union retains its full bargaining rights. In the first type of case the union, either by surrendering its demands during negotiations, or by a management prerogatives clause or a waiver clause, has abandoned the area to management's discretion. The individual grievance is no encroachment on the union, but rather serves to fill a vacuum left by the union's exclusion. In the second type of case the union is still entitled to compel bargaining. It is still the exclusive representative, if it wishes to assert that right. The individual is entitled, however, to know whether the union intends to assert its power or not, for he ought not be foreclosed from acting by the union's indifference. In this context the individual grievance compels the union either to assert its right or permit him to proceed on his own. . . .

The central problem in every collective structure is preserving the worth of the individual; protecting his interest from being unduly sacrificed in the name of the good of the group; and guarding him from oppression by unscrupulous officials or selfish majorities. These goals are achieved only through limitations on power, use of cumbersome machinery, and reduction of headlong efficiency.

This same problem exists in collective bargaining. It is lessened by the division of control between unions and management neither of whom has monolithic power and each of whom claims concern for the individual. Our awareness of the problem is blunted by our concentration on the friction and clash between the two collective parties.

For collective bargaining to function, and to serve the needs of employees for mutual aid and protection, it is necessary that unions be granted a magnitude of power to speak on behalf of all employees. This power is centered in the right of the majority union to be the exclusive representative. By virtue of this power, the union excludes the individual from determining the terms and conditions of his employment. His freedom of contract is lost, he is bound by the collective agreement.

Protecting the rights of the individual within the framework may be achieved in three ways, which are not mutually exclusive. First, the individual must be given a right to speak through his union. This is achieved by preserving within the union the essential elements of democratic process — the right to full and free participation in the making of union policy. . . . The second line of protection is to require the union to represent all employees fairly and equally. Although this gives substantial protection against blatant discrimination on the basis of race, it can not reach many subtle forms of unfairness against individuals or groups. . . .

The third line of protection against unfairness, and particularly unfairness in grievance handling, is to limit directly the union's power to represent the individual in the process of grievances. The individual is recognized as having accrued rights created by virtue of the collective agreement which the union can not destroy. . . .

The individual grievance is significant because it can provide a method of asserting and obtaining these individual rights under our collective bargaining structure. It should be tailored to meet that need. The present provisions of Taft-Hartley are not satisfactory, for they lack the clarity needed for effectiveness. Although nearly all of the results desired can reasonably be spelled out of the provision, it contains weakening ambiguities. Statutory provisions for individual grievances are important not because there are large numbers of such grievances, but because the presence of those provisions and the availability of an independent remedy stands as a warning that the individual can not be treated with impunity. The preventative value of the statute is directly proportionate to the certainty of its operation.

The objective of the statute and of decisions under the statute should be to provide a procedure which would give to the individual who processed his own grievance the same rights he would obtain if the grievance were properly processed through the union.

This standard of equality leads to some specific conclusions. First, the individual grievance should be recognized as an affirmative right. If the employer has agreed to discuss with the union certain grievances in a certain manner, he should be obligated to give equal recognition to an individual grievance. To allow the employer to refuse to deal with the individual, and even more to allow the union to extract from him a promise not to deal is to destroy completely the value of the individual grievance as a protective device. Second, the standard of equality requires that the individual be given the same recourse to arbitration as the union, and also be subject to the same requirement that it be used instead of legal action. This too, the employer should not be permitted to bargain away.

In the processing of individual grievances, the individual should be free of all intimidation, restraint, or hindrance in presenting his case. He should be allowed to present it and negotiate its adjustment without the presence or consent of the majority union. The majority union, in turn, should be notified of the adjustment and be permitted to file its own grievance in protest of the adjustment. If the individual grievance is carried to arbitration, then practical necessity requires that the majority union be allowed to intervene. Since the central concern is protecting the rights of the individual, the individual grievance ought not be allowed to become the tool of a minority union. Although the individual may need financial assistance and advice, the potentialities of disruption and abuse are too great to permit the individual to be represented by a rival union.

If these conclusions are obtained, the individual grievance will cease to be merely a sport or nuisance in the collective bargaining structure. It will become a constructive and useful device in protecting the rights of individuals from certain forms of unfairness which otherwise go unreached.

BLUMROSEN, LEGAL PROTECTION FOR CRITICAL JOB INTERESTS: UNION-MANAGEMENT AUTHORITY VERSUS EMPLOYEE AUTONOMY *

13 Rutgers Law Review 631, 651-653 (1959)

We may now turn to the task of defining the area in which individual claims will be recognized. In undertaking this task, we shall draw on the accumulation of considered judgments made by courts concerning the individual employee in the collective bargaining context, and attempt to organize these decisions into a pattern that will be a meaningful guide for future decision-making. Obviously, a court called upon to decide questions concerning individual rights will be too pressed by considerations of time and other business to weigh afresh all the considerations involved in these cases. What is essential then, is a set of guide lines derived from earlier decisions and applicable to future cases which sufficiently identify and simplify the issues which must be faced in modern context. At the same time, these guide lines must be sufficiently flexible to allow the court to deal justly with each case which comes before it.

The claims of union and employer to freedom in their joint action must be balanced with the claims of individual employees to legal protection for their "rights" under the labor agreement. A rational balance of these claims requires judicial protection for some individual employee interests, coupled with a form of relief least likely to interfere with the union and employer in running the industrial establishment, and a safety valve to take care of cases of extreme union and/or employer misconduct.

A. CRITICAL JOB INTERESTS

The idea expressed in Burley [325 U.S. 711 (1945)] that the employee may control all grievances which affect him is unworkable. The interest in union-employer freedom of decision is simply too strong for any such absolute conception of individual rights. Therefore, it is necessary to specify the type of claim in which the individual is to have legally recog-

* These excerpts of the article by Alfred W. Blumrosen are printed with the permission of the editors of the Rutgers Law Review.

nized rights, with the understanding that as to all other claims, union and employer have freedom of decision. Only those claims which are based on an existing labor agreement and are basic to the individual employment relationship should be subject to individual control. Those claims we may call *critical job interests.*

Any action which destroys the employee's claim to gainful employment is critical. Therefore, in *discharge* cases the employee must be able to secure legal protection. This same theory would justify judicial intervention where the employee complains of major disciplinary action which will substantially destroy the employment relationship. Minor disciplinary proceedings, the infliction of a suspension, or the docking of a relatively small sum of money or the like, should be left exclusively to the processes of bargaining.

An employee claim for *compensation* for work already performed should be judicially recognized on the principle of avoidance of unjust enrichment. However, the concept of compensation must be carefully limited in two ways. First, it applies only to work already performed, so as to preserve the bargaining power of the union and employer to alter conditions of employment prospectively. Secondly, it applies only to *basic* wages. This concept includes the hourly or weekly base rate, vacation and severance pay. It does not include merit increases, holiday or overtime or other premium payments. Professor Cox has vividly demonstrated the difficulties involved in the adjustment of claims concerning these payment provisions. Many union decisions to accept management action regarding these matters are based on union policies toward management which involve such complex variables as to be properly beyond judicial scrutiny. In addition, the amounts involved may be relatively small. The union needs some leeway in its day-to-day bargaining with the employer. Limitation of individual claims to "basic" wages gives that leeway. The distinction may be arbitrary, but its utility lies in leaving sufficient area for practical adjustment between union and management. If this distinction between "basic" and non-basic wages is applied to the famous Burley case, the result is adverse to the individual employees. Burley involved "penalty damages" claimed against the railroad by the employees because of failure to observe starting times. These employees were compensated for time worked. The issue is obviously a fitting matter for employer-union negotiation. The individual claim was peripheral and should have been denied on the grounds suggested here.

The third facet of the employment relation which requires judicial protection is *seniority*. Protection should be given to the acquired job status against wrongful layoff, or failure of automatic promotions. It should not extend to claims for less substantial preferences such as shift choice, starting time, or the like. Those claims should be left to intra-union politics and bargaining with the employer.

COMMENT ON THE INDIVIDUAL AND HIS GRIEVANCE

In 1935, Congress concerned itself with the role of individual employee rights in the scheme of collective bargaining. Section 9(a) of the National Labor Relations Act provided as follows: "Representatives designated or selected for the purpose of collective bargaining . . . shall be the exclusive representatives of all employees . . . for the purpose of collective bargaining in respect to rates of pay, wages, hours of employment or other conditions of employment: *Provided,* That any individual employee or a group of employees shall have the right at any time to present grievances to their employer."

The leading case under this provision was Hughes Tool Co., 56 N.L.R.B. 981 (1944), enforced, 147 F.2d 69 (5th Cir. 1945). In this case the Board discussed (p. 982) the relative roles of employer, union, and employee as follows:

"We interpret the proviso to Section 9(a) of the Act to mean that individual employees and groups of employees are permitted 'to present grievances to their employer' by appearing in behalf of themselves — although not through any labor organization other than the exclusive representative — at every stage of the grievance procedure, but that the exclusive representative is entitled to be present and negotiate at each such stage concerning the disposition to be made of the grievance. If, at any level of the established grievance procedure, there is an agreement between the employer, the exclusive representative, and the individual or group, disposition of the grievance is thereby achieved. Failing agreement of all three parties, any dissatisfied party may carry the grievance through subsequent machinery until the established grievance procedure is exhausted.

"The individual employee or group of employees cannot present grievances under any procedure except that provided in the contract, where there exists a collective agreement. . . . Only where the exclusive representative refuses to attend meetings, as prescribed in the grievance procedures established, for the purpose of negotiating in regard to the disposition of grievances presented by individuals or groups of employees, or otherwise refuses to participate in the disposition of such grievances, may the employer meet with the individuals or groups of employees alone and adjust the grievances. And any adjustment so effectuated must be consistent in its substantive aspects with the terms of any agreement which the employer may have made with the exclusive representative." [31]

In 1946, the Supreme Court decided Elgin, Joliet & Eastern Ry. v. Burley, 325 U.S. 711 (1945). In this case under the Railway Labor Act the grievances of ten employees claiming back pay were processed by the union and compromised. Not satisfied with the result, the employees sued

[31] In NLRB v. North American Aviation, Inc., 136 F.2d 898 (9th Cir. 1943), the court construed the proviso to allow the employer to process all grievances without the presence of the bargaining agent at the request of individual employees. The court approved dual methods of handling grievances — one provided by the collective agreement and the other provided by the employer's notice to his employees that he would process their grievances independently of the procedure established in the collective agreement. For an analysis of the impact of the 1947 amendments to the proviso on the pre-1947 cases, see Sherman, The Individual and His Grievance — Whose Grievance Is It? 11 U. Pitt. L. Rev. 35 (1949).

the company for back wages, and the company defended on the basis of its settlement with the union. The Court held the defense insufficient, stating (p. 738): "For an award to affect the employee's rights, therefore, more must be shown than that the collective agent appeared and purported to act for him. It must be that in some legally sufficient way he authorized it to act in his behalf."

In 1947 Congress amended the proviso to Section 9(a) by adding the following: ". . . and to have such grievances adjusted, without the intervention of the bargaining representative, as long as the adjustment is not inconsistent with the terms of a collective-bargaining contract or agreement then in effect: Provided further, That the bargaining representative has been given opportunity to be present at such adjustment."

Both the first Hughes Tool and the Elgin, Joliet cases were extensively considered by the House and Senate Labor Committees in the drafting of the 1947 amendments to the NLRA. The Senate Committee Report, S. Rep. No. 105, 80th Cong., 1st Sess. 24 (1947), stated:

"The Board has not given full effect to this right as defined in the present statute since it has adopted a doctrine that if there is a bargaining representative he must be consulted at every stage of the grievance procedure, even though the individual might prefer to exercise his right to confer with his employer alone. . . . The revised language would make clear that the employee's right to present grievances exists independently of the rights of the bargaining representative, if the bargaining representative has been given an opportunity to be present at the adjustment, unless the adjustment is contrary to the terms of the collective-bargaining agreement then in effect."

The Conference Committee Report, H.R. Rep. 510, 80th Cong., 1st Sess. 46 (1947), stated: "The existing law further provides that an individual employee or group of employees will have the right at any time to present grievances to their employer. But, as pointed out in the committee report on the bill in the House, this provision has not been construed by the Board as authorizing the employer to settle grievances thus presented.

"Both the House bill and the Senate amendment amended section 9(a) of the existing law to specifically authorize employers to settle grievances presented by individual employees or groups of employees, so long as the settlement is not inconsistent with any collective bargaining contract in effect."

The debates further indicate an intention to write into the new statute the same right of an individual over his grievance as the Elgin, Joliet decision had read into the Railway Labor Act.

As noted supra page 779, the processing of grievances is an aspect of collective bargaining. In order to reconcile the right of the employee in his grievance with the exclusive bargaining power of the union, a distinction has been drawn, under both the Railway Labor Act and the National Labor Relations Act, between "bargaining" disputes and "grievances." Thus, in West Texas Utilities Co. v. NLRB, 206 F.2d 442, 446 (D.C. Cir. 1953), cert. denied, 346 U.S. 855 (1953), the court stated: "Although any grievance may be a subject of collective bargaining, not all subjects of collective bargaining are grievances. As we view the word 'grievances' it does not encompass, for example, the setting of wage rates for a large percent of the employees in a certified bargaining unit. The word 'grievances,' in the field of industrial relations, particularly in unionized companies, usually refers to 'secondary disputes in contrast to disagreements concerning broad issues such as wage rates, hours and working conditions.' The Supreme Court, in construing the Railway Labor Act of 1934, noted that grievances are of a 'comparatively minor character' and traditionally 'affect the smaller differences which inevitably appear in the carrying out of major agreements and policies *or arise incidentally in the course of an employment.*' [18] The Fifth Circuit took a similar view in construing §9(a) of the National Labor Relations Act.[19] Nothing in the legislative history indicates that Congress intended to give 'grievances' a different meaning in §9(a) of the Labor Management Relations Act."

BLACK-CLAWSON CO. v. INTERNATIONAL ASSN. OF MACHINISTS
United States Court of Appeals, Second Circuit, 1962
313 F.2d 179

[Appeal from an order denying the right of an employee, Best, to compel arbitration of his discharge. The court first held that no such right was to be found in the language of the collective agreement.]

KAUFMAN, Circuit Judge. . . .

Appellant Best also contends that his right to compel arbitration is guaranteed by section 9(a) of the Labor Management Relations Act, 29 U.S.C. §159(a) — which authorizes the presentation and adjustment of grievances by the individual employee independently of the bargaining representative — and by the terms of the grievance procedure of the collective bargaining agreement — which adopt section 9(a) of the act and provide that any such individual adjustment be processed in accordance with the terms of the contract. We disagree and hold that section 9(a) does not confer upon an individual grievant the power, enforceable in a court of law, to compel the employer to arbitrate his grievance. . . .

Best seizes upon the first proviso to the section, which affords to the employee "the right at any time to present grievances" to the employer and to have them adjusted. Despite Congress' use of the word "right," which seems to import an indefeasible right mirrored in a duty on the part of the employer, we are convinced that the proviso was designed merely to confer upon the employee the privilege to approach his employer on personal grievances when his union reacts with hostility or apathy. Prior to the adoption of this proviso in section 9(a), the employer had cause to fear that his processing of an individual's grievance without consulting the bargaining representative would be an unfair

[18] Elgin, J. & E.R. Co. v. Burley, 1945, 325 U.S. 711, 724 (emphasis supplied).
[19] Hughes Tool Co. v. National Labor Relations Board, 5 Cir., 1945, 147 F.2d 69, 72-73; . . .

labor practice; section 9(a) made the union the exclusive representative of the employees in the bargaining unit, and section 8(a)(5) made a refusal to bargain with the exclusive representative an unfair labor practice. The proviso was apparently designed to safeguard from charges of violation of the act the employer who voluntarily processed employee grievances at the behest of the individual employee, and to reduce what many had deemed the unlimited power of the union to control the processing of grievances.

The few elucidating passages in the legislative history of section 9(a) give support to the construction here adopted. . . .

Rather than conferring an indefeasible right upon the individual employee to compel compliance with the grievance procedure up to and including any arbitration provision, section 9(a) merely set up a buffer between the employee and his union, "permitting" the employee to take his grievances to the employer, and "authorizing" the employer to hear and adjust them without running afoul of the "exclusive bargaining representative" language of the operative portion of section 9(a). This construction also best comports with the structure of the section. "The office of a proviso is seldom to create substantive rights and obligations; it carves exceptions out of what goes before." Cox, "Rights Under a Labor Agreement." 69 Harv. L. Rev. 601, 624 (1956).

As applied to the case before us, section 9(a) of the Labor Management Relations Act, and its adoption by Black-Clawson and the Union in their collective bargaining agreement, assured Best the privilege of presenting his grievance to the employer even without the cooperation of the Union, and with the consent of Black-Clawson to have those grievances adjusted, so long as the adjustment was not inconsistent with the terms of the collective agreement. See Ostrofsky v. United Steelworkers, etc., 171 F. Supp. 782, 791 (D. Md. 1959), aff'd, 273 F.2d 614 (4th Cir.), cert. denied, 363 U.S. 849 (1960); Arsenault v. General Elec. Co., 147 Conn. 130, 157 A.2d 918 (1960). See also General Cable Corp., 20 Lab. Arb. 443 (Hays, 1953).[6] Best is therefore without power to compel Black-Clawson to arbitrate the grievance stemming from his accusation of wrongful discharge. The Union is the sole agency empowered to do so by the statute and by the terms of the contract before us.

Our conclusion is dictated not merely by the terms of the collective bargaining agreement and by the language, structure, and history of sec-

---

[6] "Although the situation with respect to presentation of grievances by employees is referred to in Section 9(a) as a 'right,' the Act itself nowhere provides protection for this right. The language appears to be used in such a way as to create an exception to the employer's duty to bargain exclusively with the majority representatives. The act does not make it an unfair labor practice for the employer to refuse to entertain grievances from individual employees (Adm. Ruling, Gen. Counsel, Case No. 317 (1952), 30 L.R.R.M. 1103; Case No. 418 (1952), 31 L.R.R.M. 1039), and there seems to be no other method of enforcement available either in the Act or otherwise." 20 Lab. Arb. at 445.

See Gen. Counsel's Adm. Dec. No. 317, 30 L.R.R.M. 1103 (1952): "An individual employee is merely granted 'permission' to present a grievance. An employer is not 'required' to meet with a minority group of employees to adjust or discuss a grievance."

tion 9(a), but also by what we consider to be a sound view of labor-management relations. The union represents the employees for the purposes of negotiating and enforcing the terms of the collective bargaining agreement. This is the modern means of bringing about industrial peace and channeling the resolution of intra-plant disputes. Chaos would result if every disenchanted employee, every disturbed employee, and every employee who harbored a dislike for his employer, could harass both the union and the employer by processing grievances through the various steps of the grievance procedure and ultimately by bringing an action to compel arbitration in the face of clear contractual provisions intended to channel the enforcement remedy through the union. See Stewart v. Day & Zimmermann, Inc., 294 F.2d 7, 11 n.6 (5th Cir. 1961); Ostrofsky v. United Steelworkers, supra; . . .

If employer and union deem it consonant with the efficient handling of labor disputes to repose power in the individual employee to compel the employer to arbitrate grievances, then they may do so, by incorporating such a provision in clear language in the collective bargaining agreement. They have not done so here.

For these reasons, we affirm the judgment of the District Court.

DONNELLY v. UNITED FRUIT CO.
Supreme Court of New Jersey, 1963
40 N.J. 61, 190 A.2d 825

[The contract between United Fruit Company and the Brotherhood of Marine Officers reserved to the employer the right to discharge "for cause," and provided for a grievance procedure including arbitration. On discharge for inefficiency, Donnelly consulted the union. After investigation, the union concluded that the discharge was for proper cause, and declined to pursue the matter further. Donnelly made no effort to process the grievance with the employer himself. Instead, he brought contract actions alleging (1) discharge by the employer in violation of the contract, and (2) failure and refusal of the employer and union to process his claim of unlawful discharge in accordance with the contract grievance procedure.]

FRANCIS, Judge. . . .

The evolution of section 9(a) in its present form induces the conclusion that the employee has beneficial rights in the collective bargaining agreement which are not subject to the exclusive control of the union. Those independent rights cannot be bargained away by the employer and the union; they become integrated in the agreement as a matter of legislative policy. Their enforcement, however, is subject to the substantive terms of the agreement, and when an employee utilizes section 9(a) to secure enforcement, the union is entitled to be heard and to insist upon an adjustment conforming to the agreement. The opportunity conferred upon the bargaining representative under section 9(a) "to be present" to be meaningful cannot signify mere presence as an observer. For example, adjustment of a contract breach grievance of an individual may involve an interpretation of the contract to be applied to similar situations in the future. Elemental notions of due process, therefore, would seem to call for such optional presence by the union as will enable it to oppose a settlement inconsistent with the collective agreement. . . .

From all the foregoing, for purposes of the case before us, we conclude that an individual employee has a statutorily-vested right to present his grievance to, and to have it determined by, his employer when the union declines to process it in his behalf. "Grievance" in this context means a claim by the employee that in the application or administration of the collective agreement his rights thereunder have not been respected. Such a claim is ordinarily distinguished from collective bargaining as to rates of pay, wages, hours and conditions of employment, the purpose of which is to fix the rules of employment for the future. . . .

Thus we are brought to consideration of problems of when and how an employee may present grievances to his employer. Obviously, it should be done in the manner least likely to cause discord in the ordinary management-labor union relations. There is no doubt of the authority of employer and union to channel ordinary disputes into a system of private adjudication by means of their collective bargaining agreement. The form of that compact with respect to grievance procedure usually follows customary practice in the particular industry. As such it represents an integral adjunct of the substantive rights created by the agreement. Therefore, it should be regarded as the exclusive method of adjusting grievances, whether presented by the union or the individual employee under the auspices of section 9(a), unless some improper discrimination against the individual is inherent in the system or is likely to be brought to bear against him in the particular case by employer or union through control of the procedure.

This court is committed to the doctrine that suits at law on individual grievances allegedly arising from breach of the collective agreement should not be permitted until the stipulated private avenues of remedy are exhausted. . . .

As has been noted above, section 9(a) in bestowing on the employee the right to present his grievance personally and to have it adjusted, forbids an adjustment inconsistent with the collective bargaining agreement. Although the Congressional requirement for consistency was probably concerned primarily with substance rather than procedure, nevertheless it is entirely reasonable to conclude from the legislation that the demanded consistency also contemplated vindication of the employee's substantive right through use of the grievance procedure set forth in the agreement, unless unfeasible. Sound development of the law in this area calls for adherence to the contractual mode of processing grievances by the individual employee, as well as by the union. In our judgment such a Congressional intention floods the four corners of the statute. . . .

Moreover, requiring individual grievances to be handled through to arbitration in accordance with the agreed code of the plant not only will effectuate the Congressional purpose shown in section 9(a), but at the same time will harmonize it with the pattern of procedure commonly followed in labor-management relations. And if, perchance, in a particular case, the necessary impartiality cannot be achieved for the individual employee under the collective agreement, because of the nature or control of one or more of the steps outlined in the grievance mechanism, and the parties cannot agree upon a substitute measure, judicial inventiveness can be counted on to fill the breach. "The range of judicial inventiveness will be determined by the nature of the problem." Textile Workers Union v. Lincoln Mills, 353 U.S. at p. 457. . . .

It seems unlikely that the position outlined herein for the protection and prosecution of individual grievances will interfere unduly with normal management-union administration of the collective employee interests. . . . It leaves undisturbed the doctrine of immunity of the union from damage suits by employee members for failure or refusal to process grievances, where the failure or refusal is grounded in good faith and fair treatment toward the individual employee. At the same time, it gives necessary recognition to the federal right granted to the employee by section 9(a), but does so within the collective agreement pattern established by management and union.

It seems reasonable to assume from the relatively few reported cases that in the great majority of grievances the union fulfills its traditional role of guardian of the interests of its members by processing their claims. It is probable, also, that with section 9(a)-rights of individual employees thus implemented, there will be even fewer instances of union abstinence. The suggestion that undue burdens on union and employer will follow from such protection of workers' rights is speculation. Obviously, most grievances are adjusted in the preliminary steps of established procedure; relatively few reach formal arbitration. . . . Cases like the present one, governed as they are by the policy of the Labor Management Relations Act, limited as they are under section 9(a) to results consistent with the collective bargaining agreement, and engaged in, as they will be, under the eye of the union, will probably assist rather than prejudice tripartite harmony in labor-management relations. But, assuming the outlined implementation of section 9(a) produces some increase in presentation of grievances, in our judgment collective bargaining is sufficiently resilient to absorb the emphasized individual interest without erosion of its basic structure.

In administration, the right of the individual to process his grievance must be subject to the principle espoused by this court in Jorgensen v. Pennsylvania R.R. Co. [25 N.J. 541, 138 A.2d 24, 72 A.L.R.2d 1415 (1958)]. That is, initially, for purposes of obtaining reinstatement and back pay or simply back or lost pay where reinstatement is not asked, the individual must pursue or attempt in good faith to pursue the grievance procedure set forth in the collective bargaining contract before seeking a court remedy. Belk v. Allied Aviation Service Co. of New Jersey [315 F.2d 513]. If the union refuses to handle the matter for him or if it has a conflicting interest, the employee should request the employer to take up the grievance with him according to the contractually-prescribed mode, but with the employee in control of the procedural steps wherever necessary to achieve a just determination. On refusal, recourse may be had to the courts for specific performance of the agreement to process the dispute through to arbitration or, at the option of the employee, for damages suffered by him because of the employer's conduct (for example, discharge without cause) which gave rise to the grievance.

During the argument before us, questions were raised as to where the burden of costs would rest when, in order to obtain relief, an employee finds it necessary to "present" his grievance personally. If the matter is pressed to the final state of arbitration, decision as to expenses may be left to the arbitrator. Obviously, the union should not be saddled with costs of arbitrating worthless or petty claims of disputatious employees. On the other hand, if the employee is successful and the grievance is one which in the judgment of the arbitrator should have been handled by the union, presumably, costs would follow the course fixed in the collective agreement or usually followed by custom or practice. Further, even if the employee is unsuccessful after arbitration, if his cause is colorable and presented in good faith, and in the judgment of the arbitrator refusal of the union to press it was unfair and arbitrary, he should be relieved of costs. But if he fails and has no colorable claim of a substantial nature, he must shoulder the costs. Such treatment of expenses would be consistent with the existing union-management code of the plant and would serve to integrate further the section 9(a) right of the employee with that code. See Blumrosen, *supra* (13 Rutgers L. Rev. at 660, 661); . . .

So far as our research has taken us, amended section 9(a), and its impact on the processing of individual grievances in situations like the present one, have received practically no judicial treatment. Undoubtedly, the more recent recognition by the United States Supreme Court of enforceability of individual rights under section 301 of the Labor Management Relations Act will stimulate activity in the area. The novelty of the problem moved us to engage in the somewhat extended discussion set out above. . . .

[The court held that since Donnelly had made no effort to exercise his Section 9(a) rights, the employer was not liable for failure to process the grievance. Similarly, the unlawful discharge action failed because Donnelly had not exhausted the grievance procedure. Finally, there was no cause of action against the union because there was no showing that it had not acted in good faith in refusing to process the grievance.]

NOTES

1. In 1963 the General Counsel of the NLRB refused to process a charge that an employer committed an unfair labor practice by settling an individual's grievance without the employee being present. After noting that under the contract the individual had no right to be present after a certain step in the grievance procedure, the General Counsel said: "[E]ven assuming the applicability of the Section 9(a) proviso to this situation, the individual had been permitted to initially present his own grievance. Moreover, the legislative history of the proviso substantiated the view that it was intended to be permissive in nature insofar as employers were concerned in that it enabled them to deal with individual employees in the adjustment of grievances without violating Section 8(a)(5) but imposed no obligation upon them to do so." Administrative

Decision, General Counsel, No. SR-2721, 63-2 CCH N.L.R.B., par. 12745 (1963).

2. In Union News Co. v. Hildreth, 295 F.2d 658 (6th Cir. 1961), the company operated a lunch counter with a dozen employees. When the company sought to replace the entire crew because it believed that either food or money was being mishandled, the union objected. After prolonged negotiations, it was agreed that the company could lay off five of the employees. If thereafter the relation of food costs to gross sales improved, it would indicate that the laid-off employees were partly at fault, and they could be discharged. After the replacement, the relation of food costs to gross sales did improve and cash receipts improved. The union therefore acquiesced in the discharge of the five employees. Among them was plaintiff. Although there was no proof directly connecting plaintiff with dishonesty, the union refused to process a grievance on her behalf. In a suit by plaintiff to compel the employer to process her grievance, the court held that the company was entitled to a directed verdict. The court concluded that the union, chosen as the statutory bargaining agent of plaintiff, could properly agree with the company, as a part of the continuing bargaining process, that plaintiff was discharged for just cause under the terms of the collective bargaining agreement.

3. Where a contract required handling and adjustment of grievances by both union and management representatives at each of the three stages of a grievance procedure and the company directed "aggrieved employees" first to discuss their "problem" with the foreman for the purpose of reaching "mutual accord," the Board found that the company had unilaterally added a preliminary step which was contrary to the second proviso of Section 9(a) and contrary to the agreement itself. Such unilateral alteration of the existing grievance procedure was found to have changed the employees' terms and conditions of employment in derogation of the union's representative status, resulting in violation of Sections 8(a)(1) and 8(a)(5). Westinghouse Electric Corp., 141 N.L.R.B. 733 (1963). Enforcement was denied on the ground that there was no evidence of any actual change in the grievance procedure. Westinghouse Electric Corp. v. NLRB, 325 F.2d 126 (7th Cir. 1963). It has also been held that union officers may not invoke a grievance procedure set forth in a contract where the contractual procedure is limited to grievances filed by an aggrieved employee or the employee and his steward. Sohio Chemical Co., 141 N.L.R.B. 810 (1963).

4. State courts have decided many cases dealing with various aspects of the right of the individual in grievance procedure and arbitration. For excellent analytical surveys, see Blumrosen, Legal Protection for Critical Job Interests: Union-Management Authority Versus Employee Autonomy, 13 Rutgers L. Rev. 631 (1959); Hanslowe, Individual Rights in Collective Labor Relations, 45 Cornell L.Q. 25 (1959); Rosen, The Individual Worker in Grievance Arbitration: Still Another Look at the Problem, 24 Md. L. Rev. 233 (1964). Under the rationale of Lincoln Mills, these problems now must be decided by federal law as determined through Section 301 jurisdiction. The state court decisions may serve as a source of guidance for the development of the federal law. In addi-

tion to the various matters discussed in the Donnelly case, supra, how should the federal law deal with the following questions:

(a) If the union and the employer submit a case to arbitration which involves individual rights, may the individual intervene in the arbitration? See Iroquois Beverage Corp. v. Brewery Workers, 14 Misc. 2d 290, 159 N.Y.S.2d 256 (Sup. Ct. 1955).

(b) Is an employee who feels that the union will not do an adequate job of representing his interests in an arbitration proceeding entitled to have his own counsel present? See Soto v. Lenscraft Optical Corp., 7 App. Div. 2d 1, 180 N.Y.S.2d 388 (1st Dept. 1958).

(c) If the union and the employer submit a case to arbitration, may an individual who is affected by the award move to vacate? See Donato v. American Locomotive Co., 383 App. Div. 410, 127 N.Y.S.2d 709 (3d Dept. 1954), aff'd, 306 N.Y. 966, 120 N.E.2d 227 (1954).

5. On the impact of the Labor-Management Reporting and Disclosure Act of 1959 relating to the freedom of a union in disposing of grievances which might go to arbitration, see page 1025 infra. Consider the particular relevance of Sections 101(a)(4) and 501(a) and (b).

6. In Pittsburgh City Fire Fighters v. Barr, 408 Pa. 325, 184 A.2d 588 (1962), the trial court relied on the Elgin, Joliet distinction between "disputes concerning the making of collective agreements" and "disputes over grievances" in holding that a provision in a state statute providing for "adjustment of grievances" by a panel did not cover a broad demand by firemen for increased wages. But the Supreme Court of Pennsylvania disagreed. Although the court conceded that the term "grievances" might not apply to such a wage demand in an industrial context, it held that a different interpretation was proper under the provisions of this statute which prohibited strikes by public employees.

7. President Kennedy's Executive Order No. 10988, see page 763 supra, contains provisions relating to the establishment of grievance procedures and arbitration in the federal service, and the respective rights of individual employees and employee organizations. Sections 3(c), 6(b), and 8.

8. The Canadian Industrial Relations and Disputes Investigation Act provides that "an employee may present his personal grievance to his employer at any time." For a discussion of this provision and other emerging problems of individual rights under collective agreements in Canada, see Laskin, Collective Bargaining and Individual Rights, 6 Canadian B.J. 278 (1963).

3. *Individual's Suit on Contract*

REPUBLIC STEEL CORP. v. MADDOX
Supreme Court of the United States, 1965
379 U.S. 650, 85 Sup. Ct. 614, 13 L. Ed. 2d 580

MR. JUSTICE HARLAN delivered the opinion of the Court.

Respondent Maddox brought suit in an Alabama state court against his employer, the Republic Steel Corporation, for severance pay amounting to $694.08, allegedly owed him under the terms of the collective bargaining agreement existing between Republic and Maddox' union. Maddox had been laid off in December 1953. The collective bargaining agreement called for severance pay if the layoff was the result of a decision to close the mine, at which Maddox worked, "permanently." [1] The agreement also contained a three-step grievance procedure to be followed by binding arbitration, but Maddox made no effort to utilize this mode of redress. Instead, in August 1956, he sued for breach of the contract. At all times material to his claim, Republic was engaged in interstate commerce within the meaning of the Labor Management Relations Act, and Republic's industrial relations with Maddox and his union were subject to the provisions of that Act.

The case was tried on stipulated facts without a jury. Judgment was awarded in favor of Maddox, and the appellate courts of Alabama affirmed on the theory that state law applies to suits for severance pay since, with the employment relationships necessarily ended, no further danger of industrial strife exists warranting the application of federal labor law, Moore v. Illinois Central R. Co., 312 U.S. 630 (1941), and Transcontinental & Western Air, Inc. v. Koppal, 345 U.S. 653 (1953), cases decided under the Railway Labor Act, were cited to support the proposition. Furthermore, it was held that under Alabama law Maddox was not required to exhaust the contract grievance procedures. We granted Republic's petition for certiorari, 377 U.S. 904, to determine whether the rationale of Moore v. Illinois Central R. Co. carries over to a suit for severance pay on a contract subject to §301(a) of the Labor Management Relations Act. We conclude that the state judgment must be reversed.

I. As a general rule in cases to which federal law applies, federal labor policy requires that individual employees wishing to assert contract grievances must *attempt* use of the contract grievance procedure agreed upon by employer and union as the mode of redress.[7] If the union refuses to press or only perfunctorily presses the individual's claim, differences may arise as to the forms of redress then available. See Humphrey v. Moore, 375 U.S. 335; Labor Board v. Miranda Fuel Co., 326 F.2d 172.[8] But unless the contract provides otherwise, there can be no doubt that the

[1] The section of the contract dealing with severance allowance provided in relevant part: "When, in the sole judgment of the Company, it decides to close permanently a plant or discontinue permanently a department of a mine or plant, or substantial portion thereof and terminate the employment of individuals, an Employee whose employment is terminated either directly as a result thereof because he was not entitled to other employment with the Company under the provisions of Section 9 of this Agreement — Seniority and Subsection C of this Section 14, shall be entitled to a severance allowance in accordance with and subject to the provisions hereinafter set forth in this Section 14."

[7] Smith v. Evening News Assn., 371 U.S. 195, 196, n.1 (by implication); Belk v. Allied Aviation Service Co., 315 F.2d 513, cert. denied, 375 U.S. 847; see Cox, Rights Under a Labor Agreement, 69 Harv. L. Rev. 601, 647-648 (1956). The proviso of §9(a) of the LMRA, 29 U.S.C. §159(a), is not contra; Black-Clawson Co. v. Machinists Local, 313 F.2d 179.

[8] See, e.g., Summers, Individual Rights in Collective Agreements and Arbitration, 37 N.Y.U.L. Rev. 362 (1962); Cox, Rights Under a Labor Agreement, 69 Harv. L. Rev. 601 (1956); Note, Federal Protection of Individual Rights Under Labor Contracts, 73 Yale L.J. 1215 (1964).

employee must afford the union the opportunity to act on his behalf. Congress has expressly approved contract grievance procedures as a preferred method for settling disputes and stabilizing the "common law" of the plant. LMRA §203(d), 29 U.S.C. §173(d); §201(c), 29 U.S.C. §171-(c). Union interest in prosecuting employee grievances is clear. Such activity complements the union's status as exclusive bargaining representative by permitting it to participate actively in the continuing administration of the contract. In addition, conscientious handling of grievance claims will enhance the union's prestige with employees. Employer interests, for their part, are served by limiting the choice of remedies available to aggrieved employees. And it cannot be said, in the normal situation, that contract grievance procedures are inadequate to protect the interests of an aggrieved employee until the employee has attempted to implement the procedures and found them so.

A contrary rule which would permit an individual employee to completely sidestep available grievance procedures in favor of a law suit has little to commend it. In addition to cutting across the interests already mentioned, it would deprive employer and union of the ability to establish a uniform and exclusive method for orderly settlement of employee grievances. If a grievance procedure cannot be made exclusive, it loses much of its desirability as a method of settlement. A rule creating such a situation "would inevitably exert a disruptive influence upon both the negotiation and administration of collective agreements." Teamsters Local v. Lucas Flour Co., 369 U.S. 95, 103.

II. Once it is established that the federal rule discussed above applies to grievances in general, it should next be inquired whether the specific type of grievance here in question — one relating to severance pay — is so different in kind as to justify an exception. Moore v. Illinois Central R. Co. and Transcontinental & Western Air, Inc. v. Koppal, supra, are put forward for the proposition that it is.

In Moore, the Court ruled that a trainman was not required by the Railway Labor Act to exhaust the administrative remedies granted him by the Act before bringing suit for wrongful discharge. Mr. Justice Black, for the Court, based the decision on the use of permissive language in the Act — disputes "may be referred . . . to the . . . Adjustment Board. . . ." Mr. Justice Black wrote again in Slocum v. Delaware, L. & W.R. Co., 339 U.S. 239 (1950), a declaratory judgment suit brought in a state court by a railroad company against two unions to resolve a representation dispute. The Court held that jurisdiction of the Adjustment Board to resolve such disputes was exclusive. Moore was distinguished thus:

"Moore was discharged by the railroad. He could have challenged the validity of his discharge before the Board, seeking reinstatement and back pay. Instead he chose to accept the railroad's action in discharging him as final, thereby ceasing to be an employee, and brought suit claiming damages for breach of contract. As we there held, the Railway Labor Act does not bar courts from adjudicating such cases. A common-law or statutory action for wrongful discharge differs from any remedy which the

Board has power to provide, and does not involve questions of future relations between the railroad and its other employees." 339 U.S. 239, at 244.

This distinction was confirmed in Transcontinental & Western Air, Inc. v. Koppal, supra:

"Such [a wrongfully discharged] employee may proceed either in accordance with the administrative procedures prescribed in his employment contract or he may resort to his action at law for alleged unlawful discharge if the state courts recognize such a claim. Where the applicable law permits his recovery of damages without showing his prior exhaustion of his administrative remedies, he may so recover, as he did in the Moore litigation, supra, under Mississippi law." 345 U.S. 653, at 661.

Federal jurisdiction in both Moore and Koppal was based on diversity; federal law was not thought to apply merely by reason of the fact that the collective bargaining agreements were subject to the Railway Labor Act. Since that time the Court has made it clear that substantive federal law applies to suits on collective bargaining agreements covered by §204 of the Railway Labor Act. International Assn. of Machinists v. Central Airlines, Inc., 372 U.S. 682, and by §301(a) of the LMRA, Textile Workers v. Lincoln Mills, 353 U.S. 448. Thus a major underpinning for the continued validity of the Moore case in the field of the Railway Labor Act has been removed, and more importantly in the present context, for the extension of its rationale to suits under §301(a) of the LMRA.

We hold that any such extension is incompatible with the precepts of Lincoln Mills and cannot be accepted. Grievances depending on severance claims are not critically unlike other types of grievances. Although it is true that the employee asserting the claim will necessarily have accepted his discharge as final, it does not follow that the resolution of his claim can have no effect on future relations between the employer and other employees. Severance pay and other contract terms governing discharge are of obvious concern to all employees, and a potential cause of dispute so long as any employee maintains a continuing employment relationship. Only in the situation in which no employees represented by the union remain employed, as would be the case with a final and permanent plant shutdown, is there no possibility of a work stoppage resulting from a severance-pay claim. But even in that narrow situation, if applicable law did not require resort to contract procedures, the inability of the union and employer at the contract negotiation stage to agree upon arbitration as the exclusive method of handling permanent shutdown severance claims in all situations could have an inhibiting effect on reaching an agreement. If applicable law permitted a court suit for severance pay in any circumstances without prior recourse to available contract remedies, an employer seeking to limit the modes of redress that could be used against him could do so only by eliminating contract grievance procedures for severance-pay claims. The union would hardly favor the elimination, for it is in the union's interest to afford comprehensive protection to those it represents to participate in interpretations of the contract, and to have an arbitrator rather than a court decide such questions as whether the company has determined to "close permanently."

There are, then, positive reasons why the general federal rule should govern grievances based on severance claims as it does others. Furthermore, no positive reasons appear why the general federal rule should not apply. "Comprehensiveness is inherent in the process by which the law is to be formulated under the mandate of Lincoln Mills," and "the subject matter of §301(a) 'is peculiarly one that calls for uniform law.'" Teamsters Local v. Lucas Flour Co., 369 U.S., at 103. Maddox' suit in the present case is simply on the contract, and the remedy sought, award of $694.08, did not differ from any that the grievance procedure had power to provide. Federal law governs "suits for violation of contracts between an employer and a labor organization representing employees in an industry affecting commerce as defined in this chapter. . . ." Section 301(a) of the LMRA, 29 U.S.C. §185(a), Textile Workers v. Lincoln Mills, supra. The suit by Maddox clearly falls within the terms of the statute and within the principles of Lincoln Mills, and because we see no reason for creating an exception, we conclude that the general federal rule applies.[14]

III. The federal rule would not of course preclude Maddox' court suit if the parties to the collective bargaining agreement expressly agreed that arbitration was not the exclusive remedy. The section of this contract governing grievances provides, inter alia:

"It is the purpose of this Section to provide procedure for prompt, equitable adjustment of claimed grievances. It is understood and agreed that unless otherwise specifically specified elsewhere in this Agreement grievances to be considered hereunder must be filed within thirty days after the date on which the fact or events upon which such alleged grievance is based shall have existed or occurred. . . .

"Any Employee who has a complaint may discuss the alleged complaint with his Foreman in an attempt to settle it. Any complaint not so settled shall constitute a grievance within the meaning of this Section, 'Adjustment of Grievances.'

"Grievances shall be handled in the following manner:

"STEP 1. Between the aggrieved Employer, his Grievance Committeeman or Assistant Grievance Committeeman and the Foreman."

The procedure calls for two more grievance-committee steps capped with binding arbitration of matters not satisfactorily settled by the initial steps.

The language stating that an employee "may discuss" a complaint with his foreman is susceptible to various interpretations; the most likely is that an employee may, if he chooses, speak to his foreman himself without bringing in his grievance committeeman and formally embarking on Step 1. Use of the permissive "may" does not of itself reveal a clear understanding between the contracting parties that individual employees, unlike either the union or the employer, are free to avoid the contract proce-

---

[14] By refusing to extend Moore v. Illinois Central R. Co. to §301 suits, we do not mean to overrule it within the field of the Railway Labor Act. Consideration of such action should properly await a case presented under the Railway Labor Act in which the various distinctive features of the administrative remedies provided by that act can be appraised in context, e.g., the make-up of the Adjustment Board, the scope of review from monetary awards, and the ability of the Board to give the same remedies as could be obtained by court suit.

dure and its time limitations in favor of a judicial suit. Any doubts must be resolved against such an interpretation. See United Steelworkers v. Warrior & Gulf Navigation Co., 363 U.S. 574; Belk v. Allied Aviation Service Co., 315 F.2d 513, cert. denied, 375 U.S. 847.

Finally, Maddox suggests that it was not possible for him to make use of the grievance procedure, the first step of which called for a discussion within 30 days of his discharge with his foreman because a mine that has permanently closed has no foreman — indeed, no employees of any kind. This casuistic reading of the contract cannot be accepted. The foreman did not vanish; and it is unlikely that the union grievance procedure broke down within 30 days of Maddox' discharge. In any event, the case is before us on stipulated facts; in neither the facts nor the pleadings is there any suggestion that Maddox could not have availed himself of the grievance procedure instead of waiting nearly three years and bringing a court suit.

Reversed.

MR. JUSTICE BLACK, dissenting.

This is an ordinary, common, run-of-the-mill lawsuit for breach of contract brought by respondent Charlie Maddox, an iron miner employed by petitioner Republic Steel, to recover $694.08 of wages which he said the company owed him. . . .

This Court now . . . holds that because the contract, agreed to by the union, provided for binding arbitration of all "grievances," federal law has deprived Maddox of his right to hire his own lawyer and to sue in a court of law for the balance of wages due and has instead left him with only the remedies set out in the contract: a long, involved grievance procedure, controlled by the company and the union, followed by compulsory arbitration, with his claim put in the hands of union officials and union lawyers whether he wants them to handle it or not.

In thus deciding on its own, or deciding that Congress somehow has decided, to expand apparently without limit the kinds of claims subject to compulsory arbitration, to include even wage claims, and in thus depriving individual laborers of the right to handle their wage claims for themselves, today's decision of the Court interprets federal law in a way that is revolutionary. . . . Finally the Court, citing as its authority §301(a) of the Labor-Management Relations Act, lays down for this and future cases the flat rule that no matter what his contractual claim — or "grievance," as the Court prefers to call it — an individual laborer, even though no longer an employee, has no choice but to follow the long, time-consuming, discouraging road to arbitration set out in the union-company contract, including having the union represent him whether he wants it to or not and whether or not he is still in its good graces. And of course the Court's logic leads irresistibly to the conclusion (although it has not yet had occasion to say so) that if instead of seeking wages due on discharge an employee wants to sue his employer for unpaid wages while he is still working, he cannot do that either, but must instead wait until the union processes his claim through the interminable stages of "grievance procedure" and then turns him over to the arbitrator, whom he does not want. Employees are thus denied a judicial hearing and state courts have their ancient power to try simple breach-of-contract cases taken away from them — taken away, not by Congress, I think, but by this Court. Today's holding is in my judgment completely unprecedented, and is the brainchild of this Court's recent consistently expressed preference for arbitration over litigation and for accommodating the wishes of employers and unions in all things over the desires of individual workers. Since I do not believe that Congress has passed any law which justifies any inference at all that workers are barred from bringing and court from deciding cases like this one, and since I am not sure that it constitutionally could, it is impossible for me to concur in this decision. . . .

For the individual, whether his case is settled by a professional arbitrator or tried by a jury can make a crucial difference. Arbitration differs from judicial proceedings in many ways: arbitration carries no right to a jury trial as guaranteed by the Seventh Amendment; arbitrators need not be instructed in the law; they are not bound by rules of evidence; they need not give reasons for their awards; witnesses need not be sworn; the record of proceedings need not be complete; and judicial review, it has been held, is extremely limited. To say that because the union chose a contract providing for grievance arbitration an individual employee freely and willingly chose this method of settling any contractual claims of his own which might later arise is surely a transparent and cruel fiction. And even if the employee could with any truth be regarded as having himself agreed to such a thing, until recently this Court refused to recognize and enforce contracts under which individuals were to be denied access to courts and instead left to the comparatively standardless process of arbitration. . . . Forcing Charlie Maddox, who is out of a job, to submit his claim to arbitration is not going to promote industrial peace. Charlie Maddox is not threatening to go out in the street by himself and stage a strike against the Republic Steel Company to get his unpaid wages. Merely because this Court in Lincoln Mills has expressed its preference for arbitration when used to avoid industrial warfare by heading off violent clashes between powerful employers and powerful unions, it does not follow that §301 should be expanded to require a worker to arbitrate his wage claim or to surrender his right to bring his own suit to enforce that claim in court. Such an expansion would run counter to this Court's long-established policy of preserving the ancient, treasured right to judicial trials in independent courts according to due process of law.

The past decisions of this Court which are closest to the case before us are not Lincoln Mills and cases like it, which involved broad conflicts between unions and employers with reference to contractual terms vital to settlement of genuine employer-union disputes. The cases really in point are those which involved agreements governed by the Railway Labor Act and which expressly refused to hold that a discharged worker must pursue collective bargaining grievance procedures before suing in a court for wrongful discharge. Transcontinental & Western Air, Inc. v. Koppal, 345 U.S. 653; Moore v. Illinois Central R. Co., 312 U.S. 630. While those were wrongful-discharge cases and the suit here is for wages due on a contract after discharge, the principle of those cases is precisely applicable here since as was pointed out in Slocum v. Delaware, L. & W.R. Co., 339 U.S. 239, 244, the claim of a person no longer employed will almost never involve questions substantially affecting future relations between an employer and the remaining employees. The Court recognizes the relevance of Moore and Koppal and while declining expressly to overrule them in this case, has raised the overruling axe so high that its falling is just about as certain as the changing of the seasons. Yet although members of Congress and alert counsel for the national unions and employers are bound to have been familiar with Moore at the time the comprehensive labor statute of which §301 is a part was enacted, Congress did not see fit to disown the Moore rule and did not express a preference for a different policy with reference to individual suits on collective bargaining agreements covered by the LMRA.

The Court's opinion manifests great concern for the interests of employers and unions, but I fear not enough understanding and appreciation for an individual worker caught in the plight Maddox is in. . . . Individual workers are to take some comfort, I suppose, in the Court's statement that "it cannot be said, in the normal situation, that contract grievance procedures are inadequate to protect the interests of an aggrieved employee until the employee has attempted to implement the procedures and found them so." I think it can be said, however, and I say it. I think an employee is just as capable of trying to enforce payment of his wages or wage substitutes under a collective bargaining agreement as his union, and he certainly is more interested in this effort than any union would likely be. This is particularly true where the employee has lost his job and is most likely outside the union door looking in instead of on hand to push his claim. Examples certainly have not been wanting from which the Court might learn that often employees for one reason or another have felt themselves compelled to sue the union as a prerequisite to obtaining any help from the union at all. . . . But, says the Court, the employee attempting to recover wages owed him must, unless the collective bargaining contract of the company and the union provides otherwise, "afford the union the opportunity to act on his behalf." The Court then implies that if the union "refuses to press or only perfunctorily presses the individual's claim," there may be some form of redress available to the worker, but we are left in the dark as to what form that redress might take. It may be that the worker would be allowed to sue after he had presented his claim to the union and after he had suffered the inevitable discouragement and delay which necessarily accompanies the union's refusal to press his claim. But I cannot agree that this is the sort of remedy a worker should have to invoke to bring a simple lawsuit.

I am wholly unable to read §301 as laying any such restrictive burdens on an employee. The difference between my Brethren and me in this case, is not simply one concerning this Court's function in interpreting or formulating laws. There is also, apparently a vast difference between their philosophy and mine concerning litigation and the role of courts in our country. At least since Magna Carta people have desired to have a system of courts with set rules of procedure of their own and with certain institutional assurances of fair and unbiased resolution of controversies. It was in Magna Carta, the English Bill of Rights, and other such charters of liberty, that there originally was expressed in the English-speaking world a deep desire of people to be able to settle differences according to standard, well-known procedures in courts presided over by independent judges with jurors taken from the public. Because of these deep-seated desires, the right to sue and be sued in courts according to the "law of the land," known later as "due process of law," became recognized. That right was written into the Bill of Rights of our Constitution and in the constitutions of the States. . . . Even if it be true, which I do not concede, that Congress could force a man in this country to have his ordinary lawsuit adjudicated not under due process of law, i.e., without the constitutional safeguards of a court trial, I do not think that this Court should ever feel free to infer or imply that Congress has taken such a step until the words of the statute are written so clearly that no one who reads them can doubt. . . . Maddox has a justiciable controversy. He has not agreed since the controversy arose or even for that matter before it arose, to arbitrate it, and so he should not have the doors of the courts shut in his face. Nor do I believe that he or any other member of the union should be treated as an incompetent unable to pursue his own simple breach-of-contract losses. I cannot and do not believe any law Congress has passed provides that when a man becomes a member of a labor union in this country he thereby has somehow surrendered his own freedom and liberty to conduct his own lawsuit for wages. Of course this is not the worst kind of servitude to which a man could be subjected, but it is certainly contrary to the spirit of freedom in this country to infer from the blue that workers lose their rights to appeal to the courts for redress when they believe they are mistreated. . . .

I would affirm.

NOTES

1. Assume that (1) there is no arbitration clause in the agreement or that the clause does not cover a particular claim, and (2) the union has not validly compromised or settled the claim, the question remains as to what alleged contract violations are subject to a Section 301 suit brought by an individual employee. While some provisions of the collective agreement run in favor of employees, others just as clearly are included for the benefit of the union, and still others may be equivocal. Prior to the decision in Smith v. Evening News, supra page 904, decisions under state law had upheld the right of employees to bring contract actions on such matters as wages: Kosley v. Goldblatt, 251 F.2d 558 (7th Cir. 1958); vacation pay: Pattenge v. Wagner Iron Works, 275 Wis. 495, 82 N.W.2d 172 (1957); severance pay: Owens v. Press Publishing Co., 20 N.J. 537, 120 A.2d 442 (1956); violation of seniority rights: O'Brien v. Dade Bros., 18 N.J. 457, 114 A.2d 266 (1955).

At this point it is important to recall that in a footnote in Smith v.

Evening News, the Court stated: "The only part of the collective bargaining contract set out in this record is the no-discrimination clause. Respondent does not argue here and we need not consider the question of federal law of whether petitioner, under this contract, has standing to sue for breach of the no-discrimination clause nor do we deal with the standing of other employees to sue upon other clauses in other contracts." 371 U.S. at 201. In Humphrey v. Moore, supra page 920, the Court passed upon the employee's claim that his discharge violated the contract, but beyond that gave no indication of the scope of Section 301 jurisdiction in suits by individuals.

2. Underlying the individual's right to sue on the contract is the premise that he is entitled to rely upon the provisions of the contract which specify the terms and conditions of his employment. In Elgin, Joliet & Eastern Ry. v. Burley, 325 U.S. 711, 729 (1945), the Court stated:

"Whether or not the agent's exclusive power [recognized in the case of contract formation disputes] extends also to the settlement of grievances, in conference or in proceedings before the Board, presents . . . difficult questions. . . .

"It would be difficult to believe that Congress intended . . . to submerge wholly the individual and minority interest, with all power to act concerning them, in the collective interest and agency, not only in forming the contracts which govern their employment relation, but also in giving effect to them and to all other incidents of that relation. Acceptance of such a view would require the clearest expression of purpose. For this would mean that Congress had nullified all pre-existing rights of workers to act in relation to their employment, including perhaps even the fundamental right to consult with one's employer, except as the collective agent might permit."

At page 739, the Court went on: "To settle for the future alone, without reference to or effect upon the past, is in fact to bargain collectively, that is, to make a collective agreement. That authority is conferred independently of the power to deal with grievances, as part of the power to contract 'concerning rates of pay, rules, or working conditions.' It includes the power to make a new agreement settling for the future a dispute concerning the coverage or meaning of a pre-existing collective agreement. For the collective bargaining power is not exhausted by being once exercised; it covers changing the terms of an existing agreement as well as making one in the first place.

"But it does not cover changing them with retroactive effects upon accrued rights or claims."

This premise was put in question by Justice Goldberg in his concurring opinion in Humphrey v. Moore, supra, 375 U.S. at 352, 355: "A mutually acceptable grievance settlement between an employer and a union, which is what the decision of the Joint Committee was, cannot be challenged by an individual dissenting employee under §301(a) on the ground that the parties exceeded their contractual powers in making the settlement. . . . [While an arbitrator's powers are limited by the contract], the power of the union and the employer jointly to settle a grievance dispute is not so limited. The parties are free by joint action to modify, amend, and supplement their original collective bargaining agreement. . . . There are too many unforeseeable contingencies in a collective bargaining relationship to justify making the words of the contract the exclusive source of rights and duties. . . .

"If collective bargaining is to remain a flexible process, the power to amend by agreement and the power to interpret by agreement must be coequal.

"It is wholly inconsistent with this Court's recognition that '[t]he grievance procedure is . . . a part of the continuous collective bargaining process,' United Steelworkers of America v. Warrior & Gulf Navigation Co., 363 U.S., at 581, to limit the parties' power to settle grievances to the confines of the existing labor agreement, or to assert, as the Court now does, that an individual employee can claim that the collective bargaining contract is violated because the parties have made a grievance settlement going beyond the strict terms of the existing contract."

Compare Justice Goldberg's view with that of the Second Circuit in Black-Clawson v. Machinists, 313 F.2d 179 (2d Cir. 1962), supra page 944. If both views should eventually prevail, then neither Section 9(a) of the NLRA nor Section 301 of the LMRA would afford protection to the individual employee of contractual rights or expectations. Seemingly, only the duty of fair representation would remain. Is it sufficient to the task?

3. Under Section 13 of the Labor Court Act in Sweden, an association which has concluded a collective contract may bring an action in the Labor Court on behalf of any person who is or has been a member of the association; and a member of the association shall not himself bring an action unless he proves that the association refuses to take action in his behalf. For a discussion of individual rights under this provision of the Swedish law, see Summers, Collective Power and Individual Rights in the Collective Agreement — A Comparison of Swedish and American Law, 72 Yale L.J. 421, 443-454 (1963).

F. Review Problem

ENDERBY PROBLEM 11
(*See page 769 supra for Enderby Problem 10*)

One fine day White, industrial relations manager of the Enderby Company, gets word that the Amalgamated Workers of the World, a leftist politically oriented union, is signing up members in the plant and that it may seek an NLRB election to determine whether Local 417 of the United Rubber Workers still represents a majority. White calls Curme, president of the local, who explains that his members are indeed dissatisfied in view of all the trouble he has been having with the company, and he isn't sure just how they would vote. In view of the reputation of the AWW, White decides to do all he can to help Local 417 at this point. He offers them free office space, secretarial assistance, and the right to investigate all grievances on company time. He also suggests to Curme that maybe, after all, they should add a union shop clause to their contract, a three-year compact which still has a year to run.

White also learns that one of the chief supporters of AWW is leaving his work station frequently to talk to other employees. He decides to fire this man immediately, although the rule about obtaining permission from the foreman to leave a machine has not been strictly enforced in recent months.

O'Doul, plant superintendent, distributes a small brochure to the employees through the foreman of each department, outlining briefly all the trouble AWW has caused and quoting some of the testimony about its international president given before the McClellan Committee. Corky Constanzo requests permission to distribute some AWW literature in the plant but permission is refused by White. Corky is found passing out handbills in the company parking lot across the street from the plant in violation of a well-known broad no-solicitation rule, and he is fired. When Corky approaches Curme about filing a grievance, Curme says he wouldn't have a chance, even in arbitration. Curme turns his back and walks away.

No more is heard about AWW and everything is "coming up roses" between Local 417 and the company until, about nine months later, the company installs a large automatic curing press and lays off three of the five-man curing press crew. The men in the curing department raise particular "hell," pointing out that there are rumors of more automatic machines to come. Three grievances are filed. One is a general grievance alleging that the company should have consulted the union about anything affecting the bargaining unit as vitally as this, and that the action violated an established practice of twenty years' standing, a five-man crew having always been used on the curing press. The second grievance is filed on behalf of Mort Moskey, who has more departmental seniority than the press operator who is retained. Moskey has been a helper for the past ten years, filling in for the operator during rest periods and occasionally at lunch time. The third grievance is filed by Junior Ipavic, another helper. Ipavic has forty years of departmental seniority, but he is a little slow because of his age and a troublesome back.

At the same time Curme calls White and advises him by phone that the union intends to terminate the existing agreement at the end of the three-year term, and that he expects to negotiate a new contract which will prohibit any further inroads on the working force by installing fancy machinery without first consulting with and obtaining the consent of the union. White says, "Put it in writing," and Curme retorts, "You have the word and that's enough." Thirty-five days later White and Curme meet in a preliminary session to discuss in broad terms what the new contract should contain. White explains that the company can never agree on a provision requiring the union's consent to automation, since the right to automate is strictly a management prerogative, and the company's very existence in the highly competitive rubber business may depend on keeping up with modern processes and increasing efficiency.

Curme replies that the men have to live and if the company won't go along with something on this, a strike will be inevitable. White asks whether the Federal Mediation Service has been notified, and Curme replies that this question is too big and the mediators couldn't help.

When a formal bargaining session is held a week later, company negotiators refuse even to discuss the matter of so-called automation. The meeting breaks up when the union refuses to discuss any other terms until this important issue is settled.

When the current agreement expires, Local 417 calls a strike and about two thirds of the working force go out. Picket lines are established, and as many as twenty pickets are assigned to the main gate where they block traffic and scare some of the nonstrikers by threats. Blair, company attorney, hurries into the local court to obtain an injunction.

Three side gates, which are used by some Enderby employees and by construction employees of various contractors and subcontractors engaged in the installation of Big Mo, a large new machine which will displace at least twenty workers, are also picketed. The employees of one subcontractor refuse to cross the picket lines.

In addition, pickets appear in front of three downtown stores with signs urging customers not to buy Enderby products because the company "is replacing its men with mechanical monsters." Another sign simply says that Enderby is "unfair to organized labor." Another — "This store is unfair because it handles scab products." And another — "Enderby is a Rat Fink!"

Local 417 buys time on the local radio to make spot announcements to the effect that Enderby products may be shoddy and inferior because they are now being produced by inexperienced, nonunion labor.

The strike is finally settled when the parties agree to a clause stating that before any labor-saving machinery is installed, the matter will first be discussed and negotiated with the union. After the new agreement is signed, Curme wants to talk about Big Mo, but White says this project has gone too far and can't be stopped in any event. They do agree to meet once more, but in the meantime the men who are scheduled to be replaced by Big Mo are not called back and the work which they normally handled is temporarily contracted out to a local concern which does jobbing in this kind of work.

Local 417 files a grievance complaining that the subcontracting is in violation of the terms of the new agreement. White answers at the third step that this is also a company prerogative under its basic right to manage the business, and that there is nothing in the contract which prohibits subcontracting. When Curme appeals to arbitration, White insists that this question clearly is not arbitrable. Cooper, union attorney, files a petition in federal court to compel the company to comply with the arbitration section of the agreement.

Subsequently, when White announces that he has engaged a cleaning firm to do the office cleaning and lays off four janitors who are members of Local 417, a wildcat strike develops and Blair appears in federal court to obtain a restraining order. At the same time the janitors file a grievance, but White refuses to accept it until the men on strike return to work.

Consider all the issues raised in the light of the provisions of the Enderby Contract and the materials you have already studied in this book. Assume alternate terms for the purpose of discussion, and consider the desirability of other available courses of action.

PART FIVE

The Individual: Equal Employment Opportunity and His Relationship to the Union

A. COMPULSORY UNION MEMBERSHIP

RAILWAY EMPLOYES' DEPARTMENT, AMERICAN FEDERATION OF LABOR v. HANSON

Supreme Court of the United States, 1956
351 U.S. 225, 76 Sup. Ct. 714, 100 L. Ed. 1112

MR. JUSTICE DOUGLAS delivered the opinion of the Court.

This is a suit brought in the Nebraska courts by employees of the Union Pacific Railroad Co. against that company and labor organizations representing various groups of employees of the railroad to enjoin the application and enforcement of a union shop agreement entered into between the railroad company and the labor organizations. Plaintiffs are not members of any of the defendant labor organizations and desire not to join. Under the terms of the union shop agreement all employees of the railroad, as a condition of their continued employment, must become members of the specified union within 60 days and thereafter maintain that membership. It is alleged that failure on their part to join the union will mean the loss of their employment together with seniority, retirement, pension, and other rights.

The employees claim that the union shop agreement violates the "right to work" provision of the Nebraska Constitution (Art. XV, §13), which provides: "No person shall be denied employment because of membership in or affiliation with, or resignation or expulsion from a labor organization or because of refusal to join or affiliate with a labor organization; nor shall any individual or corporation or association of any kind enter into any contract, written or oral, to exclude persons from employment because of membership in or nonmembership in a labor organization."

They ask for an injunction restraining the railroad company from enforcing and applying the union shop agreement.

The answers deny that the Nebraska Constitution and laws control and allege that the union shop agreement is authorized by §2 Eleventh of the Railway Labor Act as amended, 64 Stat. 1238, 45 U.S.C. §152, Eleventh, which provides that notwithstanding the law of "any State," a carrier and a labor organization may make an agreement requiring all employees within a stated time to become a member of the labor organization, provided there is no discrimination against any employee and provided that membership is not denied nor terminated "for any reason other than the failure of the employee to tender the periodic dues, initiation fees, and assessments (not including fines and penalties) uniformly required as a condition of acquiring or retaining membership."

The Nebraska trial court issued an injunction. The Supreme Court of Nebraska affirmed. It held that the union shop agreement violates the First Amendment in that it deprives the employees of their freedom of association and violates the Fifth Amendment in that it requires the members to pay for many things besides the cost of collective bargaining. The Nebraska Supreme Court, therefore, held that there is no valid federal law to supersede the "right to work" provision of the Nebraska Constitution. 160 Neb. 669, 71 N.W.2d 526. The case is here by appeal. . . .

The union shop provision of the Railway Labor Act was written into the law in 1951. Prior to that date the Railway Labor Act prohibited union shop agreements. 48 Stat. 1186, 45 U.S.C. §152, Fourth and Fifth; 40 Op. Atty. Gen. 254. Those provisions were enacted in 1934 when the union shop was being used by employers to establish and maintain company unions, "thus effectively depriving a substantial number of employees of their right to bargain collectively." S. Rep. No. 2262, 81st Cong., 2d Sess., p. 3. By 1950 company unions in this field had practically disappeared. Id. Between 75 and 80% of railroad employees were members of labor organizations. H.R. Rep. No. 2811, 81st Cong., 2d Sess., p. 4. While nonunion members got the benefits of the collective bargaining of the unions, they bore "no share of the cost of obtaining such benefits." Id., at 4. As Senator Hill, who managed the bill on the floor of the Senate, said, "The question in this instance is whether those who enjoy the fruits and the benefits of the unions should make a fair contribution to the support of the unions." 96 Cong. Rec., Pt. 12, p. 16279.

The union shop provision of the Railway Labor Act is only permissive. Congress has not compelled nor required carriers and employees to enter into union shop agreements. The Supreme Court of Nebraska nevertheless took the view that justiciable questions under the First and Fifth Amendments were presented since Congress, by the union shop provision of the Railway Labor Act, sought to strike down inconsistent laws in 17 States. Cf. Hudson v. Atlantic Coast Line R. Co., 242 N.C. 650, 89 S.E.2d 441; Otten v. Baltimore & O.R. Co., 205 F.2d 58. The Supreme Court of Nebraska said, "Such action on the part of Congress is a necessary part of every union shop contract entered into on the railroads as far as these 17 States are concerned for without it such contracts could not be enforced therein." 160 Neb., at 698, 71 N.W.2d, at 547. We agree with that view. If private rights are being invaded, it is by force of an agreement made pursuant to federal law which expressly declares that state law is superseded. Cf. Smith v. Allwright, 321 U.S. 649, 663. In other words, the federal statute is the source of the power and authority by which any private rights are lost or sacrificed.[4] Cf. Steele v. Louisville & N.R. Co., 323 U.S. 192, 198-199, 204; Railroad Trainmen v. Howard, 343 U.S. 768; Public Utilities Comm'n v. Pollak, 343 U.S. 451, 462. The enactment of the federal statute authorizing union shop agreements is the governmental action on which the Constitution operates, though it takes a private agreement to invoke the federal sanction.

As already noted, the 1951 amendment, permitting the negotiation of union shop agreements, expressly allows those agreements notwithstanding any law "of any State." §2, Eleventh.[5] A union agreement made pursuant to the Railway Labor Act has, therefore, the imprimatur of the federal law upon it and, by force of the Supremacy Clause of Article VI of the Constitution, could not be made illegal nor vitiated by any provision of the laws of a State.

We come then to the merits.

In the absence of conflicting federal legislation, there can be no doubt that it is within the police power of a State to prohibit the union or the closed shop. We so held in Lincoln Union v. Northwestern Co., 335 U.S. 525, and in American Federation of Labor v. American Sash Co., 335 U.S. 538, against the challenge that local "right to work" laws, including Nebraska's violated the requirements of due process. But the power of Congress to regulate labor relations in interstate industries is likewise well-established. Congress has authority to adopt all appropriate measures to "facilitate the amicable settlement of disputes which threaten the service of the necessary agencies of interstate transportation." Texas & N.O.R. Co. v. Railway Clerks, 281 U.S. 548, 570. These measures include provisions that will encourage the settlement of disputes "by inducing collective bargaining with the true representative of the employees and by preventing such bargaining with any who do not represent them" (Virginian R. Co. v. Federation, 300 U.S. 515, 548), and that will protect the employees against discrimination or coercion which would interfere with the free exercise of their right to self-organization and representation. Labor Board v. Jones & Laughlin, 301 U.S. 1, 33. Industrial peace along the arteries of commerce is a legitimate objective; and Congress has great latitude in choosing the methods by which it is to be obtained.

The choice by the Congress of the union shop as a stabilizing force seems to us to be an allowable one. Much might be said pro and con if the policy issue were before us. Powerful arguments have been made here that the long-run interests of labor would be better served by the

---

[4] Once courts enforce the agreement the sanction of government is, of course, put behind them. See Shelley v. Kraemer, 334 U.S. 1; Hurd v. Hodge, 334 U.S. 24; Barrows v. Jackson, 346 U.S. 249.

[5] The parallel provision in §14(b) of the Taft-Hartley Act (61 Stat. 151, 29 U.S.C. §164(b)) makes the union shop agreement give way before a state law prohibiting it.

development of democratic traditions in trade unionism without the coercive element of the union or the closed shop. Mr. Justice Brandeis, who had wide experience in labor-management relations prior to his appointment to the Court, wrote forcefully against the closed shop. He feared that the closed shop would swing the pendulum in the opposite extreme and substitute "tyranny of the employee" for "tyranny of the employer." [6] But the question is one of policy with which the judiciary has no concern, as Mr. Justice Brandeis would have been the first to concede. Congress, acting within its constitutional powers, has the final say on policy issues. If it acts unwisely, the electorate can make a change. The task of the judiciary ends once it appears that the legislative measure adopted is relevant or appropriate to the constitutional power which Congress exercises. The ingredients of industrial peace and stabilized labor-management relations are numerous and complex. They may well vary from age to age and from industry to industry. What would be needful one decade might be anathema the next. The decision rests with the policy makers, not with the judiciary.

It is said that the right to work, which the Court has frequently included in the concept of "liberty" within the meaning of the Due Process Clauses (see Truax v. Raich, 239 U.S. 33; Takahashi v. Fish & Game Commission, 334 U.S. 410), may not be denied by the Congress. The question remains, however, whether the long-range interests of workers would be better served by one type of union agreement or another. That question is germane to the exercise of power under the Commerce Clause — a power that often has the quality of police regulations. See Cleveland v. United States, 329 U.S. 14, 19. One would have to be blind to history to assert that trade unionism did not enhance and strengthen the right to work. See Webb, History of Trade Unionism; Gregory, Labor and the Law. To require, rather than to induce, the beneficiaries of trade unionism to contribute to its costs may not be the wisest course. But Congress might well believe that it would help insure the right to work in and along the arteries of interstate commerce. No more has been attempted here. The only conditions to union membership authorized by §2, Eleventh of the Railway Labor Act are the payment of "periodic dues, initiation fees, and assessments." The assessments that may be lawfully imposed do not include "fines and penalties." The financial support required relates, therefore, to the work of the union in the realm of collective bargaining. No more precise allocation of union overhead to individual members seems to us to be necessary.

---

[6] See Mason, Brandeis, A Free Man's Life (1946), pp. 303-304, which quotes a letter of February 26, 1912, from Brandeis to Lincoln Steffens: ". . . But the American people should not, and will not, accept unionism if it involves the closed shop. They will not consent to the exchange of the tyranny of the employer for the tyranny of the employee. Unionism therefore cannot make a great advance until it abandons the closed shop; and it cannot accept the open shop as an alternative. The open shop means the destruction of the union.

"The advance of unionism demands therefore some relation between the employer and the employee other than either the closed or open shop, and I feel confident that we have found a solution in the preferential union shop."

The prohibition of "fines and penalties" precludes the imposition of financial burdens for disciplinary purposes. If "assessments" are in fact imposed for purposes not germane to collective bargaining,[7] a different problem would be presented.

Wide-ranged problems are tendered under the First Amendment. It is argued that the union shop agreement forces men into ideological and political associations which violate their right to freedom of conscience, freedom of association, and freedom of thought protected by the Bill of Rights.[8] It is said that once a man becomes a member of these unions

[7] A number of appellant unions have broad powers to levy assessments for unspecified purposes. For example, the bylaws of the Railroad Yardmasters of America authorize the Executive Board to "levy assessments upon all the members affected when in its opinion such assessments are necessary." §26. And §27 provides: "Local lodges may levy such assessments upon their respective memberships as may be found necessary. . . ." The General Committee of a Subordinate Division of the Order of Railroad Telegraphers is authorized "to levy such assessments upon the members employed upon the transportation company over which it has jurisdiction as may be necessary to carry on its work." Subordinate Division Statutes, §42(H). And see Constitution of the Brotherhood of Railroad Signalmen of America, Art. I, §6; Constitution of the American Railway Supervisors Association, Art. XVI, §7.

[8] The constitutions and bylaws of several appellant unions place restrictions on the individual members.

A. Some disqualify persons from membership for their political views and associations. Art. XIII, §4, of the Constitution of the Brotherhood of Maintenance of Way Employes bars from membership anyone who is a member of the Communist Party. Another constitution renders ineligible for membership any person who is "a member of the Communist Party or of any other subversive group, or who subscribes to the doctrines of any such groups." Subordinate Lodge Constitution of the International Brotherhood of Boilermakers, Iron Ship Builders, Blacksmiths, Forgers and Helpers of America, Art. VI, §1. And see Subordinate Lodge Constitution of the Brotherhood Railway Carmen of America, §6(a). Art. 16, §1 (a), of the Constitution of the Sheet Metal Workers' International Association provides: "No member of the communist party or any person who advocates the objectives thereof, and no person who belongs to or supports the policies of any other organization or group which advocates the overthrow of the United States government or the government of the Dominion of Canada by force shall be eligible" for membership.

The constitution of one of appellant unions provides that no person shall be eligible for union office "if such person associates himself with Communist, Fascist or similar organizations, or the Ku Klux Klan, or Columbians. Such eligibility shall likewise be denied where a person associates himself with, lends support or subscribes to the subversive doctrines of the organizations enumerated herein, similar organizations, or any organization or group that expounds or promotes any doctrine or philosophy inimical or subversive to the fundamental purposes of the constitution of the Government of the United States." Constitution of the Hotel & Restaurant Employees and Bartenders International Union, Art. XI, §18. The Constitution of the International Association of Machinists, Art. I, §5, provides: "A member who advocates or encourages communism, fascism, nazism, or any other totalitarian philosophy, or who, by other actions, gives support to these 'philosophies' or 'isms' is not eligible to hold office in the I.A.M."

B. The Grand Lodge Constitution of the Brotherhood Railway Carmen of America prohibits members from "interfering with legislative matters affecting national, state, territorial, dominion or provincial legislation, adversely affecting the interests of our members." §64.

he is subject to vast disciplinary control [9] and that by force of the federal Act unions now can make him conform to their ideology.

On the present record, there is no more an infringement or impairment of First Amendment rights than there would be in the case of a lawyer who by state law is required to be a member of an integrated bar. It is argued that compulsory membership will be used to impair freedom of expression. But that problem is not presented by this record. Congress endeavored to safeguard against that possibility by making explicit that no conditions to membership may be imposed except as respects "periodic dues, initiation fees, and assessments." If other conditions are in fact imposed, or if the exaction of dues, initiation fees, or assessments is used as a cover for forcing ideological conformity or other action in contravention of the First Amendment, this judgment will not prejudice the decision in that case. For we pass narrowly on §2, Eleventh of the Railway Labor Act. We only hold that the requirement for financial support of the collective-bargaining agency by all who receive the benefits of its work is within the power of Congress under the Commerce Clause and does not violate either the First or the Fifth Amendments. We express no opinion on the use of other conditions to secure or maintain membership in a labor organization operating under a union or closed shop agreement.

Reversed.

MR. JUSTICE FRANKFURTER, concurring.

The Constitution of the International Brotherhood of Electrical Workers, another of the appellant unions, forbids any member from "creating or attempting to create dissatisfaction or dissension among any of the members or among L.U.'s (Local Unions) of the I.B.E.W." Art. XXVII, §2(8). The same article and section further prohibits any member from

"(15) Attending or participating in any gathering or meeting whatsoever, held outside meetings of a L.U., at which the affairs of the L.U. are discussed, or at which conclusions are arrived at regarding the business and the affairs of a L.U., or regarding L.U. officers or a candidate or candidates for L.U. office.

"(16) Mailing, handing out, or posting cards, handbills, letters, marked ballots or political literature of any kind, or displaying streamers, banners, signs or anything else of a political nature, or being a party in any way to such being done in an effort to induce members to vote for or against any candidate or candidates for L.U. office, or candidates to conventions." And see Art. 17, §1(b), Constitution of the Sheet Metal Workers' International Association; Art. XXIV, §2, Constitution of the International Association of Machinists.

C. A number of the constitutions of appellant unions provide for the use of compulsory dues and assessments to finance union insurance and death benefit plans. See, e.g., Constitution of the International Brotherhood of Firemen and Oilers, Art. I, §22; Constitution of the Railroad Yardmasters of America, Art. VII, §4; Constitution of the International Brotherhood of Boilermakers, Iron Ship Builders, Blacksmiths, Forgers and Helpers of America, Art. VII, §2.

[9] See Summers, Disciplinary Powers of Unions (1950), 3 Ind. & Lab. Rel. Rev. 483; Summers, Disciplinary Procedures of Unions (1950), 4 Ind. & Lab. Rel. Rev. 15; Summers, Legal Limitations on Union Discipline (1951), 64 Harv. L. Rev. 1049; Aaron & Komaroff, Statutory Regulation of Internal Union Affairs (1949), 44 Ill. L. Rev. 425, 631; Wirtz, Government by Private Groups (1953), 13 La. L. Rev. 440; Williams, The Political Liberties of Labor Union Members (1954), 32 Tex. L. Rev. 826.

The provision of law now challenged is the latest exercise by Congress of its power under the Commerce Clause to promote peaceful industrial relations in the functioning of interstate railroads and thereby to further the national well-being. A mere recital of the course of history in this important field goes a long way to indicate that the main point of attack against the Act of January 10, 1951, 64 Stat. 1238, raises questions not of constitutional validity but of policy in a domain of legislation peculiarly open to conflicting views of policy. These efforts constitute a body of empiric responses by Congress to new problems or new insight for dealing with old problems.

The course of legislation affecting industrial controversies on railroads flows through these statutes: the Act of October 1, 1888, 25 Stat. 501; the Erdman Act of June 1, 1898, 30 Stat. 424, growing out of the Pullman strike of 1894, see In re Debs, 158 U.S. 564; the Newlands Act of July 15, 1913, 38 Stat. 103; the Adamson Law of September 3, 1916, 39 Stat. 721; Title III of the Transportation Act of 1920, 41 Stat. 456, 469; the Railway Labor Act of May 20, 1926, 44 Stat. 577; the Act of June 21, 1934, 48 Stat. 1185, amending the Railway Labor Act.

Nearly fifty years ago, the railroads successfully attacked the constitutionality of a vital feature of the Act of June 1, 1898, whereby Congress made it a criminal offense to bar employment in interstate railroads merely because of labor union membership. Adair v. United States, 208 U.S. 161 (1908). It is fair to say that this decision marks the nadir of denial to Congress of the power to regulate the conditions for assuring the Nation's dependence on the peaceful and effective operation of its railroads. The criticisms that the case aroused, see, e.g., Richard Olney, Discrimination Against Union Labor — Legal? 42 Amer. L. Rev. 161 (1908), and Roscoe Pound, Liberty of Contract, 18 Yale L.J. 454 (1909), were reflected in later decisions of the Court. Neither the Commerce Clause nor the Due Process Clause was thereafter conceived, at least so far as they restrain railroad labor regulation, to be confined within such doctrinaire and frozen bounds as were confined the assumptions which underlay the decision in the Adair case. Thus, the Court sustained the Adamson law, which was enacted to avert the threatened nation-wide railroad strike of 1916, Wilson v. New, 243 U.S. 332 (1917); Title III of the Transportation Act of 1920, Pennsylvania R. Co. v. Railroad Labor Board, 261 U.S. 72 (1923); and the Railway Labor Act of 1926, Texas & New Orleans R. Co. v. Brotherhood of Railway & Steamship Clerks, 281 U.S. 548 (1930); but see Railroad Retirement Board v. Alton R. Co., 295 U.S. 330 (1935).

The change in the Court's understanding of industrial problems, certainly as they affect railroads, in their bearing upon the country's commerce and all that thereby hangs, to no small degree reflected the changed attitude of the railroads towards the rôle of railroad labor unions in the discharge of the functions of railroads. As striking evidence as any of this important shift in opinion is the fact that the Railway Labor Act of 1926 came on the statute books through agreement between the railroads and the railroad unions on the need for such legislation. It is accurate to say that the railroads and the railroad unions between them wrote the Railway Labor Act of 1926 and Congress formally enacted their agreement. I doubt whether there is another instance in the history of important legislation in which acknowledgment was so candidly made by a President of the United States that agreement reached between industrial disputants regarding legislation appropriate for securing their peaceful relations should become law. "I am informed," the President reported to Congress in his annual message of December 8, 1925, "that the railroad managers and their employees have reached a substantial agreement as to what legislation is necessary to regulate and improve their relationship. Whenever they bring forward such proposals, which seem sufficient also to protect the interests of the public, they should be enacted into law." H.R. Doc. No. 2, 69th Cong., 1st Sess., p. 18. The President was Calvin Coolidge.

We have come full circle from the point of view in the Adair case. There the railroads, to repeat, successfully resisted an Act of Congress which outlawed what colloquially became known as the "yellow-dog contract." We are now asked to declare it beyond the power of Congress to authorize railroads to enter into voluntary agreements with the unions to which the overwhelming proportion of railway employees belong whereby all their workers are required to belong to such unions, provided, of course, that the unions be open unions, i.e., that membership in the unions be available on ordinary, appropriate terms. It seems to me that the constitutional objections to this legislation were conclusively and compendiously answered by Mr. Justice Holmes in his dissent in Adair v. United States, supra:

"Where there is, or generally is believed to be, an important ground of public policy for restraint the Constitution does not forbid it, whether this court agrees or disagrees with the policy pursued. It cannot be doubted that to prevent strikes, and, so far as possible, to foster its scheme of arbitration, might be deemed by Congress an important point of policy, and I think it impossible to say that Congress might not reasonably think that the provision in question would help a good deal to carry its policy along. But suppose the only effect really were to tend to bring about the complete unionizing of such railroad laborers as Congress can deal with, I think that object alone would justify the act. I quite agree that the question what and how much good labor unions do, is one on which intelligent people may differ, — I think that laboring men sometimes attribute to them advantages, as many attribute to combinations of capital disadvantages, that really are due to economic conditions of a far wider and deeper kind — but I could not pronounce it unwarranted if Congress should decide that to foster a strong union was for the best interest, not only of the men, but of the railroads and the country at large." 208 U.S., at 191-192.

The Court has put to one side situations not now before us for which the protection of the First Amendment was earnestly urged at the bar. I, too, leave them to one side.

INTERNATIONAL ASSN. OF MACHINISTS
v. STREET

Supreme Court of the United States, 1961
367 U.S. 740, 81 Sup. Ct. 1784, 6 L. Ed. 2d 1141

Mr. Justice Brennan delivered the opinion of the Court.

A group of labor organizations, appellants here, and the carriers comprising the Southern Railway System, entered into a union-shop agreement pursuant to the authority of §2, Eleventh of the Railway Labor Act. The agreement requires each of the appellees, employees of the carriers, as a condition of continued employment, to pay the appellant union representing his particular class or craft the dues, initiation fees and assessments uniformly required as a condition of acquiring or retaining union membership. The appellees, in behalf of themselves and of employees similarly situated, brought this action in the Superior Court of Bibb County, Georgia, alleging that the money each was thus compelled to pay to hold his job was in substantial part used to finance the campaigns of candidates for federal and state offices whom he opposed, and to promote the propagation of political and economic doctrines, concepts and ideologies with which he disagreed. The Superior Court found that the allegations were fully proved[2] and entered a judgment and decree enjoining the enforcement of the union-shop agreement on the ground that §2, Eleventh violates the Federal Constitution to the extent that it permits such use by the appellants of the funds

---

[2] The pertinent findings of the trial court are:

"(5) The funds so exacted from plaintiffs and the class they represent by the labor union defendants have been, and are being, used in substantial amounts by the latter to support the political campaigns of candidates for the offices of President and Vice President of the United States, and for the Senate and House of Representatives of the United States, opposed by plaintiffs and the class they represent, and also to support by direct and indirect financial contributions and expenditures the political campaigns of candidates for State and local public offices, opposed by plaintiffs and the class they represent. The said funds are so used both by each of the labor union defendants separately and by all of the labor union defendants collectively and in concert among themselves and with other organizations not parties to this action through associations, leagues, or committees formed for that purpose.

"(6) Those funds have been and are being used in substantial amounts to propagate political and economic doctrines, concepts and ideologies and to promote legislative programs opposed by plaintiffs and the class they represent. Those funds have also been and are being used in substantial amounts to impose upon plaintiffs and the class they represent, as well as upon the general public, conformity to those doctrines, concepts, ideologies and programs.

"(7) The exaction of moneys from plaintiffs and the class they represent for the purposes and activities described above is not reasonably necessary to collective bargaining or to maintaining the existence and position of said union defendants as effective bargaining agents or to inform the employees whom said defendants represent of developments of mutual interest.

"(8) The exaction of said money from plaintiffs and the class they represent, in the fashion set forth above by the labor union defendants, is pursuant to the union shop agreements and in accordance with the terms and conditions of those agreements."

exacted from employees.[3] The Supreme Court of Georgia affirmed, 215 Ga. 27, 108 S.E.2d 796.[4] . . .

I. THE HANSON DECISION

We held in Railway Employes' Dept. v. Hanson, 351 U.S. 225, that enactment of the provision of §2, Eleventh authorizing union-shop agreements between interstate railroads and unions of their employees was a valid exercise by Congress of its powers under the Commerce Clause and did not violate the First Amendment or the Due Process Clause of the Fifth Amendment. It is argued that our disposition of the First Amendment claims in Hanson disposes of appellees' constitutional claims in this case adversely to their contentions. We disagree. As appears from its history, that case decided only that §2, Eleventh, in authorizing collective agreements conditioning employees' continued employment on payment of union dues, initiation fees and assessments, did not on its face impinge upon protected rights of association. . . . When it is recalled that the action in Hanson was brought before the union-shop agreement became effective and that the appellees never thereafter showed that the unions were actually engaged in furthering political causes with which they disagreed and that their money would be used to support such activities, it becomes obvious that this Court passed merely on the constitutional validity of §2, Eleventh of the Railway Labor Act on its face, and not as applied to infringe the particularized

[3] The trial judge concluded:
"Said exaction and use of money, said union shop agreements and Section 2 (eleventh) of the Railway Labor Act and their enforcement violate the United States Constitution which in the First, Fifth, Ninth and Tenth Amendments thereto guarantees to individuals protection from such unwarranted invasion of their personal and property rights, (including freedom of association, freedom of thought, freedom of speech, freedom of press, freedom to work and their political freedom and rights) under the cloak of federal authority."
The judgment and decree provided that the appellants and the carriers "be and they hereby are perpetually enjoined from enforcing the said union shop agreements . . . and from discharging petitioners, or any member of the class they represent, for refusing to become or remain members of, or pay periodic dues, fees, or assessments to, any of the labor union defendants, provided, however, that said defendants may at any time petition the court to dissolve said injunction upon a showing that they no longer are engaging in the improper and unlawful activities described above." Judgment was also entered in favor of three of the named appellees for the amounts of dues, initiation fees and assessments paid by them.
[4] The Supreme Court of Georgia viewed the constitutional question presented for its decision as follows:
"The fundamental constitutional question is: Does the contract between the employers of the plaintiffs and the union defendants, which compels these plaintiffs, if they continue to work for the employers, to join the unions of their respective crafts, and pay dues, fees, and assessments to the unions, where a part of the same will be used to support political and economic programs and candidates for public office, which the plaintiffs not only do not approve but oppose, violate their rights of freedom of speech and deprive them of their property without due process of law under the First and Fifth Amendments to the Federal Constitution?" 215 Ga., at 43-44, 108 S.E.2d, at 807.

constitutional rights of any individual.   On such a record, the Court could not have done more, consistently with the restraints that govern us in the adjudication of constitutional questions and warn against their premature decision.   We therefore reserved decision of the constitutional questions which the appellees present in this case. . . .   Thus all that was held in Hanson was that §2, Eleventh was constitutional in its bare authorization of union-shop contracts requiring workers to give "financial support" to unions legally authorized to act as their collective bargaining agents.   We sustained this requirement — and only this requirement — embodied in the statutory authorization of agreements under which "all employees shall become members of the labor organization representing their craft or class."   We clearly passed neither upon forced association in any other aspect nor upon the issue of the use of exacted money for political causes which were opposed by the employees.

The record in this case is adequate squarely to present constitutional questions reserved in Hanson.   These are questions of the utmost gravity.   However, the restraints against unnecessary constitutional decision counsel against their determination unless we must conclude that Congress, in authorizing a union shop under §2, Eleventh, also meant that the labor organization receiving an employee's money should be free, despite that employee's objection, to spend his money for political causes which he opposes.   Federal statutes are to be so construed as to avoid serious doubt of their constitutionality. . . .   Each named appellee in this action has made known to the union representing his craft or class his dissent from the use of his money for political causes which he opposes.   We have therefore examined the legislative history of §2, Eleventh in the context of the development of unionism in the railroad industry under the regulatory scheme created by the Railway Labor Act to determine whether a construction is "fairly possible" which denies the authority to a union, over the employee's objection, to spend his money for political causes which he opposes.   We conclude that such a construction is not only "fairly possible" but entirely reasonable, and we therefore find it unnecessary to decide the correctness of the constitutional determinations made by the Georgia courts.

II.   The Rail Unions and Union Security

The history of union security in the railway industry is marked *first,* by a strong and long-standing tradition of voluntary unionism on the part of the standard rail unions; *second,* by the declaration in 1934 of a congressional policy of complete freedom of choice of employees to join or not to join a union; *third,* by the modification of the firm legislative policy against compulsion, but only as a specific response to the recognition of the expenses and burdens incurred by the unions in the administration of the complex scheme of the Railway Labor Act. . . .

A primary purpose of the major revisions made in 1934 was to strengthen the position of the labor organizations vis-à-vis the carriers, to the end of furthering the success of the basic congressional policy of self-adjustment of the industry's labor problems between carrier organizations and effective labor organizations. The unions claimed that the carriers interfered with the employees' freedom of choice of representatives by creating company unions, and otherwise attempting to undermine the employees' participation in the process of collective bargaining. Congress amended §2, Third to reinforce the prohibitions against interference with the choice of representatives, and to permit the employees to select nonemployee representatives. A new §2, Fourth was added guaranteeing employees the right to organize and bargain collectively, and Congress made it the enforceable duty of the carriers "to treat with" the representatives of the employees, §2, Ninth. See Virginian R. Co. v. System Federation, 300 U.S. 515. It was made explicit that the representative selected by a majority of any class or craft of employees should be the exclusive bargaining representative of all the employees of that craft or class. "The minority members of a craft are thus deprived by the statute of the right, which they would otherwise possess, to choose a representative of their own, and its members cannot bargain individually on behalf of themselves as to matters which are properly the subject of collective bargaining." Steele v. Louisville & N.R. Co., 323 U.S. 192, 200. "Congress has seen fit to clothe the bargaining representative with powers comparable to those possessed by a legislative body both to create and restrict the rights of those whom it represents. . . ." Id., p. 202. In addition to thus strengthening the unions' status in relation to both the carriers and the employees, the 1934 Act created the National Railroad Adjustment Board and provided that the 18 employee representatives were to be chosen by the labor organizations national in scope. §3. This Board was given jurisdiction to settle what are termed minor disputes in the railroad industry, primarily grievances arising from the application of collective bargaining agreements to particular situations. See Union Pacific R. Co. v. Price, 360 U.S. 601.

In sum, in prescribing collective bargaining as the method of settling railway disputes, in conferring upon the unions the status of exclusive representatives in the negotiation and administration of collective agreements, and in giving them representation on the statutory board to adjudicate grievances, Congress has given the unions a clearly defined and delineated role to play in effectuating the basic congressional policy of stabilizing labor relations in the industry. "It is fair to say that every stage in the evolution of this railroad labor code was progressively infused with the purpose of securing self-adjustment between the effectively organized railroads and the equally effective railroad unions and, to that end, of establishing facilities for such self-adjustment by the railroad community of its own industrial controversies. . . . The assumption as well as the aim of that Act (of 1934) is a process of permanent conference and negotiation between the carriers on the one hand and the employees through their unions on the other." Elgin, J. & E.R. Co. v. Burley, 325 U.S. 711, 752-753 (dissenting opinion).

Performance of these functions entails the expenditure of considerable funds. Moreover, this Court has held that under the statutory scheme, a union's status as exclusive bargaining representative carries with it the duty fairly and equitably to represent all employees of the craft or class, union and nonunion. Steele v. Louisville & N.R. Co., 323 U.S. 192; Tunstall v. Brotherhood of Locomotive Firemen & Enginemen, 323 U.S. 210. The principal argument made by the unions in 1950 was based on their role in this regulatory framework. They maintained that because of the expense of performing their duties in the congressional scheme, fairness justified the spreading of the costs to all employees who benefited. They thus advanced as their purpose the elimination of the "free riders" — those employees who obtained the benefits of the unions' participation in the machinery of the Act without financially supporting the unions. . . .

This argument was decisive with Congress. The House Committee Report traced the history of previous legislation in the industry and pointed out the duty of the union acting as exclusive bargaining representative to represent equally all members of the class. "Under the act, the collective-bargaining representative is required to represent the entire membership of the craft or class, including nonunion members, fairly, equitably, and in good faith. Benefits resulting from collective bargaining may not be withheld from the employees because they are not members of the union." H.R. Rep. No. 2811, 81st Cong., 2d Sess., p. 4. Observing that about 75% or 80% of all railroad employees were believed to belong to a union, the report continued: "Nonunion members, nevertheless, share in the benefits derived from collective agreements negotiated by the railway labor unions but bear no share of the cost of obtaining such benefits." Ibid. These considerations overbore the arguments in favor of the earlier policy of complete individual freedom of choice. . . . The conclusion to which this history clearly points is that §2, Eleventh contemplated compulsory unionism to force employees to share the costs of negotiating and administering collective agreements, and the costs of the adjustment and settlement of disputes. One looks in vain for any suggestion that Congress also meant in §2, Eleventh to provide the unions with a means for forcing employees, over their objection, to support political causes which they oppose.

III. THE SAFEGUARDING OF RIGHTS OF DISSENT

To the contrary, Congress incorporated safeguards in the statute to protect dissenters' interests. Congress became concerned during the hearings and debates that the union shop might be used to abridge freedom of speech and beliefs. The original proposal for authorization of the union shop was qualified in only one respect. It provided "That no such agreement shall require such condition of employment with respect to employees to whom membership is not available upon the same terms and conditions as are generally applicable to any other member. . . ." This was primarily designed to prevent discharge of employees for nonmembership where the union did not admit the employee to membership on racial grounds. See House Hearings, p. 68; Senate Hearings, pp. 22-25. But it was strenuously protested that the proposal provided no protection for an employee who disagreed with union policies or leadership. It was argued, for example, that "the right of free speech is at stake. . . . A man could feel that he was no longer able freely to express himself because he could be dismissed on account of criticism of the union. . . ." House Hearings, p. 115; see also Senate Hearings, pp. 167-169, 320. Objections of this kind led the rail unions to propose an addition to the proviso to §2, Eleventh to prevent loss of job for nonunion membership "with respect to employees to whom membership was denied or terminated for any reason other than the failure of the employee to tender the periodic dues, fees, and assessments uniformly required as a condition of acquiring or retaining membership." House Hearings, p. 247. Mr. Harrison presented this text and stated, "It is submitted that this bill with the amendment as suggested in this statement remedies the alleged abuses of compulsory union membership as claimed by the opposing witnesses, yet makes possible the elimination of the 'free rider' and the sharing of the burden of maintenance by all of the beneficiaries of union activity." House Hearings, p. 253. Mr. Harrison also sought to reassure Committee members as to the possible implications of other language of the proposed bill; he explained that "fees" meant "initiation fees," and "assessments" was intended primarily to cover the situation of a union which had only nominal dues, so that its members paid "an assessment to finance the activities of the general negotiating committee . . . it will vary month by month, based on the expenses and work of that committee." P. 257. Or, he explained, an assessment might cover convention expenses. "So we had to use the word 'assessment' in addition to dues and fees because some of the unions collect a nominal amount of dues and an assessment month after month to finance part of the activities, although in total it perhaps is no different than the dues paid in the first instance which comprehended all of those expenses." P. 258. In reporting the bill, the Senate Committee expressly noted the protective proviso, S. Rep. No. 2262, 81st Cong., 2d Sess., pp. 3-4, and affixed the Senate additional limitations. The words "not including fines and penalties" were added, to make it clear that termination of union membership for their nonpayment would not be grounds for discharge. It was also made explicit that "fees" meant "initiation fees." See 96 Cong. Rec. 16267-16268.

A congressional concern over possible impingements on the interests of individual dissenters from union policies is therefore discernible. It is true that opponents of the union shop urged that Congress should not allow it without explicitly regulating the amount of dues which might be exacted or prescribing the uses for which the dues might be expended. We may assume that Congress was also fully conversant with the long history of intensive involvement of the railroad unions in political activities. But it does not follow that §2, Eleventh places no restriction on the use of an employee's money, over his objection, to support political causes he opposes merely because Congress did not enact a comprehensive regulatory scheme governing expenditures. For it is abundantly clear that Congress did not completely abandon the policy of full freedom of choice embodied in the 1934 Act, but rather made inroads on it for the limited purpose of eliminating the problems created by the "free rider." That policy survives in §2, Eleventh in the safeguards intended to protect freedom of dissent. Congress was aware of the conflicting interests involved in the question of the union shop and sought to achieve their accommodation. . . . We respect this congressional purpose when we construe §2, Eleventh as not vesting the unions with unlimited power to spend exacted money. We are not called upon to delineate the precise limits of that power in this case. We have before us only the question whether the power is restricted to the extent of denying the unions the right, over the employee's objection, to use his money to support political causes which he opposes. Its use to support candidates for public office, and advance political programs, is not a use which helps defray the expenses of the negotiation or administration of collective agreements, or the expenses entailed in the adjustment of grievances and disputes. In other words, it is a use which falls clearly outside the reasons advanced by the unions and accepted by Congress why authority to make union-shop agreements was justified. On the other hand, it is equally clear that it is a use to support activities within the area of dissenters' interests which Congress enacted the proviso to protect. We give §2, Eleventh the construction which achieves both congressional purposes when we hold, as we do, that §2, Eleventh is to be construed to deny the unions, over an employee's objection, the power to use his exacted funds to support political causes which he opposes.[17]

We express no view as to other union expenditures objected to by an employee and not made to meet the costs of negotiation and administration of collective agreements, or the adjustment and settlement of grievances and disputes. We do not understand, in view of the findings of

---

[17] A distinction between the use of union funds for political purposes and their expenditure for nonpolitical purposes is implicit in other congressional enactments. Thus the Treasury has adopted this regulation under §162 of the Internal Revenue Code of 1954 to govern the deductibility for income-tax purposes of payments by union members to their union:

"Dues and other payments to an organization, such as a labor union or a trade association, which otherwise meet the requirements of the regulations under section 162, are deductible in full unless a substantial part of the organization's activities consists of (expenditures for lobbying purposes, for the promotion or defeat of legislation, for political campaign purposes (including the support of or opposition to any candidate for public office), or for carrying on propaganda (including advertising) related to any of the foregoing purposes). . . . If a substantial part of the activities of the organization consists of one or more of those specified, deduction will be allowed only for such portion of such dues and other payments as the taxpayer can clearly establish is attributable to activities other than those so specified. The determination as to whether such specified activities constitute a substantial part of an organization's activities shall be based on all the facts and circumstances. In no event shall special assessments or similar payments (including an increase in dues) made to any organization for any of such specified purposes be deductible." 26 CFR §1.162-15(c)(2); see also Rev. Proc. 61-10, 1961-16 Int. Rev. Bull. 49, April 17, 1961. Cf. Cammarano v. United States, 358 U.S. 498.

the Georgia courts and the question decided by the Georgia Supreme Court, that there is before us the matter of expenditures for activities in the area between the costs which led directly to the complaint as to "free riders," and the expenditures to support union political activities.[18] We are satisfied, however, that §2, Eleventh is to be interpreted to deny the unions the power claimed in this case. The appellant unions, in insisting that §2, Eleventh contemplates their use of exacted funds to support political causes objected to by the employee, would have us hold that Congress sanctioned an expansion of historical practices in the political area by the rail unions. This we decline to do. Both by tradition and, from 1934 to 1951, by force of law, the rail unions did not rely upon the compulsion of union security agreements to exact money to support the political activities in which they engage. Our construction therefore involves no curtailment of the traditional political activities of the railroad unions. It means only that those unions must not support those activities, against the expressed wishes of a dissenting employee, with his exacted money.

IV. THE APPROPRIATE REMEDY

Under our view of the statute, however, the decision of the court below was erroneous and cannot stand. The appellees who have participated in this action have in the course of it made known to their respective unions their objection to the use of their money for the support of political causes. In that circumstance, the respective unions were without power to use payments thereafter tendered by them for such political causes. However, the union-shop agreement itself is not unlawful. Railway Employes' Dept. v. Hanson, supra. The appellees therefore remain obliged, as a condition of continued employment, to make the payments to their respective unions called for by the agreement. Their right of action stems not from constitutional limitations on Congress' power to authorize the union shop, but from §2, Eleventh itself. In other words, appellees' grievance stems from the spending of their funds for purposes not authorized by the Act in the face of their objection, not from the enforcement of the union-shop agreement by the mere collection of funds. If their money were used for purposes contemplated by §2, Eleventh, the appellees would have no grievance at all. We think that an injunction restraining enforcement of the union-shop agreement is therefore plainly not a remedy appropriate to the violation of the Act's restriction on expenditures. Restraining the collection of all funds from the appellees sweeps too broadly, since their objection is only to the uses to which some of their money is put. Moreover, restraining collection of the funds as the Georgia courts have done might well interfere with the appellant unions' performance of those functions and duties which the Railway Labor Act places upon them to attain its goal of stability in the industry. Even though the lower court decree is subject to modification

---

[18] For example, many of the national labor unions maintain death benefit funds from the dues of individual members transmitted by the locals.

upon proof by the appellants of cessation of improper expenditures, in the interim the prohibition is absolute against the collection of all funds from anyone who can show that he is opposed to the expenditure of any of his money for political purposes which he disapproves. The complete shutoff of this source of income defeats the congressional plan to have all employees benefited share costs "in the realm of collective bargaining," Hanson, 351 U.S., at p. 235, and threatens the basic congressional policy of the Railway Labor Act for self-adjustments between effective carrier organizations and effective labor organizations.

Since the case must therefore be remanded to the court below for consideration of a proper remedy, we think that it is appropriate to suggest the limits within which remedial discretion may be exercised consistently with the Railway Labor Act and other relevant public policies. As indicated, an injunction against enforcement of the union shop itself through the collection of funds is unwarranted. We also think that a blanket injunction against all expenditures of funds for the disputed purposes, even one conditioned on cessation of improper expenditures, would not be a proper exercise of equitable discretion. Nor would it be proper to issue an interim or temporary blanket injunction of this character pending a final adjudication. The Norris-LaGuardia Act, 47 Stat. 70, 29 U.S.C. §§101-115, expresses a basic policy against the injunction of activities of labor unions. We have held that the Act does not deprive the federal courts of jurisdiction to enjoin compliance with various mandates of the Railway Labor Act. Virginian R. Co. v. System Federation, 300 U.S. 515; Graham v. Brotherhood of Locomotive Firemen & Enginemen, 338 U.S. 232. However, the policy of the Act suggests that the courts should hesitate to fix upon the injunctive remedy for breaches of duty owing under the labor laws unless that remedy alone can effectively guard the plaintiff's right. In Graham this Court found an injunction necessary to prevent the breach of the duty of fair representation, in order that Congress might not seem to have held out to the petitioners there "an illusory right for which it was denying them a remedy." 338 U.S., at p. 240. No such necessity for a blanket injunctive remedy because of the absence of reasonable alternatives appears here. Moreover, the fact that these expenditures are made for political activities is an additional reason for reluctance to impose such an injunctive remedy. Whatever may be the powers of Congress or the States to forbid unions altogether to make various types of political expenditures, as to which we express no opinion here,[21] many of the expenditures involved in the present case are made for the purpose of disseminating information as to candidates and programs and publicizing the positions of the unions on them. As to such expenditures an injunction would work a restraint on the expression of political ideas which might be offensive to the First Amendment. For the majority also has an interest in stating its views without being silenced by the dissenters. To attain the appropriate

[21] No contention was made below or here that any of the expenditures involved in this case were made in violation of the Federal Corrupt Practices Act, 18 U.S.C. §610, or any state corrupt practices legislation.

reconciliation between majority and dissenting interests in the area of political expression, we think the courts in administering the Act should select remedies which protect both interests to the maximum extent possible without undue impingement of one on the other.

Among possible remedies which would appear appropriate to the injury complained of, two may be enforced with a minimum of administrative difficulty[22] and with little danger of encroachment on the legitimate activities or necessary functions of the unions. Any remedies, however, would properly be granted only to employees who have made known to the union officials that they do not desire their funds to be used for political causes to which they object. The safeguards of §2, Eleventh were added for the protection of dissenters' interest, but dissent is not to be presumed — it must affirmatively be made known to the union by the dissenting employee. The union receiving money exacted from an employee under a union-shop agreement should not in fairness be subjected to sanctions in favor of an employee who makes no complaint of the use of his money for such activities. From these considerations, it follows that the present action is not a true class action, for there is no attempt to prove the existence of a class of workers who had specifically objected to the exaction of dues for political purposes. See Hansberry v. Lee, 311 U.S. 32, 44. Thus we think that only those who have identified themselves as opposed to political uses of their funds are entitled to relief in this action.

One remedy would be an injunction against expenditure for political causes opposed by each complaining employee of a sum, from those moneys to be spent by the union for political purposes, which is so much of the moneys exacted from him as is the proportion of the union's total expenditures made for such political activities to the union's total budget. The union should not be in a position to make up such sum from money paid by a nondissenter, for this would shift a disproportionate share of the costs of collective bargaining to the dissenter and have the same effect of applying his money to support such political activities. A second remedy would be restitution to each individual employee of that portion of his money which the union expended, despite his notification, for the political causes to which he had advised the union he was opposed. There should be no necessity, however, for the employee to trace his money up to and including its expenditure; if the money goes into general funds and no separate accounts of receipts and expenditures of the funds of individual employees are maintained, the portion of his money the employee would be entitled to recover would be in the same

[22] We note that the Labor-Management Reporting and Disclosure Act of 1959 requires every labor organization subject to the federal labor laws to file annually with the Secretary of Labor a financial report as to certain specified disbursements and also "other disbursements made by it including the purposes thereof. . . ." §201(b)(6). Each union is also required to maintain records in sufficient detail to supply the necessary basic information and data from which the report may be verified. §206. The information required to be contained in such report must be available to all union members. §201(c).

proportion that the expenditures for political purposes which he had advised the union he disapproved bore to the total union budget.

The judgment is reversed and the case is remanded to the court below for proceedings not inconsistent with this opinion.

Mr. Justice Douglas, concurring. . . .

The collection of dues for paying the costs of collective bargaining of which each member is a beneficiary is one thing. If, however, dues are used, or assessments are made, to promote or oppose birth control, to repeal or increase the taxes on cosmetics, to promote or oppose the admission of Red China into the United Nations, and the like, then the group compels an individual to support with his money causes beyond what gave rise to the need for group action.

I think the same must be said when union dues or assessments are used to elect a Governor, a Congressman, a Senator, or a President. . . . I do not see how that can be done, even though the objector retains his rights to campaign, to speak, to vote as he chooses. For when union funds are used for that purpose, the individual is required to finance political projects against which he may be in rebellion. The furtherance of the common cause leaves some leeway for the leadership of the group. As long as they act to promote the cause which justified bringing the group together, the individual cannot withdraw his financial support merely because he disagrees with the group's strategy. If that were allowed, we would be reversing the Hanson case, sub silentio. But since the funds here in issue are used for causes other than defraying the costs of collective bargaining, I would affirm the judgment below with modifications. Although I recognize the strength of the arguments advanced by my Brothers Black and Whittaker against giving a "proportional" relief to appellees in this case, there is the practical problem of mustering five Justices for a judgment in this case. Cf. Screws v. United States, 325 U.S. 91, 134. So I have concluded dubitante to agree to the one suggested by Mr. Justice Brennan, on the understanding that all relief granted will be confined to the six protesting employees. This suit, though called a "class" action, does not meet the requirements as the use or nonuse of any dues or assessments depends on the choice of each individual, not the group. See Hansberry v. Lee, 311 U.S. 32, 44.

Mr. Justice Whittaker, concurring in part and dissenting in part.

. . . I join Points I, II and III of the Court's opinion.

But I dissent from Point IV of the Court's opinion. In respect to that point, it seems appropriate to make the following observations. When many members pay the same amount of monthly dues into the treasury of the union which dispenses the fund for what are, under the Court's opinion, both permitted and proscribed activities, how can it be told whose dues paid for what? Let us suppose a union with two members, each paying monthly dues of three dollars, and that one does but the other does not object to his dues being expended for "proscribed activity" — whatever that phrase may mean. Of the dues for a given month, the union expends four dollars for admittedly proper activity and two dollars for "proscribed activity," answering to the objector that the two dollars spent for "proscribed activity" were not from his, but from the other's, dues. Would not the result be that the objector was thus required to pay not his one-half but three-fourths of the union's legitimate expenses? Or, has not the objector nevertheless paid a ratable part of the cost of the "proscribed activity"?

The Court suggests that a proper decree might require "restitution" to the objector of that part of his dues that is equal to the ratio of dues spent for "proscribed activity" to total dues collected by the union. But even if the Court could draw a clear line between what is and what is not "proscribed activity," the accounting and proof problems involved would make the remedy most onerous and impractical. But when there is added to this a full recognition of the practical impossibility of judicially drawing the clear line mentioned and also of the fact that the local unions which collect the dues promptly pay a part of them to the national union which, in turn, also engages in "proscribed activity," it becomes plain that the suggested restitution remedy is impossible of practical performance.

It would seem to follow that the only practical remedy possible is the one formulated by the Georgia courts, and I would approve it.

Mr. Justice Black, dissenting. . . .

I

Section 2, Eleventh of the Railway Labor Act authorizes unions and railroads to make union-shop agreements notwithstanding any other provision of state or federal law. Such a contract simply means that no person can keep a job with the contracting railroad unless he becomes a member of and pays dues to the contracting union. Neither §2, Eleventh nor any other part of the Act contains any implication or even a hint that Congress wanted to limit the purposes for which a contracting union's dues should or could be spent. All the parties to this litigation have agreed from its beginning, and still agree, that there is no such limitation in the Act. The Court nevertheless, in order to avoid constitutional questions, interprets the Act itself as barring use of dues for political purposes. In doing this I think the Court is once more "carrying the doctrine of avoiding constitutional questions to a wholly unjustifiable extreme." In fact, I think the Court is actually rewriting §2, Eleventh to make it mean exactly what Congress refused to make it mean. . . . I must consider this case on the basis of my belief as to the constitutionality of §2, Eleventh, interpreted so as to authorize compulsion of workers to pay dues to a union for use in advocating causes and political candidates that the protesting workers are against.

II

It is contended by the unions that precisely the same First Amendment question presented here was considered and decided in Railway

Employes' Dept. v. Hanson, 351 U.S. 225.　I agree that it clearly was not.　Section 2, Eleventh was challenged there before it became effective and the main grounds of attack, as our opinion noted, were that the union-shop agreement would deprive employees of their freedom of association under the First Amendment and of their property rights under the Fifth.　There were not in the Hanson case, as there are here, allegations, proof and findings that union funds regularly were being used to support political parties, candidates and economic and ideological causes to which the complaining employees were hostile. . . .　In a word, the Hanson case did not hold that the existence of union-shop contracts could be used as an excuse to force workers to associate with people they do not want to associate with, or to pay their money to support causes they detest. . . .

The Court holds that §2, Eleventh denies "unions, over an employee's objection, the power to use his exacted funds to support political causes which he opposes."　While I do not so construe §2, Eleventh, I want to make clear that I believe the First Amendment bars use of dues extorted from an employee by law for the promotion of causes, doctrines and laws that unions generally favor to help the unions, as well as any other political purposes.　I think workers have as much right to their own views about matters affecting unions as they have to views about other matters in the fields of politics and economics.　Indeed, some of their most strongly held views are apt to be precisely on the subject of unions, just as questions of law reform, court procedure, selection of judges and other aspects of the "administration of justice" give rise to some of the deepest and most irreconcilable differences among lawyers.　In my views, §2, Eleventh can constitutionally authorize no more than to make a worker pay dues to a union for the sole purpose of defraying the cost of acting as his bargaining agent.　Our Government has no more power to compel individuals to support union programs or union publications than it has to compel the support of political programs, employer programs or church programs.　And the First Amendment, fairly construed, deprives the Government of all power to make any person pay out one single penny against his will to be used in any way to advocate doctrines or views he is against, whether economic, scientific, political, religious or any other.

I would therefore hold that §2, Eleventh of the Railway Labor Act, in authorizing application of the union-shop contract to the named protesting employees who are appellees here, violates the freedom of speech guarantee of the First Amendment.

IV

The remedy: . . .

The decree requires the union to refund dues, fees and assessments paid under protest by three of the complaining employees and exempts the six complaining employees from the payment of any union dues, fees or assessments so long as funds so received are used by the union to promote causes they are against. . . . The Court's remedy is to give the wronged employees a right to a refund limited either to "the proportion of the union's total expenditures made for such political activities" or to the "proportion . . . (of) expenditures for political purposes which he had advised the union he disapproved." It may be that courts and lawyers with sufficient skill in accounting, algebra, geometry, trigonometry and calculus will be able to extract the proper microscopic answer from the voluminous and complex accounting records of the local, national and international unions involved. It seems to me, however, that while the Court's remedy may prove very lucrative to special masters, accountants and lawyers, this formula, with its attendant trial burdens, promises little hope for financial recompense to the individual workers whose First Amendment freedoms have been flagrantly violated. Undoubtedly, at the conclusion of this long exploration of accounting intricacies, many courts could with plausibility dismiss the workers' claims as de minimis when measured only in dollars and cents.

I cannot agree to treat so lightly the value of a man's constitutional right to be wholly free from any sort of governmental compulsion in the expression of opinions. . . . The three workers who paid under protest here were forced under authority of a federal statute to pay *all* current dues or lose their jobs. They should get back *all* they paid with interest. . . .

MR. JUSTICE FRANKFURTER, whom MR. JUSTICE HARLAN joins, dissenting. . . .

I completely defer to the guiding principle that this Court will abstain from entertaining a serious constitutional question when a statute may fairly be construed so as to avoid the issue, but am unable to accept the restrictive interpretation that the Court gives to §2, Eleventh of the Railway Labor Act. . . . The Court-devised precept against avoidable conflict with Congress through unnecessary constitutional adjudication is not a requirement to distort an enactment in order to escape such adjudication. Respect for the doctrine demands and only permits that we extract an interpretation which shies off constitutional controversy *provided* such interpretation is consonant with a fair reading of a statute.

And so the question before us is whether §2, Eleventh of the Railway Labor Act can untorturingly be read to bar activities of railway unions, which have bargained in accordance with federal law for a union shop, whereby they are forbidden to spend union dues for purposes that have uniformly and extensively been so long pursued as to have become commonplace, settled, conventional trade-union practices. No consideration relevant to construction sustains such a restrictive reading. . . .

. . . The aim of the 1951 legislation, clearly stated in the congressional reports, was to eliminate "free riders" in the industry — to make possible "the sharing of the burden of maintenance by all of the beneficiaries of union activity." To suggest that this language covertly meant to encompass any less than the maintenance of those activities normally engaged in by unions is to withdraw life from law and to say that Congress dealt with artificialities and not with railway unions as they were and as they functioned. . . .

For us to hold that these defendant unions may not expend their moneys for political and legislative purposes would be completely to ignore the long history of union conduct and its pervasive acceptance in our political life. American labor's initial role in shaping legislation dates back 130 years. With the coming of the AFL in 1886, labor on a national scale was committed not to act as a class party but to maintain a program of political action in furtherance of its industrial standards. British trade unions were supporting members of the House of Commons as early as 1867. The Canadian Trades Congress in 1894 debated whether political action should be the main objective of the labor force.[23] And in a recent Australian case, the High Court upheld the right of a union to expel a member who refused to pay a political levy.[24] That Britain, Canada and Australia have no explicit First Amendment is beside the point. For one thing, the freedoms safeguarded in terms in the First Amendment are deeply rooted and respected in the British tradition, and are part of legal presuppositions in Canada and Australia. And in relation to our immediate concern, the British Commonwealth experience establishes the pertinence of political means for realizing basic trade union interests.

The expenditures revealed by the AFL-CIO Executive Council Reports emphasize that labor's participation in urging legislation and candidacies is a major one. In the last three fiscal years, the Committee on Political Education (COPE) expended a total of $1,681,990.42; the AFL-CIO News cost $756,591.99; the Legislative Department reported total expenses of $741,918.24.[25] Yet the Georgia trial court has found that these funds were not reasonably related to the unions' role as collective bargaining agents. One could scarcely call this a finding of fact by which this Court is bound, or even one of law. It is a baseless dogmatic assertion that flies in the face of fact. It rests on a mere listing of unions' expenditures and an exhibit of labor publications. The passage of the Adamson Act in 1916, establishing the eight-hour day for the railroad industry, affords positive proof that labor may achieve its desired result through legislation after bargaining techniques fail. See Wilson v. New, supra, at 340-343. If higher wages and shorter hours are prime ends of a union in bargaining collectively, these goals may often be more effectively achieved by lobbying and the support of sympathetic candidates. In 1960 there were at least eighteen railway labor organizations registered as congressional lobby groups. . . .

In conclusion, then, we are asked by union members who oppose these expenditures to protect their right to free speech — although they are as free to speak as ever — against governmental action which has permitted a union elected by democratic process to bargain for a union shop and to expend the funds thereby collected for purposes which are controlled by internal union choice. To do so would be to mutilate a scheme designed

[23] Logan, Trade Unions in Canada, 59-60 (1948).
[24] William v. Hursey, 33 A.L.J.R. 269 (1959).
[25] These are the totals of the figures for 1957, 1958, and 1959 reported in Proceedings of the AFL-CIO Constitutional Convention, Vol. II, pp. 17-19 (1959) and id., pp. 17-19 (1957).

by Congress for the purpose of equitably sharing the cost of securing the benefits of union exertions; it would greatly embarrass if not frustrate conventional labor activities which have become institutionalized through time. To do so is to give constitutional sanction to doctrinaire views and to grant a miniscule claim constitutional recognition. . . .

I would reverse and remand the case for dismissal in the Georgia courts.

NOTE

On the same day that it decided the Street case, the Court handed down its decision in Lathrop v. Donohue, 367 U.S. 820 (1961). In the latter case the Wisconsin Supreme Court, pursuant to an Act of the state legislature, promulgated rules and bylaws creating an integrated state bar and requiring all lawyers practicing in the state to be members and to pay annual dues of $15. Appellant paid his dues under protest and sued for a refund, claiming that the state bar engaged in political activities which he opposed and that the rules and bylaws, by coercing his support, violated his rights under the Fourteenth Amendment. The Wisconsin Supreme Court held that compulsory enrollment in the state bar imposed only the duty to pay dues; it sustained the constitutionality of the rules and bylaws, and affirmed a judgment dismissing the complaint. The disposition of the appeal by the United States Supreme Court was scarcely conclusive, as is indicated by the following excerpt from the dissenting opinion of Mr. Justice Black (367 U.S. at 865-866):

"I do not believe that either the bench, the bar or the litigants will know what has been decided in this case — certainly I do not. Two members of the Court [Harlan and Frankfurter, JJ.], saying that 'the Constitutional issue is inescapably before us,' vote to affirm the holding of the Wisconsin Supreme Court that a State can, without violating the Federal Constitution, compel lawyers over their protest to pay dues to be used in part for the support of legislation and causes they detest. Another member [Whittaker, J.], apparently agreeing that the constitutional question is properly here, votes to affirm the holding of the Wisconsin Supreme Court because he believes that a State may constitutionally require a lawyer to pay a fee to its 'designee' as a condition to granting him the *'special privilege'* of practicing law, even though that 'designee,' over the lawyer's protest, uses part of the fee to support causes the lawyer detests. Two other members of the Court [Black and Douglas, JJ.] vote to reverse the judgment of the Wisconsin court on the ground that the constitutional question is properly here and the powers conferred on the Wisconsin State Bar by the laws of that State violate the First and Fourteenth Amendments. Finally, four members of the Court [Brennan, Clark, and Stewart, JJ., and Warren, C.J.] vote to affirm on the ground that the constitutional question is actually not here for decision at all. Thus the only proposition in this case for which there is a majority is that the constitutional question is properly here, and the five members of the Court who make up that majority express their views on this constitutional question. Yet a minority of four refuses to pass on the question and it is therefore left completely up in the air — the Court decides nothing. . . ."

BROTHERHOOD OF RAILWAY & STEAMSHIP CLERKS v. ALLEN

Supreme Court of the United States, 1963
373 U.S. 113, 83 Sup. Ct. 1158, 10 L. Ed. 2d 235

MR. JUSTICE BRENNAN delivered the opinion of the Court.

By the terms of an agreement (the Agreement) authorized by §2 Eleventh of the Railway Labor Act between the Southern Railway Company and a number of railway labor organizations including the two petitioners herein, employees of Southern are obligated, as a condition of employment, to pay the periodic dues, initiation fees and assessments uniformly required as a condition of acquiring or retaining membership in the union representing their particular class or craft.[2] The individual respondents herein are a number of such employees belonging to classes or crafts represented by petitioners.[3] When the Agreement was adopted respondents were not union members. They refused to pay petitioners any part of the moneys required under the Agreement, instead bringing this action in the Superior Court of Mecklenburg County, North Carolina, to restrain its enforcement.[4] After a trial the Superior Court

[2] Although the Agreement requires employees to become union members within the 60-day period, in fact petitioners do not insist that employees actually join the union, but regard payment of the uniform exactions required by the Agreement as complete compliance therewith.

[3] This action was commenced by 26 such employees but subsequent to the filing of the complaint 11 more were added as plaintiffs by amendment thereto; all 37 are respondents herein. Southern, which was a defendant below but disclaimed interest in the merits of the dispute between the employees and petitioners and did not appeal the Superior Court's judgment, appears in this Court as a respondent. In this opinion, the term "respondents" refers only to the individual respondents, and excludes Southern.

[4] The action was predicated in part on North Carolina's "right to work" law, which makes the union shop unlawful. N.C. Gen. Stats., §§95-78 to 95-84; but see Hudson v. Atlantic Coast Line R. Co., 242 N.C. 650, 89 S.E.2d 441. The complaint sought temporary and permanent injunctive relief on behalf of the named plaintiffs, respondents herein, and all other employees similarly situated, against Southern and every union representing employees of Southern. But the case was nonsuited as to all the defendant unions except petitioners when at trial no proof was offered that any of the plaintiffs belonged to crafts or classes other than those represented by petitioners. Also, the relief granted by the Superior Court in its final judgment was limited to "the plaintiffs, individually named as such in the caption of this case." This limitation was obviously proper and indeed required, since the instant "action is not a true class action, for there is no attempt to prove the existence of a class of workers who had specifically objected to the exaction of dues for political purposes." International Assn. of Machinists v. Street, 367 U.S. 740, 774. . . .

Upon commencement of the instant action, the plaintiffs obtained an ex parte order temporarily restraining enforcement of the union-shop agreement; after hearing, the order was continued in effect pendente lite, although it was subsequently modified to be "effective only for the protection of persons who are in-

granted an injunction upon the jury's separate findings that moneys exacted under the Agreement were used by petitioners for purposes not reasonably necessary or related to collective bargaining, namely, (1) to support or oppose legislation, (2) to influence votes in elections for public office, (3) to make campaign contributions in such elections, (4) to support the death-benefits system operated by petitioner Brotherhood of Railway Clerks. The injunction restrained petitioners "from placing any compulsion of any nature upon the [respondents] . . . whereby they . . . against their free will and choice would be required to join the Defendant Unions . . . or pay money to said Unions." It was provided, however, that upon a showing by petitioners of the proportion of expenditures from exacted funds that was reasonably necessary and related to collective bargaining, the injunction would be modified appropriately.

On appeal, the Supreme Court of North Carolina reversed, Allen v. Southern R. Co., 249 N.C. 491, 107 S.E.2d 125, holding that judgment for petitioners was required by our decision in Railway Employes' Dept. v. Hanson, 351 U.S. 225, where we held that §2 Eleventh was a valid exercise by Congress of its powers under the Commerce Clause and did not violate the First Amendment or the Due Process Clause of the Fifth. However, rehearing was granted, and pending decision thereon we decided International Assn. of Machinists v. Street, 367 U.S. 740. Upon reconsideration of the Superior Court's judgment in the light of that decision, the Supreme Court of North Carolina divided equally, which had the effect of affirming the lower court's judgment. 256 N.C. 700, 124 S.E.2d 871 (per curiam). . . . We granted certiorari, 371 U.S. 875, to consider whether the injunction granted by the Superior Court might stand consistently with our decision in Street. We reverse and remand for further proceedings not inconsistent with this opinion.

First. We held in Street "that §2, Eleventh is to be construed to deny the unions, over an employee's objection, the power to use his exacted funds to support political causes which he opposes." 367 U.S., at 768-769. Respondents' amended complaint alleges that sums exacted under the Agreement "have been and are and will be regularly and continually used by the defendant Unions to carry on, finance and pay for political activities directly at cross-purposes with the free will and choice of the plaintiffs." This allegation sufficiently states a cause of action. It would be impracticable to require a dissenting employee to allege and prove each distinct union political expenditure to which he objects; it is enough that he manifests his opposition to *any* political expenditures by the union.[5] But we made clear in Street that "dissent is not to be

---

dividually named as parties plaintiff herein or who become added by order of court as such within thirty days from date hereof." Even as modified, such relief was improper. . . .

[5] . . . In holding respondents' allegations and testimony adequately specific, we are not inconsistent with the plurality opinion in Lathrop v. Donohue, 367 U.S. 820, 845-846, where it was observed, in concluding that the question of the constitutionality of the integrated bar was not yet ripe for decision, that "(n)owhere are we clearly apprised as to the views of the appellant on any particular legisla-

presumed — it must affirmatively be made known to the union by the dissenting employee." 367 U.S., at 774. At trial, only 14 of the respondents testified that they objected to the use of exacted sums for political causes. No respondent who does not in the course of the further proceedings in this case prove that he objects to such use will be entitled to relief. This is not and cannot be a class action. See note 4, supra. "The union receiving money exacted from an employee under a union-shop agreement should not in fairness be subjected to sanctions in favor of an employee who makes no complaint of the use of his money for such activities." 367 U.S., at 774.

Second. We also held in Street that an injunction relieving dissenting employees of all obligation to pay the moneys due under an agreement authorized by §2 Eleventh was impermissible. Such employees "remain obliged, as a condition of continued employment, to make the payments to their respective unions called for by the agreement. Their . . . grievance stems from the spending of their funds for purposes not authorized by the Act in the face of their objection, not from the enforcement of the union-shop agreement by the mere collection of funds." 367 U.S., at 771. The injunction granted by the Superior Court was thus improper, even though it is subject to modification if petitioners come forward and prove the proportion of exacted funds required for purposes germane to collective bargaining. Even such a remedy, we think, "sweeps too broadly . . . (and) might well interfere with the . . . unions' performance of those functions and duties which the Railway Labor Act places upon them to attain its goal of stability in the industry." Ibid.

It also follows from Street that the Superior Court erred in granting respondents interim relief against compliance with the financial obligations imposed by the Agreement. As a result of this relief none of the respondents has taken any steps toward compliance since the suit was instituted. We think that lest the important functions of labor organizations under the Railway Labor Act be unduly impaired, dissenting employees (at least in the absence of special circumstances not shown here) can be entitled to no relief until final judgment in their favor is entered. Therefore, on remand respondents should be given a reasonable time within which they must pay to the bargaining representative of their class or craft all sums required under the Agreement, including arrears, that are owing; as to any respondent failing to do this, the action must be dismissed.

Third. We suggested in Street that among the permissible remedies for dissenting employees were "an injunction against expenditure for political causes opposed by each complaining employee of a sum, from those moneys to be spent by the union for political purposes, which is so much of the moneys exacted from him as is the proportion of the union's total expenditures made for such political activities to the union's total budget," and restitution of such a sum already exacted from the

tive issues on which the State Bar has taken a position. . . ." This observation was made in the context of *constitutional* adjudication, not statutory as here.

complainant and expended by the union over his objection. 367 U.S., at 774-775. The necessary predicate for such remedies is a division of the union's political expenditures from those germane to collective bargaining, since only the former, to the extent made from exacted funds of dissenters, are not authorized by §2 Eleventh. But at trial no evidence was offered by either side, nor was the jury required to make findings, as to the total amount of union expenditures for political purposes, the breakdown of the total union budget according to particular kinds of expenditure, or the proportion of political expenditures in the total union budget of a given period.[7] On remand, in order to frame a decree embodying the suggested remedies, two determinations will have to be made: (1) what expenditures disclosed by the record are political; (2) what percentage of total union expenditures are political expenditures. As to (1) we presently intimate no view, see note 7, supra, because here, as in Street, see 367 U.S., at 768-770, the courts below made no attempt to draw the boundary between political expenditures and those germane to collective bargaining, and it would be inappropriate for this Court to do so in the first instance and upon the present record. As to (2) the present record is insufficient to enable any calculation.

Since the unions possess the facts and records from which the proportion of political to total union expenditures can reasonably be calculated, basic considerations of fairness compel that they, not the individual employees, bear the burden of proving such proportion. Absolute precision in the calculation of such proportion is not, of course, to be expected or required; we are mindful of the difficult accounting problems that may arise. And no decree would be proper which appeared likely to infringe the unions' right to expend uniform exactions under the union-shop agreement in support of activities germane to collective bargaining and, as well, to expend nondissenters' such exactions in support of political activities.

Fourth. While adhering to the principles governing remedy which we announced in Street, see 367 U.S., at 771-775, we think it appropriate to suggest, in addition, a practical decree to which each respondent proving his right to relief would be entitled. Such a decree would order (1) the refund to him of a portion of the exacted funds in the same proportion that union political expenditures bear to total union expenditures, and (2) a reduction of future such exactions from him by the same proportion. We recognize that practical difficulties may attend a decree reducing an employee's obligations under the union-shop agreement by a fixed proportion, since the proportion of the union budget devoted to political activities may not be constant. The difficulties in judicially administered relief, although not insurmountable (a decree once entered would of course be modifiable upon a showing of changed circumstances), should, we think, encourage petitioner unions to con-

---

[7] We do conclude, however, without necessarily finding all the questions put to the jury proper for the purpose of distinguishing political expenditures from those germane to collective bargaining . . . or all the answers adequately supported by the evidence, that the verdict, fairly read, constitutes a finding for which there is adequate support in the record that petitioners use a part of the exacted funds in support of political causes.

sider the adoption by their membership of some voluntary plan by which dissenters would be afforded an internal union remedy. There is precedent for such a plan.[8] If a union agreed upon a formula for ascertaining the proportion of political expenditures in its budget, and made available a simple procedure for allowing dissenters to be excused from having to pay this proportion of moneys due from them under the union-shop agreement, prolonged and expensive litigation might well be averted. The instant action, for example, has been before the courts for 10 years and has not yet run its course. It is a lesson of our national history of industrial relations that resort to litigation to settle the rights of labor organizations and employees very often proves unsatisfactory. The courts will not shrink from affording what remedies they may, with due regard for the legitimate interests of all parties; but it is appropriate to remind the parties of the availability of more practical alternatives to litigation for the vindication of the rights and accommodation of interests here involved.

Reversed and remanded.

Mr. Justice Black, while adhering to the views he expressed in International Assn. of Machinists v. Street, 367 U.S. 740, 780-797, concurs in the judgment and opinion of the Court in this case because he believes both are in accord with the holding and opinion of the Court in the Street case.

Mr. Justice Goldberg took no part in the consideration or decision of this case.

Appendix to Opinion of the Court

The Trade Union Act of 1913, 2 & 3 Geo. V, c. 30, reads in part as follows:

---

[8] See Trade Union Act of 1913, 2 & 3 Geo. V, c. 30, reenacted by Trade Disputes and Trade Unions Act, 1946, 9 & 10 Geo. VI, c. 52; Comment, 19 U. of Chi. L. Rev. 371, 381-388 (1952); Rothschild, Government Regulation of Trade Unions in Great Britain: II, 38 Col. L. Rev. 1335, 1360-1366 (1938). Pertinent portions of the Act are set out in an Appendix at the end of this opinion. Although the Act is a legislative solution to the problem of dissenters' rights, it might be possible for unions to adopt the substantial equivalent without legislation; we do not mean to suggest, however, that the Act provides a perfect model for a plan that would conform with the discussion in this opinion and in Street, nor that all aspects of the English Act are essential, for example the actual segregation of political funds, nor that the particular boundary drawn by the Act between political expenditures and those germane to collective bargaining is necessarily sound. It may be noted that one possible solution to the problem of fluctuating union political expenditures . . . might be adoption by the union of a proportion calculated on the basis not of present political expenditures but projected future such expenditures, so as to anticipate possible fluctuations, with the dissenting employee free to contract out of this proportion of his dues and fees. Alternatively, unions might consider actually fixing a percentage ceiling of political expenditures, from which proportion dissenters could contract out. On the problem of remedies, see generally McAlister, Labor, Liberalism and Majoritarian Democracy, 31 Ford. L. Rev. 661, 687-693 (1963). Cf. Dudra, Approaches to Union Security in Switzerland, Canada, and Colombia, 86 Monthly Lab. Rev. 136 (1963).

3. — (1) The funds of a trade union shall not be applied, either directly or in conjunction with any other trade union, association, or body, or otherwise indirectly, in the furtherance of the political objects to which this section applies (without prejudice to the furtherance of any other political objects), unless the furtherance of those objects has been approved as an object of the union by a resolution for the time being in force passed on a ballot of the members of the union taken in accordance with this Act for the purpose by a majority of the members voting; and where such a resolution is in force, unless rules, to be approved, whether the union is registered or not, by the Registrar of Friendly Societies, are in force providing —

(*a*) That any payments in the furtherance of those objects are to be made out of a separate fund (in this Act referred to as the political fund of the union), and for the exemption in accordance with this Act of any member of the union from any obligation to contribute to such a fund if he gives notice in accordance with this Act that he objects to contribute; and

(*b*) That a member who is exempt from the obligation to contribute to the political fund of the union shall not be excluded from any benefits of the union, or placed in any respect either directly or indirectly under any disability or at any disadvantage as compared with other members of the union (except in relation to the control or management of the political fund) by reason of his being so exempt, and that contribution to the political fund of the union shall not be made a condition for admission to the union.

(2) If any member of a trade union alleges that he is aggrieved by a breach of any rule made in pursuance of this section, he may complain to the Registrar of Friendly Societies, and the Registrar of Friendly Societies, after giving the complainant and any representative of the union an opportunity of being heard, may, if he considers that such a breach has been committed, make such order for remedying the breach as he thinks just under the circumstances; and any such order of the Registrar shall be binding and conclusive on all parties without appeal and shall not be removable into any court of law or restrainable by injunction, and on being recorded in the county court, may be enforced as if it had been an order of the county court. . . .

(3) The political objects to which this section applies are the expenditure of money —

(*a*) on the payment of any expenses incurred either directly or indirectly by a candidate or prospective candidate for election to Parliament or to any public office, before, during, or after the election in connexion with his candidature or election; or

(*b*) on the holding of any meeting or the distribution of any literature or documents in support of any such candidate or prospective candidate; or

(*c*) on the maintenance of any person who is a member of Parliament or who holds a public office; or (*d*) in connection with the registration of electors or the selection of a candidate for Parliament or any public office; or

(*e*) on the holding of political meetings of any kind, or on the distribution of political literature or political documents of any kind, unless the main purpose of the meetings or of the distribution of the literature or documents is the furtherance of statutory objects within the meaning of this Act.

The expression "public office" in this section means the office of member of any county, county borough, district, or parish council, or board of guardians, or of any public body who have power to raise money, either directly or indirectly, by means of a rate.

(4) A resolution under this section approving political objects as an object of the union shall take effect as if it were a rule of the union and may be rescinded in the same manner and subject to the same provisions as such a rule.

(5) The provisions of this Act as to the application of the funds of a union for political purposes shall apply to a union which is in whole or in part an association or combination of other unions as if the individual members of the component unions were the members of that union and not the unions; but nothing in this Act shall prevent any such component union from collecting from any of their members who are not exempt on behalf of the association or combination any contributions to the political fund of the association or combination.

4. — (1) A ballot for the purposes of this Act shall be taken in accordance with rules of the union to be approved for the purpose, whether the union is registered or not, by the Registrar of Friendly Societies, but the Registrar of Friendly Societies shall not approve any such rules unless he is satisfied that every member has an equal right, and, if reasonably possible, a fair opportunity of voting, and that the secrecy of the ballot is properly secured.

(2) If the Registrar of Friendly Societies is satisfied, and certifies, that rules for the purpose of a ballot under this Act or rules made for other purposes of this Act which require approval by the Registrar, have been approved by a majority of members of a trade union, whether registered or not, voting for the purpose, or by a majority of delegates of such a trade union voting at a meeting called for the purpose, those rules shall have effect as rules of the union, notwithstanding that the provisions of the rules of the union as to the alteration of rules or the making of new rules have not been complied with.

5. — (1) A member of a trade union may at any time give notice, in the form set out in the Schedule to this Act or in a form to the like effect, that he objects to contribute to the political fund of the union, and, on the adoption of a resolution of the union approving the furtherance of political objects as an object of the union, notice shall be given to the members of the union acquainting them that each member has a right to be exempt from contributing to the political fund of the union, and that a form of exemption notice can be obtained by or on behalf of a member either by application at or by post from the head

office or any branch office of the union or the office of the Registrar of Friendly Societies.

Any such notice to members of the union shall be given in accordance with rules of the union approved for the purpose by the Registrar of Friendly Societies, having regard in each case to the existing practice and to the character of the union.

(2) On giving notice in accordance with this Act of his objection to contribute, a member of the union shall be exempt, so long as his notice is not withdrawn, from contributing to the political fund of the union as from the first day of January next after the notice is given, or, in the case of a notice given within one month after the notice given to members under this section on the adoption of a resolution approving the furtherance of political objects, as from the date on which the member's notice is given.

6. Effect may be given to the exemption of members to contribute to the political fund of a union either by a separate levy of contributions to that fund from the members of the union who are not exempt, and in that case the rules shall provide that no moneys of the union other than the amount raised by such separate levy shall be carried to that fund, or by relieving any members who are exempt from the payment of the whole or any part of any periodical contributions required from the members of the union towards the expenses of the union, and in that case the rules shall provide that the relief shall be given as far as possible to all members who are exempt on the occasion of the same periodical payment and for enabling each member of the union to know as respects any such periodical contribution, what portion, if any, of the sum payable by him is a contribution to the political fund of the union.

.   .   .   .   .

SCHEDULE

FORM OF EXEMPTION NOTICE

Name of Trade Union

POLITICAL FUND (EXEMPTION NOTICE)

I hereby give notice that I object to contribute to the Political Fund of the   Union, and am in consequence exempt, in manner provided by the Trade Union Act, 1913, from contributing to that fund.

A. B.
Address

day of   19

MR. JUSTICE HARLAN, concurring in part and dissenting in part.
I agree with the reversal of the interim and qualified permanent re-

lief that was granted by the state courts respecting the obligation to pay union dues. But I disagree with what in effect amounts to an affirmance of the state judgment in other respects. I believe that dismissal of this action in its entirety is called for.

International Assn. of Machinists v. Street, 367 U.S. 740, decided only two years ago, stated in unmistakable terms that a plaintiff claiming relief in an action of this kind must show two things: (1) that he had made known to the union the *particular* political candidates or causes for whose support he did not wish his union dues used; (2) that membership dues had been used for such purposes. . . .

These requirements have not been met in this case. At best all that has been alleged or proved is that the union *will* expend a part of each respondent's still-unpaid membership dues for so-called political or other purposes not connected with collective bargaining, and that each respondent would object to the use of any part of his dues for matters other than those relating to collective bargaining. None of the respondents who testified could specify any *particular* expenditure, or even class of expenditure, to which he objected.

I do not understand how, consistently with Street, the Court can now hold that "it is enough that . . . [a union member] manifests his opposition to *any* political expenditures by the union" . . . or how it can say that in so holding "we are not inconsistent with" what the plurality was at such pains to point out in Lathrop (albeit in a constitutional context), id., note 5. The truth of the matter is that the Court has departed from the strict substantive limitations of Street and has given them (and, as I see it, also that case's remedial limitations . . .) an expansive thrust which can hardly fail to increase the volume of this sort of litigation in the future.

Believing that our decisions should have more lasting power than has been accorded Street, I must respectfully dissent. I would reverse the judgment and remand the case for dismissal of the complaint.

B. ADMISSION TO UNION MEMBERSHIP

1. *The Right to Membership in the Bargaining Representative*

FRANK v. NATIONAL ALLIANCE OF BILL POSTERS
Supreme Court, New Jersey, 1916
89 N.J.L. 380, 99 Atl. 134

SWAYZE, J.

The defendants are an unincorporated organization, a trade union. They are not shown to have any property, and the plain question is whether the court will interfere by mandamus to compel the other members to receive the relator as a member. The question seems never to have been directly decided in this court. In Zeliff v. Knights of Pythias, 53 N.J. Law, 536, 22 Atl. 63, the local lodge was unincorporated, and the case turned upon the necessity of the relator seeking redress in the tribunals of the order before having recourse to the civil courts. The suggestion of the court that after appealing to the highest tribunal within the order, he might still sue for relief, and that the defendants would still be within reach of the mandatory writ, was not meant to be a decision that such writ would issue. The only authority cited was Sibley v. Carteret Club, 40 N.J. Law, 295, which was a case of a corporation, not a mere unincorporated association. The distinction between incorporated and unincorporated associations was pointed out by Vice Chancellor Emery in O'Brien v. Musical Mutual P & B Union, 64 N.J. Eq. 525, 532, 54 Atl. 150. . . . The reasons are well stated in the opinion by Jessel [in Rigby v. Connol, L.R. 14 Ch. Div. 482, 49 L.J. Ch. 328 (1880)]:

"The courts as such never dream of enforcing what I may call personal agreements, that is, agreements strictly personal in their nature, whether they are agreements of hiring and service, whether they are agreements of master and servant, or whether they are agreements for the purpose of pleasure or for the purpose of scientific pursuits, or for the purpose of charity or philanthropy. . . ."

He instances the case of a number of gentlemen meeting at each other's houses to play cards, or a number of scientific men meeting from time to time by agreement for scientific purposes. A like view was expressed by V. C. Green in Mayer v. Journeyman Stone-Cutters' Association, 47 N.J. Eq. 519, 20 Atl. 492, although the question there involved was different; two of the complainants who had never been members of the association sought to force an entrance without the aid of the court.

It would be quite impracticable for the courts to undertake to compel men to receive into their social relationships one who was personally disagreeable whether for a good or a bad reason. Property rights the court can deal with; rights in an unincorporated company are of that character, and the right of membership is ordinarily assignable. Voluntary associations are quite different. The courts can deal with property rights of such associations, if there are any, while they cannot, by a mandatory writ, intrude one man's companionship on another. The attempt to do so would be unavailing, as it would lead only to the disintegration of the association. We do not mean to deny the present relator's right to recover damages if his right to labor has been illegally interfered with. Brennan v. United Hatters, 73 N.J. Law, 9 Ann. Cas. 698. All we now decide is that mandamus is not a proper remedy.

The rule is discharged, with costs.

OLIPHANT v. BROTHERHOOD OF
LOCOMOTIVE FIREMEN AND ENGINEMEN

United States Court of Appeals, Sixth Circuit, 1958
262 F.2d 359, certiorari denied, 359 U.S. 935 (1959) [1]

PER CURIAM.

Appellants are Negro firemen who brought suit in the United States District Court for themselves and others similarly situated, seeking admission to membership in the Brotherhood of Locomotive Firemen and Enginemen whose constitution limits membership to applicants "white born." This appeal is from an order of the United States District Court denying the relief requested, for the reason that sufficient federal action was not present to subject the membership policies of the Appellee Brotherhood to judicial control. The opinion of the district court may be found at 156 F. Supp. 89; certiorari denied 355 U.S. 893.

The Brotherhood is and for many years has been designated, in accordance with the Railway Labor Act [45 U.S.C.A. §§151 et seq.], as the statutory bargaining representative for the locomotive firemen, hostlers, and hostler helpers, hereinafter collectively referred to as "firemen." A Negro fireman cannot become a member of the Brotherhood under existing provisions of the Brotherhood's Constitution, nor may any firemen who are not members of the Brotherhood attend meetings of its local lodges.

Appellants advance a double-barreled hypothesis, which roughly parallels the two judicial approaches to racial segregation in public education. Their first argument is that, inasmuch as racial exclusion from public schools is inherently a denial of the equal protection of the laws guaranteed by the Fourteenth Amendment (Brown v. Board of Education, 1954, 347 U.S. 483) and of due process of law guaranteed by the Fifth Amendment (Bolling v. Sharpe, 1954, 347 U.S. 497) it follows that denial of membership in the duly elected statutory bargaining representative, based upon race, is inherently incompatible with the rights afforded by the Fifth Amendment to the Constitution of the United States and by the equal protection and equal representation guaranteed to them by the doctrine of Steele v. Louisville and Nashville Railroad Co., 1944, 323 U.S. 192. There, the Supreme Court held that "the language of the (Railway Labor) Act . . . read in the light of the purposes of the Act, expresses the aim of Congress to impose on the bargaining representative of a craft or class of employees the duty to exercise fairly the power conferred upon it in behalf of all those for whom it acts, without hostile discrimination against them. . . ." 323 U.S. 192, 202-203. In short, appellants' first argument is that, as a matter of law, their constitutional rights and those enumerated in the Steele case are denied them as long as they are ineligible for membership in the exclusive col-

---

[1] The order denying certiorari states: "In view of the abstract context in which the questions sought to be raised are presented by this record, the petition for writ of certiorari . . . is denied." — ED.

lective bargaining agency which undertakes to represent their craft. They state in their brief: "Denial of voice and vote in the election of bargaining representatives and the formulation of bargaining objectives in and of itself denies Negro firemen equal representation."

If denial of membership in the Brotherhood is held to be not in violation of their rights as a matter of law, appellants assert that they are entitled to membership on a second and alternative ground. Cases decided under the earlier "separate but equal" doctrine of public schooling proscribed racial exclusion where in fact equal schooling was denied. See State of Missouri ex rel. Gaines v. Canada, 1938, 305 U.S. 337; Sweatt v. Painter, 1950, 339 U.S. 629. Analogizing their case to the stated doctrine, these appellants assert that the Brotherhood is in fact guilty of discriminatory practices and that the removal of the racial barrier to Brotherhood membership alone will afford them some measure of relief from discrimination.

In his carefully considered opinion, Chief Judge Paul Jones decided the facts pertaining to discrimination adversely to the contention of appellants. He stated the position of the Negro firemen to be that the "Brotherhood continues to exercise discrimination in its representation, particularly in (1) reducing the minimum mileage requirements for firemen, which has the effect of reducing the monthly income of the Negroes; (2) applying the 'gouge' rule in such a way as to reduce earnings of the Negroes; (3) applying the mileage rules to firemen and not to demoted engineers; and (4) bargaining for a compulsory retirement at age 70." (156 F. Supp. 90). The Judge continues: ". . . these alleged acts of discrimination will not be discussed in detail, but it should be noted that as to (3) above, proof was mainly in the form of opinion and was denied by Brotherhood officials, while (1), (2) and (4) are legitimate practices used by most unions for reasons other than discrimination, and since they apply to all who come within the terms of the rule involved, whether the individuals are white or colored, this court cannot state definitely that this Brotherhood adopted these practices for the purpose of discriminating against the Negroes." 156 F. Supp. 89, 90.

A meticulous examination of the detailed record in this case has been made by us, resulting in our opinion that the above findings of the district court are eminently correct and are supported by substantial evidence. There is, therefore, no occasion for further consideration of appellants' second argument.

Accordingly, we address ourselves solely to the contention advanced by the appellants that exclusion from membership in their collective bargaining representative based upon race is inherently a denial of their rights as a matter of law.

The appellee's authority as collective bargaining "representative" of the fireman craft is derived from the Railway Labor Act . . . The Brotherhood was duly elected as bargaining representative in accordance with provisions of the Act. Nowhere does the statute manifest the intention of Congress to establish criteria for membership in the bargaining representative. Nor can it be said that the attention of the

Congress was not directed to the fact that some craft members were being denied membership in certain railway labor organizations by virtue of their race. An amendment to the Act (later tabled) proposed to refuse certification to any such organization which denied membership on the basis of race. The able district judge observed: "Apparently the Act itself would not have been acceptable to the Congress if Negro membership in the agent had been required." 156 F. Supp. at page 93. The Supreme Court points out in its opinion in the Steele case, supra, that "the statute does not deny to such a bargaining labor organization the right to determine eligibility to its membership . . ." 323 U.S. at page 204. In our judgment, the language of the statute does not support reasonably any other interpretation.

A perusal of the Railway Labor Act makes it abundantly clear that no means of direct control over the actions of the agent selected by a majority of the craft was reserved by the statute to the individual employees. Apparently, the only supervision which any individual may exercise over the duly-elected bargaining representative is the threat of casting his vote in favor of a different representative at a subsequent election. The objective of Congress was industrial tranquility in the arteries of commerce. In choosing the method by which this goal could be achieved, it was deemed necessary to take from individual employees the right to negotiate their own contracts of employment. The question presented on the record before us is whether or not the Congress transcended the constitutionally protected rights of individual employees when it stripped them of their bargaining privileges as individuals and conferred that function upon a majority-elected representative, over which the individual has no direct control and in which he is not eligible for membership. It is not contended that the Negro firemen are deprived of their voting rights in the election of a bargaining representative. Their complaint is that they are a minority group whose rights are abridged, for the reason that, as a result of their ineligibility for membership in the appellee Brotherhood, they have no control over the internal affairs of the representative elected by the majority.

Although these proceedings have been punctuated by accusations of racial discrimination, it would seem that we are really concerned only with ascertaining the rights of any person who, for any reason, finds himself in a minority or out-voted status, the issue of actual discrimination by the Brotherhood having been subtracted from the issue by the findings of the district judge, as hereinbefore stated. Various facets of the collective bargaining process involving the rights of the minority have already been litigated before the Supreme Court. That tribunal has decided against the validity of agreements respecting changes of pay negotiated by individuals after pay rates had been established by collective agreement. Order of Railroad Telegraphers v. Railway Express Agency, 321 U.S. 342.

Individual contracts of employment have been held to be superseded by collective agreements subsequently entered into by the employer and the craft representative. J. I. Case Co. v. N.L.R.B., 321 U.S. 332. There, the Supreme Court discussed at length the underlying principles of the collective bargaining process, with no indication of Constitutional infirmity: "The very purpose of providing by statute for the collective agreement is to supersede the terms of separate agreements of employees with terms which reflect the strength and bargaining power and serve the welfare of the group. Its benefits and advantages are open to every employee of the represented unit, whatever the type or terms of his pre-existing contract of employment. . . . The workman is free, if he values his own bargaining position more than that of the group, to vote against representation; but the majority rules, and if it collectivizes the employment bargain, individual advantages or favors will generally in practice go in as a contribution to the collective result." 321 U.S. 332, 338, 339.

There are other decisions of the Supreme Court approving Acts of Congress which, in a limited way, interfere with the right of an individual to negotiate for employment-contract provisions palatable to his individual taste. On the subject of the power of the Congress to facilitate the flow of interstate commerce by enacting the union shop amendments to the Railway Labor Act, the highest tribunal said: "Industrial peace along the arteries of commerce is a legitimate objective; and Congress has great latitude in choosing the methods by which it is to be obtained. . . . The task of the judiciary ends once it appears that a legislative measure adopted is relevant or appropriate to the constitutional power which Congress exercises. The ingredients of industrial peace and stabilized labor-management relations are numerous and complex. They may well vary from age to age and from industry to industry. What would be needful one decade might be anathema the next. The decision rests with the policy makers, not with the judiciary." Railway Employes' Department v. Hanson, 351 U.S. 225, 233, 234.

The wisdom of this policy of judicial self-restraint was recognized here in the opinion of the United States District Court: ". . . To compel by judicial mandate membership in voluntary organizations where the Congress has knowingly and expressly permitted the bargaining agent to prescribe its own qualifications for membership would be usurping the legislative function. The Congress has entered the field of, and made provision for, labor relations and furnished means of adjusting labor disputes between employers and employees of interstate railways. For injustices due to discrimination or inadequate representation and participation to employees who are not members of the bargaining agent, the employees must look to the legislative, not the judicial branch of constitutional government." 156 F. Supp. 89, 93.

The Fifth Amendment to the Constitution of the United States protects the fundamental rights of individuals from invasion by federal governmental action. Unlike the Fourteenth, that amendment contains no equal protection guarantee. See Chas. C. Steward Machine Co. v. Davis, 1937, 301 U.S. 548, 584; Hirabayashi v. United States, 1943, 320 U.S. 81, 100. Appellants insist that we, by interpretation, should expand the due process clause of the Fifth Amendment to encompass an equal protection guarantee in the same manner that the Supreme Court recently accomplished that result in the field of public education, in Bolling v. Sharpe, 347 U.S. 497. Assuming (without deciding) that we should place such an interpretation on the Fifth Amendment, appellants, in our judgment, are still not entitled to the relief sought, for the reason that this record does not show an agency of the federal government to have been responsible for appellants' plight.

The accusing finger is pointed at the Congress. Only one analysis could tend to lay the responsibility for appellants' situation on our national legislative branch of government: that is, the violation of the Fifth Amendment by the Congress, in its enactment of the Railway Labor Act without including therein a provision requiring a labor union — when duly elected as collective bargaining representative of a craft — to extend membership privileges to all members of the craft, regardless of race. We cannot accept this fine-spun hypothesis, which charges the Congress with federal action of a type proscribed by the Fifth Amendment.

Recent decisions of the Supreme Court in the field of administration of public schooling are not analogous to the instant case. Brown v. Board of Education and Bolling v. Sharpe, supra, were predicated on the fact that *affirmative* legislation of the states and the District of Columbia, respectively, denied Negroes access to schools supported by public tax funds. These decisions are not applicable here.

The Brotherhood is a private association, whose membership policies are its own affair, and this is not an appropriate case for interposition of judicial control. A decision to the contrary could be frustrated by the simple expedient of the majority's electing directly those individuals presently designated by the union to negotiate with the employer railroads. There is no requirement that employees be represented by persons of the same race. In National Federation of Railway Workers v. National Mediation Board, 71 App. D.C. 266, 110 F.2d 529, 538, certiorari denied 310 U.S. 628; it was said that "under the Act, employees are guaranteed the right to select a common bargaining representative and that representative may be a person of any race or color (or an association made up of persons of any race or color). The quality of opportunity thus guaranteed is the complete antithesis of discrimination. To hold that colored employees could be represented only by colored persons for bargaining purposes would be to introduce into the administration of the Act the very discrimination which the Federation seeks to avoid."

For the reasons, stated herein and those found in the opinion of the United States District Judge, the judgment is affirmed.[2]

NOTES

1. The proviso to Section 8(b)(1)(A) of the NLRA states that "this paragraph [which makes it unlawful for a union to restrain or coerce employees in the exercise of Section 7 rights] shall not impair the right

[2] For a discussion of the Oliphant case and the questions raised, see Wellington, The Constitution, The Labor Union, and "Governmental Action," 70 Yale L.J. 345 (1961). — ED.

of a labor organization to prescribe its own rules with respect to the acquisition or retention of membership therein." Until recently, this proviso has operated to free unions of any NLRB supervision of admission (or expulsion) policies other than as specifically required by Section 8(a)(3)'s union-shop proviso (restrictive union membership policies may not be made grounds for discharge of an employee not a member of a union under a union-shop contract unless the employee is denied union membership because of nonpayment of dues or initiation fees) and Section 8(b)(5)'s prohibition against "excessive or discriminatory" initiation fees with respect to employees working under a union-shop contract. See, e.g., NLRB, 15th Ann. Rep. 129 (1950). However, in Hughes Tool Co., 147 N.L.R.B. No. 166 (1964), the Board rescinded the certification of a union as collective bargaining representative because, inter alia, it "discriminated on the basis of race in determining eligibility for full and equal membership, and segregated . . . members [into separate locals] on the basis of race." The Board expressly overruled its prior decisions to the contrary.

2. The Labor-Management Reporting and Disclosure Act of 1959 does not deal with the matter of admission to union membership. Title I, Bill of Rights of Members of Labor Organizations, deals only with the rights of *members*. The following amendment, proposed by Congressman Adam Clayton Powell, was defeated in the House: ". . . no labor organization shall . . . refuse membership, segregate or expel any person on the grounds of race, religion, color, sex, or national origin." 105 Cong. Rec. 15721, August 12, 1959.

For a discussion of the pertinent legislative history and the definition of "member" in Section 3(o) of the LMRDA, see Hughes v. Local 11, International Assn. of Bridge, Structural and Ornamental Ironworkers, 287 F.2d 810 (3d Cir. 1961), cert. denied, 368 U.S. 829.

2. Statutory Prohibition of Discrimination in Union Membership

CIVIL RIGHTS ACT OF 1964, TITLE VII,
§703(c) and (d) [3]
78 Stat. 255, 42 U.S.C. §2000e - 2

(c) It shall be an unlawful employment practice for a labor organization —

(1) to exclude or to expel from its membership, or otherwise to discriminate against, any individual because of his race, color, religion, sex, or national origin;

(2) to limit, segregate, or classify its membership, or to classify or fail to refuse to refer for employment any individual, in any way which would deprive or tend to deprive any individual of employ-

---

[3] The full text of Title VII ("Equal Employment Opportunity") is printed in the Reference Supplement, page 77. — Ed.

ment opportunities, or would limit such employment opportunities or otherwise adversely affect his status as an employee or as an applicant for employment, because of such individual's race, color, religion, sex, or national origin; or

(3) to cause or attempt to cause an employer to discriminate against an individual in violation of this section.

(d) It shall be an unlawful employment practice for any employer, labor organization, or joint labor-management committee controlling apprenticeship or other training or retraining, including on-the-job training programs to discriminate against any individual because of his race, color, religion, sex, or national origin in admission to, or employment in, any program established to provide apprenticeship or other training.

STATE COMMISSION FOR HUMAN RIGHTS
v. FARRELL
Supreme Court, New York, 1964
43 Misc. 2d 958, 252 N.Y.S.2d 649

MARKOWITZ, J. . . .

Pursuant to section 298 of the Executive Law, the State Commission for Human Rights has brought this proceeding seeking enforcement of its order affecting employment practices[1] in the sheet metal industry. The order of the commission, in essence, found that the respondent union, Local 28 of the Sheet Metal Workers International Association of Greater New York (hereinafter referred to as "Local 28"), and the Joint Apprenticeship Committee[2] (hereinafter referred to as "JAC")

[1] Proceedings herein were commenced by complaint of the Attorney-General of the State of New York to the commission, pursuant to section 297 of the Executive Law of the State of New York. The complaint charged violation of section 296 (subd. 1, par. [b]; subds. 1-a, 6) which provide:

"§296. Unlawful discriminatory practices.   1. It shall be an unlawful discriminatory practice: . . .

"(b) For a labor organization, because of the age, race, creed, color or national origin of any individual, to exclude or to expel from its membership such individual or to discriminate in any way against any of its members or against any employer or any individual employed by an employer.

"1-a. It shall be an unlawful discriminatory practice for an employer, labor organization, employment agency or any joint labor-management committee controlling apprentice training programs: . . .

"(b) To deny to or withhold from any person because of his race, creed, color or national origin the right to be admitted to or participate in a guidance program, an apprenticeship training program, on-the-job training program, or other occupational training or retraining program;

"(c) To discriminate against any person in his pursuit of such programs or to discriminate against such a person in the terms, conditions or privileges of such programs because of race, creed, color or national origin. . . .

"6. It shall be an unlawful discriminatory practice for any person to aid, abet, incite, compel or coerce the doing of any of the acts forbidden under this article, or to attempt to do so."

The order of the commission was issued in conformity with section 297.

[2] The Joint Apprenticeship Committee, containing equal union and employer representation, was created by the parties to supervise and control all duly quali-

denied to or withheld from qualified Negroes and other minority groups the right to be admitted to and participate in the sheet metal apprentice program, under their control, solely because of race and color. The order further found that the individual respondents herein, who are employer members of the JAC, aided and abetted the other respondents in denying qualified Negroes the right to enroll in the apprenticeship program. By separate motions, Local 28 is seeking review of said order, and the individual respondents seek to set aside said order as it affects them individually.

The commission found that Local 28, consisting of 3,300 members and 430 apprentices, has never had nor does it presently have a Negro member, nor has any Negro participated in the JAC training program. The only realistic way of becoming a member of Local 28 is through the JAC program. The commission further found that, in the most recently completed training program, 80% of the trainees were related in some manner to the members of Local 28. The commission also found that admission to the apprenticeship training program was not based upon any set of objective standards. No provision existed safeguarding any applicant against discrimination because of race, color, creed or national origin. Nor was there any provision entitling an applicant to seek review of a rejection of his application for training.

The court concludes that the findings of the commission, except as hereinafter noted, are supported by substantial evidence on the record considered as a whole. The findings are therefore conclusive (Executive Law, §298; Matter of Holland v. Edwards, 307 N.Y. 38, 44, 45; Matter of Stork Restaurant v. Boland, 282 N.Y. 256, 274). The enforcement procedures set forth in the commission's order thus are the remaining issues for consideration.

The court approaches this matter not simply as litigation between private parties, but rather views the instant proceedings as raising vital matters filled with greatest public concern. The issue herein, involving the development of nondiscriminatory shop-training programs, cannot be approached strictly within the conventional confines of an adversary proceeding. The people of this State, as well as groups throughout the country, are searching for guidelines in the handling of this volatile problem. To that end, the court enlisted the co-operation of the parties.

The court arranged conferences with all parties and governmental agencies concerned, in the hope that the desirable objectives might be achieved by conciliation and agreement rather than solely by force of law.[2a] Numerous and extended conferences were held throughout the

---

fied apprentices. It is required under the Standard Form of Union Agreement, the collective bargaining agreement governing the industry, to formulate and make operative rules to govern the conditions pertaining to duly qualified apprentices and the operation of an adequate apprentice training system.

[2a] This is in keeping with the spirit of the law against discrimination, which, rather than providing for the usual procedures for review of administrative agency determinations (see CPLR art. 78), has incorporated provisions giving

Summer in an attempt to achieve the adoption of acceptable standards for an apprentice training program which would carry out the spirit and the intent of the law against discrimination (Executive Law, art. 15) and the principles of equality which are fundamental to both our Federal and State Constitutions and systems of law. Represented and participating at the conferences were the commission, the employers, the union officials involved, the Industrial Commissioner and the Attorney-General. From time to time each of the parties requested a conference with the court, jointly or severally, while the standards for the joint apprenticeship program consonant with the court's directions were being formulated.

From the inception of these proceedings and conferences, the court advised the parties that it could not recognize any plan as acceptable unless it truly afforded every applicant for admission to the apprenticeship program equal opportunity, nor would any plan be approved that did not abolish the existing practice of favoritism because of family affiliation, or did not provide for a complete and fair review procedure, or made it economically difficult for an applicant to qualify, or incorporated unreasonable educational requirements, or which in any other way would prevent equal opportunity under objective standards or selection on any basis other than the basis of qualification alone.

The court recognized that the issue before it involved the foundations of our democracy. Judicial decisions, legislative enactments, and events in the world outside the courtroom demonstrate that today's crucial testing ground for the American system of democracy is in the area of equal rights for its Negro citizens. Equality for our minority groups — the right to equal job opportunity, the right to equal educational opportunities, the right to equal housing opportunities, and the right to vote — is the essence of democracy today. . . . There must be a moral awareness and a greater concern for human rights and dignity and the dignity of man. Industry, labor, government at all levels, and the public at large must embrace this basic concept.

The legal profession has recognized the urgency of achieving racial equality in conformity with law and order.[5] As President Johnson has

---

the Supreme Court complete jurisdiction of the proceeding and the power to grant such temporary or permanent relief as it deems just and proper (see Right to Equal Treatment: Administrative Enforcement of Antidiscrimination Legislation, 74 Harv. L. Rev, 526 et seq.).

[5] ". . . The third basic principle is that lawyers should lead in assuring the legal rights of all citizens. They are equipped by training, experience and skill to resolve disputes on a basis of reasonable adjustment, rather than emotion and violence, but they must undertake more active roles both individually and in association than heretofore. We commend the efforts of the Lawyers' Committee for Civil Rights Under Law, to resolve the nation's racial problems, and we urge all local bar associations to study what needs to be done in their own areas, and to furnish leadership in accomplishing it. The Lawyers' Committee urges local bar aid in two particular fields — establishing bi-racial committees to seek solutions to civil rights problems, and seeing that all persons in civil rights controversies can obtain competent legal counsel. When a citizen takes the law into his own hands by wilfully violating it, the result is nothing less than anarchy and must never be condoned by an emotional misjudgment that the end justifies the

recently said: "The denial of rights invites increased disorder and violence and those who would hold back progress toward equality and at the same time promise racial peace are deluding themselves and deluding the people. Orderly progress, exact enforcement of the law are the only paths to an end of racial strife." (Address to the American Bar Association, Aug. 12, 1964.)

There is perhaps no right more important for the achievement of equality than the right to learn how to perform a job. The Court of Appeals has recently noted that discrimination in employment, with its consequent economic disparities upon which other kinds of discrimination thrive, is the "main key" to the problem of ending discrimination based on race and creed. (Matter of Board of Higher Educ. of City of N.Y. v. Carter, 14 N.Y.2d 138.) Denial of the right to be trained in many industries is tantamount to denial of employment. Discrimination based upon race which effectively excludes a minority from the right to be employed in a particular industry has been condemned by the courts. (See, e.g., Kelly v. Simons, 87 N.Y.S.2d 767, 770; James v. Marinship Corp., 25 Cal. 2d 721 [1944]; Todd v. Joint Apprenticeship Comm., 223 F. Supp. 12, revd. on other grounds 332 F.2d 243 [1964]; cf. Gaynor v. Rockefeller, 21 A.D.2d 92, 100.)

Independent of judicial precedent, this court enunciates the principle that it will not countenance discrimination in job training programs which exclude the victimized minority from employment in industry. As noted above, consideration of the issue herein must realistically acknowledge the keystone position of equality in job opportunity (and as a prerequisite thereof equality in job training and apprenticeship opportunities) [7] for achievement of full equality required in our democracy. . . .

The court notes that the history of the American labor movement reveals a continuing concern by its major branches and spokesmen for the achieving of equality for all.[8] The concern of American labor for equal-

---

means. Resentment of illegal demonstrations should not be an excuse for relaxing the efforts of the white community to promote racial justice. Local bar associations can help clarify fundamental legal issues as a contribution to public discourse."

Statement unanimously adopted by the Executive Committee of the New York State Bar Association, June 15, 1964.

[7] In 1959 unemployment averages for whites were at a level of 4.6% while for nonwhites the averages were as high as 11.5%. This disparity in unemployment rates has been attributed to the inadequate participation of Negroes in apprenticeship training. The Economic Situation for Negroes in the United States, 1960 Report by U.S. Dept. of Labor. — 25% of the male Negro teenagers who are in the labor force are unemployed. (Unpublished Gov't statistics Aug. 22, 1964.)

[8] a. As early as 1866, at the convention of the National Labor Congress, it was said that if the union "be misled by prejudice or passion as to refuse to aid the spread of union principles among our fellow toilers, we would be untrue to them . . . to ourselves . . . If these general principles be correct, we must seek cooperation of the African race in America." A. C. Cameron, "The Address of The National Labor Congress to the Workingmen of the United States." (Reprinted

ity has increased with the passing years. Particularly relevant to the instant case has been the attention that the labor movement has given to the problem of discrimination in apprenticeship programs. George Meany, President of the AFL-CIO, declared before a Special Subcommittee of the House Committee on Education and Labor in 1961:[9] "What we need in this country is genuine equality of opportunity for all citizens regardless of race, creed, color or national origin. Let's grant that apprenticeships are a problem; fine, let's act on that problem. But apprenticeship is only a part of a much broader problem." [10]

In June of 1963,[11] the general presidents of the unions affiliated with the Building and Construction Trades Department, AFL-CIO, adopted a program which included the following provision: "4. With regard to the application for, or employment of apprentices, local unions shall accept and refer such applicants in accordance with their qualifications and there shall be no discrimination as to race, creed, color or national origin."

Nevertheless, discrimination does exist. It is with the effective and wise eradication of the manifestations of unwarranted prejudice in the apprenticeship program in the sheet metal industry in the City of New York that this court is concerned in the instant proceeding.

With respect to the plan proposed, Local 28 made a forceful presentation in favor of attaching some preference to those applicants who are sons or sons-in-law of present or deceased members of the Union. The court recognizes that the practice of giving some preference to applicants with filial ties to union members is widespread and dates back to the very inception of craft unions when craftsmen first joined together in guilds. The historic, economic and social reasons for the practice of filial preference and its beneficial effects have been urged by the union and examined by the court.

Under the realities of today's society, the guarantee of equal protection of the laws and the prohibition against discrimination contained in section 11 of article I of the New York Constitution requires that this

---

in Commons, et al., Documentary History of American Society, vol. 9, pp. 141-168.)

b. One year later, Uriah Stephens, of the Knights of Labor, the forerunner of the American Federation of Labor, declared that he could see ahead of him "an organization . . . that will include men and women of every craft, creed and color." (Commons, et al., vol. 2, p. 167.)

[9] United States Cong. House Comm. on Educ. and Labor, Equal Opportunity in Apprenticeship Program Hearing, 87th Cong., 1st Sess. (Aug. 1961), on H.R. 8219.

[10] The model union pledge, signed in 1962 by 116 national unions and 300 directly chartered labor unions, representing about 11 million workers, declares in unambiguous terms: "We shall seek agreement from management to write into joint apprenticeship training programs in which we participate a non-discrimination clause in regard to admission and conditions of employment of apprentices and shall see that this clause is administered in such a way as to give full and effective application of non-discrimination throughout all such training."

[11] Press Release of the Building and Construction Trades Dept., AFL-CIO, June 21, 1963, p. 2.

court refuse to sanction any plan which could be used, directly or indirectly, to discriminate against any person on the basis of race, color, creed or national origin. The 1964 amendments to the Executive Law and Labor Law apply this principle directly to the area before the court — apprenticeship training programs. The court concludes that provision in this apprenticeship training program for preference or credit because of filial relation would be illegal and unconstitutional and so advised the parties and the Industrial Commissioner.

In addition to the overriding constitutional and legislative declarations of equality, the court believes that filial preference is contrary to modern day societal objectives concerning job qualifications. No lawyer or doctor today would expect his son to receive preference by reason of family relationship in applying for admission to the Bar or for a medical license. Admission to a profession or industry based exclusively upon the applicant's qualifications to perform in the profession or industry as determined by objective criteria is to be encouraged.

The court was also concerned that the original proposed plan did not provide for adequate review procedures to an applicant, and directed appropriate amendments.

In the fourth completed draft, the parties submitted a new plan whereby an applicant, after he has exhausted his right to review before the Joint Apprenticeship Committee, may obtain further review by a member of a panel chosen by the Presiding Justice of the Appellate Division of the First Department. After consultation, the Presiding Justice graciously consented to perform this function.

The court was also concerned with the fact that educational standards higher than were reasonably necessary might be adopted. To this end, the court suggested a graduated system which would be fair to minority groups and at the same time discourage high school drop-outs, while nevertheless meeting the minimum scholastic requirements for an apprenticeship trainee. Under the court's suggestion, an apprenticeship trainee for the 1965-66 programs would be required to have completed two years of high school work or its equivalent; for the 1967-68 programs, a three-year requirement or its equivalent would be necessary, and thereafter a completed high school course or its equivalent would be mandatory. The plan as finally adopted is sufficiently flexible to meet these suggestions, and if need be will be supplemented in the final order of the court.

The question of applicant fees was also considered. In order to avert an economic barrier, it was urged by the court that such fees be kept to a minimum or even eliminated. However, it is recognized that administrative and medical examination costs might make it necessary to require an apprenticeship applicant to defray some of the expenses. Accordingly, the accepted plan adopted a provision whereby such cost would never exceed the amount of $10.

The problem pertaining to the 430 individuals on the present apprenticeship list was resolved by providing that they and all other applicants shall be accorded equal treatment in determining their eligibility to be appointed to the apprenticeship training program and be judged by the same set of objective standards. Further, it is provided that no preferential treatment shall be given to either those who apply for admission de novo or those who have applied heretofore.

Another question which remained before the court is whether the individual respondents acted as individuals or solely in their representative capacities. This is important in view of the possible sanctions. Were it not for the complete co-operation given by all of the individuals to the establishment of a nondiscriminatory joint apprenticeship training program, the court might well have found that the record was susceptible of sustaining the finding holding the individuals responsible in their individual capacities as well as in their representative capacities. The court, however, is not unaware of the private economic and social forces that operate to compel individuals to follow the course of least resistance, frequently on the theory that it is only committee responsibility and not individual responsibility which they assume. In a situation such as the present one, none of the employer members of the committee receives compensation for his services, nor do they as individuals benefit from the committee responsibility which they carry out. The court recognizes that industry/union committees are desirable, if not vital, to the harmonious working out of industry-wide labor problems. The court is convinced that the individual respondents are in favor of the underlying theory of equality of opportunity in job training. The court finds that the representatives of industry and labor act both in their individual as well as in their representative capacities. However, under the circumstances of the entire case, the court will not affirm those findings of the commission against the individuals themselves as to their prior conduct and past acts. . . .

In addition to the matters heretofore alluded to, the final plan generally provides for the selection of apprentices without regard to race, creed, color, national origin, or physical or psychological handicaps provided the latter two do not interfere with the applicant's ability to perform. Apprentices must be selected on the basis of qualifications alone, and all applicants will be afforded equal opportunity under the adopted standards. A rejected applicant is to be notified and the reasons given therefor with the right to appeal. A rejected applicant may reapply. The age prerequisites are 18 to 23 with some modifications. Medical and physical examinations are required. Aptitude tests are to be given by the New York City Testing Center or equivalent testing center. Two hundred per cent of the number of apprentices ultimately to be appointed who have achieved the highest rating in an independently conducted aptitude test will be interviewed. The interviewing board is to consist equally of representatives of labor and industry. The maximum point score one can achieve on the test will be 750, and on the interview 150. Appointments will be made solely and exclusively on the point score. The term of apprenticeship will be four years (approximately 7,000 hours) of reasonably continuous employment, divided into eight periods. On-the-job instruction will be given in specified areas, and trainees will be required to attend formal classes one day every second week with pay. Tuition fees for such instruction are provided for, as well as periodic examinations. The plan annexed hereto also embodies other aspects. Not specifically included in the plan, but agreed to by the parties, is a requirement for publicizing the program in the schools and through other channels and media making it clear that it is open to all who are interested and can meet the objective standards. The publicity requirements will be incorporated in the order to be settled hereon. The next apprenticeship class will be in January or February, 1965, and be under the plan adopted herein.

The plan herein adopted was the result of the unusual co-operative spirit on the part of the commission, industry, union officials, their respective counsel and the Attorney-General. The court expresses its appreciation to the aforenamed parties. The court accepts the plan because it is enlightened, progressive and in accordance with the principles of nondiscrimination, equality of opportunity and on the basis of qualification alone under objective standards.

It is hopefully expected from the effective implementation of this program a truly nondiscriminating union will emerge. A rare opportunity is afforded to this industry to serve as a model for others, and, by rigid adherence to the adopted standards, itself become a standard of morality and brotherhood, equal opportunity and democracy.

The objective standards herein adopted for the apprenticeship program in the sheet metal industry of New York City may well be a model for State-wide utilization by the New York State Industrial Commissioner, who is mandated to promulgate rules and regulations implementing chapter 948 of the Laws of 1964.[14]

In summary, the commission's findings and affirmative provisions of its order are adopted except as to finding No. 66 as modified and as to the cease and desist order by striking the second decretal paragraph as heretofore indicated in this opinion.

---

[14] Amendments to the Executive Law and the Labor Law of New York in relation to equality of opportunity in apprenticeship training will become effective on the 1st of September, 1964. (L. 1964, ch. 948.) Section 296 of the Executive Law is amended by adding an express provision that it shall be an unlawful discriminatory practice for any joint labor management committee controlling apprentice training programs: "(a) To select persons for an apprentice training program registered with the State of New York on any basis other than their qualifications, as determined by objective criteria which permit review."

Subdivision 5 of section 815 of the Labor Law has been concurrently amended so as to provide that suggested standards for apprenticeship agreements include: "5. Provision that apprentices shall be selected on the basis of qualifications alone, as determined by objective criteria which permit review and without any direct or indirect limitation, specification or discrimination as to race, creed, color or national origin."

These two legislative amendments along with the enactment of title 7 (Equal Employment Opportunity) of the Civil Rights Act of 1964 (78 Stat. 241 et seq., Public Law 88-352) which makes it an unlawful employment practice to discriminate on the basis of race in any apprenticeship program, evince the fact that apprentice systems have not heretofore been dedicated to the principle of equality. Both the State and Federal legislation is directed to the same end of abolishing discrimination in the apprentice programs.

At the request of the parties, the court is retaining jurisdiction. An interim order including findings consistent with this opinion will be settled hereon.[4]

NOTES

1. Would there be an unlawful employment practice under Section 703 of the Civil Rights Act of 1964, supra, *if* the qualified applicants for the Sheet Metal Apprentice Program were white, male, American-born protestants of Anglo-Saxon descent who were denied the opportunity to participate in the program solely because they were not sons or sons-in-law of present or deceased members of the union?

2. If the qualified Negro applicants in the Farrell case were denied the opportunity to participate on the ground that they were Black Muslims or that they were Communists, would there be an unlawful employment practice under Section 703? Consult Sections 703(e) and (f).

3. What is the jurisdictional relationship of a state human rights commission of the sort involved in the Farrell case and the Equal Employment Opportunity Commission created under Title VII of the CRA of 1964? See Sections 705 and 706.

C. EQUAL EMPLOYMENT OPPORTUNITY

DRAPER v. CLARK DAIRY

Superior Court, Connecticut, New Haven County, 1950
17 Conn. Supp. 93, 27 L.R.R.M. 2072

ALCORN, J. . . .

The hearing tribunal made a finding of subordinate facts from which it concluded that the employer refused employment to an applicant because of his race. Thereupon it issued an order to the employer directing that "You are hereby ordered to cease and desist forthwith from refusing to employ Oscar S. Draper of 258 Starr Street, New Haven, Conn. No appeal shall operate as a stay of this order." From that finding and order the employer has appealed under the provisions of Sec. 7407. . . .

The finding of the hearing tribunal, briefly summarized, is that the applicant, one Draper, a twenty three year old Negro, was the first to answer an advertisement inserted by Clark Dairy, the employer, in a daily newspaper reading "Boys, 18 years or over. Experience not necessary. Evening work. Apply 3 to 5 or after 6 P.M. Clark Dairy, 74 Whitney Avenue, City." Clark Dairy operates a wholesale and retail milk, ice cream, and ice cream products business and has four dairy stores. Draper was interviewed, with another colored applicant, by the store manager, and was told the advertised job was taken; but he left his name, address, telephone number, and age upon the assurance the manager would get in touch with him in the event of future openings.

---

[4] The plan approved by the court and annexed to its decision as Appendix A is omitted. — ED.

There was no discussion of the kind of employment or of the wages or hours involved.

Several other applicants later answered the advertisement and four of these, all white persons, ranging in age from eighteen to twenty-three years, secured jobs within a short space of time thereafter either as dishwasher or fountain man in the employer's milk and ice cream stores. The first of these was employed as a dishwasher some two and one-half hours after the applicant's interview. The employer had several job openings on the day Draper applied, for which no special qualifications were required other than that the applicant be eighteen years of age or older and that he be willing to work nights, and Draper met these qualifications. Subsequently, the employer's manager gave to an investigator for the commission three reasons for refusing employment to this applicant, namely that the job was filled, the applicant was too old, and the wages were too low for a man of his age. The employer had no Negro employees in any of its stores except a girl who appeared to be white. . . .

A question of intent is a question of fact, the determination of which is not reviewable unless the conclusion drawn by the trier is one which cannot reasonably be reached. . . .

The hearing tribunal saw and heard the witnesses and the Court did not. The hearing tribunal is the judge of the credibility of the witnesses. It could reject the testimony of witnesses it did not believe and base its conclusion on inferences drawn from facts which it could properly find the evidence established. Le-Blanc v. Grillo [129 Conn. 378].

The statute, §7407, in providing that "the findings of the hearing tribunal as to the facts, if supported by substantial and competent evidence shall be conclusive," must be construed to mean that the question presented by the finding in this case shall be tested on appeal by the well established principles recited. A conclusion reached by inference could not be said to be "supported by substantial and competent evidence" unless the inference satisfied those tests. An examination of the record warrants the conclusion that the finding is proper and should stand.

The third point in issue, namely, the form of the order, remains for consideration. The order appealed from — that the employer "cease and desist forthwith from refusing to employ" the applicant — is, in effect, an affirmative order to employ him now. Taken literally, it would require the employer, if no vacancy now existed, either to discharge an employee to make a place for this applicant or to create a useless job for him. It further assumes that the applicant will submit himself for employment. The record, however, does not disclose that the applicant is available for or wants the job at this time. On the contrary, the record does disclose that he had studied at a photography school following a high school education and applied for the job in issue merely as a stop-gap to have an income while waiting for an opening in his chosen work. As already stated, the order could not bind the applicant to take the job because he is not a party to the proceeding, nor is it a reasonable construction of the statute that its purpose is either to force a technically trained individual to undertake a job as dishwasher or fountain man at a soda fountain or to force the employer to discharge another employee or create such a job to make a place for him. . . .

The hearing tribunal found that the unfair employment practice in this case consisted in this employer's refusal to employ this applicant because of the latter's race.   The statute authorizes the issuance of an order, after such an unfair employment practice has been found to exist "to cease and desist from *such* unfair employment practice."   That can only mean to stop henceforth from doing the objectionable thing which has been done in the past.   The statute does not provide that, having found one unfair employment practice to have occurred, an order may issue to cease and desist in the future from refusing employment for that and every other reason, legitimate or otherwise.   Clearly, under the statute, the order must be limited to the unfair practice which has been found to exist.   It should leave the applicant free to determine whether or not he still seeks that employment.

The appeal is sustained as to the form of the order only.   The order appealed from is modified to provide as follows: "In the event that Oscar S. Draper . . . presents himself for employment, you are hereby ordered to cease and desist from refusing, because of his race, to employ him."

Enter a decree accordingly.

CIVIL RIGHTS ACT OF 1964, TITLE VII,
§703(a) and (b)
78 Stat. 255, 42 U.S.C. §2000e – 2

SEC. 703.   (a) It shall be an unlawful employment practice for an employer —

(1) to fail or refuse to hire or to discharge any individual, or otherwise to discriminate against any individual with respect to his compensation, terms, conditions, or privileges of employment, because of such individual's race, color, religion, sex, or national origin; or

(2) to limit, segregate, or classify his employees in any way which would deprive or tend to deprive any individual of employment opportunities or otherwise adversely affect his status as an employee, because of such individual's race, color, religion, sex, or national origin.

(b) It shall be an unlawful employment practice for an employment agency to fail or refuse to refer for employment, or otherwise to discriminate against, any individual because of his race, color, religion, sex, or national origin, or to classify or refer for employment any individual on the basis of his race, color, religion, sex, or national origin.

NOTES

1. Suppose that in a state which has no fair employment practices Act an employer, prior to the effective date of the CRA, established a waiting list of applicants for future employment but refused to accept

applications from nonwhites. Assuming that the employer is covered by the CRA when it became effective, may he thereafter lawfully refuse to hire an otherwise qualified nonwhite applicant because he is not on the waiting list?

2. Suppose that an employer covered by the CRA refuses to promote a Negro employee and the latter files a grievance, charging a violation of the provision in the applicable collective agreement prohibiting discrimination based on race, creed, or color. If an arbitrator rules in the employer's favor on the merits, should the grievant be barred from filing a complaint with either the state fair employment practices commission or with the Equal Employment Opportunities Commission established by the CRA? See Note, The Right to Equal Treatment: Administrative Enforcement of Antidiscrimination Legislation, 74 Harv. L. Rev. 526, 574 (1961). Cf. Spielberg Manufacturing Co., 112 N.L.R.B. 1080 (1955).

3. May an employer require as a condition of employment that all applicants pass a general ability test, uniformly administered and graded, when the demonstrable effect of such a test is to exclude the majority of Negro applicants? See CRA §703(h); Matter of Leon Myart and Motorola, Inc., 3 CCH Lab. Law Rep. (State Laws) ¶49,997.61 (Ill. Fair Employment Practices Commission, Nov. 18, 1964).

D.   INTERNAL UNION AFFAIRS

1.   *The Case Developed Law*

POLIN v. KAPLAN
Court of Appeals, New York, 1931
257 N.Y. 277, 177 N.E. 833

[The plaintiffs were members of Local No. 306 of the Moving Picture Machine Operators' Union of Greater New York, an unincorporated association. Charges were presented against them for having brought action in a state court charging the officers of the union with having violated its constitution and bylaws, for having circulated printed material charging such officers with these violations, and for failing to keep confidential the work of the union. On the basis of these charges, the union decreed fines and expulsion. Thereafter, the plaintiffs instituted these actions to have the union proceedings adjudged null and void, to procure the plaintiffs' reinstatement, and to recover damages.]

KELLOGG, J. . . .

The constitution and bylaws of an unincorporated association express the terms of a contract which define the privileges secured and the duties assumed by those who have become members. As the contracts may prescribe the precise terms upon which membership may be gained, so it conclusively defines the conditions which will entail its loss. Thus, if the contract reasonably provides that the performance of certain acts will constitute a sufficient cause for the expulsion of a member, and that charges of their performance, with notice to the member, shall be tried before a tribunal set up by the association, the provision is exclusive, and the judgment of the tribunal, rendered after a fair trial, that the member has committed the offenses charged and must be expelled, will not be reviewed by the regularly constituted courts. Belton v. Hatch, 109 N.Y. 593, 17 N.E. 225, 4 Am. St. Rep. 495; Matter of Haebler v. New York Produce Exchange, 149 N.Y. 414, 44 N.E. 87. A court "cannot review the proceedings or re-examine the merit of the expulsion." Per Miller, J., in Wilcox v. Supreme Council Royal Arcanum, 210 N.Y. 370, 376, 104 N.E. 624, 626, 52 L.R.A. (N.S.) 806. This is not to say, however, that a court will decline to interfere, if an expulsion has been decreed for acts not constituting violations of the constitution and bylaws, and not made expellable offenses thereby, either by terms expressed or implied. In such an instance, the expulsion is not within the power conferred by the contract. Accordingly, the proceedings will be set aside and the associate restored to membership. People ex rel. Bartlett v. Medical Society of Erie County, 32 N.Y. 187; Amalgamated Society of Carpenters v. Braithwaite, (1922) 2 App. Cas. 440, 470. . . .

We think also, that in every contract of association there inheres a term binding members to loyal support of the society in the attainment of its proper purposes, and that for a gross breach of this obligation the power of expulsion is impliedly conferred upon the association. It has been said by the Supreme Court of California that an association may expel a member upon one of two grounds, viz.: "First, a violation of such of the established rules of the association as have been subscribed or assented to by the members, and as provide expulsion for such violation; second, for such conduct as clearly violates the fundamental objects of the association, and if persisted in and allowed would thwart those objects or bring the association into disrepute." Otto v. Journeymen Tailors' Protective & Benevolent Union, 75 Cal. 308, 314, 17 P. 217, 219, 7 Am. St. Rep. 156. The Supreme Court of Pennsylvania has said that, if the charter of an association contains no express provision for expulsion, it may nevertheless be had if the member "has been guilty of some infamous offense, or has done some act tending to the destruction of the society." Weiss v. Musical Mut. Protective Union, 189 Pa. 446, 451, 42 A. 118, 120, 69 Am. St. Rep. 820. We subscribe to these views.

[The court found that the charges had not been sustained and that the plaintiffs were expelled "without power and illegally." Their reinstatement was ordered, and they were also found to be entitled to damages for the wages lost as result of the improper action by the union.]

HERMAN v. BERNHART and HINSHAW
(*Unreported*)

[Bernhart and Hinshaw were members in good standing of Local 47, American Federation of Musicians. Each was a studio musician of considerable experience and reputation. In February, 1958, the Federation called a strike against the motion picture producers. Shortly after commencement of the strike, the Federation announced that it would pay strike benefits (50 per cent of basic studio scale) for a period of fifteen weeks. Simultaneously, Local 47 announced that its members would continue to be bound by the same quota laws that prevailed when the former studio contract was in effect. This meant that Bernhart and Hinshaw, who were classified as studio musicians, could not accept calls from studios other than their own, could not work in television films or on live television or radio broadcasts, and could not be employed in outside dance or symphony orchestras except on a casual basis.

In March, 1958, Musicians Guild of America, an organization dual in purpose to the Federation, was organized. It eventually defeated the Federation in an NLRB election for exclusive representation rights in the studios, and executed a collective agreement with the motion picture producers. Immediately after the Guild's formation was announced, the Federation printed and distributed a form statement reading as follows:

"The payment and acceptance of strike benefits necessarily reflect a fraternal and labor union relationship of mutual aid and support.

"In view of the recently announced formation of an organized effort (Musicians Guild of America) to disrupt, divide and betray the American Federation of Musicians in the midst of a critical strike, for which benefits are being paid, it is altogether appropriate that my strike benefits from the American Federation of Musicians be accompanied by my affirmation that I am not a part of, and will not in any way associate myself with, any union or group that is dual, and hence hostile to the American Federation of Musicians."

Signing the foregoing statement was made a condition precedent to the receipt of strike benefits.

Bernhart and Hinshaw refused to sign the statement and were refused strike benefits after the first week. Their inquiries elicited the information that the requirement of signing the statement was not in the bylaws of Local 47 but was "on the direct authority of Jimmy Petrillo." The two men then announced that since they were being denied strike benefits ($160 per week), they felt themselves no longer bound by the local's quota laws. The local's secretary informed them, however, that they must abide by such laws or lose their good standing as members.

In May, 1958, Bernhart and Hinshaw filed an action in the Municipal Court of Los Angeles against the Federation and Local 47 and its officers to recover strike benefits denied them. Subsequent discussions between counsel for the plaintiffs and for Local 47 led to an agreement that the local and its officers need not answer the complaint and that the action would be maintained only against the Federation.

In July, 1958, Bernhart and Hinshaw were formally charged with violation of Article 31, Sections 2 and 5, of the Federation's bylaws. Section 2 provides: "If any member proceeds in court against any Local, before exhausting his rights in the Federation, such act shall constitute such member's resignation from membership in the Federation." Section 5 provides:

"If a member in any case where under the laws of the Federation he may appeal to the International Executive Board or a Convention of the Federation, as the case may be, involves a Local or the Federation in litigation before exhausting his right to so appeal, he shall be fined by the International Executive Board a sum of not less than $10.00 and not more than $5,000.00."

The charges were heard before a referee, Benjamin Aaron, appointed by the International President of the Federation. His recommendations were submitted to the Federation's International Executive Board, whose decision is quoted in part.]

In his report, Referee Aaron found defendants did not violate Article 31, Section 2. As for Article 31, Section 5, he recommended that the Federation take no action until the conclusion of the lawsuit they had filed against Local 47 and the Federation.

The Board has carefully examined the entire record in this case along with the referee's report and recommendations. Upon that examination and consideration we conclude that the recommendations are based on a gross misconception of the applicable by-laws and of other relevant considerations and, therefore, are constrained to reject the referee's recommendations. We have determined that defendants Bernhart and Hinshaw are both guilty on each of the two counts charged for the following reasons:

There are two elements to the offense under the by-laws, (1) the bringing of a court action and (2) failing to exhaust remedies within the Federation. The first element was, of course, conceded by Bernhart and Hinshaw in their answer. Nor was there any real contention that internal remedies had in fact been exhausted. Defendant's main assertion was that it would have been futile to exhaust them. There is no affirmative evidence in the record to show that an appeal to the Federation would not be permitted or would be futile. The record shows merely that this was the unilateral assumption of the defendants. . . .

. . . The record shows quite clearly that defendants assumed that they would not prevail on an appeal for two reasons: (1) The ruling against which they were appealing had originated with the International President; (2) The International President had expressed his strong opposition against Cecil Read [founder of Musicians Guild of America], his principles and his followers, and they were among Read's followers. These assumptions, as their attorney conceded, were "based upon probably a considerable amount of hearsay." . . .

Defendants did not establish that any unreasonable delay would be caused by requiring them to follow Federation procedures. The Federation is one of the few unions which holds annual conventions. If the Executive Board had denied defendants' appeal, they would have had the right (and the obligation before taking court action) to appeal to the convention. In 1958 this convention was begun on June 2, less than three weeks after defendants filed their suit, and less than three months after their "grievance" arose. Surely so slight a delay is not "unreasonable." This part of the allegation of defendant's answer must therefore be rejected.

We may now summarize the evidence as it appears when viewed most favorably to the defendants: They brought suit against the Local and the Federation without exhausting their internal remedies. There is no showing that it would have been futile for them to exhaust the remedies from the point of getting a fair hearing. There is no showing that there would have been an unreasonable delay in requiring them to do so. Defendants do show, however, that they *believed* that it would be futile for them to do so because they were challenging a ruling of the International President and because they were followers of Cecil Read. The question now becomes whether on these facts defendants should be found guilty of violating by-laws Article 31, Section 2 and Section 5. . . .

The referee "found" that Section 2 had not been violated because the attorney for Bernhart and Hinshaw had decided, after the suit was filed, that the Local need not answer. On this basis the referee concluded that they "really did not proceed in court against Local 47." This is patently untenable.

In common parlance one "proceeds" in court against another when one files suit naming the other as a defendant. Once the suit has been filed, even if it is immediately withdrawn, one has "proceeded," and a party can no more "unproceed" in court than he can unring a bell. The technical conception of commencing a suit accords with the common notion. "An action is commenced, within the meaning of this title, when the complaint is filed." . . . The view that the by-law is offended as soon as the complaint is filed in court is in harmony also with its purpose to keep the Local out of public conflict with its members, at least as long as it is still possible to settle the difficulty internally. This purpose would have been frustrated even if the complaint had been withdrawn the day it was filed. We find inescapable the conclusion that defendants did "proceed in court against" Local 47.

We are thus brought to the major issue in the case — whether defendants exhausted their Federation remedies within the meaning of the by-laws. The referee did not reach this question because he treated the by-law as identical with the judicial rule requiring exhaustion of internal remedies before the courts will entertain suits against membership associations. The referee's approach was clearly erroneous because the by-law has entirely different purposes than this judicial rule, and decisions under the latter cannot be the measure of a member's obligations under the by-law.

Labor unions and similar associations cannot, of course, (and do not pretend to seek to) regulate the conduct of courts. The limit of their authority and effort is to adopt and enforce rules governing their own members. Court decisions requiring exhaustion reflect a self-imposed limitation primarily based on considerations of public policy in a democratic society which frowns upon intrusion by government into the internal affairs of voluntary associations. The underlying premise of that public policy is precisely that such associations are capable of self-governance — that they can and should fairly formulate and enforce their own rules of membership. Not infrequently, where this policy is overridden by the demands and dictates of justice, the courts will disregard their self-imposed restraint and will assert jurisdiction without prior exhaustion of internal remedies.

On the other hand, no member of a union or other association may disregard or flout the lawful rules that bind all members. And no one does or can dispute the legality or propriety of a rule requiring members to attempt to resolve their grievances according to proper internal procedures before going to court. That obligation flows from the fact of membership and, though consistent with, is entirely independent of the judicial principle of self-abstention. The obligation is imposed for numerous reasons benefiting the organization as a whole, including the "aggrieved" member. It affords an opportunity for reconsideration and redress without the expense and the enduring scars of formal litigation. It enables the member and the union, in the more informal and flexible internal procedures, to work out and adjust their differences before fixed positions are taken and advanced as adversaries in public court actions. It has the advantage of keeping the organization's problems "within the family" without exposing either the arbitrary claim or arbitrary decision to humiliating public scrutiny. Above all, it preserves the fundamental values of autonomous self-rule. The almost universal adoption of this principle in association constitutions or by-laws is eloquently cogent testimony to its importance and value. . . .

. . . [I]t is clear that defendants violated both by-laws. They did not in fact exhaust their remedies within the Federation. Their defense of futility is totally without foundation in fact or proof. It was premised solely on their conjecture and suspicion that they would not prevail. This is not the test under the by-law or under any relevant judicial principle. Futility must be established as fact and must be determined by the fairness of the procedures and not by who prevails. Any other approach would, of course, completely nullify the wholesome doctrine of exhaustion of internal remedies. We reject the defenses. We find defendants guilty on both counts. . . .

We therefore rule that Defendants Bernhart and Hinshaw are each suspended for two years and each fined $2,500. The time of the suspension shall begin running when the fine has been paid.

CROSSEN v. DUFFY
Court of Appeals, Ohio, 1951
90 Ohio App. 252, 103 N.E.2d 769

[In this case the plaintiffs were charged with publishing or circulating improper campaign literature during a union election campaign in May, 1947. Fines were imposed by the union convention, and the plaintiffs brought this action to restrain the defendants from the enforcement of the penalties thus imposed.]

THOMPSON, J. . . .

. . . Examination of the facts before us impels us to hold that a member of a mutual benefit association continues to be a citizen of the United States, and the free speech guaranteed by the United States Constitution permits him freedom in criticizing his union officials, as well as his public officials generally, subject always to the limitations imposed by the laws of slander and libel. 64 Harvard Law Review 1071. In so declaring, we recognize that it is not generally the function of courts to control the policies or the internal affairs of labor unions, but the courts may and should protect the democratic processes within unions by which union policies and their leaders are determined. Upon this point, see the illuminating article entitled "Legal Limitations on Union Discipline" by Clyde W. Summers, 64 Harvard Law Review 1049, at page 1073 and also, the article by Joseph Kovner entitled "The Legal Protection of Civil Liberties Within Unions," (1948) Wisconsin Law Review, at page 18.

Particularly important seems to us the recognition that labor unions constitute a special type of mutual benefit association, standing in special relation to their members and to the state. Membership has become a frequent condition of employment, even as the right of every man to work has become increasingly recognized as one of the most valued rights of a free society. Viewing the important role of labor unions in this era, a court may well determine in a particular case that protection of their democratic processes is essential to the maintenance of our democratic government. . . .

We hold that the action of the 1949 Convention in fining plaintiffs because of publication or distribution of the handbills constituted an infringement of the right of free speech possessed by plaintiffs, calling for exercise, under the peculiar circumstances of this case, of the equity powers of this Court to protect the plaintiffs in their property rights and in their calling. . . .

In the present case, we find that a property right on the part of plaintiffs is clearly involved, since failure within thirty days to pay the fines levied would subject plaintiffs under Section 181 of the Union's Constitution to suspension from the Union. Furthermore, by Section 255 failure to pay a fine expressly deprives any member of all privileges of local membership thus entailing loss of benefits, loss of right to seek office within the Union and possible loss of work opportunities.

Numerous cases hold that where the expulsion or suspension of a member of the Union affects the individual's property rights, a court of equity will award relief to a member wrongfully expelled or suspended from the Union by decreeing his re-instatement, at least where a resort to the internal remedies within the Union would be futile, illusory or useless, or would not accord to the members in question substantial or practical justice. See the note in 168 A.L.R. 1462 entitled "Exhaustion of Remedies Within Labor Union as Condition of Resort to Civil Courts by Expelled or Suspended Member" and particularly the cases cited at page 1479.

In the court below, the trial judge in his opinion pointed out that the matter of exhaustion of remedies within the Union is not a required prerequisite to court action unless the tribunal is impartial, and in this case it was the Executive Board which brought the charges against the plaintiffs and further appeal to that Board would presumably be unavailing. Particularly, was any such gesture to be deemed futile where the objectionable actions of plaintiffs constituted support of an opposition slate and where, in the companion case being decided by this Court today [Armstrong v. Duffy, 90 Ohio App. 233, 103 N.E.2d 760], and involving attempted punishment of candidates on the rival slate, the action of the Executive Board had given evidence of intention of silencing further opposition.

Finding the plaintiffs exhausted their remedies within the Union, to the extent feasible, and finding that plantiffs' property rights were involved, we therefore conclude that the injunction prayed for should issue against the defendants in favor of the five plaintiffs in this case.

Injunction granted. Exceptions.

NOTES

1. "To justify intervention, courts have adopted two established legal principles as rationales for relief. First, they have said that membership in a labor union is a property right and must be protected against any unlawful interference. Second, they have reasoned that membership in a union creates a contract. Any improper discipline is a breach of that contract for which the law will give relief." Summers, Legal Limitations on Union Discipline, 64 Harv. L. Rev. 1049, 1051 (1951).

2. A number of exceptions have been developed by the courts to the rule that a member of a union must exhaust his internal union remedies before resorting to the courts for relief from union discipline. The exceptions include the following: (1) *lack of jurisdiction in the trial body* (the proceedings were therefore void, and there is nothing from which to appeal); (2) *improper grounds for discipline* (the grounds were either not within the union constitution or were, in any event, against public policy; the proceedings were therefore void); (3) *improper disciplinary procedure* (the provisions of the union constitution were not followed, or the specified union procedures denied a fair trial; the proceedings were therefore void); (4) *delay in appeal* (exhaustion of internal remedies would involve unreasonable delay in obtaining relief); (5) *futility of appeal* (the union tribunals to which appeal might be made are so biased as to render appeal to them a mere waste of time). These exceptions frequently overlap, and more than one may be arguably available in the particular case. See, e.g., Summers, Legal Limitations on Union Discipline, 64 Harv. L. Rev. 1049, 1086 (1951); Summers, The Law of Union Discipline: What the Courts Do in Fact, 70 Yale L.J. 173, 207 (1960); Vorenberg, Exhaustion of Intraunion Remedies, 2 Lab. L.J. 487 (1951); Annotation, 168 A.L.R. 1462 (1947).

"It is difficult to ascertain to what extent the exhaustion doctrine has really influenced results of cases and to what extent it has merely been used as make-weight in opinion-writing. First, it is always difficult to determine which of a number of different factors discussed by a court is crucial. Second, in most cases, all that is available to show what really happened in the case is the court's interpretation of the facts. It is not unnatural to expect that a court which has concluded, for example, that the plaintiff has a valid case on the merits, would state the facts so that the case appears to fit into one of the accepted formulas for avoiding the exhaustion rule." Vorenberg, supra, at 491.

2. The Labor-Management Reporting and Disclosure Act of 1959

The adoption of the Labor-Management Reporting and Disclosure Act[5] marked the first instance of substantial federal regulation of internal union affairs. Title I purports to guarantee to union members equal participation in union affairs, freedom of speech and assembly, reasonable and uniform dues, initiation fees, and assessments, freedom to sue unions and their officers, and fair treatment in disciplinary cases. Title II requires the disclosure by unions, their officers, and their employees of detailed information about financial dealings, operation of trusteeships, and private arrangements with employers. (Similar, though less stringent, requirements are imposed on employers and their agents.) Title III regulates the manner in which union trusteeships may be established and maintained, and protects the rights of members of organizations placed under trusteeship. Title IV similarly regulates the conduct of union elections, and is designed to insure the fairness of such elections, the right of equal participation as candidates and voters of all qualified union members, and the means by which illegal elections may be challenged or set aside. Title V imposes fiduciary responsibilities upon union officers and representatives, disqualifies convicted criminals and former Communists from eligibility for union office for fixed periods of time, and requires that certain union officers be bonded for the faithful discharge of their duties.

For helpful commentary upon the Act and its effects, see Aaron, The Labor-Management Reporting and Disclosure Act of 1959, Pt. I, 73 Harv. L. Rev. 851 (1960); Aaron, The Union Member's "Bill of Rights": First Two Years, 1 Industrial Relations 47 (1962); Cox, Internal Affairs of Labor Unions Under the Labor Reform Act of 1959, 58 Mich. L. Rev. 819 (1960); Previant, Have Titles I-VI of Landrum-Griffin Served the Stated Legislative Purpose? 14 Lab. L.J. 28 (1963); Rosenberg, Interpretive Problems of Title I of the Labor-Management Reporting and Disclosure Act, 16 Ind. & Lab. Rel. Rev. 405 (1963); Smith, The Labor-Management Reporting and Disclosure Act of 1959, 46 Va. L. Rev. 195 (1960); Summers, American Legislation for Union Democracy, 25 Modern L. Rev. 273 (1962); Thatcher, Rights of Individual Union Members Under Title I and Section 610 of the Landrum-Griffin Act, 52 Geo. L.J. 339 (1964); Note, Bill of Rights of Members of Labor Organizations, 1959-1964, 40 Notre Dame Law, 86 (1964).

[5] The full text of this statute is printed in the Reference Supplement, page 51.

a. EXHAUSTION OF INTERNAL UNION REMEDIES

DETROY v. AMERICAN GUILD OF VARIETY ARTISTS

United States Court of Appeals, Second Circuit, 1961
286 F.2d 75, certiorari denied, 366 U.S. 929 (1961)

LUMBARD, Chief Judge.

The appellant, manager and trainer of a troupe of chimpanzees with which he performs professionally under the name of the "Marquis Family" in theaters, night clubs, circuses, on television, and in motion pictures, instituted this proceeding under §102 of the Labor-Management Reporting and Disclosure Act of 1959, 29 U.S.C.A. §412, demanding injunctive relief and damages for an alleged violation of the procedural rights granted union members by §101(a)(5) of the Act, 29 U.S.C.A. §411(a)(5). Upon a motion for summary judgment, the district court dismissed the complaint on the ground that under §101(a)(4) the plaintiff could bring no court action against a labor union without first exhausting the internal remedies provided by the union, and that in this case the defendant union had established reasonable procedures by its constitution whereby claims against it by members could be heard within the four-month period permitted by the law.

The controversy between the appellant and the American Guild of Variety Artists, a labor union representing variety entertainers in the United States and Canada, arose out of a breach-of-contract claim made against the appellant by a resort hotel in Las Vegas, Nevada. After failing to settle the dispute by negotiation, the AGVA requested the parties to submit it to arbitration, which they did. A panel of three, one selected by each of the parties to the dispute and the third chosen by the two so designated, met in Los Angeles County, California, on January 12, 1960, and decided in favor of the hotel. The union then advised the appellant that if he did not abide by the award, it would place him on the "National Unfair List" appearing in its monthly periodical "AGVA News." The appellant replied that he intended to move to vacate the arbitration award in the California courts, but never began any such proceedings. When the three months provided by California law for vacating arbitration awards had elapsed, the union proceeded to publish the appellant's name in the August 1960 issue of the periodical under a heading which read as follows:

"Notice to Members.

"The rules require that you may not work for any employer, agent, booker or third party who is marked 'Unfair' by AGVA. Violation of these rules subjects you to disciplinary action.

"Notice to Agents.

". . . You are not authorized to book AGVA members in unfair establishments or book performers not in good standing in AGVA. Violation of rules subjects you to revocation of your franchise."

The appellant then began this proceeding in the Southern District of New York, claiming that the listing amounted to disciplinary action within the meaning of §101(a)(5) of the Labor-Management Reporting and Disclosure Act of 1959, 29 U.S.C.A. §411(a)(5), and that he was, therefore, entitled to specific written charges, a reasonable time to defend, and a full and fair hearing before having his name placed on the list.

The appellant did not, however, seek to utilize the procedure made available by Article XX of the Constitution of the AGVA. This article, entitled "Claims of Members," establishes procedures whereby claims asserted against the union are heard and determined by its Board or Executive Committee. Thus, the first issue before us now is whether the proviso in §101(a)(4), which protects the right of a union member to sue his union, "Provided, That any such member may be required to exhaust reasonable hearing procedures (but not to exceed a four-month lapse of time) within such organization, before instituting legal or administrative proceedings against such organizations or any officer thereof," required of the appellant in this case that he first have recourse to the internal procedures established by the union's constitution. The exhaustion proviso of §101(a)(4) does not appear in §102, which grants members who claim that their rights under §101 have been infringed a federal forum in which to litigate their disputes with the union. It might also appear from the rejection by the House of Representatives of H.R. 8342, the bill originally reported out of the Committee on Education and Labor, which explicitly provided for exhaustion of internal remedies in §102, that Congress did not mean to have the exhaustion doctrine apply to the rights granted by §101, except where, as in the case of the right to sue, it was expressly provided. However, the broad language of the proviso in §101(a)(4) includes suits instituted against labor unions in any court on any claim. Absent a clear directive by Congress, the policy formulated over a course of time by courts reluctant to interfere in the internal affairs of private organizations should not be superseded. We hold, therefore, that the provision in §101(a)(4) applies, as well, to suits brought in the federal courts for violations of the rights secured by §101.

Judge Dimock in this case read §101(a)(4) as imposing upon the union member an absolute duty to exhaust union remedies before applying to the federal courts. The legislative history of the section indicates, however, that Congress had no intention of establishing such a rule.[2]

_____

[2] For example, one of the authors of the bill passed by the House, Representative Griffin, expressed a clear opinion on the question. He said:

"The proviso which limits exhaustion of internal remedies is not intended to impose restrictions on a union member which do not otherwise exist, but rather to place a maximum on the length of time which may be required to exhaust such remedies. In other words, existing decisions which require, or do not require, ex-

The statute provides that any member of a labor organization "may be required" to exhaust the internal union remedies, not that he "must" or "is required to" exhaust them. When read in light of the statements made on the floor of Congress by the authors of the statute, it appears clear that the proviso was incorporated in order to preserve the exhaustion doctrine as it had developed and would continue to develop in the courts, lest it otherwise appear to be Congress' intention to have the right to sue secured by §101 abrogate the requirement of prior resort to internal procedures. In addition, the proviso dictated an outside limit beyond which the judiciary cannot extend the requirement of exhaustion — no remedy which would require proceedings exceeding four months in duration may be demanded. We therefore construe the statute to mean that a member of a labor union who attempts to institute proceedings before a court or an administrative agency may be required *by that court or agency* to exhaust internal remedies of less than four months' duration before invoking outside assistance.

Section 102, under which the appellant instituted his proceeding, provides for enforcement by federal courts of rights secured by federal law. We are not in this case, therefore, bound by the doctrine of exhaustion as developed in the New York, Nevada, or California courts with respect to suits against unions brought in the courts of those states by union members. In enforcing rights guaranteed by the new statute, whether or not similar rights would be enforced under state law by state courts, the federal courts may develop their own principles regarding the time when a union's action taken in violation of §101 is ripe for judicial intervention. Cf. Holmberg v. Armbrecht, 1946, 327 U.S. 392; Sola Electric Co. v. Jefferson Electric Co., 1942, 317 U.S. 173, 176-177. The rules formulated by various state courts may suggest helpful avenues of approach, cf. Textile Workers Union of America v. Lincoln Mills, 1957, 353 U.S. 448, 457, but the authority granted to the federal courts by Congress to secure the rights enumerated in §101 of the 1959 Act is accompanied by the duty to formulate federal law regarding a union member's obligation to exhaust the internal union remedies before seeking judicial vindication of those rights.

---

haustion of such remedies are not to be affected except as a time limit of 4 months is superimposed. Also, by use of the phrase 'reasonable hearing procedures' in the proviso, it should be clear that no obligation is imposed to exhaust procedures where it would obviously be futile or would place an undue burden on the union member." 105 Daily Cong. Rec. App. A7915 (Sept. 4, 1959).

The statement made by Senator Kennedy, who introduced the original bill to which §§101-105 were added as amendments on the Senate floor, is also representative of the attitude taken by those who instituted the legislation. He said:

"Nor is it the intent or purpose of the provision to invalidate the considerable body of State and Federal court decisions of many years standing which require, or do not require, the exhaustion of internal remedies prior to court intervention depending upon the reasonableness of such requirements in terms of the facts and circumstances of a particular case. . . . The doctrine of exhaustion of reasonable internal union remedies for violation of union laws is just as firmly established as the doctrine of exhausting reasonable administrative agency provisions prior to action by courts." 105 Daily Cong. Rec. 16414 (Sept. 3, 1959).

If we look to the substantial body of state law on the subject, we find that the general rule requiring exhaustion before resort to a court has been almost entirely swallowed up by exceptions phrased in broad terms. See Annotation 168 A.L.R. 1462 (1947); Summers, Legal Limitations on Union Discipline, 64 Harv. L. Rev. 1049, 1086-92 (1951). Rather than decide whether exhaustion is proper by determining whether the union's action can be characterized as "void" (e.g., Tesoriero v. Miller, 1949, 274 App. Div. 670, 88, N.Y.S.2d 87) or as "affecting property rights" (e.g., Local Union No. 65 of Amalgamated Sheet Metal Workers, etc. v. Nalty, 6 Cir., 1925, 7 F.2d 100), we believe it preferable to consider each case on its own facts.

The Congressionally approved policy of first permitting unions to correct their own wrongs is rooted in the desire to stimulate labor organizations to take the initiative and independently to establish honest and democratic procedures. See Cox, The Role of Law in Preserving Union Democracy, 72 Harv. L. Rev. 609, 615 (1959). Other policies, as well, underlie the exhaustion rule. The possibility that corrective action within the union will render a member's complaint moot suggests that, in the interest of conserving judicial resources, no court step in before the union is given its opportunity. Moreover, courts may find valuable the assistance provided by prior consideration of the issues by appellate union tribunals. See Summers, The Law of Union Discipline: What the Courts Do in Fact, 70 Yale L.J. 175, 207 (1960). Congress has provided a safeguard against abuse by a union of the freedom thus granted it by not requiring exhaustion of union remedies if the procedures will exceed four months in duration. But in any case, if the state of facts is such that immediate judicial relief is warranted, Congress' acceptance of the exhaustion doctrine as applied to the generality of cases should not bar an appropriate remedy in proper circumstances.

The affidavits and exhibits submitted in the district court on the motion for summary judgment establish that the only hearing given the appellant before his name was placed on the National Unfair List was that of the arbitration proceeding. The union was not a party to the arbitration, and the issue decided by the arbitrators was not whether the appellant should be disciplined by the union but whether he owed an obligation to an employer with whom he had contracted. It is undisputed that no hearing was held in which the appellant could respond to the union's intention of taking disciplinary action. Quite clearly, a hearing in which some liability between a union member and a third party is determined is not the type of hearing demanded by §101(a)(5). At no time was the appellant given the opportunity of arguing before the union's hearing board that placing him on the Unfair List exceeded the powers granted to the union by its constitution, nor could he raise other mitigating circumstances in response to an expressed intention to place his name on such a list. The facts on their face, therefore, reveal a violation of the rights guaranteed union members by §101(a)(5). If the question before us were whether the union's constitution authorized the listing of the appellant's name on an unfair list after a hearing with due procedural safeguards, a union tribunal might provide some insight to aid our decision. But no prior consideration by such a tribunal is necessary or helpful on the question whether the treatment of the appellant violated §101(a)(5).

In addition, the particular form of the disciplinary action makes it difficult for the union to provide an adequate remedy. The appellant, from the date his name appeared on the list, was virtually barred from employment by those dealing regularly with the AGVA. Since he is an independent contractor whose weekly pay varies according to the terms of the contracts he signs with his employers, the precise extent of damages suffered by the appellant as a result of the listing can never be determined. Even were the union to permit him to present his case before a review board, the board could merely order his name removed from the list and, in order to provide a more satisfactory remedy, award as damages for the period during which he was barred from employment a sum which, at best, could only be an approximation. It appears unlikely that Congress intended that its expressed desire to provide minimum safeguards against arbitrary union discipline be avoided by the union's imposition of a sanction which has its most severe effect within a four-month period, if the consequences of such action cannot be precisely measured in order to assess damages. Early judicial intervention providing an adequate remedy by means of the court's power to enjoin further violations is therefore proper.

Furthermore, when it is difficult to assess damages it is more likely that the aggrieved union member will ultimately appear in a federal court to press a damage claim. Under New York law, which might apply in this case since the headquarters of the union are in New York and the appellant's membership contract might, therefore, be deemed to have been concluded in New York, the union might be free of liability in damages for the action of one of its officers in placing the appellant's name on the National Unfair List. See, e.g., Bingham v. Bessler, 1st Dept. 1960, 10 A.D.2d 345, 199 N.Y.S.2d 681; but see Madden v. Atkins, 1958, 4 N.Y.2d 283, 174 N.Y.S.2d 633, 151 N.E.2d 73. Only the federal court, therefore, would be able to provide a damage remedy, because of §101(a)(5), for the effects of the disciplinary step taken without the minimum procedural safeguards. If it is probable that the union will grant no award or that its award will be so speculative that court proceedings will be instituted even after the remedies are exhausted, not even the policy calling for exhaustion in order to conserve judicial resources applies.

Moreover, it is by no means clear that the union's own rules afforded the appellant a remedy within the organization. The section of the union's constitution which relates to disciplinary proceedings (Article XVII) authorizes fines, censure, suspension, or expulsion pursuant to a hearing and determination made by the Board or Executive Committee of the union. An appeal may be taken from such a decision to the next following annual or special convention of the union. No provision is made anywhere for any proceeding either before or after the printing of a member's name on the National Unfair List. The union maintains that Article XX of its Constitution, entitled "Claims of Members," provides a means for reviewing the correctness of this sanction. The constitution's separate provision for disciplinary proceedings in Article XVII, however, suggests that Article XX was not intended to provide an alternate procedure for review of a union's sanctions against its members, but merely to grant a forum for other monetary claims against the union. Moreover, after the arbitration award the appellant notified the Western Regional Director of the union by telegram that he intended "appealing to the National Board," and was told in a reply letter that "the decision of the arbitrators is final and . . . you cannot appeal this to the National Board of AGVA." Although this response referred not to the disciplinary measure but to the arbitrators' decision, neither that letter nor the later notification that he was being placed on the National Unfair List notified the appellant that any specific review procedure was available. Thus, an attempt to proceed under Article XX might not have proved futile, but it would have been quite uncertain. When asserting what is clearly a violation of a federal statute, a union member should not be required to first seek out remedies which are dubious. Only resort to those expressly provided in the union's constitution or those clearly called to his attention by the union officials should be demanded of him.

Taking due account of the declared policy favoring self-regulation by unions, we nonetheless hold that where the internal union remedy is uncertain and has not been specifically brought to the attention of the disciplined party, the violation of federal law clear and undisputed, and the injury to the union member immediate and difficult to compensate by means of a subsequent money award, exhaustion of union remedies ought not to be required. The absence of any of these elements might, in light of Congressional approval of the exhaustion doctrine, call for a different result. The facts of this case, however, warrant immediate judicial intervention.

Nor can we agree with the union's claim that the listing of the appellant's name did not constitute discipline within the meaning of §10(a)-(5). If a union such as the AGVA undertakes to enforce the contracts made by its members with employers, it does so because such enforcement is to the ultimate benefit of all the members, in that it promotes stability within the industry. A breach of contract or a refusal to abide by an arbitration award, therefore, is not damaging merely to the employer but to the union as well, and the union's listing of those of its members who do violate their contracts is an act of self-protection. In thus furthering its own ends the union must abide by the rules set down for it by Congress in §101(a)(5), and any member against whom steps are taken by the union in the interest of promoting the welfare of the group is entitled to these guarantees.

In passing on the motions for summary judgment and for a temporary injunction, the district court had before it only the complaint and the affidavits of the appellant and various officers of the union. The undisputed facts of the case require that a temporary injunction issue ordering the union to remove the appellant's name from its Unfair List where it is now retained in apparent violation of §101(a)(5).

We reverse the order of the district court dismissing the complaint and remand the case with instructions to grant the temporary injunction requested by the appellant.

NOTES

1. Some interesting questions have been raised as to the meaning of the "otherwise disciplined" provision of Section 101(a)(5). In Allen v. Armored Car Chauffeurs & Guards, 185 F. Supp. 492 (D.N.J. 1960), the failure of the union to prosecute a grievance protesting the discharge of the plaintiff by the employer was held not to constitute "discipline." But see Gross v. Kennedy, 183 F. Supp. 750 (S.D.N.Y. 1960).

In Rekant v. Shochtay-Gasos Union, 320 F.2d 271 (3d Cir. 1963), rev'g 205 F. Supp. 284 (E.D. Pa. 1962), the union had passed a resolution permitting the plaintiff to share certain slaughterhouse work with other members in order to provide him with temporary employment after his own employer had gone out of business. This resolution was subsequently rescinded because of the plaintiff's unsatisfactory performance of his work and his unfriendly attitude. The court held that, in view of the plaintiff's inability to perform the work, the union's rescission of the work-sharing resolution did not constitute "discipline." "At most, the rescinding resolution was an implied and indirect reprimand or censure of appellee for his behavior . . . a mere 'slap on the wrist' " of insufficient severity to be "embraced by the 'otherwise disciplined' proviso." 320 F.2d at 277.

See generally Note, 40 Notre Dame Law. 86, 98 (1964).

2. In the Rekant case, supra note 1, one of the arguments made by the defendant union was that the jurisdiction of the district court was preempted by the jurisdiction of the NLRB. The court rejected this argument, stating (320 F.2d at 274-275):

"Even assuming that there might be elements of this case arguably subject to Sections 7 or 8 of the Taft-Hartley Act affords no basis for ousting the jurisdiction of the district court. . . .

"Congress, in enacting Section 102, has now expressly provided for the federal protection and enforcement of a union member's right to be free from certain arbitrary conduct of his union. The explicit Congressional declaration and the reasoning, in an analogous situation, of the Supreme Court in Gonzales [International Assn. of Machinists v. Gonzales, 356 U.S. 617 (1958)] establish that the district court is competent to retain jurisdiction of a Section 101(a)(5) suit even when elements of the case are arguably subject to the Board's jurisdiction." To the same effect, see Parks v. International Bhd. of Electrical Workers, 314 F.2d 886, 922 (4th Cir. 1963), cert. denied, 372 U.S. 976. But see Rinker v. Local 24, Amalgamated Lithographers, 201 F. Supp. 204 (W.D. Pa. 1962), appeal dismissed, 313 F.2d 956 (3d. Cir. 1963) (action based on alleged conspiracy to secure plaintiff's expulsion from union and discharge from employment barred because of the exclusive jurisdiction of the NLRB); Barunica v. United Hatters, Cap and Millinery Workers, 321 F.2d 764 (8th Cir. 1963) (alleged discrimination by union in refusing to refer plaintiff for employment "is subject matter exclusively vested in the Board").

MAMULA v. UNITED STEELWORKERS

Supreme Court, Pennsylvania, 1964
414 Pa. 294, 200 A.2d 306, appeal dismissed and
certiorari denied, 379 U.S. 17 (1964)

COHEN, Justice.

This is an appeal from the decree entered below dismissing appellant's amended complaint for failure to exhaust internal union remedies. Appellees are the United Steelworkers of America (International Union), Local 1211 of the United Steelworkers of America (Local Union), and various officers of Local Union.

It appears from the amended complaint that appellant formerly held the office of president in Local Union. In 1961, charges of misconduct were brought against him and after a hearing by a trial committee of Local Union, these charges were sustained and it was recommended that appellant be removed from office, fined $2,000, and be suspended from union membership until the fine was paid. When these recommendations were approved by the membership of Local Union, appellant appealed to the Executive Board of the International Union in accordance with the procedure prescribed in the International Constitution.

The Executive Board on January 20, 1962, reversed appellant's suspension from union membership and remitted the $2,000 fine, but affirmed appellant's removal from office. In addition, the Board stated that appellant should not be eligible to hold office for five years nor until he repaid $1,081.99, the amount of expense allegedly caused by his misconduct. Once this amount was tendered, however, the Board left open the possibility of decreasing the period of disqualification from office. Although the International Constitution permitted a final appeal to the International Convention of the Union which was scheduled to convene in September, 1962, appellant did not invoke this internal procedure but instead instituted the present suit complaining solely of his ineligibility to hold union office.[1] We hold that the court below correctly dismissed this action for failure of appellant to exhaust his internal union remedies.

In Falsetti v. Local Union No. 2026, United Mine Workers of America, 400 Pa. 145, 161 A.2d 882, 87 A.L.R.2d 1032 (1960), we examined at length the basis and rationale for the general rule that a member of an

---

[1] In prior litigation, appellant unsuccessfully attempted to challenge his removal from office and the election subsequently held in June, 1962, to fill this vacancy. See Mamula v. United Steelworkers of America, 409 Pa. 175, 185 A.2d 595 (1962) and Mamula v. United Steelworkers of America, 304 F.2d 108 (3d Cir. 1962), cert. denied, 371 U.S. 823 (1962). Although his amended complaint is not clear on the point, appellant states in his brief that the present action is concerned solely with his ineligibility to hold union office.

unincorporated association must first exhaust his available internal remedies before seeking judicial relief. We concluded that such a rule not only benefits the association by promoting autonomy and internal democracy, but also aids the judicial process by settling grievances internally and, where not settled internally, by supplying our courts with the considered judgment of the association tribunals. At the same time, we sought in Falsetti to protect the rights of the grievant member by establishing certain limited exceptions to the exhaustion rule where, for example, the available remedies are illusory or resort to them would be futile or unreasonably burdensome. The experience since Falsetti has not indicated any necessity for reexamining the general principles therein set forth.

In attempting to justify his failure to appeal to the International Convention, appellant makes two contentions: (1) the general exhaustion rule is inapplicable because appeal to the Convention would have been futile and unreasonably burdensome; and (2) even if the rule is applicable, it has been modified by Section 101(a)(4) of the Landrum-Griffin Act.

With regard to the first contention, appellant's complaint alleges that the disciplinary action of Local Union was directed by the international officers who are biased against him and thus further appeal would have been "illusory, futile and vain and would only afford said international union defendant opportunity for further delaying plaintiff's rights and remedies." We held in Falsetti that the grievant member must set forth facts in his complaint to support the allegation that there exists an exception to the exhaustion rule. See also Wax v. International Mailers Union, 400 Pa. 173, 161 A.2d 603 (1960). Not only has appellant failed to do this, but the admitted facts belie his contention that the bias of the international officers made an appeal to the International Convention futile.

In the first place, we have seen that appellant's appeal to the Executive Board of the International Union resulted in a reversal of his suspension from union membership and a remittance of the $2,000 fine. This fact casts considerable doubt on appellant's assertion that the internal appellate tribunals were prejudged against him. Secondly, it appears that the international officers constituted a very small percentage of the membership at the International Convention.[2] Hence even if the international officers were biased against appellant, it does not necessarily follow that the Convention would have denied him a fair hearing. See Kopke v. Ranney, 16 Wis. 2d 369, 114 N.W.2d 485, 488 (1962).

Appellant argues that the exhaustion rule is also inapplicable because it would have been unreasonably burdensome for him to appeal to the International Convention in view of the eight-month delay between the decision of the Executive Board (January, 1962) and the meeting of the Convention (September, 1962). As we indicated in Falsetti, a grievant member need not as a general matter appeal to an International Convention which does not convene for several years. However, a two or three-

[2] Of the nearly 3000 delegates at the International Convention, only 33 were international officers.

step appellate procedure is not per se unduly burdensome, nor is it possible to set forth for all situations a time limit beyond which exhaustion of internal remedies will not be demanded. Rather, an examination must be made of the special factors in each case, especially the possible prejudice caused to the grievant member from the delay in internal appellate procedures.

Applying this test to the instant case, we find that here the eight-month time period was not unreasonably burdensome. It must be remembered that the Executive Board reinstated appellant to union membership and hence there was no loss of possible employment opportunities during this period. With regard to appellant's ineligibility to hold union office, it appears that another election did not take place until sometime in 1963, well after the meeting of the International Convention. Thus no apparent harm would have resulted to appellant from insistence on an appeal to the International Convention. Particularly is this so since the right appellant seeks to protect is his right to be a candidate for office — a right *not* protected by the "Bill of Rights of Members of Labor Organizations," 29 U.S.C.A. §§411-415. We conclude, therefore, that none of the exceptions set forth in Falsetti are here applicable.

Our determination here does not mean we fail to recognize that in many instances an appeal to the International Convention is so illusory that it would be futile and unreasonably burdensome to require resort to Convention action prior to instituting suit. In fact, the whole appellate procedure of some unions is subject to the indictment of being illusory. Indeed, some new internal facility is required in some union discipline procedure — such as a public review board — which would have final jurisdiction to hear appeals from the decisions of the union. Such a board would be extremely helpful to unions, their members and the courts, and would dissipate the overtones of bias that permeates some union disciplinary action. See 73 Yale L.J. 472 (1964). Full protection of a member's individual rights of any nature is important to the concept of union democracy. Union officials should not be permitted to discipline so as to silence criticism, punish complainers and discourage reform. See Salzhandler v. Caputo, 2 Cir., 316 F.2d 445 (1963).

Appellant next contends that our exhaustion rule has been modified by Section 101(a)(4) of the Landrum-Griffin Act. That section provides as follows:

"Protection of the right to sue. — No labor organization shall limit the right of any member thereof to institute an action in any court, or in a proceeding before any administrative agency, . . . or the right of any member of a labor organization to appear as a witness in any judicial, administrative, or legislative proceeding, or to petition any legislature or to communicate with any legislator: *Provided, That any such member may be required to exhaust reasonable hearing procedures (but not to exceed a four-month lapse of time) within such organization, before instituting legal or administrative proceedings against such organizations or any officer thereof . . .*" (Emphasis supplied).

Appellant argues that the proviso clause means that courts, both state and federal, may not compel a grievant member to invoke an internal remedy which will consume more than four months. Since the appeal to the International Convention involved an eight-month delay, appellant asserts that he was not required to exhaust this remedy. We do not agree.

We read Section 101(a)(4) as a limitation upon labor organizations and not upon the judiciary. Prior to the passage of the Landrum-Griffin Act, many unions had provisions in their constitutions stating that any member who brought suit against the union without first exhausting all available internal remedies — no matter how burdensome or time-consuming — was subject to expulsion from membership. Congress' purpose in enacting Section 101(a)(4) was to invalidate such provisions, thereby protecting the union member from discipline for violation thereof, where insistence on exhaustion of remedies would be either (1) unreasonable or (2) exceed a four-month time period. Congress did not intend to alter state rules relating to exhaustion of remedies which, as we have seen, are designed to aid the courts as well as the unincorporated association. Thus while appellant could not be disciplined for bringing suit before appealing to the International Convention, the failure to exhaust this internal remedy still precludes resort to our courts.

An examination of the language of Section 101(a)(4) plainly supports this interpretation. In the first place, the section states that "(n)o labor organization" shall limit the right of any member to institute suit or to take other remedial steps. There is no reference to existing judicial limitations on the ability of members of unincorporated associations to maintain action against the association. In this connection it should be remembered that the Landrum-Griffin Act was designed to promote union democracy by protecting the rights of a union member vis-a-vis his union. In fact, Title I, of which Section 101(a)(4) is a part, is labeled the "Bill of Rights of Members of Labor Organizations" and sets forth various restrictions upon labor organizations.

Secondly, the language relied upon by appellant appears in a parenthetical clause contained in a proviso to the restrictions imposed upon labor organizations. It is highly unlikely that Congress would attempt in such cavalier manner to alter established state court rules relating to exhaustion of internal remedies.

Appellant cites two federal cases and some language contained in Falsetti in support of his interpretation of Section 101(a)(4). The federal cases[9] involved suits brought in federal court under Section 102 of the Landrum-Griffin Act to remedy alleged violations of Title I of the Act. We read those decisions as merely adopting for the federal courts an exhaustion of remedies rule patterned upon the proviso clause in Section 101(a)(4). Those cases do not mean that state courts must also adopt this exhaustion rule.

Appellant also misconstrues our language in Falsetti. In the course of discussing generally the exhaustion of remedies doctrine, we mentioned

[9] Appellant cites Harris v. International Longshoremen's Association, Local No. 1291, 321 F.2d 801 (3d Cir. 1963) and Detroy v. American Guild of Variety Artists, 286 F.2d 75 (2d Cir. 1961).

in that case the recent enactment of Section 101(a)(4) of the Landrum-Griffin Act. Since the impact of the Act upon our own exhaustion rule was not involved in the decision in Falsetti, we certainly did not intend to decide this important question at that time. Indeed, our brief discussion of Section 101(a)(4) is expressly confined to situations "to which the Act is applicable." In our decision today, we hold that Section 101(a)(4) does not alter the Pennsylvania exhaustion of remedies rule.

Since appellant has not shown any legal justification for his failure to exhaust internal union remedies, we conclude that the decree entered below must be affirmed.

ROBERTS, Justice (dissenting).

Even a highly imaginative fiction writer would have considerable difficulty conceiving a procedure more futile, frustrating and meaningless than having an individual member appear before an International Convention, consisting of approximately 3,000 delegates, to present and argue his grievances against the leadership of the union, with the expectation of moving that body to hear, understand and decide the controversy on the merits. Such exposure to the convention arena is not a reasonable pursuit of a remedy; rather, it is a compelled involvement in a vast and undefined contest. The convention is not a tribunal conducive to the fair and impartial determination of a controversy. The customary protections, rights and rules usually associated with the hearing and decisional process are totally absent. I see no reason why the litigant here should be required to travel such a hazardous and unproductive road. In no other instance is one seeking justice required to engage in such futility.

Surely, ordinary experience indicates that were a member to seek to avail himself of this doubtful opportunity to appear before such a massive forum to plead his cause, he would be engaging in a rather empty, burdensome and worthless exercise. To regard such a venture as anything but illusory is to ignore reality. No decision of this Court or any other authority requires such a result. This record does not sustain the majority's conclusion that appellant failed to exhaust his internal union remedies.

I am also unable to share the majority's interpretation of Section 101(a)(4) of the Landrum-Griffin Act and the majority's failure to apply it to this litigation. This section obviously does not alter the established substantive rule of this Commonwealth which requires exhaustion of internal union remedies. It does, however, make it unmistakably clear that "no labor organization" may delay the availability of such internal remedies for more than four months.

If appeal to the International Convention be regarded as a "remedy," as the majority holds, then clearly its availability fails to comply with the statute, since that hearing procedure was postponed more than four months.

I conclude, therefore, that appellant may not be denied relief in our courts. He has effectively exhausted all meaningful internal union remedies. Moreover, even if appeal to the International Convention be considered more than an empty gesture, as the majority holds, the Landrum-

Griffin Act requires that such appeal be available within four months of the conclusion of the prior step in the appeal process.

I dissent.

BELL, C.J., joins in this opinion.

NOTES

1. Mamula appealed his case to the United States Supreme Court. The question he sought to have answered was: Does Section 101(a)(4) of the LMRDA control or modify the exhaustion of remedies rule theretofore enforced by state equity courts in suits by members against unions? See 58 L.R.R. 32 (1964). The Court dismissed the appeal "for want of jurisdiction," then, treating the appeal papers as a petition for writ of certiorari, denied certiorari. Justice Brennan was of the view that certiorari should have been granted. Justice Goldberg took no part in the consideration. Mamula v. United Steelworkers, 379 U.S. 17 (1964).

The issue Mamula sought to present to the Supreme Court breaks down into two questions: (1) Is Section 101(a)(4) a limitation on labor unions, courts, or both? (Compare the answers to this question given by the Detroy and Mamula cases.) (2) If it is a limitation on courts, does the limitation apply only to federal courts, or does it also apply to state courts? Consult Sections 102, 103, and 603(a) of the LMRDA. See generally Summers, Pre-emption and the Labor Reform Act — Dual Rights and Remedies, 22 Ohio St. L.J. 119 (1961).

2. Does Section 101(a)(4) eliminate the union's power to screen out and dispose of grievances which might go to arbitration?

b. PROTECTIONS THROUGH UNION PROCEDURES

UNITED AUTOMOBILE WORKERS, THE UAW PUBLIC REVIEW BOARD
5-6 (1957)

Under the constitutional amendment adopted by the UAW convention, the public review board has broad powers. . . .

It is given the "authority and duty to make final and binding decisions" in all cases placed before it by aggrieved members or subordinate bodies of the UAW. Essentially these cases will involve individual members who feel they have been unfairly disciplined by their local unions and who have failed to obtain satisfaction upon appeal to the UAW executive board. Also included will be local unions which feel they have been unfairly disciplined by the international. . . .

. . . A member who has been disciplined by a trial committee of his own local must first appeal to a general membership meeting of the local union. . . . If still dissatisfied, he must within 30 days appeal to the international executive board, with a brief written summary of the case. Should he fail to get satisfaction from the international executive board, he may, if he chooses, take his appeal to the UAW convention, as before; but he may elect, instead, to go to the public review board. He can't go to both.

The constitution clearly denies to the public review board any jurisdiction over official collective bargaining policies of the UAW. In the same manner, it sharply limits the board's functions in cases involving grievances arising from the union contract.

Where the latter are involved, the public review board has jurisdiction only over charges, previously made to the international executive board, that the grievance was improperly handled because of fraud, discrimination or collusion with management. In other words, the public review board is in no way a super-substitute for local grievance machinery on contract matters.

However, complaints involving the processing of grievances are the only ones which might come before both the public review board and the convention. If the board decides it does not have jurisdiction, the appellant can take his complaint to the convention. But in doing so, he cannot raise any issue which the board threw out in dismissing the case.

The same safeguards are provided for proceedings before the public review board as for the previous trial procedure. To insure promptness, appeals must be filed within 30 days except when the UAW president extends the time in the interests of justice. A hearing is guaranteed on all charges, except when a complaint is "manifestly groundless or frivolous." All parties have the right to counsel. To discourage groundless charges, the public review board is empowered to impose a fine up to $500 and suspension from membership for three months or more upon an accuser who "acted in bad faith or with malicious intent and in a willful effort to divide and disrupt the union."

. . . The board is directed to make an annual report summarizing all appeals heard during the year, drawing attention to any activity it has found to be improper and commenting upon the steps taken by the union to correct it. This report must be published in full in the official publication of the UAW and released to the public press.

Members of the public review board are appointed by the president of the UAW, subject to the approval of the executive board and the convention. Their terms run to the following convention. Careful provision is made to insure the independence of the review board, even though its costs are paid by the UAW.

No one under the jurisdiction of the UAW or in any way employed by the union or its subordinate bodies is eligible for appointment. The board is instructed to make its own rules, hire its own staff and set up its own office, physically apart from any UAW office. The UAW executive board must provide for an annual operating budget for the public review board, including "reasonable compensation" for its members; the money is deposited quarterly to the review board's account, and the review board must arrange for an annual audit of its books for submission to the UAW secretary-treasurer and the convention.[6]

[6] For a fuller understanding of the unique and interesting UAW Public Re-

UAW PUBLIC REVIEW BOARD CASE NO. 109, 1965

Panel Sitting: Adler, Chairman; Crane, Hanrahan, and McKelvey, Members. . . .

Appellants here challenge their convictions, affirmed on review by the International Executive Board, on charges preferred by the president of their Local Union pursuant to Article 30 of the International Constitution. The charge against each was that he ". . . did violate and conduct himself in such a manner that it was detrimental to the best interests of this Union and its members . . . (by having) crossed the picket lines of this Local while on strike and proceeded to operate the plant of our striking members." At issue is the adequacy of the Local trial procedures and the jurisdiction of the Local to try appellants for the acts allegedly committed. Representatives of appellants, the International Union and Local 257 were heard in oral argument before the Board in Detroit on December 7, 1964.

I

As of May, 1962, each of appellants was an hourly-rated supervisor in the employ of the Dochler-Jarvis Company at its plant in Grand Rapids, Michigan. Bargaining unit employees at the plant are represented by UAW Local 257. Hourly-rated supervisors constitute the first line of supervision and the positions are filled by promotion from the bargaining unit. Pursuant to the Collective Agreement, hourly-rated supervisors retain seniority in the bargaining unit and hold honorable withdrawal transfer cards from the Local during their tenure as supervisor.

In May, June and July of 1962, Local 257 struck the Grand Rapids facility as a part of a nationwide strike arising out of a dispute over the terms to be included in a new master Agreement. Prior to the commencement of the strike, representatives of the Union and the Company reached certain understandings concerning the procedures which would be followed during the course of the strike. One of these was that hourly-rated supervision would be permitted to cross the picket lines and enter the various Doehler-Jarvis Plants throughout the course of the strike. Whether any agreement was also reached concerning what would be the nature of their activities, is disputed.

After the strike had been in progress for some weeks, hourly-rated supervisors at the Grand Rapids plant were instructed by their superiors to perform certain sample and close-out production work which would nor-

---

view Board, see Stieber, Oberer, and Harrington, Democracy and Public Review, A Report to the Center for the Study of Democratic Institutions (1960); Brooks, Impartial Public Review of Internal Union Disputes: Experiment in Democratic Self-Discipline, 22 Ohio St. L.J. 64 (1961); Klein, UAW Public Review Board Report, 18 Rutgers L. Rev. 304 (1964); Oberer, Voluntary Impartial Review of Labor — Some Reflections, 58 Mich. L. Rev. 55 (1958); Oberer, The Impact of the Labor-Management Reporting and Disclosure Act of 1959 on Internal Union Affairs, 11 Lab. L.J. 571 (1960). — ED.

mally have been done by members of the bargaining unit. The work was performed as instructed.

Following the conclusion of the strike, the Company found it necessary to reduce its first line supervisory staff at its Grand Rapids plant. As a result, some of the hourly-rated supervisors who crossed the picket lines and performed bargaining unit work during the course of the 1962 strike were returned to the bargaining unit. Each as he returned was charged with having committed acts detrimental to the interests of the Union by reason of his having crossed the picket lines and performed production work during the 1962 strike while holding an honorable withdrawal transfer card. That portion of the charge which pertained to the crossing of the picket line was, in every case, ultimately dropped. The trials in question occurred at various times following the conclusion of the strike. However, by stipulation of the parties the facts as developed in one of these proceedings occurring on November 7, 1963, are to apply to all appeals here pending before the Board.

II

Appellants have advanced five reasons why their convictions must be set aside: First, the Local Trial Committee was prejudiced, for one of its members stated for the record that he knew before the trial commenced the accused had committed the acts with which they were charged. Second, the verdict was contrary to the evidence in that the Local failed to offer any probative evidence to establish the charges. Third, the action of the Local taken against them was discriminatory by reason of the fact that hourly-rated supervisors at other Doehler-Jarvis plants were not similarly charged although they did the same work. Fourth, the action of the Union was contrary to a pre-strike understanding between Doehler-Jarvis and the UAW wherein it was agreed that hourly-rated supervisors would be permitted to cross the picket line and to perform limited sample and close-out production work. Finally, they maintain the Local has no jurisdiction to charge them with acts committed in a supervisory capacity.

The Union, for its part, argues that the evidence conclusively establishes that appellants operated the Plant as charged; that this conduct was clearly detrimental to the interests of the Union since it interfered with the economic pressure which the Union was at that time trying to apply to the Company; and that the Constitution expressly holds a member responsible for the acts which he commits while holding a withdrawal transfer card. The Public Review Board, it asserts, must under these circumstances affirm the convictions of appellants.

III

We are fully satisfied the Union is correct in its premise that the act of performing production work during the course of a strike is detrimental to the collective interest of its members and we so hold. The strike is simply a pressure device designed to coerce a recalcitrant employer to accepting the Union's point of view with respect to a given controversy by withholding the means of production from the employer. The success or failure of the strike as an instrument of coercion often depends in large measure upon the effectiveness of the withdrawal of the labor force in the prevention of production. If the employer, despite the absence of his normal labor force, is nevertheless able to maintain some production sufficient to satisfy at least in a minimal way his contractual obligations, he will thereby partially counter the effect of the strike and consequently diminish its effectiveness. It is clear to us therefore that appellants by assisting in the production of certain sample work and close-out runs, and thereby helping to save some of the employer's contracts, did hinder the Union in its attempt to cause the employer to yield. The critical issue, however, is not whether the Union was correct in its evaluation of the effect of appellants' acts, but whether it may properly discipline for them. We think that it may.

The relationship between member and Union is a contractual one. By joining the Union, the employee in effect contracts with the organization for it to become his exclusive collective bargaining representative. In return he agrees to become bound by the rules of the organization. Among the rules pertaining to membership in the UAW is that which is set forth in Article 17, Section 10:

"A person who has deposited his honorable withdrawal transfer card and thus resumed membership in the Union shall thereupon be subject to charges and trial for acts or conduct detrimental to the interests of the Union or its members, committed while he was out of the Union on honorable withdrawal transfer card. The provisions of Article 30 shall be applicable in such cases."

Members of the UAW therefore must be assumed to know they are held accountable to the Union for acts or conduct detrimental to the interests of the Union committed while the member holds an honorable withdrawal transfer card from the Union.

But, appellants argue, regardless of any obligation owed the Union by virtue of the holding of an honorable withdrawal transfer card, they are not answerable to the Union for acts committed in the course of the discharge of their supervisory responsibilities. The responsibility of the supervisor, they say, is wholly to management; the Union may not intervene in this relationship. Yet, they argue, to give the Union the right to impose a penalty upon a member by reason of an act pursuant to supervisory responsibility in effect confers upon it the right to exert a measure of control over the affairs of management quite beyond the rights conferred upon it by the collective bargaining agreement. A supervisor cannot serve two masters, they declare, particularly when the interests of each will often be in direct conflict. Inevitably, in their view the situation will arise where a choice will have to be made — and there is no real choice: Should he refuse to act as directed by his superior the supervisor naturally is subject to discipline, including discharge; if discharged the Union could provide him no protection. It is entirely unreasonable, they say, for the Union to expect to exact control over those to whom it can offer no protection.

Appellants' argument, it seems to us, suffers from two intrinsic weaknesses: First, they appear to hold that upon assuming supervisory positions their relationship with the Union was completely severed. This, however, was not in fact the case. Hourly-rated supervisors under the terms of the Agreement continued to retain and accumulate seniority within the bargaining unit. First line supervisors, then, were recipients of benefits under the Agreement and as a consequence had a continuing interest in the continued well-being of the collective bargaining representative. Second, appellants assume that the fines imposed upon them by their Union were an attempt by the Union to control their activities as supervisors. We believe this view to be incorrect. The Union did not attempt to determine whether appellants properly discharged their duties as supervisors, for its inquiry was strictly limited to the question of whether appellants' activity was detrimental to the interests of the Union. Nor did it, once having made the determination that appellants' acts were harmful, attempt to affect appellants' relationship with their employer. No action was taken until after each returned to the bargaining unit and then the matter was handled as a strictly internal affair. The fines imposed thus were no more than the penalty which the Union deemed appropriate to levy upon those who had damaged the collective interest of the bargaining unit by undermining its efforts to secure a more favorable Agreement.

None of the other defenses raised by appellants impresses us as having merit. There is no evidence whatsoever to establish that there was an agreement between International Union and Doehler-Jarvis that permitted limited types of bargaining unit work which might be done during the strike. Neither does their claim that the trial committee was prejudiced against them appear to be founded in fact. That the members of the trial committee may have known that appellants performed bargaining unit work would not of itself demonstrate prejudice. Knowledge *may* result in the prejudging of the question of guilt or innocence but appellants did not pursue this area of inquiry. On the issue of uniformity of union procedure, we need only observe that we know of no rule which requires autonomous locals to act with uniformity with respect to policy determinations of this sort.

Our dissenting colleague would overturn appellants' convictions because the charging parties failed to present probative evidence to establish the charges. We respectfully disagree. His conclusion is based on a premise which requires close examination; namely, that the same rigorous procedure which prevails in a court of law should obtain here — and hence the prosecution bears the exclusive responsibility for proving by acceptable means the charges on which the defendants are being tried. It is clearly evident that a lay tribunal cannot be held to the formal procedure which is followed in a court. The judges are not professionally trained in the law and the atmosphere in which such a tribunal meets is more in the nature of a meeting at which certain matters are considered than an official court operating in accordance with concepts and forms that have become crystallized and rooted in the life of a society as a result of centuries of struggle and development. The fact that work in the plant was actually done by the appellants was indeed established, though not by the legal methods honored in a court of law. Moreover, appellants, as the record shows, readily admitted and indeed defended the work they did.

The case must thus be seen in its context. Appellants of their own choice accepted promotion to supervisory posts, and thus passed from the jurisdiction of the Union into management, while retaining seniority rights in the Union. A strike was begun in May, 1962. Prior to the strike, the Union agreed that appellants as supervisory personnel would be permitted to cross picket lines during the strike. What is under dispute is the kind of activity they would be prohibited from performing while in the plant at the time of the strike.

These supervisors, though technically outside the Union, yet maintained a substantial relationship with it. Upon demotion they would resume their membership in the bargaining unit without suffering any loss in seniority. The choice they made in accepting the supervisory position, while conferring upon them the preferment in wages and prestige they evidently sought, likewise exposed them to a number of contingencies, which as responsible men they should have taken into account. The major one of these was the possibility of a strike by the bargaining unit and thus the possibility, if not likelihood, that during the strike management might call upon them for activity that would be detrimental to the Union. A strike in the labor-management field is analogous to a war in international affairs. Comfort and aid to one side is disloyalty to the other. The appellants by crossing the picket line entered what was, from the Union's point of view, a beleaguered city, an enemy post. While within the "enemy's" lines, were they doing aught that made the strike a less effectual instrument for bringing management to terms, than it otherwise might have been? A strike is not only an economic weapon; it is also a human situation. People are out of work. Anxiety and apprehension increase as the days pass. Workers' families are daily asking their provider when will they resume work, since some of the children need new clothing or the house requires repairs. Beyond the picket lines and within the plant were these supervisors, formerly their colleagues in the Union and at the plant. Is it not fair to expect in the light of such a tense situation, and since their present position was theirs by choice, that appellants on returning to full membership in the Union would present some evidence purporting to show that they did not render the kind of help to management which would prolong the strike and work to the detriment of their striking brethren?

To be sure, evidence should always be clearly and properly presented when charges are made. The procedures are of supreme significance and freedom weakens and dissolves in the absence of procedures that safeguard the rights of the accused. But appellants in the instant case did not come in without traces of suspicion generated by their own decision to accept supervisory status. There can be no reasonable doubt that they did work in the plant, though the fact was not arrived by the formal and painstaking procedure which is traditional in a court of law.

The entire arrangement whereby supervisory personnel retain seniority rights has its motivation, it appears, in the desire to broaden the opportunities for promotion from the Union's ranks. It is part of the Union's effort to advance the welfare of its members. Such an opportunity, however, should not become a means for hurting the Union's cause.

The decision of the International Executive Board is affirmed.

Concurring opinion by Member McKelvey:

In subscribing to the above opinion I should like to emphasize that I do so only because of the state of the record in this particular case. Had the appellants rested after making their motion for a directed verdict of acquittal, I would have agreed with our dissenting colleague that the charges against the appellants had not been proved and that consequently their convictions should be set aside. But since they proceeded to present their witnesses "in the interest of getting the entire facts before this tribunal" (Attorney Vana's statement in closing argument, Transcript of Local Trial, p. 168), I conclude that appellants in effect waived their procedural defense. I do not interpret our decision in this case as constituting any endorsement of the proposition that Local trial committees can base convictions upon assertions without adducing any proof whatsoever. It is only because I find that appellants here admitted the commission of the acts with which they were charged that I concur in the opinion.

Dissenting opinion of Member Hanrahan:

I think these convictions and the penalties imposed pursuant thereto should be set aside. While I do not necessarily disagree with our colleagues in their conclusion that the Union may properly discipline its member for acts which are committed in a supervisory capacity, I would not reach this issue for I am firmly of the opinion that the evidence presented by the charging party was insufficient to sustain a conviction.

In the course of his presentation, President Peterson, spokesman for the charging parties, did no more than reiterate the charges against the appellants. He stated that they crossed the picket line and that they produced castings. While he said he saw them cross picket lines, he admitted he did not see them operate the plant. He produced no witnesses who say [*sic*] them "produce castings" nor did he apparently make any effort to do so. In short, he was content to allow common knowledge of the acts, shared by all members of the Local, establish the operative facts. At the conclusion of the presentation of Local President Peterson, counsel for appellants requested that the trial committee direct that the charges be dropped for failure to introduce any probative evidence in support of the charges. This the trial committee refused to do.

It was only following the refusal of the trial committee to direct a verdict in favor of appellants, that their counsel went ahead with the presentation of the defense on behalf of the accused. Through the testimony offered by defense witnesses it was conclusively established that all of the defendants had in fact "operated" the plant as charged. Nevertheless, neither the fact that appellants' acts were a matter of common knowledge nor the fact that testimony offered on behalf of the accused conclusively established the acts beyond all doubt alters in any way the fact that the charging party failed to produce any evidence whatsoever in support of its charges.

Since appellants timely raised the issue of the adequacy of the proof presented, we must consider the record as though it contained nothing more than President Peterson's bald, unsupported assertions that the accused had done what they were charged with doing. Viewed in this respect, the case against appellants was not established and I would so hold.

Now I recognize the difficulties with which the charging party was faced in proving these particular claims. The acts took place inside the plant when all the members of the bargaining unit were outside the plant conducting a strike. The only witnesses who could testify against the accused were either their fellow defendants or members of higher supervision. A fellow-accused might be unwilling to appear against his co-defendants for fear of implicating himself, and members of higher supervision might just be unwilling to testify in a Union proceeding. There was, of course, no way for the Union to compel either group of witnesses to testify.

Against the difficulties created by the problems of proof, however, we must balance the rights of the accused. Early in its existence the Public Review Board held that every Union member accused of wrongdoing is entitled to a full and fair trial conducted in accordance with the Union's trial procedure. This we said is "to protect to the fullest the rights of an individual member against error that might more easily occur in a less formal type of hearing . . ." Appeal of Local 469 (In re Agatha Praniewicz), PRB Case No. 13.

While the Constitution of the UAW sets forth no explicit requirements concerning the trial proceeding itself, the International Union has prepared and distributed to its Locals a booklet entitled "Guide to Local Union Trials" which sets forth suggested procedures for all stages of a trial proceeding. Concerning trial procedure the Guide provides that following the opening statements:

"The accusing member shall then present evidence supporting his charge. Insofar as possible, such evidence should be limited to testimony of witnesses or presentation of authenticated documents. Witnesses should take an oath swearing to tell the truth. After each of the accusing member's witnesses has testified, the accused member may cross-examine. If a member of the Trial Committee feels that additional questions should be asked, he may ask them directly of a witness.

"The Trial Committee is not bound by the rules of evidence prevailing in courts of law but may receive any evidence — oral or documentary — that the members of the Committee would consider if they were making a decision involving an extremely important personal affair. Hearsay evidence is not excluded (hearsay evidence is given when a witness testifies about what another person has told him rather than what he did, or saw himself). Trial Committee members, of course, may consider such evidence as less weighty than direct evidence, inasmuch as the person being quoted is not present to be cross-examined."

It is plain from this that while the Guide contemplates a somewhat less rigid procedure for the presentation of evidence than would be followed in a court of law, it is to be remembered the term "trial" is used in the Constitution. Unless that word is to be deleted and replaced by the more informal term "inquiry," then such proceedings should be conducted in substantial conformity with the usual adversary type procedure the term "trial" connotes, including the basic requirement for consideration of the "evidence" produced.

This is the area in which the Local 257 proceedings involving these appellants was plainly deficient. No evidence whatsoever was produced by the accuser! Even no attempt to secure witnesses was made. Had President Peterson reported to the trial committee that he had requested members of supervision to testify then he could have made an offer of proof as to what they would have related had they appeared. Or he could perhaps have found some members who knew through conversations with others that appellants had done that with which they were accused. While "evidence" of this nature would not be admissible in a court of law, under the more liberal rules which attend a local proceeding this might have been sufficient. However, having heard no evidence the trial committee was obligated to return a verdict for the accused. By failing to do so it committed reversible error.

I do not mean to imply that I would saddle the Union trial procedures in their present form with all the procedural safeguards that attend a criminal proceeding in a court of law. I stress, however, that in order to protect the substance of justice, the forms through which justice is obtained are of material importance. In that respect the "Guide to Local Trials" should be of assistance to a trial committee.

I would reverse the decision of the International Executive Board and set aside appellants' convictions.

NOTES

1. Examination of the transcript of the trial on November 7, 1963, before the Local Trial Committee in PRB Case No. 109 discloses the following:

(a) The sole witness for the "prosecution" was the president of Local 257, Peterson. He reiterated the charges against the defendants, which were that they had acted detrimentally to the union by crossing the picket line and operating the plant. Since the charge of crossing the picket line was dropped by the union in the course of the proceedings, because of a pre-strike agreement between the union and the company permitting supervisors to cross the picket line, the critical question of fact was whether the defendants had "operated the plant," that is, done production work ordinarily performed by those on strike. Under cross-examination by Vana, the attorney for the defendants, Peterson testified that he had not seen any of the defendants doing the production work with which they were charged. Nor did he testify that he had been told by anyone that the defendants had done production work.

(b) Peterson, who presented the union's case at the trial, both as prosecutor and sole witness, presented nothing beyond the foregoing.

(c) Vana then moved that the charges against the defendants be dropped. He stated:

"It is the burden of the charging party to prove that these four men did in fact . . . operate the plant. There is no testimony under oath or otherwise that they did operate the machines. . . .

"I am not trying to be technical. Please don't think that, gentlemen and madame. I am trying to say to you this: If you all believe in justice, as I am sure you do, there's not any testimony offered to you upon which you can find these four men guilty, none at all." Transcript, Trial Committee Proceedings, p. 13.

(d) The chairman of the Local Trial Committee refused to rule on the motion that the charges be dropped (apparently not understanding what such a motion was) and requested Vana to present the testimony of the witnesses for the defendants.

(e) Vana then stated: "All right. I want it understood . . . that the presentation of witnesses and testimony of the four gentlemen charged does not in any way prejudice their rights or waive their rights on the motion just made. We are presenting this testimony only because the Trial Committee has seen fit not to rule on our motion at this time." Transcript, p. 14. He then went on to argue that the Local Trial Committee had no jurisdiction to try the defendants because none of them were employees in the bargaining unit at the time of the alleged acts, because they were required to obey the instructions of their superiors or be fired, and because the case involved the question under the National Labor Relations Act of the division between bargaining unit employees and supervisory employees.

(f) The defendants then testified and were cross-examined by Peterson in a manner amply demonstrating that they had in fact done the production work as charged. The defendants' presentation was to the effect that they had no choice but to obey the orders of management if they wished to avoid being fired, that if they were fired, the union could be of no protection to them since they were not employees within the bargaining unit, and that the production work they did actually benefited the union in that it was "close out" and "sample" work that precluded loss of important customers, thereby retaining accounts that might otherwise have gone to competitors by reason of the strike; the alternative to their doing this work would have been the hiring of permanent replacements by the company, to the detriment of the strikers, or the loss of the accounts so that the company would not have had work available for some of the strikers when the strike was terminated.

(g) During the course of Vana's closing argument to the Trial Committee, while he was speaking of the burden of proof, one member of that committee interrupted to state that there was no need of proof that the defendants had committed the offense charged since "we knew they did it." Vana asked: "Before we put in any testimony you as members of the Trial Committee knew they did it?" Answer: "Yes." Vana: "You state so on the record?" Answer: "Yes." Vana: "You knew before testimony was presented?" Answer: "Yes." Transcript, pp. 88-89.

2. Do the proceedings in PRB Case No. 109 satisfy the requirements of Section 101(a)(5) of the LMRDA? Did the Trial Committee have jurisdiction to fine the defendants for actions "detrimental to the union" committed while the defendants were part of the management team on "honorable withdrawal" from the union? Assuming that such jurisdiction existed, were the defendants accorded a "full and fair" hearing?

In this connection, to what extent should union disciplinary proceedings be analogized to criminal prosecutions? Suppose, for example, the defendants in PRB Case No. 109 had refused to testify or present any evidence. Who had the burden of proof? Were the defendants privileged against self-incrimination?

3. In Nelson v. Brotherhood of Painters, 47 L.R.R.M. 2441 (D. Minn. 1961), defendants were "tried under Robert's Rules of Order, by virtue of which each man charged would lose all rights in the union and would be considered guilty until his innocence was proved." Id. at 2442. A temporary injunction, restraining enforcement of suspensions resulting from such trials, was granted.

4. For a discussion of the elements of a fair hearing in union disciplinary proceedings, see Summers, Union Discipline: What the Courts Do in Fact, 70 Yale L.J. 175, 200 (1960).

C. FREEDOM OF SPEECH AND POLITICAL ACTIVITY

SALZHANDLER v. CAPUTO

United States Court of Appeals, Second Circuit, 1963
316 F.2d 445, certiorari denied, 375 U.S. 946 (1963)

LUMBARD, Chief Judge.

This appeal raises an important question of the rights of union members under the Labor-Management Reporting and Disclosure Act of 1959, 29 U.S.C. §§401-531: whether a union member's allegedly libelous statements regarding the handling of union funds by union officers justify disciplinary action against the member and his exclusion from any participation in the affairs of the union for five years, including speaking and voting at meetings and even attending meetings. We hold that the LMRDA protects the union member in the exercise of his right to make such charges without reprisal by the union; that any provisions of the union constitution which make such criticism, whether libelous or not, subject to union discipline are unenforceable; and that the Act allows redress for such unlawful treatment. Accordingly we reverse the judgment rendered by Judge Wham, sitting in the United States District Court for the Southern District of New York, which dismissed the union member's complaint and we remand the case for further proceedings.

Solomon Salzhandler, a member of Local 442, Brotherhood of Painters, Decorators & Paperhangers of America, brought suit in the district court following the decision of a Trial Board of the union's New York District Council No. 9 that he had untruthfully accused Isadore Webman, the president of the local, of the crime of larceny. The Trial Board found that Salzhandler's "unsupported accusations" violated the union's constitution which prohibited "conduct unbecoming a member . . ." "acts detrimental to . . . interests of the Brotherhood," "libeling, slandering . . . fellow members (or) officers of local unions" and "acts and conduct . . . inconsistent with the duties, obligations and fealty of a member." [1]

Salzhandler's complaint alleged that his charges against Webman were an exercise of his rights as a member of the union and that the action of the Trial Board was in violation of the provisions of the LMRDA under which he was entitled to relief.

The undisputed facts developed during the trial in the district court amply support Salzhandler's claims for relief.

Salzhandler was elected financial secretary of Local 442 in 1953. He was reelected thereafter and at the times in question he was serving a three-year term which was to end June 30, 1962. His weekly compensation as an officer was $35, of which $25 was salary and $10 was for expenses. The dispute giving rise to this suit was touched off in November 1960 by Salzhandler's distribution to members of Local 442 of a leaflet which accused Webman of mishandling of union funds.

Prior to the audit each July, Salzhandler obtained the checks for the auditor. In going over the union's checks in July 1960 Salzhandler noticed that two checks, one for $800 and one for $375, had been drawn to cover the expenses of Webman and one Max Schneider at two union conventions to which they were elected delegates. The $800 check, drawn on August 21, 1959 to Webman's order, was endorsed by Webman and his wife. The $375 check, drawn on March 4, 1960 to "Cash," was likewise endorsed by Webman and his wife. Schneider's endorsement did not appear on either check. Schneider had died on May 31, 1960.

On July 15, 1960 two checks, each for $6, were drawn as refunds of dues paid by Max Schneider and another deceased member. Such checks were ordinarily mailed to the widows. Webman, however, brought the two checks to Salzhandler and told him to deposit them in a special fund for the benefit of the son of Max Schneider. Salzhandler refused to do this because the checks were not endorsed. Thereafter Sol Feldman and W. Shirpin, who were trustees of the local, each endorsed one of the checks and Salzhandler made the deposit as Webman had requested. [2]

In November 1960 Salzhandler distributed to members of the local a leaflet which accused Webman of improper conduct with regard to union funds and of referring to members of the union by such names as

---

[1] Brotherhood Constitution §267(5), (6), (10) and (16).
[2] At the trial Webman testified that he had authorization from the widows.

"thieves, scabs, robbers, scabby bosses, bums, pimps, f-bums, (and) jail birds." [3] Attached to the leaflet were photostats of the four checks. With regard to the convention checks, Salzhandler wrote:

"The last convention lasted five days, Monday, August 31, to Friday, September 4, 1959. The delegates of 442 presented their credentials Monday, August 31, and on Thursday, September 3, as soon as they got the mileage fare, they disappeared. They were absent at Thursday afternoon session. The most the chairman should have gotten was a weeks pay and allowance — $250.00. The auditor's report shows he got $200 in pay and $300 in expenses — $500, or twice what was coming to him, and also $300 as expenses for the Business Agent. The check was made out to *Cash* for $800 (photostat enclosed). So was the voucher. It does not indicate that Max Schneider got any of it. The same goes for a check made out *only* to I. Webman on March 4, 1960 for another convention, where the chairman was to get $250, but got $375. It does not indicate Schneider got his share. Were the checks legal?"

The leaflet also branded Webman as a "petty robber" of the two $6 checks:

"To prove himself most unworthy of any trust, he performed the cheapest petty act ever. Two widows were refunded each $6.00 for overpayment of dues. Two checks were issued to that effect. The petty robber had two of his friends sign their names and the chairman declared these two checks as contributions to the special tax for Michael Schneider — photostats of checks enclosed."

On December 13, 1960, Webman filed charges against Salzhandler with the New York District Council No. 9 of the union, alleging that Salzhandler had violated the union constitution, §267, by libelling and slandering him in implying that he, Webman, had not reimbursed Max Schneider for convention expenses, and that he had been a "petty robber" in causing the two $6 checks to be deposited in the Michael Schneider fund, rather than being paid over to the two widows. The charge went on to state that Salzhandler was guilty of "acts and conduct inconsistent with the duties, obligations and fealty of a member or officer of the Brotherhood" and that the net effect of the leaflet was untruthfully to accuse an officer of the union of the crime of larceny. For over six hours on the evening of February 23, 1961, Salzhandler was tried by a five-member Trial Board of the District Council. As the union rules permitted, Salzhandler was represented by a union member who was not a lawyer. At the trial, Webman introduced the leaflet. Salzhandler produced the photostats and was questioned by the Trial Board. Webman's witnesses testified that the convention expenditures were approved by the membership. Salzhandler produced three witnesses who testified that Webman had called members names as alleged in the leaflet.

---

[3] Salzhandler claims that he reported these purported irregularities to the local's membership at a meeting in August 1960. He further asserts that he filed formal charges against Webman at about the same time. The defendants denied that Salzhandler had taken these actions. Judge Wham made no findings on these disputed facts.

Not until April 2, 1961 did Salzhandler receive notice of the Trial Board's decision and his removal from office and this was from a printed postal card mailed to all members:

"By a decision of the Trial Committee of District Council 9, Sol Saltzhandler (*sic*) is no longer Financial Secretary of Local Union 442."

Thereafter, on April 4, the District Council mailed to Salzhandler only the final paragraph of its five page "Decision" which read as follows:

"It is our decision that Brother Solomon Salzhandler be prohibited from participating in the affairs of L.U. 442, or of any other Local Union of the Brotherhood, or of District Council 9, for a period of five (5) years. He shall not be permitted during that period to attend meetings of L.U. 422, to vote on any matter, to have the floor at any meeting of any other Local Union affiliated with the District Council, or to be a candidate for any position in any local Union or in the District Council. In all other respects, Brother Salzhandler's rights and obligations as a member of the Brotherhood shall be continued."

Salzhandler did not receive a copy of the full opinion of the Trial Board until after this action was commenced on June 14, 1961. Meanwhile, as the union constitution required appeal within 30 days, Salzhandler filed intraunion appeals with the Secretary-Treasurer of the Council and the General Secretary-Treasurer of the Brotherhood on April 12 and 28. At the time this action was brought, plaintiff had received no word regarding said appeals.[4]

On May 15, 1961, Salzhandler attempted to attend a meeting of the local but was prevented from doing so by Webman. The complaint alleges that Webman assaulted Salzhandler and used violence in removing him.

This action was commenced in the federal court under the Labor-Management Reporting and Disclosure Act of 1959, §102, 29 U.S.C. §412, requesting a nullification of the order of the Trial Board, reinstatement in the position as financial secretary, and damages.

Judge Wham dismissed the complaint holding that the Trial Board's conclusion that the leaflet was libelous was sufficiently supported by the evidence. He went further, however, and made an independent finding that the statements were, in fact, libelous. The court held, as a matter of law, that "The rights accorded members of labor unions under Title I of the Labor-Management Reporting and Disclosure Act of 1959 . . . do not include the right of a union member to libel or slander officers of the union." We do not agree.

The LMRDA of 1959 was designed to protect the rights of union members to discuss freely and criticize the management of their unions and the conduct of their officers. The legislative history and the extensive hearings which preceded the enactment of the statute abundantly evidence the intention of the Congress to prevent union officials

---

[4] The parties are agreed that Salzhandler exhausted his intraunion remedies. We do not pass upon the question of whether, in a case such as this, the plaintiff must first exhaust his intraunion remedies.

from using their disciplinary powers to silence criticism and punish those who dare to question and complain.[5]   The statute is clear and explicit. [The court then quoted in turn Sections 101(a)(1) and (2), 102, and 609 of the statute.]

Appellees argue that just as constitutionally protected speech does not include libelous utterances, Beauharnais v. Illinois, 343 U.S. 250, 266 (1952), the speech protected by the statute likewise does not include libel and slander.   The analogy to the First Amendment is not convincing. In Beauharnais, the Supreme Court recognized the possibility that state action might stifle criticism under the guise of punishing libel.   However, because it felt that abuses could be prevented by the exercise of judicial authority, 343 U.S. at 263-264, the court sustained a state criminal libel statute.   But the union is not a political unit to whose disinterested tribunals an alleged defamer can look for an impartial review of his "crime." [6]   It is an economic action group, the success of which depends in large measure on a unity of purpose and sense of solidarity among its members.

The Trial Board in the instant case consisted of union officials, not judges.   It was a group to which the delicate problems of truth or falsehood, privilege, and "fair comment" were not familiar.   Its procedure is peculiarly unsuited for drawing the fine line between criticism and defamation, yet, were we to adopt the view of the appellees, each charge of libel would be given a trial de novo in the federal court — an impractical result not likely contemplated by Congress, see 105 Cong. Rec. 6026 (daily ed. April 25, 1959) (colloquy between Senator Goldwater and Senator Clark) — and such a Trial Board would be the final arbiter of the extent of the union member's protection under §101(a)(2).[7]

In a proviso to §101(a)(2), there are two express exceptions to the broad rule of free expression.   One relates to "the responsibility of every member toward the organization as an institution."   The other deals with interference with the union's legal and contractual obligations.

[5] The Senate Select Committee to Investigate Improper Activities in Labor-Management Relations was created to investigate improper activities in the field of labor management relations.   S. Res. 74, 85 Cong. 1st Sess., reproduced, 103 Cong. Rec. 1264-1265.   It filed a number of reports.   See S. Rept. 1417, 85th Cong. 2d Sess. (1958); S. Repts. 620, 621, 86th Cong. 1st Sess. (1959); S. Rept. 1139, 86th Cong., 2d Sess. (1960).   The legislative history of the "Bill of Rights" portion of the LMRDA is reproduced, 2 Legislative History of the Labor-Management Reporting and Disclosure Act of 1959 at 1102-1119, 1220-1239.

[6] Union discipline for libel has been characterized as a form of criminal sanction, Summers, The Law of Union Discipline.   What Courts Do in Fact, 70 Yale L.J. 175, 178 (1960).

[7] See Summers, American Legislation for Union Democracy, 25 Mod. L. Rev. 273, 287:

"The most difficult problem arises when a member is expelled for 'slandering a union officer.'   Union debates are characterized by vitriol and calumny, and campaigns for office are salted with overstated accusations.   Defining the scope of fair comment in political contests is never easy, and in this context is nearly impossible.   To allow the union to decide this issue in the first instance is to invite retaliation and repression and to frustrate one of the principal reasons for protecting this right — to enable members to oust corrupt leadership through the democratic process."

While the inclusion of only two exceptions, without more, does not mean that others were intentionally excluded, we believe that the legislative history supports the conclusion that Congress intended only those exceptions which were expressed.[8]

The expression of views by Salzhandler did not come within either exception in the proviso to §101(a)(2). The leaflet did not interfere in any way with the union's legal or contractual obligations and the union has never claimed that it did. Nor could Salzhandler's charges against Webman be construed as a violation of the "responsibility of every member toward the organization as an institution." Quite the contrary; it would seem clearly in the interest of proper and honest management of union affairs to permit members to question the manner in which the union's officials handle the union's funds and how they treat the union's members. It is that interest which motivated the enactment of the statute and which would be immeasurably frustrated were we to interpret it so as to compel each dissatisfied and questioning member to draw, at the peril of union discipline, the thin and tenuous line between what is libelous and what is not. This is especially so when we consider that the Act was designed largely to curtail such vices as the mismanagement of union funds, criticism of which by union members is always likely to be viewed by union officials as defamatory.

The union argues that there is a public interest in promoting the monolithic character of unions in their dealings with employers. But the Congress weighed this factor and decided that the desirability of protecting the democratic process within the unions outweighs any possible weakening of unions in their dealings with employers which may result from the freer expression of opinions within the unions.

The democratic and free expression of opinion in any group necessarily develops disagreements and divergent opinions. Freedom of expression would be stifled if those in power could claim that any charges against them were libelous and then proceed to discipline those responsible on a finding that the charges were false. That is precisely what Webman and the Trial Board did here when they punished Salzhandler with a five-year ban of silence and stripped him of his office.

So far as union discipline is concerned Salzhandler had a right to speak his mind and spread his opinions regarding the union's officers, regardless of whether his statements were true or false. It was wholly immaterial to Salzhandler's cause of action under the LMRDA whether he

[8] As initially introduced before the Senate, the freedom of speech section was absolute in form. See 105 Cong. Rec. 5810 (daily ed. April 22, 1959). The section was in fact passed in that form. Id. at 5827. Later the question came to be reconsidered and the free speech section was amended to include the two express exceptions. Id. at 6030 (daily ed. April 25, 1959). In effect, the section as initially passed took away the power of unions to punish for expressions of views. The subsequent amendment restored that power in only two situations.

We are referred to certain statements made during the debate in the Senate which allegedly indicate that "reasonable restraints" on speech were intended. See, e.g., 105 Cong. Rec. 6022 (daily ed. April 25, 1959) (remarks of Senator Kuchel). We find these statements to be ambiguous and we are not persuaded that exceptions other than those specified were intended.

spoke truthfully or not, and accordingly Judge Wham's views on whether Salzhandler's statements were true are beside the point. Here Salzhandler's charges against Webman related to the handling of union funds; they concerned the way the union was managed. The Congress has decided that it is in the public interest that unions be democratically governed and toward that end that discussion should be free and untrammeled and that reprisals within the union for the expression of views should be prohibited. It follows that although libelous statements may be made the basis of civil suit between those concerned, the union may not subject a member to any disciplinary action on a finding by its governing board that such statements are libelous. The district court erred in dismissing the complaint.

Accordingly, we reverse the judgment of the district court and direct entry of judgment for the plaintiff which, among other things, should assess damages and enjoin the defendants from carrying out any punishment imposed by the District Council Trial Board.

GRAND LODGE, INTERNATIONAL ASSN. OF MACHINISTS v. KING

United States Court of Appeals, Ninth Circuit, 1964
335 F.2d 340, certiorari denied, 379 U.S. 920 (1964)

BROWNING, Circuit Judge.

Plaintiffs brought suit alleging they were summarily discharged as officers of defendant union because they supported an unsuccessful candidate in a union election.[7] They sought reinstatement and damages. The district court denied defendants' motion to dismiss, and this interlocutory appeal under 28 U.S.C.A. §1292 followed.

I

The district court concluded that plaintiffs' allegation of summary dismissal stated a claim under section 101(a)(5) of the Labor-Management Reporting and Disclosure Act of 1959 . . .

---

[7] The six plaintiffs were employed by the union as "Grand Lodge Representatives" at a salary of $12,000 per year. They were appointed by the International President, who, under the union constitution, was given "full control" of them and could "assign them . . . for such particular terms and duties as shall be for the best interests" of the union. Their duties included organization, grievance representation, NLRB representation, and negotiations with employers in behalf of the union. Each of them received at the start of each year a document declaring the fact of his appointment and certifying his authority to act. The last such document, over the signatures of the International President and the General Secretary-Treasurer, specified: "This credential to remain in effect from *January 1, 1961* to *January 1, 1962* unless revoked." The plaintiffs actively supported a candidate who ran against the incumbent General Secretary-Treasurer in the 1961 election. The incumbent won the election, and the plaintiffs were notified immediately thereafter of their discharge as Grand Lodge Representatives "as of midnight July 31, 1961." See 215 F. Supp. 351, 352 (1963) (district court opinion). — ED.

We are satisfied, however, that Congress did not intend section 101(a)-(5) to preclude summary removal of a member from union office. While the Act was being considered by Congress, objection was raised to section 101(a)(5) on the ground that it would permit wrongdoing union officials to remain in control while the time-consuming "due process" requirements of the section were met.   As an alternative it was proposed that the union's power of summary discipline be retained, and that notice and hearing be required after, rather than before, disciplinary action.   This solution was rejected; instead, the objection to section 101(a)(5) was met by including limiting language in the legislative history.   The Conference Report on the Act stated that section 101-(a)(5) "applies only to suspension of membership in the union; it does not refer to suspension of a member's status as an officer in the union." Senator Kennedy, as a Senate conferee, advised the Senate that "this provision does not relate to suspension or removal from a union office. Often this step must be taken summarily to prevent dissipation or misappropriation of funds."

In deference to the "patent legislative intent" [6] it has been held with virtual unanimity[7] that section 101(a)(5) does not apply to removal or suspension from union office.[8]   We think these decisions are correct. Furthermore, we think it makes no difference what the reason for the summary removal may have been.   Congress's primary concern was that section 101(a)(5) should not bar summary removal of union officials suspected of malfeasance, but the means Congress chose to accomplish its purpose was to wholly exclude suspension or removal from union office from the category of union action to which section 101(a)(5) applied.

I I

Plaintiffs also sought to state a claim under sections 101(a)(1), 101-(a)(2), and 609 of the Act.   We think they have succeeded, and are therefore authorized by section 102 of the Act to bring a civil action in the district court for appropriate relief.

[6] Comment, Rights of Union Members: The Developing Law under the LMRDA, 48 Va. L. Rev. 78, 87 (1962).

[7] . . .

This does not necessarily mean that an officer-member summarily dismissed has no cause of action under state law.   "Violations of the federal statute are actionable in the district courts of the United States.   In all other cases improper discipline will give rise to a state cause of action, precisely as in the past.   There is no merit to the argument that the federal right is exclusive."   Cox, Internal Affairs of Labor Unions under the Labor Reform Act of 1959, 58 Mich. L. Rev. 819, 838 (1960).   See also Summers, Pre-emption and the Labor Reform Act — Dual Rights and Remedies, 22 Ohio St. L.J. 119 (1961); Jackson v. Martin Co., 180 F. Supp. 475, 481 (D. Md. 1960).   Cf. International Ass'n of Machinists v. Gonzales, 356 U.S. 617, 78 S. Ct. 923, 2 L. Ed. 2d 1018 (1958).

[8] Whether (and, if so, in what circumstances) a member who is also a union official may be "fined, suspended, expelled, or otherwise disciplined" other than by suspension or removal from his union office, without complying with §101(a)-(5), is not before us. . . .

Plaintiffs allege they were discharged because they actively supported a particular candidate for union office by meeting with other members and expressing views favorable to that candidate. Defendants concede that the right to engage in such intra-union political activity is guaranteed to members by sections 101(a)(1) and 101(a)(2) of the Act, but argue that these and other rights protected by Title I of the Act do not extend to members who are also officers of the union. However, sections 101(a)(1) and (2) apply in terms to "every member," and nothing in the statutory language excludes members who are officers.[11] Nor is there any intimation in the legislative history that Congress intended these guarantees of equal political rights and freedom of speech and assembly to be inapplicable to officer-members.[12] Indeed, the general purpose of the Act points to the contrary. The guarantees of sections 101(a)(1) and (2) were adopted to strengthen internal union democracy. To exclude officer-members from their coverage would deny protection to those best equipped to keep union government vigorously and effectively democratic. We therefore conclude that sections 101(a)(1) and (2) apply to officer-members such as plaintiffs.[14]

Section 102 (73 Stat. 523, 29 U.S.C.A. §412) provides that "[a]ny person whose rights secured by the provisions of this title have been infringed by any violation of this title may bring a civil action in a district court of the United States for such relief (including injunctions) as may be appropriate." We think it follows that plaintiffs' complaint for reinstatement and damages was sufficient to withstand dismissal for failure to state a claim upon which relief could be granted.

In any event, section 609 (73 Stat. 541, 29 U.S.C.A. §529) "makes

---

[11] This is also true of other sections of Title I. Our conclusion that §101(a)(5) is inapplicable to the present case is based upon the conclusion that one removed from office is not "otherwise disciplined" within the meaning of §101(a)(5), rather than upon a reading of the word "member" in that section as excluding officers. See note 8.

[12] Defendants call attention to the fact that as §101(a)(4) originally passed the Senate it applied to "members or officers," and the words "or officers" were deleted in conference. S. 1555, 86th Cong., 1st Sess. §101(a)(4) (1959), 1 Leg. His. LMRDA 520; H. R. 8490, 86th Con., 1st Sess. §101(a)(4) (1959), 1 Leg. His. LMRDA 877. Defendants argue that this change evidences a congressional understanding that union officers were excluded from the whole of Title I. See Judge Kalodner's opinion in Sheridan v. United Bhd. of Carpenters & Joiners, 306 F.2d 152, 156-157 (3d Cir. 1962).

The language change in §101(a)(4) was made without comment of any sort. Prior to the change, it was assumed in Senate debate that officers-members were included in §101(a)(4) (see remarks of Senator Mundt at 105 Cong. Rec. 6478 (1959), 2 Leg. His. LMRDA 1105). Thus defendants' argument requires the inference that the Conference Committee drastically narrowed the assumed coverage of §101(a)(4) with no explanation whatever. A more reasonable conclusion is that the Conference Committee recognized that the deleted words "or officers" were surplusage since as a practical matter union officers were also union members, and therefore deleted these words to conform §101(a)(4) in style with other sections of Title I which used only the inclusive word "members."

[14] The Second Circuit held §101(a)(2) applicable to an officer-member in Salzhandler v. Caputo, 316 F.2d 445 (2d Cir. 1963); Comments 77 Harv. L. Rev. 770 (1964), and 73 Yale L.J. 426 (1964). . . .

doubly secure the protection of the members in the exercise of their rights" [16] by making it unlawful for a union "to fine, suspend, expel, or otherwise discipline any of its members for exercising any right to which he is entitled under the provisions of this Act," and by providing explicitly that an action may be brought under section 102 to enforce the specific prohibitions of section 609.

Defendants argue that the words "otherwise discipline" in section 609 must be read as not including removal from union office, since the same words have that restricted meaning in section 101(a)(5). The argument is a plausible one, for it is natural to suppose that within a single statute the same words will be used with the same meaning. But it is also common experience that identical words may be used in the same statute, or even in the same section of a statute, with quite different meanings. And when they are, it is the duty of the courts to give the words "the meaning which the Legislature intended [they] should have in each instance." Atlantic Cleaners & Dyers, Inc. v. United States, 286 U.S. 427, 433 (1932).

Sections 101(a)(5) and 609 have wholly different purposes, and the difference is such as to satisfy us that although Congress did not intend the words "otherwise discipline" to include removal from union office in section 101(a)(5), it did intend the words to include such action in section 609.[20]

Section 101(a)(5) guarantees to union members, as one of several independent rights conferred upon them by Title I of the Act, that they shall be accorded procedural due process before being subjected to disciplinary action, for whatever reason. Section 609, on the other hand, has no bearing upon the procedures to be followed in disciplining union members. Section 609 appears in Title VI of the Act, a collection of sections having to do with miscellaneous administrative and enforcement matters; section 609 itself is not a source of additional independent rights, but is an enforcement provision, designed, as we have noted, to effectuate rights conferred in other sections of the Act by making it unlawful to punish members who seek to exercise such rights. Punishment for the exercise of these rights is prohibited by section 609 whether inflicted summarily or after a full panoply of procedural protections.

Congress, through the legislative history materials, imposed a limiting gloss upon the words "otherwise discipline" in section 101(a)(5) to preserve union power to summarily remove officer-members suspected of wrongdoing in order to protect unions from continuing depredations while charges are being investigated and resolved. This object is fully accomplished by reading the words "otherwise discipline" in section

[16] Salzhandler v. Caputo, 316 F.2d 445, 449 (2d Cir. 1963).

[20] ". . . [B]ecause much of the bill was written on the floor of the Senate or House of Representatives and because many sections contain calculated ambiguities or political compromises essential to secure a majority," it is particularly important, in interpreting the Labor-Management Reporting and Disclosure Act of 1959, "to seek out the underlying rationale without placing great emphasis upon close construction of the words." Cox, Internal Affairs of Labor Unions under the Labor Reform Act of 1959, 58 Mich. L. Rev. 819, 852 (1960). . . .

101(a)(5) as not including removal from union office. It would not further this purpose in any way to impose the same restriction upon the same words in section 609, since that section has nothing to do with whether or not discipline is summary. There is nothing in the legislative history to indicate that Congress wished to preserve an unrestricted power in the union to discipline officer-members (the subject matter of section 609, when discipline is imposed because of the exercise of rights under the Act), as distinguished from the power to discipline summarily (the subject matter of section 101(a)(5)). Thus, to construe section 609 to exclude from its coverage dismissal from union office would immunize a most effective weapon of reprisal against officer-members for exercising political rights guaranteed by the Act without serving any apparent legislative purpose; and, as we have noted, the members thus exposed to reprisal would be those whose uninhibited exercise of freedom of speech and assembly is most important to effective democracy in union government.[21]

Plaintiffs are appointed officials, and defendants argue that "elected officials of any private or political organization at any level have both the responsibility and the power of their positions, and . . . the burden of the responsibility carries with it the right to appoint subordinate officials to aid in the discharge of that responsibility who are in full and complete accord with the views of the elected officer." [22] Plaintiffs allege they were discharged because they exercised section 101(a)(1) and (2) rights; if defendants dispute this allegation they raise an issue of fact to be resolved at trial. We assume, however, that defendants mean to argue that successful candidates for union office must have the right to discharge appointed union officials who expressed support for their opponents. Realistically, this is simply to argue that members appointed to union office may not actively engage in union political activities while occupying such positions.

Undoubtedly a substantial argument can be made that active, partisan participation by jobholders in intra-organizational politics is a threat to good administration. Congress, in adopting the Hatch Act, endorsed this view with respect to most federal employees. Based upon this precedent, it has been suggested "that the internal political activi-

[21] It has been suggested that the right of union members to remove their officers is itself essential to the democratic self-government. Sheridan v. United Bhd. of Carpenters & Joiners, 306 F.2d 152, 158-159 (3d Cir. 1962). The power of the member-electorate to turn out elected officials for "serious misconduct" is guaranteed by §401(a) of the Act (73 Stat. 532, 29 U.S.C.A. §481(h)), and is not at issue here. And, as we have said, there is nothing to indicate that Congress believed effective union democracy required that controlling union officials have power to discharge other officers for exercising freedom of speech and assembly in internal union political affairs.

[22] To which one commentator has added, "The art of patronage is well known in political and administrative life and is equally well known and accepted for the same reasons in union life." Thatcher, Rights of Individual Union Members under Title I and Section 610 of the Landrum-Griffin Act, 52 Geo. L.J. 339, 357 (1964).

ties of full time union member employees may be regulated to prevent their use for either side in election contests . . ." [24]

It may well be that the "reasonable rules and regulations" exception of section 101(a)(1) and the similar proviso of section 101(a)(2) would permit a union to adopt the principle of "required political neutrality . . . as a sound element for efficiency," and formulate, and apply without discrimination, regulations imposing reasonable limitations upon the political activity of union jobholders. However, the defendant union has made no effort to implement such a program, and arguments in favor of doing so cannot support defendants' contention that they should be free to discharge particular union employees because they are not their political partisans.

Finally, defendants contend that to extend section 609 to dismissal from union employment would create a potential conflict of jurisdiction between the courts and the National Labor Relations Board since plaintiffs allege conduct which might constitute an unfair labor practice by the union-employer under section 8(a) of the National Labor Relations Act (29 U.S.C.A. §158(a)).[28] Congress was aware that the rights conferred by the Labor-Management Reporting and Disclosure Act of 1959 overlapped those available under state law and other federal legislation, and expressly provided that these rights were to be cumulative.[29]

The Court of Appeals for the Second Circuit has held section 609 applicable to the discharge of a union officer for exercise of section 101(a)-(2) rights.[30] There are no decisions to the contrary. We are satisfied that this is the proper construction of the statute. . . .

Affirmed.

NOTE

Suppose the plaintiffs in the Grand Lodge case had campaigned against the incumbent president of the IAM in libelous fashion. Would they be protected from termination of their appointments as members of the IAM staff by reason of the Salzhandler decision read in conjunction with that in Grand Lodge? Should they be? Consider the implications for effective conduct of union business. Is the following position sound?

"American labor . . . has become businesslike. This is so because successful union activity vis-à-vis modern industry demands businesslike, i.e., nondemocratic, organization. However unpleasant the reality, democracy is as inappropriate within the international headquarters of the UAW as it is in the front office of General Motors." Magrath, De-

---

[24] Givens, *Federal Protection of Employee Rights within Trade Unions*, 29 Fordham L. Rev. 259, 278 (1960).

[28] Office Employes Int'l Union, Local No. 11 v. N.L.R.B., 353 U.S. 313 (1957).

[29] Section 103 (73 Stat. 523 (1959), 29 U.S.C.A. §413). . . . See also Thatcher, *Rights of Individual Union Members under Title I and Section 610 of the Landrum-Griffin Act*, 52 Geo. L.J. 339, 361 (1964).

[30] Salzhandler v. Caputo, 316 F.2d 445 (2d Cir. 1963). See note 14.

mocracy in Overalls: The Futile Quest for Union Democracy, 12 Ind. & Lab. Rel. Rev. 503, 525 (1959).

d. ELECTIONS

CALHOON v. HARVEY

Supreme Court of the United States, 1964
379 U.S. 134, 85 Sup. Ct. 292, 13 L. Ed. 2d 190

MR. JUSTICE BLACK delivered the opinion of the Court.

This case raises important questions concerning the powers of the Secretary of Labor and federal courts to protect rights of employees guaranteed by the Labor-Management Reporting and Disclosure Act of 1959.

The respondents, three members of District No. 1, National Marine Engineers' Beneficial Association, filed a complaint in Federal District Court against the union, its president and its secretary-treasurer, alleging that certain provisions of the union's bylaws and national constitution violated the Act in that they infringed "the right of members of defendant District No. 1, NMEBA, to nominate candidates in elections of defendant, which right is guaranteed to each member of defendant, and to each plaintiff, by Section 101(a)(1) of the LMRDA . . ." It was alleged that §102 of Title I of the Act gave the District Court jurisdiction to adjudicate the controversy. The union bylaws complained of deprived a member of the right to nominate anyone for office but himself. The national constitution in turn provided that no member could be eligible for nomination or election to a full-time elective office unless he had been a member of the national union for five years and had served 180 days or more of seatime in each of two of the preceding three years on vessels covered by collective bargaining agreements with the national or its subsidiary bodies. On the basis of these allegations respondents asked that the union be enjoined from preparing for or conducting any election until it revised its system of elections so as to afford each of its members a fair opportunity to nominate any persons "meeting fair and reasonable eligibility requirements for any or all offices to be filled by such election."

The union moved to dismiss the complaint on the grounds that (1) the court lacked jurisdiction over the subject matter, and (2) the complaint failed to state a claim upon which relief could be granted. The District Court dismissed for want of "jurisdiction," holding that the alleged conduct of the union, even if true, failed to show a denial of the equal rights of all members of the union to vote for or nominate candidates guaranteed by §101(a)(1) of Title I of the Act, so as to give the District Court jurisdiction of the controversy under §102. The allegations, said the court, showed at most imposition of qualifications of eligibility for nomination and election so restrictive that they might violate §401(e) of Title IV by denying members a reasonable opportunity to nominate and vote for candidates. The District Court further held that it could not exercise jurisdiction to protect §401(e) rights because §402(a) of Title IV provides a remedy, declared by §403 to be "exclusive," authorizing members to vindicate such rights by challenging elections after they have been held, and then only by (1) first exhausting all remedies available with the union, (2) filing a complaint with the Secretary of Labor, who (3) may, after investigating the violation alleged in the complaint, bring suit in a United States District Court to attack the validity of the election. The Court of Appeals reversed, holding that "the complaint alleged a violation of §101(a)(1) and that federal jurisdiction existed under §102." 324 F.2d 486, 487. Because of the importance of the questions presented and conflicting views in the courts of appeals and the district courts,[10] we granted certiorari. 375 U.S. 991.

I

Jurisdiction of the District Court under §102 of Title I depends entirely upon whether this complaint showed a violation of rights guaranteed by §101(a)(1), for we disagree with the Court of Appeals' holding that jurisdiction under §102 can be upheld by reliance in whole or in part on allegations which in substance charge a breach of Title IV rights. An analysis and understanding of the meaning of §101(a)(1) and of the charges of the complaint is therefore essential to a determination of this issue. Respondents charge that the bylaws and constitutional provisions referred to above infringed their right guaranteed by §101(a)(1) to nominate candidates. The result of their allegations here, however, is an attempt to sweep into the ambit of their right to sue in federal court if they are denied an equal opportunity to nominate candidates under §101(a)(1), a right to sue if they are not allowed to nominate anyone they choose regardless of his eligibility and qualifications under union restrictions. But Title IV, not Title I, sets standards for eligibility and qualifications of candidates and officials and provides its own separate and different administrative and judicial procedure for challenging those standards. And the equal-rights language of §101(a)(1) would have to be stretched far beyond its normal meaning to hold that it guarantees members not just a right to "nominate candidates," but a right to nominate anyone, without regard to valid union rules. All that §101(a)(1) guarantees is that "[e]very member of a labor organization shall have equal rights and privileges . . . to nominate candidates, to vote in elections or referendums of the labor organization . . . and to participate in

[10] See, e.g., Mamula v. United Steelworkers, 304 F.2d 108 (C.A. 3d Cir.), cert. denied, 371 U.S. 823; Beckman v. Local No. 46 International Assn. of Bridge, Structural and Ornamental Iron Workers, 314 F.2d 848 (C.A. 7th Cir.); Robins v. Rarback, 325 F.2d 929 (C.A. 2d Cir.); Johnson v. San Diego Waiters & Bartenders Union, 190 F. Supp. 444 (D.C.S.D. Cal.); Colpo v. Highway Truck Drivers & Helpers, 201 F. Supp. 307 (D.C.D. Del.), vacated as moot, 305 F.2d 362 (C.A. 3d Cir.), cert. denied, 371 U.S. 890; Jackson v. International Longshoremen's Assn., 212 F. Supp. 79 (D.C.E.D. La).

the deliberations and voting . . . subject to reasonable rules and regulations in such organization's constitution and bylaws." Plainly, this is no more than a command that members and classes of members shall not be discriminated against in their right to nominate and vote. And Congress carefully prescribed that even this right against discrimination is "subject to reasonable rules and regulations" by the union. The complaining union members here have not been discriminated against in any way and have been denied no privilege or right to vote or nominate which the union has granted to others. They have indeed taken full advantage of the uniform rule limiting nominations by nominating themselves for office. It is true that they were denied their request to be candidates, but that denial was not a discrimination against their right to nominate, since the same qualifications were required equally of all members. Whether the eligibility requirements set by the union's constitution and by laws were reasonable and valid is a question separate and distinct from whether the right to nominate on an equal basis given by §101(a)(1) was violated. The District Court therefore was without jurisdiction to grant the relief requested here unless, as the Court of Appeals held, the *"combined* effect of the eligibility requirements and the restriction to self-nomination" are to be considered in determining whether §101(a)(1) has been violated.

II

We hold that possible violations of Title IV of the Act regarding eligibility are not relevant in determining whether or not a district court has jurisdiction under §102 of Title I of the Act. Title IV sets up a statutory scheme governing the election of union officers, fixing the terms during which they hold office, requiring that elections be by secret ballot, regulating the handling of campaign literature, requiring a reasonable opportunity for the nomination of candidates, authorizing unions to fix "reasonable qualifications uniformly imposed" for candidates, and attempting to guarantee fair union elections in which all the members are allowed to participate. Section 402 of Title IV, as has been pointed out, sets up an exclusive method for protecting Title IV rights, by permitting an individual member to file a complaint with the Secretary of Labor challenging the validity of any election because of violations of Title IV. Upon complaint the Secretary investigates and if he finds probable cause to believe that Title IV has been violated, he may file suit in the appropriate district court. It is apparent that Congress decided to utilize the special knowledge and discretion of the Secretary of Labor in order best to serve the public interest. Cf. San Diego Building Trades Council Millmen's Union, Local 2020 v. Garmon, 359 U.S. 236, 242. In so doing Congress, with one exception not here relevant, decided not to permit individuals to block or delay union elections by filing federal-court suits for violations of Title IV. Reliance on the discretion of the Secretary is in harmony with the general congressional policy to allow unions great latitude in resolving their own internal controversies, and, where that fails, to utilize the agencies of government most familiar with union problems to aid in bringing about a settlement through discussion before resort to the courts. Without setting out the lengthy legislative history which preceded the passage of this measure, it is sufficient to say that we are satisfied that the Act itself shows clearly by its structure and language that the disputes here, basically relating as they do to eligibility of candidates for office, fall squarely within Title IV of the Act and are to be resolved by the administrative and judicial procedures set out in that Title.

Accordingly, the judgment of the Court of Appeals is reversed and that of the District Court is affirmed.

Mr. Justice Douglas would affirm the judgment of the Court of Appeals for the reasons stated in its opinion as reported in 324 F.2d 486.

Mr. Justice Stewart, whom Mr. Justice Harlan joins, concurring.

This case marks the first interpretation by this Court of the significant changes wrought by the Labor-Management Reporting and Disclosure Act of 1959 increasing federal supervision of internal union affairs. At issue are subtle questions concerning the interplay between Title I and Title IV of that Act. In part, both seem to deal with the same subject matter: Title I guarantees "equal rights and privileges . . . to nominate candidates"; Title IV provides that "a reasonable opportunity shall be given for the nomination of candidates." Where the two Titles of the legislation differ most substantially is in the remedies they provide. If a Title I right is at issue, the allegedly aggrieved union member has direct, virtually immediate recourse to a federal court to obtain an adjudication of his claim and an injunction if his complaint has merit. 29 U.S.C. §402. Vindication of claims under Title IV may be much more onerous. Federal court suits can be brought only by the Secretary of Labor, and then, only after the election has been held. An additional barrier is thus placed between the union member and the federal court. Remedies shape the significance of rights, and I think the Court too casually forecloses the direct access to a federal court which the Court of Appeals held was given these respondents by Congress. . . .

The Court precludes the District Court from asserting jurisdiction over this complaint by focusing on the fact that one of the imposed restrictions speaks in terms of eligibility. And since these are "possible violations of Title IV of the Act regarding eligibility" they "are not relevant in determining whether or not a district court has jurisdiction under §102 of Title I of the Act." By this reasoning, the Court forecloses early adjudication of claims concerning participation in the election process. But there are occasions when eligibility provisions can infringe upon the right to nominate. Had the NMEBA issued a regulation that only Jesse Calhoon was eligible for office, no one could place great store on the right to self-nomination left to the rest of the membership. This Court long ago recognized the subtle ways by which election rights can be removed through discrimination at a less visible stage of the political process. The decisions in the Texas Primary Cases were founded on the belief that the equal right to vote was impaired where discrimination existed in the method of nomination. Smith v. Allwright, 321 U.S. 649; Nixon v. Herndon, 273 U.S. 536. See United States v. Classic, 313 U.S. 299. No less is the equal right to nominate infringed where onerous burdens drastically limit the candidates available for nomination. In scrutinizing devices designed to erode the franchise, the Court has shown impatience with arguments founded in the form of the device. Gomillion v. Lightfoot, 364 U.S. 339, 345. If Congress has told the courts to protect a union member from infringement of his equal right to nominate, the courts should do so whether such discrimination is sophisticated or simple-minded. Lane v. Wilson, 307 U.S. 268, 275.

After today, simply by framing its discriminatory rules in terms of eligibility, a union can immunize itself from pre-election attack in a federal court even though it makes deep incursions on the equal right of its members to nominate, to vote, and to participate in the union's internal affairs.

The Court justifies this conclusion by looking to the "structure and language" of the Act. The language is certainly not free from doubt. And the legislative history indicates that the structure can be misleading. What now constitutes Titles II through VI of the Act was substantially contained in the original bill presented to the Senate by Senator Kennedy. Title I, first introduced by Senator McClellan, was the product of doubt that the bill went far enough in guaranteeing internal democracy in union affairs. The concept of Title I — its stress on equal rights and judicial protection — was the subject of great controversy both in the Senate and in the House. Repeated attempts were made by representatives of organized labor, among other groups, to have the strict mandate of this so-called Bill of Rights modified, or eliminated altogether. Despite these efforts to remove Title I, it endured, and indeed was amended to provide stronger remedial provisions than those contained in the original version. As originally introduced, §102 would have required an aggrieved union member to make his complaint to the Secretary of Labor, exactly the remedy provided by Title IV. The Kuchel amendment, however, substituted the present provision permitting suit by an aggrieved member in a federal district court. . . . Senator Clark of Pennsylvania noted that the Kuchel amendment "takes the Federal bureaucracy out of this bill of rights and leaves its enforcement to union members aided by the courts." Leg. Hist. 1233.

Nonetheless, the Court finds a "general congressional policy" to avoid judicial resolution of internal union disputes. That policy, the Court says, was designed to limit the power of individuals to block and delay elections by seeking injunctive relief. Such an appraisal might have been accurate before the addition of Title I, but it does not explain the emphasis on prompt judicial remedies there provided. In addition to the injunctive relief authorized by §102 and the savings provisions of §103, §101(a)(4) modifies the traditional requirement of exhausting internal remedies before resort to litigation. Even §403 is not conclusive on the elimination of pre-election remedies. At the least, state court actions may be brought in advance of an election to "enforce the constitution and bylaws." And as to federal courts, it is certainly arguable that recourse through the Secretary of Labor is the exclusive remedy only after the election has been held.[6] By reading Title I rights so narrowly, and by construing Title IV to foreclose absolutely pre-election litigation in the federal courts, the Court sharply reduces meaningful protection for many of the rights which Congress was so assiduous to create.[7] By so simplifying the tangled provisions of the Act, the Court renders it virtually impossible for the aggrieved union member to gain a hearing when it is most necessary — when there is still an opportunity to make the union's rules comport with the requirements of the Act.

My difference with the Court does not reach to the disposition of this particular case. Whether stated in terms of restrictions on the right to nominate or in terms of limitations on eligibility for union office, I think the rules of a labor organization would operate illegally to curtail the members' equal right to nominate within the meaning of Title I only if those rules effectively distorted the basic democratic process. The line might be a shadowy one in some cases. But I think that in this case the respondents did not allege in their complaint nor demonstrate in their affidavits that this line was crossed. I would therefore remand the case to the District Court with directions to dismiss the complaint for failure to state a claim for relief.

NOTE

In Jennings v. Carey, 57 L.R.R.M. 2635 (D.D.C. 1964), plaintiff was a candidate for president of the International Union of Electrical, Radio & Machine Operators, AFL-CIO. Defendants were his opponent — the incumbent president, the union trustees charged with general supervision of the election, the union itself, and its secretary-treasurer.

As provided by the union's constitution, the election was conducted by mail ballot. After the balloting had been completed and all but about 6000 of the approximately 130,000 votes cast had been counted, plaintiff filed an action for injunctive relief, and obtained an order temporarily restraining the counting procedure. The complaint alleged that defendant trustees were hostile to plaintiff's candidacy and had deliber-

[6] See Summers, Pre-Emption and the Labor Reform Act — Dual Rights and Remedies, 22 Ohio St. L.J. 119, 138-139 (1961). It would be strange indeed if only state courts were available to enforce the federal law created by the Act during the pre-election period.

[7] The Court's reading of federal-court remedies available under Title I and Title IV is particularly restrictive because of the limited powers of the district judge once the balloting has occurred. Under §401(c), the court is confined to setting the election aside only if "the violation of section 401 may have affected the outcome." For the aggrieved union member, this protection may be totally inadequate. The function of nominating a candidate is not always to gain the office. A faction may be vitally interested in appearing on the ballot merely to show that it is part of the political structure of the union. Under the Court's view, until such a faction approaches majority status, judicial relief in the federal courts will be absent. See Summers, Judicial Regulation of Union Elections, 70 Yale L.J. 1221, 1257 (1961).

ately miscounted the ballots and limited plaintiff to two watchers, under conditions preventing them from ascertaining the accuracy of the count — all for the purpose of "rigging" the election in favor of the incumbent. The complaint also alleged that, absent immediate judicial intervention, defendants could use their unilateral control of the election machinery to destroy evidence of their theft of votes by substituting bogus ballots for those marked for plaintiff. Plaintiff asserted the court had jurisdiction over so much of the case as involved claims of statutory violations under Sections 401(c), 102, and 501(b) of the LMRDA; he also asserted a right to recover under the common law of the District of Columbia. By way of relief he sought an injunction against further counting, an order impounding the ballots, and a recount under the court's supervision.

The action was dismissed for lack of jurisdiction. The court disposed of the separate claims based on alleged statutory violations as follows:

Section 401(c). Suits prior to election in federal district courts are permitted only in the case of a bona fide candidate for union office seeking to enforce rights to equal treatment in the distribution of campaign literature and access to union membership lists. Suits based on failure to maintain "adequate safeguards to insure a fair election" do not fall within this category and must be brought after the election in accordance with the procedures of Section 402 of the act.

Section 102. Plaintiff was not denied the opportunity afforded equally to other members to cast his vote in the challenged election; hence there was no violation of Section 101(a)(1). The violations alleged by plaintiff occurred, if at all, under Title IV rather than under Title I; thus jurisdiction could not be founded upon Section 102. Compare Robins v. Rarback, 325 F.2d 929 (2d Cir. 1963), with Beckman v. Local 46, International Assn. of Bridge Workers, 314 F.2d 848 (7th Cir. 1963).

Section 501(a). Title IV procedures were intended by Congress to provide the exclusive remedy for violations of that title. Moreover, Section 501 suits are derivative and must be brought "for the benefit of the labor organization." Plaintiff did not allege a demand upon the union to bring the action itself; hence the complaint would have had to be dismissed in any case. See Coleman v. Brotherhood of R.R. & S.S. Clerks, 228 F. Supp. 276 (S.D.N.Y. 1964), and Penuelas v. Moreno, 198 F. Supp. 441 (S.D. Cal. 1961).

e. RIGHT TO HOLD OFFICE

BROWN v. UNITED STATES

United States Court of Appeals, Ninth Circuit, 1964
334 F.2d 488, affirmed, 33 U.S.L. Week 4603 (1965)

MERRILL, Circuit Judge.

This appeal challenges the constitutionality of §504 of the Labor-Management and Reporting Act (29 U.S.C. §504) which makes it unlawful for a member of the Communist Party to hold office in a labor union. . . .

It will be noted that the criminality is achieved in two stages: First, the holding of such office by a member of the Communist Party is prohibited as a regulation of interstate commerce; second, the violation of this regulatory prohibition is made a crime.

Section 504 was enacted in 1959 as part of the Labor-Management Reporting and Disclosure Act and is the successor of §9(h) of the Taft-Hartley Act, which was then repealed. The latter section barred the facilities of the National Labor Relations Board to any labor organization the officers of which failed to file with the Board affidavits that they were not members of or affiliated with the Communist Party.

There can be little doubt, in the light of the legislative history of §504, that it was designed to achieve the same Congressional objectives as former §9(h) and achieve them more effectively.[2] The purpose of the former section and the evils Congress intended it to combat were fully explored by the Supreme Court in American Communications Ass'n v. Douds (1950) 339 U.S. 382. There the court stated, at pages 388-389:

"One such obstruction, which it was the purpose of §9(h) of the Act to remove, was the so-called 'political strike.' Substantial amounts of evidence were presented to various committees of Congress, including the committees immediately concerned with labor legislation, that Communist leaders of labor unions had in the past and would continue in the future to subordinate legitimate trade union objectives to obstructive strikes when dictated by Party leaders, often in support of the policies of a foreign government. . . .

"It is sufficient to say that Congress had a great mass of material before it which tended to show that Communists and others proscribed by the statute had infiltrated union organizations not to support and further trade union objectives, including the advocacy of change by democratic methods, but to make them a device by which commerce and industry might be disrupted when the dictates of political policy required such action."

---

[2] See H.R. Rep. No. 741 on H.R. 8342, 86th Cong., 1st Sess., 33-35, 79 (supplementary views), I Legislative History of the Labor-Management Reporting and Disclosure Act of 1959, 791, 837. The original bill as it passed the Senate on April 25, 1959, contained no criminal disability provision relating to Communists. See S. 1555, 86th Cong., 1st Sess., §305(a) (1959), and S. Rep. No. 187 on S. 1555 at 12-13. The Senate recognized the defects of the affidavit procedure then in use, but sought to make detailed changes with respect to the time for filing, the role of the N.L.R.B. in administering the procedure, etc., while preserving the affidavit framework for control of Communists in the labor unions. S. Rep. No. 187, supra, 36-37, I Legislative History, supra, 430-432. It was the House bill, H.R. 8342, passed in July of 1959, which first contained a prohibition against Communists holding office in labor unions together with a repeal of 9(h). See §§201(3) and 504(a) of H.R. 8342, supra. In conference the House amendment to the Senate bill S. 1555 was agreed to with various substitutions, including an added criminal sanction against any labor organization or official thereof knowingly permitting any person to violate §504. See Confce. Rep. 1147 on S. 1555, 86th Cong., 1st Sess., 36 (1959), I Legislative History, supra, 940.

Section 504, then, was enacted in a continuing effort by Congress, in its regulation of interstate commerce, effectively to prevent the interruption of a free flow of commerce by political strikes.

Appellant has been a member of the Communist Party since at least 1935. In elections for the years 1959, 1960 and 1961, he was, while a party member, elected a member of the Executive Board of Local 10 (San Francisco, California) of the International Longshoremen's and Warehousemen's Union. Thereafter, while a party member, he served in this official capacity. He was thereupon indicted for a violation of §504. He was tried and convicted and this appeal is taken from judgment of conviction.

Before we reach the constitutional problems which the appeal presents, it is necessary to deal with a matter of statutory construction. Appellant contends that the executive board of the local to which he was elected is not a "governing body"; that it is not the sort of "executive board" to which the statute applies.

The court instructed the jury that the Union's executive board was an executive board within the meaning of the statute. Appellant assigns as error the action of the district court in taking this question from the jury and in refusing to instruct the jury that it had to find that the board had power to impose its policies upon the Union and thus to engage the Union in activities which might disrupt the flow of commerce.

Two questions are presented by these contentions. First, was a jury question presented as to whether or not the executive board of the Union was an "executive board or similar governing body" within the meaning of the statute? Second, if not — if this question was a question of law — was it correctly answered by the court? Upon both issues we agree with the district court.

As to the nature of the Union's board we find no factual dispute to be resolved. The constitution of Local 10, setting forth the nature and powers of the executive board, was put in evidence and was read to the jury by appellant's counsel.[3] Appellant introduced testimony to show that the executive board was primarily a recommending body whose resolutions were subject to review (and rejection) by the total membership before being translated into action.

We may accept as true all factual contentions asserted by appellant to have been established by this proof; specifically, that the board was without power on its own authority to bring about the evil with which Congress was concerned.

---

[3] The Constitution described the executive board as "the advisory board of the Local," and provided that its powers and functions were: "to adopt such measures as are deemed necessary from time to time for the good and welfare of the local, subject to the approval of the membership; . . . attend to all matters referred to it by the local, also suggest remedies for immediate and permanent benefit and report to the regular meeting; . . . dispose of communications not of interest to the local and cooperate in every way so that the business to be covered at a regular meeting may be accomplished; . . . In cases of emergency . . . to act to protect the interests and welfare of the local; . . . study the labor movement closely and formulate concrete policies to strengthen our local — said policies to be in accord with the I.L.W.U."

The true issue presented by the contentions of appellant was not as to the authority actually possessed by the Union board, but whether a board having the nature and powers specified by the local's constitution for this board, even though limited in its powers as factually contended by appellant, was an "executive board or similar governing body" within the meaning of the statute. This was a question of law.

Upon that question we note first that under the local's constitution the "executive board" was an integral part of the frame of government set up by that document for the local.

In our judgment appellant reads §504 too narrowly in attempting to confine "executive board" or "governing body" to one which, on its own authority, could take or require action threatening an interruption of commerce. While the statute was designed to strike at such interruptions its concern was not limited to those of executive authority who might by executive order accomplish such interruption. It included as well those who might by their position or office have power to influence such a result.

We note further that by specifying "any executive board" as well as "director" Congress apparently intended to include boards with a scope of authority different from that ordinarily possessed by a corporation's board of directors. By including within the prohibition all employees save those performing exclusively clerical or custodial duties, it has clearly manifested its desire to bring within the purview of §504 persons other than those who ultimately control the unions.

We also note that this Act and this section apply to persons convicted of certain crimes as well as to Communist Party members. Congress' wish to rid labor unions of racketeering and corruption by driving out criminal elements cannot reasonably be said to be restricted to upper-echelon positions of real power.

We conclude that the district court did not err in instructing the jury as it did.

This brings us to a consideration of the constitutional issue: whether criminal punishment of any and all Communist Party members who become union officers, regardless of lack of intent to bring about the evil the statute was designed to prevent or to further other unlawful aims of the Party, infringes the guarantees of the First and Fifth Amendments.

The district court, in denying motions to dismiss the indictment and for acquittal, held that no proof of specific intent of any kind was necessary under the statute and that so construed the statute was constitutional.

We turn first to a consideration of the question whether, as so construed, this regulation constitutes an impermissible restraint upon appellant's First Amendment "freedom of association for the purpose of advancing ideas and airing grievances." Bates v. Little Rock (1960) 361 U.S. 516, 523. In support of the district court judgment the Government relies upon American Communications Ass'n v. Douds, supra. There it was stated, at page 390 of 339 U.S.:

"There can be no doubt that Congress may, under its constitutional power to regulate commerce among the several States, attempt to prevent political strikes and other kinds of direct action designed to burden and interrupt the free flow of commerce."

It held that Congress could attempt to prevent Communists from serving as union officers by legislation providing that the important benefits of the National Labor Relations Act, including access to N.L.R.B. facilities, should be denied to unions having any Communist officers.

The Government urges that from this it follows that Congress, in order to make more effective its remedy for the conditions it could thus reasonably have found, could also impose personal criminal sanctions on this same general basis of political affiliation, by providing that mere membership in the Communist Party, when combined with union officership, is conclusive of guilt. We cannot agree.

At least grave doubt is cast upon such a contention by the more recent Supreme Court decisions in Scales v. United States (1961) 367 U.S. 203, and Noto v. United States (1961) 367 U.S. 290. The thrust of these decisions was that a criminal conviction for becoming a member of an organization advocating overthrow of the government — in these cases the Communist Party — can escape First Amendment condemnation only if in each case it is proved (1) that the organization was engaged in the type of advocacy, of action to accomplish overthrow, that is unprotected by the First Amendment, and (2) that the defendant was an "active" member of such an organization with a specific intent to further such unlawful purposes. The court's rejection of membership per se as a constitutionally sufficient ground of conviction was based upon the recognition, also voiced in Douds, 339 U.S. at 393,[5] that the Communist Party has both legal and illegal aims and carries on both legitimate and illegitimate activities, and the further recognition that there may be members "for whom the organization is a vehicle for the advancement of legitimate aims and policies" alone. "If there were a . . . blanket prohibition of association with a group having both legal and illegal aims," the court reasoned, "there would indeed be a real danger that legitimate political expression or association would be impaired," Scales v. United States, supra, 367 U.S. at 229, for "one in sympathy with the legitimate aims of such an organization, but not specifically intending to accomplish them by resort to violence, might be punished for his adherence to lawful and constitutionally protected purposes, because of other and unprotected purposes which he does not necessarily share." Noto v. United States, supra, 367 U.S. at 299-300.

In Douds the court, at page 400 of 339 U.S., states the problem posed by that case as follows: "In essence, the problem is one of weighing the probable effects of the statute upon the free exercise of the right of speech and assembly against the congressional determination that political strikes are evils of conduct which cause substantial harm to interstate commerce and that Communists and others identified by §9(h) pose continuing threats to that public interest when in positions of union leadership. We must, therefore, undertake the 'delicate and difficult task

---

[5] 339 U.S. at 393: "Communists, we may assume, carry on legitimate political activities."

. . . to weigh the circumstances and to appraise the substantiality of the reasons advanced in support of the regulation of the free enjoyment of the rights.' Schneider v. State, 1939, 308 U.S. 147, 161."

In discussing the extent to which the holding in Douds bears upon the present case it is essential that the dimensions of the restraint (both in that case and in ours) be examined.

In one respect the dimensions coincide: how far into the rights involved the restraint cuts.

The court in Douds, at page 402, notes: "The statute does not prevent or punish by criminal sanctions the making of a speech, the affiliation with any organization, or the holding of any belief." The restraint involved simply a loss of the right to hold union office — what the court refers to as "loss of position."

However, the court makes clear that lack of direct restraint upon Communist Party membership does not eliminate the First Amendment problem. At page 402 the court states: "But as we have noted, the fact that no direct restraint or punishment is imposed upon speech or assembly does not determine the free speech question. Under some circumstances, indirect 'discouragements' undoubtedly have the same coercive effect upon the exercise of First Amendment rights as imprisonment, fines, injunctions or taxes. A requirement that adherents of particular religious faiths or political parties wear identifying arm-bands, for example, is obviously of this nature."

That loss of position by virtue of Communist Party membership is not to be confused with the usual conflict-of-interest situation is pointed out by the court at pages 392-393:

"If no more were involved than possible loss of position, the foregoing would dispose of the case. But the more difficult problem here arises because, in drawing lines on the basis of beliefs and political affiliations, though it may be granted that the proscriptions of the statute bear a reasonable relation to the apprehended evil, congress has undeniably discouraged the lawful exercise of political freedoms as well. . . . By exerting pressures on unions to deny office to Communists and others identified therein, §9(h) undoubtedly lessens the threat to interstate commerce, but it has the further necessary effect of discouraging the exercise of political rights protected by the First Amendment. Men who hold union offices often have little choice but to renounce Communism or give up their offices. Unions which wish to do so are discouraged from electing Communists to office. To the grave and difficult problem thus presented we must now turn our attention."

In a second dimension — the quality of the restraint — the restraint confronting us is larger than that in Douds. There the court notes, at page 389:

"The unions contend that the necessary effect of §9(h) is to make it impossible for persons who cannot sign the oath to be officers of labor unions."

This the court denies, stating at page 390: "The statute does not, however, specifically forbid persons who do not sign the affidavit from holding positions of union leadership nor require their discharge from office. . . . We are, therefore, neither free to treat §9(h) as if it merely withdraws a privilege gratuitously granted by the Government, nor able to consider it a licensing statute prohibiting those persons who do not sign the affidavit from holding union office. The practicalities of the situation place the proscriptions of §9(h) somewhere between those two extremes."

The quality of the restraint in Douds was an indirect "discouragement" obtained through pressure applied to the union. In the language of the court, at page 412, it was "(t)o encourage unions to displace them (Communist Party members) from positions of great power . . ."

In our case the restraint is imposed directly upon the individual. It is not discouragement. It is one of the "extremes": flat prohibition.

In our judgment, yet a third dimension of the restraint must also be considered: the force with which it is applied. The court in Douds, at page 409, states:

"To hold that such an oath is permissible, on the other hand, is to admit that the circumstances under which one is asked to state his belief and the consequences which flow from his refusal to do so or his disclosure of a particular belief make a difference. The reason for the difference has been pointed out at some length above. First, the loss of a particular position is not the loss of life or liberty. We have noted that the distinction is one of degree, and it is for this reason that the effect of the statute in proscribing beliefs — like its effect in restraining speech or freedom of association — must be carefully weighed by the courts in determining whether the balance struck by Congress comports with the dictates of the Constitution."

Since it is the effect of a statute in restraining freedom of association with which we are concerned, we can hardly refuse to consider the consequences which are made to flow from a determined assertion of the rights in question in face of the regulation. In Douds the sanction was not a personal one; it was applied to the union, withdrawing from the union its rights to the benefits of the National Labor Relations Act. In our case, the sanction is not only personal, it is criminal. The imposing of a criminal sanction bears on the substantive quality of the restraint and poses new and different problems as to the reasonableness of the regulation. We are squarely faced with the principles enumerated in Scales and Noto.

This case, then, is far different from Douds. The restraint here bears directly upon the person of the one asserting First Amendment rights, and it does so with the duress of criminal sanctions.

It is with the personal and forceful character of the restraint in mind that we approach the question faced in Douds and which faces us here: whether, in the absence of specific intent to accomplish that which Congress seeks to prevent, there is sufficiently close relationship between the regulation and the achievement of the Congressional objective.

In Douds the court, at page 406, states:

"It is contended that the principle that statutes touching First Amendment freedoms must be narrowly drawn dictates that a statute aimed at political strikes should make the calling of such strikes unlawful but should not attempt to bring about the removal of union officers, with its attendant effect upon First Amendment rights."

This contention the court rejected, stating that "Congress should not be powerless to remove the threat, not limited to punishing the act." The court then concludes:

"While this statement may be subject to some qualification, it indicates the wide scope of congressional power to keep from the channels of commerce that which would hinder and obstruct such commerce."

In our judgment the regulation here — far broader than the threat it is designed to meet — is unreasonably broad. To relieve Congress from having to wait until it can punish the act, it is given power not simply to remove the threat but to punish it; and with no showing whatsoever that the act in fact is threatened by the person punished.

We conclude that this statute as construed by the district court constitutes an invalid restraint upon the freedom of association protected by the First Amendment.

Since §504 involves criminal punishment, we are also faced with serious problems of due process under the Fifth Amendment, which were not before the Supreme Court in Douds. The question raised by §504 is similar to that stated as follows in Scales v. United States, supra, 367 U.S. at 220: whether the section "impermissibly imputes guilt to an individual merely on the basis of his associations and sympathies, rather than because of some concrete personal involvement in criminal conduct."

Upon this question the court in Scales stated at pages 224-225:

"In our jurisprudence guilt is personal, and when the imposition of punishment on a status or on conduct can only be justified by reference to the relationship of that status or conduct to other concededly criminal activity (here advocacy of violent overthrow), that relationship must be sufficiently substantial to satisfy the concept of personal guilt in order to withstand attack under the Due Process Clause of the Fifth Amendment." And further, page 226: ". . . the enquiry here must direct itself to an analysis of the relationship between the fact of membership and the underlying substantive illegal conduct, in order to determine whether that relationship is indeed too tenuous to permit its use as the basis of criminal liability." And further, page 227: "It must indeed be recognized that a person who merely becomes a member of an illegal organization, by that 'act' alone need be doing nothing more than signifying his assent to its purposes and activities on one hand, and providing, on the other, only the sort of moral encouragement which comes from the knowledge that others believe in what the organization is doing."

In our judgment these constitutional standards of criminal imputability from association to individual are not met unless §504 could be read as restricted to party members harboring specific intent to use union office to interrupt interstate commerce or actively and purposefully participating in furtherance of illegal party activities aimed at overthrow of the Government.

It is true that in Scales and Noto the court was faced with a statute which attributed to an individual member of an organization, seemingly on the basis of membership alone, criminal conduct in which the organization was found to be engaged.

Here, it is argued, criminality is not based solely on attribution from association; there is an individually and knowingly performed act — that of becoming a union officer — for which punishment is imposed.

We feel that this is not a valid point of distinction. In Scales the defendant might have been said to have knowingly and individually violated the law through his act of association. (He was indicted for being a member of the party with knowledge of its illegal purpose.) But this was not the gist of the crime — of that which society had found offensive. The gist of the offense was the advocacy in which the organization was engaged.

So here, the gist of the offense (and, indeed, the sole basis for federal concern) lies in the anticipated efforts of the individual to use union authority or influence to bring about union action which would interfere with commerce. This, to quote from Scales, supra, is "the underlying substantive illegal conduct." It is the relationship of Communist union officers to this potential disruptive and illegal activity which alone can justify the punishment imposed by §504. In our judgment that relationship is not sufficiently substantial to justify, under the due process clause, imposition of criminal punishment on the basis of union officership combined with Communist Party membership per se.

We conclude that the relationship between the conduct or status punished and the evil intended here to be prevented is not sufficiently close or substantial to meet the requirements of either the First or Fifth Amendments unless §504 can be construed as requiring proof either that the defendant has specific intent to use his union office to attempt to disrupt interstate commerce or that he is an active member of the Communist Party with specific intent to promote unlawful party advocacy and action directed toward overthrow of the Government.

We feel it clear that this statute is not susceptible of such a limiting judicial construction.

It is true that in Dennis v. United States (1951) 341 U.S. 494, Yates v. United States (1957) 354 U.S. 298, and Scales v. United States, supra, criminal statutes, as applied to Communist activity or membership, were construed narrowly to include requirements of intent and unlawfulness of advocacy that were sufficient to remove doubts as to the constitutionality. But in each case ambiguous statutory language made such construction available.[6]

[6] Thus Dennis held that proof of intent to overthrow the Government by force was an essential element of both §2(a)(1) of the Smith Act (making it unlawful "to knowingly or willfully advocate . . . or teach" forceful overthrow of the Government), and §2(a)(3) of the Act (making it unlawful "to organize or help to

Here we are not faced with ambiguous statutory expression but with a lack of expression. The segregation of guilty from what we have held must be innocent holding of union office is not at all suggested by the statutory language. It is wholly inappropriate to consider whether scienter should be deemed essential, for the very nature of the scienter that is constitutionally necessary is hidden. No Communist Party member could know, from a reading of the statute, whether, of the many party purposes, those which he personally embraces do or do not disqualify him from union office or employment.

Not only then, is the statute overbroad. It is so wholly lacking in notice of the constitutionally essential components of the crime that it cannot be judicially narrowed.

We conclude that §504 of the Labor-Management and Reporting Act, in its imposition of criminal sanctions upon Communist Party members, must be held to conflict with the First and Fifth Amendments of the United States Constitution, and upon this ground to be void.

Reversed and remanded with instructions that judgment be set aside and the indictment dismissed.[8]

CHAMBERS, Circuit Judge (dissenting).

I agree with Judge Merrill insofar as he holds that Brown's executive board was one within the meaning of 29 U.S.C. §504 and that it was correct for the trial judge to tell the jury so. . . .

But as of now I would hold the statute constitutional. A far different case we would have if the statute proscribed a Communist party member's right to be a member of a union or to get a job.

I cannot agree that Douds, 339 U.S. 382; Bates v. Little Rock, 361 U.S. 516; Scales v. United States, 367 U.S. 203; and Noto v. United States, 367 U.S. 290, necessarily indicate we should declare §504 unconstitutional.

---

organize any society, group, or assembly of persons who teach, advocate, or encourage" such overthrow). The opinion of Chief Justice Vinson, for four members of the court, declared that implicit in the very nature of advocacy of and organization for advocacy of overthrow is an intent to bring about that overthrow. 341 U.S. at 499. Scales involved conviction under the Smith Act clause making it unlawful to become or be a member of any such society advocating or teaching overthrow of the Government, "knowing the purposes thereof." The court declared that the reasoning in Dennis "applies equally to the membership clause," and held that the clause requires proof of specific intent to further illegal and constitutionally unprotected party activities directed toward forcible overthrow of the Government. In Yates, Scales and Noto v. United States, supra, the court, by construing the word "advocate," held that the activity which is punishable by the first clause of the section and in which the organization must engage to warrant punishment of its members under the membership clause, is "advocacy 'not of . . . mere abstract doctrine of forcible overthrow, but of action to that end, by the use of language reasonably and ordinarily calculated to incite persons to . . . action' immediately or in the future." Noto v. United States, supra, 367 U.S. at 297, quoting from Yates v. United States, supra, 354 U.S. at 316.

[8] The concurring opinion of Duniway, J., and the dissenting opinion of Hamley, J., are omitted. — ED.

I shall not repeat Judge Merrill's excellent summary of the Congressional reasons for adopting §504.

All through our United States Code we find restrictions on conflicts of interest with criminal penalties therefor, only because experience has shown "a disposition to commit" on the part of executives. See 18 U.S.C. §281, §283; 38 U.S.C. §1764(a); 38 U.S.C. §1664; 18 U.S.C. §1909; 12 U.S.C. §377; 15 U.S.C. §19; 12 U.S.C. §1812; 15 U.S.C. §78(d); 49 U.S.C. §1321; and 49 U.S.C. §11. The fact that a high percentage would discharge their duties without favoritism is to no avail. "Disposition of the class of persons to commit" is enough for the proscription.

Schware v. Board of Bar Examiners, 353 U.S. 232, holds one cannot be barred from becoming a lawyer merely because one is or has been a member of the Communist party. I would suppose though that an integrated state bar act might permissibly provide that one could not be an officer of that organization if he were a Communist.

One needs a basic right to a job. One doesn't need a right to be a union officer or to be an executive with a possible conflict of interest with his government.

BARNES, Circuit Judge (dissenting).

. . . I believe that the delicate "balance struck by Congress comports with the dictates of the Constitution." The "wide scope of congressional power to keep from the channels of commerce that which would hinder and obstruct such commerce" is not, to me, violative of §504 here considered.

While a police officer or a congressional employee, under investigation, has a "right" to invoke the Fifth Amendment — he has no right to hold a particular job thereafter. Appellant herein had a right to be a certain kind of member in the Communist Party, but has no "right" to hold office in labor unions, which office directs the labor union's policy, once Congress has seen fit to refuse him such office holding. The congressional right to protect the full flow of interstate commerce must itself be protected; not at all odds, but when reasonably exercised, as I feel it here was. In this I disagree with the majority.

f.   DUES

AMERICAN FEDERATION OF MUSICIANS
v. WITTSTEIN

Supreme Court of the United States, 1964
379 U.S. 171, 85 Sup. Ct. 300, 13 L. Ed. 2d 214

MR. JUSTICE WHITE delivered the opinion of the Court.

The issue presented in these suits is whether §101(a)(3) of the Labor-Management Reporting and Disclosure Act of 1959 providing that the dues of an international union "shall not be increased . . . except . . . by majority vote of the delegates voting at a regular convention" prohibits the vote of delegates at a national convention of the union, as authorized by its constitution, to be weighted and counted according to the number of members in the local that the delegate represents.

I

The petitioner American Federation of Musicians (Federation) is an international labor organization comprising 675 locals in the United States and Canada. As with numerous other national and international labor organizations having many scattered locals of varying size, Federation's constitution and bylaws have long authorized alternative methods of ascertaining the vote of the delegates representing the locals at a union convention. Each local is entitled to one delegate for each 100 members or major fraction thereof, not to exceed three delegates from any one local. Federation's bylaws permit a voice vote of the delegates attending a convention in all cases, which is the method often used on routine non-controversial matters. When amendments to the union constitution or bylaws are at issue, however, the delegates representing the locals, upon a roll call vote, may cast as many votes as there are members in the respective locals. A roll call vote is required upon the demand of 10 delegates or five locals. All amendments to the bylaws and constitutions approved by a roll call vote are required under the constitution to be referred to a convention committee which may approve or veto the proposal.[2]

At petitioner's 1963 annual convention, a resolution increasing the per capita dues of all members, approximately 255,000, was submitted to the delegates. After the chairman ruled that two voice votes of the delegates were inconclusive, a delegate speaking on behalf of five locals requested a roll call vote in accordance with Federation's constitution. The rules governing a roll call vote were explained to the delegates. Delegates were to cast as many votes as there were members in the local that they represented. If the delegates from a given local were in disagreement, the total votes of that local were to be divided among the delegates. The roll call was taken and the recommendation carried by some 44,326 votes, with less than one-half of the delegates present voting in favor of the proposal.

Respondents, members of several locals whose delegates voted for or against the resolution at the convention, brought these suits against

[2] Article 5 of Federation's constitution provides:
"All Locals of this Federation of one hundred and fifty members or less shall be entitled to one delegate. All Locals shall be entitled to one delegate for each one hundred members or a major fraction thereof, not exceeding three delegates for any one Local, but each Local shall be entitled to one vote for each one hundred or major fraction thereof, but no Local shall cast more than ten votes, and the number each Local is entitled to shall be computed from the last report made on January 1st before the convention by the Local, according to the books of the Treasurer. On questions affecting a change in the laws, each Local may, upon roll call, cast as many votes as it has members, as per book of the Treasurer, A. F. of M. All laws so passed shall be referred to a convention committee consisting of the Executive Board, A. F. of M., and chairman of all committees, who may sanction or veto same, their action to be final. Roll call shall be demandable and had under this Article on demand of ten delegates or five Locals."

Federation and one of its locals to have the resolution declared null and void and its implementation enjoined. In the District Court, summary judgment in the consolidated actions was rendered for the respondent union members. 223 F. Supp. 27. (D.C.S.D.N.Y.) Finding that the material facts about the enactment of the dues resolution in regard to the issue under §101(a)(3)(B) were not in dispute, that court ruled that weighted voting did not comply with §101(a)(3)(B)'s requirement of approval by "majority vote of the delegates voting at a regular convention." A divided Court of Appeals affirmed. 326 F.2d 26. (C.A. 2d Cir.) Although noting that weighted voting "is to all appearances the most 'democratic' method, in the sense that each member is duly 'represented,'" it held that the plain language of §101(a)(3)(B) requires that each delegate be allowed but one vote regardless of the number of members he represents. The question being an important one of first impression under the LMRDA, we granted certiorari. 376 U.S. 942. We hold that §101(a)(3)(B) does not prohibit a weighted voting system under which delegates cast a number of votes equal to the membership of the local union from which they are elected.

I I

Under §101(a)(3)(B) an international union may increase membership dues or levy an assessment by majority vote of the members voting in a membership referendum, by majority vote of the members of the executive board, effective, however, only to the next regular convention, or "by majority vote of the delegates voting at a . . . convention." The quoted language, it is said, authorizes only one system of voting: a head count of the delegates at a convention. Just as each member and each executive board member is entitled to one vote, so too each delegate may cast only his single vote. There cannot be a majority vote of the delegates voting, the argument proceeds, unless a delegate casts but one vote, no more or less, and the affirmative votes cast add up to a majority of the delegates voting. So far the argument is based solely upon what is said to be the literal meaning of the statutory language; there is no suggestion that §101(a)(3)(B) embodies an accepted or preferable system of representation by delegates or that the provision requires any set number of delegates at a convention or any particular relationship between the size of the local and the number of representatives at the convention.

We do not think this is the only fair import of the language in §101(a)(3)(B). The section requires a majority *vote* of the delegates voting. It does not state that a dues increase must be approved by a *majority of the delegates voting* at a convention. The respondent's construction renders the key word "vote" entirely superfluous, although that word describes what is to be counted to determine a majority. The provision on its face prescribes only by whom the vote must be cast — a delegate to a convention — and the proportion of votes needed for passage — a majority of the votes cast. The statute does require that those voting at a convention be delegates, but it says nothing about the number of votes each delegate may cast. Where the "vote" cast at a convention is weighted according to the number of people the delegate represents, that vote, we think, is a vote of a delegate. We believe that a majority vote so determined in favor of a dues increase is approval by majority vote of the delegates voting at a convention.

Whatever doubts may be left by sole and plenary reliance on plain meaning are fully resolved by consideration of the legislative history behind §101(a)(3)(B) and of other provisions of the LMRDA. This section had its genesis in Senator McClellan's proposals in S. 1137, which would have required "a general vote" on rules relating to the rate of dues and initiation fees and would have required that the vote of delegates at a convention "be numerically equivalent, or proportionate, to the number of members of (each) constituent unit." [3] I Leg. Hist. 269, 278. Although S. 1137 was not reported out by the Senate Committee on Labor and Public Welfare, Senator McClellan's requirement that the voting strength of convention delegates be proportionate to the size of their constituency is significant for the reason that it was the outgrowth of the extensive hearings held by the McClellan committee which uncovered substantial evidence of various forms of internal misgovernment and abuses in several labor organizations. The findings of this committee became the primary basis for the many bills that followed its investigations, an amalgam of which ultimately became the LMRDA. In light of the fact that then as now many large unions had provisions for weighted voting by delegates at a convention, it is very clear that weighted voting was not thought to be one of these abuses or forms of misgovernment.[6]

Senate bill No. 1555, the Kennedy-Ervin bill, was favorably reported out of the Senate Committee on Labor and Public Welfare without any Bill of Rights for union members, now Title 1 of the Act, of which the provision relating to dues is a part. Senator McClellan soon introduced a comprehensive Bill of Rights provision as an amendment to S. 1555, which was adopted in the Senate by a vote of 47 to 46. In

[3] S. 1137, 86th Cong., 1st Sess., 1 Legislative History of the Labor-Management Reporting and Disclosure Act of 1959, 260, 269, 278 (1959). . . .

[6] Leiserson, American Trade Union Democracy 129-132 (1959). "Except in the few unions where locals are entitled to but one delegate with but one vote, the number of votes in a convention is always greater than the number of delegates. Although proxy voting is generally prohibited (Longshoremen and Blacksmiths are exceptions), every convention delegate casts not only his own vote, but a share of the voting strength of the local union he represents as well. This voting strength varies with the size of the locals, and the total vote of a local union may be divided among its delegates or one of them may cast all its votes. The basis of representation and the methods of basing voting strength on size of local memberships differ among the unions . . ." Id., at 129-130.

See also United States Department of Labor, Bulletin No. 1239, Union Constitution Provisions: Election and Tenure of National and International Union Officers, at 15 (G.P.O. 1958); National Industrial Conference Board, Handbook of Union Government, Structure and Procedures, Studies in Personnel Policy, No. 150, at 73 (1955).

respect to financial exactions, this amendment placed a flat limit on initiation fees and required for approval of a dues increase a majority vote of the members in the case of a local union and "a majority vote of the delegates present" at a general meeting in the case of a national or international union. It is not without significance that this language is susceptible to the same construction that is urged here in respect to §101(a)(3)(B), for it is quite clear that the author of this provision, Senator McClellan, did not intend to prohibit weighted voting. A few days later the Kuchel amendment, substituting another Bill of Rights provision, was adopted by a vote of 77 to 14. This amendment eliminated some of the more stringent requirements of Senator McClellan's Bill of Rights, such as the limit on initiation fees, and dealt with voting procedures for approval of a dues increase by a local and international union in more detail; in the case of a local, majority approval of the members was necessary, while in the case of an international, a "majority vote at a regular convention" was required. Under this language, which was said to be "taken almost verbatim from . . . the McClellan amendment," it is very clear that no question of the permissibility of weighted voting could be raised. And no one expressed the thought that the McClellan proposal on voting was being altered in this or any other respect. S. 1555 passed the Senate with the Kuchel substitute as Title 1.

The changes in §101(a)(3)(B) in the House support the conclusion that this provision does not bar weighted voting. S. 1555, as passed by the Senate, became the focus of testimony before a joint Committee of the House Committee on Education and Labor. The gist of the objections to §101(a)(3)(B) was that it failed explicitly to allow other methods of ensuring membership participation on proposals of an international or national union to increase dues, and it was too rigid in disallowing action by an executive board of the international or national union. The Committee responded by expanding the permissible methods of raising dues. As reported out in the Elliott bill, §101(a)(3)(B) allowed an international to increase dues by majority vote of the members, by majority vote of the members of an executive board, effective only until the next convention, and "by majority vote of the delegates voting at a regular convention." The Committee version was incorporated in identical language in the Landrum-Griffin bill, which prevailed on the floor of the House. In respect to his bill, Representative Griffin observed generally that the "bill of rights in our substitute is essentially the bill of rights in the form passed by the (Senate). It guarantees to union members, subject to reasonable rules and regulations, . . . that their dues and initiation fees will not be increased arbitrarily." The House Joint Conference Committee Report confirmed the view that the Senate and House versions of Title 1 contain "similar provisions." Senator Goldwater, a member of the Joint Committee that considered S. 1555 and Landrum-Griffin, stated in his textual analysis of both bills that the House version of §101(a)(3)(B) was technically preferable and that the differences were in respect to the expanded methods of approval under the House bill and the applicability of the House bill only to dues increases rather than all changes. And Senator Kuchel, the author of the Senate version of the dues proposal, and a conferee, stated that the Landrum-Griffin bill "adopted substantially the same bill of rights language" which he had earlier authored. In light of the fact that the House changes were in the direction of affording unions more latitude for raising dues and the fact that no one, in the House or Senate, perceived that the House version would restrict voting at a convention to a head count of the delegates, we think it abundantly clear that §101(a)(3)(B) was intended to guarantee a member's "right to participate in deciding upon the rate of dues, initiation fees and assessments," H.R. Rep. No. 741 on H.R. 8342, at 7, 1 Leg. Hist. 765, but not to bar a well-known system of voting embodied in many union constitutions which well serves that end.

Other provisions of the LMRDA confirm this view. Section 101(a)-(3)(B) is a part of Title 1, entitled the "Bill of Rights of Members of Labor Organizations." This Title guarantees to every member of a labor organization equal rights and privileges to vote, to attend meetings, and to participate in the deliberations and business of such meetings. Section 101(a)(3)(B) forms a part of this framework by requiring participation by all members, either directly or through their elected representatives, on certain union matters thought to be of special importance. We find nothing to indicate that Congress thought this objective would be better fulfilled by allowing a delegate to cast one vote, regardless of the size of his constituency, than by permitting him to cast a vote equal to the number of members he represents. As a part of the Act's purpose of protecting and fostering participation by the rank and file in the affairs of the union, Title IV contains elaborate statutory safeguards for the election of union officers. But nothing in that title prohibits election of union officers by delegates voting at a convention in accordance with the number of members they represent. Respondents do not demonstrate any differences between weighted voting for officers of the union and weighted voting on changes in financial exactions that would support the asserted difference in voting procedures applicable to each. It is argued that delegates may not ascertain or follow the wishes of the members in respect to dues and assessments. But few issues are more likely to arouse active opposition and general membership participation than a proposal to increase dues. Further, this argument is too broad, for it questions the validity of a system of representative union government and has little to do with the manner in which the representative's vote is counted. Section 101(a)(3)(B), as well as Title IV, authorizes a representative system of government and does not require a town meeting for action by an international or national union. To that end Congress recognized the key role of elections in the process of union self-government and surrounded it with many safeguards to provide a fair election and to guarantee membership participation.

The pervading premise of both these titles is that there should be full and active participation by the rank and file in the affairs of the union. We think our decision today that the vote of an elected delegate may reflect the size of his constituency is wholly consistent with that purpose.

Accordingly, the judgments below are reversed and the case is remanded for proceedings consistent with this opinion. . . .

THE CHIEF JUSTICE and MR. JUSTICE GOLDBERG took no part in the consideration or decision of this case.

PECK v. ASSOCIATED FOOD DISTRIBUTORS OF NEW ENGLAND

United States District Court, Massachusetts, 1965
237 F. Supp. 113

WYZANSKI, District Judge:

Plaintiffs, being members of the Associated Food Distributors of New England, Local 138, on behalf of themselves and others similarly situated, bring this class action alleging a violation of that provision, 29 U.S.C. §411(a)(3), of Title I of the Labor-Management Reporting and Disclosure Act of 1959, relating to the procedure for increasing dues and making assessments. Joined as defendants are the aforesaid local and plaintiffs' employer, The Great Atlantic & Pacific Tea Company, Inc.

Many factual issues have virtually been agreed upon in open court, following lengthy discovery and other pre-trial procedures.

At the bar of this Court, defendant union admitted that, in violation of the aforesaid Act, on October 10, 1961 it increased the monthly dues payable by its members who were A & P employees, on a part time basis, from 75 cents to $1.50; and on April 16, 1964 it imposed, effective May 1, 1964, an assessment of 25 cents upon each member. The violation in each instance consisted in the fact that, respectively, the increase and assessment were not adopted by a majority vote by secret ballot of the affected union members in good standing voting at a general or special membership meeting after reasonable notice of the intention to vote upon such question or by a majority vote of the members in good standing voting in a membership referendum conducted by secret ballot. Such conduct was an infraction of one of the so-called "bill of rights" under the Act. §101(a)(3)(A); 29 U.S.C. §411(a)(3)(A).

Probably Peck immediately objected by notifying the union, but not the employer. Other named plaintiffs are not shown to have objected by notifying anyone before this complaint was filed on July 23, 1964. No one has sought to intervene or otherwise associate himself with the named plaintiffs.

After the filing of this complaint on September 22, 1964, the then members of the union (who were admittedly not identical with those who were members on October 10, 1961 and May 1, 1964) purported to "ratify" the earlier "votes." This so-called ratification was invalid both because the persons acting had no right to speak for others, and because action initially void could not be *retroactively* cured. The September 22, 1964 action was, however, effective to bind from that date those who were then members of the local.

After the increase and also after the assessment the union notified the employer, and demanded, that thereafter the employer should make relevant check-offs. In subjective good faith, the employer did so. The employer turned over to the union all the check-offs, and kept none. It is not suggested that the employer was in any conspiracy, or had actual knowledge of the violation of the Act. Nor, on the other hand, is it claimed that the employer asked for proof of the union's compliance with the Act.

So far as concerns defendant A & P, the employer, no cause of action within the jurisdiction of this Court is shown. Were there jurisdiction over an action against it, A & P would be entitled to prevail on the merits because it was innocent of any wrongdoing, so far as appears, and retained no benefit of such wrong as there may have been.

So far as the union is concerned, its conduct having transparently violated the Act, it must be enjoined from further effectuating in any way the so-called October 10, 1961 and April 16, 1964 votes to increase dues and to impose assessments. The union's liability to make repayment presents issues which require some discussion. Money unlawfully collected from an individual against his protest, as may have been true of Peck's case, is, of course, plainly returnable. But it is argued that money collected by the union from persons who did not protest seasonably, and a fortiori from persons who did not even bother to intervene in these proceedings is inappropriate. This argument is rejected because the purpose of the Act is so plainly not merely to preclude a union from prevailing over a righteous protestant, but also to maintain discipline over the regularity of union conduct. The violations were all patent, inexcusable, and, at the furthest reach, not 3 years old when complaint was filed. All the excesses wrongfully collected are repayable, just as all amounts unlawfully withheld by an employer subject to the Federal Fair Wages and Hours legislation are in an equity proceeding subject to a judicial order requiring their repayment to the employee victims of the employer's wrong. Exact calculation presents questions of fact upon which the parties are not in agreement and therefore are appropriately set for further proceedings in accordance with the decree filed herewith.

So ordered.

g. FIDUCIARY DUTIES

HIGHWAY TRUCK DRIVERS v. COHEN

*United States District Court, Eastern District of
Pennsylvania, 1960
182 F. Supp. 608, affirmed per curiam, 284 F.2d 162
(3d Cir. 1960), certiorari denied, 365 U.S. 833 (1961)*

CLARY, District Judge.

This is a private suit brought under the recently enacted Labor-Management Reporting and Disclosure Act of 1959, Public Law 86-257 (hereinafter referred to as the "Act"), 29 U.S.C.A. §§401 et seq. That Act establishes a fiduciary responsibility on the part of officers of a labor organization (§501(a)), and further provided for a suit in a Federal district court to enforce these responsibilities (§501(b)). The present suit has been brought under §501(b) to enforce certain of these duties.

The moving parties are nine rank-and-file members of Highway Truck Drivers and Helpers, Local 107, of the International Brotherhood of Teamsters, Chauffeurs, Warehousemen and Helpers of America (hereinafter referred to as "Local 107"), who were given leave by this Court on November 12, 1959 to file a complaint against the defendants, the governing officers of Local 107. The complaint charged the defendants with a continuing mass conspiracy to cheat and defraud the union of large sums of money — the conspiracy alleged to have begun in 1954 and continued to the present time.

The defendants have yet to answer these very serious charges. Having been unsuccessful in first opposing the plaintiffs' petition for leave of this Court to sue, defendants now move to have the complaint dismissed. They are supported in this motion by counsel for Local 107, which has been allowed to intervene as a party defendant. This motion to dismiss is presently before the Court along with the plaintiffs' prayer for a preliminary injunction to prohibit the defendants from using union funds to defray the legal costs and other expenses being incurred by the defendants (and several other members of Local 107) in the defense of civil and criminal actions brought against them in the Courts of Pennsylvania and also the present suit in our own Court. The charges in these cases, in essence, grow out of the alleged activities of the defendants complained of here. The question of the preliminary injunction will be taken up after we resolve the motion to dismiss the complaint.

Section 501(a) of the new Act establishes a federal duty on the part of labor union officials to abide by the ordinary rules of fiduciary responsibility. . . .

Its complement, §501(b) authorizes suit in a federal court to enforce the duties imposed by subsection (a). . . .

On September 30, 1959 the plaintiffs filed an application for leave to sue under §501(b) and annexed the complaint which has since been filed by Order of this Court. Aside from the alleged continued expenditure of union funds to defend the criminal and civil suits brought against the defendants and others mentioned above, the only *specific* acts of misconduct alleged in this complaint relate to events occurring between June 1, 1954 (the date the defendants took office) and September 1957. The remainder of the complaint contains several *general* claims of fraud and breach of duty and alleges that such acts are continuing to the present time, and that these can only be discovered by an accounting. In light of this fact, the defendants vigorously assert that we must dismiss the complaint, since §501(a) and (b) apply prospectively only and can not be applied to acts occurring prior to September 14, 1959, the effective date of §501. . . .

[The court then discussed the retroactive application of Section 501 of the LMRDA and the alleged violations of Sections 7 and 8(a)(3) of the NLRA.]

From what has been said above, the Court holds that the statute may not be applied retroactively and that the complaint has not stated a cause of action under the provisions of the Taft-Hartley Act. Putting aside temporarily the question of injunctive relief as to expenditure of union funds for legal fees in suits now pending against the defendants, it would appear that the remainder of the action should be dismissed unless the complaint states a cause of action arising out of events subsequent to the effective date of the Act. . . . As to . . . defendants, officers and/or trustees of the local, while the complaint in general language alleges continuing misdeeds, it fails to set forth any specific act of commission or omission which occurred subsequent to the effective date of the Act.

If the only matter before the Court were the motion to dismiss discussed above, the Court might be disposed to grant the motion. However, there is another facet to the case which prevents the dismissal of the action. That facet relates to the motion for a preliminary injunction to prohibit the defendants from using union funds to defray the expense of legal fees in civil and criminal actions which have been brought against them in the Courts of Pennsylvania as well as to defray legal costs of the present action. The charges in those cases, in essence, grow out of alleged misappropriation of funds by the officers, and the plaintiffs maintain that such expenditures are in violation of the fiduciary duties imposed upon officers of a labor union by Section 501(a) of the Act, supra, and that unless such expenditures are enjoined the union will suffer irreparable harm thereby.

Shortly after the effective date of the Act and the institution of suits, criminal and civil, in the local Courts against the defendants, the union at a regular monthly meeting, with few dissenting votes, adopted a resolution authorizing the union to bear "Legal costs of such actions (against the officers) which are in reality not directed at our officers but are directed at us, the members of Local 107, our good contracts, our good wages and our good working conditions."

The question, therefore, which faces us is: Does the expenditure of union funds to pay for legal fees in the defense of both criminal and civil actions brought against the various defendant officers for an alleged conspiracy to cheat and defraud their union of large sums of money constitute a breach of that fiduciary duty imposed upon them by Section 501(a), supra, notwithstanding the purported authorization of such expenditures by a resolution of the union membership passed at a regular union meeting?

At the hearing on the preliminary injunction, it was brought out that within the limit of some four or five weeks after the adoption of the resolution the union, pursuant to the resolution, paid upwards of $25,-000 to the attorneys representing the defendants. It is also clear that counsel for the union has advised the officers that such expenditures are proper. We are, therefore, with the payment of those large sums of money already accomplished and threatened further payments about to occur, in a position factually to pass upon the merits of the plaintiffs' contention.[5]

At the outset of our discussion of this question it is necessary to make several general observations as to the construction to be given this new and far-reaching Act of Congress. We do so with caution, aware of the importance of this new legislation in the labor field and of the far-reaching effect which initial judicial interpretation of this Act must necessarily have upon its future.

The purpose of this Act is no secret. It was enacted "to eliminate or prevent improper practices on the part of labor organizations, employers, labor relations consultants, and their officers and representatives which distort and defeat the policies of the Labor Management Relations Act, 1947." §2(c). It came on the wake of Congressional findings of crime and corruption in the labor and management field §2(b).

Section 501, with which we are particularly concerned, is entitled "Fiduciary responsibility of officers of labor organizations." This section, quoted earlier, attempts to define in the broadest terms possible the duty which the new federal law imposes upon a union official. Congress made no attempt to "codify" the law in this area. It appears evident to us that they intended the federal courts to fashion a new federal labor law in this area, in much the same way that the federal courts have fashioned a new substantive law of collective bargaining contracts under §301(a) of the Taft-Hartley Act, 29 U.S.C.A. §185(a). See Textile Workers Union of America v. Lincoln Mills, 1957, 353 U.S. 448. In undertaking this task the federal courts will necessarily rely heavily upon the common law of the various states. Where that law is lacking or where it in any way conflicts with the policy expressed in our national labor laws, the latter will of course be our guide.

We then turn to Section 501, not expecting to find a detailed command or prohibition as to the particular act complained of, but rather to find a general guide which, properly developed, will lead us to an answer. We feel that that answer here must be in plaintiffs' favor.

In determining whether or not the expenditures now sought to be enjoined violate the fiduciary responsibility of an officer of a labor organization we must necessarily determine the legal effect of the September 20th Resolution. This goes to the heart of the present problem and appears to be the main ground on which the defendants seek to avoid the injunction.

The plaintiffs assert that the Resolution authorizing such expenditures is encompassed within the express prohibition of §501(a) against any

---

[5] There has been no showing on the part of the defendants, nor was it argued in defendants' brief, that defendants are responsible persons who would be able to reimburse the union for funds expended in their behalf. The sums involved are neither nominal nor minimal and in the circumstances the Court holds that a showing of irreparable harm (assuming the illegality of the payments) has been established.

"general exculpatory resolution." Although not expressly purporting to absolve the defendants of guilt, plaintiffs argue that the Resolution *in effect* does just this. Unfortunately the Act does not define the phrase "general exculpatory resolution."

The defendants take issue with the plaintiffs' interpretation. They maintain that the Resolution should be taken at face value, i.e., as a pledge of the union's faith in their officers and a pledge of financial aid to defend suits which are in reality directed at the union movement. They point to several remarks made in Congress which make it clear that this provision was not intended to restrict in any way the right of the membership to give a grant of authority — which they allege is all that the September 20th Resolution does.

A plain reading of the last sentence in §501(a) leads me to agree with the defendants, at least in their conclusion. On the other hand, it is not necessary for a resolution to read "The officers are hereby absolved of all responsibility created by the Act" before a court will strike it down as "exculpatory" under §501(a). Nor must a court accept at face value the stated purpose of a resolution when reason and common sense clearly dictate a different purpose. Nevertheless in my interpretation of §501(a), the Resolution under discussion is *not* one "purporting to relieve any [officer] of liability for breach of the duties declared by this section . . ."

We must distinguish between a resolution which purports to *authorize* action which is beyond the power of the union to do and for that reason in violation of §501(a) when done by an officer (such as the present Resolution) and a resolution which purports to *relieve* an officer of liability for breach of the duties declared in §501(a). At times this distinction may be a fine one. Very often the result will be the same. Nevertheless we feel that such a distinction should be made here unless the "exculpatory" provision is to be read as a mere "catchall" phrase.[6]

We turn then to the question of whether the September 20th Resolution is valid, i.e., conforms with the law of Pennsylvania and the Federal Labor laws. See International Union of Operating Engineers, A.F.L.-C.I.O. v. Pierce, Tex. Civ. App., 1959, 321 S.W.2d 914, at page 917-918. If it is inconsistent with either, we think it follows that the present expenditures by the defendants violate that provision in §501(a) which imposes upon them a strict duty to "expend [union funds] in accordance with its constitution and bylaws and any resolutions of the governing bodies adopted thereunder . . ." — since we read this sentence to authorize only those expenditures made pursuant to a *lawful* bylaw or resolution. . . .

The defendants argue that this Court is precluded from passing upon the merit or propriety of the Resolution in question. With this we agree. But there is a distinction between the merit of a resolution and its legal-

---

[6] We might point out in this regard that the original Senate version of the Act (i.e., The Kennedy-Ives Bill, S. Rep. No. 187, 86th Cong., First Session, 1959) contained a somewhat similar prohibition against any exculpatory resolution and *also* contained a clause prohibiting unions from paying the legal fees or fines of any person indicted or convicted of a violation of the Bill.

ity. The latter question is peculiarly within the competence of a court to pass upon and can not be abandoned finally to the organization. . . . When a serious question arises as to whether a particular act is within the legitimate aims and purposes of a labor union as expressed by its constitution and bylaws, the Court must ultimately resolve the matter so as to preserve on the one hand the rights of the union and on the other those of the individual members of that union. . . .

In answering this question of whether an act is ultra vires, we look first to the Constitution of Local 107. Article I, Section 2, sets forth the "objectives" of the organization in broad terms. These objectives might be summed up as an effort to organize workmen, to educate them, to improve their condition and to improve the industry in which they work. The defendants pointed to no more specific provision in the constitution (nor can we find any) which would authorize the type of expenditure dealt with here.

It is true that from the general objectives and purposes of a particular trade union, certain ancillary powers reasonably necessary for their attainment may be implied. In determining whether a particular act falls within this admittedly broad latitude of action, the Court must take into consideration all of the factors surrounding it, i.e., the stated purpose of the action, its immediate effect, its possible future benefit to the union, etc. This is necessary in order to determine whether the union, in light of the authority derived from its constitution, has a sufficient interest in the action to empower it to so act. If it has, a court of law will not interfere regardless of the wisdom or propriety of the act. If it has not, a court of law must intervene at the behest of a single union member. . . .

In passing upon the question of whether a union has sufficient interest in criminal and civil suits brought against various officers for the theft of union funds, to spend large sums of its money on legal fees for those officers, the Court is admittedly without a Pennsylvania case directly on point. There are, however, two interesting English cases which passed upon a similar question and which held that such expenditures were beyond the power of a union to make. Alfin v. Hewlett, 18 T.L.R. 664; Orman v. Hutt, 1 Ch. 98 (1914) (c.a.). These cases are persuasive.

Furthermore we feel that those cases involving the use of corporate funds to pay for the defense of officers charged with misconduct in office are helpful. Although this question again has not been passed upon in Pennsylvania, several other jurisdictions when faced with the problem have concluded that such expenditures are improper.[8] . . .

The only interest which Local 107 (as an organization dedicated to the objectives stated in its Constitution) would appear to have in the civil and criminal actions against these officers is an interest (1) in not

---

[8] In this regard, it is interesting to note that very recently the Pennsylvania Legislature passed a bill empowering a corporation to indemnify directors, officers and others against expenses in suits brought against them "by reason of being or having been directors or officers . . . of the corporation" *except* where he is adjudged liable for negligence or misconduct in performance of his duty. Act of April 18, 1945, P.L. 253, as amended October 13, 1959, 12 P.S. §1324.

losing the services of their officers (whom we must presume are competent) simply because someone wrongfully accuses them of misconduct, or (2) in not having men closely associated with their union (whose conduct somewhat reflects upon the union) convicted of serious wrongs when they are not in fact guilty of these wrongs, or (3) not having officers in their union accused of serious wrongs by antiunion people, simply because they are officers of a union.

Assume for a moment that one of these officers was accused of evasion of personal income taxes, would not Local 107 have exactly these same interests in the outcome of such a suit? If in such a situation, a majority of the union were to pass a resolution affirming their confidence in that officer and asserting herein that the action by the United States was in reality an attempt "to break up and destroy our union (and therefore) be it resolved that Local 107 go on record to help our (officer) in every way possible in (this) court (matter) by having Local 107 bear the legal costs of such actions which (is) in reality not directed at our (officer), but (is) directed at us, the members of Local 107, our good contracts, our good wages, and our good working conditions," a proper court of law upon an objection by a union member would independently pass upon the power of Local 107 to so spend its money, and even presuming the good faith of the membership in passing such a resolution, would properly enjoin the expenditure as outside the legitimate aims and purposes of Local 107 as expressed in its Constitution.

In light of the foregoing and upon consideration of the situation surrounding the present expenditures, in particular the nature and seriousness of the charges brought against the defendants by the State of Pennsylvania as well as by individual members of their union, the Court feels that such expenditures to pay for the legal expenses incurred by the defendant officers in the criminal and civil suits brought against them individually are expenses to be borne by the officers themselves and are beyond the power of Local 107 to make. Being beyond the powers of the union as derived from its Constitution, it follows that a mere majority vote at a regular union meeting can not authorize such expenditures. . . .

There are undoubtedly situations in which a suit against a union officer would have a direct and injurious effect upon the union itself or would in reality be directed at the union. In such a situation the union would have the power to lend its financial support to such officer. When the question of whether the union has a sufficient interest to spend large sums of money to defend such a suit arises, it must ultimately be resolved by the court. Although a court will allow wide latitude to those in control of the union, it can not, by allowing unlimited latitude, abandon the right of a minority to see that the union spends its monies in accordance with its lawful aims and purposes as expressed in its Constitution and bylaws. Particularly is this true today, when the voice of the individual employee in fixing his own wages, hours and working conditions has necessarily been surrendered to the voice of the collective bargaining unit.

There is a further reason why the present Resolution is no defense here. Aside from its validity under Pennsylvania law, it is inconsistent with the aims and purposes of the Labor-Management Reporting and Disclosure Act and violates the spirit of that Act. A stated purpose of the Act is "to *eliminate* . . . improper practices on the part of labor organizations . . . and their officers." (Emphasis added.) To allow a union officer to use the power and wealth of the very union which he is accused of pilfering, to defend himself against such charges, is totally inconsistent with Congress' effort to eliminate the undesirable element which has been uncovered in the labor-management field. To allow even a majority of members in that union to authorize such action, when, if the charges made against these defendants are true, it is these very members whom the officers have deceived, would be equally inconsistent with the Act. If some of those members have not been deceived by the defendants, but because of the immediate gains in their income and working conditions which Local 107 has won for them, they are content to accept as officers anyone who produces immediate results, regardless of what other wrongs those officers may commit in so doing, this Court would still not feel constrained to bow to their will in the light of its duty both to those members of Local 107 who place honesty above material gain as well as to the millions of others in the labor movement whose cause would be seriously injured by such an attitude.

Although we have not attempted to treat defendants' arguments individually, since we feel they are satisfactorily answered in this opinion, something should be said concerning their argument that the plaintiffs are here asking us to do that which Congress specifically refused to do when it failed to adopt Subsection 107(b) of the original Senate version of the Labor Bill (The Kennedy-Ives Bill), which specifically prohibited "both unions and employers from directly or indirectly paying or advancing the costs of defense, of any of their officers . . . who (are) indicted for . . . any violation of any provision of the Bill." S. Rep. No. 187, 86th Cong., First Session, 1959, U.S. Code Cong. and Adm. News 1959, p. 2318.

We are familiar with this argument in statutory construction. Although the value of such reasoning to discover the "intent" of Congress is often questionable, we can not of course ignore it. . . . Nevertheless there are reasons why we are not persuaded by their argument here.

First, the language contained in the Kennedy-Ives Bill is much broader than our holding in the present case. It is essential to an understanding of our position in this case that this point be made clear. That section quoted above would foreclose financial aid by the union to an officer in suits under the Act, under *any* circumstances. In our case we have expressly limited our holding *to the facts before us*. In the light of all of these facts we do not feel that the several actions brought against the defendants involve any question of sufficient interest to Local 107 to warrant their expending large sums of union money to pay the legal costs of the defendants in these suits. That Congress refused to foreclose the right of a union under *any* circumstances to lend financial aid to an officer when sued under any section of the Kennedy-Ives Bill is not, we feel, a strong argument for the conclusion that under *no* circumstances could a union be prohibited from lending financial aid to an accused officer.

Second, in none of the cases cited by the defendants to support their argument as to the conclusion to be drawn from the omission of Section 107(b) were there two distinct bills involved. Here the Act finally passed by Congress (with modification) was the Landrum-Griffin House Bill and not the Kennedy-Ives Senate Bill. Strictly speaking, the Conference Committee did not amend the final Bill as to the provision in question, since it was never contained in it to begin with. Had the Kenney-Ives Bill ultimately been adopted with Section 107(b) deleted, the defendants' argument would be more convincing.

Finally, even assuming that Congress intended to leave a union free to use its funds for the purpose of paying its officers' legal expenses in actions brought against them under the new Act, if under the law of Pennsylvania, the state in which the union membership contractual relationship arose, such expenditures are illegal, a union officer could not consistent with his duty to the union (which duties ultimately flow from its Constitution) expend union funds for this purpose. This would follow unless we interpret the omission of this prohibition as creating an affirmative federal right in a union to so spend its funds, which right is intended to supersede any state law to the contrary. We flatly reject such an interpretation of the new Act.

At the time that permission was granted to the plaintiffs to file their complaint pursuant to §501(b) of the Act (see our Order of November 12, 1959), we specifically refused to pass upon the validity of any of the legal arguments raised by the defendants. Since the reasonable time requirements of §501(b) were clearly met as to at least one phase of the complaint,[9] and there appearing to have been "good cause" shown by the plaintiffs for filing suit, the Court permitted the complaint to be filed.[10]

However, since that time we have had the benefit of extensive legal arguments on the merits of the action and as a result have reached the conclusions above set forth with regard to the retrospective application of the Act. In view of these conclusions, which in effect result in stripping plaintiffs' complaint of all but those few paragraphs which state in general terms that the defendants' unlawful activities are continuing to the present time, we are compelled to order the plaintiffs to amend their

---

[9] The union has from the outset taken the position that expenditures for counsel fees are proper in light of the Resolution. Therefore, no purpose would be served by further delay in this matter and the "reasonable time" requirement in §501(b) was met.

[10] Although the Act does not specify what is meant by "good cause" in §501(b), it would appear that such a preliminary requirement is intended as a safeguard to the union against harassing and vexatious litigation brought without merit or good faith. The fact that permission to file the complaint can be granted after an ex parte hearing would seem to support this view. The Court believed that the present suit satisfied this basic requirement.

complaint to state specific acts of misconduct in violation of §501 which have occurred *subsequent* to September 14, 1959 and which the union upon request has failed within a reasonable time to answer or otherwise correct. In the event that the plaintiffs fail to so amend within a time to be set in our order, their complaint will be dismissed with prejudice, excepting from such dismissal, of course, that part of their complaint which deals with the injunction discussed above.

A formal order will be entered enjoining the defendants from expending union funds for the defense of the cases presently pending against the defendants in either the Courts of the Commonwealth of Pennsylvania or in this Court. This ruling in no way attempts to pass upon the question of whether or not Local 107 may with propriety, by appropriate resolution, reimburse its officers for their legal expenses in the event they are exonerated from any wrongdoing in connection with the handling of union funds involved in the actions presently pending.[9]

NOTES

1. In 1961 the International Brotherhood of Teamsters amended its constitution to provide as follows:

"The international union is authorized to pay all expenses for investigating services, employment of all counsel and other necessary expenditures in any . . . cases where an officer, representative, employee, agent, or one charged with acting in behalf of the international union and/or its affiliates is charged with any violation . . . of any law or is sued in any civil action . . . (1) if a majority of the general executive board in its sole discretion determines that said charges or law suits are (A) unfounded, or (B) are politically motivated, or (C) were filed in bad faith in an attempt to embarrass or destroy the union or the union officer or representative, (2) or if a majority of the general executive board in its sole discretion determines that the expenditures should be made.

"(B) The provisions set forth in subsection (A) above shall also apply to such expenditures made by all affiliates other than local unions if the appropriate governing body of the affiliate in its sole discretion determines that the expenditures should be made.

"(C) A local union is authorized to pay any and all the above expenditures in any . . . cases where an officer, representative, employee, agent, or one charged with acting in behalf of the local union is charged with any violation . . . of any law or is sued in any civil action . . . (1) if a majority of the local executive board in its sole discretion, subject to the approval of the members present and voting at a regular meeting (or a majority of all members present and voting at all the regular, craft or divisional monthly meetings held in lieu of a single monthly regular meeting) determines that said charges or law suits are (A) unfounded, or (B) are politically motivated, or (C) were filed in bad faith in an attempt to embarrass or destroy the union or the union officer or repre-

---

[9] For an account of subsequent developments in this case, see Highway Truck Drivers v. Cohen, 334 F.2d 378 (3d Cir. 1964). — Ed.

sentative (2) or if a majority of the local executive board in its sole discretion subject to the approval of a majority of the members present and voting in a regular meeting (or a majority of all the members present and voting at all the regular, craft or divisional monthly meetings) determines that the expenditures should be made."

Is the foregoing amendment a "general exculpatory provision . . . void as against public policy" within the meaning of Section 501(a) of the LMRDA? See Highway Truck Drivers v. Cohen, 334 F.2d 378 (3d Cir. 1964).

2. Does the "good cause" prerequisite to suit under Section 501(b) preclude federal jurisdiction in a case in which plaintiff has failed to exhaust his union remedies? Compare Penuelas v. Moreno, 198 F. Supp. 441, 444-449 (S.D. Cal. 1961), with Holdeman v. Sheldon, 204 F. Supp. 890, 895-896 (S.D.N.Y. 1962), aff'd, 311 F.2d 2 (2d Cir. 1962).

h. REPORTING AND DISCLOSURE

GOLDBERG v. TRUCK DRIVERS

United States Court of Appeals, Sixth Circuit, 1961
293 F.2d 807, certiorari denied, 368 U.S. 938 (1961)

WEICK, Circuit Judge.

This case involves important questions concerning the right of the Secretary of Labor to secure judicial enforcement of subpoenas duces tecum issued by him and served on union officers in connection with an investigation he was attempting to make under the authority of Section 601 of the Labor-Management Reporting and Disclosure Act of 1959, 29 U.S.C.A. §521.

The union officers appeared in response to the subpoenas, challenged the right of the Secretary to make the investigation and refused to produce the records called for in view of legal questions which the unions and their counsel believed were involved including the constitutionality of certain sections of the Act providing for the issuance of the subpoenas. The union officers had custody of the records subpoenaed and there was no claim of any physical inability on their part to produce them.

The Secretary filed a petition in the District Court for enforcement of the subpoenas, which was denied on the ground that the Secretary had made no showing as to necessity for the investigation and because the subpoenas were too broad.

It appeared on the face of the subpoenas that they were issued in connection with "an investigation by the Bureau of Labor-Management Reports[1] involving a determination whether any person has violated any provision of the Act." The subpoenas called for the production of the following records:

All records for the period from January 1, 1959 to the present date maintained by you or under your control which contain any basic in-

---

[1] The Bureau was the duly authorized representative of the Secretary.

formation or data on matters required to be reported from which the organizational report (Form LM-1), and the financial report (Form LM-2) filed with the Secretary of Labor for Local 614, International Brotherhood of Teamsters, Chauffeurs, Warehousemen and Helpers of America may be verified, explained or clarified and checked for accuracy and completeness, in connection with all items referred to or listed in such report and all items omitted or excluded therefrom which are relevant thereto and are required to be included in said reports, such records to include but not be limited to, vouchers, worksheets, ledgers, audit reports, records of receipt of dues, fees, assessments, fines and work permits, accounts receivable, accounts payable, journals, journal vouchers, check register, payroll register and related records and all books of accounts of Local 614, related to the International Brotherhood of Teamsters, Chauffeurs, Warehousemen and Helpers of America, or other local unions affiliated with said International including all bank statements, cancelled checks, check stubs, audit reports, financial reports, records of loans, records of mortgages, records of ownership of property real and personal, deeds, records of trusts, records of investments, and all correspondence and memoranda pertaining to receipts and disbursements.

No evidence was offered in the District Court. . . .

In the District Court, the unions contended that it was obligatory on the part of the Secretary to first establish probable cause for the investigation as a condition precedent to obtaining enforcement of the subpoenas by the court.

The District Court, in its opinion denying enforcement, did not expressly use the term "probable cause," but adopted words of like import which imposed a requirement at least as stringent, namely, that the Secretary establish a basis for the investigation. The court said that there must be some "reasonable foundation or valid purpose" rather than merely looking into the records of the union in the hope of turning up something. This, in effect, was a holding that the Secretary had no right merely to investigate, but was required first to establish a probable violation of the Act.

In this Court, the unions contended that as a prerequisite to judicial enforcement of a subpoena duces tecum the Secretary "must show that he has a reasonable belief of necessity (i.e., a reasonable basis) for the investigation."

The statute required the unions to maintain the records which were subpoenaed. . . .

Power was granted to the Secretary to make an investigation by the following language:

"Investigations by Secretary; applicability of other laws

"(a) The Secretary shall have power when he believes it necessary in order to determine whether any person has violated or is about to violate any provision of this chapter (except subchapter II of this chapter) to make an investigation and in connection therewith he may enter such places and inspect such records and accounts and question such persons as he may deem necessary to enable him to determine the facts relative thereto. The Secretary may report to interested persons or officials concerning the facts required to be shown in any report required by this chapter and concerning the reasons for failure or refusal to file such a report or any other matter which he deems to be appropriate as a result of such an investigation.

"(b) For the purpose of any investigation provided for in this chapter, the provisions of sections 49 and 50 of Title 15 (relating to the attendance of witnesses and the production of books, papers, and documents), are made applicable to the jurisdiction, powers, and duties of the Secretary or any officers designated by him." 29 U.S.C.A. §521(a, b).

The pertinent provisions of Section 9 and Section 10 of the Federal Trade Commission Act which were made applicable are set forth in footnote 3.

[3] Section 9 of the Federal Trade Commission Act (15 U.S.C.A. §49) provides in pertinent part as follows:

"Documentary evidence; depositions; witnesses

"For the purposes of sections 41-46 and 47-58 of this title the commission, or its duly authorized agent or agents, shall at all reasonable times have access to, for the purpose of examination, and the right to copy any documentary evidence of any corporation being investigated or proceeded against; and the commission shall have power to require by subpoena the attendance and testimony of witnesses and the production of all such documentary evidence relating to any matter under investigation. Any member of the commission may sign subpoenas, and members and examiners of the commission may administer oaths and affirmations, examine witnesses, and receive evidence.

"Such attendance of witnesses, and the production of such documentary evidence, may be required from any place in the United States, at any designated place of hearing. And in case of disobedience to a subpoena the commission may invoke the aid of any court of the United States in requiring the attendance and testimony of witnesses and the production of documentary evidence.

"Any of the district courts of the United States within the jurisdiction of which such inquiry is carried on may, in case of contumacy or refusal to obey a subpoena issued to any corporation or other person, issue an order requiring such corporation or other person to appear before the commission, or to produce documentary evidence if so ordered, or to give evidence touching the matter in question; and any failure to obey such order of the court may be punished by such court as a contempt thereof. . . .

"No person shall be excused from attending and testifying or from producing documentary evidence before the commission or in obedience to the subpoena of the commission on the ground or for the reason that the testimony or evidence, documentary or otherwise, required of him may tend to criminate him or subject him to a penalty or forfeiture. But no natural person shall be prosecuted or subjected to any penalty or forfeiture for or on account of any transaction, matter, . . . or produce evidence, documentary or otherwise, before the commission in obedience to a subpoena issued by it: PROVIDED, That no natural person so testifying shall be exempt from prosecution and punishment for perjury committed in so testifying."

Section 10 of the Federal Trade Commission Act (15 U.S.C.A. §50) provides in pertinent part as follows:

"Offenses and penalties

"Any person who shall neglect or refuse to attend and testify, or to answer any lawful inquiry or to produce documentary evidence, if in his power to do so, in obedience to the subpoena or lawful requirement of the commission, shall be guilty of an offense and upon conviction thereof by a court of competent jurisdic-

The legislative history of the Labor-Management Reporting and Disclosure Act reveals that the original bills introduced in the House and Senate each granted power to the Secretary to make an investigation only when he had probable cause to believe that any person or labor organization had violated any provision of the Act. The probable cause requirement, however, was eliminated from the Act as it was finally passed. The reason for deleting the probable cause requirement is set forth in the minority amendments adopted by the Senate Committee on Labor and Public Welfare. It is as follows:

"Section 106(c): The Secretary shall have the power and is directed when he believes it necessary in order to determine whether anyone has violated or is about to violate a provision of this bill to make investigations.

"As originally worded, this section would have given the Secretary the authority to investigate the books and records of persons reporting under the act only when he had probable cause to believe that a person had violated provisions of the act. On the surface, the term 'probable cause' would appear to give the Secretary all the investigatory power that he needed. But the words 'probable cause' would throw a monkey wrench into the Secretary's investigatory machinery. Probable cause means more than mere suspicion that the act has been violated. To have probable cause, a person must have such evidence as would lead the ordinary prudent man to believe that the act has been violated. Consequently, every time he commenced an investigation the Secretary could be dragged into court until the question of probable cause had been decided. Under nearly every statute requiring the filing of reports, such as the Internal Revenue Act and the Fair Labor Standards Act, the Administrator can conduct 'spot check' investigations unhampered by the 'probable cause' requirement. Our amendment rewrites this section to give the Secretary investigatory power when he believes it necessary in

---

tion shall be punished by a fine of not less than $1,000 nor more than $5,000, or by imprisonment for not more than one year, or by both such fine and imprisonment.

"Any person who shall willfully make, or cause to be made any false entry or statement of fact in any report required to be made under sections 41-46 and 47-58 of this title, or who shall willfully make, or cause to be made, any false entry in any account, record, or memorandum kept by any corporation subject to said sections, or who shall willfully neglect or fail to make, or to cause to be made, full, true, and correct entries in such accounts, records, or memoranda of all facts and transactions appertaining to the business of such corporation, or who shall willfully remove out of the jurisdiction of the United States, or willfully mutilate, alter, or by any other means falsify any documentary evidence of such corporation, or who shall willfully refuse to submit to the commission or to any of its authorized agents, for the purpose of inspection and taking copies, any documentary evidence of such corporation in his possession or within his control, shall be deemed guilty of an offense against the United States, and shall be subject, upon conviction in any court of the United States of competent jurisdiction, to a fine of not less than $1,000 nor more than $5,000, or to imprisonment for a term of not more than three years, or to both such fine and imprisonment." 29 U.S.C.A. §521(a, b).

order to determine whether a violation has occurred or is about to occur." U.S. Code Congressional & Administrative News — 86th Congress, 1st Session 1959, pp. 2395, 2396.

After the bill had passed the Senate, it was sent to a Conference Committee which reported:

"Section 601 — Investigations

"The Senate bill contains a provision which directs the Secretary to conduct an investigation when he believes it necessary in order to determine whether any person has, or is about to, violate the act, or any rule or regulation authorized by the act.

"The House amendment directs the Secretary to make an investigation when he has probable cause to believe that any person has violated a provision of the act, other than title I.

"The conference substitute is similar to the Senate bill, except that the investigation authority is permissive rather than mandatory, no investigation may be made with respect to violations of rules and regulations, and the investigation authority does not extend to title I.

"The Senate bill also contains a provision authorizing the Secretary to report to interested persons concerning the facts required to be shown in reports and concerning the reasons for failure or refusal to file a report or any other matter he deems appropriate as a result of an investigation. The conference substitute adopts this provision." U.S. Code Congressional & Administrative News — 86th Congress, 1st Session 1959, p. 2508.

The legislative history of the Act is clear that Congress rejected the "probable cause" requirement because it might hamper the Secretary in the performance of his duties with respect to investigation which were imposed upon him by the Act. With such a requirement, each investigation would likely be met by a lawsuit in which the Secretary would be obliged to prove a probable violation of the Act or enforcement of subpoenas would be denied. Even if successful in his proof, the investigation by the Secretary might be delayed for months or years while the matter was being litigated in the courts. It seems to us that the court ought not to impose a condition, which Congress rejected, on the exercise of the right of the Secretary to investigate. Nor do we see any real difference between the rejected "probable cause" requirement and that of a "reasonable basis" for the investigation adopted by the District Court. While the disclosure sought must not be unreasonable or oppressive (Oklahoma Press Publishing Co. v. Walling, 327 U.S. 186, 208), this does not mean that the Secretary is obligated to establish a reasonable basis for his investigation. If the Secretary was in possession of facts establishing a probable violation he might never need to investigate. The purpose of the investigation authorized by Congress was to provide the means of discovery whereby the Secretary could determine whether the Act was being violated, or about to be violated.

All the statute required, in order for the Secretary to investigate, was that he "believe it necessary in order to determine whether any person has violated or is about to violate any provision of this chapter."

In his petition for enforcement filed in the District Court, the Secretary alleged in paragraph six that he believed it was necessary to make the investigation to determine whether any persons violated or were about to violate the law. The unions in their response to the petition (Par. I) admitted the allegations contained in paragraph six and certain other paragraphs of the petition.

. . . The trial judge commented on the fact that the Secretary did not offer any evidence to establish the reason or basis for the investigation. In our opinion, the Secretary was not required to do so. The statute was sufficient authority for him to proceed. The purpose of the investigation appeared on the face of the subpoenas. The Secretary could not very well perform his statutory duty and determine whether the Act was being violated or about to be violated without making an investigation. Requiring the Secretary to first establish a probable violation of the Act, as a condition precedent to making an investigation, effectively stripped him of his power to investigate and prevented him from determining whether the Act was being violated or about to be violated. It virtually rendered the enforcement provisions of the Act nugatory.

We believe Oklahoma Press Publishing Co. v. Walling, 327 U.S. 186, is dispositive of this issue. In upholding enforcement of a subpoena duces tecum issued by the Administrator of the Wage and Hour Division of the Department of Labor, the Court said:

"Congress has made no requirement in terms of any showing of 'probable cause'; and, in view of what has already been said, any possible constitutional requirement of that sort was satisfied by the Administrator's showing in this case, including not only the allegations concerning coverage, but also that he was proceeding with his investigation in accordance with the mandate of Congress and that the records sought were relevant to that purpose. . . .

"The result therefore sustains the Administrator's position that his investigation function, in searching out violations with a view to securing enforcement of the Act, is essentially the same as the grand jury's, or the court's in issuing other pretrial orders for the discovery of evidence, and is governed by the same limitations. These are that he shall not act arbitrarily or in excess of his statutory authority, but this does not mean that his inquiry must be 'limited . . . by . . . forecasts of the probable result of the investigation . . .' Blair v. United States, 250 U.S. 273, 282; cf. Hale v. Henkel, 201 U.S. 43. Nor is the judicial function either abused or abased, as has been suggested, by leaving to it the determination of the important questions which the Administrator's position concedes the courts may decide."

The Court was cognizant of contentions which would block an investigation at the very threshold of the inquiry stating:

"On the other hand, petitioners' view, if accepted, would stop much if not all of investigation in the public interest at the threshold of inquiry and, in the case of the Administrator, is designed avowedly to do so. This would render substantially impossible his effective discharge of the duties of investigation and enforcement which Congress has placed upon him. And if his functions could be thus blocked, so might many others of equal importance." . . .

. . . In our judgment, the District Court erred in imposing a condition on the exercise of the right granted by Congress to the Secretary to make an investigation.

It is next contended that the subpoenas duces tecum were too broad. In substance, they required production of records containing basic information or data on matters required to be reported from which the organizational reports (Form LM-1) and the financial reports (Form LM-2) filed with the Secretary by the unions may be verified, explained or clarified and checked for accuracy and completeness. These were the records which the statute required the unions to keep and were quasi-public records. Production of the records could not be resisted on the ground of self-incrimination. Shapiro v. United States, 335 U.S. 1; Wilson v. United States, 221 U.S. 361; United States v. Pulford, 6 Cir., 155 F.2d 944; Rodgers v. United States, 6 Cir., 138 F.2d 992. The unions asserted no such ground. In our opinion, it was not unreasonable to compel production of records which the law required to be kept and from which the reports filed with the Secretary were made. In no other way could the Secretary verify the reports than by examination of the records. These records were relevant to the inquiry because they would throw light on whether the reports filed by the unions with the Secretary spoke the truth. The District Court, however, had the power to impose protective restraints on the conduct of the investigation to relieve against oppression or other illegal conduct. Hunt Foods & Industries, Inc. v. Federal Trade Commission, 9 Cir., 286 F.2d 803, 811, certiorari denied 365 U.S. 877. This power was not invoked by the unions. They questioned the right of the Secretary to make the investigation.

Oklahoma Press involved a corporation. It is urged that a different rule should apply to labor unions. We think not. In United States v. White, 322 U.S. 694, a subpoena duces tecum issued by the District Court requiring a union to produce its records before a Grand Jury was resisted by a union officer on the ground that they might tend to incriminate the union or himself individually or as such officer. The Supreme Court held that this defense was not available. While White involved the Fifth Amendment, the opinion of the Court contains language which is pertinent here. The Court said:

"The fact that the state charters corporations and has visitorial powers over them provides a convenient vehicle for justification of governmental investigation of corporate books and records. Hale v. Henkel, supra; Wilson v. United States, supra. But the absence of that fact as to a particular type of organization does not lessen the public necessity for making reasonable regulations of its activities effective, nor does it confer upon such an organization the purely personal privilege against self-incrimination. Basically, the power to compel the production of the records of any organization, whether it be incorporated or not, arises out of the inherent and necessary power of the federal and state governments to enforce their laws, with the privilege against self-incrimination being limited to its historic function of protecting only the natural individual from compulsory incrimination through his own testimony or personal records."

The Court concluded:

"The union and its officers acting in their official capacity lack the privilege at all times of insulating the union's books and records against reasonable demands of governmental authorities."

Finally, the unions contend that Section 201 of the Act (29 U.S.C.A. §431), containing the provisions requiring them to file reports with the Secretary, is unconstitutional in violation of the Commerce Clause, Article I, Section 8. This contention was not passed upon by the District Court. The unions claim that the Secretary's authority to investigate is dependent upon Section 201 of the Act, and, therefore, such Section is subject to challenge in this case.

The unions concede (Brief p. 19) that Congress has the power to regulate collective bargaining activities affecting interstate commerce. N.L.R.B. v. Jones & Laughlin Steel Corp. 301 U.S. 1. They admit (Brief p. 22) that the Section would be constitutionally supportable if the reporting requirements were limited to the filing of collective bargaining agreements, reporting strike vote procedures, hiring hall practices and the like. They insist, however, that the Section contains general reporting provisions and is an attempt by Congress, using its conceded power, to legislate with respect to all of the internal affairs of the unions, which are purely local in character. They argue that if this legislation is sustained it will obliterate any meaningful distinction between federal and state authority.

The trouble with this contention is that the collective bargaining procedures and the like, which admittedly may be regulated, are not the only union activities which substantially affect interstate commerce.

Congress has made detailed findings, based on extensive investigation, which were adopted as part of the Act (29 U.S.C.A. §401). These findings, in substance, were "that the relations between employers and labor organizations and the millions of workers they represent have a substantial impact on the commerce of the Nation"; that the Federal Government has a responsibility to protect the rights of the employees; that in order to accomplish the free flow of commerce, it is necessary that labor organizations, employers and their officials maintain the highest standards of responsibility and ethical conduct in the handling of their affairs particularly as they affect labor-management relations. Congress found from its recent investigations that these high standards had not been maintained but were breached and disregarded; that it was necessary to pass the Act to eliminate or prevent improper practices which defeated the policy of the Labor-Management Relations Act of 1947, as amended, and burdened and obstructed commerce.

These findings of Congress are binding on the courts. . . .

Where, as here, the activities have a substantial effect on interstate commerce, it is not an objection that they are local in character. United States v. Darby, 312 U.S. 100; Wickard v. Filburn, 317 U.S. 111.

The Commerce Clause does not inhibit Congress in selecting the means deemed necessary for bringing out the desired conditions in the channels of interstate commerce. American Power & Light Co. v. S.E.C., 329 U.S. 90, 100.

In our opinion, Section 201 of the Act does not offend against the Commerce Clause.

The judgment of the District Court is reversed and the cause remanded with instructions to grant the petition for enforcement of the subpoenas.

i.   TRUSTEESHIPS

SECRETARY OF LABOR, REPORT TO THE CONGRESS UPON THE OPERATION OF TITLE III OF THE LABOR-MANAGEMENT REPORTING AND DISCLOSURE ACT [10]

BACKGROUND

A trusteeship is any method of supervision or control whereby a labor organization suspends the autonomy otherwise available to a subordinate body under its constitution or bylaws. The practice of imposing trusteeships by unions dates back to the 19th century, but was extremely rare until the development of strong national unions.

During hearings of the McClellan Committee it was disclosed that the power to impose trusteeship was used sometimes for the purpose of "milking" local treasuries or undemocratically controlling votes to perpetuate power. In the second and third years of the McClellan Committee hearings, legislation was proposed containing provisions to correct abuses through enforcement measures.

Provisions covering trusteeships were enacted as title III of the Labor-Management Reporting and Disclosure Act of 1959 (Public Law 86-257) on September 14, 1959. This title prescribes conditions under which trusteeships may be established and continued, requires reporting and public disclosure of their stewardship by any labor organization, makes it a crime either to count the votes of delegates of the trusteed union unless democratically elected, or to transfer funds to the supervisory body, and provides redress for the union member or subordinate body either directly in court or through the Secretary of Labor.

The discussions and committee deliberations in Congress recognized that union trusteeships, although sometimes used to control subordinated organizations illegally, most often are used to provide assistance

[10] Submitted to Congress in September, 1962, pursuant to Section 305 of the LMRDA. — ED.

to subordinates in difficulties, to assist in maintenance and stability, and to promote rather than stifle union democracy.

ADMINISTRATION

The Department's administration of title III has been guided by an awareness of these congressionally noted facts. Therefore, the Department emphasizes voluntary compliance and provides technical assistance to unions in their efforts to comply with the law. However, 306 reported trusteeships or alleged violations have been investigated thoroughly to insure that the law is being complied with. . . .

Numerous interpretations have been issued in this uncharted field, and none of them has yet been challenged in the courts. The significant interpretative problems have focused upon determining whether a trusteeship exists; whether it has been imposed or is being continued for allowable purposes; whether certain activities are prohibited during a trusteeship; the extent of the Department's enforcement authority; and the effect and application of title III's 18-month presumptive validity in civil actions.

CHARACTERISTICS OF TRUSTEESHIPS

A total of 777 trusteeships were reported to the Department of Labor during the 2½ years following enactment of the LMRDA. By the cutoff date for this study (March 13, 1962), 590 of these were terminated, leaving 187 subordinate bodies still under trusteeship. This 187 contrasts with 487 unions under trusteeship on September 14, 1959 — the effective date of the Act.

Only about one-fourth of all national unions subject to the Act have reported any trusteeships. Of the 70 organizations that have reported trusteeships, 23 had only one in effect at any time during the study period.

An analysis of the financial reports shows that the typical union under trusteeship is small, with assets of about $1,750 and annual receipts slightly in excess of $6,000. . . .

During the past 2½ years new trusteeships have continued to be imposed at a rate averaging about 10 per month and indications are that the Act has not substantially hindered national unions in the establishment of essential trusteeships.

The LMRDA states four allowable purposes for establishing trusteeships:

1. "Correcting corruption or financial malpractice." This reason has been used by parent unions to justify correction of situations ranging from minor speculations to gross mishandling of funds constituting violations of the LMRDA.

2. "Assuring the performance of collective-bargaining agreements or other duties of a bargaining representative." This was a frequently used and obviously important reason for establishing trusteeships.

3. "Restoring democratic procedures." This reason has frequently been used for trusteeships established to correct violations of the Act.

4. "Otherwise carrying out the legitimate objects of such labor organization." Included under this purpose are: *caretaker trusteeships* (accounting for about one-third of the trusteeships active during this report period), which were used when a subordinate union was relatively inactive because of the closing of a plant, a small or itinerant membership, sudden loss of leadership (e.g., by death or illness), or because it was a new local not yet able to stand on its own feet; *dissension,* a category which has shown the largest decrease in use since the LMRDA; *mismanagement,* which embraces other than financial malpractice; and *disaffiliation,* a self-explanatory reason for establishing trusteeships. . . .

Of the 487 trusteeships reported in effect on September 14, 1959, 312 were already more than 18 months old. Of the 187 trusteeships active on March 13, 1962, 74 are more than 18 months old. The most common reason for continuing those which were still active in March 1962 was the need for a "caretaker."

Analysis of the constitutions of 110 national unions having more than 10,000 members indicates that, in September 1959, 68 had specific constitutional provisions concerning the reasons for imposing trusteeships and the persons authorized to do so; 63 provided for appeals; and 57 spelled out the powers of the trustee. By May 1962, 36 of the 110 unions had amended the trusteeship provisions of their constitution or added new provisions. Most frequently they made more specific the reasons for establishment of the trusteeship and the powers of the trustee, and provided for a hearing on imposition of the trusteeship or an appeals procedure.

ENFORCEMENT

The Department has avoided a formalized procedure for processing complaints filed with the Secretary pursuant to section 304. Such complaints are investigated by the BLMR [11] and a determination on the merits of the complaint is based on the investigative findings. The parties concerned are then notified of this determination without disclosing the identity of the complainant. In cases where there is probable cause to believe that a violation has occurred, the union establishing the trusteeship is given an opportunity to take corrective action before a court action is instituted, since section 304 carries only a remedy by civil action.

BLMR has instituted investigations of 306 reported trusteeships or

[11] The Bureau of Labor-Management Reports (BLMR) was established within the Department of Labor to exercise certain delegated powers of the Secretary of Labor under the LMRDA. In 1963 the Secretary established a new Labor-Management Services Administration within the Department by Order 24-63, 28 Fed. Reg. 9172 (1963). A new Bureau of Labor-Management and Welfare-Pension Reports now carries out functions formerly performed by the BLMR and by the Office of Welfare-Pension Reports, which formerly administered the Welfare and Pension Plans Disclosure Act, 72 Stat. 997 (1958), as amended, 29 U.S.C.A. §§301-309 (1964). — ED.

alleged violations of the trusteeship provisions, of which 264 have been closed . . . Of [these,] 183 have resulted from complaints of members. Of the 264 investigations which have been closed, 199 disclosed no violations of title III. Sixty-five established violations of title III, but in each case the union imposing the trusteeship voluntarily corrected the matter. The violations found ranged from technical deficiencies in a report to illegal establishment or continuance of a trusteeship.

No basis for criminal prosecution under title III was established in these investigations, so it has not been necessary for the Secretary to go to court to enforce this title of the Act. The reports investigations, on the other hand, disclosed violations of other provisions of the act that resulted in court actions. There have, however, been several civil suits filed under title III by private individuals. The issues in these cases primarily have centered on procedural matters and the effect of statutory preservation of pre-existing State and Federal remedies. The cases are divided on the question of whether or not a union member can initiate a private suit directly without proceeding through the Secretary of Labor. U.S. district courts in California and New Jersey have held that the proper procedure to be followed by union members seeking relief under title III of the act is, first, to lodge a complaint with the Secretary.[12] Only after this remedy has been pursued, these courts have decided, may the member take his case to court. On the other hand, the U.S. district court in Maryland has held that the member has the option of either invoking the aid of the Secretary or initiating court action directly.[13]

More cases have dealt with procedural than with substantive aspects of title III. Although several cases have considered permissibility of reasons for establishing trusteeships, none has held that a trusteeship should be lifted because of illegal imposition.

The courts seem to regard prevention of secession of a local as a legitimate reason for establishing a trusteeship. They have held that a national union does not have inherent power to impose a trusteeship for this reason, but, as a practical matter, many national constitutions empower the union to prevent secession of a local. The decisions also seem to recognize the right of a national union to merge or to consolidate subordinate locals, though such an action may result in the suspension of local autonomy. So long as the governing rules of the organization authorize such action by the national, and the action is not grossly unreasonable, the statutory provisions would not appear to inhibit mergers or consolidations.

CONCLUSIONS

Operation of the trusteeship provisions of the Labor-Management Reporting and Disclosure Act during the first $2\frac{1}{2}$ years supports the following conclusions:

[12] Flaherty v. McDonald, 183 F. Supp. 300 (S.D. Cal. 1960); Rizzo v. Ammond, 182 F. Supp. 456 (D.N.J. 1960). — ED.

[13] Local 28 v. IBEW, 184 F. Supp. 649 (D. Md. 1960). — ED.

1. Establishment of trusteeships has never been a widespread practice, except in a few unions. When the Act became effective, trusteeships existed in less than 1 percent of the convened unions. Now, less than half that percentage are involved.

2. The Act has been effective in correcting the malpractices disclosed by the McClellan Committee. Further, a large number of trusteeships, while not corrupt, were unnecessarily continued and have now been terminated.

3. Since enactment of the law, many national union constitutions have been amended to provide greater safeguards against unnecessary suspension of autonomy.

4. Indications are that the Act has not substantially hindered unions from establishing essential trusteeships.

5. The reporting and disclosure of the facts surrounding trusteeships, and the active cooperation of the vast majority of unions and union officers, have resulted in substantial compliance with the law with a minimum need for enforcement.

NOTES

1. Parks v. IBEW, 314 F.2d 886 (4th Cir.), cert. denied, 372 U.S. 976 (1963), involved an action which arose out of the revocation by an international union of a local's charter, on the ground that the local had engaged in a strike without the International President's approval and contrary to his express and repeated orders not to do so. Included in the exhaustive opinion dealing with a variety of issues under the LMRDA is the following (314 F.2d at 923-924):

"The plaintiffs assert that by revoking and reissuing the charter conveying IBEW jurisdiction in the Baltimore area, the IP [International President] achieved the same objectives as he might have attained through a formal trusteeship and his action should therefore be held to have constituted the imposition of a trusteeship. So denominating the IP's action, the plaintiffs reason that the trusteeship provisions of the LMRDA have been violated.

"Preliminarily, a question to be determined is whether the District Court was empowered to exercise jurisdiction over this private action for alleged violations of Title III of the LMRDA. . . . Several district courts have interpreted this [§304(a)] to mean that individual members or subordinate bodies may not bring a civil action until full resort has been had to the administrative remedies available before the Secretary of Labor. In a litigation involving Local 28 and the IBEW, prior but pertinent to the present one, District Judge R. Dorsey Watkins had occasion to pass upon this very question. After a scholarly analysis, he concluded that, at least until the Secretary of Labor does bring suit, a private action can be maintained under §304(a) of the LMRDA. Executive Board, Local 28 IBEW v. IBEW, 184 F. Supp. 649, 653-659 (D. Md. 1960).[77] In this well reasoned view that section 304(a) does not

[77] Accord, Vars v. International Bhd. of Boilermakers, 204 F. Supp. 245, 246-247 (D. Conn. 1962); see Palisades Lodge No. 173 v. Brotherhood of Railway

require recourse to that particular administrative remedy and action of the Secretary before a private suit may be entertained, this court concurs.

"Upon review of the evidence, however, Judge Thomsen concluded that while it is possible for revocation to be used as a means of evading the trusteeship provisions of Title III, it was not proven that revocation was so used.[78] Although the question is exceedingly close, see Anderson, 'Landrum-Griffin and the Trusteeship Imbroglio,' 71 Yale L.J. 1460, 1478-85 (1962), this court is not persuaded that the District Court's disposition of the trusteeship question should be overturned."

2. In Brewery Bottlers v. International Bhd. of Teamsters, 202 F. Supp. 464 (E.D.N.Y. 1962), a local union moved to enjoin the international from effecting a merger of seven locals, including plaintiff, into two newly chartered locals, on the ground that the merger would effectuate supervision or control through which the international would suspend the autonomy otherwise available under the local's constitution and bylaws and would thus constitute a trusteeship as defined in Section 3(h) of the LMRDA, and that the alleged trusteeship was not for a permissible purpose. The court dismissed the suit for lack of jurisdiction, saying (p. 468):

"Congress has not denied a labor organization the right to merge local unions. Were the court to adopt plaintiffs' definition of a trusteeship . . . the right of a labor organization to merge locals would be permitted only '. . . for the purpose of correcting corruption or financial malpractice. . . .' Sec. 302 L.R.M.D.A., 73 Stat. 531, 29 U.S.C.A. §462. Such an interpretation would effectively frustrate the power of a labor organization to merge subordinate local unions. Nothing in the legislative history indicates a Congressional intent to curb, limit or render ineffective the power to direct merger. The desirability of merger is usually a matter of union policy dictated by economic considerations. The differences in merger and trusteeship (or receivership, or a method of supervision or control whereby a labor organization suspends autonomy) are highlighted by the anomalies that spring forth in attempting to fit a merger within the contour of Sec. 302 of the L.M.R.D.A. as delineated by Congress. For the court to go beyond the pale of the power de-

---

Clerks, 214 F. Supp. 768 (S.D.N.Y. 1960) (by implication); see also, Anderson, "Landrum-Griffin and the Trusteeship Imbroglio," 71 Yale L.J. 1460, 1498-1500 (1962). Note, 48 Va. L. Rev. 78, 96-97 (1962).

[78] At least two commentators appear to agree that revocation and reissuance of a charter should, at least under some circumstances, be held to constitute the imposition of a trusteeship. See Horowitz, "Possible Effects of LMRDA's Provisions," in Symposium on the Labor-Management Reporting and Disclosure Act of 1959 (1961), edited by Slovenko, 458, 563; Anderson, "Landrum-Griffin and the Trusteeship Imbroglio," 71 Yale L.J. 1460, 1478-85 (1962). The Department of Labor adopted the position: "that a revocation of a charter, properly conducted and in accordance with a labor organization's constitution and bylaws, does not create a trusteeship. . . . The Department has also determined that nothing in the Act prevents the creation of a new local, even though it may be composed primarily of the same individuals formerly belonging to the trusteed local that had its charter revoked." Union Trusteeships: A Report to the Congress, U.S. Dept. of Labor, BLMR (1962) 33-34.

fined in the L.R.M.D.A. to cure a real or fancied economic ill would be a usurpation of the legislative power."

3. In Flight Engineers v. Continental Air Lines, 297 F.2d 397 (9th Cir. 1961), cert. denied, 369 U.S. 871 (1962), a collateral issue involved an attempt by an international union to impose a trusteeship on one of its previously dissolved locals. Although the international's constitution was subsequently amended, it contained no provision for the establishment of trusteeships at the time of the original dissolution. The court rejected the international's claim that it had the inherent right to establish a trusteeship because the attempted dissolution threatened the "natural right of self-preservation" of the international, saying (297 F.2d at 402):

"Whatever 'inherent' power an international union formerly may have had to impose a trusteeship where the international constitution or bylaws made no provision therefor, it has had no such power since the enactment of the [LMRDA]. . . . Section 302 . . . expressly provides that such trusteeships shall be established and maintained 'only in accordance with the constitution and bylaws of the organization which has assumed trusteeship. . . .'"

4. For a review of more recent cases involving trusteeships see 1964 Report of the Committee on the Development of Law of Union Administration and Procedure, A.B.A., Section of Labor Relations Law.

INDEX

Index